EIGHTH EDITION

Notes and Resources for Teaching

The Bedford Reader

X. J. Kennedy

Dorothy M. Kennedy

Jane E. Aaron

NOTES AND RESOURCES
FOR TEACHING

THE
BEDFORD
READER

EIGHTH EDITION

NOTES AND RESOURCES FOR TEACHING

THE
BEDFORD
READER

EIGHTH EDITION

X. J. Kennedy • Dorothy M. Kennedy
Jane E. Aaron

Bedford/St. Martin's   Boston   ◆   New York

For information, write: Bedford/St. Martin's, 75 Arlington Street, Boston, MA
02116 (617-399-4000)

ISBN: 0–312–39940–5

PREFACE

In finding your way to this preface, you may already have discovered the innovations in the eighth edition of *The Bedford Reader*. (If not, they are summed up in the text's own preface.) Here we describe the various resources for teachers provided in this manual.

"Teaching with Journals and Collaboration" (p. 1). *The Bedford Reader* includes quite a bit on journal writing and small-group collaboration, and here we support the text with background on these popular techniques — benefits, pitfalls, suggestions.

"Teaching Visual Literacy" (p. 4). We suggest ways to use the chief feature of this new edition: the introductory material on critical reading of visual images and the many images appearing throughout the book.

"Using the Case Studies" (p. 7). We briefly discuss the student case studies that illustrate the rhetorical methods.

"Part One: Reading, Writing, and Research" (p. 8). This section gives an overview of the text's crucial chapters on reading and writing.

Chapter introductions. For each rhetorical chapter, we preview the method, predicting difficulties that students may have with it and suggesting various uses for the selections that illustrate the method.

Selection introductions. For each selection, we highlight what students may like (or dislike) about the piece, suggest topics for discussion and collaboration, and mark connections to other selections.

Answers to questions. For each selection, we also give answers to the questions on meaning, writing strategy, and language that follow the selection in the text.

Comments on the "Writers on Writing." For each comment by a selection author on his or her process, we suggest how the author's reported experience may be instructive for students. Note that the index at the end of the text lists each of these comments under the topic it addresses, such as choosing a subject or outlining or revising.

As always, these resources are intended not as a pedagogic *CliffsNotes* but as the notes of colleagues with whom you might care to hold a dialogue. The question answers, especially, are necessarily brief, and undoubtedly you and your students will find much to disagree with. We hope you will also find views to test and enlarge your own, questions to prompt better answers.

CONTENTS

TEACHING WITH JOURNALS AND COLLABORATION

Our users report that they often employ journal writing and small-group collaboration in their writing classes. *The Bedford Reader* and this instructor's manual support these techniques in several ways.

JOURNALS

The Bedford Reader includes a discussion of journal writing in Chapter 2 (p. 36) and a journal-writing assignment just after every selection (for example, p. 34).

More and more instructors use the journal as a teaching tool because it offers students a place to experiment with their ideas without the pressure of producing a crafted, polished essay. This opportunity for creative thinking can also lead to more provocative classroom discussions and formal essays.

One advantage of journals from the teacher's perspective is that they encourage students to share the responsibility of preparing for discussion. You can require a journal entry as part of every assignment, as the first step of writing a paper, or as an integrated part of class discussion. You can allow students to keep their entries on loose paper for easy submission or ask them to keep a notebook so they (and you) have all their entries in one place. You can use the structured journal questions we've suggested at the end of each selection, or you can allow students to write anything at all, in any direction, as long as they write something. Most instructors find that journal writing, like any other teaching technique, requires trial and error in the classroom. One teacher's pleasure is another's pain, after all; and some classes will sit slack-jawed before the same assignment that fires others into animated participation. Following are some general guidelines for those who do or want to use journals.

However often or seldom you require journal entries, try to present them in the context of other writing and discussion in the course; the danger of using journals in an unstructured way is that they can become busywork. Explain to students that it's in their best interest to use their journals as idea notebooks: safe places to record notes and impressions, grapple with difficult issues, respond to the essays in *The Bedford Reader,* and generate ideas for more formal writing assignments. They'll find that papers, discussions, and tests are easier because of the time they spend responding to what they read. Your promise not to grade the entries will guarantee more experimentation. However, you may need scheduled or surprise checks to ensure that writing is actually being committed to paper, and of course some students will be disappointed if you don't personally respond to their personal entries. One productive system is to schedule one or two submissions — emphasizing that they're just for a check in the gradebook toward a discussion grade — while encouraging unscheduled submissions for your comments on a particular entry whenever a student wants them. A student who is worried about a paper can get your early feedback, or a student who prefers writing to speaking can have a conversation with you.

Many students will be unfamiliar, even uncomfortable, with required writing that is informal and ungraded, so you may want to coax and guide them into writing. For those who are anxious about your expectations, emphasize that journals provide a free space where there are no right answers and where organization and sentence structure may simply reflect the student's train of thought. For everyone, make use of the open-ended journal assignment after every selection in the book: It asks students for personal recollections or gut responses to the selection, in an effort to help them recognize their own connection to it. Farther on, a "From Journal to Essay" writing topic asks students to hone their personal responses into structured essays, sometimes personal, often critical. You can use the journal prompt by itself to get students writing and talking. Even if you don't build journals into your course, you might find some of the prompts useful as in-class freewriting prompts or as remedies for dull discussions. Try assigning a journal entry for a particular selection and then asking volunteers to read theirs aloud and lead a discussion for five minutes or so. Try asking pairs of students to trade journals, read each other's entries on a given topic, and write responses. Try giving the journal assignments as starting points for small-group discussions.

Some students will have strong responses to the essays in *The Bedford Reader* and will not need any prompting to come up with "something to write about." Definitely encourage students to stray from our suggested avenues of response if they have another idea to explore. The main purpose of journals, after all, is to challenge students to articulate their own ideas more fully.

COLLABORATION

Working in small groups creates unique opportunities for students to examine the concepts of a course and the process of writing. Like journals, small groups are a useful testing ground for ideas and a means for exploring the nuances of issues. Often less intimidating than a whole-class discussion, a small group can provide students with a more collaborative forum for voicing their opinions. In fact, many teachers find that a major benefit of small groups is that they require all students to participate actively both as talkers and as listeners.

Small groups can augment learning in a variety of ways. Discussions might center on an opinion presented in a selection on writing style or rhetorical strategy, or on solving a problem raised by an author. (This manual's introduction to each selection suggests possible directions.) The result could be a collaborative written response that you collect or a series of brief presentations in which groups explain their responses to the rest of the class. Or, keeping it more informal, you may choose simply to roam and eavesdrop throughout the group sessions to see that groups stay focused and to discover what kinds of conclusions they are reaching.

Groups can also enhance whole-class discussions. Try having small groups spend the first fifteen minutes of class brainstorming answers to difficult questions as a precursor to a whole-class discussion. Have groups do outside research related to upcoming essays and report their findings to the class as a whole. Toward the end of the semester, you may feel confident enough in your groups to allow them to take turns planning and running class discussions.

Small groups can also be invaluable as writing workshops, to help students learn to become better readers and revisers of their own essays. Once students get to know members of their group well, they will begin to trust the feedback they receive. From brainstorming on an essay topic to providing suggestions on drafts, peer readers are often uniquely able to point out what works in an essay, what is confusing, what needs expanding, and so on.

You may have to teach students how to give this kind of feedback. Toward that end, Chapter 2 sets the stage with some words of encouragement (see p. 41). For further encouragement, try modeling a workshop process for the class, beginning with a conversation about what *constructive criticism* means. Ask a volunteer to bring copies of a draft paper to class, or copy a paper from a previous term, or even copy something of your own. Distribute copies to the class. Have the author read the paper aloud, as would occur in the small group. (If the author isn't present, ask a volunteer to read.) Ask the author to explain his or her main concerns about the essay (introduction doesn't seem to fit rest of paper, organization feels choppy, transitions awkward, and so on) — or if there is no author, take this role yourself. Then lead the whole class in a discussion of the essay, starting with what works particularly well and moving to what doesn't work. (Often, students will shy away from criticizing a peer, and you may need to get discussion going.). Give the author (you, if you're role-playing) plenty of opportunities to respond to people's comments. During the discussion, point out what works in workshopping and what doesn't. The most useful feedback will reflect the reader's understanding of the essay ("I got confused when you . . ." or "I wish you would give more details so I could see this place better" or "I don't follow your logic in paragraph 3"). *Discussion* of how to solve such problems will be more fruitful than blunt suggestions like "This passage should be cut" or "You should just rewrite this sentence like this."

Of course, negotiating personality conflicts and overcoming shyness and other qualities that can silence a small group can sometimes be tricky. To minimize these problems, have students compose a "personals" ad on an index card at the beginning of the term, explaining that they're searching for their workshop soul mates. Write a few questions on the board, such as what their strengths and weaknesses are as writers, readers, and talkers or how they respond to constructive criticism. Such self-portraits may not be entirely accurate, but they can help you group students according to complementary abilities and attitudes: You can group some who like to do research with others who like to talk in front of a large group; some who struggle to organize essays with others who feel that organizing is their biggest strength; some who are experienced in collaboration with others who aren't.

Small groups give students a chance to practice the ideas and strategies gleaned from lectures and reading. And such collaborative learning eases some of the burden on you, too: Students will not only gain a great sense of authority over their learning but also share the hot seat at the front of the room.

TEACHING VISUAL LITERACY

In this edition of *The Bedford Reader*, we provide many opportunities to incorporate the visual into writing classes: A new section in Chapter 1 extends critical thinking from texts to images; every rhetorical chapter opens with an image or related images, along with a caption that prompts students' critical responses; and four of the written selections center on images that we also reprint.

THINKING CRITICALLY ABOUT VISUAL IMAGES

In Chapter 1 on reading, we offer a detailed approach to thinking critically about visuals (pp. 27–31). Paralleling the method for evaluating written texts, the approach involves five steps: getting the big picture, analyzing, inferring, synthesizing, and evaluating. An insurance advertisement, combining photography and text, provides detailed examples of how the method can work.

Students generally like looking at images, and they often form immediate, almost visceral responses to what they see. The challenge, then, may be to guide their responses along critical pathways. For instance, they may need coaching to perceive the value of information about artists or advertisers or historical and cultural contexts — and they may need help gathering such information. In analyzing an image, they often benefit from small-group discussions in which they hear several points of view. Similarly, in the inference phase they can listen to the meanings attributed by others with different backgrounds and outlooks. Finally, as they evaluate images they may need encouragement to step back from their natural emotional responses and judge the worthiness of the image's purpose and its success in fulfilling that purpose.

CHAPTER-OPENING IMAGES

Each rhetorical chapter in Part Two opens with a visual representation of the chapter's method at work, accompanied by background information and questions about the image or images.

- A comic strip tells a humorous yet disturbing anecdote (narration, Chap. 4)
- A photograph depicts a riverside shanty (description, Chap. 5)

- A cartoon suggests outlandish cell phones of the future (example, Chap. 6)
- A well-known painting and a contemporaneous photograph play off each other (comparison and contrast, Chap. 7)
- A trailblazing photographer freeze-frames a bird in flight (process analysis, Chap. 8)
- A cartoon deconstructs a kid's bologna sandwich (division or analysis, Chap. 9)
- A poster groups artists to make a political point (classification, Chap. 10)
- A cartoon proposes a cause of gun violence (cause and effect, Chap. 11)
- A car advertisement probes the meaning of *luxury* (definition, Chap. 12)
- A public-service advertisement makes a vivid case against cigarette smoking (argument and persuasion, Chap. 13)

We anticipate that these images will inspire you and your students in several possible ways:

- Because each chapter opener shows a rhetorical method at work, it provides an additional way to introduce the method. The images may especially help students who resist or struggle with reading.
- The caption accompanying each chapter opener provides background on the image, so that students have essential information for a critical response. The questions in each caption encourage reflection and discourage snap judgments such as "I like it" or "I don't like it" or "I don't get it," and they can serve as journal or discussion prompts. Using the caption questions or your own assignments, you can devise various class or small-group projects centered on the chapter openers. For instance, the Grant Wood painting and the Ben Shahn photograph in Chapter 7 open up worlds to investigate — the backgrounds and interests of the artists, the effects of the Great Depression on farmers, the effect of medium on perception. For another example, the cartoon in Chapter 11 practically begs for a more detailed and substantiated explanation of the causes of gun violence. (At the same time, the cartoon has an undeniable punch. What are the advantages of simplifying causes?)

IMAGES ACCOMPANYING TEXT SELECTIONS

Four of *The Bedford Reader*'s text selections focus on visual images, and we print the images with the selections. In each case, the juxtaposition deepens the meaning of both the written text and the image.

- Joyce Carol Oates's poem "Edward Hopper's *Nighthawks*, 1942" (p. 165) describes and interprets Hopper's famous urban scene, which we show in full view and in a detail. "Joyce Carol Oates on Writing" comments on the making of the poem and further interprets the painting.
- Starting with a catalog illustration from FTD.com, which we reprint, Niala Maharaj and Donovan Hohn's "Thorny Truths About Flowers" (p. 285) explains the workings of the global flower trade.
- Jean Kilbourne's "'Can an Engine Pump the Valves in Your Heart?'" (p. 340) models a kind of analysis that draws conclusions from many examples of the subject — in this case, car advertisements. We reprint three of the ads Kilbourne discusses so that students can trace her thinking for themselves.

- C. Day Lewis's poem "The Expulsion: Masaccio" (p. 586) describes and analyzes a famous Renaissance fresco that we reproduce along with the poem. For many students, the subject of the expulsion from Eden will be quite familiar. They may gain the most from the poem and fresco, but all students should appreciate the intense feelings and expression of the artists.

USING THE CASE STUDIES

The Bedford Reader offers a case study in the use of each rhetorical method. These case studies fall between the chapter introductions and the selections, on pages with gray borders.

With these cases, we aim to suggest the methods' applications for purposes that students may consider more "real" than they do academic writing. Although all the case-study authors are students, they write not for their courses but for other reasons:

Reporting a car accident (narration, Chap. 4)

Advertising an apartment for sublet (description, Chap. 5)

Writing a cover letter for a job application (example, Chap. 6)

Creating a campaign poster (comparison and contrast, Chap. 7)

Explaining a fire-drill procedure (process analysis, Chap. 8)

Writing an application essay (division or analysis, Chap. 9)

Crafting a résumé (classification, Chap. 10)

Setting the record straight in a letter to the editor (cause and effect, Chap. 11)

Explaining the mission of an organization (definition, Chap. 12)

Disputing a parking ticket (argument and persuasion, Chap. 13)

The authors' purposes lead them to draw on the rhetorical methods, just as (we hope) your students will be guided by their particular purposes in using the methods.

The case studies have several possible uses. We anticipate that their main use will coincide with our chief aim in providing them — that is, to demonstrate the connection between purpose and method in real-life writing. Accordingly, we explain this connection in our introduction to each case. But this introduction also describes something of the author's process — focusing on difficulties the student overcame while working with the method — so that the cases could be used as mini-lessons in the writing process. They could also serve simply as additional examples of the methods. Or, given their practical nature, they could serve as models for letters, résumés, or other practical writing you may have your students do. To avoid pinning the cases down to a particular use, we have deliberately left them free of directions or follow-up questions.

PART ONE

READING, WRITING, AND RESEARCH

Part One of *The Bedford Reader* provides a substantial and well-illustrated discussion of reading, writing, and research documentation, with an emphasis on critical thinking. An outline of Part One follows and is followed in turn by a description of the contents.

Chapter 3: Using and Documenting Sources (p. 49)

Chapter 1 gives step-by-step instructions on attentive, critical reading, including examples of annotating a text, summarizing, and using analysis, interpretation, synthesis, and evaluation. A sample essay by M. F. K. Fisher and our commentary illustrate the steps. Then a new section shows students, again by example, how to apply their faculties for critical thinking to visual images. (For more on this topic, see p. 4 of this manual.)

Chapter 2 then details the stages of the writing process, including aids to discovery (journals, freewriting, and the rhetorical methods themselves), a stress on the thesis sentence, checklists for revising and editing, and encouragement for collaboration. This section also includes the stages of a student's response to Fisher's essay, from first journal entry through final draft. (The final draft is annotated to highlight its structure and its use of the rhetorical methods.)

Chapter 3, "Using and Documenting Sources," is the former appendix, much expanded and moved forward. It covers the critical work that students must do with sources and shows how to document sources in MLA style. A new student research paper, which is annotated, serves as a model.

You can use Chapters 1–3 in various ways, depending on your students' needs and, of course, your own inclinations. Many instructors teach directly from this material, especially when students are unfamiliar with the processes of critical reading and writing, have little experience with research, or have no other text to rely on. Other instructors ask their students to read the material on their own — it does not assume previous knowledge and so can be self-teaching. Still others select for classwork the parts they wish to stress (summary, say, or the thesis sentence) and ask students to cover the remaining sections on their own.

THE METHODS

4
NARRATION
Telling a Story

To write a short account of a personal experience is, for many freshmen, a first assignment that looks reassuring and possible to fulfill. Instructors who wish to begin in this way may assign for reading one or more of this chapter's essays by Angelou, Tan, Dillard, Alexie, and Huttmann. Four of the writers give students a sense of what a good writer can do with material perhaps much like their own: recollections and observations of ordinary experience from childhood and college days. The fifth writer, Huttmann, wrestles with difficult questions of life and death that students often find compelling. Angelou's and Tan's essays — both recalling experiences of "outsider" children in a predominantly white culture — can be paired for discussion and writing.

Not all freshmen feel comfortable writing in the first person. Some may writhe under a burden of self-consciousness. Some may feel guilty about not following the doctrine of a high-school teacher who once urged them to avoid *I*. A few members of the composition staff at Chapel Hill reported encountering this problem and, because of it, some preferred to begin their courses with *The Bedford Reader*'s chapter on description. Writing in the third person seems to give such students greater assurance about constructing that crucial first paper in which they're trying hard to please.

Chapter 1 ends with a short story. By juxtaposing Poe's "The Tell-Tale Heart" with the nonfictional narratives of the others, this chapter gives you a chance to ask, "How does fiction differ from nonfiction?" One difference, clearly, is that a fiction writer has the power to enter heads and explore the thoughts of characters.

NARRATION IN OTHER CHAPTERS.   Many selections later in *The Bedford Reader* rely heavily on narration to make a point, even as they develop mainly or at least partly by other methods.

Part Two

Brad Manning, "Arm Wrestling with My Father"
Sarah Vowell, "Shooting Dad"

Jhumpa Lahiri, "Indian Takeout"
Joyce Carol Oates, "Edward Hopper's *Nighthawks*, 1942"
Brent Staples, "Black Men and Public Space"
Dave Barry, "Batting Clean-Up and Striking Out"
David Sedaris, "Remembering My Childhood on the Continent of Africa"
Alice Walker, "Everyday Use"
Don DeLillo, "Videotape"
Michael Kroll, "The Unquiet Death of Robert Harris"
William F. Buckley, Jr., "Why Don't We Complain?"
Laura Fraser, "Why I Stopped Being a Vegetarian"

Part Three

Sandra Cisneros, "Only Daughter"
Judith Ortiz Cofer, "Silent Dancing"
Maxine Hong Kingston, "No Name Woman"
John McPhee, "Silk Parachute"
George Orwell, "Shooting an Elephant"
Richard Rodriguez, "Aria: A Memoir of a Bilingual Childhood"
E. B. White, "Once More to the Lake"
Terry Tempest Williams, "The Clan of One-Breasted Women"
Virginia Woolf, "The Death of the Moth"

MAYA ANGELOU

Champion of the World

A story within a story, Maya Angelou's suspenseful narrative invites attention to both its method and its matter. Inside the story of what happens in the general store (told in the first person, as Angelou looks back to her childhood), we follow the story of the Louis-Carnera fight. Suspense builds from the beginning, in the introductory glimpse of the people crowding in eagerly, in the "apprehensive mood" compared to a sky "streaked with lightning" (par. 2), and in the scraps of conversation. Larger events of the history of civil rights form a background to this narrative — for example, the fact that African Americans were not safe at night, although we learn this only at the end of the story.

You might begin by asking students what they know of the career of Joe Louis. (In some classes no one may know of him.) You could break the class into groups of three or four and have them research what it meant in the 1930s for an African American to become a prominent and universally admired athlete. Come up with a few contextual categories: Louis's career overall; other firsthand reminiscences of boxing in the 1930s; African American life in the 1930s. Each group could then present its findings for five to ten minutes, ending with a whole-class discussion of Angelou's memoir. (Note: If this sort of background research is something you'd like to have students do fairly regularly, you might consider rotating the responsibility so that just one group works and reports on any given essay.)

Audio aids: Angelou reads excerpts from *I Know Why the Caged Bird Sings* on a set of tape cassettes with the same title, produced by Random House Audiobooks. On another recording, *Maya Angelou Reading Her Poetry* (Tapes for Readers), she talks energetically about the same memoir and recalls a three-year period in her childhood when she refused to speak. Both recordings may be ordered from the American Audio Prose Library, P.O. Box 842, Columbia, MO 65205; telephone 1-800-447-2275.

QUESTIONS ON MEANING

1. Like the rest of the autobiography from which this selection is taken, "Champion of the World" seems written for a dual purpose: to recall vivid and significant moments of the author's life and to reveal the ironic situation of African Americans in America in the 1930s: able to become world champions but not able to walk a country road at night. This irony is given great weight by being placed at the end the story.

2–3. As Angelou indicates in much of her story, and especially in paragraphs 16 and 17, the pride of the race depends on the fight. Not only pride but a whole future rides on the outcome: "If Joe lost we were back in slavery [. . .]." Everyone in the store believes this, but the author's view is not so simple. Obviously she doesn't share the notion that if Joe Louis lost it would be clear that "God Himself hated us"; she is exaggerating the assumptions of the people in the store to emphasize the ideological importance of the fight.

4. The error makes untrue a small corner of the story (and might distract people who recognize it), but the fact that Angelou mixed up Louis's fights does not discredit what she reports experiencing.

QUESTIONS ON WRITING STRATEGY

1. Every sentence in the first paragraph contributes to our sense of the importance of the coming events. Note that, with space inside the store at such a premium, children (except infants and toddlers who could fit on a lap) are banished to the porch outside.

2. From paragraph 1 we feel anticipation and a tension that mounts to a crisis in paragraph 15, when the contender rains blows on Louis and staggers him. Short, punchy sentences add speed and force to Angelou's account: "We didn't breathe. We didn't hope. We waited" (par. 18 — and, incidentally, a good example of parallelism). The whole device of telling the story of the fight through a radio announcer's spiel is particularly effective because, as Angelou makes clear, the listeners in the store hang on the announcer's every word. Using radio as a medium in storytelling can increase suspense by leaving much to the imagination.

   Anyone familiar with the history of boxing will predict the winner as soon as the name of Joe Louis emerges; others may not be sure until Louis rallies in paragraph 20.

3. Students who sense the irony will probably express it in any of several ways. Some will say that despite all the hopes and dreams bound up in the fight, Louis's victory hasn't delivered his people. Maybe Louis is the strongest man in the ring, but African Americans in rural Arkansas are still vulnerable. Angelou's irony in the final line is so strong that it is practically sarcasm. Isn't there a suggestion, too, that on this particular night some whites, resenting the Louis victory, will be out to punish any African Americans they can find alone or in small numbers?

4. Here, as everywhere, direct quotation lends immediacy to any scene an author creates.
5. The descriptive details in paragraph 27 — drinking Coke "like ambrosia," eating candy "like Christmas," boys "blowing their breath in front of themselves like proud smokers" — move the story ahead and re-create the special joy and pride of the occasion.

QUESTIONS ON LANGUAGE

1. Singing commercials for razor blades; sales pitches designed to "string" the listener along. It is possible that Angelou finds irony in the sponsor's product, too, since a racist, stereotypical view of poor African Americans might have them fighting with razors or razor blades.
2. Nonstandard English here makes the people gathered in the store come alive for us. (This story offers a great opportunity to point out the occasional high value of nonstandard English. The comments in pars. 4 and 8 are so well put that they're hard to forget.)
3. The definition of *white lightning* is hard to find in standard dictionaries. *The Dictionary of American Slang* defines it as "cheap, inferior, home-made, or bootleg whisky, usually uncolored corn whisky."

MAYA ANGELOU ON WRITING

Here are some responses to the questions for discussion.

1. What Angelou means by *rhythm* won't be easily defined, but for her, finding the rhythm of a subject is that early stage all writers go through when first preparing to write. It means (we'd guess) getting a sense of the size and shape of a subject — or perhaps working up some feeling for it.
2. Writing twelve or fourteen pages of longhand notes, setting down all she knows about the subject, may seem to some students an excessive amount of toil. But Angelou invites the observation that the more work you do before you write, the easier it is to write.

AMY TAN

Fish Cheeks

Amy Tan is one of the best-known Chinese American writers on the current scene. This brief, amusing piece about a shock between two cultures is a good example of how much can be accomplished in very little space. Every detail contributes to the contrast between the two families and their cultures.

In this edition we have paired "Fish Cheeks" with Maya Angelou's "Champion of the World." Both essays illuminate the experience of being an outsider in America and the ways family can ameliorate or exacerbate a child's grappling with social identity.

Some students may take offense at Tan's use of stereotypes for humor, while others may see her Asian Americanness as exempting her from criticism on those grounds. If this issue is controversial in your class, consider setting up small-group debates on the "political correctness" of the essay.

Students who enjoy Tan's story should be encouraged to look further into Tan's works — *The Joy Luck Club* (1989), *The Kitchen God's Wife* (1991), *The Hundred Secret Senses* (1995), and *The Bonesetter's Daughter* (2001). Another valuable look at the Chinese American experience is Maxine Hong Kingston's *The Woman Warrior* (1976), a portion of which is reprinted on page 609.

QUESTIONS ON MEANING

1. Tan believes that her family will embarrass her.
2. Tan's mother wants to teach her not to be ashamed of her Chineseness, not to become completely Americanized. "Your only shame is to have shame" (par. 7).
3. Tan is ashamed of her background, referring to her family's "shabby Chinese Christmas" and "noisy Chinese relatives who lacked proper American manners" (par. 2). She resents her mother at the time, but eventually learns to appreciate the lesson she has taught her.
4. Tan's purpose is to amuse and entertain, yes, but possibly also to thank her mother and to impart her lesson to the reader.

QUESTIONS ON WRITING STRATEGY

1. Tan sets us up for a story right away. We know immediately that we're going to hear an anecdote about the minister's cute son —and an ethnic conflict.
2. The narrative progression is straightforward; each paragraph starts with a transition that places us in time: "the winter I turned fourteen" (par. 1); "When I found out" (2); "On Christmas Eve" (3); "And then" (4); "Dinner" (5); "At the end of the meal" (6); "After everyone had gone" (7); "And even though I didn't agree with her then" (8). This gives a sense of constant forward momentum to the story.
3. The irony lies in the narrator's inability to acknowledge or realize that the dishes she has described with such disgust in paragraph 3 are in fact her favorites. The Chinese Tan and the American Tan conflict with each other.
4. The descriptive paragraph is meant to be humorous and entertaining, and it will probably have the desired effect on non-Chinese readers: to make clear the culture shock the narrator thinks the minister's family will experience. (Some readers, though, may relish the description.)

QUESTIONS ON LANGUAGE

1. The comparison is amusing because the minister's son is compared to a chaste female figure even though it's a first crush and the narrator is "in love"; it also underscores both the cultural and nonsexual nature of her love.

2. Tan's language is typical of a young adolescent girl: "my mother had outdone herself" (par. 3); "Robert grunted hello, and I pretended he was not worthy of existence" (4); "Dinner threw me deeper into despair," "I wanted to disappear" (5).
3. Tofu (a curd of soybean milk) comes from the Chinese *dòu*, "bean," and *fū*, "curdled." Once exotic in the United States, tofu is now a staple of many American diets.

AMY TAN ON WRITING

Tan provides a lesson in turning a negative into a positive, from her initial difficulties with language to her acceptance of the richness her many Englishes give her voice. Many readers have been consistently impressed with her ear for dialogue. If you have second-generation students in your classroom, they may have strong opinions on the fairness of standardized testing and the reasons why more children of immigrants enter the precise scientific fields than the subjective field of English. Incidentally, Tan's comments bear comparison with Richard Rodriguez's "Aria" (p. 639). Both deal with the conflicts for bilingual children between the private and public realms.

ANNIE DILLARD
The Chase

This portrait of childhood beautifully captures the energy and idealism of youth. It originally appeared as a chapter in *An American Childhood* (1987), which one reviewer described as being "less about a coming-to-age than about a coming-to-consciousness, a consciousness so heightened by what appears to be an overactive autonomic nervous system that one sometimes fears her nerves will burst through her skin."

The narration of the chase itself (pars. 10–15) is an excellent model for students' own narrative writing. Point out the rhetorical devices Dillard uses to vary the narration and to make the chase seem endless (such as asyndeton, repetition, use of the plural in par. 13).

The story is also a good example of how narration can be used in the service of a larger theme, with implications that go beyond the events recounted. Dillard does more than simply tell a story; she makes an interesting observation about the death of enthusiasm.

Students might want to share in small groups their reactions to Dillard's contrast between a child's and an adult's point of view. Some may find Dillard's description of adulthood overly cynical and her portrait of childhood romanticized. Others may recall a time when they themselves expected more from life, when their own senses of joy were greater. (Or they may have experienced moments when they suddenly caught themselves thinking or speaking like their parents.) Encourage students to discuss their reactions to this theme and to come up with other examples of it from literature and movies.

QUESTIONS ON MEANING

1. Dillard wants to show how a harmless chase can take on epic propor-
    tions in the mind of a child. She wants to point out valuable qualities of
    childhood lost in adulthood: energy and wholeheartedness.
2. No. This driver is exceptional, the only one who has ever left his car (par.
    9).
3. The pursuer is the only adult the narrator has encountered who "knew
    what I thought only children who trained at football knew: that you have
    to fling yourself at what you're doing, you have to point yourself, forget
    yourself, aim, dive" (par. 13). At the end of the chase he "comes down to
    earth" (19), addressing the children in the banal, perfunctory tones of an
    ordinary adult. Dillard is disillusioned because of the gap between her
    ideals and reality.
4. Nothing can live up to the glorious moment that was the chase. The
    pursuer has resumed the role of just another adult, parroting the words
    all adults are required to say at such moments.

QUESTIONS ON WRITING STRATEGY

1. Football serves as a metaphor for life in the story: Everything you do, you
    have to tackle, giving 100 percent of yourself.
2. From football to baseball, from baseball to snowball throwing: These tran-
    sitions contribute to the essay's coherence. Baseball is a logical link be-
    tween football (another boys' sport) and snowball throwing, in which the
    throwing arm is all-important. The lesson Dillard has learned from play-
    ing sports is carried over to a more general lesson about life.
3. Far from weakening the narrative, this is the story's epiphany, where
    Dillard explains the larger meaning the chase was to take on.
4. Dillard's narration seamlessly combines the articulateness and sophisti-
    cation of an adult interpreter with a child's view of the events taking
    place.
5. Adults are lazy and take shortcuts. ("Any normal adult would have quit,
    having sprung us into flight and made his point," par. 10.) Unlike chil-
    dren playing football, adults are unwilling to fling themselves "whole-
    heartedly" (1) into things. With their "normal righteous anger" and "usual
    common sense" (20), they are victims of habit and routine. Children are
    willing to go all out; they know that life is "all or nothing" (1). (See also
    the second writing suggestion.)

QUESTIONS ON LANGUAGE

1. Dillard uses language with religious connotations to describe her pur-
    suer. Besides "exalting" and "righteous," she also uses "glory" (par. 19)
    and "sainted" (21).
2. The children, though playing together, exhibit a "natural solitude" (par.
    5). While being chased they are at once "exhilarated" and "dismayed"
    (14). The man chasing them is referred to as "our pursuer, our captor"
    and "our hero" (16). Dillard portrays childhood as a time of confusion
    and contradiction.
3. The sentence indicates how long and complicated the chase was and
    helps to bring the pursuer back down to earth. It is also anticlimactic
    after the imaginative digression about the Panama Canal and the lyrical

tribute to the pursuer that precede it. It is a typically banal, "adult" question.

ANNIE DILLARD ON WRITING

Any student who has ever become tangled in a long, complicated sentence and gone around in circles, losing track of an idea, will find sense in Dillard's remark that short sentences "can get you out of big trouble." If we teach sentence combining, we sometimes risk creating monsters; some students — often the best ones — may try to make a sentence carry too much weight. But Dillard's advice shouldn't be construed as urging us to write in nothing but short, simple sentences, sounding like a first-grade reader as a result. A good point to suggest: Mix up your sentences; vary them in length. And don't worry at all about your sentences while you write a draft; deal with them when you edit.

SHERMAN ALEXIE
Indian Education

In this impressionistic piece, Sherman Alexie charts both the plight of Native Americans living on reservations and his own escape from that plight through application to his schoolwork and sheer willpower. You might begin discussion by asking the class to enumerate the problems that Alexie suggests Native Americans face: poverty, alcohol and drug addiction, prejudice, an overriding sense of helplessness and failure. Students might then consider the personal qualities they see in the writer that helped him overcome such adverse circumstances. Make sure that students recognize Alexie's deep sense of ambivalence as he gradually says "good-bye to my tribe, to all the Indian girls and women I might have loved, to all the Indian men who might have called me cousin, even brother" (par. 46).

Some discussion should certainly focus on Alexie's rather unorthodox narrative method. Students should consider the effect of the series of vignettes, one for each school year, often concluding with a concise comment on Alexie's emotional response. The accumulation of these brief incidents gives the essay much of its power and suggests Alexie's overriding themes of personal triumph and cultural loss. This aspect of the piece could be the subject of small-group discussion.

Students interested in exploring more of Alexie's prose (he is also a poet) can be referred to his short-story collections *Reservation Blues* (1995) and *The Toughest Indian in the World* (2000). In addition, Alexie wrote the screenplay for the independent film *Smoke Signals*, which is available on videocassette and DVD; you might consider screening portions of this film to shed light on reservation life. Alexie also has a Web site at *http://www.fallsapart.com*.

QUESTIONS ON MEANING

1. The overall impression from incidents reported for almost every year is bleak and hopeless. The lives of reservation residents are marked by violence, substance abuse, hunger, discrimination, and despair.
2. The teacher in second grade exhibits overt prejudice, and Alexie shows examples of negative stereotypes of Indians in the seventh and ninth grades. His purpose is to show the many obstacles to success faced by Native Americans on and off reservations, obstacles he himself had to struggle to overcome.
3. While Alexie is, to some extent, describing the formal education of an Indian both on and off the reservation, his title refers more generally to the ways Native Americans are taught to believe that they are second-class citizens, that they have no right to achievement, that their customs have no value, and that they are by nature the source of their own failures.
4. In the first grade Alexie is made fun of by his Indian friends because his hair is too short. His teacher in the second grade insists that his parents cut his braids, but they actively defy her. In the twelfth grade Alexie's graduation cap doesn't fit because of the length of his hair. Hair seems a symbol of Indianness here, of maintaining traditions in defiance of the views and actions of non-Indians. As valedictorian of his white high school, Alexie obviously had conformed to white standards of behavior, but he also wore his hair long in an act of rebellion that tied him to his culture.

QUESTIONS ON WRITING STRATEGY

1. One striking effect of Alexie's technique is that it allows each section to have its own definite conclusion, adding punch to each individual anecdote. It also allows Alexie to present a series of incidents that are closely and clearly related by theme but that wouldn't flow seamlessly from one into another. To have run the sections together with transitional expressions would have more narrowly limited the kinds of stories Alexie could tell. In addition, the unconventional form can be seen as an expression of Alexie's own unconventionality.
2. The conclusions draw each incident to a close and point up the purpose of each incident. In some cases they simply cap the story being told: In the sections on the first and fourth grades, for instance, the final paragraphs provide humorous comments. In the sections on the sixth, eighth, and tenth grades, the conclusions offer morals that grow out of the stories told. In the sections on the third, fifth, seventh, eleventh, and twelfth grades, the conclusions add a poignant or reflective note. These variations keep the stories fresh, avoiding the monotony of, for example, ending each section with a moral.
3. In the seventh grade Alexie seems to be opening up to the world of non-Indians, reluctantly "saying good-bye to my tribe." He will go on in eighth grade to enter the white school where he will excel outside of his native culture.
4. The final image of the essay is of Alexie's contemporaries on the reservation fulfilling the stereotype of Native Americans as low achievers and alcoholics. Many, Alexie suggests, are given little other choice.
5. Comparison and contrast can be found in "Fifth Grade" (between Alexie and his cousin), in "Eighth Grade" (between the white girls starving them-

selves to stay thin and the unwilling starvation of those on the reservation), and in "Twelfth Grade" (between Alexie's graduation from the white school and his contemporaries' graduation from the reservation school). In each case the contrasts point up the difficulties faced by Indians on the reservation.

QUESTIONS ON LANGUAGE

1. The teacher spoke of Indians in a derogatory, dismissive manner. Alexie asserts his pride and defiance in the next paragraph: "*I am Indian. Indian, I am.*"
2. Alexie evidently means that he was isolated in silence when he moved to the white school off the reservation. By exaggerating the isolation, the hyperbole emphasizes the lonely distance he felt from the familiar people and traditions of his culture and between himself and the people now surrounding him.
3. The newspaper headline "Indians Lose Again" refers to the basketball team Alexie played on, but for Alexie it applies to him and all Native Americans.
4. The balance sharpens the difference between Alexie and his contemporaries on the reservation: While he enjoys the possibilities and science of basketball (par. 29), his cousin enjoys the distraction of drugs (31); while Alexie looks "toward the future" (70), his poorly educated former classmates, with limited prospects, look "back toward tradition" (72).
5. As class *valedictorian,* Alexie was the highest-ranking student in his class, responsible for the farewell speech at graduation. The word comes from the Latin *valē,* "farewell."

SHERMAN ALEXIE ON WRITING

Alexie speaks and writes freely about his role as an "American Indian Writer." The quotations we've selected emphasize the mix of humor and pain evident in "Indian Education" and his other writing. Most students will be familiar with "the Earth Mother and Shaman Man thing" that colors much writing by and about Native Americans. Indeed, it may color students' own impressions of Indian life, so that Alexie's depiction comes as a surprise.

BARBARA HUTTMANN

A Crime of Compassion

Huttmann's essay is a tough, no-nonsense account of the horror of disease and the greater horror of artificially prolonging it by refusing a patient a natural death. The essay is as much an example of argument by emotional appeal as it is of narration. (For example, Huttmann gives away the ending of her story in par. 3, thereby eliminating any element of suspense.) Huttmann's detailed personal anecdote adds tremendous ethical appeal to her argument, and even students who disagree with her on principle may have a hard time objecting to her individual act.

This essay should inspire lively discussion among students. For freewriting at the beginning of class or as a journal entry at home, have students respond to the journal-writing part of the first writing suggestion; then have a few read their opinions aloud in small groups or as a whole class. If opinions are divergent enough, you may want to stage a debate on whether or not Huttmann made the right choice. If time permits, consider assigning four or five students a joint research project for extra credit. Have them go to the library and hunt down recent articles on euthanasia, or on the specific case of Dr. Jack Kevorkian, and present their findings (in fifteen to twenty minutes) to the rest of the class.

QUESTIONS ON MEANING

1. Huttmann's purpose is both personal and social. She wants to argue that artificially sustaining a patient's life is not always the most humane thing to do. At the same time, she wants to justify her own choice through narrative.
2. A crime is usually anything but a compassionate act.
3. She may be accused of murder. By "legal twilight zone" she means that the law is fuzzy on these matters or that this is what the law requires, but irrationally.
4. Even though she is confident she did the right thing, Huttmann understands that she may be technically guilty in the eyes of the law: "Perhaps I am guilty" (par. 18).
5. The thesis is in the last paragraph: We do not have the right to die, and until we do we all could face Mac's fate.

QUESTIONS ON WRITING STRATEGY

1. Huttmann begins the essay with a shock effect. We immediately think of the "evil nurses" one hears about who deliberately kill their patients. We question this as soon as Huttmann begins to speak in her own voice, in paragraph 3.
2. The tone is objective but not distant; Huttmann writes with the matter-of-factness of someone used to dealing with death but who is not entirely insensitive to it. She describes the details of Mac's disease objectively in paragraphs 7 and 8, but admits to being "riddled [. . .] with guilt" (par. 13).
3. It immediately establishes the inevitability of Mac's death. Trying to stave it off has become a preposterous undertaking.
4. Huttmann's argument is that, in some instances, we should be able to choose when we want to die. Life should not be saved at any cost. Narrative makes this abstract idea concrete.

QUESTIONS ON LANGUAGE

1. *Resuscitate* ("restore consciousness or life") is a word with a complicated etymology. According to *The American Heritage Dictionary*, it comes from the Latin *resuscitāre*, which combines *re* ("backward") plus *suscitāre* ("to

stir up"), which itself combines *sub* ("below, under") plus *citāre* ("to set in motion"), which returns to the Indo-European root *kei* ("to set in motion").

2. *Newsweek* is a general-interest magazine whose readers would not be especially well versed in medical terms.
3. "Favorite" (par. 3), "young," "witty" (4), "I loved him" (5). Huttmann's argument is strengthened by the fact that Mac is not just any patient: His life meant something to her.
4. The metaphor of the fatted calf and the hungry vultures conveys the vulnerability of a talk-show guest.

EDGAR ALLAN POE

The Tell-Tale Heart

In this classic tale of terror, a rationalizing madman recounts a murder, and in so doing unintentionally reveals his paranoia and feelings of guilt. The first-person narration leaves it to the reader to separate what is real from what occurs only in the narrator's imagination.

Poe was one of the first literary critics and one of the first theorists of the short-story form. In "The Importance of the Single Effect in a Prose Tale," which we have excerpted in "Edgar Allan Poe on Writing," Poe sets forth the theory that the unity of a "single effect" is the essential quality of all successful short fiction. He maintains that the short story (or "prose tale"), which can be read in a single sitting, is perfectly adapted to the "exaltation of the soul which cannot be long sustained." The short story form allows writers to create unity of impression, and calls for highly structured fiction: "In the whole composition there should be no word written, of which the tendency, direct or indirect, is not to the one pre-established design."

Here is an in-class exercise that will allow students to test out Poe's ideas: Split your class into two or four groups. Each group will collaborate on a brief (two- to three-page) short story based on an identical plot. (Assign a simple plot familiar to everyone, such as that of a fairy tale or fable.) One or two groups will write the story collectively; the other one or two will assign different parts of the story to different students. At the end of class, read the stories aloud and discuss the results of close versus piecemeal collaboration. (If you have four groups, have students guess which kind of collaboration created each story.)

QUESTIONS ON MEANING

1. The narrator claims that the acuteness of his senses and the rationality of his actions prove his sanity. For example: "The disease had sharpened my senses — not destroyed — not dulled them" (par. 1); "Madmen know nothing. But you should have seen *me*. You should have seen how wisely I proceeded — with what caution — with what foresight — with what dissimulation I went to work! [. . .] Would a madman have been so wise as

this?" (3); "And now have I not told you that what you mistake for madness is but over-acuteness of the senses?" (10); "If still you think me
mad, you will think so no longer when I describe the wise precautions I
took for the concealment of the body" (12). The narrator's claims to sanity are of course unconvincing (see the second writing suggestion).

2. The narrator (perhaps falsely) projects his own neuroses onto the old
   man.
3. The narrator does this out of bravado, in the "wild audacity of my perfect
   triumph" (par. 16).
4. The narrator is paranoid. He thinks the officers can hear the beating
   heart and are playing games with him.
5. Poe's main purpose is to entertain through terror, but at the same time
   he examines the effects of guilty paranoia.

QUESTIONS ON WRITING STRATEGY

1. The first paragraph introduces the voice of the narrator and establishes
   the atmosphere of the story. We learn that the narrator is mad and defensive about it. The reader's curiosity is piqued.
2. The narrator's addressing the reader directly draws the reader into the
   story, as if hearing it face to face from the narrator.
3. The shutters were closed to deter robbers, but because they prevented
   the old man from seeing the narrator enter the room, they ended up
   being the death of him.
4. The story is being told from the point of view of the police. The use of the
   past perfect tense shows that this is an example of free indirect discourse. Each clause of the last sentence could be preceded by "The officers said that. . . ."
5. There is a movement from silence, to noise, back to silence again, a cre-
   scendo, then a decrescendo. Poe sets off the loudness of the heartbeat
   ("It grew louder, I say, louder every moment!") against the otherwise extreme silence of the room ("I [. . .] kept still. I scarcely breathed"). The
   silence and loudness become simultaneous; the heartbeat (actually heard
   only in the narrator's imagination) is the only noise in the house: "And
   now at the dead hour of the night, amid the dreadful silence of that old
   house, so strange a noise as this excited me to uncontrollable terror. Yet,
   for some minutes longer I refrained and stood still. But the beating grew
   louder, louder! I thought the heart must burst." The pressure thus builds
   until the narrator's paranoia gets the best of him, and the silence is
   broken by his scream, joined by the old man's: Imagined noise becomes
   real noise. With the old man dead, the paragraph ends in silence.

QUESTIONS ON LANGUAGE

1. The repetition increases the immediacy of the narrative, giving it an in-
   cantatory, oral quality. It also contributes to the portrait of the narrator's
   insanity.
2. An hour hand would be too slow to convey the slowness of the narrator's
   hand, a second hand too fast. Other examples of figures of speech are
   the comparison of the old man's eye to that of a vulture and the expression "my blood ran cold" (par. 2); the comparison of the ray of light to
   "the thread of a spider" (8) and the heartbeat to a watch enveloped in
   cotton (10).

3. Italics add emphasis and in this story increase the sense that the narrator is speaking directly to us. We hear the emphasis of speech, the hysteria of the narrator.

4. *Tattoo* and *mark* in Poe's usage mean, respectively, "a rhythmic drumming or beating" and "to attend to."

EDGAR ALLAN POE ON WRITING

Poe sounds as if he's explaining a process ("he then combines," "his first step"), but we're quite sure that he did *not* expect the first sentence to be perfect at first writing. The point that students shouldn't miss is that the final story has a single effect, and it's evident from the first sentence.

5
DESCRIPTION
Writing with Your Senses

Because most instructors make much of descriptive writing, this chapter offers an ample choice of illustrations. Students tend to think of descriptive writing as a kind of still-life painting in words: An apple or a banana sits on a table and you write about it. In this chapter, we strive to demonstrate that, on the contrary, description can involve the testimony of all the senses. All the prose writers employ description in fresh and engaging ways. And the poet — Joyce Carol Oates — examines with careful eyes the smallest details of a painting, Edward Hopper's *Nighthawks* (reproduced along with the poem).

For our pairing in this chapter, we have chosen Brad Manning's "Arm Wrestling with My Father" (Manning wrote the essay as a college freshman) and Sarah Vowell's "Shooting Dad." Both authors look at their fathers, but otherwise their views (and their descriptions) are quite different. Note that each essay is followed by a "Connections" writing suggestion involving the other.

DESCRIPTION IN OTHER CHAPTERS. In introducing the method of description, we stress its uses in all kinds of writing. For proof, we can offer up every essay in the book. Here are other *Bedford Reader* essays (outside this chapter) in which description plays a large role:

John McPhee, "Silk Parachute"
George Orwell, "Shooting an Elephant"
Richard Rodriguez, "Aria: A Memoir of a Bilingual Childhood"
E. B. White, "Once More to the Lake"
Terry Tempest Williams, "The Clan of One-Breasted Women"
Virginia Woolf, "The Death of the Moth"

BRAD MANNING

Arm Wrestling with My Father

Manning's essay specifically addresses the male experience by exploring how masculine ideals (such as strong, silent, athletic) can affect father-son relations. Most students will have something to say about the general difficulties of parent-child communication, and you may want to extend discussion to how Manning's personal experience represents larger issues. That men communicate nonverbally and women verbally is a commonly held belief. Ask students whether they agree with this gender generalization. Is it easier, more common, more acceptable, for mothers to talk openly with their daughters than for fathers with their sons? What about mothers and sons, fathers and daughters? (For a take on the latter relationship, Sarah Vowell's "Shooting Dad," the essay following this one.) Students may need encouragement to complicate their answers to these questions with specific reasons for their generalizations.

To enhance class discussion, small groups could initially be asked to spend ten to fifteen minutes brainstorming stereotypes about a particular gendered parent/child relationship: one group working with fathers and sons, one with mothers and daughters, and so on (you could even throw stepparents into the mix). When the class reassembles, groups should both respond to each other's ideas and connect their claims to the relationship and standard of communication that Manning describes with his father.

QUESTIONS ON MEANING

1. Manning's father communicates through gestures rather than words.
2. They have learned primarily that they don't have to compete to express affection and that there are many different kinds of communication.
3. Clearly, Manning has always felt loved, but he recognizes that these challenges *show* that his father loves him.
4. His purpose is definitely to express love for his father. In a larger context, he also wants to suggest the strength of a nonverbal relationship between fathers and sons.

QUESTIONS ON WRITING STRATEGY

1. Manning begins with his bitterness to set us up for the emotional progress of the essay, which moves from frustration and anger to acceptance (all responses to various arm-wrestling competitions).

2. These options suggest that he believes they have both learned something about new avenues of communication. We aren't supposed to predict anything; just knowing options exist shows progress is being made.
3. Manning compares the thrill of hooking his first big fish (par. 10) to the sense of accomplishment he initially felt when he realized that he was going to win his first arm-wrestling match with his father. Although both events are exciting firsts that suggest the approach toward manhood, Manning is a little sorry in both cases to know that he can defeat (kill?) a worthy and longtime foe: "I wanted to win but I did not want to see him lose" (9); "when you finally think you've got him, you want to let him go, cut the line, keep the legend alive" (10). Still, these poetic and self-sacrificing impulses stand in contrast to the end of this wrestling match, which Manning, despite his regrets, won't lose on purpose (11).
4. The narrative progresses through events that demonstrate Manning's boyish powerlessness: his "whole upper body pushing down in hope of winning," his father would "grin with his eyes fixed on me," Manning would "start to cheat and use both hands," his brother once even tried to help, and yet "the man would win." The description emphasizes the contrast between the boy and the man in terms of size ("tiny shoulders" and "little legs" are no match for the man's "calm, unmoving forearm"); effort (the father "not seeming to notice his own arm" while the boy's "greatest efforts" were useless); and power (the father's arm moves "steadily [. . .] regardless of the opposition").

QUESTIONS ON LANGUAGE

1. *Competition* suggests sportsmanship, organized rivalry with a goal, rather than the discordant clash of wills that *conflict* suggests.
2. This reduces the father to just the arm, giving the reader a greater sense of how large a role the father's arms play in characterizing the man as a whole. The image of him as "the arm" suggests both his competitiveness and his protectiveness (par. 4).
3. Manning still feels competitive with his father, but is loath to sacrifice his sense of being protected by a father who is stronger than he is.
4. *Mononucleosis* is a disease involving a high white-blood-cell count, causing fever, weakness, swollen lymph nodes, and a sore throat.

BRAD MANNING ON WRITING

Manning has some good advice for college writers, especially about taking the time to plan and revise and working for one's own voice. Students who struggle to write may dispute Manning's implication that writing can be a better means of self-expression than speaking. You might reinforce Manning's message that writing, unlike speaking, provides a chance to build and shape thought.

SARAH VOWELL

Shooting Dad

To begin discussion of this essay, consider the particular cleverness of Vowell's title: Her father is literally a "shooting dad" (a dad whose pastime is shooting firearms), and, in her conclusion, Vowell says that after his death the family will fulfill his request to bag his ashes and shoot them from his cannon (thus, the family will be literally "shooting Dad").

If you pair this with the previous essay, Brad Manning's "Arm Wrestling with My Father," consider asking students to compare and contrast the father-child relationships these two writers present. One interesting difference is that Manning focuses much more overtly on the love he feels for his father and his father's love for him than Vowell does in describing her relationship with her father. Why might this be less of an issue for Vowell? How would students characterize Vowell's feelings for her father and his feelings for her? Her portrait is for the most part quite affectionate, but she also treats her father with considerable humor, poking fun at his various foibles. Despite their differences, as Vowell has grown older she and her father seem to have developed an easygoing relationship, with little if any of the unspoken baggage Manning describes between himself and his father. Do students think this a reflection more of gender, age, or basic family dynamics? (Note that Vowell's family seems far less "shy" than the family Manning describes.)

Another focus of discussion might be Vowell's highly polished comic tone, her delightful way of casually tossing in a verbal joke — having "to move revolvers out of my way to make room for a bowl of Rice Krispies" (par. 3), for example, or referring to her father's shop as "a tetanus shot waiting to happen" (7). You could divide students into groups, have each group analyze Vowell's essay for further examples, and then report on their findings and how the examples contribute to the persona Vowell presents in this essay. What relationship does she establish with her readers?

QUESTIONS ON MEANING

1. Throughout their lives, Vowell and her father have been at odds over political issues and divided in their interests — she the liberal, he the conservative; she antigun, he progun; she artistic, he mechanical. The division is made explicit in paragraphs 1–2, 5, 7–8, and 13.

2. Vowell writes that both her parents grew up in controlling households "where children were considered puppets and/or slaves" (par. 12). In reaction to the rigidity of his own parents, her father wanted his children to have the freedom to make their own choices. We see him, then, as fundamentally open-minded.

3. Vowell had reached a point in adulthood where she wanted to connect more closely with her father and decided that sharing in this major project of his was a good place to start — particularly since it represents "a map of all his obsessions" (par. 19). She isn't bothered by her father's cannon as she is by other guns because "it is a completely ceremonial object" (30), not a weapon that could readily be used to harm others. Also, she enjoys the noise it makes and the way its smoke fills the air.

4. Vowell's father is proud to be the descendant of reactionaries and renegades and enjoys recalling tales of his "nefarious" ancestors. His slyly ornery streak helps explain his outspoken individualism.

5. Vowell's purpose seems to be to trace her evolving view of her father, from seeing him as her polar opposite to realizing that they have more in common — in terms of being "smart-alecky loners with goofy projects and weird equipment" (par. 29) — than she ever expected. She creates the impression of a man who is exasperating, obsessive in his beliefs and habits, but somehow endearing, finally, because of his idiosyncratic devotion to "his art" (31).

QUESTIONS ON WRITING STRATEGY

1. The anecdote demonstrates in a nutshell her father's penchant for guns and his tendency to behave as he sees fit. It also shows that, even at eleven, Vowell saw things completely differently and welcomed the restrictions that town life would place on her father's behavior.

2. The paragraph provides a bit of humor with its suggestion that boyfriends feared Vowell just might shoot them if they betrayed her. It also acts as a transition into the following paragraph, where Vowell admits that she has only shot a gun once in her life. While this aside doesn't contribute directly to the portrait of Vowell's father, it does bring in outsiders' views of her father's guns.

3. The final sentence suggests the depth of Vowell's feelings for her father: When he dies, she will and wants to feel pain. The double meaning of "hurt" — the pain of the cannon noise and the pain of loss — ties together the threads of guns and father and sharply etches Vowell's love for her father.

4. Comparison and contrast is found in paragraphs 1–2, 6–7, 13, and 29. The method is important to show how different Vowell believed herself and her father to be until she came to share one of his pleasures and realized that they were surprisingly alike.

QUESTIONS ON LANGUAGE

1. Shooting crows is clearly not "a national pastime, like baseball and apple pie." Vowell points up the irony of her father's statement by stating her own preference.

2. Repeating the word "six" asks the reader to focus on the young age of the twins when they were first allowed to shoot a gun. The short final sentence neatly summarizes, by contrast, Vowell's own bad experience of shooting.

3. In personification and similes, Vowell says the gun "kicked little me back to the ground like a bully, like a foe." It's not just big and heavy and dangerous to others but malevolent to her, "an evil presence."

4. *Pharaohlike* (par. 18) will not show up in students' dictionaries, though of course *pharaoh* will ("a king of ancient Egypt; a tyrant"). Vowell alludes to the biblical story of Moses, in which the ruler of Egypt ordered all Hebrew boy babies killed.

SARAH VOWELL ON WRITING

Most students won't share Vowell's experience of writing for radio and print, but they will know some frustrations of getting thoughts into writing and they may, like Vowell, have experienced distinct advantages and disadvantages in speaking and in writing. For instance, in speaking, as Vowell says, you can leave some things unsaid and can be a bit slapdash. But in writing you don't have to face your audience and can take time to work out your ideas.

JHUMPA LAHIRI

Indian Takeout

Jhumpa Lahiri's essay is a wonderful example of description almost purely for the sake of description. Lahiri's purpose seems less to make some larger point about human nature or humanity than to offer readers a detailed sensory account of the Indian foodstuffs and cooking utensils so cherished by her immigrant family. Lovingly packed into their spacious "Food Suitcase" each time the family returned from Calcutta, these provisions helped tie them to their native culture, so foreign to the United States of Lahiri's childhood.

The essay provides an excellent chance for students to examine the language of description. Individually or in small groups, they might look at Lahiri's use of adjectives, adverbs, and descriptive phrases. Or you might ask them to analyze the ways Lahiri appeals to all the senses here — not only to sight, taste, and smell, as one would expect in writing about food, but also to sound and touch (for example, in par. 3, her father's "sucking" on mango pits and her mother's relishing "sticky" orange sweets).

"Indian Takeout" is also suffused with a sharp sense of nostalgia: not only Lahiri's parents' nostalgia for the foods they grew up with but also their and Lahiri's later nostalgia for earlier days when the Food Suitcase — no longer needed because Indian foods are available in the United States — played so important a role in their lives (pars. 8–9). Students might consider why nostalgia has a central place when writers describe things important to them in the past.

Lahiri's collection of short stories, *Interpreter of Maladies*, won the Pulitzer Prize for fiction in 2000. If the book is available in your library, you might share some passages with students as further examples of this writer's descriptive powers.

QUESTIONS ON MEANING

1. Like true pirates, who raided towns for any loot they could carry away, Lahiri's parents raided — in a manner of speaking — the bazaars and markets of Calcutta for the native foodstuffs then unavailable in Rhode Island. Sometimes they even included fresh produce, which it is illegal to

bring into the United States, and smuggled their "plunder" past customs inspectors by tying it up securely in a padlocked bag (par. 4).

2. This food was, as Lahiri writes in paragraph 3, "the food of their childhood, the food they had been deprived of" as American immigrants. They missed the flavors of their homeland.

3. The modest meal was appropriate because the family felt melancholy on their return, missing the family and ways of life they had enjoyed during their stay in Calcutta. Her mother made "food to mirror our mood."

4. The parents no longer need to bring food back from India because they can now purchase most things in the United States. Although certainly convenient, the availability of Indian foods also brings "some sadness" (par. 8), presumably for the lost pirating adventure.

5. Lahiri apparently intends to share with readers the pleasure and comfort her family took in buying, transporting, preparing, and eating Indian foods. She could assume that readers of *Food and Wine* would be interested in food of all types and would want vivid descriptions of tastes and other sensations.

QUESTIONS ON WRITING STRATEGY

1. Lahiri's opening reference to her parents as "former pirates" is a way of piquing readers' interest. Her parents were not, of course, pirates in a literal sense, but the analogy makes for a dramatic start to the essay.

2. Paragraph 6 describes what the family took with them to Calcutta from the United States. Lahiri might have omitted the paragraph, but it answers a question many readers would have ("What did they take to India?"). Chronologically, the information would precede paragraph 3, but there it would distract from the essay's narrowing focus on Indian foods. Lahiri presumably placed the information where she thought it would be least disruptive.

3. The conclusion (par. 9) refers to the "pirating ways" of Lahiri's parents. The echo of the pirating image in the introduction draws a string around the essay, providing a satisfying sense of closure.

4. Paragraph 4 is process analysis because it explains a series of actions that were carried out in the same way every time the family returned from India. (Narration retells singular events.) Here, the process analysis adds vivid sensory details, from the "bare-chested, [. . .] cross-legged" father to the "salty, crunchy snack mix."

QUESTIONS ON LANGUAGE

1. "Indian takeout" generally refers to prepared food bought at an Indian restaurant and eaten elsewhere. In context, however, the title refers punningly to the family's bringing food out of India and into the United States.

2. As the vocabulary list in the next question indicates, Lahiri takes for granted readers' knowledge of some foods that are fairly common to Americans, such as lentils and cumin. She is careful to describe foods and utensils that Americans may not know, some in greater detail than others — for example, *boti* and *sil-nora* are easier to visualize than *karhais* (par. 5).

3. *Portmanteau* is an old-fashioned word meaning a large traveling case for clothes. It comes from the French words *porter*, "to carry," and *manteau*,

"a cloak"). A *portmanteau word* is one that combines two other words in form and meaning, as *smog* combines *smoke* and *fog*.

JHUMPA LAHIRI ON WRITING

Like many writers, Lahiri reports taking refuge in her imagination from problems in the real world — shyness and the immigrant's feeling of not belonging. Rather than nurse her wounds, Lahiri sought a "vital experience" in observation and in self-expression. Perhaps some students will recognize themselves in Lahiri's self-description and try out the therapeutic and transformative effects of writing for themselves.

JOAN DIDION

Marrying Absurd

Joan Didion is a novelist and a journalist well known for her searching insights into the quirks of American life. In this essay she describes the Las Vegas wedding with her usual vivid yet economical detail.

Students may or may not agree with Didion's label of "absurd" to describe the Las Vegas wedding; but even those who crave kitsch should appreciate the careful way she builds this portrait to emphasize the ridiculous. After discussing Didion's style and tone, you can give students a chance to try their hand at these techniques by having them collaboratively write a similar portrait of some place or situation that they consider absurd. Working in groups of three or four, students should be able to write a couple of paragraphs of detailed description during a class period. They should think carefully about what aspects of their subject are most ripe for satire or exaggeration and what details will economically convey their sense of the situation. (They — and you — will probably want to hear what all the groups have written when these portraits are done.)

Students who are interested in the Las Vegas environment might wish to look into *Learning from Las Vegas*, by Robert Venturi, Denise Scott Brown, and Stephen Izenour (1972). A good source of interviews with Didion and critical essays on her work is *Joan Didion: Essays and Conversations*, edited by Ellen G. Friedman (1984).

QUESTIONS ON MEANING

1. The practical reason is that Nevada requires no blood test or waiting period (see par. 1). Also, Las Vegas's unreality — its sense of being an adult playground "merchandising 'niceness'" (4) — might be attractive to some marrying couples.
2. Everything is open twenty-four hours a day. Also, Las Vegas is profoundly isolated from what we think of as "real life."

3. Didion states her thesis in paragraph 4: "Las Vegas is merchandising 'niceness,' the facsimile of proper ritual, to children who do not know how else to find it."
4. Didion seems sympathetic to her subjects in a way; she also seems extremely detached from them.

QUESTIONS ON WRITING STRATEGY

1. Didion's descriptions primarily appeal to the visual sense, perhaps because her thesis is that the Las Vegas wedding industry is all about appearance.
2. Didion uses quotation (par. 1); anecdote (3 and 4); dialogue (3 and 4); descriptive details and images (throughout).
3. Didion's point of view is detached. When discussing the phenomenon of the Las Vegas wedding in a general way, she uses the pronoun *one*. Only when she is describing her personal observations and interactions does she use the pronoun *I*.
4. The essay's dominant impression is of Las Vegas as glittery, isolated, and superficial. The couples who marry there, as Didion depicts them, are looking for something real but find only a sham.
5. The process is this: Get to Las Vegas. Pay the fee and obtain a license. Choose a wedding chapel and "costumes." Attend the brief ceremony. Celebrate.

QUESTIONS ON LANGUAGE

1. Didion's diction is much more formal than the diction used by those she describes, as shown by the contrast with the dialogue she reports. This sets her apart from her subjects and lends authority to her analysis.
2. The essay's tone is ironic and detached. Ask students to look closely at paragraph 3, for instance, where Didion writes that "marriage, like craps, is a game to be played when the table seems hot."
3. The ads and slogans show how the industry is selling a veneer of respectability, exaggerated decorum, "niceness."
4. "Panglossian" alludes to the incurably optimistic Dr. Pangloss in Voltaire's *Candide*.
5. "Chinchilla" (a fur), "bouvardia" (a fragrant flower), and "*peau de soie*" (a soft silk) are right out of the highly detailed bridal literature.

JOAN DIDION ON WRITING

Didion's comments on writing seem apt from a writer noted for observation. She has, though, been criticized for lacking a framework, for writing without a point. Do details as carefully selected and well written as Didion's make their own point, or does she have some other responsibility as a writer?

Students may be surprised at Didion's assertion about the relation between meaning ("the picture") and grammar, especially if they believe (as many students seem to) that grammar is somehow extrinsic to meaning, the frightening "rules" meant to be applied to already-expressed meaning.

JOYCE CAROL OATES
Edward Hopper's Nighthawks, *1942*

When assigning this poem, also ask students to look carefully at the reproduction and detail of Hopper's painting that accompanies it. You might even ask students to complete a variation of the "Journal Writing" suggestion in which they jot down their own responses to the painting before reading the poem.

In class discussion, a central question for students is what they see as Oates's larger theme in the poem. Oates goes well beyond simply describing the scene of the painting and those peopling it — and even beyond imagining its characters' thoughts and feelings (although these are presented quite vividly). Implicitly, she is contemplating the painting as a work of art in which "time is never going to budge" (line 37), in which the word *still* has the connotations both of "not moving" and of "not changing," even being trapped in the moment the artist has created. In Oates's hands the image could be a metaphor for the human condition ("so why isn't he happier?" [60]).

Your library can probably provide you with other works by Hopper either in books about the artist or on slides, and numerous online links to Hopper images can be found at *http://www.artcyclopedia.com/artists/ hopper_edward.html.* You may also want to bring to class a color reproduction of *Nighthawks* to share with students.

QUESTIONS ON MEANING

1. The couple are in the midst of an extramarital affair. The man has apparently left his wife (line 7), but he's done that before and gone back (15–19, 28–30, 39–41). He's relieved but, in the end, not happy (60). The woman's thoughts dwell on her mistrust of the man (7–8) as she works herself up not to be hurt by him again (37–41, 45–47).

2. Various interpretations are possible, of course. Perhaps the poem's speaker poses the question about the painting itself; none of the figures in the painting would seem to have this wider perspective. The setting of the picture seems to have the characteristics of a dream — "so much that's wide, still, mute, horizontal" (lines 23–24).

3. Two possible interpretations stand out. The figures in any painting are caught forever in a particular moment, still and silent, so Oates could be urging her readers to contemplate the larger idea of art and its permanency. And Oates also pictures a relationship that is stagnant, going nowhere (although the man is blind to this fact at the moment), which may be interpreted as a fact of the human condition.

QUESTIONS ON WRITING STRATEGY

1. Oates describes the painting in lines 1–6, 8–10, 22–27, and 54–56. She uses these details as a springboard, imagining what they reveal about the characters or how the characters respond to them: for instance, "And she's thinking / the light in this place is too bright, probably / not very

flattering, she hates it when her lipstick / wears off and her makeup gets caked" (30–34). Oates's purpose is not so much to render the physical details of the painting as to describe the situation those details could be illuminating, as well as to parallel the situation with the idea of artistic creation.

2. In lines 14–15 the woman thinks of her lover's guilt as "an actual smell, sweaty, rancid, like / dirty socks," and in lines 52–53 she recalls him "burying his hot face in her neck, between her cool / breasts." The man, in contrast, is "not the kind to talk much" (20), and his thoughts lack imagery: "he's thinking / thank God he made the right move at last" (20–21), "he's feeling pretty good, [. . .] this time he's sure / as hell going to make it work, he owes it to her / and to himself" (27–30), "he's thinking he's the luckiest man in the world" (59).

3. Oates runs sentences and phrases together with few pauses, in a stream of consciousness that builds to the italicized sentence ending line 44.

4. The man's thoughts and, particularly, the woman's thoughts are essentially narrative, and through them the reader can infer the larger narrative of their past relationship. The painting suggests a story to Oates, so she needs narration to relate it.

QUESTIONS ON LANGUAGE

1. *Rancid*, from the Latin *rancēre* ("to have a rank, unpleasant smell"), is a particularly effective word, its sound mimicking its meaning. One almost curls one's lip when saying it.

2. Oates clearly sees these two as a couple of tough characters, not at all refined or even admirable. Who else would be sitting in a coffee shop on a deserted street in the middle of the night?

3. "Relief" implies escape from a bad situation, whether from his unhappy home life or from his girlfriend's anger. It suggests looking back at something unpleasant rather than looking forward to something good.

JOYCE CAROL OATES ON WRITING

Both the prolific and the protean Joyce Carol Oates reveal themselves in her essay about her poem about a painting: Oates likes to communicate, and she has much to say in many different ways. This explicit analysis illuminates the painting and also Oates's description of it in her poem. Some students may at first have difficulty penetrating Oates's brief essay, but they should get the point that she wrote the poem for just the reason that most people write anything: to find meaning ("The poem enters the painting as a way of animating what cannot be animated; a way of delving into the painting's mystery").

6
EXAMPLE
Pointing to Instances

Some essays in this chapter use only a few examples; others use many. They all show the ways examples can pin down and give meaning to generalizations.

Barbara Lazear Ascher's and Anna Quindlen's essays are connected by theme as well as by method: Both treat homelessness, what it means, how to confront it. Bill Bryson's "Design Flaws" wins the hearts of technophobes with examples of things that don't work as they should. William Safire's "Fulminations" presents not his own peeves but those of scientists at the misuses of their terms. And finally, Brent Staples's personal memoir, "Black Men and Public Space," is an essay that arouses keen interest and lively discussion.

Some students find difficulty in seeing the difference between giving an example and giving evidence to support a general statement. The latter is a larger concern, in which example is only one strategy. It may help to explain that, usually, an example backs up a general statement ("There have been many fine woman runners: Grete Waitz . . .") but that not everything supporting a general statement is an example. Statistics and other data, factual statements, expert opinions, and quotations also serve as evidence. The distinction may not be worth losing sleep over, but if a class has trouble seeing it, ask them to take a more painstaking look at "The Method" at the beginning of this chapter.

EXAMPLE IN OTHER CHAPTERS. Every essay in this book uses examples — a point that students may benefit from hearing. The following list includes essays outside this chapter that center on one or more examples:

Part Two

Sherman Alexie, "Indian Education"
Barbara Huttmann, "A Crime of Compassion"
Jhumpa Lahiri, "Indian Takeout"
Joan Didion, "Marrying Absurd"
Suzanne Britt, "Neat People vs. Sloppy People"
Dave Barry, "Batting Clean-Up and Striking Out"
Judy Brady, "I Want a Wife"
Armin A. Brott, "Not All Men Are Sly Foxes"
Jean Kilbourne, "'Can an Engine Pump the Valves in Your Heart?'"
Russell Baker, "The Plot Against People"
Deborah Tannen, "But What Do You Mean?"
Stephen King, "'Ever Et Raw Meat?'"

BARBARA LAZEAR ASCHER

On Compassion

Ascher's essay on responding compassionately to human desperation forms a pair with the next essay, Anna Quindlen's "Homeless." Both concern the prevalent and disturbing condition of homelessness. The headnote to Ascher's essay anticipates students' possible objections that Ascher's essay is just a "New York story." Are what we think of as big-city problems really national problems?

The third writing suggestion gives students a chance to do research into and write about the rights of the homeless — to supplement the evidence of their own experience with facts, expert opinions, and so on. Students could research collaboratively, with small groups focusing on each of the following questions to cover more ground: How widespread is homelessness in your area? What are local attitudes toward the homeless? What provisions are made for the homeless? Are the homeless thought of differently on the national level? Each group could report its findings back to the class. (Note: If this sort of research is something you'd like to have students do fairly regularly, you might consider rotating the responsibility so that just one group works and reports on any given essay.)

QUESTIONS ON MEANING

1. They are examples of poor, unkempt, somewhat frightening, and probably homeless human beings.
2. Ascher's thesis isn't stated outright but appears to be something like this: The proximity and visibility of "the helpless" create disgust and fear, but they are also conditions that "give birth to empathy, the mother of compassion." Ascher's purpose is to heighten readers' awareness of this point, perhaps to make them more tolerant.

3. The homeless may be moved off the streets into hospitals and shelters. To Ascher, the humanity of the idea is mitigated by its less noble goal of burying the problem.
4. She is, shall we say, cautiously optimistic. Exposure to "There but" situations worked for the Greeks, but then they could walk away when the play was over. We, Ascher implies, must stay and deal with the problem.

QUESTIONS ON WRITING STRATEGY

1. Examples precede generalizations, probably because the examples are dramatic and draw the reader into the essay.
2. The author assumes readers who are economically comfortable: "We" are the bystanders with nice clothes, enough food, and homes to live in.
3. Ascher says charitably, or perhaps ironically, that the bystanders "daydream"; one man plays with his shoe. The people seem to represent all those who "look away" from the homeless to anyplace else.
4. Students' answers will vary.

QUESTIONS ON LANGUAGE

1. According to *The American Heritage Dictionary*, compassion is "the deep feeling of sharing the suffering of another, together with the inclination to give aid or support or to show mercy" (from Latin *com* + *pati*, "to bear with"). Empathy is "identification with and understanding of another's situation, feelings, and motives" (from Greek *empatheia*, "passion"). Empathy is thus the first half of compassion, which goes further to involve aid, support, or mercy.
2. Ascher uses *stay* as a transitive verb ("stay the cold"), whereas students may know it only as an intransitive verb ("stay in school") or even as a noun ("stay of execution"). The word comes from the Latin *stare*, "to stand."
3. London during Charles Dickens's time (he lived 1812–70) was a city of sharp contrasts between rich and poor.
4. Ascher's description is mainly objective, although she indicates sympathy for the first man (he has "carefully plaited dreadlocks," he walks with "the shuffle of the forgotten ones," he resembles "a bridegroom waiting at the altar"), and the unsparing detail in the description of both men is obviously intended to push us close to them.

BARBARA LAZEAR ASCHER ON WRITING

Ascher's comments on writing "tight" reinforce our own advice about coming to a point and writing concisely. The questions for discussion encourage students to explore in more detail just what makes writing tight, versus Ascher's opposing term "excessive," and how the former benefits readers.

ANNA QUINDLEN
Homeless

In this direct, personal essay, Quindlen uses detailed examples to explore what it is to be without a home. The third question on meaning provides a likely occasion for class discussion of the importance of a home and what a home *is*.

Barbara Lazear Ascher's "On Compassion" complements Quindlen's essay. A "Connections" writing suggestion after each essay helps students compare them. The collaborative research suggestion we provide for Ascher's essay (p. 36 of this manual) could be equally useful for Quindlen's, if you are not planning to use the essays together and you think your students may need more background on the issue of homelessness. If they already have this background, you might use Quindlen's essay as a springboard for discussing practical measures to help solve the problem. Working in groups of three or four, students could discuss the practicalities of Quindlen's claim that nothing but a home will solve the problems of the homeless: With this as a premise, what can be done to achieve this goal? Fifteen minutes of collaborative brainstorming on this question should give students enough time to prepare for a whole-class discussion of the issues Quindlen raises.

QUESTIONS ON MEANING

1. Quindlen's thesis (in pars. 8–9) is that abstraction from particular human beings to "issues" may distance us from problems and impede their solution — in this case, solving homelessness with homes.
2. The key is in paragraph 8: "The homeless" distances us from the problem suffered by particular people with particular needs.
3. Having a place to live makes you "somebody" (par. 2); it provides "certainty, stability, predictability, privacy" (4), and "pride of ownership" (7). Students' opinions about the importance of a home will vary. This question and the fourth writing suggestion provide good opportunities to discuss just what a home is, anyway: a house or an apartment? a room in a dorm? a heating grate?

QUESTIONS ON WRITING STRATEGY

1. Quindlen might have begun with a statement of her opinion (among other options), but the story of Ann draws the reader in and illustrates Quindlen's point. It also, perhaps even more important, reinforces Quindlen's argument that we should focus more on particular people with particular problems.
2. The examples bring Quindlen to earth and magnify the loss suffered by the homeless.
3. The author assumes that the reader has a home and feels strongly about it. Some students may not feel as strongly about having a home as Quindlen does. In paragraph 7, she addresses readers' likely assumption that shelters are better than the streets.

4. She wants readers to agree that nothing short of homes will solve the problems of homeless people.

QUESTIONS ON LANGUAGE

1. It invests her opinion with passion and urgency.
2. Not only do our hearts reside in and take nourishment from our homes, but we can show heart by providing homes for those who lack them.
3. *Crux* is a Latin word meaning "cross." In English it is a critical point or essential feature.

ANNA QUINDLEN ON WRITING

Analyzing the differences between Quindlen's essay and a conventional news report (the second question for discussion) may engage students. To us, the myriad differences come down to "My God" (par. 9): Such a fervently personal exclamation would never appear in straight news, not even in feature writing. Other examples include statements of belief, such as "You are where you live" (par. 2) and "That [a home] is everything" (4), or personal details, such as the Irish grandfather (3) and the beloved hot-water heater (4).

BILL BRYSON

Design Flaws

Not all students will identify with Bill Bryson's irritation at poorly designed consumer products, but they will certainly spot this essay as a sterling example of writing with examples. You might point out that to support his central point that many "everyday items [. . .] are ill thought out" (par. 11) Bryson offers one extended example (2–6), two more briefly developed examples (7–8, 9), and, finally, a list of additional examples (11).

Bryson clearly exaggerates, as is evident from the very outset. Yet underlying this humor is a real criticism of the fact that, in his view, many products — and especially electronics — are often not designed with easy or convenient use as a primary consideration. Ask students if they have design complaints of their own, starting perhaps with the design of something on campus.

Bryson's essay also offers an occasion to consider how humor works in writing. As anyone can attest who has ever tried to explain a joke, explaining humor is no easy task, but still the effort can be illuminating. After they've read the essay, have students divide into small groups to consider what they find funniest in Bryson's writing (our favorite is his send-up of auto design in par. 8). Then ask each group to report back to the class with an analysis of this instance of humor. Based on such discussion, students can at least learn what tickles other people, and that may help them understand what tickles them.

QUESTIONS ON MEANING

1. Bryson's purpose is partly to entertain (see the discussion of tone under "Questions on Language"), but he believes he has a legitimate gripe (a "serious inquiry," par. 2) about consumer products that are designed in ways that make them difficult or even impossible to use. Bryson states his thesis at the end of paragraph 10.
2. He uses the shoes for contrast: They are designed (even overdesigned) to the last detail with the runner's needs in mind, while less specialized products are simply "ill thought out" (par. 11).
3. Bryson complains that computer keyboards have too many keys most people never use, encourage typing errors and overwriting of correct text, and lack a key for the fraction $1/2$. Students might question whether the elaborate process Bryson describes for inserting the fraction is really necessary, since one can easily type "1 slash 2."

QUESTIONS ON WRITING STRATEGY

1. Bryson offers three detailed examples (his computer keyboard, the shallow container on his car's dashboard, and videocassette recorders) and also lists several others in paragraph 11. We'd say yes, he supports his generalization.
2. Bryson seems to assume that his readers share his frustrations with poorly designed products — that readers are with him in his experiences and complaints. This assumption is most obvious in paragraph 9: "Now I am not going to prattle on about how impossible it is to program the typical VCR because you know that already."
3. By acknowledging that some contemporary products are well designed (even causing "gratitude and wonder"), Bryson makes it clear that he's not a complete curmudgeon who opposes all design efforts. Thus his complaints seem more legitimate. (See also the first question on language, below.)
4. In each case, design flaws (cause) lead to a product or one of its features being difficult or impossible to use (effect).

QUESTIONS ON LANGUAGE

1. As noted earlier, Bryson's acknowledgment that some contemporary products have great value to him helps to overcome any "old guy" tone, and his persistent exaggeration keeps the tone humorous (for instance, his son's "sixty-one hundred pairs of running shoes," par. 1). We'd characterize the tone as perplexed ("I haven't the faintest idea," 4) and lightly whiny ("Nor will I observe how irritating it is that you must cross the room and get down on your stomach to confirm that [the VCR] is actually recording," 9).
2. Bryson shifts from formal, somewhat inflated language ("seemingly limitless range of scrupulously engineered, biomechanically efficient footwear") to highly informal slang ("why does my keyboard suck?"). The effect is to surprise readers while setting up his subject and establishing his humorous tone.
3. There is obviously no Dodge model called the "Excreta"; although it sounds as if it might be the name of a real car, the linguistic association with *excrement* is meant to be a joke.

4. In philosophy, a *metaphysical question* deals with essential reality or the nature of being. In paragraph 5 Bryson comically poses such a question by asking whether a "Pause" key that does nothing "is therefore doing its job."

BILL BRYSON ON WRITING

We couldn't resist Bryson's acerbic comments on spelling checkers, believing that students can benefit from every reminder about the inadequacies of the programs. Admittedly, Bryson's checker seems to have been particularly bad, but the point remains. In our last question, we mean of course to lead students to conclude that their own careful proofreading is the best remedy for spelling errors.

WILLIAM SAFIRE

Fulminations

William Safire's essay addresses language errors of which even many careful speakers and writers are guilty: the everyday misuses of specialized terms such as *organic* and *quantum*. You might want to give students a chance before they read the essay to discuss how they define the terms and uses Safire focuses on — *organic* food, the *epicenter* of an event or place, *exponential* growth, a *quantum* jump, the *synergy* of a corporation, and so on. (Such discussion could initially take place in small groups, each perhaps focusing on one or two terms and then reporting back their definitions to the whole class.) Many students will have encountered these terms used popularly to mean exactly what Safire's experts argue they do not mean technically. With this awareness, students can better appreciate what these experts are "fulminating" about.

As part of your discussion, you might want to ask students why such popular misuses (and, in the case of *architect*, such misappropriations) so offend the specialists who use the terms in their strict technical (or traditional) senses. Do they have good reasons to protect their terms, or are they just nitpickers? If you have any linguistic *bêtes noires* of your own — *comprise* to mean *compose*, for example, or *anxious* to mean *eager* — you might bring them up and explain your reasons.

QUESTIONS ON MEANING

1. "The specialists are in open rebellion at the theft of their vocabularies" (par. 1) — the theft, it becomes clear, having been perpetrated mostly by the general public.
2. A *fulmination*, from the Latin for "to strike with lightning," is a vehement, even violent, denunciation of a serious infraction. Safire's title and the uses of the term in paragraphs 1, 2, and 16 exaggerate: The complaints of the specialists hardly constitute true fulminations. Safire achieves a humorous effect, somewhat at the expense of the specialists.

3. *Organic:* not food grown without chemicals, but life based on hydrocar-
    bons (pars. 2–4). *Epicenter:* not "the most center," but the surface of the
    earth directly above an earthquake's center or possibly directly below a
    bomb explosion (5–6). *Exponential:* not rapid, but proportional to size (7–
    8). *Quantum:* not extremely large, but quick, leaping.
4. *Myopic* means "nearsighted," able to see close and not far, but it's often
    misused to mean "can't see what's right in front of you." *Beg the question*
    means to assume as true what you are claiming (and should be proving),
    but it's often misused to mean something like "demand that we ask the
    question," as in "Your saying you're hungry begs the question of where to
    eat."

QUESTIONS ON WRITING STRATEGY

1. Safire's purpose is to share the complaints of specialists regarding the
    popular misuse of technical terms, so it is appropriate to quote the exact
    comments of the specialists.
2. Transitions can be found at the beginnings of paragraphs 3 ("Right on"),
    5 ("too"), 7 ("these terms"), 9 ("however"), 12 ("too"), and 16 ("other fields").
3. Readers of the *New York Times Magazine* would of course be well edu-
    cated and would have a general, rather than a specialized, interest in
    language. (Readers of Safire's regular column might have a higher than
    average general interest.) Safire's tone and examples definitely assume
    an educated audience (for example, the deliberately formal, almost
    highfalutin opening paragraph and the impressive academic credentials
    of most of his correspondents).
4. Throughout, Safire contrasts the popular misuses of the terms he dis-
    cusses with their precise technical meanings.

QUESTIONS ON LANGUAGE

1. *Nonagenarian* may be the least familiar word Safire uses, unless stu-
    dents have very elderly relatives. From the Latin *nonaginta*, "ninety," the
    word refers to a person in his or her tenth decade.
2. In all four examples Safire plays on the specialists' subject. In paragraph
    5 geologists criticize "lay writers with rocks in their heads" — rocks, of
    course, being geologists' subject. In paragraph 7 "a totality of mathema-
    ticians" plays on their "totaling" activity. In paragraph 13 an architect's
    complaint is "superstructured" by a project engineer, a person who de-
    signs structures. And in paragraph 16 ophthalmologists — doctors who
    specialize in eyes — "narrow their eyes" at "nearsighted" use of *myopic*,
    which means "nearsighted."
3. To help students get Safire's joke, we translate the French *bêtes noires* in
    a footnote. Both "This is my pet, Peeve" and "meet my *bête, Noire*" main-
    tain the word order of the original expression and name the troubling
    object with the second word in the expression.

WILLIAM SAFIRE ON WRITING

Many students will have asked the question Safire attributes to his readers ("Who the hell are you to say?"), if not about Safire then about other lan-

guage authorities they've encountered — parents, dictionaries, teachers. Safire's answer is refreshingly blunt.

We were somewhat hesitant to print Safire's statement that the self-conscious writer is "a nerd, a schnook, and a wimp" because of course some students will count themselves as self-conscious writers. We went ahead because of the further point Safire makes, which we hope will give heart to these students — that simply caring can carry one across this line from self-conscious to conscious, into possession of the language.

BRENT STAPLES

Black Men and Public Space

As Brent Staples demonstrates, the most gripping and convincing examples are often brief anecdotes. In this essay, examples of Staples's discovery — of the "alienation that comes of being ever the suspect" — take up most of the room. In addition, Staples gives examples of "tough guys" who died in street violence (par. 7) and precautions he takes to appear less threatening (11–12). His vivid opening paragraph, with its opening sentence pretending that he is a killer, deserves special scrutiny.

For collaborative work on this essay, we suggest focusing on just what public space is and what happens to us when we enter it. Students might try to define *public space* by coming up with examples and discovering what the examples have in common. How do they feel different in private and in public space? Once they have their examples and definitions, the groups could reassemble as a class to arrive at a generally accepted definition.

As an alternative, you could encourage students to explore their own feelings about public space. Are there places they feel more or less welcome, safe, at home? The "Journal Writing" topic after the essay gives students an opportunity to explore such questions. They might also find it helpful to generate a list of generalizations in small groups. What does it mean to be a student, a woman, a man, a member of a particular religious or ethnic group, and so on in American public spaces? Working in small groups, students will probably feel freer to discuss their experiences; you might even consider dividing the groups along gender lines for those women and men who might be reluctant to speak up.

QUESTIONS ON MEANING

1. Your students will state the author's purpose variously. Staples writes to communicate his experience as a black man of whom others are needlessly frightened. He writes to explain his discovery that, when mistaken for a criminal, it is wiser not to react with rage but to take precautions to appear less threatening. However the writer's purpose is put, this is a piece of personal experience and observation; we do not see Staples trying to predict the future or proposing any long-term solutions.

2. If we keep on reading, we find Staples acknowledging that women are often the victims of street violence, some of it perpetrated by young African American males. He believes, though, that reports have been exaggerated. He takes pains to make clear that he isn't dangerous. He considers himself not a tough guy but a "softy" who hates to cut up a raw chicken (par. 2); he has shrunk from street fights (6); his own brother and others have been killed in "episodes of bravado" (7).

3. By using it in this context, Staples gives the word *survivor* fresh connotations. Usually it suggests rugged strength, ability to endure, and so on, but here Staples helps us to understand that, in an area of gang warfare, knifings, and murders, timidity is a form of self-preservation.

QUESTIONS ON WRITING STRATEGY

1. Staples convinces by giving examples: anecdotes from his own experience (pars. 1, 5, 8, 9) and that of another African American male (10).

2. The examples are set forth in detail too rich to seem a mere bare-bones list. The similar nature of all the examples lends the essay coherence and, to give it even more, Staples uses transitions skillfully. In nearly every paragraph, the opening sentence is transitional, and transitional phrases indicate time: "One day," "Another time," "a couple of summers ago."

3. Beginning with the scene of a near-empty street at night and a frightened woman fleeing him, Staples dramatizes his thesis and immediately sets forth a typical, recurrent situation.

QUESTIONS ON LANGUAGE

1. As we have seen, Staples's essay uses a narrative hook at the start and, to make the hook grab hard, the writer deliberately misleads us. The word *victim* leads us to take him for a self-confessed criminal. By the end of the paragraph, we doubt our impression, and in his second paragraph, Staples explains that he is harmless, can hardly take a knife to a chicken. If we look back on the opening paragraph, we see the discrepancy between the word *victim* and reality. In truth, the fleeing woman is mistaken and fearful, a person on whom the innocent narrator has no designs. This discrepancy makes clear the writer's ironic attitude. As the essay proceeds, he expresses a mingling of anger, humor, and resignation.

2. We admire Staples's use of that fine old formal word *constitutionals*, "walks taken for health." Like the expression "robust constitution," though, it seems a throwback to another era.

3. Students will have fun defining *dicey* ("risky, unpredictable"), recalling that shooting dice is, of course, a game of chance.

BRENT STAPLES ON WRITING

Staples provides a clear and enlightening illustration of how writing generates ideas, instead of simply recording them, as most inexperienced writers seem to believe. His comparison of essay- and news-writing is related: The work begins in the details, in the data, the observations, the feelings — in the facts, as Staples says. The big picture depends on the details.

7
COMPARISON AND CONTRAST
Setting Things Side by Side

Many students have an irrational dread of the method of comparison and contrast, perhaps acquired from meeting it on essay examinations. We do our best to reassure them (in "The Method") that it is manageable with a little planning. The chapter offers extra help with outlining; we try to take some of the mystique out of it, and we urge the student not to feel a slave to a mere charting of letters and numerals. For a short paper, the formal outline — of the Roman numeral *I*, capital *A* variety — is surely more trouble than it's worth. But in writing any paper that compares and contrasts, a plan to follow, at least a rough plan, is especially useful.

Suzanne Britt's "Neat People vs. Sloppy People" is easy reading, but it makes sharp comments on human behavior. We've paired it with another humorous piece on human behavior, Dave Barry's "Batting Clean-Up and Striking Out." Both essays contrast neatniks and others, but they explain the differences differently.

Keeping up the humor, David Sedaris's essay, "Remembering My Childhood on the Continent of Africa," amusingly contrasts the writer's dull life in an American suburb with his friend's garishly textured life as the child of a nomadic diplomat. The next two essays in this chapter are more serious, though not somber. Bruce Catton's "Grant and Lee" remains a classic example of a method clearly serving a writer's purpose. And Nancy Mairs's "Disability" uses comparison to argue for greater representation of disabled persons in the media. Finally, Alice Walker's story "Everyday Use" contrasts, through the eyes of their mother, a daughter who has gone far and one who never left.

For introducing the method of comparison and contrast, here's a lightweight illustration possibly worth reading to your class. At least it suggests that in comparing and contrasting, a writer has to consider a whole series of points. Craig Hosmer, a Republican and, at the time, representative from California's thirty-second district, introduced the following advice into the *Congressional Record* for October 1, 1974. (We found this item in *American Humor: An Interdisciplinary Newsletter*, Fall 1983, and offer it in a slightly abbreviated version, the better to illustrate comparison and contrast.)

How to Tell Republicans from Democrats

Republicans employ exterminators.
Democrats step on bugs.

Democrats name their children after popular sports figures, politicians, and entertainers.
Republican children are named after their parents or grandparents, according to where the money is.

Republicans tend to keep their shades drawn, although there is seldom any reason why they should.
Democrats ought to, but don't.

Republicans study the financial pages of the newspaper.
Democrats put them in the bottom of the bird cage.

Democrats buy most books that have been banned somewhere.
Republicans form censorship committees and read them as a group.

Democrats give their worn-out clothes to those less fortunate.
Republicans wear theirs.

Democrats raise Airedales, kids, and taxes.
Republicans raise dahlias, Dalmatians, and eyebrows.

Democrats eat the fish they catch.
Republicans hang them on the wall.

Republicans sleep in twin beds — some even in separate rooms.
That is why there are more Democrats.

COMPARISON AND CONTRAST IN OTHER CHAPTERS.   A number of essays elsewhere in the book also develop by comparison and contrast:

Part Two

Sherman Alexie, "Indian Education"
Brad Manning, "Arm Wrestling with My Father"
Sarah Vowell, "Shooting Dad"
Anna Quindlen, "Homeless"
Armin A. Brott, "Not All Men Are Sly Foxes"
Deborah Tannen, "But What Do You Mean?"
Gloria Naylor, "The Meanings of a Word"
Christine Leong, "Being a Chink"
Marie Winn, "TV Addiction"
Laura Fraser, "Why I Stopped Being a Vegetarian"

Part Three

Maxine Hong Kingston, "No Name Woman"
Richard Rodriguez, "Aria: A Memoir of a Bilingual Childhood"
Cornel West, "Race Matters"
E. B. White, "Once More to the Lake"

SUZANNE BRITT

Neat People vs. Sloppy People

Whatever Suzanne Britt believes, she believes wholeheartedly. Then she merrily sets out to convince her readers that she's right. A danger in teaching this essay, perhaps, is that students without Britt's skill may be inspired to emulate her slapdash unreasonableness without quite achieving the desired effect. Some students, though, just might surprise you with the delightful writing they can produce with this essay as their inspiration.

Small groups can be useful for helping students through the brainstorming part of writing an essay. Students might appreciate having time to talk about the points of comparison they have come up with in preparing to write an essay for either of our first two writing suggestions. Group members can help each other expand their lists of comparative points and find the details that will bring these points to life.

QUESTIONS ON MEANING

1. Whoever said it failed to perceive Britt's humor.
2. Britt is hardly impartial. It's easy to see that her sympathies lie with sloppy people and that she considers herself one of them. Mostly, she writes to amuse and entertain.
3. "As always" means what it says. Yes, Britt is saying — with tongue only partially in cheek — the distinctions among people are moral.

QUESTIONS ON WRITING STRATEGY

1. Britt's tone is blunt, assured, and, of course, hyperbolic. The tone is established from the start: "Neat people are lazier and meaner than sloppy people." Words and phrases that illustrate the tone abound throughout the essay.
2. Britt finds no similarities at all between the two. Had she mentioned any, her essay would be less exaggerated and would therefore lose some of its force. Writers who aren't exaggerating might give short shift to similarities, too, if they are obvious or irrelevant.
3. These broad statements are generalizations because they make conclusive assertions on the basis of some evidence — although, of course, Britt is deliberately exaggerating whatever evidence she has. By using so many generalizations, Britt compounds the outrageous nature of her essay. Her humor derives from her being unfair to neat people and finding no fault at all with their opposites.
4. The examples do specify the kinds of behavior Britt has in mind, but they are themselves generalizations about the two kinds of people. They illustrate behavior but not particular persons.

QUESTIONS ON LANGUAGE

1. *The American Heritage Dictionary* tells us that *métier* is a word that be- gan as the Latin *ministerium* ("occupation") and then became Vulgar Latin *misterium* and Old French *mestier* before assuming its present spelling and meaning ("specialty") in modern French and English.
2. The word is not to be understood literally, but humorously, as are *recti- tude, stupendous* (par. 2), *excavation* (5), and *vicious* (9). Students may argue for one or two others that they perceive are not to be taken liter- ally.

SUZANNE BRITT ON WRITING

Here are some responses to the questions for discussion.

1. Britt doesn't offer much specific advice for the student assigned to write about Guatemala. But the method she urges, it seems, is to study the subject long enough to discover some personal connection or interest in it.
2. Britt's first paragraph yields at least two metaphors ("You have to suck out all the marrow of whatever you do" and "My answer is rock bottom and hard") and a simile ("silence falls like prayers across the room"). More colorful still are the similes two paragraphs later, in which the student is advised to gather "your life around you as a mother hen gath- ers her brood, as a queen settles the folds in her purple robes." There's hyperbole, too, in the next paragraph: "an interminable afternoon in a biology lab."
3. What is the *tone* of Britt's remarks? Though she regards writing with humor and zest, and doesn't take it in grim earnest, clearly she deeply cares about it. In the end, she equates it with an act of faith.

DAVE BARRY

Batting Clean-Up and Striking Out

Dave Barry is one of America's best known and most prolific humorists, and his essay makes a perfect companion piece to Suzanne Britt's. Both writ- ers rely on exaggeration and generalization to make readers laugh.

Students respond differently to humor based on stereotypes. While some will see this kind of humor as cathartic, others will be annoyed or even an- gered by it. The second through fourth writing suggestions all ask students to respond to Barry's use of stereotypes for their humorous potential. In addi- tion, you may want to give students a chance to express their reactions in class. Encourage those who were offended by the essay to voice and clarify their objections; encourage those who enjoyed the essay to defend it.

QUESTIONS ON MEANING

1. Barry's purpose is to entertain and amuse. His humor is characterized by broad generalizations (such as the first sentence); tall tales (the "hormonal secretion" and the Pompeii example, par. 2); exaggeration ("clumps large enough to support agriculture," 2; "bacteria you could enter in a rodeo," 3); self-effacement ("an important project on the Etch-a-Sketch" and the pajamas anecdote, 4); and a tongue-in-cheek tone ("my specific family unit" and "Standard Male Cleaning Implements," 3; "a sensitive and caring kind of guy," 4; "human relationships or something," 8).
2. Barry is anything but objective. He is clearly writing from a male point of view, and he understands male behavior. However, his tone is far too facetious for the essay to be taken as a justification of boorish behavior. He makes as much fun of himself as of anyone else.
3. Barry seems to take the differences between the sexes as a given. He is less interested in reconciliation than in exploiting gender misunderstandings for their humorous potential.

QUESTIONS ON WRITING STRATEGY

1. A subject-by-subject organization would have undermined Barry's examples, which depend on the interaction of women and men to make their point.
2. From the first ironic sentence we know to take everything Barry says with a grain of salt.
3. The second half of Barry's thesis sentence is in paragraph 5: "The opposite side of the dirt coin, of course, is sports. This is an area where men tend to feel very sensitive and women tend to be extremely callous." Students (and teachers) may disagree over whether the divided thesis sentence helps or hurts. A single, early sentence might have tied the parts together, but it also would have stolen an element of surprise from the essay.
4. Barry effectively appropriates the force of Poe's story, giving his own anecdote an added dimension. The incongruity of Poe's horror story and Barry's domestic scene produces a comic effect.
5. This example is obviously invented. Its purpose is not to persuade but, like everything else in the essay, to amuse.

QUESTIONS ON LANGUAGE

1. Students sensitive to its connotation may object to Barry's use of *prattled* to describe the women's talk, even though he clearly intends it humorously. The word means "to talk idly or meaninglessly" and comes from a Dutch word, *praten,* with the same meaning.
2. The breathless, digressive nature of the sentence adds to the humor of the anecdote. It has the oral quality of someone gossiping on the telephone.
3. Again, the orality of the text is increased. We can hear the emphasis in Barry's voice, the near hysteria of "*during a World Series Game*" (par. 6), the sports-announcer tone of "Annual Fall Classic."
4. By using *males*, Barry creates an anthropological distance between himself and his subject.

DAVE BARRY ON WRITING

Writing is a serious job for this humor writer, and students may be surprised at how difficult it can be for a funny man to wring a laugh from a reader. We appreciate Barry's observation that writing is, to quote Edison on genius, "one percent inspiration and ninety-nine percent perspiration." We also appreciate Barry's insistence that experience helps, a lesson that students may learn themselves as they gain more practice writing.

DAVID SEDARIS

Remembering My Childhood on the Continent of Africa

This essay is humorist David Sedaris's account of the exotic childhood and adolescent experiences of his friend Hugh — who grew up in various African outposts as the son of a US diplomat — as contrasted with Sedaris's far more mundane youth in suburban North Carolina. Students may initially have some trouble with Sedaris's subtle irony. You could begin discussion by asking class members whether they think Sedaris truly wishes he could have traded places with Hugh, whose youth, while "fascinating" in retrospect (par. 13), was in fact marked by some pretty gruesome and dangerous events. Sedaris admits that he can't acknowledge this fact because it means "I should have been happy with what I had" (21). Instead he retreats into fantasy, safely appropriating the stories he has heard from Hugh as memories of his own.

To pursue this question further, you could divide the class into small groups and have each group analyze the essay for evidence of Sedaris's clear awareness that Hugh's childhood "was not as glamorous as it sounds" (12). In reporting back their findings to the class, each group could consider what Sedaris seems to be suggesting about his own personality.

Sedaris's reading of *Me Talk Pretty One Day*, from which this essay comes, is available on audiotape and CD. Students may enjoy his distinctive delivery, familiar to anyone who has heard him on National Public Radio.

QUESTIONS ON MEANING

1. Sedaris contrasts his own "unspeakably dull" middle-class American childhood (par. 8) with the much more exotic and eventful childhood of his friend Hugh, who, as the son of a diplomat, grew up in various countries in Africa.
2. The thesis might seem to be that Sedaris's life was dull compared to Hugh's (par. 8) or that Sedaris makes up for his dull life by appropriating Hugh's (21). But hovering over all, just hinted, is the larger idea that Hugh's childhood, while much more exciting than Sedaris's and food for resentment and imagination, had terrible costs that Sedaris would not have wanted to pay.

3. Sedaris's envy is essentially ironic because many of Hugh's childhood experiences seem pretty lonely and harrowing, beginning with the field trip to the slaughterhouse. This is true even when Sedaris writes of something that one might indeed be envious of: For example, Hugh's family had servants, but they included guards with machetes (par. 11), suggesting that the family was always in danger. In paragraph 21 Sedaris notes that while he was longing for more exotic adventures as a child, Hugh ("[s]omeone unknown to me" at the time) was probably longing for something more normal.

QUESTIONS ON WRITING STRATEGY

1. Sedaris's point-by-point organization can be outlined as follows: comparison of field trips (pars. 1–7); of daily life (8); of access to popular culture, specifically movies and the circumstances of viewing them (9–10); of servants and security (11); of dangerous experiences (12–13); of meeting a celebrity (14); of Sedaris's ten-day visit with his senile grandmother and Hugh's two years living with strangers (15–19); and of vacations (20–21).
2. A monkey is a particularly exotic pet that many children might long to own. Hugh's monkey comes to represent for Sedaris everything that he envies about Hugh's childhood.
3. The opening conversation establishes the relationship between Sedaris and Hugh and particularly the fact that Hugh seems unfazed by his odd experiences. This opening also makes clear that Sedaris has had many such conversations with Hugh, on which he bases his knowledge of Hugh's experiences.
4. Sedaris narrates stories from his own life and from Hugh's to point up how different their experiences have been.

QUESTIONS ON LANGUAGE

1. The second and third, fourth and fifth, and sixth and seventh sentences in the paragraph are parallel in structure, which highlights the contrast that concludes each sentence. As Sedaris wittily puts it, "The verbs are the same, but [Hugh] definitely wins the prize when it comes to nouns and objects."
2. The term "petty thief" emphasizes the self-deprecating portrait that Sedaris has presented throughout. His use of Hugh's memories represents no "spiritual symbiosis" but is merely a way for Sedaris to live vicariously through the other man's experiences.
3. Almost any paragraph will provide examples of specific, concrete language. In paragraph 6 examples include "low-ceilinged concrete building," "small white piglet," "its dainty hooves clicking against the concrete floor," "class gathered in a circle," "turned from face to face," "drew a pistol from his back pocket, held it against the animal's temple, and shot the piglet, execution-style," "Blood-spattered, frightened children wept."
4. *Symbiosis*, from the Greek word for "living together," implies the intimate union of two dissimilar types.

DAVID SEDARIS ON WRITING

You might take a poll of the students in your class: How many have ever used a typewriter? Sedaris's animus against the computer and love of the typewriter probably grows quainter by the day, but we like what he says about the *feel* of writing, the sense "that you're actually building something."

BRUCE CATTON

Grant and Lee: A Study in Contrasts

If ever that weary term *classic* applied to an essay, this is it. Where can you find a neater illustration of comparison and contrast? First Catton contrasts the two generals, then he compares them — gracefully moving from broad generalizations to specific evidence. Introducing the essay, you might remind students that they know a good deal about Grant and Lee already (or reveal that they need more knowledge). If your campus is far from Virginia, you may wish to acquaint the class with the connotations of *tidewater Virginia* (old family name, wealth, landowning, patrician). (See the third question on language.) A small group of students could research Virginia, the generals, and the Civil War and present their findings as a counterpoint to Catton's observations. (Note: If this sort of research is something you'd like to have students do fairly regularly, you might consider rotating the responsibility so that just one group works and reports on any given essay.)

QUESTIONS ON MEANING

1. Catton's central purpose is to explain how Grant and Lee stood for opposing social forces. Though he remarks in paragraph 13 that the two generals differed in personality, he doesn't expand on this observation. The qualities he cites (daring, resourcefulness, and so on) seem traits not of personality but of character.
2. Lee, an aristocrat from tidewater Virginia, believed in a leisure class of landowners responsible to their community and obliged to be models of strength and virtue. Grant, son of a frontier tanner, held with self-reliance, competition, and a society in which the most resourceful will rise. Lee's first loyalty was to his native soil; Grant's was to the nation. Lee's commitment was to the agrarian society of the past; Grant's, to an urban industrial future.
3. Both had "utter tenacity and fidelity," "daring and resourcefulness." Most important, both possessed the ability to turn quickly from war to peace. They made possible a reconciliation of North and South, for which all later Americans are indebted to them.
4. Each by nature was a warrior of "utter tenacity and fidelity" (par. 14), who fought for the ideals of his people (10–11).

QUESTIONS ON WRITING STRATEGY

1. *American Story* is a collection addressed to general readers with a special interest in American history. Catton doesn't assume a profound knowledge of the Civil War on their part, but he does assume that the campaigns of Petersburg, Second Manassas, Chancellorsville, and Vicksburg (in pars. 14–15) will be at least somewhat familiar to his readers.

2. Catton rounds out his essay by so doing; he stresses his point (made in his opening paragraph) that at Appomattox "a great new chapter" in American life began.

3. By arranging the essay to show that Grant and Lee, despite their profound differences of background and outlook, agreed on one essential, Catton saves his most important point for last. This structure makes the point more effectively than if Catton had begun by asserting that Grant and Lee were much alike and had then spent the body of his essay differentiating between them. Important points often stand out more when the reader is left with them.

4. Catton's view of Grant (who was "everything Lee was not") is stated in paragraphs 7–12, an extended contrast. His comparison of the two men, considerably shorter, begins in paragraph 13 and continues to the end of the essay. Students may be told to expect that, in expository writing, differences will often require more words to explain than similarities. No law requires that a writer give equal space to both.

5. Nearly every paragraph begins with a sentence containing some transition: sometimes no more than a word or phrase, such as "these men," "they," "each man," referring back to both Grant and Lee. Some transitions are explicitly comparative, such as "on the other hand" (par. 11). The most crucial sentence of transition is the one that opens paragraph 13: "Yet it was not all contrast, after all" — announcing the start of Catton's comparison.

6. The tone is sympathetic, admiring, and respectful. By imagining Lee with lance and banner, Catton hints that he finds the general's chivalric ideals a bit preposterous. But he is referring back to the point he makes in paragraph 5: Lee's way of life descended from "the age of knighthood." That he thinks its values outdated doesn't mean he finds them silly, nor that he mocks Lee for being their representative.

7. The classification broadens the significance of the comparison from two generals to the whole population. The analysis provides Catton with his points of comparison, his differences and similarities.

QUESTIONS ON LANGUAGE

1. Like most figures of speech, Catton's add vigor and concreteness to his prose. They include the metaphor of "two conflicting currents" (par. 3); the metaphor of an age "transplanted" (5); the metaphor of the "past that had settled into grooves" (8); the metaphors of the nation's expanding horizons and of the "dollars-and-cents stake" (9); the metaphor of Grant's seeing the Union as the ground under his feet (11); the personification of Grant as "the modern man emerging," the metaphor of the stage, and that of Lee as a knight with banner and lance (12); the metaphor of Grant and Lee as two battered boxers, each able to "remain on his feet and lift his two fists" (14).

2. *Poignant*, from the French verb *poindre* ("to sting"), means "sharply painful to the feelings; piercing or wounding." Clearly it is a stronger and

more energetic word here than *touching, sad,* or *teary.* You might care to remind students (if you aren't tired of it) of Twain's remark about the right word being the lightning; the almost right word, the lightning bug.

3. Eastern Virginia's tidewater region, the low-lying coastal plain bisected by Chesapeake Bay, is so named because tidal water flows up its bays, inlets, and rivers. It is the area of the oldest colonial settlements (including Jamestown, Yorktown, and Williamsburg), where large plantations were established.

4. *Aristocratic* refers to a privileged class responsible for the well-being of the people it served as leaders.

5. Context will supply these meanings almost as well as a dictionary. This might be an opportune moment to point out that you don't expect students to interrupt their reading of an essay fourteen times to rummage a dictionary. They usually can figure out the sense of words they don't know if they pay attention to other words in the neighborhood. Those they can't figure out they can circle and save up for a one-time trip to the dictionary.

BRUCE CATTON ON WRITING

In response to the questions: According to Jensen, concentration and getting up early in the morning made Catton the writer he was. And Catton the writer, it would seem, criticized his own work as unsparingly as Catton the editor criticized the work of others.

NANCY MAIRS

Disability

This essay may stimulate intense discussions, as students reexamine their own attitudes toward persons with disabilities. How true do students find Mairs's assessment of the "invisibility" of the disabled in our culture? Ask students to keep a log for one day, noting any references to or images of the physically challenged that they encounter. Have them share their findings in small groups. This activity should help them warm up for a full class discussion that seeks to understand the effects of "invisibility" on everyone, the "temporarily abled" and disabled alike.

Your campus may have an office or department devoted to the concerns of students and staff with disabilities. It could be productive to invite someone from that office to give a brief talk to your class about the experiences of the physically challenged at your institution.

QUESTIONS ON MEANING

1. It shows the woman as one-dimensional, dominated by the fit male doctor, and confined by her illness.

2. The advertiser's dream — someone who loves to buy things and would listen attentively to sales pitches.

3. Images of the physically challenged would help the nondisabled realize their connection to the disabled, would be fair, would bolster the self-esteem of persons with disabilities, and might actually help to sell things.

4. The media should treat "disability as a normal characteristic" (par. 7) because disability does not entirely define a person (4), its effacement from the media undermines the self-esteem of the disabled (6), and positive representation would help broaden the outlook of the "Temporarily Abled" and help prepare them for disability (7).

5. Mairs's purpose is to bring an injustice to the reader's attention, showing how people with disabilities are erased from public awareness.

QUESTIONS ON WRITING STRATEGY

1. Mairs compares herself with a disabled woman in a TV drama (pars. 2–4) and compares the effects on the disabled and the nondisabled of not showing disabled persons in the media (6–7). The comparisons clarify that disabled persons are otherwise "normal" and doubly reinforce Mairs's thesis.

2. "I haven't noticed any woman like me on television" (par. 1); "physical disability [. . .] doesn't devour one wholly" (4); if disability "is effaced completely," the viewer "won't feel threatened" (5); "This kind of effacement or isolation has painful, even dangerous consequences" (6). Students are likely to find Mairs's generalizations valid: Her assessment of television images would dovetail with theirs, and her authority as one who knows what it is to be disabled is unassailable.

3. Mairs defines her own characteristics (par. 1), then states that she cannot find them on TV. By using the word "Actually" (2), Mairs juxtaposes her generalization with one possible exception — which proves not to be one after all.

4. Mairs's tone is partly humorous: "I'm easy to spot even in a crowd" (par. 1), "sucking breath mints and splashing on cologne and swigging wine coolers" (6). But it is also serious: "effacement or isolation has painful, even dangerous consequences" (6). Mairs's humor makes her essay more accessible; her seriousness underscores the gravity of her topic.

5. Mairs gives examples of television shows that depict the disabled as powerless (pars. 2–3); of the products she uses (tampons, mouthwash, lotions, bleach [4]); of ads in which the disabled could appear (5). The examples are ordinary, everyday ones. The effect of the examples is to show how the disabled could be made part of the television world.

QUESTIONS ON LANGUAGE

1. Mairs's irony exposes the ridiculousness of the attitudes she opposes. Another example: "an illness-of-the week like the daily special at your local diner" (par. 2).

2. Multiple sclerosis is a progressively degenerative disease in which the coatings of the body's nerves decay. As nerve impulses stop being transmitted, the person with multiple sclerosis loses control of his or her movements.

3. Mairs chooses the word *effaced* to describe the disabled, rather than *erased*, making a distinction between something that has been covered up and something that has been removed.

4. The connotations are negative. Mairs is forestalling any nervous, eva-
    sive, or hostile reactions from her readers.
5. The "Temporarily Abled" are people without disabilities. Some disabled
    persons use this phrase to show how arbitrary fitness and disability are
    and how disability might befall an able-bodied person at any time.

ALICE WALKER

Everyday Use

Before students read Alice Walker's well-known short story, you may want
to provide them with a bit of historical background. "Everyday Use" was originally published in 1973, after the first wave of the civil rights movement,
when many younger African Americans were beginning to take advantage of
newly won educational and economic opportunities while also embracing their
cultural heritage both as Africans and as descendants of slaves. Yet in many
parts of the country — and especially in the Deep South, where the story takes
place — old ways died hard. It is against this backdrop that Dee's return to
her mother's rural home should be read.

A central question to pose in discussing the story is "Where do one's sympathies lie?" Dee clearly comes off as pretentious and self-centered — even
callous in her dealings with her family — but just as clearly she represents "a
new day" for African Americans (par. 81) and a leap forward from a mother
who cannot "even imagine [. . .] looking a strange white man in the eye" (6).
And while the mother and Maggie are admirable in their purity, simplicity,
and loving devotion to each other, they are also mired in a past social order
that keeps them impoverished and severely limits the scope of their world.
Students should come to see that it is a testament to Walker's imaginative
powers that the story offers no simple sense of who might be right and who
might be wrong.

You could have students discuss in small groups how they respond to the
characters, and, more specifically, whether they agree with Dee that the family quilts should be preserved essentially as works of art instead of being put
to "everyday use." Groups could then report on any differences of opinion and
the source of these differences, which could lead to a larger class discussion
of the story's multiple layers.

QUESTIONS ON MEANING

1. The explicit contrast, made by the mother, is that between the two daugh-
    ters: Maggie is shy, awkward, "not bright," and rather plain, but also
    sweet-natured and devoted to her family, while Dee is outspoken, styl-
    ish, intelligent, and attractive, but sharp-tongued and self-centered. The
    more implicit contrast (suggested by much that Dee says, including her
    parting words in par. 81) is that between the traditional lifestyle and
    attitudes of the mother and Maggie and the more "progressive" view of
    Dee.

2.   She regards the name Dee (from "Dicie") as a legacy of slavery because slaveholders gave their slaves Anglicized names. Like many African Americans, she takes on a new name with roots in African languages. At the same time, however, her given name is part of a family tradition that goes back for many generations, as the narrator makes clear, so her change of name can be seen as a denial of that tradition.

3.   Dee presumably wants pictures of the house to show friends how she grew up and how her family still lives — proof, in a sense, of her "black" authenticity. The quilts also represent something she can display as representative of her black heritage. It is ironic that, as a teenager, Dee hated the house she grew up in (par. 10) and thought the quilts "old-fashioned, out of style," refusing one when her mother offered it before she left for college (67).

4.   Dee charges in paragraph 66 that Maggie would put their grandmother's quilts to "everyday use," rather than treat them with respect, even as works of art. Her mother retorts that maybe the quilts should be put to use. Walker's title suggests that such objects of "everyday use" have a special value and importance in tying those who use them to their heritage. She implies that those, like Dee, who look at them as artifacts have lost such a direct connection to their heritage.

QUESTIONS ON WRITING STRATEGY

1.   Walker seems both to be celebrating the simple integrity of the mother and Maggie and to be suggesting that African Americans like Dee, who have made social and economic gains because of the civil rights movement, have at the same time lost a straightforward, uncomplicated connection to their roots.

2.   The story opens with the mother saying that the front yard of her house "is more comfortable than most people know" as a place to sit. It ends with the mother and Maggie sitting in the front yard, "just enjoying" before they go to bed. The story's opening and closing thus reinforce the admirable simplicity of the characters.

3.   Walker describes the yard (par. 1), the narrator (5), Maggie (7, 9), the house (14), Dee and her boyfriend (19–21), the churn (54), the quilts (55), and Maggie again (75).

QUESTIONS ON LANGUAGE

1.   Students might find some of the mother's language unlikely for one with a second-grade education (par. 13) — for instance, "You've no doubt seen those TV shows where the child who has 'made it' is confronted, as a surprise, by her own mother and father" (3). Mostly, however, she uses simple sentence constructions and words to express complex perceptions and feelings.

2.   The dash indicates the interruption of the mother's musings by the arrival of Dee and her friend. The exclamation point suggests how strongly she has anticipated their arrival. The second part of the sentence achieves an interesting effect by shifting from reverie into the story's current time.

3.   These references show that the mother sees Dee as putting on airs with her name change.

4.   *Clabber* is sour milk, short for *bonny clabber*, from the Gaelic *bainne clabair*.

ALICE WALKER ON WRITING

Classroom discussion might well focus on Walker's idea of writing as a tool for correcting injustices. It's possible that students who are in general not keen on writing might come to see some point in it if they're made aware of its usefulness as a tool. Walker's view of writing as a healing activity is also interesting. Probably most students have not yet written enough to know whether or not they could heal themselves by writing. If anyone in the class is in a position to say that Alice Walker is right on this point, however, the resulting discussion might be a lively one, and students might be encouraged to try writing as therapy the next time they need restoring.

8
PROCESS ANALYSIS
Explaining Step by Step

By assigning only two essays from this chapter, you can provide your students with illustrations of both kinds of process analysis: the "how-to" kind (Lucinda Rosenfeld's advice on dumping a friend) and the "how something happens" kind (Jessica Mitford on how a corpse is embalmed, Horace Miner on American "body rituals," or Niala Maharaj and Donovan Hohn on the production of flowers). Linnea Saukko's "How to Poison the Earth" falls in between: Saukko provides a directive process analysis, but she does not wish anyone to follow her instructions.

The pair in this chapter is Mitford and Miner — two detailed and amusing analyses of processes the authors see as peculiarly American. (We debated whether to give away Miner's joke in the essay headnote and decided not to, though we did hint broadly. For students who arrive at the end without recognizing themselves, we ask them in the first question on meaning to examine the word *Nacirema*.)

Incidentally, the opening of this chapter explains the *analysis* part of process analysis. We continue to introduce process analysis *before* analysis (Chap. 9), because we expect that many students find the former easier to understand. Process analysis thus becomes a way into analysis. But if you'd rather cover analysis itself first, nothing in the text discussion or essays will impede you.

PROCESS ANALYSIS IN OTHER CHAPTERS. Somewhat surprisingly because it is a method serving such specific purposes, process analysis comes in handy for a number of the writers represented in other chapters of the book.

Part Two

Brad Manning, "Arm Wrestling with My Father"
Jhumpa Lahiri, "Indian Takeout"
Deborah Tannen, "But What Do You Mean?"
Stephanie Ericsson, "The Ways We Lie"
William Lutz, "The World of Doublespeak"
Gina Kolata, "Probing Disease Clusters"
Atul Gawande, "The Cancer-Cluster Myth"
Marie Winn, "TV Addiction"
Peter Singer, "The Singer Solution to World Poverty"

LINNEA SAUKKO

How to Poison the Earth

It won't take students long to realize that Saukko's essay is an impas-
sioned plea for sanity on the part of those whose actions are contributing to
the pollution of the earth. Though it is mainly a directive process analysis, no
one is expected to follow the directions. Clearly what the author hopes is just
the reverse: that readers will make every effort to stop those who are already,
and all too effectively, poisoning the earth.

With this essay, students might be asked to do a little research into the
issues — questioning why environmental destruction is permitted, whom it
benefits, what its elimination might cost, and what its alternatives are. (The
second writing suggestion can be helpful in this regard.) If students are themselves well informed about the issues, the discussion that results might be
one of the liveliest of the year.

Saukko's technique — giving advice precisely opposite to what she really
hopes will happen — is so effective that students may find themselves inspired
to imitate her. While the method can be particularly forceful, duplicating her
deadpan irony will not be so simple. You can give students practice at managing this tricky tone by asking them to work in pairs or threes to write a short
how-to essay of their own. Have them consider carefully *why* Saukko's essay
works so well and then try their own hands at giving advice in this backward
way. (You may need to remind them that they will likely be more successful if
they choose a subject that they know a lot about.)

QUESTIONS ON MEANING

1. Saukko's purpose is to warn readers about threats to the future of our
    planet, and she has done her homework. She has taken the trouble to
    collect statistics and other information. She knows the names and
    strengths of the pollutants she mentions. She is familiar with the meth-
    ods by which wastes are disposed of, oil wells are drilled, pesticides are
    applied, and bombs are tested. Her satire is all the more biting for being
    buttressed by facts.
2. Students will find the mechanisms explained succinctly in paragraphs
    5–7.
3. Saukko mentions disposal of nuclear wastes and toxic chemicals through
    deep-well and shallow-well injection, the location of dumps and landfills
    where their poisons can spread, pesticide use, ocean dumping, indus-
    trial air pollution, and nuclear bomb testing as practices detrimental to
    the environment.

QUESTIONS ON WRITING STRATEGY

1. Clearly Saukko doesn't expect individual readers to carry out her instructions. Her point is that these dangerous exercises are already routine — practiced by corporations and by local, state, and federal governments on our behalf — and ought to be stopped.
2. Saukko introduces her essay effectively with some generalizations about poisoning the earth and then, starting with paragraph 2, moves more or less geographically, as water does, from land to ocean to air. The organization is effective because it corresponds with a natural order.
3. The people most likely to respond to this essay are those who share Saukko's concern about the future of the earth.
4. The tone is ironic, as almost every sentence demonstrates. Typically, satire depends on such irony to attack its subject.
5. The examples Saukko uses — nuclear wastes, PCB, DDT, nuclear fallout — are perhaps the most poisonous. Among the pollutants she doesn't mention, lead emissions from automobiles, carbon particles from smokestacks, and carbon dioxide from diverse sources come immediately to mind.

QUESTIONS ON LANGUAGE

1. All are dripping with irony.
2. One of the things students would do well to note about the word *nuclear* is its pronunciation. A number of people in the United States still speak of "nucular" war, "nucular" power, and the like, just because they've heard it wrong and never looked closely enough at the word to get it right.

LINNEA SAUKKO ON WRITING

Perhaps one of the reasons that Linnea Saukko's essay won a Bedford Prize for Student Writing was her feeling for the subject. Those writers who pick a subject about which they care passionately tend to write well. Students who know that are off to a running start.

LUCINDA ROSENFELD

How to Dump a Friend

Rosenfeld's tone in this essay is flip (as well as hip), but the writer nonetheless offers serious, useful advice about ending friendships, based in part on consultations with relationship experts (see pars. 8 and 15). How does Rosenfeld achieve the balance she does here? Students should see that she reserves her most outrageous humor for over-the-top examples of how and how not to end a friendship ("It really hurt my feelings when you blew off my blessing ceremony to attend a breathing workshop" [par. 6]). Underlying her joking here is the sensible idea that one ought to respect the feelings of the other person when breaking off a friendship.

Students can test Rosenfeld's advice by working in pairs or small groups to role-play interaction between a "breaker-upper" and a "dumpee." They might determine first what category the dumpee belongs to (see "Other Methods" under "Questions on Writing Strategy"), the motivation for the breakup, and where the conversation is taking place. Then volunteers could share their dialogues with the class, who might evaluate their effectiveness based on Rosenfeld's advice.

QUESTIONS ON MEANING

1. The first stage is to decide on one's approach based on one's relationship with the person, one's reasons for breaking off the friendship, and the friend's personality (pars. 6–11). The second stage is to determine the means for delivering the message (12–13). And the third stage is to give the friend a chance to respond.
2. Breaking off a relationship in which "time and emotion have been invested" (par. 6) requires some sort of explanation. E-mail is "just impersonal enough to suggest that you don't care and never did" (13). Both suggest that Rosenfeld believes we should respect the feelings of people with whom we have been friends.
3. The dumped friend will likely tell mutual friends if you have been too brutal in breaking off the friendship, and these friends will likely side with the offended party, seeing you as the bad guy.
4. In part, doing so allows Rosenfeld to end on a somewhat more positive note. In addition, the advice from psychologist Martin Devine is thought provoking and, Rosenfeld evidently feels, worth her readers' consideration.

QUESTIONS ON WRITING STRATEGY

1. Opinions may differ somewhat about Rosenfeld's purpose. Rosenfeld clearly means the essay to be entertaining — a decidedly humorous and light-hearted approach to the subject — but she also seems to be offering readers serious advice, obviously based on the opinions of several experts.
2. Fundamentally, she assumes that her readers have been in the situation of wanting to break off friendships but have found it difficult to do so except by the "silent treatment." Moreover, her tone and diction assume a fairly sophisticated audience, and her examples in paragraphs 1 and 15 assume a fairly young audience.
3. Rosenfeld's opening provides a vivid, witty example of the kind of annoying, needy friend whom most readers would also want to dump. Her conclusion echoes her opening by referring again to the telephone ringing. Note that her final advice here — to ignore the friend until he or she gets the picture — comically belies the advice she offers throughout the essay.
4. In paragraphs 6–11 Rosenfeld classifies types of friends one might want to dump: acquaintances, simply annoying friends, friends who have seriously offended one, friends who might react vindictively, and friends with whom one has other friends in common. One must approach a breakup with each type of friend in a different way.

QUESTIONS ON LANGUAGE

1. Rosenfeld's tone here is breezy and casual, reflected in the informality of much of her language: "blowing off a friend" (par. 2), "huge wimps" (4), "cut bait" (5), and "pretty hairy" (9), for example. Yet students will probably notice that she uses more complex diction as well, often for the effect of exaggeration — for example, "parasitic" and "metastasizing" (2) and "passive-aggressive" (3). This juxtaposition of different levels of diction (see "vindictive psycho" in par. 10) provides part of the essay's humor.
2. Most obviously, the gender alternatives make it clear that Rosenfeld's process applies to both female and male dumpees. The phrase also creates an air of pseudoexpertise.
3. With such examples, Rosenfeld establishes that she is not entirely serious, that she is exaggerating for comic effect.
4. *Passive-aggressive* refers to a common personality disorder that is marked by resistance to social and personal responsibility. Passive-aggressive types "act out" by giving the impression they will cooperate while covertly refusing to do what is expected or required of them.

NIALA MAHARAJ AND DONOVAN HOHN
Thorny Truths About Flowers

To open class discussion of this exposé of the international flower trade, you might ask students what information presented by the authors they found most surprising and what information they found most disturbing. Then you could move on to discuss this piece as an example of investigative journalism, in-depth research into a subject in order to make readers aware of events or abuses that were previously unreported. (The following essay, Jessica Mitford's "Behind the Formaldehyde Curtain," is another good example of investigative journalism.) Ask students: Is it important for reporters to seek out such information and share it with readers? Why, or why not?

Students may be intrigued by the way Maharaj and Hohn use the FTD advertisement as a centerpiece and reference point, their commentary posing an ironic contrast to the ad. Such an eye-opening "Annotation" is a monthly feature in *Harper's* magazine. If you have access to the magazine, you might share four or five other "Annotation" features with your class. Have students in small groups analyze one and then report back to the class on its subject, its method, and how it is similar to and different from the one by Maharaj and Hohn.

QUESTIONS ON MEANING

1. The thesis might be stated as follows: "The process of producing flowers for the world market involves significant genetic engineering (par. 1), the exploitation of poor countries by richer ones (2), the use of dangerous pesticides that harm workers (3), and a vast consumption — even depletion — of natural resources, such as oil and water (4)."

2. Genetically engineered flowers do not represent natural blooms but are designed by "fashion experts and marketing consultants" to serve the needs of "global commerce."

3. They are showing that US florists can make a significant profit on foreign-grown flowers, buying for "less than $10" and selling for $86.99.

QUESTIONS ON WRITING STRATEGY

1. The opening quotation reinforces the authors' point about genetically engineered flowers: Such flowers are produced not by a nature who "loves us" but by an industry that exploits both workers and consumers.

2. With the greeting of "Happy Valentine's Day!" the authors ironically suggest that knowing readers, now better informed about the flower trade, should not think of cut flowers as representing a "happy holiday" at all.

3. The numbers show the extent to which US consumers are complicit with the flower industry in exploiting poor countries, their workers, and their natural resources.

4. Among other elements, the authors imply a persuasive thesis (see number 1 under "Questions on Meaning"), provide copious evidence to support their claims, reason carefully between evidence and claims, and use language forcefully to support their claims (for example, "poorly ventilated greenhouses producing [. . .] pesticide-laden roses," par. 3).

QUESTIONS ON LANGUAGE

1. The term *Third World* was originally coined to refer to nations that were not part of either the non-Communist bloc (mainly the United States and Western Europe) or the Soviet-dominated Communist bloc. Today, the term refers more generally to poor nations with economies based mostly on agriculture, without significant manufacturing or technological capabilities, and with generally poor education and health care.

2. The unattractive image of a vase filled with fuel oil stands in ironic contrast to the pictured vase filled with flowers.

3. A "thorny" issue is one marked by difficulties or controversy; roses, one of the subjects here, also have thorns, of course.

4. *Hieroglyphs* are the characters used in systems of pictographic writing, such as that of ancient Egypt. Goethe's meaning (or his translator's) is the more general "symbol."

JESSICA MITFORD

Behind the Formaldehyde Curtain

For that soporific class that sits and looks at you, here is a likely rouser. If Mitford can't get any response out of them, they're in a league with her Mr. Jones, and you might as well devote the rest of the course to silent study periods. Sometimes, it is true, a class confronted with this essay will just sit there like people in whose midst a large firecracker has been hurled, watching it sputter. Give them time to respond with five or ten minutes to freewrite about whatever Mitford's essay first inspires them to say. Then have them trade papers in groups of three or four, read the papers, and discuss their responses to each other. You can turn these smaller group discussions into a whole-class conversation whenever it seems appropriate.

Teaching Mitford's essay invites one possible danger: that someone in the class, having recently experienced the death of a loved one, will find Mitford's macabre humor cruel and offensive. We once received a painful letter from a student in Wenatchee, Washington, who complained bitterly about this "hideous" essay. "My husband was crushed in a logging accident," she wrote. "If Mitford also learned a little about grief, she would know that those people who view a body have an easier time with grief than those who don't. She wouldn't hate funeral directors. I guess Mitford would have had me view my husband's mangled body, but I'm glad the funeral director prepared his body for viewing."

How can you answer such a protest? Before assigning this essay for reading, you might ask the class whether anyone present has suffered a death in the family. At least warn students what to expect. Anyone recently bereaved might be given the option of skipping both Mitford's essay and the class discussion. If a student in mourning reads Mitford's essay anyway and protests its seeming callousness, you might see whether that student feels impelled to write a personal response to Mitford and her essay — as our correspondent did so effectively. The first and fourth writing suggestions may be helpful.

The painstaking legwork that Mitford did before she wrote *The American Way of Death* is documented in *Poison Penmanship: The Gentle Art of Muckraking* (1979). Much of her information came from professional journals, such as *Casket & Sunnyside, Mortuary Management,* and *Concept: The Journal of Creative Ideas for Cemeteries.* While laying stress on the value of such research, Mitford adds that a muckraker profits from sheer luck. A friend happened to recall a conversation with an undertaker when she was arranging for her brother-in-law's funeral. She had insisted on the cheapest redwood coffin available, but the undertaker objected. The deceased was too tall to fit into it; a costly coffin was required. When she continued to insist, the undertaker said, "Oh, all right, we'll use the redwood, but we'll have to cut off his feet." This grim example of high-pressure sales tactics supplied Mitford's book with one of its "more shining jewels."

When Mitford first showed her analysis of the embalming process (as a manuscript chapter for *The American Way of Death*) to her British and her American publishers, "it was met with instantaneous and thunderous disapproval from the editors on both sides of the Atlantic; this chapter is too revolting — it must go, they said." She insisted on keeping it, and lost the publishers. A year after Simon & Schuster brought out the book, she recalls, "those selfsame embalming passages were chosen for inclusion in a college textbook on writing. Well! Of course I felt vindicated. The obvious moral is that although *some* editors can *sometimes* perform wonders in improving your work, in the last analysis your own judgment must prevail" (from *Poison Penmanship,* pp. 22–23).

QUESTIONS ON MEANING

1. In case anyone finds this essay repulsive and resents your assigning it, we suggest you begin by inviting reactions of all kinds. Let students kick the essay about, and, if they hate it, encourage them to say why. Almost certainly some will find it hilarious and will defend it as humor. Others will probably say that they didn't like it, that it's unpleasant, but that it tells truth we ought to know. You'll usually get more reactions if you are slow to advance your own. If the sense of the meeting should be vehemently against this essay, you may care to stick up for it (or you may want to skip on to the next selection in a hurry). But if, as is likely, most students are intrigued by it, they'll indicate this by their reactions, and your ensuing class discussion can ride on this momentum.

2. She speculates that perhaps undertakers keep it secret for fear that patrons, knowing what it is, wouldn't want it done (par. 6).

3. "To make the corpse presentable for viewing in a suitably costly container" (par. 2). Most of the usual obstacles to presentability are itemized in paragraphs 14–18: the effects of mutilation, emaciation, and disease.

4. If the subject was not dead, the undertaker will have killed him.

5. Her purpose is to attack the custom of embalming (and to chide the society that permits it). Mitford finds Americans "docile" and "ignorant" in tolerating such a procedure (par. 4). From her concluding paragraphs (23–27), we infer that she would urge Americans not to embalm, to admit the fact of death, and to bury the dead in closed coffins, as is done in much of the rest of the Western world.

QUESTIONS ON WRITING STRATEGY

1. Mitford's tone is cheerful scorn. Her verbs for the treatments inflicted on the corpse — "sprayed," "sliced," "pierced," "pickled," and so on — clearly show that she regards the process as ridiculous. The ironic phrase "suitably costly container" strongly hints that she regards morticians as racketeers.

2. She is determined to show that if we knew what embalming and restoration entailed — its every detail — we wouldn't stand for it.

3. The body becomes a character in her drama — whether it is that of an adult or a child.

4. Mitford's opening sentence indicates the start of a time sequence, and students should easily be able to find the ensuing time-markers. Her favorites are the small words "next" and "now," and most of the paragraphs about Mr. Jones contain one or the other.

5. There are four stages: The body is laid in the morgue (par. 7); the blood is drained and replaced by embalming fluid (11); the teeth are scrubbed and eye caps are applied (12); a trocar is employed and "cavity fluid" introduced (13).

6. Her audience is American general readers, whom she distinguishes from "funeral men" in paragraph 6.

7. The quotation in paragraph 3 suggests that embalming (and all it entails) may be illegal; the one in paragraph 10 suggests that dolling up the corpse is more important to the mortician than possibly saving a life. Mr. Kriege (quoted in par. 22) makes the undertaker sound like a funeral football coach, in whose hands the corpse is a helpless ball. In offering these quotations, Mitford hangs the ethics and professional behavior of

morticians by their own words, and once more questions the desirability of embalming.

8. The groups are "surgery" tools, tissue chemicals, restorative cosmetics and plasters, and props and stabilizers. The groups make the catalog of equipment and supplies more intelligible and reinforce Mitford's point about the pretentions and absurdities of the process.

QUESTIONS ON LANGUAGE

1. By alluding to the Prince of Denmark's speech with skull in hand (*Hamlet* 5.1), Mitford suggests that perhaps Yorick's "counterpart of today" is another luckless jester or clown. This theatrical allusion also enforces her metaphor of the drama that begins and the curtain that must be lifted.

2. Mitford delights in citing undertakers' euphemisms. The morticians, she implies, dislike plain words — in paragraph 20, she quotes one who warns against creating the impression "that the body is in a box" (which, of course, is fact). There seems an ironic discrepancy between the attitudes expressed in the last two sentences and Mitford's own view. A funeral, she implies, shouldn't be a "real pleasure" but an occasion for grief. Death isn't an opposing football team.

3. To the general reader, these brand names carry unpleasant connotations, and a lively class discussion may be devoted to unraveling what these are. Lyf-Lyk tint seems cutesy in its spelling, like some drugstore cosmetic item. Other brand names seem practical and unfeeling: Throop Foot Positioner, Armstrong Face Former and Denture Replacer. Porto-Lift and the Glide Easy casket carriage stress slickness and efficiency. Classic Beauty Ultra Metal Casket Bier seems absurdly grand. Mitford's purpose is to attack our sympathy and tolerance for the undertaker's art, and certainly these names rub us the wrong way.

4. "Dermasurgeon" (par. 8) is a euphemism Mitford especially relishes. Although it tries to dignify the mortician, Mitford points out how (unlike the surgeon he imitates) the embalmer acquired his training in a quick post–high-school course.

JESSICA MITFORD ON WRITING

Surprisingly often, authors are in total agreement when they discuss the art of writing. Mitford is clearly on the side of all those who say that to write well, you have to care deeply about your subject. (We love that British phrase "besotted by.") Like so many writers, both amateur and professional, she knows that writing is hard work. Like George Orwell, muckraker Mitford sees writing as a valuable tool for righting the world's wrongs.

From what Mitford says about her research for *The American Way of Death*, students can learn how important it is to get the facts straight when doing an exposé. The author makes clear as well that in writing, as in most other activities, a sense of humor is a valuable asset.

HORACE MINER

Body Ritual Among the Nacirema

Like Jessica Mitford's essay, with which it is paired, "Body Ritual Among the Nacirema" uses process analysis to critique aspects of American culture, specifically our obsession with appearance and the body (see the fourth writing suggestion). Both essays are excellent ways to encourage students to look critically at the culture in which they live.

Because Miner parodies the style and tone of anthropologists like himself, some students may at first find the essay difficult. You might warn them of what to expect (without giving away the gimmick, of course), urging them to soldier on even if they have trouble with the language. Once Miner's intention becomes clear, they will find the language more transparent.

Many students will have already given much thought to body image. Interested students might do a group presentation on body image in advertising, comparing today's images with those from the 1950s, when Miner's essay was written. For the sake of practicality, students will probably want to limit their research to magazines or other print media.

If you have multinational students in your class, why not discuss (without putting anyone on the spot) what American culture looks like from an outsider's point of view? American students who have spent time abroad will also be able to contribute.

QUESTIONS ON MEANING

1. Answers will vary, of course. "North American group" (par. 2) is the first hint. Most students will probably catch on somewhere during the description of the "shrines" (4–8).
2. Miner wants to show the small distance between ourselves and "primitive" cultures; to criticize the American obsession with the body (see the second writing suggestion); and to check the smugness of anthropologists (see the third writing suggestion).
3. The stereotype that doctors' handwriting is illegible.
4. Magic is usually attributed to primitive cultures. This narrows the gulf between Americans and the members of such cultures, whose behavior we often consider more irrational or ignorant than our own.

QUESTIONS ON WRITING STRATEGY

1. Obtaining medication from doctors and pharmacists (par. 6), storing old medication in a medicine cabinet (7), washing (8), brushing teeth (10), visiting the dentist (11–12), shaving (12), drying hair (12), going to the hospital (13–16), going to a therapist (17), cosmetic procedures such as dieting (18), sexual customs and childbirth (19).
2. Authenticity: These make the essay seem like a genuine journal article. Students may balk at the opening, so it may help to escort them through it, stressing its purpose.

3. Anthropologists are doubly satirized in the essay: as anthropologists and as members of American society. They are in a better position to appreciate the parody of their jargon and tone. Students may find both somewhat off-putting but should still appreciate the clinical view of anthropologists' methods.
4. Signs of age: the generic *he* and *man*, with its implicit assumption that dentists and doctors are always men; weekly hair drying by women (par. 12), recalling women's periodic visits to a hairdresser. Otherwise, the "rituals" are the same. In fact, Americans today are even more concerned with the body (dieting, fitness, cosmetic surgery, and so on) than in the 1950s. (The second writing suggestion gives students a chance to explore this topic further.)
5. Such definitions abound: bathroom as a "shrine" (par. 4), medicine as a "charm" (7), sink as "font" (8), dentists as "holy-mouth-men" (9), dental equipment as "augers, awls, probes, and prods" (11), hair dryers as "small ovens" (12), nurses as "vestal maidens" (13), thermometers as "magic wands" (16). The effect is one of defamiliarization: The reader is forced to look at everyday things in a different light.

QUESTIONS ON LANGUAGE

1. Besides the fact that *Nacirema* is *American* spelled backwards, it also sounds like an exotic tribe somewhere in the underdeveloped world.
2. We are still living in an age of magic. We have just as many superstitions as so-called primitive peoples, and they serve us in the same ways.
3. "Wattle and daub" is a construction technique involving a framework of woven rods and twigs overlaid and plastered with clay. It is cruder than, but resembles, common American timber-framed construction with the spaces filled with laths.

9
DIVISION OR ANALYSIS
Slicing into Parts

Division and classification have long been combined and confused in composition textbooks, so it is no wonder that some authors, some teachers, and many students cannot tell them apart. The true loser has seemed to be division. Indeed, some texts dispose of division as the mere servant of classification, the operation required to sort (divide) things into classes.

At the same time, freshman writing classes are absorbed in critical thinking, reading, and writing. Scholarly journals, textbooks, and teachers are inventing and experimenting with ways to teach these crucial skills. Yet all along we have had the means to introduce the skills through the Cinderella of the division and classification pair. Though generally treated, when treated at all, as a simple cutting operation, division is of course *analysis*. And what is analysis but the basis of criticism?

We have tried to rescue division/analysis and give it useful work in the composition course. We have, most noticeably, given the method its own chapter (and classification *its* own), in which we stress analytic thinking and discuss critical thinking. We have also made much more explicit the analytical underpinnings of the other methods of development, including (but not only) classification. (Two of these related methods — comparison-contrast and process analysis — continue to be covered before this chapter on the theory that they may be more familiar and accessible to students, even without explicit discussion of analysis. Of course, you may change the order of chapters if you see it differently.)

We continue to pair Judy Brady's provocative "I Want a Wife" with Armin A. Brott's "Not All Men Are Sly Foxes," an interesting (if indirect) rejoinder to what many see as Brady's stereotyping of men. Brott's essay also forms a bridge from simple division to critical analysis, illustrated by Shelby Steele's "Notes from the Hip-Hop Underground," Emily Prager's "Our Barbies, Ourselves," and Jean Kilbourne's "'Can an Engine Pump the Valves in Your Heart?'" All three of these pieces analyze aspects of popular culture, so that students may bring their own experiences and views to bear. The chapter ends with Jamaica Kincaid's famous short story "Girl," which ties back to Brady and Brott as it enumerates the responsibilities of a young woman.

DIVISION OR ANALYSIS IN OTHER CHAPTERS. The following list includes selections elsewhere in the book that rcly significantly on division or analysis. We have kept the list as short and useful as we could, but in doing so we have omitted many essays in which you (and your students) may find good examples of this pervasive method.

Part Two

Part Three

JUDY BRADY

I Want a Wife

In the late 1980s newspapers and magazines quoted an instantly famous remark attributed to the actress Joan Collins after her divorce from musician Peter Holm. Declaring that her bitter public divorce battle had soured her on remarrying, Collins is also said to have quipped, "I don't need a husband, I need a wife." But we suspect that the credit for originating this epigram belongs to Judy Brady.

Instructors who have taught this essay in earlier editions report that it's a trusty class-rouser, evoking lively comments and a few intense disputes. Does Brady overstate her case in "I Want a Wife"? Some students, reading her essay in the new millennium, may think so. Perhaps their skepticism indicates real advances in the status of women since Brady first wrote in 1972. Do wives today play roles as humble and exacting as the one Brady details here? Are

men as well as women freer today to depart from prescribed patterns of behavior? Are women still as angry as Brady was? Note that similar questions
are addressed in the third writing suggestion. Armin A. Brott's "Not All Men
Are Sly Foxes" implicitly counters some of Brady's attitudes toward men, so
the two essays together create an even stronger basis for discussion and writing.

Give students some time to consider the above questions by having them
collaboratively update Brady's essay: What are the requirements of a wife
these days? Students can replace "wife" with "husband," "girlfriend," or "boyfriend" if they prefer. You might ask a few groups to read their responses
aloud to the class as a way to open discussion of Brady's essay.

QUESTIONS ON MEANING

1. The essay lists them all. In general, the duties of a wife seem to entail
    making life easy and comfortable for everyone in the family — except the
    wife herself.
2. What it all boils down to, in Brady's view, is that husbands shoulder
    whatever responsibilities they want to assume. All others they assign to
    their wives.
3. The thesis is implied: Wives are not persons but conveniences whose
    subservient roles have been fashioned by husbands.
4. Answers will vary. Are all men as demanding and insensitive as the com-
    posite male chauvinist Brady draws? Are there fewer who resemble him
    nowadays than there were in 1972, when the essay was first published?
    The class might like to consider the extent to which traditional roles
    have changed in the past decade.

QUESTIONS ON WRITING STRATEGY

1. Because the author's name clearly indicates that she is a woman, the
    title is a surefire attention-getter.
2. The first two paragraphs establish Brady's credentials, position her es-
    say in the real world, and show from the outset that wishing for a wife is
    not uncommon — among men.
3. Brady's tone is sardonic.
4. Avoiding the pronoun, though a bit awkward here and there, contributes
    greatly to the irony of "I Want a Wife." It dehumanizes a wife; she is not a
    woman but a thing to be used.
5. The principle of analysis is determined by the thesis: The role of a wife
    can be divided into jobs that serve others, especially the husband. Other
    principles of analysis might be the jobs a wife does that require brainpower
    or the satisfactions of the role of wife —but these, of course, would pro-
    duce entirely different essays.
6. Readers of *Ms.* have feminist leanings. To us, the essay's observations of
    husbands and wives remain fresh: "Supermom" is, after all, a recent
    coinage. However, not everyone will agree.
7. The groups of duties are nurse-governess (par. 3), maid (4), confidante
    (5), social planner (6), and sex object (7). Today, "bread winner" might
    get more play than Brady gives it (par. 3).

QUESTIONS ON LANGUAGE

1. It emphasizes the selfishness and the demanding tone of the words. The words themselves reduce a wife to the level of a possession.
2. You might be able to elicit a definition of *monogamy* by asking your class to list other words they know that contain *mono-* and to list what all the definitions have in common.
3. The essay's diction is appropriate, the words easy for any intelligent reader to understand. The repetition of "I want a wife" and the author's use of short sentences give the essay a staccato beat that underscores the anger behind it.

ARMIN A. BROTT

Not All Men Are Sly Foxes

Brott's essay uses examples from children's books to explore what he sees as a larger social problem: stereotyping fathers as nonnurturing. You might begin discussion by asking students for examples of "good" and "bad" dads, from TV shows, movies, and children's books other than the ones Brott mentions. Is Brott blowing the problem out of proportion? If not, what are the practical consequences of this stereotype — are "bad" fathers excused on the grounds that "men are just that way"?

Many students will give examples from personal experience, which can segue into critical discussion of cultural assumptions. Does Brott need more evidence? different kinds of evidence? Are there factors that refute his claims? Where do students' own generalizations come from?

Students will probably not take issue with Brott's claim that fathers should be (and often are) nurturing. Still, it might be useful to give them some time to imagine that children's books wield even *more* cultural authority than Brott claims — that the stories children read program the adults they become. Stressing their grave responsibility, have small groups outline the ideal children's story, focusing on mother, father, child. They should assign an animal to each and carefully consider the implications of each choice. As a whole class, compare the stories and the values each promotes. Then discuss whether these images could change our society.

QUESTIONS ON MEANING

1. "Ignoring men who share equally in raising their children, and continuing to show nothing but part-time or no-time fathers is only going to create yet another generation of men who have been told since boyhood — albeit subtly — that mothers are the truer parents and that fathers play, at best, a secondary role in the home" (par. 9).
2. Brott assumes his readers have kids, or at least are familiar with kids' books, and that they know or are responsible fathers.

3. The pictures show a close emotional connection between baby and mother but not between baby and father. This is important because the book is for children who are too young to read and who therefore probably learn at least as much from the book's pictures as from its text.
4. This call-to-action aligns all parents together, proposing a plan that discourages passive acceptance of a negative stereotype.

QUESTIONS ON WRITING STRATEGY

1. His principle of analysis is the image of fathers in children's books. Elements he identifies are women's versus men's roles in households and with children, fathers' neglectfulness and sloppiness, fathers' absence, and fathers' physical remoteness.
2. This reference connects children's books to the parents who read them. It also shows how pervasive negative stereotypes of fathers are.
3. Mother Goose is "a successful entrepreneur" who serves "homemade" meals in "pretty porcelain cups." Sly Fox is "unemployed"; his children are "filthy, hungry pups" living in a "grimy hovel," a space "littered with bones." One parent is a working, single mother who cooks and cares for her children; the other is an unemployed father who can't even be bothered to clean up his hovel.

QUESTIONS ON LANGUAGE

1. Caregivers take care of physical needs, while nurturers also love, cuddle, and make emotional connections with a child.
2. The tone is generally reasonable but occasionally plaintive ("Don't the fathers care? Do they even have fathers?" par. 5) and occasionally determined ("I need my answers," 5; "Let's finish the job," 9).
3. Brott's analysis hinges on his sense of the subtlety of stereotyping. Students may be interested to know that the word *subtle* can mean elusive, obscure, perceptive, expert, artful, or crafty. Brott uses it more in the last sense, suggesting an insidious element to something seemingly innocuous.

SHELBY STEELE

Notes from the Hip-Hop Underground

Steele's essay on hip-hop music may surprise both the music's fans and its detractors if they perceive that he is excusing or even championing its notorious images of violence and misogyny. What Steele actually says is that hip-hop compensates for the grim realities of the black underclass, where it had its roots, and now also for the alienation and powerlessness felt by many of its white fans. It is, in short, a symptom of a problem rather than the problem itself. This is less a defense of hip-hop than it is a condemnation of a society in which "family life is eroded either by welfare and drugs or by the stresses and indulgences of middle-class life" (par. 14).

You might raise the question of whether Steele believes that the image of the "Bad Nigger" among hip-hoppers themselves — especially those who make fortunes with it — is essentially a pose or a role rather than a true reflection of their lives. What are their motives as artists/entertainers?

If you have both fans and detractors of hip-hop music in your class, you could organize a debate between them, giving both sides some time to prepare outside of class so that each group can bring in examples of songs to support its side. After hearing these presentations, other class members could offer comments of their own and even vote for the more persuasive case.

QUESTIONS ON MEANING

1. The "Bad Nigger," according to Steele's first paragraph, developed out of slave culture as one who "flaunts the constraints, laws and taboos that bind a person in slavery." He is "unbound and contemptuous," and his actions, particularly against white women, "assert the broadest possible freedom"; indifferent to any feeling, he is "revolution incarnate." He also "lives out a compensatory grandiosity" of exaggerated arrogance, masculinity, and sexuality (par. 2). He was, for slaves, "the imagination's compensation for the all-to-real impotence and confinement" that they endured.
2. Hip-hop artists have adopted the persona of the BN "in all his sneering and inflated masculinity" (par. 3) as a way of appealing to adolescent rebellion (4). The contradiction is that successful rap artists are, in fact, wealthy businessmen who must "act out" this image of rebelliousness.
3. Steele sets up his thesis with a question in paragraph 6, answered in paragraph 7: The BN image "has become the MTV generation's metaphor for rebellion" (6) because "many of today's youth ironically share with yesterday's slave [. . .] a need for myths and images that compensate for a sense of alienation and ineffectuality" (7). Steele goes on to explain his thesis by suggesting that contemporary social and cultural forces — high rates of divorce and single-parent households, two-career families, ineffectual institutions outside the home — have created a generation of young people, notably in the white middle class, who ironically share with slaves a crippling sense of alienation and helplessness and for whom the image of the BN is a source of solace and empowerment.
4. Poverty, illegitimacy, and the absence of strong father figures led children of the 1960s into an alienation so "withering" that "[n]ot even the blues" could express their hurt. Growing out of this, rappers updated the BN as an image immune to any sort of feeling in a way that "has nothing to do with race. In rap, the BN nurtures indifference toward those he is most likely to love" (par. 13).

QUESTIONS ON WRITING STRATEGY

1. Steele's principle of analysis is the elements of hip-hop's BN image that appeal to white and black youths. His thesis asserts generally that these elements "compensate for a sense of alienation and ineffectuality" (par. 7).
2. Writing for the *Wall Street Journal*, Steele must assume a fairly conservative, conventional audience who sees rap "as yet more evidence of America's decline" (par. 6). His purpose is to suggest that the popularity

of rap confirms the conservative argument about the erosion of family life. Rap itself is not the problem; it is merely an artistic expression of the alienation so many young people feel.

3. Steele compares Eminem and Dostoyevsky to make the point that images of individuals alienated from society — and the sociopathology this alienation drives them to — have a long literary history. He plants Eminem in this tradition as a way of legitimizing his work.

4. He wants his readers from the start to view the image of the BN from the slave's perspective — that is, as a positive, empowering myth for those who are powerless.

5. Throughout, Steele suggests causal connections: between the powerlessness of slaves and the creation of the BN image, between young people's sense of alienation and the popularity of rap, between larger social forces and the alienation that marks contemporary youth.

QUESTIONS ON LANGUAGE

1. The BN is immune to feeling, so it is ironic that he would warm anyone's soul.

2. Clark, of course, is the aging, white, nice-guy popular-music promoter whose career began in the 1950s — about as far from the "gangsta" image of the rapper as one can get.

3. Steele probably uses the abbreviation to avoid the repeated offense of the word *nigger*. It might be worth speculating on whether this choice was Steele's independently or was suggested by the *Wall Street Journal* editors.

4. *Decimation*, from the Latin *decem*, or "ten," literally means the destruction of a tenth part of something — as of an army during battle — but it has come to mean simply large-scale destruction.

SHELBY STEELE ON WRITING

Steele's epiphany listening to the radio is of course unique, but it seems to us that what happened next is not so unique. Students, too, are learning to write out of their private selves into public discourse and in the process are finding that writing can help them think about both realms.

EMILY PRAGER

Our Barbies, Ourselves

This essay may initially put off some of the men in your class: What do they care about a girl's doll? Yet even if your students have never owned or played with Barbie, they'll be interested in Prager's lighthearted yet thought-provoking look at the way that masculine and feminine ideals are created and internalized. (Introducing this essay in the context of men's and women's *mutual* influence on gender ideals may help.)

In preparation for discussing this essay, students could collaboratively devise a portrait of the ideal woman and man in America today. What qualities do we find most valuable or important in men? in women? Who might be said to represent this ideal today? Are there different sets of standards? Who decides them? In groups of four or five, students should be able to generate a list of ideal qualities in about ten minutes (half the class focusing on the male, half focusing on the female). Will these two prototypes be a happy couple?

QUESTIONS ON MEANING

1. She is referring not just to Barbie's looks, but also to the fact that we understand and crave Barbie's looks because she is a product of male-defined notions of female beauty.
2. Certainly these claims are exaggerated, but Prager's point is that Barbie's influence lasts far beyond childhood.
3. In paragraph 6 she defines a feminist as "her own person," a "liberated woman, a gal on the move," "sexual." The definition is no doubt somewhat ironic.
4. Barbie is not an appropriate female role model or even an innocent toy, but an object created by a man to embody his and other men's damaging ideal of women.

QUESTIONS ON WRITING STRATEGY

1. Prager focuses on Barbie's physical appearance, such as her large breasts and tiny waist (pars. 2–3, 5–7); her accessories, such as high heels, condos, and Ken (4–6); her personality and attitude toward life (6); and her sexuality (7). Through these elements, Barbie is transformed from a harmless toy into a dangerous influence on girls' self-images and ambitions.
2. The women are Zsa Zsa Gabor, a certain kind of glamorous woman who loves men, whom some men love (pars. 1, 5); Madame Alexander, a famous doll designer (6); Elizabeth Taylor, actress and renowned feminine beauty even as a child (6); Jackie Kennedy, perfect wife and mother (6). All are traditional women in one way or another, yet only Zsa Zsa is consistent with Barbie.
3. These questions concentrate readers' attention on the main issues Prager wants them to consider, involving readers in her inquiry.
4. Barbie's "sexual equipment" is "obvious" while Ken's is not. This discrepancy leads to a mystification of male sexuality and a sense of female loneliness and isolation. She suggests this mystery may also imply male power or dignity, which is greater than that of women.

QUESTIONS ON LANGUAGE

1. "King," rather than "queen," implies that women were still conscious of male standards of beauty even as feminism was taking hold.
2. She's "masculine" in the sense that she's hard and unyielding — not what little girls, unswayed, would seek in a doll. There's no contradiction because her "masculine," "phallic" quality reflects her being designed by a man to suit men's interest.
3. It suggests conservative ideals, financial success, business interests, and ambition — an ideal as unrealistic in its way as that represented by either Madame Alexander dolls or Barbie.

4. Prager's use of the word *totemic* to describe Barbie is suggestive in its implication that Barbie has become a valuable cultural icon, a symbol of the feminine ideals revered by our culture. Much the way a totem pole is used to tell the most important stories of a family history, Barbie (for many) has become a symbol of the most important attributes of woman.

EMILY PRAGER ON WRITING

Although Prager's comments are not specifically about her own writing process and are, to be sure, a bit intemperate, we couldn't resist printing them because of the truth that glows through. Prager's support of reading as a "fantastic turn-on" and of reading and writing together as a means to discover "personal freedom" may turn the heads of a few students who feel the two activities are "dry, dull, meaningless, academic."

JEAN KILBOURNE

"Can an Engine Pump the Valves in Your Heart?"

This lively take on automobile advertising provides a very clear example of analysis, with an explicit thesis and a straightforward structure in which the elements of the advertising appeals are readily revealed. The subject should also prove engaging to most students, for whom advertising and the car culture are ubiquitous.

You might begin discussion by dividing students into groups and asking each group to generate a list of things that people look for in a car. Then, as a class, combine the lists, writing the various items on the board. Using this list, have students consider the extent to which the ads Kilbourne describes appeal to the actual desires of consumers, whether directly or metaphorically. Do these advertisers seem to know their target audience, or are they essentially off the mark?

Some students may resist the notion that advertising is significant — that they are influenced by ads, including car ads, or that, as Kilbourne states in her last paragraph, ads "have a cumulative direction and a cumulative impact," creating "a world in which things are becoming ever more, and people ever less, important." The "Journal Writing" prompt and "From Journal to Essay" writing topic are intended to get students thinking about how advertising has influenced them. To bring this thinking into class discussion, you might point up a key contrast between the car-culture ideal (for instance, the freedom of the open road) and the reality of life with cars (traffic-clogged roadways). Which of these does car advertising emphasize? Why?

QUESTIONS ON MEANING

1. Kilbourne's thesis is two-part: Car ads, stressing romance and rebellion (par. 1), are an example of an increasing emphasis on things and an increasing de-emphasis on the people who own things (22).
2. Car ads appeal to romance or rebellion. Specific romantic appeals: equating "buying a car [with] falling in love and getting married" (pars. 2–5), offering "the automotive equivalent of a one-night stand" (6–8), offering "a substitute for sex" (9–10), depicting a "passionate relationship [. . .] between the car and the sky or the car and the road" (11–12). Specific rebellion appeals: suggesting "control and competition" (13–16), encouraging "overidentification of owners with their automobiles" (17–18), identifying the car with "the self" (19–21). Students may also note that within the subtypes Kilbourne sometimes includes further breakdowns, such as "cars [. . .] more likely to be true-blue and loyal than our mates" (5) and cars seen as male sex objects and as female sex objects (7, 8).
3. Students' opinions will vary, of course. Some may think the thesis adequately supported by the sheer volume of Kilbourne's examples and their repeated illustration of cars substituting for people. Other students may resist the underlying notion that advertising matters at all or that it can negatively affect consumers' self-images.

QUESTIONS ON WRITING STRATEGY

1. Kilbourne's principle of analysis is the appeal made by car ads to consumers. She identifies a twofold appeal (romanticism and rebellion) with multiple elements (love, constancy, reliability, etc.).
2. Examples of transitions include "In ad after ad" (par. 2), "however" (6), "not only as [. . .] but as" (9), "no longer necessary at all" (11), "also" (13), "often" (17), and "Some ads go even further" (19).
3. In paragraph 3 the parenthetical phrase comments on the ad. In 6, two parentheses offer quotations that support the previous statements. In 10, the parenthesis expands the thought. In 22, the parenthesis recalls a phrase from an ad previously cited that exemplifies the point.
4. These questions emphasize the absurdity of the ads' suggestions and promises.
5. Two other methods stand out: examples of ads and description of the examples. Without both of these, Kilbourne's thesis would float unconvincingly in abstraction. Some students might also note classification in the two main types of appeal and their numerous subtypes.

QUESTIONS ON LANGUAGE

1. Kilbourne clearly finds most of the language overblown, often disconnected from reality, sometimes silly, and always highly manipulative. One example, in paragraph 4: "surely the solution can't be to fall in love with our cars." Other examples appear in paragraphs 10, 11, 13, 14, 15, 16, 21, and 22.
2. After one particularly "sexy" ad, Kilbourne writes tongue in cheek, she "longed for a cigarette ad" (par. 11) — a take on the stereotype of wanting a cigarette after lovemaking. Again, the suggestion is that the sexiness of the ad is absurd.

3. The phrase "so to speak" emphasizes the pun on the word "overkill": It is used both for its usual meaning ("excessive," "beyond what is required") and as an ironic comment on the ad for the "car from hell" that "looks like an ad for a slasher film."

4. A *siren song* is an alluring or seductive appeal, particularly one that is deceptive. In Greek mythology, Sirens are part-human female sea creatures that sing beguilingly, luring sailors to wreck their ships on hidden shoals.

JAMAICA KINCAID

Girl

Students may need a little guidance on how to read and understand this lyrical and evocative piece of fiction. They may complain that as a story, it unfolds much less clearly and logically than, say, the narrative essays in Chapter 4. For those who resist the unorthodox style, you might ask someone to read the story aloud, or do so yourself (see the fourth question on language). The story's form helps emphasize the mother and daughter's relationship.

Students will certainly notice that this story is not set in the United States. Encourage them in small groups to locate the details that make this fact obvious. How does the "foreignness" of the location help or hinder understanding of the story? Are there things in "Girl" that suggest the universal experience of growing up? How would they rewrite this story to capture the lessons their parents repeat?

QUESTIONS ON MEANING

1. These are any boys who hang around without enough to do — boys without motivation. She should avoid them because, presumably, they would be interested in "ruining" her.

2. Such a woman is one who isn't respected or trustworthy and who is probably the "slut" the mother keeps gloomily predicting the girl will be.

3. A life full of risk, danger, and vigilance — risks including miscooked food and bad sex, dangers including becoming pregnant and becoming a "slut," vigilance with household chores, social obligations, health, and personal morality.

QUESTIONS ON WRITING STRATEGY

1. This single sentence reads like an unbroken litany of advice. The method works because it echoes a parent's nagging, suggesting that this could be either a hypothetical conversation — all a mother needs to tell a daughter growing up — or a real one.

2. The italicized sections quote the girl, so we know that she *does* speak occasionally, that she is listening, and that she is a good girl ("*But I don't*

sing benna on Sundays"). We also know she can hardly get a word in and is mostly ignored.

3.   This advice lightens with a little laugh the heavy sense of obligation conveyed by all the other advice. If it were the last line, it might detract from the seriousness of the rest of the piece.

4.   These categories include how to wash, cook, sew, iron, sing, grow food, sweep, smile, set the table, interact with men, and make medicine. The categories show that the roles of woman are methodical, not random, and should be appreciated for their subtlety, efficiency, and complexity.

QUESTIONS ON LANGUAGE

1.   These multiple explanations suggest the nuances of woman's work, the level of detail a woman must know, and the care she must take to avoid being a "slut."

2.   This is a girl who is on the verge of womanhood, being coached in how to give up tomboy habits.

3.   The story is redolent with words and expressions of the Caribbean. The words most likely to be unfamiliar to American readers have been defined in footnotes.

4.   You might ask a volunteer to read the story aloud or do so yourself. The story is different in voice, and Vaughn's "singing" seems apt.

JAMAICA KINCAID ON WRITING

Kincaid's interview centers on the process of finding herself through writing. Her lonely childhood, impotence in the face of her mother's hold over her, and eventual rebellion are themes students may recognize from their own lives. The fact that she embarked on writing as an act of courage, in defiance of her own reservations and the anticipated criticism of others, should reassure beginning writers who question their own creativity and ability. This essay could spur a good "Why write?" discussion. It also shows how their origins, as painful as they may be, provide some writers with marvelous and abundant material for their art.

10
CLASSIFICATION
Sorting into Kinds

In our general comments on Chapter 9, we explain our reasons for divorcing the hoary pair of division and classification. Our reasons have mainly to do with salvaging division/analysis, but benefits accrue to classification, too. For one thing, it doesn't have to compete for attention (ours, yours, students'), so it's much clearer. For another, we can provide more illustrations.

The essays in this chapter range from humorous to serious, reflecting the classifications we find in the publications we read. Russell Baker contributes a well-known humorous piece of curmudgeonly confusion over our material possessions. Then four writers look at how we communicate: Deborah Tannen examines the different conversational styles of men and women; Stephen King sorts the comments he gets from his readers; and Stephanie Ericsson and William Lutz look at the language of lies and obfuscation, respectively.

Troubleshooting: All our efforts to keep division/analysis and classification separate and equal are hampered by the inescapable fact that *divide* is sometimes taken to mean *classify*, as in "Divide the students into groups." You might want to point out this issue directly to students if you think the terminology will confuse them. We maintain that division/analysis treats a singular, whole, coherent subject (a camera, a theory, a poem), whereas classification treats a plural, numerous subject (cameras, theories, poems).

The confusion between division and classification may account for the tendency of some students to "classify" by taking a single item (say, the television show *Friends*) and placing it in a category (say, situation comedies). We'd explain that they haven't classified anything; they have just filed an item in a pigeonhole. If they'll remember that classification begins not with one thing but with several things, they may avoid much perplexity.

CLASSIFICATION IN OTHER CHAPTERS. Essays developed predominantly by classification are fairly common, but in support of other methods it tends to develop only a paragraph or two. The relatively short list of essays below includes those that use classification more intensively.

Part Two

Jhumpa Lahiri, "Indian Takeout"
Suzanne Britt, "Neat People vs. Sloppy People"
Bruce Catton, "Grant and Lee: A Study in Contrasts"
Judy Brady, "I Want a Wife"
Armin A. Brott, "Not All Men Are Sly Foxes"
Jean Kilbourne, "'Can an Engine Pump the Valves in Your Heart?'"

RUSSELL BAKER

The Plot Against People

In this essay, the well-known humorist Russell Baker makes a common use of classification — for humor. Baker takes a wry look at the universal human feeling that the material world is conspiring against us. Ask the class to come up with more examples of things that "have it in" for people.

Writing humor is difficult, as students who have tried can attest. Give students an opportunity to try their hands at a collaborative essay modeled on Baker's. What conspiracy theories can the class generate? (These might include the school's conspiracy to keep students from registering for any of the classes they most need, the local market's conspiracy to run out of Diet Coke when you most need one, and so on.) Make a list of ideas on the board, and have small groups of students write a short essay describing this conspiracy in detail. You might ask the groups to read their finished products.

Students who enjoy Baker's approach can be encouraged to look into some of his collections, such as *Poor Russell's Almanac* (1972) and *So This Is Depravity* (1980).

QUESTIONS ON MEANING

1. Baker's thesis is stated in paragraph 1. His larger meaning is that inanimate objects conspire to frustrate humans.
2. The reason may be that objects are doing humans a favor (par. 11) or that they are "incredibly stupid" (12).
3. He may also want to point out how ridiculous we are when we become infuriated with inanimate things.
4. By not working, thus "conditioning him never to expect anything of them."

QUESTIONS ON WRITING STRATEGY

1. Baker classifies objects by the ways they thwart human wishes. He might have included things that work for a while and then break, or even things that work fine; but his use of extreme cases adds to the essay's humor.
2. "Any object capable of breaking down at the moment when it is most needed will do so" (par. 2); "A furnace [. . .] will invariably break down [. . .]" (10); "Thereafter, they never work again" (13). (Students will, of course, find others.) Hyperbole establishes Baker's comic tone of exasperation.

3. His pseudoscientific classification, with its dogmatic assertion of the three categories of objects, is a parody of intellectual authority. The pseudo-philosophical discussion of spiritual "peace" in the conclusion reinforces the essay's mock-serious tone.
4. Baker's little stories (the cunning automobile of paragraph 3, or paragraph 8's climbing pliers) capture the reader's attention. Shared experiences provide a sense of recognition and help make the essay funny.

QUESTIONS ON LANGUAGE

1. The vocabulary words highlighted here all contribute to the essay's mock-serious tone. In general, the essay's diction is quite simple.
2. Clever, malicious, plotting. Its effect is to personify the automobile.
3. The general terms make the shared experiences more universal. Had Baker used *I*, he might have seemed more of a crank, less persuasive.

RUSSELL BAKER ON WRITING

What do lead pencils, Shakespeare, eternal quests, cave writing, dreaming, Luddites, and cornpone politicians have to do with computers? In Russell Baker's fertile mind, everything and nothing. In addition to enjoying the fun of the piece, students may be interested in noting how he cleverly shows a mind in the act of composition. Stream-of-consciousness writing has been used more often in confessions, but with some behind-the-scenes crafting, Baker demonstrates its humorous potential.

DEBORAH TANNEN

But What Do You Mean?

The linguist Deborah Tannen came into national prominence with *You Just Don't Understand*, a book about misunderstandings between men and women in conversation. Since then, she has continued to disseminate much of her research through the mass media, trying to help people solve the communication problems of daily life. Oliver Sacks, another intellectual who often addresses a general audience, wrote of *You Just Don't Understand*: "Deborah Tannen combines a novelist's ear for the way people speak with a rare power of original analysis. It is this that makes her an extraordinary sociolinguist, and it is this that makes her book such a fascinating look at that crucial social cement, conversation."

This is one essay that students should be able to apply easily to their own lives, although the men in your class may be more resistant than the women. The essay will certainly evoke a wide range of student response, which should lead to lively class discussion.

Here is an in-class exercise to test Tannen's theories: Ask students to bring in dialogues that illustrate conflict from novels, plays, or movie scripts, deleting characters' names and direct references to gender. Have students read the dialogues out loud and try to guess characters' genders, justifying their choices. Encourage students to look for instances of Tannen's seven categories of miscommunication in the dialogues. (A variation is to cross-cast the dialogues, with women reading men's lines and vice versa, and see if they are still believable.)

QUESTIONS ON MEANING

1. Tannen is pointing out the areas of communication in which misunderstandings between the sexes are most frequent. She seems to hope that a better understanding of how men's and women's communication styles differ will help eliminate such misunderstandings. A secondary purpose is to show women how their problems in the workplace may be linked to their style of communication.
2. Much of what we say is based on pure protocol, which serves as a kind of social cement. We're not so much communicating facts as establishing a rapport with the other person. This speech is often so automatic and predictable that we aren't even aware of what we're saying. (See also the journal prompt and first writing suggestion.)
3. "Many of the conversational rituals common among women are designed to take the other person's feelings into account, while many of the conversational rituals common among men are designed to maintain the one-up position, or at least avoid appearing one-down" (par. 2).
4. "Thank you" is not always used as an expression of gratitude, but is simply a ritual, "an automatic conversation starter and closer" (par. 15). An answer of "You're welcome" results in an imbalance between the speakers.

QUESTIONS ON WRITING STRATEGY

1. Tannen uses these characters as examples of the points she is making. She adds variety to the essay by referring to people alternately by their first names (real or fictitious) and by their functions ("a well-known columnist," par. 4; "a woman manager I know," 13). These characters are ciphers, empty vessels in the service of Tannen's argument, and as such do not need to be described in detail. Tannen reveals only what is relevant to her point. (See also the next question.)
2. That the columnist is well known makes her apology all the more unexpected, less likely to be chalked up to insecurity.
3. Because the essay appeared in *Redbook*, a women's magazine, Tannen uses *you* to address women readers: "What's important is to be aware of how often you say you're sorry (and why), and to monitor your speech based on the reaction you get" (par. 9); "Although you may never enjoy verbal sparring, some women find it helpful to learn how to do it" (19). (Tannen takes a broader approach in *Talking from 9 to 5*, the book intended for a male *and* female audience from which this essay was excerpted.)
4. (1) *Apologies*: Women apologize more than men. They see apology as a way of keeping both speakers on an equal footing, of sharing responsibility. Men take apologies at face value, seeing them as self-deprecating. (2) *Criticism*: Women tend to soften criticism more than men. Men prefer "straight answers." (3) *Thank-yous*: Women say "thank you" more often,

as a ritual. Men take "thank you," like "I'm sorry," more literally. (4) *Fighting*: Men see conversation as a battleground, stating their ideas and criticizing those of others in the strongest possible terms. Women often perceive this approach as a personal attack. (5) *Praise*: Women often assume that the absence of praise is the equivalent of criticism. For men, in contrast, praise is often implied when no criticism is given. Women who ask for criticism may really be asking for praise, but men will give them what they ask for. (6) *Complaints*: Women complain as a way of bonding with others. Men see these complaints as a call for a solution. (7) *Jokes*: "[T]he most common form of humor among men is razzing, teasing, and mock-hostile attacks, while among women it's self-mocking. Women often mistake men's teasing as genuinely hostile. Men often mistake women's mock self-deprecation as truly putting themselves down."

QUESTIONS ON LANGUAGE

1. The humor here relies on exaggeration. It usually refers to finishing off a suffering animal.
2. Tannen uses the metaphor of a gun: criticism as shooting.
3. These verbs liven up the essay and inspire a strong visual or auditory impression. Other examples are "*leapt* into a critical response" (par. 10) and "*poke* holes" (17).
4. Note Tannen's vocabulary of physical and verbal conflict: "contentious," "hedge," "sparring," "rebuttal," "retorted," as well as "disadvantage" (par. 2), "attack" (18), and "enemy" (19). You might discuss whether Tannen loads her case with such words, perhaps exaggerating the conflicts between genders.

DEBORAH TANNEN ON WRITING

Students may not be aware of the debate about the personal in scholarly writing, but many have probably been told at some time not to use *I* in their academic papers. Tannen suggests why and also argues in favor of the first person on scholarly grounds. Students in the natural and applied sciences may be more likely than others in the class to resist Tannen's argument, contending that they don't write about personal interactions. Uncovering resistance and getting a discussion going are of course the aims of the first follow-up question. For the second one, collaboration in small groups is ideal: Working together, students will find it easier to draft the third-person or first-person passage and then revise it, seeing firsthand what the differences are.

STEPHEN KING

"Ever Et Raw Meat?"

This quirky essay by Stephen King gives a "normal" voice to the renowned master of horror and the paranormal. It may be hard to keep students from rehashing lurid scenes from *The Shining* or *Dolores Claiborne*.

King's humor in this essay relies on the assumption that his readers will sympathize with the trials of fame, but some students may be antagonistic to King's satiric treatment of his audience. Is there a difference between the audience for this essay, the people who read King's novels, and the readers who pose the questions King lists? (To direct students who wish to explore the issue of King's attitudes and his obligations to his reading public, see the third writing topic.)

King's frequent references to his fiction suggest that the readers of the essay are also readers of his books. If you have time, assign one of King's novels or screenplays to each of several small groups *before* students read King's essay. Give all the groups the same topic for postreading discussion: "Questions *I'd* like to ask Stephen King." We'll wager that some questions will be as unusual as the ones King reports.

QUESTIONS ON MEANING

1. The thesis is in the second and third sentences. His purpose seems to be primarily entertainment: King pokes fun at the questions he has been asked and asks readers to join in. King may also want to convey the difficulty of transforming himself from private creator to public personality — macabre imagination aside, he's just your average guy. (See also the second question on writing strategy.)
2. They are complicated or illogical questions that King has no "real answers" for and that thus make him uncomfortable.
3. Like flagellation, King's book signings represent a self-sacrifice or punishment in the name of a greater good, in this case, making himself available to his fans and promoting his books.

QUESTIONS ON WRITING STRATEGY

1. "One-of-a-kind Questions" are unique and uniquely strange. "Old Standards" are tiresomely familiar. "Real Weirdies" are frequently asked, like "Old Standards," but they are puzzling and unanswerable.
2. As noted in the answer to the first question on meaning, King sees himself as allied with his readers, who he seems to expect will share his amusement and surprise at the silly, ill-worded, and illogical questions. One tip-off is the sarcastic asides in parentheses in paragraphs 11–19. At the same time, King also must expect his readers to appreciate the dilemma of a writer confronted with the unanswerable "weirdies" about his craft (for example, pars. 22, 28, 29).
3. At the end of his essay, King suggests that he does not just tolerate but also appreciates genuine questions seeking real answers.

4. The examples all display the readers' sense of their entitlement to ask King questions. Since they have bought the books he has published, he has become in part theirs.

QUESTIONS ON LANGUAGE

1. *Self-abnegation* may be the least familiar word on this list to students. *Abnegate* comes from Latin *ab*, "away from," and *negave*, "to deny," and means "renounce." *Self-abnegation* means "renouncing of self-interest."
2. Addressing readers directly is like touching their elbows to get their attention and establish connection.
3. This metaphor suggests an automatic answer requiring no thought, like a form letter.

STEPHEN KING ON WRITING

We hope that students will see how King's thoughts can apply to their writing as well as to his. Knowing from experience that the writing will come, keeping an eye on your audience but pursuing your own vision — these are valuable gains that students can also expect as they continue to write.

STEPHANIE ERICSSON
The Ways We Lie

Lying and being lied to are universal human experiences. This selection offers a thoughtful look at lying that should inspire lively class discussion. One way to begin work on the essay is to ask students to give their definitions of *lying*. Write the responses on the board, and invite students to challenge each other's definitions. What consensus does the class reach? What are the points of contention?

Ericsson admits that sometimes we lie for reasons that seem almost virtuous — to protect someone else's feelings, for example. How justifiable are the various kinds of lies she lists? Divide the class into five groups and have each group look closely at two sections of the essay, two kinds of lies. From what perspectives are these examples of unexcusable lies? Who would assert that they were necessary, valid, or reasonable manipulations of the truth? Once these points of view are established, ask each group to come up with a comprehensive definition of a *lie*. How do the groups' definitions differ depending on which sections the students were examining?

We pair Ericsson's essay with William Lutz's "The World of Doublespeak," a complementary examination of lies. Many of the questions raised about Ericsson's essay can be raised about Lutz's as well.

Some longer works on this topic are *Lying: Moral Choice in Public and Private Life*, by Sisela Bok (1978), and the title essay in *On Lies, Secrets, and Silence*, by Adrienne Rich (1979).

QUESTIONS ON MEANING

1. Ericsson's thesis is that the lies we tell in everyday life, however seemingly unimportant and even necessary, cause us to lose our sensitivity to larger, more damaging lies.
2. No, it would not be possible to eliminate lies completely. Ericsson's experience (par. 4) supports this, as do the benefits of different lies, such as the sergeant's lie to help a soldier's family (9), the dismissal to help ration a parent's energy (31), the delusion to help us function despite the possibility of global disaster (33).
3. Eliminating lies might help ourselves and others to perceive reality clearly; it would be more just; and it would sharpen our awareness of the lies we are told.
4. The purpose is to examine the roles that lying plays in our lives and its effect of dulling our insistence on the truth.

QUESTIONS ON WRITING STRATEGY

1. She's not casting blame, since she's as much a liar as any of her readers. She puts herself eye-to-eye with her readers.
2. Answers will vary. The epigraphs could be judged on pithiness, wit, relation to the category following, and other criteria. Some of our favorites: Cicero before paragraph 14, Freehill before 23, Wilde before 26, Hoffer before 32, Shaw before 35.
3. Ericsson's message: As much as possible, tell yourself the truth and insist on it in others, or the "moral garbage" will become "invisible." Her conclusion is very effective, we think — it clearly shows the relation of the everyday lie to the Big Lie and urges that honesty begin where she has been showing lies begin, with each of us individually.
4. Answers will vary. Some of Ericsson's most pointed definitions are those of the white lie ("a vote of no confidence" par. 8), the stereotype ("a candy bar of misinformation instead of a balanced meal," 21), and delusion ("an adhesive to keep the status quo intact," 34). Some highly effective examples are the illustrations of groupthink with Pearl Harbor (24–25), out-and-out lies with her nephew's assertion that "murderers" broke the fence (26), and delusion with alcoholics (33).

QUESTIONS ON LANGUAGE

1. The internal disease of cancer (the lies we tell ourselves and others) affects our perception of the external garbage we're floating in (the lies told to us).
2. The tone, to us, seems more appropriate in the first passage than in the second. It may be strong to say that the Catholic Church was a "co-perpetrator" with Porter (par. 13), but its actions were deceitful and harmful. Ericsson's feelings about the "omission of Lilith from the Bible" (20) are a little harder to credit. The events she mentions are the subject of extensive scholarly inquiry and far from proved, and imputing contemporary motives to ancient people is ahistorical. (Still, the issue is a live one: Just in recent years, the church has condemned the elevation of the goddess by some of its members.)
3. Ericsson's most highly charged language seems to come in her discussion of religion: Note "pedophilia," the sexual abuse of children (par. 12),

"co-perpetrator" (13) in her treatment of the Father Porter scandal, "misogynists" and "patriarchal" (20) in her inquiry into the suppression of Lilith.

4. The adult-children-of-alcoholics movement, as represented by groups like Al-Anon, may not be familiar to your class. The movement aims to empower, through support groups and literature dealing with shared problems, those whose parents were or are alcoholics.

STEPHANIE ERICSSON ON WRITING

We provide Ericsson's brief comments on writing-as-therapy because we like her idea about the "blank white page": It "will never contradict you, never ignore you, and never judge you." These could be encouraging words to students who are just beginning to experiment with journal writing, especially those (and there are many) who have trouble shaking their own internal censors or their sense of an audience besides themselves.

WILLIAM LUTZ
The World of Doublespeak

William Lutz is a leading figure in the campaign against the dishonest language that he (and others) call doublespeak. This essay, extracted from the first chapter of his book-length treatment of the subject, both defines the term and classifies its varieties. The many, many examples will leave students in no doubt about the meaning of doublespeak and should make it relatively easy for them to spot it.

One problem with doublespeak is that it often relies on multisyllabic words and complicated syntax. As a result, the most example-heavy parts of Lutz's essay may be difficult reading for some students. Lutz himself practices what he preaches, writing clearly and concisely, but you may want to warn students that some passages in the essay require patience.

Probably the best way to make this essay immediate and significant for students is to have them locate doublespeak in what they read and hear. Indeed, you may want to ask them to try the journal-writing assignment as soon as they've read the essay and to bring their examples to class. Even if each student contributes only one or two examples, you'll have a good collection. Working as a whole class or in small groups to sort their examples into Lutz's categories, students will be writing a continuation of the essay.

We pair Lutz's essay with the previous one, Stephanie Ericsson's "The Ways We Lie." Ericsson deals with explicit lies, Lutz with a more subtle form of deception, but both authors look at how we use language to avoid the truth. The fourth writing topic following each essay can be used as an assignment or to spark discussion.

QUESTIONS ON MEANING

1. Lutz's thesis might be stated briefly as follows: The four kinds of doublespeak all include language "that avoids or shifts responsibility, language that is at variance with its real or purported meaning" (the quotation is from par. 2). The thesis accumulates over paragraphs 2–3, with the addition of the intention to classify in paragraph 5.
2. Paragraph 4 offers the following questions: "Who is saying what to whom, under what conditions and circumstances, with what intent, and with what results?" These questions locate the motivation for dishonesty that would indicate doublespeak.
3. The greatest danger is that, as in Orwell's *1984*, doublespeak will lead to the "control of reality through language" (par. 23). Doublespeak "alter[s] our perception of reality and corrupt[s] our thinking. [. . .] [It] breeds suspicion, cynicism, distrust, and, ultimately, hostility" (22). It can "infect and eventually destroy the function of language" (23).
4. Lutz clearly assumes an educated reader, someone able to perceive the fundamental dishonesty in his examples. At the same time, his careful classification, scores of examples, and extensive discussion of the dangers indicate that he believes his reader probably is not sensitive to doublespeak and needs help to recognize it.

QUESTIONS ON WRITING STRATEGY

1. Lutz's principle of classification is the intention of doublespeakers. Those who use euphemisms are trying to "mislead or deceive" (par. 7) with inoffensive words. Those who use jargon seek to give their words "an air of profundity, authority, and prestige" (10). Those who use gobbledygook or bureaucratese are bent on "overwhelming the audience with words" (13). And those who use inflated language seek "to make the ordinary seem extraordinary; [. . .] to make the simple seem complex" (17).
2. Greenspan's second comment is surprising because he acknowledges that he is deliberately unclear. With the quotation, Lutz shows that doublespeak is intentional.
3. Many of Lutz's examples are dated, and some students may at first think that doublespeak is an old, not a current, problem. The first writing suggestion, asking students to find current examples of their own, should help them see that doublespeak is no less a problem now than it was two decades ago.
4. Definition appears mainly in paragraphs 2 and 3 and in the explanations of each kind of doublespeak (pars. 5 and 7, 9–10, 13, 17). Cause and effect also figures in the explanation of categories, as Lutz gives the intentions of doublespeakers, but mainly it develops the last section of the essay (20–23). The definition, of course, clarifies Lutz's subject and his categories. The cause and effect shows what is at stake with this dishonest language.

QUESTIONS ON LANGUAGE

1. Lutz's language provides a good foil to the quotations of doublespeak: He uses plain language and relatively simple syntax.
2. The words listed all have negative connotations, suggesting undesirable or even dangerous effects of doublespeak. More neutral language would

not make Lutz's point as sharply. For just a few examples, see paragraph 1.

3. *Taboo* now refers to a prohibition against the use or practice of something. The word comes from the Tongan word *tabu*, an adjective meaning "set apart, consecrated to a special use or purpose." Captain Cook traveled to Tonga in 1777; his widely read narrative of his experiences, including an explanation of *tabu*, brought the term into common use in England.

WILLIAM LUTZ ON WRITING

Students may be encouraged to see recognizable behaviors, particularly procrastination, in a successful writer. Students aren't writing whole books for their classes, of course, but Lutz's advice, scaled down, should remind them that they needn't try to write an essay all at once, only a few paragraphs. The longer students wait to write a paper, the greater the chance they will have to do it in one sitting and will be daunted by the task.

The writer and humorist Fran Lebowitz once joked that being a writer was a bit like being a perpetual student . . . except you can't write a book the night before it is due. "I know," Lebowitz deadpanned, "because I tried twice."

11

CAUSE AND EFFECT

Asking Why

As you know, the matter of cause and effect can plunge a class into many complexities, and it can sometimes lead to fruitless wrangles. Still, many instructors find that this chapter leads to unusually satisfying results.

We start off with two complementary essays, Gina Kolata's "Probing Disease Clusters" and Atul Gawande's "The Cancer-Cluster Myth." In this pair, the subject matter is nearly identical, with the differences lying in depth of investigation and explanation. Then follow two essays that seem always to get a rise out of students: Gore Vidal's "Drugs," which recommends legalization, and Meghan Daum's "Safe-Sex Lies," about the effects of AIDS awareness on the author's twenty-something generation. Finally, in Don DeLillo's short story "Videotape," the narrator tries to understand his obsession with a tape of a murder.

We have endeavored to clarify the difference between process analysis and cause-and-effect analysis, a frequent source of confusion for students. Process asks *how;* cause and effect asks *why.* Further, process deals with events that are repeated or repeatable or even just theoretically repeatable (like the creation of the Grand Canyon); cause and effect deals with singular events, one-time happenings.

Studying cause and effect can lead to a discussion of common errors in reasoning, as we indicate in this chapter when we touch on the fallacy of *post hoc.* If you wish to bring up logical fallacies, a few are listed, defined, and illustrated in Chapter 13 on argument and persuasion (pp. 508–09). Perhaps it might be enough at this point merely to call students' attention to them. Cause and effect may be complicated enough without trying to tackle logical fallacies at the same time.

CAUSE AND EFFECT IN OTHER CHAPTERS. The following list of essays is quite lengthy, but it would have been much longer — perhaps including the entire table of contents — if we had included all the pieces in which cause and effect plays any note. In the essays we do list, the method provides significant support for the writer's ideas.

Part Two

Sherman Alexie, "Indian Education"
Barbara Huttmann, "A Crime of Compassion"
Brad Manning, "Arm Wrestling with My Father"
Sarah Vowell, "Shooting Dad"
Barbara Lazear Ascher, "On Compassion"

Bill Bryson, "Design Flaws"
Brent Staples, "Black Men and Public Space"
Bruce Catton, "Grant and Lee: A Study in Contrasts"
Nancy Mairs, "Disability"
Linnea Saukko, "How to Poison the Earth"
Niala Maharaj and Donovan Hohn, "Thorny Truths About Flowers"
Armin A. Brott, "Not All Men Are Sly Foxes"
Shelby Steele, "Notes from the Hip-Hop Underground"
Deborah Tannen, "But What Do You Mean?"
Stephanie Ericsson, "The Ways We Lie"
William Lutz, "The World of Doublespeak"
Gloria Naylor, "The Meanings of a Word"
Marie Winn, "TV Addiction"
H. L. Mencken, "The Penalty of Death"
Chitra Divakaruni, "Live Free and Starve"
Peter Singer, "The Singer Solution to World Poverty"
William F. Buckley, Jr., "Why Don't We Complain?"
Laura Fraser, "Why I Stopped Being a Vegetarian"
Colleen Wenke, "Too Much Pressure"

Part Three

Sandra Cisneros, "Only Daughter"
Stephen Jay Gould, "Sex, Drugs, Disasters, and the Extinction of Dino-
    saurs"
Maxine Hong Kingston, "No Name Woman"
George Orwell, "Shooting an Elephant"
Richard Rodriguez, "Aria: A Memoir of a Bilingual Childhood"
Jonathan Swift, "A Modest Proposal"
Cornel West, "Race Matters"
Terry Tempest Williams, "The Clan of One-Breasted Women"

GINA KOLATA

Probing Disease Clusters

Kolata's report from the *New York Times* and Atul Gawande's "The Cancer-Cluster Myth," with which it is paired, both suggest how hard it can be to
establish firm cause-and-effect relationships. The difficulty is especially marked
when the apparent effect is a seeming pattern that is in fact random, with no
distinct cause. Distinguishing between genuine and illusory cause-and-effect
patterns is especially fraught in the case of disease clusters.

As part of your discussion, you might have students think about other
such random patterns and the rush to find causal explanations. For example,
suppose a community has a larger than usual number of teenage traffic fa-
talities over the course of a year. Commentators point out that the local school
district dropped driver-education courses four years earlier — hence the greater
number of accidents by teenage drivers. Ask students whether this proposed
cause-and-effect relationship can be proved. They should realize that it can't
be — that correlations or associations (par. 16) are not proof. Even if driver-

education courses were reinstated and teenage traffic accidents subsequently fell, the connection would only be an association, not a certain cause-and-effect relationship.

Once they understand this concept clearly, students in small groups could work together to come up with other examples and then share these with the rest of the class.

QUESTIONS ON MEANING

1. A disease cluster is a higher than normal incidence of a particular disease within a particular area. Residents of the area may believe that the cluster is caused by some toxin in the air, water, or other part of the environment and that it will continue to make people ill.
2. The clustered diseases are common and the toxins appear in other areas without clusters, so the cluster could be a chance occurrence (pars. 10–11); it is difficult "to draw the boundaries of a cluster" (12); "other exposures" could have caused the clusters (16).
3. A statistician is generally a mathematician who specializes in manipulating and analyzing data about populations. Disease clusters are themselves statistical constructs, as are their links to possible causes. According to Kolata, many statisticians believe that statistical analyses of small populations can provide only limited results and that most clusters are the result of "random chance."

QUESTIONS ON WRITING STRATEGY

1. Kolata's purpose is to explain why disease clusters, as painful and frustrating as they are for victims to bear, generally cannot be linked definitively by scientists to specific environmental causes. Writing for an audience of newspaper readers, Kolata presents specific details and quotations from experts to develop these two points.
2. Kolata cites the experts mainly to borrow their authority for her essay and to present professional views of disease clusters.
3. Kolata opens with the example of the high incidence of autism in a small New Jersey town and discusses a leukemia cluster in Woburn, Massachusetts, the subject of a recent film (par. 6). She contrasts these with clusters involving coal miners, asbestos workers, and others, which were clearly linked to toxins because the "chemical exposure was enormous, and the disease was extraordinarily rare" (8–9). The examples underline which disease clusters can and can't be traced.

QUESTIONS ON LANGUAGE

1. In the folk tale, a boy cried "Wolf!" several times when there was actually no danger from a wolf. When at last he called because a wolf did threaten, no one believed him. For epidemiologists, most disease clusters are similarly false alarms. Judging from the attitudes Kolata goes on to report, the repetition of the false alarms is also increasing the skepticism of the professionals.
2. Two conditions in "association" merely occur in sequence or at the same time. A cause-and-effect relationship may exist, but not necessarily. (A

similar question comes up with Gawande's essay, over the word "corre-lation." See number 4 under "Questions on Meaning," p. 434 of the text.)

3. Even Kolata's *New York Times* readers might be unfamiliar with the term *mesothelioma*. It is a rare form of lung cancer.

GINA KOLATA ON WRITING

Kolata's stress on digging beneath the surface of others' opinions seems useful for students who are having perhaps their first experiences with re-search writing. In fact, all of her points about a reporter's job seem relevant to students' work, especially if the work involves interviews and other original research.

ATUL GAWANDE

The Cancer-Cluster Myth

Like Gina Kolata's "Probing Disease Clusters," with which it is paired, "The Cancer-Cluster Myth" makes the point that some apparent "patterns" that seem to have a causal connection are, more plausibly, simply random occurrences. Ultimately, students should realize that cause-and-effect analy-sis can be a tricky business and should be approached with great care.

Gawande offers a number of examples of the "almost irresistible" (par. 11) human tendency to perceive clusters or patterns where they don't, in fact, exist. Give students some time to talk about and make sense of what Gawande introduces as "the Belief in the Law of Small Numbers" — that is, the "system-atic error in human judgment" that leads us mistakenly to see a pattern in a small set of numbers. Students should see Gawande's basic point here: Most neighborhood "cancer clusters" occur on such a small scale that they cannot be traced to a single source — unlike, say, cancers associated with the use of tobacco products, which occur across a much broader spectrum of the popu-lation.

Based on the advice offered in the final paragraphs of the essay, you might have students in small groups draft a set of guidelines for public-health offi-cials who have to deal with citizens fearful of a "cancer cluster" in their com-munity.

QUESTIONS ON MEANING

1. In paragraph 4 Gawande attributes the increase to the media attention received by several high-profile cases of cancer clusters and to the in-creasing availability of "data on potential toxic sites" and "local cancer rates."
2. Scientists have been successful at locating "the causes of other kinds of disease clusters," so why not local cancer clusters (par. 6)? See also num-ber 5 under "Questions on Writing Strategy."

3. The fallacy is that, like a phony "sharpshooter" who after the fact draws a bull's-eye around the places hit, people notice a seemingly high incidence of cases first and then "define the population base around them." However, within small populations randomly high levels of common cancers may easily occur. The fallacy distorts the level of danger.

4. Correlations may seem to be related because they occur together in statistically significant ways, but they are in the end mere statistics, not demonstrated causes and effects. (A similar distinction comes up in Kolata's essay, with the word "association." See number 2 under "Questions on Language," p. 425 of the text.)

5. Gawande's thesis is stated in several different ways: "Given the exceedingly poor success rate of such investigations [into cancer clusters], epidemiologists tend to be skeptical about their worth" (par. 5); "scientists have hardly any way to distinguish the 'true' cancer cluster that's worth investigating from the crowd of cluster impostors" (14); "This isn't to say that carcinogens in the local environment can't raise cancer rates; it's just that such increases disappear in all the background variation that occurs in small populations. [. . .] [C]orrelations inevitably turn up. Yet, years later, in case after case, nothing definite is confirmed" (16). In the last two paragraphs, Gawande extends his thesis to recommend responding to public concerns despite the scientific findings: Public education can eliminate the demand for most cluster investigations (17), and some investigations should simply go ahead (18).

QUESTIONS ON WRITING STRATEGY

1. While the essay is clearly explanatory, Gawande seems to want to persuade readers that the clusters are a "myth" and at the same time persuade scientists and government officials to take the public's concerns seriously.

2. The introduction reinforces Gawande's point that the number of reported cancer clusters has been growing significantly.

3. The personal note suggests that Gawande has a stake in residential cancer-cluster research, so his conclusion that most such research is fruitless may carry more weight.

4. Gawande wants to make the point that health officials cannot ignore the public's concerns, that "acting on public concerns" by investigating apparent cancer clusters may be the best way to "maintain public trust."

5. The four groups are outbreak clusters, occupational clusters, medical clusters, and neighborhood clusters. Explaining the successes in identifying the causes of the first three kinds helps Gawande explain why the last kind does not engender the same success.

QUESTIONS ON LANGUAGE

1. First-year college students may find these paragraphs a bit difficult to follow, but Gawande does clearly define his terms and carefully explain the progress of cancers. Students should recognize that most of Gawande's language would be accessible to the educated readers of *The New Yorker*.

2. The Minnesota epidemiologist's strong condemnation of "wasting" taxpayers' dollars on researching residential cancer clusters goes further than Gawande himself does in arguing against the research, and it is offset by Minnesota's efforts at public education.

3. *Carcinogens* are any substances that produce cancers. The word comes from the Greek *karkinos*, "crab." The Latin word *cancer* also means "crab." Some tumors that resulted from cancers were thought to resemble crabs.

ATUL GAWANDE ON WRITING

Students may at first find Gawande's experiences remote from their own. Nonetheless, we reprint Gawande's remarks for two reasons: First, because he stresses, once again, that writing is a way of thinking; second, because his airing of his own mistakes, and the response he got, is a sterling example of writing as communication.

GORE VIDAL

Drugs

Vidal's radical solution to the problem of drug addiction in the United States, and his charge that the government was responsible for the deaths of some New York drug users, may cause some students to sputter with objections. The discussion is usually lively.

Vidal is optimistic about the effects of legalizing drugs in the United States, but he does not give examples of countries (Holland, for example) that have already begun to do so. For small-group work, you could ask students to extend and update Vidal's essay with research of their own. One group could research legalization in other countries; another could research current prominent support for legalization; a third could research statistics on drug use and crime; and so on. Researching the prolegalization position will give students experience in preparing a case based on cause and effect. Further, since most students probably will not agree with Vidal (prolegalization is usually a minority view), this research will help prepare them to support and defend their own views with evidence as well as feeling.

As an alternative to an admittedly time-consuming research project, you could simply divide students according to their beliefs about whether drugs should be legalized. Then give them fifteen minutes or so to prepare to argue in favor of the *opposite side* (that is, those who are for will have to argue against, and vice versa). Although such a debate probably will not sustain itself for very long, the experience will encourage students to consider the opposition in formulating their own views.

An informative debate between two scholars on the subject of drug legalization occurred in the pages of *The Public Interest*, Summer 1988: Ethan Nadelmann, "The Case for Legalization," and John Kaplan, "Taking Drugs Seriously."

QUESTIONS ON MEANING

1. Vidal's purpose is evidently to explain how he believes most drug trafficking and addiction in this country could be stopped. The chief cause
of our vast drug problem, he claims, is that drugs are illegal and thus
doubly tempting to many people. His explanation is terse, clear, and
biting. (We might also say that Vidal aims to convince readers of his
position, but he undermines that purpose himself with "Will anything
sensible be done? Of course not," par. 12.)

2. Vidal, claiming that the Bureau of Narcotics would be superfluous if
drug laws were eased, believes that self-preservation figures in the
bureau's antidrug position. He also contends in paragraph 12 that Americans are endowed with a puritanical desire to punish sin and with a love
of moneymaking. Both tendencies, he suggests, find expression in illegal
drug trafficking and in efforts to combat it. What Vidal too cavalierly
ignores, perhaps, are the very real dangers that many drug users inflict
on themselves and on others. It might occur to some that not all the
perils would disappear with legalization.

3. Vidal's essay makes several now-dated references (the "silent majority"
and Richard Nixon, par. 4; fear of "Commies" and "murmuring 'groovy,'"
5). And Vidal's radical zeal may strike some students as outdated. But
Vidal is hardly addressing a dead issue: Drugs are a worse problem now
than in 1970. In some quarters, the increase in drug abuse has intensi-
fied calls for legalization. In other quarters, it has made legalization seem
more absurd.

QUESTIONS ON WRITING STRATEGY

1. Vidal's essay displays a sarcastic wit. Of the many examples, why not
encourage students to cite just a few?
   a. Reference to "the popular Fu Manchu theory" in paragraph 2.
   b. The parenthetical statement in paragraph 3 about persecution being
   some people's idea of happiness.
   c. Vidal's explanation of the "silent majority" (par. 4).
   d. The author's exaggerated view in paragraph 5 of the public's expected
   reaction to his views.
   e. Reference to Congress's "divine mission to stamp out Demon Rum"
   (par. 7).
   f. The mention of "friendly playground pushers" (par. 11).
   g. The barbs in paragraph 12: "Of course not" in answer to the rhetorical
   question, and Vidal's unflattering picture of the professional politi-
   cian.

2. Most notably in paragraph 5, Vidal anticipates many of his readers' probable objections. By demonstrating that he is already aware of their arguments, he succeeds in defusing them a bit.

3. "Is everyone reasonably sane?" (par. 6) anticipates yet another possible
objection to the author's plan, thus reducing its power to damage his
views. In paragraph 9 the questions, by suggesting the most likely sus-
pects, set the reader up for Vidal's surprise answer. In paragraph 12 the
author apparently asks the question so that he can answer it for the
reader.

4. Combined with the Prohibition analogy (par. 7), the example does have
weight. Vidal does not give data to support his assertion that the US
government was in essence responsible for the deaths. He does mention

other possible causes (Mafiosi, parental permissiveness, bad examples like Timothy Leary), but, in rejecting them, he may open himself to the charge of oversimplification, especially in the absence of data. Yet he is analyzing the cause(s) of a specific situation, for which there may indeed have been a single dominant cause. Vidal is hardly alone in charging that US drug policy sometimes worsens the drug problem — for instance, by picking on easier targets such as marijuana distributors and thus pushing users to harder drugs. (Note that this passage in the essay is also the subject of the second writing suggestion.)

QUESTIONS ON LANGUAGE

1. A *mainliner* is a slang term for someone who injects a drug into a principal vein. Like most slang, this is colorful coinage; originally a *main line*, according to *Merriam-Webster's Collegiate Dictionary*, was "a principal highway or railroad line."
2. The phrase is heavy with irony. Nixon was never known as a wit, even an underestimated one. Vidal ascribes to Nixon a knowledge he surely did not have about the origins of his famous phrase.

GORE VIDAL ON WRITING

Here, if students need it — and many do, at least occasionally — is evidence that writing can be fun. Interesting to us is Vidal's declaration that he no longer plans his work in advance. In this he is perhaps more like a poet than like most nonfiction writers. No one who reads what writers say about their craft can think that there is just one way to write and that everyone ought to master it. We have to acknowledge how unique each approach to writing is.

MEGHAN DAUM

Safe-Sex Lies

Many or most of your students will be unable to remember a time before AIDS. This provocative essay challenges received notions about safe sex that have become almost dogma, especially that everyone is at equal risk of contracting the AIDS virus and that everyone should be equally vigilant against it. Daum's analyses of the treatment of AIDS in popular culture and advertising are excellent models of a critical reading of the media. In this respect the essay might be taught alongside Jean Kilbourne's "'Can an Engine Pump the Valves in Your Heart?'" and Tom Wolfe's "Pornoviolence."

Daum's analysis of the Benetton ad could be a good springboard for a class discussion of media representations of AIDS or, if you prefer, a more general discussion of media manipulation. You might ask students to bring in advertisements from magazines and discuss them in small groups. Each group could be responsible for presenting a close critical reading of one ad, a reading perhaps informed by one of the readings suggested below.

For further reading on the media's treatment of AIDS, you might suggest Simon Watney's *Policing Desire: Aids, Pornography, and the Media* (1987). Another source is Douglas Crimp's anthology, *AIDS: Cultural Analysis/Cultural Activism* (1988). Randy Shilts's *And the Band Played On*, which has been made into a film, gives a journalistic account of the early reception of the disease.

Students who want to look further into representation in advertising could be steered toward the works of Marshall McLuhan, in particular *The Mechanical Bride* (1951) and *The Medium Is the Message* (1967). Mark Crispin Miller's *Boxed In* (1988) contains sharply observed essays on *Family Feud, Cosby,* Zest soap ads, and other topics. Another recent inquiry into image manipulation is Carol Moog's *"Are They Selling Her Lips?" — Advertising and Identity* (1990).

QUESTIONS ON MEANING

1. Daum is trying to expose what she sees as a double hypocrisy: By overstating the threat of AIDS to low-risk groups, the media lose their credibility in the eyes of educated young adults, who can see through the hype. The young adults' response to media lies is to engage in unsafe behavior, which they in turn feel compelled to lie about. This atmosphere of lies and mistrust is potentially more harmful than the virus itself. Daum specifically says, "[T]here is no solution" (par. 10), although she presumably believes that greater honesty about the risk of AIDS to heterosexuals would improve the situation.

2. "My suspicion is, in fact, that very few of us — 'us' being the demographic profile frequently charged with thinking we're immortal, the population accused of being cynical and lazy and weak — have really responded to the AIDS crisis the way the Federal Government and educators would like us to believe. My guess is that we're all but ignoring it and that almost anyone who claims otherwise is lying" (par. 3).

3. The fear of contracting the AIDS virus is outweighed by a sense that sexual freedom is a "right."

4. The discourse on AIDS has become as slick as a music video. Style is more important than content, as in the case of the Benetton ad, which is conceived as a "work of art," open to any interpretation. Overexposure to AIDS propaganda has deadened its persuasiveness.

QUESTIONS ON WRITING STRATEGY

1. By exaggerating the threat of AIDS to heterosexuals who don't use IV drugs, the media lose credibility with the members of this group who are sophisticated enough to "filter out" the hype (par. 9). Because these people no longer know whom or what to believe, they eventually give in and have unprotected sex. But they lie about their behavior to others because they don't want to be confronted with the risks they're taking. Thus they feel ashamed, guilty, mistrustful, and dishonest.

2. Daum's tone is frank and confessional with a dose of dark irony. For instance, as early as the first sentence she tells us, "I have been tested for HIV three times" (par. 1). She goes on to admit: "I am terrified of this

disease" (1); "I've gone into more than a few relationships with the safest of intentions and discarded them after the fourth or fifth encounter" (3); "We find ourselves wondering about these things over dinner dates. We look for any hints of homosexual tendencies, any references to a hypodermic moment" (6). Examples of her irony abound: "I [. . .] don't take pity on heroin-addicted bass players by going to bed with them in the hopes of being thanked in the liner notes of their first major independent release"; "they'd seen it happen, oh, yes, they had"; "didn't quite explain how to use dental dams"; "fistfuls of condoms" (1); "AIDS-concerned citizen" (5); "It's a bummer on a grand scale" (10).

3.   She establishes herself as honest and up-front, giving an impression of having nothing to hide. She also creates a bond with readers who have been in the same situation.

4.   She is clearly targeting readers who share her "demographic profile" (par. 1) — that is, young, middle- to upper-class heterosexuals who don't use IV drugs. But the urgency of her essay and the care with which she explains causes and effects make it clear that she is also targeting the other readers of the *Times* — the ones who don't already know this situation.

5.   The ad, presumably with the best of multicultural intentions, is putting a false face on the disease. By implying that AIDS is a straight white disease, the ad does a disservice both to straight white people and to the people who are most at risk.

QUESTIONS ON LANGUAGE

1.   A *mantra*, in Hinduism and Buddhism, is a sacred utterance (a syllable, word, or verse) considered to possess mystical or spiritual efficacy. Repetition of a mantra representing a concept or deity is said to evoke the very essence or presence that it represents. The word comes from Sanskrit, meaning "sacred counsel" or "formula." In English the word is usually used ironically or pejoratively to suggest overuse of or excessive dependence on a phrase or an idea.

2.   Daum is forming a bond with her audience by evoking a common experience. The use of *those* suggests that we all know what she's talking about, that we've all been in the same situation.

3.   The informal language seems quite appropriate to us. In the first two examples, it re-creates the experience of hearing and receiving the words of "health service counselors." Elsewhere, it is fresh and youthful, emphasizing that this is a problem of young adults.

DON DeLILLO

Videotape

DeLillo's riveting short story is an unusual work of fiction. It focuses less on the central incident viewed on tape — a serial killer's random shooting of a driver — than on the narrator's responses to the constant replay of the tape on television. You might begin discussion by asking students what the narrator himself wonders: Why does he find the tape so compelling? For the narrator, the shooting and its unintentional capture on videotape become a metaphor for the randomness, the precariousness, of life. He finds in the tape a sort of hyperreality — "a channeled path through time, to give things a shape and a destiny" (par. 19) — and its effect is enhanced by the fact that it was recorded by a child, an "innocent."

The incident is fictional, of course — there was no "Texas Highway Killer" — but you might want to have students consider the way DeLillo's careful use of detail creates the feel of reality, of something that might easily have happened in contemporary life. (For instance, in par. 33: "This is either the tenth or eleventh homicide committed by the Texas Highway Killer. The number is uncertain because the police believe that one of the shootings may have been a copycat crime.")

As another way of analyzing the story, you could divide students into small groups and have each group consider a different strand of meaning or imagery that runs throughout: the idea of the randomness of life, the role of the girl who made the videotape, the power of video itself, the narrator's relationship to his wife, the impact of the media. Then groups could report their findings to the class.

QUESTIONS ON MEANING

1. The girl is like an innocent bystander observing the killing; she has gotten "lost and wandered clear-eyed into horror" (par. 22). The speaker feels, in a sense, that he sees what happens on the tape through the eyes of this innocent girl (27).
2. He wants his wife to watch because the violence is real (par. 28) and because of a certain aggressiveness, a wish for her to see firsthand "the risk of existing" (31).
3. The narrator says that the killer "commits the crimes as if they were a form of taped-and-played event. The crimes are inseparable from the idea of taping and playing [. . .] cheap mass production, the sequence of repeated images and victims, stark and glary and more or less unremarkable." The narrator connects the possibility of playback with the serial killer's repeated and usually similar murders. He may be implying that relentlessly repeatable videotape, like the duplicated crimes of a serial killer, robs events of their singularity and their potential to grow and change in recollection and imagination.

QUESTIONS ON WRITING STRATEGY

1. The reasons given: the tape's relentlessness and "crude power" (pars. 11–13); its heightened reality (14, 28); its ability "to give things a shape and destiny" (19); the randomness of what happens, "something here that speaks to you directly, saying terrible things about forces beyond your control" (21); and, finally, "Seeing someone at the moment he dies, dying unexpectedly [. . .] is reason alone to stay fixed to the screen. It is instructional [. . .]. It demonstrates an elemental truth, that every breath you take has two possible endings" (36) — that is, any one of us could be killed at any minute.

2. We learn in paragraph 4 that the video involves a victim, in 9 that it records a homicide, in 20 that a gun was shot, in 24 that the driver was shot, in 26 that the video is shown on TV, in 33 that the killer is a serial killer. Slowly doling out information creates a questioning suspense in the reader's mind about what happened and also intensifies the sense of immediacy in the narrator's delivery: He seems to be speaking in real time.

3. The second-person pronoun shows some attempt on the narrator's part to create distance between himself and his own dubious behavior. At the same time, it draws the reader into the events of the story and universalizes the response to the random death.

4. The present tense gives the story immediacy. It also suggests the "present tense" of watching a videotape, where events occur before our eyes even though they happened in the past.

5. Description is necessary to show what occurs on the videotape: the ordinariness of the man driving the car, the jolt when he is shot, his leaning into the door, the twist of his head, the drift of the car toward the guardrail, and the "split-second blur" before the tape ends.

QUESTIONS ON LANGUAGE

1. Other such references include "aimless" (par. 11); "the random, [. . .] the accidental" (13); "The chance quality of the encounter" and "Random energies that approach a common point" (21); "this is the risk of existing" (31); "a crime designed for random taping" (34); and "an elemental truth, that every breath you take has two possible endings" (36). Both life and death, the speaker suggests, are random events over which we have little control.

2. The ordinariness of the scene at the beginning is echoed in the ordinariness the crime has for the serial killer.

3. The narrator seems to be questioning the ability of language to describe what happens on the videotape. Its awful reality is overwhelming.

4. A *slapstick* is literally a device consisting of two flat pieces of board linked together so that they slap loudly against each other when they hit something. Stage comedians used slapsticks to increase the sound of a blow (generally to the buttocks) that would, in fact, result in little pain. The term now refers to any sort of broad physical comedy, particularly if it includes mock violence, pratfalls, and the like.

DON DeLILLO ON WRITING

Like most of us, student writers tend to want to use every word they produce, so that cutting can be torture. DeLillo gives a good lesson on the will to discard. His technique for isolating paragraphs on separate pages is one many writing texts recommend as a way to help students focus on chunks of meaning. It may not lead students to quite the intensity of focus that DeLillo finds, but just learning that such intensity is possible may be eye opening.

12
DEFINITION
Tracing a Boundary

"When they come to definition," said the late Richard Beal, an author of textbooks, a director of composition, and our sage adviser, "most authors of rhetorically organized readers seem not to know what it is nor what to do about it."

Definition, he suggested, is not in itself a distinct and separate expository method, but a catchall name for a kind of explaining that involves whatever method or methods it can use. It would break with tradition, Beal said, to place definition last among methods of exposition. Then the instructor might use it to review all the rest.

We hope that this ordering of the book's contents proves useful to you. You will also find the book carefully distinguishing a short definition (the kind found in a dictionary), a stipulative definition (the kind that pins down an essential term in a paragraph or two), and extended definition (the kind found in whole essays).

All the essays in this chapter trace the shape of a definite territory and attempt to set forth its nature. In the paired selections, Gloria Naylor and Christine Leong demonstrate how words change meanings in different contexts: Each explores the alterations in a derogatory word for her race depending on who uses it. (As a bonus, Leong, a student, responds directly to Naylor — thus modeling a common writing assignment.) George F. Will then disputes a definition of *egalitarian* that he believes casts the United States in an inaccurately negative light. Marie Winn concisely limns the problem of TV addiction, proving that it is an addiction as disabling as that to drugs or alcohol. And Bruno Bettelheim's "The Holocaust," a classic, provides a measured, somber definition of the title word.

DEFINITION IN OTHER CHAPTERS. To keep the following list short, we have included only the selections that focus on definition, especially those using the kind of extended definition stressed in this chapter's introduction and examples.

Part Two

Barbara Lazear Ascher, "On Compassion"
Anna Quindlen, "Homeless"
William Safire, "Fulminations"
Nancy Mairs, "Disability"
Judy Brady, "I Want a Wife"
Jamaica Kincaid, "Girl"

GLORIA NAYLOR

The Meanings of a Word

In this essay Naylor maintains that context determines interpretation. Many students will disagree with this assertion, arguing that language carries its own meaning, so it might be useful to open up this issue right away. Students will certainly agree that saying something like "It was all my fault" means something completely different depending on whether uttered with sincerity or with sarcasm. Can students think of other instances when they have relied on inflection to convey meaning? Have they manipulated language — through exaggerations or half-truths, for example — for their own benefit? Stephanie Ericsson's "The Ways We Lie" (p. 389) provides another perspective on how we can (and often do) twist language to suit ourselves.

Part of Naylor's point, too, is that speech can be more precise (or more nuanced) than writing. How do writers overcome (or try to overcome) the limitations of written language? Students can explore the connections among tone, context, and meaning. Give groups fifteen or twenty minutes to look over essays they have already read this semester, in search of sentences, ideas, or passages that might be easily misinterpreted if read out of context. (It will be helpful if you read aloud a few examples as models. Promising examples appear in Barbara Huttmann's "A Crime of Compassion," Chap. 4; Anna Quindlen's "Homeless," Chap. 6; Jessica Mitford's "Behind the Formaldehyde Curtain," Chap. 8; and Meghan Daum's "Safe-Sex Lies," Chap. 11.) Have students identify different interpretations for an isolated excerpt as well as interpretations for the excerpt when considered in the context of the entire selection. After each group explains its examples, the class will be better prepared for a discussion of writing strategies and/or Naylor's sense of the multiple meanings of language.

QUESTIONS ON MEANING

1. Written language, with less inflection and immediacy, doesn't offer the variety and richness of spoken language.
2. This was the first time it sounded offensive, so it was the first time she was shocked enough to really notice — "hear" — it.
3. They took a derogatory term and redefined it, gaining power from using it as a form both of praise and of informed condemnation rather than simply as a term of prejudice.

4. She wants to show how the meanings of a word change with the context in which it is used. (See the next question.)

QUESTIONS ON WRITING STRATEGY

1. Naylor holds that spoken language is richer and more powerful than written language and that the power of words derives from their context. The rest of the essay presents examples of these assertions in uses of *nigger*. To us, the opening is a bit flat and perhaps unnecessary: The assertions are well made through the examples. But some students may appreciate the initial overview.
2. These last sentences make clear that despite the empowering use of the word within her family and community, her mother knows Naylor will face more uses of the word in a racist context. It also suggests a protective bond between Naylor and her mother.
3. Paragraphs 3, 14, and 15 discuss racist uses of the term: They sandwich nonracist uses, as the African American experience is sandwiched by racism. At the same time, the discussion of nonracist uses is longer, emphasizing the positive.
4. They suggest how the word might be used in a sentence, so that the audience can get a sense of different inflections. Through them, Naylor tries to add a spoken component to written language.

QUESTIONS ON LANGUAGE

1. The old question is "Which came first, the chicken or the egg?" This debate helps Naylor show the circular ways that language and reality influence one another.
2. They identify, respectively, a sex-crazed woman and a person sexually interested in corpses. Both connote perversion, twistedness. Naylor uses the words to emphasize the unfamiliarity of *nigger*, but she implies with them just how venomous was the little boy's insult.
3. The religious connotations of *mecca* suggest a sense of reverence for a place that offers a retreat from daily strife. *Mecca* can be understood both in a religious sense (a spiritual center in Islam) and in a secular sense (a center for people who share a common interest). Describing the grandmother's house as a *mecca* identifies it as a safe and spiritual gathering place.

GLORIA NAYLOR ON WRITING

Naylor's remarks could fuel a discussion about the literary canon — what's included, what's excluded, who decides. Naylor turned a perceived disadvantage, a dearth of "approved" African American literature, into an advantage by deciding to help right the wrong herself. When she says she attempts to "articulate experiences that want articulating," she evokes many silenced forebears.

CHRISTINE LEONG
Being a Chink

Leong's essay is clearly modeled on Gloria Naylor's "The Meanings of a Word" (p. 468). Like Naylor, Leong explores the power to be gained from refusing to allow words, especially those originally intended as demeaning or offensive, to have fixed meanings. For students who resist the idea that language is flexible and that context often determines meaning, you might wish to consider some of the suggestions and questions we pose in the introduction to Naylor's essay.

Deborah Tannen's "But What Do You Mean?" (p. 372) is another interesting counterpart to this essay; both discuss ways that communication relies on mutual assumptions about the meanings of words. In clusters of three or four, students could brainstorm a list of groups that have "private" language. (Students may need to be reminded that groups may be defined not just by race, ethnicity, or gender, but also by age, occupation, marital status, education, hobby, and so on.) How does knowing the private language create a position of power for a speaker or a listener?

QUESTIONS ON MEANING

1. Leong explains *chink* in paragraph 10: a label that describes specific external characteristics but not internal ones.
2. For this group of friends, the word has become a way to comfort each other by acknowledging the way they have all had to deal with racism (par. 11).
3. Her purpose is the last one listed: Although her essay does both of the other things to some degree, Leong wants to show the reader how the flexible nature of language allows for power through redefining racist terms. You know this from the conjunction of her first and last paragraphs.

QUESTIONS ON WRITING STRATEGY

1. Both essays have an introduction on language and meaning, a story that starts "I remember the first time" and a conclusion that explains the power in co-opting racist terms. Leong places her experiences in the context of racist issues generally and of Naylor's reading of them specifically.
2. Leong builds suspense as she sifts through the trash. Ending with the envelope accomplishes several things: The envelope is both grouped with other forgotten rubbish and set apart by its racist inscription.
3. This example sets up the parallel between Naylor's family's redefinition of *nigger* and Leong's redefinition of *chink*, enhancing Leong's explanation of the way she and her friends dealt with the label and their reasons for doing so.
4. To make clear that they are consciously subverting the original meaning of *chink* and not misunderstanding it.

5. She assumes the slur is directed at her father and she is outraged on his behalf.

QUESTIONS ON LANGUAGE

1. Words like "imposed," "small," "weak," "insignificant," "paralyze," and "belittle" all suggest that racist language is debilitating.
2. This characterization of their use of *chink* suggests affection, gentleness, and mutual understanding, almost like a nickname — all of which are in contrast to racist uses.
3. Students should notice how careful Leong is with the language of labels: In terms of both race and gender, she is very politic, using "Caucasian" instead of "white," and "human" or "person" instead of "man." You might ask students how this care contributes to her essay's message.

CHRISTINE LEONG ON WRITING

Leong's insistence on the writer's personal involvement in writing is refreshing, especially coming from a student. Your students may be surprised by Leong's assertion that inspiration counts more than grammar and sense in reaching readers. With "Being a Chink" and her comments on writing — both not only correct but sensible — Leong makes a strong case for clarity informed by passion.

GEORGE F. WILL

The Equity of Inequality

George F. Will's central point here is that growing income disparities between the rich and the poor in the United States do not mean that the country is becoming less egalitarian, moving away from its ideals. The argument is based on an assumption that students should be able to identify — namely, that all Americans have access to "equal opportunity for striving" (par. 5), that, to use the current cliché, "the playing field is level." As Will states in his conclusion, our society "offers upward mobility equally to all who accept its rewarding disciplines."

If students disagree over Will's essay, you might set up a debate. Divide students with similar beliefs into small groups, and have members of each group prepare an argument for their side. Then have each group appoint a representative or two to argue its case before the class and to respond to arguments presented by the opposing side. As a writing assignment, you might have students analyze what they see as the central terms of the debate and whether it is possible for the two sides to reach common ground.

QUESTIONS ON MEANING

1. The thesis is stated at the end of the essay: "[I]ncreasingly unequal so-
    cial rewards can conduce to a more truly egalitarian society, one that
    offers upward mobility equally to all who accept its rewarding disciplines."
2. The writer for the *New York Times* implies that, in an egalitarian society,
    wealth is distributed relatively equally, that great disparities do not exist
    between the rich and the poor. Will argues that equality, "sensibly un-
    derstood" from the perspective of most Americans, involves not "equality
    of outcomes" (par. 5) or "equality of condition" (6), but rather equality of
    opportunity to achieve wealth. For Will, *egalitarian* means equal in op-
    portunity, not wealth (par. 11). The presence of great wealth in the United
    States should act as an incentive to those without it.
3. Will suggests that the "solutions" that might be offered to lessen the
    disparities between the rich and the poor (par. 8) would be unacceptable
    for other reasons.
4. Individuals should do what "society as a whole" should do, defer gratifi-
    cation and gain education (par. 10).

QUESTIONS ON WRITING STRATEGY

1. The anecdote shows, as Will says, that "much depends on how a thing is
    presented." Will's purpose is to re-present statistics about income dis-
    parities in order to dispute the *New York Times* statement that "rather
    than being an egalitarian society, the United States has become the most
    economically stratified of industrial nations" (par. 2).
2. True. The most obvious clue to Will's assumption is his diction, which is
    clearly directed at educated, economically savvy readers familiar with
    such concepts as "market economy" (par. 7), "progressive taxation" (8),
    "portfolios" (8), "knowledge-based economy" (9), "deregulated global
    economy" (10), and "mobile capital" (10). In addition, encouraging "the
    deferral of gratification" does not provide less well-off people with spe-
    cific advice.
3. Will is writing about the effects of income disparity in the United States.
    While the *Times* writer sees disparity as leading to a society that is de-
    creasingly egalitarian, Will believes that disparity provides "an incentive
    to rational behavior [on the part of those who aren't wealthy] in contem-
    porary economic conditions" (par. 2). The "solutions" that would reduce
    income disparity (8) would undermine the incentives "for the rising gen-
    eration to take education seriously as a decisive shaper of individuals'
    destinies" (9).

QUESTIONS ON LANGUAGE

1. An "equitable" distribution of wealth is one based on fairness and impar-
    tiality — not an equal distribution among citizens but one according to
    their merits or abilities. Will accuses the *Times* writer of politicizing the
    term "equitable," using it as a synonym for "equal"; he further argues
    that most Americans do not value "equal" distribution of wealth — that
    is, giving everyone roughly the same amount of wealth — but rather the
    "equitable" distribution of wealth.

2. Will wants it known that he accepts the studies only provisionally, for the sake of the argument he's constructing about values. He implies that he doubts the findings.
3. Will means that those who accept the "disciplines" of thrift and education will be "rewarded" with "upward mobility."
4. Will uses the verb *conduce* — "lead" or "contribute," from the Latin — in paragraphs 8 and 11. Students might consider why Will chose this word over the more straightforward *lead.*

GEORGE F. WILL ON WRITING

Will's comments on writing tools are slight but suggestive, raising thoughts about the relationship between the physical act of writing and the mental act. For some students, as for Will, writing longhand may intensify the creative process. For others, particularly those for whom handwriting is difficult, the computer may seem much more liberating.

MARIE WINN

TV Addiction

Television is probably near and dear to many of your students, and you may find that many of them resist Winn's analysis. On the flip side, everyone has something to say about this ubiquitous appliance. Is it addictive? damaging? instructive? a harmless source of pleasure? (It may be fun to ask students to cite specific shows to support their general statements.)

You may want to open the discussion by reading the following quotation from a 1944 *Scientific American:* "Television offers the soundest basis for world peace that has yet been presented. Peace must be created on the bulwark of understanding. International television networks will knit together the peoples of the world in bonds of mutual respect." Ask whether TV has lived up to the initial hopes for the medium. Or have small groups brainstorm the pros and cons of television, with a shared goal of finding holes in Winn's essay (or of proving that there are none).

QUESTIONS ON MEANING

1. The former is a habit, perhaps, but not a detrimental or destructive obsession that the person can't get out of. The main distinction is provided in paragraph 3: An addict can't live without the source of pleasure.
2. The answer comes in the last sentence of her essay: There *are* viewers who are serious addicts.
3. Excessive TV watching blots out the real world (par. 7), distorts one's sense of time (10), weakens relationships (10), and produces viewers who can't stop watching (8) and who put off other, often important, activities (9). (See also the fourth question on writing strategy.)

4. No. In the last sentence of paragraph 9, she says nothing is less worth-while.

QUESTIONS ON WRITING STRATEGY

1. By stipulating her understanding of *addiction*, Winn makes her terms perfectly clear and also, through comparison with TV addiction, strengthens her case.
2. This delay forces readers to propose potential answers, speculate, consider the issue, and become more engaged than if they were simply told her answer.
3. Quotation marks add to her credibility by making it seem that she's not just theorizing but has actually observed these behaviors and heard people talking about TV in these terms.
4. Like drug or alcohol addiction, TV addiction erases the "real world," is passive, and is not controllable (par. 7); it is unproductive (8); it distorts time and hurts relationships (10). Winn does not identify any differences.

QUESTIONS ON LANGUAGE

1. These words imply that an addiction is a bodily need — as opposed to a mere desire — like that for food or sleep.
2. This metaphor suggests a permanent circling, like a plane forever floating above its destination.
3. Note how Winn's word choice emphasizes the addict as almost inhuman: "will-less" (par. 8), an "organism" whose life is "distorted" (4), and "dehumanized" (5).

MARIE WINN ON WRITING

You may find Winn's statement about writing, with its emphasis on the joys of "mouse milking," one of the most valuable in the book. Students sometimes need to be reminded that revision is important. When they see that even professionals have to do it, and that some of them enjoy it, they may be more willing to spend more time than usual polishing their own first drafts.

That professionals may also hate part of what they do, as Winn confesses she does, may come as a revelation. We hope that your students will not decide they hate writing after reading Winn's statement, but that they will simply be more aware than before that writing is hard work for almost everyone who does it, even published authors. That authors persist anyhow, and often succeed, might even prove to be encouraging. At least it shows that the job of putting words together on the page is ultimately accomplished.

BRUNO BETTELHEIM
The Holocaust

Normally, we do not like to print parts of essays, but we make an exception in this case because Bettelheim's definition is such a powerful example of the method. He makes the problem of definition much more than a historical issue, too: It is about us, today.

Bettelheim's notion of language as a tool for emotional distancing might remind students of other examples of this phenomenon, such as our romantic film images of How the West Was Won (John Wayne, tough man in *Rio Bravo*, has been replaced by Kevin Costner in *Dances With Wolves* — both equally scripted to present a certain version of history). What other aspects of our history, politics, or personal relations do we cover over or pretty up with careful use of language? What is the motivation for these moves: sensitivity, shame, fear, loathing, or what? Have students work in pairs or small groups to come up with examples of language that protects people from uncomfortable truths. As a whole, can the class come up with any generalizations based on these examples? (You might also have students read or reread Stephanie Ericsson's "The Ways We Lie" and William Lutz's "The World of Doublespeak," both of which address dishonest language.)

QUESTIONS ON MEANING

1. *Holocaust* allows us to distance ourselves from the emotional reality of the event (par. 1). It and other "linguistic circumlocutions" (roundabout or evasive expressions) provide "psychological relief" (9) but rob the victims of their true fate (10).
2. The purpose seems plain: to stop the use of the term *holocaust*.
3. "We dwell on the tiny minority who did exercise some choice" (par. 10).
4. Bettelheim clearly prefers *murder:* "mass murder most foul" (par. 1); "vile mass murder" and "most vicious of mass murders" (3); and so on.

QUESTIONS ON WRITING STRATEGY

1. Etymologies and dictionary definitions appear in paragraphs 3 and 6. They support Bettelheim's argument by proving that the words are misused.
2. Paragraph 8 says just what happened to the murder victims, a necessary corrective to the sidestepping of *holocaust*.
3. The tone is serious and smoldering. See, for instance, the words "entirely false" (par. 3); "sacrilege" and "profanation" (4); "robs" and "denies" (9); "unfair" (10).
4. The repetition or restatement is certainly deliberate and seems to serve two purposes: It emphasizes important points, and it lends Bettelheim's argument the force of other forms that use repetition or restatement, such as prayers, sermons, and inspirational speeches.
5. The thesis is stated at the end of paragraph 2: "We should give [murder] its true designation and not hide it behind polite, erudite terms created

out of classical words." The evidence is mostly semantic: *holocaust, martyr,* and *genocide* are not "true designations."

QUESTIONS ON LANGUAGE

1. Bettelheim uses blunt, no-escape words: "murder" (throughout); "asphyxiated" (pars. 5, 8); "corpses were burned" (5); "gassed" (6); "slaughtered" (7); "brutalized," "clothes torn from their naked bodies," "herded," "piled," "last breath of air" (8).
2. *We,* including both the author and his reader, aligns the author with his audience and includes him among those who abuse the language. It mitigates the harshness of the criticism.
3. A *neologism,* students may not know, is a newly minted word; and indeed, as Bettelheim asserts, *genocide* was coined after World War II. In 1949, the United Nations declared it a crime under international law.

13
ARGUMENT AND PERSUASION
Stating Opinions and Proposals

Argument and persuasion are often difficult for students to master, so the introduction to this chapter is more detailed than the others. We spell out the elements of argument, explain the Toulmin method (data, claim, warrant) as well as inductive and deductive reasoning, cover the most common fallacies, and (in the section headed "The Process") discuss possible structures for arguments.

This chapter includes two sets of paired pieces, rather than one pair as in the other chapters. In the first, H. L. Mencken's "The Penalty of Death" and Michael Kroll's "The Unquiet Death of Robert Harris," the two authors take opposite sides in the debate over capital punishment. In the second pair, Chitra Divakaruni's "Live Free and Starve" and Peter Singer's "The Singer Solution to World Poverty," the writers address poverty: how to alleviate it, and how not to.

The three following essays fly solo. The always popular "Why Don't We Complain?" by William F. Buckley, Jr., answers the title question with a grave warning. "Why I Stopped Being a Vegetarian," by Laura Fraser, argues for meat eating mainly on social grounds. And "Too Much Pressure," by the student Colleen Wenke, locates a cause for increased cheating in schools.

By the way, the persuasive power of humor should be clear from the selections by H. L. Mencken and William F. Buckley, Jr.

ARGUMENT AND PERSUASION IN OTHER CHAPTERS. This chapter provides enough selections to teach an introduction to persuasive writing. If you need still more, however, the list below includes a number of notable arguments.

Part Two

Barbara Huttmann, "A Crime of Compassion"
Anna Quindlen, "Homeless"
Nancy Mairs, "Disability"
Linnea Saukko, "How to Poison the Earth"
Niala Maharaj and Donovan Hohn, "Thorny Truths About Flowers"
Judy Brady, "I Want a Wife"
Armin A. Brott, "Not All Men Are Sly Foxes"
Shelby Steele, "Notes from the Hip-Hop Underground"
William Lutz, "The World of Doublespeak"
Atul Gawande, "The Cancer-Cluster Myth"
Gore Vidal, "Drugs"
Meghan Daum, "Safe-Sex Lies"

H. L. MENCKEN

The Penalty of Death

Whether or not Mencken persuades his readers to favor capital punishment, at least he provides a cogent explanation for its continuing existence.
His essay begins with a deft and masterly demonstration of that effective strata-
gem, the summation and dismissal of opposing arguments.

Students may need a warning that Mencken, although to some degree
serious, is not arguing in grim earnest. A professional entertainer and a play-
ful disturber of the peace, he delighted in baiting reformers ("uplifters," in his
term) and offending the faithful. In paragraph 2 he can't resist an obviously
specious argument from an analogy that a more responsible debater might
have resisted. "Make 'em laugh" is clearly one of the author's concerns along
with "Make 'em think."

Mencken's essay voices a strong support for capital punishment as long
as it is meted out justly (only for crimes deliberately beyond the bounds of
"ordinary homicides") and in a humanely efficient manner. Recent critics of
the practice, however, argue that this sort of justice is not possible until the
injustices of the legal system as a whole — its disproportionate punishment of
African American men, for example — are redressed. What do students know
about this issue that might have some bearing on how they read Mencken's
essay? Have small groups research different aspects of capital punishment
and put together an annotated bibliography of the sources they find. The class
as a whole would then have an extensive pool of resources to use in writing a
more formal paper.

Laura Ashouri, a student in Gainesville, Florida, wrote us a deeply felt
protest after she read "The Penalty of Death" in a previous edition. Why, she
wanted to know, did we have to include an essay so sympathetic to capital
punishment? Couldn't we at least include another essay as a foil to Mencken's?
This we have done, with Michael Kroll's disturbing eyewitness account of a
convicted murderer's trip to the gas chamber. The two essays together represent a wide range of approaches to the death penalty.

The publication of *The Diary of H. L. Mencken* in 1989 revealed thoughts
of Mencken's that can only be considered bigoted about blacks, Jews, and

others. No doubt we would like our heroes untarnished, especially by the taint of intolerance. Mencken, alas, does not oblige. It's interesting that he forbade the publication of his diary — maybe because he was sorry for the bigoted comments. Certainly, as his defenders have pointed out, racial and ethnic epithets and stereotypes were more common (and accepted, however blindly) in Mencken's day. Does this excuse him?

QUESTIONS ON MEANING

1. The hanging of people is an "ancient art," which some executioners practice proudly (par. 2). An execution brings satisfaction and happiness to the criminal's victim (or, we presume, to the victim's surviving relatives). It also brings "grateful relief" to the public at large (3). The first reason seems to us the weakest. Students may well find that Mencken has just one central reason for supporting capital punishment: his belief that it affords *katharsis.* His thesis is stated in paragraph 6: Death is a "just and proper punishment" for "the taking of human life" because it is cathartic.
2. Safeguarding society is one further reason, certainly. We have trouble thinking of any other solid reasons, ourselves. To fulfill an ancient tradition? To create jobs for chaplains and hangmen? To supply matter for playwrights and scriptwriters (*The Last Mile, Dead Man Walking*)?
3. For people "openly defiant of all civilized order" and who deliberately take human life (par. 6).
4. That it is habitually delayed (par. 7).

QUESTIONS ON WRITING STRATEGY

1. Wry and outrageous, we'd call it. Examples: his likening of capital punishment to a tack on a teacher's chair (par. 3), "even saints reach for their sidearms" and the story of A and B (4), the euphemism "wafting the criminal to realms of bliss" (6), God's ability to forgive "a whole herd of murderers in a millionth of a second" (8). Those students who found no humor in Mitford's essay (p. 290) will probably find none in Mencken's, either. In their light approaches to grim subjects, the two may be compared.
2. He lists the main arguments of the opposition.
3. Some students may think that Mencken's sympathy for those awaiting death strengthens his argument because it conveys compassion and balance. Other students may think that this concern lays Mencken open to the charge that if he is so all-fired concerned about human suffering, he is inconsistent in his willingness to see people die merely to give others satisfaction.
4. We think he expects agreement, though he begins by recognizing that many don't see things his way.
5. The analogies are between executioners and others with unpleasant jobs (par. 2) and between execution and putting a tack on a teacher's chair. Both analogies seem false — the similarities, such as they are, do not justify the comparison. But we suspect Mencken knew as much and used the analogies in any event, for the dual purpose of gaining ground and adding levity.
6. Mencken defines *katharsis* (par. 3) by saying what it is not (that is, revenge) and by giving an example (the students' glee at the teacher's pain). He then applies the term to capital punishment (4–6).

QUESTIONS ON LANGUAGE

1. *Uplifters*, a pejorative word like *do-gooders*, suggests that opponents of the death penalty would lift the rest of society up to their own high moral standards. Calling one's opponents a name — a kind of ad hominem argument — doesn't strengthen an argument but probably resonates with those who already share the author's views.
2. Mencken loves to strut his Latinate vocabulary for the fun of it, and some of his recondite words have simple synonyms: *salubrious* ("healthful"), *pruritus* ("itching"), *mandamuses* ("court writs").
3. The phrase dignifies the hangman's job by attributing to it a long tradition and a high degree of skill.
4. To our ears, Mencken's generic "man" and "men" do date the essay, but they don't weaken it. This question may give your students a chance (if they need one) to note and debate this usage.

H. L. MENCKEN ON WRITING

The last paragraph is the one worth examining as an illustration of Mencken's writing at its colorful best. His metaphors are worth a moment of admiration: Thought, before it is captured in writing, is either fine wine or mush. Here, much as he does in "The Penalty of Death," Mencken advances a serious idea as if it were a joke.

MICHAEL KROLL

The Unquiet Death of Robert Harris

We have included this argument against the death penalty as a response to Mencken's essay. While Mencken's approach is rational and abstract (he even refers to people as A, B, and C), Kroll puts a human face on the issue of capital punishment, and his appeal is more emotional than rational.

Although this is a controversial subject, students will probably be able to discuss it more abstractly (if not more calmly) than issues that hit closer to home. Class discussion will be more fruitful if students have done some soul searching ahead of time. Consider assigning the first writing suggestion, which asks students to crystallize their feelings about capital punishment into an argument, before bringing up the issue in class. You might give a small group of students the task of going to the library and looking up your state's record on capital punishment: Is the death penalty in force? Has it ever been? What is the number of executions per year?

Several films dealing with capital punishment may interest students, including the fairly recent *Dead Man Walking*. An informal screening of such a film could be a good opportunity for an out-of-class get-together.

QUESTIONS ON MEANING

1. Kroll seems to be proposing, if not the abolition of the death penalty, at least a more humane and less public method of carrying it out.
2. The executioner had to wait for the Supreme Court to decide whether or not to overturn the stays granted by the court of appeals. Harris's fate is being decided on, in a manner reminiscent of Kafka, by a host of unseen judges.
3. Kroll clearly thinks the appeals are substantial enough to warrant postponement of the execution. This can be inferred from his suggestion that Harris's brother was too easily exculpated and his insistence on the fact that ten judges signed two of the stays.
4. It's hard to know how to read this last sentence, and there is no "right" answer. Irony certainly figures in the contrast between the beauty of the sunrise and the experience Kroll has just had. The question is whether the irony is bitter or hesitantly optimistic.
5. Kroll certainly opposes the way this particular execution was handled, execution by gas in general, and execution as public spectacle. His indictment of "the cold-blooded killing of a human being" (par. 24) may indicate opposition to the death penalty in all cases.

QUESTIONS ON WRITING STRATEGY

1. The first two times (pars. 9 and 16), Kroll explains, with the benefit of hindsight, the delays in the execution. In paragraph 24 Kroll breaks with the narrative to make his most explicit argument against the way his friend was put to death.
2. Kroll's calm tone in describing a Kafkaesque experience makes him seem reasonable even as his bias is quite clear.
3. Kroll's appeal is more emotional than rational, emphasizing the cruelty of his friend's death, the emotions experienced by his friends and family, and the insensitivity of the prison staff.
4. The families seem cartoonish in their callousness. Kroll is bitter about society's sanctification of victims' families and feels a need to provide an opposing, if lopsided, perspective.
5. This violent description serves in effect as an argument against death by cyanide poisoning.
6. By putting a human face on the "villain," Kroll renders the debate over the death penalty less abstract. The narrative strengthens an emotional appeal, showing the execution as "indescribably ugly" and revealing the point of view of the dying man and those close to him.

QUESTIONS ON LANGUAGE

1. *Barbaric* comes from the Latin *barbarus* and originally referred to foreign peoples whom the Romans considered to be inferior to themselves. *Webster's* defines *barbaric* as "possessing or characteristic of a cultural level more complex than primitive savagery but less sophisticated than advanced civilization." In common usage, the word means wild, marked by a lack of restraint, bizarre, primitive, or unsophisticated.
2. Crittendon sees the execution as a public spectacle; Kroll says he sounds like "the operator of the Jungle Cruise at Disneyland" (par. 2). The job title is euphemistic; "public information officer" sounds like a PR job at a large corporation.

3. The tone is ironic. The language of "escorts" and "invitations" makes the execution seem like a party or a dance.
4. Kroll tends to select speech that puts the prison officials in the worst possible light. Crittendon comes across as self-important (par. 1). Martinez treats Harris's brother like a criminal (5, 6). All the other communication is brusque and monosyllabic ("Now," 10; "Okay [. . .]. Let's go," 12), as if Harris's friends were themselves inmates (Kroll refers to their "marching orders," 8).

CHITRA DIVAKARUNI
Live Free and Starve

Chitra Divakaruni's own observations of child labor contribute to a thought-provoking argument against America's attempt to stop child labor abroad without also taking responsibility for the terrible deprivation that sends children into labor in the first place. That "without also" is crucial for students to understand: Divakaruni may argue *against* a bill banning goods produced with child labor, but she certainly does not argue *for* child labor. For readers inclined to favor American action on unjust labor practices and similar issues of human rights around the world, Divakaruni's paragraph 5 presents a warning not to evaluate others' situations from a strictly American perspective. In the end, the author suggests the kinds of measures Americans would need to take if they really want to help child laborers.

"Live Free and Starve" provides an excellent chance to discuss emotional appeals in argument. Ask students to mark places in the essay where Divakaruni works to touch the emotions of readers, and then in class spend some time at the board noting the relevant passages. Small groups of students could each analyze one of the passages: What beliefs and values does Divakaruni appeal to? How accurate is she in gauging her readers' sympathies? Do the appeals work to strengthen her argument? (If you would like students to write on Divakaruni's emotional appeals, see the third writing suggestion.)

In this edition, we pair "Live Free and Starve" with the next essay, Peter Singer's "The Singer Solution to World Poverty." Both essays grapple with how to ease suffering in the world, though in most respects they are quite different.

QUESTIONS ON MEANING

1. Divakaruni wants to make her readers think with greater complexity about the solutions available — or not available — for the problem of child labor in Third World countries. The title alerts the readers that the author's perspective is perhaps unusual. The brief paragraph 2 makes it clear that she disagrees with the House's solution. Then in paragraph 4 she begins to explain why.

2. Third World countries are the developing nations of Asia, Africa, and Latin America. The term comes from the Cold War: The first and second worlds were the non-Communist and Communist industrialized nations.

3. Divakaruni means that most Americans have already met their survival needs (for "bread," as she puts it) and thus can afford the relative luxury of seeking freedom and other needs at the top of the pyramid.

4. The children lack "food and clothing and medication," there are no schools for them, their governments can't provide these things, and ultimately no one takes responsibility for them.

QUESTIONS ON WRITING STRATEGY

1. Divakaruni acknowledges her audience's likely views most notably in "It is true that child labor is a terrible thing" (par. 3); "It is easy for us in America," "solutions that make excellent sense — in the context of our society," "Even we immigrants," and "it seems inconceivable to us" (5); "I would not disagree with anyone who says that it was hardly a desirable existence for a child" (6); "Exploitation, you might be thinking" (7); and "Are we [. . .] willing to shoulder that burden? [. . .] that responsibility?" (8).

2. The last paragraph makes very clear the responsibilities Americans must take on, beyond passing trade bans, if they truly want to help child laborers.

3. In telling the detailed story of one child, Divakaruni grounds her argument in a specific case. She establishes her authority as an observer of child labor abroad, and an open-eyed and sympathetic observer at that. Though Nimai had a life that was "hardly a desirable existence for a child," he still was better off, Divakaruni contends, than the nonworking children in his village.

QUESTIONS ON LANGUAGE

1. The survival of the families is so borderline that caring for their own children could ruin them.

2. The words show compassion — "ribs sticking out," "hunger was too much to bear," "ate whatever they could find," "knew they'd be beaten for it."

3. *Blithe* has roots in Old Saxon, Middle Dutch, Old High German, and Old Norse. It earlier referred to the outward expression of a kindly feeling but has come to mean "heedless or careless, unaware of the full implications of an act."

CHITRA DIVAKARUNI ON WRITING

For Chitra Divakaruni, social activism broadens and sensitizes her and is thus a boon to her writing. Our questions prompt students to consider just what a writer gains from having her or his "preconceptions" challenged and from understanding the lives of others. The questions could open up a discussion of critical thinking, not just about others' ideas but about one's own as well.

PETER SINGER

The Singer Solution to World Poverty

The philosopher Peter Singer is notoriously controversial, often reviled, for his ethical stands on human and animal rights. This essay should not prove upsetting, just provocative: Lively class discussion should greet Singer's argument that "[w]hatever money you're spending on luxuries, not necessities, should be given away" to the world's poor (par. 22). You could start things off by asking students whether and why they accept the premise of Singer's hypothetical analogy concerning Bob, the Bugatti owner — that allowing the child to be killed by the runaway train rather than sacrificing his expensive car is "gravely wrong" (7–8). Then consider the question Singer raises about Bob in paragraph 16: "How far past losing the Bugatti should he go?" How great must his potential sacrifice be that it overrides saving the life of the child?

Singer's emphasis on the life of a child ties in with the preceding essay, Chitra Divakaruni's "Live Free and Starve." What is a child's life worth? How miserable should a child's life be allowed to be? What should happen when there's a trade-off between life itself and the quality of the life?

Another interesting question raised by Singer's essay is how we distinguish a luxury from a necessity. Food is obviously a necessity, but is steak? Transportation is obviously a necessity for most people, but how expensive must a car be before it becomes a luxury? You might have students in small groups draw up lists of things common to most American households that they all agree are necessities or luxuries and then compile master lists for class discussion.

If no one in class brings up one of the more obvious problems with Singer's argument, you might want to do so yourself: If consumer spending were so drastically curtailed, what might be the consequences for the American economy, for unemployment rates, and so forth? And this leads directly into the larger question of Singer's purpose. Students should ultimately recognize that the success of this essay depends less on its persuading readers to give so much to the world's poor than it does on making readers see that "living a morally decent life [is] extremely arduous" (23).

QUESTIONS ON MEANING

1. Singer hints at his thesis at the end of paragraph 3, but he doesn't state it specifically until the end of paragraph 22: "Whatever money you're spending on luxuries, not necessities, should be given away."
2. Singer makes it clear he doesn't really expect readers to act on his thesis. Rather, his purpose is to make readers think twice when spending money on luxuries, knowing they could have used that money to help poor children: "knowing where we should be going is the first step toward heading in that direction" (par. 23).
3. Someone who would sell a child for organ transplants when that child is present shows a "chilling kind of heartlessness; it is much easier to ignore an appeal for money to help children [one] will never meet" (par. 5).

Also, this person would have to "mislead the child [and] initiate the chain of events imperiling [that child]" (9). Bob belongs in the other group because "the child [Bob] was sacrificing for his own material comfort [. . .] was a complete stranger to him and too far away to relate to in an intimate, personal way."

4. Singer means the extreme examples to encourage the reader to consider "the level of sacrifice that you would demand of Bob, and then think about how much money you would have to give away in order to make a sacrifice that is roughly equal to that."

QUESTIONS ON WRITING STRATEGY

1. Writing for the *New York Times Magazine*, Singer naturally assumes an educated, affluent audience to whom the figures he bandies about (for example, household income of $50,000 or $100,000) would apply. Students who don't have even $200 to spare may or may not see themselves as exempt from Singer's argument.

2. At the beginning of paragraph 15 Singer pretends to assume that readers have followed his suggestion at the end of paragraph 14, interrupting their reading to call UNICEF or Oxfam America and donate $200. Of course, he doesn't really expect readers to have done this, but he wants them at least to realize how easily they could have done so and to ask themselves why they didn't.

3. In paragraphs 18–21 Singer raises the kinds of objections he expects readers to make to his proposal: that faced with doing so much, readers will do nothing; that if everyone contributed his or her fair share, no one would be obligated to give so much; that such aid should be the responsibility of government. He then goes on to refute these objections.

4. Singer's argument is based on deductive reasoning. His syllogism can be summarized roughly as follows: Bob should sacrifice his Bugatti to save the life of a child. Bob's sacrifice of his Bugatti corresponds to people in affluent countries giving up luxuries to save poor children. Therefore, people in affluent countries should give up luxuries to save poor children.

5. Singer's questions challenge readers to think about their beliefs and how they should most ethically act on those beliefs.

6. Singer establishes three main sets of comparisons: between financially comfortable US readers and Dora, the *Central Station* character (pars. 3–5); between readers and Bob, the Bugatti owner (mainly 9–14, 17); and between Dora and Bob (9).

QUESTIONS ON LANGUAGE

1. Singer provides a brief definition: A "utilitarian ethic" is a code or standard of behavior "that judges whether acts are right or wrong by their consequences." An expanded definition: One's actions are "right" when they result in the broadest positive outcomes (or the fewest negative outcomes), and they are "wrong" when they primarily benefit the actor at the expense of others.

2. "Fair share" is a familiar phrase, generally accepted as a standard of behavior. Singer stresses that doing only one's fair share may seem reasonable and even moral, but according to a utilitarian ethic it is not, because it will not prevent deaths.

3. Singer writes that "living a morally decent life" can be "arduous," from the Latin *arduus*, "high," "steep," or "difficult." His implication is that such a life requires constant struggle.

PETER SINGER ON WRITING

We find Singer's comments interesting because his aims — to be clear, to be blunt — are so evident in "The Singer Solution to World Poverty." For one example, the list of vocabulary words with Singer's essay (number 3 under "Questions on Language") is quite short considering the subject and the author's background. And the argument itself could hardly be more straightforward.

We hope the statement we quote about a disabled infant won't distract students from the point Singer makes about clearing the fog from discourse about ethics. Certainly, Singer's views are highly debatable, but his fearlessness is not.

WILLIAM F. BUCKLEY, JR.

Why Don't We Complain?

Buckley is at the same time an engaging storyteller and a formidable debater. In "Why Don't We Complain?" the author's narrative skill helps support his argument that by failing to complain about small indignities, Americans risk diminution of their personal freedom.

What injustices, recent political moves, inedible meals, rude clerks, or intolerant teachers would your students most like to complain about? You can turn the second writing suggestion into a full-class activity by having students generate a list of grievances on the board and then divide themselves into groups according to which offense they feel most strongly about. Allow the groups to write a collaborative letter of complaint, which all the members should sign and the group should mail. (You might want to make copies of all of them for the class.) How long has it been since members of the class last registered a formal complaint? Do they agree with Buckley's assessment of why?

QUESTIONS ON MEANING

1. The author was so intimidated by his seatmate's resentful stare that he thought better of creating a fuss about the overheated railroad car. In paragraph 5 he gives three reasons for his failure to complain to the theater manager about the out-of-focus movie.
2. In paragraph 19 Buckley succinctly blames "our increased sense of helplessness in an age of technology and centralized political and economic power." He amplifies the statement in this paragraph and in paragraphs 20–22.

3. Buckley views the political apathy of Americans as an outgrowth of their feeling of general helplessness (par. 19). The less we are able to accomplish as individuals, the more we resign ourselves to government control.

4. Buckley's thesis is stated most fully in paragraph 19: "I think the observable reluctance of the majority of Americans to assert themselves in minor matters is related to our increased sense of helplessness in an age of technology and centralized political and economic power." His purpose is to entertain, in part, but by that route to persuade readers to complain more, lest we become "automatons, incapable of feeling" (par. 22).

QUESTIONS ON WRITING STRATEGY

1. By admitting that he is as much at fault as any other American, the author strengthens his case. Sharing the blame, Buckley lessens the discomfort his readers might experience if the author were preaching to them.

2. Buckley's audience, while nonspecialized, is apparently educated, for his essay contains a generous number of polysyllabic words.

3. Buckley's argument appeals to both reason and emotion. The closest reasoning appears in paragraphs 19 and 20, where the author seeks causes and forges a connection between acquiescence in the face of small annoyances and "our notorious political apathy." He appeals to emotion in, for instance, paragraph 22: "We shall have become automatons."

4. Buckley says (par. 17) that he regards the Jiggs episode as "a reversal": Certainly it does nothing to prove his point. He includes it, no doubt, for the humor and to ingratiate himself with his audience. Perhaps also he is acknowledging that complaints sometimes go awry.

QUESTIONS ON LANGUAGE

1. *Hectoring* means "bullying," and derives from Hector, the Trojan prince in Homer's *Iliad*.

2. The use of the upper case in this instance helps define the whole concept of authority. The big *A* lends the word authority, so to speak, and a certain ominous force.

3. The allusion is to Caspar Milquetoast, the quaking hero in H. T. Webster's newspaper cartoon, "The Timid Soul," which ran in daily and Sunday newspapers from 1924 into the 1950s. Caspar was named for milk toast, "a bland dish of hot buttered toast in warm milk, often associated with frail persons" (*The American Heritage Dictionary*).

WILLIAM F. BUCKLEY, JR., ON WRITING

Buckley says that he writes because it is easier than introspection. But it can't be overlooked that Buckley is a prolific and persuasive critic and advocate: He has ideas about where we are and should be headed, and he has the means to express them.

You may want to emphasize in class the point that, in his views on revision, Buckley differs greatly from most other writers of stature. Students probably wish that writing were as speedy for them as it can be for Buckley. Unless they have an intellect the equal of Buckley's and can write equally well, however, you'll probably want to encourage them to take the time needed for clear and convincing expression.

LAURA FRASER

Why I Stopped Being a Vegetarian

Nonvegetarians may enjoy Fraser's clever, self-deprecating take on the fundamental hypocrisy of her fifteen years as a vegetarian (or at least a "pesco-ovo-lacto vegetarian"). Vegetarians in the class — especially vegans — should be given a chance to rebut Fraser's arguments based on their own beliefs and experiences. Ask students what they see as Fraser's central argument for not eliminating meat completely from one's diet. She says that unless one is indeed a strict vegan, also eschewing eggs and milk and leather and wool, then to force others to accommodate one's meatless diet is "selfish" (par. 21) and based on an unearned sense of moral superiority (3). Moreover, humans are arguably omnivores who require some meat for a truly balanced diet. (It should be noted, of course, that Fraser also clearly suggests that meat should be eaten in much greater moderation than it is by most Americans [17].)

As a small-group activity, you could have students investigate the eating habits of students on your campus. Each group should devise a plan for observing places to eat both on and near campus, with members reporting back their individual findings and then the group as a whole drafting a brief report. These group reports could then be compared in class.

QUESTIONS ON MEANING

1. The arguments are that not eating meat is good for one's health, that it doesn't require animals to be killed, and that it means the depletion of fewer environmental resources. Fraser counters the first by noting that, while her cholesterol level was quite low, she was still fifteen pounds overweight despite her meatless diet; the second by noting her hypocrisy in eating fish and wearing leather goods; and the third by suggesting that environmental concerns could be alleviated if Americans simply ate less meat.
2. Fraser's thesis is stated at the end of the essay: "If eating is a socially conscious act, you have to be conscious of the society of your fellow *Homo sapiens* along with the animals. And we humans, as it happens, are omnivores." The thesis encompasses Fraser's two strongest arguments against vegetarianism: Vegetarians often selfishly inconvenience others or behave in ways that seem rude because of their self-imposed dictary restrictions; and human bodies are designed for a diet of meat *and* plants. Fraser's third reason is that meat tastes good (par. 18).
3. Fraser partly means to entertain readers with the saga of her transformation from "pesco-ovo-lacto-vegetarian" to "omnivore," as is clear from her witty, self-deprecating observations of behavior. But she is also sug-

gesting that many vegetarians share her hypocrisy in eating fish and wearing leather and that they may see themselves as "morally superior to all those bloodthirsty carnivores" (par. 3) when, in fact, "you have to be conscious of the society of your fellow *Homo sapiens* along with the animals" (21).

QUESTIONS ON WRITING STRATEGY

1. See number 3 under "Questions on Meaning." Fraser's shift in her final paragraph to the second person *you* and her closing comment that humans are omnivores both suggest that she is writing of (and to) vegetarians more broadly. Some students — particularly any vegetarians in your class — may feel that Fraser's focus on herself does limit the applicability of her argument because not all vegetarians believe or behave as she does.
2. Fraser's tone through much of the essay is essentially humorous as she pokes fun at herself as a sort of knee-jerk vegetarian whose convictions weren't all that strong to begin with. Her tone begins to turn more serious in paragraph 16 as she takes on the environmental argument, acknowledges her craving for meat, and suggests that vegetarians can be "antisocial." Most readers will probably enjoy her humor even if they don't accept her more serious points.
3. Fraser uses herself as an example of the kind of vegetarian she is implicitly criticizing — one who refuses to eat meat out of a sense of moral superiority but who nonetheless readily compromises these principles by eating eggs, dairy products, and fish and by wearing leather.

QUESTIONS ON LANGUAGE

1. Fraser stresses the hypocrisy of adding Italian bacon to her vegetarian diet and of turning a blind eye to whether a dish was prepared with chicken broth (which is made from a cooked chicken). She alludes to the military's "Don't Ask, Don't Tell" policy regarding gay service members.
2. Fraser suggests that rather than vegetables she ate mainly cheese, a product made with animal milk — and so she was not strictly vegetarian. The effect, again, is humorously to point out hypocrisy.
3. Doctors inoculate patients against disease; Fraser uses the word punningly in context to express her disregard for her doctor's advice that she lose weight. Similarly, "recycle" is used as a sort of pun, here to make antivegetarian behavior seem otherwise virtuous.
4. *Hedonistic,* from the Greek *hedone,* "pleasure," describes a way of life based primarily on the pursuit of physical pleasure. It is the opposite of *ascetic,* from the Greek *askein,* "to work or exercise," which describes a way of life involving strict self-denial and austerity.

LAURA FRASER ON WRITING

Fraser makes a good case for journal writing and especially for using a journal to find one's own voice. Students who are having their first experiences with journal writing may need encouragement like Fraser's to let go and experiment with voice and then to apply what they gain to their public writing.

COLLEEN WENKE
Too Much Pressure

This student essay on the prevalence of cheating among today's students will likely strike close to home for most members of your class. As a prelude to discussion, you might have students in small groups list examples of cheating they have encountered among their peers in high school and college. What seem to be the most common forms of cheating? Is copying homework as bad as cribbing someone else's answers for a test? And what about those students who allow other students to copy their homework or provide test questions or answers? Are they cheaters, too?

If you have a mix of younger and older students, you might ask if their experiences bear out the contention of the experts quoted by Wenke that cheating is more prevalent and acceptable among students now than it was in generations past. What percentage of high-school classmates do they think regularly cheated? Does the same hold true in college? What leads students to cheat? Does your class agree with Wenke that the pressure for grades is a primary cause? Or are there other reasons? Will any students admit to having cheated?

A larger question for discussion is what can be done to discourage cheating. If your college has guidelines for dealing with students caught cheating, this would be a good opportunity to discuss them in depth. It is also a good time to discuss plagiarism of published sources, though Wenke doesn't specifically mention it.

QUESTIONS ON MEANING

1. Wenke writes that students today who cheat are generally "college-bound overachievers [. . .] who are trying to juggle too many activities" (par. 6) and who are facing "too much competition" and "increased pressure to do well." Moreover, penalties for cheating are not strong enough to act as deterrents, particularly when students are more and more concerned about getting "the best grades so that they can get into the best schools and get the highest-paying jobs" (7). Increasingly, students believe that people who cheat are the ones who get ahead in life, so they find cheating "acceptable [. . .] as long as you don't get caught and you are getting As" (8). Thus, even students who would not normally cheat believe they must in order not to be at a disadvantage.
2. Wenke believes that cheating in school will carry over when today's students become business leaders and politicians: "In all likelihood they will not stop cheating once they get to the top" (par. 10).
3. Schools should put less emphasis on grades and more on the value of education for its own sake, on replenishing "the thirst for knowledge [. . .] in a student's mind" (par. 10).

QUESTIONS ON WRITING STRATEGY

1. Wenke's opening anecdote effectively conveys the pressure on students to resort to cheating in order to avoid bad grades. Her use of the pronoun *you* here suggests that she is writing at least in part to fellow students and that she wants other readers to experience firsthand the pressures students face.
2. Wenke uses sources to establish the extent to which students today actually do cheat (pars. 4, 8), to support the idea that much cheating results from the desire to get into good schools and then prosperous careers (7), and to establish that most students feel they have to cheat to compete (8–9). She also cites one writer's analysis of the causes of the increase in cheating in order to expand on his assertions (5).
3. Wenke's admission demonstrates her assertion that even those students who find cheating reprehensible feel compelled to do it at times to keep up with other students who cheat habitually. Students may differ over whether the admission enhances Wenke's ethical appeal. It makes her credible (she admits cheating) but also undermines her credibility (she has cheated).
4. Responses will vary. Some students, for instance, may think Wenke deemphasizes the moral dimension of cheating.

QUESTIONS ON LANGUAGE

1. Examples of colloquial language include "a big fat F" (par. 1), "pull [a grade]" (2), "big deal" (3), "sucked into" (9), "in a jam" (9), and "cheat sheets" (9). Such language lends the essay the authenticity of a student's voice, although some readers may find it inconsistent with Wenke's generally more formal tone.
2. An *oxymoron* is a combination of contradictory words, often for poetic effect ("deafening silence," for example, or "sweet sorrow"). Wenke suggests that in the future no businessman will be honest — the two words will have become contradictory.
3. *Integrity*, from the Latin *integer,* "whole" or "complete," can refer to a state of being complete or undivided (as in the integrity of a geometric form) or to a condition that is sound or unimpaired (as in the integrity of a mechanical system). Wenke uses it in its more common sense of "adherence to a code of moral or ethical values."

PART THREE

MIXING THE METHODS

In this part of the book we provide an anthology, arranged alphabetically by author, of fifteen works by very well-known writers. The collection has a dual purpose. First, we want to widen the tight focus of the previous ten chapters so that students see the methods as a kit of tools to be used *in combination* as the need arises. All fifteen selections demonstrate just this flexibility in approach, narrating here, comparing there, analyzing a process for a couple of paragraphs, defining a term when helpful. The headnote to each selection lists the methods the author most relies on, pointing to specific paragraphs. And the introduction to Part Three gives students a list of questions — a kind of crib sheet of the methods — that they can use to explore or focus any subject.

The second goal of this anthology is to give you more leeway in your assignments. You can teach this part as a "mixing the methods" unit, of course, but you can also pluck out individual selections for any number of uses. If you want to show how a particular method works with other methods, you can point to, say, the cause and effect in Kingston's "No Name Woman" or the description in White's "Once More to the Lake." If you're just seeking another example of a particular method, you can turn to, say, King's "I Have a Dream" for argument and persuasion or Orwell's "Shooting an Elephant" for narration. If you think students will respond to the thematic pairing of White's "Once More to the Lake" with Brad Manning's "Arm Wrestling with My Father" (in Chap. 5), you can assign them together.

We have highlighted the possible links in several ways. As we mentioned above, the headnote to each essay in this part itemizes the main methods used by the author. Among the writing suggestions for each selection in this part is at least one "Connections" topic that pulls in an essay from Part Two. For more general thematic links among selections, we provide a "Thematic Table of Contents" just after the book's main contents. And here in this manual, the discussion of each method ends with a list of selections elsewhere in the book, including Part Three, that illustrate the method.

SANDRA CISNEROS
Only Daughter

This much-reprinted essay is sure to resonate with any students who have shared Cisneros's frustrations with a parent's lack of support for their interests and goals. For students who are children of immigrants, the essay may be especially affecting because cultural differences often exacerbate the normal parent-child conflicts.

Two possible approaches to discussing this essay: Focus on how your students define *success* and the degree to which their families contribute to that definition, directly or indirectly; or focus on how differences between parents and children nourish or thwart the children. For either approach, students will be drawing on their own experiences, so small groups may encourage freer discussion than a whole-class setting. Hearing their classmates' experiences and ideas will broaden students' own perspectives and prepare them for work on the first, second, and third writing suggestions.

QUESTIONS ON MEANING

1. Cisneros's main purpose is to show how being her father's only daughter and living with her father's indifference to her writing contributed to her choice of writing as a career.
2. Being the only daughter left Cisneros to herself (par. 3), allowed her to attend college (4), allowed her to major in English and "putter about" with writing (5), led her to seek her father's approval (7–8), and (she implies) led her to seek recognition (12).
3. All writers are "trying to woo" a public. Cisneros describes her father and the public as "uninterested in reading" and as those she is writing "about and for."
4. Cisneros had succeeded, finally, in impressing her father with her writing. She had won her "public" (par. 8).

QUESTIONS ON WRITING STRATEGY

1. Cisneros seems to be writing for an audience wider than Mexican Americans: She takes pains to explain the effects of being the only daughter in a Mexican American family, and she translates all the Spanish words she uses.
2. We can infer that Cisneros writes serious literature. The implicit contrast between her work and her father's reading material is particularly illuminating.
3. The opening definition establishes the range of formative experiences that Cisneros goes on to explain in more detail. To us, it is quite effective.
4. The incident was obviously crucial to Cisneros, as her last sentence makes clear. By recalling it in great detail, down to the "one black sock and a plastic urinal" in her father's bedroom (par. 18), she conveys both her own heightened awareness at the time and the suspense of eliciting her father's reaction.

QUESTIONS ON LANGUAGE

1. "Only daughter" expresses the specialness of being unique and perhaps the loneliness of being sisterless. "*Only* a daughter" retracts some of the specialness by implying that a daughter is not as good as a son.
2. Cisneros expresses some resentment in "As if he deserved a medal from the state" (par. 11). Her word "erased" to describe her feeling and her "tug at my father's sleeve" (12) convey the hurt she experienced and the urgency she brought to correcting her father.
3. *Philandering* has had an interesting history. Originally from the Greek word for a woman who loves her husband (*phil-*, "love," and *andr-*, "man"), it came to mean "loving" generally and now refers to the behavior of a man who has casual sexual affairs.

SANDRA CISNEROS ON WRITING

There's more evidence of the rhythmic possibilities for the bilingual writer in Cisneros's fiction than in "Only Daughter." Still, students might comment on how they're affected by the use of Spanish words in the essay. In class, bilingual students may offer their sense of how their versatility has affected their prose. How do they handle the issue of "translation" for an audience? How much are they required to translate?

JUDITH ORTIZ COFER

Silent Dancing

Judith Ortiz Cofer's essay navigates complicated terrain, memory shaped by dreams, old film, dialogue with parents, and details accumulated as a child. Together, these elements work to provide a rich portrait of Cofer's singular experience and also of a larger experience, that of Puerto Ricans who came to this country in the 1950s and 1960s.

Ask students to work together in small groups in order to arrive at an understanding of how the essay's interlocking pieces fit together. The first question on writing strategy can help because it points to Cofer's use of italics and small print to distinguish the films and the dreams.

Students who are intrigued by Cofer's Latina perspective may want to read more of Cofer's writing, such as the book *Silent Dancing*, or one of the following: *Reclaiming Medusa: Short Stories by Contemporary Puerto Rican Women*, edited by Diana Velez (1988), Julia Alvarez's *How the Garcia Girls Lost Their Accents* (1991), or Laura Esquivel's *Like Water for Chocolate* (1992). A film based on Esquivel's book was released in 1993 and is available on video.

QUESTIONS ON MEANING

1. Cofer wants the reader to understand the cultural shifts that accompanied Puerto Ricans' immigration to the United States and especially the way she as a girl experienced them.
2. Cofer's father's experience with racist landlords (pars. 5–8) and his insistence on assimilating as quickly as possible (12–14) suggest that he longed to be accepted into mainstream America. The fact that Cofer's mother could not read English (13) and the comfort "El building" offered her (12) demonstrate her fear that living outside the Puerto Rican community would be lonely and difficult.
3. Cofer says in paragraph 24 that the speeches are from her dreams, but she has tuned her remembered dreams to a very likely representation of the speech of these relatives. When the *tiá política* recalls "the comment your mother made to a neighbor" about a baby flushed down the toilet (par. 27), the details resonate as genuine.

QUESTIONS ON WRITING STRATEGY

1. Passages in italics describe the film, placing the reader in a darkened room where the focus is not on the full sweep of Cofer's past but on a specific night and the importance of the film that resulted. The smaller type presents imagined speeches reconstructed from Cofer's dreams. Separating these passages from the regular text distinguishes Cofer's own memories from the other kinds of recollection. By highlighting them, Cofer heightens their importance in her story.
2. Perhaps along with "nostalgic," "comical and sad" seems a fair description of the essay's dominant impression and its overall tone.
3. The dialogue conveys authenticity and intimacy.
4. Cofer was obviously sensitive and observant. She was also curious, as evidenced by her banging on shared pipes (par. 4).
5. The three women represent the transition from Puerto Rican to American, from the newly arrived girlfriend through the more adapted mother to the eagerly Americanized cousin.

QUESTIONS ON LANGUAGE

1. Like the silent dancing Cofer watches onscreen, memory can be both dreamlike and incomplete.
2. The simile illustrates the importance and value of music to the people Cofer remembers from childhood.
3. *Adept*, meaning "well versed" or "skilled," is from the Latin *adeptus*, "having attained."

JUDITH ORTIZ COFER ON WRITING

This is a brief but powerful statement on family as a source of growth *and* of material for writing. The transformation from one's origins to maturity may be more marked for an immigrant because it corresponds to a cultural sea change, but "accepting the terms necessary for survival" is essential to anyone's successful adulthood.

C. DAY LEWIS

The Expulsion: Masaccio

This thematically complex poem may give students some difficulty, so you will need to encourage them to read it closely, paying attention to the reproduction of the painting on which it is based and being sure to look up the meanings of any unfamiliar words. If you have students who are not familiar with the biblical story of Adam and Eve and their expulsion from the Garden of Eden, you'll need to provide this background information as well, perhaps by reading Chapter 3 of Genesis to the class.

One way of beginning discussion of the poem is to share the following characterization of the poet made by a recent biographer and critic of his work, Albert Gelpi: "Instead of living for an afterlife, for heaven in the Christian sense, Day Lewis tried to ask, 'What about making a good society now?'" Day Lewis's poem is clearly based on a religious theme, but is it about spirituality or humanism or both?

After discussing the meaning questions, you might have students in small groups analyze how Day Lewis uses end rhyme and partial end rhyme: Lines 5 and 7 contain the first end rhymes in the poem, and beginning with lines 9 and 10 each pair of lines ends in rhyme or near rhyme. Though not always obvious because the lines vary in meter and length, the content of these rhymes and near rhymes adds to the poem's resonance: for example, "loss/toys" (lines 11–12), "god's/goads" (15–16), "wish/flesh" (17–18), "die/humanity" (21–22).

QUESTIONS ON MEANING

1. Students' interpretations may differ, but the main idea seems to be stated near the end of the poem: Masaccio's fresco depicts both childish shame and the moment of awareness of mortality, which separates humans from other animals.
2. Day Lewis's contrast of the "dear old garden god" with the more austere "accusing cosmic voice" and the opening image of a supreme being responsible for a devastating flood and the massacre of innocent people (*pogrom* refers more specifically to the massacre of Jews, as during the Holocaust) suggest a vision of God as wrathful or indifferent. One effect of this is to render Adam and Eve — and their human descendants — more sympathetic in their "fallen" state.
3. "More" here seems to refer to knowledge, an understanding of the cosmos and our place in it.

QUESTIONS ON WRITING STRATEGY

1. Notably missing is any mention of the serpent, Satan, the force of evil that tempted Eve into tasting, then sharing, the forbidden fruit. The serpent is not shown in the fresco, of course. Day Lewis seems to have wanted to stress the direct relationship between Adam and Eve and God, and he may have wanted to de-emphasize Adam and Eve's guilt (note "innocent fault" in line 12).

2. The description of Adam and Eve in the painting (lines 1–8 and echoed in line 19) provides the source for Day Lewis's musings on the "tragedy" of their expulsion from Paradise. As Day Lewis describes them, Masaccio depicts the two with overwhelming sympathy.
3. Day Lewis focuses on the "naked grief" in the behavior and posture of the figures (lines 1–2, 19), the encircling leaves (3), the faces full of "desolation" and shame (4–8), Adam's and Eve's childlike innocence (10–14, 29), the sword-bearing angel (15–16). These elements contribute clearly to a depiction of "childish tragedy" (19). Some students might observe that seeing the transformation (20–21) in the fresco requires as well some knowledge of the event's background and significance.

QUESTIONS ON LANGUAGE

1. The three nouns can be read as Adam's descending vision of himself: first as Eve's "lord," then as her "accomplice" in tasting the forbidden fruit, and finally as her "dupe," when he realizes the consequences of what he has done.
2. Day Lewis is suggesting both that Masaccio "paints [for] us," as viewers, a particular vision of the scene and that he "paints us," all humanity, as represented by Adam and Eve.
3. "Put on" here could mean "donned": Adam and Eve (and humanity) subsequently clothed themselves to cover their nakedness. More abstractly, by acquiring awareness of mortality Adam and Eve acquired the mantle of humanity.
4. Day Lewis uses *pickets* in an interesting way. As a verb (his use), the word means "encloses" or "secures." The sword — apparently the one wielded by the angel in the fresco — encloses Paradise as a fence made of pickets (sharpened stakes or posts) encloses a garden.

C. DAY LEWIS ON WRITING

Day Lewis writes about writing poetry, and what he says will certainly interest the poets in your class. But many of Day Lewis's points apply to prose, too, as our questions try to show. Students, especially the more conscious writers, may appreciate the humor in the fishing analogy — the patient waiting, the lure of false hope, the luck of a catch.

STEPHEN JAY GOULD

Sex, Drugs, Disasters, and the Extinction of Dinosaurs

Why did the dinosaurs vanish? Students intrigued by this perennial puzzle will warm to this essay, in which Gould sets forth much solid learning in a light-handed style. Gould tries to justify his flamboyant title in his third paragraph. Sex, drugs, and violence are "the primally fascinating themes of our culture," and for each there is a corresponding, widely held (or once widely held) hypothesis to account for the dinosaurs' disappearance. Gould not only analyzes these three answers to the question, but dismisses two of them as "silly" and supports the third as the most probable.

What other kinds of unanswered (or unanswerable) questions might students explore in an essay modeled on Gould's? Have the class generate as many potential questions as they can and write them on the board. Working in groups of three or four, students should choose a question on which to focus a collaborative essay. As a group, they can generate as many hypotheses as possible to answer this question. Each group member can have the responsibility to research one possibility, and the whole group can come together to write the essay.

QUESTIONS ON MEANING

1. A good scientific hypothesis is testable: It can generate both refuting and confirming evidence. It throws light on other subjects, even remote ones (par. 4). But useless speculation cannot be tested, nor can it be supported by evidence. It leads to no conclusions; it remains merely "an intriguing idea" (5).
2. On the whole, Gould's essay supports hypothesis number 3, "disasters," in paragraph 5. But Gould's thesis is larger: that one of the three hypotheses "represents science at its grandest and most useful."
3. Gould's procedure is to set forth the three explanations one at a time: the testicular theory (pars. 8–12), the overdose theory (13–14), and the asteroid or comet theory (15–16). Then he dismisses the first (18–19) and the second (20) as useless speculations.
4. Gould spends the rest of his essay in showing how the third idea is the only one that has gone anywhere, and that it lends credence to the speculation about the aftermath of nuclear holocaust.

QUESTIONS ON WRITING STRATEGY

1. "Hit parade of primal fascination" (par. 17), Gould's allusion to the old radio show "Your Hit Parade" (or *Hit Parader*, a magazine of song lyrics), makes clear that he regards some theories as no more substantial than passing crazes in popular music. The phrase "testicular frying" (18) — suggesting a mess of "Texas strawberries" sautéed in butter, or something — seems an archly comic dismissal of the theory. These phrases are ironic, practically sarcastic.
2. Why not read aloud "Do Not Go Gentle into That Good Night," from Dylan Thomas's *Collected Poems*, or in many anthologies? It's only nineteen lines long. Students don't have to know the poem, but if they do they'll better appreciate Gould's ironic humor. They'll need to be told that Thomas is addressing his dying father, urging the old man to resist death.
3. A diagram of the causal chain (pars. 15–16) might look like this:

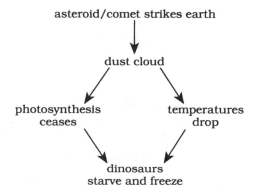

4. The process analyses explain how science works (pars. 4–5) and how each of the three theories explains the extinction of the dinosaurs (9–12, 14, 16). Without the first instance, we would not understand Gould's criteria for evaluating the three theories. Without the other instances, we would not understand the theories themselves.

QUESTIONS ON LANGUAGE

1. Separate from what? Separate from all else on earth at the time when the dinosaurs died. The problem, as Gould sees it, is not merely what happened to the dinosaurs, but what phenomenon could have occurred on earth at that moment about 65 million years ago.
2. In the vocabulary list, only *photosynthesis* and *paleontology* are specialized terms from science. We hesitated to call attention to many others that Gould uses, for the essay is slightly heavy with them: Cretaceous, plankton, invertebrates, ammonites (par. 6); amino-acid-based alkaloids, detoxify (14); iridium (21); indigenous volcanism, isotopes, spherules (24). Some of these words, however, Gould defines briefly as soon as he uses them.

STEPHEN JAY GOULD ON WRITING

Like most science writers, Gould was himself a scientist. But he strived to make science accessible to nonscientists without oversimplifying. Like most writers (not just scientists), Gould wrote to learn as well as to teach. He also, like any good writer, wrote about what interested and excited him. In his case, it was evolutionary theory. Your students can judge how successfully Gould reaches readers who are not themselves scientists. Instructors of English may appreciate the fact that Gould quotes poetry, too.

MARTIN LUTHER KING, JR.

I Have a Dream

Although Dr. King's speech was meant to be heard aloud, it remains impressive on the page, and it supplies a splendid illustration of a proposal that appeals to emotion. You will probably wish to point out, however, that some of its strategies are directed primarily toward listeners: the strong use of repetition, parallelism, and direct references to the audience.

Your students will better appreciate the power of this speech if they see or at least hear it as delivered by King in 1963. (Your school library may well have the speech on video or audiotape, or a reference librarian can point you toward an appropriate Web source.) Have students in small groups discuss the differences between reading and hearing this speech. Alternately, have a group of students listen to the speech and make a presentation to the rest of the class, playing certain brief selections and commenting on the differences in hearing versus reading. How is hearing and reading King's speech the same as or different from hearing and reading Jamaica Kincaid's "Girl" (Chap. 9)? What rhetorical techniques mark these works as speech-oriented?

QUESTIONS ON MEANING

1. The purpose is to inspire its hearers, despite their setbacks and disappointments, to go on working for civil rights.
2. African American people have yet to receive the freedom and the justice that the nation's founders guaranteed.
3. While King praises the rise of black activism, he believes it can advance its cause by nonviolent means, as he makes clear in this paragraph.
4. King recalls both early American history and the present occasion in his opening paragraph and in paragraphs 3 and 5.

QUESTIONS ON WRITING STRATEGY

1. Besides directly addressing his followers (in pars. 6–8), King employs parallelism in phrases such as "from the dark and desolate valley of segregation to the sunlit path of racial justice" (4). Still more impressively, he builds parallel structures by repeating phrases and clauses, lending them tremendous emphasis. This strategy informs much of the essay. In paragraph 2 there is a refrain ("One hundred years later"), and in paragraph 4 another (*"Now* is the time"). Most powerful of all are "I have a dream" (11–18) and "Let freedom ring" (20–27) — repeated again and again, at the start of each paragraph.
2. Paragraph 6.
3. Though he begins by recalling the past and its disappointments, he devotes by far the largest part of his speech to the future, in his extended description of his dream (pars. 10–27).
4. King's reasonableness is especially evident in his condemnation of bitterness and violence (par. 6). His personal authority — having been discriminated against and failing, having led demonstrations and achieving victories — combines with his rhetoric to give the speech its power.

5. In paragraph 2 the metaphors strengthen King's connection with the African Americans in his audience by showing his understanding of his race's hobbled, outcast state. In paragraph 4 the extended metaphor of the promissory note gives an argument by analogy, linking African American history to something concrete. The remaining metaphors in this paragraph intensify King's urgent appeal by contrasting what is with what could (and should) be.

QUESTIONS ON LANGUAGE

1. King uses concrete words in much of his imagery: the metaphors of "manacles" and "chains" (par. 2), that of the "check" (4), the visualization of the "governor's lips" (16). But for most of the speech his diction is largely abstract, as seems necessary to encompass two centuries of the past and the whole of the future.
2. King employs many figures, some biblical in connotation. Besides those noted in question 5 above and in the preceding question, they include "summer of [. . .] discontent" (5), an echo from Shakespeare ("Now is the winter of our discontent / Made glorious summer by this sun of York" — the opening lines of *Richard III*); "the palace of justice," "the cup of bitterness" (6); "justice rolls down like waters" and "righteousness like a mighty stream" (7); "storms of persecution" and "winds of police brutality" (8); "valley of despair" (9); the "heat of injustice and oppression" and the "oasis of freedom and justice" (13); the topographical references in paragraph 18; the "mountain of despair" and the "stone of hope" (19); and the "symphony of brotherhood" (19).
3. There seems freshness in King's application of *curvaceous* to California mountain peaks, instead of to (as in the usual cliché) Hollywood film goddesses.

MAXINE HONG KINGSTON
No Name Woman

Students are usually moved by Kingston's evocation of a haunting childhood story. Ask them to describe their own reactions to the tale of Kingston's aunt. Does it seem completely alien, from a world far away, or more immediate? Does it hold students' imaginations?

Kingston's books *The Woman Warrior* and *China Men* are sources of further mystery and understanding about Chinese *and* American culture. In addition, a number of films have depicted Chinese village life: *Ju Dou, Raise the Red Lantern,* and *To Live* are a few available on videotape. Students who are interested in the films might consider writing a comparative paper on the role of women, for example, in Kingston's essay and in one of the films. How important is the medium to the message? What do the two media say in common? Another use of the films, given their complicated imagery, is to assign a collaborative paper. Interested students could watch one film together, discuss it, and prepare a comparison between it and Kingston's essay, addressing the questions above.

QUESTIONS ON MEANING

1. Kingston and her mother share the purpose of telling a riveting story. Kingston's purpose is also self-examination and an inquiry into Chinese cultural attitudes; her mother's is also to instill these cultural attitudes into her.
2. Her aunt's husband could not have been the child's father (par. 3). Kingston posits two possible fathers: a man who "commanded [the aunt] to be with him" (15), and a man she herself was drawn to (21).
3. It is meant to warn her against adultery and, by extension, sexuality.
4. Kingston is haunted by her Chinese heritage; she seeks "ancestral help" (par. 22). Her aunt is a powerful representative of that heritage, an example of its grip on women and their emotions. Her life and death are a profound "family secret" that transcends Kingston's own immediate family.

QUESTIONS ON WRITING STRATEGY

1. Kingston's family and other older Chinese would be unlikely to read the essay: Kingston does address Chinese Americans directly (par. 12), and her detailed descriptions of Chinese and Chinese American culture indicate that she is trying to explain them to other Americans. Older Chinese, and particularly her family, would be shocked that she is breaking the silence about her aunt. Chinese Americans would see themselves and their own "haunting" in her story. Other Americans might be enlightened about the complexity and power the Chinese heritage holds.
2. The story of the aunt is supposed to be kept secret by the mother. The mother's tale is supposed to be kept secret by Kingston but is instead examined minutely in this essay. Kingston's telling the secret of her aunt's story is an act of rebellion equivalent to her aunt's. Thus, the opening line presages all the themes of the essay (and creates suspense as well).
3. The effect is to intensify the confusion of reality and truth and to show the subjective nature of memory and family history. Kingston creates this effect in passages such as "I want her fear to have lasted just as long as rape lasted" (par. 18), "I hope that the man my aunt loved appreciated a smooth brow" (25), and "She may have gone to the pigsty as a last act of responsibility" (44). You might want to draw students' attention to places where Kingston's different sources are intertwined — for example, "My mother spoke about the raid as if she had seen it, when she and my aunt, a daughter-in-law to a different household, should not have been living together at all" (19).
4. The details in paragraphs 15–18 tell a much bleaker story: "She obeyed him" (par. 16), "No one talked sex, ever" (18). The details in paragraphs 21–28 are those of a more romantic tale: "she often worked at herself in the mirror" (23), "my aunt combed individuality into her bob" (25), "she dreamed of a lover for the fifteen days of New Year's" (28). Kingston seems more caught up in the romantic version of the story, in her aunt's desire and need to rebel.
5. Her aunt may have been "commanded [. . .] to lie with" the father of her child (par. 15), or she may have "let dreams grow" and "offered us up for a charm that vanished" (21). The raid may have been organized by her

rapist (16) or by villagers who were "speeding up the circling of events" (39). She may have killed her child because it was "a foreign growth that sickened her every day" (43) or because "Mothers who love their children take them along" (46). In the end, Kingston concludes that her aunt's suicide was caused by her feelings of imprisonment within the conventions of village life.

QUESTIONS ON LANGUAGE

1. Kingston's poetic language shows how deeply she responds to her Chinese heritage and its tales. Some striking phrases include "a protruding melon of a stomach" (par. 3), "the heavy, deep-rooted women were to maintain the past against the flood" (20), "women looked like great sea snails" (27), "violence could open up a black hole, a maelstrom that pulled in the sky" (37).
2. You may want to explain the "commensal" tradition (par. 19), in which food is shared by the generations of an extended family. The idea of food and its allocation is central to societies, like China's, where resources are stretched to their utmost. Kingston underscores this in paragraph 15, when she describes her ancestors as "people who hatch their own chicks and eat the embryos and the heads for delicacies and boil the feet in vinegar for party food, leaving only the gravel, eating even the gizzard lining."
3. Kingston blurs the distinction between history and her interpretation of it.

MAXINE HONG KINGSTON ON WRITING

In this interview, Kingston discloses a profound belief in the power of writing to generate writing, even to bring order and meaning to one's life. Some students may have had this experience of writing, and perhaps they can confirm Kingston's words for students who haven't. (Students often don't realize that the turmoil of writing can actually be productive.) Kingston also slips in a small warning: It's fine to let yourself go in drafting, but eventually the "intellectual" (Kingston seems to mean "critical") side must kick in for revision.

JOHN McPHEE

Silk Parachute

McPhee's essay provides a strong example of source material every student has access to: memories from childhood. Much of the delight in McPhee's essay comes from placing these memories within the context of our litigious culture, denying memory, refusing to acknowledge facts. The contrast creates a balanced, diplomatic, tender, and humorous portrait of McPhee's mother. Writing exercises and discussions that encourage students to draw on their own memories may draw students into this brief, entertaining essay.

In the previous edition, we used McPhee's essay to illustrate the method of example — an unusual one that lacks a stated generalization or thesis for the examples to relate to. Indeed, the only generalization McPhee offers comes through the example and metaphor of the parachute in the final paragraph. You may want to discuss the absence of a stated thesis in class, aided by the first question on writing strategy. Then divide students into small groups and ask each one to come up with a sentence or at most two that state the gist of McPhee's characterization of his mother. If each group reports its statement back to the whole class, the ensuing discussion could be a good lesson in thesis building.

QUESTIONS ON MEANING

1. The proverb says that not only McPhee himself but also his mother will be tarnished by his bad behavior.
2. The comment displays pride and faith in McPhee's writing, as well as humor. In the footnote to paragraph 17, we have given the pronunciation of *Knopf* so that students see the joke in the mother's "k-nock."
3. McPhee's memories demonstrate his mother's reliability and grace, and the parachute captures both. The toy "never failed" — just as his mother responded to every difficulty of parenting with patience and grit. "Even if you abused it, whacked it really hard — gracefully, lightly, it floated back to you" — just as McPhee's mother was always there for him no matter what challenges he presented.

QUESTIONS ON WRITING STRATEGY

1. One simple generalization, drawn from the examples: McPhee's mother was stern, protective, humorous, generous, and thoughtful. As noted in the answer to question 3 on meaning, McPhee provides a kind of metaphysical generalization in the final sentence. To us, the absence of an explicit thesis statement strengthens the essay by involving the reader in building a generalization.
2. McPhee pretends to deny or not recall events in which his behavior was bad and in which his mother punished or spoke sharply to him. The childlike denials, couched in adult language, are familiar and funny.
3. The vividness of McPhee's details is more believable than his denial, of course, and his reporting of later events (without denials) proves him to have an excellent memory for his childhood.
4. The essay first details the "half-truths, prevarications, false allegations, inaccuracies, innuendoes and canards" (par. 16), relating all in a tone of disbelief and distance. After that, the tone is touched with tenderness and awe. Examples include "My mother knew what to do about that" and "elegant spyglass" (18) and "My mother figured out," "stood there in the icy wind," "fabulous toy," "gracefully, lightly, it floated back to you" (19).
5. McPhee uses narration and description in paragraphs 7–14 (the anecdote about the sandwich), 18 (the trip to the theater), and 19 (the visit to LaGuardia Field to watch airplanes, the purchase of the silk parachute and the author's delight in playing with it). The first anecdote reflects his mother's strong will and iron hand with her son, while the latter two suggest her concern, empathy, and indulgence.

QUESTIONS ON LANGUAGE

1. The phrase "Mister Man" provides a note of humor and authenticity to the dialogue. Most students will be able to recount similar mock-formal names their parents used to indicate frustration and a no-nonsense attitude, such as "missy" and "young man."
2. Applied to the parachute, the words connote physical action. Applied to McPhee's mother (about whom we know nothing physical), they connote traits of character and emotional response.
3. *Guffaws* comes from a Scottish onomatopoetic word. It's related to *gawf*, a loud noisy laugh, also Scottish in origin.

JOHN McPHEE ON WRITING

We have quoted two of McPhee's helpful explanations of his writing process from the many he has given. The article in which the quoted statements appear provides a fascinating look at the concerns and habits of a master, including McPhee's comments on criticisms and possible rewrites of his work. See Douglas Vipond and Russell A. Hunt, "The Strange Case of the Queen-Post Truss: John McPhee on Writing and Reading," *College Composition and Communication* 42.2 (1991): 200–10.

GEORGE ORWELL

Shooting an Elephant

Orwell's gripping narrative, told with vivid detail and an appealing self-effacement, tends to stick in the memory of anyone who studies it. Orwell's elegant prose may at first put some students off, but even they will soon enough be caught up in the narrator's tale.

Indelible as it is, the essay may strike students as remote from their concerns because it takes place in a country and a time far from their own. If you find this response, point out that the essay tells of doing what seems necessary, even what's wrong, to save face. Governments and their representatives everywhere, including our own, commit dubious actions for just this reason. The second writing suggestion can help students discover the relation between Orwell's experience and their own: Ask students to scour newspapers and TV news programs for examples of contemporary face-saving among public officials. In small groups, each student could present one such example for discussion of the perpetrator's likely motives as well as the effects of such behavior.

QUESTIONS ON MEANING

1. Orwell explains that he took his .44 Winchester with him because "the noise might be useful *in terrorem*" (par. 3). His borrowing the elephant

rifle later (4) seems a wise precaution because the elephant had killed a man. As he explains in paragraph 5, the rifle was for self-defense only.

2. The answer is twofold. He had to save face — that was the more important reason. But, as he mentions in paragraph 9, his being a bad shot also influenced his behavior by injecting an element of fear.

3. He expresses the epiphany most clearly and vehemently in paragraph 7: "I perceived in this moment that when the white man turns tyrant it is his own freedom that he destroys." And so on to the end of the paragraph.

4. The coolie's death put the young Orwell "legally in the right." By the time he wrote "Shooting an Elephant," though, Orwell was no longer motivated by any need to save face. He had the courage to tell his story truthfully and unsparingly, awful as it was. It seems clear that the mature Orwell did not share his younger self's view of the coolie's death.

5. Orwell's purpose is clearly to show, through his experience of shooting the elephant, how the need to save face motivates — indeed, compels — the actions of himself and every other imperialist.

QUESTIONS ON WRITING STRATEGY

1. These paragraphs, because they reveal so much about the author's feelings toward his job and toward the Burmese who made it difficult, shed light on the complex motives that resulted in the unnecessary shooting. They also, perhaps, somewhat justify the author's behavior — to himself and to us.

2. He explains the circumstances best in his opening paragraphs. He had come to hate imperialism and all that it stood for. Still, because it was his job, he had to do "the dirty work of Empire." Adding to his misery was the abuse he and his English compatriots had to endure from the Burmese.

3. With hindsight, Orwell has a broader and deeper perspective on the events. At the time, he was bitter, embarrassed, and a little afraid. In retrospect, he can see his foolishness and the tyranny he helped to further.

4. The paragraphs seem to unfold almost in real time, and the details of the wounded elephant are excruciating. We understand, almost too plainly, Orwell's horror at his act.

5. The Burmese are portrayed as both detestable (spitting on European women, yelling "with hideous laughter," "sneering") and pitiable ("wretched prisoners huddling in the stinking cages," "gray, cowed faces," "scarred buttocks"). The contradiction makes Orwell's position "perplexing and upsetting."

QUESTIONS ON LANGUAGE

1. The term refers to the annual period during which a male elephant is most sexually aroused and is often violent.

2. Some examples: "chucked up my job" (par. 2), "had taken the wrong direction" (3), "rubbish van" (3), "had come suddenly upon him round the corner of the hut" (4), "I ought not to shoot him" (6), and various uses of *got*, such as "I had got to do it" (7), "I had got to shoot" (7), and "I had got to act quickly" (8).

3. *Sahib* is a title of respect from the Urdu use of the Arabic *cahib*, meaning "friend."

GEORGE ORWELL ON WRITING

This is a grim account of the writing process! "Writing a book is a horrible, exhausting struggle, like a long bout of some painful illness." But students who have suffered when writing even a brief paper may take heart from Orwell's account of his agonies.

Orwell's remark about the need to efface one's own personality (cited in the second discussion question) echoes similar advice given by T. S. Eliot in his familiar essay "Tradition and the Individual Talent" (1919). Blasting the Romantic poets' notion of writing as self-expression, Eliot finds the poet obligated to do something more interesting than vent personal emotions. He adds: "But, of course, only those who have personality and emotions to express know what it means to want to escape from these things."

Orwell here stresses the importance of writing both to achieve something readable and beautiful and — more important, because it affects the artistry of the finished work — writing to improve society.

RICHARD RODRIGUEZ

Aria:
A Memoir of a Bilingual Childhood

Rodriguez, in sensuous detail, recalls from his childhood the pleasures and pains of growing up speaking Spanish in surroundings where English was the official language. Spanish was the family language; its use at home came to signify warmth and security, a way for the Rodriguez family to separate themselves from the difficulties encountered in the English-speaking world around them. Yet Rodriguez has come to feel that recent efforts to provide bilingual education in the public schools for Spanish-speaking children are misguided. To prolong their dependence on Spanish, he insists, is to relegate them for an unnecessarily long time to the ranks of the disadvantaged.

Not all reviewers of *Hunger of Memory* sided with Rodriguez on this point. For a differing view of the book by a fellow Mexican American (like Rodriguez, the holder of a doctorate in English), see the attack in the *American Book Review* (May–June 1983) by Cordelia Candelaria. Although Candelaria thinks Rodriguez has a right to his opinions (he is against not only bilingual schooling but also affirmative action), she objects to his being regarded as a spokesperson for Mexican Americans. She disputes, too, his assumption that good schooling inevitably leads to a loss of one's ethnic identity. Her own experience was otherwise: "My normal adolescent estrangement from family was never permanent."

Bilingual education continues to be controversial, of course. A writing suggestion encourages students to grapple with the issue and could be used as the basis of class discussion. You could also have students work in pairs or threes to locate another opinion on the subject to complement or refute Rodriguez's. What is the basis of this other perspective? How does it agree with or answer Rodriguez's claims? Have each group briefly explain its findings. Can the class as a whole come up with a sort of map of the debate?

QUESTIONS ON MEANING

1. Rodriguez objects to bilingual education in the schools for those children whose native language is not English. He introduces his view in paragraph 4, then returns to it in paragraphs 19–20 and 38–39. The author believes that by slowing down the Spanish-speaking child's assimilation into the cultural mainstream, bilingual education does a disservice.

2. In paragraphs 12 and 13 the author probes his ambivalent reactions. Though his parents always managed to understand and communicate necessary information, their son, in spite of himself, felt unsettled and occasionally embarrassed by their difficulties.

3. The author makes an important distinction between "sounds" and "words." For the child Rodriguez, the sounds of the Spanish language were synonymous with intimacy, with family, with home (pars. 8 and 14). Before he learned words in English, the gringos' sounds seemed to him exotic and polysyllabic, loud and confident, firm and clear, nasal and high (10). The sounds of Spanish constituted a private language. English was a public language. When he says he was a child longer than most, he means that for a longer time than most children he heard language in terms of sounds. His progress toward comprehending and using the words of public language was slow.

4. There was a somewhat troubling diminution of their togetherness. What Rodriguez doesn't acknowledge is that the loosening of family ties is an inevitable development in all families, regardless of their language. To the author, separation, language, and his growing inattention to "sounds" seem inextricably bound together.

5. The child Rodriguez was miserable over having to speak English. As an adult, the author was grateful to the nuns who had insisted that he learn English.

QUESTIONS ON WRITING STRATEGY

1. It offers the reader much necessary background: where and when the author's childhood experiences occurred, the facts that as a first-grader Rodriguez knew very little English and that his family included three siblings, two of them older than he was. Furthermore, "I remember," by promising a story at the outset, immediately captures the reader's interest.

2. It is hard to argue against what someone has learned through personal experience. The author's memories, therefore, strengthen his arguments against bilingual education. The autobiographical paragraphs in "Aria" do more, however. The insights they provide into the heart of a sensitive child lend the essay a touching, elegiac aura hard to forget.

3. In paragraph 1 the books brought home from school by his Spanish-speaking older siblings remain unread on the table. In paragraph 40, where Rodriguez writes about life in his house after he has learned English, the important detail about the schoolbooks is that, instead of remaining tightly closed, they are now being read. The child is fully Americanized, Rodriguez maintains, because he has mastered the English language.

4. Advocates of bilingual education — and their numbers are significant — would find much to criticize in "Aria." We think it would be hard even for them not to find much to praise as well.
5. English is "loud, booming," "high, nasal," "birdlike," "chirping" (par. 10). Spanish is embracing (14), "light and free," "fast," "twirling" (18), "tender" (33), "singsong" (37). The English sounds are unpleasant, the Spanish pleasant.
6. From his narrative, we know Rodriguez to be very sensitive, highly intelligent, thoughtful. His fairness might be questioned: He states but barely examines the opposing view. But since, as he says, bilingual education was well entrenched when he wrote, he may not have felt much obligation to present that side of the debate.

QUESTIONS ON LANGUAGE

1. Shy students might find it interesting that the word *diffident* came into Middle English from the Latin *dis-* ("not") and *fidere* ("to trust"). The present participle was *diffidens*. *Diffidere* literally meant "to mistrust." *Diffident* now means "lacking self-confidence; timid" (*The American Heritage Dictionary*).
2. For Rodriguez, Spanish was a private language and English was a public language. He insists that educators do a disservice to children whose native language is not English unless they oblige those children to learn English at the outset. To be unable to use the public language, Rodriguez maintains, is to be doubly disadvantaged.
3. He means that increasingly he was able to understand what he heard. He had always understood Spanish, of course. But it was even more important to his future that he hear English as *words*, not as interesting but useless sounds.

RICHARD RODRIGUEZ ON WRITING

Rodriguez is particularly adept at describing the conflicting feelings that writers sometimes experience when they look back over words they wrote long ago. In some cases he "cannot remember having written them." Some of his other words, conversely, "recall the very day they were composed" (par. 4).

The eloquent plea in the concluding paragraph deserves attention. The quality of a writer's audience, Rodriguez indicates, is tremendously important.

To stimulate class discussion about Rodriguez's comments, you may want to ask some of the following questions in addition to those that appear in the book:

1. For Rodriguez, what does writing have to do with *need*? (In a sense, Rodriguez wrote because he had to. "I began writing to stay alive — not as a job, but to stay alive," par. 3. For him, writing is serious business. His attitude supports what good teachers and good writers know: The best writing comes from those with something they are burning to say.)
2. What is "universality" in novels and essays? Describe in your own words the "paradox" that sometimes produces it. (Universality is that quality in literature that reaches out to every member of a diverse audience. The paradox, according to Rodriguez, is that writers who achieve universal

appeal are generally those who are the most individual [par. 5]. Compare this statement with E. B. White's in "E. B. White on Writing" [p. 677], on the same subject.)

JONATHAN SWIFT
A Modest Proposal

That Swift is being ironic in proposing this monstrous solution to the problems of Ireland usually dawns slowly on a few students. It will be a highly entertaining class wherein someone thinks Swift is serious. From Swift's essay a perfectly straightforward argument for Christian charity may be inferred. For a contemporary satiric essay that depends on irony, see Linnea Saukko's "How to Poison the Earth" (Chap. 8).

The irony of Swift's essay is masterful and inspiring. Students who would like to imitate Swift's tone would benefit from feedback on their attempts. Try assigning the class a single paragraph written in a tone of heavy irony. (You may wish to leave the subject up to students, or integrate this with the first writing suggestion.) Give students time in class to read their paragraphs aloud in small groups (it will help if every student in the group has a copy) and to discuss how they might revise their work to improve the tone and the point(s) they are making.

QUESTIONS ON MEANING

1. Swift is proposing that Irish poor sell their year-old children to the rich for meat.
2. Swift is calling for charity and compassion. Some specific alternatives for relieving poverty are given in Swift's list of "other expedients," paragraph 29.
3. Swift's essay calls attention to both the plight of the poor in Ireland and the hardheartedness of their oppressors.
4. Swift's image of the begging mothers and their children immediately arouses readers' sympathy and prepares them to react with horror against the "modest" proposal.
5. Objections should be obvious, unless one regards a human being as an animal to be butchered.

QUESTIONS ON WRITING STRATEGY

1. The author writes as a reasonable, kind, serious do-gooder, impatient with the failure of those in power to do anything about the problem.
2. Swift does this effectively by calling his proposal "modest," by citing authorities and experts to back him up (such as the "very knowing American," par. 9), by carefully listing the advantages of the proposal (21–28), by his concern that the flesh would spoil if exported (31), and by professing at the end that he doesn't stand to make a penny himself.

3. Probably not until paragraph 9.
4. Surely to our feelings. Most of the reasonable arguments are deliberately monstrous, although other convincing points appeal to reason in paragraph 29.
5. The process analysis makes us study the proposal in its every gruesome particular. It forces our noses into the proposal, and thus into the plight of the Irish poor, in a way mere generalities would not have. The cause and effect specifies the ways in which the proposal will achieve its goals, summarized in paragraph 33 as "advancing our trade, providing for infants, relieving the poor, and giving some pleasure to the rich."

QUESTIONS ON LANGUAGE

1. The words from breeding and butchery include "dam" (par. 4); "breed" (10); "carcass" (14); "flay" (15); "dressing them hot" (16); "mares in foal [. . .] ready to farrow" (26); "barreled beef [. . .] bacon" (27); and "customers for infants' flesh" (28).
2. Swift's vocabulary is extensive. When they read "A Modest Proposal," students may have to use their dictionaries more than they usually do when reading an essay. The exercise may increase their vocabularies.

JONATHAN SWIFT ON WRITING

Though dated, Swift's advice still makes sense. To be sure, when Swift set forth his fable of the spider and the bee in *The Battle of the Books*, he was writing in defense of the Roman classics, the study of which, needless to say, has been greatly curtailed since the early eighteenth century. Immediately after we quote his celebrated fable, we attempt to translate it into terms useful to the student, but we'll have to admit that our translation somewhat betrays the original. Still, Swift's advice to writers — don't just spin cobwebs out of your own entrails — can be taken as another argument for writers' paying attention to the world beyond their heads. You'll find comparable advice in the Writers on Writing feature by George Orwell (p. 637).

CORNEL WEST

Race Matters

Depending on the political makeup of your class, you may get cheers or resistance in response to this piece. The African American scholar West wants to jolt readers out of any complacent belief that racial progress in the United States has removed race as a significant problem both here and internationally. Aimed as much at affluent black readers as at white readers, the essay stands as an indictment of a society in which people of color are still disproportionately poor, undereducated, incarcerated, and subject to police brutality. It is also an attack on "the ever-expanding market culture that puts everything and everyone up for sale" (par. 7) and a call for greater "environmental, consumers', and workers' protections" (11) throughout the world.

To help students understand what troubles West, you might have them consider the statistical evidence he offers to support his contentions: that "black people consume 12 percent of illegal drugs in America yet suffer nearly 70 percent of its convictions" (par. 4), that "the top 1 percent [of Americans] have wealth equivalent to the bottom 95 percent" (6), and that "roughly 40 percent of black children [live] in poverty and almost 10 percent of all black young adult men [are] in prison" (10). Then have them take note of those issues for which he provides no statistics but which are generally accepted as problems in much of the African American community, from racial profiling (4) to decrepit schools (5).

If students object that West only describes the problem of continued racial injustice without offering any solutions, remind them that this is the preface to an entire book in which he does go on to suggest concrete changes.

QUESTIONS ON MEANING

1. West states his thesis at the beginning of paragraph 11: "As we enter the twenty-first century, we must connect the urgent black domestic issues to pressing class and gender issues in the corporate globalization around the world." West's purpose seems to be to lead readers to see that racial discrimination — even oppression — is still a serious problem in the United States and to argue that this is largely a result both of "plutocratic, patriarchal, pigmentocratic realities" (par. 6) and of failed black leadership (9–10).

2. Continuing problems, according to West, include "racial profiling, [disproportionate] drug convictions [. . .] and death-row executions," along with "unemployment levels, infant mortality rates, special education placements, and psychic depression treatments" (par. 4). He also mentions "[d]ecrepit schools, inadequate health care, unavailable childcare, and too few jobs with a living wage" (5) and "black uncivil combat zones" and "black nihilism and collective suicide" (8). He attributes these problems to growing disparities of wealth in the United States, which pit classes against each other; to "the expansion of unaccountable corporate power in the economy and government and the unleashing of arbitrary police power in poor communities of color" (5); and to an unrestrained "market culture" and an overriding emphasis on "[i]ndividual success" (7).

3. West believes that black leaders "give in too quickly and sell out too easily" (9) and "downplay the black youth realities at the expense of black professional advancement" (10). He believes black leaders are neglecting to focus on the underprivileged because it is unpopular to do so within the white mainstream.

4. West sees a direct link between the oppression of poor African Americans (and other minorities) in the United States and the oppression of poor people and women in the developing world. We must face the problem at home, he implies, before we can face the equally pressing problem worldwide.

QUESTIONS ON WRITING STRATEGY

1. West argues that this legacy of oppression — one few would deny — "has left its indelible mark on all spheres of American life" and that "the problem of the twenty-first century remains the problem of the color line" (par. 1).

2. Students may have different thoughts here, but our sense is that West writes for a broad audience. He does, however, seem to be addressing African American leaders in paragraphs 9–10.

3. West relies on cause and effect particularly in paragraphs 5–10, where he focuses on both the causes and the consequences of the continuing oppression of poor African Americans. His point is to make clear to readers that discrimination remains a serious social problem deserving attention.

4. West contrasts African American communities in the past — "highly nurturing, caring, loving, and self-respecting" (par. 8), even in the face of more overt discrimination — with today's "uncivil combat zones" (8), where blacks prey on blacks. His point is that this transformation has resulted from "strong market forces and vicious white supremacist (and male supremacist, heterosexist) stereotypes that disproportionately shape black perceptions and practice" (8).

QUESTIONS ON LANGUAGE

1. West's tone is forceful, almost angry, some would say strident. It comes from words such as "American barbarism" and "vicious" (par. 1) and driving sentences such as the very first one: "Black people in the United States differ from all other modern people owing to the unprecedented levels of unregulated and unrestrained violence directed at them." Students will surely differ over whether the tone works or not, their opinions no doubt correlating directly with their acceptance of West's views.

2. West uses the word *matters* both as a noun (as in "matters of race") and as a verb (as in "the subject of race matters in any discussion of democracy, gender, and class").

3. West means there are no positive choices, only negative choices that differ little from one another. You might discuss with students the appropriateness of West's use of this cliché.

4. *Apartheid* — from the Dutch *apart*, "separate," and *-heid*, "-hood" — was the South African policy of segregation of nonwhites from whites. Like others, West applies the term to segregation outside South Africa, specifically in the United States fifty years ago.

E. B. WHITE

Once More to the Lake

Among White's essays, this is one of the most often reprinted. In July 1941 White made a pilgrimage back to the Belgrade Lakes, northwest of Augusta, Maine, together with his young son, Joel. "This place is as American as a drink of Coca Cola," he wrote to his wife, Katharine. "The white collar family having its annual liberty. I must say it seems sort of good" (*Letters of E. B. White* [1976], p. 215). After his return to civilization, White produced "Once More to the Lake" for a column he was then contributing to *Harper's* magazine. Too marvelous to be a reasonable model for most student writers, the

essay can encourage them to believe that their own memories are worth recording and can interest others. "Once More to the Lake" exhibits a whole
array of rhetorical methods, too: description, narration, exemplification, comparison and contrast, even process analysis.

Of course, it is White's description — of place, people, feelings — that is
most inimitable, but students can try their hand in a small way at first. Give
them a one-paragraph writing assignment — even with a word limit, if you
desire — to describe a place that is highly familiar to them. Working in small
groups, students can read aloud their paragraphs and get feedback on how
they might revise them to make the images more vivid, the phrasing more
precise, the details more developed. (This will work best if students bring copies of their paragraphs for the other members of their group.) Fine-tuning
their own writing on this small scale should give students the confidence to
undertake larger writing projects (like those in "Suggestions for Writing").

QUESTIONS ON MEANING

1. White senses that nothing essential at the lake has changed; besides, he
    sustains the illusion that his son is himself as a boy and that he has
    become his own father (par. 4 and later passages).
2. Once, inboard motors had made a sleepy sound; today, the outboards
    seem "petulant, irritable." A central detail: "this was the note that jarred,
    the one thing that would sometimes break the illusion and set the years
    moving."
3. White's son is engaged by the same attractions: the joy of getting up
    early and going off by himself in a boat (par. 4), the fun of learning tricks
    with a motor (10). But the essay sets forth an insight that is White's
    alone, and the boy is not portrayed in any clear detail until the final
    paragraph.
4. White's purpose, made explicit in the final paragraph, is to set forth a
    theme: that although time at the lake seems to have stood still, time for
    the writer has been passing. He has aged and he will die like his father
    before him.

QUESTIONS ON WRITING STRATEGY

1. The repetitions help set forth the central theme of the essay. (In question
    4 above we suggest one way of stating it.)
2. Beautifully arranged, this essay doesn't completely unfold its purpose
    until its final line. By a multitude of details, we have been lulled into
    accepting the illusion that time stands still. Suddenly, in one unforget-
    table image, White invokes reality. The feeling of donning an ice-cold
    bathing suit is a familiar sensation from childhood, but the cold of the
    suit also suggests the cold of the grave.
3. Young readers, we trust, will understand and appreciate it, too. Ask them.
    Students may not be greatly excited by White's slowly unfolding account
    at first, but most do warm to it.
4. The author's tone, sometimes gently humorous, in general is nostalgic,
    even dreamlike — as if he were viewing the lake and his early adventures
    there through a gentle haze.
5. White's images appeal to all five senses. They capture the smells of bed-
    room and wet woods (par. 2); the sight of a dragonfly, the boat, and its

contents (5); the sounds of motors (10); the taste of donuts dipped in sugar (11); and the tactile sense of damp moss in the bait can (5), of the "soggy, icy" bathing trunks (13).

6. The comparison, notably between White's childhood experiences and his son's, contains the essay's theme of time and mortality.

QUESTIONS ON LANGUAGE

1. For the word *cultist* (par. 6), it may be worth pointing out that White apparently means an enthusiast for cleanliness.
2. The diction may sound exaggerated, but "unique" and "holy" describe the way the lake appears to White in memory.
3. White's description of a thunderstorm is only one of the essay's rich array of figurative language. The lake in early morning preserves "the stillness of the cathedral" (par. 2). Waves keep "chucking the rowboat under the chin" (5). In paragraph 10 a one-cylinder engine was like a wild animal "eating out of your hand," and a boat could approach a dock like a charging bull. In paragraph 11 a steamboat used to look like a Ubangi, and a drink of soda pop would backfire like an engine. In paragraph 12 the storm becomes a wild concert, and the generations are linked "in a strong indestructible chain." The essay ends in a splendid metaphor.

E. B. WHITE ON WRITING

For aspiring writers — probably every class has at least one or two — E. B. White's advice must be among the most encouraging in existence. To the discouraged seventeen-year-old who wrote to him, White simply said, "Write." What eager aspirants might fail to notice at first glance is White's confession that he wrote "half a million words" before trying to get any of them into print. This statement comes as a cool, refreshing breeze in a world where too many people try to get published before they are ready.

E. B. White isn't big on market tips, either. His whole point is that if you really care about what you write, if you really work at it until it's as good as it can be, someone will want to read it. Clearly, not every aspiring writer was born with a gift equal to White's. Still, we hope you agree that one of the most helpful things you can impress upon students is that their writing will be better if they care about what they're saying.

TERRY TEMPEST WILLIAMS

The Clan of One-Breasted Women

This essay falls into two distinct sections, and having students define the focus of each section would be a good place to begin class discussion. In paragraphs 1–38, Williams — a Mormon native of Utah — writes about the high incidence of breast cancer among the women in her family beginning in the 1960s. She goes on to link these cancers, and those of other Utahans, to nuclear fallout from above-ground atomic testing — a link the US government initially denied and later was legally absolved of responsibility for on grounds of "sovereign immunity."

The second section (pars. 39–58) describes civil disobedience against atomic testing, which continued to take place underground. Williams first dreams that "women from all over the world" came together like benign witches in the wilderness to "reclaim the desert for the sake of their children, for the sake of the land," while a few miles away the earth itself smoldered (39–42). Then the dream merges into the protest Williams was part of, ending in her arrest and release and her empowerment.

The transition from dream to reality in paragraphs 39 to 49 is complex and worth some analysis. Students in small groups might consider Williams's technique here, noting what she describes that is clearly dreamlike, what she describes that seems actually to have happened, and what she describes that lies somewhere in between dream and reality.

Students may be interested to know that in 1992, the year after Williams published this essay in her book *Refuge*, the government abandoned underground atomic testing in Nevada. Ironically, although the test site is still officially off-limits, the Department of Energy now conducts closely supervised tours for civilians who wish to visit it. An account of such a tour by students from the University of Arizona, including photographs, is online at *http://www.lpl.arizona.edu/grad/fieldtrips/NTS/*.

QUESTIONS ON MEANING

1. After noting that breast cancer is usually attributed to heredity, a poor diet, and childlessness or bearing children after age thirty, Williams makes the point that — except for heredity, perhaps — these factors do not apply to her Mormon family. She goes on later in the essay to suggest that residents of Utah, where rates of cancer are high, do have in common their exposure to high levels of radioactive fallout between 1951 and 1962, so that living there could have been a greater hazard than any other factor.

2. Williams refers to the US government's deceit in denying that atomic testing in Nevada posed any risk to nearby residents. Williams, like most Utahans, had not questioned the testing until her father reminded her of the family's immediate exposure in 1957.

3. Williams's point is to show that, sound as the case was, as determined by the lower court, it was not upheld in higher courts because they preferred the historical precedent of government immunity — according to Williams, an outdated precedent.

4. Her evidence is basically the high incidence of breast cancer among family members after 1960 and the absence of other clear risk factors (par. 5), along with the fact that her mother's cancer was first manifest fourteen years after her 1957 exposure, the time one expert says radiation cancer takes to appear (36).

5. The women were protesting the government's continuing atomic testing in the Nevada desert, which now takes place underground, because they believed such testing still posed a risk to humans and the environment.

QUESTIONS ON WRITING STRATEGY

1. Williams's thesis is that the US government should take responsibility for human cancers that can be attributed to past atomic testing and should cease current atomic testing. Williams no doubt believed the thesis was obvious. But she may also have thought a bald statement would be out of keeping with her incremental approach. Her essay, though argumentative, is not a formal argument.
2. The quotation shows how meekly many Utahans, particularly Mormons, responded to their plight. Even under the circumstances, Irene Allen would not blame the government.
3. The dream foreshadows Williams's actual experience and heightens it, emphasizing the women's intense relationship to the land, their inner power, and their dramatic appearance as "apparitions" (par. 46). The reality would inevitably be far more mundane.
4. Williams uses narration and description to relate the impact of her mother's surgery (pars. 6-12), the conversation with her father that led to her making a connection between atomic testing and the cancer in her family (12–19), her dream (39–48), and the actual circumstances of the women's civil disobedience, subsequent arrest, and release into the desert (50–58). These stories convey both the way her parents accept their fate and Williams's own act of defiance and protest. The description — mainly in paragraphs 16, 32, 39, 41–45, and 56 — highlights the beauty of the desert, the horror of nuclear explosion, and the sad gruesomeness of death from cancer.
5. Although not a conventional argument — Williams doesn't even state her thesis — her essay clearly criticizes past and current government policies on atomic testing and is meant to persuade readers of the rightness of these views.

QUESTIONS ON LANGUAGE

1. "Clan" implies both Williams's extended family, many of whom have suffered breast cancer, and the "clan" of women more generally, who will fight for that which affirms and enhances life as opposed to agents of death and suffering.
2. The Shoshone song ties the women in the dream to a long Native American tradition of respect and reverence for the earth and its creatures. It can also be seen as an ironically peaceful "war chant."
3. Williams here suggests that what is "born" of underground nuclear testing is actually an agent of death and that the process is a bastardization of the earth's natural processes.
4. Williams means that she will use pen and paper, her abilities as a writer, to fight against nuclear testing — as she does in this essay.
5. *Absolute monarchs* are kings and other sovereign rulers whose very word is law. Any challenge results in punishment for treason, and they are immune from legal punishment for actions of their own.

TERRY TEMPEST WILLIAMS ON WRITING

We like Williams's stress on writing as questioning, as following a path of exploration to find answers. Perhaps her statements will help students who believe they must know everything before they begin to write or that their writing must be the last word on a subject.

TOM WOLFE

Pornoviolence

Can anyone have missed seeing the *National Enquirer, Star, Weekly World News,* or other tabloids Wolfe mentions? (Can anyone be so lucky?) Displayed at supermarket checkout counters and piled high in drugstore newsstands, they're hard to dodge. Why not buy one, bring it to class, and ask students to analyze the headlines' evident purposes? Which stories apparently offer *pornoviolence,* and which make other appeals? Other familiar appeals are to the reader's curiosity about the private lives of celebrities: "Burp! Liz Has a Big-ee Mac-ee Attack in China," "Princess Roasts the Rumps of Her Royal Spoiled Brats." Some stories offer simple belly laughs: "World's Loudest Snorer! ('It's like Sleeping with a Freight Train,' Says Wife.)" An occasional story will offer advice: fad diets, panaceas, arthritis remedies, "Health Insurance for Pets Can Save You Big $$." Some offer vicarious satisfaction to the frustrated: One tale in the *News* tells of a seventy-three-year-old disabled woman who beats up a burglar with the aid of brass knuckles; another, of a man who applies a hammer to the offices of the IRS.

Not only newsstand fare but an evening's viewing of prime time television proves that Wolfe's essay has not, since its 1976 appearance, turned any less true. Students, from their vast knowledge of TV and film, can be invited to supply more recent examples of pornoviolence. Have students work in groups to draw up a "Top Ten" list of the pornoviolent from any other source that seems appropriate: tabloid press, movies, TV, and popular music seem the likeliest. What are the most gratuitous examples? Do students find pornoviolence as disturbing as Wolfe does?

And where does it all lead? Wolfe's final paragraph, with its prediction based on the example of the late Roman Empire (boys and girls "suited up, gaily cutting a sequence of dwarfs and feebles down to short ribs"), is deeply unsettling in this age of schoolyard massacres. Ask students: What is the effect of the violence in the media, especially the sort that Wolfe describes? It's a big question, to be sure, but one certain to elicit response. You may be able to sidestep the actual cause-and-effect of violence (a complicated, perhaps unanswerable issue, at least in a composition classroom) and focus discussion instead on the question of censorship: Should media violence be censored? If so, what exactly should be censored, and for what audience? (See also the first writing suggestion.)

Wolfe's New Journalism style may surprise students encountering it for the first time. For a sampling of lively writing by Wolfe and others, direct students to the anthology Wolfe edited with E. W. Johnson, *The New Journalism* (1973).

QUESTIONS ON MEANING

1. The third would be our pick. The fifth would seem at least a subsidiary purpose.
2. Perhaps the main purpose of such an article is to make readers shift their gum to a different corner of their mouths and mumble "Wow!" or "Holy Gee!" — whatever will sell papers.
3. The point of view is that of the aggressor (par. 25).
4. The power to dish out violence renders the aggressor an important person, at the top of the status heap (at least in his or her own eyes).
5. Since Wolfe condemns pornoviolence, he implies his condemnation of *In Cold Blood* for promising (and delivering) gore. Capote, he strongly hints, is teasing the reader with a "grisly dangle" — using bait to lure along the bloodthirsty (par. 29).
6. You can make a case, we think, for calling Wolfe's tone one of "savage indignation." In his view, Americans are growing more and more bloodthirsty. Like Swift (p. 653), he appeals to our better natures by humorously provoking our outrage and disgust.

QUESTIONS ON WRITING STRATEGY

1. Students who were baffled by that opening were within their rights, but they should have tumbled to what was going on by the end of paragraph 7 or 8. The irony in those social introductions lies in the discrepancy between the horror of the headlines and the bland, cheery occasion for which they served as cards of identity. Wolfe's introduction uses a narrative hook to haul in readers. It makes them wonder, What's happening? What's all this about? — and obliges them to keep reading in order to find the explanation.
2. The paragraph serves to support Wolfe's claim that the convention of *National Enquirer* stringers was unique. Odd (or dully similar) as those other affairs may have been, "none has ever been quite like this."
3. Sorrowfully comic, amusedly bemused, savagely indignant, Wolfe's closing line implies that, in the name of freedom and pleasure, still worse is in store.
4. Paragraph 17 springs the short definition. Had Wolfe given it immediately, in paragraph 1, he wouldn't have been able to use that fine "What's happening?" narrative hook.
5. Both the examples (of the Kennedy assassination in pars. 21–23 and of James Bond in par. 30) illustrate the mainstreaming of pornoviolence. The Kennedy example shows how pornoviolence favors the aggressor. The Bond example, with its comparison to the Lone Ranger, dispels the notion that Bond is outside the system and thus shows that pornoviolence is firmly entrenched in "the bureaucratic middle class."

QUESTIONS ON LANGUAGE

1. He gives us the Greek derivation of the word and, from that, a literal definition.
2. When we go to school we undergo training; our attentions are fixed and directed; we are innocents obliged to become knowledgeable; and so on. We play the role of the schoolchild when we watch TV, too. (Wolfe may be alluding as well to the Texas School Book Depository from which Oswald shot Kennedy.)

3. The terms, of course, come from psychiatry. A classic joke may help students recall the difference between a sadist and a masochist: A masochist hands a sadist a sledgehammer, stoops low, points to the top of his own head, and invites: "Hit me." With gleaming eyes, the sadist lifts the hammer and prepares to slam it down, while the masochist, with a silly grin, waits eagerly. Then the sadist stops. He thinks. He lowers the hammer. "No," he says with a leer. "No, I won't."
4. The phrase "Them-those walls" is of course nonstandard, uneducated English, the speech of "Low Rent bums" (par. 30).
5. See, for only one example, paragraph 17: "people [. . .] blowing brains out, and getting even with all those bastards."
6. Wolfe indicates that the cowardly emperor didn't want to risk any return blows from the fighters and cripples. Evidently, as his name suggests, Commodus was a human crock of crud.

TOM WOLFE ON WRITING

Wolfe may write fast, but of course he isn't advocating sloppy writing. Essential to his method is that long period of time spent in preparation: doing research and reporting, carefully planning. His reliance on an outline, and his insistence that outlining *is* writing, is somewhat unusual among the authors quoted in this book.

Perhaps Wolfe's strategy of setting himself a quota will be useful to students in writing a term paper, or even a shorter paper. Suggestion: Instead of demanding of themselves ten typewritten pages a day, they might demand a half page an hour.

VIRGINIA WOOLF

The Death of the Moth

Virginia Woolf's essay provides a stunning example of the power of observation. Students may well recognize the impulse to observe everything else around them when their work interferes with a gorgeous day: "Such vigor came rolling in from the fields and the down beyond that it was difficult to keep the eyes strictly turned upon the book" (par. 1). Asking students to contribute specific moments of distraction from their own work or studies may help them relate to the careful attention Woolf gives the moth.

The process of establishing links between observation of a specific thing and a refreshed understanding of the world can be a productive focus for discussion. Ask students to spend some time writing in their journals to establish links between observation and larger understanding. The first writing suggestion can get them started. Their efforts will prepare them for a discussion of Woolf's strategies.

By the way, the depth and power of Woolf's essay is especially astonishing in the light of what Leonard Woolf tells us in his note to the posthumous collection in which the essay first appeared. He notes that the essay did not receive the laborious revisions for which Virginia Woolf is known. She wrote this one out in longhand (her usual practice) and then merely typed it over once. Leonard Woolf (in his usual practice with Virginia's work while she was alive) "punctuated [it] and corrected obvious verbal mistakes." "The Death of the Moth," then, is but a lightly edited first draft.

QUESTIONS ON MEANING

1. Woolf uses the moth's death to reflect on life and death, the energy of the one and the inevitability of the other. She also comments, through her admiration and her pity, on the value of living to potential.
2. In constant, agitated activity, the moth is pitiable because it is so energetic and yet so small and insignificant.
3. The moth's plight seems to represent that of human beings, hurrying through a limited share of the world for a limited time. The moth, though, takes better advantage of life: He can "show us the true nature of life" (par. 3).
4. Woolf's attitude becomes somber in the face of the "power [. . .] massed outside, indifferent, impersonal, not attending to anything in particular" — in short, in the face of death and especially its blank inevitability.

QUESTIONS ON WRITING STRATEGY

1. It is a subjective description, filtered through and dominated by Woolf's feelings. For instance, Woolf endows the moth with human traits and importance: He seems content with life (par. 1); he enjoys his activities with zest (2); he serves as a messenger to show us how to live (3); he is pitiable (2, 3, 4, 5). In short, he symbolizes our own living and dying.
2. The opening paragraph both creates a benign, even cheerful mood and backdrop and sets off the moth's tininess and frailty.
3. Woolf relies almost exclusively on visual imagery, even though a trapped and then dying moth presumably made some noise and the mid-September air must have had some odor. But the visual emphasis seems appropriate, for the whole essay centers on Woolf's equation of life and light.
4. In paragraph 1 the moth is an unexciting creature, but by paragraph 2 the energy outside has transferred inside to the moth, and in paragraph 3 only the moth commands attention. In paragraph 4, though, the moth becomes boring. Then his struggle makes him diverting and again riveting. In paragraph 5 what is outside seems opposed to the moth, and his death is not only riveting but heartrending and wondrous.

QUESTIONS ON LANGUAGE

1. In paragraph 5 Woolf's sentences are shorter than before, creating a quicker pace to match the moth's struggle and Woolf's own fearful excitement. The energy outside has changed from "benignant" to "a power [. . .] massed outside, indifferent, impersonal." The moth, meanwhile, has become almost heroic, making "extraordinary efforts," a "superb [. . .] protest," "a gigantic effort."
2. The synonyms for the moth reflect Woolf's on-again, off-again interest in and sympathy for the moth. Examples: "the present specimen" (par. 1);

"a thread of vital light" (2); "a tiny bead of pure life" (3); "queer spectacle," "machine" (4); "little hay-colored moth," "tiny legs," "insignificant little creature," "minute wayside triumph" (5).

3. *Zest*, here "spirited pleasure," is adapted from the now-obsolete French *zeste*, referring to the peel of a lemon or orange. In English the original meaning is retained in one sense of *zest*, "orange or lemon peel." The later sense is derived from a figurative use of the earlier: the experience of piquancy.

VIRGINIA WOOLF ON WRITING

Woolf's own experience with "freewriting" and her advice about it to a young writer should dovetail nicely with most instruction on the writing process. We think she's quite serious about the need to let loose — and quite right, too, as thousands of students and we ourselves have learned.

Business Communication

Sixth Edition

A.C. "Buddy" Krizan
Murray State University

Patricia Merrier
University of Minnesota—Duluth

Carol Larson Jones
California State University—Pomona

THOMSON
™
SOUTH-WESTERN

Australia · Canada · Mexico · Singapore · Spain · United Kingdom · United States

THOMSON

SOUTH-WESTERN

Business Communication, 6e
A.C. "Buddy " Krizan, Patricia Merrier, Carol Larson Jones

VP/Editorial Director:
Jack W. Calhoun

VP/Editor-in-Chief:
George Werthman

Acquisitions Editor:
Jennifer Codner

Developmental Editor:
Taney Wilkins

Production Editor:
Tamborah E. Moore

Marketing Manager:
Larry Qualls

Media Technology Editor:
Jim Rice

Media Production Editor:
Kelly Reid

Manufacturing Coordinator:
Diane Lohman

Production House:
Pre-Press Company, Inc.

Printer:
RR Donnelley-Willard, OH

Design Manager:
Chris A. Miller

Internal Design:
Chris A. Miller

Cover Design:
Beckmeyer Design

Cover Images:
Getty Images

Library of Congress Control Number:
2003110012

ISBN: 0-324-27225-1 package
(core text + Student CD + InfoTrac)

ISBN: 0-324-27226-X
(core text only)

ISBN: 0-324-22536-9 ISE package
(International Student Edition core text
+ Student CD + InfoTrac)

ISBN: 0-324-22537-7
(ISE core text only)

ISBN: 0-324-27236-7
(CD only)

Brief Contents

THOMSON
★
SOUTH-WESTERN

Dear Friends and Colleagues:

As authors of *Business Communication*, Sixth Edition, we are extremely grateful to users of previous editions. We appreciate the feedback that you provided, which has helped us mold the sixth edition into what it is today. *Business Communication*, Sixth Edition, maintains the approach that has appealed to users for many years, presenting basic business communication fundamentals using practical applications. Our book is carefully designed to assist students in achieving academic and career success through the development of strong communication skills.

As in previous editions, this revision centers around the traditional content of an introductory business communication course. In-depth discussion of current communication topics includes workplace diversity, technology, correspondence applications, proposals, business plans, special reports, visual aids, teamwork, interpersonal communication, listening and nonverbal messages, presentation skills, and employment communication.

At the end of the course using this book, adopters will understand and possess the skills needed to implement solid business communication.

Good luck on your instructional endeavor and, as always, we welcome your feedback.

Sincerely,

Buddy Krizan

Patricia Merrier

Carol Jones

New and Hallmark Features

FREE WITH NEW COPIES OF 6E — A STUDENT CD

This distinctive and valuable tool was created with students in mind. The CD contains a set of unique PowerPoint® slides specifically created for students, as well as true/false and multiple-choice quizzes and discussion questions for each chapter. In addition, the CD has a section containing more than 50 practice sentences with grammatical errors. It provides students the opportunity to e-mail their answers to their instructor. The CD also provides answers to the questions so students know immediately which concepts and chapters require more review. Finally, we have included links to the book to support the Website, as well as important and relevant content on business etiquette, time management, and other useful information. We think you will agree, the Student CD is an invaluable tool!

• WORKPLACE DIVERSITY

An entire chapter is devoted to communicating effectively with diverse cultures, key strategies for global business communication, and guidelines for working with an interpreter to overcome language barriers. In our ever-expanding workplace, these skills will be absolutely critical to achieving success.

LEARNING OBJECTIVE
Describe guidelines
for working with an
interpreter or translator
to overcome language
barriers. ⑤

Guidelines for Working with Interpreters

If English is your only language and your receiver does not know English, then you must use an interpreter for oral communication. Unless expatriates or transnational executives are proficient in the languages of countries where they do business, they will likely use interpreters in some of their business interactions. Keep these considerations in mind when working with an interpreter.

AVOID COMPLEX LANGUAGE AND FOCUS ON THE RECEIVER

When working with an interpreter, avoid long introductory phrases, parenthetical elements, interjections, and complex and compound sentences. As you prepare to use an interpreter, give special attention to the parts of your message that may be difficult to ~~~ of these difficult parts to help ensure your receiver's

• TECHNOLOGY, LEGAL, AND ETHICAL CONSIDERATIONS

In-depth discussions of ethical and legal considerations for communication, vital communication technology trends, and planning and composing messages are woven throughout the text.

LEARNING OBJECTIVE
Describe communi-
cation technology
trends and legal and
ethical issues related to
technology. ②

Technology-Related Legal and Ethical Issues

In this section of the chapter, you will learn about legal and ethical considerations for the use of communication technology. Technology brings with it a number of legal and ethical issues. These issues pertain to copyright and privacy, as well as to employee behavior and organizational actions.

Cell Phones and Other Mobile Devices

NOTE 3.16
Users of mobile computer devices should respect the rights and safety of others.

Ethical and legal issues pertinent to the use of cell phones, PDAs, and other telecommunication mobile devices are evolving as rapidly as the technology itself. Issues center around using these devices in a manner that respects the rights, safety, and privacy of others. Legislatures have considered laws restricting the use of cell phones in automobiles, citing the danger of driver distraction during phone conversations. To date, federal laws banning cell phone usage while driving have not emerged in the United States, but some states restrict use in automobiles to hands-free phones.

NOTE 3.17
A heuristic guide is a rule of thumb based

Use of mobile devices to conduct business on the road or in public places, however, would not require laws if individuals practiced courtesy, respect, and concern for the ~~~ **heuristic** or experiential guide for individ

- ## LET'S TALK BUSINESS
  Businesspeople relate information about the value of strong communication skills in the business world. This feature brings immediate relevance to students and motivates their interest in the subject.

- ## MARGIN NOTES
  Summaries of text material greatly aid student comprehension, enhance their exam preparation time, and provide a review and reinforcement of chapter concepts.

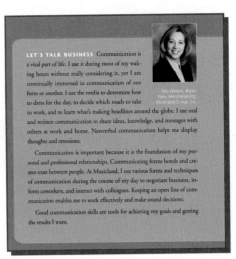

LET'S TALK BUSINESS Communication is a vital part of life. I use it during most of my waking hours without really considering it, yet I am continually immersed in communication of one form or another. I use the media to determine how to dress for the day, to decide which roads to take to work, and to learn what's making headlines around the globe. I use oral and written communication to share ideas, knowledge, and messages with others at work and home. Nonverbal communication helps me display thoughts and emotions.

Communication is important because it is the foundation of my personal and professional relationships. Communicating forms bonds and creates trust between people. At Musicland, I use various forms and techniques of communication during the course of my day to negotiate business, inform coworkers, and interact with colleagues. Keeping an open line of communication enables me to work effectively and make sound decisions.

Good communication skills are tools for achieving my goals and getting the results I want.

Tana Benson, Buyer, Video Merchandising, Musicland Group, Inc.

> **NOTE 1.8**
> The sender should make it easy for the receiver to respond.

- ## TIPS AND HINTS
  This feature offers advice that business professionals can use in their daily communication situations.

TIPS AND HINTS

Suggestions for Telecommuters

- Keep in frequent e-mail or phone contact with fellow workers.
- Go to the office for staff meetings at least once a week or on a regular schedule.
- Create a productive office work environment in your home.

- Arrange meetings with clients in a business location.
- Plan a reasonable work schedule. Be fair to your employer and to yourself.

- ## COMMUNICATION NOTE
  This unique feature relays interesting and relevant information related to chapter content and real-world business experiences. Students will find these interesting and easily applicable to chapter content.

COMMUNICATION NOTE

Definition of Business Communication The word communication comes from the Latin Word *communis*, which means common. When individuals communicate, they try to establish a common understanding between or among themselves. **Business communication** is the process of establishing a common understanding between or among people within a business environment.

NOTE 1.4
Effective communication benefits you and the organization.

Effective communication is essential to both you and the organization for which you work. The material in this book is designed to help you improve your ability to communicate. This chapter focuses on the goals, patterns, and process of communication. It also addresses communication barriers and ways to remove them. Later chapters provide more details about meeting the challenges of communicating in a business environment.

LEARNING OBJECTIVE
List and explain the goals of business communication.

② Goals of Business Communication

Effective business communication involves both the sender and the receiver, but the sender ... for achieving the four basic **goals of business communication**:

• COMMUNICATION QUOTE

Comments from experienced professionals as well as individuals beginning their careers provide real-life application and bring students into close contact with the business world.

COMMUNICATION QUOTE

Owning a small business is like having a small child to nurture and work with so it grows and develops. Good communication on a daily basis is of utmost importance. Never assume employees are going to perform all tasks you need done unless they have clear instructions.

—Betty Lou Marsaa, Owner, Betty Lou's Health Foods, Inc. (Photo courtesy of Jeff Frey & Associates Photography)

• BUSINESS CASES

Chapters 6 through 10 contain end-of-chapter case problems. The cases give students a chance to apply their knowledge on topics such as communicating ethically, teamwork, and technology as they demonstrate how to respond to the case situation. Students are introduced to situations they may face in the real-world and are challenged to react or respond to the issue.

Case Problems

Persuasive Requests

1. Your company has selected FreeMed Insurance to provide your employees a plan that takes advantage of tax laws. Individuals enrolling in the plan can pay their share of certain insurance premiums tax-free. The plan also permits employees to set aside money tax-free to help pay for expenses not covered by medical insurance. As director of human services, write a memo that would persuade employees to attend a meeting in which FreeMed personnel would be available to explain this tax-saving plan.
2. You are the business manager of Missouri Ostrich, Inc. The company's primary income comes from selling ostriches. The ostrich market, however, is not well established. A $25,000 payment on a loan is due on April 15, and you are unable to make the payment. Write a letter to Ruben Hurwitz, Loan Officer, Houston County Bank,

Persuasive Messages   **CHAPTER 9**

• NEEDS WORK/LOOKS GOOD ILLUSTRATIONS

This extremely useful feature offers a direct comparison of good examples and those that "Need Work." The correspondence chapters include ethical and unethical messages, good and poor application letters, and good and poor sales messages.

Numerous "Needs Work" and "Looks Good" examples aid students in composing successful business messages.

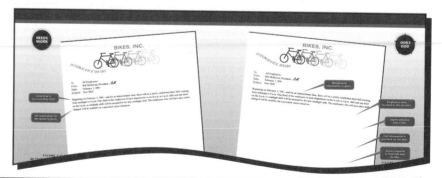

• EASY TO READ AND UNDERSTAND

An important and hallmark feature of *Business Communication* is the well-written, concise, and easy-to-understand material. Students at a variety of academic levels use and appreciate the book.

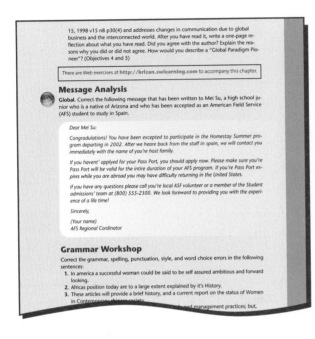

• END-OF-CHAPTER ACTIVITIES

Challenging activities, message analysis in real-world situations, and grammar workshop activities provide numerous opportunities for students to apply their knowledge.

• DESIGNATED ICONS

Thoroughly revised end-of-chapter material utilizes all new icons designating Technology, Ethics, Collaboration, and Global topics to help students and instructors identify key areas and important focal points for their study.

Technology   Ethics   Collaboration   Global

• DOCUMENTATION APPENDIX

A strong appendix includes guidelines for APA and MLA as well as guidance for documenting Web, CD-ROM, and other technology sources. This feature also provides students with a valuable reference for citing outside sources in papers and reports.

Comprehensive Learning Package

INSTRUCTIONAL RESOURCES

INSTRUCTOR'S RESOURCE CD-ROM (ISBN 0324272324)

This wonderful instructor resource includes all-new Small Business School Video clips with accompanying discussion questions and case information; PowerPoint® slides—a great enhancement tool for stimulating classroom lectures; ExamView testing software, allowing instructors to create appropriate and challenging quizzes and tests; and the Instructor's Manual files, all in one easy to use CD.

INSTRUCTOR'S MANUAL (ISBN 0324272286)

The Instructor's Manual provides resources to increase the teaching and learning value of *Business Communication*. This useful manual includes teaching tips, activities, and guidelines for classroom discussion. Also included in the Instructor's Manual are the solutions to the Study Guide.

TRANSPARENCY ACETATES (ISBN 0324272316)

A full set of transparencies is provided for use in the classroom.

PRINTED TEST BANK (ISBN 0324272294)

The printed test bank is available for use in conjunction with, or in place of, the ExamView software. The combination allows for the most flexible testing system yet.

WEBTUTOR™ ADVANTAGE FOR *BUSINESS COMMUNICATION*, SIXTH EDITION

This online learning aid available in WebCT™, Blackboard®, and eCollege allows your class to practice and apply their knowledge in an online environment developed with your students in mind and is especially useful for distance education. This interactive online learning aid provides reinforcement that helps students grasp the concepts presented throughout *Business Communication*.

INSTRUCTOR'S SUPPORT WEB SITE: HTTP://KRIZAN.SWLEARNING.COM

Provides text resources such as downloadable files for the Instructor's Manuals, PowerPoint® slides, Solutions to the Study Guide, Solutions for Web activities, and Transparency masters to support *Business Communication*. All of these useful supplements are available at your fingertips through the Instructor's Resource Web site.

STUDENT RESOURCES

STUDENT CD

The student CD is FREE with new books and contains a set of unique PowerPoint® slides specifically created for students, as well as true/false and multiple-choice quizzes and discussion questions for each chapter. In addition, the CD provides a section containing more than 50 practice sentences containing grammatical errors. The FREE Student CD is an invaluable tool for any student.

INFOTRAC® COLLEGE EDITION

InfoTrac College Edition is fully integrated into the sixth edition for easy classroom and homework usage. Application Exercises at the end of each chapter contain at least one question that asks students to access InfoTrac and read a specific article or search for articles on a particular topic. The InfoTrac passcode bound in to new copies of the sixth edition gives students access to a dependable, familiar database of publications. Whenever students use it, they can feel comfortable that they will find a wide selection of reliable, timely information. Searching is made simple and once your students find the right articles, they can read them, print them, receive them via e-mail, or mark them for future retrieval.

STUDY GUIDE (ISBN 0324272308)

The Study Guide provides a thorough supply of supplementary questions and activities to prepare students for tests and exams. The Study Guide would be useful to any student requiring extra practice and quizzing and is especially useful for distance learning courses.

STUDENT WEB SITE AT HTTP://KRIZAN.SWLEARNING.COM

An innovative and comprehensive student site contains Web exercises for each chapter in the book as well as text links organized by chapter. "E-mail it!" and "Click on It!" features involve the students in activities that require application of the concepts learned within the chapters. The comprehensive new Web site adds depth and challenges your students to do more than simply "surf" the Web.

About the Authors

DR. A. C. "BUDDY" KRIZAN is a professor emeritus in the College of Business and Public Affairs at Murray State University, Murray, Kentucky. Formerly, he served as assistant dean, department chair, and professor in the College of Business and Public Affairs. He began teaching business communication courses, seminars, and workshops in 1977. He has conducted research on a variety of topics including basic business communication, resume content, visual aids, proposals, and written and oral messages. He has served in leadership positions for national, state, and local professional organizations. Buddy has made presentations at numerous professional conferences and has published in many professional journals.

DR. PAT MERRIER is a professor in the Finance/MIS Department at the University of Minnesota, Duluth. She has worked as an administrative service professional in both the public and private sector and has taught at both secondary and collegiate levels. Pat has honed her communication skills through these experiences and through leadership on campus and in the Duluth community. She has also served on the boards of several professional organizations. Pat enjoys collaborating on interdisciplinary research projects; her work has been published in a variety of journals.

DR. CAROL LARSON JONES is a professor in the Management and Human Resources Department at California State Polytechnic University, Pomona, in Pomona, California. Carol has been instrumental in developing innovative approaches to teaching communication skills and principles of management at the high school, community college, and university levels for more than 25 years. Her current research, writing, and presentation areas include international education, diversity in the workplace, women in development, internships, English as a second language, and groupware. Carol has made presentations at numerous professional conferences and has been published in many professional journals. She has traveled, studied, and worked in China, Swaziland, Hong Kong, Vietnam, and various European countries. Carol has served in leadership positions for national, state, and local professional organizations.

Contributing Author Joyce Logan, University of Kentucky

We gratefully acknowledge Joyce Logan's contributions to *Business Communication*, Sixth Edition. Joyce authored several chapters for this edition. From planning through editing page proof Joyce was a creative, motivated, detail-oriented professional who understands what it means to be a team member.

Acknowledgments

We appreciate the support of the following individuals who have reviewed and offered creative and useful suggestions for improving *Business Communication*:

Freda Mays, Western Kentucky University

Jeff Phillips, Northwood University

Karen Tussey, Southwestern Community College

Jan Wulf, Southeast Community College

Barb Mesley, Graceland College

Marcel Robles, University of North Dakota

Mary Beth Robbins, Herzing College

Jane Troop, Fullerton College

Steve Iman, California State Polytechnic University

Linda Cresap, Minot State University

Karl Smart, Central Michigan University

Andrew Halford, Paducah Community College

Bonnie Edwards, Mesabi Range Community & Technical College

Randall Waller, Baylor University

Annette Wyandotte, Indiana University Southeast

Maria W. Warren, University of West Florida

Wayne Moore, Indiana University of Pennsylvania

Greg Drummer, Stone Child College

Vincent C. Trof, Providence College

Anne Beebe, Lansing Community College

Janel Bloch, Iowa State University

Roosevelt D. Butler, The College of New Jersey

Elizabeth H. Campbell, Kettering University

William B. Chapel, Michigan Technological University

Ophelia Clark, City College San Francisco

Patricia A. LaRosa, California State University

Kenneth L. Mitchell, Southeastern Louisiana University

Jeffrey G. Phillips, Northwood University

Terry D. Roach, Arkansas State University

Janet C. Adams, Mankato State University

Marilyn Beebe, Kirkwood Community College

Thomas G. Beery, Lima Technical College

Bette J. Carpenter, West Texas A&M University

Johnnie E. Drake, Jr., TESST, Electronics and Computer Institute

Laura C. Gilliam, Western Piedmont Community College

Barbara Hagler, Southern Illinois University

Richard Lacy, California State University, Fresno

Lorita Langdon, Columbus State Community College

Paul Martello, Bryant & Stratton Business Institute

John F. Mastriani, El Paso Community College

Diana S. McKowen, Indiana University at Bloomington

Wayne A. Moore, Indiana University of Pennsylvania

Richard David Ramsey, Southeastern Louisiana University

Deborah Rankins, Southern Ohio College

Peggy L. Schultz, Trumbull Business College

Jean Anna Sellers, Fort Hays State University

Tom Seymour, Minot State University

Jane M. Thompson, Solano Community College

Anna R. Trexler, Southern Arkansas University

Marion Stanton Webb, Cleveland State University

Buddy Krizan   Patricia Merrier   Carol Larson Jones

HOW 10 (ISBN 0324178824) by James L. and Lyn R. Clark
Since 1975, *HOW* and its subsequent editions have been a
prominent reference source for business writers, office personnel,
and students. With every new edition, *HOW* has kept pace with
changes in language and the business environment, striving to
provide a useful and easy-to-understand reference manual for all
professionals involved in organizational operations. It includes
detailed and precise information for writing, formatting, and
transmitting communications. Unlike other reference books,
HOW 10 is tailored for writing style, grammar, mechanics,
and techniques in a business/office environment. This text can
be used as a stand-alone reference or as a supplement.

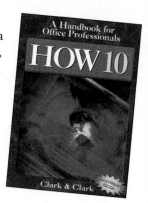

EMPLOYMENT STRATEGIES FOR CAREER SUCCESS
(ISBN 0324200056) by Robert Rasberry

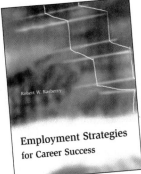

Robert Rasberry's first edition of *Employment Strategies for Career Success* provides
students a thorough look at how to manage a successful career search. This
practical book covers all aspects of career searches including negotiations, the
case interview, and confronting nervousness in interviewing. This book can be
a useful tool for any student or executive as they strategically search for career
fulfillment.

CREATING DYNAMIC MULTIMEDIA PRESENTATIONS USING MICROSOFT® POWERPOINT®, SECOND EDITION
(ISBN 032418767X) by Carol Lehman

This brief book focuses on creating dynamic presentations
using Microsoft PowerPoint. It goes beyond the traditional
step-by-step manual by exploring specific design techniques
that lead to superior PowerPoint presentations. Lessons and
exercises are built around Microsoft PowerPoint XP and
allow students the full benefit of the latest PowerPoint
functionality and features. The content also includes
explanations compatible with PowerPoint 97.

WOW (ISBN 032401385X) by Dana Loewy and Teeanna Rizkallah
Writer's On-line Workshop (WOW,) formerly known as *PoWER: Professional Writer's
Electronic Reference*, is designed to help users accurately assess their current skill
level and refine their understanding of business English and business communication.
Users start by taking the self-assessment to aid in diagnosing their current skills.
The results of the self-assessment directs users to specific business English or
business communication lessons that require further review. The modules within
the *Writer's On-line Workshop* are designed to allow users to review a concept, see
an example of the concept, and then practice utilizing the concept presented in
that module. *Writer's On-line Workshop* offers convenient 24-hour, online access
to a wealth of communication-based resources.

Part 1

The Communication Environment

1

Business Communication Foundations

LEARNING OBJECTIVES

①

Explain why business communication is important to individuals and organizations.

②

List and explain the goals of business communication.

③

Describe the patterns of business communication.

④

Explain the communication process.

⑤

Identify communication barriers and describe ways to remove them.

Tara Benson, Buyer, Video Merchandising, Musicland Group, Inc.

LET'S TALK BUSINESS Communication is a vital part of life. I use it during most of my waking hours without really considering it, yet I am continually immersed in communication of one form or another. I use the media to determine how to dress for the day, to decide which roads to take to work, and to learn what's making headlines around the globe. I use oral and written communication to share ideas, knowledge, and messages with others at work and home. Nonverbal communication helps me display thoughts and emotions.

Communication is important because it is the foundation of my personal and professional relationships. Communicating forms bonds and creates trust between people. At Musicland, I use various forms and techniques of communication during the course of my day to negotiate business, inform coworkers, and interact with colleagues. Keeping an open line of communication enables me to work effectively and make sound decisions.

Good communication skills are tools for achieving my goals and getting the results I want.

As Tara Benson notes in Let's Talk Business, people spend the majority of their waking hours communicating. Because it is used so extensively, communication is one of the most important skills you can develop. How well you read, listen, speak, and write will affect the quality of your personal relationships and, as shown in Figure 1.1, help determine the progress you make in your career.

NOTE 1.1
Individuals spend most of their time communicating.

The Importance of Communicating Effectively

- **Getting Jobs You Want** Effective communication will make it possible for you to design a powerful resume, compose a persuasive application letter, interview with poise and confidence, and get the job you want.
- **Gaining Promotions** Moving ahead in your career depends on communicating your technical competence to others and maintaining effective relationships with them.
- **Providing Leadership** Your ability to motivate and help others achieve rests on your understanding of human nature and on mastering communication skills.
- **Being Productive on the Job** Work performance is enhanced by your ability to listen effectively, speak clearly, and write competently.
- **Relating Positively to Others** Successful business and personal relationships depend on mutual trust and respect; communicating ethically, with concern and compassion, is essential.
- **Assuring the Success of Your Organization** Your organization will succeed only if it has the support of its constituencies—support that comes from effectively communicating with customers or clients about the organization's products or services.

FIGURE 1.1
Key Ways in Which Communicating Effectively Is Important to You

Research with business professionals reveals that effective communication ranks high among the skills necessary to succeed in business. The number and types of work-related communication activities in which a person engages depend on his or her field and level of responsibility. For example, telemarketers spend the majority of their work hours placing calls to prospective customers; entry-level tax accountants devote the majority of their time to entering and manipulating data; public relations specialists gather information and write news releases; and human resource managers attend meetings, train employees, and prepare reports.

Businesses must have effective internal and external communication in order to succeed. Internal operations depend on the day-to-day exchange of information among employees. Performance objectives, job instructions, financial data, customer orders, inventory data, production problems and solutions, and employee production reports illustrate the range of *internal communication* exchanged in the course of business. Organizations accomplish long-range planning and strategic decision making by relying on research, reports, proposals, conferences, evaluations, and projections.

External communication builds goodwill, brings in orders, and ensures continued existence and growth. Day-to-day external communications include sales calls, product advertisements, news releases, employment notices, bank transactions, and periodic reports to governmental agencies. External communications that have a long-range impact include new product announcements, plant expansion plans, contributions to community activities, and annual reports.

As you can see from these examples, most business communication is **transactional;** it involves a give-and-take relationship between the sender and the receiver(s) in order to establish a common understanding. This interaction is the primary feature that distinguishes business writing from journalistic or creative writing.

LEARNING OBJECTIVE

1

Explain why business communication is important to individuals and organizations.

NOTE 1.2
Communication is a necessary workplace skill.

NOTE 1.3
How and when you communicate varies by field.

Definition of Business Communication The word communication comes from the Latin Word *communis*, which means common. When individuals communicate, they try to establish a common understanding between or among themselves. **Business communication** is the process of establishing a common understanding between or among people within a business environment.

Effective communication is essential to both you and the organization for which you work. The material in this book is designed to help you improve your ability to communicate. This chapter focuses on the goals, patterns, and process of communication. It also addresses communication barriers and ways to remove them. Later chapters provide more details about meeting the challenges of communicating in a business environment.

②

Goals of Business Communication

Effective business communication involves both the sender and the receiver, but the sender must take responsibility for achieving the four basic **goals of business communication**:

[1] Receiver understanding

[2] Receiver response

[3] Favorable relationship

[4] Organizational goodwill

The sender must take responsibility for achieving the four goals of business communication. Keep these goals in mind and assume responsibility for accomplishing them every time you initiate or respond to a message.

Receiver Understanding

The first goal of business communication, **receiver understanding,** is the most important. The message must be so clear that the receiver understands it *as the sender means it to be understood.*

For communication to be successful, the sender and receiver must achieve shared meaning. Suppose a supervisor sent an e-mail to a subordinate saying, "No one plans for a meeting like you do." Should the worker react with pleasure or disappointment? Is the supervisor praising or criticizing the worker's attention to detail? The message is too vague to guarantee receiver understanding. If a worker says "I'll need time off to travel to my cousin's wedding," the sender and receiver might have different ideas about the length, type, and timing of the leave. The message would be clearer if the worker were to say, "I will be taking vacation August 5, 6, and 7." Company policy and the work relationship between the sender and receiver would dictate whether the sender included the reason for the absence as part of the written or spoken message.

It is a challenge for the sender to achieve the goal of receiver understanding. To develop a clear message, the sender must consider the following four issues, which are discussed in detail later in this chapter:

- Receiver characteristics
- Message form and content
- Receiver feedback
- Communication barriers

Receiver Response

The second goal of business communication is receiver response. The **receiver response** may be positive, neutral, or negative. It may be conveyed through words, actions, or both. The situation will determine what is appropriate. If the chair of a committee distributes a memo announcing the time and date of a meeting, those who receive the memo may act in any of four ways. They may (1) notify the chair that they will attend, (2) notify the chair that they will be unable to attend, (3) attend without having notified the chair in advance, or (4) miss the meeting without providing advance notice. The first three actions achieve the goal of receiver response; the fourth does not.

Because this goal is achieved when the receiver demonstrates his or her understanding of the message by providing an appropriate response, a sender should assist the receiver to respond. The wording of the message should encourage response. In a face-to-face conversation, the sender (speaker) can ask the receiver (listener) if he or she understands the message. Further, the sender can ask directly for a specific response.

When written messages are used, the sender can encourage a response by asking questions, enclosing a reply envelope, asking the receiver to telephone, or using any one of many other possibilities. For example, suppose a publisher receives a mail order for a cookbook, but the customer does not specify hard or soft binding. To get the information needed to fill the order, the clerk could phone; send an e-mail message; or write an inquiry letter and enclose a postage-paid, self-addressed reply card on which the customer can simply check the type of binding desired.

Favorable Relationship

The third goal of business communication—**favorable relationship**—focuses on the people involved in the communication process. To establish a strong business relationship, the sender and the receiver should relate to each other in three important ways: positively, personally, and professionally. They must create and maintain a favorable relationship.

Both the sender and the receiver will benefit from a favorable relationship. If the sender manufactures goods or provides services, a favorable relationship might mean job satisfaction, increased sales, and more profits. If the sender is a customer, a favorable relationship could lead to a continued source of supply, better prices, and assistance if problems develop.

The sender should assume primary responsibility for creating and maintaining a favorable relationship. Some of the ways the sender can do this include the following:

- Using positive wording
- Stressing the receiver's interests and benefits
- Doing more than is expected

For example, suppose you have to refuse to work overtime on Wednesday. If you simply say "No," you will do little to promote a favorable relationship with your supervisor. By offering to work overtime on Thursday or by finding someone who is willing

NOTE 1.7
Second goal: Receiver provides necessary response.

NOTE 1.8
The sender should make it easy for the receiver to respond.

NOTE 1.9
Third goal: Sender and receiver have a favorable relationship.

to work Wednesday, however, you will have helped your supervisor; you will have taken a positive approach and done more than was expected.

Organizational Goodwill

NOTE 1.10
Fourth goal: Organizational goodwill.

The fourth goal of business communication stresses benefit to the organization. The goodwill of customers or clients is essential to any business or organization. If a company has the goodwill of its customers, it has their confidence and often their continuing willingness to buy its products or services. The more goodwill a company has, the more successful it can be.

Senders of messages have a responsibility to try to increase goodwill for their organizations. They do so by ensuring that their communications reflect positively on the quality of the company's products, services, and personnel.

Communication helps foster positive relationships between people and the organizations they represent.

©LEFT LANE PRODUCTIONS/CORBIS

An example of an employee building goodwill for an organization is found in the handling of returned merchandise. If store policy dictates that employees should accept returned merchandise even when the customer doesn't have a receipt, the employee could say: "Would you prefer a refund or a replacement?" After the customer has chosen, the employee should complete the transaction quickly and courteously. Doing so might lead to repeat business for the company and enhance its reputation. This behavior allows the employee to generate goodwill for the store and achieve the fourth goal of business communication—**organizational goodwill**.

LEARNING OBJECTIVE
Describe the patterns of business communication.

③ Patterns of Business Communication

As communicators strive to achieve the four goals of business communication, they send and receive messages that are both internal and external to their organizations. Some of these messages are formal, some are informal. Some messages are work related, others are personal. As Christopher Zenk illustrates in the Communication Quote, internal communication is critical to his work at Accenture.

Internal Communication Patterns

As shown in Figure 1.2, organizational communication can flow vertically, horizontally, or through a network. In **vertical** communication, messages flow upward or downward along a path referred to as the "chain of command." Reports and proposals commonly follow an upward path; policy statements, plans, directives, and instructions typically follow a downward path. As Betty Lou Marsaa notes in her Communication Quote, giving clear instructions is important in vertical communication. **Horizontal** message flow occurs between workers or units of comparable status who need to share data or coordinate efforts. In **network** communication, information flows freely among those who have a

NOTE 1.11
Organizational communication flows in all directions.

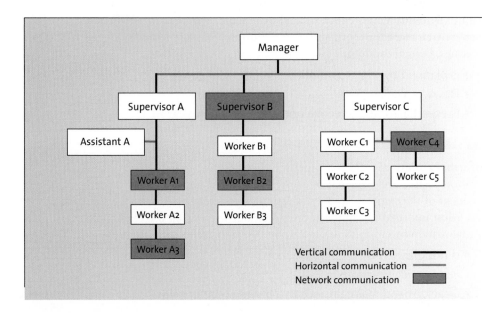

FIGURE 1.2
Business Communication Patterns

common bond that goes beyond the participants' role or unit within the organization. Members' roles or status within the organization will generally have the greatest influence in vertical communication and the least influence in network communication.

NOTE 1.12
Networks may be planned or unplanned.

A network may be a planned part of the business operation or it may arise from informal interactions. An example of a planned network is a project team formed to develop and market a new product. An informal network could consist of employees who share interests outside the workplace. Organization-based informal networks, such as company-sponsored softball teams, can be powerful. Members can discuss work-related issues outside the traditional communication structure and then combine efforts to influence the direction of the organization. Personal networks such as those consisting of friends and relatives, classmates and faculty, current and former employers, and current and former coworkers are important sources of professional and personal support.

Regardless of the direction in which it flows, communication may have a formal, an informal, or a serial pattern. In this section, formal and informal refer to the nature of a communication, not the writing or speaking style used to convey a message. You'll learn more about communication style in later chapters.

FORMAL COMMUNICATION

NOTE 1.13
Formal communication is business related.

Formal communication is business related, possibly with some personal touches. It can be written (memo, report, policy) or oral (speech, meeting). Most organizations keep written records of formal oral communication—copies of speeches, minutes of meetings. Formal communication

- Is planned by the organization
- Flows in all directions
- Is essential for the effective operation of the business

INFORMAL COMMUNICATION

NOTE 1.14
Informal communication can be business related or personal.

Informal communication—sometimes referred to as a grapevine—consists of both business-related and personal information. Rumors about who is to become the new president of the company and a discussion of yesterday's baseball scores are two examples. Most informal communication is oral, but widespread use of e-mail has made informal written communication more popular. Informal communication

- Is not planned by the organization
- Flows in all directions
- Develops and maintains positive human relationships

The following Communication Note provides additional information about the advantages of cultivating an organizational grapevine.

SERIAL COMMUNICATION

A great deal of the information flowing vertically and horizontally within an organization involves three or more individuals. For example, job instructions are developed by managers and transmitted to the supervisors who report to them. The supervisors, in turn, transmit the instructions to the workers under their direction. This communication pattern is called **serial communication.**

NOTE 1.15
Serial communication is chain transmission of information.

In serial communication, messages are usually changed—sometimes dramatically— as they are sent from one member of the chain to another. Because each sender may omit, modify, or add details to the message as he or she relays it, special precautions are necessary. Four techniques will assist in maintaining the accuracy of and achieving understanding with serial communication:

Senders should	Receivers should
• Keep the message simple	• Take notes
• Request feedback	• Repeat the message

Although serial communication is typically oral, e-mail has increased its presence in written form. The ability to forward messages without paraphrasing them minimizes or eliminates the distortion customary in oral serial messages. This advantage is lost, however, when those who receive the message add to or comment on it before passing it along. Having to read the additional information can place a burden on the receiver.

NOTE 1.16
Serial communication may be oral or written.

External Communication Patterns

NOTE 1.17
Organizations communicate with many external publics.

External communication flows between a business organization and the entities with which it interacts. Companies have many external contacts such as customers, suppliers, competitors, the media, governmental agencies, and the general public. These contacts may be domestic or international. The information that flows between a business and its external receivers can be either written or oral. Letters, reports, orders, invoices, and Web pages illustrate external written communication; telephone calls and advertisements broadcast over radio or television are examples of external oral communication.

NOTE 1.18
External communication can be formal or informal.

Although external communication is typically formal, it may occur informally as well. Whenever an employee comments about work-related matters to someone not affiliated with the organization, informal external communication has occurred. The external audience could be a neighbor, a friend, someone to whom the worker has just been introduced at a party, or someone who accidentally overhears a conversation. Employees represent their organizations both on and off the job; therefore, they should demonstrate good communication skills in their professional and their social interactions.

Literally thousands of formal and informal communications take place every day. Effective communication enhances both individual and organizational success.

The Communication Process

LEARNING OBJECTIVE
Explain the communication process.
(4)

Understanding the communication process can help you become a better communicator. The following sections focus on the components of the communication process model and ways to implement the model successfully.

A Communication Process Model

The best way to study the communication process is to analyze a model of it. An understanding of the communication process model shown in Figure 1.3 will strengthen your performance as a communicator.

The communication process model operates in an environment that includes the sender, the message, the receiver, feedback, and communication barriers. The **communication environment** includes all things perceived by the participants in that environment; namely, all things perceived by the senses—seeing, hearing, touching, smelling, and tasting.

FIGURE 1.3
A Communication
Process Model

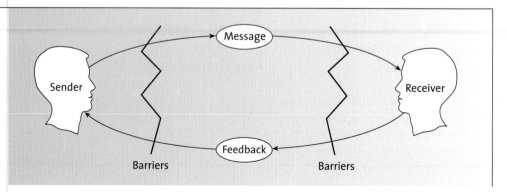

The communication environment is complex and distracting. Overcoming distractions is necessary to achieve the goals of business communication. In addition, communicators must recognize that each organization has its own culture, a personality that affects the communication environment and the way the communication process is implemented. Leaders (past and present), traditions, attitudes, and philosophies determine each organization's culture. An organization may be formal, as indicated by conservative clothing, limited access to leaders, and a preference for written communication. On the other hand, an organization may be informal—casual dress, open-door policies, and a preference for oral communication. Other factors influencing the culture are the organization's values relating to diversity, seniority, friendliness, teamwork, individuality, and ethics. An organization's culture can be dynamic, changing with its size and leadership. Effective business communicators adapt to and positively influence the development of their organizations' cultures.

NOTE 1.19
An organization's culture affects its communication environment.

Sender's and Receiver's Roles

The sender and the receiver have important responsibilities in the communication process. If both fulfill their roles, the communication will be successful.

SENDER'S ROLE

In the communication process the sender initiates the message. The sender may be a writer, a speaker, or one who simply gestures. The **sender's role** in the communication process includes (1) selecting the type of message, (2) analyzing the receiver, (3) using the you–viewpoint, (4) encouraging feedback, and (5) removing communication barriers.

NOTE 1.20
Both sender and receiver have important roles.

RECEIVER'S ROLE

The receiver is the listener, reader, or observer in the communication process. The **receiver's role** includes (1) listening or reading carefully, (2) being open to different types of senders and to new ideas, (3) making notes when necessary, (4) providing appropriate feedback to the sender, and (5) asking questions to clarify the message.

Remember, the sender has a greater responsibility for the success of communication than does the receiver. How you can successfully fulfill your role as the initiator of the communication process is discussed in detail in the sections that follow.

Communication Types and Channels

There are two types of communication: verbal and nonverbal. **Verbal** communication uses words; **nonverbal** communication does not. Although many people associate the term only with spoken words, verbal communication actually includes both written and oral messages.

All communications travel from their sender to their receiver(s) through **channels**. Written message channels include memos, letters, e-mail, notes, reports, telegrams, newsletters, and news releases. These items may include diagrams, drawings, charts, and tables. Oral message channels take many forms including face-to-face conversations, telephone conversations, voice mail, in-person conferences, video conferences, and speeches.

Senders must consider several things as they prepare to select the type of message they will send and the channel through which they will send it. Answering the questions listed in the following Tips and Hints will help you when you must make those choices.

NOTE 1.21
Messages may be
• Written
• Oral
• Nonverbal

Selecting Message Type and Channel

When selecting the type of message to be used and the channel through which it will pass, ask yourself the following questions:

- **Do I need a permanent record of this communication?** If yes, choose a letter (external audience), a memo (internal audience), an e-mail message (either internal or external audience), or a report (either internal or external audience). Written messages can have historic and legal value.
- **Will my receiver(s) readily accept the message?** If yes, a written message is appropriate. If no, oral communication is preferred. The ability to convey emotion and to react to feedback make face-to-face oral communication the best format for persuading receivers or conveying bad news. The size of and distance from the audience must also be considered.
- **Where and how large is the audience for the message?** Face-to-face oral communication can be effective if the sender and receiver(s) are in the same location. A telephone call may work if the number of receivers is small. Written com-

munication works best when it is impractical to bring receivers together or when the message doesn't warrant the personal touch of face-to-face communication.

- **Is the message long or complex?** If yes, select written communication. The writer can draft and revise the message before it is sent, and the receiver can refer to it as often as necessary to understand the message. Visual aids may supplement the written text.
- **Is timeliness a factor?** Do I need immediate feedback? Use face-to-face or telephone communication for urgent messages or when immediate feedback is important. In some circumstances, e-mail and fax may be viable alternatives. Letters or memos are often used to confirm messages conveyed orally.
- **Is credibility a concern?** Written messages are perceived as being more credible than oral messages. E-mail messages have less credibility than documents displayed on an organization's letterhead or presented as a report.

NOTE 1.22
Nonverbal communication is powerful.

Nonverbal messages can be conveyed by both people and objects. The human channels through which these messages pass include gestures and facial expressions. Object-based nonverbal message channels include the appearance and layout of a document and the audio and visual clarity of a videotaped presentation. Nonverbal communication supplements verbal communication. As noted in the following Communication Note, nonverbal communication can be powerful. When there is a conflict between a speaker's words and actions or between a document's contents and appearance, the receiver will most likely believe the nonverbal message.

Analysis of the Receiver for the You–Viewpoint

NOTE 1.23
The sender must analyze the receiver for the you–viewpoint.

The sender's most important task in the communication process is to analyze the receiver for the you–viewpoint. The **you–viewpoint** means that the sender gives primary consideration to the receiver's point of view when composing and sending messages. This is the most powerful concept in business communication, the key to achieving common understanding. To use the you–viewpoint, you must first analyze your receiver.

ANALYZING THE RECEIVER

No two receivers are alike. You must learn as much as possible about how a particular receiver or group of receivers thinks and feels, in general and with respect to the

Nonverbal Communication Can Help Servers Get Better Tips **Although the size of the check is the major factor in determining the amount of a tip, it is by no means the only factor. Consider the following nonverbal communication methods that have been shown to produce tips for servers:**

- Squatting at the table to look customers in the eye
- Smiling
- Touching diners on the shoulder
- Placing the check on a tray decorated with a credit card logo
- Writing *thank you* on the check
- Bringing candy with the check

Drawing a happy face on the back of the check also boosts tips . . . but only for female servers; male servers who apply this technique decrease their take!

Reprinted with the permission of The Associated Press

situation about which you will communicate. Specifically, you must analyze the receiver(s) in four areas—knowledge, interests, attitudes, and emotional reaction.

KNOWLEDGE

Begin the analysis with a review of each receiver's education and experience. Some of the questions you might ask are

- What is my receiver's highest level of education?
- Does my receiver have education specifically related to the topic of my message?
- How much work experience does my receiver have?
- How much of my receiver's work experience relates to the specific topic of my message?
- Does the receiver have prior experience interacting with me? with my organization?

Answers to these questions will help you decide the vocabulary level of your message, the extent to which you will be able to include technical terms, and the amount of detail the receiver will require.

INTERESTS

Second, analyze the receiver's interests. The sender will want to ask the following questions:

- What are the receiver's concerns? needs?
- Does the receiver have a particular motive? seek a particular outcome?

A receiver's position and level of authority may influence the nature of her or his interest in a situation. For example, an employee responsible for production will have a greater interest in the technical details of machine repair than will the manager to

NOTE 1.24
Analyze the receiver's knowledge.

NOTE 1.25
Analyze the receiver's interests.

NOTE 1.26
Position and level of authority affect interests.

whom he or she reports. The manager's primary interests may be the timing and cost of the solution. A careful analysis of your receiver's interest will help you determine what content to include in your message and the approach you take in organizing it.

ATTITUDES

Third, examine the attitudes of the receiver. You'll want to ask the following questions:

- What values, beliefs, biases, and viewpoints does the receiver have?
- What words or symbols will make a positive impression on the receiver? a negative impression?
- What ideas can be used effectively to communicate with this receiver?

Among the many attributes that can affect receiver attitudes are status, power, personality, expectations, nationality, and culture. Let us use the last attribute—culture—as an example. Generally speaking, people raised in the Japanese culture prefer to communicate indirectly. Therefore, a person of Japanese heritage might use the phrase "very difficult" rather than say "No." Those raised according the the German culture, on the other hand, favor directness; they tend to get to the point at the beginning of or very early in the message.

Culture can influence communications within a country as well as those that cross its borders. The population of the United States includes those with Hispanic, Asian, African, Native American, Polish, and many other heritages. Cultural diversity exists in other countries as well. Citizens of Canada, for example, have strong ties to the customs and traditions of England, Scotland, Ireland, France, India, Africa, Russia, and many other countries.

Knowing about a receiver's cultural heritage and nationality will help achieve the you–viewpoint in both verbal and nonverbal communication. The meaning of a gesture can vary dramatically from country to country and among cultures. An up/down nod of the head may be interpreted as *yes* in some cultures and as *no* in others. Using white paper as giftwrap will signal *joy* in some cultures, *death* in others. You will learn more about culture and workplace diversity in Chapter 2.

EMOTIONAL REACTION

Finally, anticipate the receiver's emotional reaction to your message. Will the message make the receiver happy? make the receiver angry? leave the receiver unaffected? Your assessment will assist you in determining whether you should use a direct or an indirect approach. In most cultures, people will accept pleasant or neutral messages when you give the main point in your opening (direct approach). A message that could disappoint or anger a receiver, however, might gain greater acceptance if the sender offers an explanation, reason, or other supporting information before giving the main point (indirect approach).

Analyzing your receiver will assist you in every communication situation. It will enable you to make effective use of one of the most important concepts of business communication—the you–viewpoint.

USING THE YOU–VIEWPOINT

Using the you–viewpoint requires that you understand your receiver's point of view. It means that you will give your receiver's knowledge, interests, attitudes, and emotional reaction primary consideration as you develop and send your message. To achieve the goals of business communication—understanding, response, relationship, and good-will—the sender should always use the you–viewpoint.

Your analysis of the receiver will enable use of the you–viewpoint. You can use your understanding of the receiver's knowledge to influence the ideas you include and the amount of explanation you give. In addition, you will be able to use words the receiver will understand and accept. You can design the message to address the receiver's concerns, needs, and motivations. Determining your receiver's attitudes will assist you in avoiding or carefully handling negative situations. Finally, anticipating your receiver's emotional reaction will influence whether you use a direct or an indirect approach in your message.

If you are sending the same message to a group of receivers and you want to achieve the business communication goals with every member of that group, each individual in the group must be analyzed as fully as possible. Then, if the receivers are of equal importance to your goals, you must compose the message for the member(s) of the group with the least knowledge about, the least interest in, and the greatest emotional opposition to the subject.

NOTE 1.31
Members of a group of receivers must be individually analyzed.

The opposite of the you–viewpoint is the I–viewpoint, which includes the me–, my–, our–, and we–viewpoints. The **I–viewpoint** means the sender composes messages from his or her point of view instead of the receiver's point of view. Poor communicators use the I–viewpoint and choose message content based on their own knowledge, interests, attitudes, and emotional reaction. Only rarely will an I–viewpoint message achieve the goals of business communication.

NOTE 1.32
I–viewpoint messages are rarely effective.

Examine these contrasting examples of sentences from opposite viewpoints:

I–Viewpoint	You–Viewpoint
I think your report is excellent.	You wrote an excellent report.
I am really excited about your having earned your CPA.	Congratulations for earning your CPA!
You simply do not understand what I am saying.	Perhaps an example will help make the instructions clearer.

As these examples show, you–viewpoint messages respect and emphasize the receiver's perceptions and feelings. Note that *I* in some of the I–viewpoint examples has been changed to *you* and *your* in the you–viewpoint examples. This type of change seems obvious, but the you–viewpoint requires much more than simple word changes. It requires that the message be receiver-centered, not self-centered. It requires that you emphasize the receiver's interests and benefits rather than your own. When you use the you–viewpoint, the receiver is apt to respond positively to both you and the content of your message. Although using the you–viewpoint may mean you sometimes write passively, the results are worth it.

NOTE 1.33
Messages should be receiver centered.

The recommendation that you use the you–viewpoint in your messages does not suggest that you ignore basic values or compromise ethics. Complimenting someone just so he or she will do what you want is inappropriate. Sincerity, honesty, and forthrightness are basic to all successful business communication.

It will be helpful now to look at an example of a message written in the you–viewpoint. The goal of the message in Figure 1.4 is to persuade readers.

NOTE 1.34
Be honest and forthright when you communicate.

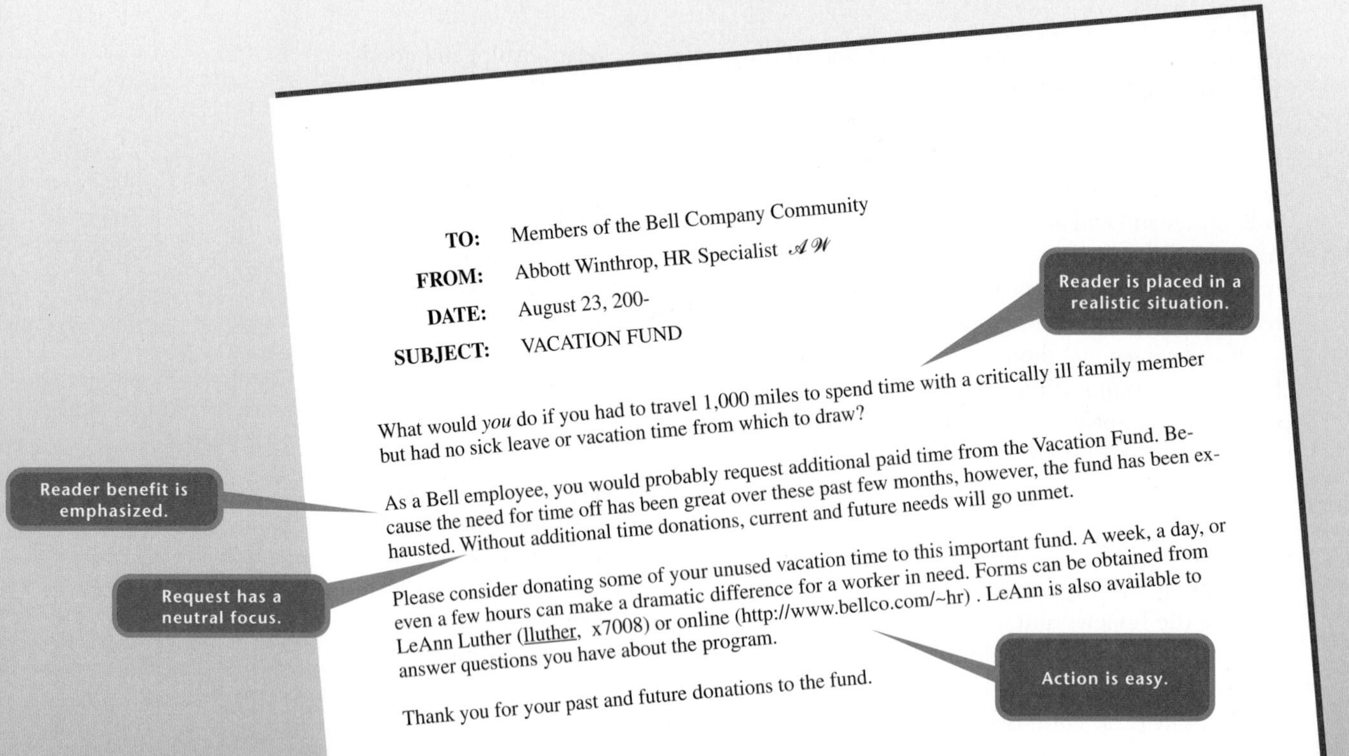

FIGURE 1.4
Interoffice Memo
Written from
Reader's Viewpoint

The memo content reads:

TO: Members of the Bell Company Community

FROM: Abbott Winthrop, HR Specialist *A W*

DATE: August 23, 200-

SUBJECT: VACATION FUND

What would *you* do if you had to travel 1,000 miles to spend time with a critically ill family member but had no sick leave or vacation time from which to draw?

As a Bell employee, you would probably request additional paid time from the Vacation Fund. Because the need for time off has been great over these past few months, however, the fund has been exhausted. Without additional time donations, current and future needs will go unmet.

Please consider donating some of your unused vacation time to this important fund. A week, a day, or even a few hours can make a dramatic difference for a worker in need. Forms can be obtained from LeAnn Luther (lluther, x7008) or online (http://www.bellco.com/~hr) . LeAnn is also available to answer questions you have about the program.

Thank you for your past and future donations to the fund.

Callout labels: "Reader is placed in a realistic situation." / "Reader benefit is emphasized." / "Request has a neutral focus." / "Action is easy."

Providing for Feedback

The sender's role in implementing the communication process includes providing for **feedback** from the receiver. Recall that appropriate receiver response is one of the goals of business communication. To achieve this goal, you can

- Ask directly or indirectly for the response
- Assist the receiver in giving the response

NOTE 1.35
Feedback is essential
to confirm receiver
understanding.

When a job applicant submits a letter and a resume to a company, he or she wants the receiver to respond by extending an invitation to interview for a job. To make it easier for the receiver to respond, the sender should be sure the message clearly asks for an interview and includes a telephone number and address where the sender can be reached easily. In a written sales message, the sender should ask for the order and provide a toll-free telephone number, an e-mail address, or an easy-to-use order form. If the communication is oral, the sender can ask tactfully whether the receiver understands the message or has any questions. In critical situations the sender might ask the receiver to repeat the message and explain his or her understanding of it. When speaking to a group, a sender can gain feedback by observing the audience, asking questions, or administering an evaluation. Because the most important goal of business communication is that the receiver understand the message, feedback from the receiver to the sender is essential to confirm that understanding.

Communication Barriers

Although knowledge of the communication process and skill in implementing it are basic to effective communication, the sender must also deal with barriers that interfere with the communication process. A **communication barrier** is any factor that interferes with the success of the communication process (see Figure 1.3). These barriers may occur between any two of the communication process steps or may affect all the steps in the process. The most crucial barriers are discussed in the next sections.

Word Choice

Choosing words that are too difficult, too technical, or too easy for your receiver can be a communication barrier. If words are too difficult or too technical, the receiver may not understand them; if they are too simple, the reader could become bored or be insulted. In either case, the message falls short of meeting its goals. As you will recall, analyzing the receiver will lead to determining the vocabulary level of the message. Therefore, senders must be careful to choose the correct words for their messages. Refer to Business English Seminar E for examples of many words that are easily confused or frequently misused.

Word choice is also a consideration when communicating with receivers for whom English is not the primary language. These receivers may not be familiar with *colloquial* English—the casual or informal way in which the language may be used.

Denotative Versus Connotative Meaning

A receiver and a sender may attach different meanings to the words used in a message. A **denotation** is the specific dictionary definition for a word. A **connotation** is any other meaning a word suggests to a receiver based on his or her experiences, interests, attitudes, and emotions. Connotative meanings can also be the result of slang or sarcasm. Senders should analyze their receivers as thoroughly as possible to determine what connotations those receivers might attach to specific words.

If you said to one of your subordinates, "Well, that certainly was fast work!" you may have meant the work was completed in less time than you expected. The receiver, however, may attach a different meaning to the statement. Based on what he or she is thinking and feeling at the moment, the receiver may think you meant the work was slow, was done too quickly, or was done improperly. Other specific examples of connotations versus denotations include the following:

Word	Possible Meanings	
assertive	energetic	pushy
compromise	adjust	give in
equitable	fair	equal
frugal	thrifty	cheap
funny	humorous	unusual

Implications and Inferences

An **implication** is a meaning given through connotation rather than through specific details. An **inference** is a conclusion drawn from connotation rather than specific

NOTE 1.36
Barriers interfere with the communication process.

NOTE 1.37
Communication Barrier 1: Poor word choice.

NOTE 1.38
Communication Barrier 2: Differing connotation.

NOTE 1.39
Communication Barrier 3: Inappropriate implications and inferences.

details. Although inferences and implications need not occur as a set, a speaker who *implies* something can cause a receiver to *infer* a meaning different from what was intended. For example, a person who says that his work is undervalued may mean to suggest that he doesn't get enough positive feedback from his supervisor. Without specific detail, however, the receiver of the message might infer that the speaker believes his salary isn't high enough. To guard against this communication barrier, senders should always use specific language and receivers should clarify meaning by asking questions.

Implications may be made and inferences may be drawn from actions as well as words. For example, suppose that two employees laugh as their supervisor passes. The supervisor may infer that the workers are making fun of her or him. The workers, however, may have wanted to signal that their morale is high or, more likely, to signal nothing at all.

In spite of the problems they can cause, inferences and implications play a role in workplace communication. Intelligent and appropriate inferences are essential to initiative and follow-through on the job; implying rather than directly stating bad news can soften its impact on the receiver. The challenge is to ensure that inferences and implications are appropriate. Carefully analyzing the receiver and situation will help you to meet this challenge.

Punctuation, Spelling, Grammar, and Sentence Structure

NOTE 1.40
Communication
Barrier 4: Incorrect
grammar, spelling,
punctuation, and sentence structure.

Incorrect grammar and poor sentence structure could hinder the receiver's understanding of a spoken or written message. Punctuation and spelling errors may create barriers to understanding a written message. As the number of errors increases, readers often stop reading for content and begin editing. The ultimate result could be that the sender loses credibility. The errors suggest that the person who sent the message either does not know the basics of the language or was too careless to correct the problems. Neither explanation creates a positive impression of the person who sent the message. The following Communication Note describes a situation that had both monetary and image implications for a firm.

COMMUNICATION NOTE

Errors Have $ and Image Implications A vice president for the firm that prepared a plaque to be presented to actor James Earl Jones at a celebration of civil rights leader Dr. Martin Luther King, Jr. described the error as "a very unfortunate mistake." The problem? The plaque read "Thank you James Earl Ray for keeping the dream alive." Ray was the person convicted of assassinating Dr. King.

Event sponsors declined the engraver's offer to redo the plaque and accused the company of being "culturally insensitive." Another company was located, and the damaged plaque was repaired in time to be presented at the celebration.

Reprinted with the permission of The Associated Press.

Type of Message

NOTE 1.41
Communication
Barrier 5: Wrong
type of message.

Selecting a message type appropriate to the situation is essential to communication success. For example, communicating complex job instructions orally will most likely fail because the receiver must rely solely on his or her memory of what was said—or per-

B.C.

haps memory plus sketchy notes. A written message to which the worker can refer as needed will achieve better results. An in-person oral message is desirable when resolving a conflict between employees. Both the sender and the receiver can take full advantage of the nonverbal cues that accompany the spoken words.

If the message is a report on an evaluation of alternative manufacturing processes, the type of message will depend on who will receive it. The report may be written or oral, long or short, technical or simple; graphic aids might be used to support verbal content. Often, more than one type of message can be used for the same communication situation.

Generally, the higher the level in an organization to which a message is sent, the more concise the message should be. Top managers view time as a precious commodity; therefore, a brief summary may be more suitable than a long, detailed report. Managers who have greater involvement with operating procedures may derive greater benefits from long, technical messages.

Appearance of the Message

The appearance of a message affects its readability and influences a receiver's acceptance of its content. Smudges, sloppy corrections, light print, wrinkled paper, and poor handwriting may distract the reader and become barriers to effective communication. Using emoticons and keying text only in uppercase letters can be barriers in e-mail. Senders should examine every document before it is sent to ensure that its appearance does not interfere with its potential for success.

NOTE 1.42
Communication Barrier 6: Poor appearance of written message.

Appearance of the Sender

The credibility of an oral message can be reduced if the appearance of the sender is unattractive or unacceptable to the receiver. In addition, unintended nonverbal signals can distract a receiver and influence the way an oral message is received. For example, if you smile when you sympathetically give bad news, your motives may be suspect.

If the credibility of the message is questioned, the quality of the receiver's understanding, acceptance, and response will be reduced. For success in oral business communication, senders should be sure that their dress, cleanliness, and facial and body movements are appropriate to their professions and to the communication situations they encounter. Wearing a tuxedo to a beach party is as inappropriate as wearing a swimsuit to the office.

NOTE 1.43
Communication Barrier 7: Poor appearance of speaker.

Environmental Factors

The environment in which communication occurs can interfere with the success of a message. A noisy machine in an area where a supervisor is trying to speak with an employee

NOTE 1.44
Communication Barrier 8: Distracting environmental factors.

can become a distracting environmental factor. When a supervisor's desk separates him or her from a worker during a meeting, the desk can intimidate the worker and limit his or her ability to respond to the message. Other examples of environmental factors that can serve as barriers to effective communication include room temperature, odor, light, color, and distance.

The sender has the responsibility to try to eliminate environmental factors that are communication barriers. If the room in which an oral presentation is to be given is too warm, the sender should try to get the thermostat turned down or to have the windows opened. If the receiver cannot see to read a message because of limited light, the sender should arrange for more light. Environmental barriers can usually be eliminated or reduced, often before communication begins.

Receiver's Capability

If the receiver has a physical or mental disability that causes a communication barrier, the sender should recognize this in choosing message type and channel. The receiver may have a hearing impairment or a learning disability. The sender can remove or compensate for such barriers in the communication process by carefully selecting the form of the message and by providing for appropriate feedback mechanisms. Most of the solutions are clear choices. Increased volume, printed text, or a sign language interpreter can help overcome the potential barrier of a hearing impairment. When a visual impairment threatens the success of a written message, print can be enlarged or the message can be given orally.

In recent years considerable progress has been made in providing for full participation of persons with disabilities in all fields. Effective communicators will focus on their receivers' abilities and will work with receivers to ensure communication success.

Listening

Failure to listen is a common barrier to successful oral communication. Listening effectively is not easy. One reason listening is challenging is that most people speak 100 to 200 words a minute but are capable of listening to material of average difficulty at 500 or more words a minute. This difference allows listeners' minds to wander to topics other than the message. In addition, listeners may tune out a speaker and begin thinking about how they will respond to the message. Listening is a skill that can and must be learned.

Senders can use several methods to overcome poor listening as a communication barrier. Receivers can be reminded to listen carefully, or they can be asked questions periodically to determine the extent of their comprehension. In some circumstances a poor listener may be encouraged to study and learn improved listening skills. One of the most effective ways to remove poor listening as a barrier to communication is to improve the quality of the message and the way in which it is conveyed. Thoroughly analyzing the audience before designing the message will help a sender plan, organize, and deliver an appropriate oral message.

Other Communication Barriers

Several of the most common communication barriers and ways to remove them have been discussed in the preceding sections. In attempting to improve your communication effectiveness, you must also eliminate other barriers. For example, some receiver-related communication barriers include lack of interest, lack of knowledge, different cultural perceptions, language difficulty, emotional state, and bias. The sender must do everything possible to remove these receiver-related communication barriers. Information in Tips and Hints will help overcome barriers associated with cultural differences.

Summary of Learning Objectives

Explain why business communication is important to individuals and organizations.

Business communication is the process of establishing a common understanding between or among people within a business environment. Good communication skills help individuals enhance self-esteem, become effective employees, and advance in their careers. The quality of an organization's internal and external communications affects its success.

List and explain the goals of business communication.

Business communication has four goals: (1) Receiver understanding—the receiver understands the message as the sender intended it to be understood. (2) Receiver response—the receiver demonstrates his or her understanding of a message by providing an appropriate response. (3) Favorable relationship—the people involved in the process relate to each other positively, personally, and professionally. (4) Organizational goodwill—the receiver has confidence in the sender's organization and is willing to continue the business relationship.

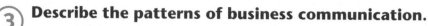

③ Describe the patterns of business communication.

Business communication may be internal or external, formal or informal, work related or personal. Messages may flow vertically upward from workers, downward from managers, or horizontally between or among workers who report to the same supervisor. Serial communication can occur in either horizontal or vertical communication. Messages can also flow diagonally between or among workers regardless of unit or status. The diagonal pattern is known as a network. The grapevine is one type of informal network communication.

④ Explain the communication process.

Communication occurs in an open environment that includes the sender, the message, the receiver, feedback, and communication barriers. The sender will analyze the receiver and then design a message that reflects what was learned through that analysis. The message should focus on the receiver's interests, encourage feedback, and eliminate or minimize communication barriers. The receiver must listen or read carefully and be open to senders and to their ideas; making notes, asking questions, and providing feedback are also part of the receiver's role in the process.

⑤ Identify communication barriers and describe ways to remove them.

The primary barrier to effective communication is failure to use the you–viewpoint. Other barriers include word choice; punctuation, spelling, grammar, and sentence structure; appearance of the sender or the message; environmental factors; type of message; receiver capability; and listening. Analyzing the receiver and taking the you–viewpoint will eliminate or minimize these and other communication barriers that might arise.

Discussion Questions

1. Why are both internal and external communication important to an organization? (Objectives 1 and 3)
2. Name the four goals of business communication. Identify the one that is the most important, and explain why it has this distinction. (Objective 2)
3. How can assessing a receiver's knowledge help a message sender overcome word choice as a communication barrier? (Objectives 2 and 5)
4. **Technology.** How have technologies such as e-mail and voice mail affected grapevine communication? (Objective 3)
5. Discuss the networks to which you belong. Identify the basis for the network—the thing the members have in common. (Objective 3)
6. Based on your work or school experience, discuss how roles or status have influenced the way in which people communicated. (Objective 3)
7. Assume that you've just accepted a part-time job that will require you to work Tuesday and Thursday evenings, all day on Saturday, and from noon to closing on Sun-

day. The income from the job will enable you to remain in school. Analyze each of the following people to help you determine how to tell them your good news: (Objective 4)

   a. Your parents, who expect you to attend your grandparents' 65th wedding anniversary celebration three weeks from Sunday.

   b. Elena, your study partner, who works Monday, Wednesday, and Friday nights. You and she had planned to spend this Sunday studying for a major exam you'll both take at 8 a.m. on Monday. Elena hasn't pressed you to repay the $27 you borrowed two months ago.

   c. Terry, your eight-year-old "buddy" in a mentoring program for disadvantaged youth. You've promised to be Terry's guest at the circus this Saturday afternoon; Terry earned the tickets in a school read-a-thon.

8. Describe a communication situation you have experienced or observed that succeeded because the sender and the receiver were able to identify and remove potential communication barriers. The situation need not be work related. (Objectives 4 and 5)

9. Is it possible to use the you–viewpoint and transmit ethical messages? Discuss. (Objective 5)

10. How does each of the following sayings relate to communication? (Objectives 2, 3, and 5)

   a. A picture is worth a thousand words.

   b. Sticks and stones can break my bones, but words will never hurt me.

   c. Seeing is believing.

   d. Actions speak louder than words.

Application Exercises

1. **InfoTrac. E-mail.** Informal mentoring has a long history of helping new workers become acquainted with the communication environment and style within an organization. More recently, formal mentoring programs have emerged to accomplish this purpose and more. Learn more about formal mentoring programs by reading InfoTrac article A20825427, "Mentoring Programs: They're an Inexpensive Way to Tap Your Company's Talent to Groom Future Leaders," by Karen Hildebrand. Then, send your instructor an e-mail in which you respond to the following questions:

   a. Why does mentoring pair people who don't have a supervisory relationship with one another?

   b. What role does communication play in the meetings between mentor and mentee?

   c. How does "feedback" contribute to the mentoring process?

2. **Teamwork.** Form a four-person team. Have each team member select one of the business communication goals and prepare a one-minute presentation that explains and illustrates it. Practice, then join with another group and make the presentations to each other. (Objective 2)

3. **Teamwork.** Obtain a copy of your school's administrative organization chart. As a group, identify the vertical and horizontal communication patterns suggested by the structure. Then, interview one of the administrators to learn about whether/how network (diagonal) communication occurs within the structure. As your instructor directs, report your results in a one-page memo or orally to the class.

4. Select an appropriate message type and channel for each of the following situations. Justify your choices. (Objective 3)

a. Effective the first of next month, the cost of dependent coverage under your company's group insurance policy will rise. Your task is to inform 300 employees who work at the three facilities in your state.

b. You want to invite the new manager in your division to have lunch with you today. The manager works on another floor of your building.

c. An employee you supervise has been named Volunteer of the Year in your community.

d. A sweater shown on page 6 of your company's fall catalog is no longer available in green. You want to persuade those who order the item to select another color.

e. The proposal you have written must reach your client's office by 3 p.m. today. Your offices are in the same community.

5. Analyze the receiver's knowledge, interests, attitudes, and emotional state in the following communication situation: (Objective 4)

You are a public accountant writing a letter to Wilson Brooks, a contractor who builds homes. Mr. Brooks prepares his own tax returns with occasional assistance from your firm. He has had last year's return, which he prepared himself, audited by the Internal Revenue Service (IRS). The IRS did not allow some of the deductions Mr. Brooks listed; therefore, he has been told he owes $3,750 in additional taxes. Mr. Brooks has sent you a copy of the IRS audit report. He asks you to review the report and advise him on what he should do.

6. Modify the following sentences to make them reflect the you–viewpoint. Be sure not to change the meaning of the sentences in your revised versions. (Objective 4)

a. The meeting time has been changed from 4 p.m. to 3 p.m.; don't be late.

b. I have enclosed a postage-paid reply card for you to use when ordering from us.

c. We have received your order and a check for the amount you owe for the merchandise.

d. I set extremely high standards for myself and for those who work for me; your work isn't meeting my standards.

e. What did you do to this CD player? I'll have to charge you at least $200 to repair it.

f. Be quiet and listen to these important instructions.

g. He always seems to interrupt while others are talking.

h. Your request for a promotion is denied. Talk to me again next month.

i. Don't be late again. Give the monthly reports to Amanda no later than the 20th of the month.

j. Make no mistakes. The report must be completely accurate.

7. Words and phrases can have connotative meanings not only in business communication but also in classroom communication. For each item in the following list, identify what a teacher might mean when he or she speaks the word or phrase and what a student might interpret it to mean when he or she hears it during class. (Objective 5)

a. Okay.

b. Are there any questions?

c. This is important.

d. You need to . . . (study, do your homework)

8. **Global.** Select a culture other than your own. Gather information on that culture's values, attitudes, biases, and viewpoints. As your instructor directs, interview a student or faculty member from another culture or use Internet or library resources to conduct your research. Share your findings with the class. (Objective 5)

9. Observe a clerk, cafeteria worker, or custodial worker at your school. Record the number of nonverbal messages he or she conveys in five minutes. Identify each cue as positive or negative. (Objective 5)

10. **E-mail. Teamwork.** Think about a supervisor or teacher you would describe as your favorite.

   a. Make a list of the things that make her or him stand apart from others you have known (e.g., Is he or she a good listener? Does she or he respond to your verbal and nonverbal feedback?).

   b. Work with another member of the class. Exchange your lists; use e-mail if available. What items appear on both your and your partner's list? Which items relate to the ability to communicate well? What do your findings tell you about how the ability to communicate well influences someone's perception of you?

   c. Work alone. Summarize your findings and conclusions in an e-mail to your instructor. Be sure your message is constructed using correct grammar, spelling, punctuation, and sentence structure. (Objectives 1, 2, and 5)

There are Web exercises at **http://krizan.swlearning.com** to accompany this chapter.

Message Analysis

Correct the content and word choice errors in the following business memo:

TO: Staff
FROM: Manager
DATE: June 1, 200–
SUBJECT: BUSINESS COMMUNICATION

Yesterday, I attended a seminar on business communication. The speaker introduced me to some principals and techniques, and I want to pass some of his advise on to you. Specifically, pay attention to the items below:

- *Always analyze the situation. You'll get farther if you focus on yourself—use the You–Viewpoint!*
- *Use lots of technical words; readers are impressed by them.*
- *Long messages are better then brief ones because you may include more details.*
- *Don't waste time proofreading e-mail; its meant to be quick and dirty, and you can always send another one if you make a mistake.*

You may already have known these things, but a reminder never hurts. Discuss these items between yourselves, and let me know if you have any questions.

Grammar Workshop

Correct the grammar, spelling, punctuation, style, and word choice errors in the following sentences:

1. Sheridan's entire collection of mens' cardigans are also on sale.
2. Its a secret between him and I.
3. Murray Jefferson who joined the firm just 18 months ago has been named Quality Control manger.
4. The attornies tried to clearly explain the terms of the settlement to their client.

5. If you would like to order a subscription for a friend, record his name and address on the enclosed card and mail it to us now, we'll bill you later.
6. The meating sight has been changed form Sams' office too Conference room A, therefore, more people can attend.
7. Joan Bob and Alicia was selected to be the departments represenatives to the counsel.
8. While their outward appearance remains relatively unchanged designers note that lockers are larger more durable and can be customized for special purposes.
9. Any staff member who may come into contract with a biohazard during their duties, should have access to protective devices such as gloves masks and goggles.
10. The short term outlook is dim however long term projections are positive.

Workplace Diversity

Kelley Sloane, Vice President, Marketing, Exstream™ Software

LET'S TALK BUSINESS Today's eGeneration is a growing community of consumers demanding higher quality and individualized treatment in a 24/7 world. From their paper correspondence (statements, invoices, and notifications) to cyber media (the Web, cell phones, and interactive kiosks), they expect personalized information on demand and in real time. Companies around the world must be prepared to connect with the eGeneration through high quality, fully personalized customer communications in print and on the Internet.

Customers want only the information that matters to them. Whether your company needs to send prospectuses, proposals, statements, direct marketing, letters, or insurance benefit booklets, staying ahead of the competition means being able to maximize all customer touch points with high quality, relevant, and timely communications—delivered electronically or in print, according to your customers' preferences.

LEARNING OBJECTIVES

① *Explain why creating a multicultural workforce and communicating effectively with diverse cultures are important for businesses.*

② *Describe core dimensions of culture in the workplace and how a multicultural environment affects communication.*

③ *Explain basic guidelines for communicating in a multicultural environment.*

④ *Describe challenges and key strategies for multinational and global business communication.*

⑤ *Describe guidelines for working with an interpreter or translator to overcome language barriers.*

The contemporary business world brings together diverse groups of people through multinational corporations, communication technology, and an increasingly multicul- tural population within national boundaries. The eGeneration described by Kelley Sloane in Let's Talk Business represents some of the changes taking place in customs, habits, and expectations for communication. Later in the chapter, you will find an ex- ample of a communication disconnect between a middle-aged manager and a younger employee who sends an electronic greeting card.

Diversity in the workplace is a reality. **Diversity** means differences. In this chapter, you will study about cultural differences and the effects of these differences on commu- nication. Customers, clients, and employees represent diverse cultures, whether in do- mestic or global business environments. In a mobile society with almost instant elec- tronic global communication, business success depends on people who can communicate effectively with individuals from a variety of cultural backgrounds. Diver- sity is good for business, and major business corporations are making diversity initiatives a priority. **Diversity initiatives** are strategies that recognize and value human differences in the workplace and develop a workforce that can communicate effectively in a multi- cultural environment. Examples include orientation to cultural differences, diversity- related career training, languages, diversity recruiting, and community outreach.

Human resource professionals from companies in the Fortune 1000 and Fortune's Top 100 Companies to Work For[1] reported in a 2001 survey that 79 percent of diver- sity initiatives are housed in human resource departments, 14 percent are in separate diversity departments, and 7 percent in other departments. The average dollar amount of the HR budget spent on diversity is $239,000. The average budget for separate di- versity departments is $1.5 million, ranging from a low of $30,000 up to $5.1 million. As shown in Figure 2.1, these executives indicate that diversity initiatives affect the bot- tom line by improving corporate culture, employee recruitment, client relations, and employee retention. In addition, attention to diversity decreases complaints and litiga- tion and helps prepare companies to move into emerging markets. Dealing effectively with cultural diversity affects business profitability.

FIGURE 2.1
How Diversity Initiatives Help an Organization Keep a Competitive Advantage

	Percent Responding $n=106$
Improves corporate culture	83
Improves employee morale	79
Higher retention of employees	76
Easier recruitment of employees	75
Decreases complaints and litigation	68
Increases creativity	59
Decreases interpersonal conflict among employees	58
Enables the organization to move into emerging markets	57
Improves client relations	55
Increases productivity	52
Improves the organization's bottom line	49
Maximizes brand identity	34
Reduces training costs	13

Reprinted with permission of Society for Human Resource Management (SHRM®)/Fortune Survey on Impact of Diversity Initiatives on the Bottom Line, 2001.

[1] Society for Human Resource Management, "Impact of Diversity Initiatives on the Bottom Line," pp. 9 and 11, 2001.

Opportunities for increased profits motivate large corporations, and even some small businesses, to expand their world trade. This expansion increases multicultural and multinational communication. Business operations across national borders can result in increased productivity at low costs, thereby increasing profit. In addition to branch operations in more than one country, businesses also increase profit margins by exporting their products to other countries or importing products for sale. Multinational and global business communication requires special strategies for negotiating and establishing good relationships.

The prefix **multi-**, specifically defined, means multiple, many, or more than two—or in some cases, more than one. Because of an increasing number of business interactions among people of different cultures and nationalities, the terms used in this chapter to describe communication diversity are *multicultural* and *multinational*. **Multicultural business communication** refers to the transmission of information among businesspeople from different cultures, whether within national boundaries or across national boundaries. **Culture** means the customary beliefs, social norms, values, and material traits of a racial, ethnic, religious, or social group. These beliefs and values become an integrated behavior pattern that is transmitted from generation to generation. *Multicultural communication* implies interactions with individuals or groups who represent diversity in race, ethnicity, gender, age, disability, sexual orientation, or religion. The term **multinational communication** describes interactions across national boundaries; that is, communication among citizens of different countries. A **global perspective** extends beyond multicultural or multinational to a world marketplace.

In this chapter, communication is described for both multicultural and multinational business environments. As you study this information, keep in mind the values of diversity and the contributions that an understanding of individual differences make to business success. The first part of the chapter addresses cultural change and guidelines for multicultural communication. The last part includes a discussion of multinational and global business environments and key strategies for communicating in these environments. As a student, you are already interacting in a multicultural environment. In all likelihood, you will be communicating in a multinational, and even global, business environment at some point in your business career.

NOTE 2.3
Increased profits encourage businesses to expand to multinational and global markets.

NOTE 2.4
Multicultural communication means communication with many cultures; multinational communication is interaction across national boundaries.

Multicultural Business Communication

Changes in workforce demographics create an increasingly diverse business environment. Figure 2.2 illustrates cultural diversity in businesses in the United States. Changes reported by these major corporations show that the number of African Americans, Asians/Pacific Islanders, Hispanics/Latins, and females increased more than 50 percent over five years. The highest percentages of decrease were for Caucasian/white and males. More subtle cultural differences such as sexual orientation, workers over 40, employees with disabilities, and employees with English as a second language may be underreported in these statistics. The high percentages in Figure 2.2 for *Don't know* suggest that these percentages may be inaccurate.

The workplace environment includes employees and customers with a wide range of needs, interests, and abilities. Understanding differences and responding effectively are critical to communication and successful business operations. If diversity is not understood and valued, discrimination may result. Analysis of the multicultural dimensions of diversity helps the business communicator transmit messages that are

LEARNING OBJECTIVE
2
Describe core dimensions of culture in the workplace and how a multicultural environment affects communication.

FIGURE 2.2
Demographic Workforce
Changes over the Past
Five Years: As Reported
in 2001 by Fortune 1000
and Fortune's Top 100
Companies to Work For

Percent Responding Demographic Changes

	n	Increased	Decreased	Same	Don't know
African American (not Hispanic)	112	61	7	25	7
Asian/Pacific Islander	111	52	4	31	14
Caucasian/White (not Hispanic)	108	31	28	34	7
Hispanic/Latin	112	56	5	30	9
Native American/American Indian or Alaska native	110	24	4	53	20
Females	112	58	5	29	8
Males	109	27	24	41	8
Gays/lesbians/transgendered	112	16	2	3	80
Workers over 40	110	30	6	23	42
Employees with disabilities	111	15	1	32	51
Employees with English as a 2nd language	111	24	0	14	61

Reprinted with permission of Society for Human Resource Management (SHRM®)/Fortune Survey on Impact of Diversity Initiatives on the Bottom Line, 2001.

understandable and acceptable. The differences between and among individuals are numerous. The following sections focus on five core dimensions of cultural diversity that affect how persons view the world, what they value, and how others perceive them. These dimensions are ethnicity, race, gender, age, and physical challenges.

Ethnicity and Race

Ethnicity is a term that relates to common racial, national, tribal, religious, linguistic, or cultural origin or background for a large group of people. **Race** refers to traits transmissible by descent and sufficient to identify a distinct group of people. Ethnicity and race are two of the core dimensions of a multicultural environment. Telecommunication advances and rapid travel have increased communication with individuals of diverse ethnic and racial backgrounds.

NOTE 2.5
Ethnic and racial
demographics are chang-
ing in the United States.

Ethnic and racial demographic changes are taking place in the United States. According to census data, the Asian population had the greatest percentage increase from 1990 to 2000 (74.3%), followed by the percentage of increase in Hispanic populations (57.9%). By 2010, projections show the Hispanic population having the greatest increase in percentage of the U.S. population. These same projections show that the white population percentage, which has been decreasing since 1980, will continue to decrease. The percentage of black people in the population can be expected to remain at about the same level. Currently, approximately 10 percent of U.S. residents are foreign born. Immigration laws from 1965 to 1990 brought increased diversity, and the number of foreign-born residents almost tripled from 1970 to 2000—from 10 million to 28 million.

In addition to cultural differences among racial and ethnic groups, individuals within each group have differences. For example, people within a particular group may be new immigrants, have come from urban or rural populations, and represent regional language or cultural differences. Chinese and Japanese have been residents in this country since the early 1900s, but Vietnamese, Laotians, and Cambodians became residents only 25 to 30 years ago. Hispanic people share an ethnicity but represent a variety of racial groups. They may be Mexicans, Puerto Ricans, Cubans, South and Central

Americans, or others. Deep-seated cultural differences that affect communication underlie obvious cultural variations such as language or physical characteristics.

AWARENESS OF CULTURAL DIFFERENCES

The first step to becoming an effective multicultural communicator is an awareness of self in a specific culture.[2] To see others as individuals who represent one of many variations rather than as a deviation requires seeing yourself in specific terms—family heritage, customs, gender, beliefs, and values. Understanding these myriad aspects of your own culture and their effect on your perceptions and behavior are key to understanding the meaning of culture. When interacting with persons who have different cultural backgrounds, characteristics, beliefs, and values from yours, you do not know the specificity of details that you have with your own culture. Unknown aspects of other cultures affect communication and require sensitivity and respect, as well as a willingness to learn about other cultures and to accept and appreciate differences.

NOTE 2.6
Awareness of your culture is the first step to effective multicultural communication.

COMMUNICATION NOTE

Effective multicultural communicators—
- Learn about their own culture and recognize that cultural heritage affects perceptions and expectations of others.
- Seek to understand cultural backgrounds when interacting with others and respect their values, beliefs, and communication patterns.
- Consider culture as an element of the you-viewpoint for communication.

LANGUAGE DIVERSITY

As early as 1990, almost one in five persons five years of age and above in households in the United States either spoke a language at home other than English or did not speak English "very well." More than 3,000 different languages are spoken throughout the world. More than 200 different languages are spoken in India alone. Considering all of the dialects in the world, some linguists estimate that there are at least 10,000 variations of languages. If you are not skilled in the use of your receiver's primary language, you are facing your first major challenge in multicultural business communication.

NOTE 2.7
Language differences can be a barrier to communication.

An increase in multicultural and multinational interactions presents language challenges. This means that organizations communicate with large numbers of people who speak languages other than English—employees, clients, customers, suppliers, and government personnel. Voices speaking languages other than English can be heard in public places almost anywhere in the United States. Also, this language diversity is illustrated by the printing of product directions in more than one language and the posting of universal symbols on road signs along highways. Although English has become the language of business in many countries, the increased contacts with persons whose native language is not English make bilingualism a valuable workplace skill.

Because of different meanings that translated English words may have in another language, a businessperson with knowledge of language and language subtleties is a business asset. A number of examples can be found of past experiences of U.S. companies that had communication difficulties because of a lack of knowledge of another culture's

[2] Patricia Digh, "Culture? What Culture?" *Association Management*, 53(2), pp. 42–47, 2001.

language. Pepsi Cola's slogan "Pepsi Comes Alive" was not received well in Taiwan because the Chinese translation means "Pepsi Brings Your Ancestors Back from the Grave." In the Middle East an American company was marketing tomato paste but learned that "tomato paste" translated into Arabic meant "tomato glue."

NOTE 2.8
Words may have different meanings in different languages.

There are other examples of a word being appropriate in one language and not in another. A U.S. trade magazine promoting gift sales in Germany used the English word *gift* in its title. Unfortunately, the word "gift" in German means "poison." The trade magazine did not effectively achieve its objective of selling gifts in Germany. A foreign company inappropriately selected EMU for the name of its airline that flew to Australia. An emu is an Australian bird that cannot fly, hardly an appropriate name for an airline.

Even the use of parts of speech varies in different languages. In Japanese, the verb is at the end of a sentence. This enables Japanese speakers to begin to express a thought and watch the receiver's reaction. Depending on how the receiver is reacting to the message, the verb may be changed, thereby changing the whole meaning of the sentence. For example, a Japanese speaker might start to say, "Please go away from me now," but end up saying "Please stay with me now" by changing the verb, which is said last.

An American company caused itself considerable communication problems in Germany by insisting that all its employees call each other by their first names. This made Germans uncomfortable because they do not use first names even with close business associates. In Germany, the use of first names is reserved for intimate friends and relatives. Forcing the Germans to adopt an American custom caused stress that seriously reduced the quality of communication in the German-based American operation.

COMMUNICATION QUOTE

As a student majoring in international economics and foreign language, I have used my language skills to participate in a multistate network of land-grant universities that supplies Spanish language broadcast programs through the Internet. I was born in Brazil and speak Portuguese but also learned Spanish as a child, so it was easy for me to help with the radio broadcast that provides information to address the information needs of the Hispanic people. With today's instant communication with persons in nations all over the world, I believe that speaking more than one language will increase my opportunities for business success.

—Nara De Sa Guimaraes, University of Kentucky (Photo courtesy of Nara De Sa Guimaraes)

NONVERBAL COMMUNICATION

A sender's nonverbal signals influence the receiver's understanding and acceptance of a message. In multicultural business communication, nonverbal signals vary as much as spoken languages do. Nonverbal greetings vary from a bow to a handshake, or from a hug to an upward flick of the eyebrows. When communicating with different cultures, be observant and learn the meanings of nonverbal communication signals such as facial expressions, social distance when conversing, and hand gestures.

NOTE 2.9
Misunderstood nonverbal signals cause communication problems.

Not understanding cultural differences in nonverbal messages causes communication problems. For example, in Germany if an American were to signal *one* by holding up the index finger, it would be understood as *two*. Consequently, if the American is ordering a train ticket in Germany by raising the index finger, he is likely to get two tickets instead of one. In Japan, crossing your legs by placing one foot or ankle on the knee of the other leg is impolite or vulgar. The preferred way of sitting in Japan is with both feet on the floor with knees held fairly close together. Thumbs up in America means approval but in Iran and Ghana it is a vulgar gesture. In addition, the social distance or individual space that is needed for comfort in communication by persons varies in different cultures. If people stand too close when conversing, people from some cultures may feel uncomfortable; although in other cultures, conversations may be almost nose to nose.

PERSPECTIVES ON CULTURAL DIVERSITY

Racial or ethnic distinctions other than language are many and varied. These distinctions may be observed in how people dress, the food they eat, the holidays they observe, what they value, and how they relate to other people. The cultural mix of people throughout the world blurs some differences but others remain. Sociologists classify aspects of social culture into *material* and *nonmaterial culture*.[3] **Material culture** includes objects such as clothing, houses, equipment, art, and tools. **Nonmaterial culture** is abstract and refers to values, beliefs, language, symbols, and norms and sanctions. Material culture is most likely to change as a result of increased interaction of cultures, while nonmaterial culture is deeply embedded in tradition and religion and is likely to remain distinct. An example of material culture change is dress. Western jeans may be worn in Japan or a sari garment in the United States, but Afghanistan women continue to wear a burka in public places. Although the burka is a material object, it is linked with religious and social tradition (nonmaterial culture) and, therefore, is resistant to change.

Cultural relativism is a term that describes different standards of right and wrong for different cultures. A natural tendency is to assume that your cultural beliefs, values, and behaviors are normal and that the ways of other cultures are not. **Ethnocentrism** is the inherent belief that one's own group and culture are superior. Differences may seem peculiar, strange, and even wrong. As you study other cultures, however, you should realize that there is not necessarily one right or wrong way to do something but rather many different, but equally correct, ways.

People use **stereotypes**, simplistic beliefs about the typical behaviors or characteristics of a particular group of people, to help them understand the messages those individuals are sending. Although numerous resources describe cultural characteristics of specific ethnic groups, such as the examples given in this chapter, these descriptions should be regarded as general in nature. They may be descriptive of a large number of persons in that group but not descriptive of others. The tendency to stereotype groups of people should be recognized; strictly categorizing individuals on the basis of simplistic expectations based on stereotypes should be avoided. Studying reliable sources to learn about different customs and values can be helpful if you use this knowledge as a beginning point to understand the needs and interests of individuals with whom you communicate.

NOTE 2.10
Nonmaterial culture changes much more slowly than material culture.

NOTE 2.11
Ethnocentrism is the belief that your culture is superior to others.

NOTE 2.12
Stereotypes are simplistic beliefs about characteristics and are not reliable.

---

[3] Linda Schneider and Arnold Silverman, *Global Sociology: Introducing Five Contemporary Societies*, 2nd ed., Boston: McGraw-Hill, 2000.

Diversity Pays Off Diversity is about more than color and gender, although that's how it's frequently measured. It's about all the differences that make us unique in terms of lifestyles and challenges as well as skills and contributions.

—Business Special Report, *Computerworld, 35*(25), June 18, 2001, p. 32

One way to study cultural variations is to determine where the behaviors and values might be placed on a continuum from high to low for uncertainty avoidance and for their view of human relationships.[4] **Cultures with high avoidance of uncertainty** depend on formal rules, details, and specific plans. They are likely to believe in absolute truth and expect high expertise. Rituals and ceremonials are important. On the other hand, **low uncertainty avoidance** prefers few rules, tolerates generalizations and deviance, seeks individual opinions, has less ritualization and ceremony, and accepts relativity of beliefs. Cultural groups or individuals may be at any point on the continuum from high to low.

The **human relationship cultural perspective** pertains to whether a culture is individualistic or collectivist. Those with an **individualistic perspective** tend to make decisions based on individual needs and place a higher importance on the individual than the group. On the other hand, **collectivist cultures** focus on the group and place a high value on relationships. Chinese and Japanese cultures tend to be high on the collectivist and uncertainty avoidance continuum while persons in Canada, the United States, or Germany are likely to be individualistic and more comfortable with uncertainty and ambiguity.

Business conduct in cultures that emphasize relationships, tradition, ceremony, and social rules requires an indirect approach. Initially, time is spent in social conversation and rituals such as handshakes and an exchange of business cards. In general, businesspeople in the United States value straightforward communication—the direct approach—and may become impatient with time spent in lengthy relationship building before "getting down to business."

To become an effective multicultural communicator, keep an open mind and learn as much as possible about your own cultural identity and biases and become familiar with other cultures, beliefs, and customs. Individuals within a culture vary although many have similar tastes in food and clothing and hold common values and possess similar attitudes, opinions, and beliefs. To achieve effective multicultural communication, go beyond stereotypes and learn about the cultural background of individuals with whom you are communicating. With the myriad ethnic backgrounds of people with whom you work and do business, how is it possible to communicate effectively? Keep a few basic guidelines in mind and continue to learn about different ethnic and racial cultures.

Gender

Organizations in the United States have made significant progress in valuing and promoting women in the workplace, but barriers to advancement persist for women in some businesses. In 2000, census figures showed that approximately 80 percent of women between the ages of 25 and 54 worked full time in a salaried position. Figure

[4] Geert Hofstede's Cultural Value Dimensions, retrieved July 4, 2002, from *http://www2.andrews.edu/~tidwell/bsad560/Hofstede.html*

2.3 shows percentages of men and women in selected occupations in the civilian workforce as of March 2000.

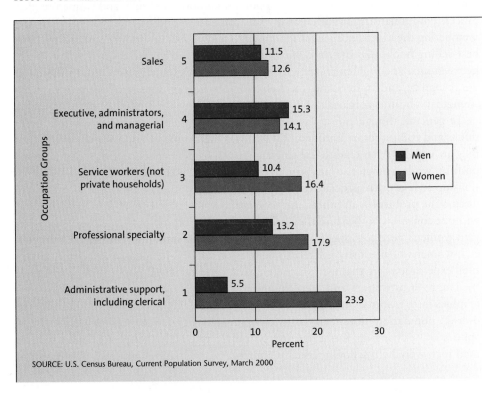

FIGURE 2.3
Selected Occupation Groups of the Employed Civilian Population by Sex: March 2000 (Percent of employed civilians aged 16 and older)

SOURCE: U.S. Census Bureau, Current Population Survey, March 2000

The numbers of men still predominate in a number of professional highly paid fields such as engineering and science. However, companies such as IBM recognize the need to appeal to women and minorities for the engineering and information technology workforce. In a competitive market for high-tech talent, increasing and retaining the number of women and minorities has become a priority. IBM has added initiatives to seek diversity when filling technology positions. With a minority population in the United States of 83 million people who have buying power of more than $1 trillion,

NOTE 2.15
Customers expect to see people like themselves at every level of the business.

IBM's vice president of workforce diversity in Armonk, New York, says that "Diversity is the bridge between the workplace and the marketplace; customers need to be able to look into IBM and see people like them at every level, from the mailroom to the boardroom."[5]

NOTE 2.16
Men and women's roles are changing; the glass ceiling has cracked.

Cultural stereotypes of men and women still exist, but traditional perceptions of men's and women's roles are changing. The glass ceiling persists as a barrier to advancement for women to some high-level positions, but the glass ceiling has cracked; more women are moving up the corporate ladder. Jeanne Lambert, CEO, Cerida Corp., has experienced some incidents of sexism. She gives an example of a sales meeting that she and a male sales executive held with a prospect who directed all questions to the male sales executive.[6] Her response to this incident was to ask the male sales executive and the male vice president to make further calls on the prospect to ensure that the company could win the account. She noted that being in the minority sometimes creates challenges but that "man or woman, CEOs face just one objective: growing a successful business. And doing so requires the use of all the tools and resources available to you, including both the men and women I work with on a day-to-day basis."

GENDER DIFFERENCES

Research documents some evidence of gender behavior differences. For example, a recent study from Stanford University supports the notion that men and women tend to process emotional stimuli differently, with women responding more intensely and remembering the experience longer than men.[7] John Gray, author of the *New York Times* best-selling book *Men Are from Mars, Women Are from Venus* notes that relationships between men and women are extremely complex; however, it is okay to be different if we recognize and understand the behavior of the opposite sex. Both sexes bring strengths to business organizations.

NOTE 2.17
In general, women and men communicate differently.

In general, though not always true, men and women are motivated by different things and communicate in different ways. This has nothing to do with whether or not they are equals.[8] Men tend to use language to assert independence and maintain group position while women use language to create connections and relationships. The relationship style is often associated with women. In decision making, women are likely to discuss the problem with others and seek input; whereas, men may make the decision without consultation because they believe it is their job to do so. Men sometimes regard women's need for input as inability to make a decision, not realizing that, in general, women's first priority is likely to be relationships while men's may be status. Cultural expectations are that men should be strong and decisive.

NOTE 2.18
More women than men earn bachelor's and master's degrees.

The roles of women and men change with each generation. Census 2000 demographics in the United States show females outnumbering males by six million. In the over-25 population more men than women are college graduates; however, this trend appears to be changing. In the age group from 25 to 29 a higher percentage of women than men were high school graduates and college graduates. Currently, 57 percent of

[5] Beth Stakepole, "Stopping Diversity from Walking Away: IBM Programs Work at Keeping Women and Minority Techies in House," *eWeek*, May 14, 2001, p. 63.

[6] Jeanne Lambert, "Estrogen vs. Testosterone: What Will Win in the Boardroom," *Boston Business Journal*, 21(32), September 14, 2001, p. 39.

[7] Paul Racer, Associated Press, "Why Women NEVER Forget Marital Spats," *Lexington Herald-Leader*, July 23, 2002, p. 1.

[8] Candy Tymson, "Business Communication: How to Bridge the Gender Gap," *Journal of Banking and Financial Services*, 115(3), June 2001, p. 18.

Sally Forth

college and university graduates across the United States are women.[9] More women than men receive bachelor's and master's degrees, but they receive fewer doctorate and professional degrees. The predominance of women earning master's degrees portends a shift in percentages of advanced degrees in favor of women. Having females better educated than males could have long-term implications for social change.

Deeply rooted cultural attitudes toward the appropriate roles of men and women vary markedly throughout the world. Although gender differences are de-emphasized in business in the United States, women—simply because of gender—find conducting business in some countries practically impossible. In general, developed nations are more accepting of women in business, while opportunities for women in lesser-developed nations may be practically nonexistent. Businesswomen must analyze carefully the cultural attitudes toward females in those countries where they want to do business. Based on this analysis, women must adjust their language and nonverbal behavior and project an indirect approach. In some countries and some situations, women may need to use men as intermediaries to do business. Men also must adapt to other cultures, although not to the extent required of women in countries with strict rules for women's appearance and propriety in public interactions.

SEXUAL HARASSMENT

Business communication between the sexes calls for a clear understanding of remarks and actions that could be construed as sexual harassment. **Sexual harassment** is unwelcome behavior of a sexual nature or with sexual overtones and may occur for men as well as women. Legally, either of the following conditions constitutes sexual harassment:[10]

- **Quid pro quo** (exchange something for something). Quid pro quo occurs when threats or rewards affect employment decisions based on whether the person submits to or rejects sexual demands.

- **Hostile environment.** This results from unwelcome sexual conduct that creates an offensive environment and interferes with a person's job performance or causes intimidation.

Quid pro quo is applicable when rejecting advances could be used for hiring, firing, promotion, or evaluation. Examples of quid pro quo would be a supervisor who persists

NOTE 2.19
Quid pro quo is an exchange of one thing for another.

---

[9] Michael A. Fletcher, "57 Percent of College Graduates Are Women," reprinted from the *Washington Post* by the *Lexington Herald-Leader*, June 26, 2002, p. 1.

[10] *Preventing Sexual Harassment*, 1999, and *How to Recognize and Prevent Sexual Harassment in the Workplace*, 2002, Old Saybrook, CT: Business & Legal Reports, Inc.

Sexual Harassment A single incident or isolated incidents of offensive sexual conduct or remarks generally do not create an abusive environment unless the conduct is quite severe. With quid pro quo a single incident is sufficient for action.

—Equal Employment Opportunity Commission

NOTE 2.20
In business interactions, avoid remarks or actions that have sexual connotations.

with unwelcome advances toward an employee, or an employee who threatens to use friendship with the supervisor to influence a coworker's evaluation if advances are rejected.

A hostile environment can be frequent interactions that have sexual connotations, such as comments and jokes with sexual innuendoes, as well as touching that may be viewed as inappropriate and of a sexual nature. Examples of problem behavior that could be interpreted as creating a hostile environment include a comment on clothing such as "That sweater really makes you look sexy," a joke with crude language or sexual content, an e-mail with a crude joke or pornography, a sexually graphic calendar posted in the workplace, or an action such as brushing against a coworker each time you walk by. A hostile environment depends on the feelings of the *recipient* about unwelcome behavior and the *extent* to which it becomes an intimidating or offensive work situation.

The victim of sexual harassment should make it clear that offensive comments or actions are unwelcome. This may be by verbal or nonverbal behaviors such as evident annoyance or pushing the person away. However, failure to do so does not absolve the offender of guilt as long as the sexual banter or horseplay was not responded to in kind. A victim of continued offensive behavior should promptly report the harassment to the proper person in the organization.

NOTE 2.21
The law requires a workplace free of sexual harassment.

Employers have a dual responsibility. They are held responsible not only for their own actions but also for ensuring a work environment free of sexual harassment. The relationship between an employer and employee or a supervisor and subordinate merits special care to avoid careless remarks, as well as intentional actions, that may be perceived as affecting the employment relationship or creating a hostile environment. When harassment comes from an employer or supervisor, the recipient may be reluctant to object to the behavior for fear of reprisals or the potential for a negative influence on employment decisions.

Litigation over sexual discrimination and sexual harassment constitutes one in five civil lawsuits in the U.S. federal courts.[11] This represents four times as many as ten years ago. In 1998 the Supreme Court ruled that employers have a stronger defense in discrimination suits if "they take proactive steps to control loss and manage risk." However, not all state courts apply this decision and sometimes hold that employers are "strictly liable for the harassing conduct of supervisors."

Fear of sexual harassment charges should not prevent forming friendships in the workplace. Respect for each individual is the key to positive relationships. Good-natured fun is different from sexual harassment. But keep in mind that what one person views as friendly banter another may view as harassment. Cultural background and experiences affect an individual's viewpoint on appropriate or inappropriate language and behavior.

NOTE 2.22
Avoid calling attention to race and ethnicity, gender, age, or physical limitations.

Just as is true with ethnicity and race, neither women nor men wish to be treated as "different" in the work setting. Most customers or coworkers prefer that special attention not be called to their differences—whether race, ethnicity, gender, age, or physical limitation.

[11] "Women in Suits: Sexual Discrimination," *The Economist*, March 2, 2002.

Workplace Communication Relevant to Gender

Avoid being overly sensitive or defensive about comments by others; referring to women or men in a disrespectful manner, making sexual remarks or behaving in a sexually suggestive manner that may be offensive to others, telling off-color jokes or e-mailing them to coworkers, using stereotypical expressions directed to women such as "girls in the office" or "helpless women" and words such as "stud" or "wimpy" to men, describing women or men by appearance or age rather than accomplishment, and overemphasizing differences between men and women.

Instead keep the emphasis on individuals rather than gender, refer to men or women with terminology that does not emphasize gender (*executive* or *manager* may be a better choice than businessman), keep sexual language and innuendoes out of the workplace, recognize the value and contributions of both men and women to the organization, and show respect for and sensitivity to the feelings and values of all persons with whom you work.

Age

Age is another core dimension of diversity that is perceived differently based on cultural background and experiences. Differences may exist in attitudes toward and treatment of persons perceived to be young or old. Some cultures associate aging with senility and loss of skills while others show special respect for wisdom gained by maturity and experience. Likewise, some groups may disregard young workers' abilities because of youth and inexperience.

One in five persons in the United States is 55 or older, compared to one in ten at the beginning of the 20th century. The Census Bureau projects that by 2010 the number will be one in four. This means that senior adults are an important consumer market. In addition, labor force projections reflect expectations that as the number of healthy seniors increases and the pool of younger workers decreases, persons over 55 will stay in the workforce longer than in previous years. Figure 2.4 shows census figures for labor force participation rates for men and women over 55.

NOTE 2.23
One in five people in the United States is 55 or over.

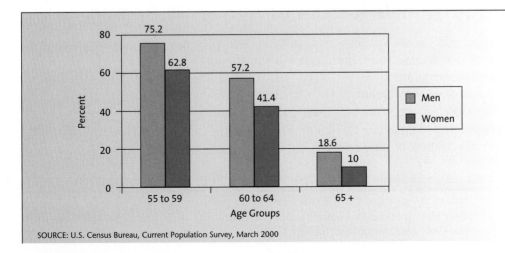

SOURCE: U.S. Census Bureau, Current Population Survey, March 2000

FIGURE 2.4
Workforce Participation Rates by Persons 55 and Older

(Percent of population in each age group)

The Age Discrimination in Employment Act of 1967 (ADEA) as amended in 1978 and 1986 prohibits forced retirement of employees and protects people over 40 from discrimination based on age. To help convince American companies of advantages to hiring older workers, the American Association of Retired Persons (AARP) conducts research and advocacy programs. In a population with fewer young persons entering the labor force, it is likely that companies will be looking for ways to hire and retain senior workers as well as young people.

In recent years some advertising firms have looked for young employees based on a presumption that senior citizens are out of touch with technology.[12] However, senior staff have important skills to contribute and can learn to use technology. Other businesses, such as accounting and management consultancy, reward long-term employees because clients are willing to pay higher fees for experience.

COMMUNICATION NOTE

Generation Communication Disconnect Is there a new generation gap? A disconnect between managers and their younger charges? Consider this real-life exchange, noted in a new book by consultants Lynne C. Lancaster and David Stillman. A middle-aged manager had come to the aid of a younger employee on a project. The cadet took the time to send a thank-you note, but it was an electronic version, which failed to impress his mentor. "I get a card that basically costs nothing and required no effort to send, after I gave so much," she groused. "Am I supposed to be flattered by that?"

—Andrea Sachs, "Generation Hex: A New Book Identifies Four Age Groups Warring at Work," *Time*, *159*(10), March 11, 2002, p. Y22.

NOTE 2.24
Focus on individuals, not their age.

Think of colleagues and customers as individuals, regardless of age. Telling a customer over 50 that she needs to choose an item with large print so that she can see it easily is unlikely to sell the item unless she has mentioned a problem with eyesight. Also, asking, "Now that you have tried this product, what do the elderly think about it" is likely to be received negatively.

TIPS AND HINTS

Communication That Focuses on Individuals instead of Age

Avoid using terminology that refers to old age, infirmity, youth, inexperience, or that depersonalizes the individual; using terms such as elderly, aged, old, geriatric, girl, boy, young man or young woman; pitying or being overly concerned for effects of age; talking to seniors or young workers using a tone or language that implies they are children; or treating them differently from others.

Instead refer to persons without reference to age; if age references are required, use age categories such as employees under 30 or over 55 or use terms such as seniors; respect their strengths and abilities; and treat everyone respectfully as individuals.

[12] Jeremy Barwick, "Age of Experience: The Marketing Industry Only Has Eyes for Young Recruits But at What Cost," *The Financial Times*, February 19, 2002, p. 40.

At the other end of the working age spectrum, young people, especially in their 20s, may have trouble getting a first job because they are viewed as immature, although they can bring enthusiasm and new ideas to the work setting. In the workplace, thoughtless remarks that refer to youth or inexperience show disrespect for young workers. Expecting them to run errands or do tasks that no one else wants to do is inconsiderate, and comments to young customers about unusual dress, body art, or makeup may be offensive.

Individuals with Disabilities

U.S. census figures show approximately one in five adults has some type of disability; among those aged 45 to 54, 23 percent have a disability. In the workforce, disabilities usually mean one or more of the following physically challenging conditions:

- Use of a wheelchair, cane, crutches, or walker
- Difficulty in seeing, hearing, speaking, or performing physical activities

Individuals with physically challenging or limiting conditions frequently are patronized and judged based on ignorance and irrational fears and concerns. Attention is given to their disabilities rather than their abilities. Passage of the Americans with Disabilities Act (ADA) was a major step toward removing unreasonable barriers to these individuals. The intent of the legislation is to help prevent discrimination against qualified employees who have physically challenging conditions and to make facilities accessible to persons who have disabilities. The ADA prohibits discrimination in employment against a qualified individual with a disability and includes a provision that reasonable accommodations must be made for workers who have disabilities when such accommodations would not impose undue hardship on the organization. In addition, public accommodations such as hotels, restaurants, theaters, stores, offices, transit stations, museums, parks, schools, social service agencies and gyms must not discriminate against individuals with disabilities.

NOTE 2.25
Focus on abilities, not disabilities.

COMMUNICATION NOTE

The ADA Says . . . No individual shall be discriminated against on the basis of disability in the full and equal enjoyment of the goods, services, facilities, privileges, advantages, or accommodations of any place of public accommodation. In the workplace, reasonable accommodation is required for workers with disabilities when such accommodations would not impose an *undue hardship.*

—Americans with Disabilities Act, *ADA in Brief*

Effective communication avoids pitying or patronizing physically challenged employees or customers. Most people are well intentioned but do not know how to respond to persons who have disabilities. Individuals with disabling conditions may be limited in some functional aspect but often can compensate for the disability through the use of devices or personal strengths. Observable evidence of a disability does not imply incompetence; instead, it may be simply a limiting factor that can be overcome through various means. Recognize the strengths of individuals and realize that all individuals deserve the same respect and professionalism in business communication.

Communicating with Individuals Who Have Physical Limitations

Avoid using terms such as handicapped or disabled person, AIDS victim, the disabled, cripple, and deaf and dumb; leaning on a wheelchair or pushing the wheelchair unless asked to do so; giving assistance to any individual with a disability without asking first; pretending you understand what was said if you did not; and treating individuals as children or as incompetent.

Instead emphasize the individual's ability rather than the disability; if required to refer to the limiting condition, use terms such as *a person who uses a wheelchair, person living with AIDS or HIV, persons with disabilities,* or *a person with a speech disability*; these terms keep the focus on the individual. Some

limitations may require communication adjustments. To get on the same eye level when talking more than a few minutes with a person in a wheelchair, sit during the conversation. Use verbal cues to give direction for a person who is blind—verbalize the stair, curb, or a chair location (*Be ready to step down; the stairs are three steps in front of you.*); offer assistance by letting a blind person grasp your left arm. When talking with a person who is deaf, enunciate clearly to permit lip reading; use a combination of gestures, facial expressions, and note passing; if necessary, use an interpreter but speak directly to the person rather than the interpreter.

Guidelines for Multicultural Business Communication

LEARNING OBJECTIVE

Explain basic guidelines for communicating in a multicultural environment.

③

Respect for and sensitivity to the feelings and cultural behavior of others is a basic premise for effective communication and is consistent with the you–viewpoint as described in Chapter 1. Analyzing communication receivers in a multicultural environment extends to understanding that cultural variations exist in languages, values and beliefs, symbols and gestures, religions, and social norms.

NOTE 2.26
With political correctness, use good judgment and mutual respect.

Recent attention to altering language and changing traditional word usage to avoid offensive language (referred to as **political correctness**) is, at times, an overreaction intended to conform to expectations of others. Good judgment and mutual respect should prevail. No one should be overly sensitive to words if their good intent is evident. You must recognize that no one is completely objective because cultural background and experiences affect expectations of others and behavior toward others.

Your goal for effective multicultural communication is to achieve normal business communication without cultural prejudice. This means having the ability to communicate comfortably and naturally while eliminating barriers by understanding cultural differences. This section gives guidelines for improving multicultural communication.

Review Business Communication Principles

In any multicultural communication situation, the basic business communication knowledge you have gained already will apply. A review of that knowledge should be your first step in preparing to communicate in a multicultural business environment.

NOTE 2.27
Apply principles of business communication.

As you will recall, the goals of business communication given in Chapter 1 include achieving a shared meaning between sender and receiver, achieving an appropriate receiver response, establishing a favorable relationship between sender and receiver, and building goodwill for your organization. These goals will be a part of your multicultural business communication effort. In addition, the communication process will be the same—analyze your receiver and use the you–viewpoint, select the appropriate form of message, provide for feedback, and remove communication barriers.

Analyze Your Own Culture

Remember that a starting point in relating effectively to others is to know your own culture. The next step for successful multicultural communication is understanding how others view your culture. People everywhere use comparisons, evaluations, and categories to assimilate and understand the messages they receive. This process, called **perception**, uses personal knowledge and experience to interpret and give meaning to the world. Understanding other cultural perceptions is crucial to communication.

Understanding the practices of your own culture will help you to understand and relate successfully to the practices of other cultures. The following analysis describes some perceptions about Americans (a term used worldwide to refer to a citizen of the United States). This mainstream culture consists of people who prefer to communicate in the English language and who are inclined to use the direct plan of communication (versus the indirect plan). Americans are generally friendly and informal. They are likely to greet you by your first name and shake your hand with a firm grip and pumping action. They tend to have a strong sense of humor and laugh and smile frequently.[13]

Americans are inclined to be time conscious, frank, and outspoken. Eye contact while conversing is considered a sign of strength and honesty. Americans tend to have a greater need for personal space than do some other cultures—usually keeping at least two to three feet minimum distance between themselves and others—and tend to limit personal touching of each other in public. An individual's freedom to achieve is valued highly; and work, activity, and progress are valued in their own right.

Recognize that these characteristics generally attributed to Americans do not apply to many other cultures nor do they apply to all Americans. In some cultures, these characteristics are regarded as offensive. As you communicate with people from different cultures, you will note common basic human needs: physical, safety and security, and social affiliation needs. However, there are sharp differences in values, tastes, beliefs, and behaviors.

Be Open to and Accepting of Other Cultures

As you think about your own culture, you begin to sense that it represents one way—and not the only way—to believe and to do things. This understanding is essential in order to

NOTE 2.28
Analyze and recognize customary practices of your own culture.

NOTE 2.29
Americans generally prefer the direct style of communication.

---

[13] This cultural analysis was based on *Culturegram* © 1999; Lillian H. Chaney and Jeanette S. Martin, *International Business Communication*, 2000; Roger E. Axtell, *The Do's and Taboos of International Trade*, 1994.

communicate successfully with people of other cultures who believe and do things differently. With your involvement in a diverse multicultural business environment, you will want to adopt an open, accepting attitude toward the differences in others.

NOTE 2.30
Learn about and accept the differences of other cultures.

How can you be open and accepting? Be open to learning about the other culture with which you are interacting. Be open to different foods, to different ways of doing things, and to different beliefs. For example, in a number of countries the value placed on time differs from the importance placed on it in the United States. In the United States, people are time conscious and rush to meet deadlines and appointments; in some other countries such as Mexico and Latin America, the pace is slower and time may not be a priority. Be accepting of other people's needs for indirectness in communicating (as in Asia), and for the use of titles and last names instead of first names (as in Europe). Be open to and accepting of the different ways people of other cultures think and feel. Learn to tolerate and cope with ambiguity. Understand that information can be interpreted in different ways.

NOTE 2.31
Be careful not to misread communication because of cultural differences.

Be patient, but do not be condescending. Be understanding of differences. Do not rush to an early judgment about the way a conversation or business deal is going. You may be misreading a communication situation because of cultural differences. Ask questions. Ask if you are being understood. Obtain feedback.

Your success in multicultural communication will depend largely on your ability to be open to and accepting of differences in others. Only then can you communicate the you–viewpoint without cultural prejudice.

Learn About Other Cultures and Apply What You Learn

Learning and applying what you learn about different cultures is the *key guideline* for effective multicultural communication. There is, of course, much to be learned about another culture. Do not let the volume of information overwhelm you. Anything you learn will be helpful and will strengthen your ability to communicate.

Culture is an abstract and complex concept that has interrelated and intertwined elements. Because much of culture is hidden from view, cultural differences can be intricate, subtle, and difficult to learn. Cultural understanding consists of both factual knowledge and interpretive knowledge.

NOTE 2.32
Learning about other cultures and knowing their languages improve communication.

A basic recommendation in learning about other cultures is to learn as much as you can of that culture's language. Ideally, you would be able to speak and write the other culture's language fluently. This may not be possible, but learn as much as you can. Learn at least greetings, courtesy words, and the basic positive and negative signals. Learn the few basic phrases that represent typical words used in your communication. For example, learn how to say "We want to do business with you," if that is appropriate.

You should not only learn as much as possible of the other culture's language, but you should also use what you know in your oral and written messages. Your receivers will appreciate your efforts. They will be understanding and accepting of deficiencies in your use of their language.

NOTE 2.33
Learn about habits, negotiation, and acceptable and nonacceptable behaviors.

A second aspect of learning about another culture is to learn as much as possible about the people of that culture. This aspect of learning includes a wide range of information from how the people think to the foods they eat. Understanding, as well as recognizing the ways people think, is also important. Try to learn how people relate to each other, their food and apparel preferences, the hours that comprise their workday and days for their workweek, their negotiation style, their business ethics, acceptable and unacceptable topics of discussion, and acceptable and unacceptable nonverbal gestures. When you have acquired information about the other culture, analyze it in the following ways: How is it similar to your culture? How is it different? How can you best bridge these differences? By applying the information gained in this analysis—and with practice—you can become an effective multicultural communicator.

Consider Language Needs

Most multicultural business communication is conducted in the English language. This is true not only in this country but also throughout the world.

NOTE 2.34
Keep the message simple: speak clearly and precisely.

The extensive use of English as the primary multicultural business language is fortunate for English-speaking citizens; however, it is important to recognize that for most people in the world English is a second language. As mentioned earlier, U.S. census data show this to be true also of many people who live and work in this country. For people for whom English is not their primary language, their degree of facility with the English language and their understanding of its context will govern communication effectiveness. Apply the following Tips and Hints to avoid miscommunication.

TIPS AND HINTS

Communicating with Individuals Who Speak English as a Second Language

Avoid jargon, slang, and colloquial expressions that may be unfamiliar such as *back to square one, piece of cake, red tape, ballpark figure,* and *the bottom line*; accents or speech mannerisms that may be a communication barrier; speaking too rapidly; or speaking so slowly and simply that your language becomes childlike and condescending.

Instead recognize that language capabilities vary; make language adjustments based on the individual's language skill; enunciate clearly and pronounce words precisely; speak at a normal, conversational volume.

Multinational or Global Business Communication

Business operations across national boundaries require a greater adaptation to cultural boundaries than conducting business within one country. The terms *multinational, international,* and *global business* often are used as synonymous terms. As noted at the beginning of this chapter, multinational rather than international is used here to emphasize the prevalence of businesses that operate in multiple locations outside of the home country. Global operations may be distinguished from operations that are international or multinational, particularly from the perspective of global marketing. According to this perspective, **multinational marketing** results from extensive asset development abroad with operations in a number of foreign countries and strategies adapted to each specific location.[14] Conversely, **global marketing** creates and integrates one strategy for a product, service, or company that is flexible enough to be applied throughout the world market. Although technology facilitates communication across national boundaries, employees may travel to sites in other countries to do business, live in them to do

LEARNING OBJECTIVE
④ Describe challenges and key strategies for multinational and global business communication.

NOTE 2.35
Multinational marketing uses a strategy for each location; global marketing uses one worldwide.

[14] Jeannet Hennessey, *Global Marketing Strategies*, Boston: Houghton Mifflin, 2001.

business, or a combination of both. Multinational and global business operations usually have executives or other employees who operate outside of the home country at least part of their time.

NOTE 2.36
Business hours and
workdays vary among
countries.

Differences in business hours affect conducting business across national borders. You might be able to leave a voice-mail message, but you cannot talk to a person on the telephone, for instance, if that business is not open. Time variations exist because of the international time zones. A 6- to 9-hour time difference between European or Asian countries and the United States allows little or no overlap in normal business hours. Also, many countries in warmer climates tend to close their offices in the middle of the day for the main meal and for rest.

The days of the week that businesses operate vary around the world. In the United States most business offices operate Monday through Friday. In Korea the workweek is Monday through Saturday, and possibly Sunday. In contrast the workweek in Saudi Arabia and other Islamic countries is Saturday through Wednesday, with Thursday and Friday as the days off. Friday is the Islamic day of rest and worship.

*Office hours in businesses
around the world vary
considerably, making
transaction of business
difficult. For example,
when it is 8 A.M. in New
York City, it is 10 P.M. the
next day in Beijing, China.*

©A. RAMEY/PHOTOEDIT

NOTE 2.37
Doing business outside
your home country
requires behavior
changes.

Effective communication when managing differences of country, culture, language, and values from a location outside your home country calls for changes in assumptions that you make about yourself and others. This creates both stimulating and frustrating experiences.[15] Old ways don't work and things take longer, you have to think about everything, nothing is simple, some things don't make sense, and you have difficulty understanding others and being understood.

The remainder of this chapter provides information pertinent to multinational and global business communication and gives examples of communicating and conducting business with four major trading partners of the United States. Two of these countries, Japan and Germany, are industrial, long-standing trade partners. The other two, China

---

[15] Morgan W. McCall, Jr., and George P. Hollenbeck, *Developing Global Executives*, Boston: Harvard Business School Press, 2002.

and Mexico, are emerging as major players in world trade. Information in these examples should be used only generally because national conditions change rapidly, and the world marketplace is complex. Successful multinational business communication will take place only when you continue to learn about the countries and the individuals with whom you are doing business. You can learn about other countries through Internet research at **http://www.infoplease.com/countries/html** or **http://www.cia.gov/cia/publications/ factbook/geos/ja.html**. Another Internet source can be found using the Yahoo! directory for *countries* under *Regional* (**http://dir.yahoo.com/regional/countries**). In addition, you can find information about specific countries using an encyclopedia.

Communicating in Japan

Japan consists of four main islands and has numerous business operations that cross boundaries with the United States. The land is mountainous, and most of the population lives in only one fifth of the total area. Japan, the second largest world economy,[16] is a major economic world player and has experienced the stress inherent in a culture with an emphasis on work and highly structured social institutions. Although perceived by others as a major power in the global economy, the Japanese feel vulnerable to outside forces. The country has no oil, has few raw materials, and imports most of its meat and grain.

When conducting business with the Japanese, you should be gracious and diplomatic. In Japan, greeting your host by bowing and then shaking hands are important gestures. Because status and hierarchy are important in Japan, exchanging business cards helps to define relationships. Job titles assist in judging relative status, and businesspeople meeting for the first time exchange business cards almost without speaking. The cards contain names, titles, and organizations. They should be printed in Japanese on one side and English on the other and should be presented with both hands. Once occupational statuses

NOTE 2.38
In Japan status and relationships affect how people communicate.

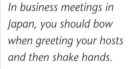

In business meetings in Japan, you should bow when greeting your hosts and then shake hands.

---

[16] The cultural analysis was based on Linda Schneider and Arnold Silverman, *Global Sociology*, 2000; Eric N. Berkowitz, Roger A. Kerin, Steven W. Hartley, and William Rudelius, *Marketing*, 6th ed., and Jeannet Hennessey, *Global Market Strategies*, 2001.

are established in the meeting, the Japanese know how to treat others based on each individual's status. Assessing higher or lower status determines how low you should bow in greeting or taking leave and the words used to address others. The Japanese language structure provides different verbs and pronouns to use based on the status, age, gender, and intimacy of the person spoken to or referred to and the speaker.

NOTE 2.39
Punctuality is important for appointments in Japan.

Appointments should be arranged in advance, and punctuality is important for both business and social engagements. Japanese prefer indirectness in business transactions and may seem to agree with you to avoid offending you. Do not let this courtesy mislead you into believing that agreement is set. The agreement is not finalized until it is written and signed. Businesspeople in Japan want to spend time in the meeting clarifying the relationships of the trading partners and discussing the details of the business arrangement. Many times the actual terms are agreed to during informal social gatherings.

Japanese tend to be modest, respectful of superiors, and loyal to their organizations. They value their privacy and resent direct questioning about their personal life. Saving face is important, and *face* means the image the person has in his or her social groups. Positive comments add to social standing, and negative comments lower it. Most Japanese prefer being called with their last name followed by the word *san;* for example, *Tanaka-san* for *Mr. Tanaka.* Courtesy, humility, patience, and relationship building are key to successful communication in Japan.

Communicating in Germany

Germany is Western Europe's richest and most populous nation and, therefore, is a key member of the continent's economic, political, and defense organizations.[17] Although ranking third (after the United States and Japan) as the most technologically powerful economy, Germany struggles with high non-wage benefit costs for workers, long-term unemployment problems, and large outlays for social security. Modernization and integration of the eastern Germany economy with western Germany continues to present challenges. However, the restructuring of corporations and growing capital markets are expected to enable Germany to meet the challenges.

NOTE 2.40
Germans are formal and direct; they do not appreciate social small talk.

Germans are known for their seriousness, love of order, and respect for authority. They place a high value on hard work and social responsibility. Promptness, formality, and getting right to business are important for business meetings. Social small talk is not appreciated. They appreciate directness, logic, and individualism; however, they see it as their duty to obey laws and correct others that they see disobeying a law. For example, they use an honor system for deposit of bus fares, and passengers will hiss a stranger who fails to put in the money. Germans like to make all rules explicit and do

COMMUNICATION NOTE

Germans Respond Coldly to Wal-Mart Wal-Mart, the world's number one retailer, ran into culture shock when it opened the super-sized, friendly stores in Germany. German customers recoiled when employees greeted them in the aisles. Customers, used to fending for themselves, resisted when cashiers tried to pack their purchases in free plastic bags. They viewed the "synthetic friendliness" as an attempt to sell something.

Based on an article by Daniel Rubin, Knight Ridder Newspapers, December 2000

---

[17] The cultural analysis was based on *CIA Government Factbook*, retrieved 8/10/02 from *http://www.cia.gov/cia/publications*, and Linda Schneider and Arnold Silverman, *Global Sociology*, 2000.

not rely on informal understandings. Businesspeople require a great deal of technical information before making a decision. Germans tend to be outspoken and blunt and see their behavior as simple honesty.

Business appointments should be made well in advance. Titles and last names should be used. Greetings mean firm handshakes with all of those present. Business cards are exchanged—English on one side and German on the other. In meetings, focus on agreed-on goals. Germans are likely to be inquisitive and want to hear the supporting evidence for a new idea or procedure. They enjoy vigorous discussion based on logical reasoning. First, you may want to present a new proposal to the top German executive for approval. Then, that executive can either present the proposal to other Germans on your behalf or endorse your presentation after you have made it. This approval by a German executive can increase the credibility of your proposal with other Germans and reduce the amount of time spent justifying it.

NOTE 2.41
Germans expect technical details and supporting justification for a proposal.

Communicating in China

China is emerging as a major force in the world economy.[18] In 2001 the United States was the leading market for Chinese exports and ranked fourth in the percentage of imports supplied to China. The country is called the *People's Republic of China* or simply *China*. Hong Kong is a part of China; however, the relationship with Taiwan is a sensitive political issue and should not be mentioned in conversation.

Businesses must be adept in communicating with their Chinese counterparts if they wish to take advantage of their increasing consumer buying power. Chinese are formal and use the full title of guests for introductions. A slight bow accompanied by a handshake is appropriate when meeting. Business cards should be printed in English on one side and Chinese on the other and presented with both hands.

NOTE 2.42
In China use formality, full titles, and a bow with a handshake.

Businesspeople should schedule appointments in China in advance and arrive at meetings on time. Chinese customarily take a long time to make up their minds, so do not expect a quick business decision. Even after what appears to be a final decision, be prepared for a change in plans.

Western businesspeople may have difficulty understanding Chinese rituals of leave taking. In the Western culture, a few minutes of small talk generally precede leaving; however, Chinese may stand up suddenly and say "I'm sorry to have taken up so much of your time" or "Tomorrow you will have to get up early." Relating the reason for leaving to the other person may seem odd but results from their orientation to the needs, wishes, and expectations of others. The Chinese show a high level of courtesy and modesty.

Yes or *no* in the Chinese language does not always mean that. Instead of showing agreement, *Yes* means *OK, I want to respect you and not offend you.* Instead of *no* Chinese will say *impossible, perhaps,* or *maybe.* Common phrases are *we will consider it* or *we will study it.* Their communication style is indirect, particularly when conveying negative messages. They may use a claim of ignorance to gain information. Frequently, they let it be known that they are negotiating with the competition and may sign contracts but may not act as if they are bound by the agreement.

NOTE 2.43
Chinese prefer indirect communication, and *yes* or *no* vary in meaning.

Communication strategies include using an intermediary to moderate discussion—one who can be neutral, using firmness only when necessary, referring to the

---

[18] The cultural analysis was based on Linda Schneider and Arnold Silverman, *Global Sociology*, 2000; Boye Lafayette De Mente, "Asian Business Codewords," *Chinese Etiquette and Ethics in Business,* July 2002; and Wei-lin Dou and George William Clark, Jr., "Appreciating the Diversity in Multicultural Communication Styles," *Business Forum, (54)*8, Winter-Spring 2000.

relationship rather than to self, and being sensitive to the nonverbal signals that you send. Recognize that business in China has a social and political as well as economic content and be knowledgeable and flexible in adapting to the environment. Be honest and frank in responses. If any misunderstanding arises, address it or the Chinese will assume that you approve. Be sincere and show goodwill but be consistent in making points and positions clear. Say nice things about China and your country and emphasize that a successful relationship will be beneficial for both countries. When making a presentation, prepare summary copies in both the English and Chinese languages to distribute at the beginning of the meeting.

Communicating in Mexico

Mexico borders the United States; and, as a participant in the North American Free Trade Agreement (NAFTA), has attracted considerable international investment with increased output into the U.S. free trade market. Mexicans are part of the Hispanic subculture and with a growing Hispanic population in the United States, Spanish and English labels are beginning to appear on products in parts of the western and southwestern United States. With Mexico's proximity and its status as a major emerging market, the importance of effective business communication with Mexico is great. To understand and relate to Mexico's business goals and procedures call for an understanding of its history and core cultural values.[19]

Mexico is a collectivist country with high value placed on the family. Families are the center of Mexican culture; the extended family may include cousins, loyal employees, and servants, as well as children. The welfare of the community takes precedence over the welfare of an individual. Relationships are important to Mexicans, and trust is critical to business relationships. In Mexico, make personal contact and establish rapport to initiate business. Extended face-to-face communication is important for establishing relationships and building trust.

Mexican Spanish is elegant and melodious with long, florid phrasing that expresses respect, honor, affection, and emotion. Business communication is likely to be eloquent and personal. Mexican business documents carry a personal tone and are less precise in giving specific goals, requests, or completion dates. Figure 2.5 is an example from a Mexican business letter that illustrates this personal tone and florid phrasing. Mexicans accept uncertainty as a part of life and believe in the importance of today because history shows the uncertainty of tomorrow. Promises and long-term agreements might not be viewed as sincere commitments. An acceptance of power differences based on social and economic class, as well as rank, age, and gender, results in differential treatment from businesspeople when the communicators are from different power strata.

From this description, you can see a contrast between the way business is conducted in Mexico and the U.S. preference for a bottom-line, direct, specific, and efficient conduct of business transactions. However, changes are taking place in communication practices by some Mexican businesses due to the influence of corporations such as General Electric and IBM who conduct operations in Mexico. In addition, current education texts cover some business communication principles similar to those taught in the United States. Even with these changes, building relationships through personal contact continues to be important.

[19] This cultural analysis was based on Linda Schneider and Arnold Silverman, *Global Sociology*, 2000, and Elizabeth Tebeaux, "Designing Written Business Communication Along the Shifting Cultural Continuum: The New Face of Mexico," *Journal of Business and Technical Communication, 13*(1), January 1999.

Emphasizes relationship

First Paragraph

Because of the relationship that exists between us, it is my pleasure to greet you and present for your consideration the special services in Consulting and Executive Training that are offered by Grupo Empresarial SIA, which have as their object to support your organization in the achievement of the objectives of competitiveness and leadership that are demanded by the economic and social environment in which we actually live.

Ending Paragraph

We would feel very honored to have the opportunity to discuss personally with you the solutions we would be able to propose to you, and by which we would be in contact with you or the person that you indicate to us, in order to agree upon an interview in this respect.

Shows courtesy and honor

Indicates need for personal contact

From Elizabeth Tebeaux, "Designing Written Business Communication Along the Shifting Cultural Continuum," *Journal of Business and Technical Communication*, 13(1), January 1999, p. 65. Reprinted with permission.

FIGURE 2.5
Sample Beginning and Ending Paragraphs of a Mexican Business Letter

Communication Strategies for Multinational and Global Business

The brief sketches of four trading partners of the United States, as described in the previous section, introduced you to some of the traditional culture and communication strategies for conducting business in or with these countries. Remember that these descriptions are too general to capture the experience of conducting business as an *expatriate*, someone living and working in a country different from your own, or even as a *transnational* who travels abroad to work across national borders for short periods of time. Companies with operations outside the home country must have executives who can conduct business in countries other than their own.

4 LEARNING OBJECTIVE
Describe challenges and key strategies for multinational and global business communication.

NOTE 2.46
Expatriates live in a foreign country; transnationals travel across national borders.

Surveys of 101 global executives from 36 different countries gathered their perspectives of strategies for succeeding in global business. According to one executive, "Managing in another culture requires that you dig out the local culture and incorporate it to give credibility to what you do."[20] Numerous contextual and organizational factors make business communication for global executives complex and uncertain but not impossible. Figure 2.6 summarizes advice from these global executives identified as successful by their companies.

NOTE 2.47
Global business communication is complex and uncertain but not impossible.

[20] Morgan W. McCall, Jr., and George P. Hollenbeck, *Developing Global Executives*, Boston: Harvard Business School Press, 2002.

FIGURE 2.6
Advice from Global Executives

- **Develop your expertise.** Focus early on building technical, function, or specific business skills.
- **Go early.** Take advantage of opportunities for task forces, business travel, and international and education experiences.
- **Just do it—take a risk.** Be willing to move from the comfortable to the uncomfortable, from the familiar to the strange. If you want to do it, just do it!
- **Don't confine yourself to business.** Experience the cultural variety outside the office. Understand the context in which you work.
- **Be open to learning.** The *what* may be the same but the *how* will be different. Be adaptable and open to learn.
- **Focus on business results.** Don't forget that performance matters—no cultural excuses for business failures.
- **Maintain your networks.** Keep your contacts with colleagues, within and outside of your organization. Well-maintained networks are a safety net.
- **Take care of your family.** Distance from home makes maintaining supportive relationships especially important to personal and business success.

Adapted from Morgan W. McCall, Jr., and George P. Hollenbeck, *Developing Global Executives*, Harvard Business School Press, 2002, pp. 206–210. (Reprinted with permission)

Communicating effectively in multinational business environments requires flexibility, a desire to learn, the ability to be sensitive and adapt to practices and traditions in a foreign setting, and the ability to exhibit appropriate sensitivity to the many differences in overseas locations. In addition, temper firmness and business savvy with grace, kindness, and a sense of humor; build relationships and friendships; and network through international societies and trade groups.

Guidelines for Working with Interpreters

LEARNING OBJECTIVE 5
Describe guidelines for working with an interpreter or translator to overcome language barriers.

If English is your only language and your receiver does not know English, then you must use an interpreter for oral communication. Unless expatriates or transnational executives are proficient in the languages of countries where they do business, they will likely use interpreters in some of their business interactions. Keep these considerations in mind when working with an interpreter.

AVOID COMPLEX LANGUAGE AND FOCUS ON THE RECEIVER

When working with an interpreter, avoid long introductory phrases, parenthetical elements, interjections, and complex and compound sentences. As you prepare to use an interpreter, give special attention to the parts of your message that may be difficult to convey. Develop clear illustrations of these difficult parts to help ensure your receiver's understanding.

NOTE 2.48
When using an interpreter, talk directly to the person addressed, not to the interpreter.

Avoid talking to your interpreter during your meeting. Talk directly to your receiver while keeping your interpreter in the corner of your eye. Permit your interpreter to explain your remarks if necessary, and encourage your receiver to ask questions if you sense you are not being understood clearly. Remain calm and poised. Concentrate on your receiver's interests and not on yourself or your interpreter.

PRACTICE WITH YOUR INTERPRETER

If possible, learn your interpreter's preferred ways of operating—in complete thought units, in short phrases, or word by word. You and your interpreter will be a team. Practice improves any team effort, so you will want to rehearse your cooperative effort with an interpreter.

Guidelines for Working with Translators

Translators are used for written messages that are received or sent in a language other than your own. Translation from one language to another requires a skilled, qualified translator. The following guidelines can be helpful.

SELECTION OF QUALIFIED TRANSLATORS

Most people who have read instructions accompanying products manufactured overseas know the difficulty of translating from one language to another—generally, languages cannot be translated verbatim. The translator must be both competent in the languages involved and qualified in the subject matter so that the *meaning of the message* is conveyed to the receiver, *not just the words*. In addition, computerized language translation software can be of value when translating letters, memos, sales literature, and other business messages. Speech recognition and translation software can assist in customizing documents in a particular language.

NOTE 2.49
Translators must convey the meaning, not just the words.

PROVIDE FOR BACK TRANSLATION OF YOUR WRITTEN MESSAGES

Check for translation errors; that is, have a second translator convert the message back into English for verification of its meaning. Back translation is a technique for obtaining essential feedback and preventing many translation errors.

Summary of Learning Objectives

Explain why creating a multicultural workforce and communicating effectively with diverse cultures are important for businesses.

Population diversity in this country is increasing. This cultural diversity, as well as more business communication across national borders, makes effective communication with people from different cultures essential to business success. Profitability is affected by business initiatives directed toward employing and retaining a diverse staff that can communicate both internally and externally with individuals representing multicultural and multinational needs and interests.

Describe core dimensions of culture in the workplace and how a multicultural environment affects communication.

Ethnicity, race, gender, age, and individuals with disabilities represent five core cultural dimensions in the population and in the workplace. The cultural background of experiences for each of these groups of people, along with cultural variations within each group, affects their beliefs, values, behaviors, and perceptions of others. Assuming the you–viewpoint and understanding the receiver's needs and interests are critical to avoid miscommunication and to achieve the desired message response. Learning about these core dimensions in a multicultural environment will help avoid miscommunication and improve your ability to relate to individual needs and interests.

③ Explain basic guidelines for communicating in a multicultural business environment.

Effective communicators must apply business communication principles—analyze your receiver and use the you–viewpoint, select the appropriate form of message, provide for feedback, and remove communication barriers. A lack of understanding of culture is a communication barrier. To improve communication in a multicultural business environment, first you need to understand your own culture and how it affects your perceptions of others. This helps you to be open to and accepting of other cultures and to recognize that different ways of doing things are not wrong and that each individual has abilities that can make contributions in the conduct of business. In addition, you should continue learning about different cultures and how to overcome cultural and language barriers to effective communication.

④ Describe challenges and key strategies for multinational and global business communication.

Multinational and global business operations increase the complexity and uncertainty of communication. Communicating across national boundaries usually means not only written and oral communication through telecommunication and mail service but also traveling abroad to do business as a transnational or living and working as an expatriate in another country. Doing business in or with another country presents many challenges to your familiar habits and ways of doing things. This requires learning how to interact in a different social environment as well as how to accommodate local business behavior and communication practices. Key strategies include developing your expertise in working with other cultures by being open to opportunities to do so, maintaining focus on business performance, and experiencing the cultural environment to understand the context of business. In addition, develop networks of colleagues inside and outside the business setting, while maintaining concern for your own personal support networks.

⑤ Describe guidelines for working with an interpreter or translator to overcome language barriers.

When using an interpreter, keep the language simple and develop clear illustrations of difficult parts of the message. Talk to the receiver and permit your interpreter to explain remarks. View you and your interpreter as a team and practice together to achieve the best results. For written messages, select a translator competent both in the language and how the receiver will interpret the words. Translation involves more than verbatim word conversion. Use of a second translator to convert the message back to English can help verify its meaning.

Discussion Questions

1. How does employing and retaining a diverse staff benefit a business? (Objective 1)
2. Define multicultural business communication and multinational business communication. (Objectives 1 and 2)
3. List the five core dimensions of cultural diversity and explain them. Why is understanding these cultural dimensions important to business communication? (Objective 2)
4. Explain how cultural backgrounds and experiences affect business communication. (Objective 2)
5. What is the goal of multicultural communication? Discuss the meaning of this goal. (Objectives 2 and 3)
6. Describe four guidelines for effective multicultural business communication. (Objective 3)
7. Explain the terms stereotype, cultural relativism, and ethnocentrism. (Objectives 3 and 4)

8. **Global.** What is the difference between a global and a transnational business executive? (Objective 4)

9. **Global.** How do you think that technology has affected multinational and global business communication? (Objectives 4 and 5)
10. Describe the difference between an interpreter and a translator, and give two guidelines for working with each. (Objective 5)

Application Exercises

1. **Teamwork.** Form groups of four to seven people. Discuss the importance of diversity initiatives in businesses. Plan an agenda for a seminar that could help people in a business understand the needs and interests of people representing different cultures. (Objective 1)

2. **E-mail. Global.** Research information on the Internet that will enable you to analyze the culture in a country other than the four countries studied in this chapter (Japan, Germany, China, and Mexico). Give particular attention in your analysis to the information about the culture or geography of the country that would affect communication. From your information, prepare a report with word processing and e-mail it to your instructor or post it on a class electronic bulletin board if one is available. Use subheadings similar to those below for major topics. (Objectives 2, 3, and 4)
   a. Business customs
   b. National holidays
   c. Time
   d. Transportation modes
   e. Foods and tipping customs
   f. Languages

3. **Technology. Global. Ethics.** Interview a student, a businessperson, or a visiting lecturer who is a native of another country or who has spent extensive time in a particular country other than the United States. Prepare a report using presentation software such as PowerPoint. Ask the following questions. (Objectives 1, 3, and 5)
   a. How do the people of this country perceive U.S. citizens?
   b. Describe the style of speaking or writing. Is it direct or indirect?
   c. Give examples of business behavior that are considered appropriate and ethical.
   d. Give an example of a social behavior that is considered unethical in that country.

e. Describe a typical meal and the food and mealtime etiquette.

f. What advice would you give someone going to that country to live and work?

g. What would be the most difficult adjustment to make when moving to that country?

4. **Global.** Contact an international center at a university (visit, call, or send e-mail). Ask about a study abroad or work abroad program. Develop and present your findings to your class. (Objectives 4 and 5)

5. **Teamwork. Ethics.** Form groups of four to seven students each. Assign each group a specific culture from among the following: ethnicity, race, gender, age, or individuals with disabilities. Each group is to ask the following questions of three people for each of the five core cultural dimensions. Summarize responses by specific ethnicity, race, gender, age, or disability for each person interviewed but do not identify names. Write a report of your findings. (Objectives 1, 2, and 3)

a. Give an example of a time when you thought that you were mistreated because of your ethnicity, race, gender, age, or physical condition.

b. What do you consider the most important values passed on to you from your parents and grandparents?

c. Has anyone used words that were offensive to you because of your ethnicity, race, gender, age, or physical condition? If so, what were they and what was your reaction? Why do you think the person used these words?

d. When you are with a group that does not include anyone of your ethnicity, race, gender, age group, or physical condition, how do you prefer to be treated?

6. **Teamwork.** Form a group of two to three students and discuss how age affects communication. Obtain three articles on age and present a copy of these articles to your teacher. Make a presentation to your class members on your findings. (Objective 2)

7. **E-mail.** Draft and send an e-mail note to your instructor on the importance of understanding one's own culture. Give five examples of business behaviors that are descriptive of North Americans. (Objectives 2 and 3)

8. **Teamwork.** With a partner read alternate sentences from the following paragraph aloud to each other.

> ehT qaimtimg also qroved that, sa well sa being a great humter, Cro-Wagmom Nam saw a comsiberadle artist. He dah flourisheb ta a tine whem eno fo eht terridle Ice Ages saw dlotting out much fo Euroqe. He dah estadlisheb hinself amb fought wilb aminals rof livimg sqace. eH surviveb eht ditter colb, amb left beeq bown umber groumb nenorials fo his yaw fo life!

Discuss with one another the difficulty that you had reading this passage and how you tried to compensate to understand what you were reading. Compare this to a person who may have dyslexia or have a vision problem or a person reading English as a second language. Make a list of ways that you and your partner find experience in trying to read this passage to be similar to or different from reading a message written in a language that you are just beginning to learn. (Objectives 2 and 3)

9. **Ethics.** Read the following statements and write a paragraph for each that describes what you believe would be ethical behavior in response to the situation. (Objectives 1, 2, and 3)

a. You observe a person humiliating someone or acting inappropriately.

b. You are part of a group of friends sharing casual conversation when one member of the group begins to use derogatory language and speak in a way that shows extreme cultural bias toward an international student who walks by your group.

10. **InfoTrac.** Use InfoTrac to locate and read "Communicators Go Global," by Cynthia L. Lemper (article A21244395). This article comes from *Communication World,* September

15, 1998 v15 n8 p30(4) and addresses changes in communication due to global business and the interconnected world. After you have read it, write a one-page reflection about what you have read. Did you agree with the author? Explain the reasons why you did or did not agree. How would you describe a "Global Paradigm Pioneer"? (Objectives 4 and 5)

There are Web exercises at **http://krizan.swlearning.com** to accompany this chapter.

Message Analysis

Global. Correct the following message that has been written to Mei Su, a high school junior who is a native of Arizona and who has been accepted as an American Field Service (AFS) student to study in Spain.

Dear Mei Su:

Congradulations! You have been excepted to participate in the Homestay Summer program departing in 2002. After we heare back from the staff in spain, we will contact you immediately with the name of you're host family.

If you havent' applyed for your Pass Port, you should apply now. Please make sure you're Pass Port will be valid for the intire duration of your AFS program. If you're Pass Port expires while you are abroad you may have difficulty returning in the United States.

If you have any questions please call you're local ASF volunteer or a member of the Student admissions' team at (800) 555-2300. We look foreward to providing you with the experience of a life time!

Sincerely,

(Your name)
AFS Regional Cordinator

Grammar Workshop

Correct the grammar, spelling, punctuation, style, and word choice errors in the following sentences:

1. In america a successful woman could be said to be self assured ambitious and forward looking.
2. Africas position today are to a large extent explained by it's History.
3. These articles will provide a brief history, and a current report on the status of Women in Contemporary chinese society.
4. Cultural differences effect not only values attitude and management practices; but, also impact the process of information gathering.
5. Many articles has been written over the past few years about public school Reform.
6. Denmark was the location for the 1997 world Conference.
7. The university of Mining and metallurgy is located in Krakow polland.
8. Bronx is the only one of New York citys five boroughs on the mainland of the United States.
9. The cite of the devestation of the twin towers of the World Trade Center in N.Y. should have a appropriate memorial.
10. Africa is the only continent in all four hemispheres Northern Southern eastern and Western.

3

Technological, Legal, and Ethical Considerations

Jose Palma, General Manager, CompUSA

LET'S TALK BUSINESS Today's manager relies on technology: cellular phones, pagers, portable computers, and the World Wide Web. On any given day, I have access to a virtual network that allows me to check numbers, inventory valuations, and profit and loss statements. At any time, I can call my staff and let them be proactive to respond to our performance. Business can be conducted remotely from anywhere in the United States.

In using technology to keep in touch, however, it is important to remember that interpersonal communication is also essential. Technology cannot replace the person-to-person contact. At times because of its brevity or impersonal nature, technology takes away the human touch that is so important to achieving goals in any business. For example, your employer may send an e-mail about important opportunities within your business, but these opportunities may be lost if you do not sense the urgency or importance of the request. A phone call instead of electronic mail would communicate its importance. For any business to succeed, communication cannot be complete without the personal element.

Jose Palma in Let's Talk Business describes his use of *high tech* as a routine part of business operations. However, the daily use of communication technology such as cell phones, e-mail, the Internet, and fax machines creates a fast-paced, and at times impersonal, system of relaying messages. In the midst of all of this technology, Palma cautions against losing the human element as people increasingly rely on electronic communication in business operations. He underscores the importance of selecting the best communication medium for the message. These comments call attention to the limitations of e-mail for understanding the sender's meaning as accurately as hearing a voice or observing body language in personal interaction. They also emphasize the you–viewpoint and how messages affect the behavior of others.

Consideration, respect, and responsible behavior in interacting with others are the foundations of both ethical and legal behavior. **Legal issues** pertain to *laws* and represent *standards of behavior valued by society*. **Ethical issues** relate to *value systems* and *cultural beliefs* that determine *individual and organizational standards of behavior* for interaction with others. Governments enact laws to prevent or to address behavior of individuals or organizations that is unacceptable to society or endangers the welfare of others.

LEARNING OBJECTIVE
(1) *Distinguish between legal and ethical issues.*

NOTE 3.1
Legal issues are standards of society. Ethical issues are individual and organizational values.

This chapter describes technology trends in communication and alerts you to legal and ethical considerations for business communication. A theme throughout the chapter is how technology and legal and ethical issues affect interactions with others and reinforce the importance of building relationships, creating goodwill, and maintaining trust based on ethical behavior and integrity.

The first part of this chapter covers technology trends, followed by legal and ethical issues pertinent to communication technology. The next section describes legal and ethical issues for a variety of business transactions and gives guidance for developing a code of conduct for ethical behavior. The chapter concludes with a discussion of planning and composing messages that meet legal and ethical standards for an organization and its members.

Technology Trends

Technology plays a major role in business communication. Technology advances are increasing the speed and volume of text messages and e-mail that can be handled away from the office. Wireless communication technology gives mobile access to data through a variety of portable communication devices. Further innovation in computer chip technology, as well as advances in software and hardware, can be expected to make communication, through text and voice, easier and faster than ever before. In addition, electronic commerce (e-commerce) has become a part of daily life.

LEARNING OBJECTIVE
(2) *Describe communication technology trends and legal and ethical issues related to technology.*

Wireless Technology and Mobile Communication

Broad area coverage and competitive rates make cell phones extremely popular not only for business but also for personal use. Cellular service has become so widespread and popular that many people use it as their only phone service. At least 400 million cell phones are sold each year worldwide.[1] Features such as color screens, camera phones, Internet browsing, and e-mail are already on the market. Cell phone popularity provides

[1] Brian Bergstein, "Microsoft Wants to Provide 'Smart' Cell Operating Systems," *Lexington Herald Leader*, 17 January 2003, Metro final edition, sec. C, p. 2, cols. 4–6.

an incentive for the telecommunication industry to continue improving Internet transmission of text messages and data to the wireless cellular system.

Wireless technology uses either low-powered infrared beams or radio frequency transmission for two-way voice or data transmission. This telecommunication technology enables users to connect communication devices without wires or cables. Typically, infrared beams send small amounts of data between devices in close proximity. However, *free-space optics (FSO)* can send infrared beams through the open air for distances up to four miles.[2] FSO technology helped maintain vital communication in New York City in 2001 after the attack on the World Trade Center.

Radio frequency (RF) is the most widely used wireless communication technology; cellular phone systems operate with radio frequencies. RF transmission uses a variety of wireless technologies. *Wireless local area networks (WLANs)* use RF transmission signals to allow portable computer devices to remain connected to a network and transmit data while moving to different locations.

The third generation of wireless technology, known as **3G**, is emerging. This technology will enable rapid and effective transmission of data as well as voice messages and *video streaming*. **Video streaming** plays video in real time as it is downloaded from the Internet and requires a fast computer and fast Internet connection. Estimates are that 3G will be able to transmit data at rates up to 2 megabytes (about 500,000 words) per second. In 2003 DaimlerChrysler exhibited a Mercedes Benz S-class equipped with a Third-Generation Universal Mobile Telecommunications System (3G-UMTS) capable of video conferencing and delivering e-mail and live television, as well as detailed maps for navigation.[3]

A **personal digital assistant (PDA)** is a pocket-sized computer for recording appointments, connecting with the Internet, using wireless text messaging, and handling e-mail. Initially, handling e-mail was awkward with the PDA; accessing e-mail took a long time because transmission included all undeleted messages from the desktop. New hardware and software can delete e-mails received prior to a certain date and can show the e-mails as read or unread, just as they are shown on your desktop e-mail inbox. Keyboards are available which can be connected to the PDA to enable speedier data entry than using a stylus to press keys on the PDA screen. Rapid changes in technology are difficult to predict, but 3G could bring a convergence of PDA devices with multitasking cellular phones.

Global positioning system (GPS) satellite technology is available as a wireless communication device on automobiles and also on handheld PDAs. Operating on a

NOTE 3.2
Cellular phone systems use radio frequencies.

NOTE 3.3
3G is third-generation wireless communication.

NOTE 3.4
PDAs are pocket-sized computers.

---

[2] Mark Ciampa, "Teaching Wireless Technology," *Business Education Forum*, 57:1 (October 2002), 47–49.
[3] "High-tech Gear Turns Mercedes into Road Office," *Jakarta Post*, 19 January 2003, (EBSCO HOST database, Business Source Premier), 1–2.

A PDA with a global positioning system provides driving directions to locations in its address book.

system of 24 satellites that can show a user's exact location, GPS gives turn-by-turn voice directions to any location in its computerized address book, an asset to the mobile businessperson.

Tablet PCs, portable computers that can process handwriting, have been on the computing scene previously with limited sales, but new models aimed at business note taking are returning to the market. These machines enable writing with cursive or block letters, or a combination of both, on a touch-sensitive screen. An optional standard keyboard can be connected.

Technology Research

What does the future hold for changes in communication technology? A number of advances are underway; others may develop rapidly.

Computing power depends on the amount of data that can be compressed into a microchip. Chipmakers such as Intel, Hewlett-Packard, and IBM are focusing on **nanotechnology**, a scientific effort to develop practical items by manipulating matter smaller than 100 *nanometers*.[4] A **nanometer** is one billionth of a meter. Three or four atoms in a row would equal a nanometer.

Nanotechnology arranges molecules precisely to make complex structures. Microchip researchers are stringing together tiny molecules to create chips one-hundredth of the size of today's chips. At the same time, other researchers in Japan and the United States are trying to increase computer chip power by developing a *three-dimensional (3D) chip*.[5] The **3D chip** would increase storage surface by using a cylinder or pillar shape.

NOTE 3.5
A 3D chip has greater memory storage because of its shape.

[4] Gina Miller, "The Basics of Nanotechnology," *Nanotechnology Industries,* 9 February 2000, *<http://www. nanoindustries.com/essays/basicsofnano.html>* (25 January 2003).

[5] Benjamin Fulford, "Another Dimension: Chipmakers Chase 3-D," 22 July 2002, *<http://www.forbes.com>* search 3D microchip, (20 June 2003).

NOTE 3.6
Speech-recognition soft-
ware being developed
uses voice inflections
to interpret meaning
and intent.

Another area of computer research is the interface of speech with computer input and output. **Voice recognition software** that captures spoken sounds and converts them to digital signals and into printed words has been on the market for a number of years. Improvements are ongoing to make the human voice an accurate and viable means of data input. However, researchers are also developing speech recognition software that can detect differences in pitch, timing, and amplitude to improve the message receiver's understanding of the sender's meaning and intent for the message. The war on terrorism accelerated this research in the United States. Accurate interpretation of message intent could help gauge the seriousness of computer-intercepted conversations and improve response to potential threats. This software capability holds potential for business usage by increasing the accuracy of text transcripts of voice-generated data.

Another area of speech-related research is the development of computer-generated speech for use with portable devices that can improve communication for persons with speech or other physical limitations. With a mouse click, the user can generate speech that reads e-mail or other messages aloud.

High Tech and the You–Viewpoint

Technology makes available an overwhelming amount of information and enables rapid transmission of messages. However, when you need to speak to a person but connect to automated answering messages, technology seems impersonal and frustrating. A call that you place to a business or other organization is more likely to connect to a recorded message than to a person. There are exceptions; some companies continue to have employees answer calls personally as part of their belief in personal service—another way to demonstrate the you–viewpoint. Almost everyone can recall getting caught in a seemingly endless loop of "press 1 if . . . press 2 if. . ." You probably felt the same as Cathy does in the following cartoon. As a communicator, remember that the impression of your organization depends not only on the message content but also on the media used to communicate it.

Cathy

NOTE 3.7
E-commerce is buying
and selling of goods
and services via
the Internet.

Electronic Commerce

Electronic commerce (e-commerce) has become an accepted way to shop. **E-commerce** is the buying and selling of goods and services over the Internet. Over one-quarter of large businesses nationwide sell their products and services through the Internet. Shopping and buying on the Internet have become commonplace for everything from bobble-head dolls to automobiles.

Internet-based commerce appeals to businesses because of its virtually unlimited market expansion. More than 50 percent of all U.S. households now have computers and, although numbers are smaller in other countries, the growth of the Internet literally makes the world an e-commerce market. In fact, online sales are forecast to be between $100 billion and $600 billion early in the 21st century—and that prediction came before passage of the electronic signature law in the summer of 2000. Success in the international marketplace depends not only on technology but also on the ability to communicate effectively.

E-commerce offers a wide range of services and products for delivery to homes, offices, or other locations. Forecasters suggest that nearly one-quarter of all household expenditures will occur in cyberspace by the year 2005. How do customers pay? Payment is by credit card or through a preestablished account that stores personal information on a secure site. The thought of sending a credit card number across the Internet makes some people reluctant to participate in e-commerce; however, safeguards for the security of information through *encrypting* private information such as the buyer's credit card number help allay this concern. **Encrypting** is an encoding system used to protect the privacy of messages. As customers become more comfortable with the idea of ordering and paying for goods and services through the Internet, business communicators can expect to process more of their messages electronically. Inquiries and complaints, for example, will arrive and receive a response via e-mail.

Many customers will not speak English, or English will be their second language. In fact, some Internet watchers believe that people in other countries may learn English not through formal training but rather through their use of the Internet. Translation programs can assist in interpreting and responding to messages in languages other than English; but, as noted in Chapter 2, awareness of and sensitivity to cultural differences and the subtleties of language translation will remain extremely important.

NOTE 3.8
Encrypting is an encoding system for ensuring privacy of information.

NOTE 3.9
Translation software helps with multinational e-commerce messages.

Business Applications of Technology

Organizations are increasingly dependent on computers and other technological devices to handle the volume and complexity of information communicated through daily operations. This section describes a number of technology applications to business communication.

LEARNING OBJECTIVE
(2) *Describe communication technology trends and legal and ethical issues related to technology.*

Business and Organization Web Pages

The number of businesses and other organizations that maintain Web sites on the Internet continues to increase. A Web presence provides an advertising medium that helps potential customers learn about the organization. The Web site may include an e-mail address that, with a mouse click, opens an e-mail message form addressed to the organization or an official in the organization. Even officials in those companies not selling services or products via e-commerce see a Web site as important for the company image.

Careful planning, design, and management of Web sites are important considerations. Chapters 4 and 5 provide information about applying business communication principles to Web page design.

NOTE 3.10
The number of business and organization Web sites is increasing.

Internet Research

Expanded Internet use means that business professionals may find themselves using the Internet for both *primary* and *secondary* research. **Primary research** refers to gathering data from original sources to gain knowledge about a problem or question; **secondary research** involves locating and studying information gathered by other researchers. Market research is an example of primary research; reading about previous marketing studies is secondary research.

NOTE 3.11
Web-based surveys can be quickly and accurately summarized.

Conducting surveys through the Internet is not unusual. Collecting data electronically expedites analysis because the researcher does not have to enter and proofread the data items; computerized totals come directly from respondents' entries. Web-based surveys for market research eliminate interviewer errors and inconsistencies and can be posted on a secure Web site with respondents directed to the site from banner advertisements or e-mail invitations. These surveys can be multimedia with video clips, graphics, and text and be designed for easy response with a click of the mouse.

TIPS AND HINTS

Etiquette for Primary Internet Research

- Keep the questionnaire format easy to use. The response should be to the right of statements or questions because the normal eye movement across the page is from left to right. Make the survey response easy to make with a click of the mouse.
- Use only survey items essential to answer your research questions. Short, simple surveys yield higher return rates. Save the responder's time as well as your own.

- Make sure the survey goes only to persons who agree to participate. Unwelcome mass mailings of survey instruments to e-mail lists are discourteous to the receivers.
- Set up a Web site for the survey and invite persons to participate, either with a banner on your Web site or an e-mail invitation to a selected list.

Online database research has become a preferred method of locating published information. Universities and other public libraries offer full-text journal articles and other publications online through a variety of resource databases. Libraries pay a subscription fee for each database, which has a collection of periodical articles or research reports. Library patrons access these databases from in-house library computers or through usernames and passwords for off-site access. For example, the username may be the person's last name, and the password may be the number on a magnetic strip of the individual's library card. Some states, such as Kentucky, have a statewide virtual library that provides online access to an array of full-text materials. Statewide virtual libraries may recognize library access codes from library cards issued by public libraries throughout the state.

Intranets and Collaborative Projects

NOTE 3.12
An intranet is for internal business communication.

Most businesses use an organization-only computer network called an **intranet** for internal communications. Businesses with such systems enable their employees to move information, exchange ideas, and discuss strategy electronically within the company without going through the Internet. The primary reason for establishing an intranet is the security of having a *firewall* to protect company information from outside intruders, hackers, or others with destructive motives.

As organizations increase their use of cross-functional teams, collaboration on projects, reports, and proposals increases. **Collaborative writing software** facilitates group writing. The product allows several users to work on the same electronic document rather than on a printed or electronically transmitted (e-mail attachment) copy of the document.

Collaborative writing may be *interactive* (**synchronous**) or *independent* (**asynchronous**). When collaboration is **interactive**, two or more people work with the same document at the same time and see changes as they are made. The document resides on a host computer used by one of the participants, referred to as the host. To contribute to the document, each person signals the host, who determines the sequence in which participants will access the document. Interactive collaborative writing sessions resemble meetings in that they must be prearranged. In addition, only the host has access to the document between sessions.

For **independent collaborative writing**, the document resides on a computer location that may be accessed at any time by anyone in the writing group. This type of collaboration has the advantage of permitting writers to work on the document at their convenience. The disadvantage is that writers must also check periodically to see what changes their coauthors have made. For this reason, writers tend to rely on strikeout and redline techniques or shading to mark the changes. A task-tracking function on word processing software can be used to underline changes and line through deletions automatically as the changes are entered. Selection of a font color such as red for the changes makes them highly visible.

Collaborative writing software is one element of a larger software category called **groupware.** Other features available in groupware include shared scheduling and project tracking. When members of a group each have access to other members' schedules, meetings are easier to arrange. Project management has similar advantages. Updates can be entered by one person and quickly seen by all people who are working on the project.

NOTE 3.13
Collaborative software is a type of groupware.

Video Conferencing

Technology makes video conferencing a viable alternative to face-to-face meetings. Persons in scattered locations can participate in meetings without travel expense to meet in one location. Special software, a video camera, and a computer at the multiple locations create the ability to use a whiteboard for notes, see a document online, and watch facial expressions of participants.[6]

Telecommuting

Use of computer networks opened opportunities for *telecommuting* employees. Employees often prefer the flexibility offered by working as a telecommuter. However, according to Stephanie Armour in *USA Today*, telecommuting is stuck in the slow lane and hasn't lived up to expectations. **Telecommuting** is working from a location other than the office where business is usually conducted. Although anyone who communicates with his or her office from a car, public telephone, hotel, or client's office might

NOTE 3.14
Telecommuting employees work in a location other than the company office.

[6] John Brandon, "Genesys Meeting Center 2.0," *Laptop Mobile Solutions for Business and Life*, November 2002, 20.

be defined as a telecommuter, the term is more widely applied to those who work from their home. Telecommuters access data and communicate with clients, colleagues, and supervisors electronically.

For organizations doing business across time zones, telecommuting enhances communication by allowing people to talk more conveniently early in the morning or late at night. Increased productivity, reduced employee turnover, and reduced need for costly office space are among the reasons businesses permit employees to telecommute.

Despite its advantages, telecommuting can promote worker isolation. To minimize the impact telecommuting can have on worker-worker, worker-supervisor, or worker-organization relationships, telecommuters may spend one day a week (or some other pattern) in the office. This structure permits organizations to schedule employee face-to-face meetings and to facilitate interpersonal teamwork.

NOTE 3.15
Telecommuting can cause worker isolation.

TIPS AND HINTS

Suggestions for Telecommuters

- Keep in frequent e-mail or phone contact with fellow workers.
- Go to the office for staff meetings at least once a week or on a regular schedule.
- Create a productive office work environment in your home.

- Arrange meetings with clients in a business location.
- Plan a reasonable work schedule. Be fair to your employer and to yourself.

LEARNING OBJECTIVE

Describe communi-cation technology trends and legal and ethical issues related to technology.

② Technology-Related Legal and Ethical Issues

In this section of the chapter, you will learn about legal and ethical considerations for the use of communication technology. Technology brings with it a number of legal and ethical issues. These issues pertain to copyright and privacy, as well as to employee behavior and organizational actions.

Cell Phones and Other Mobile Devices

NOTE 3.16
Users of mobile computer devices should respect the rights and safety of others.

Ethical and legal issues pertinent to the use of cell phones, PDAs, and other telecommunication mobile devices are evolving as rapidly as the technology itself. Issues center around using these devices in a manner that respects the rights, safety, and privacy of others. Legislatures have considered laws restricting the use of cell phones in automobiles, citing the danger of driver distraction during phone conversations. To date, federal laws banning cell phone usage while driving have not emerged in the United States, but some states restrict use in automobiles to hands-free phones.

NOTE 3.17
A heuristic guide is a rule of thumb based on experience.

Use of mobile devices to conduct business on the road or in public places, however, would not require laws if individuals practiced courtesy, respect, and concern for the safety of persons around them. A common **heuristic** or experiential guide for individual rights says that *your rights end where the other person's begin.* In other words, if your behavior becomes excessively intrusive or dangerous to others, your conduct exceeds your rights.

Mobile communication devices offer many positive benefits; remember to balance these benefits with respect for the people around you. The following Tips and Hints suggests etiquette practices to guide cell phone use in public places.

E-Mail Messages and the Internet

Whether their employees work on site or off, organizations must be sure they use technology appropriately. Misuse of e-mail and Internet resources not only threatens productivity and creates legal concerns but also endangers the company's image.

Productivity issues stem from workers' easy access to e-mail and the Internet. Access to and curiosity about these services, which are provided to facilitate business transactions, create the temptation to waste time. When workers exchange e-mail with family and friends, forward jokes to coworkers and others, play games, engage in day trading, or just surf the Web, they are not engaged in activities that promote the organization or its mission.

Legal concerns about misuse of e-mail and the Internet relate to liability and privacy. Most employers want to trust employees and respect their privacy, but they fear the organization will be liable for the content of e-mail messages. Computer systems can retain messages long after they have been deleted from the user's mailbox. Gossip, derogatory comments, lewd or obscene messages or graphics, harassing messages, or any number of other items could be retrieved from e-mail files and used as evidence in court cases. In addition, having such messages originate or circulate within the workplace negatively affects the organization's responsibility for a harassment-free environment and could ultimately tarnish its good image and decrease productivity.

Even business-related e-mail can haunt an individual or organization, as demonstrated in the antitrust case against Microsoft in the late 1990s. In this case, e-mail exchanged by Bill Gates and his staff was retrieved and used as evidence against Microsoft. In 2002, an internal e-mail that resulted in shredded documents from an Enron audit became part of legal actions against the company and its accounting firm.

Recognize that e-mail is not private. Your employer can monitor it, computer hackers can intercept it, your adversary in a legal action can review it, law enforcement agents who suspect a crime can obtain it, and your Internet provider can retrieve a copy

NOTE 3.18
Misuse of e-mail and the Internet threatens productivity and creates legal problems.

NOTE 3.19
E-mail messages and Internet sites accessed are not private; others can retrieve them.

of it from the e-mail server. U.S. federal code gives a governmental agency authority under state or federal criminal procedures to secure a warrant and require communication service providers to disclose the contents of an electronic communication. Illegal use of the Internet, whether from business or a home computer, is subject to disclosure and may be used as evidence of a crime. Visiting pornographic Web sites on work time is likely to get you fired; accessing and sending child pornography is a crime, whether from work, home, or a computer in any other location.

The fear of litigation and the concern over wasted time prompts some organizations to monitor workers' use of electronic resources. Special network and e-mail software programs exist for just this purpose.

The Fourth Amendment against unreasonable governmental searches and seizures pertains to public workplaces. A Supreme Court case, *O'Conner v. Ortega* 480 U.S. 709 (1987), ruled that a *public employee*'s privacy in his office must be balanced with the employer's right to conduct a reasonable search based on the circumstances. A "reasonableness test" examined whether the search was *justified at its inception*, meaning that there was reason to suspect that evidence would be found of employee misconduct or that access and retrieval of the file was necessary in the employee's absence. The other part of the test examined the scope of the investigation; that is, its relation to the objectives of the search and its reasonableness when weighed against the nature of the misconduct.

Private employers are not subject to the Fourth Amendment restrictions; however, such searches should be based on reasonable suspicion or legitimate business needs, and care should be taken to disclose the contents only in clearly permissible instances. Employers often have a legitimate need to search an employee's e-mail, voice mail, or other electronically stored messages. The Electronic Privacy Act gives an employer the right to access an employee's e-mail and voice-mail messages that are maintained on a system *provided by the employer.*

The final word of advice for employees is to treat e-mail, voice mail, and other electronic messages as if they will be public knowledge. Confine messages to business and limit the time you spend communicating with family and friends while you are at work. Accessing pornographic Web sites, sending sexually suggestive messages, or revealing company trade secrets is a recipe for losing your job and may result in legal charges.

Organizations often choose to develop clear policies on the use of e-mail and other company resources. Such policies become a part of the employee handbook and alert employees that their Internet log of sites visited and their e-mail and voice-mail messages are not private. Employers should obtain legal advice on the wording of such policies. The Tips and Hints that follows gives some suggestions for policy content.

Some companies make employment contingent on a prospective employee's willingness to sign a statement saying that she or he has read, understands, and accepts the organization's computer-use policy. Organizations may embed a statement about technology misuse into the system's log-on procedure; users may not proceed without acknowledging the message and the warning that their computer activities may be monitored.

Other Technology Privacy Issues

Internet research is controversial. Technology makes it feasible to gather data about computer users without their knowledge or permission, a practice that many consider unethical and an invasion of individual privacy. As experienced computer users know, many e-commerce sites use tracking software that stores information about you on your computer in a brief text file called a **cookie**. This stored file can be read each time you

NOTE 3.20
Employers have a legal right to monitor e-mail on company computers.

NOTE 3.21
Treat electronic messages as if they are public knowledge.

NOTE 3.22
Some companies require employees to sign a computer-use policy.

Content for Policies on E-mail and the Internet

- Be aware that employee e-mail is a part of business records and subject to review in legal actions or reasonable suspicion of misconduct that may damage the reputation of the organization.
- Don't send animated greeting cards through business e-mail. These messages consume a high volume of processor memory; too many of these greetings (particularly around holidays) could disable the company network.
- Adhere to professional conduct in the use of e-mail and the Internet. Accessing pornographic sites or sending obscene or sexually suggestive messages can result in disciplinary penalties or termination of employment and could become the basis for legal action.
- Treat business e-mail messages and the use of the Internet as you would the business phone. Keep personal use to a minimum.
- Avoid viruses by deleting e-mail attachments unopened if they come from an unknown source.
- Direct questions about proper use of technology to management or other appropriate personnel.

visit their site; it enables you to be greeted by name when you return to the Web site and may include your encrypted credit card information to eliminate the need for re-entry of data on subsequent orders. Objections arise because advertisers on the net may secure information from these files to track your preferences and online shopping habits. To allay concerns about cookies, organizations frequently include a privacy statement on their Web sites that explains the type of data gathered and their use.

Bulk e-mail with multiple copies of the same message going to multiple persons who, given a choice, would not want to receive them is **spam**. Most mass mailing of advertising on the Internet is spam. These mass mailings often advertise questionable products, schemes for making money, or services that are only marginally legal. Much of it comes from developing countries.[7] Responding to spam usually leads to more spam and can lead to harassment and identity theft or attempts to steal your credit card number.

> **NOTE 3.23**
> Spam is mass mailing of a message to persons unlikely to want it.

A National Do Not Call Registry prohibits telemarketing calls to market goods or services to consumers who register. Calls to persons on this registry may be subject to fines up to $11,000 per call. Exceptions include groups such as charities and political organizations and calls from a business to a customer who made a purchase within the last 18 months unless the customer asked not to be called again. Organizations should abide by no-call restrictions. In addition to ethical and legal issues, persistent telemarketing and spam can damage the company's image due to angry reactions to unwanted contacts.

Copyright

Original works of authorship—including written works, art, music, photographs, multimedia, and computer software—qualify for *copyright*. **Copyright** is a legal right of the

> **NOTE 3.24**
> Copyright is the legal right of the owner of original works to control distribution.

[7] "Frequently Asked Questions: General Questions about Spam," *Frequently Asked Questions*, n.d., <http://www.spamstopshere.com/faq.htm>(25 January 2003).

owner to control reproduction, distribution, and sale of the work. Legal use of copyrighted material obtained from the Internet follows the same fair-use guidelines as are applicable to printed, electronic, or other types of work. Copyright law grants a right of *fair use* to the public. Fair use is a privilege, but there is no legally binding answer that defines fair use in a specific instance. Legal interpretations depend on circumstances of the particular use and relate to four factors:

[1] Purpose and character of use (including whether it is for nonprofit educational use or of a commercial nature). Nonprofit or educational use is most favorable for fair use. Commercial purposes are most likely to be weighed against fair use and require permission by the owner.

[2] Nature of the copyrighted work (fact or fiction). Information that is general knowledge or factual material may be fair use even if published; whereas, imaginative, creative work and unpublished work tips the balance toward control of use by the owner.

[3] The amount and portion of the work used in relation to the copyrighted work (no exact percentage). A small amount of a large document is most likely to favor fair use.

[4] The effect of the use on the potential market for or value of the copyrighted work. If use of the work competes or takes away sales from the original work or avoids payments for permission in an established permission market, this effect is a consideration against fair use.

NOTE 3.25
When unsure of fair use of copyrighted material, request the owner's permission.

If you are quoting material, be sure to quote it accurately and give credit to the source. Further, you cannot be certain the material is free of copyright just because you do not see a copyright notice on the material. In most cases, protected work would have the symbol © or the word Copyright followed by the year, but this designation is no longer essential for a person or organization to prove a copyright violation. When in doubt, request permission to use quoted material.

NOTE 3.26
Facts and general knowledge are not subject to copyright.

You do not have to cite a source for information that is general knowledge, such as "communicators should be sure their messages are ethical and legal." You can say that on your own even though you might have read it in a book or in some other publication. Copyright laws do not apply to public domain works; works that are not original; U.S. government materials; or ideas, processes, methods, or systems (not original) described in copyrighted works.

NOTE 3.27
Plagiarism means stealing ideas and words; paraphrasing is restating others' ideas without giving credit.

Plagiarism means stealing and using someone else's ideas or words as your own without giving the other person(s) credit as the source. This theft of ideas or words takes place by using exact quotes or by paraphrasing. **Paraphrasing** is restating ideas (in your own words) but retaining the original meaning. Cite the source when you quote another person's words or ideas and when you reword passages that express someone else's ideas unless those ideas are facts or general knowledge. Paraphrasing or rewording another person's material and making it appear to be your original work is unethical even when it is not illegal. Avoid these problems by (1) understanding and obeying the copyright laws, (2) giving credit to others when using their ideas or words, or (3) not using others' ideas and words.

Illegal copying of software is **software piracy** and can result in severe legal penalties. You can copy software that is freeware. Shareware restricts copying. Copyright laws and the fair-use doctrine are complex. Most libraries have the material published by the copyright office on these topics. Business communicators must make themselves aware of the laws and guidelines that apply to their messages.

Computer Fraud

Illegal uses of the Internet include attempting to gain unauthorized access to the computer systems of others or deliberately attempting to disrupt the computer system or destroy data by spreading computer viruses or other means. Federal code defines as a fraud intentional unauthorized computer access to a wide variety of computer records (such as government agency computers and computers involved in interstate or foreign communication) to gain information or extort money or other value, or to intentionally cause damage.

Computer viruses and worms have disrupted businesses and Internet connections. A **virus** is a program that may attach itself to a file and replicate itself, corrupt the data of the invaded file, or attempt to crash the machine. Viruses range from harmless simple programs to those that corrupt files and cause the system to crash. A **worm** is a type of computer virus that invades a computer, stealing its resources and using networks to spread itself.

Organizations should make sure their computer systems have firewalls and filters to protect their data. Another reason for such protection is the capability that exists for hackers or terrorists to damage targeted Internet sites by millions of requests for information launched by a small program sent from an unsuspecting third-party unprotected computer site. The unsuspecting owner could be liable for damages. The Communication Note that follows warns of cell phones as the next frontier for viruses.

NOTE 3.28
Computer hackers and persons who send computer viruses and worms commit computer fraud.

COMMUNICATION NOTE

Cell Phone Viruses The next frontier in virus mischief is the mobile phone. Such a virus could instruct the phone to call the White House or the police with a hoax message or forward your personal address book to a telemarketing firm. Cell phone owners in Japan and Europe have already experienced such problems.

Adapted from an Associated Press article by Jim Krane, "Cell Phones Prone to Viruses," March 10, 2002.

Web-Site Linking

A common Web-site practice is *linking* to other Web sites without obtaining permission from the owner of the linked page. The culture of Web-site usage has accepted this practice; however, as Web sites become more commercially important as e-commerce, this practice may change. Use of copyrighted or trademark-protected text or images from a linked page, an artist's work, links to internal pages rather than the Web home page, and links to copyrighted works or defamatory material have become subjects of legal action. If you capture graphics from another Web site, make sure that you obtain permission for copyrighted material.

Links to internal pages in a Web site create a problem not only with a risk that the Web master will change internal pages but also because the visitor to the page will not see the Web owner's home page. The symbol or text that the viewer clicks to go to the linked site is called a **hot zone**. Selecting the wording or the symbol used as a hot zone should be done with caution. The following Tips and Hints box gives suggestions for linking to other Web sites but is not intended as legal advice. Consult an attorney for specific legal questions.

NOTE 3.29
Most Web-site links should be to the Web home page.

NOTE 3.30
Don't use others' logo, trademark, or product design as a link "hot" zone.

Tips and Hints for Web Site Links

- Use plain-text names (without description) as the "hot" zone for a link. Describing the link may lead to allegations of inaccurate or misleading statements. Do not use the logo, product design, slogan, or trademark of others as a "hot" zone.
- Link to the home page. Bypassing the home page to go to internal pages keeps the viewer from seeing advertising and reduces advertising revenue based on the number of "hits" to the page. If you wish to link to an internal page, request permission from the owner of the linked page.

- Add a Terms and Conditions statement to your Web site that includes Web-site usage policies and a disclaimer that you cannot control the content of third-party Web sites that link to your Web site. Also, you may state that you visited the Web sites that are linked to your sites before linking but that you do not control their content and that such content changes frequently.

Adapted from "Internet Legal Issues: Linking" by Lloyd L. Rich, © 1999 Publishing Law Center. Retrieved September 16, 2002 from *http://www.findlaw.com*.

E-Commerce

NOTE 3.31
Legal jurisdiction relates to court authority applicable to the conduct of business.

A legal issue for e-commerce is court jurisdiction that governs the conduct of the business. Companies that conduct business across state lines or with foreign residents in other countries may come under the jurisdiction of those courts. Legal counsel should be consulted to determine jurisdiction. *Starmedia Network, Inc. v. Star Media, Inc.*, resulted in a determination in 2001 of sufficient minimum contacts to be subject to New York court jurisdiction. Although their interstate commerce business did not take on-line orders or sell products directly over the Internet, they did provide customers with access through a password to certain confidential information. This was determined to be an exchange of information through e-mail.

Electronic signatures facilitate contractual arrangements through e-commerce. A federal electronic signature law endorsed electronic signatures that could be logically associated with a record and executed by encryption technology. Courts have upheld "click-through" agreements for consumer assent to a contract and conditions.

LEARNING OBJECTIVE
Discuss legal considerations for business communication.

③ # Legal Considerations for Business Messages

You and your organization could be sued or prosecuted if you violate the law in your business messages. Thousands or even millions of dollars could be lost. Prison terms might result. Recent legal problems of major companies like WorldCom and Enron underscore the loss of public confidence and serious effects of business decisions that violate laws and ethical principles. To assure the legality of your written or oral communication, you must be aware of laws, court decisions, and administrative regulations that apply to those messages. Ignorance of the law does not excuse violators.

NOTE 3.32
Consult an attorney when unsure about legality of message content.

If you are unsure about the legality of a message's content, you should consult an attorney or other authority. Many companies have attorneys available to employees. In addition, some company officials—personnel officers, purchasing agents, and others—have specialized knowledge of legal requirements in their areas of responsibility.

This section of the chapter reviews some important legal considerations for contracts, employment communication, and defamation and fraud. This information can alert you to situations that have legal implications for business communication.

Contract Communication

Both oral and written communication with your company's customers must meet the requirements of several laws. Among the most important forms of communication is the **contract**, a legally binding agreement between two or more parties. A proposal or offer by one party and acceptance by the other party or parties creates a contract. The contract may involve completing a particular action, providing a particular thing, or refraining from doing something.

NOTE 3.33
A contract is a legally binding agreement.

An enforceable contract may result from an exchange of letters—one that makes a clear and definite offer and another that accepts the offer without making conditions on the acceptance—or a series of letters that makes clear that the parties have reached agreement about material elements of the contract. A contract does not have to be written in a letter or on a particular form if it includes essential elements of the agreement and has the necessary signatures. A valid contract must have the following elements:

• Offer and acceptance
• Competency of parties
• Legality of subject matter
• Consideration (the price, motive, or promise exchanged)

Businesses generally use the services of a lawyer or forms reviewed by a lawyer for all but the simplest type of contract. Examples of contracts are agreements for the sale of goods or services, transfer of property or interests in property, and contracts of employment.

"PLAIN ENGLISH" LAWS

Several states have "plain English" laws requiring that contracts be written so consumers can understand them. Some states specify readability levels, average number of syllables per word, layout, size of print, and other content details. These laws require careful analysis of a contract's content. Other states have more general guidelines, such as requiring contracts to contain understandable words, short sentences, and short paragraphs. The principles of business communication given in Chapter 4 will help you meet the requirements of "plain English" laws.

WARRANTIES AND GUARANTEES

Federal law requires the manufacturer or seller to stand behind a purchase of a major product. A warranty must be available for the purchaser to read at the time of purchase. The Uniform Commercial Code, the Consumer Product Warranty Act, the Federal Trade Commission Improvement Act, and similar legislation cover **express warranties** (promises made willingly by the seller) and **implied warranties** (promises created by law). An example of an express warranty is a manufacturer's written promise to replace a product during the first year if it proves defective due to quality of construction or materials. An example of an implied warranty is that the product must be satisfactory for the purpose intended. Promises to consumers and others can be made orally or in writing, so be sure you warrant only to the extent you intend.

NOTE 3.34
Warranties are of two types: express and implied.

©JOSÉ LUIS PELAEZ, INC./CORBIS

Credit and Collection Communication

Many state and federal laws specify the responsibilities of businesses in issuing credit and collecting debts. Here are some of the important federal laws.

EQUAL CREDIT OPPORTUNITY ACT

This law requires that credit be equally available to all creditworthy customers. It also covers how creditworthiness is determined. Credit grantors cannot discriminate on the basis of race, color, religion, gender, or national origin. Credit decisions cannot be based on age (if of legal age for a binding contract) or marital status.

FAIR CREDIT BILLING ACT

This law protects credit card users against false charges made to their accounts. The act specifies in detail those procedures that consumers and creditors must follow to resolve problems.

FAIR DEBT COLLECTION ACT

This law specifies in detail what debt collectors can and cannot do. The law defines a **debt collector** as a person, other than the creditor, who regularly collects debts from others. Although the law does not forgive any legitimate debt, it requires that debt collectors treat the debtor fairly. A collector may make contacts through mail, telephone, telegram, or fax but cannot make contact at unreasonable times or places, such as before 8 a.m. or after 9 p.m., unless agreed to by the debtor.

FEDERAL TRUTH-IN-LENDING ACT

Full disclosure of credit terms to consumers is a requirement in this law. Lenders and creditors must clearly disclose service charges, finance charges, and the effective annual interest rate. The law covers how the terms and conditions of loans must be specified—such as number of payments and due dates of payments. It also gives the borrower a right to cancel within three business days after signing a contract.

NOTE 3.36
The terms and conditions of loans must be specified.

Employment Communication

Managers, supervisors, and employees need to know the legal requirements affecting employment communication. The following laws specify much of what can and cannot be said or written about employees.

THE CIVIL RIGHTS ACT

This law and its amendments prohibit discrimination in employment. Hiring, firing, compensation, and other conditions of employment cannot be based on race, color, religion, gender, or national origin. This law, first passed in 1964 and since amended, is landmark legislation. Every business communicator should be aware of its requirements. Affirmative action programs have evolved from the Civil Rights Act; the Equal Employment Opportunity Act; and other extensive federal, state, and local employment regulations.

THE AGE DISCRIMINATION IN EMPLOYMENT ACT (ADEA)

The ADEA deals with a shift in the age demographics of the American workforce. The ADEA prohibits discrimination against workers over 40 years of age. This act requires due diligence, record keeping, and documentation on the part of employers in firing employees. **Due diligence** is defined as the care that a reasonable person under the same circumstances would use; due diligence entails reasonable but not exhaustive efforts to act in accordance with the law.

NOTE 3.37
The ADEA prohibits discrimination in employment for workers over 40.

LABOR-MANAGEMENT RELATIONS ACT

This law guides communication between managers and workers, particularly as it concerns unions, and prevents employment discrimination based on union activity. The National Labor Relations Board provides details regarding its implementation; its Web home page is http://www.nlrb.gov.

THE PRIVACY ACT

Employees can access information about themselves as a result of this law. It also limits the use of personnel information to the purpose for which it was collected. For example, it is important when serving as a reference that you respond only to specific requests that have been approved by the employee. Further, your comments should relate only to documented job performance. Any reference should be objective, given in good faith, and without malice.

NOTE 3.38
Employees can access information about themselves that their employer maintains.

FAMILY EDUCATIONAL RIGHTS AND PRIVACY ACT (FERPA)

This law protects the privacy of information directly connected to a student and includes student records in any media—computer media, video or audiotape, film, microfilm, microfiche, or written records. FERPA requires written permission from a parent or from the student (if 18 or older) before disclosing any personally identifiable information contained in educational records. Exceptions provided by regulation permit disclosure to a limited set of persons or institutions such as official parties in connection with financial aid, accrediting agencies, or in response to a court order or subpoena.

AMERICANS WITH DISABILITIES ACT

This 1990 act, covering some 43 million Americans with disabilities, is referred to as the most important employment legislation since Title VII of the Civil Rights Act. This law makes it illegal to discriminate against people with disabilities in regard to hiring, firing, compensation, training, and advancement. Communicators must be aware of language that the courts might rule discriminatory, such as job descriptions and advertisements calling for *high energy level, able-bodied,* and so forth. The law covers both physical and mental disabilities. Persons with disabilities are qualified applicants or employees if they *can perform the essential functions of the job*. Human resource personnel refer to essential job functions as **bona fide occupational qualifications (BFOQ).**

An employer cannot eliminate a qualified applicant from equal consideration for employment if the applicant can perform the essential job functions with reasonable accommodation for the disability. For example, an administrative assistant with a hearing disability could have an amplifier added to the phone to make it possible to handle telephone calls. The amplifier would be a reasonable accommodation; and if this candidate is employed, the ADA requires the employer to provide it.

FAMILY AND MEDICAL LEAVE ACT (FMLA)

NOTE 3.39
FMLA recognizes the rights of parents and other caregivers to take unpaid work leave to care for family members.

The FMLA was passed in 1993. This law recognizes the responsibility of employees to care for seriously ill family members, to recuperate from their own serious illness, or to care for a new baby or newly adopted child. Certain employers must allow up to 12 weeks per year of unpaid leave for this purpose. The FMLA applies to employers who have 50 or more employees, including part time. The covered individual must have been an employee for a year and worked at least 1,250 hours during the 12 months before the leave. The law describes certain restrictions concerning scheduling and notice requirements and proof of illness.

Defamation and Fraud

Common law and other legislation cover such important legal considerations as defamation and fraud. These laws restrict what you say about other persons that may damage their reputation or cause financial loss because of misleading or false information.

DEFAMATION

NOTE 3.40
Defamation results from written or oral statements that injure another person.

The law does not permit you to make statements that injure the reputation or character of another person. Such statements, called **defamation**, are libelous (written) or slanderous (oral). To be considered defamation, the statements must be false, made for or read by a third person, and must cause injury. A publication that injures a corporation's credit, property, or business is libelous, also. In certain situations, true statements may be considered defamation if they are made with the intent of harming the other person. In most cases, someone other than the person defamed must read a letter before its contents can be grounds for a court action for libel.

FRAUD

Lying that causes another person monetary damage is called **fraud**. Fraud can be committed by words or conduct and includes false advertising and false endorsement of products or services. Fraud exists when these conditions are proven:

- A communicator misrepresents or conceals a material fact.
- The misrepresentation was made knowingly or with a reckless disregard for the truth.
- The misrepresentation was made with the intent to deceive.
- The deceived person relied on the false statement.
- The deceived person incurred monetary damage.

Ethical Considerations and Codes of Conduct

Ethical communication is essential to successful individuals and organizations. Effective interpersonal relationships are built on trust, honesty, and fairness. Promises made are kept. Fair disclosure of information is provided. Acceptable organizational values should be shared and promoted.

Being ethical is enlightened self-interest. You will pay far more in time, money, and effort to repair the damage caused by false messages than truthful, forthcoming messages would cost in the first place. In addition, it is not always possible to repair the damage caused by an unethical message. Your credibility is likely to be lost, your interpersonal relationships destroyed, and your career impaired.

An Ethical Communicator

How can you be sure you are an ethical communicator? First, you determine exactly what ethical communication is. Second, you adopt principles or develop systems that work best for you in choosing ethical content for your messages.

DEFINING ETHICAL COMMUNICATION

The word **ethics** is derived from the Greek word *ethos,* meaning character. Being ethical means doing what is right to achieve what is good. In business communication what is right refers to the responsibility to include information in your messages that ought to be there. What is good refers to the end result of the communication. The ethical end result is to strive for the highest good attainable for all of those involved in the communication. Therefore, **ethical communication** strives for the highest good for all involved and provides information that is fully adequate for the circumstance, truthful in every sense, and not deceptive in any way.

CHOOSING ETHICAL CONTENT FOR YOUR MESSAGES

Choosing ethical content for messages requires the same analytical and practical skills as does sound business leadership. Being ethical in your communication requires that you determine—from among all the alternatives—the right and good information in given situations. Figures 3.1 and 3.2 show contrasting choices for message content.

NEEDS WORK

BIKES, INC.

INTEROFFICE MEMO

To: All Employees
From: Bill McKeiver, President *BM*
Date: February 1, 200–
Subject: New Shift

Beginning on February 3, 200–, and for an indeterminate time, there will be a newly established third shift running from midnight to 8 a.m. One-third of the employees in each department on the 8 a.m. to 4 p.m. shift and one third on the 4 p.m. to midnight shift will be assigned to the new midnight shift. The employees who will have their shifts changed will be notified via a paycheck insert tomorrow.

> Lend time is unreasonably short

> No explanation for the action is given.

FIGURE 3.1
An Unethical Message

Ethics in Business

NOTE 3.44
Only a small percentage of business and professional people are unethical.

Today we frequently learn about unethical behavior in business and government through the news media. Insider trading, bribery, misleading advertising, misrepresentation of facts, cover-ups, and stonewalling seem to be common practice.

In fact, only a small percentage of business and professional people behave in unethical ways. Those who are unethical rarely succeed in the long run, and most of them are not successful even in the short run. Businesses complete millions of transactions daily based on trust and honesty. They advertise merchandise fairly, they receive orders and ship high-quality products, and make payments on time. If businesses and their customers do not relate this way, business survival is doubtful.

Global Business Ethics

In our global economy, managers face new issues on how to operate ethically in foreign lands. To conduct business ethically in another culture, managers must be aware of that culture's values and ethics. Companies must help managers distinguish between practices that are wrong and those that are merely different. A Web site for business ethics

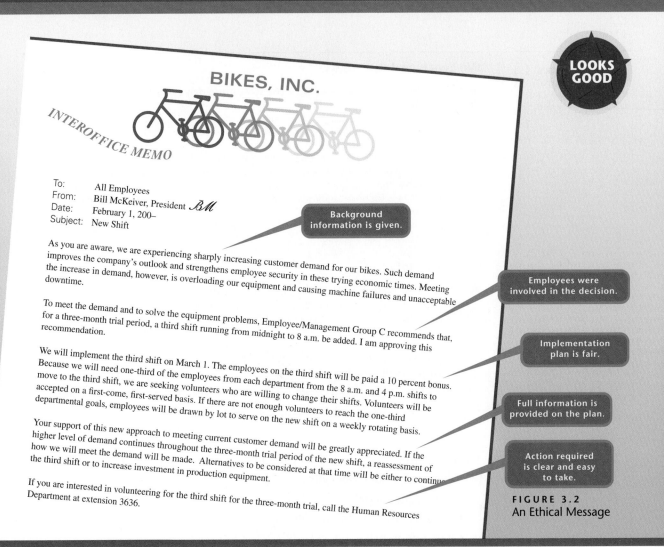

LOOKS GOOD

BIKES, INC.

INTEROFFICE MEMO

To: All Employees
From: Bill McKeiver, President *BM*
Date: February 1, 200–
Subject: New Shift

> **Background information is given.**

As you are aware, we are experiencing sharply increasing customer demand for our bikes. Such demand improves the company's outlook and strengthens employee security in these trying economic times. Meeting the increase in demand, however, is overloading our equipment and causing machine failures and unacceptable downtime.

To meet the demand and to solve the equipment problems, Employee/Management Group C recommends that, for a three-month trial period, a third shift running from midnight to 8 a.m. be added. I am approving this recommendation.

> **Employees were involved in the decision.**

We will implement the third shift on March 1. The employees on the third shift will be paid a 10 percent bonus. Because we will need one-third of the employees from each department from the 8 a.m. and 4 p.m. shifts to move to the third shift, we are seeking volunteers who are willing to change their shifts. Volunteers will be accepted on a first-come, first-served basis. If there are not enough volunteers to reach the one-third departmental goals, employees will be drawn by lot to serve on the new shift on a weekly rotating basis.

> **Implementation plan is fair.**

Your support of this new approach to meeting current customer demand will be greatly appreciated. If the higher level of demand continues throughout the three-month trial period of the new shift, a reassessment of how we will meet the demand will be made. Alternatives to be considered at that time will be either to continue the third shift or to increase investment in production equipment.

> **Full information is provided on the plan.**

If you are interested in volunteering for the third shift for the three-month trial, call the Human Resources Department at extension 3636.

> **Action required is clear and easy to take.**

FIGURE 3.2
An Ethical Message

in different countries, as well as a philosophical approach to international corporate ethics, can be found at the Web home page for the Joseph M. Katz Graduate School of Business at the University of Pittsburgh, http://www.pitt.edu/~ethics/.

Business Ethics Codes of Conduct

The most successful businesses are managed and operated by ethical employees. Research shows that today about 90 percent of all Fortune 500 companies have codes of ethics to help guide their employees' behavior. Codes of conduct must provide clear direction about ethical behavior when the temptation to behave unethically is strongest. The pronouncement in a code of conduct that bribery is unacceptable is useless unless accompanied by guidelines for gift giving and suggested employee responses to unethical situations such as offers of bribes. Executives must practice the ethical standards outlined in the code of conduct if the company is to have a successful ethics program.

Texas Instruments (TI) is an example of a company with a long-standing code of ethics. TI published its first written code of ethics in 1961 and has revised it several times to reflect business environment changes. Figure 3.3 on page 80 shows a portion of the TI Code of Ethics. TI employees receive a copy of the TI Ethics Quick

NOTE 3.45
The most successful businesses have ethical employees.

FIGURE 3.3
Excerpt from Texas
Instruments Code
of Ethics

We Learn and Create By:

Understanding that impatience with the status quo drives business and personal growth.

- Working together with trust to achieve superior results.
- Recruiting, training, promoting and rewarding people based on their performance and contribution.
- Encouraging open, honest and candid communications.
- Maintaining a professional work environment that is both satisfying and rewarding.
- Giving recognition and credit appropriately and frequently.
- Valuing all TIers for their contributions without regard to their position or level within the organization.
- Understanding that working together successfully may depend upon our willingness to trust someone else to take the lead.

We Act Boldly By:

Pioneering new business directions and opportunities.

- Striving to win aggressively and doing so with the highest standards of ethics.
- Taking responsible risks, managing those risks and learning from our experiences.
- Promoting workplace flexibility to make TI the employer of choice for the most creative and innovative people.
- Seeking out new perspectives and ideas through a diverse workforce.
- Recognizing that we succeed or fail together.

"Integrity," Ethics at TI, Texas Instruments. Retrieved 9/16/02 from *http://www.ti.com*. Permission granted courtesy of Texas Instruments.

Test on a business-card size mini-pamphlet to carry with them. This test consists of the following questions and advice:[8]

- Is the action legal?
- Does it comply with our values?
- If you do it, will you feel bad?
- How will it look in the newspaper?
- If you know it's wrong, don't do it!
- If you're not sure, ask.
- Keep asking until you get an answer.

NOTE 3.46
A company's code of
conduct provides direc-
tion for ethical behavior.

Many companies have training sessions to discuss ethics codes and explain procedures for compliance. Ethics codes can be in employee handbooks and placed on the company's Web site. In addition, corporations may provide a toll-free hot line for employees to obtain advice on ethical matters. Ethics is not just a U.S. issue. A Web site for the Institute of Business Ethics (IBE) in England gives guidelines for content of a code of business practice and ethics and how to make codes of conduct effective. The site may be found at http://www.ibe.org.uk/code.htm. Most businesses now realize the importance of a strong sense of individual and corporate values. The following examples of ethical and unethical communication illustrate the importance of business ethics.

[8] "Ethics at TI," *Texas Instruments> Company Information>Corporate Citzenship*, 1995–2003, <*http://www. ti.com/corp/docs/company/citizen/ethics/quicktest.shtml*> (26 January 2003).

A HUMAN RESOURCE CASE

In the mid-1990s a lawsuit by African-American Texaco employees alleged illegal racial discrimination practices in hiring and promotion. Two years after the filing of this suit, a public relations nightmare developed when the *New York Times* reported an audiotape recording of several high-level Texaco executives using racial slurs and derogatory metaphors. An examination of events by the Equal Employment Opportunity Commission ensued and, as a result, Texaco agreed to a $176.1 million class-action settlement. A research study of the economic damages suffered by Texaco shareholders as a result of the lawsuit and the negative publicity showed an estimated total loss in excess of $500 million.[9]

A GLOBAL CASE

Levi Strauss, located in San Francisco, California, had a supplier that posed an ethical problem. The Tan family, a large supplier for Levi Strauss, allegedly forced 1,200 Chinese and Filipino women to work 74 hours per week in guarded compounds in the Mariana Islands. Levi Strauss, after repeated warnings—good examples of ethical messages—to the Tans, broke off the business arrangement. The story of Levi Strauss has numerous examples of how the company applies its key values in meeting consumer needs. A comprehensive code of conduct ensures that individuals making the company's products "anywhere in the world will do so in safe and healthy working conditions and be treated with dignity and respect."[10]

NOTE 3.47
Employee actions should be compatible with the company ethical code.

A PRODUCT CASE

A review of the way Johnson & Johnson and its managers faced an ethical situation may illustrate how most businesses should operate. In 1982 an unknown criminal poisoned Tylenol capsules, which led to the deaths of seven people. Unaware of the cause of the deaths, Johnson & Johnson managers based their ethical and decisive reactions to this crisis on the company's 45-year-old credo, which can be accessed on its Web site at http://www.jnj.com. Underlying this credo is the belief that business is a moral undertaking for the benefit of society, with responsibilities that go far beyond sales and profits.

Johnson & Johnson developed communications to alert the public and medical community, removed all Tylenol capsules from stores, halted production, and cooperated with the media and public health officials. Society was well served by this private company. Its managers' ethical behavior was the foundation for the comeback of Tylenol in new tamper-proof containers. Less than six months after the tragedy, Johnson & Johnson had regained 70 percent of its previous market and Tylenol was again available to the public. The Johnson & Johnson story is a model of ethical managerial decisions and communication.

ETHICAL DECISIONS

In many communication situations, you will be faced with gray areas. Most situations are complex, and few decisions are entirely right or entirely wrong. There may be

NOTE 3.48
Ethical standards guide decisions for gray areas of right or wrong.

---

[9] Stephen W. Pruitt and Leonard L. Nethercutt, "The Texaco Racial Discrimination Case and Shareholder Wealth," *Journal of Labor Research*, 23:4 (Fall 2002), (EBSCO HOST database, Business Source Premier), 1–5.

[10] Levi Strauss & Co., Vision & Values, "Integrity—Doing the Right Thing," (2001), <*http://www.levistrauss. com*> (13 October 2002).

competing interests among your superiors, subordinates, customers, suppliers, stockholders, and others. Ethical principles and systems that can help you make decisions on ethical content for your messages are presented in the following sections. In her Communication Quote, Whitney Calvert describes challenges businesspeople face for ethical conduct and suggests two guides for meeting these challenges.

An Ethical Situation—Communicating about Coca-Cola's Downsizing Program

As you study the principles and systems for making ethical decisions, think about the following example. The Coca-Cola Company's significant restructuring of its operations in January 2000 involved the largest downsizing of employees in its 113-year history.[11] Assume that you are Douglas Daft, the company's president and chief operating officer, responsible for developing and transmitting messages that will announce to various receivers that the company has a suffered a loss for the fourth quarter and plans a layoff of 6,000 employees. The job cuts include about 2,500 in Atlanta and affect nearly 21 percent of the company's 29,000 employees in the global workforce.[12] The receivers of your messages will include the company's current employees, businesspeople in the communities where the company is located and where the employees live, suppliers to the company, local and state government officials, managers and supervisors within the company, the company's stockholders, the company's customers, and the general public.

NOTE 3.49
Respond to the receivers' needs for information.

Reflect on the receivers' needs in this communication situation. Assume the you–viewpoint. The employees need to know about the company downsizing several months in advance so they can search for other jobs. The local community and government officials need to know so they can seek other industries to replace the lost jobs and tax income. The suppliers need to know so they can seek replacement customers. The company managers and stockholders want a smooth transition and need the

[11] Betsy McKay and Joann S. Lublin, "Coke Planning Sweeping Job Reductions," *The Wall Street Journal*, 26 January 2000, sec. A, p. 3 , cols. 1–3.

[12] Henry Unger, "Coke CEO Says Growth Targets Are Out of Reach," *Knight Ridder/Tribune Business News*, 26 January 2000, (InfoTrac database, Gale Group and Thomson Learning), 1.

restructuring program to boost Coca-Cola's reputation and market leadership. The company needs to maintain a positive image with its customers and the general public.

How do you decide what is the *right information* that ought to be in your messages to these receivers? How do you resolve what is the *highest good* attainable for all those involved? After the following ethical principles for planning and developing messages are presented in the next section, the Coca-Cola downsizing communication situation will be analyzed.

Legal and Ethical Messages

LEARNING OBJECTIVE

⑤ *Explain how legal and ethical consider-ations are an integral part of planning, com-posing, and sending messages.*

Some of the ethical principles and systems that have worked well for others are pro-vided in the following sections. These principles and systems can help you be an ethical communicator. Choose among these suggestions to find the one or the combination that works best for you. Use the principles and systems you choose on a daily basis to ensure that your business messages are ethical.

The Golden Rule

The Golden Rule is "Do unto others as you would have them do unto you." This time-tested guide exemplifies the you–viewpoint. It calls for you to assume that you are the other person and from that perspective consider what should be done. This simply stated, fundamental moral imperative is a helpful, ethical principle for many business communicators. They analyze the communication problems facing them. Then they analyze the alternative content they could select for their messages. They choose con-tent that will provide the full disclosure, truth, and straightforwardness that they would want to have. Full disclosure and straightforwardness implies providing more informa-tion than technically necessary to avoid a lie as the following cartoon illustrates.

NOTE 3.50
Analyze message content based on ethical principles.

Zits

The Social-Utility Concept

The concept of social utility provides a systematic approach to ethics. To determine ethical content for a message using this approach, you first list all alternative content from which you could choose. You then consider the positive and negative impact of each of the alternatives on all those your message affects. Those content alternatives that produce the greatest good and the least harm for all affected are chosen for inclu-sion in the message. Using this approach, self-interest is overridden by the requirement that everyone's good be counted equally.

NOTE 3.51
Social-utility principles consider both positive and negative impact on receivers.

The Universal-Law Concept

Using the universal-law approach, the actions and the alternatives that could be chosen for message content are categorized as good or evil for society as a whole. The question the business communicator asks is, "Would I be willing to require all others in the same circumstances to send the same kind of message I am sending?" The answer has to be yes. You would have to be willing, for the welfare and betterment of society, to establish a universal law requiring all others to behave as you are behaving.

An Analysis of the Example Ethical Situation— Communicating about Coca-Cola's Downsizing Program

To determine whether a situation is ethical, consider these three steps: First, you should make sure that your message content meets applicable community and society standards of behavior. Second, you should make sure your message is legal. Third, you should apply your own personal values to the content.

Let's apply the ethical principles and systems given in this chapter to the Coca-Cola Company's downsizing situation described earlier. As you will recall, you are the manager responsible for announcing Coca-Cola's downsizing to various receivers.

The ethical issues in this communication situation involve competing interests. The company's managers and stockholders want a cost-effective downsizing that does not involve employee turmoil. The company's employees will need to find other jobs. Government officials will be concerned about lost tax revenue and community development. Suppliers will be concerned about replacing lost business. The company's customers will need a new source of supply. Finally, the public at large will have a general interest.

When do you send the messages? What information do you include in different messages for different receivers? How do you best achieve the highest good for all those involved in the communication?

Application of ethical principles and systems can guide you to develop ethical messages that contain full information and provide the greatest good to all receivers. With some assumptions about detailed facts in this communication situation, here are logical, ethical decisions regarding your messages:

- The messages will go out at the same time. They will be sent several months in advance of the downsizing to give the large number of people who will be affected time to take corrective actions.

- A truthful, open explanation of how the downsizing and restructuring are intended to streamline the company will be given. Information will be shared on how the changes in the company's organization will enable Coca-Cola's line managers around the world more autonomy to provide better service to their markets.[13]

- Information will be provided to the company's employees and managers to assist them in the transition. Departing Coca-Cola employees will leave with one of the more generous severance packages in recent history. The $800 million in severance benefits will also provide affected employees with resume, job search, and other out-placement services.[14]

---

[13] Constance I. Hays, "Coca-Cola to Cut 20% of Its Staff After Woes at Home and Abroad," *The New York Times,* 27 January 2000, sec. A, p. 1, cols. 1–2 & p. 6, cols. 1–2.

[14] Tammy Joyner, "Coke Tries to Soften Blow of Layoffs with Generous Severance Package," *Knight Ridder/Tribune Business News,* 26 January 2000, (InfoTrac database, Gale Group and Thomson Learning), 1–2.

- The company's stockholders and managers will be reminded of how the timing and content of the messages—to employees, customers, the general public, and others—best serve the company's long-term interests. The move is aimed at cutting costs and boosting earnings. Coca-Cola said completion of the restructuring will yield about $300 million in annual cost savings.

Final Comments on Ethical Behavior

In today's environment, public perception of business ethics may be at an all-time low, largely due to stock fiascoes of major corporations, with devastating effects on employees and public investors in contrast to large financial gains for CEOs and other organizational insiders. These corporation failures brought increased governmental scrutiny and legislation. In addition, the media focus on the effects of these actions on society, as well as public opinion, should bring a reexamination of ethical as well as legal issues for organizations and individuals.

Being ethical in your communication is not only essential and the right thing to do, it is also contagious. Others will follow your lead when they observe the success you experience in interpersonal relationships and in your career. Applying ethical principles and laws requires human judgment and interpretation.

Summary of Learning Objectives

Distinguish between legal and ethical issues.

Legal issues pertain to laws that are enforced through court systems and which represent standards of behavior valued by society. Ethical issues relate to value systems and cultural beliefs of individuals and organizations that determine their standards of behavior.

Describe communication technology trends and legal and ethical issues related to technology.

Technology is moving toward more portable and wireless systems, faster and higher capacity chips for computers, faster messaging and e-mail transmission to cell phones, and improvements in speech and handwriting recognition software. Continued growth is expected for the use of e-commerce, cell phones, Web sites, and the Internet. Legal and ethical technology issues relate to respect for the rights of others for privacy, protection of copyrighted works, and court jurisdiction of interstate and international commerce. In addition, laws can be broken and ethics breached by accessing pornographic Web sites or using business e-mail for personal use, sexually explicit language, or crude jokes.

Discuss legal considerations for business communication.

The contents of messages must be both legal and ethical. When in doubt about legal questions, consult an attorney. Contracts, credit and collection letters, and employment communication are subject to a variety of laws, legal codes, and requirements. Further, defamation and fraud can result from false statements that injure another person.

(4) Describe ethical considerations for communication and explain how codes of conduct help organizations promote ethical behavior and gain credibility.

Ethical communication means determining the right thing to do and demonstrating fairness and respect for the message receiver. Trust and honesty, fairness in advertising, and not harming others by withholding important information are a part of communication ethics. Ethical behavior means not only staying within the law but also being consistent with your own value system and your company's code of conduct. A code of conduct publicly announces the values and beliefs of the organization and makes company expectations a part of the work culture. Making this guide for conduct publicly available increases public respect for the business and its employees.

(5) Explain how legal and ethical considerations are an integral part of planning, composing, and sending messages.

Planning, composing, and sending messages requires constant adherence to legal and ethical principles. Is the message content accurate and complete? Have you considered what the receiver needs to know? Have you selected a medium that is appropriate for the message and that will be favorably received? Does the message reflect the community and society standards of behavior and the organization's ethical standards? Is it legal? Does it meet your own personal value system? Apply ethical principles and codes of conduct to all of your business messages. Consider these principles when planning your messages.

Discussion Questions

1. Define ethics and explain the difference between legal and ethical issues. (Objective 1 and Objective 4)
2. Describe three wireless technology devices that enable sending and receiving messages. (Objective 2)
3. Explain two types of research to increase computer power. (Objective 1)
4. **Internet.** What change in e-commerce increased public confidence in shopping and buying through the Internet? What other technology changes could cause growth in e-commerce? (Objective 2)
5. What is the difference between primary and secondary research? Give an example of how the Internet can help with each type of research. (Objective 2)
6. Describe two ethical considerations for using cell phones. (Objective 2)
7. Describe two types of laws that affect agreements between two or more parties. (Objective 3)
8. Explain why you agree or disagree with this statement: "Only a small percentage of business and professional people behave in unethical ways." (Objective 4)
9. Explain the universal-law concept as a guide to ethical messages, and give an example of how this law could apply in communication about pollution from a company's manufacturing process. (Objective 5)
10. How can a code of conduct by a business or other organization help employees to make ethical decisions? (Objective 4)

Application Exercises

1. **Ethics. E-mail.** Assume that you are in college and your roommate is a "computer whiz." She tells you about once being able to get access to the bank's database in her hometown, explaining that no harm was done because she didn't steal anything but just wanted to see if it could be done. Since coming to the university, she has tried to get access to the campus registrar's database of student records. Develop a list of points for your discussion with her of the legal and ethical implications of her actions. E-mail the list to your instructor. (Objective 2)

2. **Ethics. Teamwork.** Form a team of three to five students. For one week, each of you will listen to a television news show or read the daily newspaper to identify situations reported in the news that have legal or ethical implications for communication. At the end of the week, meet together and make a list of the situations your team observed. As a team use a group consensus technique to select five issues for a discussion of the legal and ethical implications. Consider the individual opinions that may arise when discussing what is or is not ethical. Remember that individual ethical standards and opinions about ethics may differ; not everyone agrees about what is ethical. (Objectives 3 and 5)

3. **Ethics. Internet. Teamwork.** From the five issues identified in the activity above, meet with your team and write three questions about the situation that you need to research further to understand the legal and ethical implications for action in these situations. Use the Internet for this research. As a team, develop a summary of what the team learned about each issue, and present your findings to the class. (Objectives 1, 3, and 5)

4. **E-mail. Ethics.** Send an e-mail message to your instructor describing an ethical or legal communication that you had to handle at your job or in the classroom. Apply the ethical principles described in this chapter to the situation. (Objective 5)

5. **E-mail. Ethics.** A friend gives you a copy that he has made of a software program that he purchased. Is this a legal or ethical issue or both? Explain your answer in an e-mail sent to your instructor. (Objectives 1 and 2)

6. **Global. Ethics. Internet.** Assume that you are a good friend of an executive of a company that markets widgets in the Bahamas. You have stock in this company and your friend casually mentions that the widget is becoming obsolete. Nothing is mentioned about your stock. Is it legal for you to call your stockbroker and sell your stock? Is it ethical? Research the topic *insider stock trading* on the Internet. Write your answer to these two questions, explaining your answers based on your research. (Objectives 1 and 3)

7. **Ethics. E-mail.** Evaluate this statement using the TI Ethics Quick Test and the Code of Conduct from Figure 3.3: "It is better to steal from the stockholders of a company than the public because it will receive less media attention." Summarize your evaluation and post it to a class electronic discussion board, if one is available, or send it as an e-mail attachment to your instructor and members of your class. (Objectives 1, 3, and 4)

8. **Ethics.** For each of the following behaviors, explain whether it is illegal and/or unethical and what effect the behavior could have on an employee and the employer. (Objectives 1, 2, and 3)
   a. Sending sexually-explicit jokes to fellow employees using company e-mail.
   b. Taking personal calls on your own cell phone or pager while at work.
   c. Copying company software for home use.
   d. Blaming a technology glitch for an error that you made.
   e. Using the office copier to make 150 copies of your social club's newsletter.

f. Taking home pens and paper from the office for other than work tasks for your company.

g. Overstating an expense item on a travel expense report for reimbursement.

h. Inflating the sales price and giving a kickback to a customer.

i. Shopping on the Internet at work for personal items.

j. Using a cell phone to transact business while traveling in a company car.

k. Using an employer's stationery when applying for a job with another firm.

 9. **Ethics.** Assume that a section of the company policy where you work conflicts with your own individual value system. When a situation arises that requires application of this policy for a communication that you are to write, which ethical guide would you follow? What would be the likely consequences? Form a team of three to five students to discuss this question. Summarize your conclusions to share with the class. (Objective 4)

10. **Ethics.** Company officials searching for a way to avoid bankruptcy raised cash with off-the-balance-sheet loans and overstated results by inflating capital expenses and hiding the debt. The company's stock traded on Wall Street. Evaluate the actions taken to avoid bankruptcy. Use the guidelines from this chapter for your evaluation. (Objective 1, 3, 4, and 5)

 11. **Ethics. E-mail.** John Kenneth Galbraith is quoted as saying "The salary of the chief executive of the large corporation is not a market reward for achievement. It is frequently in the nature of a warm personal gesture by the individual to himself."[15] Collaborate with another classmate to write a reaction paragraph that considers the quote and the ethical and legal issues related to it. (Objectives 4 and 5).

 12. **Ethics. E-mail.** A civil right is an enforceable right or privilege. Breach of this right can result in legal charges. Laws protect freedom of speech, press, assembly, the right to vote, and the right to equality in public places. A newspaper prints a story based on an unsubstantiated source that proves to be false but is damaging to the reputation of a local business official. Is the story protected by freedom of the press from charges of defamation or fraud? Prepare a brief slide presentation explaining your answer. Send the slide presentation to your teacher as an e-mail attachment. (Objectives 3 and 5).

13. An automobile manufacturer planned to sell cars directly to consumers through the Internet. Texas law prohibited auto manufacturers from acting in the capacity of dealers. If cars are sold to Texas consumers via the Web, is the action subject to Texas courts? Explain how laws of legal jurisdiction apply to this manufacturer's car sales. (Objectives 3 and 5)

 14. **Ethics.** A bank charges extra fees to Hispanic customers for opening and maintaining a checking account without meeting the bank's minimum deposit amount. The account has no check writing privileges although it was advertised to Hispanics as a checking account. Customers must go to the bank to make a withdrawal. Each deposit or withdrawal from the account costs the customer $1.50. Write a letter to the Better Business Bureau explaining why you believe this action may be unethical or illegal. (Objectives 1, 3, and 5).

 15. **Ethics. Teamwork.** A manager of a department store tries to follow a company policy that prohibits off-the-clock work requirements of employees; however, store managers have to keep payroll costs below a target set by headquarters and overtime pay is against policy. The store manager decides that the only way to control payroll costs is to require employees to stay at work 30 minutes each day after they clock out to

[15] Susan Ratcliffe (ed.), *The Oxford Dictionary of Phrase, Saying, and Quotation*, 2nd ed., (New York: Oxford University Press, 2002), col. 1, item 46, p. 54.

straighten merchandise for the next day. After all, she reasons, the two company policies are in conflict with one another. Write a paragraph explaining why you believe the action is or is not unethical or illegal. Exchange papers with a classmate and critique each other's response. (Objectives 1, 3, 4, and 5)

16. **Ethics.** A pharmaceutical company hides indications of a drug's dangerous side effects and delays sending a message to physicians about possible effects until six months after research documented serious illness or death from use of the drug. Describe in writing your beliefs of the actions that the manufacturer should have taken to send messages that could have saved lives or prevented serious injury. Explain whether you believe a pharmaceutical company has an obligation to the public greater, equal to, or less than manufacturers of automobiles. (Objectives 1, 3, 4, and 5)

17. **Ethics.** A friend of a college football coach faxed the coach a description of plays from a rival team's play book. The coach's team was scheduled to play the rival team the next week. The coach accepted the plays and used them in preparation for the game. In a group of three to five people, decide whether you believe the actions of the friend and the coach to be ethical. Explain the reason for the decision. (Objectives 1, 2, and 5)

18. **InfoTrac. Ethics. Internet.** Use InfoTrac to access an article in *Maclean's*, June 19, 2000, p. 40, titled "Who Owns Knowledge?" by Diane Francis (Article No. A62736801). Read the article and answer the following questions: (Objectives 1, 2, and 5)
    a. Do you believe that the intent of the program to help fellow impoverished Filipinos steal free access to the Internet makes the behavior ethical?
    b. Explain your beliefs about whether equity of access to computer technology is a justifiable argument in this case.
    c. Debate the issue of property rights and copyright versus open access of Internet material for the benefit of society.

19. **InfoTrac. Ethics.** Access from InfoTrac the article "New Technology Strains Ethics" from *USA Today*, June 1999, Volume 127 (article A54821978). Review the responses of workers to "Unethical Acts in the Workplace." Compare your responses to those of the workers. Answer the following questions: (Objective 5)
    a. How many of these acts do you believe are unethical?
    b. Have you committed at least one of them?
    c. Explain why these actions would not meet one of these guides for legal and ethical messages: the Golden Rule, the Social-Utility Concept, or the Universal-Law Concept.

20. Obtain a sample contract. Identify the four essential elements applicable to this contract. (Objective 3)
    a. Offer and acceptance
    b. Competency of parties
    c. Legality of subject matter
    d. Consideration

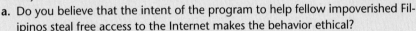

There are Web exercises at **http://krizan.swlearning.com** to accompany this chapter.

Message Analysis

Based on what you have learned in this chapter about codes of conduct, revise the following letter that explains the General Standards of Conduct for State Government Employees. Reword for a positive tone, as well as clarity and completeness. Edit your letter carefully before submitting it to your instructor. Assume that this letter is to be signed and returned as evidence that the employee has seen the policy.

Dear Employee:

It is my duty to inform you that every employee is required to sign this letter and return it no later than one week after it is received. You should know that your actions will be monitored while you work for this organizations. The Public code of Conduct recognised that public servant work is for the benefit of the people and is a trust based on concent of its citizens. Citizens are to have trust in the integrety of there government. Therefore, the following general statements of required behavoir are presented:

- *Don't take bribes. Be independent and impartial in decisions.*

- *Don't make decisions and policies outside of established goverment processes.*

- *Don't comit behavioral actions that destroy public confidence.*

- *Do not engage in conflict of interest deals*

- *Don't use public property—technology, copiers, telephones, etc. for private use.*

If you do any of these actions you will be found out and will be fired without an opportunity for explaination.

Have a good day!!!!

Respectfully Yours

Grammar Workshop

1. A System of morale principals is a definition of the word Ethics.
2. The ABC Journal publishs articles on Business Communications.
3. Effective english teachers learn the students how to write, speaking and listen.
4. Basic communications skills is fundmental for successful work in the business-field.
5. If I was president of the Company, I'ld make everyday a "casual, dress day.
6. Me and Rob was going to play golf last Saturday; but canceled since we heard about the severe thunderstorm's warning.
7. Your technology skills should be brushing up.
8. A code of conduct can helped a company to build a solid repute.
9. If you brake the law, you can axpect to be punish.
10. New technology hardwear keeps getting fast and grater.

Part *2*

Effective Communication Development

4

Principles of Business Communication

LEARNING OBJECTIVES

①

Identify words that your receiver(s) will understand and that will elicit the intended response.

②

Discuss the elements that create clear, concise, and effective sentences.

③

Develop clear, concise, logical, coherent, and effective paragraphs.

④

Use available alternatives to assure unbiased language in business messages.

⑤

Apply your own composing style to personalize your messages.

A. Michelle Jones, Client Service Associate, Bank One

LET'S TALK BUSINESS As a client service associate for Bank One, I understand the importance of oral and written communication. Success in business depends on building positive relationships with clients. In today's multicultural society, understanding the diversity of backgrounds, interests, and needs is essential to good customer service. Listening to each client's needs, communicating clearly, and always being willing to take that extra step to be helpful builds trust that leads to a long-term relationship between the customer and the bank. A smile and a helpful attitude are understood and appreciated, regardless of differences in language, age, gender, or ethnic background. Use simple, conversational words that do not stereotype people and that reflect a genuine interest in each person as an individual.

Being able to communicate effectively, either orally or in writing, depends on understanding the business client and responding to each situation from the client's point of view. In today's competitive business environment, improving communication with clientele promotes business success.

PHOTO COURTESY OF A. MICHELLE JONES

Michelle Jones reminds us that business success depends on effective communication and that simple, conversational words and the you–viewpoint promote such communication. As you study this chapter, you will see how these principles apply to word choice, sentence construction, and paragraph development. The best way to improve your ability to compose effective business messages, whether oral or written, is to apply these principles of business communication.

A basic principle is to keep your message short and simple. Communicators remember this principle by its initials, KISS, which stands for Keep It Short and Simple. Application of this principle means using short and simple words, sentences, and paragraphs to compose your business messages. As a result, your messages will be concise, easy to understand, and straightforward.

To communicate effectively, adopt a businesslike, friendly, and easy-to-understand style consistent with the KISS principle. Composing short, effective messages takes extra time but is worth it to you and your receiver. Competent communicators build customer relations and goodwill.

NOTE 4.1
Keep business messages short and simple.

Choosing Words

Words are the smallest units of messages. Give attention to each word you choose to be sure it is the most effective one. An **effective word** is one that your receiver will understand and that will elicit the response you want. You can improve your ability to choose words by (1) using a dictionary and a thesaurus and (2) following the six principles of business communication described in this section.

LEARNING OBJECTIVE

1

Identify words that your receiver(s) will understand and that will elicit the intended response.

Use a Dictionary and a Thesaurus

The two most valuable resources for the business communicator are a dictionary and a thesaurus. Use of these tools can increase your power to choose the most appropriate words for each of your messages.

A **dictionary** is a word reference and gives word meanings, acceptable spelling(s), hyphenation, capitalization, pronunciation(s), and synonym(s). Dictionaries may be in book or electronic format. Dictionary software can be installed on your computer or read from a CD. In addition, dictionary Web sites can be found on the Internet by using a search engine. Some of these Web sites require a subscription fee for full use; others allow use without a cost. An example of a dictionary Web site can be found at http://www.onelook.com. Specialized dictionaries for areas such as technology can be found also on the Internet.

A dictionary is helpful in choosing correct words. Similar words are confusing and, therefore, at times are misused. Examples of such words are *effect* and *affect, capital* and *capitol, principal* and *principle, continuous* and *continual,* and *further* and *farther.* See Business English Seminar E for an extensive list of easily confused words.

A **thesaurus** provides synonyms and different shades of meanings. If you have an idea you want to express, use a thesaurus to check for words that represent the idea and find several alternative words that you can use. Each choice usually has a slightly different connotation. A thesaurus can provide the simplest and most precise words for your message. Most word processing programs include thesaurus and spell-check functions.

NOTE 4.2
Use a dictionary to select words.

NOTE 4.3
Use a thesaurus to find synonyms.

© JOSÉ LUIS PELAEZ, INC./CORBIS

A dictionary and a thesaurus should be readily accessible when composing messages. These two references help you choose words and avoid overuse of the same word by providing **synonyms** (alternative words with similar meanings). In addition to using these references, apply the following six principles to select words for effective messages.

Principle 1: Choose Understandable Words

The first principle of word selection is to choose words that your receiver will understand. Prior to composing your messages, you should analyze your receiver's knowledge, interests, attitudes, and emotional reaction. Keep in mind the importance of the you–viewpoint. When you select words understandable to your reader and consider the reader's attitudes and emotional reaction, you are applying the you–viewpoint. Mentally, you are viewing the message from the receiver's perspective and anticipating the receiver's information needs and responses.

An **understandable word** is one that is in your receiver's vocabulary. Consider your receiver's educational level and knowledge of the message topic. The words that will communicate best are those slightly below the receiver's vocabulary level. Examples in the following list of words labeled *More Understandable* are an appropriate choice for most receivers. These words help you maintain a conversational tone to the message.

Less Understandable	More Understandable
abdicate	resign
amble	walk
apprehend	arrest
ascend	climb
demonstrate	show
emulate	copy
exonerate	clear
expedite	rush
facilitate	help
finality	end
gregarious	sociable
incite	provoke
incriminate	blame
initiate	start
prerogative	right
petulant	rude
utilize	use
verbalize	say
zealot	fanatic

The words listed under *More Understandable* in the previous examples are generic for most readers. Notice their brevity and conversational tone. Also, word choice requires selection of technical word usage. **Technical words** are terms that have a special meaning in a particular field.

Appropriate choice of technical words is a special consideration in choosing understandable words. Technical words assist in conveying precise, meaningful messages among certain receivers and senders. For example, between two accountants the use of the words *accrued liabilities* will be understandable. Using these technical words enables accountants to be more precise and efficient than using nontechnical language. For most of us, though, *accrued liabilities* is not as understandable as *debts that have not yet been recorded on our books*. Here are some other examples of technical and nontechnical words:

NOTE 4.5
Understandable words are generally simpler and shorter.

Technical Words	Nontechnical Words
acceleration clause	immediate repayment demand for late loan payments
amenities	features of the property
arrears	an unpaid debt
brief	summary of a legal case
capital-intensive	requiring large sums of money
cerebellum	lower part of the brain
COLA	cost of living adjustment to income
de facto	actual
equity	owner's value beyond debt
gelding	neutered male horse
font	typeface or print style for characters

(continued)

(continued)

Technical Words	Nontechnical Words
freeware	free software
haute couture	high fashion
juried	judged
symposium	conference
synchronous	at the same time
underwriter	sponsor or insurer

NOTE 4.6
Appropriate technical words are those in your receiver's vocabulary.

You will want to use only those technical words that are in your receiver's vocabulary. To do otherwise reduces the receiver's understanding of your message. If you are not sure if a technical word is in your receiver's vocabulary, do not use it.

In summary, you can best choose understandable words by selecting simple words, short words, and technical words appropriate to the receiver. The example words shown below under *More Understandable* are for a receiver who is a typical high school graduate and who has no particular knowledge of the topic.

Less Understandable	More Understandable
She should be on the qui vive.	She should be alert.
Benito formulated the manifesto.	Benito prepared the statement.
Have you ever met a philodox?	Have you ever met a person who likes to hear himself talk?
The altercation between Hilda and Lupe originated following dissension.	The fight between Hilda and Lupe began after a quarrel.
Midori demanded the prerogative to establish her own docket.	Midori demanded the right to set her own schedule.
Mea culpa.	I am at fault.
The boys on the corner were deadbeat after working all day.	The boys on the corner were exhausted after working all day.

The Communication Note captures the importance of Principle 1. For a message to be effective, the receiver must understand its meaning and intent.

COMMUNICATION NOTE

"Strive for Clarity in All Your Correspondence" Whatever your purpose for writing, your first and premier goal should be to gain your readers' understanding.

From *Essential Assistant*, 15:7 (July 2002), 7

Principle 2: Use Specific, Precise Words

NOTE 4.7
Use specific and precise words.

Specific words are clear and precise in meaning. In your business messages use words that are clear and that will leave no question in your receiver's mind about the intended meaning. Words selected for your message should be so precise that they accurately mirror what you want the receiver to understand.

Vague or **abstract words** are indefinite words; they do not have a specific meaning that is the same for each receiver of the message. Vague words are not precise; they are the opposite of specific words. **Abstract words** may be nouns that identify an idea, emotion, quality, or belief. Examples are *thought*, *beauty*, and *miracle*. Because people differ in opinions and feelings, abstract nouns have different meanings for different people. Also, some adjectives and adverbs do not have the same meaning for different people. For example, the word *some* in the previous sentence is an adjective. How much is *some*? Is it 5, 10, or 50? The message receiver cannot be sure; therefore, *some* is vague and imprecise in meaning. A speaker or writer who uses the adverb *very*, intends to emphasize the word the adjective modifies. However, *very* is imprecise and does little or nothing to help the message receiver interpret the meaning. Additional words add preciseness to meaning only if they provide meaningful, specific details that help interpret the meaning.

Vague or abstract words can create wrong or confusing meanings in your receiver's mind. They state a general idea but leave the precise meaning to the receiver's interpretation. Give preference to specific and precise words in your business messages. Here are examples of vague or abstract words and ways to make them specific and precise:

NOTE 4.8
Vague or abstract words mean different things to different people.

Vague	Specific
many	1,000 or 500 to 1,000
early	5 a.m.
hot	100 degrees Fahrenheit
most	89.9 percent
others	College of Business Administration students
poor student	has a 1.6 grade point average (4.0 = A)
very rich	a millionaire
soon	7 p.m. Tuesday
furniture	an oak desk

Notice in the preceding examples how adding a few words makes the meaning precise. These additions to the length of your message are worth the clarity that you gain. The Rugrats cartoon shows how confusing words can be.

Principle 3: Choose Strong Words

A **strong word** is one that creates a vivid image in the receiver's mind. In the English language verbs are the strongest words, and nouns are next in strength. (See Business English Seminar A for a review of the parts of speech.)

Give preference to verbs and nouns in your business messages. The strongest verbs are those that express action (run, play, work, explain) rather than a state of being (is, are, was, were). Use state-of-being verbs sparingly; words of action present a strong, meaningful picture in the receiver's mind. Think of these action verbs and specific nouns as power words. **Power words** have a distinct meaning and create a visual image in the mind of the receiver. Adjectives and adverbs that make a noun or verb specific give preciseness and clarity; however, if they are vague terms (i.e., very, many, few, some, often), they distract the receiver from the main points of the message. Furthermore, overuse of adjectives and adverbs reduces their effectiveness and results in overstating a point or position. To have an impact, business messages should convey objectivity without exaggeration.

Overuse of prepositions and prepositional phrases distracts from the message. Eliminate those that are unnecessary.

A sender who communicates with clarity and forcefulness is described as "a person of few words," "the strong, silent type," "straight to the point," and "clear as a bell." A short, powerful message composed of power words will get the attention of your receiver. Note how changing word usage in these examples creates a stronger message and presents a clearer mental image.

Weak Nouns and Verbs	Strong Nouns and Verbs
The conflict is ongoing.	The war rages on.
The situation was creating contention.	The problem created conflict.
He dived into the water.	He plunged into the waves.

Weak Adjectives and Adverbs	Strong Adjectives and Adverbs
Her dress is pink.	She wore a rose-colored dress.
Many individuals were at the reception.	Fifty people attended the reception.
I very nearly died.	I almost died.

Unnecessary Prepositions or Phrases	Simple, Direct Statement
I ran the copies off on the printer.	I printed the copies.
The market sold the item free of a duty charge.	The market sold the item duty free.
Did you pay out rent for the storage space?	Did you rent the storage space?

Although Principle 3 advocates a preference for strong words, at times you will want to soften a message with weaker words. This is particularly true for a message that is bad news for your receiver. If you have to discuss a problem with a coworker, you will build better human relations and more acceptance of your message if you use the weaker word *situation* instead of the stronger word *problem*. (In Chapter 8 you will study how word choice can help to gain acceptance for a negative message.)

Principle 4: Emphasize Positive Words

NOTE 4.12
Effective communicators
have a positive,
can-do attitude.

A positive, *can-do* attitude is one of the most important attributes you can have in business. Having that attitude is just the first step. Communicate a *can-do* message to your receivers by selecting positive words and avoiding negative words. A **positive word** is one that conveys optimism and confidence. **Negative words** trigger unpleasant emotional feelings for receivers.

Positive words in a message help achieve business communication goals of securing the needed response, maintaining a favorable relationship, and gaining goodwill. Here are examples of negative words you should avoid using when possible:

N O T E 4 . 1 3
Positive words help achieve message goals.

Negative Words

contradict	disapprove	deny	thwart	failed
complaint	accuse	stingy	hateful	not
don't	disgust	discouraging	wrong	angry
problem	obnoxious	blame	improper	neglected
impossible	flunked	trouble	disaster	insensitive
never	unhappy	sorry	regret	no

These examples show that unpleasant and negative words are strong words. On occasion, you will want to use negative words for emphasis. An example would be a letter to a vendor to replace a lamp broken in shipment. The tone of the letter should be positive, but negative words can emphasize the loss. A sentence might read: "The lamp was broken when it arrived. The glass base was shattered, and the lampshade was torn. The box in which it was shipped was mashed almost flat." Although the words *broken*, *shattered*, and *mashed* are negative, they emphasize the condition of the lamp when it arrived.

As the next examples show, however, you will convey a positive attitude and the you–viewpoint more effectively if you emphasize what can be done rather than what cannot be done. Selecting positive words and avoiding negative ones help promote good professional and personal relationships.

Negative Phrasings	Positive Phrasings
I cannot attend the meeting today.	I will be available tomorrow for a meeting.
The item you ordered is not in stock.	We will fill your order on December 5.
You will not regret your decision.	You will be pleased with your decision.
We are not open until later.	We open at 10 a.m.
Gloria is never happy before 7 a.m.	Gloria is happy only after 7 a.m.
The gas tank is half empty.	The gas tank is half full.
You will not be enrolled at UCSB until after December 2004.	You will be enrolled at UCSB as of January 2005.
I regret to advise that we must decline the refund for your defective lawn mower.	Our professional staff will repair your lawn mower.

Principle 5: Avoid Overused Words

An **overused word** is one used so much in normal conversation or in business messages that it has lost its effectiveness. The continued use of such words makes messages less

N O T E 4 . 1 4
Overused words have lost their effectiveness.

Employees who develop a positive, can-do attitude become better communicators.

precise and less understandable. Because we hear them often, overused words make messages less interesting. Avoid these and other overused words:

Overused Words and Phrases

win-win	it goes without saying	you know
awesome	below the belt	like
really	wannabe	OK or okay
random	interface	dude
change agent	down to the wire	rightsizing
nice	by leaps and bounds	slamdunk
level playing field	out of the loop	razor thin
synergy	thinking outside the box	lean and mean
bottom line	impact (as a verb)	get over it
paradigm	wow	in denial

Principle 6: Avoid Obsolete Words

NOTE 4.15
Obsolete words are pompous, dull, or stiff.

An **obsolete word** is one that is out-of-date, pompous, dull, or stiff. Business messages in past years used these formal, unnatural words and expressions; and they continue to appear in some of today's business messages. Everyday conversation does not use these words, and they should not be used in business communication.

The use of obsolete words makes a written or oral message formal, stilted, and pompous. The following are examples of obsolete words and phrases that you should avoid:

Obsolete Words and Phrases

Enclosed please find	permit me to say	as per	pleased to inform
permit us to remind	enclosed herewith	hereby advise	thanking you, I remain
mind your p's and q's	thanking you in advance	your kind favor	in regard to
regret to advise	I hereby send	wish to advise	
trusting you will	take the liberty of	tower of strength	we remain

Obsolete expressions are stilted and unnatural. As you read the previous examples, you quickly realize that most people do not use obsolete words in their everyday conversations. However, some people use them in their writing or public speaking because they view a written message or a speech as formal. Such obsolete words should be avoided in all business messages. Conversational language communicates best with receivers.

Developing Sentences

In the first part of this chapter you learned how to choose effective words. Now you are ready to study the principles that will guide you in combining those words into effective sentences. Businesspeople prefer concise, efficient, effective communication. To be successful, you will want to use clear, short sentences that are in the active voice and that emphasize your most important points. The following are principles for developing clear sentences.

Principle 1: Compose Clear Sentences

Using the principles discussed in the preceding sections for choosing words will help you compose clear sentences. A **clear sentence** uses words that are understandable, precise, strong, and positive. In addition, clear sentences have unity; that is, they normally contain one main idea and have related words placed close to one another. Finally, clear sentences are grammatically correct.

GIVE SENTENCES UNITY

A sentence that has **sentence unity** communicates one main idea—one main thought. At times you may want to include ideas that support the main idea. The general rule, however, is one thought, one sentence. If you have two main thoughts, construct two separate sentences. Examine these contrasting examples of sentences without unity and with unity:

Lacks Unity	Has Unity
University students will receive notice of a change in the Small Business minor; and the Small Business Web site, which provides information for managers of small businesses, will show this change in the minor and list the new requirements.	University students will receive notice of a change in the Small Business minor. The Small Business Web site, which provides information for managers of small businesses, will show this change in the minor and list the new requirements.

LEARNING OBJECTIVE

2 *Discuss the elements that create clear, concise, and effective sentences.*

NOTE 4.16
Use short, clear sentences; active voice; and appropriate emphasis.

NOTE 4.17
Compose clear sentences with understandable, precise, strong, and positive words.

NOTE 4.18
Clear sentences have unity.

Separating the two subjects—*University students* and Small Business Web site—made each sentence clearer and gave each subject more emphasis.

KEEP RELATED WORDS TOGETHER

NOTE 4.19
Place related words close together in sentences.

Words, phrases, or clauses that describe or limit other words, phrases, or clauses are **modifiers**. Modifiers should be placed close to the words they modify. For the sentence to be clear, the word or words described or limited by the modifier must be obvious. Each of the following Unclear Relationship examples shows in italics both the modifier and word(s) that could be confused, followed by the question in the reader's mind.

Unclear Relationship	Clear Relationship
When I give you the *test* and raise my *hand*, start taking *it*. (Take my hand or the test?)	When I raise my hand, start taking the test that I gave to you.
Luke *will submit* his resume *after he talks with Mark* for the professional trainer position *on Friday*. (Will he talk to Mark on Friday or submit his resume on Friday?)	After talking with Mark, Luke will submit his resume on Friday for the professional trainer position.
Sue and Jim laid the *plans* on the table where *they* remained for two weeks. (The plans remained for two weeks or Sue and Jim remained for two weeks?)	The plans remained on the table for two weeks after Sue and Jim laid them there.

USE CORRECT GRAMMAR

NOTE 4.20
Clear sentences are grammatically correct.

Clear sentences are grammatically correct. All parts of a sentence should agree. The subject and verb should agree in number—plural or singular. Pronouns should agree with their antecedents in three ways—number, gender, and clear relationship. A clear relationship between the pronoun and its **antecedent** (the word to which it refers) means that there is no question about which word in the sentence is the antecedent.

Beetle Bailey

Another important form of agreement is **parallelism**—using the same grammatical form for parts of sentences that serve the same purpose. Correct grammar is discussed in Business English Seminars A and B. The Beetle Bailey cartoon shows Sarge using the same word as an adjective and its –*ly* form as an adverb. Although we can only imagine what that word is, the two words do not serve the same purpose and, therefore, do not require parallel form!

Grammatically correct sentences have agreement of subject and verb, agreement of pronoun and antecedent, and parallel structure of similar sentence components. The sections that follow illustrate each of these grammatical rules for sentences. Study the following examples; you can use the Internet to review additional examples of pronoun usage in the InfoTrac database in Article A87457704, "Master Those Problem Pronouns."

Agreement of Subject and Verb

The *quarterback* and his offensive *team* always *play* to win. (plural subject; plural verb)

The *price* of stamps, as well as postal cards, *changes* often. (singular subject; singular verb)

Agreement of Pronoun and Antecedent

The *company* increased *its* number of subsidiaries. (singular antecedent; singular pronoun)

Students expected *their* grades to be posted promptly. (plural antecedent, plural pronoun)

The *woman* followed *her* career plan to obtain the position. (feminine antecedent and pronoun)

Mary and *John* attended *their* high school reunions. (Plural subject, plural antecedent, and plural pronoun; both genders and a generic gender pronoun)

Because only five people attended the *meeting* and the *conference* started on time, *it* should be rescheduled. (Unclear antecedent. Should the meeting or the conference be rescheduled?)

Only five people attended the *meeting*, and *it* should be rescheduled. The conference started on time. (Clear relationship between the pronoun and its antecedent)

Parallel Structure

The defendant in the case said that *he was despondent* over his wife's death, *he was without employment*, and *he was under a doctor's care* for depression. (parallel clauses)

The company president asked for an audit, notified employees to update accounts, and *called an accountant* to schedule the audit. (parallel verb structures)

Principle 2: Use Short Sentences

A short sentence is more effective than a long sentence. Generally, short sentences are easier to understand.

The average length for your sentences depends on your receiver's ability to understand. Keep the sentences short if the receiver has limited knowledge of the topic. Sentence length varies within a message, but short sentences should average 15 to 20 words. The following Communication Note gives a guide for sentence length. Generally, you

NOTE 4.21
Use short sentences.
They are understandable.

should use sentences of longer-than-average length only in messages for receivers with a high degree of knowledge about the message content.

NOTE 4.22
Vary sentence length for interest.

Vary the length of your sentences to provide interest and to eliminate the dull, choppy effect of too many short sentences. At times, you need a long sentence to cover the main idea or the relationship of ideas; but be sure that the meaning is clear. Any sentence that is 30 words or longer is considered a long sentence and should be examined for clarity. Read the sentence aloud to yourself to check its clarity.

A **complete sentence** usually has at least two words—a subject and a verb—and expresses a complete thought. For example, *Paul laughed* is a complete sentence, but *When I started my car* is not a sentence because the thought is incomplete. Words or phrases that are commands, assertions, or exclamations but are understood as a complete thought can be written as sentences in informal writing or in business letters but not in formal business reports. Examples of these self-contained words include *Best wishes, Great, Yes,* or *Wait!* Words, phrases, or clauses that are **sentence fragments** and do not express a complete thought may be used in informal conversation but should not be used in written communication. Examples of these sentence fragments are *In the near future, Anyway,* or *When I return from my trip to Mexico.*

Give preference to short sentences because they have several advantages. They are less complex and, therefore, easier to understand. They are efficient and take less time for the reader or listener. Short sentences are businesslike—concise, clear, and to the point. Omit unnecessary words and limit sentence content to one major idea to shorten long sentences.

OMIT UNNECESSARY WORDS

NOTE 4.23
Compose short sentences by omitting unnecessary words.

An **unnecessary word** is one that is not essential to the meaning of the sentence. Clear and concise sentences are lean. They have only *essential* words. When composing sentences, read each sentence carefully to eliminate unnecessary prepositions, prepositional phrases, and other nonessential words. Compare these examples:

Wordy	Lean
There were five women who attended.	Five women attended.
Automation of the workplace is a critical and necessary activity to make it more effective and efficient in the future.	Workplace automation is essential to improving future productivity.
On the occasion of the company's 10th anniversary, all of its customers were contacted and invited to a gala celebration.	The company invited all of its customers to a 10th anniversary celebration.

(continued)

(continued)

Wordy	Lean
I met the accountant on only one occasion.	I met the accountant once.
Now seems to be an appropriate time to restructure our own organization to prepare ourselves for the competitive marketplace of tomorrow.	Restructuring our organization now will prepare us for tomorrow's competitive marketplace.
Print out the copies of this report before tomorrow when I have to present it to the board.	Print copies of this report before my board presentation tomorrow.
He went up to my house where I live in the east end of the city.	He went to my residence in the city's east end.

LIMIT CONTENT

As you will recall, clear sentences convey one main idea. If you have a sentence that is 30 words or longer, you may want to divide it into two or more sentences. Examine the unity of the sentence to see if it is appropriate to divide it further. Remember, you want just one thought unit for most sentences.

NOTE 4.24
Limit content to achieve short sentences.

Excessive Sentence Content	Simplified Sentence Content
On today's visit to IBM, we were happy to have the opportunity to be introduced to Kim Lea; she presented some of the new information on new notebook computers. If you have any questions about these notebook computers, feel free to call her at IBM.	On today's visit to IBM, we met Kim Lea, who presented information on new notebook computers. If you have questions about these computers call her at IBM.
When you come to the office, contact the manager before attending the meeting; this contact will enable you to become familiar with the agenda for the purpose of being prepared to participate in the discussion.	When you arrive at the office, contact the manager to get the agenda before you attend the meeting. This agenda will help you prepare for the discussion.

One technique for changing long sentences to short sentences is to change commas or semicolons to periods when possible. This was done in the previous examples. Unnecessary words were omitted also. Often you can modify phrases and dependent clauses so that they can stand alone as short sentences.

Principle 3: Prefer Active Voice in Sentences

Sentences using an active-voice verb communicate more clearly, concisely, and forcefully than those in the passive voice. In the **active voice** the subject of the sentence is the actor; in the **passive voice** the subject is the receiver of the action. For example, *Gloria issued the teaching schedules* (active voice) versus *The teaching schedules were issued by Gloria* (passive voice). The active voice emphasizes Gloria and the action.

NOTE 4.25
Prefer active voice. It is
clear, concise, and
forceful.

The active voice is more direct, stronger, and more vigorous than the passive voice. The active voice usually requires fewer words and results in clear, concise sentences. Use active voice for most sentences. Consider the advantages of the active voice over the passive voice in these contrasting examples:

Passive	Active
The audit was performed by a local company.	A local company performed the audit.
The $1,000 fine was paid by the guilty party.	The guilty party paid the $1,000 fine.
Profits have increased this year at Disney.	Disney reported increased profits this year.
The automobile was purchased from John Coldiron.	John Coldiron sold the automobile.

NOTE 4.26
Passive voice can be used
for variety and for de-
emphasizing ideas.

Although these examples clearly show the power, liveliness, and conciseness of active voice, passive voice may be appropriate when you want to emphasize the result of the action or when you want to de-emphasize negative or unpleasant ideas. For example, when a customer's order is more important than who shipped it, the passive voice is appropriate:

Active: The department store delivered the clothing on schedule.

Passive: The clothing was delivered on schedule.

Passive voice emphasizes the customer's order and reflects the you–viewpoint. Further, in the passive voice the doer of the action—the vendor—is de-emphasized and appropriately left unnamed.

In the next example you can see how active voice seems to place blame. Passive voice reduces the negative impression and permits you to leave the doer of the action unnamed.

Active: The department store delivered your clothing late.

Passive: Your clothing was delivered late.

You can make limited use of passive voice to provide variety and interest in your messages and to emphasize the receiver rather than the doer of the action. However, because of its advantages, active voice should be dominant in your business messages.

Principle 4: Give Sentences Appropriate Emphasis

Giving your sentences **appropriate emphasis** means emphasizing the important ideas and de-emphasizing the unimportant ideas. Every speaker or writer wants a particular message understood by the receiver. As you develop each sentence in a message, ask yourself, "Should the main idea of this sentence be emphasized or de-emphasized?" Then design the sentence to give the appropriate emphasis.

You can emphasize or de-emphasize an idea in several other ways: Use sentence length, use location within the sentence, use sentence structure, repeat key words, tell the reader what is important, be specific or general, use format, and use mechanical means. Each of these ways is discussed and illustrated in the following sections.

USE LENGTH

Short sentences emphasize content; long sentences de-emphasize content. Use short sentences to give your ideas emphasis. Compare these examples:

The team planned to go to the meeting that will be held on Friday at 7 p.m.

The team planned to attend Friday's 7 p.m. meeting.

The important content of the message—*Friday's meeting*—receives emphasis in the short sentence. The longer version not only changes the main idea to a dependent clause but also includes unnecessary, distracting words.

NOTE 4.28
Length: Short sentences emphasize; long sentences de-emphasize.

USE LOCATION

Beginnings and endings of sentences are the locations of greatest emphasis. What ideas are stressed in these sentences?

Larry received a raise.

Larry's salary was raised from $30,000 per year to $35,000 per year.

Larry's outstanding performance resulted in a raise.

Larry is emphasized in all three sentences. Larry's raise also receives emphasis in the first sentence by its location at the end. The fact that Larry is now earning $35,000 receives emphasis in the second sentence. Finally, in the third sentence Larry's outstanding performance is emphasized, as well as his raise.

Sentence beginnings compete for attention with the words that follow them; endings compete for attention with words that precede them. Words in the middle of sentences, however, have to compete with both the preceding and following words and, therefore, are de-emphasized. For example:

The new position requires a transfer to another facility, but it affords an excellent opportunity for advancement.

Dumsile received her SAT scores; the scores for the ACT test, which was taken earlier, should be sent to her next week.

In the first sentence, *a transfer to another facility* is de-emphasized by its location. In the second sentence, *which was taken earlier* is de-emphasized. Location is an excellent way to give appropriate emphasis.

NOTE 4.29
Location: Beginnings and endings emphasize; middles de-emphasize.

USE SENTENCE STRUCTURE

You give the greatest emphasis to an idea by placing it in a short, simple sentence. If you want to show a relationship between ideas, emphasize main ideas by placing them in independent clauses and de-emphasize other ideas by placing them in dependent clauses. The independent clause is similar to the short sentence; it could stand alone as a complete sentence. Dependent clauses are not complete thoughts; they do not make sense stated without the rest of the sentence. (See Business English Seminar B for a discussion of sentence structure.)

The two short sentences that follow give approximately the same emphasis to two main ideas: the *six-figure salary* and *consider opportunities.*

I prefer to earn a salary in the low six figures. I would consider opportunities at a lower level.

NOTE 4.30
Structure: Independent clauses emphasize ideas; dependent clauses de-emphasize them.

If you want the two ideas to share emphasis—each receiving a reduced amount—you can organize them into a compound sentence:

> I prefer to earn a salary in the low six figures, but I would consider opportunities at a lower level.

By organizing these two ideas into one complex sentence, however, one idea can be emphasized and one de-emphasized. This sentence structure is called **subordination**. Organizing your sentences using subordination of ideas gives you flexibility in composing your messages. Examine the varying emphases in the following examples:

> Although I prefer to earn a salary in the low six figures, I would consider opportunities at a lower level.

> Although I would consider opportunities at a lower level, I prefer a salary in the low six figures.

In the first example, the idea of considering opportunities at a lower level is emphasized by being placed in an independent clause. In the second sentence, the primary idea of a salary in the low six figures gets the attention as an independent clause.

REPEAT KEY WORDS

Main ideas represented by key words can be emphasized by repeating those words within a sentence. Note the emphasis given *defective* and *radio* in this sentence from a customer complaint:

> The radio I purchased from you is defective; please replace this defective radio immediately.

Here is another example of emphasis through repetition of the same root word in different forms:

> Les and Tim flew to Costa Rica on a Boeing 767; the Boeing 767 is a safe plane.

Repetition of key words also provides coherence and movement in a sentence. Coherence and thought flow are discussed later in this chapter.

TELL THE RECEIVER WHAT IS IMPORTANT

NOTE 4.33
Explicitness: You can tell
the receiver what is im-
portant and what is
unimportant.

You can tell your receiver that an idea is important or unimportant by your word choice. For example:

> High grades and high SAT scores are *critical* for gaining acceptance at a top university.

> Of *less concern* is that the flight to Krakow, Poland, will be delayed.

Of course, you can use different words and constructions to indicate the importance of an idea. You can refer to ideas with such words as *significant, of (no) consequence, (not) a concern, high* (or *low) priority, (not) critical, fundamental,* and *(non)essential.* Your thesaurus will be helpful in choosing words to tell your receiver that one idea is important and another unimportant.

BE SPECIFIC OR GENERAL

NOTE 4.34
Specification: Specific
words emphasize; gen-
eral words de-emphasize.

Another way to give appropriate emphasis is to use specific words to emphasize ideas and to use general words to de-emphasize ideas. Here are examples of how this works:

Specific: Craig Jones bought a new *white Porsche Boxter*.

General: Craig Jones bought a new *car*.

Specific: I like to *run*, *swim*, and *bicycle*.

General: I like to *exercise*.

USE FORMAT

NOTE 4.35
Format: Emphasize ideas with punctuation and lists.

The way you arrange and punctuate a sentence can give emphasis to selected ideas. One way to highlight an idea is to separate it from other information in the sentence. Consider this example:

One factor is always key at any successful fund-raising event—food!

"Food" stands out because it is set off with a dash and an exclamation point. Dashes, colons, and exclamation points are strong punctuation marks and can be used to emphasize ideas. Ideas can be de-emphasized by setting them off with commas or parentheses, which are weaker punctuation marks. Ideas set off from the sentence with commas or parentheses are explanations that could be omitted without changing the meaning of the sentence; they add detail to the sentence.

A vertical numbered or lettered list attracts more attention than a list of items simply set off by commas in regular sentence format. This example shows how you can emphasize points by putting them in a numbered list:

The major conclusions of the study indicate that effective online delivery of instruction has these elements:

[1] An orientation session.

[2] Student-to-student interaction.

[3] Frequent communication and feedback from the instructor.

USE MECHANICAL MEANS

NOTE 4.36
Mechanics: Emphasize with underlining, type, color, and other mechanical means.

You can emphasize ideas through mechanical means in a variety of ways. You can *italicize* or use **boldface** type. You can use a different color to highlight selected ideas. The previous sentence and the illustrations and marginal notes in this book are examples of the effective use of color. Other mechanical means include type size, typeface, uppercase letters, bullets, arrows, and circles.

Overuse of format or mechanical means to emphasize ideas reduces their effectiveness and distracts from the ideas expressed. Reserve their use in letters and memorandums for special situations. The use of mechanical means to emphasize ideas is more common in advertisements, reports, and visual aids.

You can emphasize and de-emphasize ideas as you develop effective sentences. Applying and practicing the principles described in this section will help you strengthen your business communication skills.

Forming Paragraphs

LEARNING OBJECTIVE
③
Develop clear, concise, logical, coherent, and effective paragraphs.

Organizing sentences into meaningful paragraphs is an important part of composing a message. Organization of paragraph content helps your receiver understand the message and its intent. You can form effective paragraphs by following five basic principles for paragraph construction. These principles will guide you in determining paragraph length, unity, organization, emphasis, and coherence.

Principle 1: Use Short Paragraphs

You will want to use short paragraphs in your business messages. A **short paragraph** helps your receivers organize their thoughts, increases understanding of the message, and appears more inviting to the receiver than a long paragraph. Long paragraphs are more complex, are more difficult to read, and are harder to comprehend than short paragraphs. Receivers are more likely to read short paragraphs than long paragraphs.

In business letter and memo writing, short paragraphs average *four to five lines*. If any paragraph in a letter or memo is eight lines or more, it is long and should be examined carefully to see if it can be shortened or divided. Usually, business letters and memos are read quickly, and short paragraphs aid receiver understanding. A short message helps the receiver quickly understand its main thought. Billy, in the Family Circus cartoon on the next page, shows that he can shorten a long message and clarify the main point with only a few words.

Business reports are likely to be studied carefully, and the paragraphs can be somewhat longer, but not much longer than those in a letter or memo. In business report writing, short paragraphs should average six to seven lines. Twelve lines or more in any paragraph in a report is a signal that it is long, and its unity (see Principle 2) should be examined carefully. Criteria for a short paragraph for business letters, memos, and business reports are shown in the following Communication Note. These guidelines for the lengths of paragraphs in business messages are recommended averages and should vary, as needed, to accommodate content and to promote reader interest.

COMMUNICATION NOTE

How Long Is a Short Paragraph?

Business Letters and Memos

- A short paragraph can have *1 line.*
- Short paragraphs will average *4 to 5 lines.*
- Long paragraphs are *8 lines or more.*

Business Reports

- A short paragraph can have *2 lines.*
- Short paragraphs will average *6 to 7 lines.*
- Long paragraphs are *12 lines or more.*

In most business letters, memos, and reports, the first and last paragraphs are shorter than the middle paragraphs. Often the first and last paragraphs in letters and memos are one to three lines long and consist of only one or two sentences. In reports the first and last paragraphs may be somewhat longer. Short opening and closing paragraphs are inviting to the reader. They add emphasis to the message's beginning and ending ideas. In Parts 3 and 4 of this book, there are several examples of letters, memos, and reports. Notice the paragraph lengths in these written messages as you study these chapters.

THE FAMILY CIRCUS   By Bil Keane

7-3
©2002 Bil Keane, Inc.
Dist. by King Features Synd.
www.familycircus.com

"If I was Jefferson, instead of all those words, I'd have written: 'That's it, King! We're outta here!'"

Principle 2: Give Paragraphs Unity

Paragraphs should have unity. **Paragraph unity** means that all the sentences in a paragraph relate to one topic. The topic should be covered adequately; however, if the paragraph becomes too long, it should be divided into two or more logical parts. Examine the following paragraphs:

NOTE 4.42
Clear paragraphs have unity.

Lacks Unity

The baseball game had reached a crucial point. A large crowd had been at the park all afternoon. The weather had been muggy. Vendors were selling hot dogs and soft drinks.

Has Unity

The baseball game had reached a crucial point. It was the bottom of the ninth inning and the score was tied. Two batters were out. The third was at the plate, and the pitcher had already thrown two strikes and three balls. Yes, this was the most exciting time in the game.

Giving unity to paragraphs is sometimes more difficult than the preceding examples imply. The following example lacks unity. Can you determine why?

Lacks Unity

To save time, the College of Business has proposed that all professors submit their professional development plans online. The new procedure will require all professional development plans to follow the same format. Format consistency will save time for reviewers of the professional development plans. All College of Business faculty members must publish one refereed article per year and make two presentations at professional conferences.

Did you note that the fourth sentence did not relate directly to the paragraph's main topic? If you did, you are right. The main topic was saving time by submitting professional development plans online. The fourth sentence shifted the topic to publishing a refereed article and making presentations. The fourth sentence is a separate topic that requires its own paragraph or paragraphs.

Principle 3: Organize Paragraphs Logically

NOTE 4.43
Organize paragraphs logically using the direct or the indirect plans.

NOTE 4.44
Present positive or neutral news using the direct plan.

NOTE 4.45
Present negative news or persuasion using the indirect plan.

NOTE 4.46
The topic sentence presents the main point of the paragraph.

NOTE 4.47
The first sentence should be topical or transitional.

Paragraphs can be organized logically using one of two basic plans: the direct plan (deductive approach) or the indirect plan (inductive approach). In the **direct plan** the main idea is presented in the first sentence of the paragraph, and details follow in succeeding sentences. In the **indirect plan** details are presented first, and the main idea comes later in the paragraph.

The content determines which plan—direct or indirect—you will use. Positive news and neutral news can best be presented using the direct plan. Getting directly to the main point and following it with details help orient the reader to the content.

Negative news or persuasive news can be presented best by using the indirect plan. This approach enables message details at the beginning to pave the way for an unpleasant main point, an unfavorable recommendation, or a request for action.

The sentence that presents the main point of a paragraph is called the **topic sentence**. The topic sentence announces the main idea to the reader, or it summarizes the content of the main idea. In the direct plan, the topic sentence is like a headline and will be the first sentence, as it is in this paragraph. With the indirect plan, the topic sentence will be placed later in the paragraph.

As a general rule, the first sentence in a paragraph should be either the topic sentence or a transitional sentence. How to provide transition (movement) in a first sentence will be explained later, under Principle 5. Unless there is an important reason to locate it elsewhere in the paragraph, the topic sentence should be placed first in business messages.

The Communication Note that follows gives examples of the two basic plans. The topic sentences are italicized to show their location in each paragraph.

COMMUNICATION NOTE

Topic Sentence Location in Direct and Indirect Plan

Direct Plan (Topic Sentence First)
Most chief business executives rate business communication as the most important skill a manager can possess. A recent survey of business executives showed that 80 percent of the respondents thought business communication was a manager's most important skill. The remaining 20 percent of the respondents rated business communication second to technical skill. The survey was conducted using a random sample of the presidents of the Fortune 500 companies.

Indirect Plan (Topic Sentence Within)
Gain the edge in 2001! *Call 1.888.555.2387 and enroll in the International Training Certificate program today.* The International Training Certificate program offers certification for conducting business with people from (1) Asian cultures, (2) European cultures, and (3) Hispanic cultures.

Indirect Plan (Topic Sentence Last)
Spring is just around the corner. This means that vacation time is almost upon us. When you think about planning your vacation for this year, think of us. *Call the Newport Coast Travel Agency at 949.555.1234, and let us send you the "Summer Vacation Planner's Guide."*

In summary, paragraphs can be organized logically using the direct or the indirect plan. Generally, the direct plan is recommended for good news and neutral news; and the indirect plan is recommended for bad news and persuasion.

Principle 4: Give Paragraphs Appropriate Emphasis

As you will recall from this chapter's section on sentences, giving *appropriate emphasis* means emphasizing the important ideas and de-emphasizing the unimportant ideas. Many of the same ways for giving appropriate emphasis to sentences apply to giving appropriate emphasis to paragraph content. The Communication Note summarizes applicable ways to give emphasis.

NOTE 4.48
Give paragraphs appropriate emphasis using paragraph design.

COMMUNICATION NOTE

Six Ways to Emphasize Ideas

Length: Using short paragraphs emphasizes content, and using long paragraphs de-emphasizes content.

Location: Placing ideas at the beginning or ending of paragraphs gives the greatest emphasis. The middle of a paragraph is the location of least emphasis.

Repetition: Repeating key words throughout the paragraph can emphasize the ideas represented by those words.

Explicitness: Telling your reader that an idea is important or unimportant emphasizes it.

Format: Arranging and punctuating paragraphs in certain ways give emphasis. Call attention to ideas by using such things as punctuation, lists, or wider margins.

Mechanics: Emphasizing ideas can be done by mechanical means: underlining, boldface type, color, type size, typeface, uppercase letters, bullets, arrows, or circles.

Principle 5: Provide Paragraph Coherence

Providing **coherence** between and within paragraphs means having a smooth thought flow from one sentence or paragraph to the next one. You want to encourage your receiver's thoughts to move smoothly and logically through the message. The primary way to assure coherence is to organize paragraphs logically using the direct or indirect plans discussed in Principle 3.

Also, you can use transitional words and tie-in sentences to provide for coherence between and within paragraphs. Hints for successfully adopting these suggestions follow.

NOTE 4.49
Smooth thought flow provides paragraph coherence.

USE TRANSITIONAL WORDS

A **transitional word** is a helpful bridge from one idea to the next. Transitional words help receivers see where you are leading them, why you are leading them there, and what to expect when they get there. Transitional words provide coherence by holding ideas together logically.

For example, suppose you present an idea in one sentence and you want to expand on that idea in the next sentence. By using transitional words such as *in addition,*

NOTE 4.50
Provide coherence with transitional words.

furthermore, and *also* at the beginning of the second sentence, you help receivers see the relationship between ideas. The following example shows this kind of bridging between two sentences:

Adding Information

Monica is a proficient writer. *In addition,* she is an excellent speaker.

Various transitional words provide coherence for different situations. The following Communication Note gives some examples.

COMMUNICATION NOTE

Transitional Words Bridge Ideas

Contrasts: but, however, by contrast, nevertheless, on the other hand, on the one hand, from another viewpoint

Examples: for example, to illustrate, for instance, that is, as follows, like, in illustration

Sequence: first, second, third; one, two, three; also, in addition, finally; next, then, finally; to sum up; in conclusion

Emphasis: significantly, primarily, most important, particularly, especially, in fact, indeed, above all

Conclusions: therefore, thus, so, consequently, as a result, accordingly, hence

Exclusions: except, neither . . . nor, except that, all but, except for, all except

Additions: in addition, furthermore, also, and, similarly, moreover, as well as, too

---

USE TIE-IN SENTENCES

NOTE 4.51
Provide coherence with tie-in sentences.

A **tie-in sentence** helps your receiver move from one aspect of the subject to the next. When using the tie-in sentence technique for coherence, repeat the same subject one or more times. To develop tie-in sentences, you can paraphrase the subject, repeat key words that describe the subject, or use pronouns that refer to the subject. Examples of tie-in sentences using these approaches are as follows:

Paraphrasing: The information system in the Sheldon Hotel is *used extensively* for decision making. Because of this *high rate of use,* it is imperative that the data in the information system be up-to-date.

Repeating Key Words: Ernesto Garcia found that direct mail is a *cost-effective technique* for selling magazine subscriptions. Telemarketing is another proven *cost-effective technique* for promoting subscription sales.

Using Pronoun Reference: *Students* submitting applications to MBA programs must register for the GMAT test by April 1. *They* will receive confirmation of *their* registration by May 1.

Using Unbiased Language

The use of unbiased language is a final and important consideration in the composition of business messages. Fair and balanced treatment of all individuals regardless of race, gender, culture, age, ability, religion, or socioeconomic status is essential in a democracy. Such treatment is vital to the maintenance of favorable human relationships.

You will want to avoid all words that have unfavorable denotations or connotations in their reflection on any individuals. The use of such language will offend not only those to whom the references are made but also other persons. Respect for the dignity and worth of all persons is compatible with being a responsible citizen. To increase your effectiveness as a business communicator, analyze your messages to eliminate any biased language.

Roger Rydell, a Lexmark Vice President for Corporate Communications, uses the customer's perspective to plan content for Web sites that meet the needs of an international audience. How does his Communication Quote apply the you–viewpoint?

NOTE 4.52
Use unbiased language in your messages.

COMMUNICATION QUOTE

Customers around the globe are looking for seamless access to both product and purchase information. They want to know what your products can do for them and where they can obtain those products easily and efficiently. Web sites need to offer this seamless information access, followed with flawless execution. Web sites that are intuitive have a distinct advantage over those that require numerous words and clicks to get to the end game. They should be both role and task oriented. Above all, they should clearly reinforce the brand position you are trying to convey. Visitors want to know they've come to the right place and that they can count on everything you stand for in other venues.

—Roger Rydell, Vice President, Corporate Communications, Lexmark (Photo courtesy of Roger Rydell)

AVOID GENDER-BIASED LANGUAGE

Using unbiased gender language is a special challenge because of the structure of the English language. The English language implies stereotyping of males and females because of the generic use of masculine singular pronouns—pronouns used to represent both men and women—and the generic use of the word *man*. Fortunately, the structure of our language does not stereotype individuals on the basis of race, age, or religion.

Some English language listeners and readers subconsciously tend to picture a male when words such as *man, he,* or *chairman* are used. This is true even though such words are used generically—used to represent both men and women. These images should be avoided in your business messages. The examples shown on the next page suggest the availability of alternatives to words implying gender stereotyping:

LEARNING OBJECTIVE
4 Use available alternatives to assure unbiased language in business messages.

NOTE 4.53
Generic masculine words in the English language imply gender stereotyping.

Biased	Unbiased
businessman	businessperson, business executive, manager
chairman	chairperson, moderator, chair, group leader
policeman	police officer
salesman	salesperson or sales agent, representative, or associate
executives and their wives	executives and their spouses
mankind	humanity, people, human race
manned	staffed
mailman	mail carrier, letter carrier
Each chairman must submit his program to the membership committee.	Each chair must submit a program to the membership committee.
When a student carries a computer to class, she is able to take notes easily.	When students carry computers to class, they are able to take notes easily.
If an employee is late, give him one warning.	Give one warning to an employee who is late.
the ladies and the men	the women and the men, the ladies and the gentlemen
Gentlemen: Dear Sirs: (letter salutations)	Ladies and Gentlemen: (or avoid salutation by using the Simplified Block Letter style shown in Appendix A)

AVOID OTHER-BIASED LANGUAGE

NOTE 4.54
Avoid negative stereotypes.

To be sure that you treat people of different races and cultures in a bias-free manner, avoid negative stereotypes of any group. Chapter 2 gave guidelines for avoiding stereotypical language. A key point in respecting diversity is to think of people as individuals and avoid categorizing them by describing their special characteristics. Unless a description of the individual or group is essential to the message meaning, omit references to race, religion, age, or disability. For example, leave out the terms in italics in the following sentences: "The *Jewish* investor from New York City funded the construction of the regional mall." "The *white* teacher spoke to the inner-city youth." "The *old* man exercised in the mall."

NOTE 4.55
Use no language that belittles, offends, embarrasses, or denigrates other persons.

If reference to race or ethnic background is required, use terms that do not have unfavorable connotations. For example, African American is preferred to Negro; people of color is preferred to colored people. Individuals from Mexico may prefer the term Hispanic as an ethnic description. Senior is preferable to elderly or older person. When referring to persons with disabilities, use people-first language and focus on the person, not the disability. Thus, use *person with AIDS* instead of *AIDS patient* and *person with mental illness* instead of a *mentally ill woman* (or *man*).

"Do Not . . ."

- Use any language that belittles, offends, embarrasses, or denigrates other persons.
- Imply that a person of a different classification (race, gender, religion, culture, age, socioeconomic level, or physical or mental condition) is inferior simply because he or she is of that classification.
- Imply by your language that a person of another status is rigid, lazy, stupid, slow, devious, shrewd, dishonest, fanatical, or cold.
- Attribute superior qualities to persons of a certain status.

Composing with Style

The most effective business communicators use the principles in this chapter. You, too, should find them effective. Another important dimension of your communication is your personality. Your writing and speaking should reflect the interesting, unique person you are.

Be yourself. Use words and combinations of words that not only are understood by your receiver but also reveal who you are—words that give life and distinction to your message. Many combinations of words will send the same basic message to your receiver. Use the words that communicate clearly and concisely and that reflect your personality.

One of America's outstanding orators, Patrick Henry (1736–1799), showed what can be accomplished with style. The first sentence shows how he might have made one of his famous statements; the second sentence is what he actually said:

Not This: If I can't have freedom, then I would rather not live.

But This: Give me liberty, or give me death!

One of the leaders in advocating full rights for women, Susan B. Anthony (1820–1906), was extremely effective in awakening the American nation to inequities based on gender. Contrast the way she might have expressed her basic belief in equality for women with the way she actually expressed it:

Not This: There is no reason to give women fewer rights than we give men.

But This: Men, their rights and nothing more; women, their rights and nothing less.

Another powerful communicator who moved Americans, Martin Luther King, Jr. (1929–1968), used the principles of communication coupled with his own unique selection of words. What he could have said and what he did say are sharply contrasted in the following illustration:

Not This: It is hard for others to hold you down if you never give them the chance.

But This: A man can't ride your back unless it's bent.

Finally, from another effective writer and speaker, John F. Kennedy (1917–1963), we have this contrast in what could have been said and what was said:

Not This: Do not inquire about what you can get the government to do for you; instead, find out what you can do for the government.

But This: Ask not what your country can do for you; ask what you can do for your country.

LEARNING OBJECTIVE

(5) *Apply your own composing style to personalize your messages.*

NOTE 4.56
Compose messages that reflect *you.*

Effective communicators give thought and time to what they say and write. You, too, with study and effort, can improve your ability to be an effective communicator in your professional career and your personal life. Remember to use the you–viewpoint, apply the principles of business communication, and be yourself—you will then be a powerful business communicator.

The checklist in the Communication Note that follows will help you apply the principles of business communication. When drafting and revising messages, use the checklist to help you refine the content and structure.

Summary of Learning Objectives

(1) Identify words that your receiver(s) will understand and that will elicit the intended response.

Words are the smallest units of messages, and you will want to choose the most effective words for your messages. The six principles of choosing words are (1) choose understandable words; (2) use specific, precise words; (3) choose strong words; (4) emphasize positive words; (5) avoid overused words; and (6) avoid obsolete words. The two most valuable resources for the business communicator are the dictionary and the thesaurus. You need both accessible when composing messages.

(2) Discuss the elements that create clear, concise, and effective sentences.

Businesspeople prefer concise, efficient, effective communication; therefore, you will want to use clear, short sentences that use the active voice and that have appropriate emphasis. The four principles of developing sentences are (1) compose clear, grammatically correct sentences with unity and clear relationships between words and ideas; (2) use short sentences because they are more understandable than long sentences; (3) use active voice in sentences with the subject doing the action; and (4) give your sentences appropriate emphasis by using sentence length, location, structure, key word repetition, format, and other sentence design elements.

Develop clear, concise, logical, coherent, and effective paragraphs.

Combining sentences into paragraphs is an important part of composing a message. Paragraphs help the receiver organize the thoughts and understand the message. The five principles for effective paragraphs are (1) use short paragraphs because they are easy to understand; (2) give paragraphs unity, which means that all the sentences in a paragraph relate to one topic; (3) organize paragraphs logically using the direct or indirect plan; (4) give paragraphs appropriate emphasis by stressing the important ideas and de-emphasizing the unimportant ideas; and (5) provide for smooth thought flow for paragraph coherence.

Use available alternatives to assure unbiased language in business messages.

Message analysis includes assuring unbiased language for fair and balanced treatment of all individuals regardless of race, gender, culture, age, ability, religion, or socioeconomic status. You will want to avoid all words that have unfavorable denotations or connotations in their reflection on any individuals.

Apply your own composing style to personalize your messages.

The most effective business communicators use the principles that have been reviewed in this chapter. There is one other important dimension of your communication—your personality. Use words and combinations of words that not only are understood by your receiver but also reveal who you are—words that give life and distinction to your message.

Discussion Questions

1. Define the KISS principle of business communication and address the advantages of its use. (Objective 1)
2. Explain how a dictionary and thesaurus can help you be a more effective communicator. (Objective 1)
3. Define "technical words" and explain how you would make decisions about their use in your business messages. (Objective 1)
4. Give three examples of vague or abstract words and how they could be made more specific. (Objective 1)
5. Describe three characteristics of grammatically correct sentences. (Objective 2)
6. Why are short sentences preferred in business communication? How can sentences be shortened? (Objective 2)
7. Discuss when to use active voice and when to use passive voice in sentences. Write a sentence in passive voice then change the sentence to active voice. (Objective 2)

8. Explain why a sender should use short paragraphs in business messages. Tell what the average length of short paragraphs should be for (a) letters and memos and (b) reports. (Objective 3)
9. Discuss why and how unbiased language should be used in business messages. (Objective 4)
10. How can you follow the principles of business communication in your composing efforts and still reflect your own personality in your messages? (Objective 5)

Application Exercises

E-mail. For each principle of business communication listed, follow the directions given for its exercise. Keep the basic meaning contained in each of the exercises, and use examples that are different from those in this chapter. Use a dictionary and a thesaurus to assist you in these exercises. Assume that your receiver is a high school graduate with a tenth- to eleventh-grade vocabulary level and no particular technical expertise. Reword sentences as necessary for clarity. E-mail your responses to your instructor.

Principles of Word Usage

Principle 1: Choose Understandable Words (Objective 1)

1. **Select simple words.** Use an online dictionary or word processing thesaurus to select simpler words to replace these difficult words: (a) mesmerize, (b) exemplary, (c) garner, (d) protocol, (e) decorum, (f) illicit, (g) adversary, (h) jeopardy, (i) segregate, (j) advocate, (k) beguile, (l) impeccable, (m) propriety, (n) proponent, (o) sequester.
2. **Use short words.** Use a word processing thesaurus to select short words to replace these long words: (a) whimsical, (b) facsimile, (c) consolidate, (d) reproduction, (e) reasonable, (f) confederate, (g) vacillation, (h) prerogative, (i) clandestine, (j) amalgamate, (k) representation, (l) incorporate, (m) surreptitious, (n) lackadaisical, (o) capacitate.
3. **Use appropriate nontechnical words.** Use an online dictionary or word processing thesaurus to select nontechnical words to replace each of these technical words: (a) dividend, (b) prosthesis, (c) equity, (d) hypothesis, (e) asset, (f) invoice, (g) accounts payable, (h) tabloid, (i) theology, (j) debug, (k) carcinoma, (l) accounts receivable, (m) generate, (n) chronicle, (o) matriculate.

Principle 2: Use Specific Words (Objective 1)

Select specific words to replace these vague words: (a) book, (b) industry, (c) building, (d) equipment, (e) nice, (f) flower, (g) soon, (h) early, (i) transportation, (j) periodically, (k) car, (l) tree, (m) airline, (n) slow, (o) country.

Principle 3: Prefer Strong Words (Objective 1)

Teamwork. Work with another student to select power words to replace these weak words: (a) let go, (b) remiss, (c) inexpensive, (d) request, (e) suggest, (f) refrain, (g) purchase, (h) decline, and (i) resist.

Principle 4: Emphasize Positive Words (Objective 1)

List five positive words to use in business messages and five negative words to avoid using.

Principle 5: Avoid Overused Words (Objective 1)

List five overused words or phrases a sender should avoid using.

Principle 6: Avoid Obsolete Words (Objective 1)

Develop three sentences using obsolete words or phrases. Rewrite these sentences avoiding the use of the obsolete words or phrases.

Principles of Effective Sentences

InfoTrac. Before completing the exercises for sentence construction, read InfoTrac article A9240410611, "Word Usage Rules for Writing Strong Memos & Reports," from *Essential Assistant*, October 2002. This article provides additional help for sentence clarity.

Principle 1: Compose Clear Sentences (Objective 2)

1. **Give sentences unity.** Rewrite the following long sentences. Divide them into a number of sentences, each of which possesses unity.
   a. The art show is scheduled to be given on the 14th of November if all art work is submitted in a timely fashion; however, if the artists submit their work late, we may have to reschedule the show for a date at sometime later in the future but only time will tell.
   b. The farmers' market is held each Saturday on a street in the downtown area when people come in from all around the city to buy fresh fruit and vegetables; the city budget is insufficient to support a special building for the market but everyone believes the market is important to the economy.

2. **Keep related words together.** Revise the following sentences to show a clear relationship between the modifiers and the words they modify:
   a. E-mail work journals are due by 5 p.m. each Wednesday promptly.
   b. To all employees the cards must be given before Monday.
   c. The fax machine needed repair which was purchased last year.
   d. Postal mail is losing customers to e-mail because it is slower.
   e. The newspapers fell through the bars because they were wet.

Principle 2: Use Short Sentences (Objective 2)

Shorten the following sentences by omitting unnecessary words and limiting content:
1. We received your letter of January 15 on company letterhead and responded to it in as quick a fashion as possible.
2. As head of the human resources department, Mr. Srinivas was happy to have been asked and have the opportunity to be a part of an interview team for applicants for the new position.
3. Our services include a logistic audit to evaluate your transportation department, warehouse operation, and the ability to get your products to market.
4. Our goal is to affect your bottom line directly in a positive manner.
5. I will call you within the next several days to see when we might schedule an exploratory meeting.
6. The prices that are for the nonfat variety of milk are going up in cost.

Principle 3: Prefer Active Voice in Sentences (Objective 2)

Change the verbs in the following sentences from passive voice to active voice:
1. A lecture must be prepared by the professor.
2. The deed of trust must be signed by the owner of the property.
3. Proposals are to be prepared in triplicate.
4. The information was faxed to Brunswick Company on Thursday by Cindy Greene.
5. The cross-country race was won by Liz Morse.

Principle 4: Give Sentences Appropriate Emphasis (Objective 2)

Teamwork. Work with another student to create two sentences for each situation. Add details, as needed.
1. **Use length.** You want to help students at a local high school understand the importance of performing well on their upcoming ACT test for college admission. Emphasize this point by the length of your sentences.

2. **Use location.** You want to stress to students the importance of attending every class session. Emphasize this point at the beginning of your sentences.
3. **Use sentence structure.** You have to tell a group of jazz band students that they have not been accepted to perform at Disneyland. Use sentence structure to de-emphasize the *no* in your sentences.

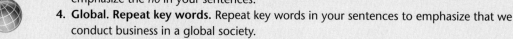

4. **Global. Repeat key words.** Repeat key words in your sentences to emphasize that we conduct business in a global society.
5. **Be specific or general.** Be general in your sentences to de-emphasize the grade that you received on your chemistry final.
6. **Use format.** Use format in your sentences to emphasize the number of students in your graduating class who will be continuing their education.
7. **Use mechanical means.** Use mechanical means in your sentences to emphasize the importance of attending the business education seminar at the Marriott Hotel.

Principles of Paragraph Development

Principle 1: Use Short Paragraphs (Objective 3)

Write a one- to three-sentence opening paragraph of a business letter for each situation below.

1. Ask for a refund for a book that you are returning because it was damaged in shipment.
2. Thank a customer for prompt payment of each month's invoice. Assume the customer has been buying from your department store for five years.
3. Explain to the host of a reception for your employer why you will be unable to attend.
4. Request a personal leave day to attend the funeral of a close friend.
5. Ask your supervisor to talk with a coworker who continually makes you uncomfortable by using derogatory language about your appearance. You have asked the coworker not to do this, but your requests have been ignored.

Principle 2: Give Paragraphs Unity (Objective 3)

Indicate the sentence that does not belong in each of the following paragraphs:

1. Business communication instruction offers students an important opportunity. This is a chance to strengthen the most critical skill they can possess—the ability to communicate. Managers say that strong communication skills are essential to success. Specifically, this success depends on several subskills. Included in these subskills is knowing how to develop a business message from the you–viewpoint. In addition, understanding how to communicate constructive criticism is crucial to managerial success. Basic to managerial achievement, however, is knowing how to budget and plan for future changes.
2. Colleges have an increasing number of students applying for admission. Over the next ten years, enrollment projections show the number of applicants will increase by 25 percent. This influx of students is called Tidal Wave 2. Students like college. The colleges are building more classrooms and hiring more professors to accommodate more students.

Principle 3: Organize Paragraphs Logically (Objective 3)

Using the direct plan, indicate the most logical order of these two groups of sentences by listing their letters in that order:

1. **a.** This new marketing plan should increase sales significantly.
   b. The increased sales will justify the intensive planning effort.
   c. The vice president for sales approved the new marketing plan.
   d. I think you will agree that the planning effort was worthwhile.

2. **a.** The facts in your request clearly supported your position.
   b. Your request to attend the conference is approved.
   c. Report these expenses to me when you return.
   d. Please keep a careful record of your travel expenses.

Principle 4: Give Paragraphs Appropriate Emphasis (Objective 3)
1. Create a paragraph that emphasizes the importance of getting a college education and de-emphasizes the time commitment that is required.
2. Create a paragraph that emphasizes the importance of having a computer connected to the Internet for use in your homework and de-emphasizes the cost of making the arrangements for Internet service and purchasing the equipment.

Principle 5: Provide Paragraph Coherence (Objective 3)
Using the indirect plan, indicate the most coherent order for these sentences by listing their letters in that order:
1. **a.** Why should you join the National Business Education Association?
   b. Don't wait. Join NBEA today!
   c. You will receive valuable publications.
   d. In addition, you can exchange ideas with other teachers.
2. **a.** The University of Michigan has offered Jean Almarez a teaching contract.
   b. She received her bachelor of science degree from the University of Loyola and her Ph.D. from the University of Illinois.
   c. Dr. Almarez is excited about her new position as associate professor.
   d. She loves to sing and dance.
   e. Dr. Almarez has taught management for more than ten years.

Comprehensive Exercise 1

Teamwork. Form a group of two to three students and use your creativity to rewrite the following sentences. While retaining the basic meaning of the original version, be sure to draw on your own unique personalities in determining the wording of the revised versions. Present your rewritten sentences to your instructor. (Objective 5)
1. Communication skills are important for success in business.
2. Using the Internet is important for students today.
3. Teamwork is important in business.
4. Last year was the best ever for the Corona del Mar girls' cross-country team.
5. The dress cannot be returned to the department store; the tags have been torn off and the dress has been worn.
6. Being ethical is important for many reasons.
7. Preparing for retirement is important to all individuals.
8. Achieving financial stability is important for each and every person.
9. Learning a foreign language is essential for conducting business abroad.
10. The key variables of performance are ability, motivation, clarity of expectations, and opportunity.

Comprehensive Exercise 2

Change the language to improve the following sentences and to ensure unbiased references to race, gender, culture, age, or disability. (Objective 4)
1. Jack is confined to a wheelchair. (*Hint*: Avoid emphasizing the limitation of the disability.)
2. That the company merged with a small company that was owned by an older, white female was the headline of the news release. (*Hint*: Avoid emphasizing age, race, and gender when it is not essential to the main point of the message.)

3. The exercise program was developed for handicapped people. (*Hint*: Avoid emphasizing the limitations of the disability.)

4. The elderly executives of major companies and their wives regularly attend the Chamber of Commerce annual banquet. (*Hint*: Avoid language that is limiting or implies bias.)

5. This is obviously man's work. (*Hint*: Avoid language that is demeaning, patronizing, or limiting.)

6. The mathematics student should determine which type of problem gives him the most difficulty and then ask the instructor for help. (*Hint*: Avoid language that implies stereotyping.)

7. Dear Sirs: Please accept my application for the position as human resources manager. (*Hint*: Avoid language that implies stereotyping.)

Comprehensive Exercise 3

Follow the directions in each exercise below:

1. **Teamwork.** Using unbiased gender language is a special challenge because of the structure of the English language. Form a group of four or five students and develop a list of ten biased words and the unbiased alternatives. Develop a sentence for each of the words and their alternatives.

2. **E-mail.** Send an e-mail message to your instructor explaining why you took the class. Apply the principles of business communication that you studied in this chapter.

3. **InfoTrac.** Use the Internet and InfoTrac to locate and read "Tips for Business Writing," Article A90754935. Plan and write a short essay to present orally (2 minute) to the class. You should tell why you agree or disagree with the quote in the last paragraph in the article about planning before writing.

4. **InfoTrac.** Use the Internet and InfoTrac to locate and read "Writing Clearly and Forcefully," by W. H. Weiss, article A80853855. After reading the article, send an e-mail to your teacher answering the following questions:

   a. What three ideas from the article will help you write clearly?

   b. What three ideas from the article will help you write forcefully?

   c. What three ideas from the article will help you write effective memos?

   d. What is one statement in the article that you disbelieve or find of little help?

There are Web exercises at **http://krizan.swlearning.com** to accompany this chapter.

Message Analysis

The following message follows a direct plan of organization. Rewrite it using an indirect plan, a positive tone, and simple language.

Dear Valued Customer:

We will be unable to bill your Internet service to your local telephone bill effective January 1, 2005. If we don't receive your credit card billing information before December 31, you may experience difficulty accessing the Internet.

Important: To ensure continued access to your e-mail and dial-up account, please call (800) 987-5000 (select the billing option) so that we may switch your account to credit card billing before December 31. Representatives are available to assist you Monday–Friday from 7 a.m. to 10 p.m. and Saturday 8 a.m. to 5 p.m. Eastern time.

We look forward to your continued business and look forward to hearing from you before December 31. Thank you for choosing our company to provide your Internet service.

Sincerely,

Grammar Workshop

Correct the grammar, spelling, punctuation, style, and word choice errors in the following sentences:

1. Sandy arrived to their class late and set at the back of the classroom so that she could leave before class ended.
2. Before going Sally packed her back pack laid out her clothes and read one chapter in Phyllis A. Whitneys book Start Flight.
3. Shiori Sakamoto PhD has been reserching the April 1912 the fatal voyage of the titantic.
4. The guitar players strolled between the diners in the spanish restaurant.
5. Jose interrupted a private discussion among Patty and me.
6. All students had his resumes already to submit in at the beginning of english 101.
7. Mr. Ringi Nisimura a Financial Advisor gives people advise on money matters.
8. What is the amount of June graduates?
9. Todays computer technology, and presentation software increases flexibility, capability and editing power.
10. Women works in both traditional and non traditional tecknical education jobs.

5

Print and Electronic Messages

LEARNING OBJECTIVES

① Identify the advantages and disadvantages of written messages.

② Use a three-step process to develop effective business messages.

③ Describe how to determine the vocabulary level of business messages.

④ Explain how to develop effective e-mail and Web pages.

Ilene Levin and Steve Goldfine, Owners, Goldin Properties Midwest LLC

LET'S TALK BUSINESS We are the managing partners of a company operating five lodging facilities. All facilities are located 1½ to 4 hours from our office. It is important for us to be in frequent contact with our on-site managers, often several times per day, communicating company policies, instituting and monitoring programs, and helping them resolve problems. We rely heavily on various communication media: telephone, fax, and increasingly the computer—especially the use of e-mail. With a business that operates 24/7, e-mail allows us to send detailed messages directly to the managers and allows them to respond no matter the time of day or night. The use of e-mail has become increasingly important in our business as partner Ilene Levin has speech problems that make the use of the telephone difficult.

Successful communicators like those featured in this chapter's Let's Talk Business approach writing as a process that includes selecting the appropriate type of message; being aware of the vocabulary level at which they write; and planning, drafting, and finalizing their work. As business owners, Ilene Levin and Steve Goldfine know that output quality is directly related to input quality, and they are willing to do what it takes to achieve the goals of business communication. In this chapter, you will study and apply the techniques associated with developing print and electronic written messages. In later chapters, you will learn how to plan for effective oral communication.

The Advantages and Disadvantages of Written Messages

LEARNING OBJECTIVE
1 Identify the advantages and disadvantages of written messages.

When faced with a situation that requires communication, your first decision will be whether to convey the message orally or in writing. Each method has advantages and disadvantages. The advantages of written messages are that they

- Provide a permanent record that can be filed and referred to in the future.
- Can be reread and studied, which is important if a message is long, is complex, or has been written in anger.
- Can be revised and edited to ensure they adhere to the principles of business communication.
- Can have legal value.

NOTE 5.1
Written messages have advantages and disadvantages.

The disadvantages of written messages are that they

- Are generally transmitted slowly; e-mail and fax are notable exceptions.
- Are viewed as being more formal, in part because they are permanent.
- Do not lend themselves to quick or thorough feedback because there are few nonverbal cues and because the sender and receiver are in different locations.
- Require storage, which can be time-consuming and expensive.

In contrast, oral messages can be transmitted quickly, are considered to have a more personal tone, and allow for immediate feedback. Because oral messages do not provide a permanent record, however, receivers have limited time to reflect on them. These factors make oral messages unsuitable for complex material.

Developing Written Business Messages

LEARNING OBJECTIVE
2 Use a three-step process to develop effective business messages.

The process for developing written business messages consists of the following three steps:

[1] Planning

[2] Drafting

[3] Finalizing

NOTE 5.2
The three steps are plan, draft, and finalize

Carrying out this process may take from a few seconds for routine letters, memos, or e-mail to several days for a long written report or a Web page. Following the process is essential for developing effective business messages.

Step 1: Plan the Message

NOTE 5.3
Begin by planning the message.

The steps taken before putting words on paper or entering them into a computer are called **planning** or **prewriting**. This process incorporates and applies topics covered in Chapter 1, "Business Communication Foundations," and Chapter 4, "Principles of Business Communication."

ANALYZE THE COMMUNICATION SITUATION

NOTE 5.4
Assess the communication situation.

Your first planning task is to decide what is involved in the specific communication situation. When analyzing the communication situation, you will want to ask yourself the following general questions:

- Who will receive the message?
- Will he or she be the final receiver or an intermediate reader?
- What are the physical and political constraints under which I am operating?
- What does the receiver need to know?
- What action do I want my receiver to take?

NOTE 5.5
Ask general and specific questions.

Specific questions you might ask when analyzing the communication situation include the following:

- Is the receiver internal or external to the organization?
- Has the receiver asked specific questions I must answer?
- Will my receiver view my message as positive? negative? persuasive? mixed?
- What is the relationship between me and my receiver? between our organizations?
- Is my message part of an ongoing dialogue, or does it introduce a new topic?

ESTABLISH PRIMARY AND SECONDARY PURPOSES

NOTE 5.6
Your primary and secondary purposes should relate to the business communication goals.

After analyzing the communication situation, you will establish the primary and secondary purposes of your message. This will be done within the framework of the four business communication goals:

[1] Receiver understanding

[2] Necessary receiver response

[3] Favorable relationship

[4] Organizational goodwill

The message's main idea is the primary purpose, and its supporting ideas are the secondary purposes. For example, assume that you can say *yes* to a department head's request to hire three temporary staff members. This positive message will be sent to someone you know well. The memo or e-mail will include the *yes*, plus additional information about items such as hiring procedures, timelines, and salary level. Figure 5.1 shows how your purposes might appear for this communication situation.

NOTE 5.7
Message purposes can be simple or involved.

Another example shows how establishing primary and secondary purposes for a specific message can be more involved. Assume that the message you are developing is a written annual departmental report. The message may include positive, neutral, negative, and persuasive information. The receivers of the report could include employees who report to you, managers at your level in other departments, and upper-level man-

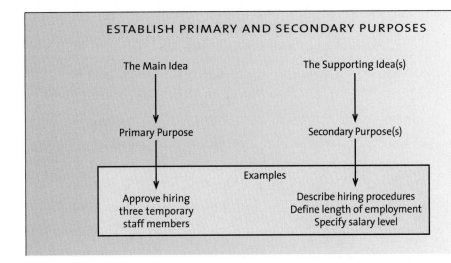

FIGURE 5.1
Simple Message
Purposes

agers. The primary and secondary purposes for your departmental report might be as shown in Figure 5.2.

When you have analyzed the communication situation and have determined the primary and secondary purposes of the message, you are ready to analyze your receivers to enable you to use the you–viewpoint. Because this step is discussed fully in Chapter 1, only a brief summary of it is given here.

ANALYZE THE RECEIVER

For some communication situations, you will know the receiver of your message so well that little or no analysis will be necessary. By contrast, it may be necessary for you to do a careful, detailed analysis of the receiver in other communication situations. Whether your analysis of the receiver requires a limited or an extensive amount of research, the approach is the same. You analyze your receiver in four areas—knowledge, interests, attitudes, and emotional reaction—as shown in Figure 5.3.

If you have multiple receivers, you need to analyze each person. For example, if you are writing a memo to five people in your office, analyze the knowledge, interests, attitudes, and potential emotional reaction of each of them. To achieve its goals and purposes, your message must be understandable to the receiver with the least amount of

NOTE 5.8
Analyze receivers for their knowledge, interests, attitudes, and emotional reactions.

NOTE 5.9
A message must be composed so all receivers can understand it.

Involved Message Purposes

Primary Purposes

1. To document clearly the department's accomplishments for 200–.
2. To persuade upper management to meet the department's future needs.

Secondary Purposes

1. To instill pride of accomplishment in the department's employees.
2. To inform managers at your own level of the department's activities and needs.
3. To inform upper management of the contributions your department and its employees have made.
4. To convince upper management to finance the department's continuing operation and proposed projects.
5. To maintain favorable relationships with others.
6. To build organizational goodwill for the department.

FIGURE 5.2
Involved Message
Purposes

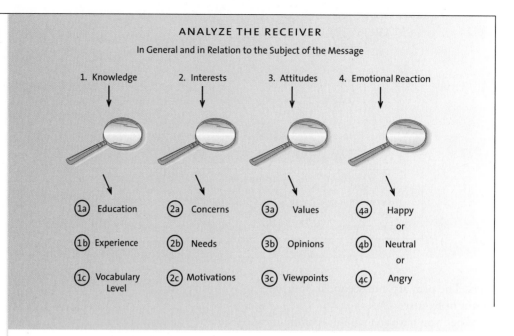

FIGURE 5.3
Analysis of the Receiver

ANALYZE THE RECEIVER

In General and in Relation to the Subject of the Message

1. Knowledge   2. Interests   3. Attitudes   4. Emotional Reaction

(1a) Education	(2a) Concerns	(3a) Values	(4a) Happy
			or
(1b) Experience	(2b) Needs	(3b) Opinions	(4b) Neutral
			or
(1c) Vocabulary Level	(2c) Motivations	(3c) Viewpoints	(4c) Angry

subject knowledge, the lowest vocabulary level, and the most emotional opposition without insulting or being condescending to other receivers.

Your analysis of the receiver will give you important information about the receiver's vocabulary, interests, possible biases, and emotional reaction. From your analysis you can determine the ideas, words, and approaches that communicate best in the situation you face.

SELECT THE TYPE OF MESSAGE

NOTE 5.10
Select the best type of message for the situation.

Written messages can be formatted as e-mail, letters, memos, written reports, or other document types. In addition, they can be handwritten, typed, or keyed into a computer and printed. Format and style will vary with the situation. Memos are used exclusively for internal communication; letters, e-mail, and reports may have either an internal or an external audience.

SELECT AN ORGANIZATIONAL PLAN

Business messages may be organized by either the direct (deductive) plan or the indirect (inductive) plan. These two plans have many variations. In Parts 3 and 5 of this text, alternative ways to use the direct and indirect approaches are discussed. The direct and indirect plans for messages are shown in Figure 5.4.

NOTE 5.11
Match the organizational plan to the receiver's perception of the message.

The **direct plan** attempts to achieve the primary purpose of the message by placing the main idea in the opening. The details supporting or explaining the primary purpose follow the opening. The **indirect plan** opens on neutral ground or on a point of agreement. The sender then provides supporting reasons or explanations that lead to the main idea, which is presented later in the message. Although research has shown that in most situations the direct plan is more effective for positive or neutral information and the indirect plan is more effective for negative information or persuasion, you will want to do a thorough analysis of your receiver before selecting the organizational plan. Variables such as age, gender, and culture will be factors in your decision.

FIGURE 5.4
Organizational Plans for
Messages

```
To:       Lian Lian Jian              To:       Peggy Kelley
From:     Peggy Kelley               From:     Lian Lian Jian
Date:     December 5, 200–           Date:     January 5, 200–
Subject:  Conference Fees            Subject:  Conference Reimbursement
              MAIN IDEA
_____             _____
_____             _____
_____                     _____

_____                       MAIN IDEA
_____             _____
_____             _____
_____                     _____
                                    _____
_____
_____                     _____
```

Direct Plan
Use for Positive or
Neutral Messages

Indirect Plan
Use for Negative or
Persuasive Messages

After selecting the type of message you will use and the organizational plan for your message, you are ready to outline message content.

OUTLINE THE MESSAGE CONTENT

In outlining message content, you are organizing your ideas for the message. You can use the traditional outline form (I., A., 1., a.), write each main point and its related ideas on an index card, brainstorm, or use cluster diagramming. The traditional outline and index card methods work well when you have a clear idea of what to write;

NOTE 5.12
Organize your ideas.

©TONY FREEMAN/PHOTOEDIT, INC.

Employees engaged in brainstorming.

FIGURE 5.5
Brainstorming the Message Content on a Claim Letter

Purpose of message:
Reject request for refund on piano.
Maintain customer's business.
Increase organizational goodwill.

3623 Happy Valley Lane
Lafayette, CA 94549
April 24, 200–

Ideas for Content: Express appreciation for purchase. (1)
Neutral spending – "do all we can." (2)
Recommend purchase of $125.95 for foam baffles. (7)
Thank for making Yamaha part of their life. (8)
Amount of savings – $4,000. (4)

Mr. Richard Spear
Store Manager
Pacific Fields Piano
1800 Mount Diablo Blvd.
Lafayette, CA 94549

Dear Mr. Spear:

I want my money back on the G2F PE Yamaha acoustic piano I bought from you during your "Winter Sale." After I had the piano delivered, my neighbors complained that my son's piano practicing made too much noise. This piano will not work in this house! Please send me the refund check for $13,899.75, and I will have Orange Coast Piano Movers return it to your Lafayette store.

Sincerely,

Ronalee Reid

Ronalee Reid

Volume purchases/cut overhead. (5)

Reinforce purchase decision. (3)
No–All sales final. (6)

NOTE 5.13
Brainstorm alone or as part of a group.

NOTE 5.14
Evaluate and sequence ideas.

brainstorming and cluster diagramming work best when generating ideas and determining how they relate to one another.

Brainstorming means listing or jotting ideas without evaluating or sequencing them. It is a stream-of-consciousness process that can be done alone or with a group and can be completed in various ways. If you are working alone, you could randomly list ideas you think you will include in your message. When working in a group, the person designated as recorder could write ideas on a flipchart and post the lists where all can see and react to them. If you are responding to a message, you could make notes on the incoming letter or memo. When all ideas have been listed, review them to determine what should be added, deleted, or modified. Finally, number the ideas to show the sequence in which you will use them. Figure 5.5 illustrates how the brainstorming technique can be applied to the preparation of a claim refusal. In this example, the number in parentheses following each idea shows its sequence within the message.

NOTE 5.15
Cluster diagramming groups ideas as they are generated.

Another technique for outlining message content is **cluster diagramming**. With this technique, ideas are grouped as they are introduced. The main idea is placed in the center, and the key concepts are placed in various locations around it. As ideas are generated, they are written near the key concept to which they relate. After all ideas have been recorded, they are reviewed. Duplicate ideas are deleted; new ideas are added. Finally, lines are drawn to connect related ideas. Each cluster of ideas becomes a section of the letter or report.

After completing the sequencing of ideas, you are ready to draft the message.

Step 2: Draft the Message

Using your mental or recorded notes from the outlining process, you draft the message. Apply the principles of business communication, use the you–viewpoint, and focus on content. At this stage, getting something in writing is more important than generating perfect copy. Experienced writers know that the clearest, most effective communication results from revising and editing message drafts. Issues concerning spelling, grammar, and mechanics will be addressed during the finalizing process.

Even with good planning, experienced writers sometimes encounter **writer's block**—difficulty in putting thoughts into words. The Tips and Hints feature contains suggestions to help overcome this challenging situation.

NOTE 5.16
You may have one or more drafts.

NOTE 5.17
Tackle writer's block.

TIPS AND HINTS

Overcoming Writer's Block

When the words aren't flowing freely or when your mind seems as blank as the computer screen or paper before you, try these techniques for overcoming writer's block:

- Divide the writing project into smaller parts. Completing a series of smaller tasks will give you the feeling of accomplishment.
- Start somewhere other than the beginning of the document. Write the middle or end and then fill in the remaining material.
- Change writing methods. Switch between pen and computer, or try a voice recorder. Some people find talking easier than writing.
- Be sure you have pen and paper or a tape recorder handy at all times. Good ideas often

arise when you least expect them, and you'll want to have access to the tools to record them.
- Write during the time of day when you're most productive; be sure to allow a reasonable block of time.
- Take a brief break. A change of scenery, a drink of water, or a breath of fresh air can help clear the cobwebs.
- Have music playing in the background. If you're anxious or stressed, use soothing music; if you lack motivation, select upbeat tunes.
- Ask a colleague for assistance. The conversation process may help you formulate ideas.

Step 3: Finalize the Message

Finalizing a message involves proofreading the document to determine where it needs to be revised and edited. Revising and editing are similar processes with different objectives. Revising focuses on content; editing focuses on mechanics.

NOTE 5.18
The clearest messages result from revising and editing drafts.

REVISE THE MESSAGE

When a writer revises a message, he or she makes changes to its content. To determine what changes to make, read the message—aloud—from your receiver's point of view. Ask whether the primary and secondary purposes have been achieved. Check that you have used the chosen organizational plan effectively. Determine whether better transitions or bulleted lists would help make your message more clear. Check to see that the principles of business communication have been applied. Verify that all necessary information is included and accurate. Finally, think about the visual image the message creates.

If you detect any weaknesses in the message, make changes to add strength. This is your opportunity to improve your word choice, sentence development, and paragraph formation. In addition, revising gives you another chance to add distinctiveness—a part of your personality—to the message.

The ability to insert, delete, move, and copy text is essential to revising efficiently, and word processing software helps writers accomplish these tasks with ease. However, unless writers cut and paste carefully, they may find that their messages say something other than what they intended.

Word processing software allows writers to move quickly and easily from one part of a document to another while revising their message—for example, from the top of the page to the bottom or from page 43 to page 5. Movement also may be linked to words or phrases. Writers can find the next or every occurrence of a character, word, or phrase. When combined with a replace function, the find feature becomes a powerful revision tool, but one that must be used with care. Unless users precisely define what is to be replaced, they may create a problem in addition to solving one. Imagine directing the software to replace all occurrences of *his* with *his and her* only to find that *This idea has merit* becomes *This and her idea has merit.*

Word processing software also can assist writers in choosing words and emphasizing text. A **thesaurus** helps writers select appropriate words by suggesting a variety of alternatives. Its use helps avoid word repetition and brings variety to word choice. For emphasis, text may be displayed using **bold,** <u>underscore</u>, *italic,* or other enhancement features. Type fonts (styles) and pitch (size) can be changed. Margins may be widened or narrowed. Tables can be created. Boxes or other borders can be placed around text. Symbols or images may be inserted to draw a reader's attention to important items. Writers who have access to color printers should determine whether using color will enhance the communication and, if so, how much of which color(s) is appropriate. The following Tips and Hints feature contains information about colors and their meanings.

TIPS AND HINTS

What Colors Mean

Empirical and scientific evidence points to the belief that color impacts not only our eyes but also our senses and our minds. As you create or design print and electronic documents, consider the following possible meanings your receivers may associate with the colors you choose.

Blue:	patience, guidance, happiness, change
Brown:	earthiness, concentration
Green:	money, growth, prosperity
Orange:	energy
Pink:	romance, friendship

Purple:	power
Red:	strength, passion, courage, health
Silver:	stability
White:	peace, truth-seeking, protection
Yellow:	intelligence, activity, creativity, togetherness

Some colors have significance within a culture. If your message is designed to reach a person or group within a particular culture, include color as part of your audience analysis.

With so many options available, writers must choose wisely. Using too many enhancements could deter rather than facilitate successful communication. Decide what you want to accomplish and then choose the best feature that helps you reach your goal. In other words, analyze your receiver and the communication situation.

EDIT THE MESSAGE

After a message has been revised, it must be edited. During the editing process, the writer proofreads the message to determine whether it is mechanically correct. The writer checks to be sure there are no errors in format, spelling, grammar, punctuation, spelling, or style.

A **spell checker** assists with, *but does not replace,* careful proofreading. A spell checker will not detect an error that results in the correct spelling of another word (e.g., *thin* for *than*). Recent versions of word processing software automatically correct certain types of errors. If a writer keys *te* rather than *the,* the software detects and corrects the error. The software also automatically changes the first letter of a sentence from lowercase to uppercase if the writer makes such an oversight. Users may choose to turn off these features when keying material that is intentionally contrary to the rules.

A **style checker** analyzes a document and alerts the writer to potential problems with sentence length, vocabulary level, word choice (e.g., *affect* for *effect*), punctuation, and passive voice. The software does not, however, correct the errors. The writer retains responsibility for ensuring that style errors do not create communication barriers. Although they are a good writing aid, style checkers are not perfect; they may question things that are correct or fail to question things that are incorrect. Writers always should be sure they have applied the principles of business communication.

The steps in the finalizing process are iterative—one or more of the steps may need to be repeated before the message is ready to sign and send. As they go through these iterations, many writers find that the tasks associated with finalizing a message are best accomplished by printing a copy of the document and using symbols to indicate the location and nature of the changes they will make. Standard symbols for editing and revising are shown in Figure 5.6. These symbols are especially helpful if the person who writes the message is not the one who prepares the final document. In this circumstance, the symbols themselves become a valuable communication tool. Learn to use these symbols in your revising, editing, and proofreading efforts.

The results of editing and revising can be seen in Figures 5.7 and 5.8 on pages 138–139. Figure 5.7 shows the draft of a message; Figure 5.8 shows the final version. Note the clarity, power, and you–viewpoint that have been added by applying the principles of business communication while revising the message and the grammar and punctuation errors that were eliminated during editing.

PROOFREAD THE MESSAGE

Proofreading is an activity used several times during the process of finalizing a document. Proofreading occurs during and after revising and editing. The process involves (1) reading the message for content and (2) reading it again for correct spelling, grammar, and punctuation. Some proofreaders can find more spelling errors by reading the copy backwards.

Proofreading procedures include the following steps:

[1] If you are using a word processing program, use your spell checker and grammar checker to check for errors. Next, proofread the copy on screen and print a copy of the document in double-spaced format.

[2] Proofread the copy by reading the document aloud from beginning to end, focusing on the content. Reread the document looking for spelling errors, grammatical errors, punctuation errors, and style errors. Pay special attention to personal

NOTE 5.22
Edit to achieve mechanical correctness.

NOTE 5.23
Spell checkers and style checkers assist with proofreading.

NOTE 5.24
To aid communication between message preparer and originator, use editing symbols.

NOTE 5.25
Give the editing and revising tasks highest priority.

NOTE 5.26
Proofread during and after revising and editing.

FIGURE 5.6
Editing Symbols

EDITING SYMBOLS

Defined		Examples
Paragraph	¶	¶ Begin a new paragraph at this point.
Insert a character	∧	Insᵉrt a letter here.
Delete	ℓ	Delete these words.
Do not change	stet	Disregard the previous correction.
Transpose	tr	To transpose is to around turn.
Move to the left	[	[Move this copy to the left.
Move to the right	]	M]ove this copy to the right.
No paragraph	no ¶	no ¶ Do not begin a new paragraph here.
Delete and close up.	⌒	Delete the hyphen from pre-empt and close the space.
Set in caps	Caps or ≡	a sentence begins with a capital letter.
Set in lower case	lc or /	This Word should not be capitalized.
Insert a period	⊙	Insert a period ⊙
Quotation marks	⌄/ ⌄\	Quotation marks and
Comma	⌃	a comma should be placed here he said.
Insert space	#	Space between these words.
Apostrophe	⌄	An apostrophe is whats needed here.
Hyphen	=	Add a hyphen to African American
Close up	⌣	Close the extra space.
Use superior figure	↓	Footnote this sentence. ↓
Set in italic	italic or _____	Set the words, sine qua non, in italics.
Move up	⊓	This word is too low.
Move down	⊔	This word is too high.

names, numbers, addresses, information in brackets, words displayed in uppercase letters, and unusual words.

[3] After you have completed proofreading the document, ask a colleague or associate to proofread the document. It helps to have another person proofread the document because you will be tired of looking at it. If you have columns of numbers, consider reading the document aloud with a partner.

[4] Make the corrections as required and then reprint the document for an additional reading.

Several proven procedures and techniques for effective proofreading can be found in books at the library. You may also check the Online Writing Lab (OWL) at the Purdue University Web site at http://owl.english.purdue.edu/ or the Resources for Writers Web site by Jack Lynch at http://andromeda.rutgers.edu/~jlynch/ for additional guidelines on proven methods of proofreading.

NOTE 5.27
Proofread before signing and sending every document.

Proofreading is not a glamorous activity, but it is a critically important one. Errors detract from the clarity of the message and reduce your credibility in the mind of the receiver. Therefore, you or some other competent person should proofread each message carefully. As the one who submits the report or signs the letter or memo, you have the ultimate responsibility for both the content and the accuracy. *No document should be signed or sent—electronically or by more traditional methods—without proofreading it to be sure it is accurate and error-free.*

You may revise and edit some messages many times. Continue revising, editing, and proofreading until you have a clear, concise, businesslike, error-free message that reflects the you–viewpoint.

Determining Vocabulary Level

LEARNING OBJECTIVE
3
Describe how to determine the vocabulary level of business messages.

Message analysis is an aspect of writing related to developing effective business messages. Control the vocabulary level of your messages so that it fits your receivers. As you know, one of your primary concerns in composing effective business messages is using a vocabulary level that your receiver will understand. **Vocabulary level**, as used in this book, refers to the level of difficulty of the words and combinations of words in messages.

NOTE 5.28
Message analysis includes determining vocabulary level to assure receiver understanding.

Readability Formulas

Readability formulas can be used to calculate vocabulary levels for your messages. These formulas—such as the Gunning, Flesch, Dale-Chall, and Fry—are described in materials available in most libraries or on the Web. They generally measure the average length of sentences and the percentage of "difficult" words. Although the counting necessary to use the formulas can be done manually, several of the formulas have been computerized and can be used easily with electronic media. Many grammar-checker software programs are able to calculate the vocabulary level of your message.

NOTE 5.29
Readability formulas can be used to check vocabulary levels.

Readability Ratings

The vocabulary-level ratings obtained from readability formulas generally reflect the approximate grade level a person would need to understand the written material. For example, a rating of 12 would mean that a person would have to be able to read at the twelfth-grade level to comprehend the material fully.

NOTE 5.30
Readability ratings show approximate grade level.

Readability analysis does not check the actual words you use or the manner in which you combine those words into sentences. An analysis will not show whether the writing is accurate or inaccurate, interesting or dull, valuable or not valuable to a receiver. Use readability ratings as guides, and use common sense in applying them.

NOTE 5.31
Common sense must be used with readability ratings.

A message may have a low readability rating because it uses short words and short sentences even though it uses difficult technical words. By contrast, a message may have a high readability rating because it uses long words and long sentences, even though

Pacific Fields Piano

1800 Mount Diablo Blvd.
Lafayette, CA 94549
(714) 283-5000

May 1, 200–

Mrs. Ronalee Reid
3623 Happy Valley Lane
Lafayette, CA 94549

Dear Mrs. Reid:

We appreciate your recent purchase of a G2F PE Yamaha acoustic piano. You certainly have chosen an extremely high-quality parlor grand piano that will give you many years of joy and satisfaction. A Yamaha piano is the instrument chosen by many of the world's top artists. We want to ensure that enjoyment is possible.

You made a good decision when you bought a G2F PE Yamaha acoustic piano during the Pacific Fields Piano "Winter Sale." The tremendous savings you got on this sale totaling almost $4,000 were made possible in two ways: We (1) buy merchandise in large volumes whenever we can, and (2) cut overhead and pass the savings on to our customers.

One of the ways we cut overhead is to make all sales final on items purchased during the "Winter Sale." We make every effort to be sure all our customers are aware of this policy by noting it in all advertisements and posting signs throughout the store.

You will be very glad to learn that you can easily make the piano quieter by purchasing a set of foam baffles. These foam baffles are installed under the piano between the ribs in order to quiet the sound. For $125.95 you can purchase the foam baffles that have complete directions and guides for installation. You can either "do-it yourself" or have one of our technicians take care of it for you at cost. Please call us collect at (714) 555-9011 and tell us your preference.

Once again, thank you for making Yamaha part of your life.

Sincerely yours,

Richard Spear

Richard Spear, Manager
Keyboard Division

FIGURE 5.7
Draft Message

the sentences are easy to understand and the words are familiar. In addition, an appropriate grade level for a message does not necessarily guarantee that the message will communicate effectively. An inappropriate grade-level rating for a message, however, does mean that the message should be examined for word choice and sentence length.

Vocabulary Levels

As you compose a message for a given communication situation, keep in mind the estimated vocabulary level of your receiver. A message written at too high a vocabulary level will not be understood. A message written at too low a vocabulary level will either insult your receiver or fail to hold his or her attention and interest. Business messages written at the eighth- to twelfth-grade levels will communicate clearly with most receivers.

Readability formulas are important tools for analyzing your messages. Use these tools regularly to analyze the vocabulary levels of form letters or memos, newsletters, speeches, magazines, books, and similar materials that will be read (or heard) by many

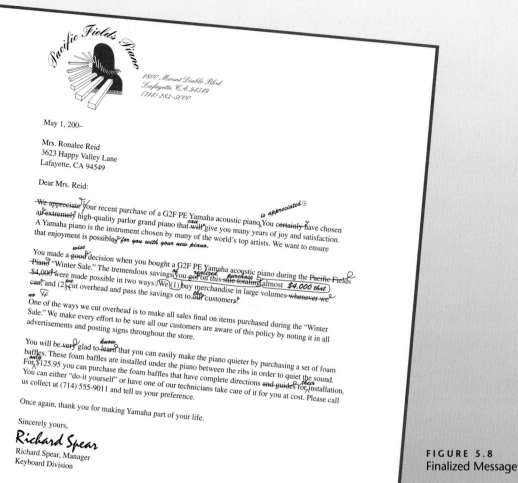

FIGURE 5.8
Finalized Message

receivers. Use these tools periodically to check the vocabulary levels of your messages to only one receiver.

Developing Electronic Messages

Advances in technology have enabled people to communicate in ways previously not possible. In this section, you will explore concepts and techniques associated with writing for two of these technology-driven media—e-mail and Internet Web pages.

When two or more computers are linked to facilitate information transfers, they form a **network.** The **Internet** is the world's largest network, but rather than linking individual computers, it links computer networks.

Created in the 1960s, the Internet began as a tool for communication among employees of various government agencies, especially research scientists. Today, the Internet is an international communication medium used by educators, businesses, nonprofit

LEARNING OBJECTIVE
(4) *Explain how to develop effective e-mail and Web pages.*

NOTE 5.33
The Internet is a worldwide network.

organizations, and private citizens. One of the factors contributing to the popularity of the Internet was the inception of the **World Wide Web.**

NOTE 5.34
The Web makes Internet access easy.

The Web, which originated at the European Center for Nuclear Research (CERN) in Geneva, Switzerland, has made the Internet more accessible to those who want to tap its resources. Users navigate the system via a *browser* and rely on *hyperlinks* (electronic pointers) to move from one *site* (location) to another.

E-mail represents the most common Internet application. The Internet can, however, be used for many other purposes, including research. Information about how to use the Internet as a research tool, how to develop an effective search strategy, how to recognize a credible source, and how to cite Internet resources can be found in Chapter 10. Chapter 16 includes information about how the Internet can be used to research potential employers and be a channel through which people apply for employment.

Electronic Mail

NOTE 5.35
E-mail is the most common Internet application.

One of the most common questions business professionals ask today is "What's your e-mail address?" The reason for the query is simple—e-mail represents a fast, efficient, relatively inexpensive method of exchanging messages. Users may select stand-alone or network versions of commercial packages, subscribe to a service, or obtain free e-mail through the Internet.

NOTE 5.36
Speed and convenience contribute to e-mail's popularity.

Once used primarily as an informal method of communicating with friends, family, and colleagues, e-mail has evolved into a high-level official communication method. Many individuals and organizations have found that they receive more e-mail than they do print mail. Some business organizations and schools—perhaps yours—now use e-mail rather than paper as an official method of communicating with employees and students.

NOTE 5.37
Use the plan/draft/finalize method when developing e-mail.

Whether content is embedded within the text of a message or created separately and conveyed as an attachment, e-mail is becoming the medium of choice for message transmission. The result is that writing has become an important part of nearly everyone's job. Because of its role in official business communication, e-mail is developed using the same three-step plan as other written messages—plan, draft, and finalize. These steps were thoroughly described earlier in this chapter, so that discussion will not be repeated here. Rather, this section will focus on the e-mail features and guidelines that will help you complete those steps.

E-mail Features

E-mail systems may be internal or external. Internal systems allow users to communicate only *within* an organization. External systems allow users to communicate with others in the same organization or, by using the Internet, to channel messages to users outside the organization.

NOTE 5.38
E-mails and memos have a similar format.

E-mail resembles a memo. The software automatically enters the sender's name and records the date and time of the message. The writer enters the receiver's name and the subject. Salutations, closings, and signatures are not needed, but many users include them to make the message seem more personal.

NOTE 5.39
Signature blocks provide information about how to contact the writer.

Another feature used to personalize e-mail is a **signature block,** a segment of text appended to the end of a message. Signature blocks are like electronic business cards. They typically include the writer's name and information seen on letterhead stationery—company name, mailing address, phone, e-mail address, and fax number. Also, they may contain other things, such as a quote. Writers should choose carefully when selecting what to include in a signature block. The text goes with *every* message that is sent and, unless deleted by the receiver, stays with the message if it is forwarded.

E-mail programs vary in the number and sophistication of mail management tools they include. In order to derive the greatest benefit from the software, writers should be thoroughly familiar with the programs they use. One common management tool is an **address book.** This feature offers writers the opportunity to store the e-mail addresses of those with whom they frequently exchange messages. To access the address, the writer uses an **alias,** a code or short version of the name. The same concept allows writers to group the mailing addresses of several receivers and enter an identifier to retrieve all of them. For example, rather than entering the full address for each budget committee member every time a message is to be sent, the committee chair might record all information only once and then retrieve it by keying "Budget Cmte" or a similar alias. Your instructor probably uses a feature like this when sending messages to your class.

NOTE 5.40
Aliases save time when sending one message to many receivers.

Another useful e-mail feature is auto response. When you are away from the office and unable to respond, **auto response** alerts those who send e-mail to you that you will not be able to respond immediately.

E-mail programs can have many of the same features found in word processing software. Users can check spelling as well as move and copy passages. Writers can format messages by adjusting margins and can use emphasis features such as bold, italic, and underscore. These emphasis features, however, are useful only when senders and receivers use the same software program.

Certain emphasis features have a special connotation in e-mail. Anything displayed entirely in uppercase letters, for example, suggests the sender is shouting at the receiver. Exclamation points, when used often or in a series (!!!), suggest greater volume. To intensify a portion of a message, a sender may *place the text within asterisks.* Other methods of incorporating emotion into informal business messages are illustrated in the following Communication Note.

NOTE 5.41
Emphasis techniques can have special meaning in e-mail.

COMMUNICATION NOTE

Help Your Reader "Hear" Your E-mail By its nature e-mail communication encourages a personal, informal style of writing, a feature most people view as attractive. Writers get into trouble, however, when they assume that readers actually can hear their voices. Although e-mail may be more like oral communication than traditional forms of written communication, it's still writing, not speaking. Your reader cannot hear the inflection of your voice.

To guard against this type of misunderstanding, take this simple precaution: Include a goodwill statement in every message you send. Rather than write "Please come prepared to discuss the report," for example, add another sentence: "As always, I value your experience and insight."

Rather than "Fine," write "Fine. Happy to do it." Rather than "Well, you did it again. Would you mind adapting your presentation for our board?" write "Well, you did it again. Great job! Would you mind adapting . . ."

A goodwill statement is like an insurance policy. It protects you from being misunderstood. Including it reduces the risk of miscommunication when you are writing quickly.

Reprinted with permission of the author, Stephen Wilbers. You can visit his Web page at *http://www.wilbers.com.*

NOTE 5.42
Business e-mail deserves
the same attention as
other business messages.

If you've used e-mail to communicate only with friends or family, or if you've heard that grammar and spelling aren't important in e-mail, the statements in the preceding section might make you wonder why e-mail software has *any* editing features. The reason is simple: In business communication, the only difference between an e-mail message and a paper message is the channel through which it is transmitted. When e-mail is used in a business setting, the extent to which a writer edits a message depends on his or her analysis of the situation and the receiver.

E-mail Guidelines

NOTE 5.43
Set high standards for
e-mail quality.

Those who receive business e-mail from you will judge both you and your organization by the quality of your messages. You will want to create and maintain a professional image. Using the following guidelines will help you apply the same high standards to business-related e-mail that you apply to paper messages:

- **Make the subject line count.** Use the subject line to convey your real message to your receiver. For example, if you are asking the reader for a favor, your subject line might be "Request with Deadline."

- **Keep the subject line short.** Some systems limit display space, and you won't want your subject line to be truncated (cut). If you forward a message, change the subject line or it could become a cumbersome mess of commands such as "FW: RE: FW: FW: RE: Budget Update."

- **Cover only one topic in each message.** Limiting yourself to one topic allows you to use the subject line effectively, helps ensure that each item gets the attention it deserves, and permits the receiver to take action on each message and then delete it.

- **Make your message inviting.** Use short line lengths, short paragraphs, conversational language, and traditional format.

  using all lowercase lettersfailing to correct typographical errrs and omitting punctuation may mean you can create messages faster but it makes the message hard to read readers are accustomed to seeing material in a mixture of characters and use punctuation to guide them through a message varying from what is normal affects comprehension.

  Take the time to correct errors or your readers may find your message as difficult to read as you found the previous paragraph.

- **Use position wisely and keep messages brief.** Deliver the most important information in the opening sentence or paragraph. If the message is longer than one screen, the receiver might not bother reading it. If you need to transmit lengthy documents via e-mail, use the attachment feature. Be sure your message directs the receiver to critical parts of your attachment.

- **Use attachments carefully.** Not all computer programs are compatible when it comes to attachments. Confirm in advance that your receiver has the software necessary to access what you send. If you're sending a text file, for example, tell the receiver what program you used to create it. Opening a Corel WordPerfect file using Microsoft Word can result in a message that resembles hieroglyphics. When you have multiple attachments, consider sending them separately. Some e-mail programs don't support multiple attachments. Also, be sure to include the attachment! Completing that task before writing the message will ensure you don't have to send a second message just to convey the attachment.

- **Hold your temper.** Remember, you're communicating with a person, not a machine. Don't send messages when you're angry or upset. If you feel the need to vent, write the text of the message then let it *and you* rest for at least 24 hours before adding the receiver information and sending the message.

Close to Home

Unfortunately, Lyle had already sent nasty e-mails to his boss, three vice-presidents and the CEO.

- **Eliminate emoticons; use abbreviations and initialisms wisely.** **Emoticons** are the symbols [e.g., :)-smile] writers use to reflect emotion; use them only in personal e-mail. **Abbreviations** are shortened forms of words (e.g., Feb. for February). **Initialisms** are letter combinations that substitute for words (e.g., BTW for by the way or QFR for Quarterly Financial Report). A good abbreviation is one your receiver will recognize quickly and interpret correctly. Learn and use the abbreviations and initialisms your organization has adopted.

- **Know when *not* to use e-mail.** Because it lacks the cues supplied by body language, voice tones, and shared environment, e-mail lacks the communication richness of a face-to-face or telephone communication and the formality or authority of a letter. Consider other communication channels when messages are time sensitive (scheduling or canceling a meeting on short notice), when the message is simple and the receiver is nearby

NOTE 5.45
E-mail is inappropriate in some situations.

(cubicle-to-cubicle conversation), when the topic merits face-to-face discussion (performance appraisals, negotiations, grievance settlements), or when the message contains content that will have significant emotional impact on the receiver (e.g., job termination). Requests or claims submitted by e-mail, however, may be refused by e-mail; the decision rests on the emotional stake the receiver has in the situation.

- **Choose "reply" or "reply to all" as appropriate to the situation.** Ensure that your message gets to its target audience and no one else.

- **Set the context for your response.** Edit the subject line *(Request Response–Yes!),* recap the original message, or include some or all of the original message in your reply. Most e-mail programs distinguish between old and new text by placing a > or other symbol before each line of text retained from the original message.

- **Avoid e-mail chains.** Replying to or forwarding e-mail messages without deleting unnecessary text from earlier messages creates an e-mail chain. Long chains increase the chance that confidential or potentially embarrassing material will reach an unintended audience. Long chains also waste reader time and use storage space needlessly.

- **Respect confidentiality.** Never forward confidential information unless you are authorized to do so. If you receive a blind copy (BCC), recognize that the primary receiver doesn't know you also received the message. Do not mention the message to the primary receiver or to anyone else. If you don't want your message forwarded to others, explicitly request that it remain confidential.

NOTE 5.46
Proofread e-mail before sending it.

- **Proofread the message before you send it.** Most systems do not allow messages to be canceled or retrieved after a user gives the *send* command. To make matters worse, it takes just a few keystrokes for the receiver to forward the message to one, a few, or literally thousands of additional receivers.

As Sherri Novitsky points out in her Communication Quote, electronic messages require the same attention to planning and development as do letters and memos.

COMMUNICATION QUOTE

As Administrative Director of the Metropolitan Rehabilitation Services, Inc. for seventeen years, I have witnessed few technological advances that have impacted the way we communicate as radically as the advent of e-mail. I have noticed that e-mail is often used in lieu of a "telephone conversation," with the author inaccurately assuming the same level of privacy. This cavalier attitude towards e-mail is typically inconsequential; however, in cases where the information is privileged or thoughtless, there can be repercussions. It is our policy to treat e-mail as we would any other business correspondence, taking care to ensure the information being sent is accurate with regard to both context and content. This approach alleviates embarrassment not only to the author but the corporation as well.

—Sherri Novitsky, Administrative Director, Metropolitan Rehabilitation Services (Photo courtesy of Sherri Novitsky)

The speed by which e-mail can be transmitted has led communicators to expect quick responses to their messages. Courteous e-mail users check their messages once or twice every day and strive to respond within 24 hours. They read items once and decide whether to respond immediately, delete the message, or move the message to a project-related folder. E-mail users are also careful about viewing attachments they receive. Computer viruses are often sent as e-mail attachments; when the attachments are opened, the virus is activated. Unless your employer directs you to delete all attachments received from sources outside the company, a good rule is to save the attachment as a file so that virus detection software can be applied.

NOTE 5.47
Be a courteous e-mail user.

Web Sites and Web Pages

A **Web site** is the name given to a group of related Web pages. The opening screen or **home page** of a Web site acts as a table of contents. From this screen, users link to other pages or sites by clicking on icons or phrases designed for that purpose. The convenience and speed of this process relate directly to the way in which the page is organized.

NOTE 5.48
A Web site may have one or more pages.

Building an effective Web site involves five steps:

NOTE 5.49
Be sure your Web site is effective.

[1] **Determine the purpose and audience.** Web sites may have one or more purposes. Sites are designed to inform, persuade, and/or entertain. Each site owner also hopes to generate goodwill. If a site has more than one purpose, separate pages should be devoted to each. Once you have determined why your site exists, you are ready to decide to whom it is going to be directed. Although your site may be accessible to the world of Internet users, you should define your target audience. Knowing your audience will help you determine your site's content and design.

One characteristic common to all Web audiences is that they spend most of their time scanning material. If they don't find what they want quickly—within the first minute—they will probably leave your site and may never return. To help the audience find what they want and find it fast, you will want to use short headings (3–5 words), short sentences (15–20 words), short paragraphs (4–5 lines), and short summaries (30–40 words).

[2] **Develop the content.** Site content may consist of original material or material supplemented by links to other sites. Most people who search the Internet are seeking information; a site that contains only links won't meet their primary need and won't be visited frequently. Materials you prepare yourself should adhere to the principles of business communication. They should also be prepared with full respect for copyright, fair use, and intellectual property rights. If you establish links to other sites, be sure those sites meet your high standards. Those who view your site will construct an image of you based not only on what you prepare but on where you might direct them.

[3] **Design the site.** Organization is the key to site design, and an outline will help you create an easy-to-navigate site. Visiting other sites can help, too. The Tips and Hints box on page 146 contains items to consider when designing a site.

[4] **Tackle technical issues.** Every Web page is an HTML document. Users may write their own HTML, create it using commercial software, or hire a commercial service to perform the task. To be accessible to readers, each site must have a URL and reside on a computer equipped with server software and connected to the Internet.

[5] **Update the site.** Web sites need regular maintenance to retain their value. The site's contents will determine how frequently updates are needed, but quarterly

reviews are the outside limit. During an update, verify that all sites to which you link are still active and appropriate; software is available to assist with this task.

Guidelines for Designing a Web Site

Following these guidelines when designing a site can ensure that your receiver will get your message:

- **Label your page.** Place the title, purpose, and creation/update date near the top, where it will get strong emphasis.
- **Format carefully.** Minimize the number of horizontal and vertical lines; they make the page look busy. Use headlines to summarize topics or to list elements, so your reader can scan your document and locate the desired information quickly. If your site has multiple pages, use the same format on all pages to give your site an identity or image. Keeping navigational information (e.g., "return to home page," "back," "next") in the same place will assist your readers. Encourage feedback and make action easy; provide your e-mail address as a link.

If the site is for an organization, include a mailing address and phone number.

- **Use graphics wisely.** A few well-chosen graphics add interest; too many add to the load time. The longer a visitor has to wait before being able to read or use the page, the greater the likelihood he or she will leave and not return to the site. Consider providing a text-only version of your page. If you take images from other sources, do so ethically—respect copyrights and get permission when necessary.
- **Select appropriate emphasis techniques.** Bold and italics are generally more effective than blinking text. Colors should complement each other. Background patterns, if used, should be subtle and not detract from the readability of the page. Be sure the font style and size lend themselves to easy reading.

Summary of Learning Objectives

(1) Identify the advantages and disadvantages of written messages.

Written messages provide a permanent record, accommodate lengthy and complex content, can be reread and studied, and can be edited and revised. Unfortunately, they are also transmitted slowly, are more formal, produce delayed and reduced feedback, and require storage.

(2) Use a three-step process to develop effective business messages.

The three-step process for developing business messages is simple but critical to your success in communicating. The three steps are as follows:

Step 1: Plan the Message. Planning involves asking general and specific questions to assess the communication situation, establishing primary and secondary purposes, analyzing the receiver, selecting the type of message, selecting an organizational plan, and outlining the message.

Step 2: Draft the Message. The second step in developing an effective written business message is to put thoughts into a written draft—an effort that focuses on getting something on paper rather than on format, spelling, grammar, and mechanics. Writer's block may occur during this process, but it is a problem that can be overcome.

Step 3: Finalize the Message. The third step in developing an effective business message involves revising, editing, and proofreading the document. Word processing software can be a valuable tool in this process.

Describe how to determine the vocabulary level of business messages.

③

Using a vocabulary level that your receiver will understand is a primary concern in composing effective business messages. Vocabulary level, as used in this book, refers to the level of difficulty of the words and combinations of words in messages.

Any of several readability formulas can be used to calculate vocabulary levels for your messages. Many grammar-checker programs are able to calculate the vocabulary level of your message. Business messages written at the eighth- to twelfth-grade levels will communicate clearly with most receivers.

Explain how to develop effective e-mail and Web pages.

④

E-mail and Web pages are electronically transmitted written messages. Although they may be created to meet personal goals, they also play a critical role in business. When used for business purposes, e-mail and Web documents should be developed following the same planning, drafting, and finalizing process used for letters, memos, and reports.

Discussion Questions

1. Compare written and oral messages on the factors listed below. Which earns the higher rating? Why? (Objective 1)
   a. permanence
   b. tone
   c. ability to be edited
   d. feedback
2. Describe how to analyze a communication situation. (Objective 2)
3. Discuss how word processing software programs affect the drafting of messages. (Objective 2)
4. How has e-mail changed your expectations about communication turnaround time? For each situation below, indicate how long you would expect to wait for a reply. (Objective 4)
   a. An e-mail message to your business communication instructor, sent at noon on Wednesday, inquiring about an assignment due Thursday.
   b. An e-mail to your accounting instructor, sent at noon on Wednesday, inquiring about problems due on Thursday.
   c. A product inquiry submitted to the e-mail address given on a manufacturer's home page.
   d. An e-mail to your best friend, a student at a different school.
   e. An e-mail complaint about a product you purchased over the Internet.

Take part in a class discussion during which you discuss your responses and your reasons for them.

5. Explain why spell checkers and style checkers do not replace proofreading. (Objective 2)

6. Explain the importance of vocabulary level in composing effective business messages. (Objective 3)

7. What are readability formulas? Why should writers use them? (Objective 3)

8. What advice would you give to someone who consistently deletes the text of incoming e-mail before adding a one- or two-word reply? (Objective 4)

9. Is it ethical to send blind copies of e-mail? Is it unethical to forward them to others? Discuss. (Objective 4)

10. List and explain two guidelines to follow when creating e-mail and one to follow when replying to e-mail. (Objective 4)

11. Why is audience analysis important when designing a Web page? (Objective 4)

12. Discuss how the statement "Luck is what happens when preparation meets opportunity" applies to the topics in this chapter. (Objectives 2 and 4)

Application Exercises

1. Briefly describe (a) three specific situations in which you would choose to use written communication and (b) three specific situations in which you would choose to use oral communication. Give a printed copy of the descriptions to your instructor. (Objective 1)

2. **Global.** Interview a person of another culture. Describe for the interviewee the direct and indirect plans for organizing messages as they are explained in this chapter. Ask the interviewee the following questions: (Objective 2)
   a. Which organizational plan is used for most messages in your culture?
   b. What types of messages in your culture use the direct plan?
   c. What types of messages in your culture use the indirect plan?
   Report your findings to the class.

3. In conjunction with the launch of a new product line, your 30-person company will host an open house on the third Wednesday of next month. You have been asked to announce the event to your firm's employees and to the community. Analyze the two groups of receivers and then outline the who, what, when, where, and why information you would include in the message to each group. As your instructor directs, submit your e-mail or use it as a springboard to class discussion. (Objective 2)

4. **Ethics. Teamwork.** In a group of three to five students, brainstorm the challenges that one faces being ethical in business. Record your ideas on a flipchart or other large sheet of paper and post them where other class members can see them. As a class, discuss the challenges identified by the groups. (Objective 2)

5. Use the spell-check feature of your word processing program to check for errors in the following paragraph. Compare the results with errors you find as you proofread the text. (Objective 2)

> *Paula were working a loan in the jewelry department. Tree choppers approached the counter while he was rapping an other customers' pack age. Max, the stationary department clerk, offered to provide assistants. Pauline expected. All six customs were served quickly.*

6. Revise and edit the following message so that it communicates more clearly and concisely to a middle-level American receiver: (Objectives 2 and 3)

> *It is excruciatingly apparent that in order to ascend to the new heights of sales and to achieve the new sales quotas the salesmen and saleswomen must dramatically and definitely augment their labors.*
>
> *Here are the things they must execute whenever: (a) Get out in the field more of the time (b) practice, perform, rehearse, and improve their presentations that they make. This will ultimately result in more—more commissions for them and more income over expenses or profit, for the organization.*

7. During the past few weeks, you've received many—too many—e-mails that contain chain letters, jokes, recipes, and other nonbusiness material. An occasional message of this nature is a nice diversion and can enhance morale within an organization, but too many clog the system and reduce productivity. Prepare an e-mail message that politely but firmly asks the senders of these messages to stop. Send the message to your instructor. (Objective 4)

8. **Teamwork.** Work with one other student. Exchange the messages you wrote in Exercise 7 and read them silently, then aloud. Discuss whether and how the tone you thought you used in your message paralleled the tone the receiver conveyed when he or she read the message aloud. What, if anything, should be done to improve the message? (Objective 4)

9. **InfoTrac.** According to an August 2001 *Communication World* article by Gerald Goldhaber, over three billion work-related e-mails are sent every day in the United States. Use InfoTrac to access the article (Article No. A78404403) and learn more about how this volume of e-mail affects productivity. After reading the article, answer the following questions: (Objective 4)
    a. For what types of messages is e-mail not desirable?
    b. How has extensive use of e-mail affected interpersonal communication skills such as listening and conversation?
    c. The article cites the dollar costs associated with poor e-mail management. What advice would you give business owners who wished to reduce these costs by improving their e-mail management?

10. **Teamwork.** Form a four-person group consisting of two subgroups. Each subgroup will find an appropriate substitute for the words in the following list. One subgroup will use a traditional (book) thesaurus, the other the electronic thesaurus feature of a word processing software program. Both subgroups should record the time it takes to accomplish the task. Compile the findings of the two subgroups into a visual that compares the two methods. (Objective 2)

a. archaic	f. exemplify
b. monumental	g. preposterous
c. veritable	h. assimilate
d. sundry	i. ubiquitous
e. irritable	j. ameliorate

11. **Teamwork.** Form a four-person group. Have each person in the group ask five students and five office workers to identify three things they like and three things they dislike about e-mail. Summarize your responses in a memo to your instructor. (Objective 4)

12. **Global. Internet.** Access the home page of two companies based in countries other than the United States and two similar companies in the United States (e.g., financial institutions, airlines). In which ways do the home pages for companies based outside the United States differ from those for companies based in the United States? Did any of the companies make their pages available in languages other than English? Present your results in a memo to your instructor. (Objective 4)

13. J. J. Peak plans to send the following e-mail to his new boss, someone who has been with the company only three weeks. Knowing this is a business message and that J. J. hasn't had much time to develop a casual, working relationship with his new boss, convert the message to one more appropriate to the situation. Send the revised document to your instructor as an attachment to an e-mail, indicating what is attached. If you are unfamiliar with the initialisms and emoticons used in this message, first try to interpret them based on context, then ask your instructor.

> THX 4 reviewing the proposal I plan 2 submit 2 Mears, Inc. YOU CERTAINLY MADE LOTS OF SUGGESTIONS!!! :'(FYI the dew date is 4.1. Then TPTB at Mears will do a pelim screening & invite 3 bidrs to make F2F presentations. I'll let ya know ASAP after I hear from em. FWIW I think r chances are xlnt :-D If u have any ??? plz call. TAFN T2UL8R

There are Web exercises at **http://krizan.swlearning.com** to accompany this chapter.

Message Analysis

Using what you have learned in this chapter and previous chapters, revise and edit the following letter. Be sure to proofread the document before submitting it to your instructor.

> Dear Sirs:
>
> It is with a great deel of pleasure and personnel enthusiasm that I communicate to you the introduction of a new insurance policy written and designed exclusively for the small businesses run by businessmen in our iner city area. Our Chairmen will be holding a special conference to explane the covrage on February 30.
>
> This knew policy is written for small businesses only so if you have sales over $250K per year and purchase this policy we might have to report you're attempt to the authorities. This policy not only offers the small businessmen the coverage they need and have been asking for, but it also is offered at a very low price.
>
> You're business is greatley appreciated! We are glad you choose Protection Mutual for your Insurance needs. For your convient in replying to let us know if you may attend the session conducted by our Chairman in February, we have enclose is a postage-payed, addressed form.
>
> Very Sinerly Yours

Grammar Workshop

Correct the grammar, punctuation, spelling, style, and word choice errors in the following sentences:

1. Thank you for excepting my invitation to speak at next months' meeting of the Assoc. For Electronic Commerce [ACE].
2. 52% of the respondents indicated they plan to lease there next car, 38 percent plan to bye.
3. Before opening a Exit Door on a Air Plane look thru a window too check for smoke and fire.
4. Mr. Siders said Julia me and Jim did a well job planning the knew member social.
5. While on vacation my office was re-modeled.
6. The attornies adviced us too seek an injunction.
7. Each member was asked to return their ballots by December 15th.
8. Did Melissa say that "I should bring the package on her desk to the mailroom?".
9. Rob and Sams' business did so well last quarter that each of the firm's workers recieved a 300 dollar bonus.
10. The environmental impact report lead us to quickly decide against purchasing the land.

Part 3

Correspondence Applications

6

Positive and Neutral Messages

Dick Anderson,
BellSouth Corporation

LET'S TALK BUSINESS In my role as President—Customer Markets for BellSouth Corporation, I use verbal and nonverbal communication skills daily to deliver a positive or neutral message. As an example, I might speak to the industry press regarding the introduction of a new BellSouth product or service or discuss with a major client the advantages of BellSouth as a communications provider, both of which rely on the ability to emphasize the positive.

My responsibilities include leadership of all domestic sales and marketing operations with $18 billion in annual revenue. With customers, it is essential to be able to present information concisely and with confidence, offer an explanation, personalize the appeal, and then close with conviction. It is essential because your competitor may have used the same approach to position its offer earlier in the day.

Equally, BellSouth's sales associates use the direct approach to describe BellSouth's position in the market and the prospects for our future.

In a world increasingly dependent on e-business, concise e-mail messages are essential to success. E-mail has the power to shorten decision cycles by conveying needed information without the normal protocols around hierarchy. It is most effective for decisions when it conveys only the most critical facts and advocates a decision or point of view.

A **positive** or **neutral message** conveys pleasant, favorable, or neutral information to the receiver. Such a message may (1) inquire about a service, a product, or a person; (2) approve a request that has been made of you or your organization; (3) announce an upcoming sale or a new product; or (4) be used in internal communication to announce promotions, expansions, salary increases, or improvements in fringe benefits. The receiver will be getting information that is favorable or neutral and will accept easily the contents of the message. The message should be constructed using the direct plan so the receiver can readily see the benefits. As illustrated in the following Communication Note, communicating information in a positive manner can be beneficial.

LEARNING OBJECTIVE
(1) *Describe positive and neutral messages.*

NOTE 6.1
Positive and neutral messages give favorable or neutral information.

COMMUNICATION NOTE

Keeping Track of Guests Marriott International uses special customer management software to send positive messages in an effort to keep customers happy and, hopefully, keep them coming back. In 1998, this approach helped generate an additional $55 million for the large hotel chain.

Marriott's software allows hotel representatives to pull together information from a number of internal departments and various resorts on any particular returning guest. Representatives then can use this information to send positive messages regarding that guest's unique needs. Imagine how customers feel when they contact the Marriott and the agent already knows what type of room they require, whether they need a rental car, which special events or activities to offer to book for them, and more. This kind of information frees the customer from hours of planning and can leave the guest with a wonderful feeling.

Hotel agents are also beginning to use this customer information to market Marriott properties around the world to guests. Individual customers aren't the only ones benefiting from Marriott's new technology. Businesses are also finding it easier to use the Marriott. With their needs on file, activity planners can leave it to the Marriott to do all the legwork.

Adapted from Amy Borrus's "How Marriott Never Forgets a Guest," *Business Week Online*, February 21, 2000.

Claim messages are also discussed in this chapter because they follow a plan similar to that used for positive information. Even though claim messages may communicate bad news—the sender indicates that he or she has been wronged—receivers should welcome them because they assist in improving products or services. Claim messages are strengthened when written in the direct plan format.

Use the Direct Plan for Positive and Neutral Messages

The **direct plan** should be used in transmitting all positive and neutral messages, written and oral. The direct plan will immediately give the good or neutral information to the receiver, who will then respond favorably to the remainder of the message. An advantage of this plan is that the receiver knows at once that the message conveys information that

NOTE 6.2
The direct plan increases the likelihood that the receiver will read the entire message.

is beneficial (or at least not harmful). If the positive or neutral information—the purpose of the message—is not at the beginning, the receiver may lose interest and not finish the message.

NOTE 6.3
The direct plan gets the receiver in a positive frame of mind.

Another advantage of giving the positive or neutral information at the beginning of the message is to put the receiver in an agreeable frame of mind before presenting an explanation of the conditions related to the positive or neutral information. The explanation will have a much better chance of acceptance if the receiver is in a good mood rather than in an apprehensive state.

LEARNING OBJECTIVE
Describe the four specific guidelines for using the direct plan.

② How to Use the Direct Plan

You should incorporate into your positive and neutral messages the business communication fundamentals that were presented in Chapters 1, 3, and 5. In particular, analyze your receiver and use the you–viewpoint, as discussed in Chapter 1. The four stages in the direct plan for presenting positive or neutral information are detailed in Figure 6.1.

NOTE 6.4
The direct plan has specific steps.

FIGURE 6.1
Direct Plan Outline

Direct Plan for Positive and Neutral Messages

I. The **Opening**
  A. Give the positive or neutral information.
  B. Be optimistic.
  C. Provide coherence.
  D. Use emphasis techniques.
  E. Stress receiver interests and benefits.

II. The **Explanation**
  A. Present related information.
  B. Be objective.
  C. Be concise.
  D. Be positive.

III. The **Sales Appeal** (if appropriate)
  A. Personalize appeal.
  B. Suggest alternatives if appropriate.
  C. Aim for quick action.

IV. The **Friendly Close**
  A. Build goodwill.
  B. Be concise.
  C. Be positive.
  D. Express appreciation.

The direct plan is used for a variety of positive messages—approved adjustments, requests, credit applications, and employment applications; favorable decisions; or any other favorable information. The direct plan is also used for neutral information and claim messages. The content of the message must be decided before the direct plan can be implemented.

NOTE 6.5
The content of the message is developed after the situation is analyzed and its purposes are determined.

The situation must be analyzed and the primary and secondary purposes of the communication determined before any message can be composed. If the primary purpose is transmitting positive or neutral information, the direct plan should be used in organizing the message. Before composing a positive or neutral message, you must answer the following questions:

- What is the most favorable information?
- How will this information benefit the receiver?
- What additional information should be given to the receiver?
- Would a convincing sales appeal be appropriate in this message?
- What friendly message can be transmitted in the close to build goodwill?

Once you have determined the purpose and content, you are ready to implement the direct plan. The parts of the direct plan outline are discussed in the following sections, and the most important considerations are reviewed.

Opening

In the direct plan, the memo or letter should give the positive or neutral information in the **opening**—subject line or the first paragraph of the message. Especially in a memo or e-mail, the subject line can be used to convey the good news. Give the positive information immediately, be optimistic, provide coherence, use emphasis techniques, and stress receiver interests or benefits.

NOTE 6.6
In the direct plan, messages begin with positive or neutral information.

The first sentence of the first paragraph should contain the information that will be most beneficial to the receiver. Only positive words should be used in describing the information. The paragraph should be short for emphasis. The receiver's interest will be aroused if the benefits of the good information are stressed in the opening. For coherence, information should be provided so that the receiver will know which request, order, contract, or previous transaction is being discussed. This identification may be placed in a reference line.

Explanation

The second part of a message using the direct plan should contain the explanation. The **explanation** presents any additional information that relates to the positive or neutral information presented in the first paragraph. The explanation is factual and, therefore, needs to be presented in an objective manner. It should be concise but still contain all the details the receiver needs. The explanation should be written optimistically.

NOTE 6.7
The supporting explanation should follow the positive or neutral opening.

Sales Appeal

The **sales appeal** is the portion of a message in which the writer attempts to persuade the reader to take a specific action. It can be effective in many positive and neutral messages, but it is not appropriate in all of them. Situations in which a sales appeal should be used include letters approving charge accounts, letters informing students that they have been accepted into a program, and messages approving claims. Situations in which a sales appeal would not be appropriate include claim letters and messages agreeing to speak at a meeting.

NOTE 6.8
The sales appeal should be used when appropriate.

The sales appeal, if used, should come after the explanation. Depending on its length and nature, the sales appeal may be placed in a paragraph by itself or combined with the closing paragraph. Adapt the appeal to the situation; if possible and desirable, provide alternatives for the receiver. The sales appeal may tell about an upcoming sale or a new product. Personalize the appeal to convince the receiver that it is in his or her best interest to take immediate action.

NOTE 6.9
The sales appeal should follow the explanation.

Friendly Close

NOTE 6.10
A properly written close builds goodwill.

The **friendly close** is the final paragraph of a message. Its primary purpose is to build goodwill. Goodwill is built by being personal and optimistic. The close may express appreciation for an employee's past service or for a customer's business. The close may move to a related subject, or it may unify the message by referring to the good information given in the first paragraph. The close in a positive or neutral message is normally short and avoids clichés.

LEARNING OBJECTIVE
③
Distinguish between poor and good positive and neutral messages.

③ Implementing the Direct Plan

The direct plan is illustrated in the following case, which shows the development of a positive information letter to a customer. You could follow this same plan when organizing your thoughts prior to telephoning a customer. Here are the details of the communication situation.

NOTE 6.11
A communication case will help illustrate how to compose positive information messages.

THE JAMES THOMAS CASE

James Thomas recently retired from Hard Rock Gas Company. He was employed by Hard Rock for more than 30 years, during which he held various administrative positions. The company has decided to establish an endowed scholarship in Mr. Thomas' name that each year would award $5,000 to a student. You are director of human resources for Hard Rock. You will write a letter to Mr. Thomas informing him of this scholarship and asking him to develop the selection criteria. The human resources department will need details such as the academic major, the GPA, ACT or SAT score, financial need, and class standing. In addition, you will need to ask Mr. Thomas if he or one of his family members wishes to serve on the selection committee.

Students will be awarded the James N. Thomas Endowed Scholarship.

©CHARLES GUPTON/CORBIS

The first step in writing is to analyze the situation and determine the purpose and content that will most effectively accomplish the objective of the communication. In the James Thomas letter, the objective is to transmit positive information—the establishment of a scholarship. For this situation the ideas should be developed and organized using the direct plan. The following sections illustrate how the content of the positive information letter could be developed. Each section discusses a stage of the direct plan and presents an example of *poor writing* and an example of *good writing*.

Peanuts

Open with the Positive Information

A **poor** opening presenting the positive information follows:

- The Hard Rock Board of Directors had its quarterly meeting yesterday. Its members have directed me to inform you that a scholarship will be established in your name.

This poorly written opening stresses the writer's interest instead of the receiver's interest and benefits. Note that the positive information, the establishment of a scholarship, is not given until the second sentence and that the scholarship is not clearly described. The paragraph is also written in a stiff, impersonal manner rather than in a positive, friendly style. After reading the opening, James will be neither excited nor eager to read about the scholarship.

The following would be a **good** opening for this case problem:

- To honor you for your many years of dedicated service, a James N. Thomas Endowed Scholarship awarding $5,000 a year will be established. The Hard Rock Board of Directors created this scholarship at its quarterly meeting yesterday.

In contrast to the poorly written opening, this paragraph meets all the requirements of properly presenting positive information in a message. It opens with positive information, and the you–viewpoint is emphasized. The establishment of a scholarship is specifically identified in two sentences, thus providing coherence. Because this first paragraph has a positive, personal tone, James will be excited about reading the rest of the message.

Provide an Explanation

The next step in composing a message using the direct plan is to present an explanation of the conditions under which the positive information—the establishment of a scholarship—will be carried out.

A **poor** way to present an explanation to James follows:

- I need to know what you want to include in the guidelines for the $5,000 scholarship. I need to know who should receive the scholarship each year.

NOTE 6.12
The example of a poor opening lacks the you–viewpoint.

NOTE 6.13
The good opening meets all requirements for presenting positive news.

NOTE 6.14
The poor explanation lacks the you–viewpoint, is negative, and does not give a specific deadline for the guidelines.

NEEDS WORK

Hard Rock Gas Company
3478 Lamar Avenue
Houston, TX 77025-1135
(713) 555-6391 Fax (713) 555-2833

November 14, 200–

Mr. James N. Thomas
690 Bishop Drive
San Angelo, TX 76901

Dear Jim:

Weak positive news.

The Hard Rock Board of Directors had its quarterly meeting yesterday. Its members have directed me to inform you that a scholarship will be established in your name.

Explanation is impersonal and negative.

I need to know what you want to include in the guidelines for the $5,000 scholarship. I need to know who should receive the scholarship each year. We have never established a scholarship fund before, so I don't know what all you need to include in the guidelines. I do need these guidelines soon.

Sales appeal is presented in a harsh tone.

We will use a selection committee to pick someone for the scholarship. Since you are retired and have plenty of free time, why don't you serve on the committee?

Don't forget that I need the guidelines by the end of the month. I cannot establish the scholarship until you let me know how you want the guidelines written.

Impersonal close.

Sincerely,

Charles Giese

Charles Giese
Vice President

FIGURE 6.2
Example of a *Poor*
Positive Message

We have never established a scholarship fund before, so I don't know what all you need to include in the guidelines. I do need these guidelines soon.

The style of this poor explanation is similar to the style of the poor opening; it stresses the writer's interests rather than the receiver's benefits. Lack of a you–viewpoint and the tone of the message make the explanation negative. The explanation should contain all relevant facts so that the receiver will not have any questions. In this example, no assistance is given concerning the types of information to include in the guidelines. The explanation could be made more concise by stating that you would be willing to meet with James to develop the guidelines.

In contrast, a **good** explanation follows:

NOTE 6.15
The good example meets all requirements for a positive explanation.

- This $5,000 endowed scholarship bearing your name will be awarded each year to a student from the university or college of your choice who meets the guidelines that you establish. The following information should be included in the guidelines: specific major of the recipient, required minimum GPA, required minimum ACT score, and classification of the recipient (incoming freshman or upperclassman).

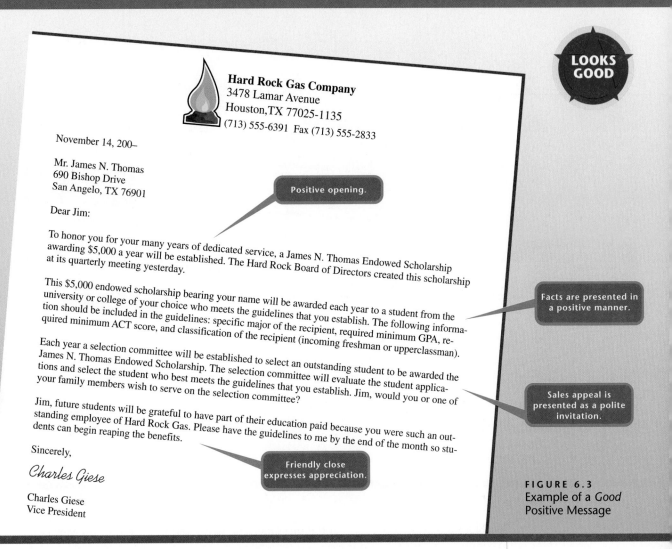

Hard Rock Gas Company
3478 Lamar Avenue
Houston, TX 77025-1135
(713) 555-6391 Fax (713) 555-2833

November 14, 200–

Mr. James N. Thomas
690 Bishop Drive
San Angelo, TX 76901

Dear Jim:

Positive opening.

To honor you for your many years of dedicated service, a James N. Thomas Endowed Scholarship awarding $5,000 a year will be established. The Hard Rock Board of Directors created this scholarship at its quarterly meeting yesterday.

This $5,000 endowed scholarship bearing your name will be awarded each year to a student from the university or college of your choice who meets the guidelines that you establish. The following information should be included in the guidelines: specific major of the recipient, required minimum GPA, required minimum ACT score, and classification of the recipient (incoming freshman or upperclassman).

Facts are presented in a positive manner.

Each year a selection committee will be established to select an outstanding student to be awarded the James N. Thomas Endowed Scholarship. The selection committee will evaluate the student applications and select the student who best meets the guidelines that you establish. Jim, would you or one of your family members wish to serve on the selection committee?

Sales appeal is presented as a polite invitation.

Jim, future students will be grateful to have part of their education paid because you were such an outstanding employee of Hard Rock Gas. Please have the guidelines to me by the end of the month so students can begin reaping the benefits.

Sincerely,

Charles Giese

Charles Giese
Vice President

Friendly close expresses appreciation.

LOOKS GOOD

FIGURE 6.3
Example of a *Good* Positive Message

This explanation presents the facts in an objective way and answers the receiver's questions. The paragraph is written positively. It contains enough information so that the receiver understands the conditions of the positive information. After presenting the explanation, the writer should consider using a sales appeal.

Consider a Sales Appeal
A sales appeal should be used whenever a writer attempts to obtain additional business from the receiver. The sales appeal, depending on its length and nature, may be written as a separate paragraph(s) or as part of the final paragraph of the letter. Topics for sales appeal may include information about additional services that the business may provide, an upcoming sale, or a new product.

In this case the following is an example of a **poor** appeal for James to serve on the selection committee:

- We will use a selection committee to pick someone for the scholarship. Since you are retired and have plenty of free time, why don't you serve on the committee?

NOTE 6.16
The poor example of a sales appeal is cold and impersonal.

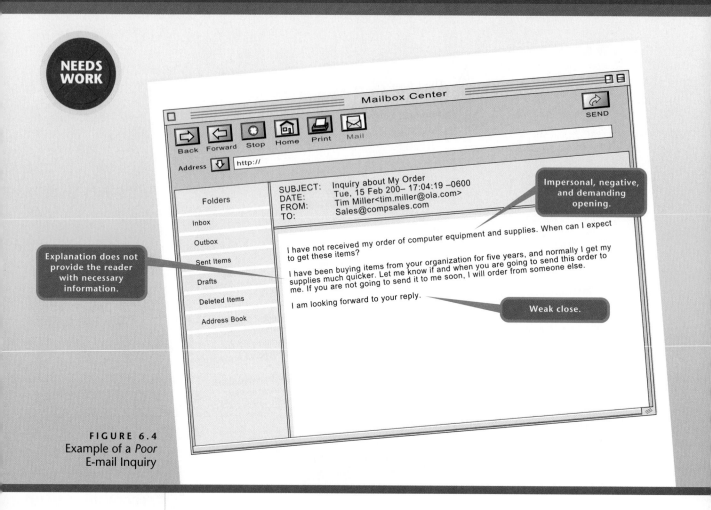

Mailbox Center

SEND

Back Forward Stop Home Print Mail

Address http://

Folders

Inbox

Outbox

Sent Items

Drafts

Deleted Items

Address Book

SUBJECT: Inquiry about My Order
DATE: Tue, 15 Feb 200– 17:04:19 –0600
FROM: Tim Miller<tim.miller@ola.com>
TO: Sales@compsales.com

Impersonal, negative, and demanding opening.

I have not received my order of computer equipment and supplies. When can I expect to get these items?

I have been buying items from your organization for five years, and normally I get my supplies much quicker. Let me know if and when you are going to send this order to me. If you are not going to send it to me soon, I will order from someone else.

I am looking forward to your reply.

Weak close.

Explanation does not provide the reader with necessary information.

FIGURE 6.4
Example of a *Poor*
E-mail Inquiry

Note the impersonal tone of the message. The writer did not use the you–viewpoint in the sales appeal, and the second sentence is more likely to discourage than encourage James to serve on the committee.

NOTE 6.17
The good example of a sales appeal is positive and personalized.

- Each year a selection committee will be established to select an outstanding student to be awarded the James N. Thomas Endowed Scholarship. The selection committee will evaluate the student applications and select the student who best meets the guidelines that you establish. Jim, would you or one of your family members wish to serve on the selection committee?

This example of a **good** sales appeal is written in a personalized way; it encourages James to serve on the selection committee. It briefly explains the purpose of the committee, and it politely asks James whether he or a member of his family would be willing to serve on the committee.

End Your Letter with a Friendly Close
A positive or neutral message should conclude with a friendly close that builds goodwill. A **poor** close, such as the one that follows, would guarantee ill will:

NOTE 6.18
The example of a poor close is negative and does not build goodwill.

- Don't forget that I need the guidelines by the end of the month. I cannot establish the scholarship until you let me know how you want the guidelines written.

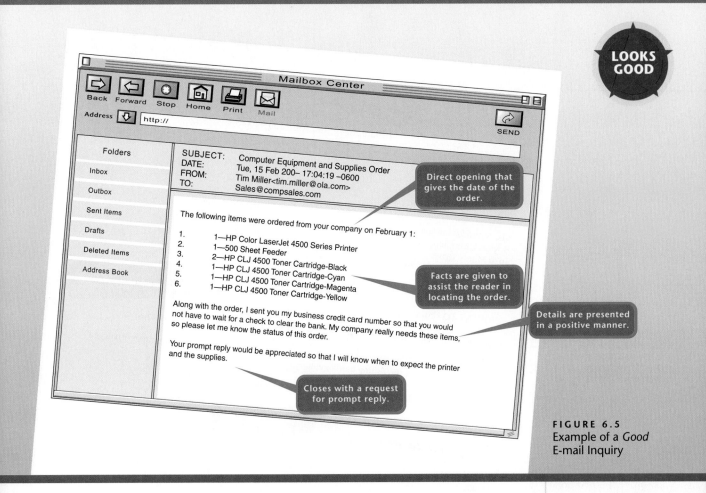

FIGURE 6.5
Example of a *Good*
E-mail Inquiry

The callout labels in the figure read:

- Direct opening that gives the date of the order.
- Facts are given to assist the reader in locating the order.
- Details are presented in a positive manner.
- Closes with a request for prompt reply.

The e-mail message shown in the figure reads:

Mailbox Center

Back Forward Stop Home Print Mail

Address http://

SEND

Folders

Inbox
Outbox
Sent Items
Drafts
Deleted Items
Address Book

SUBJECT: Computer Equipment and Supplies Order
DATE: Tue, 15 Feb 200– 17:04:19 –0600
FROM: Tim Miller<tim.miller@ola.com>
TO: Sales@compsales.com

The following items were ordered from your company on February 1:

1. 1—HP Color LaserJet 4500 Series Printer
2. 1—500 Sheet Feeder
3. 2—HP CLJ 4500 Toner Cartridge-Black
4. 1—HP CLJ 4500 Toner Cartridge-Cyan
5. 1—HP CLJ 4500 Toner Cartridge-Magenta
6. 1—HP CLJ 4500 Toner Cartridge-Yellow

Along with the order, I sent you my business credit card number so that you would not have to wait for a check to clear the bank. My company really needs these items, so please let me know the status of this order.

Your prompt reply would be appreciated so that I will know when to expect the printer and the supplies.

An example of a **good** friendly close that will do much to establish goodwill follows:

- Jim, future students will be grateful to have part of their education paid because you were such an outstanding employee of Hard Rock Gas. Please have the guidelines to me by the end of the month so students can begin reaping the benefits.

This friendly close is written in a positive, personalized, and concise way. Appreciation is shown for James's long service.

Summary—Poor and Good Messages to James Thomas

Poor and good messages are used to demonstrate how effective positive messages are written. The *poor* paragraphs are combined as a letter in Figure 6.2. This **poor** message fails to use the direct plan for positive information and fails to incorporate the communication fundamentals that are presented in Chapters 1, 3, and 5.

Employee goodwill is promoted in the positive letter shown in Figure 6.3. This letter combines the *good* paragraphs. It integrates communication fundamentals into the direct plan message to produce an effective business communication.

An unsolicited positive message has been used to illustrate how the direct plan is used to communicate a positive message. To demonstrate further how the direct approach is used in actual business correspondence situations, several other examples of good and poor positive and neutral messages are presented in the following pages.

NOTE 6.19
The example of a good close is friendly and builds goodwill.

NEEDS WORK

Gun & Rod Club

706 Happy Time Trail
Mountain Home, AR 72653-3185
(501) 555-5219 Fax (501) 555-7729

July 20, 200-

Ms. Teresa Livingston
Boys & Girls Club
1620 Milroy Drive
Mountain Home, AR 72653

Dear Teresa:

REQUEST TO USE LAKE

> Approval is not given in first paragraph.

I have received your request dated July 14 to use our lake for your annual fishing tournament.

> Not written from you–viewpoint. Explanation is not clear.

Our members are glad that your organization wants to host a fishing tournament for underprivileged children. We will allow the fishing tournament.

I hope you organize the tournament so that no child is injured while fishing.

> Inappropriate close.

Sincerely,

Jack McClendon

Jack McClendon
Manager

FIGURE 6.6
Example of a *Poor* Request Approval Letter

LEARNING OBJECTIVE
④
Prepare competently a variety of positive and neutral messages using the direct plan.

Inquiries

Businesspeople periodically make routine requests for information. Routine **inquiries** are neutral messages that require no persuasion and, therefore, should be written using the direct plan. These inquiries may be about a product, a service, or a person.

A message of inquiry must be written so that the writer will obtain all the information necessary to make a decision about a product, service, or person. Consider what you or your company needs to know and ask specific questions. Your letter of inquiry should be written so that the receiver can reply easily, quickly, and completely.

An inquiry about products or services should make the receiver of the message glad to respond. The inquiry may include only one sentence requesting a pamphlet or catalog, or it may have several paragraphs in which questions are asked. If several questions are asked, listing and numbering them will aid the receiver in responding. Use the direct plan outline by presenting your request and stating the reason for it (if necessary) in the opening paragraph. In the second part of your message, give enough information so that the receiver can respond intelligently. Close your message by requesting action. Inquiries usually do not have a sales appeal section.

NOTE 6.20
Use the direct plan with inquiries because persuasion is not needed.

NOTE 6.21
Inquiries should ask specific questions.

NOTE 6.22
The message receiver should be glad to receive an inquiry about products or services.

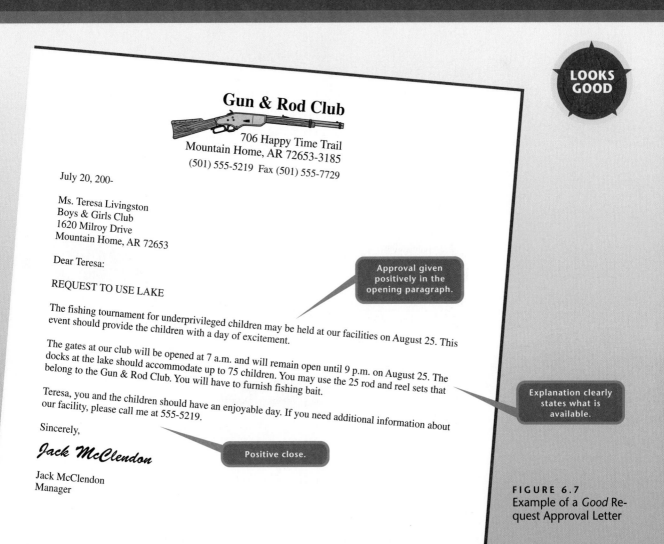

Gun & Rod Club

706 Happy Time Trail
Mountain Home, AR 72653-3185
(501) 555-5219 Fax (501) 555-7729

July 20, 200-

Ms. Teresa Livingston
Boys & Girls Club
1620 Milroy Drive
Mountain Home, AR 72653

Dear Teresa:

REQUEST TO USE LAKE

The fishing tournament for underprivileged children may be held at our facilities on August 25. This event should provide the children with a day of excitement.

(callout: Approval given positively in the opening paragraph.)

The gates at our club will be opened at 7 a.m. and will remain open until 9 p.m. on August 25. The docks at the lake should accommodate up to 75 children. You may use the 25 rod and reel sets that belong to the Gun & Rod Club. You will have to furnish fishing bait.

(callout: Explanation clearly states what is available.)

Teresa, you and the children should have an enjoyable day. If you need additional information about our facility, please call me at 555-5219.

Sincerely,

Jack McClendon

(callout: Positive close.)

Jack McClendon
Manager

(badge: LOOKS GOOD)

FIGURE 6.7
Example of a *Good* Request Approval Letter

Figure 6.4 is an example of a **poor** inquiry in the form of an e-mail requesting the status of a purchase order. The inquiry is not specific enough to enable the sales department to respond with the information Tim Miller needs to make a decision. It would be difficult for the sales department to determine when the order was placed, what items were ordered, why they have not been sent, or when Tim Miller may expect to receive the order.

The letter in Figure 6.5 is an example of a **good** inquiry in the form of an e-mail requesting the status of a purchase order. The letter starts by stating the date that the original order was placed. Sufficient information is provided to the sales department so that it can provide the necessary details in its reply. The listed and numbered items make it easier for the sales department to respond. The close is positive and encourages a prompt reply.

An inquiry about a person must be made carefully to protect the rights of the individual. You should ask only questions that are relevant to the situation. Information obtained should be kept confidential. State whether the person about whom you are inquiring authorized your request. Begin your inquiry by clearly identifying the person and stating your need for the information. The explanation should contain relevant facts—pertinent information that the individual shared with you, requirements that

NOTE 6.23
Inquiries about persons should include only relevant questions and should promise confidentiality.

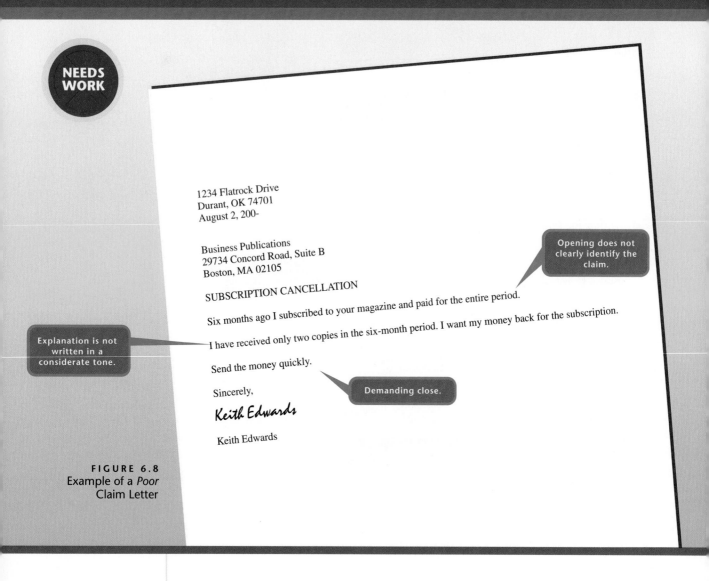

NEEDS WORK

1234 Flatrock Drive
Durant, OK 74701
August 2, 200-

Business Publications
29734 Concord Road, Suite B
Boston, MA 02105

SUBSCRIPTION CANCELLATION

Six months ago I subscribed to your magazine and paid for the entire period.

I have received only two copies in the six-month period. I want my money back for the subscription.

Send the money quickly.

Sincerely,

Keith Edwards

Keith Edwards

Opening does not clearly identify the claim.

Explanation is not written in a considerate tone.

Demanding close.

FIGURE 6.8
Example of a *Poor* Claim Letter

must be met (job, loan, award, etc.), or questions that you need answered. Close by stating that you would appreciate the receiver's sharing the information and by promising to keep the information confidential.

Request Approvals

NOTE 6.24
Most business requests are approved.

A **request** is a message expressing the writer's needs or desires; it usually asks for a response. A request differs from an inquiry by seeking action rather than seeking information. Managers of business organizations receive requests from their customers, their employees, and others. These requests may include, for example, a request from an employee for a six-month parenting leave or a request from a civic organization for the manager to speak at a conference. Requests should be carefully considered and approved whenever feasible.

NOTE 6.25
Goodwill can be improved with proper handling of requests.

The proper handling of a request can build goodwill for an organization. For instance, approval of a parenting leave will gain goodwill for the organization. Accepting

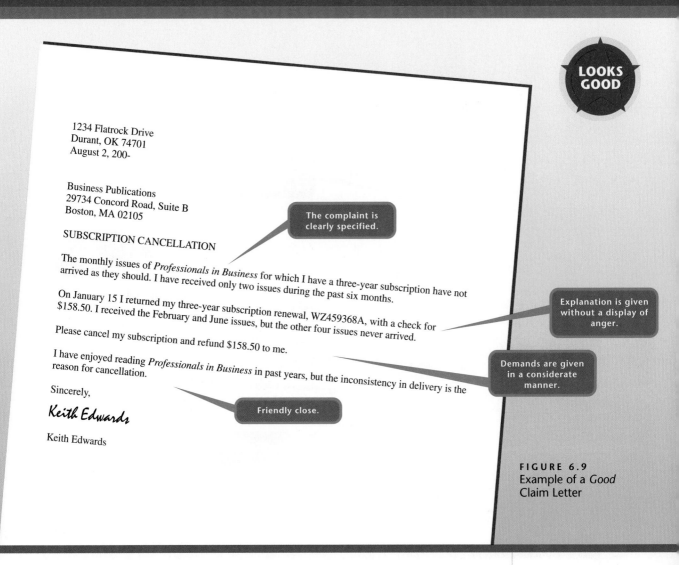

1234 Flatrock Drive
Durant, OK 74701
August 2, 200-

Business Publications
29734 Concord Road, Suite B
Boston, MA 02105

SUBSCRIPTION CANCELLATION

The monthly issues of *Professionals in Business* for which I have a three-year subscription have not arrived as they should. I have received only two issues during the past six months.

The complaint is clearly specified.

On January 15 I returned my three-year subscription renewal, WZ459368A, with a check for $158.50. I received the February and June issues, but the other four issues never arrived.

Explanation is given without a display of anger.

Please cancel my subscription and refund $158.50 to me.

Demands are given in a considerate manner.

I have enjoyed reading *Professionals in Business* in past years, but the inconsistency in delivery is the reason for cancellation.

Sincerely,

Keith Edwards

Keith Edwards

Friendly close.

LOOKS GOOD

FIGURE 6.9
Example of a *Good* Claim Letter

an invitation to speak at a meeting of a civic organization can build goodwill for the company among those attending the meeting. The acceptance letter should convey enthusiasm about the prospect of appearing before the group; it should in no way indicate a duty to perform a community service. The acceptance letter should emphasize the positive aspects of accepting the invitation to speak.

To illustrate how the direct plan can be used in a positive message communicating approval of a request, assume that you are the manager of the Gun & Rod Club. Teresa Livingston, director of the Boys & Girls Club, has requested the use of your lake. This request will allow underprivileged children to experience a character-building day. Because you want to build goodwill, you will write a letter to Teresa approving her request and providing details.

A **poor** approval letter for this request is shown in Figure 6.6. It does little to build goodwill for the Gun & Rod Club. Note the absence of the you–viewpoint. Also, notice that the positive information is not given until the second paragraph.

The **good** letter in Figure 6.7 uses the direct plan and should influence positively Teresa's attitude toward the Gun & Rod Club. It gives Teresa the positive information

NOTE 6.26
Request approvals should stress the positive news.

Business Publications

29734 Concord Road, Suite B
Boston, MA 02105

> Facts are presented in a happy manner with a third line added.

August 19, 200-

Mr. Keith Edwards
1234 Flatrock Drive
Durant, OK 74701

Dear Mr. Edwards:

> Negative opening that doesn't approve the claim.

We are sorry that you have not received all the magazines that we sent you. They must have been lost in the postal system.

> Awarding the claim should be in the first paragraph; explanation sounds accusatory.

We will send you the $158.50 you requested. We have researched your situation and have found that all six issues were sent to your home address; therefore, we will have to use another method of delivering our publications.

> Clumsy sales appeal; should not have to return a card.

Would you like to give us another chance? If so, we can send you free three months of *Professionals in Business* if you return the enclosed postcard.

We are sorry about your subscription and will get the $158.50 in the mail soon.

> Negative final apology.

Sincerely,

Wilfred Schroeder

Wilfred Schroeder
Circulation Editor

Enc.

FIGURE 6.10
Example of a *Poor* Adjustment Letter

---

in the first sentence. The second paragraph presents an explanation that is factual, positive, and concise. A friendly close is given in the final paragraph. A sales appeal—the optional third step in the direct plan—is not appropriate for this situation.

Claims

NOTE 6.27
Claims take many forms.

Claims include requests for merchandise exchange, for refunds on defective or damaged merchandise, and for remedies for unsatisfactory service or work. Your complaint receives greatest emphasis when presented as the first item in the message. Generally, the receiver wants the claim information so that he or she can make necessary corrections as soon as possible. For this reason, and to give strength to your claim, use the direct plan.

NOTE 6.28
Claims are presented using the direct plan.

The plan for claim messages can be adapted easily from the direct plan used for positive and neutral information shown in Figure 6.1. Present the claim in an objective way, without displaying anger and without placing blame on the receiver. The *opening* should present immediately the claim and its impact. The impact could in-

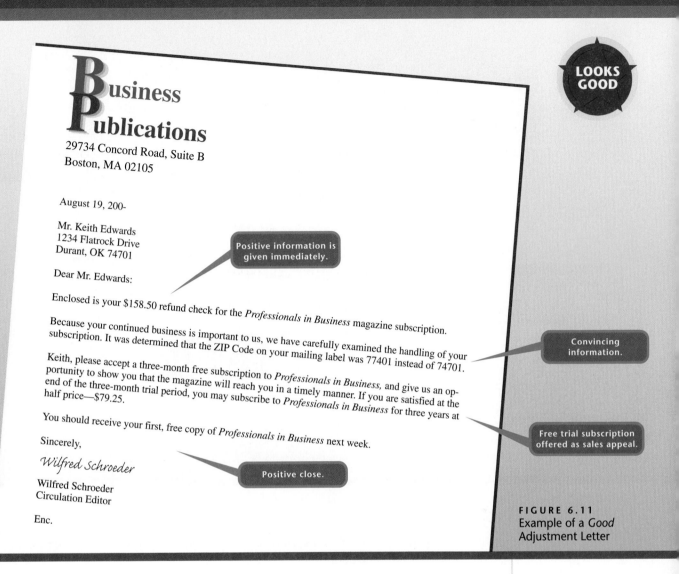

Business Publications

29734 Concord Road, Suite B
Boston, MA 02105

August 19, 200-

Mr. Keith Edwards
1234 Flatrock Drive
Durant, OK 74701

Dear Mr. Edwards:

Enclosed is your $158.50 refund check for the *Professionals in Business* magazine subscription.

[Positive information is given immediately.]

Because your continued business is important to us, we have carefully examined the handling of your subscription. It was determined that the ZIP Code on your mailing label was 77401 instead of 74701.

[Convincing information.]

Keith, please accept a three-month free subscription to *Professionals in Business,* and give us an opportunity to show you that the magazine will reach you in a timely manner. If you are satisfied at the end of the three-month trial period, you may subscribe to *Professionals in Business* for three years at half price—$79.25.

[Free trial subscription offered as sales appeal.]

You should receive your first, free copy of *Professionals in Business* next week.

Sincerely,

Wilfred Schroeder

Wilfred Schroeder
Circulation Editor

Enc.

[Positive close.]

[LOOKS GOOD]

FIGURE 6.11
Example of a *Good* Adjustment Letter

clude the inconveniences suffered and identification of specific damages. The *explanation* should provide all necessary additional background that relates to the claim. In this section provide facts supporting the claim, describe actions that have been taken, and enclose relevant documents (invoices, etc.). In addition, you should specify actions that you want the receiver to take and set a deadline by which corrective action should be taken. There would be no *sales appeal* in a claim letter. Finally, the *friendly close* should be optimistic.

Figure 6.8 is an example of a **poor** claim letter from an individual who has not received all issues of his magazine subscription. Note that the main objective of the letter—not receiving magazines—did not appear until the second paragraph. Also note that the letter is harsh in its request. In addition, the claim was not clearly identified— the publication and the subscription period. The receiver needs this information to process the claim. Lastly, this letter is not written in a considerate tone.

A preferred letter for the same situation is shown in Figure 6.9, an example of the **good** use of the direct plan for a claim. This letter is objective and courteous. The problem is specified in the opening. A concise explanation of the circumstances is given in

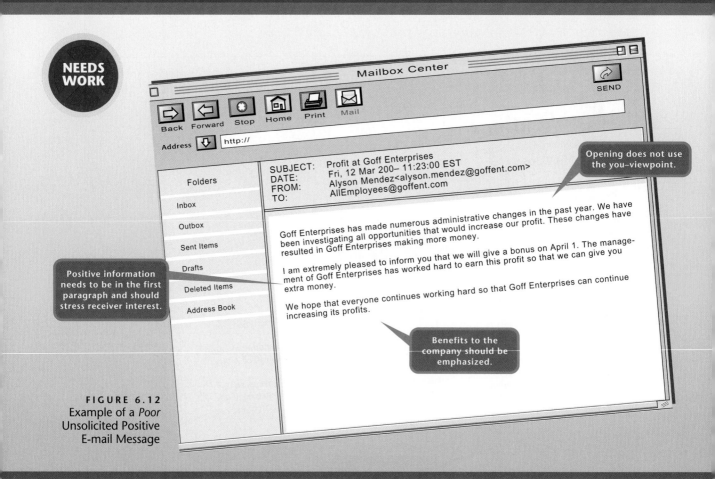

NEEDS WORK

Mailbox Center

Back Forward Stop Home Print Mail SEND

Address http://

Folders

Inbox

Outbox

Sent Items

Drafts

Deleted Items

Address Book

SUBJECT: Profit at Goff Enterprises
DATE: Fri, 12 Mar 200– 11:23:00 EST
FROM: Alyson Mendez<alyson.mendez@goffent.com>
TO: AllEmployees@goffent.com

Goff Enterprises has made numerous administrative changes in the past year. We have been investigating all opportunities that would increase our profit. These changes have resulted in Goff Enterprises making more money.

I am extremely pleased to inform you that we will give a bonus on April 1. The management of Goff Enterprises has worked hard to earn this profit so that we can give you extra money.

We hope that everyone continues working hard so that Goff Enterprises can continue increasing its profits.

> Opening does not use the you–viewpoint.

> Positive information needs to be in the first paragraph and should stress receiver interest.

> Benefits to the company should be emphasized.

FIGURE 6.12
Example of a *Poor*
Unsolicited Positive
E-mail Message

the second paragraph. A request for cancellation is given politely in the third paragraph. The close is friendly and optimistic.

Adjustments

NOTE 6.29
Legitimate claims should be approved quickly.

Business firms that receive claim messages should respond to them quickly in order to maintain the goodwill of the customer. A positive response to a claim is known as an **adjustment**. If there is any doubt about the legitimacy of a claim, the customer usually receives the benefit of the doubt.

NOTE 6.30
Use the direct plan for adjustment letters.

A letter approving a claim is positive information and should use the direct plan. The letter should begin with the positive information—the adjustment. This immediate positive information will aid in eliminating any negative feelings the customer has toward the company. The explanation should be convincing to regain the customer's confidence. An effective, personalized sales appeal gives the company an opportunity to emphasize to the customer the quality of its products or services. To avoid ending on a negative note, an adjustment letter should never close with an apology.

An example of a **poor** adjustment response to the claim letter about the magazines that were not received is shown in Figure 6.10. This letter does not get to the positive information until the second paragraph. The explanation places the blame on the

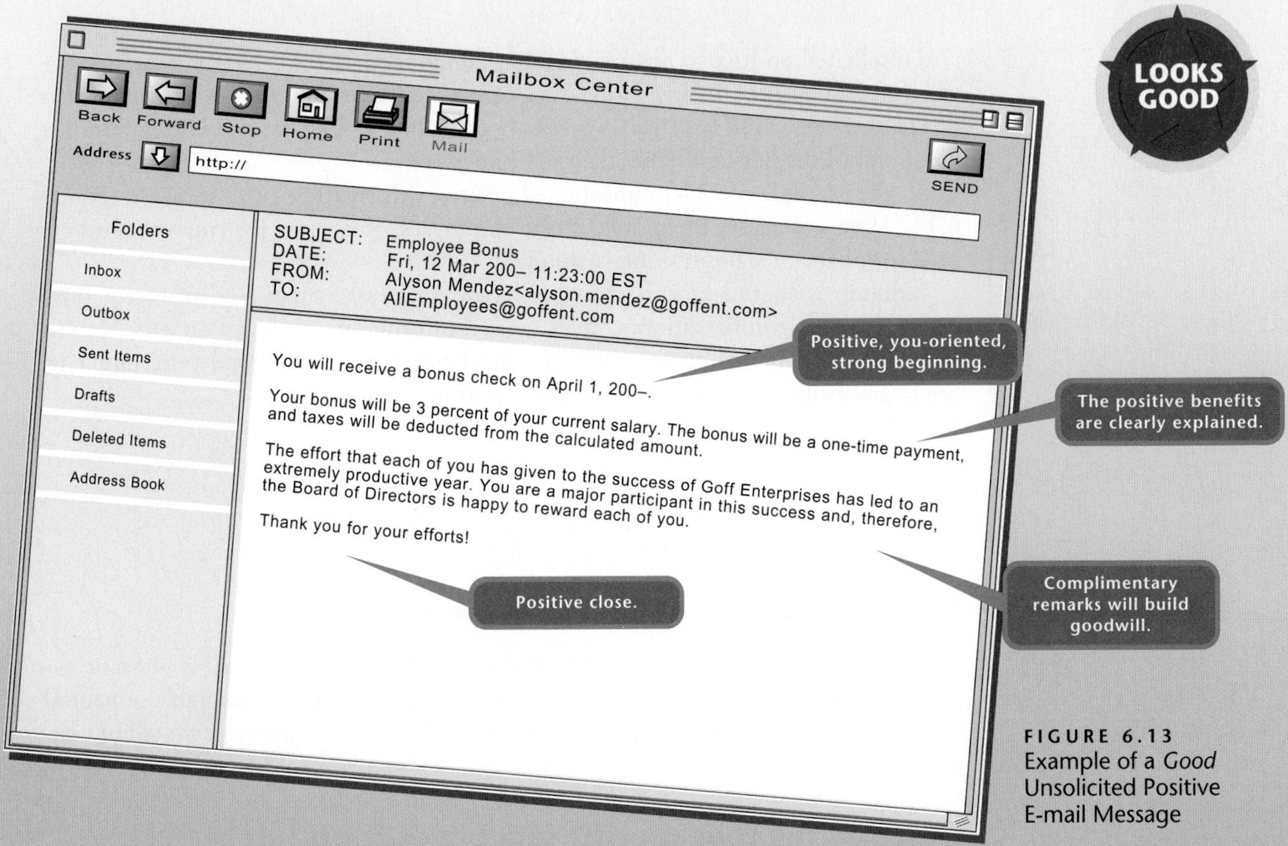
LOOKS GOOD
Mailbox Center
Back
Forward
Stop
Home
Print
Mail
Address
http://
SEND
Folders
Inbox
Outbox
Sent Items
Drafts
Deleted Items
Address Book
SUBJECT: Employee Bonus
DATE: Fri, 12 Mar 200– 11:23:00 EST
FROM: Alyson Mendez<alyson.mendez@goffent.com>
TO: AllEmployees@goffent.com
You will receive a bonus check on April 1, 200–.
Your bonus will be 3 percent of your current salary. The bonus will be a one-time payment, and taxes will be deducted from the calculated amount.
The effort that each of you has given to the success of Goff Enterprises has led to an extremely productive year. You are a major participant in this success and, therefore, the Board of Directors is happy to reward each of you.
Thank you for your efforts!
Positive, you-oriented, strong beginning.
The positive benefits are clearly explained.
Complimentary remarks will build goodwill.
Positive close.

FIGURE 6.13
Example of a *Good* Unsolicited Positive E-mail Message

postal system and is not convincing. The repeated references to the trouble continually remind the receiver of the negative aspects of the situation. The hollow apology in the close does not build the goodwill of the customer. The you–viewpoint is absent from the letter.

An example of a **good** letter approving an adjustment is shown in Figure 6.11. Note that this letter begins immediately with the positive information. The explanation emphasizes not the wrong itself but what was done to correct the wrong. This explanation should help regain the customer's confidence. In the third paragraph, the writer offers a free subscription that could demonstrate a timely delivery of the magazine. The close ends the letter on a happy, positive note.

Unsolicited Positive and Neutral Messages

An **unsolicited positive** or **neutral message** is a communication initiated by an organization. Examples of unsolicited positive or neutral messages to customers may include an announcement of new products or services, notification of new hours of operation, reductions in prices of merchandise, relocation to a new building, or employment of new customer representatives. Unsolicited positive messages to employees may announce new fringe benefits, an unscheduled pay increase, or a promotion.

NOTE 6.31
Businesses send both internal and external unsolicited positive or neutral messages.

Unsolicited positive or neutral messages should employ the direct approach. In the example in Figure 6.12, Alyson misses an opportunity to build on the goodwill that was gained when Goff Enterprises gave everyone a bonus. The letter is written from the viewpoint of the business rather than the employees.

In the example of a good unsolicited positive information letter shown in Figure 6.13, Alyson increases the morale of the employees. Note how the you–viewpoint is used to enhance the positive information.

NOTE 6.32
Use of the direct plan in positive and neutral messages increases their effectiveness.

Skillfully used, the direct plan is appropriate for messages that request information, convey favorable information, convey neutral information, or make or settle claims. With the direct plan, effective messages can increase employee morale, promote customer goodwill, and positively affect those who receive them.

Summary of Learning Objectives

① Describe positive and neutral messages.

A positive or neutral message conveys to the receiver information that is pleasant, favorable, or neutral. The receiver will be getting information that is favorable or neutral and will accept the contents of the message easily; therefore, the message should be constructed using the direct plan.

② Describe the four specific guidelines for using the direct plan.

Open the letter or memo with the positive or neutral information. In the opening paragraph be optimistic, provide coherence, use emphasis techniques, and stress receiver interests or benefits. In the second part of the message, the explanation, present additional information that relates to the positive or neutral information that was presented in the first paragraph. Present the explanation in a concise and objective manner but still include all details that the receiver needs. In the third section, the sales appeal, attempt to persuade the reader to take a specific, desired action. Not all messages need a sales appeal. Complete the message with a friendly close. Build goodwill by being personal and optimistic.

③ Distinguish between poor and good positive and neutral messages.

A good positive and neutral message stresses the reader's interest, the you–viewpoint; a poor message stresses the writer's interest, the I–viewpoint. A good message is written in a positive and friendly style instead of an impersonal manner. The explanation in a good message is concise but gives necessary details; whereas, the explanation in a poor message does not contain all relevant facts. A good message uses the you–viewpoint to appeal for additional business; whereas, a poor message will be more impersonal. A good message concludes with a friendly close that builds goodwill.

Prepare competently a variety of positive and neutral messages using the direct plan.

Incorporate the communication fundamentals in a direct plan when preparing inquiries, request approvals, claims, adjustments, and unsolicited positive and neutral messages. Present the information optimistically using the you–viewpoint. Use the direct plan: (1) Opening—start with the main idea of the message. (2) Explanation—present additional information concisely but completely. (3) Sales Appeal—persuade reader to take specific action that is on a related item. (4) Close—build goodwill by being personal and optimistic.

Discussion Questions

1. Discuss factors that should be considered in selecting the medium to use for transmitting positive or neutral information. (Objective 1)
2. **E-mail.** Explain how e-mail can aid in positive and neutral messages. (Objective 1)
3. Identify and discuss three characteristics of the explanation section of the direct plan. (Objective 2)
4. **Ethics.** Describe the process to follow when gathering information about a person to ensure that the individual's rights are protected. (Objective 2)
5. Explain why a positive message should use the direct plan. (Objective 2)
6. Which of the following paragraphs would be more appropriate for the sales appeal of a request approval? Explain why. (Objective 3)

   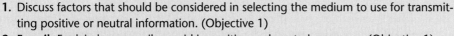

   Mr. Williams, I want to invite you to our annual sale. We have many new appliances that would look nice in your home. We are giving our customers a 25 percent discount during this sale.

   Mr. Williams, you may be interested in browsing through our store and selecting from the many washers, dryers, freezers, dishwashers, etc. that would complement the refrigerator that you recently purchased. These appliances are now being featured during our annual 25 percent off sale. You may be especially interested in the new Model 450 flat-screen television that is being offered at a 35 percent discount during this sale.

7. Explain why the following paragraph would be weak in opening a request approval letter: (Objective 3)

   Your interest in obtaining a membership in the Calloway Country Club is appreciated. You have been a valuable asset to our community during the five years you have lived here.

8. What is an unsolicited positive message, and why should the direct plan be used in developing it? (Objective 4)
9. What benefits can be gained from an effective sales appeal in an adjustment message? (Objective 4)
10. Discuss five characteristics of an inquiry. (Objective 4)

Application Exercises

1. **E-mail.** Develop a message that could be sent via e-mail to business students at your school inviting them to attend a meeting of a student professional organization. You may include details such as a guest speaker, free pizza, or any other activity that would be attractive to the students. E-mail a copy of this message to your instructor. (Objective 3)

2. **InfoTrac.** Excessive employee turnover can be costly; therefore, companies are devising methods to reduce turnover. The Young and Lundberg study at Cornell University looked at what companies are doing to make new employees feel more at ease. Read InfoTrac article A19075395, "Creating a Good First Day on the Job: Allaying Newcomers' Anxiety with Positive Messages." Respond to the following questions in a memo addressed to your instructor:

   a. How are newcomers made to feel welcome within their new companies?
   b. What negative experiences did newcomers encounter?
   c. What example was given of contrasts causing shock to new employee socialization?
   d. Young and Lundberg stated that other studies have focused on unmet expectations. What unmet expectations were measured in these studies?

3. Visit with an officer of a service organization (e.g., Lion's Club, Rotary) in your community and ask how the organization recruits new members. Be prepared to present your findings to the class. (Objective 3)

4. **Teamwork.** Form a team of three or four students and develop a questionnaire to determine why students selected their majors and why they chose to attend your school. Have each member of the team survey at least ten students and combine the results for the team. Write one memo from the team to the instructor reporting the results of the survey. (Objective 4)

5. **E-mail.** You are the regional manager of 11 video stores. Assume your instructor is the manager of one of the stores in your region. The employees of your instructor's store have had the lowest absentee record in the region for the past two quarters. Send an e-mail to your instructor acknowledging this accomplishment. Consider the four parts of a direct plan when preparing this message. (Objective 4)

There are Web exercises at **http://krizan.swlearning.com** to accompany this chapter.

Case Problems

Inquiries

1. You have recently been elected vice president for programs of Young Business Professionals of America. This organization has approximately 1,500 members and holds a national conference in a major U.S. city each year. The major responsibility for the vice president for programs is to plan and coordinate the national conference.

   Develop a form letter that could be sent to the vice presidents who coordinated the last five conferences. Ask these individuals for advice in beginning your preparations. Some of the questions you may want to include are pitfalls in the preparations, types of committees that you should form to assist you in planning the conference, tips on negotiating with hotels, advice on whom to ask and whom to avoid as keynote speakers, and travel arrangements.

2. **Teamwork.** Brian's Food Service is expanding its catering division. It needs an additional enclosed truck with a refrigeration unit; several propane ovens to keep food

warm; and storage shelves and cabinets for supplies, serving trays, linens, and food items. Form a committee of three students to develop an inquiry that could be sent to several custom vehicle dealers requesting a design for this vehicle. Be sure to include details to make this a complete inquiry.

3. **Global.** Mandy McKinney would like to take her husband, Paul, on a vacation to Germany for their tenth wedding anniversary. She is doing all the planning for this event so she can surprise him with the trip. She will need to contact the Tourist Information Office, Schumannstrasse 27, 50201, Salzburg, Germany, for information and land costs. Write a letter that Mandy McKinney could use to obtain pertinent information. Be sure to include necessary details to make this a complete inquiry.

4. You and a friend are considering a safari to Africa. You have heard that True Adventures of New Orleans, Louisiana, provides excellent safaris. You need to know the cost (including airfare), equipment required, length of the safari, success rate of the safari, immunization requirements, and visa information. Write a letter to True Adventures obtaining this and other pertinent information.

5. **E-mail.** You are interested in buying a basset hound. Develop a message that could be sent via e-mail to a dog breeder obtaining information on any basset hounds that he or she may have for sale. Information you wish to obtain includes the age of the dog, the gender of the dog, its color pattern, its pedigree, and the price. After adding details to make the message complete, send it via e-mail to your instructor.

Request Approvals

6. This past spring your organization constructed a Wellness Center for use by all employees. After the center was in operation for several weeks, the employees requested that their lunch hour be extended to 1½ hours to allow more time to exercise, to shower, and to eat a quick lunch. You, as director of human resources, realize the benefits that the employees are gaining from the center. After conferring with top management, you must now write a memo to all employees informing them that they can take a 1½-hour lunch break to use the Wellness Center but will have to make up the extra half hour by starting at 7:30 a.m. or by working until 5 p.m. Give the memo to your instructor.

7. Tanya Schmidt has requested a three-month leave of absence to care for her uncle who has been diagnosed with terminal cancer. Tanya has been a faithful employee for nine years. Write her a memo approving her request. Add necessary facts to make the memo complete.

8. **E-mail.** You are the office manager for Family Care Clinic. Today you received an e-mail from Charley Hess who explained that he was billed $60 for a physician's office visit on May 11. He did not see Dr. George Clark, a physician at the clinic, on May 11 because he was out of town on vacation the first 15 days of May. He requests that his account be credited for the $60 office visit. After checking your records, you determine that Mr. Hess is correct. Prepare an e-mail confirming the error and telling Mr. Hess that his account will be credited. Send the message to your instructor via e-mail.

9. ElectroCon, an electrical contracting company, has been in operation for one year. It has requested a line of credit of $100,000 from Mesquite Supply. You have a leaflet describing payment for line-of-credit accounts. As finance manager of Mesquite Supply, write ElectroCon approving its request and including this leaflet. Be sure to include necessary details to make this letter complete.

10. As director of customer service for Harvey's, a regional department store, you receive the following letter from Salley Standfast:

I opened an account with your store on September 28 and charged merchandise in the amount of $74. On December 4 I called your billing office to find out why I had not received a statement. I learned that you had been sending the statement to the wrong address. I was told that my account balance is now $114 due to interest and late fees.

Because you were sending the statement to the wrong address, I do not feel obligated to pay interest and late fees. I am enclosing a check for $74, which was the original charge. Please adjust my account so that my balance is $0.

Write a letter to Salley approving her request. Supply details to make this a complete request approval.

Claims

11. Wilson Chemicals sent $1,188 to Executive Seminars for six employees to attend a two-day hazardous waste handling seminar. After the registration forms and fees for this seminar were submitted, Executive Seminars changed the date for the seminar. Wilson Chemicals will be unable to release the six employees for the seminar during the new dates. Write a letter to Executive Seminars requesting a refund for $1,188. Be sure to supply details.

12. **E-mail.** Six months ago you entered into a one-year contract with Waldo's Fitness Center. In the past two months much of the equipment has not been working properly. In addition, many days the facility has been too hot to work out because of faulty air conditioning. You have spoken to the local manager about receiving a refund for the unused portion of the contract, but he is unable to release you from your contract. E-mail a message to your instructor that could be sent to the home office of Waldo's Fitness Center requesting a refund for the remaining six months of the contract.

13. This past summer you purchased by mail order from MicroCompu an Executive 900 microcomputer for home use. The microcomputer has 128 MB of RAM and a 20 GB hard drive. You purchased this microcomputer primarily for its speed. While using a statistical package on the computer, you found that it did not make the calculations faster than the Executive 800 microcomputer you replaced. Write a letter to MicroCompu explaining that you want to return the microcomputer and be refunded the $895 that you paid for it. Supply details that are necessary to make a complete claim letter.

14. As manager of Thurman Furniture, you ordered ten sets of brocade pinch-pleated drapes to use in displays. When the drapes arrived from Lillie's Window Fashions, you thought they appeared to be a lighter weight fabric than advertised. The sample swatch given you by Lillie's sales representative is also a higher quality material. Write a claim letter requesting a full refund and asking for instructions on how to return the merchandise. Supply details to make this a complete claim letter.

15. Approximately three months ago you purchased a MovieWatcher DVD player that came with a one-year warranty. After watching a movie, you cannot get the player to eject the disk. When you took the DVD player to an authorized repair shop, you overheard another customer complaining about a similar problem. Not wanting to "get stuck" with a faulty machine when the warranty expires, you decide not to have the machine repaired but return the player for a full refund. Write a letter to MovieWatcher requesting this refund. Be sure to include details to make this letter complete.

Adjustments

16. Clean Air Appliances manufactures freestanding gas ranges. Ted's Appliances purchased three of the ranges and has sold one. This range was converted to propane on installation. Ted's customer is unhappy with the oven's performance. The customer states that the oven is very erratic. Sometimes the food is burned and other times the food is underdone. Ted's service representative has tried unsuccessfully to adjust the

oven's thermostat. Due to this poor performance, Ted's would like to return all three ranges. You feel the problem is with the conversion to propane but are willing to accept the return. Write a complete letter containing a sales appeal section to Ted's Appliances giving your decision.

17. Dave Barr, owner of Barr Hardware, has contacted your company about a shipment of 500 bags of lawn fertilizer that he received last week. He stated that 48 bags were torn and not saleable. He would like a refund of $200 for the damaged merchandise. As manager of Rapid Grow Fertilizer, write a complete letter to Dave refunding his $200.

18. Scott Reynolds purchased a new Water Tiger jet ski. He is dissatisfied with its performance because it will not go fast enough, and it is too bumpy in rough water. He returned it to the dealer for a full refund. The dealer has contacted you, the jet ski manufacturer, asking if a full refund can be made on the Water Tiger that has been used for 22 hours. Write a letter to the dealer approving the request. Supply details to make a complete adjustment.

19. Oscar's Sportswear creates designer shirts. Recently, Marty's Sporting Goods purchased a dozen shirts from Oscar's. Marty's has returned one of the shirts for tests because one of its customers reported that his shirt shrunk. Marty's would like to return the other 11 shirts for full credit. The test failed to find proof of shrinkage, but you will be willing to accept the return of the shirts to maintain your good relationship with Marty's. Write a letter to Marty's explaining your decision.

20. Roscoe's Personalized Printing specializes in customized printing of items used for business advertisements. Jennifer Fairbanks designed an unusual calendar to be given to her customers during the holiday season. In October Ms. Fairbanks phoned in an order for 11,000 calendars. You shipped these calendars to her in early December. On January 9, you receive a letter from Ms. Fairbanks stating that she ordered only 7,000 calendars. She is willing to pay $3,500 for the calendars but not the $5,500 you charged her. You believe that she ordered more calendars than she needed; however, you are willing to adjust her bill to continue getting her business. Write a letter to Ms. Fairbanks explaining your decision to adjust the charge in her account to $3,500, and add details to make the letter complete.

Unsolicited Positive and Neutral Messages

21. You are chief of information systems at the Bank of Newberry. Due to increased demands on information processing, you have decided to divide the division of administrative services into two units: administrative services and telecommunications. Send a memo to Margaret Collins confirming the oral agreement appointing her as head of the telecommunications division.

22. Harry Ferguson has served the city of Paris in various capacities during the past 25 years. The Allegro Foundation Board of Directors has decided to honor Mr. Ferguson by naming him Citizen of the Year. This award will be given to Mr. Ferguson at a banquet honoring him. Write a letter informing Mr. Ferguson of Allegro's decision. Add necessary information.

23. Last month a severe thunderstorm in the area interrupted cable reception for three days. As director of public relations for Trinity Cablecomm, you need to prepare a message that could be inserted in the monthly statement for all Trinity subscribers. This message should restore subscriber confidence in Trinity. The cable company is giving credit for three days' service; the credit will appear on next month's statement. Provide details to make this message complete.

24. The Board of Directors of the City Library has added activities for the summer. These additional activities include an 8 a.m. story hour and a 6 p.m. children's theater

production. The children's theater production will change weekly. As secretary of the board, write a letter that could be sent to all of the area schools announcing these activities. A flyer describing the theater productions is being developed by the Children's Art Guild and will be included in your letter.

25. The Faith Mission is a nonprofit organization that accepts donations of food, clothing, furniture, household items, and cash to be distributed to persons in the community who are in need of assistance. As director of Faith Mission, prepare a form letter to thank donors for their contributions. Provide spacing in the letter to individualize the donation.

Message Analysis

Correct the following message that has been written to Amber Henderson, who has been approved for a credit card with Cisco Financial Institution:

The Cisco Financial Institution's credit card may be used in most business establishments throughout the state. We have been in existence for more than 20 years.

Our credit committee approved your application for a credit card today. We are certainly glad that we can serve someone like you. The Cisco credit card has a 9 percent interest rate for the first year. This rate will change at the end of the first year and may be higher. The payment for your credit card is due by the 10th of each month. When you don't make the minimum payment by the 10th, you will be assessed a 1 percent penalty.

I want to invite you to use your credit card whenever you can. We will consider changing your credit limit of $1,000 as soon as you have shown that you can make payments on time.

We are glad that you are doing business with us. If there is anything else I can do, please call.

Grammar Workshop

Correct the grammar, spelling, punctuation, style, and word choice errors in the following sentences:

1. Last week one of the forty band members reports that his instrument was stole during the Marching Contest.
2. The alteration shop repaired the zipper in Ted's trouser within 1 hour.
3. The interior decorater select drapes that complimented the pattern of the sofa.
4. Becky used her capitol for collateral in purchasing the apartment building after she was ensured that the property would appreciate in value.
5. Of much greater influence however on the golfers scores were the high wind.
6. Once your cleaning shores have been completed you can go to the movies or the golf course.
7. Despite being Chief Executive of a $50 million-a-year business Marty drove a 1967 pick up truck.
8. Both the internet and the Fax is a tool that business graduates must understand to be successful.
9. The Historic preservation act of 1966 established the National Register of historic places and made it difficult for Federal Agencies to harm registered landmarks.
10. Can I leave if it starts snowing so that I can get home safe.

Goodwill Messages

7

Andrea Holle,
Edward Jones

LET'S TALK BUSINESS As an Edward Jones investment representative, I send goodwill messages to extend birthday wishes, get well wishes, condolences, and congratulations.

Goodwill messages help build relationships in which selling investments is more enjoyable. I strengthen current relationships with my clients and build future business prospects by sending Thanksgiving notes, telling my clients I appreciate their business, or birthday cards telling them I remember their special day.

It is essential to build a strong relationship with all business contacts since the financial business is very competitive. Contacting business associates or clients in their time of need or at a time of celebration will strengthen your business relationships and set you apart from your competitors. Sending sincere messages to your clientele conveys that you appreciate their business.

LEARNING OBJECTIVES

① *Describe goodwill messages.*

② *Compose the six common types of goodwill messages.*

③ *Describe the criteria for selecting the style for a goodwill message.*

In previous chapters it has been suggested that one maintains good relationships with receivers by personalizing positive, neutral, negative, and persuasive messages. Andrea Holle uses goodwill messages to maintain and build good relationships with her clients. The use of goodwill messages provides Ms. Holle with an edge over her competitors.

A **goodwill message** is written to communicate your concern and interest. Sending a goodwill message shows that you care about the receiver. Avoid canceling the positive effects by inserting statements that will cause the receiver to think you are simply trying to further a business relationship. Your goodwill messages should cause your receiver to form a positive opinion of you—the sender of the message. Timeliness is of utmost importance; goodwill messages should be sent as soon as you learn of the incident or event.

Types of Goodwill Messages

The types of goodwill messages are congratulations, condolence, appreciation, invitation, holiday greetings, and welcome.

Congratulations

Everyone enjoys receiving praise. A message that praises the receiver for an accomplishment or an achievement is referred to as a message of congratulations. One of the reasons that congratulatory messages are so effective in building goodwill is that organizations and businesspeople do not use them very often. Congratulatory messages may be as formal as a typewritten letter about a promotion or as informal as a handwritten note attached to a newspaper clipping of a birth announcement.

A letter of congratulations may be presented along with a plaque or a pin.

©NETWORK PRODUCTIONS/INDEX STOCK IMAGERY

Congratulatory messages are sent both to individuals and organizations. Occasions that warrant such messages may be either personal or business in nature. A congratulatory message may be sent to an individual on the occasion of a business-related accomplishment, such as attaining the highest sales for the month, retiring after 30 years of

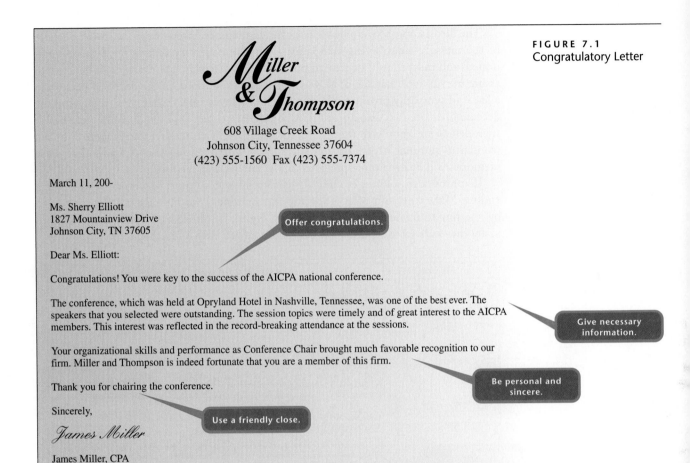

FIGURE 7.1
Congratulatory Letter

Miller & Thompson

608 Village Creek Road
Johnson City, Tennessee 37604
(423) 555-1560 Fax (423) 555-7374

March 11, 200-

Ms. Sherry Elliott
1827 Mountainview Drive
Johnson City, TN 37605

Dear Ms. Elliott:

Offer congratulations.

Congratulations! You were key to the success of the AICPA national conference.

The conference, which was held at Opryland Hotel in Nashville, Tennessee, was one of the best ever. The speakers that you selected were outstanding. The session topics were timely and of great interest to the AICPA members. This interest was reflected in the record-breaking attendance at the sessions.

Give necessary information.

Your organizational skills and performance as Conference Chair brought much favorable recognition to our firm. Miller and Thompson is indeed fortunate that you are a member of this firm.

Be personal and sincere.

Thank you for chairing the conference.

Sincerely,

James Miller

Use a friendly close.

James Miller, CPA
Senior Partner

service, or receiving a promotion. You also may send a congratulatory message to an individual for a personal event, such as a birthday, an engagement, a marriage, a birth, or an election to office in a social or civic organization. A business firm could receive a message of congratulations for expansion of its company, relocation to a new building, announcement of a new product, or celebration of an anniversary.

Congratulatory business messages should be written in a personal, sincere manner. A direct approach should be used by immediately mentioning the honor or accomplishment. The message should focus on the receiver from start to finish. A closing that refers to the writer's assistance to the receiver in his or her achievement diminishes goodwill. A congratulatory letter to an individual who had great success in organizing a national conference is shown in Figure 7.1.

NOTE 7.3
Use the direct approach in composing a congratulatory message.

Condolence

A letter of **condolence** or sympathy is difficult to write because it deals with misfortune. When written properly, however, the message should leave no doubt about your empathy. More important, it should help ease the pain felt by the receiver.

Messages of sympathy may be sent for an illness, death, natural disaster, or other misfortune. They may be typewritten or handwritten, or they may be in the form of a printed card. Handwritten messages are by far the most personal and will be the most appreciated.

NOTE 7.4
Messages of condolence must be sincere.

The direct approach should be used for condolence letters. Begin with the purpose of the message—conveying sympathy. Only the necessary details need to be mentioned, and these should be treated positively and sincerely. For example, it is better to assure the survivor that she or he was appreciated and loved by the deceased person, in a letter of sympathy prompted by the death of a loved one, rather than eulogizing the deceased person. It is also appropriate to mention a personal detail of the deceased if such details are known to the writer; for example, "I remember your mention of the wonderful summer vacations you spent with your grandmother. I know that these memories will be even more precious to you now and in the future."

If appropriate, a letter of condolence can offer assistance; however, avoid a cliché ending. Make sure your offer is specific and genuine. Your message may be concluded by referring to the future in a positive way. Figure 7.2 shows an e-mail sent to a friend in another state whose mother has been hospitalized with a life-threatening illness.

FIGURE 7.2
Condolence Message

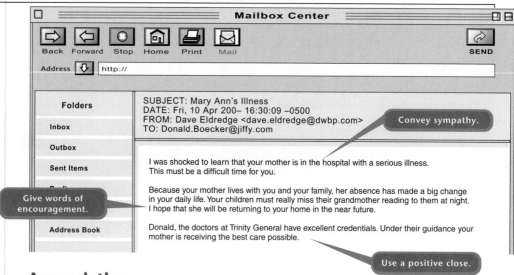

Appreciation

Most people do not expect rewards for acts of kindness or thoughtfulness; however, we all enjoy knowing that our efforts are appreciated.

A letter of **appreciation** may be sent for long-time thoughtfulness or for a one-time favor. Some examples of individuals who have shown sustained thoughtfulness include a long-standing, loyal customer; a faithful employee; a friend who has consistently recommended a company and brought it many customers; and a volunteer who has generously contributed time and effort to charitable causes. Letters expressing thanks to such persons are always appropriate. Examples of letters of gratitude for one-time favors include a complimentary letter from a customer to a service department, a letter to a guest speaker who has given an excellent presentation, a letter to a new customer, a letter to a new member of an organization, and a letter to someone who has found a lost article and returned it to the owner.

Letters of appreciation should follow the direct approach. The good news—the expression of gratitude—should be given in the first paragraph and be followed by supporting evidence in the second or succeeding paragraphs. The letter should conclude with a comment of appreciation in the final paragraph; however, different words should be used in the opening and closing paragraphs. The thought of the letter, not the length of the letter, is the important consideration. A letter thanking a volunteer for participating in a fund-raising phonathon is shown in Figure 7.3.

FIGURE 7.3
Letter of Appreciation

MSY
MAIN STREET YOUTH

480 Main Street
Terra Ceia, FL 34250-1240
(813) 555-6635
Fax (813) 555-4389

March 6, 200-

William Taylor
4284 Starfish Drive
Terra Ceia, FL 34250-1221

Dear Bill,

> Say thank you.

Thank you for participating in the Main Street Youth Phonathon, which culminated on March 3. This four-week event provided more than $150,000 in pledges to Main Street Youth, Inc. This figure represents a 41 percent increase over last year's total.

This increase will enable members of Main Street Youth to attend sporting events, concerts, children's theater productions, and other enrichment activities. Also, much needed playground equipment will be purchased with some of the money.

> Give supporting comments.

A level of success such as this could not have been achieved without your support and that of other volunteers. Thanks again for your contribution to the success of the 200- MSY Phonathon.

Sincerely,

Emily Lacewell

> Express appreciation.

Emily Lacewell
Phonathon Director

Invitation

A business **invitation** is a request for an individual's presence and is used in various situations. Inviting employees to a small social gathering, asking prominent community members to attend a fund-raising event, and inviting civic leaders and selected customers to a company open house are all examples of invitations that are used in the business community. An invitation to a semi-annual membership meeting is shown in Figure 7.4.

An invitation may be handwritten, typed on company stationery, or printed. It should include all the necessary details such as the date, time, place, suggested dress, and whether the receiver may bring a guest. Be sensitive to diverse living arrangements (guest versus spouse). In order to plan efficiently, an invitation should include an *RSVP*; that is, a request for a reply to the invitation. The RSVP should specify the method by which to respond and the date by which the response is requested:

NOTE 7.8
An invitation may be formal or informal.

RSVP 555-7803   or   Regrets only
by October 31   555-6249

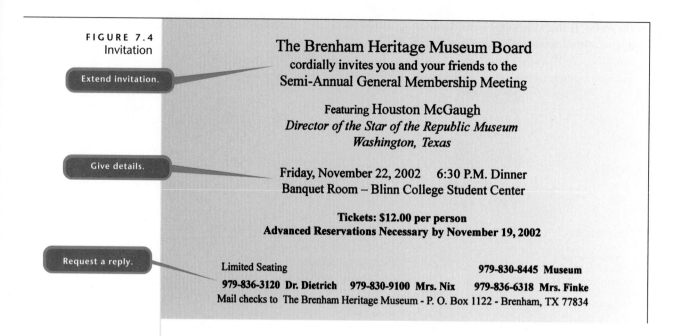

FIGURE 7.4
Invitation

Extend invitation.

Give details.

Request a reply.

The Brenham Heritage Museum Board
cordially invites you and your friends to the
Semi-Annual General Membership Meeting

Featuring Houston McGaugh
Director of the Star of the Republic Museum
Washington, Texas

Friday, November 22, 2002   6:30 P.M. Dinner
Banquet Room – Blinn College Student Center

Tickets: $12.00 per person
Advanced Reservations Necessary by November 19, 2002

Limited Seating   979-830-8445 Museum
979-836-3120 Dr. Dietrich   979-830-9100 Mrs. Nix   979-836-6318 Mrs. Finke
Mail checks to The Brenham Heritage Museum - P. O. Box 1122 - Brenham, TX 77834

COMMUNICATION NOTE

Responding to an RSVP Is Important! Today's casual society creates havoc for planners of social events. Many individuals fail to respond to an invitation and the host or hostess has difficulty in properly planning the event. Hosts or hostesses enclose a stamped, self-addressed card with the invitation; set up a Web site to take *RSVPs*; or include phone numbers and deadlines for replying; and *still* people do not respond. Telling the host or hostess that you will be attending and then not showing up is equally rude.

Adapted from Maria Puente, "Mom Was Right: It's Rude Not to RSVP," *USA Today, http://www. usatoday.com/life/2002,* June 17, 2002.

Holiday Greeting

NOTE 7.9
Holiday greetings may
be sent to celebrate
festive seasons.

A **holiday greeting** may be sent before or during any festive season. New Year's Day, Easter, Labor Day, Thanksgiving, Hanukkah, and Christmas are holidays generally celebrated in the United States. Businesses participating in international trade should be aware of and acknowledge appropriate holidays in the countries where they have employees, customers, or suppliers.

Many companies send season's greetings cards to customers or suppliers. The majority of letters and cards sent during December now say "Holiday Greetings" rather than "Merry Christmas" because of diversity in the workplace. These greetings usually have the company name printed on the card. Executives and sales representatives may use a different kind of company card on which they can write personalized greetings to business friends and colleagues. Some companies send distinctively designed cards that bear the company name and logo. This type of card is impressive because it is unique to the organization sending it. Individualized holiday greeting letters are sent by some business firms.

Figure 7.5 shows the Thanksgiving message Andrea Holle sent to the clients she referred to in the Let's Talk Business section at the beginning of this chapter. Along with extending wishes for a happy holiday season, the letter anticipates prosperity.

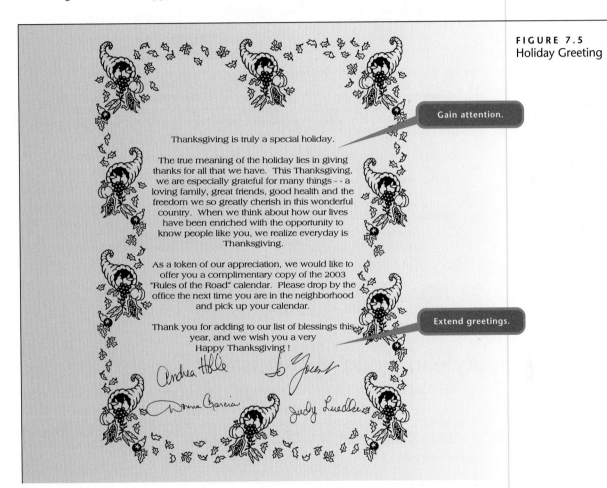

FIGURE 7.5
Holiday Greeting

Welcome

A **welcome** message is used to greet new employees, new customers, and newcomers to a community. Many cities have organizations, such as the Welcome Wagon, that send welcome letters to persons moving into the community. A new employee welcome is aimed at familiarizing new employees with the company and at building goodwill. Figure 7.6 is an example of such a letter.

Welcome letters are frequently sent to new customers, particularly to those who are establishing credit with the business. These messages are used to congratulate the customer on opening a charge account with the business and to offer an incentive to the new customer to make a purchase soon.

NOTE 7.10
Welcome letters are appropriate for new employees, customers, or community members.

FIGURE 7.6
Welcome Letter

Harris, Locke & Williams, Inc.

1638 Pebble Valley Lane
Evansville , IN 47701-1426

(477) 555-5218
Fax (477) 555-6831

August 3, 200–

Ms. Carolyn Fields
538 Hillcrest Drive
Evansville, IN 47712

Dear Carolyn:

Welcome employee.

Welcome! You have selected an excellent company with which to begin your professional career.

Provide information.

Harris, Locke, & Williams, Inc., is a well-established company with an outstanding reputation. The company places trust in its employees, and they are encouraged to use innovative ideas in meeting their daily challenges. Our employees are so satisfied with their jobs that we have one of the lowest employee turnover rates in the industry.

As you were informed during your employment interview, Harris, Locke, & Williams, Inc., provides its employees with excellent fringe benefits. Please contact Jennifer Wolfe at extension 3279 to set up an appointment to learn how these benefits can be of value to you.

Carolyn, our company is very pleased that you have selected us. We hope that you have many successful and rewarding years with us. If I can be of any assistance, please let me know.

Sincerely,

Harry Standfast

Show appreciation.

Harry Standfast
Human Resources Manager

(3) # Style in Goodwill Messages

A goodwill message is an effective way to build a positive relationship with a customer, an employee, or a supplier. Style is important in accomplishing the purpose of the communication. Goodwill messages come in many forms. The following Communication Note describes how technology has enabled individuals from around the world to send goodwill messages.

COMMUNICATION NOTE

Congratulatory Radio Messages to the Queen of England The North Terrace of Windsor Castle was the site of a special golden jubilee amateur radio station. This radio station in its first six days of operation enabled 24,500 people from 130 countries to send congratulatory messages to Queen Elizabeth II on her Golden Jubilee.

Adapted from "Her Majesty the Queen Receives 24,500 Goodwill Messages from around the World," Radio Society of Great Britain, *http://www.rsgb.org,* August 25, 2002.

Handwritten Versus Typewritten Versus Printed Messages

You must decide whether a goodwill message should be handwritten, typewritten, or printed. A handwritten note is appropriate in times of sorrow, but a printed invitation to a formal social function is preferred, whether it is for a small wedding or a dinner and dance for several hundred people. A typewritten message is normally used to welcome a customer or employee to a business. The form that is most effective for conveying your message should be the basis of your decision.

Card Versus Letter versus E-mail

Using a commercially produced card is less time consuming and frequently is more suitable than a typed letter. A short, handwritten note on a holiday greeting card or a sympathy card may mean more to the receiver than a long, formal letter. However, a typewritten welcome letter to a new credit customer is the preferred business style. Messages sent via e-mail are gaining popularity rapidly as a means of delivering goodwill to employees, customers, and friends. E-mail is inexpensive and timely; however, e-mail messages may not convey the same personal sentiment as other goodwill messages.

NOTE 7.12
Whether to send a card or a letter depends on the occasion.

Familiarity Versus Formality

The formality of a goodwill message depends on the purpose of the message you are sending and on how well you know the receiver. Put yourself in the place of the receiver and write a message that you would like to receive—whether the message must, of necessity, be phrased in formal language or whether the nature of the message permits you to be relaxed and informal.

NOTE 7.13
How well you know the receiver dictates the formality of the message.

Summary of Learning Objectives

Describe goodwill messages.

A goodwill message is written to show that you care about the receiver. Goodwill messages should not be used as sales messages. Goodwill messages must be sent promptly.

Compose the six common types of goodwill messages.

The types of goodwill messages are congratulations, condolence, appreciation, invitation, holiday greetings, and welcome. A message of congratulations praises the receiver for an accomplishment or an achievement. Messages of condolence or sympathy may be sent for an illness, death, natural disaster, or other misfortune. Letters of appreciation are sent to acknowledge thoughtfulness. A business invitation is a request for an individual's presence. An invitation may be handwritten, typed, or printed. Holiday greeting messages may be sent during any festive season. A welcome message is used to greet new employees, new customers, and newcomers to a community or an organization. All goodwill messages are organized using the direct approach.

Describe the criteria for selecting the style for a goodwill message.

Style is important in accomplishing the purpose of the communication. A goodwill message may be handwritten, typewritten, or printed. A handwritten note is appropriate in times of sorrow, but a printed invitation is preferred for a social function. A typewritten message is normally used to welcome a customer or employee to a business. Commercially produced cards generally are used for brief personal messages, whereas typewritten letters are used more often for less personal goodwill messages. The purpose of the goodwill message and your familiarity with the receiver determine the formality of the message.

Discussion Questions

1. Describe similarities and differences between goodwill messages and positive messages. (Objective 1 and Chapter 6)
2. What is an *RSVP* and why should you respond to it? (Objective 2)
3. Discuss the three major elements that should be included in an appreciation message. (Objective 2)
4. What written form is most effective for conveying a condolence message? Why? (Objective 2)
5. Describe the content that should be included in an invitation. (Objective 2)
6. Discuss the criteria that should be considered when deciding whether to use a handwritten note, a typewritten message, or a printed style for goodwill messages. (Objective 3)
7. Should goodwill messages be written using formal or informal language? Explain. (Objective 3)

Application Exercises

1. Select a business in your community and interview a supervisor to learn how he or she handles condolences with employees, with customers and clients (both long-term and new), and with community leaders who are not customers or clients. Obtain copies of the messages, if possible, and report your findings to the class. (Objective 1)

2. Describe to the class any goodwill message that you have received from businesspersons. Was it successful? How could it have been improved? (Objective 2)
3. **InfoTrac. E-mail.** Events following the destruction of the World Trade Center in 2001 and a general decline in economic conditions in 2001 and 2002 caused Americans to reconsider whether and how they would send holiday greetings. Heidi Prescott discusses this uncertainty in InfoTrac article CJ80834298, "Americans Hesitant to Send Holiday Greetings through Mail." Read the InfoTrac article and respond to the following questions via e-mail to your instructor:
   a. What are the strengths of e-cards?
   b. What is the major disadvantage of e-cards?
   c. Describe the safety guidelines recommended by the U.S. Postal Service to those receiving paper cards in the mail.
   d. According to a marketing research firm that conducted a national survey for American Greetings and Hallmark, what percentage of respondents plan to send the same number of holiday cards this season as they did last season? (Objective 2)

4. **Teamwork.** Divide into teams of three students and design a brochure that could be used to welcome new students to your college. Be prepared to promote your brochure in a class contest that will select the best one to be forwarded to the dean. (Objective 2)
5. **E-mail.** Your instructor has been hospitalized for emergency surgery and is now recovering at home. He or she can access e-mail. Compose an appropriate message and send it to your instructor using e-mail. (Objective 3)

Case Problems

Congratulations

1. James Ferguson, your information systems manager, was recently named by the Information Systems Association (ISA) as the Outstanding Information Systems Manager of the year in the United States. As the human resources manager in your company, write a letter to James congratulating him on his accomplishment. Add details to make this a complete letter.

2. You are the human resources manager in your company, and you belong to several professional organizations. Yesterday, you read in *Professional Managers,* a newsletter from one of the organizations, that Theresa Goodman has been promoted to president of her company. Write a letter to Theresa, a longtime friend, congratulating her on the promotion. Add details to make this a complete letter.

3. David Mikulcik, owner of The Green House, has developed a new variety of rose. Its blossoms are turquoise and it has an unusually sweet smell. David has been working on this project since graduating from college 15 years ago. Write a letter to David congratulating him on his accomplishment. Add details to make this a complete letter.

4. You and Joan Hightower were best friends in high school. After graduating, Joan married and moved to another state. About three years ago Joan's husband died after a lingering illness. You have learned that Joan has remarried. Write Joan a complete letter congratulating her on her marriage.

Condolence

5. You are the executive director for the chamber of commerce in your town. Last week a group of tourists ate contaminated turkey in a local restaurant, and 14 of them were hospitalized. Local health department officials determined that the contamination was the fault of the food supplier and not of the restaurant. However, the incident has attracted much negative media attention and has resulted in greatly reduced business. The restaurant, Ethel's, is owned by one of your chamber members. Write a letter to Ethel Thompson, expressing your condolences and asking her how you can be of assistance. Add details to make this a complete letter.

6. Chris Norris and you were friends in college. Chris became a high school coach after graduation. You read in the newspaper that Chris's team was defeated at the state championship game. Write a letter to Chris expressing your condolence. Add details.

7. Sure Tuff Tires has operated a plant in your community for 27 years. Yesterday, it was announced in the local paper that the plant will close at the end of the year. This unexpected shutdown will affect the company's 600 employees, many of whom are not eligible for retirement. Write a letter to the editor of the local paper expressing your company's concern for Sure Tuff's employees. Add details to make this a complete letter.

8. You are the owner of a dude ranch. Roger Lockett reserved the ranch for 45 family members. The family chartered a bus to come to your ranch. On the way, the bus was involved in an accident in which two family members were killed and several were injured. Write Roger a letter expressing your sympathy. Add details to make this a complete letter.

Appreciation

9. Margie Boldt, an accounting professor, has been of great assistance in getting you a job after your graduation from college with a degree in accounting. She wrote several letters of recommendation and gave you names of several contacts. One of these contacts resulted in your present job. Write a letter of appreciation to Margie, and send a copy of the letter to the dean of your school. Add details to make this a complete letter.

10. You are program coordinator for Young Urban Professionals. Chris Madden spoke on "Professionalism" to your organization. Supply supporting details and write a letter thanking him for his presentation.

11. **Global.** Elizabeth Morton spent a semester with your family as an exchange student from Australia. Six months after Elizabeth returned home, you and your family spent two weeks with Elizabeth and her family. Write a letter thanking the Morton family for their hospitality. Add details.

12. **E-mail.** A Relay for Life celebration was held this past weekend in your town. The celebration was extremely successful and raised more than $200,000 to fight cancer.

Five of your employees have been involved with organizing this project for the past four months. Develop a message that could be sent via e-mail to the employees; be sure to supply details. Send this message to your instructor.

Invitation

13. Dr. Eva Schultz, a noted botanist, is scheduled to present a program at city hall on October 12, 200–; the admission will be $5 per person. Dr. Schultz has recently returned from South America and will present a program on the plight of the rain forest. Compose an invitation that could be placed in the local newspaper advertising this program. Supply details to make this a complete message.

14. Bluebonnet Electric is having an open house to celebrate moving into a new facility. Write a form letter that can be personalized and sent to all customers inviting them to the open house.

15. The Sunnyvale Heritage Museum is unveiling a new artifact exhibit of medical equipment used in the 1800s. This exhibit may attract new members for the museum. Write an invitation that could be sent to the 500 people on the list supplied to you by the local chamber of commerce.

16. The president of your organization, Kern Alexander, is retiring after 32 years of service. A dinner honoring him for his long service to the company, community, and region will be held on September 24. One of his closest friends, Kristi Urquhart, lives in a community 200 miles away. Write a letter inviting her to the dinner and asking her to present a brief tribute to Kern. Remind her that many others will be giving similar presentations, so she must keep her remarks brief.

Holiday Greeting

17. **E-mail.** The American Flag Company would like to send a Flag Day greeting to its customers. Prepare a message that could be sent via e-mail to its customers.

18. The local Boys and Girls Club is hosting a House of Fear for Halloween. It will be held on Halloween night and the Friday and Saturday prior to Halloween. The admission to the House of Fear is $5. Design a flyer that could be duplicated and distributed to the schools in the area.

19. Red Rose Ice Cream is holding a one-mile fun run followed by an ice cream social on Labor Day. All individuals participating in the fun run at 10 a.m. will receive a free T-shirt. Everyone in town is invited to the ice cream social from noon to 2 p.m. at Jackson Park. Design a notice that could be placed in a local newspaper to advertise the festivities. Include a registration form for the fun run, and note that there is no entry fee.

20. As owner of Indian Hills Landscape, you would like to place an Arbor Day greeting in the local newspaper. Design an appropriate message that could be used. Make it attractive to gain readers' attention.

Welcome

21. Randi Sawyer has been approved for a credit card from your company. Her card has a credit limit of $2,000. Write a letter that could be used to welcome Randi. Include a brochure that was prepared earlier describing the details of the credit card.

22. The Health Academy opened last month and is rapidly expanding its membership. Prepare a form letter that could be used to welcome all of its new members. Be creative and add details.

23. Businesses in your area are interested in building better relationships with students from your college. As executive director of the chamber of commerce in your town, you need to prepare a flyer announcing a free pizza party for all students. This flyer will be given to students at registration. Be creative and add details to make this a complete flyer.

24. You are the president of the Tri-City Industrial Foundation. You have been successful in getting Little Toy Machines, a toy manufacturer, to relocate to your community. This factory will provide employment for 325 people. Write a letter to the president, Roy Stevens, welcoming him and his company.

There are Web exercises at **http://krizan.swlearning.com** to accompany this chapter.

Message Analysis

Correct and strengthen the following message that has been written to invite supporters to a post-election party:

Jack Galante is having an election night party, after the polls close, at the Williams Cabin on Berlin Road. He will provide the drinks but is short on deserts. Spread the word because I know I will leave someone out and we cannot have that.

Grammar Workshop

Correct the grammar, spelling, punctuation, style, and word choice errors in the following sentences:

1. The tornado blew a tree on Douglas car; twisted the television antenna on Joys' house; and flattened Bob's and Reba's home.
2. The hunters shall feed the deers in the park each week.
3. The instructor asked the computor students why they had doubled spaced they're reports.
4. Sara Redden the company President met with the board of directors in the morning, and played golf with Amy in the afternoon prior to leaving for Tulsa.
5. Erosion occured as rainwater run out of the gutter, however; the rain was needed bad due to the draught.
6. Nancy eat her lunch and then Nancy returned to work.
7. Get these legal documents to Mr. McDaniels's whose in the office next door.
8. In order to meet more frequently the world war II Aviators changed it's meetings from monthly to bi-monthly.
9. To receive service in the lube department you have to be wrote up by 7:30.
10. Wow. The St. Louis zoo has numerous exotic monkies, colorful peasants, and sleek tigers.

8

Negative Messages

LEARNING OBJECTIVES

Describe the nature of negative messages.

List the advantages of using the indirect plan for effective communication of negative information.

Describe the five specific guidelines for using the indirect plan.

Prepare competently a variety of negative messages using the indirect plan.

Prepare negative messages using the direct plan when it is appropriate.

Tim Farmer, Co-owner, ComputerLand of Paducah, Kentucky

LET'S TALK BUSINESS As a business owner, I am faced with a difficult customer from time to time. The old saying in the retail industry is "the customer is always right." Sometimes, however, it seems impossible to satisfy customers. No matter what action the business takes, it is never enough to please some customers. When the business or the customer is unhappy, the business stands at a crossroads with a difficult decision. Do you continue to do all that you can to try to accommodate a customer at any cost? Or, do you decide to end the relationship?

Let me share a situation in which I believe it would be in the best interest of a business to sever the relationship with the customer and describe the communication I would use in handling this situation. In some instances, customers routinely do not pay their bills in a timely manner even after they are sent several past-due statements. At this time, it becomes necessary to begin sending the customers several letters stating that their account is past due. The first letter I use begins and ends with a positive paragraph thanking the customer for his or her business. However, the second and third letters I send are more direct and usually state my negative message in the opening paragraph. After these conventional attempts have been made to rectify the problem, more drastic measures may be required, such as writing a letter indicating my company's desire to end the relationship.

Letters of this nature are the hardest ones to write considering the company may have had a long-standing relationship with the customer. Nevertheless, a final letter to sever the partnership between the business and customer is sometimes inevitable. In this final letter, I begin by thanking the customer for his or her business and conclude by stating my desire to end the business relationship. Furthermore, I describe with detail the circumstances that led to this difficult decision.

If negative messages are written properly, your image and your company's image will remain positive.

A **negative message** is one that is likely to be viewed as unpleasant, disappointing, or unfavorable by the receiver. A negative message, for example, may be written to refuse a request that has been made of you or your organization. The message may provide information about a change in policy that employees do not particularly favor or a price increase that customers prefer to avoid.

As Tim Farmer states in the Let's Talk Business section, a negative message is a challenge to compose. At the same time, it is an opportunity for you as a writer or speaker to resolve a common business problem successfully. You can even win a friend for yourself or a customer for your organization with an effectively conveyed negative message.

LEARNING OBJECTIVE

1

Describe the nature of negative messages.

Use the Indirect Plan for Negative Messages

LEARNING OBJECTIVE

2

List the advantages of using the indirect plan for effective communication of negative information.

The general strategy for conveying all types of negative messages is to use the indirect plan. With the indirect plan, the sentence or the section of the message that conveys the disappointing idea follows reasons that explain why you must refuse a request or why you must provide unfavorable information. The indirect plan prepares your receivers for the negative information. Research has shown that receivers are more accepting of negative information when they have been prepared to receive it.

Important advantages of the indirect plan are that it enables receivers (1) to accept the negative information you must give them and (2) to maintain a satisfactory relationship with you.

The indirect plan has these advantages because it maintains calm through its gradual approach. It gives time for the receiver's anxiety to subside. The indirect plan affords the opportunity for reason to prevail and for understanding to develop. If the negative information is given first, the receiver may ignore the rest of the message; even a fair, reasonable explanation following the bad news may never be accepted.

If your message is written or spoken thoughtfully and carefully in the you–viewpoint, the receiver may even agree that the negative information is appropriate and acceptable. An effective presentation of the message may show clearly that the negative information is, in fact, in the best interest of the receiver. It may represent a decision that benefits the receiver. The achievement of a positive receiver reaction is your goal in preparing negative messages.

NOTE 8.1
The indirect plan prepares the receiver for negative news.

NOTE 8.2
The indirect plan enables receivers to accept negative information and to maintain their relationship with you.

NOTE 8.3
The indirect plan
• Maintains calm
• Permits reason to prevail
• Changes a negative situation to a positive one

How to Use the Indirect Plan

LEARNING OBJECTIVE

3

Describe the five specific guidelines for using the indirect plan.

In this section specific guides for using the indirect plan for writing negative messages are given. In addition, you will want to use the fundamentals of effective business communication that are presented in Chapters 1, 3, and 4. Figure 8.1 outlines the steps and specific guides for using the indirect plan to present negative information.

The indirect plan can be used effectively for a variety of written and oral negative messages—refused claims, refused requests, unfavorable decisions, or unsolicited unpleasant information. Written messages are shown in this chapter to illustrate clearly the use of the indirect plan for negative messages.

FIGURE 8.1
Indirect Plan Outline

Indirect Plan for Negative Messages

I. The **Opening Buffer**
   A. Provides coherence.
   B. Builds goodwill.
   C. Is positive.
   D. Maintains neutrality.
   E. Introduces the explanation.

II. The **Logical Explanation**
   A. Relates to the opening buffer.
   B. Presents convincing reasoning.
   C. Stresses receiver interests and benefits.
   D. Uses de-emphasis techniques.
   E. Is positive.

III. The **Negative Information**
   A. Relates to the logical explanation.
   B. Implies or gives negative information explicitly.
   C. Uses de-emphasis techniques.
   D. Gives negative information quickly.
   E. Is positive.
   F. Says what can be done (not what cannot).
   G. Avoids an apology.

IV. The **Constructive Follow-up**
   A. Provides an alternative solution.
   B. Gives additional reasoning.

V. The **Friendly Close**
   A. Builds goodwill.
   B. Personalizes the close.
   C. Stays off the negative subject.
   D. Is warm.
   E. Is optimistic.

Determination of Content

NOTE 8.4
Analyze the situation
before implementing
the indirect plan.

Each communication situation must first be analyzed to determine (1) primary and secondary purposes and (2) the basic content of the message. As you plan and draft an unpleasant message, you will want to answer the following questions: What ideas can I use in the opening to establish coherence and build goodwill in this particular situation? Why is it in the receiver's interest for me to refuse the request or present the unfavorable information? Is there an alternative course of action that I can recommend to this receiver? What friendly message can I convey in the off-the-subject close?

Once you have determined the purposes and content of the negative message, you are ready to implement the indirect plan. In the following sections, the indirect plan outline is discussed; and the most important considerations are reviewed.

Opening Buffer

NOTE 8.5
Use the opening
buffer to
• Provide coherence
• Build goodwill
• Be positive
• Maintain neutrality
• Introduce the
explanation

In the indirect plan, the opening buffer should meet the following requirements: provide coherence, build goodwill, be positive, maintain neutrality, and introduce the explanation. The opening buffer usually will consist of one to three sentences. It will serve as the first paragraph in a memo or a letter.

To provide coherence, the opening buffer puts you and your receiver on the same wavelength. The negative message is tied to a previous conversation, a point of agreement, a memo or letter received earlier, a prior transaction, or some other common ground.

You will want to build goodwill by using courteous, polite words such as *thank you, please,* and *I appreciate,* and by keeping the receiver's interests central to your opening buffer. Use positive words; avoid negative words. Using positive words helps set a favorable tone and makes your message more acceptable to the receiver. It is possible, in fact desirable, to compose negative messages without using a single negative word.

The two final requirements for a good opening buffer—maintaining neutrality and introducing the explanation—are closely related. You will want your receiver to read through the opening buffer into the logical explanation that follows. You do not want to suggest the negative information in the opening. Therefore, the opening buffer should not imply either a yes or a no. It should not lead the receiver in either direction; it should be neutral.

The final requirement of the opening buffer is to set the stage for the explanation, that is, introduce the explanation. In the last sentence of the buffer, give your receiver some indication of the thrust of the explanation. In effect, give the receiver the "headline" for the explanation that follows in the next paragraph(s). This sets up the strategy for the logical explanation, which is the next part of your message, and it assists in providing coherence.

Logical Explanation

The second part of the indirect plan is the logical explanation. In a memo or letter, the logical explanation usually begins after the opening buffer and often can be handled in one paragraph. If the explanation is short, the negative information may be included in the same paragraph. In some situations the constructive follow-up can immediately follow the negative information in the same paragraph. This technique buries the negative news in the middle of a paragraph. In other written message situations, the logical explanation may be so long that it requires two or more paragraphs.

One of the most important aspects of the indirect plan is that the reasoning that justifies the negative information is presented *before* the actual negative information. After the opening buffer, you present the reasons explaining why you must convey the negative information. If at all possible, these reasons should show how the negative information will be in the best interest of your receiver. This reasoning, in order to be effective, must be presented in a calm, convincing, and pleasant manner using the you–viewpoint. The following Communication Note indicates that company policy, without explanation, should not be used as justification for bad news.

NOTE 8.6
Logical explanation follows the opening buffer and precedes the negative information.

NOTE 8.7
The logical explanation
• Justifies the negative information
• Provides coherence
• Presents convincing reasoning
• Uses rules of emphasis
• Accents positive wording

COMMUNICATION NOTE

Company Policy Is NOT Justification Company policy, in and of itself, is not sufficient justification for negative news. Readers could argue that the policy should be changed or that their situation deserves an exception. Writers should explain the reason behind the policy.

The specific requirements for the logical explanation are that it relates coherently to the opening buffer, presents convincing reasoning, stresses receiver interests and benefits, uses emphasis techniques, and is positive.

The opening buffer will have introduced the explanation. The beginning of the logical explanation should use coherence techniques to relate it to the opening and to facilitate the flow of thought. You may use repetition of key words, a tie-in sentence, or some other coherence technique to ensure that the logical explanation follows the opening.

The convincing reasoning, which supports the unfavorable information, should be composed with the receiver's interests or benefits as the focal points. The receiver's favorable reactions to the words you choose will be your goal. In fact, if at the end of the reasoning the receiver agrees that the negative information represents the best alternative in this situation, you will have composed the ideal negative message.

Although the ideal logical explanation presents the reasoning in terms of receiver benefit, circumstances will not always permit you to compose the ideal message. You may have to base your reasoning on what is fair for all concerned. Also, occasionally confidentiality precludes giving any specific reasons. In these situations, you will want to communicate convincingly and persuasively that the matter was carefully considered in the interest of the receiver before the decision was reached.

You will want to use rules of emphasis in the logical explanation. Start with the points that are most favorable to your receiver; and, as you move deeper into the paragraph, deal with the least favorable aspects of your reasoning.

Finally, the logical explanation should be positive. Avoid all negative words. For example, use *situation* instead of *problem* and *needed change* instead of *correction*. In referring to the negative information, avoid such words as *failure, cannot, trouble, inadequate*, and *defective*.

Negative Information

NOTE 8.8
The negative information follows the logical explanation.

After the opening buffer and the logical explanation, you are ready to present the negative information. This step in the indirect plan consists of the request refusal, unfavorable decision, or other disappointing information. If the opening buffer and the logical explanation have been effective, receivers will be expecting the negative information. In fact, in most circumstances, it is possible for you to prepare your receivers so well that they will easily accept the information, refusal, or decision.

NOTE 8.9
Be sure negative information is clear.

The primary goal in presenting negative information is to be sure that the receiver clearly understands this part of your message. In communicating with Americans, Europeans, Australians, and others with similar cultures, you will want to imply or state explicitly your decision. Wording such as "therefore, it would seem better for you to follow the company policy" may leave a question in the mind of your receiver. With this lack of clarity, the receiver may think that the decision is still up for discussion or that he or she could decide what to do. However, in many parts of the world—Asia and Latin America, for example—people prefer a lack of clarity because it makes the moment more pleasant.

COMMUNICATION NOTE

Tell It Like It Is Bad news often occurs in business; however, when communicated properly, bad news can result in earning respect from employees. Bad news should be communicated immediately to avoid rumors that can lead to half-truths. Bad news may be communicated informally but not lightheartedly.

Adapted from Maggie Rauch's "And the Bad News Is...," *Sales and Marketing Management*, January 2001. Retrieved through InfoTrac-College.com.

Even with cultures that prefer more directness and clarity, it is desirable in most situations to imply the negative information. It softens the bad news and permits you to present negative information in a positive manner. For example, "Smoking is permitted in the hallways only" is much more acceptable to most people than "Smoking is prohibited in the classrooms and offices." These statements both say basically the same thing; the first just says it positively. For effective communication of negative information, it is better to say what can be done rather than what cannot be done.

In some situations the negative information should be given in explicit terms. These are the times when you believe that an implied refusal would not be strong enough or might be misunderstood by your receiver. In the case of rejecting admission to a college, for example, it may not be possible to imply the refusal. In this type of situation, it is better to present the logical explanation and then explicitly state the refusal in clear terms, such as "therefore, the committee has not approved your application for admission." This wording can leave no doubt in the receiver's mind. In most cases, though, you will want to imply the negative information to reduce its emphasis.

The recommended placement of the negative information section of the message is immediately following the logical explanation. In a written message, never place the negative information in a separate paragraph. In order to de-emphasize the negative information, place it in the middle of a paragraph. The negative news may be followed by an additional reason or suggested alternative(s). This placement would tuck the negative information inside the paragraph and de-emphasize it.

The negative information should be given in as few words as possible. Ideally, you can further de-emphasize the unfavorable news by placing it in a dependent clause. As in all sections of a negative message, you will want to use positive words and avoid negative words—say what can be done and not what cannot be done. Also, in most cases you will want to avoid apologies throughout the message because they only call further attention to the negativeness of the situation. Do not use apologies such as, "I am sorry I must refuse your request."

In summary, negative information is implied or stated explicitly, follows the logical explanation, uses techniques to de-emphasize it, is given quickly, is positive, says what can be done, and avoids apologies. After giving the negative information, your next step in the indirect plan is to provide constructive follow-up.

Constructive Follow-Up

In the constructive follow-up section of a negative message, you provide other solutions to the problem or, if that is not possible, you give an additional reason justifying the unfavorable news.

For example, one good way to strengthen your communication and to build improved relations is to do more than is expected by offering an alternative solution to the receiver. If you were asked to return to your high school on October 24 to speak to seniors about attending college and your schedule would not permit you to do so, you could suggest an alternative speaker or an alternative date. Even though you have to refuse the request, your suggested alternative may solve the problem and maintain effective relationships. In the case of adjustment refusals, you can make a special offer or resell the customer on the product or service.

If you cannot suggest an alternative or offer a solution to the problem, it will be important for you to save part of the logical explanation and place it following the

NOTE 8.10
Stress what can be done (not what cannot be done).

NOTE 8.11
De-emphasize the negative information by placing it in the middle of a paragraph.

NOTE 8.12
State the negative information quickly and positively.

NOTE 8.13
Avoid an apology.

NOTE 8.14
Constructive follow-up consists of other solutions or additional justification.

negative information. This helps the receiver accept the bad news by de-emphasizing its importance and giving him or her additional justification for it.

Friendly Close

NOTE 8.15
The friendly close
• Builds goodwill
• Is off the subject

The friendly close moves the receiver's mind away from the problem—the negative information—and provides an opportunity to build goodwill. If you must refuse a customer credit, you will want him or her to continue to buy with cash. If you have to refuse an employee's request, you will want to maintain goodwill and not reduce the employee's productivity.

You can build goodwill in the friendly close by ensuring that it is personalized, off the subject, warm, and optimistic. The wording of the friendly close should fit the receiver and the particular situation. The close should relate to the topic while avoiding the bad news. It could make further reference to the constructive follow-up, or it could express appreciation to a customer for his or her business.

The friendly close should not include anything that reminds the receiver of the negative information you have given. It should be off the subject of the negative information. The friendly close should not include an apology such as, "Again, let me say how sorry I am that we cannot honor your claim." This only reminds the receiver of the problem. The close can include any friendly remark appropriate to your receiver. The prime requirement for the friendly close is to regain the goodwill that may have been lost due to the negative information.

Implementing the Indirect Plan

NOTE 8.16
A communication situation will help illustrate how to compose negative messages.

The step-by-step development of a memo to employees who must be given negative information shows clearly how the indirect plan works. Although negative messages often are best presented orally, a written message will be developed for this case to illustrate the content. Here are the details of the communication situation.

THE KREBS FURNITURE CASE

Krebs Furniture has manufacturing plants in six locations within the United States. Its Georgetown, Texas, plant manufactures collectible reproductions and has been operating for 35 years. It currently has 150 employees who have excellent fringe benefits and earn above-average salaries for the Georgetown area. Krebs began its operation in Georgetown with 12 employees and steadily grew to more than 250 employees. About five years ago competition in producing collectible reproductions, especially from international companies, increased tremendously. This competition forced Krebs to downsize its workforce to its present size of 150 employees. Now Krebs' management, realizing that it cannot compete with the lower production costs due to the low wages that international companies pay, has decided to close its Georgetown plant at the end of the year. Your task is to write a memo conveying the negative information to the employees and, at the same time, to make that information acceptable and maybe even desirable for them.

Determine Appropriate Content

The primary purpose of your memo to Krebs' employees will be to convey clearly the negative information, and the secondary purpose is to make that information acceptable and maybe even desirable for them. The content of the memo must be developed and organized for each step in the indirect plan. Examples of *poor* and *good* content you could decide to use are illustrated in the following sections.

Write an Effective Opening Buffer

The five qualities of a good opening buffer described previously can best be illustrated for this communication situation through contrasting examples. An example of a **poor** opening buffer for a memo to Krebs' employees follows:

- It is my unfortunate duty to inform you that Krebs Furniture is closing its plant in Georgetown, Texas, on December 31, 200–.

In analyzing this poor opening buffer, note the lack of you–viewpoint and absence of goodwill. Also, the receivers' interests are ignored. Finally, this opening buffer reveals the negative information, the closing of the plant, immediately. There is no motivation for the employees to read the logical explanation that is to follow the opening.

An example of a **good** opening buffer for this situation follows:

- Krebs Furniture has been operating a plant in Georgetown for 35 years. During these years you have produced high-quality furniture that our customers have been proud to place in their homes. Your dedication to our company has made it possible for us to offer excellent benefits and above-average salaries.

In contrast to the poor opening buffer, this paragraph effectively meets all the requirements of a good buffer for a negative message. Coherence and goodwill are built by reminding the employees that they have received excellent salaries and fringe benefits.

Goodwill is further built through commending the employees for the high-quality product they have produced. This good opening buffer is neutral—it does not disclose the plant closing. It introduces in a positive manner the logical explanation by mentioning salaries and fringe benefits that result in high production costs.

Provide a Convincing Logical Explanation

The next step in the indirect plan is to build on the opening buffer with a logical explanation justifying the negative information.

A **poor** logical explanation to Krebs' employees might read as follows:

- I know that this plant closing comes at a bad time. However, there is no good time for employees to lose their jobs. Krebs cannot continue losing money at this plant because of the high wages and excellent fringe benefits that you receive. This continuous loss is not fair to the employees at the other five plants that are making a profit. The closing of this plant will give us the opportunity to pay higher dividends to our stockholders.

This logical explanation shows—as did the poor opening buffer—a lack of positive wording and you–viewpoint. This poorly worded explanation is negative and ignores receivers' interests. The statement "However, there is no good time for employees to lose their jobs" will sound unsympathetic to individuals losing their jobs. Inability to pay "higher dividends" is not convincing reasoning to use in this explanation.

Conversely, a **good** logical explanation for this communication situation could read as follows:

- You have been rewarded with excellent salaries and benefits for producing high-quality furniture. Our company is facing the challenge of maintaining our high-quality products at a competitive price while providing excellent

NOTE 8.17
The poor opening starts with negative information and lacks the you–viewpoint.

NOTE 8.18
The good opening meets all requirements for an effective buffer.

NOTE 8.19
The poor logical explanation fails to justify the negative information.

NOTE 8.20
This example meets all requirements for a good logical explanation.

salaries and security for employees. International companies can produce collectible reproductions at a much lower cost due to the availability of cheaper labor in their locations.

This logical explanation coherently follows the good opening buffer by picking up on the ideas "excellent salaries and benefits" and "producing quality furniture." The most positive ideas are presented early in the paragraph with a gradual movement to less positive ideas. This is an effective use of the rules of emphasis.

After reading this logical explanation, the employees may not understand how the low wages paid by international companies have caused them to lose their jobs, but at least they will believe you have presented them with a fair, logical explanation. They will be prepared for the negative information that will be presented to them later in the paragraph.

Give Negative Information Positively

A **poor** way to tell the employees that the plant is closing follows:

- It is my unfortunate duty to inform you that Krebs Furniture is closing its plant in Georgetown, Texas, on December 31, 200–. I know that this plant closing comes at a bad time.

NOTE 8.21
This poor presentation states the negative information immediately.

The letter begins with the negative, harsh words "unfortunate duty to inform you. . . ." The second paragraph begins in the I–viewpoint rather than the you–viewpoint. The letter overemphasizes the problem by using negative words *(unfortunate, closing,* and *bad)* in both paragraphs.

A **good** way to inform the employees of the plant closing follows:

- After analyzing production costs at all plants, management has decided to close its Georgetown plant on December 31. The other five Krebs' plants will continue producing furniture.

NOTE 8.22
This good presentation de-emphasizes the negative information.

This negative information is presented at the end of the logical explanation paragraph. The plant closing is de-emphasized by being placed within the explanation. Instead of an apology, which would emphasize the negativeness of the situation, the explanation paragraph ends with a statement using positive words that should give hope to the employees for employment at another Krebs' plant.

Because you prepared the employees to receive negative information, this plant closing will likely be acceptable to them. In fact, as suggested earlier, they may prefer the alternative solution that you will give them in the next paragraph—the constructive follow-up. They will also know you respect them because you took the time to explain the decision to close the plant.

Assist the Receiver with Constructive Follow-up

Is there an alternative solution you can suggest to the Krebs' employees in this communication situation? The following is an example of a **poor** constructive follow-up section of your memo to the employees:

- I hope you find another job soon.

NOTE 8.23
The poor constructive follow-up example does not really help, whereas the good example does more than is expected.

A **good** constructive follow-up section would be:

- Krebs has five manufacturing plants that are in need of good employees. Employees at the Georgetown plant will be given priority for filling vacancies at

A manager's justification can make negative information acceptable and the decision preferable.

the other plants. Human resources personnel from the five plants will be here next week to discuss employment opportunities and interview employees interested in these open positions. Attached is a flyer describing activities at each of these plants and times for interviews with human resources personnel.

This constructive follow-up suggests a possible solution for the Krebs' employees. If it is not the solution the employees want, it is at least one employment opportunity for them. Note that the good suggested alternative is longer than the poor suggested alternative. This is often true of the you–viewpoint when writing or speaking. In effective business communication, the additional effort and additional words are worthwhile.

Build Goodwill in a Friendly Close
The last part of the indirect plan is the friendly close. A **poor** friendly close for the employees' memo might read this way:

- Again, let me say I am sorry that the Georgetown plant has to close. If I can be of any further help, please let me know.

Obviously, the apology serves no purpose other than to remind the employees of the negative information they have received. In fact, the negative information is re-emphasized. Also, the last sentence in the poor example sounds condescending and seems hollow.

A **good** friendly close for the employees' memo is as follows:

- Please contact my secretary, Pam, at extension 4196, if you would like to schedule an interview with a representative from one of the plants. Moving to another plant appears to be a good alternative for many of you. Your excellent work is appreciated, and I hope you stay with Krebs Furniture for many years to come!

This paragraph meets all the requirements of a friendly close. It builds goodwill. It is personalized, warm, and optimistic. It also meets the important requirement of being off the subject—it does not refer to the negative information.

NOTE 8.24
The poor friendly close contains an apology.

NOTE 8.25
The good friendly close is in the you–viewpoint and builds goodwill.

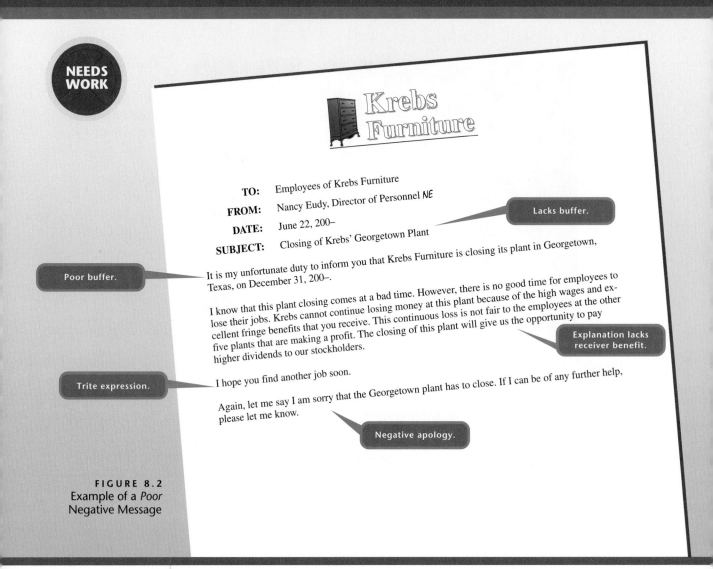

NEEDS WORK

Krebs Furniture

TO: Employees of Krebs Furniture

FROM: Nancy Eudy, Director of Personnel *NE*

DATE: June 22, 200–

SUBJECT: Closing of Krebs' Georgetown Plant

It is my unfortunate duty to inform you that Krebs Furniture is closing its plant in Georgetown, Texas, on December 31, 200–.

I know that this plant closing comes at a bad time. However, there is no good time for employees to lose their jobs. Krebs cannot continue losing money at this plant because of the high wages and excellent fringe benefits that you receive. This continuous loss is not fair to the employees at the other five plants that are making a profit. The closing of this plant will give us the opportunity to pay higher dividends to our stockholders.

I hope you find another job soon.

Again, let me say I am sorry that the Georgetown plant has to close. If I can be of any further help, please let me know.

Callout labels: Lacks buffer. | Poor buffer. | Explanation lacks receiver benefit. | Trite expression. | Negative apology.

FIGURE 8.2
Example of a *Poor* Negative Message

NOTE 8.26
Contrasting memos to employees of Krebs Furniture are presented in Figures 8.2 and 8.3.

Summary—Poor and Good Memos to the Krebs' Employees

In reviewing how to write effective negative messages, two example memos—one poor and one good—have been presented. Both of these memos carry the negative information about the plant closing. The **poor** memo (see Figure 8.2) shows a failure to use proven communication guides that enhance understanding and acceptance of negative messages. The poor memo also fails to use the indirect plan to present the message.

The **good** memo to the employees shown in Figure 8.3 incorporates the recommended guidelines for effective business communication. The good memo shows how the indirect plan, properly implemented, builds goodwill and improves human relations.

To illustrate further how the guides apply to actual business situations, several other examples of poor and good negative messages are examined in the following pages.

Krebs Furniture

TO: Employees of Krebs Furniture

FROM: Nancy Eudy, Director of Personnel *NE*

DATE: June 22, 200–

SUBJECT: Krebs' Georgetown Plant

> Positive reference.

Krebs Furniture has been operating a plant in Georgetown for 35 years. During these years you have produced quality furniture that our customers have been proud to place in their homes. Your dedication to our company has made it possible for us to offer excellent benefits and above-average salaries.

> Good opening buffer.

You have been rewarded with excellent salaries and benefits for producing quality furniture. Our company is facing the challenge of maintaining our quality products at a competitive price while providing excellent salaries and security for employees. International companies can produce collectible reproductions at a much lower cost due to the availability of cheaper labor in their locations. After analyzing production costs at all plants, management has decided to close its Georgetown plant on December 31. The other five Krebs' plants will continue producing furniture.

> You–viewpoint is reassuring; negative information is de-emphasized.

Krebs has five manufacturing plants that are in need of good employees. Employees at the Georgetown plant will be given priority for filling vacancies at the other plants. Human resources personnel from the five plants will be here next week to discuss opportunities and interview employees interested in these open positions. Attached is a flyer describing activities at each of these plants and times for interviews with human resources personnel.

> Alternative is suggested.

Please contact my secretary, Pam, at extension 4196, if you would like to schedule an interview for a position with one of the plants. It appears to be a good alternative for many of our employees. Your excellent work is appreciated, and I hope you stay with Krebs Furniture for many years to come!

Attachment

> Goodwill and off-the-subject close.

FIGURE 8.3
Example of a *Good*
Negative Message

Request Refusals

Business firms frequently receive requests—for example, a request from a senior citizens' organization for a contribution to its greenhouse project or a request from a local Boy Scout troop to use a bank's community meeting room on the first Wednesday night of each month. Many of these requests are reasonable, and companies will want to respond positively.

Sometimes, however, a **request refusal**—a denial of something asked for—must be sent. For example, the company receiving the senior citizens' request may budget all charitable contributions once a year; therefore, no allocation is available at the time of the request. The company must then refuse this worthy request—at least at this time. The constructive follow-up in this negative message might be that the company will be glad to consider the request when the next budget is planned.

NOTE 8.27
Some requests must be refused.

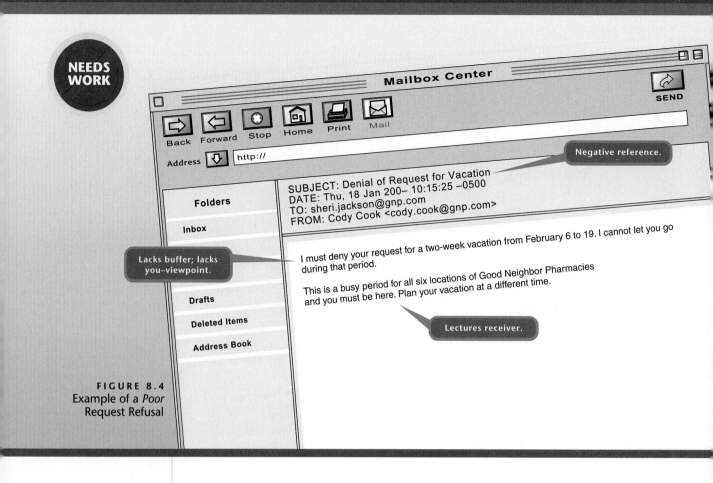

FIGURE 8.4
Example of a *Poor*
Request Refusal

NEEDS
WORK

Mailbox Center

SEND

Back Forward Stop Home Print Mail

Address http://

Negative reference.

SUBJECT: Denial of Request for Vacation
DATE: Thu, 18 Jan 200– 10:15:25 –0500
TO: sheri.jackson@gnp.com
FROM: Cody Cook <cody.cook@gnp.com>

Folders

Inbox

Lacks buffer; lacks
you–viewpoint.

I must deny your request for a two-week vacation from February 6 to 19. I cannot let you go
during that period.

This is a busy period for all six locations of Good Neighbor Pharmacies
and you must be here. Plan your vacation at a different time.

Drafts

Deleted Items

Address Book

Lectures receiver.

NOTE 8.28
Use the indirect plan for
refusals.

In the case of the local Boy Scout troop's request to use the bank's meeting room, this kind of use may be exactly the type the bank intended for the meeting room. However, if the room is scheduled for use by the League of Women Voters on the first Wednesday night of each month, the bank must refuse the request. The bank, if possible, will suggest an alternative night for the Boy Scouts.

In any request refusal situation, it will be important to a business to maintain goodwill. At the same time, the business has to send a message that the receiver does not want to receive. Effective use of the indirect plan will make the refusal more acceptable.

Here is another situation that illustrates the use of the indirect plan for a request refusal: Assume that you are the owner of six Good Neighbor Pharmacies in the area. You receive an e-mail from Sheri Jackson, department manager, who is requesting a vacation for the period from February 6 to 19. Each year your pharmacies do their annual inventories during the first two weeks of February. No one is permitted to take a vacation during this period. You must send an e-mail to Sheri denying her request for vacation during the inventory period. Figure 8.4 shows a **poor** e-mail message for this situation.

The **good** e-mail message for this request refusal, shown in Figure 8.5, builds goodwill by explaining the situation and suggesting an alternative for Sheri.

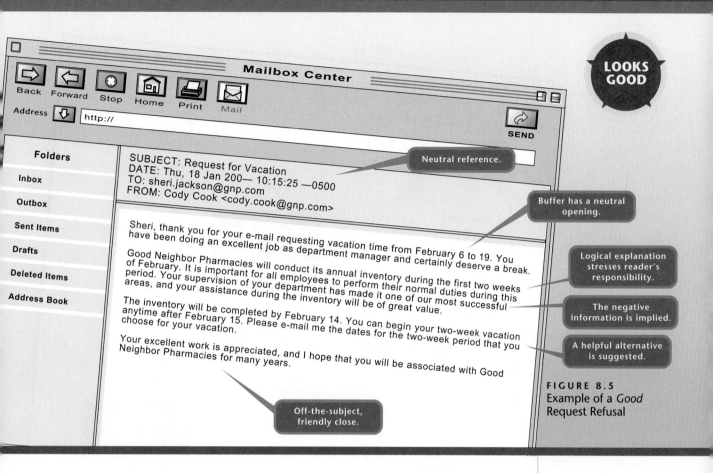

Mailbox Center

Back Forward Stop Home Print Mail

Address http://

SEND

Folders

Inbox

Outbox

Sent Items

Drafts

Deleted Items

Address Book

SUBJECT: Request for Vacation
DATE: Thu, 18 Jan 200— 10:15:25 —0500
TO: sheri.jackson@gnp.com
FROM: Cody Cook <cody.cook@gnp.com>

Sheri, thank you for your e-mail requesting vacation time from February 6 to 19. You have been doing an excellent job as department manager and certainly deserve a break.

Good Neighbor Pharmacies will conduct its annual inventory during the first two weeks of February. It is important for all employees to perform their normal duties during this period. Your supervision of your department has made it one of our most successful areas, and your assistance during the inventory will be of great value.

The inventory will be completed by February 14. You can begin your two-week vacation anytime after February 15. Please e-mail me the dates for the two-week period that you choose for your vacation.

Your excellent work is appreciated, and I hope that you will be associated with Good Neighbor Pharmacies for many years.

Callouts:
- Neutral reference.
- Buffer has a neutral opening.
- Logical explanation stresses reader's responsibility.
- The negative information is implied.
- A helpful alternative is suggested.
- Off-the-subject, friendly close.

LOOKS GOOD

FIGURE 8.5
Example of a *Good* Request Refusal

Adjustment Refusals

Handling customer claims is a common task for most business firms. These claims include requests to exchange merchandise, requests for refunds, requests that work be corrected, and other requests for adjustments. Most of these claims are approved because they are legitimate. However, some requests for adjustment must be denied, and an adjustment refusal message must be sent. Adjustment refusals are negative messages for the customer. They are necessary when the customer is at fault or when the vendor has done all that can reasonably or legally be expected.

An adjustment refusal message requires your best communication skills because it is bad news to the receiver. You have to refuse the claim and at the same time retain

NOTE 8.29
Businesses try to retain customers when making refusals.

Karen's
Kreations

2640 Poidres Lane • Dallas, TX 75236-2721
(214) 555-3265 • Fax (214) 555-7381

March 18, 200–

Ms. Renee Black
Susie's Fashions
1438 Commerce Street
Marion, IL 62959-4143

Gives negative information first; is negative; talks down to the receiver.

Dear Ms. Black:

We are sorry we cannot honor your request to return the 24 dresses that you recently purchased from us. You can see that these dresses are made of a high-quality material.

Explanation is not in the you–viewpoint and is illogical.

We feel sure that with a little effort, you can sell these dresses. We have been making dresses for a long time, and all of our customers are always satisfied. We have sold you dresses before, and you were able to sell them. Our profit would be reduced if we allowed our customers to return dresses without their trying to sell them. I am sure you can understand why we can't let you return these dresses.

Again, let us say we are sorry that you will not be allowed to return these dresses. Don't forget to place your order for fall dresses no later than July 1.

Negative final apology; constructive follow-up is poorly written and out of sequence.

Sincerely yours,

Michelle Miller

Michelle Miller
Marketing Manager

tp

FIGURE 8.6
Example of a *Poor* Adjustment Refusal Letter

the customer. You may refuse the request for adjustment and even try to sell the customer more merchandise or service. All this is happening when the customer is probably angry, disappointed, or inconvenienced.

You will want to use the indirect plan effectively for the presentation of this negative information. As a case in point, consider a customer who wants to return 24 dresses that do not meet her expectations. Figure 8.6 shows a **poor** letter in which the dress manufacturer fails to implement the indirect plan and probably makes an enemy.

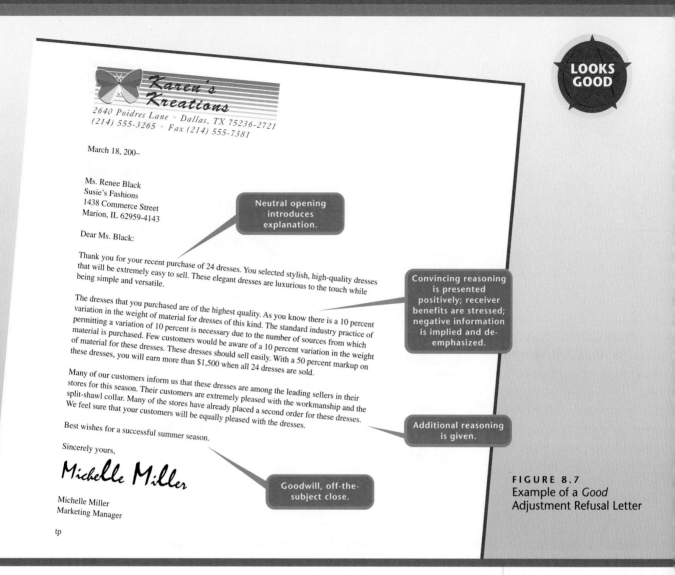

Karen's Kreations

2640 Poidres Lane • Dallas, TX 75236-2721
(214) 555-3265 • Fax (214) 555-7381

March 18, 200–

Ms. Renee Black
Susie's Fashions
1438 Commerce Street
Marion, IL 62959-4143

Dear Ms. Black:

Thank you for your recent purchase of 24 dresses. You selected stylish, high-quality dresses that will be extremely easy to sell. These elegant dresses are luxurious to the touch while being simple and versatile.

[Neutral opening introduces explanation.]

The dresses that you purchased are of the highest quality. As you know there is a 10 percent variation in the weight of material for dresses of this kind. The standard industry practice of permitting a variation of 10 percent is necessary due to the number of sources from which material is purchased. Few customers would be aware of a 10 percent variation in the weight of material for these dresses. These dresses should sell easily. With a 50 percent markup on these dresses, you will earn more than $1,500 when all 24 dresses are sold.

[Convincing reasoning is presented positively; receiver benefits are stressed; negative information is implied and de-emphasized.]

Many of our customers inform us that these dresses are among the leading sellers in their stores for this season. Their customers are extremely pleased with the workmanship and the split-shawl collar. Many of the stores have already placed a second order for these dresses. We feel sure that your customers will be equally pleased with the dresses.

[Additional reasoning is given.]

Best wishes for a successful summer season.

Sincerely yours,

Michelle Miller

Michelle Miller
Marketing Manager

[Goodwill, off-the-subject close.]

tp

[LOOKS GOOD]

FIGURE 8.7
Example of a *Good*
Adjustment Refusal Letter

On the other hand, the same basic message can be written using the indirect plan and result in keeping a good customer. Figure 8.7 is a **good** example of how this letter refusing the return of the dresses could be written.

Credit Refusals

Buying on credit is common today. Most businesses permit and even encourage qualified customers to buy on credit. It is a strategy that increases sales. The discussion in this section is more relevant to in-store credit cards than national or international bank cards.

Customers who have good credit ratings or who have sufficient assets for collateral will be granted credit. Customers who have problems paying their bills or who own

NOTE 8.30
Buying on credit is common.

March 10, 200-

Clowers Plumbing
2154 Industrial Road
Shreveport, LA 71109

Dear Mr. Clowers:

I am sorry to inform you that your application for a line of credit with Shreveport Supply cannot be approved at this time. We would like to extend you a line of credit; however, a credit check shows that you owe too much money.

The competition among plumbers in our area makes it difficult for small plumbing firms to survive. We cannot take a chance on extending credit to a company that is heavily in debt. We hope that your company does not fail, but we can't take a chance.

Again, let me say that I am sorry that we cannot extend a line of credit to your company. If you need any plumbing supplies, please use Shreveport Supply.

Sincerely,

George Campbell

George Campbell
Credit Manager

jpt

Gives bad information; is not in the you–viewpoint.

Not personalized; is not in the you–viewpoint; sounds negative.

Negative final apology; poor reselling.

FIGURE 8.8
Example of a *Poor* Credit
Refusal Letter

NOTE 8.31
Credit refusals usually
are in the customer's
interest.

nothing of sufficient value to use as collateral may be refused credit. A message rejecting a request for credit is called a **credit refusal**.

Business firms attempt to communicate credit refusals in a manner that makes the answer acceptable to the customer. Businesses want to do this out of common decency and also because they want to continue to serve the customer on a cash basis if possible.

Credit refusals are communicated in the following four basic ways: (1) personalized letters, (2) form letters, (3) telephone calls, or (4) face-to-face conversations. In all these cases the indirect plan is used for communicating the credit refusal.

Figure 8.8 is a **poor** example of a personalized letter in which a supply house denies a customer's application for a line of credit. The indirect plan is not used in this letter.

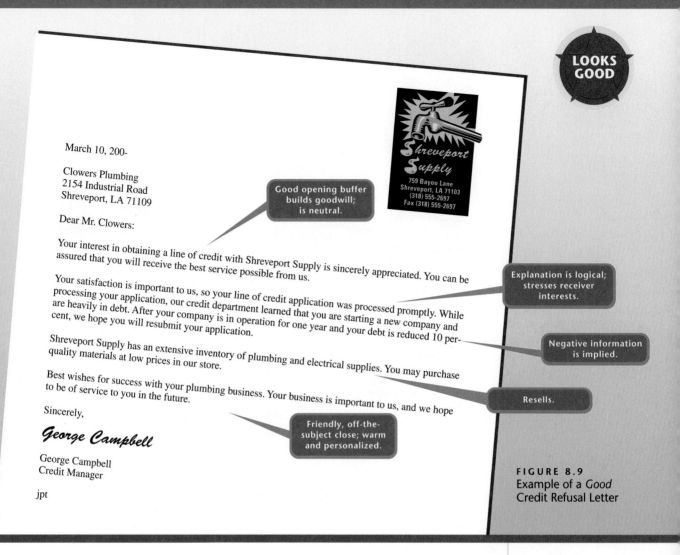

March 10, 200-

Clowers Plumbing
2154 Industrial Road
Shreveport, LA 71109

Dear Mr. Clowers:

Your interest in obtaining a line of credit with Shreveport Supply is sincerely appreciated. You can be assured that you will receive the best service possible from us.

Your satisfaction is important to us, so your line of credit application was processed promptly. While processing your application, our credit department learned that you are starting a new company and are heavily in debt. After your company is in operation for one year and your debt is reduced 10 percent, we hope you will resubmit your application.

Shreveport Supply has an extensive inventory of plumbing and electrical supplies. You may purchase quality materials at low prices in our store.

Best wishes for success with your plumbing business. Your business is important to us, and we hope to be of service to you in the future.

Sincerely,

George Campbell

George Campbell
Credit Manager

jpt

Good opening buffer builds goodwill; is neutral.

Explanation is logical; stresses receiver interests.

Negative information is implied.

Resells.

Friendly, off-the-subject close; warm and personalized.

FIGURE 8.9
Example of a *Good* Credit Refusal Letter

An improved letter for this circumstance is shown in Figure 8.9, a **good** example of the use of the indirect plan for a credit refusal. A mutually satisfactory business relationship could develop from this credit refusal.

Unsolicited Negative Messages

Not all negative messages are in response to a request or an inquiry. An **unsolicited negative message** is a bad news message initiated by the sender. Examples of such unsolicited negative messages include communications about price increases for products or services, budget reductions, and staff reductions (layoffs). These messages are especially difficult to compose because they initiate the bad news.

NOTE 8.32
Sometimes businesses must initiate negative messages.

INTEROFFICE MEMO

Gizmos & Doodads, Inc.

DATE: November 15, 200–
TO: Sales Representatives
FROM: Mei-ling Sheng, Production Manager
SUBJECT: Recall of Defective Doll

I hate to tell you that you will have to contact all of the stores in your area and inform them that they must return Longneck the Giraffe.

I know that this recall comes at a bad time. Most of the stores will have these dolls on their shelves and will be mad at you for having to rearrange their displays. We must get these dolls back since we have determined that children may easily remove the heads and possibly swallow them. This problem can result in many lawsuits and many dollars in damages.

Again, let me say that I am sorry that you will have to spend your valuable time informing the stores about this recall. If there is anything that I can do, please contact me.

kt

> Opening gives unfavorable information explicitly and negatively.

> Lacks you–viewpoint (receiver's interest is ignored); negative.

> Close is not off the subject; limited offer to help.

FIGURE 8.10
Example of a *Poor* Unsolicited Negative Memo

In Figure 8.10, you can feel the negative impact of the **poor** interoffice memo informing sales representatives of a product recall. The indirect plan and the guides for its implementation were not used.

Figure 8.11, a **good** example of an unsolicited negative message, shows how the same information can be conveyed in a more acceptable manner. Sale representatives are not going to be happy about having to inform their customers that a toy is being recalled, but at least the situation is more acceptable when the indirect plan is used. There is no need for a communicator to anger, disturb, or hurt receivers—intentionally or inadvertently—through poorly conveyed messages.

INTEROFFICE MEMO

DATE: November 15, 200–
TO: Sales Representatives
FROM: Mei-ling Sheng, Production Manager
SUBJECT: Longneck the Giraffe Doll

> Good opening buffer builds coherence; is positive; sets the stage for the explanation.

You have done an outstanding job in selling our products for the upcoming holiday season. Your efforts have contributed to Gizmos & Doodads' having its most profitable year ever. Our toys attract children's interest and make your job of selling much easier.

> Convincing logical reasoning precedes the negative information.

As you know, Gizmos & Doodads does extensive research and throughly tests all of its products before releasing them to the public. One phase of the testing involves putting the toy in the hands of hundreds of children. After the children keep the toy for a month, the toy is sent back to the lab for additional testing. In spite of this extensive testing, sometimes problems with these toys will not appear until after they have been distributed nationwide. This is the case with Longneck the Giraffe. All of these dolls must be returned to our warehouse because under extreme conditions the heads may become loose.

> Negative information is de-emphasized by its position in the paragraph.

Gizmos & Doodads has decided to release Patty the Panda to replace Longneck. Notify us of the stores wanting this replacement doll, and we will ship the dolls via overnight express with no shipping cost to the stores. The return shipping costs for Longneck will also be paid by Gizmos & Doodads.

> Receiver's interests are stressed in the helpful alternative solution.

This holiday season will be an appropriate ending to a banner year. By working together we can all look forward to good years ahead.

kt

> Friendly close is warm and optimistic.

FIGURE 8.11
Example of a *Good* Unsolicited Negative Memo

Use the Direct Plan for Negative Messages When Appropriate

LEARNING OBJECTIVE
(5) *Prepare negative messages using the direct plan when it is appropriate.*

NOTE 8.33
The direct plan gives negative information first.

You are already familiar with the direct plan for message preparation; that is, the main idea of the message is conveyed in the first sentences. On some occasions the direct plan is used for negative messages—when the negative information is given first. Your analysis of the situation and the receiver will help you determine when you can use the direct plan.

You may use the direct plan when you know your receiver prefers to learn the bad news first and the reasons or rationale for it later. For example, if your receiver's personality is the type that prefers directness, use the direct approach.

Likewise, in online customer relations situations, the responder should use the same style as the person making the request—if the request is direct, the response should be, too, even if it's negative news.

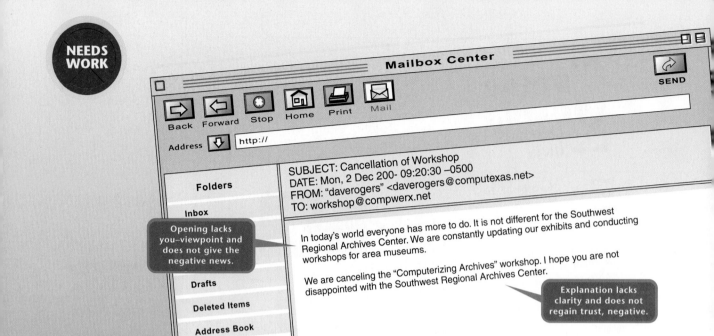

FIGURE 8.12
Example of a *Poor* Negative Message Using the Direct Plan

Text inside the figure:

NEEDS WORK

Mailbox Center

Back   Forward   Stop   Home   Print   Mail

SEND

Address http://

Folders

Inbox

Drafts

Deleted Items

Address Book

SUBJECT: Cancellation of Workshop
DATE: Mon, 2 Dec 200- 09:20:30 –0500
FROM: "daverogers" <daverogers@computexas.net>
TO: workshop@compwerx.net

In today's world everyone has more to do. It is not different for the Southwest Regional Archives Center. We are constantly updating our exhibits and conducting workshops for area museums.

We are canceling the "Computerizing Archives" workshop. I hope you are not disappointed with the Southwest Regional Archives Center.

Opening lacks you–viewpoint and does not give the negative news.

Explanation lacks clarity and does not regain trust, negative.

Another instance in which the direct plan may be used is when you want to emphasize how sorry you are about the negative situation. An example of this is a sympathy note sent regarding a death or tragedy.

You may also use the direct plan when the negative information is routine and will not be upsetting to your receiver. For example, a receiver will not be upset to learn that a nonessential meeting has been canceled. A message canceling the meeting should use the direct approach. Figures 8.12 and 8.13 are examples of **poor** and **good** uses of the direct plan in e-mail messages to cancel a nonessential meeting at the Southwest Regional Archives Center. The poor message may confuse the receiver while the good message should regain trust and build goodwill.

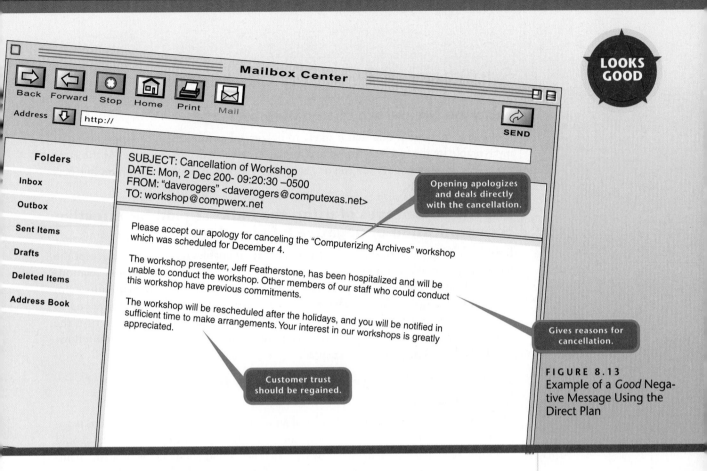

Mailbox Center

Back Forward Stop Home Print Mail

Address http://

SEND

Folders

Inbox

Outbox

Sent Items

Drafts

Deleted Items

Address Book

SUBJECT: Cancellation of Workshop
DATE: Mon, 2 Dec 200- 09:20:30 –0500
FROM: "daverogers" <daverogers @computexas.net>
TO: workshop@compwerx.net

Please accept our apology for canceling the "Computerizing Archives" workshop which was scheduled for December 4.

The workshop presenter, Jeff Featherstone, has been hospitalized and will be unable to conduct the workshop. Other members of our staff who could conduct this workshop have previous commitments.

The workshop will be rescheduled after the holidays, and you will be notified in sufficient time to make arrangements. Your interest in our workshops is greatly appreciated.

> Opening apologizes and deals directly with the cancellation.

> Gives reasons for cancellation.

> Customer trust should be regained.

FIGURE 8.13
Example of a *Good* Negative Message Using the Direct Plan

Another instance in which the direct plan may be used for negative messages is when the negative information needs to be emphasized. In the chapter opening, Tim Farmer says that he uses the direct plan in the second and third letters he sends to customers who do not pay their past-due bills. The direct plan emphasizes the negative message that Tim must send in these situations.

In most negative message situations, however, you will want to use the indirect order of presentation because of its many advantages.

Summary of Learning Objectives

(1) Describe the nature of negative messages.

A negative message is one that is likely to be viewed as unpleasant, disappointing, or unfavorable by the receiver. A negative message is a challenge to compose. At the same time, it is an opportunity for you as a writer or speaker to resolve a common business problem successfully.

(2) List the advantages of using the indirect plan for effective communication of negative information.

Important advantages of the indirect plan are that it enables receivers (1) to accept the negative information you must give them and (2) to maintain a satisfactory relationship with you. The indirect plan has these advantages because it maintains calm through its gradual approach. The indirect plan affords the opportunity for reason to prevail and for understanding to develop. If the negative information is given first, the receiver may ignore the rest of the message; even a fair, reasonable explanation following the bad news may never be accepted.

(3) Describe the five specific guidelines for using the indirect plan.

Messages using the indirect plan consist of an opening buffer, logical explanation, negative information, constructive follow-up, and friendly close. The opening buffer should meet the following requirements: provide coherence, build goodwill, be positive, maintain neutrality, and introduce the explanation. The logical explanation usually begins after the opening buffer and often can be handled in one paragraph. The negative information follows the logical explanation and is short—normally one sentence. It may be implied or given in explicit terms and should be de-emphasized. Solutions are provided or additional justification of the unfavorable information is given in the constructive follow-up section. The friendly close should be personalized, off the subject, warm, and optimistic. The friendly close should move the receiver's mind away from the negative news.

(4) Prepare competently a variety of negative messages using the indirect plan.

Incorporate the communication fundamentals in an indirect plan when preparing request refusals, adjustment refusals, credit refusals, and unsolicited negative messages. You should present the information positively using the you–viewpoint. Organize the message in the following order: opening buffer, logical explanation, negative information, constructive follow-up, and friendly close.

(5) Prepare negative messages using the direct plan when it is appropriate.

Analyze the situation and the receiver to determine when the direct plan should be used with a negative message. Use the direct plan when you know your receiver prefers to learn the bad news before the reason(s) for it. It may also be used when the negative information is routine and will not be upsetting to your receiver. When using the direct plan with negative messages, start the message with the negative information and follow with the explanation.

Discussion Questions

1. What benefits may a writer gain by effectively composing a negative message? (Objective 1)
2. What are possible consequences when the indirect plan is not followed and the negative information is given at the beginning of the message? (Objective 2)
3. How can a writer use a friendly close to build goodwill? (Objective 3)
4. Describe how to ensure that the logical explanation coherently follows the opening. (Objective 3)
5. Describe how to present convincing reasoning and use emphasis techniques in the logical explanation. (Objective 3)
6. What is the difference between an adjustment refusal and a request refusal? (Objective 4)
7. If a person is a bad credit risk, why shouldn't a writer simply begin the negative message by telling the receiver that he or she doesn't meet the minimum credit standards of the company? (Objective 4)
8. What are the four basic ways that credit refusals are communicated? (Objective 4)
9. Describe a circumstance where a businessperson would have to transmit an unsolicited negative message. (Objective 4)
10. Are there any circumstances under which a writer would present the negative information before giving a buffer or explanation? Explain. (Objective 5)

Application Exercises

1. Analyze the following sentences for their effectiveness in opening a negative message organized by the indirect approach: (Objective 3)
   a. Your credit history prevents us from issuing you a credit card.
   b. Thank you for your interest in the show, "Patsy Cline Returns to the Ryman."
   c. Your check for four Super Bowl tickets is enclosed.
   d. When you were hired, you were told that you could not take vacation the first two weeks in April.
   e. Your registration for the computer application workshop has been received.
2. Interview three instructors and ask them how they would respond to a student in the following situation. *A student who will fail your course comes to your office and asks if he or she will pass the course.* Be prepared to report your findings to the class. As a student, how would you prefer to be notified? (Objective 1)

3. **InfoTrac. E-mail. Global.** Positive wording in business communication is highly recommended; however, using negative wording can be effective in certain situations. The strategy of using negative wording is discussed in InfoTrac article A56336323, "Negative Messages as Strategic Communication: A Case Study of a New Zealand Company's Annual Executive Letter." Read the InfoTrac article and respond to the following questions in an e-mail message to your instructor:
   a. What are the short-term objectives of focusing on negatives in the annual executive letter of the small New Zealand business discussed in the article?
   b. In what type of business was the New Zealand company involved?
   c. What are some real problems that the company faced but were not addressed in the executive letter?
   d. Why did the writer focus on minor problems instead of good news?
4. Change the following statements to reflect what can be done instead of what cannot be done: (Objective 3)
   a. No smoking in this building.

b. Don't touch any of the artwork.

c. No refunds will be made without the sales slip.

d. This telephone cannot be used for personal calls.

e. The computer lab is closed on Saturdays and Sundays.

5. Contact the loan officer at a local bank and ask him or her what is the most effective way to convey negative information to a customer. Be prepared to share your findings with the class. (Objective 2)

6. Select one of the five parts of an indirect plan for negative messages, and prepare yourself for a class debate. Attempt to convince the class that the part you selected is the most important in effectively delivering negative messages. (Objective 2)

7. Ask a businessperson or an instructor at your school in what situations he or she uses the direct approach in conveying negative information. Share your findings with the class. (Objective 5)

8. **E-mail.** Your instructor has asked you to speak to the faculty club at your school. Your speech is to be about the benefits of belonging to a student organization. You are unable to make the presentation. Send an e-mail message to your instructor declining the invitation. Add any necessary details. Remember that you will need this instructor to write a recommendation letter for you. (Objective 4)

There are Web exercises at **http://krizan.swlearning.com** to accompany this chapter.

Case Problems

Request Refusals

1. You are the owner of Brian's Gourmet Diner, a low-cost, high-quality restaurant. Last week Angie Laird, a representative from Single Parents Association (SPA), visited your establishment and spoke to you about being affiliated with SPA. Businesses that are associated with SPA pay a small monthly fee and give members belonging to SPA a 20 percent discount on purchases. Supposedly, belonging to SPA would increase your customer base. Today you receive a letter from Angie asking you once again to become a SPA affiliate. You have thought about affiliating with SPA and have decided against it. Your diner is doing quite well, and giving the 20 percent discount to members would definitely cut into your profit margins. Write a letter to Angie declining the offer without offending her or appearing to be self-serving. Add any necessary details.

2. **E-mail.** The Colonial Apartment complex in your town is one year old and has a heated swimming pool, a fully furnished exercise room, and a party room. Its pet policy allows only cats. Jennifer Wolf is interested in renting one of the units. She has e-mailed you, the apartment manager, requesting an exception to the policy that would allow her to move into the unit with her two birds. Compose an e-mail reply that would deny the exception to the pet policy; send your message to your instructor.

3. **Global.** Citizens International is a global service organization. One of its service projects is sponsoring students from other countries. Christopher Blair, president of the Winnipeg Chapter of Citizens International, has written requesting that your chapter sponsor Sally Cannon, a high school junior, for the upcoming school year. Your chapter has committed to sponsor a student from Genoa, Italy, and it only sponsors one student per year. Write a letter to Christopher denying his request but offering to sponsor someone the following year. Add details to make your letter complete.

4. You have accepted a volunteer job as editor of your professional journal. One of the undesirable parts of the job is to send rejection letters to persons who have submitted articles for publication. Many of these articles are well written but do not contain ap-

propriate content for the journal. The letter must be written so that it will not offend the writer, who is a member of your professional organization. Write a form letter that would deny publication in your journal.

5. **Teamwork. Ethical/Legal.** You have just learned that one salesperson at Replacement Windows, Inc., has been promising customers installation dates that could not possibly be met. To get the sale, Kyle lets the customer request any date he or she wants.

   The owner has terminated Kyle because of his unethical behavior and has you (sales manager) and four of your staff meet to write a form letter suitable for sending to the customers involved. Your writing team's challenge is to compose an effective message that will convey the negative information that you cannot install the windows on the dates promised. In addition, you will try to keep their business. Your installation schedule will permit you to install the windows approximately three months after the promised date. Add details to make this a complete request refusal letter.

6. You are the manager of a franchise for Pizza Stores, Inc. An executive of a manufacturing plant near your restaurant has asked you whether he may have his employees attend a pizza party at your restaurant at 9 p.m. on Thursday. You would have to close your restaurant two hours early to accommodate the large number of his employees. Because you do not feel it is possible for you to close your restaurant to the public two hours early, you will have to turn down the request. You would be glad, however, to cater a pizza party at some other location. You can do this in the manufacturer's plant, at the community center, or at some other location of the executive's choosing. Write a letter to the executive that will turn down his request and keep the business. Add any necessary details.

Adjustment Refusals

7. Angela and Richard Little have been remodeling their house for more than a year. About six months ago they special ordered a prefabricated countertop with a 3-inch lip that goes against the back wall. While visiting with some friends, they learned that a Formica countertop would be better. They contacted your company, Woodson Supply, and stated that they wanted to exchange the original countertop for a Formica countertop. As general manager you have to deny their request. The prefabricated countertop was cut specifically to their measurements and would be next to impossible to sell to someone else. As an alternative, you may offer the Formica countertop at your cost. Write a letter to Angela and Richard giving them your decision. You do not want to lose their business in the future.

8. Mary and Tom Nance purchased a travel trailer from you at Vacation Vehicles one year ago and have used this trailer for many long trips. They would like to exchange the old trailer for a new one because the axle makes a squealing noise. Write them a letter denying their request; however, tell them that you are willing to replace the bearings at no cost to them.

9. Nine months ago Sandra Tucker purchased a computerized sewing machine by mail order from Kunkel Enterprises. The sewing machine was sold with a six-month limited warranty. Sandra has returned the sewing machine to Kunkel's because its stitching was poor and the tension could not be adjusted to correct the problem. She has requested a new replacement machine. Write a letter to Sandra denying her request, but offer to repair the machine at a cost of $90 to Sandra.

10. You are the owner of Tuff Built Implements, a firm that sells farm machinery to equipment dealers. You receive a letter from Tieman Tractors, an equipment dealer, who sold one of your medium-size tractors to Ken Robertson. After using the tractor for one season, Ken has returned the tractor to Tieman Tractors and demanded a full refund. While investigating the transaction, you learn that Ken purchased a new 22-foot field cultivator and was unable to pull it with the Tuff Built tractor that he had pur-

chased a year earlier. The tractor was not designed to pull implements as large as the 22-foot cultivator. Write a positive, courteous adjustment refusal letter to Tieman Tractors. Suggest to them that Mr. Robertson use a smaller cultivator or trade his medium-size tractor for a larger model. You are willing to sell Tieman Tractors one of your larger tractors at a greatly reduced price.

11. Frank Electronics sells televisions, radios, CD players, cell phones, and other electronics equipment. In addition to operating his retail store, Frank publishes a catalog each month. Part of the catalog is devoted to clearance merchandise. Frank has received many returns of catalog clearance sale merchandise even though it clearly states in the catalog that it is not possible to return merchandise that has been purchased from the clearance sale section of the catalog. Prepare a form letter that Frank could use to deny the claims for clearance sale merchandise.

12. Billy Ray's Ready Mix delivers a variety of concrete, sand, rock, gravel, fill dirt, and so forth. Its 60-truck fleet makes deliveries in six counties. As manager of Billy Ray's, you received from Jack Drum a huge order for fill dirt. He was planning to build a shopping mall on 40 acres of undeveloped land. For two months you delivered fill dirt to the location and leveled the land. One week after billing Mr. Drum for your work, you receive a letter from him stating that he will not pay the charges because he was expecting topsoil and not fill dirt. He had changed his mind about building a shopping mall and had decided instead to construct a par 3 golf course. A golf course needs grass, and it will not grow on fill dirt. Write a letter to Mr. Drum informing him that he is responsible for the work done because fill dirt was requested in the original order. You may suggest that he replace the top 12 inches of fill dirt with topsoil.

Credit Refusals

13. You are the owner of Dale's Clothiers for Men, a business designed to serve white-collar professionals. The policy of your store is to provide credit cards for individuals who have good jobs and excellent credit. One day you receive an application from Jason Williams, a full-time graduate student at your local university. Jason went from high school to college then to graduate school without ever working full time. He has few assets but not many liabilities since his parents paid for all of his expenses until he started graduate school. He is scheduled to graduate with an MBA in a year. You have decided to refuse his application but do not want to alienate him because he may become a good customer after graduation. Write him a refusal letter adding necessary details.

14. Billy Davis has applied for a $9,000 loan to buy a pre-owned automobile. As credit manager of A-1 Finance Corporation, you learn during a credit check that Billy is behind on payments for several credit cards, a home mortgage, and child support. He does not meet the qualifications of a good credit risk with your corporation. Write Billy telling him that you must refuse his credit request on the $9,000 automobile. Add necessary details.

 15. **E-mail.** You are the loan officer for LuckyOnes Bank. Your bank accepts and processes online loan applications. Shane and Karen Fletcher have sent an e-mail asking about LuckyOnes approving a $200,000 loan application to build a weekend home in the country. They purchased a $300,000 home in town three years ago with a loan from your bank. Shane is an account executive and Karen is a systems analyst. Both jobs pay well; however, the Fletchers are spending beyond their means. Periodically they are late in making payments on their home and two sports cars. You would like to keep them as customers, but at this time you must send them an e-mail denying the loan for the weekend home. Prepare the message, adding details, and send the message via e-mail to your instructor.

16. As loan officer of Sierra National Bank, you receive a loan application from Scenic Air Tours. Scenic is a small company that provides helicopter tours of the surrounding

scenic area. It currently has two helicopters. The company would like to purchase three to five used helicopters and has requested a loan for $2 million. Due to the unreliability of used aircraft, you must deny Scenic's request for the loan. Write a letter that will maintain this company's business with the bank but will refuse this particular loan.

17. Lynn Cooper has moved into your town and is interested in becoming a painting contractor. She has requested a line of credit with your home decorating store. The problem with her application for the line of credit is that her information is sketchy. You have been unable to contact her references, and she has refused to furnish you her employment history. You would like to do business with Ms. Cooper on a cash basis but cannot approve a line of credit until you obtain more creditable information. Write a letter to Ms. Cooper denying her line of credit but encouraging her to buy on a cash basis. Add necessary details.

18. You are the owner of Oliver's Food Market, a small grocery store. Oliver's success has been largely due to its personable and friendly service. Over the past 20 years you have not accepted credit cards but have allowed your faithful customers to charge their groceries until the end of the month. Recently, two large chain groceries have moved into town forcing you to lower your prices to remain competitive. Reducing the price of your groceries has greatly cut into your profit margin. As you analyze your entire operation, you determine that permitting customers to charge for 30 days is becoming too costly; therefore, you decide to terminate your credit plan at the end of next month. Write your customers informing them that as of the end of the month, you will no longer permit customers to charge their purchases. Add details.

Unsolicited Negative Messages

19. Place yourself in the position of the plant manager of Mighty Pressure Compressors, Inc. Your sales representative in Texas, Victoria Morales, sold one of your largest and most powerful air compressors to Mesquite Drilling Company. Victoria promised the purchasing manager of Mesquite Drilling, Charles Harrell, that the air compressor would be delivered in two weeks; however, due to the increased drilling of oil and gas wells, you have a backlog of deliveries and will not be able to deliver the compressor for at least 90 days. You do not want to lose this order or jeopardize any future business with Mesquite Drilling. Write Mr. Harrell a letter explaining the delay in delivery of his compressor. Add information to make the letter realistic.

20. You are the owner of Jimmy's Electric, a small electrical construction company. Because of reduction of building in the area, it is necessary that you terminate Milton Young's employment. He is an excellent worker who has been with your company for nine months. Develop an outline that you could use when talking with Milton about his termination. You would like to see him come back to work for you when building conditions improve.

21. You are the administrative manager of Sunnyvale Medical Center. The center has 28 doctors with various specialties. A popular family physician, Dr. Linda Seabolt, is moving to an out-of-state hospital at the end of June. The center has another family physician, Dr. Ali Raj, and is searching for an additional family physician. Write a form letter that could be sent to all of Dr. Seabolt's patients informing them of her departure and encouraging them to see Dr. Raj or the new doctor when he or she arrives. Add information to make the letter realistic.

 22. **Teamwork. Global.** You have over 2,000 wholesale dealers in Canada who regularly buy high school graduation rings from your U.S. company. Price levels for these rings have increased only at the rate of inflation during the past four years. Because of the increase in the world price of gold over the past 24 months, your company is going to have to increase the price level of your ring line by 12 percent. Work with a writing team from management to write the form letter that will maintain the goodwill of

your customers, keep their business, and help them accept your bad news. Add details to make the letter complete.

23. For the past ten years Boone, Texas, has held a Freedom Fest celebration during the Fourth of July week. One of the highlights of Freedom Fest has been a performance by a country and western entertainer followed by a fireworks display. Fans attending the performance paid a small fee, and the rest of the expenses were paid by a local company. This company has informed you, the Boone city manager, that it will no longer sponsor the event. As city manager you need to write a negative message that could be put in the local newspaper stating that this year's Freedom Fest will not feature an entertainer.

24. You are manager of Gerald's Home Improvement Center. Your 20,000-square-foot building is one of the largest in the area. To escape the weather, many individuals use your facility for their daily walking exercise. The number of people using your facility has increased to a point that it is interfering with your business. Write a notice that could be placed in the local newspaper explaining that walkers will no longer be able to use your facility for exercise. Word the notice so you do not offend anyone.

Message Analysis

Steve Armstrong, one of your marketing representatives has ten years of experience, two with your company. He has written you requesting a promotion to sales director. Steve has been a marginal employee for the entire time he has been with your company; however, as he gains experience and maturity, he has potential for being an excellent employee. Edit and revise the following memo that could be sent to Steve denying his promotion request:

> I cannot believe that you think you are ready to be promoted to sales director. This position requires interpersonal skills, initiative, and complete honesty. You have a difficult time in communicating with others and must be given detailed instructions in order for you to complete a job. In the past three months you have had your travel expense voucher returned twice because it had been padded. I am sure you will work on these problems so the next time a position opens, you will be better prepared.

Grammar Workshop

Correct the grammar, spelling, punctuation, and word choice errors in the following sentences:

1. Transportation and a car is provided for you, when you spend three or more days at our luxurious resort.
2. The doctors patient were having surgery at 9 am.
3. Saras' graph compliments the text in her report.
4. Although drinking stations for walkers and joggers was added to the trails it remain an ecologically-sound facility.
5. Nearly three-fourths of the fruit crop were lost due to the extreme cold temperatures.
6. The requirements for the class included an oral report; writing a two page executive summary; and a final exam.
7. Pat and Bonnie were the first to excuse theirselves from the meeting, so that they could go golfing.
8. Representatives of Cummins High School headed by the varsity cheerleaders are encouraging local businesses to get behind the Wildcats for their State Championship Game.
9. After completing a three day inventory of the stock Darcy finds a 10% shortage.
10. Judy appeared relaxed at the musical as she looked contented at her class.

Persuasive Messages

9

LEARNING
OBJECTIVES

①

Describe a persuasive message.

②

List the purposes of a persuasive message.

③

Describe the four specific guidelines for using the indirect plan for persuasion.

④

Write different kinds of persuasive messages using the indirect plan.

⑤

Write messages that are used for the various stages of collection.

*David E. Alexander,
Vice Chairman—Area
Practices and
Management
Committee Member
Ernst & Young LLP*

LET'S TALK BUSINESS From my early years at Ernst & Young as a staff accountant to my current role as vice chair, the power and importance of effective communication have been constantly reinforced. Persuasive messages are a part of everyone's daily business because we are all in "sales." We may not be directly involved in selling products or services to external customers, but success requires that each of us be able to "sell" ideas to our internal customers—those we report to, our peers, and those who report to us. In fact, I have found that I often have to "sell" my internal customers and gain their acceptance before I can work on taking new ideas, products, and services to our client market.

For me, the starting point in developing a persuasive message is a thorough understanding of my audience and what they value. If I am making a presentation to a potential client, I always take the time to research the company and its decision makers to understand what business challenges they are facing. My goal is to construct and communicate a message that will lead to a positive impact on their business. I clearly communicate the value of my message in terms they can relate to—cost savings, increased profits, better efficiency, and improved market strength.

Once I've developed the framework of a message, I find it helpful to get the input of others who can enhance the communication. An objective third party may be used to identify potential points of confusion or gaps in information that I have overlooked.

Finally, make your persuasive message concise. Over-communicating can be just as ineffective as under-communicating. Your brevity will be appreciated by your busy audience and hopefully rewarded with the response you seek.

A **persuasive message** is (1) a request for action when you believe the receiver may be unknowing, disinterested, or unwilling, or (2) a communication to try to change the opinion of a receiver. These messages will be viewed as neither positive nor negative by the receiver.

Persuasive messages are used in both internal and external communication. Examples of persuasive messages in internal communication include a speech asking employees to volunteer to work on upcoming weekends, an employee's memo to a manager requesting that the organization initiate a flextime policy, an employee's recommendation or proposal to establish a day care center, and a letter to employees requesting donations for a charity the company endorses.

A **sales message** is a communication that includes a description of a product, its benefits, available options and models, price, and related services. It is the most common persuasive message in external communication. Other examples of persuasive messages used in external communication include a telephone call to ask the manager of another company to be the keynote speaker at an annual banquet or a letter to persuade readers to respond to a questionnaire. Persuasive messages also include letters requesting employment with an organization.

In the Let's Talk Business section, David Alexander supports the idea that persuasive messages must be designed to convince receivers that taking the requested action is in their best interest. The supporting facts in the message must be presented as useful or profitable to the receiver. Persuasive messages should usually be presented using an indirect approach.

NOTE 9.1
Persuasive messages are used to convince receivers to take action or change an opinion.

NOTE 9.2
Persuasive messages are used for a variety of purposes in internal and external communication.

NOTE 9.3
Receivers will have to be convinced that it is in their best interest to take action.

Use the Indirect Plan for Persuasive Messages

The *indirect plan* should be used for messages that attempt to convince the receiver to take an action. The advantage of using the indirect plan for persuasive messages is that it enables the sender to present first the benefits that the receiver may gain from fulfilling the request. This approach puts the receiver in the proper frame of mind to consider the request. If the request were given prior to the explanation, the receiver might form objections that would be difficult to overcome. The receiver also might not read the part of the letter that contains the benefits. The indirect plan does require the use of more words than the direct plan, but the result is worth the additional words.

If the message is positively constructed in the you–viewpoint, the receiver will more likely be in a positive mood to consider the value of the entire message and will more likely agree with its contents. An effective presentation will associate the message with the motivating factors in the receiver's mind.

NOTE 9.4
The indirect plan assists in convincing a receiver to take action and accept the message.

NOTE 9.5
The you–viewpoint should be used.

LEARNING OBJECTIVE

*List the purposes
of a persuasive
message.*

(2)

How to Use the Indirect Plan

Analyzing your receiver is especially important when planning a persuasive message. You will have to anticipate what motivates the receiver—his or her goals, values, and needs. You must then build your persuasive message around these factors using the you–viewpoint. Do this by stressing the receiver's interests and benefits.

The two primary purposes of a persuasive message are (1) to get the receiver to read or listen to the entire message, and then (2) to have the receiver react positively to the request. These purposes are more easily achieved when the indirect plan is used in constructing the message. The specific guides for using the indirect plan to construct persuasive messages are shown in Figure 9.1.

The indirect plan can be used for a variety of persuasive messages—requests, recommendations, special claims, sales, collection, and employment. The organization and development of the first five types of persuasive messages are discussed in this chapter, and employment messages are covered in Chapter 17. An analysis of the indirect plan for persuasion will be helpful prior to discussing the construction of five sample persuasive messages.

NOTE 9.6
Carefully analyze the receiver to determine motivational factors.

NOTE 9.7
Purposes of a persuasive message are to have the receiver consider the entire message and then to take requested action.

INDIRECT PLAN FOR PERSUASION

I. Attention
  A. Attract the receiver's attention in opening sentence.
  B. Cause the receiver to read or to listen to rest of message.
  C. Be positive and brief.

II. Interest
  A. Build on attention gained in the opening.
  B. Show benefits to the receiver.
  C. Motivate the receiver to continue reading.

III. Desire
  A. Build on the receiver's attention and interest by providing proof of benefits.
  B. Re-emphasize benefits to the receiver.
  C. Downplay any negative points or obstacles.

IV. Action
  A. Motivate the receiver to take immediate action.
  B. Be positive.
  C. Make action easy.

FIGURE 9.1
Indirect Plan Outline for Persuasion

NOTE 9.8
Persuasive messages include requests, recommendations, special claims, sales, collection, and employment.

Attention

The opening in any persuasive message must attract the receiver's attention. A persuasive message is successful only when the receiver takes the desired action. The desired action is not likely to be taken unless the receiver is motivated to read or listen to the entire message. An attention-getting opening increases the chances that the receiver will read or listen to the entire message and then take the desired action.

The receiver's attention must be captured in the opening sentence. It is important that the opening be concise and positive. In a well-planned persuasive message, the receiver's curiosity is aroused when a message opens with an interesting point. When a positive emotion is aroused, the receiver will continue reading.

Many different methods have been used successfully by communicators to capture the receiver's attention. These methods include using mechanical devices (such as color or drawings), the receiver's name in the sentence, rhetorical questions (for example, "Would you enjoy a weekend of skiing in Aspen?"), and interjections. The you–viewpoint must be considered when organizing the content of the message. Any method that gets the receiver's attention may be used if it is relevant to the topic of the message and is not trite or high pressure. Gimmicks may be used but should not give the receiver the impression that an attempt is being made to mislead him or her. For example, beginning a letter with

LEARNING OBJECTIVE
③
Describe the four specific guidelines for using the indirect plan for persuasion.

NOTE 9.9
Get the receiver's attention immediately.

NOTE 9.10
Senders use different techniques to gain receivers' attention.

"Your investment of $10 may grow to a million dollars by the end of the year" will probably cause the receiver to read no further because the message is unrealistic.

Interest

NOTE 9.11
To hold interest, make the receiver aware of the benefits of taking the action.

You must hold the receiver's interest after his or her attention is gained. Expand the topic of the first paragraph while maintaining the interest of the receiver. Interest will be maintained when the receiver sees benefits for himself or herself. When taking the requested action will result in several benefits to the receiver, the benefits may be emphasized by listing them. The receiver may hesitate to take the desired action unless he or she clearly sees the value of taking such action. Using the proper mechanical device for presenting the message can affect receivers' interest. The Communication Note below demonstrates how the improper selection of a mechanical device to deliver a message can negatively affect the receiver's interest.

COMMUNICATION NOTE

Importance of Proper Packaging of a Message The Wisconsin legislature passed a $1 billion tax relief package that included $700 million in sales tax rebates to 2.5 million taxpayers. The rebate checks were mailed as postcard-sized items that were mistaken for junk mail by many recipients. Many of the recipients improperly disposed of the rebate checks.

When this problem was brought to the attention of the Wisconsin Revenue Department, it redesigned the checks for easier identification. The replacement checks were sent in a blue, business-sized envelope, which was easier for recipients to identify.

Adapted from "Replacement Rebate Checks Being Sent," *Duluth News-Tribune*, January 21, 2000.

Desire

NOTE 9.12
Providing proof of the benefits and values increases a receiver's desire to take action.

Once you have the receiver's attention and interest, offer proof of the benefits the receiver can gain. Doing so will motivate the receiver to take the requested action. Remember, the purpose of the persuasive message is to move the receiver to take the desired action. Details of the message are used to intensify the interest of and create desire in the receiver. Anticipate the receiver's negative reactions to avoid the desired action; attempt to overcome these feelings by showing proof of the benefits. Facts and figures can be valuable but should not be overused. Too many numbers or testimonials will confuse or bore the receiver.

The *interest* and the *desire* sections of a persuasive message may be combined by listing a benefit and then immediately providing proof of that benefit. This arrangement would be used until all the pertinent benefits have been discussed.

Action

NOTE 9.13
The receiver should feel that taking the action is a logical conclusion.

You are ready to ask the receiver to take immediate action once you have built his or her interest and desire. The action you request of the receiver should be a logical next step. This action should be requested in a direct and positive manner. As Gregg Appel points out in the Communication Quote that follows, persuasive messages must always have the tone of authority.

Business persuasive messages must be concise with a clear and consistent message. Messages must always have the tone of authority. Simple messages are usually better than messages with some type of underlying meaning. The result of the message must have a direct action.

—Gregg Appel, President, Appel Motors, Inc. (Photo courtesy of Gregg Appel)

Ensure that minimal effort is required for the receiver to take the necessary action. Ask for a simple action such as checking a choice and returning an enclosed card rather than for a time-consuming action such as writing an entire letter.

When the desired action is required by a certain date, be sure that this date is clearly stated. If no time limit is involved, encourage the receiver to act quickly.

Many techniques can be used to influence the receiver to take the desired action immediately. A sales letter can offer coupons to be redeemed, specify a date that the offer ends, or suggest that supplies are limited. Collection letters can offer assurance that the receiver's credit will not be damaged if payment is received by a certain date. Including the receiver's name in a drawing for a free prize if he or she returns a questionnaire can be used with requests. All these techniques are effective if the receiver feels no undue pressure and sees value in what is offered.

NOTE 9.14
Make it easy to take the action.

NOTE 9.15
If a deadline is necessary, give it.

Implementing the Indirect Plan

The use of the indirect plan for persuasion will be illustrated through the development of a manager's request to an employee asking her to transfer to a new facility. Here are details of the communication case problem.

NOTE 9.16
A communication case will help illustrate a way to compose persuasive messages.

THE JERI MATTHEWS CASE

Jeri Matthews has been a computer specialist for Samson Foods Distribution in Jackson, Tennessee, for seven years. Samson Foods is opening a new distribution center in Little Rock, Arkansas, this fall. The vice president for operations recently spoke to Jeri about the new facility. At that time, he did not tell Jeri about the possibility of her transferring to Little Rock. Now, he would like Jeri to make a lateral transfer to Little Rock and assume the duties of computer analyst. It would not be a promotion for Jeri nor would there be an increase in pay; however, the company will pay moving expenses and a relocation allowance. Jeri would have to move to a new city and get a system operating for the new distribution center.

As is the case in developing all business messages, you must first analyze the situation to determine the content that will best accomplish the purpose of the communication. The following sections show how the content of the Jeri Matthews memo may be developed. Each section discusses a stage of the indirect plan for persuasive messages and presents an example of poor writing and then an example of good writing.

Capture the Receiver's Attention

The first step in writing a persuasive message is to capture the receiver's attention. A **poor** way of gaining Jeri's attention is shown here:

NOTE 9.17
The poor opening is negative and impersonal.

- The new distribution center for Samson Foods in Little Rock, Arkansas, needs a computer analyst. You have been working with computers for a long time and should take this job.

This poorly written opening paragraph begins by immediately telling Jeri that she should transfer to a new location and take a different job. It may get her attention but not in a positive way. The paragraph is impersonal and shows a lack of appreciation for Jeri's service with the company. She may be reluctant to continue reading the memo if she immediately senses that the company may be taking advantage of her.

In contrast, a **good** opening to gain Jeri's attention follows:

NOTE 9.18
The good opening is positive and personal.

- Your work as a computer specialist has been outstanding for the past seven years. You have stayed current with computer technology through your continuing education at the University of Memphis, and you have done an excellent job in applying this knowledge to your position at Samson Foods.

This good opening gains Jeri's attention by recognizing her longtime dedication to the organization. This paragraph uses both a positive approach and the you–viewpoint. It should interest her because it praises her for her previous service. Everyone likes to receive recognition, and this acknowledgment of her efforts should motivate Jeri to read the remaining portion of the memo with an open mind.

Build the Receiver's Interest

After you have captured the receiver's attention, concentrate on building his or her interest in accepting the request. A **poor** way of building Jeri's interest follows:

NOTE 9.19
The poor message lacks a you–viewpoint.

- This job is not a promotion. You would continue earning the same salary that you presently make. Samson Foods has been looking for a competent computer analyst, and your record shows that you could become one.

This poor attempt to build the receiver's interest is similar to that of the poor opening in that it focuses on the negative and trivializes her transfer. The paragraph is cold and lacks a you–viewpoint; it is of no help in building Jeri's interest in accepting the transfer.

A **good** paragraph, which should build Jeri's interest, follows:

NOTE 9.20
The good message aids in building receiver's interest.

- As I mentioned to you last week during our discussion, Samson Foods is opening a distribution center in Little Rock, Arkansas. This distribution center will be fully operational by November 1, 200–. The center needs a computer analyst who has experience in the foods distribution industry. The possibility of promotion is great at our new facility, even though your transfer would not mean an immediate promotion. On a personal note, Little Rock is the capital of Arkansas, and you will find museums, theaters, and other cultural activities unique to metropolitan areas.

This good paragraph describes in a positive manner the opening of the new center and a benefit of the transfer. Jeri's interest, now stimulated, will peak in the next paragraph.

Funky Winkerbean

Promote Desire in the Receiver

This section should emphasize the benefits that Jeri would receive by taking the requested action and attempt to overcome any negative thoughts that Jeri may have. A **poor** attempt to create desire is illustrated here:

- I know that this job would present many challenges, but you could learn from them. It is always interesting and educational when starting an operation in a new location. I know that you would have to leave many friends and relatives in Jackson; however, you can make new friends in Little Rock.

This approach will do little to motivate the reader to accept the transfer. The paragraph is written from the sender's point of view—not from the receiver's. Jeri will look at the transfer as nothing more than having to move and having to learn a new job.

A **good** attempt to stimulate Jeri's desire to accept the transfer follows:

- The facility in Little Rock will have state-of-the-art equipment. You would be involved in planning and implementing the distribution operations for the southeast region of Samson Foods. Your moving expenses will be paid by Samson Foods, and you will receive a moving allowance of $1,000.

The benefits that Jeri can gain from the transfer are clearly explained in the good example. The negative aspect of the transfer—that she will have to move to a new city—is handled in a positive way. Jeri should now be looking forward to accepting the transfer.

Request Action from the Receiver

Once Jeri has been motivated to accept the transfer, request that she do so immediately. Jeri's action of accepting the transfer should be made as easy as possible for her.

A **poor** example of requesting action is shown here:

- Jeri, if you decide to accept this job as computer analyst in Little Rock, please send me a letter of acceptance. Make sure that you let me know if you don't want the new position so I can get someone else.

This paragraph does little to motivate Jeri to accept the transfer. The you–viewpoint is absent. The paragraph is negative; it emphasizes the alternative that she does not have to accept the transfer.

A **good** example of requesting action may be written as follows:

- Jeri, please accept the computer analyst position in our Little Rock distribution center. Your acceptance will be an exciting opportunity for you to be part of the implementation of a new site, and your expertise will make a major contribution to its success. Please e-mail your response to me no later than August 25 at dmartin@samsonfoods.com.

NOTE 9.21
The arguments in this poor example are presented from a selfish point of view.

NOTE 9.22
This good example points out the benefits to the receiver.

NOTE 9.23
This poor request for action is presented in a negative manner.

NOTE 9.24
This good example makes it easy for receiver to take action.

NEEDS WORK

Samson Foods Distribution

TO:	Jeri Matthews
FROM:	David Martin *DM*
DATE:	August 3, 200–
SUBJECT:	Opening in Little Rock Center

The new distribution center for Samson Foods in Little Rock, Arkansas, needs a computer analyst. You have been working with computers for a long time and should take this job.

This job is not a promotion. You would continue earning the same salary that you presently make. Samson Foods has been looking for a competent computer analyst, and your record shows that you could become one.

I know that this job would present many challenges, but you could learn from them. It is always interesting and educational when starting an operation in a new location. I know that you would have to leave many friends and relatives in Jackson; however, you can make new friends in Little Rock.

Jeri, if you decide to accept this job as computer analyst in Little Rock, please send me a letter of acceptance. Make sure that you let me know if you don't want the new position so I can get someone else.

jh

Gains attention negatively.

Fails to show benefits.

Emphasizes obstacles.

Fails to motivate receiver.

FIGURE 9.2
Example of a *Poor* Persuasive Message

Notice the direct, positive approach used in this paragraph. Accepting the transfer is made easy for Jeri; she can simply e-mail her acceptance.

Summary—Poor and Good Messages to Jeri Matthews

Good and poor persuasive messages have been illustrated. The poor paragraphs are combined as a memo in Figure 9.2. This persuasive request does not follow the indirect plan outline as shown in Figure 9.1.

The chances of Jeri's accepting the transfer are improved in the good message shown in Figure 9.3. This effective persuasive message follows the guidelines described earlier in this chapter.

This case problem shows how the indirect plan can be effective in communicating persuasive messages. To help you better understand the use of the indirect plan in organizing persuasive messages, several examples of both good and poor messages are illustrated in the following pages.

Samson Foods Distribution

TO: Jeri Matthews
FROM: David Martin *DM*
DATE: August 3, 200–
SUBJECT: Opening in Little Rock Center

> Focuses attention on receiver.

Your work as a computer specialist has been outstanding for the past seven years. You have stayed current with computer technology through your continuing education at the University of Memphis, and you have done an excellent job in applying this knowledge to your position at Samson Foods.

> Continues building interest and keeps attention that was gained in first paragraph.

As I mentioned to you last week during our discussion, Samson Foods is opening a distribution center in Little Rock, Arkansas. This distribution center will be fully operational by November 1, 200–. The center needs a computer analyst who has experience in the foods distribution industry. The possibility of promotion is great at our new facility, even though your transfer would not mean an immediate promotion. On a personal note, Little Rock is the capital of Arkansas, and you will find museums, theaters, and other cultural activities unique to metropolitan areas.

> Emphasizes proof of benefits to receiver.

The facility in Little Rock will have state-of-the-art equipment. You would be involved in planning and implementing the distribution operations for the southeast region of Samson Foods. Your moving expenses will be paid by Samson Foods, and you will receive a moving allowance of $1,000.

> Motivates receiver and makes taking action easy.

Jeri, please accept the computer analyst position in our Little Rock distribution center. Your acceptance will be an exciting opportunity for you to be part of the implementation of a new site, and your expertise will make a major contribution to its success. Please e-mail your response to me no later than August 25 at dmartin@samsonfoods.com.

jh

FIGURE 9.3
Example of a *Good* Persuasive Message

Persuasive Requests

Organizations use both simple requests and complex requests. The simple request was discussed in Chapter 6 and should be constructed with the direct plan. The **complex request** is a persuasive message because in it you will have to convince the receiver to take action. The complex request should use the indirect plan.

In this section we will be concerned only with complex (persuasive) requests. Examples of persuasive requests are those that seek an increase in a department's budget, ask for a donation to a community organization, look for participants for a research project, desire a change in a work schedule, and recruit volunteers.

LEARNING OBJECTIVE
④ *Write different kinds of persuasive messages using the indirect plan.*

NOTE 9.25
Organizational plans for requests may be
• Simple—direct
• Complex—indirect

Heart Research Center
474 Park Lane, Suite 210
San Diego, CA 92145-2314
(619) 555-1922 • (619) 555-3781

March 14, 200-

(INDIVIDUALIZED INSIDE ADDRESS)

Dear **(NAME)**:

Impersonal—does not gain attention.

The Heart Research Center does all kinds of research. We need individuals to serve as guinea pigs for our research.

Selfish—does little to build interest.

We want to conduct this research so that we can continue receiving federal grants. Our research may eventually lead to a healthier society.

If you want to participate in our study, read the enclosed brochure that gives all the details.

Sincerely,

Lori McKeever

Lori McKeever
Research Coordinator

Vague—difficult for receiver to take action.

sm

Enclosure

FIGURE 9.4
Example of a *Poor* Persuasive Request

Figure 9.4 shows a **poor** persuasive request to individuals to participate in a heart research study. This example does not create any receiver interest. The memo is written in the I–viewpoint rather than in the you–viewpoint. The individuals will have little motivation to participate in this study.

Figure 9.5 shows a **good** persuasive request written in the you–viewpoint. The message creates receiver motivation to participate in the heart research study. The letter gains attention, builds interest, creates desire, and makes taking action easy.

The following table summarizes the approach used for the two types of requests:

NOTE 9.26
Recommendations are best when organized in the indirect persuasive plan.

Request	Approach
simple or routine	direct
persuasive or complex	indirect

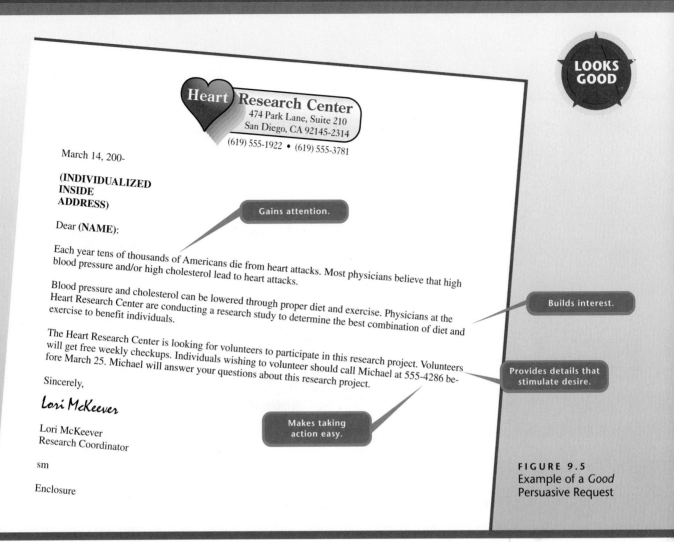

FIGURE 9.5
Example of a *Good*
Persuasive Request

Within the figure:

LOOKS GOOD

Heart Research Center
474 Park Lane, Suite 210
San Diego, CA 92145-2314
(619) 555-1922 • (619) 555-3781

March 14, 200-

**(INDIVIDUALIZED
INSIDE
ADDRESS)**

Dear **(NAME)**:

Each year tens of thousands of Americans die from heart attacks. Most physicians believe that high blood pressure and/or high cholesterol lead to heart attacks.

Blood pressure and cholesterol can be lowered through proper diet and exercise. Physicians at the Heart Research Center are conducting a research study to determine the best combination of diet and exercise to benefit individuals.

The Heart Research Center is looking for volunteers to participate in this research project. Volunteers will get free weekly checkups. Individuals wishing to volunteer should call Michael at 555-4286 before March 25. Michael will answer your questions about this research project.

Sincerely,

Lori McKeever

Lori McKeever
Research Coordinator

sm

Enclosure

Callouts:
- Gains attention.
- Builds interest.
- Provides details that stimulate desire.
- Makes taking action easy.

Recommendations

A **recommendation** is a message that attempts to persuade the receiver to take an action proposed by the sender. Individuals in business, government, and civic organizations periodically submit recommendations to receivers who are above, below, and at their organizational level. Recommendations are most effective when the indirect persuasive plan is employed. Examples of recommendations that should use the indirect plan include a company officer advising the firm to replace obsolete equipment, a manager changing a company policy, a civic leader using a tract of land for a city park rather than a housing project, and an individual seeking employment.

Figure 9.6 shows a **poor** recommendation from Derrick Martin, a vice president, to Steve Allen, the president. Derrick is responding to a memo from Steve Allen concerning renovation. Derrick probably will not be successful in his recommendation if the poor memo is submitted. This memo is not written with the you–viewpoint. It also displays bitterness, which hinders communication. In addition, the memo is not written using the indirect plan—the key to successful persuasive messages.

ALLENIndustries, Inc.

TO: Steve Allen, President

FROM: Derrick Martin, Vice President *DM*

DATE: October 11, 200–

SUBJECT: Renovation of Facilities

You should not even consider renovating our present facilities. It will cost so much money and you will still have an old, outdated building.

Renovation of this building is ridiculous. We could have a new building that would be modern and attractive; however, if you want to renovate the present building, we can do it. We will have to move to a temporary site during the construction.

If you decide to go ahead with this renovation, I will begin planning the move to a temporary location.

gw

> Negatively influences receiver.

> Displays negative attitude; does not show benefits.

> Begrudgingly accepts responsibility.

FIGURE 9.6
Example of a *Poor* Recommendation Memo

The **good** memo in Figure 9.7 should increase the chances that Steve Allen will proceed with the proposed renovation. Note how the indirect persuasive plan presents the *benefits*—improved production and increased employee morale—before the *recommendation*. This memo gains the president's attention in the opening, uses the you–viewpoint in presenting the reasons supporting the recommendation, and presents the recommendation in a positive, professional manner.

Special Claims

NOTE 9.27
Special claims should use the indirect plan.

Special claims are unique and should use the indirect persuasive plan. Routine claims use the direct plan and are discussed in Chapter 6. **Special** or **nonroutine claims** are those in which the fault is disputable. The sender may need to convince the receiver that the adjustment or refund is appropriate.

Examples of special claims that should be organized as persuasive messages include the following: You want a roofing contractor, who has guaranteed his work, to replace the shingles on your office building because they are not aligned properly. A trans-

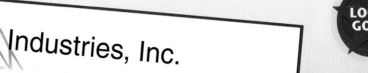

ALLEN Industries, Inc.

TO: Steve Allen, President
FROM: Derrick Martin, Vice President *DM*
DATE: October 11, 200–
SUBJECT: Renovation of Facilities

Allen Industries has become one of the most successful businesses in the state. It has more than doubled its sales and profit in the past three years. This success is expected to continue in the future.

> Gains the manager's attention.

I agree with you that the increased volume of business has resulted in Allen Industries' facilities being inadequate. Renovation of our facilities would greatly benefit our company. Enlarging the facility would aid production and contribute to increased sales. Attractive, modern offices will boost the morale of our employees.

> Builds interest.

Relocation of our operation during renovation can be accomplished easily if we follow the proposed relocation plan that I have attached to this memo. Interruption of production should be minimal during the renovation process. Employees will readily accept this relocation plan because they look forward to the increased efficiency of the renovated facilities.

> Stimulates desire.

I recommend that you proceed with the renovation plan that you proposed.

> Gives a recommendation.

gw

Enclosure

FIGURE 9.7
Example of a *Good* Recommendation Memo

portation company has purchased a fleet of 25 trucks, 20 of which had their transmissions replaced in the first six months. The company wants the manufacturer to absorb the cost of the new transmissions. A work of art, which was purchased for $50,000, was found to be a forgery; the buyer demands reimbursement from the gallery that sold it.

Figure 9.8 is a **poor** special claim letter from Terry McNichols, owner of Terry's Antiques. Terry purchased an antique doll that was of lesser quality than advertised. Terry is upset and it shows in the letter. The receiver's attention may be gained in the opening paragraph but not in a way that will get the desired reaction. Terry clearly does not give the necessary details. The entire letter is negative, which will irritate the receiver and hinder getting the desired action—a refund.

The letter in Figure 9.9 covers the same situation but is a **good** message. Notice how Terry shows the receiver the benefits to be gained by adjusting the purchase price of the doll. The tone of this letter remains calm and explains the necessary details for the receiver. The positive approach will encourage cooperation from the receiver. Terry is courteous throughout the complaint but emphasizes that the doll is of lesser quality than advertised. Notice that the receiver may fax a response.

NEEDS WORK

TERRY'S
ANTIQUES
1230 MAGNOLIA DRIVE, GREENSBORO, GA 30642-1252
(404) 555-6891   FAX (404) 555-7733

February 23, 200–

Ms. Marie Coltharp
Wholesale Antiques & Collectibles
3245 Bayou Circle
Houston, TX 77040-2132

Dear Ms. Coltharp:

> **Is negative.**

I want the $2,700 back for the doll that I ordered because it is not of the quality that you promised.

> **Shows anger.**

You promised that the doll was of museum quality. It is NOT! Someone painted over several of the bad spots trying to hide the chips that the doll had. Your sorry antique may make me lose a good customer.

I want you to either send me back my $2,700 and I will return the doll, or I will keep the doll and you refund me $300 because it is not of the quality that you promised. I need you to let me know quickly so that I can tell my customer.

> **Demands action rather than makes a request.**

Sincerely,

Terry McNichols

Terry McNichols
Owner

FIGURE 9.8
Example of a *Poor* Special Claim Letter

The following table summarizes the approach used for the two types of claims:

Claim	Approach
simple or routine	direct
special or nonroutine	indirect

NOTE 9.28
Most sales messages are prepared by advertising professionals.

NOTE 9.29
A careful analysis of the product or service should be completed before composing the sales material.

Sales Messages

Sales messages come in many different forms, such as letters, brochures, leaflets, catalogs, radio and television commercials, and billboards. Most of these messages are prepared by advertising professionals; however, you may one day be asked to compose one.

Before you compose a sales message, know the product or service you are going to sell. Know its strengths, its weaknesses, its competitors, and its market. As you com-

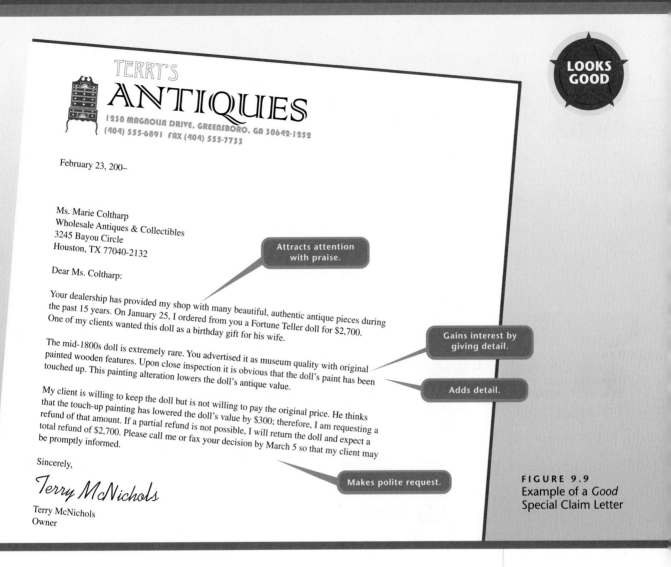

FIGURE 9.9
Example of a *Good*
Special Claim Letter

The letter in the figure reads:

Terry's ANTIQUES
1230 MAGNOLIA DRIVE, GREENSBORO, GA 30642-1252
(404) 555-6891 FAX (404) 555-7755

February 23, 200–

Ms. Marie Coltharp
Wholesale Antiques & Collectibles
3245 Bayou Circle
Houston, TX 77040-2132

Dear Ms. Coltharp:

Your dealership has provided my shop with many beautiful, authentic antique pieces during the past 15 years. On January 25, I ordered from you a Fortune Teller doll for $2,700. One of my clients wanted this doll as a birthday gift for his wife.

The mid-1800s doll is extremely rare. You advertised it as museum quality with original painted wooden features. Upon close inspection it is obvious that the doll's paint has been touched up. This painting alteration lowers the doll's antique value.

My client is willing to keep the doll but is not willing to pay the original price. He thinks that the touch-up painting has lowered the doll's value by $300; therefore, I am requesting a refund of that amount. If a partial refund is not possible, I will return the doll and expect a total refund of $2,700. Please call me or fax your decision by March 5 so that my client may be promptly informed.

Sincerely,

Terry McNichols

Terry McNichols
Owner

Annotations: Attracts attention with praise. / Gains interest by giving detail. / Adds detail. / Makes polite request.

LOOKS GOOD

---

pose the message, emphasize the strengths and omit any mention of weaknesses. Your market should be researched carefully to determine how to appeal to your customers and to get their business.

Various techniques are used in sales messages to gain the receiver's attention: color, sentence fragments, catchy slogans, famous quotations, testimonials from celebrities, and descriptions of benefits. A salutation is frequently omitted from the message.

Once you gain the receiver's attention, you must maintain his or her interest to ensure that the entire message is read or heard. A careful analysis of the receiver is critical in preparing the message from the receiver's point of view. Extra care must be taken in the analysis of the receiver because sales messages are usually prepared for multiple receivers.

A **poor** sales message to the Russells about a golfing vacation is shown in Figure 9.10. This message is not written from the you–viewpoint. The letter fails to point out the benefits of the vacation resort. The resort's features are given, but Ms. Burgess does it in a negative manner. The request for action is weak. How should the customer "let us know"?

NOTE 9.30
Receiver's attention is gained through different techniques.

NOTE 9.31
An interested receiver will hear or read the entire message.

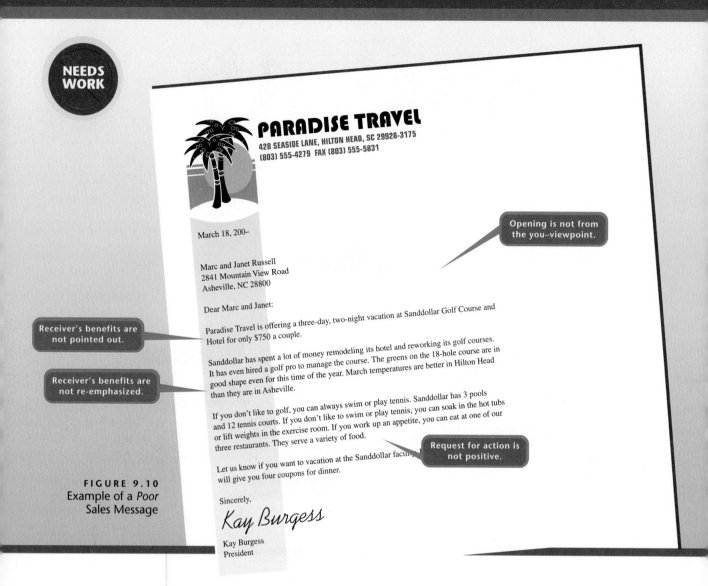

PARADISE TRAVEL
428 SEASIDE LANE, HILTON HEAD, SC 29928-3175
(803) 555-4279 FAX (803) 555-5831

March 18, 200–

Marc and Janet Russell
2841 Mountain View Road
Asheville, NC 28800

Dear Marc and Janet:

Paradise Travel is offering a three-day, two-night vacation at Sanddollar Golf Course and Hotel for only $750 a couple.

Sanddollar has spent a lot of money remodeling its hotel and reworking its golf courses. It has even hired a golf pro to manage the course. The greens on the 18-hole course are in good shape even for this time of the year. March temperatures are better in Hilton Head than they are in Asheville.

If you don't like to golf, you can always swim or play tennis. Sanddollar has 3 pools and 12 tennis courts. If you don't like to swim or play tennis, you can soak in the hot tubs or lift weights in the exercise room. If you work up an appetite, you can eat at one of our three restaurants. They serve a variety of food.

Let us know if you want to vacation at the Sanddollar facil... will give you four coupons for dinner.

Sincerely,

Kay Burgess

Kay Burgess
President

Opening is not from the you–viewpoint.

Receiver's benefits are not pointed out.

Receiver's benefits are not re-emphasized.

Request for action is not positive.

FIGURE 9.10
Example of a *Poor* Sales Message

A **good** sales letter is shown in Figure 9.11. Note how this letter stresses the benefits that the Russells will gain from the "Spring Fling." The subject line is effective in gaining the reader's attention. Mentioning golf and relaxation will build interest. Notice how the letter integrates the golf course and the other facilities of the vacation resort. Ms. Burgess makes it easy for the Russells to take action—to reserve their room.

LEARNING OBJECTIVE (5)
Write messages that are used for the various stages of collection.

Collection Messages

NOTE 9.32
Collection messages are designed to collect money and retain goodwill.
NOTE 9.33
Collection messages are written in three stages.

A collection message is used by businesses to collect overdue accounts. The two purposes of collection messages are (1) to collect the money due and (2) to retain goodwill with the customer.

Collection messages, generally, are written in three stages—reminder, appeal, and warning. Each stage is progressively more persuasive, and each stage has several steps.

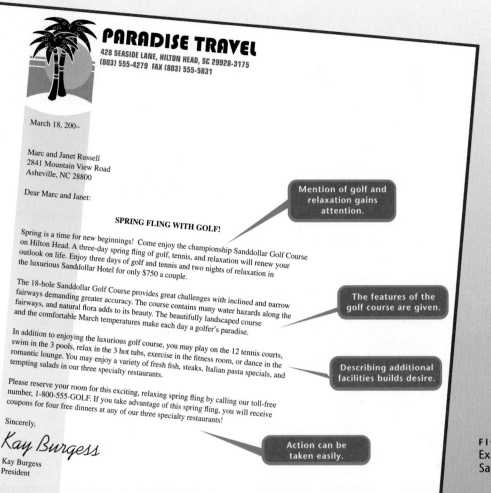

FIGURE 9.11
Example of a *Good*
Sales Message

The number of steps in each stage will vary according to the type of business involved and the credit rating of the customer.

Reminder Stage

The reminder stage is for customers who intend to pay but just need a reminder. The **reminder** is a simple and sometimes comical message intended to get a receiver to pay a bill. Collection messages in this category are direct and friendly; they must never offend the receiver. These messages are normally only short notes or a sticker on a bill.

Examples of collection messages in the reminder stage include the following:

Past Due

Reminder

Please Remit

NOTE 9.34
The reminder stage is for customers who forgot to pay.

NOTE 9.35
Comical sticker can be used as a reminder

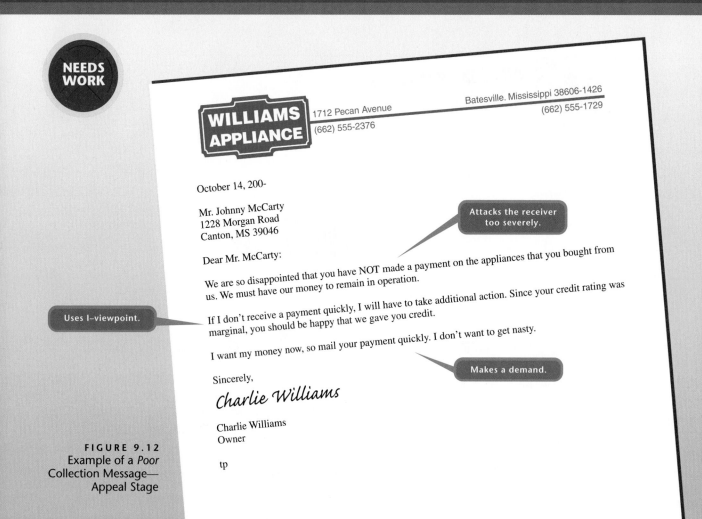

FIGURE 9.12
Example of a *Poor*
Collection Message—
Appeal Stage

Messages in the reminder stage are very courteous because failure to make a payment is often only an oversight. A harsh reminder may well alienate a customer who had intended to pay on time. If the reminder fails, the collection process will proceed to the appeal stage.

Appeal Stage

NOTE 9.36
The appeal stage must effectively persuade the receiver.

An **appeal** is stronger than a first-stage message because the customer has failed to heed the reminder notice. You need to analyze the customer carefully before writing a letter of appeal. You will have to select the type of appeal that will persuade the customer to pay. You may appeal to the customer's pride, credit rating, morality, or reputation. Once you have selected the type of appeal to use, construct the message using the indirect persuasive outline.

A **poor** collection letter in the appeal stage is shown in Figure 9.12. This letter is too harsh. It is written from the writer's point of view and will cause anger, which will reduce rather than increase the chances of collection. Necessary details such as the amount due are not furnished.

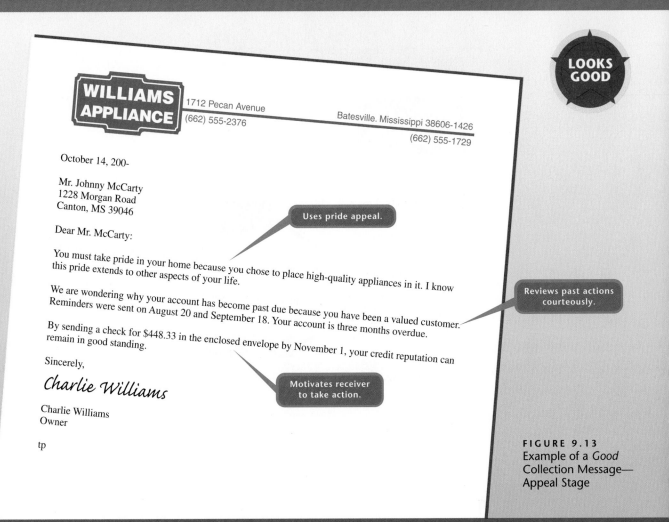

LOOKS GOOD

WILLIAMS APPLIANCE
1712 Pecan Avenue
(662) 555-2376
Batesville, Mississippi 38606-1426
(662) 555-1729

October 14, 200-

Mr. Johnny McCarty
1228 Morgan Road
Canton, MS 39046

Dear Mr. McCarty:

You must take pride in your home because you chose to place high-quality appliances in it. I know this pride extends to other aspects of your life.

We are wondering why your account has become past due because you have been a valued customer. Reminders were sent on August 20 and September 18. Your account is three months overdue.

By sending a check for $448.33 in the enclosed envelope by November 1, your credit reputation can remain in good standing.

Sincerely,

Charlie Williams

Charlie Williams
Owner

tp

Uses pride appeal.

Reviews past actions courteously.

Motivates receiver to take action.

FIGURE 9.13
Example of a *Good* Collection Message— Appeal Stage

The **good** collection letter in Figure 9.13 is recommended for the appeal stage. It is written in a positive, courteous tone. The opening paragraph will get the customer's attention by appealing to his pride. The customer should believe that the store is trying to help him maintain his excellent credit reputation. The store's chances of collecting are greatly increased with this letter.

Warning Stage

Reminders and appeals may not succeed in collecting all past-due bills. When these efforts fail, you must move into the final stage—warning. Until now, you were interested in maintaining the customer's goodwill while trying to collect. When the warning stage is reached, you are interested only in collecting the past-due amount.

A **warning** is the last opportunity for a customer to pay an account before it is transferred to a collection agency, a credit bureau, or an attorney. Use the direct plan to develop your message for this stage. Sending the warning letter by registered mail— so a signature is required—stresses the importance of the message and creates a sense of urgency.

NOTE 9.37
The warning stage is used only when the other stages have failed.

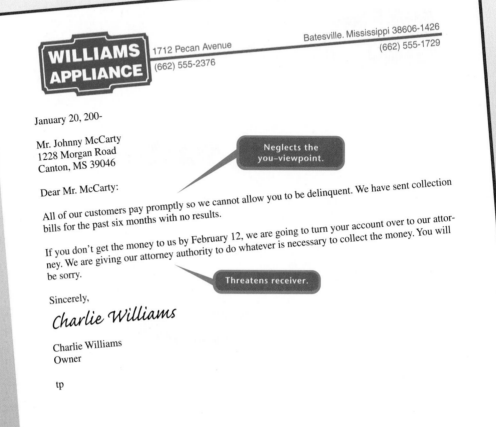

FIGURE 9.14
Example of a *Poor*
Collection Message—
Warning Stage

A **poor** warning stage collection message is shown in Figure 9.14. In this poor example, the customer will be inclined to resist because Mr. Williams does not get directly to the warning in a firm manner without displaying anger. Notice that the amount due is never given. The use of threats is illegal and will not increase the writer's chances of collection.

Figure 9.15 shows how a **good** collection letter in the warning stage should be written. This letter gets directly to the main idea—the customer's account is past due, and no attempt is being made to correct the problem. Facts are presented in a positive tone with no sign of anger. In the last paragraph, the customer is told exactly what must be done to avoid legal action.

Finally, let us summarize the approach that is used in each stage of collection messages:

Stage	Approach
reminder	direct
appeal	indirect
warning	direct

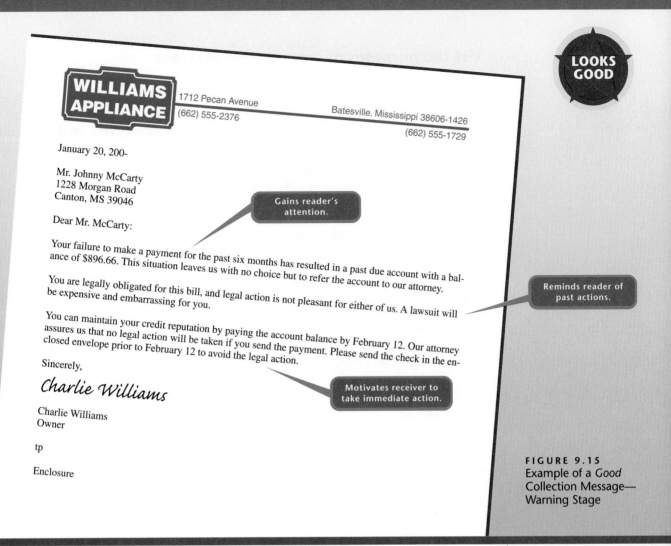

FIGURE 9.15
Example of a *Good*
Collection Message—
Warning Stage

Your use of the indirect plan outline will enable you to compose effective persuasive messages. The ability to do so will serve you well throughout your career.

Summary of Learning Objectives

Describe a persuasive message.

A persuasive message is (1) a request for action when you believe the receiver may be unknowing, disinterested, or unwilling, or (2) a communication to try to change the opinion of a receiver. These messages will be viewed as neither positive nor negative by the receiver and may be used in both internal and external communication. The supporting facts of persuasive messages must convince receivers that taking the requested action is in their best interest. Persuasive messages should almost always be presented using an indirect approach.

(2) List the purposes of a persuasive message.

The two primary purposes of a persuasive message are (1) to get the receiver to read or listen to the entire message, and then (2) to have the receiver react positively to the request.

(3) Describe the four specific guidelines for using the indirect plan for persuasion.

The four parts of an indirect plan for a persuasive message are the following: (1) Attention—the receiver's attention must be gained in the opening to ensure the message is read or heard. (2) Interest—benefits must be shown to hold the receiver's interest. (3) Desire—providing proof of the benefits will motivate the receiver to take action. (4) Action—make it easy for the receiver to take action and motivate him or her to take the action quickly.

(4) Write different kinds of persuasive messages using the indirect plan.

Use the indirect plan when preparing complex (persuasive) requests, recommendations, special claims, sales messages, some collection messages, and employment messages. The indirect plan for persuasion includes attention, interest, desire, and action.

(5) Write messages that are used for the various stages of collection.

The three stages normally used in collection messages are reminder, appeal, and warning. The reminder stage is a short, direct, polite message to a customer who simply forgot to pay. In the appeal stage, use the indirect plan for persuasion. When the other stages fail to collect, move to the warning stage. Messages in the warning stage are constructed using the direct plan and are not concerned about maintaining the receiver's goodwill.

Discussion Questions

1. What is a persuasive message? How does anticipated receiver reaction influence the organizational plan used to write a persuasive message? (Objective 1)
2. Why is analyzing your receiver important when planning a persuasive message? (Objective 2)
3. Describe different techniques that a sender may use to gain a receiver's attention in a persuasive message. What techniques should be avoided? (Objective 3)
4. Briefly describe the plan that should be used in organizing most persuasive messages. (Objective 3)
5. You have been advised by one of your better employees that another company may be calling you for a recommendation about him or her. Develop an outline you could use during the conversation with the propective employer. (Objective 4)
6. Explain why the following paragraph would be ineffective as the final paragraph of a letter to Becky trying to convince her to assume the duties of newsletter editor. Rewrite the paragraph to be more effective. (Objective 4)

> *Becky, if you feel that you can spare the time to be newsletter editor, I would appreciate your writing a letter stating so. Make sure that you let me know because if you don't accept, I will have to find someone else.*

7. Should you respond to all requests by using the same organizational plan? Explain. (Objective 4)

8. Explain why the following paragraph would be ineffective in opening a sales message. Rewrite the paragraph to be more effective. (Objective 4)

We need to sell many briefcases. Our warehouse is full, and bills need to be paid.

9. What are the purposes of collection messages? (Objective 5)

10. Are the objectives the same for all three stages of collection messages? Explain your answer. (Objective 5)

Application Exercises

1. Visit a business in your community and ask how the business uses recommendation letters when hiring new employees. Are there specific qualities, positive or negative, that the business uses to select the new employee? Be prepared to discuss your findings in class. (Objective 3)

2. Discuss several situations in which someone tried to persuade you to do something. Analyze the strengths and weaknesses of these oral or written messages. (Objective 3)

3. **InfoTrac.** Use InfoTrac to access article A78640278, "The Sales Letter Will Work if You Get It Write," by Jeffrey Gitomer. Read the article and answer the following questions:
   a. How should the sender of a sales message sign his or her name?
   b. What would be something extra or unexpected to include in a sales message?
   c. When writing a sales letter, where should you place the purpose of your letter?
   d. Can a product be oversold in a sales letter? Explain. (Objective 4)

4. Write a memo to your instructor recommending that students be permitted to work in teams to prepare class projects. (Objective 4)

5. Write an article that could be used in your school newspaper for recruiting new members to your communication club. (Objective 4)

6. **E-mail.** All of your grades in your business communication class except one have been good. The poor grade came at a time during which you were extremely busy with extracurricular activities. This one poor grade may lower your average for the class by one letter. Send a persuasive e-mail to your instructor asking that he or she permit you to do an additional assignment for extra credit. Use facts to support your persuasive message. (Objective 4)

There are Web exercises at **http://krizan.swlearning.com** to accompany this chapter.

Case Problems

Persuasive Requests

1. Your company has selected FreeMed Insurance to provide your employees a plan that takes advantage of tax laws. Individuals enrolling in the plan can pay their share of certain insurance premiums tax-free. The plan also permits employees to set aside money tax-free to help pay for expenses not covered by medical insurance. As director of human services, write a memo that would persuade employees to attend a meeting in which FreeMed personnel would be available to explain this tax-saving plan.

2. You are the business manager of Missouri Ostrich, Inc. The company's primary income comes from selling ostriches. The ostrich market, however, is not well established. A $25,000 payment on a loan is due on April 15, and you are unable to make the payment. Write a letter to Ruben Hurwitz, Loan Officer, Houston County Bank,

Mountain Grove, Missouri 65711-1402, requesting that payment be postponed for three months. You have some good birds that will be ready for sale in three months. Ruben will need to be persuaded because ostrich farming is new and risky.

3. Star Electric has provided electricity to the area for many years. Recently Star upgraded all of its wiring to fiber optics and is expanding into digital cable services. As marketing manager for Star Electric, write a letter that could be sent to residents in the area persuading them to take advantage of these services. These letters may be sent to current as well as potential electrical customers. Add details to make it a complete letter.

4. **Global.** You are program director for the student economics organization on your campus. You have done such an outstanding job that you have been asked to obtain the keynote speaker for this year's state conference. You would like to get an economist from Germany. Write a letter to the head of the economics department at the University of Heidelberg in Germany requesting that he or she furnish a speaker at no cost, except travel-related expenses, for the state conference. Add details needed to make this a complete request.

5. You live on the corner of 15th and Vine Street. There have been a number of minor accidents in the past six months. You are concerned because several children in the neighborhood ride their bikes on this corner. Write a letter to the city manager, Ray Cantu, requesting the intersection be made into a four-way stop.

Recommendations

6. Alyssa Johnston has been working for you as a communication specialist for seven years. She is interested in advancing to a more challenging job, but your organization currently has no room for advancement. She has applied for the director of public relations position at Freeman International and has requested that you write a letter of recommendation for her. She has been an excellent employee for you, and you do not want to lose her; however, you feel obligated to write her a letter that would influence Freeman International to hire her. Write a complete letter of recommendation for her.

7. You are the president of the student government association for your school. Numerous students have complained of difficulty in finding parking spaces on campus. You have noticed an empty parking lot behind a vacant building one block from campus. Write a letter to the owner recommending that students be permitted to park on the lot during the week.

8. Samantha Clark was employed by your firm during the summer. She is attending college in your city and is applying for the William Bennett Scholarship. She has asked you to write a letter of recommendation for her. Add details to make the letter convincing and realistic.

9. The city in which you go to school needs a new administration building. One location being considered for the building site is a public park in the downtown area. If this park area is used, many beautiful old trees would be destroyed. An alternative location would be property owned by the city at the edge of town. Write a recommendation letter to the city officials persuading them to select the alternative site. Add details.

10. Tom Wilson is president of the local chapter of Business Leaders of the Future. He is interested in becoming the National President of Business Leaders of the Future. He has asked you to write a letter recommending him to the nominating committee. Supply details.

Special Claims

11. You and a friend have saved for a year to take a cruise during spring break. You contacted a reputable travel agency and purchased a five-day luxury cruise for $1,950. The cruise was a disaster. The rooms were too small, the food tasted as if it were cooked in the college cafeteria, the ship was too crowded, and the service was awful.

Write a special claims letter to your travel agency requesting a full refund for the cruise. Add details.

12. You hired Kane Lawn Service, a new company, to install lawn sprinklers and landscape the area surrounding your office building. Kane installed the sprinklers but did little to improve the appearance of the area around your building. The company billed your business $18,500 for the work. You have checked with other businesses who have had similar work done by other landscapers and found they were charged about $10,000. You selected Kane because it was a new company trying to get established in lawn service. Write a special claims letter to Kane requesting an adjustment in the cost to approximately $10,000.

13. You purchased a computer online and discovered when you unpacked it that it did not work. You called the company's technical support division and spoke to Rebecca Manning. On hearing the symptoms, Rebecca stated that the power supply was faulty and recommended that you return the CPU. When the replacement unit arrived, the monitor did not work. Experiencing these problems, you decide to return the entire computer for a full refund. Write a letter to CompuCo requesting a refund for the computer, including shipping costs. Add details to make the letter complete.

14. Mayes's Leadership analyzes a company and then provides personnel training seminars to improve the organization's operating efficiency. As human resources director, you hired Mayes's Leadership to improve the morale and reduce absenteeism. Mayes's conducted many seminars for all levels of employees and managers over a three-month period. Nine months later you have noticed no significant improvement. In fact, absenteeism has increased and morale is at an all-time low. Write a letter to Mayes's Leadership requesting a refund of $95,000 for its consultant work. Add details.

15. You and your siblings planned a party on October 12 for your parents' 25th wedding anniversary. As part of this celebration, you made a verbal agreement with The Emotions to play live music for four hours. They charged $3,000 of which you gave them $1,500 as a down payment. On October 12, The Emotions did not show. When you contacted them, you found that they thought they were booked for October 19. Write a letter asking them to refund your $1,500 down payment.

Sales Messages

16. The service organization, We Care, is having a Demolition Derby for a fund-raiser. You have been asked to develop a sales message that could be placed in the local newspaper. Add details and be creative so that the ad will attract spectators to the event.

17. **Teamwork. Global.** You are a member of your school's Humanities Student Association, which has decided to organize a retired-persons' tour to the Black Forest of Germany for its service project. Several tasks must be accomplished for this project. Your tasks include the following:
    a. Contact a travel agency or airline to obtain airfare information.
    b. E-mail a tourist information office in one of the towns in the Black Forest area to obtain necessary information for developing a sales letter about the tour.
    c. Find the exchange rate for German deutsche marks to U.S. dollars.
    d. Write a form letter that could be sent to the retired people in the area advertising this tour. The letter should include the cost of the tour (airline tickets, lodging, food, and ground transportation). Have interested individuals send a deposit for the tour.

18. Arnold's Fitness Center provides a complete program for a healthy body. It offers aerobic classes, seminars on nutrition and stress management, weight training, and a variety of exercise equipment. Arnold's has hired you to create a flyer announcing a program for students interested in building and maintaining a healthy body. This flyer

will be placed on various bulletin boards on your campus encouraging students to enroll in the program. Create this flyer adding details.

19. Your student business organization has been contacted by Claudia's, a clothing boutique, for help in promoting a Valentine's Day sale. Claudia's would like your organization to sell coupons for $5 each. The boutique would be closed one evening, and the only way a person could enter the store would be with this coupon. In addition to admitting the person, the coupon would entitle the customer to free refreshments and a 25 percent discount on all purchases. Claudia's would donate all of the coupon monies to your organization. Design an advertisement that could be used in the local or school paper to help your organization with this fund-raiser.

20. Andy Gatts is starting Andy's Web Creations, a small business that will build Web pages for organizations. Andy's can customize Web pages to meet the needs of a client's organization—as complex or as simple as desired. Fees to create Web pages are based on an hourly rate. Write a letter that Andy can send to organizations in the area inviting them to investigate his services. Add details.

Collection Messages

21. Patsy Simmons owns a large condominium complex. Approximately two years ago she hired Jimmy Gee, a local plumber, to renovate the plumbing in the complex. Jimmy completed the renovation and sent her an invoice for $32,500. Patsy has not paid any of the charges and has not responded to any of the numerous appeals that Jimmy sent her. Jimmy would like you to write a letter to Patsy asking for the money and informing her that if the money is not received within three weeks, he is going to contact his attorney. Add details to make this a complete warning letter.

22. Kent Fulsom has been a credit customer of Thurman Furniture Store for eight years. He is a good customer but periodically fails to make payments on his account. He is currently four months past due ($235.81); several reminders have produced no response. As credit manager of Thurman's, write an appeal collection letter to Kent requesting payment.

23. Mary Lou's Family Cooking has been operating for 25 years. Several chain restaurants have moved into the area resulting in a highly competitive market. Mary Lou's currently owes an $18,750 balance for grocery products to Hillman's Wholesale. Payment is eight months past due. Because the bill has not been paid, you changed the policy for this restaurant to pay for all groceries on delivery. This policy has worked well, but Mary Lou's has made no payment toward the $18,750 past-due balance. Write a letter that will encourage the restaurant to begin paying on the past-due amount. You realize that it may take a year to reduce the balance to zero.

24. Hal Montgomery purchased a ring from your jewelry store when he became engaged to Kimberly Fairbanks, the daughter of a prominent family in the community. The financial agreement that Hal signed when he purchased the ring stated that Hal would pay $550 down and $150 a month until the account was paid in full. The balance on the account is $1,450, and Hal has made no payment during the last eight months. Your appeal letters to him have produced no response, and he has not done any other business with your store. Write a letter to Hal informing him that he must pay the entire balance on the account or the debt will be turned over to a collection agency.

25. You are a new employee for Chapel Hill Gas Company. Your supervisor has asked you to use your creative talents in developing a simple message that could be used to remind customers to pay their bill that was overlooked. You want your message to be courteous and not alienate the customer.

Message Analysis

Correct the errors in the following letter that has been written to Bill and Emily Chadwick, who have not made a payment for the past five months on their home bought through Habitat for Humanity:

> *When are you going to begin making your monthly house payment? Since you moved into the house we at Habitat for Humanity remodeled for you, you have made only two payments on it.*
>
> *We at Habitat want our money. We made it clear to you that you were geting a good deal by paying the low 2% interest rate. We were able to provide this low rate because our Habitat members worked on the house for free and many of the materials were donated. We know that you were happy to get the lovely home for such low cost that we would hate to take it away from you. However, you must start making payments immediately or else we will have to give the house to someone else.*
>
> *We will be expecting to get your $260 check to cover this month's $210 payment and $50 to be applied to the past-due balance by March 15 or we will have to take other action.*

Grammar Workshop

Correct the grammar, spelling, punctuation, and word choice errors in the following sentences:

1. Employers expects employees to have writing skills that clearly communicates information.
2. Different cultures interpret gestures in different ways therefore care should be taken in using gestures.
3. Young investors that want a good retirement should invest in Stocks Bonds and Mutual Funds.
4. Last month Ricardo speak at Universities in Oxford, Mississippi, Dallas, Texas, Grand Forks, North Dakota, and Duluth, Minnesota.
5. Susan's parents could not hardly wait to congratulate her for graduating with Honors.
6. Voters have been turning out in steady numbers to cast early ballots in the Ennis School Districts $35 million bond election.
7. Harold set at the desk and begun his paper that was dew tommorrow.
8. Jose' learned to talk english in a class that he took at midwest college.
9. Troy ran the marathon and 100 meter dash threw the javelin and discus and participated in the mile relay during the Spring Meet.
10. Robert and Lisa Wilson are happy and proud of the arrival of their first, great, grandchild Zoe Frances that was born March 9.

Part

4

Written Report Applications

10 Business Research and Report Writing

LET'S TALK BUSINESS As a tax manager in a CPA firm, I conduct research as an integral part of my day-to-day responsibilities. Tax laws and cases related to them sometimes change on a daily basis, so we must do research before we can give a client advice about a certain tax position. In addition, we have to stay on top of all changes in the tax law in order to make sure our clients are not paying excess taxes.

Connie Cushing, CPA, Manager, O'Sullivan Hicks Patton, LLP

In this fast-moving, high technology society, it is imperative that CPA firms have online Internet access to a tax service that is updated daily. Knowing how to do effective, thorough research both online and by using printed tax service materials, law books, and tax books is very high in our criteria for job promotion.

Research and report writing are common activities in business. As Connie Cushing indicates in Let's Talk Business, research helps her advise clients about tax issues. Research can have other purposes, too. For example, it can be used to develop procedures, to test products, to explore markets, or to gather opinions. The results of research may be reported orally or in writing, informally or formally, to internal or external audiences.

Regardless of their purpose or destination, reports must be based on thorough, accurate, ethical research. Because the information gathered through business research becomes the basis for decisions by managers, research reports must be written and formatted to ensure readability and understanding. This chapter, which builds on the communication basics introduced in earlier chapters, is devoted to discussing research techniques and report writing, including formatting. Techniques for making effective oral presentations are discussed in Chapter 15. Because visual aids may be used in both oral and written communication, that topic is covered separately, in Chapter 12.

LEARNING OBJECTIVE

1

Identify and use the five steps for conducting research.

NOTE 10.1
Research has many uses in business.

Research Techniques

The systematic procedures used to conduct a business study are called **research methods**. Those who expect to pursue careers in any business field should know how to plan and conduct a research project.

NOTE 10.2
There is a common, overall approach for conducting business research.

The Steps in Conducting Research

The five steps in conducting research are

[1] Plan the research.

[2] Gather information.

[3] Analyze the information.

[4] Determine solution(s).

[5] Write the report.

Plan the Research

Planning the research includes stating the problem, setting the boundaries, identifying and analyzing the audience, and deciding on the procedures to be followed.

STATING THE PROBLEM

The **statement of the problem** is a clear, accurate, description of what is to be studied. Prior to finalizing the problem statement, managers or other key people might discuss what the research should accomplish or agree to conduct a preliminary investigation. Examining files, talking with employees, reading similar reports, speaking with vendors, or making inquiries are activities that could help the researcher(s) clarify what needs to be done. Here are examples of problem statements for studies:

NOTE 10.3
Problem statements can use either the statement or the question form.

- Determine ways to improve employee morale.
- Design a new procedure for processing online orders.
- What is the best city in which to locate a Southwest regional distribution center?
- Should we replace paper towel dispensers with air dryers in all public rest rooms?

Discussions held before research begins help clarify project goals.

Notice that the first two examples are statements whereas the last two examples are questions. Either form is appropriate.

SETTING THE BOUNDARIES OF THE RESEARCH

NOTE 10.4
What factors will you research?

Research needs to have boundaries. The scope, time schedule, and budget affect these boundaries for the project.

Scope The **scope** of the research is determined by the factors that will be studied. It is best to limit the amount of information you will gather to the most needed and most important factors. The factors for one of the problem statements given previously might look like this:

Statement of Problem: Determine ways to improve employee morale.

Factors:

[1] Salaries   [4] Work hours

[2] Fringe benefits   [5] Evaluation procedures

[3] Work assignments   [6] Recognition programs

You could research many other factors relative to improving employee morale, and you might want to consider some of them later. However, a clear and reasonable scope must be defined for every research project.

NOTE 10.5
What time schedule will you follow?

Time Schedule The person who assigns the project and the person who conducts the research should agree on a completion date. The schedule is set by working back from the report deadline. The **time schedule** should show the major steps in the research and report writing process and when each is to be completed. Figure 10.1 illustrates a time schedule known as a **Gantt chart**.

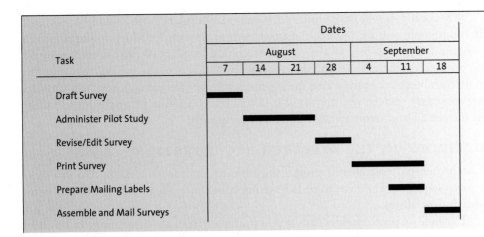

FIGURE 10.1
Gantt Chart

Task	Dates						
	August				September		
	7	14	21	28	4	11	18
Draft Survey							
Administer Pilot Study							
Revise/Edit Survey							
Print Survey							
Prepare Mailing Labels							
Assemble and Mail Surveys							

As you view the chart, notice that several tasks can be worked on at the same time. For example, you can prepare mailing labels while the survey document is being printed. Time schedules should include enough detail for everyone associated with the project to understand exactly what is to be done and when.

Budget All studies cost money. Even studies that are conducted within an organization will have some costs above normal operating expenses.

A large organization may use a charge-back system to bill one department for having work done by another. For example, if you are conducting a survey for the human resources department, the graphic arts department might charge your unit for printing the questionnaire and the final report. In addition, the information systems department might charge for processing the survey results. Other research costs could be incurred for items such as personnel time, supplies, and postage. All costs should be estimated and a budget approved before work begins.

NOTE 10.6
How much will the research cost?

DETERMINING THE AUDIENCE

Effective communication depends on using the you–viewpoint in all written and oral messages. This is certainly true for written reports. As Rob Duff notes in his Communication Quote, the way in which you write the results of your research should be determined by your readers' knowledge, interests, attitudes, and emotional reactions—the key factors in audience analysis.

NOTE 10.7
Analyze the primary and secondary receivers.

COMMUNICATION QUOTE

In my industry (consulting) many companies emphasize delivering documents with high "thud factors." In other words, if a report or study doesn't make a "thud" when a client drops it on her desk, she won't think she got her money's worth. This is based on the belief that an idea is not "professional" if it's not wrapped with the weight of many words. Effective communication, however, is as much an exercise in determining what to exclude from what you say or write as it is about determining what to include.

—Robb Duff, Principal Consultant, AVT Consulting, LLC. (Photo courtesy of Robb Duff)

When a report will have primary and secondary readers, both should be analyzed. If, for example, you are a financial manager writing a report for which colleagues in the field are primary readers, you can use the technical language of finance because it will be understood by other financial managers. If members of the general management staff, members of the production management staff, general employees, or stockholders are secondary readers, you may want to define your terms the first time you use them or include a list of terms and definitions as an appendix.

DECIDING ON THE RESEARCH PROCEDURES

NOTE 10.8
Outline the steps in the project.

Comprehensive research will result if the project is outlined and completed in a step-by-step sequence. The steps to be followed in completing the project are known as **research procedures**.

Deciding on procedures for each step in your research means determining exactly how to carry out that step. Although the procedures you actually select will vary from project to project, the following can serve as an example of things you may wish to consider:

- Will I invest the money and time required to gather current data?
- Will I use information that is already printed about the topic?
- Will I survey employees?
- Will I seek information from outside the company?
- Will I use a computer to gather or analyze the information?
- Will the report be printed internally or externally?

NOTE 10.9
Surveys must have validity and reliability.

When conducting research, you may want to seek the advice of one or more specialists. If, for example, you are going to use statistical procedures to analyze survey data, you could seek the help of a statistician. He or she can assist with sample selection and help ensure that your survey has validity and reliability. **Validity** means the survey measures what it intended to measure; **reliability** means the survey is likely to produce consistent results.

Gather Information

NOTE 10.10
Information sources can be primary or secondary.

You may gather information for your research from one or more sources. There are two types of information sources: secondary and primary. **Secondary sources** of information are the published materials on the topic. **Primary sources** include individuals, company files, observations, and experiments.

If your research requires gathering information from both primary and secondary sources, gather secondary source information first. The published information may contain good ideas on what primary information you should gather and how to gather it.

SECONDARY SOURCES OF INFORMATION

Published materials on most topics are readily available in company, public, and college libraries. Experienced reference librarians can provide valuable assistance in finding published information that will be helpful in your research. They can direct you to print or electronic indexes, catalogs, reference books, government documents, computer databases, and other helpful secondary sources of information.

NOTE 10.11
Carefully evaluate all sources.

When gathering secondary information, be sure to evaluate the sources carefully. Not all information found in print or available through the Internet is accurate. When examining a print source, consider the following items:

One Big Happy

- *Timeliness.* Is the information current?
- *Relevance.* Is the information related to the specific topic I am researching?
- *Approach.* Is the work an opinion piece or a research report? Are opinions supported by facts or research? Is the research complete and thorough? Was appropriate methodology used to conduct the study? Is the research unbiased?
- *Outlet.* Is the publication reputable? Was a review process used to screen the work for publication? Who are the reviewers? What are their qualifications?
- *Author.* Is the author an authority in this particular area of research? What are his or her credentials and reputation in the field?

Because no one controls who posts what to the Internet, you will want to consider the following if your secondary information source is a Web site:

- *Type/Purpose.* Is the site a personal page or one geared toward advocacy, marketing, information, or news? For help in distinguishing among the categories, consult the Harvard University Widener Library site at http://www. widener.edu/Wolfgram-Memorial-Library/ and access the section on evaluating Web pages.
- *Sponsor.* Is the page owner a group, organization, institution, corporation, or government agency?
- *Perspective.* Does either the author or the sponsor bring a bias to what is posted at the site?
- *Author/Contact Information.* Who wrote or gathered the materials? What credentials does the person or group possess? Can the credentials be verified?
- *Completeness.* Does the site include up-to-date links to other relevant sites? Are links purely internal (same site), exclusively external (outside site), or mixed?
- *Attribution.* Is the information contained at the site original? If not, have the authors appropriately cited their sources?
- *Timeliness.* How current is the information? When was the site last updated?

Many university libraries offer advice to students about how to evaluate Web sites. In addition to the Widener Library site mentioned previously, you may find the site http://thorplus.lib.purdue.edu/%7Etechman/eval.html to be useful.

Traditional Searches An assortment of reference materials can be used in conducting library research: handbooks, almanacs, yearbooks, encyclopedias, dictionaries, books, periodicals, reports, directories, government publications, and audiovisual materials. Figure 10.2 briefly explains each source.

FIGURE 10.2
Traditional Reference
Sources

Reference Sources Used in Conducting Research

Handbooks and Almanacs	These sources can assist you in developing a brief topic overview. Examples include *AMA Management Handbook, Handbook for Business Writing, Handbook of Accounting and Auditing, The Real Estate Handbook, The World Almanac and Book of Facts,* and *Insurance Almanac.*
Yearbooks and Encyclopedias	These reference materials cover a full range of business topics. Most yearbooks are published annually and include statistical information and important events during the year. Encyclopedias include histories of important events and people, definitions of terms, and comprehensive coverage of various subjects. Examples include *Business Statistics, Statistical Yearbook, Collier's Encyclopedia, Encyclopedia Americana, The Encyclopedia of Associations, Encyclopedia Britannica,* and *Encyclopedia of Business Information Sources.*
Dictionaries	Dictionaries provide brief definitions. Examples include *New Webster's Dictionary of the English Language, Webster's Unabridged Dictionary, Dictionary of Business and Management,* and *The Business Dictionary.*
Books	Hundreds of business books are published annually. For recommendations, consult a book review publication such as *Bibliographic Guide to Business and Economics, Subject Guide to Books in Print, Business Periodicals Index,* or *Publisher's Weekly.*
Periodical Literature	When searching for periodical literature, begin with a subject index. *Business Week, Forbes, Fortune, The Economist, Financial Times,* and *Wall Street Journal* all have subject indexes.
Reports	Corporate annual reports, market research reports, and various census reports are published for private, limited circulation and may be obtained directly from the company to which they apply.
Directories	Business directories provide entries for companies, products, and individuals. Directories are considered essential for marketers and others who are prospecting. Examples include *Directory of Directories, AT&T Toll Free 800 Directory, Mail Order Business Directory, Standard & Poor's 500 Directory,* and *Official Airline Guide.*
Government Publications	The United States government is one of the largest publishers of business information. The subject areas are varied. *Guide to Popular U.S. Government Publications, Directory of Government Document Collections & Librarians,* and *Free Publications from U.S. Government Agencies* illustrate the range of available government publications.
Audiovisual Materials	Audiovisual materials include motion pictures, filmstrips, videocassettes, videodiscs, slides, transparencies, computer programs, and audiocassettes. Audiovisual materials are available from sources such as *Ambrose Video Publishing, Inc., AV Market Place, Books on Cassette,* and *Dartnell.*

Adapted from Ernest L. Maier, Anthony J. Faria, Peter Kaatyrude, Elizabeth Wood, *The Business Library and How to Use It*, Detroit, Mich.: Omnigraphics, Inc., 1996.

©MICHAEL NEWMAN/PHOTOEDIT, INC.

Secondary research encompasses both traditional and electronic sources.

Computerized Searches Of particular value to businesspeople today are computerized searches of published information on a given topic. Most reference librarians can assist you in searches that quickly give you an up-to-date bibliography of materials on your topic. In addition, they can guide you to databases that have periodicals available in full text.

Computerized sources can be categorized as either commercial or open access. As the name implies, **commercial sources** require users to pay for materials, which may be provided online or as a CD. Many business periodicals, newspapers, and journals offer subscriptions to online versions of their publications. In addition, professional associations may make databases or other resources available to members either free or for a modest fee. Professional organizations may also sponsor newsgroups, listservs, or chat rooms where members can pose questions. Although these online forums can provide leads to reputable sources, they are seldom viewed as credible in and of themselves.

Open-access sources are available free to anyone who has access to the Web. Because anyone can publish anything and post it on the Web, finding good material related to your topic can be challenging unless you have a search strategy. Begin by using a **subject directory**, a hierarchically organized index of subject categories similar to those found in books. These indexes will help direct you to the Web site with information on your research topic.

Once the appropriate subject is identified, an in-depth search can be completed using a search engine. **Search engines**, also referred to as *spiders* or *crawlers,* require the use of keywords pertinent to your area of research. Although all search engines perform the same task, it is unlikely that any two will produce identical results. If you do not obtain the results you want from one search engine, try others.

Because of the growth in the number of search engines, **multithreaded**, or "**meta**," search engines have been developed. Users enter their query only once, and the engine searches multiple databases concurrently.

More information about search engines, metasearch engines, and Internet directories is available at sites such as Search Engine Watch, **http://www.searchenginewatch.com**, or Search Engine Showdown, **http://www.searchenginesshowdown.com**. Clearly defining the research topic will help you select the keywords to use during a search. Most

NOTE 10.12
Reference librarians can assist you in locating print and electronic sources.

NOTE 10.13
Some computerized sources are free; others have access fees.

NOTE 10.14
Subject directories are similar to indexes in a book.

computer searches follow the principles of Boolean logic, which relies on three operators: *OR, AND,* and *NOT.* Search engine sites typically offer suggestions on how to use these operators effectively.

When you find a good source, either record the Universal Resource Locator (URL) or save it as a bookmark on your browser. Keep all of your bookmarks in a booklist that acts as a personal menu.

NOTE 10.15
Accurately cite all sources.

Be sure that you get complete bibliographic information on published materials while you work with them so that it will be available for footnotes or text citations and the bibliography. Most published materials are copyrighted. You may have to obtain permission to use such information, and you will be required to give credit to the originator as the source. **Plagiarism** is using someone else's ideas or words without giving him or her credit. To avoid plagiarism you must correctly document information found in all data sources including the Web. Information on documenting sources is given in Appendix B. Plagiarism and paraphrasing are also discussed in the copyright and fair-use communication sections of Chapter 3.

PRIMARY SOURCES OF INFORMATION

NOTE 10.16
Primary sources provide unpublished information about the topic.

Your research may require gathering original information—information about your topic that has not been published previously. This primary information may come

---

COMMUNICATION NOTE

The Audit Interview As part of their work at client sites, auditors may be called on to interview people about operations and procedures, about internal controls and, occasionally, about the honesty and integrity of management and employees. The following ten steps help auditors frame and conduct constructive audit interviews.

1. *Prepare.* Review relevant documents and make notes about the areas to explore.
2. *Think as you go.* For greatest flexibility, work from a list of key points rather than a list of complete questions.
3. *Watch nonverbal behavior.* People behave differently when relaxed than when stressed. Watch how people behave when asked easy questions; then, compare that behavior with that exhibited when the questions get tough.
4. *Set the tone.* Prepare an introduction that creates a professional impression, enlists cooperation, and explains the nature of your inquiry.
5. *Pace your questions.* Begin by asking easy questions; establish a comfortable rapport without having the interviewee become put off or suspicious.
6. *Do more listening than talking.* You need to give information to get information, but speak only about 25 percent of the time.
7. *Be straightforward.* Be honest and open. If you are "cagey," your subject may become withdrawn or defensive.
8. *Take your time.* Trust your instincts; keep pressing—in a nice way—for answers.
9. *Double-check the facts.* Near the end of the interview, recap what's been said to ensure you've got the story right.
10. *Get it in writing.* If the interviewee admits to wrongdoing, get it in writing then and there.

Adapted from "Ten Steps to a Top-Notch Interview" by Joseph T. Wells; *Journal of Accountancy,* 00218448, November 2002, Vol. 194, Issue 5.

from an examination of original company records, a survey of knowledgeable individuals, a focus group, an observation of an activity, an experiment, or as described in the Communication Note on the previous page, an interview.

Original records and files are obvious sources of historical information that may be helpful to you. Other sources of primary information—surveys, focus groups, observations, and experiments—may not be as obvious.

Surveys To gather opinions and facts from individuals, you can survey them. Surveys can be conducted face to face, by telephone, by mail, or electronically. One of the most common survey methods is described in the following Communication Note.

NOTE 10.17
Surveying people is a way to get primary information.

COMMUNICATION NOTE

Getting Feedback about Customer Service One of the most common methods of getting feedback about the quality of customer service is the comment card.

- In restaurants, cards are placed in containers on tables or presented to diners with their bill. Cards may be left at the restaurant immediately after the dining experience or completed and returned at a later date.
- Lodgers may find comment cards on the desk or night table in their guest room or have the card presented with their bill at checkout. The procedure for returning the card parallels that used at restaurants—cards may be left at the checkout desk or completed and returned after departure.
- Retail store associates may present comment cards to shoppers immediately after completing a purchase transaction or include a card with the merchandise receipt.

Comment cards work well in situations where transactions are quick and uncomplicated. Mail or telephone surveys are the preferred methods for getting customer service feedback in situations where transactions are lengthy or complex.

Each survey method has advantages and disadvantages. Compared with other survey methods, face-to-face interviews are expensive. Personnel must be trained, scheduling and conducting the interviews is time-consuming, and transportation can be costly. The process does, however, produce the most in-depth responses.

Telephone surveys can be conducted fairly quickly and can be relatively inexpensive if done within a local calling range. Those who conduct the interviews generally read from a script and are cautioned not to deviate from it, so training costs are minimized. Response rates for telephone surveys will generally be higher than for those conducted by mail, but establishing credibility can be challenging in an era when reactions to telemarketing are negative.

Because they require fewer people to conduct them, mail surveys are generally less expensive than telephone or face-to-face surveys. The process is quite slow; it can take months to get an acceptable number of responses, even with follow-up mailings to those who don't respond to the initial mailing.

Electronic surveys may be conducted online through a Web site or via e-mail. In a Web-based survey, e-mail is sent to potential respondents inviting them to complete the survey located at a particular URL. This method enables the researcher to incorporate color, graphics, and audio features into the survey. In addition, the software used to create the survey can be programmed to collect data automatically and to generate

NOTE 10.18
E-mail and Web-based surveys are becoming popular.

Trained personnel conduct in-person surveys.

©SPENCER GRANT/PHOTOEDIT, INC.

ongoing data summaries. See Figure 10.3 for an example of an online questionnaire used by AmericanWest Bank to get feedback from its customers.

The simplest way to conduct an e-mail survey is to embed the questions into a message that is sent to potential respondents. Receivers are told to use the reply function and answer the questions as they scroll through the message. The simplicity of this method is offset by the limits placed on the researcher's ability to incorporate emphasis techniques such as type font and size variations, color, and graphics into the document. Pretesting the survey is essential to ensure alignment is maintained through transmission and to verify that entering a response will not adversely affect the format of subsequent items.

One way to overcome concerns about format is to send the survey as an e-mail attachment. The respondent can download the attachment and use a word processing program to respond. The completed survey can then be sent as an e-mail attachment to a "reply" message. The number and complexity of steps in this process may deter people from responding. Another, perhaps stronger, deterrent is the respondent's fear of infecting his or her computer with a virus passed through an e-mail attachment.

Regardless of whether e-mail surveys are embedded or attached, their response rate could be negatively affected by the lack of anonymity associated with e-mail transmissions. In addition, e-mail is very easy to ignore or delete, especially if it spans multiple screens.

When designing a questionnaire, be sure to follow the principles of business communication. The following guidelines may also be useful:

NOTE 10.19
Questionnaires used in surveys should be developed carefully.

- *Develop the survey questions from the factors being studied.* In a survey to assess employee morale, you might develop questions to seek opinions or facts about employee salaries, fringe benefits, work hours, and so forth.

FIGURE 10.3
On-line Questionnaire

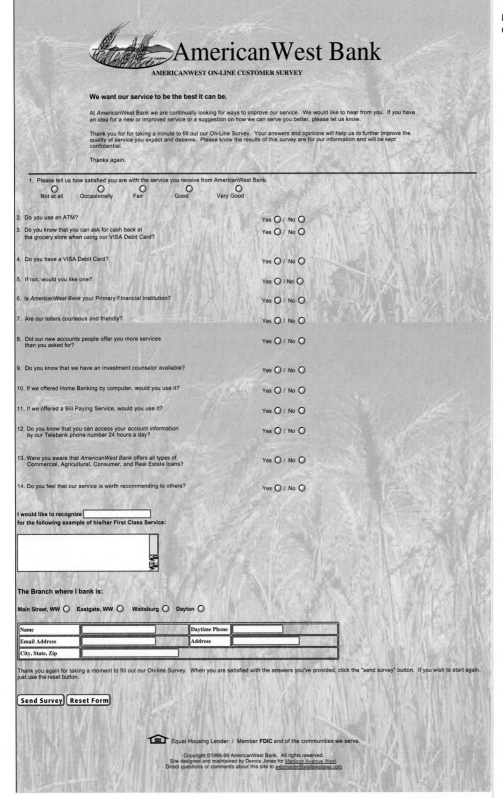

- *Sequence questions appropriately.* Start your questionnaire with easy questions that will encourage respondents to continue. Group similar topics. For example, put all questions on salaries in the same section. Arrange questions in logical order—the way people commonly think of the topics.

- *Use clear questions.* Phrase each item so that it will be interpreted uniformly by all respondents. A question such as "What kind of car do you own?" is vague. Based on the respondents' interpretations, the answers could be *convertible, Chevrolet, sports, foreign,* and so on. An example of a clearer way to obtain specific information is, "Please indicate the name of the manufacturer of the car you drive most often."

- *Ask only for relevant demographic data.* If factors such as age, gender, marital status, income, and so on won't be used in your analysis, don't ask respondents to provide the data.

NOTE 10.20
Leading questions produce biased responses.

- *Avoid leading questions.* Leading questions influence respondents to give a biased answer. Questions such as, "Would it be a good idea to improve the arrangement of our work hours?" will likely be biased toward a yes answer. A better method would be to ask the respondent to rate his or her satisfaction with current work hours. The rating could be along a numeric (e.g., 5 high, 1 low) or verbal (e.g., very satisfied, satisfied, dissatisfied, or very dissatisfied) indicator known as a **Likert scale**.

- *Provide for all expected responses in the answer options.* When it is not possible to be inclusive, use an "other" option and encourage respondents to write an explanation.

- *Avoid skip-and-jump directions.* For example, "If your answer to Question 9 is no, skip Questions 10, 11, and 12 and go directly to Question 13. If your answer is yes, also answer Question 10, but skip 11 and 12 if you do not have children."

NOTE 10.21
The two basic types of questions are open-ended and forced-answer.

- *Choose the appropriate type of question.* Forced-answer questions will outnumber open-ended questions in mail, telephone, and electronic surveys; the opposite is true in face-to-face interviews. **Open-ended questions** let respondents answer in their own words. These kinds of questions must be worded carefully in order to obtain the desired information. Data obtained through open-ended questions can be difficult to interpret and analyze, which is why forced-answer questions are used wherever possible. In the

Blondie

forced-answer question style, the researcher provides possible answers to the questions, and the respondents choose among the alternatives. The possible answers should be discrete; that is, use 25–29, 30–34, 35–39 instead of 25–30, 30–35, 35–40. Provide lines or boxes for easy check-mark answers. The lines or boxes for the responses should precede the possible answers.

Once the survey has been drafted, field test or "pilot" it. The feedback you get from this process will assist you in revising the document prior to distribution.

Brief, attractively designed documents accompanied by a message that explains the purpose of the survey help to convey a professional image and encourage receivers to respond. One sheet of paper (8½ × 11, 11 × 14, or 11 × 17) printed on both sides and folded to resemble four "book" pages is more inviting than four single-sided, stapled pages. Including a confidentiality statement similar to that shown in Figure 10.4 also encourages receivers to reply and enables the researcher to code the questionnaires so that reminders or follow-up requests can be sent to those who do not respond.

NOTE 10.22
Questionnaires should encourage response.

No. *56*

Your individual responses will be kept confidential; data will be reported only in the aggregate. The number on this form will be used only to follow up with nonrespondents. Once an acceptable number of responses has been received, all documents linking surveys to respondents will be destroyed.

FIGURE 10.4
Confidentiality Statement

To save time and money, researchers usually send surveys to a selected number of people who are representative of a larger group. This type of survey is called a **sample survey**. A statistician can help determine how to select the sample, how many surveys to distribute, and the minimum number of responses necessary to draw conclusions about the entire group from responses provided by the sample.

NOTE 10.23
Surveys are usually conducted using samples.

Focus Groups When you are seeking ideas or feedback in qualitative rather than quantitative format, focus groups are an appropriate research method. These groups, frequently used in market research, involve 6 to 12 participants and a moderator. Clearly defined research objectives; thoughtful, well-prepared questions; unbiased, randomly selected participants representative of the target audience; and a trained moderator are critical success factors. A comfortable site that creates a relaxed atmosphere also contributes to success.

NOTE 10.24
Focus groups solicit qualitative data.

Under the guidance of the moderator, the group discusses a series of ideas or issues—the focus. The moderator must ensure that everyone's thoughts are heard and that no one is influenced by others in the group. The task of keeping records also falls to the moderator. Note taking is kept to a minimum during the session so that the moderator can concentrate on what is being said and keep the discussion flowing in an appropriate direction. Immediately after the session, he or she will summarize the positive and negative points that arose during the discussion. Reviewing a video- or audiotape of the session—made with full knowledge of the participants—makes this task easier. Information from the notes and tape(s) will be used when the moderator prepares his or her report.

Online Focus Groups Judith Langer is president of Langer Associates, Inc., a qualitative research firm that has conducted some online research and plans more investigation of the medium. While recognizing that online focus groups have advantages, Langer acknowledges that questions need to be answered through further research. Among the questions she raises are these:

- Are respondents who they really say they are? Is the information they provide when signing up on the database or at the time of screening for a particular focus group true? How can we be sure that someone else hasn't substituted for them?
- How often should online respondents participate? Some may be signing up regularly because they enjoy the experience and/or the incentives.
- Are online focus groups less likely to be free of group dynamics bias than in-person ones, or do they just have different dynamics?
- Does the anonymity of a screen name make online respondents more honest, saying what's really on their minds rather than being polite? Are they more open about sensitive subjects? And is the bluntness and so-called *flaming* in chat rooms true candor or just rudeness?
- Are focus groups in this interactive medium truly interactive? How much moderator-respondent and respondent-respondent interaction really takes place if respondents are busy keying?
- Can researchers and observers gain a clear sense of individual respondents the way they can in physical observation?
- What ways can be found to encourage respondents to give longer answers rather than one- and two-sentence replies?
- How much is lost by the absence of body language and vocal inflection?

Taken from Judith Langer, "'On' and 'Offline' Focus Groups: Claims, Questions," *Marketing News* 34 (12), June 5, 2000, p. H38.

Although most focus groups are in-person events, online focus groups are possible. The technique is fairly new, however; and, as detailed in the above Communication Note above, several questions about it are yet to be answered.

NOTE 10.25
Observations may be used to gather primary information.

Observations Observation is another way to gather primary information for a research project. This technique involves one or more observers watching and recording facts about an activity. Although the observation technique can incur high personnel costs, it is a way to obtain precise information.

A common use of the observation technique is to gather information on how a worker operates a machine in a factory. The worker's repetitive movements might be timed, production records maintained, and conclusions drawn about the efficiency of the procedures. Similarly, observers might be posted in selected areas of cities to count out-of-state cars in order to get a measure of tourist traffic. Many managers and employers use informal observation to obtain information that is helpful to them in performing their jobs. This kind of information, although not scientifically obtained, can be of value in a limited way.

The observation technique requires careful control. All observers must look for the same thing and record their observations in the same way for the information to be of comparative value. Proper control requires that observers and subjects do not interact.

Experiments The last way to gather primary information for a research project is the experiment. Experiments in business are usually used to compare two ways of doing something so that the better way can be identified. For example, employees in one plant might be placed on a four-day workweek, while employees in another plant would be kept on a five-day workweek. The employees in the two plants would then be observed and surveyed periodically to determine their productivity and their satisfaction with work hours.

Another approach would be to conduct a presurvey and a postsurvey of a group of employees that you plan to change from a five-day workweek to a four-day workweek. In this approach, employees who are on a five-day workweek could be asked a series of questions about the effect their work schedule has on their productivity and job satisfaction. Then their five-day workweek would be changed to a four-day workweek. After three months, the employees would be asked the same set of questions they were asked before their work schedule was changed. Then the two sets of answers would be compared.

Experiments are not as common in business as they are in scientific laboratories, but experiments do have their uses. **Experiments** are used usually to compare two ways of doing something in similar settings. In an experiment, you can easily compare the old way with the new way, compare Method A with Method B, or test-market a new product. Experiments can be expensive. Carefully designed and controlled experiments, however, have provided businesspeople with much valuable information.

As explained in the previous sections, business research often involves gathering information from or about people. As the following Communication Note points out, the research should be designed to protect its subjects.

NOTE 10.26
The observation technique must be carefully controlled.

NOTE 10.27
Experiments may be conducted to gather primary information.

NOTE 10.28
Experiments are a good way to make comparisons.

COMMUNICATION NOTE

Research Oversight Business research is not the only type of research that must be designed with care. Faculty at colleges and universities also engage in research. Schools that have faculty engaged in research involving human or animal subjects will have policies governing such research. Those policies, which are designed to protect the subjects, are typically monitored by a committee or board that reviews the research procedures.

If your school is among those where faculty engage in research, you will want to learn more about its research policies and review procedures. Specifically, you will want to ask about whether and how the policies affect research projects conducted by students as part of their coursework.

Analyze the Information

NOTE 10.29
Analysis may be a short and clear or a long and complex process.

Once you have planned your research and gathered information, you are ready to begin your analysis. The information you gathered may speak for itself. It may clearly say yes to adopting a new procedure or product. The information you gathered may clearly say that employees overwhelmingly prefer the four-day to the five-day workweek. Under these circumstances, the analysis may take only a few minutes. On the other hand, you may have gathered a great amount of complex information. It may take you days, weeks, or months to complete the analysis.

NOTE 10.30
Analysis should be objective.

The word **analysis** means to look at the parts of things separately or in relationship to the whole. The various parts of your information are compared and contrasted in an effort to try to develop new or better ideas. Separate facts and figures are interpreted by explaining what they mean—what significance they have. You will not want personal bias of any kind to enter into the analysis. Use your brain power—objectively and unemotionally.

For example, if you were doing research to determine which computer to buy for your office, you would collect information on the type of work you are currently doing and the kinds of work you want to do. Next you would gather information on computers, including cost, software compatibility, speed of operation, machine capacity, machine dependability, maintenance availability, potential for upgrading, and other factors. Then you would compare the machines to determine how well they can do what you want done, what their potential is, how dependable they are, and so on. Once you have completed the analysis, you would be ready to determine solutions.

Determine Solution(s)

NOTE 10.31
Solutions may consist of conclusions and recommendations.

Based on your analysis, you will be ready to offer a solution or solutions to the problem you have been researching. Your solution will be framed as conclusions and recommendations.

A **conclusion** is an inference drawn from the facts; it is a reasoned judgment that you make from your analysis. If you were to select the most important ideas suggested by your analysis, these ideas would be your conclusions. Based on your conclusions, you could state the research answer or **recommendation**—the research solution. In formal studies and reports, you can draw conclusions from your analysis and state them separately from the recommendation(s).

The conclusions and recommendations must be based on the findings and your objective analysis, not your personal opinion of what a good solution would be. Your conclusions and recommendations for a report might look like this:

Conclusions

- Procedure B appears significantly more cost-effective than Procedure A in the two installations studied.
- Dependable equipment for implementing Procedure B on a wide-scale basis is not currently available.
- The XYZ Manufacturing Company currently has in stock 20 Model 3CA machines that can be used to implement Procedure B.
- The XYZ Manufacturing Company projects that it will have 500 Model 3CAs available within six months.

Recommendations

- Immediately lease the 20 Model 3CAs from XYZ and continue to compare Procedure A with Procedure B for three more months.
- Enter an option to purchase 500 Model 3CAs from the XYZ Manufacturing Company.
- If the additional research continues to show that Procedure B is significantly more cost-effective than Procedure A, exercise the option with XYZ to purchase the 500 Model 3CAs.

Write the Report

The final step in a research project is to write the report. This is an important step because you will want to present your results effectively. The writing process for reports parallels that for other messages. You will plan, draft, and finalize your report before submitting it.

The time and effort spent in researching and writing a report are wasted unless the report is read and understood. The probability that a report will be read and understood is increased when certain principles of formatting are followed. The remainder of this chapter discusses the various report types and the formatting principles to follow for effective report preparation.

NOTE 10.32
Written reports must be readable and understandable.

Report Types and Characteristics

Written reports vary from short, informal reports to long, formal reports. The language can vary from conversational, first-person language to highly structured, third-person language. This section provides a brief introduction to informal and formal reports; each type is then discussed individually.

Informal reports are generally brief. They can consist of a body and a title page or a body only; informal reports are often formatted as memos or letters. **Memo reports** communicate information to individuals within an organization. This style is used primarily for reporting routine information concerning day-to-day operations or to provide a written record. **Letter reports** use a letter format to present information and make recommendations to individuals outside an organization; a subject line may be used to identify the topic of the report. When formatted as correspondence, informal reports use side headings to guide the reader from topic to topic. This type of report rarely contains graphic aids and seldom draws on material from secondary sources. Informal reports are usually written in the first person (I recommend that . . .).

A **formal report** may consist of all or some of the following parts: title page, authorization message, transmittal message, table of contents, list of illustrations, abstract, body, glossary, appendix, and bibliography. The body of the report will span several pages and include multiple levels of headings. Content could be drawn from primary and/or secondary sources. Visual aids assist readers to interpret information presented as text. Formal reports are usually written in the third person (It is recommended that . . .). Recent trends, however, suggest that informality is acceptable in formal reports. The degree of formality is determined after the report originator has analyzed the receiver(s).

LEARNING OBJECTIVE
(2)
Distinguish between formal and informal reports.

LEARNING OBJECTIVE
(6)
Write formal and informal reports.

NOTE 10.33
Informal reports are shorter and less structured than formal reports.

LEARNING OBJECTIVE ③
Identify the types of informal reports.

LEARNING OBJECTIVE ⑥
Write formal and informal reports.

NOTE 10.34
Significant events and changes in a project are reported in a progress report.

Informal Written Reports

In business, the informal report is used much more frequently than the formal report. There are many different types of informal reports; three of the most common—progress, periodic, and technical—are discussed in the following sections. Some informal reports may fall into more than one of these categories. For example, a report could be classified as technical and periodic.

Progress Reports

A **progress report** (also called a *status report*) is used to inform readers about the status of a particular project. A report that flows upward within the organization assists managers in monitoring and making decisions about the project; one that flows downward or horizontally keeps participants or other interested persons informed. The report should inform the reader about the work that has been accomplished, the work that is being done currently, and the work that is scheduled to be done in the next reporting period. Any significant progress or problems should be discussed in the report. The frequency of the reports will depend on the type or nature of the project being discussed. An example of a progress report in memo form is shown in Figure 10.5.

Periodic Reports

A **periodic report** provides managers with statistical information at regularly scheduled intervals. These intervals may be daily, weekly, monthly, quarterly, or annually. Periodic reports

---

FIGURE 10.5
Progress Report

SANBORG MANUFACTURING

835 West Lake Road
Sparks, GA 31647-0137

Telephone (478) 555-3340
Fax (478) 555-3350

DATE: May 16, 200-
TO: All Employees
FROM: Matt Prima, Community Campaign Coordinator *MP*
SUBJECT: Campaign Update

Thanks to the generosity of Sanborg's employees, nearly $20,000 has been contributed during the first month of this year's Community Campaign. As shown in the following table, we are ahead of last year's totals and well on our way to achieving our $35,000 goal.

Department	Last Year			This Year		
	Donor #	Donor %	$	Donor #	Donor %	$
Accounting	10	56	1,175	11	65	1,230
Administration	31	65	3,565	30	64	3,685
IS	7	78	700	9	73	1,040
Maintenance	21	58	525	24	53	860
Marketing	19	46	3,180	33	57	4,020
Production	115	83	8,625	106	83	8,125
R&D	17	93	1,020	14	78	935

The campaign ends June 15, so please return your pledge form soon. If you've misplaced your form, phone Joan Ruprecht at 3367.

FIGURE 10.6
Periodic Report

DAILY SECURITY CHECK OF FACILITIES		
FAIRCHILD, INC.		
FACILITY	**TIME**	**RESULTS**
Conference Room		
Dining Area		
Human Resources		
Accounting		
Purchasing		
Advertising		
Laboratory		
Assembly Room		
Warehouse #1		
Warehouse #2		
Warehouse #3		
Parking Lot		
OFFICER'S NAME		
OFFICER'S ID NO.		
DATE		
OTHER INFO.		

follow no set format; many organizations use preprinted forms. A form used to indicate the security status of facilities is shown in Figure 10.6.

Technical Reports

A **technical report** conveys specialized or scientific information. There are no standard formats or organizational plans for technical reports. However, organizations will often specify particular formats and plans to be used for internal reports. Standardized formats make it easy for readers to scan reports for information of particular interest to them. An example of a technical report in letter format is shown in Figure 10.7 on page 270.

Technical terms need not be defined when a technical report is prepared for someone familiar with the terminology. If the reader does not have the appropriate technical expertise, however, words used in the report must be clarified. A good rule to follow is to remember the principles of business communication discussed in Chapter 4.

NOTE 10.35
Technical terms must be defined if they are likely to be misunderstood by the reader.

FIGURE 10.7
Technical Report

KIRKPATRICK TESTING/SERVICE

3477 Ridgeway Road, Chicago, IL 60602-3109
Telephone (224) 555-4490 Fax (224) 555-7861

November 17, 200-

Bridgewater Advertising Company
316A Willow Building
567 Main Street
Carbondale, IL 62901

TESTING RESULTS

On November 10, technicians collected carpet dust samples from various locations in your office
complex. Samples were sealed and delivered to our laboratory where they were examined.

Results

Sample No.	Location	CFU*/Gram	Primary Organisms	
1A	Reception Area	590,000 CFU/gm	Cladosporium Alternaris Other	90% <10% <10%
2A	Weber's Office	700,000 CFU/gm	Cladosporium Alternaris Other	90% <10% < 5%
3A	Jenkins' Office	800,000 CFU/gm	Cladosporium Alternaris Other	86% <10% <10%

*CFU=Colony Forming Units

Recommendations

Based on these results we recommend that the carpet be removed and tile or wood flooring
be installed. New flooring should reduce the allergy-like reactions you and your employees
have been experiencing. If you have questions about the data or this recommendation,
please phone.

K. P. Yuli

K. P. Yuli
Industrial Hygenist

Formal Written Reports

A formal report is prepared for and read by individuals in top levels of management
and possibly individuals outside the writer's organization. It may take from several
weeks to several months to research and write the report. These activities can be completed by one person or by a team.

A formal report generally contains three major divisions: the preliminary section, the body, and the supplementary section. A formal report may contain all or some of the following parts:

Parts of Formal Reports

[1] Preliminary Section
   a. Title Page
   b. Letter or Memo of Transmittal
   c. Table of Contents
   d. List of Illustrations
   e. Executive Summary

[2] Body
   a. Introduction
   b. Procedures
   c. Findings
   d. Analysis
   e. Conclusions
   f. Recommendations

[3] Supplementary Section
   a. Glossary
   b. Appendix
   c. Bibliography or Reference List

Figure 10.10 (see pages 280–291) contains an actual business report that features many of the parts described in the following sections. Although the report's authors adopted a format different from the one described in this chapter, the document is visually appealing and easy to follow; the style is consistent throughout. Appendix C contains a report that illustrates the content and format guidelines described in this chapter. This report is also visually appealing and formatted for readability. Although different in style, the reports have one thing in common—both were written to meet the needs of their audience.

Preliminary Section

The **preliminary section** contains all the parts of a report that precede the body. The specific preliminary pages included in the report will vary with the formality of the report. A discussion of the individual parts follows.

TITLE PAGE

A **title page** typically contains the title of the report; the writer's name, title, and department; and the date of submission. The name of the person or company receiving the report is used when reports are prepared for clients or others outside the organization. The title should indicate the purpose and content of the report.

Some organizations have specific guidelines for the preparation of title pages; others permit artistic freedom. If specific guidelines do not exist, the traditional format may be the best choice. In traditional format, each line on the title page is centered horizontally

NOTE 10.36
A formal report normally is written for upper management.

NOTE 10.37
All formal reports should contain a title page.

with equal vertical spacing between items. Titles containing more than one line are single spaced. The title should be all capitals; other lines may be either all capitals or initial capitals.

LETTER OR MEMO OF TRANSMITTAL

NOTE 10.38
A letter or memo of transmittal conveys and introduces the report.

The **letter** or **memo of transmittal**, if used, introduces the report to the reader. A report to readers outside the organization would contain a letter, whereas reports for internal use would contain a memo. In more formal reports, a preface or foreword may be used.

The letter or memo of transmittal should be concise and may be subjective—that is, the writer may offer a suggestion or opinion not supported by data. It may contain personal comments. The letter or memo may also refer readers to parts of the report of special interest or suggest special uses of the information. In general, any item worthy of discussion may be included in the letter or memo of transmittal. The message typically ends with a statement expressing appreciation for the opportunity to participate in the project.

TABLE OF CONTENTS

NOTE 10.39
Use a table of contents only when a report exceeds four pages.

A **table of contents** lists all major sections that follow it and the page on which each begins. Its purpose is to aid the reader in quickly locating specific information in the report. A table of contents normally is not used in reports of fewer than five pages. Section heads should be listed exactly as they appear in the body and should be connected to the page number by leaders (horizontally spaced periods). Page numbers are optional for subheadings. The table of contents normally is prepared after the report is typed or printed in its final form.

LIST OF ILLUSTRATIONS

NOTE 10.40
A list of illustrations summarizes the visual aids used in the report.

Visual aids are identified in a **list of illustrations**. The list may be on the same page as the table of contents, or it may begin on the page following the table of contents if the report contains more than four illustrations. The list of illustrations uses the same format as the table of contents, with illustration captions instead of section heads. A report may group all visual aids into one list of illustrations, or it may group each type (table, chart, graph, etc.) separately. This section is normally prepared after the report is keyed or printed in its final form.

EXECUTIVE SUMMARY

NOTE 10.41
An executive summary is a capsule form of the report.

An **executive summary** is a brief version of the report; it restates each section of the report in abbreviated form with an emphasis on findings, conclusions, and recommendations. Other common names for an executive summary are *summary, abstract, overview,* and *synopsis.*

The summary, which is approximately 10 percent of the length of the report up to a limit of two single-spaced pages, saves readers time by providing an overview of its contents. Reports that include a synopsis in the letter of transmittal generally do not contain an executive summary. Figure 10.8 illustrates an executive summary.

Body

NOTE 10.42
The body of a report may use the direct or the indirect approach.

Most formal reports will contain all the information presented in the sections discussed in this part of the chapter; however, some of the sections may be combined. The mate-

Introduction and Executive Summary

South Shore Investment Consulting, Inc. has been retained by the Bell University Foundation, Inc. (the Foundation) to conduct an Asset Allocation Modeling Study for the Foundation's endowed and other assets with a long-term investment horizon. The Investment Committee is seeking to determine the most efficient and effective portfolio construction to enable the foundation to meet its long-term growth and spending objectives.

Returns for all asset classes during the recent 10 to 15 years have been high relative to historic norms. South Shore believes that the returns realized in the traditional domestic stock and bond markets over the last decade are unlikely to be repeated into the next decade. The Investment Committee has expressed a desire to evaluate the alternative allocation strategies that might be appropriate for assets that will be invested in the Foundation's Long-Term Investment Pool and explore the benefits of continuing to utilize diversifying asset classes such as international equities and small cap domestic equities.

Following a brief review of the asset modeling process (Section II), South Shore presents an analysis of the Foundation's current asset allocation and four alternative asset allocations for consideration. It is generally accepted that the asset allocation maintained by an investor is by far the most important determinant of the returns and volatility of returns (risk) experienced over time. Although other investment policy–related issues and the selection of quality investment managers are also important, South Shore considers the selection of an appropriate long-term strategic asset allocation to be the most important issue under consideration.

The following observations summarize the analysis:

- The results of the analysis support maintaining significant equity exposure and increasing diversification among equity subsectors. With the exception of the most aggressively postured alternative allocation strategy, each of the allocations exhibits a higher return per unit of risk compared to the Current Portfolio due to the benefit of increased diversification.

- The use of a reasonable exposure to asset classes which are not closely correlated with domestic stocks and bonds can increase expected portfolio return while decreasing downside risk.

- The study supports the expectation that increasing total equity exposure increases the probability of achieving higher returns in exchange for greater volatility. The results of the study indicate that, even with as much as 80 percent of total assets dedicated to the equity sector, there is a high probability of achieving a positive rate of return over periods of five years or longer.

- Two primary long-term investment objectives for the Foundation's endowed assets are 1) growth net of inflation and 2) growth in spending. By diversifying and maintaining a significant equity exposure, the Foundation has a high probability of achieving a level of investment returns over long investment horizons, which would support the attainment of these objectives.

South Shore Investment Consulting, Inc.   Bell University Foundation, Inc.

Reprinted with permission; organization name and consultant's identification have been changed.

---

rial in the body may be presented using the direct or the indirect approach. The conclusions, recommendations, or both come at the beginning of the body when the direct approach is used; they come at the end of the body in the indirect approach.

INTRODUCTION

The **introduction** provides adequate background concerning the study so that the reader can understand the scope and sequence of the report.

BACKGROUND

The introduction often begins with the **background**, a general description of the problem that was studied, and the main issues involved in it. The background leads to the statement of the problem.

Statement of the Problem The **statement of the problem** clearly identifies the specific problem that was researched. The statement should be brief but informative.

Purpose of the Study The **purpose of the study** indicates why the study was conducted. The purpose should help convince the reader of the worthiness of the report. The purpose may be stated as a question ("Which insurance company will best serve our needs?") or as a statement ("The purpose of this study is to provide information for the selection of the insurance company with the most effective plan.").

NOTE 10.45
The purpose provides the reason for the study.

Scope The **scope** of the research is defined by the main factors that were studied and generally appears next in the introductory section. It lets the reader know the extent of the research. Boundaries set by the researcher as well as factors over which the researcher had no control are listed in this section of the introduction. These limitations can include lack of resources, lack of time, or geographic boundaries.

Related Literature **Related literature** is material collected while doing research on a topic being studied. A review of related literature may be included in the introduction if only a limited amount of literature is available about the topic. A separate section should be used when extensive amounts of related literature are reviewed.

Unfamiliar Terms Definitions of terms unfamiliar to the reader can be included in the introductory section. When many terms need to be defined, however, a glossary should be included in the supplementary section.

PROCEDURES

NOTE 10.46
The steps used in conducting the study are described in the procedures section.

The **procedures**, or methodology, section describes the steps taken in conducting the study. One purpose of this section is to allow readers to determine whether all aspects of the problem were adequately investigated. This section can also be used by another researcher to conduct a similar study that could validate or disprove the results of the original study.

FINDINGS

NOTE 10.47
The results of the study are presented in the findings section.

Findings are results discovered during the research. This section should be presented in a factual and objective manner without personal opinions or interpretations. Present all findings—positive and negative. Visual aids such as those presented in Chapter 12 can be used to assist the writer in communicating the findings of the study.

ANALYSIS

NOTE 10.48
Significant outcomes and relationships are discussed in the analysis section.

The **analysis** section contains the writer's interpretation of the qualitative or quantitative assessment of the findings. If prior research on the topic exists, the writer compares its results with the findings of the current study. Information in the analysis section assists the reader in determining which relationships are important. In a brief report, writers may describe and discuss their findings in one section.

CONCLUSIONS

NOTE 10.49
Conclusions are drawn from the findings of the study.

A **conclusion** is a statement of reasoning made by a researcher after a thorough investigation. The findings and analysis should support or substantiate the conclusions. In many studies, conclusions are summary statements of the content of the analysis section. No new data should be presented in this section. A study may have one or several conclusions. Because these statements become the basis for the writer's recommendations, the two sections may be combined.

RECOMMENDATIONS

A **recommendation** is the writer's suggestion to the reader as to the action(s) that should be taken to solve the problem that was studied. Recommendations should develop logically from the findings, analysis, and conclusions of the study. A study can result in one or more recommendations. If three or more recommendations are presented, they can be listed and numbered. This section may contain only the recommendations, or it may contain both the recommendations and the supportive reasoning for their development.

NOTE 10.50
Recommendations are based on conclusions.

Supplementary Section

The final section of a written report contains material that relates indirectly to the main topic of the study. This section may consist of one or more subsections, such as a glossary, an appendix, and a bibliography or reference list.

GLOSSARY

A **glossary** is an alphabetic list of terms used in the report with a brief definition of each. It is used only when numerous unfamiliar terms are included in the text. When the report contains only a few specialized terms, the writer should define them in the introduction or when they first occur in the text.

NOTE 10.51
Unfamiliar terms are defined in the glossary.

APPENDIX

An **appendix** contains related information excluded from the body to improve its readability. When appending two or more items, label each separately and identify it with a capital letter:

Appendix A: Computer Printout of Daily Sales
Appendix B: Sample Follow-up Letter

All appendixes should be referred to in the body of the report. If the material is not referred to in the body, it is not relevant enough to be included as an appendix. Some items commonly included as appendixes include questionnaires, computer printouts, follow-up letters, reports of similar studies, working papers, intricate tables, and supporting material.

NOTE 10.52
Indirectly related material is placed in an appendix.

BIBLIOGRAPHY OR REFERENCE LIST

A **bibliography** is an alphabetic list of all references used as sources of information in the study, including those that do not appear in footnotes or text citations. A **reference list** includes only those sources cited in the text of the report. Consult Appendix B or a reference manual for information on how to display entries for various sources.

NOTE 10.53
References are listed in a bibliography or reference list.

Mechanics of Formal Reports

The mechanics of a written report—format, spacing, and so forth—are as important as the mechanics of a letter or memo in that they make the first impression on the reader.

LEARNING OBJECTIVE
5
List the advantages of correct report formatting.

The reader's first impression of the report will be based on its appearance. A negative first impression may increase the time it takes for a reader to gain confidence in the report writer's credibility.

When preparing the document, the writer must consider general guidelines of report mechanics as well as the guidelines and policies of the organization. The primary consideration in the physical presentation of a written report is that the mechanics improve the readability of the report. Paragraphs averaging six to seven lines make it easy for the reader to concentrate on the written material. Proper spacing between paragraphs and correct margins make it easy for the reader to follow the material. Headings lead the reader from one section to the next by announcing the next topic.

Cover

NOTE 10.55
The cover provides
information and
protects the report.

The **cover** protects the contents of the report; therefore, it is often constructed of lightweight card stock. Information can be printed on the cover or displayed through a cutout section (window). The cover should be attractive and may contain an appropriate picture or drawing that will add to the impact of the report. Many organizations use preprinted covers on which the author can place the variable information. The items generally displayed on a report cover are the title, the name of the author, and the date the report was submitted. Normally, the title is in uppercase letters, and the author's name has initial capital letters. Covers usually are used only on long, formal reports.

Margins

NOTE 10.56
Margins add to the
attractiveness of the
report.

Proper **margins** are important because they create the white space that makes the report visually appealing to the reader. As a general rule, report margins should be 1 inch on all sides. However, reports that are bound at the left should have a $1\frac{1}{2}$ inch left margin, and reports that are bound at the top should have a 2-inch top margin. Preliminary parts, supplementary parts, and the opening page of major sections typically have larger (2-inch) top margins.

Spacing

NOTE 10.57
Most reports are single
spaced, but double
spacing is acceptable.

Reports may be **single spaced** or **double spaced**. The trend in business organizations is toward single spacing to reduce the number of sheets of paper that have to be handled. In reports using double spacing, paragraph indentations should be $\frac{1}{2}$ inch from the left margin; no space is added between paragraphs. Single-spaced reports should be double spaced between paragraphs; indenting the first line of the paragraph is optional.

Headings

NOTE 10.58
Structural or informative
headings may be used.

Appropriate headings help the reader follow the report organization and enable him or her to refer quickly to specific sections within the report. Sections that are of little interest can be skipped or scanned quickly.

Headings may be either informative or structural. An **informative heading** indicates the content of a section and orients readers so that they can more easily understand the material. A **structural heading** emphasizes the functional sections within the report. Once the type of heading is selected, it should be used consistently throughout the report. An example of each follows:

NOTE 10.54
The outward appearance
of a report influences the
reader of the report.

Informative Heading

CUSTOMERS' ATTITUDES TOWARD TELEVISION AS
AN ADVERTISING MEDIUM

Structural Heading

FINDINGS

The ways headings are presented vary according to the style manual used by the organization. Regardless of the method selected, consistency of presentation is vital. An explanation of one widely accepted method follows.

First-level headings (main headings) are centered on the page in uppercase letters. Main headings may be printed in boldface uppercase letters but preferably not in uppercase letters and underscored. **Second-level headings** (side headings) begin at the left margin, and the first letter of each main word is capitalized. Side headings are often italicized, underlined, or boldfaced for emphasis. The **third-level heading** (paragraph heading) begins one-half inch from the left margin, has the first letter capitalized, ends with a period, and is underlined or boldfaced. An example of this method is shown in Figure 10.9.

The headings at each level must be constructed so that they are grammatically parallel. For example, all first-level headings must be parallel; however, first-level headings do not have to be parallel with second-level headings. In the following example, the second-level headings are parallel, but the first-level headings are not:

INCOME FOR FIRST QUARTER

Rent
Dividends

WAYS THAT FIRST QUARTER INCOME IS SPENT

Wages
Insurance
Travel

This example could be corrected by changing "WAYS THAT FIRST QUARTER INCOME IS SPENT" to "EXPENSES FOR FIRST QUARTER."

The rules of outlining should be followed when preparing headings in a written report. That is, when second- or third-level headings are used, each level must have at least two entries.

All first- and second-level headings within a report should be set off from preceding and following text by a double space. Text for sections with third-level headings begins two spaces after the period in the heading. This method of organizing headings is shown in Figure 10.9.

Footnotes or Citations

Footnotes or citations must be used to give credit to the source of quoted or paraphrased material. Reports in the business community do not contain as many footnotes or text citations as reports in other fields because business reports usually contain only

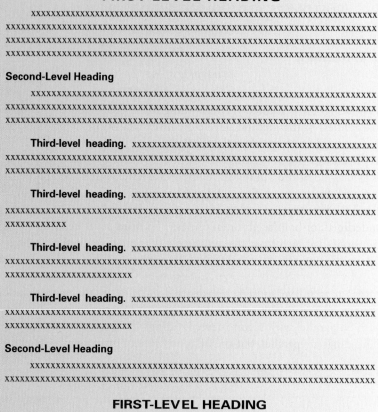

FIGURE 10.9
Levels of Headings

NOTE 10.61
Commonly used
footnoting methods are
• Traditional
• Contemporary

information that is based on data gathered through primary research. Two commonly used methods for citing sources follow.

The traditional method of footnoting is convenient for the reader when a report contains information gathered from a number of sources. Material to be footnoted is marked by an Arabic numeral that is placed at the end of the quoted material and raised $\frac{1}{2}$ line (superscript). The footnote numbers begin with 1 and are consecutive throughout the report. The footnote is separated from the text by a 1-inch or 2-inch horizontal rule beginning at the left margin 1 line below the last line of the text material. The footnote is typed or printed on the second line under the rule; it is single spaced, with the first line indented $\frac{1}{2}$ inch from the left margin. The superscript number identification precedes the citation.

The footnoting feature of word processing software makes enumeration and placement easy, but the report writer must still ensure that the citation is complete and correct. Information contained in traditional footnotes varies depending on the source—book, periodical, encyclopedia, government publication, newspaper, or unpublished material. An example of a traditional footnote follows:

The number of new oil wells being drilled has decreased by 10 percent from the number drilled last year.[1] There will be a shortage of oil products if the trend of drilling fewer wells continues for the rest of this decade.

---
[1] A. W. Hodde, "Oil Production in 1997," *Petroleum Quarterly* 9 (1998), p. 8.

A contemporary method of citing sources of information within the text uses the author's name and date in parentheses instead of a footnote at the bottom of the page (see Appendix B). If a direct quotation of text or statistics is used, the page number is included in the parentheses. For information about the source, a reader would refer to the bibliography. An example of this method follows:

> The number of new oil wells being drilled has decreased by 10 percent from the number drilled last year (Hodde, 1998, p. 8). There will be a shortage of oil products if the trend of drilling fewer wells continues for the rest of this decade.

See Appendix B for a more detailed description of procedures to follow when constructing citations.

Page Numbers

Pages in reports of only one or two pages do not have to be numbered. Pages in long reports should be numbered consecutively. Preliminary pages (pages prior to the body of a report) should be numbered by placing small Roman numerals (ii, iii, iv, etc.) at the center of the page, 1 inch from the bottom, beginning with the second page. The title page is considered page i, even though no page number is displayed.

The body of the report should begin as page 1, identified with Arabic numerals (1, 2, 3, 4, etc.). For each section or chapter that is started on a separate page, the page number should be centered 1 inch from the bottom. On the remaining pages of unbound or left-bound reports, the number should be placed on the fourth line from the top of the page in the right margin; on top-bound reports the page number should be centered and 1 inch from the bottom edge of the page. The page numbering feature of word processing software simplifies the placement process. An example of a formal report appears in Figure 10.10.

NOTE 10.62
Reports containing more than two pages should be numbered.

FIGURE 10.10
Formal Report

IMPACT STUDY:

Duluth Botanical Gardens/Conservatory

Date:
August 30, 1999

Richard Lichty
with Jean Jacobson
and Arnela Smajlovic

Bureau of Business and
Economic Research
University of Minnesota Duluth

FIGURE 10.10
Formal Report
cont.

IMPACT STUDY:
Duluth Botanical Gardens/Conservatory

August 30, 1999

In this study:

-2-

FIGURE 10.10
Formal Report
cont.

INTRODUCTION

This study was requested by the Bayfront Visions citizens' group to muster impact data for presentation to the Duluth City Council and planning committee in support of a proposal to build a conservatory and botanical garden for Duluth in the area known as the Bayfront. Assumptions for new visitors and other tourism-related impacts are discussed below but represent preliminary notions about possible numbers. Data are supplied and analysis is accomplished by the IMPLAN software model and data.

BACKGROUND

THE IMPACT MODEL AND DATA

IMPLAN Professional is an economic impact assessment modeling system. IMPLAN allows the user to build economic models to estimate the impacts of economic changes in their states, counties, or communities. The IMPLAN system is comprised of two pieces purchased separately. The first is the IMPLAN Professional software. The second piece is the IMPLAN database. You need both software and data to create an economic impact model. Software IMPLAN Professional® is an economic impact assessment software system. IMPLANPro®, combined with MIG databases, allows the user to develop local level input-output models that can estimate the economic impact of new firms moving into an area, professional sports teams, recreation and tourism, and many more activities.

DATABASE COMPONENTS

IMPLAN databases consist of the following components: Employment; Industry Output; Value Added; Employee Compensation; Proprietary Income; Other Property Type Income; Indirect Business Taxes; and more.

DATABASE SOURCES

- U.S. Bureau of Economic Analysis Benchmark I/O Accounts of the U.S.
- U.S. Bureau of Economic Analysis Output Estimates
- U.S. Bureau of Economic Analysis REIS Program
- U.S. Bureau of Labor Statistics ES202 Program
- U.S. Bureau of Labor Statistics Consumer Expenditure Survey
- U.S. Census Bureau County Business Patterns
- U.S. Census Bureau Deciennial Census and Population Surveys
- U.S. Census Bureau Economic Censuses and Surveys
- U.S. Department of Agriculture
- U.S. Geological Survey

-3-

FIGURE 10.10
Formal Report
cont.

THE NATURE OF IMPACTS

Assumptions:

Several assumptions are necessary in any impact analysis. This was especially true in the case of the tourism impact analysis of the proposed Duluth Botanical Gardens/ Conservatory since time and money did not allow for surveys or other methods aimed at fine-tuning the analysis.

The following assumptions apply to the impacts here reported:

- **Production, Not Sales**

  The impacts reported here are based on production, not sales. This is a common approach using the models and tools used for this analysis.

  What does this mean? The primary implications from these assumptions are for retail and wholesale trade. An example might help: If I buy a car from a local car dealer for $20,000, how much was produced in Duluth? Well, the car dealer did not manufacture the car. So we can deduct $15,000 or so that went to Detroit or Japan. Perhaps the owners do not reside in Duluth. We can deduct their earnings from profit that goes to wherever they reside. That leaves local salespeople, maintenance people, for a local impact.

  We call that proportion of total sales by the car dealership in our example *margins*. Margins represent the contribution to local production by the local dealership. This means that the output impacts will be much less than the total sales impact. However, the output impact is a true production impact upon which decisions can be made. Since tourism deals mostly with retail establishments, to use sales as an estimator is misleading relative to the true impact.

- **Employment Assumptions**

  Employment figures are based on Department of Commerce definitions. This means that a part-time employee is counted as one employee. There are no adjustments toward full-time equivalent measures.

  Once again, this assumption has its greatest effect on sectors such as retail trade. Retail trade hires a significant number of part-time employees. This means that any impact measure in this sector will be inflated when compared to full-time equivalent definitions.

  Another required assumption for employment impacts is that there is no excess capacity in the community. New levels of sales require new employees, and we are assuming these new employees are available. Any other assumption would require more time and budget than is available for this analysis.

-4-

FIGURE 10.10
Formal Report
cont.

- **The Source of Margins**

  For this analysis, the margins were initially taken from the default values contained in IMPLAN. Each was then reviewed based on other data, such as the Census of Retail Trade, Department of Commerce and a few adjustments were made.

- **Prices in 1996 Dollars**

  The most recent IMPLAN model contains a database based on 1996 information. This is taken as the base year for this analysis. An inflation rate of 2 percent is then factored into the model for each year of the analysis. All figures provided were deflated by this factor. Of course, if there is a desire to have the impacts stated in current dollars, the factor can be added back in.

- **High and Low Assumptions for New Visitor Days**

  Probably the most heroic assumption regards tourists. It is difficult to understand what motivates a tourist to come into our region without surveys of our major markets. These markets pretty much follow Interstate 35, with the Twin Cities being our biggest customers, Iowa coming second, Missouri third, and so on. There is some evidence that Chicago residents are increasing in number for our tourist base.

  Our assumption is that one major motivator for tourism in the region is to see the Lake and related environment offered by Duluth. The landscape proposal being analyzed here maximizes this exposure.

  Why is this important? Because only new tourist expenditures should be included in any tourism project impact statement. If a new operation only results in a tourist spending money in one Duluth store instead of another, the net impact is zero.

  For this initial impact study, we present high and low assumptions: a high of 70,000 new visitor days for Duluth because of this operation, or a low of 35,000 new visitor days for Duluth because of this operation. For occupancy we assume that an average stay in a hotel/motel is one night.

- **Personal Tax Assumptions**

  It is important to note that tax impacts extend beyond those directly paid by employees of the operation. Impacts include the indirect and induced (see below) effects from an initial change in activity. Even if an assumed operation resulted in no direct tax impacts from its own operations, the indirect and induced effects could be quite large.

  The tax impact model assumptions for this study come from the IMPLAN tax impact structure, as built into the IMPLAN Pro 2.0 model and data.

-5-

FIGURE 10.10
Formal Report
cont.

- **Other Assumptions**

  There are several other assumptions associated with the IMPLAN model used in this analysis. The reader is referred to the *IMPLAN User's Guide* for a list of these assumptions.

TYPES OF MULTIPLIERS

There are several types of multipliers used in this analysis, specifically, the Direct, the Indirect, and the Induced. The total of these three make up the Total Impact. In the impact data to be presented, all of these impacts will be listed.

The following definitions apply:

- **Direct**

  The direct impact comes from the operation itself. Remember that, in the case of retail or service operations, margins constitute the basis for direct impact estimates.

- **Indirect**

  The indirect impacts stem from the interaction between the facility and other local businesses. The interaction comes from the facilities purchases of locally produced producers. Only purchases and sales from *local* businesses count in this calculation.

  It is important to note that the purchases by the facility under consideration are the direct impacts. The indirect impacts come from these second-round businesses purchasing needed local goods and services in order to provide for the increased production in the region as a result of the initial, direct expenditures. Then third round increases in activity occur, fourth round, and so on until the multiplier has played itself out.

- **Induced**

  Induced impacts stem from the earnings of employees in each round of impact activity. Employees spend a portion of their personal income in the region, creating rounds of induced activity.

- **Total**

  The total impact is simply the direct, plus the indirect, plus the induced impacts.

TYPES OF MEASURES

Our impact estimates include the following measures: output, employment, personal income, and personal taxes. Each will be described in a sentence:

-6-

FIGURE 10.10
Formal Report
cont.

- **Output**

    Output impacts represent the new direct, indirect, and induced *production* from local industries as a result of the new facility. Output is generally not the same as sales, as discussed above.

- **Employment**

    Employment impacts are the direct, indirect, and induced impacts from industry activity in the region as a result of the new operation. Remember, an employee is an employee, whether full- or part-time.

- **Personal Income**

    Personal income impacts are the direct, indirect, and induced impacts from industry activity in the region as a result of the new operation. Personal income includes employee compensation plus proprietorís income if the proprietor is a local individual.

- **Taxes**

    Tax impacts are based on household factors and on indirect taxes. Household taxes include personal taxes and property taxes, as well as estimates of various other income based taxes. Indirect taxes include sales taxes and excise taxes. All tax estimates are for state and local taxes. Federal taxes are not included.

IMPACTS FROM CONSTRUCTION

The construction associated with this project is assumed to take place in the year 2000. All construction expenditure estimates were provided by the supporters of this development plan. We then discounted these estimates to 1996 dollars based on the 2 percent per annum inflation rate assumed for this project. The initial assumptions for this impact were a total construction cost of $7,250,000. Of course, the construction impacts are for one year only and do not extend into the future.

Table 1 presents the direct, indirect, and induced impacts from the assumed construction activity.

Table 1: Construction

	Direct*	Indirect*	Induced*	Total*
Labor Income	$2,040,403	$815,031	$776,467	$3,631,900
Output Impact	$6,643,396	$2,086,144	$1,900,508	$10,630,04
Employment	74.6	34.6	36.1	145.3
*1996 dollars				

-7-

IMPACTS FROM OPERATIONS

FIGURE 10.10
Formal Report
cont.

The operations associated with this project are assumed to begin in the year 2001. The impacts listed here are for that one year. The assumption is that the operations impact would continue indefinitely into the future. The initial assumptions for this impact were a total operations cost of $1,514,400.

Table 2 presents the direct, indirect, and induced impacts from the operations assumptions.

Table 2: Operations

	Direct*	Indirect*	Induced*	Total*
Labor Income	$417,876	$143,425	$152,633	$713,934
Output Impact	$1,057,774	$392,216	$373,589	$1,823,579
Employment	19.5	6.2	7.1	32.7
*1996 dollars				

IMPACTS (HIGH, MEDIUM, AND LOW ASSUMPTIONS) FROM NEW VISITOR DAYS

Table 3 reflects high (70,000), medium (35,000), and low (10,000) assumptions of additional visitor days for the region to take advantage of this new park. This number would begin with the operations in the year 2001. The expenditures of these tourists are assumed to concentrate in a few local industries. Impacted industry sectors included are retail, eating and drinking, lodging, advertising, theater, sports, motion pictures, transportation, food stores, banking, and Rental.

Remember that the direct impact on retail trade is based on margins, not on sales. Table 3 presents the direct, indirect, and induced impacts from the new tourism in the region.

Table 3: Tourism

	Direct*	Indirect*	Induced*	Total*
HIGH:				
Labor Income	$2,106,985	$702,055	$763,852	$3,572,892
Output Impact	$6,314,169	$2,010,325	$1,869,630	$10,194,124
Employment	144.3	30.8	35.5	210.6
MEDIUM:				
Labor Income	$394,613	$138,324	$144,920	$677,857
Output Income	$1,240,351	$398,739	$354,710	$1,993,800
Employment	29.9	6.1	6.7	42.7
LOW				
Labor Income	$925,417	$300,759	$333,429	$1,559,605
Output	$2,758,642	$861,954	$816,114	$4,436,709
Employment	62.2	13.1	15.5	90.8
*1996 dollars				

-8-

FIGURE 10.10
Formal Report
cont.

IMPACT FROM TAXES

Table 4 presents the household-based tax impact and indirect business-tax impact in the region.

Table 4: Tax Impact

	Household-Based Taxes	Indirect Business Tax
Construction	$133,307	$329,611
Operations	$25,812	$46,352
Tourism (High)	$128,849	$534,370
Tourism (Medium)	$24,454	$110,601
Tourism (Low)	$6,987	$31,600
High TOTAL	$287,968	$910,333
Medium TOTAL	$183,573	$486,564
Low TOTAL	$166,106	$407,563

-9-

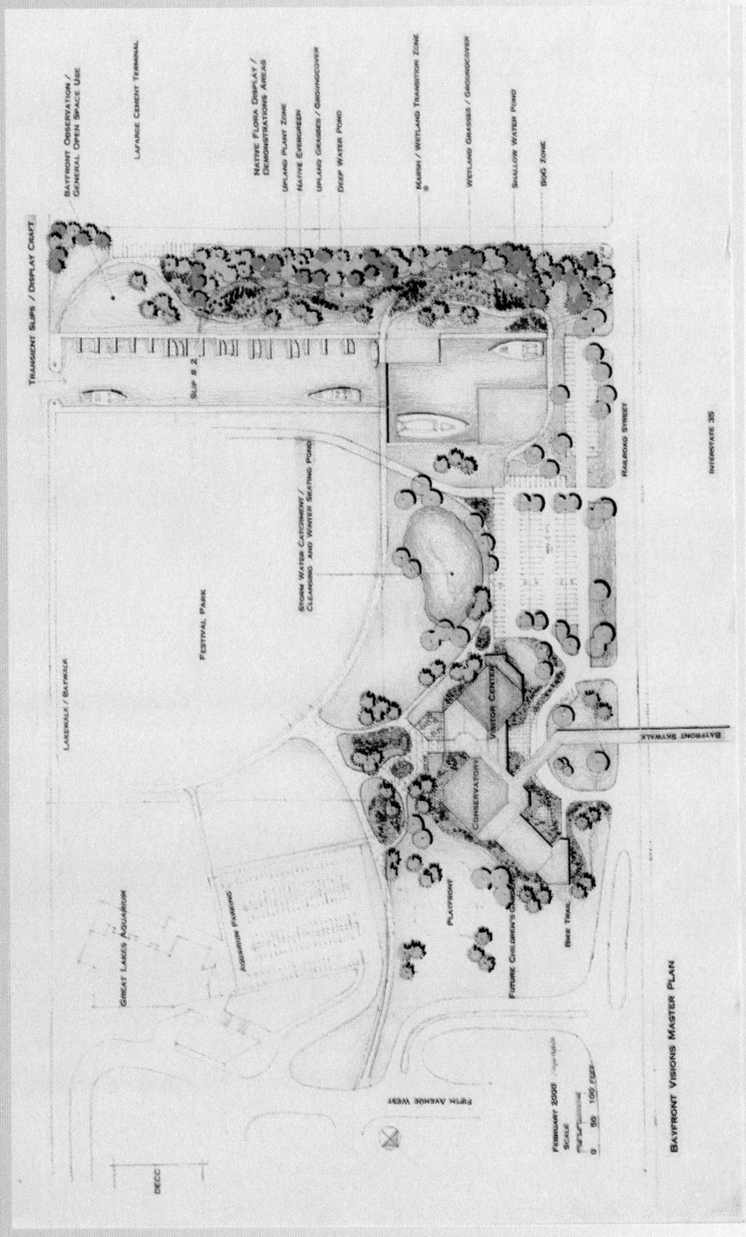

Figure 1 Bayfront Visions Master Plan, prepared by Bayfront Visions Group, April 1999

FIGURE 10.10
Formal Report
cont.

FIGURE 10.10
Formal Report
cont.

REFERENCES

Data and Software:

Minnesota IMPLAN Group, Inc., IMPLAN System (1996 data and
    software), 1940 South Greeley Street, Suite 101, Stillwater, MN 55082,
    http://www.implan.com, 1997.

Written Guide:

Olson, Doug and Scott Lindall, "IMPLAN Professional Software, Analysis,
    and Data Guide," Minnesota IMPLAN Group, Inc., 1940 South Greeley
    Street, Suite 101, Stillwater, MN 55082, http://www.implan.com, 1996.

-11-

FIGURE 10.10
Formal Report
cont.

APPENDIXES AND SUPPORTING IMPLAN DATA

For Appendixes and Supporting IMPLAN Data Tables please see
    the UMD Bureau of Business and Economic Research, including:

Tourism (High, Medium, and Low Assumptions)
    Labor Income Impact, Output Impact, Employment Impact, Tax Impact
Construction
    Labor Income Impact, Output Impact, Employment Impact, Tax Impact
Operations
    Labor Income Impact, Output Impact, Employment Impact, Tax Impact

-12-

Summary of Learning Objectives

(1) Identify and use the five steps for conducting research.

The five steps in conducting research are: (1) *Plan the research.* Planning the research includes stating the problem, setting the boundaries, determining the readership, and deciding on the procedures to be followed. (2) *Gather information.* You may gather information for your research from one or more sources. There are two basic types of information sources: secondary and primary. The Web has become an essential tool for conducting research. (3) *Analyze the information.* The purpose of the analysis is to make sense, objectively, of the information you have gathered. You will not want personal bias of any kind to enter into the analysis. (4) *Determine the solution(s).* Based on your analysis, you will be ready to offer a solution or solutions to the problem you have been researching. For formal studies and reports, you may draw conclusions from your analysis and state them separately from the recommendation(s). (5) *Write the report.* The final step in a research project is to write the report. It is an important step; you will want to present your results effectively.

(2) Distinguish between formal and informal reports.

A formal report may consist of all or some of the following parts: title page, transmittal message, table of contents, list of illustrations, abstract, body, glossary, appendix, and bibliography or reference list. An informal report may consist of a title page and body or of a body only; it may also be formatted as correspondence. Formal reports are usually written in the third person, but informality is becoming more acceptable; informal reports are usually written in the first person. Both formal and informal reports use headings to guide the reader through the document.

(3) Identify the types of informal reports.

The three most common informal reports are progress, periodic, and technical. A progress report informs readers about the status of a particular project. A periodic report provides managers with statistical information at regularly scheduled intervals. A technical report conveys specialized or scientific information.

(4) Describe the components of a formal report.

The report cover, which contains the report title and author's name, protects the contents of the report. Report margins are generally 1 inch on all sides. Reports may be single spaced or double spaced. Single spaced reports should be double spaced between paragraphs. Headings may be informative or structural. Informative headings indicate the content of a forthcoming section; structural headings emphasize the functional sections within the report. Footnotes give credit to the source of quoted or paraphrased material. Pages of short reports need not be numbered; pages of long reports should be numbered. Preliminary pages are normally numbered with Roman numerals, whereas pages containing the body and supplementary parts of the report are numbered with Arabic numerals.

List the advantages of correct report formatting.

Correct report formatting will cause the reader to have a good first impression of the report. It decreases the time necessary for a reader to gain confidence in the report writer's credibility. Formatting a written report properly will improve its readability. Properly formatted reports help the reader follow the organization of the material by using appropriate headings.

Write formal and informal reports.

Informal reports are normally written in the first person. They usually do not contain visual aids or material from secondary sources and may be formatted as letters or memos.

Discussion Questions

1. List the five steps in conducting research and explain each step. (Objective 1)
2. How can a report writer meet the needs of both primary and secondary readers? Give a specific example. (Objective 1)
3. What factors should a researcher consider when assessing the value of traditional and computerized secondary sources? (Objective 1)
4. Distinguish between primary and secondary sources. Give an example of each. (Objective 1)
5. What factors should a researcher consider when using a focus group? (Objective 1)
6. How do formal and informal reports differ? (Objective 2)
7. What format options exist for informal reports? (Objective 2)
8. What information should be included in a progress report? (Objective 3)
9. How does an organization benefit from establishing a standard format for its technical reports? (Objective 3)
10. List and briefly describe the three major divisions of a formal report. (Objective 4)
11. How does the purpose of an executive summary differ from the purpose of a letter of transmittal? Objective 4)
12. How does a writer determine whether to include material within the body of a report or as an appendix to the report? (Objective 4)
13. Explain when to use Roman numerals and when to use Arabic numbers in a formal report. (Objective 5)
14. Distinguish between a structural heading and an informative heading. Give an example of each. (Objective 5)
15. Explain why correctly formatting a report improves its readability. (Objective 5)

Application Exercises

1. **Teamwork.** Form teams of no more than five people. Each team will select an important current issue or problem on the campus. As directed by your instructor, do one or more of the following:
   a. Design a research study that either surveys student attitudes about the issue or investigates the problem and proposes a solution.
   b. Submit a memo to your instructor in which you identify your topic, outline your research plan, and ask for authorization to complete the study.
   c. Submit a progress report to your instructor at the midpoint of your research.
   d. Prepare and submit a formal report to your instructor. (Objectives 1 through 6)

2. Indicate what would be (a) an appropriate statement of the problem and (b) an appropriate list of factors for comparative research of the relative cost-effectiveness of two procedures for processing employment application forms in a human resources office. (Objective 1)

3. The small company for which you work manufactures and sells camping equipment. Recently, the company's management team decided to expand its sales efforts to include e-commerce. Barbara Kramer, the owner of the company, has read various articles indicating that consumers are dissatisfied with the merchandise return policies used by companies that sell online. She has asked you to prepare a report that provides information about merchandise return policies. State the problem, list the research factors, and indicate the way you would gather data. (Objective 1)

4. **InfoTrac.** Annual reports are formal reports used to communicate with various audiences. Learn more about the contents of annual reports and tips for making them readable by accessing InfoTrac Article A87944609, "A More Effective Annual Report," by Christopher Doyle and InfoTrac Article A59950515, "How to Use Plain English Writing Annual Reports," by Carol Worth. After reading the articles, answer the following questions:
   a. According to Mr. Doyle, who is the primary audience for an annual report?
   b. What tips does Mr. Doyle offer for achieving clarity in an annual report?
   c. What advice does Ms. Worth give to help achieve a favorable tone in the letter from the chair?
   d. What publication is available to help annual report writers create readable documents?
   e. How does the material in these articles parallel the principles of business communication? (Objective 2)

5. **Teamwork.** As directed by your instructor, complete one or more of the following activities:
   a. Form teams to develop a questionnaire that could be used to survey student opinions on the quality of student advisement in your school. (Objective 1)
   b. Pilot-test, revise, and then administer the questionnaire developed in Application Exercise 5a to the students in three business classes. Tabulate the students' responses and analyze the data. As your instructor directs, report your findings in a memo or an oral report. (Objectives 1, 3, and 6)
   c. Repeat Exercise 5a using the focus group technique. As your instructor directs, report your findings in a memo or an oral report. (Objectives 1, 3, and 6)

6. Contact the manager of a local grocery store and obtain permission to observe customers as they pass through the checkout line during set times over a three-day period. Your goal is to obtain data to determine whether plastic or paper bags are preferred. Incorporate other relevant factors into your observation. Report your results in a memo report to your instructor and in a letter report to the store manager. (Objectives 1, 3, and 6)

7. **Teamwork.** Work with two or three of your classmates to design an experiment to determine how people react to receiving compliments. After getting feedback on your design from members of another team, conduct your experiment. Submit an informal report to your instructor. (Objectives 1, 3, and 6)

8. **Teamwork.** Your instructor will place you in a group and delegate to that group the task of designing an online questionnaire to gather data about college students' preferences within the following topic areas:

a. Breakfast food
b. Music
c. Leisure reading material
d. Videos/Movies
e. Vehicles

f. Pizza topping(s)
g. Candy
h. TV shows
i. Clothing color
j. Spring break destination

Present your survey to the class. Modify the survey based on class feedback, and present a copy to your instructor. (Objective 1)

9. **Internet.** The increased use of computers within your organization has prompted your supervisor, R. J. Tibbs, to become concerned about repetitive strain injury (RSI). R. J. has asked you to research the topic; specifically, she is interested in information on prevention, symptoms, and treatment. Use traditional and/or computerized search techniques to gather your information, then prepare an informal report. (Objectives 1, 3, and 6)

10. Review the online or print copy of a corporation's annual report. Prepare an outline of the report using its major headings and subheadings as your guide. Submit your outline to your instructor. (Objectives 4 and 5)

Case Problems

1. The employees of Hazel Savings have asked about the possibility of classes being offered on-site. Upon inquiring at State College, you learn that up to two classes could be taught if enough students enroll to make the classes cost-effective. A survey was taken; 131 of Hazel Savings' 162 employees responded. The results follow. Write a memo report to the human resources director, Teresa Trevino, giving the results of the investigation and your recommendations.

1. *What courses would you be interested in taking? (Give your top 3 choices as 1, 2, and 3.)*

	1	2	3
Business communication	14	14	17
Human relations	28	9	16
Computer applications	32	17	14
Financial accounting	9	23	18
Marketing	7	22	8

2. *What would be the best day for the class?*

Monday	15
Tuesday	52
Wednesday	32
Thursday	32
Friday	0

3. *What would be the most convenient time for the class?*

7 a.m.	12
5 p.m.	41
6 p.m.	52
7 p.m.	26

2. Northeastern Savings and Loan's contract with its insurance company lapses in four months. It is trying to determine its employees' attitudes toward medical coverage. Following are the results of a survey to which 89 of the 105 employees responded.

The responses have been organized into three groups—single persons, individuals with one dependent, and individuals with two or more dependents. Use the data to prepare a report that could be sent to the company's president.

	Single	1 Dependent	2+ Dependents
1. Which type of coverage is best?			
a. Employee only	25	5	1
b. Family plan	5	16	37
2. What coverage(s) should be available? (Check all that apply.)			
a. Basic medical	30	21	38
b. Major medical	30	21	38
c. Hospitalization	30	21	38
d. Dental	16	12	32
e. Optical	9	7	32
f. Prescriptions	20	15	25
3. What limit should a policy place on out-of-pocket expenses?			
a. $ 500	21	13	31
b. $1,000	6	5	6
c. $2,500	1	1	1
d. $5,000	2	2	0
4. Should the company offer a menu insurance program in which an employee can choose the type of coverage desired?			
a. Yes	28	19	37
b. No	2	1	2
5. Which would you prefer?			
a. Minimum coverage— company pays premium	22	12	25
b. Increased coverage— employees shares in paying premium	8	9	13
6. What should be the maximum premium that the employee must pay each month?			
a. $ 0	23	13	30
b. $ 25	5	2	4
c. $ 50	1	4	2
d. $100	1	2	2

3. As program planner for the local entertainment league, you surveyed your 396 season ticket holders to determine what plays they are interested in seeing during the following season. You listed the play possibilities and asked respondents to indicate their interest level in each (1 = low; 4 = high). Although patrons prefer musicals, past experience dictates that a schedule that excludes comedy and drama results in lower-than-average attendance. This year, you also wanted to gather information about when ticket holders prefer to have performances. Data from 302 respondents is summarized below. Analyze the data and prepare a memo report to the entertainment league's president, Mildred Babcock, who will use the information when she negotiates with agents. (Numbers may not total 302 due to incomplete responses on some survey returns.)

Plays	1	2	3	4
1776	57	55	101	86
A Chorus Line	17	77	73	135
A Flea in Her Ear	209	53	25	13
A Streetcar Named Desire	12	73	183	31
Ah, Wilderness?	113	45	74	70
Barefoot in the Park	93	72	81	55
Cabaret	4	60	124	110
Cats	2	35	83	181
Charley's Aunt	161	52	71	18
Chicago	71	49	79	103
City of Angels	77	84	58	78
Conversations with My Father	44	134	67	48
Dancing at Lughnasa	44	81	148	29
Death of a Salesman	76	72	80	74
Eleemosynary	55	207	27	10
Fiddler on the Roof	114	59	103	26
Grease	1	39	258	4
Hamlet	70	79	77	75
How to Succeed in Business without Really Trying	93	144	56	3
Inherit the Wind	31	127	126	18
Jeckyll & Hyde	102	87	76	35
Jelly's Last Jam	40	94	86	78
Les Miserables	103	157	30	2
Little Shop of Horrors	183	11	56	52
Lost in Yonkers	149	51	91	11
Man of La Mancha	79	86	77	60
Peter Pan	21	96	133	52
Rent	3	34	111	153
Show Boat	16	237	25	24
Six Degrees of Separation	98	78	82	41
South Pacific	64	170	46	16
Stomp	121	32	126	23
The Fantasticks	80	200	16	4
The Secret Garden	68	64	96	74
The Sound of Music	94	163	23	17
The Sunshine Boys	108	104	79	11
The Glass Menagerie	111	103	80	1
The Last Night of Ballyhoo	90	46	43	116
The Lion King	36	6	92	168
The Phantom of the Opera	14	63	173	52
The King and I	53	116	63	64
The Homecoming	134	122	27	19
Victor/Victoria	22	89	146	44

Scheduling Preferences: Days	1	2	3	4
Monday	273	26	3	1
Tuesday	132	8	129	33
Wednesday	45	10	68	177

Scheduling Preferences: Days, cont.	1	2	3	4
Thursday	6	92	63	109
Friday	206	74	16	4
Saturday (matinee)	244	51	8	0
Saturday (evening)	20	9	253	19
Sunday (matinee)	237	20	32	13
Sunday (evening)	84	6	157	55

Scheduling Preferences: Months	1	2	3	4
September	37	102	114	49
October	22	70	144	64
November	55	110	103	34
December	193	19	85	5
January	88	100	112	2
February	16	130	133	22
March	82	64	76	79
April	71	80	85	64
May	55	83	70	93
June	122	86	58	36

4. You are an administrative trainee at The Babcock Inn, a 200-room hotel catering to business travelers. Three months ago, the hotel began leaving comment cards in guest rooms. Instructions on the form direct guests to place completed surveys in a box in the lobby. Data for the past month follow.

FACTOR	Excellent	Very Good	Average	Poor	N/A
Service at Check-in	211	367	88	9	
Service at Check-out	93	214	101	3	264
Room Cleanliness	59	293	312	11	
Restaurant/Lounge	28	133	169	17	328
Overall Rating	121	365	183	6	

A few of the guests took time to make comments. You've consolidated them into the following list. The number of people who responded with like comments is shown in parentheses.

Coffeepot was not cleaned.

Check-in was slow. (11)

The type of room I requested was not available.

Room had towels but no washcloths; it took 30 minutes to get them after I phoned.

Great stay! I'll be back.

Servers were courteous, listened to and honored my special requests.

Food was mediocre. (6)

Buffet was not available at 6 a.m. (3)

Speedy check-in. (8)

The first room to which I was assigned was occupied. (2)

Clean, quiet, comfortable. (15)

Jerry Hajak, the manager and your supervisor, tells you that only about 15 percent of the hotel's guests take time to return the form, and some of them do not answer all the questions. When he asked you to analyze the data for last month, Jerry also asked you to offer suggestions on what The Babcock can do to encourage more guests to respond. Prepare an informal report.

5. **Ethics.** Barnard's Industrial Supply is attempting to improve its image. It is conducting a workshop on ethical business practices. A questionnaire sent to employees asking them to rate selected aspects of their behavior as *Never, Rarely, Sometimes,* and *Often* was returned by 243 of Barnard's 287 employees. Use the following results to write a memo report that could be distributed to the employees at the workshop.

In the past five years I have

	Never	Rarely	Sometimes	Often
1. Taken money illegally from the company	227	16	1	1
2. Withheld truth to cover my mistakes	76	87	59	21
3. Withheld truth to cover others' mistakes	54	63	103	23
4. Reported hours that weren't worked	198	12	24	9
5. Made personal long-distance calls on business phones	17	53	97	76
6. Taken supplies for personal use	51	17	42	133
7. Given false reasons for missing work	36	69	107	31
8. Used unethical behavior to make a sale	202	21	9	11
9. Submitted false expenses for travel	164	33	28	18
10. Stayed past break or lunch periods	8	14	168	53
11. Used equipment for personal projects	21	37	149	36
12. Made illegal copies of software	104	52	71	16

6. You serve on the Professional Development Committee of a national association in your field. Your group recently sponsored a regional seminar on a pertinent topic in that field. The all-day seminar, held at a large hotel, featured a keynote speaker, a panel, and four small-group sessions scheduled so that each participant could attend two. Refreshments were provided during registration as well as during morning and afternoon breaks, but participants were responsible for their own lunch. Over 300 people attended; 214 of them took time to complete and return the seminar evaluation form included in their registration packet. You have been asked to analyze the results of the evaluation and report to the Committee. Create information appropriate to your field (e.g., seminar title, speakers, topics, location). The survey results follow:

	(Very High) 5	4	3	2	1 (Very Low)
Facility	3	17	37	136	21
Keynote Speaker	99	66	41	8	0
Panel (overall)	28	152	31	0	0
Panelist 1	47	113	51	0	0
Panelist 2	0	1	22	143	45
Panelist 3	53	117	39	2	0
Session 1a	94	16	3	0	0
Session 1b	26	41	18	0	0
Session 2a	16	37	10	2	0
Session 2b	23	59	1	0	0
Registration	24	43	119	18	0
Breaks	29	54	71	0	0

Comments (number of similar responses):

Registration table was understaffed during the 30 minutes just before the meeting began. (33)

Serve something other than sweets. (12)

Serve sodas at the morning break. (17)

Need a larger area for registration or a separate area for refreshments. (3)

Session 1a was overcrowded. Those standing in the back couldn't hear. (47)

Moderator lost control of the panel. (5)

Panelist 2 dominated the discussion; he was insulting to other panelists and audience. (71)

AV in Session 2b was inadequate. (4)

Keynote speaker was excellent; she set a positive tone for the day. (18)

Afternoon break needs to be longer; couldn't get refreshments and move to next session. (23)

The panel topic was controversial. Both sides of the issue needed to be presented . . . calmly and logically. (3)

7. The human resources department surveyed Elite Accounting's 74 employees to determine how best to structure the workweek. The results of the survey follow. Write a memo report to the company president, Connie Trevathan, giving the results of the survey and your recommendations.

	Number of Respondents
1. *Preference for 4-day or 5-day week:*	
Four 10-hour days	*53*
Five 8-hour days	*18*
No preference	*3*
2. *Work hours preferred if 8-hour days with 1-hour lunch break:*	
7 a.m. to 4 p.m.	*4*
8 a.m. to 5 p.m.	*15*
9 a.m. to 6 p.m.	*4*
All work 10 a.m. to 3 p.m., flexible hours for other 4	*48*
No preference	*3*
3. *Work hours preferred if 10-hour days with 1-hour lunch break:*	
6 a.m. to 5 p.m.	*3*
7 a.m. to 6 p.m.	*14*
8 a.m. to 7 p.m.	*4*
All work 9 a.m. to 4 p.m., flexible hours for other 4	*50*
No preference	*3*

8. As a field associate for a national marketing research firm, you surveyed 50 women to learn whether they perceived the scent of several hand and body lotions to be (a) appropriately named and (b) attractively packaged. Summarize the results of your research in an informal report that will be sent to the national office with your raw data. The question and coding schemes used in the interviews are as follows:

Age: 1 = under 25   2 = 25–34   3 = 35–44   4 = 45–54   5 = 55 or over

Educational level: 1 = high school   2 = some postsecondary   3 = associate degree or certificate   4 = bachelor's degree   5 = graduate degree

Fragrance rating: 1 = low 5 = high

Attractive packaging: 1 = yes 2 = no

Respondent Number	Age	Educ. Level	Almond Blush	Rose Garden	Mountain Spring	Rainwater Fresh	Autumn Day	Package Rating
1	1	4	5	3	1	1	2	1
2	4	2	3	3	5	2	2	2
3	3	3	4	5	5	1	3	1
4	4	4	5	3	2	1	4	1
5	4	5	3	1	4	5	2	2
6	2	3	5	1	1	4	5	1
7	3	3	4	4	4	3	3	2
8	2	1	5	5	4	4	1	2
9	5	3	3	4	2	2	5	1
10	4	4	2	4	5	3	3	1
11	1	1	3	3	3	3	3	2
12	3	1	2	3	4	4	2	2
13	3	2	4	5	5	1	2	2
14	2	4	2	4	2	4	1	2
15	3	1	4	5	5	5	4	1
16	5	1	3	3	2	4	5	1
17	4	4	4	3	2	3	1	1
18	1	2	2	3	4	4	4	1
19	4	2	2	4	3	5	5	2
20	2	4	2	2	3	4	5	1
21	2	4	3	3	4	5	2	1
22	1	2	1	1	3	4	2	2
23	1	3	4	3	5	5	4	1
24	2	3	4	4	1	1	2	2
25	4	5	3	3	1	2	5	2
26	1	1	2	2	4	3	5	1
27	1	2	3	4	5	5	3	2
28	1	3	2	2	4	3	5	1
29	3	1	5	5	5	5	5	1
30	2	4	2	3	2	1	2	2
31	5	4	3	3	3	3	3	2
32	1	3	2	4	5	5	1	1
33	3	3	3	3	4	1	2	1
34	4	3	5	4	5	3	4	1
35	1	2	2	2	3	3	2	2
36	5	3	5	5	3	3	5	1
37	2	1	3	3	3	3	3	2
38	1	4	2	2	2	4	5	1
39	3	1	5	4	3	5	4	1
40	2	2	5	4	1	1	1	2
41	5	5	5	3	2	2	1	1
42	3	2	4	5	4	3	2	2
43	1	1	1	2	3	2	1	1
44	2	3	5	5	3	4	2	1

Respondent Number	Age	Educ. Level	Almond Blush	Rose Garden	Mountain Spring	Rainwater Fresh	Autumn Day	Package Rating
45	5	2	3	4	3	4	4	1
46	4	2	1	3	5	3	2	2
47	4	1	2	2	4	4	5	1
48	5	4	2	4	3	3	4	2
49	2	5	3	2	4	3	4	2
50	1	2	3	3	4	2	3	2

There are Web exercises at **http://krizan.swlearning.com** to accompany this chapter.

Message Analysis

Format the following text as a short, informal report. Give the report a descriptive title, organize the text logically, develop transitions, write a summary, and insert headings where appropriate. Correct grammar, punctuation, and spelling errors.

Business travel is becoming increasingly complex. Deadlines, delayed or canceled flights, crowded airports and airplanes, and hotel stays are just a few of the challenges travelors face. These suggestions presented in this report may help weary travelers to cope with the stress and meet those challenges. If your flight is canceled, call your travel agent or the airline to get a new reservation. By doing this, you will avoide the crowds at the airport ticket counters. If you have carry-on bags, ask to be seeded near the rear of the aircraft; You board first and have easier time stowing your bags. Become familiar with the local laws and customs of the countries to which you are traveling. Make telephone calls through a hotels' in-room telephone service is very expensive. For cheaper rates, use a long distance calling card. When staying in a hotel, try to stay between the second and seventh floor. This can help to avoid break-ins while remaining in reach of emergency ladders. Always be sure to request automatic locks when renting a car. These are a valuable safety measure when driving and parking in unfamiliar areas. If you regularly travel to the some destination investigate corperate housing for stays of more then a week. You can go home for the weekends and still keep the lower rates. To minimize the expensive refueling charges when renting a car, note the location of a gas station as you leave the airport. When you returning the car, you will nowhere to refuel. Keep clothing wrinkle free by rolling articles in dry-cleaning bags when packing. Learn the carry-on bag size restrictions of the airlines you use before you get to the gate and have to forefit your bag. If you loose your passport while traveling internationally, immediately contact the Embassy or Consulate for assistance right away. Make photocopies of your prescriptions for medicines and eye-glasses, as well as credit cards. This will speed the process of obtaining new ones while on the road. Always be sure to keep a copy of your ID and/or passport in your luggage and at home in case of theft or loss. Place any breakable items, like perfume or cologne, in bubble warp and sealed plastic bags prior to packing to protect them and avoid a mess in the event that they should break. Avoid isolated phones payphones or ones in dimly-lit areas. Face outward while calling to stay alert to possible intruders, and hang onto your belongings. When boarding your flight or checking into your hotel room, always note the location of emergency exist.

Grammar Workshop

Correct the grammar, spelling, punctuation, style, and word choice errors in the following sentences:

1. Miss Beth Hustad and here husband Mark well attend the Opening Ceremonies at the 2004 summer olympics.
2. Can I take you the check and paperwork to your house?
3. Carpal tunnel syndrome is an repetitious, stress injury that effects the nerves in the hands.
4. What is the name of that cozy bussling café on St Charles street in Seattle?
5. Sherri will of coarse reimbursed you fore yore business related expanses.
6. Although ice cream comes in many, exhotic flavors Celeste choses vanilla.
7. A senior citizen will receive a free nights lodging when they join our travel club.
8. The news paper re-porter will phone again latter if she has anymore quotations about the emerger.
9. No topic is mere passionately contested then how to raise children correct; and many parents' find that the government and themedia undermine parental authority.
10. Did Donna say why less people are accepted to attend this years' meeting than last years'.

11

Proposals, Business Plans, and Special Reports

Sean M. Dean and Steven M. Dastoor, Co-owners, Citon Computer Corp.

LET'S TALK BUSINESS Proposals are key to our business success. We wrote about 200 the first year we were in business; now, seven years later, we write over 3,000 proposals a year. Each of those proposals must be designed for the prospective client for whom it is prepared. Audience analysis is essential to determining what will best meet the customer's needs. Clear, complete proposals help to establish us and our business as professional, organized, and reliable.

Typically, the proposals we prepare fall into three categories.

Project Proposals These lengthy documents describe the scope of the work we will do and the timeline we will follow.

Complete System Proposals By providing thorough descriptions and itemizing costs, we allow potential customers to compare the quality and price of our equipment against that of other vendors.

Individual Component Proposals These brief proposals focus on replacement devices or on accessories the customer may want to use with an existing system.

Service has and will continue to be our competitive advantage. Service begins with submitting a high-quality proposal.

Formal reports are not the only structured documents used within organizations. Proposals and business plans fall into this category, as do a variety of special reports. Each of these document types is discussed in this chapter.

Proposals

LEARNING OBJECTIVE
1
Identify the different types of proposals.

A **proposal** is a persuasive message in which a writer analyzes a problem and recommends a solution. The problem may be a need for equipment, services, research, a plan of action, or other things. The recommended solution may be products, personnel, a business study, a description of work to be performed, or other outcomes. As Sean Dean and Steven Dastoor show in Let's Talk Business, proposals are common in business, and it is important that they be clear, be concise, and meet reader expectations.

NOTE 11.1
Proposals analyze problems and provide solutions.

Businesspeople look for initiative. They welcome suggestions about how to change things for the better. Customers and suppliers want to receive proposals that will benefit them and you. Successful organizations depend on the creation of ideas that will improve productivity and profitability.

NOTE 11.2
Proposals present ideas for improving productivity and profitability.

Proposals are gambles. They take time to develop and they often are rejected. Some proposal developers believe that they are doing well if they win acceptance of one of every ten proposals. Effective proposal writers are risk takers; they assess the probability of success and then decide whether to proceed.

Types of Proposals

Proposals can be external or internal, solicited or unsolicited, formal or informal.

NOTE 11.3
Proposals may be
• External or internal
• Solicited or unsolicited
• Formal or informal

External proposals go outside an organization to current or prospective customers, to government agencies, or to private agencies and foundations. These messages include proposals to supply products at given prices, to build roads, or to perform audits. This category also encompasses requests for grants of money or goods to support the work of not-for-profit agencies or other groups hoping to meet some societal or humanitarian need. Such requests are submitted to foundations established solely for the purpose of funding projects in areas such as the arts, education, the environment, or human services. They are submitted also to corporations, whose missions often include returning a portion of their profits to the communities or regions in which they do business.

Receiving approval of external proposals is essential to the success of many for-profit and not-for-profit organizations. Libraries and the Web are sources of information and sample proposals. For example, the site at http://www.npguides.org provides advice and sample proposals to public and private agencies; the site at http://www.foundations.org/grantmakers.html offers links to the sites of corporate and private foundations.

Proposals sent to others within an organization are **internal proposals**. These can be proposals to solve problems or to meet needs by improving procedures, changing products, adding personnel, reorganizing departments, expanding facilities, reducing budgets, or making other changes. Ideas for internal improvement, creatively developed and effectively presented, are the lifeblood of organizations.

A **solicited proposal** is prepared in response to a request for proposal (RFP). The solicitation may be made face-to-face, by telephone, or in writing. Solicited proposals are generally submitted externally. When responding to solicitations for proposals, writers must provide all the requested information and use the specified format. Failure to do so may eliminate the proposal from consideration.

Blondie

Proposals prepared at the writer's initiative rather than in response to an RFP are called **unsolicited proposals**. These proposals represent an independent analysis of another's problems or needs and the creation of possible solutions. Unsolicited proposals may be internal or external. When submitting proposals to foundations or government agencies, writers must match the goals of the writer's organization to those of the foundation or agency.

Informal proposals generally take the form of letters (external) or memos (internal). Some foundations, corporations, and government agencies encourage or require proposal writers to submit preproposals or letters of inquiry. These documents, which are submitted without attachments, provide a succinct description of the project. After review, the funding agency either rejects the proposal or directs the writer to submit a full proposal.

Qualities of a Successful Proposal

Successful proposals have qualities that separate them from unsuccessful proposals. Although success sometimes depends on factors such as luck, politics, timing, and reputation, most proposals must have excellent content and be presented clearly to be accepted. The following qualities usually are required for a successful proposal:

- The purpose of the proposal is stated clearly.
- The problem or need is understood and defined clearly.
- The solution is innovative and presented convincingly.
- The benefits outweigh the costs.
- The personnel implementing the solution are qualified.
- The solution can be achieved on a timely basis.
- The proposal is honest, factual, realistic, and objective.
- The presentation is professional and attractive.

To convey these qualities in the proposal, the writer must carefully analyze the situation and the receivers, use the you–viewpoint, and apply the principles of business communication.

The proposal should be a powerful, persuasive message. The receivers are going to be looking for the benefits to them, their department, the company, the community, the society, or some other group to which they belong. The proposal should get the receivers' attention, show clearly the benefits of accepting the proposal, give proof of those benefits, and motivate favorable action.

The Elements of a Formal Proposal

Items contained in a proposal vary with the situation and the reader. As you'll learn by reading the Communication Notes below and on page 308, an audit proposal and a grant proposal are similar but not identical.

A successful proposal contains essential elements or parts. In solicited proposals, the elements are specified in the RFP. Careful and complete responses should be made to all the elements requested in the RFP. If you think elements necessary to the acceptance of your proposal are missing from the RFP, then you should try to work those parts into the specified format. In unsolicited proposals, you must decide which elements to include. What follows is a list of possible proposal elements:

NOTE 11.6
Successful proposals contain specific elements.

- Cover letter or memo
- Title page or cover
- Reference to authorization
- Table of contents
- List of illustrations
- Proposal summary
- Purpose
- Problem or need
- Background
- Benefits of the proposal

The Grant Proposal A grant proposal must convince the prospective donor of two things: (1) that a problem or need of significant magnitude exists and (2) that the applicant agency has the means and the imagination to solve the problem or meet the need.

When no specific format or guidelines are provided by the funding source, assume the proposal should be no more than 15 single-spaced pages and that it should include the following:

- Summary (½ page)
- Qualifications of the organization (1–2 pages)
- Problem statement or needs assessment (3–4 pages)
- Program goals and objectives (1–2 pages)
- Methodology (4+ pages)
- Evaluation (1–2 pages)
- Future funding (½ page)
- Budget
- Appendixes

The proposal is submitted with a 1–2 page cover letter addressed to the person responsible for the funding program. The letter provides a brief overview of the organization and its purpose, includes the reason for the request and the amount (if required by the funder), and provides the name and phone number of a contact at the requesting organization. The letter should be signed by someone who can speak with authority on behalf of the organization.

Excerpted from material at *http://www.silcom.com/~paladin/promaster.html*. Used with permission of the Center for Nonprofit Management, Los Angeles. Adaptations and enhancement by The Paladin Group.

- Description of the solution
- Evaluation plan
- Qualifications of personnel
- Time schedule
- Cost
- Glossary
- Appendixes
- Reference list

Although all these elements are important for many large proposals, the key elements are the purpose, problem or need, benefits of implementing the solution, description of the solution, qualifications of personnel, time schedule, and cost. All the proposal elements are described in the following sections.

COVER LETTER OR MEMO

NOTE 11.7
The cover letter or memo highlights the contents and encourages action.

The **cover letter** or **memo**, also referred to as a *transmittal message,* introduces the proposal to the reader. A letter is used for an external proposal and a memo for an internal proposal. The cover letter or memo should include content that provides coherence for the reader, reviews the highlights of the proposal, and encourages action.

TITLE PAGE OR COVER

The information contained on the **title page** or **cover** of a proposal can include the title of the proposal, name and location of the receiver, name and location of the submitter, date of submission, principal investigator, proposed cost, and proposed duration of the project. The title should be concise, preferably under ten words. Consider which of the six "W and H" questions—what? when? where? who? why? how?—must be answered by the title. The title of the proposal should attract the reader's attention and, because it will be used to identify the proposal, it should be easy to remember. Eliminate meaningless words such as "A Study of" or "An Examination of"; use descriptive adjective–noun combinations.

REFERENCE TO AUTHORIZATION

If the proposal is solicited, the request should be noted in a **reference to authorization**—the permission or request for the proposal. The information contained in the reference to authorization depends on the RFP. For an informal or short RFP, the reference could be as simple as listing the RFP number on the cover or including a line in the cover letter or memo that says "This proposal is in response to your telephone call of May 5, 200–." For a formal RFP, the reference to authorization could be one or more pages following the title page or cover. A lengthy RFP may require an abstract as a reference to authorization.

NOTE 11.8
If the proposal is solicited, its authorization should be noted.

TABLE OF CONTENTS

The **table of contents** lists the titles and page numbers of all the major sections of the proposal. It will assist in orienting readers and will serve as an aid to locating specific information. The names and page numbers of the appendixes are also included in the table of contents.

LIST OF ILLUSTRATIONS

The titles and page numbers of any tables, figures, graphs, or other illustrations are placed in a **list of illustrations** immediately following the table of contents.

PROPOSAL SUMMARY

The **proposal summary** is the proposal in capsule form. This section, which contains the most vital information from each of the major sections of the proposal, is prepared after the proposal has been written. It should be short. The summary is designed to give busy people a quick but complete overview of the proposal. For short proposals the summary may be just a paragraph. For a long proposal of 100 to 500 pages, the summary might be 1 to 10 pages. If the RFP specifies a length, be sure to make the summary that length and no longer.

NOTE 11.9
The summary provides an overview of the proposal.

PURPOSE

Following the summary, the actual proposal begins. The purpose should be stated first. The **purpose statement** helps the reader understand clearly (1) the reason you are making the proposal and (2) the nature of the proposal—how it will accomplish the purpose. Example purpose statements follow:

> This is a proposal to reduce manufacturing costs 10 percent by replacing the Assembly Line A conveyor system.

NOTE 11.10
The purpose statement clearly describes the reason for and nature of the proposal.

The purpose of this proposal is to increase sales by adding commission sales personnel.

The purpose of this proposal is to improve the quality of life of Middleton's senior citizens by securing funding and constructing a senior center adjacent to the community library.

These purpose statements may stand alone or they may be followed by brief explanations. The amount of explanation given depends on the reader's knowledge and his or her need for information.

PROBLEM OR NEED

NOTE 11.11
State the problem being solved or the need being met.

The next section should describe the problem being solved or the need being met. This section should use coherence techniques to link it to the section in which the purpose was stated. For example, the first purpose statement given in the previous section might be followed by a problem statement such as the following:

Manufacturing costs for the second quarter are up 5 percent over the first quarter. Most of this cost increase can be attributed to the new labor agreement that became effective March 1. To meet competition, we must find new ways to reduce manufacturing costs.

BACKGROUND

NOTE 11.12
Limit background information to what the reader needs.

If necessary for your reader's complete understanding, you should provide background data on the problem. The background section may be combined with the problem/need section or, if both sections are long, it can be presented separately. In the **background** section, you may explain the problem—how it developed, its magnitude, and the consequences if nothing is done.

BENEFITS OF THE PROPOSAL

NOTE 11.13
Benefits of implementing the solution must outweigh the costs.

The benefits of the proposal are important. **Benefits of the proposal** represent the outcomes of the implementation of the proposed solution. The benefits must be stated in the you–viewpoint; they must clearly serve the interests of the reader and/or the reader's organization. The benefits must outweigh their cost. (The cost data will be given later in the proposal.) If your proposal is competing with other proposals, the benefits you cite must be more cost-effective than your competitors' benefits for your proposal to be the winning one.

When presenting the benefits of the proposal, use the emphasis techniques discussed in Chapter 4, but be careful not to overstate the benefits. Make them concrete, realistic, and honest.

DESCRIPTION OF THE SOLUTION

Because the solution to the problem is the most important section in the proposal, it will likely be the largest section. This part of the proposal must tie coherently to the information given previously in the proposal. The writer must refer to the purpose, the problem or need, and the benefits of the proposal. The solution must be presented so clearly that readers will understand it and be convinced that it achieves the purpose, solves the problem, and provides the benefits cited earlier.

The description of the solution should specify what you are proposing be done, who will do it, when it will be done, where it is to be done, how it will be done, and why it should be done. As mentioned earlier, proposals submitted in response to an RFP must provide all the information called for in the request.

You will want to stress the innovative aspects of your proposal, the special nature of the resources you are recommending, and the strength of your solution's rationale. Show how these features of your proposal fit your reader's needs or mission. A good way to do this is to relate your solutions directly to each of the benefits given earlier. Those benefits might be listed individually, with each followed by an appropriate part of the description of the solution. The intent is to show clearly that (1) you have carefully thought through all aspects of the proposed solution; (2) it represents a realistic, feasible, and desirable way of solving the problem or meeting the need; and (3) you, your department, or your organization are capable of implementing the solution.

NOTE 11.14
Be sure the description is realistic and persuasive.

EVALUATION PLAN

If appropriate for your proposal, you will want to include an evaluation plan. The **evaluation plan** is a way to measure the degree of success achieved if your proposal is implemented. The evaluation plan could consist of a record-keeping system; a review by a panel of experts; statistical analysis procedures; a reporting system; or any number of control, analysis, measurement, or judgment techniques.

An evaluation plan is a major element in proposals for research studies. In other proposals, such as increased staffing proposals, the evaluation system might be an employee performance review procedure already in place. In this case, only a brief reference to the existing plan would be needed.

NOTE 11.15
An evaluation plan provides a way to judge the success of proposal implementation.

QUALIFICATIONS OF PERSONNEL

In the qualifications of personnel section, you provide biographical information about each key participant involved in implementing the proposal. You show his or her qualifications to provide the services proposed. The information should include the education, experience, accomplishments, successes, and evidence of achievement that directly relate to each participant's involvement in the proposed solution. You are justifying to the reader that these persons are fully qualified to serve in their assigned roles. The appropriate types of data are discussed in detail in the "Resume" section of Chapter 16.

Depending on the nature of the proposal, the amount of data presented for each individual will vary from a few lines to several pages. In some proposals, brief summaries are presented in the qualifications of personnel section and full resumes are provided in an appendix. If you are responding to an RFP, provide exactly the amount and type of personnel information specified.

TIME SCHEDULE

The time schedule shows when activity is to start and when it is to be completed. For simple proposals, the time schedule may consist of a listing of activities and their beginning and ending dates. For elaborate proposals, it may be necessary to use more complex task-time analysis charts such as Gantt, PERT (Program Evaluation Review Technique), or Milestone.

If you need assistance in selecting a time-schedule format, most libraries have good reference materials you can use. Your responsibility in this section is to show the reader a realistic time schedule.

COST

The cost or the price of the proposed solution is shown next. This section may be labeled *Cost, Prices, Budget,* or given another appropriate title. The cost may be presented in logical parts, such as personnel, supplies, equipment, and facilities; or it may be organized by benefits, parts of the description of the solution, time phases, or other appropriate categories.

The cost of the proposed solution must cover your expenses and, if appropriate, a profit. It also must be reasonable in relation to the benefits and the products or services to be provided. If you are following the guidelines in an RFP, the format for the cost section will likely be specified and should be used.

GLOSSARY

Based on a careful analysis of your readers, you may decide to include a glossary in your proposal. A **glossary** lists alphabetically the unfamiliar terms used in the proposal and gives their definitions. Include a glossary only when many unfamiliar, specialized, or technical terms have to be used. When there are only a few such terms, define them the first time they are used.

APPENDIXES

NOTE 11.16
Complex supporting information is shown in the appendixes.

To keep the body of the proposal as short and readable as possible, it is sometimes appropriate to place complex supporting information in an appendix. An **appendix** contains items that are indirectly related to the proposal but are excluded from the body to improve readability.

It was suggested earlier that resumes of key personnel might appropriately be placed in an appendix. Other information that might be placed in appendixes includes your organization's history, product specifications, records of past successes with similar projects, letters of support, details that support information in the description section, a questionnaire to be used for the proposed research, or other supporting and reference materials.

NOTE 11.17
Limit appendixes to information that is essential to the reader's needs.

An RFP may specify what appendixes are to be included. Be sure to include only those appendixes essential to the reader's understanding and decision making. If the proposal becomes too bulky, it will be less acceptable to a potential approver, funder, or purchaser.

REFERENCE LIST

If you think it strengthens your case, include a reference list in the proposal. A **reference list** is an alphabetical listing of all sources of information in the proposal, including those items presented as text citations or footnotes.

Writing a Proposal

The task of writing a long, complex proposal may be assigned to a team. When proposal writing is a collaborative effort, it is important to have one chief writer—someone who will be responsible for ensuring consistency and coherence within the document. As suggested in Tips and Hints on the next page, a solo author may ask others to read the proposal before it is finalized and submitted.

Whether written by one person or a team, proposals—like correspondence and reports—require planning. The principles of business communication must be applied as the document is drafted, revised, and edited.

Format, too, plays a part in readability and can help to generate interest in the proposal. Headings, margin notes, bullet points, outlines, charts, and diagrams can serve as road signs to guide the reader. White space can help to highlight important items.

Figure 11.1 is an example of a **poor** internal proposal. This chapter's suggestions for writing successful proposals are not implemented in this memo. An improved proposal for the same situation is shown in Figure 11.2. This example of a **good** informal proposal follows the guidelines for developing and writing successful proposals.

Figure 11.3 is an example of the text of a **good** external proposal submitted by Goodwill Industries, a not-for-profit agency, to secure funding to hire a consultant to guide it through a strategic planning activity. The remaining parts of the report—including forms, budget, transmittal messages, and final report—are available at the Web site for this book, http://krizan.swlearning.com.

Proposals are the way that new ideas are conveyed to decision makers. Most of the recommendations in this section on proposals apply to both written and oral proposals. Successful businesspeople develop and submit many proposals in their careers. They are not deterred by rejections. Instead, they follow the suggestion in Tips and Hints and try to improve their skills. They keep developing and submitting proposals and realize professional and personal gains when their proposals are accepted.

NOTE 11.18
Use format to enhance readability.

NOTE 11.19
Well-written proposals can help you advance your career.

Business Plans

A **business plan** is a special type of proposal, one designed to persuade a financial institution or a private party to invest money to support a particular venture. The investment may be in a start-up company or in a business that wishes to expand. The

LEARNING OBJECTIVE

③ *Draft a business plan.*

VALLEY PUBLISHING COMPANY

1222 Century Drive   Logan, Utah 84341   Tel: (435) 555-0366   Fax: (435) 555-6630

August 2, 200-

TO: VPC Board of Directors

FROM: Milly Vincent, Public Relations Director *MV*

SUBJECT: **MEETING ROOMS**

> Subject line is not specific.

Based on the number of phone calls and letters I've received during the past few months, I think it would be a good idea if we let folks from the community use our meeting rooms. Now that the Mountain Community Club is gone and the library is being remodeled, someone has to step up to fill the gap, and I think it should be us. What would we gain by letting groups meet here? Good PR . . . something no organization ever has too much of.

> Purpose statement is weak; problem is vague.

Let me know soon whether you like this idea, and I'll gather the data needed to determine how much we should charge for our rooms.

> Benefits and costs are neither clear nor emphasized.

FIGURE 11.1
Example of a *Poor* Internal Proposal

NOTE 11.20
Business plans are special-purpose proposals.

plan provides all the information necessary for the project to be evaluated by the funding source.

This section contains a brief description of what a business plan contains and offers several presentation suggestions. When faced with the task of developing a business plan, most people consult an accountant or a business development specialist. Numerous print and electronic resources are also available to provide background information beyond what is available here. In addition, agencies such as the Small Business Administration

VALLEY PUBLISHING COMPANY

1222 Century Drive   Logan, Utah 84341   Tel: (435) 555-0366   Fax: (435) 555-6630

August 2, 200-

TO: VPC Board of Directors

FROM: Milly Vincent, Public Relations Director *mv*

SUBJECT: PROPOSAL TO CHANGE FACILITY-USE POLICY

> **Subject is clear.**

VPC could enhance its public image and strengthen relationships with its employees by permitting outside groups to use the company's meeting rooms.

> **Purpose is clear and focuses on benefits.**

Background

During a typical three-month period, VPC receives one or two requests to use its meeting rooms. These requests come from employees, customers, and representatives of the general public. In accordance with Policy No. 102, which was enacted for financial and liability reasons, we refuse these requests.

> **Background sets context for the problem and solution.**

Problem

> **Problem is stated clearly.**

In the three-month period May 1 through July 31, we received 27 requests to use our facilities. Thirteen of these requests came from our employees or from representatives of organizations that VPC supports through financial or in-kind donations.

The increased request activity can, at least in part, be attributed to the fact that two popular meeting sites are no longer available: Fire destroyed The Mountain Community Center in April, and Central Library began a major remodeling project in mid-June.

Recommendation

> **Benefits are clear; costs are specific.**

I recommend that we make our three main-floor meeting rooms available to local groups between 6 and 10 p.m. weekdays on a cost-recovery basis until other facilities are again available (approximately nine months). By doing so, we will provide a valuable public service and build on our already strong reputation in the community.

Information gathered from our insurance carrier, our maintenance manager, and our security chief suggests that a $35 per hour fee will cover our costs.

If you approve this recommendation, I will issue a news release, notify those whose requests have been processed that our policy has changed, and draft internal procedures for your review.

> **Subsequent action is identified.**

LOOKS GOOD

FIGURE 11.2
Example of a *Good* Internal Proposal

(SBA) provide free or low-cost services. The SBA's Web site at http:// www.sba.gov is one of many online that provide sample business plans.

Although the actual format and organization may vary, a business plan will contain the following elements:

- *Executive summary.* The executive summary describes the highlights of the plan and helps capture the interest of the reader. It provides a brief, crisp introduction that discusses the nature of the business and its proposed

NOTE 11.21
Financial institutions expect business plans to contain certain information.

FIGURE 11.3
Example of *Good*
External Proposal

GOODWILL
INDUSTRIES
Vocational
Enterprises, Inc.

80th
ANNIVERSARY
1919–1999

700 Garfield Avenue   Duluth, Minnesota 55802
Tel: (218) 555-6351   Fax: (218) 555-8108   E-mail: goodwillduluth@servegroup.com

A Funding Request to the Duluth-Superior Area Community Foundation for a facilitator to guide Goodwill Industries through the development of a strategic plan

1. GENERAL INFORMATION

1999 marks the 80th anniversary of Goodwill Industries in Duluth, Minnesota. In North America there are 187 chapters of Goodwill Industries, all of which are members of Goodwill Industries International (GII), headquartered in Bethesda, Maryland. Minnesota has two chapters of Goodwill Industries: Duluth and St. Paul.

Goodwill Industries in Duluth has a territory assigned by GII consisting of 25 counties in Minnesota, or approximately the northern half of the state, and the top four northwest counties in Wisconsin. The agency's annual operating budget is approximately $4,000,000 with 50 percent of its operating revenue coming from the sale of recycled household items in eight thrift stores located throughout its territory.

Goodwill's mission is to provide vocational evaluation, training, extended employment, job placement, and related vocational rehabilitation services to persons with disabilities and others with barriers to employment. The agency serves approximately 300 people annually with the majority of clients being served in the Extended Employment Program. The primary disability served is mental retardation, followed by mental illness. Other disabilities typically include cerebral palsy, epilepsy, learning disability, and traumatic brain injury. A variety of training and employment opportunities is available to clients within the facility, including industrial sewing, wood working, assembly and packaging, and the manufacture of rubber stamps. Community-based training and employment opportunities are found in janitorial and lawn maintenance work, food growing, and frozen food processing.

2. PROJECT INFORMATION

A. NEED FOR THE PROGRAM

Goodwill Industries does not have a strategic plan in place guiding the agency. With the recent change in executive directors in September 1998, the time is ideal for the development of one. The process would take between six and nine months. A facilitator with a broad knowledge of the community would enhance Goodwill's ability to identify the unmet employment and training needs of people with disabilities and/or disadvantaged backgrounds in northern Minnesota and northwest Wisconsin. The process will analyze the agency's internal strengths and weaknesses in addition to external opportunities and threats. Goodwill Industries needs to develop a long-range programmatic vision to provide a framework for its programs of service to people experiencing barriers to employment. The result of the strategic planning process will be an agency with a renewed commitment to serve the community and an enhanced capability to help people with special needs become self-sufficient through employment.

B. TARGET POPULATION AND INTENDED BENEFICIARIES

For the 1997–1998 program year, Goodwill provided vocational services to 184 unduplicated people with disabilities or special needs. Mental retardation comprised the largest disability group at 39 percent, and mental illness was second at 24 percent. The remaining 37 percent of clients served included those with learning disabilities, seizures, cerebral palsy, chemical dependency, hearing impairments, visual impairments, cardiac conditions, arthritis, diabetes, physical disabilities, and traumatic brain injury. A community needs assessment will most likely broaden the types and numbers of people served. One of the keys to Goodwill's longevity and success has been its ability to be flexible and to develop programming to meet changing community needs.

FIGURE 11.3
Example of *Good*
External Proposal
cont.

C. ANTICIPATED RESULTS

The outcome of a strategic planning process would be an organization with an enhanced management capability and an improved communication system. The organization would have a refocused mission, most likely encompassing a broader range of community needs. In turn, the long-range stability and strength of the organization would be enhanced through the establishment of goals leading to steady growth and diversification. Overall agency morale would increase as the natural creativity of staff members is given full expression. In addition, the strategic planning process will produce an agency road map for the future and a means to measure progress toward mutually agreed upon goals and objectives.

D. PLAN OF ACTION

A strategic planning committee has been formed composed of board members, staff, and volunteers. The strategic planning process would take between six and nine months. The facilitator would guide the organization through the eight steps in the strategic planning process as follows:

1. **Situation Audit**
   Assist the agency in interpreting its operating environment by examining agency history, territory demographics, and current financial position. Assist in the clarification of agency core values and the development of a long-range programmatic vision, using observations, trend analysis, and feedback from stakeholders.

2. **Community Needs Assessment**
   Assist the agency in determining the employment and training needs of people with disabilities or disadvantaged backgrounds in the community. Guide the development and implementation of surveys and other vehicles to reach stakeholders for their opinions and observations of Goodwill Industries. Conduct research on existing community needs studies of people with disabilities or disadvantaged backgrounds.

3. **Risk Analysis**
   Lead the organization in an analysis of its internal strengths and weaknesses and external opportunities and threats.

4. **Mission Statement**
   Guide the organization through a reexamination of its mission statement. Help define the mission narrowly enough to encompass existing programming and funding sources yet broad enough to allow for growth and diversification.

5. **Determination of Organizational Objectives**
   Assist in the development of programmatic and operational goals and objectives in line with the overall mission of the organization.

6. **Development of Action Steps**
   Provide guidance in the development of action steps and strategies required to achieve objectives.

7. **Implementation**
   Give guidance and direction to the organization on how to gain cooperation and acceptance of the strategic plan among staff, clients, and board members. Provide a framework for linking annual planning and short-term activities with the achievement of long-term strategic goals.

8. **Evaluation of Plan**
   Assist in the development of a process for ongoing evaluation and revision of the strategic plan.

3. PLAN FOR EVALUATING THE PROJECT

A review of the strategic plan would be part of the annual agency planning and budgeting process. Progress or difficulties in achieving stated goals and objectives would be discussed at the Board of Directors meetings on an annual basis. The plan would be updated on an as-needed basis following periodic reviews by the Board of Directors.

location; how much funding you need and why; and the time period in which money is needed.

- *Ownership/management/staffing.* This section describes the proposed ownership and legal structure; it gives information about the experience, skills, training, and qualifications of key personnel.
- *Product/service/market identification.* When describing the products or services, identify the size, location, demographics, and other relevant information about your market. Explain your pricing strategy and how you plan to advertise and market the product or service.
- *Administration/production factors.* Next, provide information about equipment and facilities, production techniques, quality control mechanisms, management structure, accounting systems and controls, and any other factors specific to your product or service.
- *Growth and development potential and plans.* Present a one- or two-year projection linked to improving or expanding products, services, or markets. Describe changes in required staffing; and identify additional investment that might be required.
- *Financial information.* Provide detailed, realistic information about how much the project will cost, money that will be provided through other sources, and what financial security you can offer lenders. Develop a one-year monthly operating budget and cash flow projection. Forecast a first-year return on investment. Identify the breakeven point. Supply projected income statements and balance sheets for two years.
- *Appendixes.* Documents that relate to or further explain or support the plan are included in an appendix or appendixes. Resumes of key personnel, letters of intent, and copies of contracts or leases are among the items that may be included.

As you can tell from the item descriptions, the business plan is a complex document—one that poses a writing challenge. As Steve Schneberger notes in the Communication Quote on page 319, success depends in part on your ability to present (sell) your ideas clearly and convincingly.

Like other forms of business writing, the business plan should reflect the principles of business communication and show evidence of thorough planning. As a persuasive message crafted to sell your idea, the plan should contain the attention, interest, desire, and action elements described in Chapter 9 and be designed to reflect a professional image. The Tips and Hints on page 320 offers suggestions related to these topics.

Many universities, economic development agencies, and other organizations conduct business plan competitions and award cash prizes to those who write what judges deem to be outstanding business plans. Business owner Eric Goerdt, who authored an award-winning plan, offers his thoughts in the Communication Quote on page 320. The statement of purpose displayed in Figure 11.4 is taken from Mr. Goerdt's plan, which is available at the Web site for this book, http://krizan.swlearning.com.

LEARNING OBJECTIVE
Report the proceedings of a meeting effectively through the use of minutes.
(4)

Special Reports

Some business reports require special content or format considerations. Four common special reports are minutes, policies, news releases, and performance appraisals.

It is difficult to overstate the value of a well-thought-out and well-written business plan. Perhaps the most common use of the written business plan is in the procurement of the financing needed to start or expand a business. In many cases, the loan applicant meets with and presents the loan request to a single loan officer, but loan approvals may be issued only after a higher lending authority such as a senior lender, a loan committee, or a board of directors (and sometimes all three) has reviewed and approved the loan request. In some instances, the specific loan request may be eligible for assistance under one of a number of entrepreneurial loan programs or perhaps the request will be approved only if it qualifies under one of the loan guaranty programs.

Circumstances such as these are not uncommon, and when they arise, the availability of a thoroughly conceived and well-written business plan will increase the likelihood that the entrepreneur's story will be accurately communicated to all parties involved, with minimal loss of critical content. The following advice is offered to business plan writers:

[1] Be thorough. Seek and use all available resources as you research and write your plan. The perspective gained from sharing ideas with individuals whose profession regularly involves them in this type of activity will produce a better business plan, one that is viewed by the reader as realistic, easy to comprehend, and devoid of mistakes and redundancies.

[2] Include all key assumptions used in preparing financial projections. Support for the assumptions should also be included whenever the reason for their selection is not obvious.

[3] Strive for accuracy. If the reader discovers inaccuracies or unfounded statements, he or she may question the writer/entrepreneur's competence. In some cases, inaccuracy could be interpreted as an intentional attempt to mislead the reader. Obviously, neither of these conclusions is desirable from the writer's perspective.

[4] Be enthusiastic. While your plan must come across as reasonable and realistic, your commitment and enthusiasm for your project must also be conveyed to the reader.

—Steve Schneberger, Vice President, Commercial Loans, National Bank of Commerce.
(Photo courtesy of Jeff Frey and Associates)

Minutes

Minutes are an official report of the proceedings of a meeting. They serve as an official record, assist in refreshing memories of participants, provide information to individuals who were not present, and help prepare members for upcoming meetings.

As pointed out in the Communication Note on page 320, recording word-for-word minutes can be a costly venture. Therefore, unless law or policy mandate that verbatim record be kept, minutes should be reported in summary form.

NOTE 11.22
Only pertinent information should be included in minutes.

Minutes should be concise and accurately report all pertinent information. All motions and resolutions should be recorded word-for-word as presented. Individuals presenting motions and resolutions should be identified by name in the minutes. It is important to indicate that a motion was seconded, but the name of the individual who

NAME AND STATEMENT OF PURPOSE

FIGURE 11.4
Business Plan
Statement of Purpose

Northern Waters Smokehaus
Eric and Lynn Goerdt, Sole Proprietors
Superior, Wisconsin 54880

Statement of Purpose

Northern Waters Smokehaus is committed to providing premium smoked salmon and other quality handmade products to the communities of Superior and Duluth. We are committed to providing a quality of life for the owners and employees and being an asset to the business community in Superior.

Reprinted with permission; some names and contact information have been modified. The remainder of the business plan is available at *http://krizan.swlearning.com*

seconds a motion need not be recorded. The outcome—approval or defeat—should be included also.

The following parts normally are included in minutes:

- Committee or organization name
- Date, time, and location of the meeting
- List of those who attended
- Reference to approval of last meeting's minutes
- Chronological record of the meeting
- Time of adjournment
- Signature of the secretary and/or chairperson

These parts will vary depending on the purpose and formality of the meeting. Style will also vary based on the parliamentary authority used by the group. Figure 11.5 shows an example of minutes for a meeting of a committee of a national organization.

Policies

LEARNING OBJECTIVE
Develop clear policy statements.
(5)

A **policy statement** serves as a guideline for employees, customers, or others to follow.

Policy statements affecting employees normally will be assembled into a manual. This manual can be used to orient new employees and can serve as a reference for long-time employees. Policies affecting customers may be posted in a highly visible location or printed on transaction documents. A retail store's return policy, for example, could be printed on a cash register receipt or on a card that is attached to the receipt at the time of sale. An emergency closing policy such as the one shown in Figure 11.6 might be contained in a manual, posted at a prominent place in the building, and/or posted to the organization's Web site.

NOTE 11.23
Policies should be broad for managerial personnel and specific for nonmanagerial personnel.

Policy statements should be written in the third person and should be clear, concise, and complete. Policies written for managerial personnel are broad guides that allow flexibility, whereas policies for nonmanagerial personnel are narrower and more restrictive.

News Releases

LEARNING OBJECTIVE
Write an effective news release.
(6)

A **news release** is a special business report containing information that will be of interest to the public. News releases need to be newsworthy, accurate, timely, concise, and positive. Common subjects for news releases include promotions, business expansion, employee layoffs, and introduction of new products.

NOTE 11.24
News releases should be written in the inverted pyramid format.

The **inverted pyramid format** should be used for news releases. The inverted pyramid format begins with a summary lead that tells who, what, where, when, and sometimes why or how. Develop the body of the release by giving the details in descending order of importance. This organizational pattern respects both news agency personnel, who will cut material from the bottom to meet space constraints, and the general public, who may not read or listen to the entire story because of time constraints.

The news release should be double spaced with the company's name and address typed or printed at the top. The contact person's name and telephone number also should be on the news release. Special instructions ("FOR IMMEDIATE RELEASE," "FOR RELEASE ON MAY 2") should be typed in all capital letters at the top. The release text is immediately preceded by city, state, and date. A news release should end with "-30-" or "###" beneath the last line to inform the news agency that the release is

FIGURE 11.5
Minutes of a Meeting

Membership Affairs Committee (MAC)
Minutes
August 5–6, 2000
Chicago, Illinois

The following were present for all or part of the meeting:

Members: Phil Brigham (Chair), Sylvia Cotting, Adam Dougherty, Seth Finch, Tonya Hawkins, Julia Lloyd, Walter Murphy. **Staff:** Mike Castro, Elsa Craig, Don Patberg. **Guests:** Jim Elwood, Jeremy Vieth, Vince Vincent.

Meeting Details
The Committee met in executive session from 9 a.m. until noon on Saturday, August 5, and from 8:30 a.m. until 11:30 a.m. on Sunday, August 6. The Subcommittees on Member Services (MS), Member Recruitment/Retention (MRR), and Membership Categories/Dues (MCD) met separately from 1:30 p.m. until 4:30 p.m. on Saturday, August 5.

1. **Approval of Minutes of the May 14–15, 2000, Meeting**
   The minutes were approved with one correction: page 3, ". . . The conference will be held in Arlington, Texas, . . ." [Cotting/Finch/unanimous]

2. **Chair's Report**
   Brigham reviewed what MS/MRR Joint Task Force has done on insurance benefits. Dougherty suggested the group investigate long-term care insurance.

   Brigham referred to a letter from the Committee on Professional Affairs (CPA), which plans to survey members under age 40. MAC was invited to suggest topics. The matter was referred to the MRR, which will be asked to report at the next meeting.

3. **Membership Certificate Presentation**
   Jeremy Vieth of the Board of Directors made a presentation about membership certificates. During discussion, a question arose about whether years as a student affiliate were counted when a member applied for emeritus status. The matter was referred to the MCD for discussion.

4. **Committee Web Site**
   Patberg reviewed the Committee Web site. He encouraged members to look at the Web site (www.membership.acu.org/mac). A counter and "mail to" links have been added; surveys can be conducted through the site. The Committee asked staff to consider the following questions and report at the next meeting:
   1. Should Committee and Subcommittee minutes go on the Web page?
   2. How should page traffic be tracked?
   3. Will inserting meta tags improve searchability?
   4. Who reviews content? How often?

5. **Subcommittee Reports**
   Membership Services—Tonya Hawkins, Chair
   ACTION: Support the Subcommittee recommendations for expanding the nontechnical members' benefits in 2001 and 2002 to include worldwide Internet access. [Hawkins/Vieth/unanimous]

   Member Recruitment/Retention—Julia Lloyd, Chair
   ACTION: Accept the Subcommittee recommendation that a notebook be awarded to 10-year members and a pen to 25-year members and that both bear the association logo and year milestone. [Lloyd/Murphy/passed]

   Membership Categories/Dues—Sylvia Cotting, Chair
   No recommendations were forwarded for Committee action.

Mike Craig

Mike Craig

FIGURE 11.6
Policy Statement

Winter County Library	Policy: 37 Passed: 01/08/1990 Modified: 11/12/2001

EMERGENCY CLOSINGS

This policy shall apply in the event of an emergency such as severe weather, utility failure, fire, or terrorism.

- **The safety of library personnel and patrons will be the primary consideration in the decision to close.**

- **The Director or Assistant Director, working in collaboration with public safety departments and emergency service providers, shall have the authority to close the facility.**

- **In the event of a closure, the Director or Assistant Director shall notify local news media.**

- **In the event of a closure, the Director or Assistant Director shall prepare and submit a closure report to the Library Board of Trustees.**

complete; for releases longer than one page, "more" should be printed on the bottom of each page that is to be continued. Figure 11.7 shows a sample news release.

Performance Appraisals

LEARNING OBJECTIVE ⑦
Prepare a construc-tive performance appraisal.

NOTE 11.25
Performance appraisals help the employee and the organization.

A **performance appraisal** reports a supervisor's evaluation of an employees' job performance. The appraisal is a tool for helping to improve subpar performance and for identifying leadership potential. A written appraisal is prepared, then discussed with the worker before becoming part of his or her employment record. Often the employee is asked to sign the appraisal to acknowledge that the supervisor has discussed it with him or her. Employees who disagree with the supervisor's appraisal may have an opportunity to write a response and have it included in the file, too. Information contained in Chapter 13 will be useful in preparing for and conducting the performance appraisal meeting.

No employee should be surprised by information contained in a written performance appraisal. Good management practice dictates that duties and expectations be conveyed to employees in advance and that informal feedback—praise, criticism, and suggestions for improvement—become a routine part of supervision. Nevertheless, supervisors must approach the writing of a performance appraisal as they would any other business document. They must identify the purpose, analyze the receiver, and select the appropriate approach.

An evaluation that will be received positively or neutrally should follow the direct pattern; evaluations that contain negative news should be presented indirectly. Because the appraisal will become the basis for human resource decisions such as pay raises, promotions, discipline, and terminations, assessments must be supported by

FIGURE 11.7
News Release

APPLEGATE Manufacturing, Inc.
P.O. Box 7329, Huntington, WV 25714-7329, (304) 555-4156

NEWS RELEASE

FOR IMMEDIATE RELEASE

Applegate Manufacturing Declares Dividends

Huntington, WV (April 13, 200–) Applegate Manufacturing, Inc. announced today that its Board of Directors declared a quarterly dividend of $0.175 a share on the company's Common Stock and $0.875 a share on its Preferred Stock, both payable April 15, 200–, to stockholders of record on March 16, 200–.

Applegate Manufacturing is a leading North American plastics manufacturer specializing in products used in food packaging. Based in Huntington, West Virginia, the company also has facilities in El Paso, Texas, and Salem, Oregon.

CONTACT:

Walter Henry
304.555.4082
W.Henry@applegate.paper.net

###

A supervisor and worker discuss the worker's performance appraisal.

©MICHAEL NEWMAN/PHOTOEDIT, INC.

factual evidence. Saying "Paul has submitted 4 of his last 6 monthly reports 3 to 10 days after they were due" is more descriptive than "Paul does not submit reports in a timely manner."

Brevity is also a factor in preparing performance appraisals. Many organizations have developed forms that supervisors must use, and space is usually limited. If necessary, the writer should continue his or her comments on another sheet and attach it to the form. The organization may ask that the worker sign both the form and the supplement. An honest appraisal, devoid of humor and sarcasm, is most effective. Omit comments such as "He sets low standards and consistently fails to achieve them." Figure 11.8 represents one section of a performance appraisal.

FIGURE 11.8
Performance Appraisal

Performance Appraisal

Employee: Barbara Wriggly	**Department:** Administration

Duty: Employee is responsible for greeting visitors, issuing visitor badges, and notifying employees that their guests have arrived.

Standard: Visitors should be greeted within 30 seconds after entering the lobby. No guests should pass beyond the lobby without a visitor badge. No guests should pass beyond the lobby without an employee escort.

Evaluation: Barb performs her duties efficiently. Guests are greeted in a timely manner and served in the sequence in which they arrive. Her smile and the warm, friendly tone of her voice create a positive impression on our guests. Barb needs to ensure that she exhibits these positive traits in her interactions with employees as well as guests. During the past three months, I have received calls from four employees expressing concern that Barb has become sharp with them if she must phone them more than once. They fear that guests may hear her and react negatively.

Action/ Follow-up: Barb and I will develop several strategies for handling delays and review their effectiveness after two weeks and again after six weeks.

Employee's Signature: *Barbara Wriggly*   Supervisor's Signature: M. P. Arb
Date Reviewed: June 16, 200–

Summary of Learning Objectives

① Identify the different types of proposals.

A proposal is an analysis of a problem and a recommendation for a solution. The recommended solution may be products or personnel, a business study, work to be performed, or any of several other ways of solving a problem. Proposals may be external or internal, solicited or unsolicited, formal or informal. External proposals can be directed to prospective clients, government agencies, or private agencies/foundations.

Write formal and informal proposals.

Proposals are common in business and must be written as persuasive messages designed to win the reader's approval of the writer's recommendation. Successful proposals must have excellent content and be clearly presented.

Draft a business plan.

A business plan is a proposal for funding to start or expand a business. The proposal will provide information about the people, products, potential, and financing of the business. A realistic, well-thought-out, well-written business plan has the greatest opportunity for success.

Report the proceedings of a meeting effectively through the use of minutes.

Minutes of a meeting should be brief and contain only relevant information. Motions and resolutions should be recorded exactly as presented. The name of the individual presenting a motion or resolution should be included in the minutes along with the outcome of the motion.

Develop clear policy statements.

Policy statements serve as guidelines for the operation of a business. They should be clear, concise, and complete.

Write an effective news release.

News releases should be written in the inverted pyramid format. The body should contain the important facts first and least important facts last. It should not contain a conclusion.

Prepare a constructive performance appraisal.

Performance appraisals provide feedback to workers and help them improve their performance. They typically become the basis for human resource decisions such as pay raises, promotions, discipline, and termination. Statements should be concise, clear, and concrete. Comments should be organized directly for positive, neutral evaluations and indirectly for negative evaluations. A written evaluation should be discussed with and signed by the worker to show he or she has reviewed it.

Discussion Questions

1. Define and explain the various types of proposals. (Objective 1)
2. Discuss the qualities of successful proposals. (Objective 2)
3. How does the purpose of a proposal's cover letter or memo differ from the purpose of the proposal's summary? (Objective 2)

4. Explain the role format plays in proposal writing. (Objective 2)
5. What is a business plan? For whom is it prepared? (Objective 3)
6. Briefly describe the nature of the materials included within a business plan. (Objective 3)
7. What items typically are included in the minutes of a meeting? (Objective 4)
8. What purposes do policy manuals serve in organizations? (Objective 5)
9. What is the inverted pyramid format? Why is it used when composing news releases? (Objective 6)
10. What is a performance appraisal? What purpose does it serve? (Objective 7)

Application Exercises

1. **Internet. Teamwork.** Individually or as a group, develop a proposal on one of the following topics. If possible, use the Web to research the topic. The proposal is to be sent to the dean or president of your college, as appropriate for the topic. (Objectives 1 and 2)
   a. Requiring all students to have laptop computers
   b. Establishing a "Club Member of the Term" award
   c. Instituting a career shadowing program in local businesses
   d. Requiring all business students to complete an internship
   e. Operating on a four-day school week
   f. Installing baby diaper-changing stations in all (male and female) restrooms
   g. Requiring all business students to complete 200 hours of volunteer work
   h. Increasing summer school offerings
   i. Sponsoring a blood drive
   j. Sponsoring a "Business Jeopardy" competition among student organizations

2. **Internet. Teamwork.** Write an informal proposal to your instructor in which you recommend that your business communication course be offered on the Internet. Think carefully about the purpose, the problem, and the benefits of this proposal. Use a Web search engine to locate other schools that offer courses on the Internet. Consider working with a team to brainstorm the recommended action. (Objective 2)
3. Interview the development officer at your school, the director of a not-for-profit group within your community, or the director of a local foundation to learn about the proposals they write or fund. Report your findings to the class. (Objectives 2 and 3)
4. Write a complete proposal using all 18 proposal elements discussed in this chapter. The subject of your proposal can be (a) combating fatigue by allowing workers to take short naps during the work day or (b) instituting self-appraisal or peer review as part of the performance evaluation process within the organization. (Objectives 2 and 7)

5. **Internet.** You volunteer at a Boys and Girls Club in your community. The playground equipment at the club is old and potentially unsafe. You've decided to explore the possibility of applying for foundation funding to buy and install new playground equipment. Use the Internet to locate three foundations that fund proposals of this nature.
   a. Prepare a memo to the club's director, Myron Tulley. Report your findings and volunteer to prepare the grant proposal.
   b. Prepare a grant proposal that meets the guidelines of one of the foundations. (Objectives 1 and 2)

6. **Teamwork.** Work with two or three students who are pursuing the same degree as you and design an Internet-based business. As your instructor directs, prepare all or selected parts of a business plan designed to obtain the funding necessary to start your business. (Objective 3)

7. A copy of the minutes of the Butler Insurance Company Fringe Benefits Committee meeting follows. List the items that have been omitted from the minutes. (Objective 4)

> *MINUTES*
>
> *FRINGE BENEFITS COMMITTEE*
>
> *The meeting was called to order at 10:30 a.m. on April 18, 200–.*
>
> *Copies of the last meeting's minutes were distributed.*
>
> *Ms. Carson presented a proposal on the new procedures for vacations. Mr. Wilson moved that the proposal be approved.*
>
> *The committee unanimously approved the motion.*
>
> *The proposal for adding dental insurance to the family policy was defeated by a 5 to 2 vote.*
>
> *The president appointed Mr. Thomas to gather information on eye care insurance. He was directed to report his findings at the next committee meeting.*
>
> *The meeting was adjourned at 11:15 a.m.*

8. **Internet/E-mail.** Many organizations and local government bodies now post minutes of their meetings on the Web. Check to see whether organizations to which you belong or the city in which you reside has adopted this policy. Report your findings to your instructor in an e-mail and, if one or more of these groups have not adopted this policy, prepare an informal proposal suggesting that one of them do so. Submit your proposal not only to your instructor but also to the organization or government body. (Objectives 1, 2, and 4)

9. **InfoTrac.** The suggestions included in InfoTrac article A78800765, "Meeting of the Minutes: Writing Meeting Minutes," by Philip Vasallo (Summer 2001) can help novice minute takers reduce the stress associated with recording notes. Access and read the article. As your instructor directs, prepare written answers to the following questions or use them as a basis for class discussion:
   a. Why do people who write for a living dislike recording minutes?
   b. What is the focus of minutes within an organizational setting?
   c. What can the minute taker do before, during, and after the meeting to ensure that he or she does the note taking task well? (Objective 4)

10. **E-mail.** Write (or e-mail) three businesses and request copies of their policy on reimbursing employees for business-related travel. Summarize your findings in a memo to your instructor. Describe the format of the policies, including whether they are numbered, dated, and so on. (Objective 5)

11. A student organization to which you belong recently returned from its national conference. One of the highlights of the conference was announcement of "Chapter of the Year"—and your group won! Prepare an appropriate news release; add details to make the release interesting. (Objective 6)

12. Work with three or four of your classmates to develop a job description for business communication students. Then, prepare a performance appraisal that discusses how or whether you meet the standards. Include recommendations for self-improvement. (Objective 7)

There are Web exercises at **http://krizan.swlearning.com** to accompany this chapter.

Message Analysis

Rewrite and improve the quality of the following policy statement. Implement the guidelines given in this chapter.

Due to the increasing litter problem on the head quarters building, the following poster policy is in effect. This affects all posters, flyers, handbills, and other publicity materials posted on the walls. ANY POSTER, NOT APPROVED OR LACKING INFORMATION WILL BE TAKEN DOWN. See the Public Relations Office manager for detales; the Hr director can give special approval of items that do not fit these criterion.

1. *All posters must contain the following information:*
   - *Sponsoring Organization (internal grapes take priority)*
   - *Time of the event*
   - *Place of the event*
   - *Cost to attend the event*
   - *Who the event is open to*

2. *Posters must not exceet a size of 22 x 14.*

3. *Each poster must be individually stamped and initialed by the Pr receptionist.*

Posting

1. *Posters can only be only posted in one of the approved posting locations. See Approved Posting Areas.*

2. *Posters CAN NOT be put on department bulletin boards, painted surfaces, wood surfaces, wall-papered surfaces, metal surface, glass surfaces, directional signs*

3. *Masking tape is the only adhesive you can use. Other tapes or poster mounts are not permeated.*

4. *Please remove posters after the even has occured. This will help keep advertising activities effective and keep the accumulation of posters to a minimum.*

Grammar Workshop

Correct the grammar, spelling, punctuation, style, and word choice errors in the following sentences:

1. If you're a conservative invester look for stocks with high credit ratings well established records and stability.
2. In edition to being a means of transportation the automobile has also become a cymbal of freedom.
3. Your card and note is setting hear on my desk waiting for a reply.
4. Each of the travelers must have their Passport ready for examination when we enter France.
5. Did Sal say it was him whom forgot to turn the copier off before leaving the office last night.
6. Jody planes to ask for a four % raise, but will be happy if she receives 3.
7. After you pass the class we will reimburse your tuition and fees; the from you must complete fill out is availabe at the HR websight.
8. Dolores Huerta—one of the 1st women involved in union leadership, cofounded the United farm workers Union with Cesar Chavez.
9. Cicily chose verticle blinds for her office which will be installed early next month.
10. Sasha Gordev president of the International club will precide at this years' Feast of Nations Celebration which will be held on Saturday May 04th.

Visual Aids

Jim Thomas, Vice-President/General Manager, Eastern Division Operations, Trussway Ltd.

LET'S TALK BUSINESS As a manager for one of the nation's leading engineered wood products companies, I use visual aids to help organize and simplify the information I present. Visuals provide order and sequence to information documents, as well as maintain subject continuity. Whether I am discussing market data, financial information, sales figures, or any other aspect of our company's goals, visual aids are used to underscore the highlights of key ideas. Visual aids keep me focused and prevent the omission of key points of information.

Graphs, statistical information, and financial data presented visually to our management group reduce misinterpretation and give our operations team a and clearer message. Visual aids play a vital role in giving confidence to our sales and management staff when they make presentations to important clients. Visual aids add realism by giving our company the ability to import graphics.

Visual aids add the sight component to our company's business needs. Engineering and technical information can be explained, understood, and retained far easier when visual aids are used as a component of communication. Our financial team uses visual aids to communicate and compare budget information from profit-and-loss statements to actual performance. Our procurement department uses visual aids to track historical data so that market cycles can be monitored and purchases made at opportune times. Our human resources staff provides management with graphs and charts to track employee data that can visually help solve issues that might take days to interpret through timely statistical computations. Organizational charts and flowcharts are used to provide an understanding of our company's management structure, process and procedure information, and job-flow information.

A **visual aid** is an illustration used to clarify points in and improve comprehension of material in a written report or business presentation. Visual aids may be in the form of tables, graphs, charts, drawings, photographs, diagrams, or maps. As Jim Thomas indicates in Let's Talk Business, visual aids are used to complement and simplify the communication. Visual aids for written reports may reduce the volume of text, but they do not eliminate the written material completely. Visual aids can clarify complex data in an oral presentation without lengthy explanation.

Use of Visual Aids

When used properly, visual aids can be helpful in effectively communicating ideas. Indiscriminate use of visual aids may impede rather than promote communication. The selection of effective visuals requires a basic knowledge of the purposes of visual aids and the design elements of these visuals, as well as careful consideration of how they will be used to complement the written or spoken word.

Purposes of Visual Aids

Visual aids can complement your communication by summarizing complex figures in charts and graphs, by identifying your company through the use of a drawing or photograph for a logo, by showing relationships in a chart, by indicating trends in a graph, or by abstracting in a table details that are too cumbersome for written text or oral presentation. Appropriate placement and identification of visual aids will enhance the effectiveness of your communication.

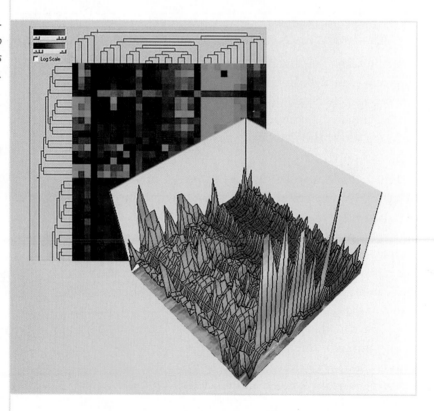

Placement of Visual Aids in a Written Report

LEARNING OBJECTIVE
② *Label visual aids properly, and explain where to place them within a report.*

Visual aids (also referred to as *illustrations*) must be placed in appropriate locations to enhance the message of the written report. Illustrations that directly relate to the topic should be placed within the written text. A small illustration, less than one-half page, should be placed after the first reference to the aid, preferably on the same page. A large illustration, one-half to one page, should be placed on the page following the first mention of the illustration. Avoid dividing a visual aid between two pages. It is more desirable to place the entire illustration on one page, separate from the copy, than to divide it.

NOTE 12.4
Reports are improved when visual aids are placed in proper locations.

Illustrations that indirectly relate to the copy may be of interest to only a few readers. These illustrations will add unnecessary bulk to the body of the report and should be placed in an appendix.

You should refer to a visual aid within the written text of the report prior to its appearance. This reference is a powerful tool—it guides the reader to the items you want to stress. The reference may be nothing more than "as shown in Graph 2" or "(see Table 3, page 12)." A reference to a visual aid should be subtle and not distract the reader's attention from the material being read.

NOTE 12.5
Illustrations should be referred to in a report before they appear.

Identification of Visual Aids in a Written Report

All formal visual aids within a written report should be identified by appropriate titles. The title of a visual aid should describe its contents. The title should contain enough detail so that the reader can understand the visual aid without reading the text of the report, but it should not be extremely lengthy. You should consider the five Ws—who, what, when, where, and why—and use those that will make the title most clear.

NOTE 12.6
Illustrations must have titles.

Methods of numbering visual aids vary. One method is to call all visual aids *illustrations* and number them with either Arabic or Roman numerals. A second method is to divide the graphic aids into two categories and use Roman numerals for *tables* and Arabic numerals for *figures* (all illustrations other than tables grouped together). A variation of the second method is to categorize and number each type of figure separately (chart, diagram, graph, etc.) but still use Arabic numerals for identification.

Visual aids should be numbered consecutively. However, if there is only one visual aid in a report, it need not be numbered. If the report contains more than one section or chapter, the illustrations may be numbered consecutively throughout the report (Figure 1, Figure 2, etc.); or they may be numbered consecutively by sections or chapters (Figure 1.1, Figure 1.2, Figure 2.1, etc.). The most important consideration in numbering illustrations is consistency.

NOTE 12.7
Illustrations must be numbered in a consistent manner.

Illustration titles may be printed either in uppercase or in uppercase and lowercase letters. Traditionally, titles were placed above tables and below all other illustrations. Today, businesses use either location. As in the numbering of illustrations, consistency is the important guideline in title placement.

NOTE 12.8
Titles may be placed above or below illustrations.

Identification of Visual Aids Sources

The same consideration for acknowledging sources of text material should be used in acknowledging sources of visual aids. A **source note** is used whenever content is obtained from another source. The source note normally consists of the word *source* in uppercase letters followed by a colon and the source. An example of an illustration using material from a report written by Toshi Okano follows:

NOTE 12.9
Source notes have to be used for illustrations obtained from others.

SOURCE: *Toshi Okano Report*, January 11, 2004, p. 17.

Although a source note usually is placed a double space below the illustration, it may be placed under the title of the illustration. When the content of an illustration is originated by the writer, no source note is required.

Development of Visual Aids

Effective communication depends in part on the selection of the most appropriate visual aid for a specific situation. You must be knowledgeable about the various types of illustrations so you can select the one that will most effectively convey information under specific conditions. The most frequently used visual aids in business reports are tables, charts, and graphs.

LEARNING OBJECTIVE

Construct tables and the three most common types of charts.

③

Tables

A **table** is a display of words and numbers arranged in columns and rows. The data in tables should be presented in an orderly arrangement for easy and clear reference. In addition to the title, a table includes column headings and row identifiers in the first column that classify the categories of data in each row. These column headings and row identifiers need to describe the data clearly but should be short so they do not detract from the data.

NOTE 12.10
Tables show data arranged in columns and rows.

Statistical information can be presented more effectively in a table than in text material. To illustrate this point, consider the following information:

> Jason's investment in the stock market was reduced drastically in 2003. His investments in various companies in 2002 and 2003 were: Dell Computers—$4,585 and $4,110; Eastman Kodak—$8,659 and $5,327; Johnson & Johnson—$13,284 and $11,831; Kraft Foods—$3,250 and $2,105; Monsanto—$13,294 and $9,240; Procter & Gamble—$9,945 and $7,276; Qwest Communications—$17,310 and $6,384; Reebok—$6,397 and $4,839; Tyson Foods—$12,629 and $9,435; and Wrigley—$14,530 and $11,292. Part of this decrease was from thesale of stock; however, much of it was because of the declining stock market.

This statistical information would be communicated more effectively if presented in a table, as shown in Figure 12.1. The statistical information in the 2003 column is listed from high to low. Readers can interpret data more easily when the numbers are listed in some order, high to low or low to high, rather than randomly.

When information to be presented in a table requires numerous columns, the table may be constructed horizontally (landscape orientation) on the page rather than vertically. Figure 12.2 is a table printed with landscape orientation.

Charts

NOTE 12.11
Pie charts, flowcharts, and organization charts commonly are used in business reports.

The three types of charts commonly used in business reports are organization charts, flowcharts, and pie charts. None of these charts needs lengthy text interpretation. The first two types, organization charts and flowcharts, clearly present relationships and procedures. The pie chart is used to illustrate the proportion of a part to the whole.

FIGURE 12.1
Table

Jason's investment in the stock market was reduced drastically in 2003. His investments in various companies in 2002 and 2003 were:

Jason's Stock Investments

Stock Holdings	2002	2003
Johnson & Johnson	$13,284	$11,831
Wrigley	14,530	11,292
Tyson Foods	12,629	9,435
Monsanto	13,294	9,240
Procter & Gamble	9,945	7,276
Qwest Communications	17,310	6,384
Eastman Kodak	8,659	5,327
Reebok	6,397	4,839
Dell Computers	4,585	4,110
Kraft Foods	3,250	2,105
Totals	$103,883	$71,839

Part of this decrease was from the sale of stock; however, much of it was because of the declining stock market.

ORGANIZATION CHARTS

An **organization chart** shows lines of authority among the various positions within an organization. This type of chart illustrates the relationships among departments and among personnel within the departments. The chart may depict the entire organization or a selected portion of it. The senior position is placed at the top of the chart. Other positions are placed on the chart in descending order of authority. These positions are connected by solid lines if they are line positions with authority over other positions, and by broken or dotted lines if they are advisory or staff positions. An example of an organization chart is shown in Figure 12.3.

NOTE 12.12
An organization chart shows lines of authority and relationships within an organization.

FLOWCHARTS

A **flowchart** may be used to illustrate step-by-step progression through complicated procedures. Such procedures could include the steps needed to manufacture a product, the route that a form follows when processed in an office, or the steps in a computer program.

Complicated written instructions are more easily understood when accompanied by a flowchart. Each step of the procedure needs to be included, but the chart should not be so detailed that it becomes difficult to understand. Boxes of various shapes are connected by arrows to illustrate the direction that the action flows during the procedure. The size of a box is determined by the number of words in the label and does not indicate the importance of that particular portion of the procedure. A flowchart displaying the procedure used to take blood pressure is shown in Figure 12.4.

NOTE 12.13
Flowcharts simplify the interpretation of complicated procedures.

PIE CHARTS

A **pie chart** can be used to show how the parts of a whole are distributed and how the parts relate to each other. To make the chart easy to read, begin slicing the pie at the twelve o'clock position and continue in a clockwise direction. The pieces should be arranged in descending order of size. If several smaller pieces are combined into an "Other" category, this piece should be placed last. "Other" should never be the largest segment. Label individual pieces by showing the quantity, or percentage, of each piece.

NOTE 12.14
A pie chart is a circle; its slices show the relationships of the parts to a whole.

FIGURE 12.2
Table with Landscape Orientation

**Percentage of Membership Attendance at Young
Business Leaders' Meetings by District in 200—**

District	Jan.	Feb.	Mar.	Apr.	May	June	July	Aug.	Sep.	Oct.	Nov.	Dec.	Average
I	65	72	83	64	75	64	41	46	64	77	64	59	64.5
II	79	84	87	91	84	82	84	85	93	95	90	88	86.8
III	59	82	69	74	83	68	74	75	84	80	74	58	73.3
IV	85	86	85	87	87	85	84	84	87	85	86	89	85.8
V	91	88	92	91	90	87	85	92	91	91	92	90	90.0
VI	56	59	63	67	59	50	48	51	47	54	56	48	54.8
VII	80	78	82	82	79	73	71	80	83	85	84	79	79.7
VIII	64	76	63	73	62	59	57	53	64	66	76	72	65.4
IX	87	91	89	90	89	85	86	85	91	90	89	88	88.3
AVERAGE	74.0	79.6	79.2	79.9	78.7	72.6	70.0	72.3	78.2	80.3	79.0	74.6	76.5

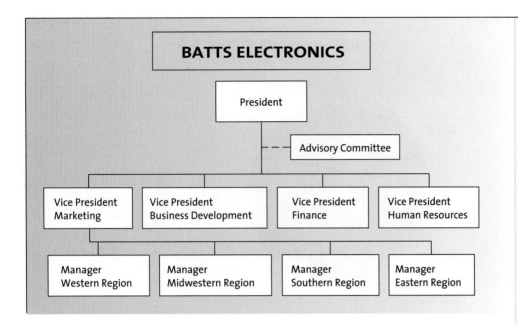

FIGURE 12.3
Organization Chart

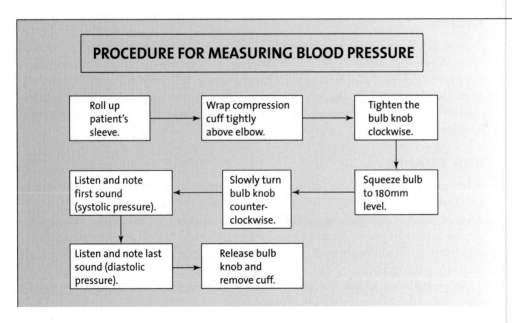

FIGURE 12.4
Flowchart

Pie charts are easy for most readers to understand, but remember certain considera-tion when constructing them. All pie charts within a report should be the same size. A pie chart should contain from two to eight pieces. When more than eight pieces are used, a pie chart becomes unclear. The percentages shown in a pie chart need to total 100.

When a writer wants to emphasize a specific segment, an exploded pie chart may be used. In an **exploded pie chart**, one segment is separated from the rest of the chart for emphasis. Figure 12.5 shows Patsy's Investment Portfolio, with the category "Mutual Funds" being emphasized.

NOTE 12.15
Exploded pie charts are used to emphasize one segment.

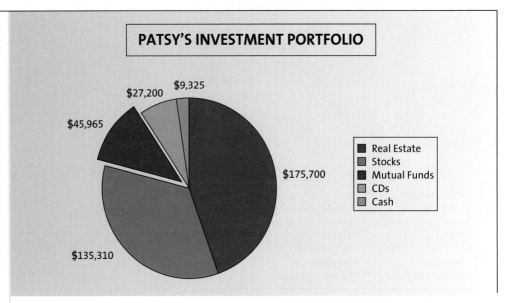

FIGURE 12.5
Exploded Pie Chart

PATSY'S INVESTMENT PORTFOLIO

$27,200
$9,325
$45,965
$175,700
$135,310

- Real Estate
- Stocks
- Mutual Funds
- CDs
- Cash

LEARNING OBJECTIVE
Construct the various types of graphs.

④

NOTE 12.16
Graphs show relationships among variables and should not have a complex design.

NOTE 12.17
Comparisons of quantitative differences can be shown in bar graphs.

NOTE 12.18
The length or height of a bar indicates quantity in a simple bar graph.

NOTE 12.19
Several quantitative variables can be compared on one multiple-bar graph.

Graphs

A graph is a drawing that represents the relationships of quantities or qualities to each other. A graph provides a convenient medium through which data can be compared. Graphs should use a simple design so that the reader can easily interpret the information. Using complex graphs will confuse rather than impress readers. The most frequently used graphs in business organizations are bar and line. These types of graphs have several variations.

BAR GRAPHS

A **bar graph** can be effective in comparing differences in quantities. These differences are illustrated graphically by changes in the lengths of the bars. Bar graphs may be constructed either horizontally or vertically. The most widely used bar graphs include simple, broken, multiple, stacked, and positive-negative. All bar graphs except a positive-negative one should begin with zero at the bottom or extreme left and use the same increments throughout.

In a **simple bar graph**, the length or height of a bar indicates quantity. You should use a bar width that makes a good visual impression. The width of individual bars should be the same throughout a graph. Bar graphs may be presented either vertically or horizontally. A simple horizontal bar graph is shown in Figure 12.6.

Graphs depicting very large amounts may make it impractical to include the entire amounts. In such cases a **broken-bar graph**, as shown in Figure 12.7, may be used.

A **multiple-bar graph** is used to compare several quantitative areas at one time on a single graph. Cross-hatching, shading, or color variation can be used to distinguish among bars representing different areas. Bars should be labeled, or a legend should be included on the graph to identify the different cross-hatching, shading, or color variations. The graph will become cluttered and difficult to read if more than four areas are compared on one graph. Figure 12.8 shows a multiple-bar graph.

FIGURE 12.6
Horizontal Bar Graph

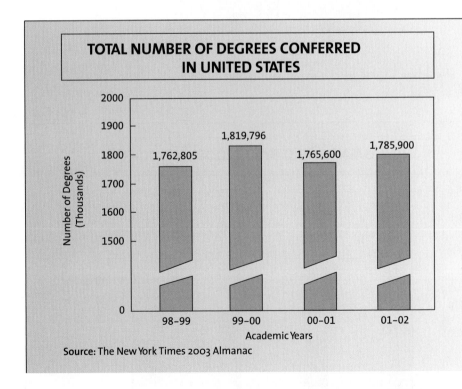

PAID ATTENDANCE BY AGE GROUP FOR ROUGH WATER SLIDE FOR JULY

Attendance (Thousands)

Age Groups:
- Over 60 Years
- 26–60 Years
- 19–25 Years
- 13–18 Years
- 6–12 Years
- Under 6 Years

FIGURE 12.7
Broken-Bar Graph

TOTAL NUMBER OF DEGREES CONFERRED IN UNITED STATES

Number of Degrees (Thousands)

- 98–99: 1,762,805
- 99–00: 1,819,796
- 00–01: 1,765,600
- 01–02: 1,785,900

Academic Years

Source: The New York Times 2003 Almanac

NOTE 12.20
A stacked-bar graph
shows differences in val-
ues within variables.

Elements within a variable may be illustrated in a **stacked-bar graph**. This type of graph is useful in demonstrating differences in values within variables by dividing each bar into its parts. Values should be included for each part, and the parts should be differentiated and identified as in multiple-bar graphs. A stacked-bar graph is shown in Figure 12.9.

FIGURE 12.8
Multiple-Bar Graph

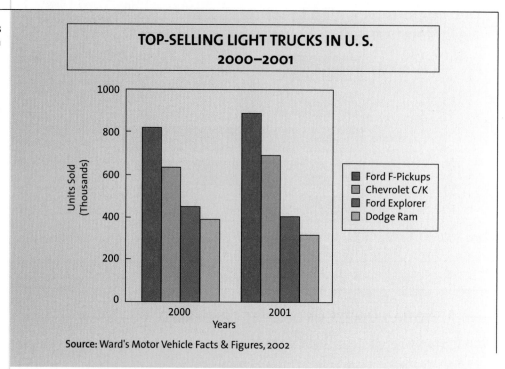

FIGURE 12.9
Stacked-Bar Graph

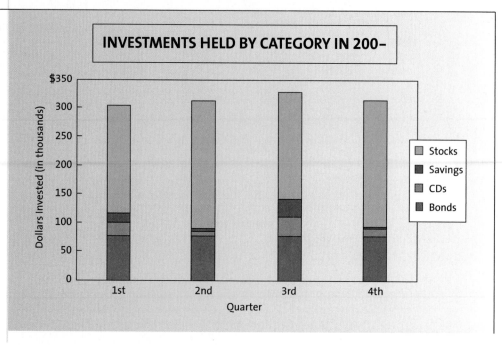

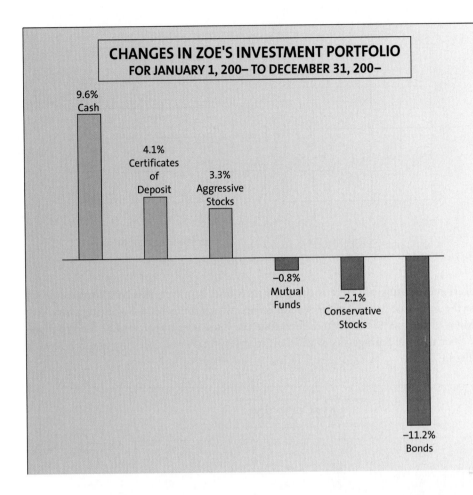

FIGURE 12.10
Positive-Negative
Bar Graph

CHANGES IN ZOE'S INVESTMENT PORTFOLIO
FOR JANUARY 1, 200– TO DECEMBER 31, 200–

9.6%
Cash

4.1%
Certificates
of
Deposit

3.3%
Aggressive
Stocks

–0.8%
Mutual
Funds

–2.1%
Conservative
Stocks

–11.2%
Bonds

A **positive-negative bar graph** shows plus or minus deviations from a fixed refer-ence point. The bars go up or down from this fixed reference point. Relationships be-tween positive and negative values can be illustrated clearly using a positive-negative bar graph as shown in Figure 12.10.

LINE GRAPHS

A **line graph** is used to illustrate changes over time. Trends can be effectively portrayed by showing variations within each time period.

A line graph is constructed by drawing a line on an equally divided grid, with the horizontal reference line called the *x*-axis and the vertical reference line called the *y*-axis. The interval between each vertical and horizontal line depends on the data being illus-trated. The grid lines may or may not appear on the finished version of the line graph. All the data need to be included to give an accurate and informative illustration. If the data are excessive, the grid may be broken by a slash or by wavy lines as shown in Figure 12.11.

A line graph can include either a single line or multiple lines. A **single-line graph** depicts movement of one variable. Shading or color may be used in a single-line graph to add emphasis. A **multiple-line graph** is used to illustrate changes in more than one value. The lines can be differentiated easily by using dotted, broken, and solid lines or by changing the symbols (triangle, square, circle, and diamond) for each line. Some

NOTE 12.21
A positive-negative bar graph can show compar-ison of variable values that fall above or below a reference point.

NOTE 12.22
Line graphs show changes over time.

NOTE 12.23
Changes in several values can be shown at one time on a multiple-line graph.

FIGURE 12.11
Broken Scales on
Line Graphs

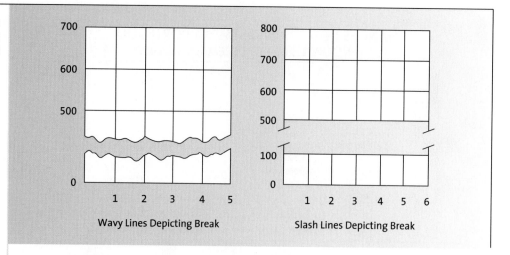

writers prefer using a different color for each line; however, this technique requires that the report be printed using several colors, which increases the printing costs. Regardless of the method used to differentiate the lines, a legend should be used to identify lines that are ambiguous or difficult to interpret. A multiple-line graph is shown in Figure 12.12.

FIGURE 12.12
Multiple-Line Graph

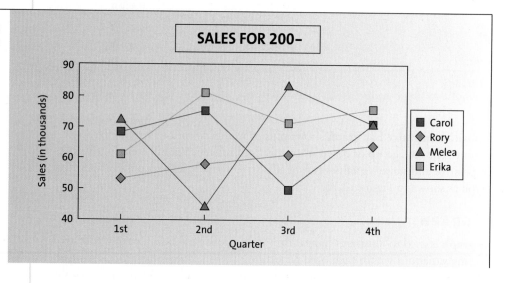

LEARNING OBJECTIVE

Describe how mis-
cellaneous visual
aids are used.

(5)

NOTE 12.24
Consider using an illus-
tration that complements
the written text.

Miscellaneous Visual Aids

Although the most commonly used visual aids are tables, charts, and graphs, these are not the only effective visual aids that can be used in reports. Graphic aids such as maps, photographs, pictographs, and drawings are used infrequently, but they can be extremely effective in conveying specific messages at appropriate times. Many of these visual aids may be obtained from Web sites. Any relevant visual aid that clarifies and strengthens the communication should be considered for use in a report or presentation.

A **map** can be effective in helping a receiver visualize geographic relationships. The complexity of maps ranges from simple sketches to detailed, multicolored presentations. The content of the map determines the size of the visual aid. Notice how the states containing a larger number of Omicron Delta Kappa circles (chapters) are differentiated from the states with only a few circles (chapters) on the map in Figure 12.13.

A **pictograph** is similar to a bar graph in that it emphasizes differences in statistical data, but it differs in that it uses images of items or symbols instead of bars. All the images or symbols should be the same size to avoid distorting their values. The pictograph in Figure 12.14 graphically accentuates the increase in personal computer sales over a period of time.

A personal touch can be added to a written report or an oral presentation by including a **photograph** of a facility, product, or employee. The Communication Note on page 344 describes one method of effectively using photographs. In order to enhance communication, the photograph must be clear and well planned. A mistake often made in the use of photographs is including too much material. If a photograph shows something extremely large or extremely small, a reference point should be included. A coin or a pin can be a useful reference point for small items, and a person can be a good reference point in a photograph of a large item. A photograph can be used to stimulate interest in a topic such as vacationing at a resort.

A **drawing** may be the most effective means of communicating a complicated idea or procedure. A photograph may not be desirable because it would contain clutter that would distract from the idea to be communicated. A drawing can omit the clutter and

NOTE 12.25
Maps can help the reader understand geographic details.

NOTE 12.26
Pictographs use images to emphasize differences in quantitative data.

NOTE 12.27
Photos used as graphic aids should not contain too much material.

NOTE 12.28
Drawings can be used to emphasize one point within a procedure.

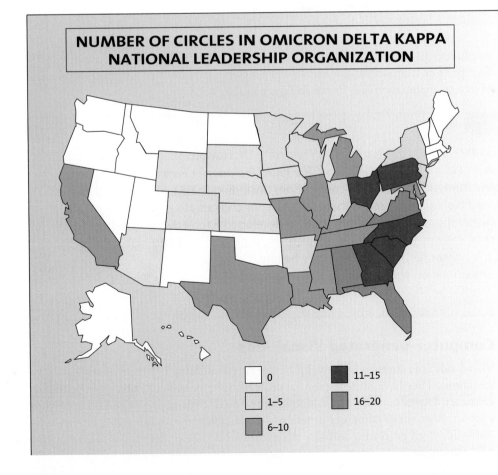

NUMBER OF CIRCLES IN OMICRON DELTA KAPPA NATIONAL LEADERSHIP ORGANIZATION

- 0
- 1–5
- 6–10
- 11–15
- 16–20

FIGURE 12.13
Map

FIGURE 12.14
Pictograph Showing
Personal Computer Sales

PERSONAL COMPUTER SALES

800,000 Personal
Computer Unit Sales

1985   1990   1995   2000

Source: The New York Times 2003 Almanac

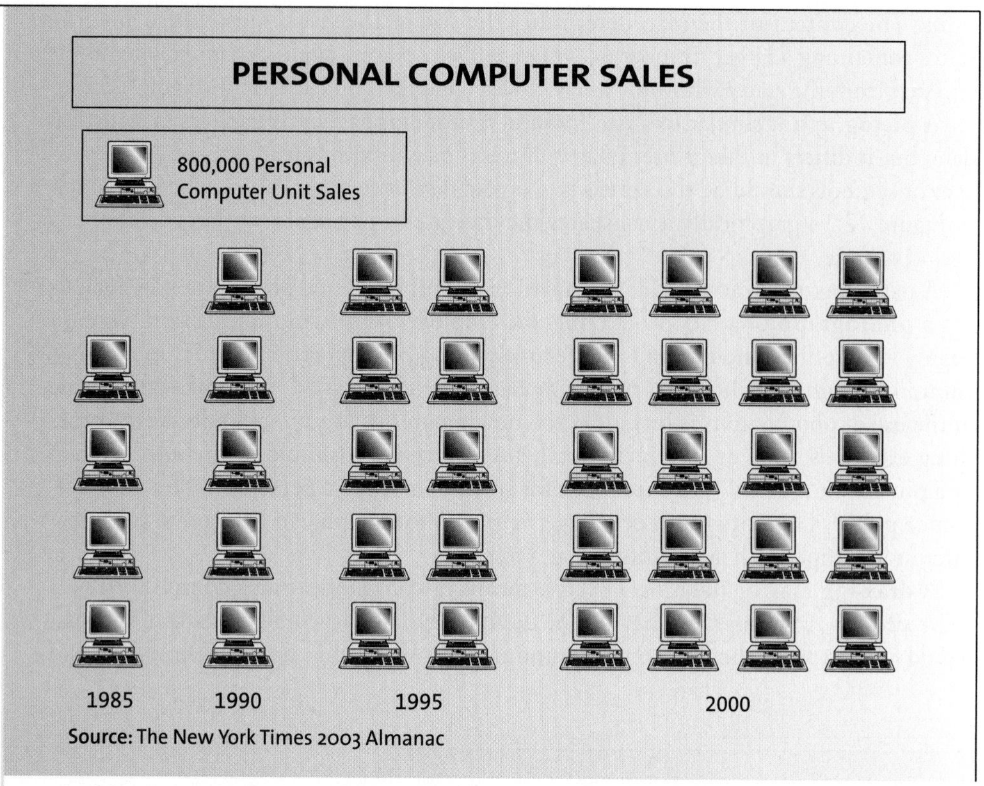

emphasize the desired details in an idea or procedure. Furthermore, a drawing can reflect parts or components not visible when viewing the "finished" product. A drawing of part of an automobile is shown in Figure 12.15.

COMMUNICATION NOTE

Using Pictures in a Weight-Loss Program Dr. Howard Shapiro is the author of *Dr. Shapiro's Picture Perfect Weight Loss: The Visual Program for Permanent Weight Loss.* The book features about 100 food comparisons, including snacks, lunches, and dinners out, and highlights the foods that are the better choices. His patients found that calorie-comparison lists are boring, so he developed a food display program for his patients. Patients who don't know much about portion sizes and high-calorie foods find the photographs in the book very helpful.

Adapted from Nanci Hellmich, "A Picture Is Worth a Thousand Pounds: Visual Aids Are a Slimming Tool," *USA Today.com*, April 3, 2000.

Computer-Generated Visual Aids

NOTE 12.29
Computers have simplified the creation of visual aids.

Visual aids are extremely powerful tools for supplementing written text and oral presentations. They have become more popular because technology makes them easier to construct. Digital cameras and scanners may be used to insert photos and other art into a report. Also, many computer programs are available that can integrate graphics software with word processing software to develop an easy-to-understand and informative communication.

Photograph used to promote a resort

FIGURE 12.15
Drawing of Part of an
Automobile

The keyboard and mouse are used to input data. The software uses the data to produce pie charts or other types of visual aids.

©PETER KORNICKER/CORBIS

Graphics software programs are easy to use. The originator needs only to enter the raw data and select the type of visual aid desired. The computer will create the chart or graph selected. These visual aids may be printed using several colors, depending on the type of software and printer.

Using graphics software, the originator can produce visual aids from the simple to the sophisticated. A spreadsheet may be used to display raw data. Current spreadsheet software permits the user to change fonts and to bold or shade data to emphasize selected figures in the spreadsheet. Graphs and tables that are produced using spreadsheet programs can also be imported into word processing or desktop publishing programs. Figure 12.16 shows a spreadsheet prepared using Microsoft Excel.

. NOTE 12.30
Clip art can make reports more attractive.

The appearance of reports can be improved by the use of **clip art**, prepackaged art images designed to be used with word processing, presentation graphics, or desktop publishing programs. Clip art is included in most word processing, presentation graphics, and desktop publishing programs. It may also be purchased separately and imported. Clip art program files normally are grouped into categories, such as business, travel, history, automobiles, airplanes, or holidays. Examples of clip art are shown in Figure 12.17.

Graphics software packages such as Microsoft Excel, Lotus 1-2-3, Harvard Graphics, Freelance Graphics, Aldus Persuasion, Corel Draw!, Claris McDraw, Charisma, and GraphShow can easily produce bar graphs, line graphs, pie charts, area charts, and combination charts. Most software programs permit the creation of several variations of each type of visual aid, such as stacked-bar graphs or exploded pie charts.

NOTE 12.31
A variety of visuals can be produced with different software packages.

More sophisticated software programs have additional options: Photographs may be printed in a report; the size of graphic aids may vary; lines, curves, and geometric

Maggie Moneybag's Personal Worth

Personal Assets	Jan. 2002	Jan. 2003	Jan. 2004
House	$130,000	$135,000	$137,500
Home Furnishings	5,000	4,500	4,250
Automobile	11,000	10,000	9,000
Truck	14,500	14,000	13,750
Insurance—Cash Value	9,500	10,200	10,500
Total Personal Assets	170,000	173,700	175,000
Investments			
Stocks	215,000	245,000	310,000
Mutual Funds	145,000	155,225	159,825
Undeveloped Land	45,000	70,000	95,000
IRA	60,150	62,325	61,250
Bonds	12,000	13,000	13,520
Art Collection	6,000	6,000	6,000
Savings Account	6,500	5,100	5,750
Total Investments	489,650	556,650	651,345
TOTAL ASSETS	$659,650	$730,350	$826,345
Liabilities			
Loan—Home	$112,750	$110,925	$109,850
Loan—Undev. Land	30,630	28,710	27,450
Loan—Truck	12,840	11,980	11,170
Credit Cards	875	1,120	1,250
TOTAL LIABILITIES	$157,095	$152,735	$149,720
NET WORTH	$502,555	$577,615	$676,625

FIGURE 12.16
Excel Spreadsheet

FIGURE 12.17
Examples of Clip Art

shapes may be created instantly; main headings and captions with special fonts may be inserted; and color and patterns may be added. The software programs allow the user to size, rotate, flip, recolor, and distort digitally-stored drawings or photographs to enhance the written report or oral presentation.

Once data are entered into a software program, different graphs and charts can be generated easily. A spreadsheet was used to generate a line graph for the data in Figure 12.18. An originator using the same data can enter different commands to generate a bar graph instead.

NOTE 12.32
Different styles of graphs and charts can be created without rekeying data.

FIGURE 12.18
Line and Bar Graphs
Using Identical Data

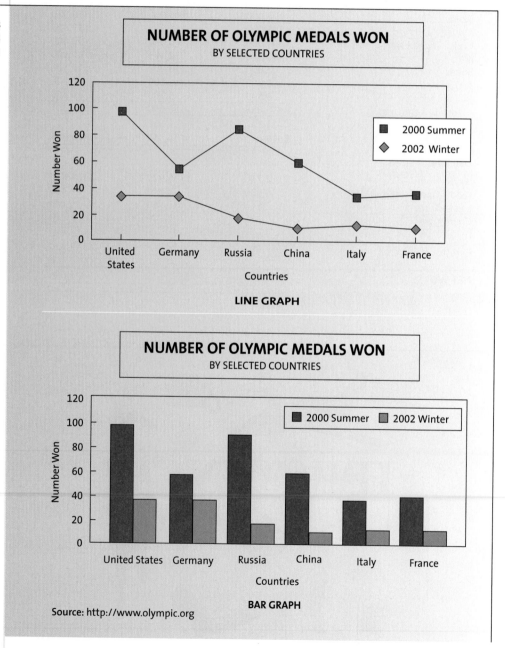

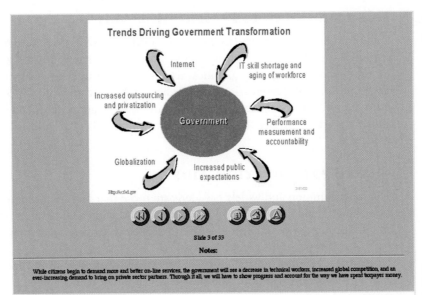

Key points may be projected for emphasis.

An advantage of using a simple graphics software program is that little training is required to produce a visual aid. A disadvantage of using a simple program is that the visual aid produced may not be exactly what is desired. For instance, some elementary graphics software programs do not begin pie charts with the largest piece at the twelve o'clock position. Also, a simple program may limit the number of characters that may be included in the titles or captions of the visual aid. Care should be taken in selecting a graphics software program so that it will meet the communicator's needs.

NOTE 12.33
Know the advantages and disadvantages of the computer software program.

Selection of Appropriate Visual Aids

The purpose of a visual aid is to complement the text or presentation by communicating information quickly. Presenting accurate data in a clear and organized manner is important. The receiver will have little difficulty in interpreting the data when the appropriate visual aid is selected.

Comparisons of quantities in data are best illustrated by bar graphs. For instance, a report comparing the various fixed costs with the assorted variable costs can be complemented by the use of bar graphs.

NOTE 12.34
Compare quantities in bar graphs.

If a report or presentation discusses trends in quantitative data over a period of time, a line graph would be the most appropriate visual aid. A multiple-line graph is also an effective device for showing changes in two or more related variables. A company comparing the sales trends for its four salespeople can effectively utilize a line graph.

NOTE 12.35
Illustrate trends in line graphs.

Pie charts are used to show the relationships between the parts and the whole. Budgets are commonly displayed in pie charts in order to illustrate the proportion each item is to the entire budget.

NOTE 12.36
Show relationships with pie charts.

Flowcharts illustrate steps within a procedure. A new employee can easily learn the flow of a work order within an organization by carefully studying a well-designed flowchart.

NOTE 12.37
Illustrate steps with flowcharts.

Careful selection of the appropriate visual aid may enhance the effectiveness of a written report or oral presentation. The length of the written text can be reduced by the use of a well-chosen graphic aid. Many times it is easier to interpret a visual aid than to struggle through pages of written text.

LEARNING OBJECTIVE
Select the appropri-
ate type of visual aid
to complement an oral
presentation.

⑥

Select Appropriate Presentation Aids

Unlike a written report, which draws only on the receiver's sense of sight, an oral presentation can draw on sound, sight, touch, taste, and smell. Most speakers will find sound (audio) and sight (visual) most useful. Whether used separately or in combination (multimedia), presentation aids can be an asset in conveying a message. They can make it more understandable. They can spark interest, add variety, and help to hold an audience's attention. See the Tips and Hints on page 351 for guidelines on designing visual aids.

VISUAL PRESENTATION AIDS

The most common and widely used aids are those that require the audience to look at something. Handouts, flip charts, posters, objects, whiteboards, slides, transparencies, and projection devices fall into this category. A brief description of each follows.

Handouts Handouts can be used to present an outline or to illustrate points from your presentation. Distribute handouts in advance that you will refer to during the presentation. Handouts containing complex supplementary material should be distributed after your presentation. Although listeners can concentrate better on your comments if they do not have to worry about taking notes, using too many handouts can be distracting.

NOTE 12.39
Distribute simple hand-
outs before and during
your presentation and
detailed ones after.

Flip Charts This economical, easy-to-use aid works best with small groups. Charts can be prepared in advance or spontaneously, as part of an interaction with the audience. Their advantage in interactive settings is that each sheet can be posted for reference and serve as a tangible sign of accomplishments. Prepared charts should be designed on paper first, then transferred to the flip chart pad. Penciled notes added when the chart is finished can help remind you of key points you wish to make. Remember that charts require some sort of stand; be sure the pad you select fits the stand.

Posters Posters can be used for text, charts, graphs, and pictographs; they work especially well for blueprints and drawings. Be sure to consider how the posters will be displayed and whether they will be visible during the entire presentation or revealed as they are used. You may also need a pointer to help highlight important items.

NOTE 12.41
Models and physical
objects can strengthen
a presentation.

Objects In many business presentations you will have something to display either in final or model form. If the physical objects or models used as visual aids are not large enough for every member of the audience to see, consider giving each member an object or circulating one or more of the items among audience members. Introducing the sensory dimension of touch into your presentation can reinforce what you have to say, but it does detract from active listening. Before making objects available to your audience, consider both the benefits and costs to your overall presentation.

NOTE 12.42
You can use a white-
board to develop a con-
cept while you speak.

Whiteboards Whiteboards, either stationary or portable, are the modern-day version of the chalkboards common in most classrooms. The flexibility associated with whiteboards makes them desirable for meetings or other interactive, small-group sessions. Printing legibly is slow and cumbersome, however, and means that the writer's back is to the audience a great deal of the time.

Slides Slides can be a colorful and professional-looking presentation aid that works well with groups of various sizes. Depending on the detail of the material to be presented, however, the time and talent necessary to prepare and produce the slides can be substantial. In addition, (1) someone must dim and restore the lights at appropriate times, (2) it is harder to keep the audience attentive, (3) the projector could malfunction, and (4) the speaker could have difficulty using the remote control or communicating with the assistant who will operate the projector. Although not major obstacles to using slides, these factors must be considered.

NOTE 12.43
Slides can be colorful and professional, but preparation may be time consuming and costly.

Transparencies Overhead transparencies, also known as foils or acetates, have long been an inexpensive presentation tool for use with groups of various sizes. They can be prepared in advance using markers, printers, or photocopiers. Markers can also be used to add to or create transparencies as part of a presentation. As with slides, transparencies carry the disadvantages associated with using a projector and operating in a darkened room.

NOTE 12.44
Transparencies are widely used visual aids.

Projection Devices These presentation tools enable images displayed on a computer monitor to be projected for viewing by a larger audience. Some units link the computer directly to the projector; others use a panel placed on an overhead projector. In either case, the user may create or manipulate computer files as the audience watches. This presentation aid works well in meetings where groups attempt to answer what-if questions. However, technical problems with any of the equipment can bring a quick halt to even the most best-prepared presentation.

NOTE 12.45
Projection panels are used to display computer images.

TIPS AND HINTS

Designing Presentation Aids

- Display only one idea on each visual. Use progressive disclosure to move through elements of a complex concept.
- Select an overall style and use it on all your visual aids. Consistency will help your audience stay focused on what you have to say. Introduce the style in an opening slide that includes the title of your presentation and other information (your name, your organization's name, the date, etc.) the audience might need.
- Choose print style and size carefully. Thick, straight characters are easier to read than thin, curved ones. Mixing uppercase and lowercase letters saves space and, because it is a familiar style, makes text easier to read. Using the "6 by 6" rule—six lines of no more than six words each—puts font size for keyed material in the 40- to 50-point range.
- Use color to emphasize material. Choose a feature color for main ideas; use one or two complementary colors to accent sub-points. Remember that about 10 percent of the male population is red-green color sensitive and that pastels are hard to read, especially from a distance. Background colors must also be considered; a dark background in a darkened room will encourage drowsiness.
- Computer graphics (background patterns, clip art, etc.) should be used when they enhance the presentation. Gimmicks are not a substitute for content.
- Proofread! Even small errors can embarrass you and portray a poor image of your organization.
- Plan ahead. Finish the project well ahead of the presentation date. Allow time to redo visuals that don't satisfy you. If you are relying on in-house or commercial services, respect their schedules.

AUDIO PRESENTATION AIDS

NOTE 12.46
Audio aids should be
used selectively.

Variety and impact are made possible by supplementing your oral presentation with an audio aid. Cassette tapes are the most common audio aid; CDs also fall into this category. Whatever the medium, the recording quality must be high and the volume sufficient to enable all members of the audience to hear without strain or discomfort. Because audio aids are, in a sense, disembodied sounds, use them sparingly. An audience can tire quickly of simply listening to sound and not having visual stimuli.

MULTIMEDIA AIDS

NOTE 12.47
Multimedia aids require
audience members to
use more than one sense.

Multimedia aids have the capacity to incorporate text, graphics, sound, and animation into a presentation. The most basic multimedia device is a videotape; the most sophisticated device utilizes presentation graphics software on a PC linked to the Internet. Each aid is described in the following paragraphs.

NOTE 12.48
Videotapes should be
not only shown but also
discussed.

Videotapes Speakers who use videotapes rely heavily on professionally prepared materials and honor all copyright restrictions. The monitor(s) used during the presentation must be strategically placed and adjusted for appropriate contrast and volume. The speaker must tell the audience the purpose of the tape before showing it and summarize the main points after viewing it. Long tapes should be shown in segments separated by discussions. For the comfort of audience members, keep the lights dimmed during discussions between segments.

NOTE 12.49
Presentation graphics
software offers creation
ease and presentation
variety.

Presentation Graphics Software This comprehensive aid allows speakers to create, edit, and give presentations using sophisticated computer technology. The ease with which these presentations can be created and the variety they offer make them desirable for small- to medium-sized groups (100 or fewer). The disadvantage of needing a darkened room for clear viewing is often offset by the ability to incorporate sound and motion into the presentation.

NOTE 12.50
Use presentation graph-
ics software to create
• Slides (images)
• Outlines
• Speaker's notes
• Audience handouts

A number of presentation graphics software programs are available either as separate products or as part of integrated packages. Materials used in the presentation may be keyed directly into the program or copied from another file created, for example, using word processing or spreadsheet software. Although each software program approaches the task differently, all are capable of producing slides, outlines, speaker's notes, and audience handouts.

A **slide** is a one-page visual image. In business, the most common slide format consists of a heading and various levels of subheadings. Each subheading level is marked by a **bullet**, a symbol designed to capture attention and show the beginning of a new item. Different emphasis techniques (font, pitch, color, bold, underscore, italics, etc.) can mark each subheading level. Users may create their own slide format or choose from among many template formats included in the software. Formats may be altered from slide to slide, but a better approach is to select one format, called a **master**, and retain it throughout the presentation. As each item is entered into the slide, the software automatically adjusts it to meet the preset format. Items such as a company logo or the speaker's name may also be imbedded into a master. Figure 12.19 shows a slide created using Microsoft PowerPoint.

To obtain an overview of the presentation, a speaker can generate an **outline**, a sequential listing of the slides and their content. Because the outline and creation modes

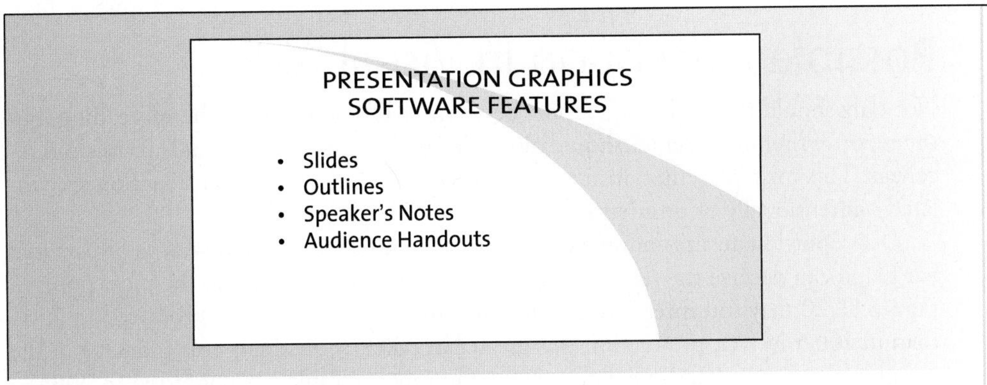

FIGURE 12.19
Presentation Graphic
Slide

PRESENTATION GRAPHICS
SOFTWARE FEATURES

- Slides
- Outlines
- Speaker's Notes
- Audience Handouts

are so closely aligned, a user can add, delete, or modify slides while in one function and have them automatically reflected in the other.

A software feature called **speaker's notes** allows the user to add comments to each slide—comments that may be displayed on the screen during rehearsals and removed during the actual presentation. The printed notes will appear either beside or below a copy of the slide. Notes may also be added by hand after printing.

Finally, one or more slides can be printed on a page as an **audience handout** or **take-away**. Distributing your visuals as a handout gives those attending the presentation an accurate record of the materials that were used and the opportunity to add their own notes about the topic.

Once the basic elements of a presentation have been created, the user can focus on how the software's more powerful features might be used to enhance the presentation. Specifically, the speaker needs to decide whether sound, fades, dissolves, or similar transition techniques will be incorporated into the presentation. A speaker may, for example, decide to use progressive disclosure and reveal the subtopics of a bulleted listing one by one. Sound could be used to signal the addition of an item, or the old item could fade into the background as the new item emerges. When moving from one topic to another, the old image could slowly dissolve. For a lighter effect, a user might choose to have an animated object or character erase the text or to have a gloved hand appear to tear away the old slide. Some software programs offer pre-animated templates. In either case, the user may choose the speed at which a transition takes place. Options are many and varied; creativity and the topic will help a speaker decide which to use without detracting from content.

At various points during the presentation, the speaker may wish to draw on other media sources. This can be accomplished by including **hyperlinks**, a method of moving to and immediately accessing another source. The links are displayed as icons (images) on a slide. When clicked (activated), the image causes the computer to point to a different location in its resource base. By using hyperlinks, presenters may access and manipulate a spreadsheet or database, visit one or more Web sites, conduct an Internet search, or engage in any number of other interactive activities.

Although presentation graphics software offers users a host of options, presenters must remember that equipment and software at the presentation site must be compatible with that used to create the presentation. If Internet resources are to be used, for example, a network connection must be available. Speakers must also prepare for unexpected equipment or network failures.

NOTE 12.51
Sound and animation can be incorporated into a presentation.

NOTE 12.52
Access to other sources makes interactive sessions possible.

7 Possible Deception in Visual Aids

Not only should the reader of a report be aware that visual aids can be misleading, but the report writer or presenter should also be careful not to use visual aids to mislead receivers. This misrepresentation may occur if certain principles of construction are violated—intentionally or unintentionally.

Disproportionate sizes of images in a pictograph or inconsistent widths of bars in a bar graph can deceive the receivers of a message. A receiver scanning the pictograph in Figure 12.20 may interpret it to mean that more motorcycles were produced in 2003 than in 2002; in fact, production was greater in 2002. Individuals only glancing at the bar graph in Figure 12.20 may perceive the number of diplomas conferred in 2003 as being larger than in 2002; however, the diplomas conferred represented by the two bars are of equal value. Specific principles must be followed in creating and interpreting pictographs and bar graphs. In a pictograph, the number of images, not their size, determines the value; and in a bar graph, the height or length of the bar, not the width, determines the value.

NOTE 12.53
Visual aids can mislead a reader.

NOTE 12.54
Bars should be of the same width.

FIGURE 12.20
Deception Caused by Changing Width or Size

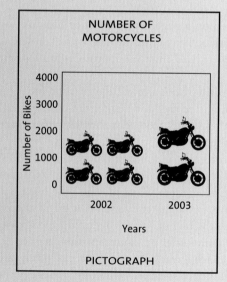
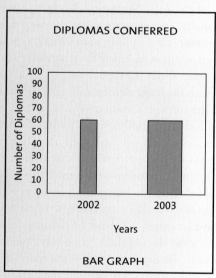

NOTE 12.55
Pieces of pie charts need to be drawn to correct proportion.

NOTE 12.56
The reference point of all bar graphs should be zero.

NOTE 12.57
Grid increments should be of consistent value throughout a line graph.

An originator could deceive a receiver into thinking the sales tax in Pie Chart A of Figure 12.21 is one fifth of the tax revenue; it is actually one third. Pie Chart B in Figure 12.21 displays the proportions correctly. The size of each piece of a pie chart must be in the same proportion to the whole pie as is the value of the part to the total value.

Another method of deceptive illustration is beginning the bottom of the bars in a bar graph at a point other than zero. This method exaggerates the differences between the individual bars. A company can lead its stockholders to believe that the company has experienced significant growth in sales during the three quarters shown in Graph A of Figure 12.22; Graph B better represents the true sales of the company.

Improper construction of a line graph can also deceive the receiver. Inconsistent intervals on the *y*-axis can make changes appear greater or lesser than they actually are. Notice that in Figure 12.23 that the $30,000 increase between 2000 and 2004 appears greater than the $100,000 decrease between 1998 and 1999.

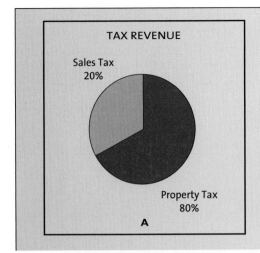
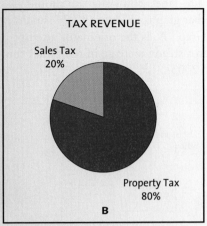

FIGURE 12.21
Pie Charts Showing
Disproportionate and
Correct Division

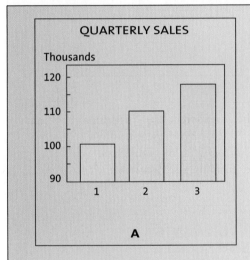
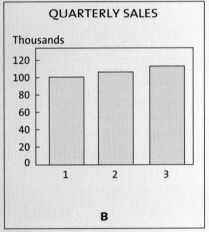

FIGURE 12.22
Deception Caused by
Not Starting Baseline
at Zero

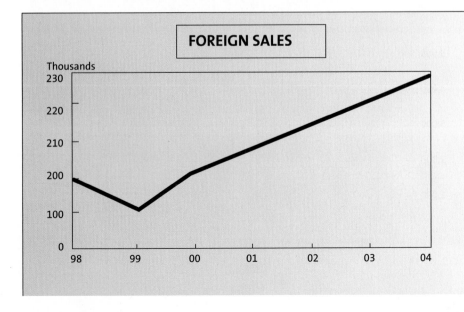

FIGURE 12.23
Inconsistent Increments
on a Line Graph

The labels of a visual aid should also be critically evaluated. A receiver looking at the bar graphs in Figure 12.24 should question why the odd years have been omitted in Graph A. Is the originator attempting to make the receiver believe that there has been a steady increase in the values throughout the period? What happened in 2001 and 2003?

FIGURE 12.24
Intentional Omission
of Data

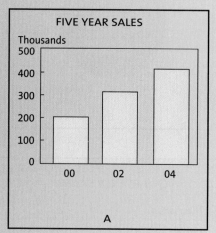

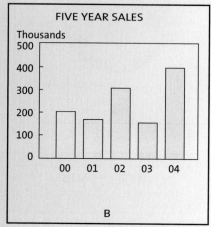

Text references to visual aids should be considered, too. Suppose a report reads, "Student enrollments, as shown in Figure 12.25, have grown steadily during the four years." Would the reader assume that all three types of enrollments have grown or would the reader assume that only graduate enrollments have grown?

FIGURE 12.25
Stacked-Bar Graph
Showing Student
Enrollments

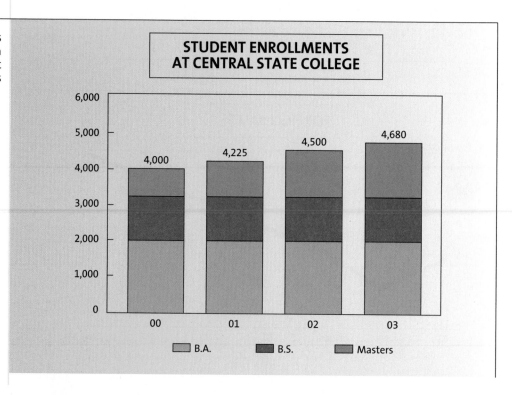

The selection of appropriate visual aids and accurate descriptions of them are of equal importance to successful communication.

NOTE 12.58
The written text must accurately describe the visual aid.

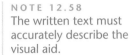

Summary of Learning Objectives

Describe the purposes of visual aids in written and oral communication.

Communication can be improved by summarizing complex figures in charts and graphs, by identifying your company through the use of a drawing or photograph for a logo, by showing relationships in a chart, by indicating trends in a graph, or by abstracting cumbersome details in a table.

Label visual aids properly, and explain where to place within a report.

All formal visual aids should be identified by appropriate titles that describe their contents. Consider the five Ws (who, what, when, where, and why) when developing the title. Illustration titles may be printed either in uppercase or in uppercase and lowercase letters and may appear above or below the visual aid. Visual aids should be numbered consecutively, but methods of numbering them vary. When only one visual aid appears in a report, it need not be numbered. The most important consideration in labeling illustrations is consistency. Place illustrations that directly relate to the topic with the written text. A small illustration, less than one-half page, should be placed after the first reference to the aid, preferably on the same page. A large illustration, one-half to one page, should be placed on the page following the first mention of the illustration. Avoid dividing a visual aid between two pages. Place illustrations that are indirectly related to the topic in an appendix at the end of the text.

Construct tables and the three most common types of charts.

Words and numbers should be arranged systematically in columns and rows in a table. The table should contain a title, a heading for the first column that classifies the categories of data in each row, and a heading for each additional column. An organization chart depicts the relationships among departments and of personnel within the departments. Positions are connected by solid lines if they are line positions with authority over other positions and by broken or dotted lines if they are advisory or staff positions. A flowchart may be used to illustrate step-by-step progression through complicated procedures. Boxes of various shapes are connected by arrows to illustrate the direction that the action follows during the procedure. A pie chart can be used to show how the parts of a whole are distributed and how the parts relate to each other. The pie chart should begin at the twelve o'clock position and continue in a clockwise direction. The pieces should be arranged in descending order of size with the category "other" appearing in the last position.

(4) Construct the various types of graphs.

A bar graph can be effective in comparing differences in quantities by changing the lengths of the bars. In a simple bar graph, the length or height of a bar indicates quantity. Graphs depicting very large amounts may make it impractical to include the entire amounts. In such cases a broken-bar graph may be used. A multiple-bar graph is used to compare several quantitative areas at one time on a single graph. Cross-hatching, shading, or color variation can be used to distinguish among bars representing different areas. A stacked-bar graph can be used to demonstrate differences in values within variables by dividing each bar into its parts. A positive-negative bar graph shows plus or minus deviations from a fixed reference point. The bars go up or down from this fixed reference point. A line graph is constructed by drawing a line on an equally divided grid, with the horizontal reference line called the x-axis and the vertical reference line called the y-axis. A line graph can include either a single line or multiple lines. A single-line graph depicts movement of one variable whereas a multiple-line graph is used to illustrate changes in more than one value. The lines can be differentiated easily by using dotted, broken, and solid lines.

(5) Describe how miscellaneous visual aids are used.

A map can help a reader visualize geographic relationships. A pictograph is similar to a bar graph in that it emphasizes differences in statistical data, but it differs in that it uses images of items or symbols instead of bars. A personal touch can be added to a business report by including a photograph of a facility, product, or employee. A drawing may communicate a complicated idea or procedure by omitting clutter and emphasizing details in an idea or procedure.

(6) Select the appropriate type of visual aid to complement an oral presentation.

Handouts can be used to illustrate points in a presentation. Flip charts can be prepared in advance or as part of an interaction with the audience. Posters can be developed for most visual aids and work well for blueprints and drawings. Actual objects can be displayed during a presentation, and presenters can write on whiteboards. Slides can be effective with large audiences while a transparency is an inexpensive presentation tool. When a computer is available, projection devices can be used effectively. Multimedia aids can incorporate text, graphics, sound, and animation into a presentation.

(7) Explain how receivers can avoid being deceived by visual aids.

To avoid being deceived, receivers must remember that in a pictograph, the number of images, not their size, determines the value; and in a bar graph, the height or length of the bar, not the width, determines the value. Receivers also should remember that each piece of a pie chart must be in the same proportion to the whole pie as is the value of the part to the total value. When looking at a bar graph, readers should be aware that the bars must begin at zero to avoid exaggerating the differences between the individual bars. Intervals on the y-axis of a line graph must be consistent to avoid changes appearing greater or lesser than they actually are. The labels of a visual aid should also be critically evaluated.

Discussion Questions

1. How can visual aids complement your business reports? (Objective 1)
2. You are writing a report that includes visual aids. Where would you place the visual aids in the report? Explain why you chose these placements. (Objective 2)
3. When should a source note be used, and where is it normally placed? (Objective 2)
4. You have been hired as a consultant for a restaurant to improve the efficiency of its operation. During your investigation you find that the business serves many more customers on certain days of the week than on other days. In your report you need to illustrate which days are busy and which days are slow. What type of visual aid would best illustrate your findings? Describe how you would construct the visual aid. (Objective 3 or 4)
5. Explain how to present statistical data in a business report table. What parts are necessary to make a table complete? (Objective 3)
6. What are the purposes of the three types of charts commonly used in business reports? (Objective 3)
7. Compare a stacked-bar graph with a positive-negative bar graph. (Objective 4)
8. Describe how graphics software programs can be used to improve a written report. (Objective 5)
9. Name and explain three visual presentation aids a speaker might use when giving an oral presentation. (Objective 6)

10. **Ethics.** Are ethics involved in the construction of visual aids for business reports? Discuss what readers should consider when analyzing visual aids in a report. (Objective 7)

Application Exercises

1. Locate annual reports from three major corporations. Analyze the various visual aids in each of the annual reports. Include in your analysis the placement of the aids, their labels, references to them in the report, and their appropriateness. (Objective 2)
2. Prepare a visual aid that shows the steps you must take in conducting research. (Objective 3)
3. Construct a visual aid that best illustrates the time you have spent each week studying for each of your classes during the past three weeks. (Objective 4)
4. Select the most appropriate visual aid to illustrate each of the following. Give justification for each of your selections. (Objectives 3, 4, and 5)
   a. Annual change in buffalo population after relocating the herd to a state park
   b. Arrangement of flowers in a vase
   c. Comparison of the number of students in a school by grade level over a five-year period
   d. Average rainfall for major cities in the United States
   e. Dow Jones Industrial Averages in relation to Dow Jones Bond Averages for a six-month period
   f. Procedure that students must follow to register for classes
   g. Damage to an automobile that was involved in an accident
   h. The number of freshmen, sophomores, juniors, and seniors attending a college
5. Construct the visual aid that best illustrates the data for each of the following situations. Create your own titles and labels. Write the introduction to the aid. Be sure to direct your reader to some aspect of the data and refer to the illustration by number. (Objectives 2, 3, and 4)

a. The attendance at the Tigers' soccer games in 200–

Game 1	78	Game 4	130
Game 2	121	Game 5	108
Game 3	159	Game 6	98

b. The number of employees in each department at Allan's Electrical

Administrative support	2
Service	8
Residential	6
Commercial	14
Accounting	1
Management	4

c. Income earned in a day at Cherokee Hills Steak House

Appetizers	$ 1,200
Beverages	5,200
Carryouts	450
Desserts	510
Entrees	11,900
Sandwiches	730

d. Average annual return on Nanci's investments

	Growth & Income	Growth	Aggressive Growth
2000	19.3%	25.4%	31.7%
2001	21.6%	23.8%	21.0%
2002	19.7%	24.6%	24.6%
2003	16.5%	25.1%	19.9%

e. Golf scores for the month of May

May 2	Bob	93	May 23	Bob	97
	Fred	89		Fred	89
	Ralph	98		Ralph	96
May 9	Bob	86	May 30	Bob	89
	Fred	91		Fred	84
	Ralph	103		Ralph	94
May 16	Bob	90			
	Fred	90			
	Ralph	94			

6. Construct a visual aid that most effectively illustrates how the various U.S. tax amounts compare with each other. The receipts of the taxes, in millions, may be the following: (Objective 3)

Individual income	$590,157
Corporation income	157,088
Social insurance	484,474
Excise	97,485
Estate and gift	84,764
Miscellaneous	63,928

7. E-mail. Construct a visual aid showing the grades you have in this course. Send the visual aid in an e-mail message to your instructor. (Objective 4)

8. Global. Teamwork. Divide into groups of three and perform a library search to determine the five leading wheat-exporting countries for the past year and for ten years ago. Ascertain the principal language that is spoken in each of the countries. Construct a visual aid that could be used in a report discussing languages used in leading agricultural nations. (Objectives 3, and 4)

9. **InfoTrac.** When learning report writing, a reader's ability to understand note taking can be enhanced through the use of maps. Read InfoTrac article A15667871, "Using Maps to Teach Note Taking and Outlining for Report Writing," by Florence Pieronek. Answer the following questions:

    a. What are two important stages that a writer needs to perform prior to writing a report?

    b. When using a map to teach note taking, what criteria should be used to select an "easy" map?

    c. What are two strategies for teaching about the structure of descriptive expository prose?

There are Web exercises at **http://krizan.swlearning.com** to accompany this chapter.

Message Analysis

Rewrite and improve the quality of the following paragraph. Use a visual aid that would be appropriate for the paragraph.

> *Individuals have been going to movies at a fast pace this summer. Many movies have been released this summer.* The six newest movies with their gross income are: Cream Puff Express, $270,000; Metroman, $61,800,000; Murder After 12, $51,600,000; The Perfect Vacation, $12,325,000; The Mad Musician, $70,000,000; Hounds and Kittens, $62,500,000. *It looks as if* The Mad Musician *will outperform all the rest of the movies this summer.*

Grammar Workshop

Correct the grammar, spelling, punctuation, style, and word choice errors in the following sentences:

1. If it rains tommorrow we will stay home, how ever if it doesn't we will go to the beach.
2. The entrances to the Trinity Memorial Hospital intensive care unit is located on the 1st floor for patiences convenience.
3. The folage in the lobby is replaced annualy by the university greenhouse club.
4. The personal manager wants you to carefully reconsider you're decision to submit your request for retirement.
5. Jon is the slower reader in his class so his instructor cent him to the libary for their speed reading class.
6. The computer programmer is a real smart person that can make a computer do almost anything.
7. Nancy was late in meeting her appointment because she had sat her alarm for 6.00 pm instead of 6.00 am.
8. Either Brian or Bill will leave their car at the airport, when they attend the super bowl at New Orleans.
9. Why did the Administration fire Dr. Fumiko Hayashi Assistant Professor of Foreign Language?
10. You can excess leading edge cases published by top researchers at our new web sight.

13

Interpersonal Communication and Teamwork

Amy Rosvold,
Business Analyst,
Fair, Isaac

LET'S TALK BUSINESS As a software engineering lead at Fair, Isaac, one of my responsibilities is to document the requirements needed to create a new product or to update an existing product. This involves using teleconferences to communicate with and gain consensus from a wide array of coworkers, from very technical computer programmers to very nontechnical marketing folks.

It is very common during teleconferences to encounter periods of silence. While a few seconds of silence may feel like an eternity to the facilitator, it does not to the participants. Resist the temptation to fill "dead air" by starting sentences with "Ahhh" or "Ummm." Always gather your thoughts before you speak. Use silence to your advantage. Ask for feedback, invite questions, or use my mantra: Silence Is Acceptance!

Facilitating teleconferences presents a unique set of challenges. Because you do not have the benefit of visual cues, you must work even harder to achieve effective oral communication. You can successfully conquer teleconferencing challenges with perseverance, patience and, most importantly, *practice.*

The ability to create positive business relationships with colleagues, clients, and others is an important skill. In her work at Fair, Isaac, Amy Rosvold faces the challenge of developing those relationships with people over long distances. To be successful, Amy needs excellent interpersonal communication skills. Interpersonal communication—what it is and how it is used in business settings—is one of the topics we explore in this chapter.

The Elements of Interpersonal Communication

LEARNING OBJECTIVE
1 Identify the components of interpersonal communication.

Interpersonal communication is the term applied to the verbal and nonverbal interactions in one-on-one or small-group settings. "People skills" and "soft skills" are terms often used to describe someone's interpersonal abilities.

Interpersonal communication is a cornerstone in what social scientists refer to as the **communication climate**—the quality of the personal relationships that exist within an organization. The communication climate reflects the workers' perceptions of whether the organization trusts, respects, and values them—factors related to job satisfaction and commitment. Interpersonal communication is linked to leadership potential, a quality employers seek in those they hire. Therefore, one key to success in business is learning to create a positive communication climate.

Interpersonal skills have always played a role in business, but that role grew in importance as the United States moved from an industrial to a service-oriented economy. Service thrives on positive working relationships between coworkers, departments, and organizations. Recall that developing and maintaining these relationships is a goal of business communication.

Workplace diversity, globalization, organizational restructuring, worker specialization, and technology contribute to the current emphasis on interpersonal skills. Workplace diversity and globalization call on workers to be aware of and sensitive to the ways in which an individual's culture affects his or her attitudes and actions in the office. Organizational restructuring, often resulting in downsizing, has redistributed the workload and placed pressure on those who remain. Worker specialization increases the likelihood that senders and receivers won't speak the same technical language. Technology has increased the speed at which work is processed and reduced the number of face-to-face encounters. Failure to recognize and adapt to these factors can create communication barriers.

Interpersonal communication skills exhibit themselves in the style with which people write and speak. Techniques for enhancing your written communication skills are covered in the correspondence section of this book. Here, we focus on how listening, speaking, and nonverbal communication are used to build positive relationships, to give and receive criticism comfortably, to manage conflict effectively, and to be an effective team member.

NOTE 13.1
Interpersonal communication skills are used in one-on-one and small-group interactions.

NOTE 13.2
Organizations that demonstrate trust, respect, and value of workers have a good communication climate.

LEARNING OBJECTIVE
2 Enhance your ability to build positive relationships.

Positive Relationships

Positive relationships don't just happen. They are built over time, and they require ongoing maintenance. Trust and respect are key elements in building and maintaining relationships. As noted in the Communication Note on page 364, efforts to convey respect can be undermined by the way in which we communicate.

NOTE 13.3
Positive relationships don't happen by chance.

Communicate Respect, Not Disrespect Respecting others makes them feel safe; when people feel safe, they are more productive. You can improve your ability to communicate respect by avoiding these communication traps:

Sarcasm: Even when it's cute or clever, sarcasm can be perceived as an attack and is unwelcome.

Impatience: Showing impatience demeans the receiver. Patience is productive.

Distraction: When you're distracted, you suggest that you don't care as much about the receiver as you do about someone or something else. Lack of attention is insulting and creates distance, which is unproductive.

Minimization: You minimize an issue when you brush it aside. Issues must be acknowledged and discussed. High-priority issues will get the attention they deserve, but smaller issues won't be ignored.

Adapted from "Four Communication Rules to Maximize Productivity," by Lawrence M. Kohn and Robert N. Kohn; *Accounting Today*, July 23, 2001; p. 8. Used with permission.

This section focuses on three topics related to building and maintaining positive relationships—conversations, office politics, and relationship repair.

Conversations

NOTE 13.4
Relationships begin with cautious conversation.

Relationships generally begin with conversations. At first, the interaction will probably be cautious. Then, as trust and comfort grow, participants begin to reveal more of their personalities and to share information about their lives. People begin to connect on intellectual, personal, and emotional levels. At the office, this may mean speaking about family or friends, hopes and fears, and problems and solutions. The nature and extent of the topics discussed will vary with each relationship. A worker might share less with a superior or subordinate than with a colleague, and more with one colleague than another. The key elements are trust and comfort.

NOTE 13.5
Workplace relationship patterns parallel personal relationship patterns.

This pattern of trust and sharing in the workplace parallels that used in other parts of life. Consider your best friend. How did you meet? What were your early conversations about? What do you discuss now? Do you share things with one friend that you do not talk about with another? The patterns you observe in your school and social life will be evident in your work life as well.

One-to-one oral communication, including conversation, is a valuable business tool. In fact, it is probably the most important form of interaction used in business. It occurs in both structured and social business settings, it is essential to good customer service, and it forms the foundation for workplace interactions among employees. More critical business decisions are made during conversations between two people than in any other forum.

Whether conversations occur in person, via the telephone, or during a computer-based video conference, they are constantly changing situations. Sometimes you will be a message sender; sometimes you will be a receiver. Therefore, you must listen carefully (Chapter 14), continually analyze your receiver (Chapter 1), and adjust your delivery based on feedback (Chapter 1). In addition, you must apply the principles of business communication (Chapter 4). The success of a conversation also depends on using care in developing and sending the message and on eliminating communication barriers that threaten the conversation (Chapter 1).

Before we identify factors associated exclusively with successful face-to-face and successful telephone conversations, we must understand the conversation process.

THE CONVERSATION PROCESS

Conversations generally take place in five stages:

[1] Greeting

[2] Introduction

[3] Exchange

[4] Summary

[5] Closing

Greeting The greeting opens the channel for a conversation. "Hello," "Good morning," and "Jose, this is Marla" are verbal greetings; a wave and a smile are nonverbal greetings.

Through gestures, tone, and words, you provide information about your relationship with the receiver. Smiling warmly, extending your hand, and saying "Hi, Bob. It's good to see you again" portrays a very different relationship than does a stern face and a curtly uttered "Hello." Similarly, you might greet a coworker or personal friend by saying "Yo, Mary" but choose "Good afternoon, Mrs. Baumann" for a prospective client or the president of your firm.

Whatever your relationship with the receiver, be sure that the tone of your greeting matches the tone of your message. A positive, upbeat, carefree greeting would not be a good match for a message conveying bad news. Once the greeting has occurred, the conversation moves to the introduction stage.

Introduction During this stage, the person initiating the conversation previews what will follow. Introductions should be brief and informative. "Tony, you've had experience with just-in-time inventory systems. What do you see as their strengths?" alerts the receiver to the topic of the conversation and helps frame the context for his or her role in it.

An introduction may be direct or indirect. For example, if you believe you deserve an above-average increase in salary and your analysis of your boss tells you she or he prefers the direct approach, introduce your conversation topic by saying "Considering my performance this past year, I think that I deserve an above-average raise. Can we discuss this?" Your introduction makes your position on the topic clear. On the other hand, when a division manager needs to discuss a budget cut with a department supervisor, he or she might say "We need to discuss your department's budget request." This introduction defines the topic, provides a buffer to the negative news, and serves as a smooth transition between the greeting and the exchange, the third stage of the process.

Exchange As the word *exchange* implies, the business of a conversation is conducted in a give-and-take format. During this stage of the process, the purpose of the conversation comes to the forefront. For example:

NOTE 13.6
Conversations occur in stages.

NOTE 13.7
Greetings consist of words and actions.

NOTE 13.8
Introductory remarks should be brief yet informative.

NOTE 13.9
Business is transacted during the exchange.

	Elaine:	Jack, are you free to meet with Ced and me at 2 tomorrow afternoon? We need to discuss plans for this year's division retreat.
	Jack:	Possibly. How much time will we need? I know I have a staff meeting at 3.
	Elaine:	Thirty or forty minutes should do it.
	Jack:	OK. I'll put it on my calendar. Will you confirm with Ced?
	Elaine:	Sure.

In this example, the exchange is brief and direct. In another situation, the exchange might be longer and use the indirect approach. Specific techniques for a productive exchange are offered in the "Keys for Successful Face-to-Face Conversations" section below.

NOTE 13.10
The summary recaps the exchange or leads to the close.

Summary The fourth stage in the conversation process, the summary, allows the parties to reflect on the exchange, to recap the items discussed during a long or complex exchange, and to signal that a conversation is ending. This stage of the process does for the end of a conversation what the introduction does for the beginning: It serves as a bridge.

Either the sender or the receiver may summarize a conversation. By saying "Please have the revised budget on my desk by Friday morning" or "Call me if you have questions," a supervisor signals to a worker that their budget conversation is about to end. By saying, "I'll make the changes we've agreed to and have the revised budget on your desk by Friday morning," the employee indicates readiness to end the exchange and move to the final stage, the closing.

NOTE 13.11
The closing should be cordial.

Closing The closing is the cordial conclusion to the conversation. Depending on the situation, the closing may be verbal, nonverbal, or a combination of the two. After finalizing a sale with a new customer, for example, a sales representative might say, "It's been a pleasure doing business with you, Mr. Maestas. I'll process the order today and phone you about a week after the printer has been installed to be sure you're satisfied with it. Good-bye." The wording makes it clear the conversation has ended; the process has been completed.

Whether spontaneous or planned, successful conversations are honest, objective, sincere, and reasonable. Effective interpersonal relations and communications depend on these attributes. The process and techniques described in this section apply to all conversations; those described in the next two sections relate to special forms of conversation—face-to-face and telephone.

NOTE 13.12
Work to make conversations productive.

Keys for Successful Face-to-Face Conversations Face-to-face conversations have an advantage over written and telephone communication because both the sender and receiver can use nonverbal cues to help them interpret a message. As Carl Svendsen notes in the Communication Quote, the ability to converse with clients, agency representatives, and colleagues is key to his work as a public accountant. The following techniques will help make a face-to-face exchange productive:

- Carefully choose the location.
- Minimize interruptions.
- Speak effectively.
- Send clear, appropriate nonverbal cues.
- Ask questions.

My job as a certified public accountant requires me to be in contact with people on a daily basis. Whether I am consulting a client on an accounting or tax issue, presenting a client situation to a regulating authority, or discussing a current project with another staff member or partner, I always need to communicate the issues in a clear, concise, and professional manner. Many individuals and small business owners do not understand the complexities involved in accounting, and public accountants need to have the ability to break technical issues into simpler terms. The ability to do this is key to serving the client, adding value to our services, and projecting a good image for the firm. None of these things could be accomplished without effective interpersonal communication.

—Carl Svendsen, CPA, Eikill and Schilling, Ltd. (Photo courtesy of Jeff Frey and Associates)

- Accommodate diversity.
- Listen with your ears and eyes.

Carefully Choose the Location Conversations may take place in your office, in someone else's office, or at a neutral site. The purpose of the meeting should dictate the site and seating arrangement. Furniture can be a barrier to open communication. In a small office, a chair placed beside the desk creates a more welcoming atmosphere than does a chair placed opposite the desk. When you are uncomfortable with the seating arrangement in an office other than your own, ask politely to change it; do not move chairs without permission.

Restaurants are neutral sites that provide the opportunity for both social and business interaction. When meeting a business associate at a restaurant, select a table away from major traffic flows and wait for your guest there. Seat yourself across the table from your guest; be sure the guest has the seat with the fewest distractions.

Minimize Interruptions Interruptions affect your ability to hold a meaningful conversation. Ask staff to intercept telephone calls, have your calls transferred directly to voice mail, or simply let your phone ring. Keep your office door partially or fully closed to discourage interruptions. When off-site, turn off your pager or set it to signal messages by vibrating rather than ringing. Make similar adjustments to your cellular phone.

Speak Effectively Strong, effective messages are short and simple. Always think before you speak, and structure your sentences so that the receiver will understand them. Most receivers want to hear only those details they need to understand the message. They react favorably to the ideas of a sender who is concise and to the point without being abrupt. People also appreciate having others call them by name. The Tips and Hints box on page 368 provides helpful suggestions on this topic.

Vary your pitch, speed, and volume to hold your listener's interest and to emphasize important points. Enunciate words clearly and pronounce them correctly. Eliminate vocal distractions such as *um* and *ah.* Avoid vocal gestures that show impatience (humming, speaking abnormally fast) or do not support your message (sighing).

NOTE 13.13
Place furniture to encourage open communication.

NOTE 13.14
Give the conversation your full attention.

NOTE 13.15
Apply the principles of business communication.

The Importance of a Name

A person's name is his or her most important possession. Until asked to do otherwise, use the courtesy title and surname of customers, clients, or people who hold positions above yours within your organization. Address peers or others in the organization by their given name.

When you forget someone's name, be open and honest; admit your memory lapse. The specific approach you take will depend on the situation. When someone who phones you fails to give her or his name and you are unable to identify the caller by voice or from context, apologize and ask the caller's name. If the individual approaches you and addresses you by name, say, "It's good to see you again. I remember meeting you (indicate event or time) but don't recall your name." To initiate a conversation, begin by introducing yourself and reminding the person about where and when you met. Use the same strategy if you begin conversing with someone and sense he or she doesn't remember your name. Comfort, not embarrassment, is your goal.

Your purpose, analysis of the situation, and analysis of the receiver will guide you in determining how assertive you should be. Remember, though, that assertiveness does not mean aggressiveness; assertiveness does not alienate others. Be assertive by stating your views in a clear, straightforward manner appropriate to the circumstance.

NOTE 13.16
Control your emotions.

In business relationships people are expected to be calm, cool, and controlled, so keep your emotions in check. It is possible to disagree without being disagreeable. Successful businesspeople do not argue, they discuss. They avoid sarcasm, vulgarity, and inappropriate tears or laughter. They don't embarrass themselves or others.

NOTE 13.17
Use nonverbal cues that match the situation.

Send Clear, Appropriate Nonverbal Cues If appropriate to the situation, smile. When you offer someone a genuine smile, you show acceptance and build trust. People speak more freely when they feel safe, and a smile conveys safety.

Generally, the gestures and other movements used during conversations are smaller and more subtle than those used when speaking before a group. The proximity of the person or group with whom you are conversing makes your facial expressions more noticeable. Be sure any touch is appropriate to the situation and the person. Touch can be perceived to signal playfulness, control, support, gratitude, affection, intimidation, harassment, aggression, or other motives. Respect the personal space of those with whom you speak.

Limited eye contact may be thought to signify dishonesty, fear, or lack of interest—all barriers to effective communication. Recall that the appropriate level of eye contact varies among cultures. Let your receiver and the circumstances govern your behavior.

NOTE 13.18
Use questions to obtain facts and learn about feelings.

Ask Questions One of the best ways to encourage another person to communicate is to ask questions. Carefully structured questions can help you gather facts, determine your receiver's needs, and encourage dialogue. Good communicators understand and use both closed- and open-ended questions.

NOTE 13.19
Use closed- and open-ended questions.

A **closed-ended question** is designed to produce a one- or two-word answer; this type of question works best for fact finding. An **open-ended question** requires a longer answer and promotes a dialogue. Use this type of question when you want expanded answers or background information. Open-ended questions also work well when your receiver or the situation is emotional.

If, for example, you are trying to help a subordinate improve the quality of his or her work, you will have a more meaningful exchange if you ask "What can I do to help you do a better job?" than by asking "Do you need help to do your job?" The open-ended question invites the employee to suggest things that each of you can do to improve the work. In this situation, the closed-ended question invites a one-word response—and resentment or anger. Conversely, if you need to know when a contract was signed, you will get the data you want faster by asking "What is the signature date on the contract with Recore?" than by asking "What's the history of the Recore contract?"

Once you've asked a question, give the receiver time to respond. Fast-paced questioning could be perceived as interrogation, which will stifle rather than stimulate discussion. Refer to the following Tips and Hints box for information on the part questions play in social conversation.

Social Conversations

Questions play a role in conversations during business-related social functions. A good host or hostess will introduce guests to one another and, as part of the introduction, will offer information on which discussion can commence. For example, a host might say "Selina, this is Yuri, who just returned from a business trip to London." Turning to Yuri, the host might then say "Selina enjoys theater and has seen productions in New York and in London."

Savvy conversationalists ask receiver-centered questions that respect an individual's privacy. They might ask people where they work but not what they paid for their house or what they earn. People interested in developing positive relationships avoid hot-button topics—those that will evoke emotional responses or provoke confrontation. Religion and politics are classic examples. When the person with whom you are speaking introduces a topic you don't wish to discuss, simply listen, make a noncommittal response such as "That's interesting," and then change the subject to something noncontroversial.

Accommodate Diversity Recognize and accommodate cultural or other differences during your conversations. Consider language differences; nonverbal communication differences; and factors such as values, attitudes, religion, political systems, and social orders. Be alert to and sensitive about physical and other disabilities that affect communication. Chapter 2 provides information about various cultures. The Tips and Hints box on page 370 provides helpful information about communicating with people who have various disabilities.

Listen with Your Ears and Eyes When people are conversing, they often think about what they are going to say next instead of listening to what the other person has to say. By giving the speaker your full attention, you can participate effectively in the conversation and make the other person believe she or he is important and interesting.

Giving the speaker your full attention will allow you to "hear" both verbal and nonverbal cues. Any deviation from the person's normal speech pattern and nonverbal behavior must be considered in the context of the situation. Negative words or an angry tone may signal disagreement or fear; a fast pace may signal enthusiasm, excitement, or anxiety. Darting eye movements, frequent shifts of body weight, and changes in

NOTE 13.20
Attentive listening shows your interest in the speaker.

Tips for Communicating with People Who Have Disabilities

When a person has a . . .	You should . . .
Visual impairment	• Speak directly to the person, not through an interpreter or other person unless requested to do so. Ask how he or she communicates best and honor the preference. • Introduce yourself and others. Give names, titles, and locations (e.g., "To my right is Greg Peters, project director"). Tell the person when someone joins, leaves, or changes location within the group. • Accept that "I'll see you later" and other colloquial expressions containing sight terms will not be viewed as offensive.
Hearing impairment	• Use a light touch on the shoulder, a wave, or other signal to gain attention. • Minimize visual distractions, including bright sunlight. • Look directly at the person. Keep your hands away from your face. • Speak clearly and rephrase if necessary. Write your message if further clarification is needed. • Accept that "Did you hear?" and other colloquial expressions containing sound terms will not be viewed as offensive.
Mobility impairment or other physical disability	• Ask whether assistance is needed, and wait for a response before taking action. Carefully follow all instructions. • Create a comfortable viewing angle for someone who uses a wheelchair. Eye level is best but, if you must stand, move back enough to minimize the angle without having to raise your voice to be heard. • Offer to shake hands. People who have limited use of their right arm or hand or who use an artificial limb often use their left hand in greetings.
Speech impairment	• Try to speak in a quiet location. • Be patient. Allow the speaker to finish sentences; don't complete them for him or her. • Paraphrase and ask if you have understood what's been said. Ask to have statements repeated when you don't understand what has been said.

posture must also be interpreted. You may tell an employee that you have decided to give a desirable assignment to a coworker. If the employee's shoulders slump or if he or she becomes teary-eyed while saying "Fine. Good." you know that the employee does not view your decision as either fine or good. Feelings must be addressed before you can move forward with business discussions.

To verify or acknowledge what you hear, paraphrase the message or ask relevant questions. Repeating what was said will help you retain what you have heard. When the speaker pauses, count to three before you speak. Interruptions can destroy the comfortable atmosphere you want to create, but a carefully placed "You seem frustrated," or "So, what you said is . . ." can keep the line of communication open.

Empathy means understanding how a person feels; it does not mean you agree with how the person feels. Listening with empathy is especially important when someone comes to you with a problem. After the problem has been described, ask how you can help. Offer advice only when encouraged to do so. Sometimes just listening is all the help the person needs.

Keys for Successful Telephone Conversations

The telephone is important for sending and receiving business messages and can be valuable in building interpersonal relationships. For some message receivers, the entire image of a company rests solely on the quality of their telephone interactions with representatives of the organization. The following will help you improve the quality of your telephone conversations:

- Use the telephone equipment and system properly.
- Be businesslike.
- Be considerate.

Use the Telephone Equipment and System Properly

Hold the telephone mouthpiece one to two inches from your mouth and talk directly into it. Speech faults, accents, and other sounds are magnified during telephone conversations. Never chew gum, eat, or drink while on the phone; remove earrings, bracelets, and similar jewelry before placing or receiving a call. Know how to transfer calls, arrange conference calls, use a speaker phone, set up callbacks, and use other special features of your system. Employees who are not able to use the company telephone system properly will be perceived as inefficient, as will the organization.

Be Businesslike

When the telephone rings, be ready to talk when you answer; end all conversations with others in your office. Identify yourself immediately. Some phone systems produce a different ringing sound or have a screen display code to indicate whether a call originated inside or outside the organization. You may wish to include your organization and department name only for calls from outside the organization.

As you speak, create and hold a mental image of the person you call. This technique will help you to maintain a businesslike manner. The method will also help keep the conversation receiver-centered and your voice conversational. Because you cannot be seen, your voice has to carry the whole message and convey its tone. Use the caller's name and cordial terms such as *please, thank you,* and *I appreciate.* Remember to smile; the tone of your voice is more pleasant when you smile.

If the caller is angry or has a complaint, stay calm. Realize that the caller is upset with a situation or policy, not with you personally. When you or your company has made an error, acknowledge it without placing blame or making excuses; then, move on. Do what you can to correct the problem; if you promise action, set a reasonable time frame and do what you promise.

After the conversation has ended, let the caller hang up first. This simple gesture reinforces the impression that the caller is important and has your undivided attention.

NOTE 13.21
Paraphrasing helps you clarify and retain what you hear.

NOTE 13.22
Listen with empathy.

NOTE 13.23
Telephone conversations are important business tools.

NOTE 13.24
The telephone amplifies sounds.

It also minimizes the need for a second call because the sender thought of something else to say but was cut off before he or she could do so.

When you place a call, the telephone may be answered by a support staff member or channeled to a voice mail system. Be prepared to leave a clear, complete message that includes at least your name, your phone number, and the purpose of your call. Be sure to pronounce and spell your name clearly; slow down when giving your phone number.

Whether at home or at the office, be sure your outgoing message is current and complete. Resist the temptation to record a generic "I'm unavailable to take your call" message; provide your callers with real information about when you will be available to take or return calls. Invite your caller to leave a message. Be sure, too, that your message is businesslike. Friends or family members may enjoy a humorous greeting, but a client or prospective employer could view the greeting—and you—as unprofessional. Also, international callers may be confused by messages using colloquial English or by messages recorded at a faster than normal speaking rate. Read the Tips and Hints box on page 373 to learn about telephone communication with those who speak with foreign accents.

Be Considerate Place your own calls. Having an assistant place your calls and then keeping the called party waiting while you get on the line makes it appear that you believe your time is more valuable than the receiver's. Such a procedure is inconsiderate and gets the conversation off to a bad start.

When taking calls, answer on the first ring, if possible, but certainly no later than the third. When you must ask a caller to wait while you gather information, return at 15- to 30-second intervals to report your progress and assure him or her that you will be back to the conversation as soon as possible. If it becomes obvious that your off-phone efforts will take longer than a minute or two, offer to return the call at a specified time. Be sure to keep a pencil and notepad close to the telephone. Before using a speaker phone, ask whether the other person objects; honor the person's preference for privacy.

Office Politics

Office politics is the name given to the competitive environment created whenever three or more people work in an organization. The competition may be for tangibles such as equipment, pay raises, promotions, or office space; it may also be for intangibles such as status or influence. Any workplace action that represents an informal attempt to protect self-interest, meet personal needs, and advance personal goals could be termed office politics. The way in which office politics affects a relationship depends on the situation and the people involved—sometimes it can be benign; other times, incendiary.

Each of us may want to believe that the workplace is fair and that gains come solely through hard work. We may want to believe that we can trust everyone, that comments can be made without fear of retaliation, and that statements made in confidence will remain confidential. We want to believe that rules exist and that everyone will follow them. In reality, that is not the case. Written rules seldom address competitive strategies and, even when they do, bending and breaking occur. These comments may sound cynical, but they are not meant to be. Their purpose is to introduce a topic that can best be described as a gray area in communication, an area dependent as much on perception as on fact. Consider the following example.

NOTE 13.25
Create meaningful voice-mail messages.

NOTE 13.26
Placing and taking your own calls is efficient and courteous.

NOTE 13.27
The office is a competitive environment with its own politics.

Tips for Handling Telephone Conversations with People Who Have Foreign Accents

Call it simple kindness or call it common sense, but learning to deal with accents that are foreign to you can definitely be good for business. More than one million legal immigrants enter the United States each year, and most of them have one thing in common: English is their second language. This population represents a sizable market for any corporation selling products or services in the United States.

The phone calls you answer may be from people whose accents are unfamiliar to you. Here are six easy points to remember when dealing with a foreign accent:

[1] Don't pretend to understand. If you don't understand the caller, it's perfectly okay to say gently that you're having a little difficulty understanding him or her. Ask the caller to slow down so you can get all the information correct.

[2] Don't rush. Rushing threatens callers. Listen to the caller's pattern of speech. You'll be able to pick up key words. Repeat the key words to them; they'll appreciate the fact that you're really listening.

[3] Don't shout. The difficulty is with language, not volume.

[4] Don't repeat unnecessarily. People with an accent usually speak two or more languages, so it will take them a little longer to go through the thought process: their native language for thinking, English for communicating with you. Repeating the same word over and over to be sure they understand is unnecessary.

[5] Don't be rude. If you've ever told a caller, "I can't understand you," or "Huh?" or even "What did you say?" you've been a little rude, whether you intended that or not. It's much better to stop, take full responsibility, and explain you're having difficulty understanding. Say, "If you'll repeat it for me again, I'll be able to help you." It's a subtle difference, but a key one.

[6] Do keep a job aid available. If most of the calls you receive are predominantly from one particular ethnic group, keep a list with a few commonly used phrases near your phone. For example, in Spanish "Uno momento, por favor" means "one moment, please." Even if you pronounce it poorly, this phrase would be appreciated by a Latino whom you are having difficulty understanding. You can then pause and bring someone to the phone who can help.

Adapted from materials produced by American Media Incorporated, 4900 University Avenue, West Des Moines, IA 50266-6769; used with permission.

B. J. and Shawn worked in different units of a large organization. B. J. had been with the company for about two years and worked in an entry-level position; positive performance reviews resulted in pay raises and increased levels of responsibility but no promotion. Shawn had been with the company for over ten years and managed a growing division. The two, both of whom were interested in physical fitness, had no real interaction until they joined a new health club near their homes. Over the next several months, their common interest outside the office led to conversations at work. People began to notice and, when B. J. applied for and was hired for a supervisory position in Shawn's division, people began to talk. "It's office politics," they said, "B. J. didn't earn that promotion. At least six people in Shawn's division are more qualified. B. J. was hired just because of their friendship. Shawn didn't even know who B. J. was until they met at that health club. I heard that B. J. joined that health club because several managers belonged."

Was the meeting between B. J. and Shawn coincidence or strategy? Was their friendship genuine or contrived? Did Shawn hire B. J. because of qualifications or friendship? Was the promotion a function of networking? office politics? neither? both? The answers are anything but clear.

One thing is clear: Because people are human and have emotions, politics exist in every organization. Once you acknowledge the reality, you can assess the political landscape—who's who and how things get done—and decide at what level to participate. The choices run along a continuum anchored by "light" and "heavy," but there are no standard definitions of the type of behavior associated with each. Light participation in one organization may consist of participating in the grapevine only when the information is not destructive to someone. In another organization, light participation may involve identifying one or two strengths of an influential manager and supporting and playing to those strengths.

Ronna Lichtenberg, author of *Work Would Be Great if It Weren't for People,* contends that skill alone is insufficient for survival in today's organizations; people must be good at office politics, too.[1] This view is shared by others, among them Rebecca Luhn Wolfe, author of *Office Politics: Positive Results from Fair Practices,* who advocates practical, ethical choices based on five rules:[2]

[1] Understand your corporate culture. Follow policy unless you are in a position to change it.

[2] Know when to hold and when to fold. Each is appropriate depending on the situation; be flexible.

[3] Believe in win-win situations. Being able to negotiate a solution can help you survive.

[4] Play fair. Respect yourself and others.

[5] Think first, act later. Results will be better if based on reason rather than emotion.

You probably won't be able to assess the political environment in an organization until you begin working there. If you find yourself working in an organization where the politics don't match your beliefs or ability to play, you may benefit by changing employers.

Relationship Repair

Sometimes, despite the good intentions of those involved, relationships are damaged. Rather than let pride or indifference cause them to walk away from a damaged relationship, effective communicators take steps to rebuild it.

The obvious thing to do, of course, is apologize. Sometimes a simple "I'm sorry" is all that's needed. When this simple statement doesn't accomplish its goal, however, the speaker must make an additional effort. Acknowledging that he or she played a part in the failure is an option, but the speaker must do so sincerely and without expectation that the receiver will also claim responsibility. Relinquishing dual responsibility is a sacrifice that demonstrates the speaker's commitment to rebuilding the relationship.

Depending on what caused the relationship to weaken, actions may be the glue that's needed to mend it. This is especially true when the relationship has a history of broken promises. Actions can replace or complement an apology or acknowledgment.

Finally, both parties must let go of the problem that caused the relationship failure. Until they do, the relationship cannot regain its strength or grow stronger.

[1] "Office Politics," *Executive Excellence,* October 1998, p. 14.
[2] Rebecca Luhn Wolfe, *Office Politics: Positive Results from Fair Practices,* Menlo Park, CA: Crisp, 1997.

NOTE 13.28
Assess the political environment in the organization.

NOTE 13.29
With effort, damaged relationships can be repaired.

Non Sequitur

Criticism

LEARNING OBJECTIVE

③ *Give criticism effectively and receive it appropriately.*

Praise is easy to give and nice to receive. For most people, the opposite is true of criticism. Despite our dislike for it, criticism is a fact of workplace life. Therefore, it is important that we learn to deliver it effectively and accept it without becoming defensive.

Giving Criticism

The following list contains suggestions to help you maximize the chances of having your receiver understand and accept criticism:

- Be sure you have the authority to critique the receiver. If you don't, he or she will most likely reject the criticism and resent you for delivering it.
- Criticize one relevant concern at a time. People become overwhelmed, confused, or dejected when faced with a long list of complaints. Be assertive but consistent. Repeat and clarify the issues, but do not argue about them.
- Check your facts. Avoid using absolute words such as *never* and *always*. If your receiver identifies even one small element of your concern as being false, he or she could focus on it, argue about it, and move the conversation

NOTE 13.30
Criticism contributes to improved performance.

NOTE 13.31
Receiver understanding and acceptance are the goals.

away from the issue at hand. Once a sender's credibility on an issue is tainted, the goal cannot be accomplished.

- Criticize privately and calmly, preferably face-to-face. Criticism is difficult enough to receive without being embarrassed in the process. Give the receiver an opportunity to retain his or her dignity and to use every available verbal and nonverbal cue. Be sure no one interrupts your meeting with a phone call or office visit.

- Offer only constructive criticism. Comments that are clear, specific, and show receiver benefit will be most effective. Rather than say "Your proposal is disorganized, contains computational errors, and is a writing disaster" say "All the elements of a good proposal are here, they just need to be re-ordered. By placing the strongest element first, we can capture and hold the reader's attention. Double-check your figures and be sure grammar and punctuation are correct." Vague, self-serving suggestions could cause the receiver to feel anxiety or doubt.

NOTE 13.32
Focus on the receiver; use the you–viewpoint.

- Use the you–viewpoint; criticize the action or item, not the person. "Being abrupt with a customer portrays the company as uncaring" or "You'll make a more positive personal and corporate impression if you are courteous with customers" works better than "You are abrupt with customers."

- Be sure the receiver knows your criticism in one area won't cloud your overall judgment of him or her. Show respect and appreciation for what the person has done in other areas. By scheduling the meeting for early in the week or early in the day, you will have opportunities to see the individual in positive, reassuring situations shortly after the meeting. Criticize personal items (e.g., hygiene, dress) only when they relate to work performance.

- If appropriate, accept partial responsibility for the problem. An introduction such as "Perhaps my directions weren't clear" can temper the impact of the criticism that follows.

- Be aware of the verbal and nonverbal cues that accompany your message. Use a conversational pace and tone. Use "blameless" gestures. Pointing with a pen or your finger, for example, creates an aura of accusation.

NOTE 13.33
Allow the receiver to absorb and respond.

- Allow the receiver time to process and respond. Even when the receiver knows the purpose of the meeting is to discuss behavior or work performance, hearing the message may have an emotional impact. Accept silence and emotional displays. Listen actively and empathetically. When people believe they have been heard and understood, they are less defensive.

Receiving Criticism

NOTE 13.34
Accept criticism without becoming defensive.

Perhaps the only thing more difficult than giving criticism is receiving it. When faced with criticism, people generally respond with "fight or flight" behavior. Fighting manifests itself as defensive, argumentative, or counterattack remarks. Fleeing can be physical (e.g., avoiding face-to-face or telephone contact) or mental (e.g., tuning out). In the long run, neither method solves the problem as effectively as (1) agreeing with the criticism or (2) seeking more information.

NOTE 13.35
Agree with the facts; influence the perception they create.

Agreeing Criticism can be based on facts, perceptions, or both. If, for example, your supervisor identifies computational errors in your work, he or she may perceive these facts as being related to inability or carelessness. Arguing about the facts (computational errors) is futile, but you can redirect the perception by pointing out that these errors are the exception, not the rule, in your work performance. You can also acknowledge that you understand why he or she might feel you let him or her down. Acknowledging the other person's feelings doesn't mean you agree with them. Say what you will do to minimize the likelihood the problem will be repeated.

Seeking More Information Showing interest in what prompts the criticism can help you decide how to fix whatever prompted it. To that end, consider doing the following:

NOTE 13.36
Clarify the concern by seeking more information.

- Ask for specific examples. "Can you show me where the errors are?"
- Describe a situation and ask whether it illustrates the problem. "Does the formula error in the spreadsheet I prepared on the Miller account illustrate your concern?"
- Paraphrase the criticism to focus on an outcome. "Are you saying that when my work contains errors it creates problems for the people who must use it?"
- Ask how you can improve. "Other than proofreading more carefully, do you have specific suggestions that might help me?"

After receiving criticism, be sure to take action to remedy the situation. If the critic's suggestions result in improvement, thank him or her; if problems persist, ask for another opportunity to discuss the situation.

Conflict

LEARNING OBJECTIVE
④ *Describe techniques for resolving conflicts.*

NOTE 13.37
Conflict can arise from various sources.

Conflict is inevitable. To deny it is to prove it. Conflict can occur in your personal life or at work. In the workplace, conflict may arise between you and a coworker, between two employees you supervise, between your department and another, or between your organization and a customer or client.

Conflict can arise from differences in personalities (e.g., extrovert and introvert), goals or expectations, values or beliefs, circumstances (e.g., money and time), or facts (e.g., different sources). Conflicts associated with values and beliefs tend to be the most difficult to resolve because they are so deeply rooted. When faced with conflict, you have four options:

- **Yield.** This approach should be used when the issue is less important to one person than to the other or when maintaining the relationship is more important than the issue. It is also the logical approach when one person knows he or she can't win or wants to bank a favor.
- **Compromise.** This approach works best when the parties have some areas of agreement on which a mutually agreeable solution can be built or, as in yielding, when the relationship is more important than the issue.
- **Overpower.** This approach should be used only in an emergency or when the issue is more important than the relationship.
- **Collaborate.** This approach requires people to work together. It fits best in situations that may repeat themselves or when the relationship has been long-term.

NOTE 13.38
Responses to conflict
vary by person and
situation.

As you can see by these descriptions, the option that could work best will vary with the situation and the people involved. This is true within as well as across cultures. When Tinsley[3] analyzed responses that Japanese, German, and American managers gave to a hypothetical conflict scenario, she learned that (1) Japanese managers preferred deferring to status power more than German and American managers; (2) German managers rated applying regulations and integrating interests equally; (3) Germans' preference for applying regulations was greater than that of American and Japanese managers; and (4) American managers preferred integrating interests more than did German and Japanese managers. Research by Morris, et al.[4] found that U.S. managers, because of their relatively high value on individual achievement, rely on a competing style of conflict resolution. Chinese managers, on the other hand, rely on an avoiding style because of their relatively high value on conformity and tradition.

Conflict may be healthy or destructive. At its best, conflict fosters creative thinking and the opportunity to improve. Healthy conflict is marked by the ability to disagree on one issue while working collaboratively on others. At its worst, conflict sabotages relationships, destroys morale, and polarizes people. Unhealthy conflict is not issue specific; it transcends both time and situations. Fortunately, destructive conflicts can be resolved. The techniques that follow can be used either when you are directly involved in the conflict or when you are an outside party with a vested interest in seeing it resolved.

General Techniques for Handling Conflicts

Several conflict resolution techniques apply to situations in which you are a participant and to those in which you are facilitator:

- **Act promptly.** The longer a problem goes unattended, the greater the chance it will escalate into a major issue. If the conflict involves emotions, the parties will need 24 to 48 hours to cool off.
- **Schedule a meeting.** Whenever possible, meet face to face so that the participants can take advantage of nonverbal cues. Choose a neutral location so neither party has a territorial advantage.
- **Use active listening.** Every conflict has two sides, and each person fervently believes his or hers is the accurate or "right" side. Both people want to be heard and understood. Before a conflict can be resolved, both parties must be able to separate what happened from how they feel about it. Paraphrasing can be valuable in this effort.
- **Focus on the problem, not the person.** Laying blame delays resolution. The parties must respect themselves and each other.
- **Brainstorm solutions.** Look for win-win opportunities; negotiate if necessary.
- **Formalize the solution.** Putting the solution on paper allows both parties the opportunity to see as well as hear it and minimizes the likelihood that they will later disagree on the solution.
- **Implement the solution and set a date for follow-up.** The follow-up creates an air of accountability.

[3] C. Tinsley, "Models of Conflict Resolution in Japanese, German, and American Cultures," *Journal of Applied Psychology*, 83, 1998, pp. 316–323.

[4] M. W. Morris, et al., "Conflict Management Style: Accounting for Cross-National Differences," *Journal of International Business Studies*, 29, 4, 1998, pp. 729–747.

When You Are Involved

One person in a conflict must initiate resolution. Although some perceive the person who takes the first step as the weaker party, others believe he or she is the stronger. In the workplace, the latter is more likely to be true.

Before you approach the other person, critically analyze the situation and your role in it. If you don't know the basis for your position, you won't be able to explain it. Bring your emotions under control; place organizational goals above personal goals.

When you approach the other person, do so with sincerity. Issue an invitation rather than a directive. Telling the other person that you must meet will create more tension.

During the meeting, let the other person tell his or her story first. Paraphrase to verify that you understand both facts and feelings. Ask for specific examples and facts, but choose your words and tone carefully. Getting angry, arguing, telling the person how he or she should feel, making statements that ridicule or criticize the other person, or telling him or her to be quiet and listen will make the situation worse. As you listen, look for areas of agreement. When you tell your story, begin by citing areas on which you agree. Then move to those on which resolution will be necessary. If the list is short or simple, begin immediately to look for solutions. If the list is long or complex, schedule a second meeting with the understanding that you'll each come to it with possible solutions.

When You Are a Facilitator

As a supervisor or manager, you will have responsibility for building a team, a group that will work with each other and with you to achieve goals. Productivity declines, lowered morale, absenteeism, accidents, and emotional outbursts are all signs that conflict may exist. When conflict emerges within your group, you have an obligation to see that it is resolved before it escalates.

You may learn about a conflict by (1) observing it, (2) being told of it by one or both parties involved in it, or (3) being informed by a third party. Sometimes intensity can be mistaken for conflict; simply hearing raised voices isn't sufficient to presume conflict exists. If you believe you observe conflict or are told of it by a third party, document it.

If one party to a conflict tells you about it, the situation is more tenuous. You must acknowledge what you are told without giving the impression that you agree with the person. Taking sides or giving the impression that you are taking sides creates animosity and enemies. Similarly, you must refrain from placing blame or forcing the parties to apologize. Trying to identify who is at fault is unproductive; it causes you to look backward rather than forward. Being forced to apologize humiliates the parties and can increase the animosity between them.

Regardless of how you learn about a conflict, deal with it in private. Invite the parties to meet with you separately and then together. Use the individual meetings to ascertain the real source of the conflict and its severity. Sometimes people argue about secondary concerns. Unless the key issue is identified and resolved, it will resurface. Use the group meeting to encourage teamwork and problem solving. During the joint meeting, the facilitator acts as an emcee; he or she introduces topics, clarifies, refocuses, and summarizes. Remember that your goal is to help the parties resolve their disagreement. If you approach the situation with the goal of saving or rescuing, you could cause resentment.

NOTE 13.41
Take the first step.

NOTE 13.42
Listen before speaking.

NOTE 13.43
Left unattended, conflict will escalate.

LEARNING OBJECTIVE

Develop the skills
associated with
leading and participating
in teams.

(5) # Teamwork

Teamwork has permeated the corporate and nonprofit sectors of American organizations. The concept is simple—by working together, people can accomplish more than any individual can achieve by working alone—but the execution can be complex. A successful team requires persistence, energy, and focus on the part of the team leader and the team participants. Because teams are so common, you should know about the various types of teams, know how teamwork benefits you and the organization, be aware of the conditions that must exist for effective teamwork, and learn how to be a good team leader and a good team member.

NOTE 13.44
Together **E**veryone
Achieves **M**ore.

Types of Teams

NOTE 13.45
Teams may be categorized by type.

Teams can generally be categorized as being self-managed, process-improvement, or cross-functional.

SELF-MANAGED TEAMS

Teams that have a great deal of autonomy are considered to be self-directed or self-managed. Self-managed teams are ongoing groups with decision-making authority for virtually every aspect of product production or service delivery. Their responsibilities generally include planning daily work as well as hiring, firing, and training. This structure exists in organizations that have adopted teamwork as an operational model.

PROCESS-IMPROVEMENT TEAMS

As the name implies, process-improvement teams are charged with making changes to a process. Their focus may be increasing quality, reducing costs, providing speedier service, or eliminating redundancy. Once changes have been proposed and/or implemented, the team is disbanded.

CROSS-FUNCTIONAL TEAMS

Members of these teams are drawn from various functional areas and charged with accomplishing a particular task, completing a particular process, or providing ongoing input about various issues. This type of team draws its strength from the perspectives and diverse viewpoints its members can present.

Benefits and Drawbacks of Teamwork

Teams have both advantages and disadvantages.

NOTE 13.46
Teams have personal and organizational impact.

On a personal level, participating on a team can help you increase your knowledge of the organization, broaden your perspective of areas within the business, develop a sense of camaraderie with coworkers, be more visible within the organization, learn about the various management styles used by team leaders, and improve your own project management skills.

At the organizational level, teams help corporations gain a competitive advantage. In addition, they can help increase productivity, improve communication, encourage creativity, facilitate problem solving, and increase the quality of decisions. As Julie Tapp notes in the Communication Quote on page 381, good communication helps team members achieve organizational goals.

Interpersonal communication skills are critical in my role as an analyst. As a member of a project team working to develop an automated system, the analyst is responsible for identifying and bridging gaps between business expectations and requirements. Effective listening, as well as good oral and nonverbal communication skills, are essential; they help the project team define the business requirements and manage business expectations. Ultimately, this will aid in the design and development of a system that meets the company's needs.

—Julie Tapp, Analyst, Federated Insurance. (Photo courtesy of Julie Tapp)

The negatives of working in a group include loss of control, pressure to conform, and uneven distribution of workload, a phenomenon also known as "free riding" or "social loafing." With effective team leadership and participation, these disadvantages can be neutralized or eliminated.

Conditions for Effective Teamwork

For teams to function effectively, the following conditions must exist:

- **Communication must be open and honest.** Members must trust and respect one another. Ideas should be offered freely and listened to with patience and courtesy. Decisions should be based on an idea's merits, not on the popularity or power of the person who offers it. Personal attacks reduce the comfort level within the team and can promote retaliation or reduced participation.

- **The team must be cohesive.** Members must share and be committed to the team's goals and vision. When some members are excluded, the spirit of cooperation is threatened. Members must be free to interact with each other and with the leader.

- **Growth should be fostered.** The needs of the individual, the team, and the organization must be considered. At the individual level, participation should offer the opportunity for personal and professional growth. Keeping the group to a workable size helps make this happen. When teams exceed ten members, communication and coordination pose challenges. Balanced contributions are more difficult to achieve in a large team; some members may even try to be anonymous.

- **Accomplishments must be recognized.** When teams achieve their goals, they should be recognized for their accomplishment. All members—not just the leader—should receive recognition.

NOTE 13.47
Communication, cohesiveness, and potential for growth foster team success.

Meeting Leadership and Participation

Meetings are the common vehicle through which teams plan, report, and coordinate efforts toward reaching their goals. Depending on their jobs and the industries in which they work, managers report spending anywhere from 30 to 60 percent of their time in meetings. Unfortunately, many businesspeople view meetings as boring, intrusive time wasters.

NOTE 13.48
Meetings are vehicles for sharing information and solving problems.

Knowing how to lead and participate in meetings is, therefore, essential to helping you make them worthwhile, productive experiences. The suggestions offered in the following Communication Note may also be useful.

KEYS FOR EFFECTIVE SMALL-GROUP MEETING LEADERSHIP

Sometimes effective teams arise naturally; more often, they need guidance and leadership. The person primarily responsible for the success of a team is the leader. The keys for successful small-group leadership are presented in the following paragraphs.

NOTE 13.49
The way a group operates is influenced by its purpose.

Determine the Purpose of the Group The scope of the group's responsibility and authority must be defined. Will it make recommendations, or does it have the power to act? Is the group an ongoing one, designed to share information and solve problems as they arise, or is it a special team formed to brainstorm solutions to a specific dilemma? The purpose of a group will influence the way in which it accomplishes its work. Therefore, the leader must ensure that the group's purpose is clear, communicated to, and understood by all members.

Determine the Purpose of Each Meeting Planning, brainstorming, sharing information, solving problems, and training are among the reasons for which meetings may be held. Groups that meet regularly (e.g., weekly meeting of department managers) may have more than one purpose for each meeting. Members might share information about human resources needs and, at the same meeting, brainstorm about ways in which space may be reallocated.

NOTE 13.50
Hold meetings only when necessary.

Before scheduling a face-to-face meeting, be sure it needs to be held. Meetings, even regularly scheduled weekly or monthly meetings, should be canceled if no issues need to be discussed or no decisions need to be made. Consider, too, whether another format might better serve the group. A two- or three-person conversation, an e-mail, or a telephone conference might be more efficient. Although face-to-face meetings have a social dimension, socializing should not be the only reason for meeting.

All too often, people are invited to meetings because the leader doesn't want them to feel left out. Although appropriate in many settings, courtesy is insufficient reason for including someone at a meeting. The larger the group, the less productive the session will be. Limit attendance to those who are instrumental in achieving the group's goals.

NOTE 13.51
Keep groups to a manageable size.

Plan the Meeting Agenda The group leader must prepare the meeting agenda carefully. The topics to be discussed should be listed in some logical order, in a sequence that serves the purpose of the group. For a formal meeting, copies of the agenda and all related materials should be distributed a few days in advance of the meeting so that the members can prepare. When the volume of attachments is small, e-mail is a suitable distribution method. Outlines for two styles of agenda are presented in Figure 13.1. Either could be modified to include the name of the person responsible for each item and to indicate the approximate time to be devoted to each item. For informal meetings with very limited scope, a telephone message describing the date, time, place, and topic may be sufficient.

NOTE 13.52
Prepare and distribute agenda and related materials in advance.

Traditional Agenda	**Functional Agenda**
Group Name Time, Day, and Date of Meeting Location	Group Name Time, Day, and Date of Meeting Location
Participants and Guests Call to Order Minutes of Previous Meeting Reports of Standing Committees Reports of Special (ad hoc) Committees Old Business New Business Announcements Adjournment	Participants and Guests Action Items Discussion Items Information Items

FIGURE 13.1
Sample Agenda Outlines

The time at which a meeting is held can have an effect on its success. Scheduling a meeting for early morning (e.g., 8:15 a.m.) suggests importance; starting at an off-hour time (e.g., 10:45 a.m.) encourages punctuality; selecting an odd starting time (e.g., 1:17 p.m.) captures interest; and scheduling meetings for times just before lunch or at the end of the day encourages timely adjournment. Finally, keep meetings brief. Attention and interest wane after about 45 minutes. If meetings must be longer than an hour, schedule a short break, then reconvene.

NOTE 13.53
Weigh the effects of start time, end time, and duration.

The first time a group gathers, list the names of participants on the agenda. Be sure to list the names of guests any time they attend. Knowing who will attend a meeting helps the participants plan for the event.

Select and Prepare the Meeting Facility Most routine business meetings are held on-site. Off-site meetings encourage efficiency by minimizing interruptions such as telephone calls; the rental, transportation, and time costs may, however, make them desirable primarily for sessions devoted to strategic planning or similar purposes.

NOTE 13.54
Consider site options.

The group leader or a support staff member should arrange for the meeting room and be sure that it is properly prepared. Items to be considered include adequate seating; writing surfaces and supplies; extra copies of the agenda and related materials; room temperature and ventilation; audiovisual equipment, cords, and power sources; lighting and location of light switches; and refreshments. Preparations should be completed well in advance of the meeting and checked about an hour before the meeting starts. The leader should arrive a few minutes early to make a final check of the facility.

Lead the Group Discussion

NOTE 13.55
Lead the discussion to achieve the group's purpose.

During the meeting, the primary role of the leader is to assist the group in achieving its purpose. This means keeping the group focused on its tasks and not allowing the discussion to stray to unrelated topics. It also means moving from one item on the agenda to the next in a timely manner without stifling adequate discussion. The leader must discourage private discussions among members. Asking members to share their comments with the entire group could bring new insights to the topic or discourage future side conversations. Another strategy is to stop the meeting until the side discussions cease.

A good group leader actually talks very little during a meeting. Rather, he or she serves as a facilitator, a catalyst—someone who motivates participants to work together effectively and who secures group decisions after adequate discussion. Unless the leader anticipates having to exercise authority during a meeting, she or he should sit among the members rather than at the head of the conference table.

Encourage Appropriate Participation

NOTE 13.56
Encourage meaningful contributions.

The group leader is responsible for eliciting the best contributions possible from each participant. The first Tips and Hints box on page 385 lists ways to encourage members to participate in discussions. She or he should create an environment in which ideas are offered freely and responded to constructively. Whenever anyone presents an idea, ask the others to indicate its strengths as well as its weaknesses and to suggest specific ways to eliminate the weaknesses. If the group is a committee formed of employees from different levels in an organization, some higher-level people might intimidate some of the lower-level people. Avoid creating this situation. While formed into a group with a specific purpose, all employees should be considered equal in order to obtain effective contributions from all participants.

Be Time Conscious

NOTE 13.57
Be aware of time without discouraging discussion.

The group leader should start and adjourn the meeting on time. Periodically, the leader may need to remind the group of its time constraints. Comments on time must be made judiciously, however, or they will restrict discussion.

Be sure to stick to the agenda. Allowing a member to introduce topics not on the agenda usually results in hasty, uninformed decision making. The group is disadvantaged because only the person who introduces the new topic has had adequate time to prepare to discuss it. Manipulative group members may try to use this tactic to advance a personal or hidden agenda. Such behavior destroys team unity.

Just before the meeting ends, summarize what has been accomplished and clearly state who is to do what by when. If appropriate, set the date of the next meeting.

Resolve Group Conflicts

NOTE 13.58
Resolve conflicts before they damage teamwork.

Often participants in group meetings take opposing positions. This is natural and healthy. When disagreements intensify, however, they can lead to animosity or hostility and destroy a group's ability to work as a team. The leader must resolve conflicts before they reach a destructive level. When conflicts arise within your group, follow the suggestions in the second Tips and Hints box on page 385.

Tips for Encouraging Appropriate Participation in Discussions

When members speak too much

[1] Thank the speaker, summarize his or her views (this shows you've listened), and invite another member to speak.

[2] Stress to the whole group that it is important for everyone to have an equal chance to comment.

[3] Suggest that the group is beginning to cover the same territory again and that it needs to move on.

[4] Remind the whole group at the start of the meeting that participation should be uniform.

[5] Sit next to the perpetually dominant person to make it more difficult for him or her to get the leader's attention.

[6] Ask the talkative person to serve as recorder so he or she has less time to participate.

[7] Speak with the member individually after the meeting.

When members speak too little

[1] Ask direct questions; draw on the individual's particular expertise relative to the topic.

[2] Have one member summarize the ideas presented by another speaker.

[3] Ask members for their viewpoints on several safe topics before seeking input on controversial items.

[4] Speak to members individually outside the meeting setting. Tell them that their contributions have value and ask what could be done to make them more active participants.

Tips for Resolving Group Conflicts

The first task in conflict resolution is to be sure the basic issue in the disagreement is clear. If the conflict continues after the issue is clarified, the leader has several options including the following:

[1] Take a vote, leaving the decision to majority rule.

[2] Postpone discussion, giving time for reflection.

[3] Submit the conflict to an arbitrator, such as a superior officer in the company.

[4] Create subgroups and ask each to work independently for 10 to 15 minutes. When the time ends, ask each group to report its proposed solution or compromise.

[5] Move to the next agenda item after deciding the conflict is not worthy of the group's time.

Maintain Appropriate Records The leader should ensure that a record of the group's activities is maintained. Some groups conduct highly structured meetings. These groups closely follow the rules of parliamentary procedure and keep detailed records. Most business meetings, however, are less structured. Decisions are reached by consensus rather than by vote. If motions are made, they typically follow discussion rather than precede it.

Depending on the formality of the group, photocopying notes made on the agenda may be a sufficient record. If a more formal written record must be maintained, delegate the recording task to someone who isn't part of the group. Having a support staff member or other individual take notes gives members the opportunity for full participation

NOTE 13.59
Appropriate records must be maintained and shared in a timely manner.

without distraction. If staff support isn't available, the leader should keep the record or ask a member to do so. The member may volunteer, be elected, or agree to serve when asked. In groups that meet regularly, the task of recording and distributing minutes is often rotated among members. Another option is to have major points or actions listed on newsprint or flip charts during the meeting so that all members can see and agree on what is to be recorded. Minutes are then prepared from these notes. Suggestions for preparing traditional minutes for group meetings are given in Chapter 11.

Minutes or notes should be distributed promptly following each meeting. This procedure will enable members to note any corrections while the meeting is still fresh in mind. Minutes of one meeting also serve as a platform from which the agenda for a subsequent meeting can be developed. E-mail can be an effective tool for distributing and receiving feedback about meeting records.

The fluid nature of business suggests that someone may be the leader of one group and a participant in another. To be effective, the business professional must recognize and accept his or her role in each situation.

KEYS FOR SUCCESSFUL SMALL-GROUP MEETING PARTICIPATION

The following keys for successful small-group participation will increase your effectiveness in team meetings.

NOTE 13.60
Participation requires preparation.

Prepare to Participate Every member of a team should learn as much as possible about the group's purpose. If an agenda is provided in advance, information can be gathered on each topic to ensure intelligent participation. All available background information should be studied.

NOTE 13.61
Leave personal and work-related problems behind.

Participate Appropriately Members should arrive on time and be ready to devote their full attention to the meeting. Other work-related problems should be set aside temporarily. Members should participate by making clear, concise comments; asking relevant questions; and voting on issues. Participants must maintain objectivity in their comments and control their emotions. Lively debate is healthy; arguments are destructive. Honesty must permeate all discussions. Withholding information is unethical.

NOTE 13.62
Concentrate on what speakers say.

Listen Effectively Meetings can challenge listening skills. Group members will spend most of their time listening to other participants' comments and must strive to keep their concentration. Members should not have side conversations, gaze into space, or exhibit other behavior that detracts from effective listening. Participants can be surprised when, without warning, a speaker asks them what they think. Listeners must be ready to become speakers at any time.

Take Thorough Notes Bring paper and a pen (or an electronic device that allows you to take notes) to every meeting. Use them to record key words, ideas, dates, and activities. Using an outline format will help you take notes while still being an active participant in discussions.

NOTE 13.63
Be courteous and fair to speakers.

Be Courteous Participants must respect the rights and opinions of others. Opinions should be expressed tactfully, avoiding any indication of self-righteousness. By accepting different viewpoints and by being willing to discuss them, participants can help encourage open discussion. Members should not interrupt, even when the speaker pauses midthought. Avoid sarcasm; use humor carefully.

Other Meeting Formats

Now and in the future, we can expect more work to be accomplished by **virtual teams**—people who are connected via e-mail, groupware, and conferencing software. As shown in the following Communication Note, participation in virtual teams is forecast to grow in the next few years.

NOTE 13.64
Alternative formats can be effective.

COMMUNICATION NOTE

Teamwork, Past and Future What a difference a decade can make! As you review the data in the following table, consider the type of work in which you might be engaged in the year 2010.

Factor	Year 2000	Year 2010
Time spent working alone	40%	30%
Time spent working with others in the same time zone and same place	15%	5%
Time spent working in a different place at the same time	15%	25%
Time spent working at a different place and different time	30%	40%

Source: Gartner "The Deployee: At the Forefront of Workforce Transformation," July 11, 2002, Regina Castonato I Diane Morello; used with permission.

One advantage of virtual teams is that groups can transcend the boundaries of time and location. A company with offices in North America and Europe can establish teams with members on the two continents and effectively lengthen the workday by having the project handed from one team to another across time zones.

Virtual teams also level status differences that can occur when people representing various levels within an organization meet in person. As a result, ideas are more likely to be evaluated on merit; team members contribute more often and more freely because they feel a certain level of anonymity when communicating electronically. In addition, the convenience of these meetings often means that more people can contribute; better decisions may result from broader input as well as from ready access to files and other materials.

Although some managers perceive that motivation and morale building are more difficult in virtual teams, computer technology has been so well integrated into our personal and professional lives that concerns about the ability to create team spirit without face-to-face meetings is waning. People now initiate and maintain relationships via the Internet.

The following paragraphs describe four common ways in which technology can be used in virtual teams.

E-MAIL AND GROUPWARE

E-mail and groupware (calendaring/scheduling, real-time meetings, bulletin boards, group document handling, and project tracking) support the work of virtual teams by allowing team members to exchange messages and share documents.

NOTE 13.65
Technology supports virtual teams.

AUDIO CONFERENCING

NOTE 13.66
Audio conferences use modified meeting procedures.

Audio conferences use telephone technology to link participants. The typical audio conference begins with a roll call to determine whether all participants are online and whether the connection is clear. Next, the leader verifies that all participants have received the agenda and appropriate supplementary materials. If not, accommodations must be made (fax or e-mail the materials; summarize materials as items are presented). Once these tasks have been accomplished, the group works through the agenda.

Because members cannot see one another and may not recognize a speaker's voice, participants should introduce themselves every time they speak. Speaker identification also helps the recorder keep accurate notes. If a member must leave the call for any reason, he or she should announce the departure.

Although audio conferences do not permit use of visual cues, the absence of eye contact sometimes makes people more willing to speak. For some people, meetings are more free and less intimidating in this mode.

VIDEO CONFERENCING

NOTE 13.67
Video conferences permit long-distance, face-to-face communication.

Video conferencing is the electronic version of a long-distance, face-to-face meeting. It is preferred over audio conferencing when the meeting involves bargaining, persuasion, images, or complex topics. The ability to see participants' faces and observe their body language enhances the communication.

In order to take part in a video conference, each meeting participant must be at a site equipped with a camera, microphone, and viewing screen. Depending on the organization, the site may be an individual's office, a conference room, or a commercial facility. The equipment the individual uses may be a simple, relatively inexpensive PC-based system or a costly, highly sophisticated system requiring special operating equipment and technical support personnel. The quality of the picture and the number of sites that can be displayed simultaneously vary with the nature of the equipment.

NOTE 13.68
Whether basic or sophisticated, equipment should be tested in advance.

Regardless of the site or the nature of the equipment, the procedures for conducting a video conference parallel those used to conduct an audio conference. The meeting begins with a roll call to ensure that all group members are connected and that the equipment works properly. If participants are not familiar with one another, each displays a large-print name card at his or her station. The meeting then proceeds according to the agenda and within the framework of the technology used to link the sites.

ELECTRONIC MEETINGS

Group decision support system (GDSS) software combines the power of networked personal computers with specialized software to enable teams to work together better and faster whether at the same site or at different locations. The number of participants is limited only by the number of stations on the network.

NOTE 13.69
Electronic meetings allow anonymous input.

GDSS meetings begin with members signing in and, if the group is meeting for the first time, entering a brief biographical sketch describing the skills and experiences they bring to the meeting. This process parallels the oral introductions common in face-to-face meetings. Unlike oral introductions, which may be forgotten soon after they are made, the biographical sketches are stored and made available to members throughout the meeting. The constant availability of information doesn't

Video conferencing allows participants to take advantage of nonverbal cues.

end with personal sketches. Participants may also use their computers to retrieve data from any other source normally accessible through the network used to link group members.

As the meeting progresses and issues arise, participants offer facts or opinions by keying them at their PCs. When a member is satisfied with the message, he or she submits it. All submissions are anonymous, so members are less reluctant to participate. Contributions are evaluated and responded to solely on their merit.

A facilitator receives all comments and, unless directed to screen them, makes them available to all group members. The method used to view the shared comments varies with the situation in which the group operates. If members are gathered in a room designed specifically for GDSS meetings, items are projected on a large screen for all to see. If members are working from remote PCs, comments are displayed on their computer screens. Contributions may be made (keyed) simultaneously, not sequentially as in oral communication. This means that the pace of the meeting is more rapid than in other formats.

Voting, too, can be accomplished quickly and easily. In fact, the ease with which votes can be taken encourages groups to use methods other than the traditional yes or no vote. Allocation, multiple choice, and ranking votes can be tallied and analyzed almost effortlessly.

When the meeting ends, all input is automatically stored on the computer, replacing minutes as the permanent record of the meeting. The record can be printed or saved to disk for future reference.

Whether the meetings you attend are conducted face-to-face or by another method, be sure to follow the techniques associated with good meeting leadership and participation.

NOTE 13.70
Electronic meetings can be fast paced.

(6) # Writing Teams

So far, information in this chapter has focused on skills other than writing. Sometimes, though, the product or outcome of teamwork is a written document such as a long report or a complex proposal. Therefore, it seems appropriate to comment on writing teams in this chapter.

The Writing Team

The composition of a writing team varies with the task to be accomplished. For one message, the team might be you and your boss; for another message, the team might consist of persons from various departments, computer and research specialists, and an editor.

NOTE 13.72

Writing teams have the same characteristics and challenges as other teams.

Regardless of its size and membership, a writing team will face the same challenges and use the same communication skills as those of teams formed for other purposes. Members must communicate well verbally and nonverbally. They must be effective listeners. Effective group dynamics have to prevail during team meetings. Team members must respect each other and have complementary skills. In a shared writing effort, team members must be open to constructive criticism and be able to disagree with each other without being disagreeable. A group loyalty must develop. Team members must understand the writing process and be able to implement it. They have to agree on a schedule and adhere to it.

Productive collaborative writing depends on an effective team effort that competently implements the planning and composing process. In the appropriate communication situation, collaborative writing can result in a message that is comprehensive, accurate, and concrete—a message that is more powerful than an individual could develop.

The Team Writing Process

In team writing, the planning and composing process described in Chapter 5 is usually carried out in the following manner:

Step 1: **Plan.** Step 1 is a group effort. Team members analyze the communication situation and agree on the primary and secondary purposes. They also analyze the receiver and agree about the organizational structure to use, identify the reader benefits to include, and brainstorm for content.

Step 2: **Draft.** When two or more people meet to draft a document, the process becomes inefficient. Different thinking and writing styles prolong the process and actually reduce the quality of the product. Therefore, one team member refines the broad concepts developed during the group planning process, seeks data as necessary, and drafts the document.

Step 3: **Finalize.** Revising, editing, and proofreading responsibilities are split. The person who drafts the document shares it (electronically or in paper form) with members of the team. Each member suggests changes to content and organization and notes typographical, grammar, punctuation, and style errors. When documents are shared electronically, members see all suggestions offered by other team members; when paper is the medium, changes are generally referred to the draft's author. The document may go through several iterations of revising and editing before the group meets to review the final product.

Summary of Learning Objectives

Identify the components of interpersonal communication.

①

Interpersonal communication refers to the verbal and nonverbal interactions in one-to-one or small-group settings. Listening, speaking, and nonverbal communication are the primary elements of a person's "people skills," but writing can also reflect them. Interpersonal communication has a major influence on the communication climate of an organization.

Enhance your ability to build positive relationships.

②

Conversations, the core of positive relationships, follow a five-step process: greeting, introduction, exchange, summary, and closing. The effectiveness of a conversation can be enhanced when participants pay attention to the location, minimize interruptions, speak skillfully, send appropriate nonverbal cues, ask questions, listen for words and emotions, and accommodate diversity. Efficient and effective equipment operation, consideration, and a businesslike manner will help make telephone conversations and voice mail messages successful. Conversations are part of office politics, a competitive environment that affects an interpersonal relationship. Once damaged, a relationship can be repaired by words and/or actions only if both parties are willing to let go of the problem that caused the damage.

Give criticism effectively and receive it appropriately.

③

Criticism that is given constructively and received without being defensive can help an individual grow. Criticism should be given in private and be limited to documented, relevant, work-related concerns. Focus attention on the behavior, not the person; don't let criticism in one area cloud your judgment in another. Accept partial responsibility if appropriate. Use and read nonverbal cues carefully; allow the receiver time to consider and respond to the message. Agreeing and seeking more information are strategies to use when receiving criticism.

Describe techniques for resolving conflicts.

④

When faced with conflict, people have four options: yield, compromise, overpower, or collaborate. The option chosen will vary with the people and situation; culture is a factor. Techniques that apply both to participants and to facilitators are acting promptly, scheduling the meeting, using active listening, focusing on the problem, brainstorming solutions, formalizing the solution, and implementing and following up on the solution. When a participant initiates resolution, he or she should first do a self-assessment, then sincerely approach the other person. Active listening combined with paraphrasing should reveal areas of agreement as well as areas to be resolved. Both parties should be involved in developing a solution. Techniques used to facilitate conflict resolution will vary depending on how the facilitator learned of the conflict but generally include arranging a meeting; introducing topics; and clarifying, refocusing, and summarizing discussions and agreements.

⑤ Develop the skills associated with leading and participating in teams.

Teams—whether self-managed, process-improvement, or cross-functional—have personal and organizational advantages and disadvantages. To be effective, a team must engage in open, honest communication; be cohesive; foster growth; and be recognized for their achievements. Meetings are the vehicle through which teams plan, report on, and coordinate efforts to achieve goals. Both the leader and the participants have responsibilities in ensuring that meetings are productive. Although most business meetings are face-to-face gatherings, other formats are possible.

⑥ Describe the features of and process used by a writing team.

Successful collaborative writing depends on the ability of the writing team members, the dynamics of the writing team, group loyalty, and the ability of the members to agree on a schedule and adhere to it. The tasks associated with the three-step writing process are completed either individually or as a group.

Discussion Questions

1. What is "communication climate"? Why is it important? (Objective 1)
2. List and explain two factors that contribute to the need for employees to have good interpersonal skills. (Objective 1)
3. Distinguish between being assertive and being aggressive during a conversation. (Objective 2)
4. Explain why it is important to learn and use your receiver's name during a conversation. (Objective 2)
5. Name the two types of questions and give an example of each. (Objective 2)
6. Explain how to "hear" verbal and nonverbal cues. (Objective 2)
7. How can relationships be repaired? (Objective 2)
8. What role does the you–viewpoint play in giving criticism? (Objective 3)
9. How can a receiver seek more information about criticism he or she receives? (Objective 3)
10. What four options do people have when faced with conflict? Explain. (Objective 4)
11. What steps should you take to resolve a conflict in which you are a participant? (Objective 4)
12. How is someone who facilitates a conflict like an emcee? (Objective 4)
13. How do individuals benefit by team participation? (Objective 5)
14. Briefly describe what a meeting leader and participant should do before, during, and after a meeting. (Objective 5)
15. Define team writing and explain how teams approach the three-step writing process. (Objective 6)

Application Exercises

1. Interview five people. Ask each to describe the features he or she most appreciates in a best friend and a good boss. During a class discussion, combine your findings with those of other class members, paying special attention to those findings you would consider interpersonal skills. (Objective 1)

2. Convert the list prepared in Exercise 1 into a self-assessment. For each item, rate yourself on a 5-point scale, where 1 = poor and 5 = excellent. Identify two items on which you wish to improve and make a personal commitment to do so. (Objective 2)

3. **Teamwork.** As best as possible, create and complete this scenario within your classroom or another room at your school: You are attending the social that precedes the business meeting of the local chapter of the Society for the Betterment of Management. Your instructor will give you a card indicating the role you are to take (e.g., officer, membership committee member or chair, speaker, speaker's spouse/guest, prospective member, new member, other member, founding member). Take on this role as you mingle within the group and engage in conversation with individuals or small groups. Remember to introduce yourself or others as appropriate. Spend 15 to 20 minutes in this activity, then discuss the exercise as a class. (Objective 2)

4. **Ethics.** Picture yourself as the author of the "Ask Andy" column in your company newsletter. This month, you receive a letter from Edna, who writes "I'm tired of all the office politics here. I think that those who participate in office politics are unethical. Do you agree?" Respond to "Edna the Ethical Engineer." (Objective 2)

5. **Teamwork.** Another "Ask Andy" writer (see Exercise 4) says, "My boss is always suggesting ways for me to do my job better. When I mentioned this to my brother, he said that giving criticism is part of my supervisor's job. What do you think?" Prepare the response you'll include in your column. Address your response to "Criticized Chris." (Objective 3)

6. **Teamwork.** As your instructor directs, role-play one or more of the following situations in which you are required to give constructive criticism: (Objective 3)

   a. One of the workers in your office has complained to you that another worker has offensive foot odor. You have checked the facts and must now discuss the problem with the second worker and agree on a way to solve it.

   b. Clerks in the retail store you manage were encouraged to participate in the mall's Halloween festivities by wearing costumes to work. One person has chosen to wear something you believe is inappropriate to the image of your store. Handle the situation.

   c. During the past month, several customers have hinted that one of your customer service representatives treated them rudely. Convey the message to the representative.

7. **Teamwork.** Conduct a classroom "tug-of-war" on one of the following items or a controversial issue at your school: (Objective 4)

   a. Dress code for business students at your university

   b. Employer's right to monitor workers' e-mail

8. **Teamwork.** Recall a recent conflict in which you were involved. How did you behave? Did you allow the other person to treat you as if you had little or no value (passively)? Did you treat the other person as though he or she had little or no value (aggressively)? Did you handle the situation with mutual respect (assertively)? Plan a three- to four-minute presentation that (1) describes the situation, (2) explains how you reacted, and (3) suggests how the encounter might have ended had you behaved differently. Working in small groups as assigned by your instructor, give your presentation. (Objective 4)

9. **InfoTrac.** Virtual teams are growing as an organizational phenomenon. To learn more about how virtual teams are managed, read Carla Joinson's June 2002 article, "Managing Virtual Teams: Keeping Members on the Same Page Without Being in the Same Place Poses Challenges for Managers." This *HRMagazine* article can be accessed through InfoTrac (article 87461019). After reading the article, prepare a memo to your instructor in which you answer the following questions: (Objective 5)

   a. Why do companies form virtual teams?

   b. In what types of industries or situations are virtual teams undesirable?

   c. What worker characteristics blend well with participation in virtual teams?

   d. What can managers do to have their virtual teams emulate the attributes of co-located teams?

10. Hold an in-class debate on one or more of the following statements: (Objective 5)

    a. Participating in work teams takes away from a person's real job.

    b. Teams hide a member's individual accomplishments.

    c. Teams are a management fad.

11. **E-mail.** "Free riders," people who don't contribute to a team's success but share in the credit given for team accomplishments, are often cited as a problem in school-based group projects. What can the leader of a student team do to minimize or eliminate the free-rider problem? What can team members do to minimize or eliminate the free-rider problem? Send your suggestions to your instructor in an e-mail.

12. **Teamwork. E-mail.** Work with one other student in your class. Identify and arrange to attend a regularly scheduled meeting of some group (e.g., student organization, faculty/staff committee, professional society) at your school or in your community. (Objectives 5 and 6)

    a. Prepare a written report that describes the extent to which the leader and participants followed the guidelines presented in this chapter.

    b. E-mail to your instructor a message in which you describe how you and your teammate divided the work on this project.

There are Web exercises at **http://krizan.swlearning.com** to accompany this chapter.

Message Analysis

Arrange the following items into the agenda for a meeting. Use the functional format. Correct typographical errors.

> Bob Harman (chair)
> January 1/16
> Approve minute of last Week's meating
> Hillary Patberg (guest; staff representative to benefits task force; guest)
> Sybil Hutchinson—need to decide on property insurance cararier
> 2–3 a.m.
> Chad Donald—update on computer upgrades
> Art Westberg wants us to review the equipment acquisition procedure
> Wilma Marvin—will have recommmendations from benifits task force
> next Tuesday
> Conference Room B
> Budget Committee
> Distribute budget planning forms for next fiscal year; fist draft due March 22

Grammar Workshop

Correct the grammar, spelling, punctuation, style, and word choice errors in the following sentences:

1. Mr. Maki enquired if the crowd had disbursed.
2. The polls show people thing the irs has made process toward improving it's level fo consumer service
3. A mix of stocks bonds and short term reserves will help you achieve a secure financial future.
4. Built in 2002 four approximately $15.9 million dollars the River Road development contains 224 one, two, and three-bedroom apartments in seven three-story bldgs..
5. Everybody whom attended the demonstration were able to get their questions answered during the ten minute question:answer section that followed the 20 minute presentation.
6. For your convienence I have inclosed a coupon good for a ten % discount which means you'll pay only 13.95 for a full-year of "The Money Manager's Guide".
7. Unless a major new customer can be found our 37000 foot bldg will be vacated indefanitely; and, two hundred people will loose they're jobs.
8. 4,400 companies—about 1/3 of those operating within the State has less then 5 hundred employees.
9. General Supremes' C.E.O. & major shareholder Gaylor court will announce that the company has filed an Initial Public Offering to rays $25 million dollars.
10. This money saving offfer is only valid thru April 31.

Part

5

Oral and Nonverbal Communication

14

Listening and Nonverbal Messages

LET'S TALK BUSINESS Approximately 65 percent of the 6,500 employees in our health care organization are organized under one of 28 bargaining agreements. Therefore, I am presented with many occasions where listening and nonverbal communication take place at the bargaining table.

Jerry Zanko, Manager of Employee & Labor Relations, SMDC

During traditional, adversarial bargaining, silence may be used as a strategy. Participants simply do not respond to positions or comments of the other party. Silence is accompanied by lack of body movement. This behavior sends a message that allows for jockeying, which is important in seeming to get what you want without giving up your issue.

In the more candid interest-based bargaining model, open and honest verbal communication is supported by nonverbal communication. Words, facial expressions, gestures, and body position reflect the participants' desire to solve problems and reach agreement.

In either case, listening—genuine listening—must be worked at. You can understand the *why* behind an issue only if you listen. If you expend your effort in formulating your reply before the other party has fully presented its issue, you lose an opportunity for progress in negotiations, an opportunity that may not present itself again.

The significant roles of written communication have been stressed in the preceding chapters of this book. However, the importance of listening and nonverbal communication should not be overlooked. Successful businesspeople communicate orally with many different people who have varying abilities to communicate effectively. Chapter 13 introduced speaking, listening, and nonverbal communication as components of interpersonal communication and teamwork. In this chapter, we will explore listening and nonverbal communication in greater depth. Chapter 15 discusses how to communicate orally and how to prepare and deliver formal presentations.

NOTE 14.1
Information is acquired through listening.

Listening

People have various reasons for listening. They listen to enjoy entertainment, to gain information, to receive instructions, to hear complaints, and to show respect. The situations in which listening takes place also vary. Listening can occur (1) in one-on-one telephone or face-to-face conversations; (2) in a small group, such as a few supervisors receiving instructions from their manager; and (3) in a large group, such as an audience listening to a keynote speech at a conference. Jerry Zanko, the HR professional quoted in Let's Talk Business, uses listening in collective bargaining sessions—small-group meetings designed to exchange information and reach agreement about terms and conditions of employment. One-to-one conversations are also part of his daily routine, and he is called on frequently to speak to student or professional groups.

Hearing versus Listening

Hearing is a physical process; listening is a mental one. For example, you may have attended a class session during which the instructor gave directions for completing a report or project. Later, as you began preparing the assignment, you realized that you could not recall the details needed to complete the work. You *heard* the instructions but did not *listen* to them. Listening involves comprehending and retaining what is heard.

Ineffective listening occurs in the workplace as well as in the classroom. Consider the situation where George, an office manager, is told to develop his unit's budget for the next year by using a 3 percent revenue decrease. George heard the instructions but did not listen to them and created his budget using a 3 percent increase. His supervisor was not impressed. George needs to learn how to use the entire listening process.

LEARNING OBJECTIVE
1 *Distinguish between hearing and listening.*

NOTE 14.2
Hearing is not the same as listening.

The Listening Process

The listening process consists of four elements. Hearing is one of these elements; the other three are filtering, interpreting, and recalling. Figure 14.1 shows the four elements of the listening process.

LEARNING OBJECTIVE
2 *Describe the four elements of the listening process.*

Hearing ⟶ Filtering ⟶ Interpreting ⟶ Recalling

FIGURE 14.1
The Listening Process

HEARING

The first element in the listening process, **hearing**, is a physiological process. When we hear, our auditory nerves are stimulated by sound waves. Everyone hears sounds unless he or she has a hearing impairment.

NOTE 14.3
Hearing is a physiological process.

FILTERING

NOTE 14.4
Filtering eliminates
unwanted stimuli.

The second element in the listening process, **filtering**, is the elimination of unwanted stimuli. Filtering allows a listener to focus on stimuli that are of specific interest. Consider an example illustrating both unwanted and wanted stimuli: Suppose someone attending a meeting on insurance benefits is seated near an open window through which the aroma from a nearby fast-food restaurant is wafting, making the listener hungry. The unwanted stimulus is the food aroma, and the wanted stimulus is the speaker's information about insurance. An individual has difficulty concentrating on an oral message when his or her filtering process is unable to eliminate or at least minimize distracting stimuli.

INTERPRETING

NOTE 14.5
Stimuli are interpreted
and assigned meanings
by the receiver.

The third element of the listening process is interpreting. When **interpreting**, the listener's mind assigns meaning to the stimuli. Listeners tend to consider nonverbal cues as well as verbal cues when interpreting oral messages. In addition, a speaker's prior comments and actions are considered when interpreting present messages. As pointed out in Chapter 1, it is important for the receiver to interpret the stimuli in the way the sender intended. As noted in the following Communication Quote, listeners must interpret more than just the speaker's words.

COMMUNICATION QUOTE

As a Compliance Officer/Analyst, I investigate a variety of compliance/legal concerns. This occurs both on a proactive (surveillance) and reactive (allegations of wrongdoing) basis. The position has elements of being a police officer, social worker, judge, and jury. My group determines and delivers corrective and developmental counseling and recommends discipline, which can include fines, suspension, and termination. Asking questions and then listening—not only for facts but also for emotions—is important. I must always remember that talking is the antithesis of listening.

—William Ellis, Compliance Analyst, American Express. (Photo courtesy of William Ellis)

RECALLING

NOTE 14.6
Proper association im-
proves recall ability.

The fourth element, **recalling**, involves remembering at a later time the information that was interpreted earlier. The success of this element depends heavily on the association (relationship) placed on the stimuli during the interpretation phase.

The success of the listening process depends on all four elements. If one of the elements is omitted or fails to function properly, the entire listening process is jeopardized. To ensure that the listening process is carried out properly, certain guidelines need to be followed.

LEARNING OBJECTIVE

List the guidelines
for effective
listening.

③

Guidelines for Effective Listening

Most people think they are good listeners, and perhaps they are—at least some of the time. Although listening is more of an art than a science, it is a process that can be improved if the receiver takes an active role. The following guidelines can help you to improve your listening skills.

To be a successful listener, you need to take an active role in the listening process.

CONCENTRATE ON THE MESSAGE

People normally speak at 100 to 200 words a minute. Listeners, however, are capable of hearing up to 500 words a minute. This mismatch between speaking and listening speeds makes it necessary for people to concentrate diligently in order to listen effectively. If you do not concentrate, your mind may wander to another topic.

NOTE 14.7
Concentrate on the main concepts, but be aware of hidden meanings.

One concentration technique is mentally summarizing the message. This technique is especially important when the speech is not well organized or when the speaker has a heavy accent. Also, you should concentrate on the main points the speaker is trying to convey. Look for hidden messages. Determine whether the speaker is using facts, opinions, or inferences. Do not allow the speaker's physical appearance or vocal qualities to affect your concentration. Focusing on the message will assist you in overcoming barriers that may interfere with your hearing the entire message.

DETERMINE THE PURPOSE OF THE MESSAGE

Oral messages have purposes, as do written messages. As a listener, you need to determine the purpose of the oral message so that you can decide on the mode that you will use when listening. The three modes commonly used to listen to messages are cautious listening, skimming, and scanning.

NOTE 14.8
The three modes of listening are cautious listening, skimming, and scanning.

Cautious Listening This mode, **cautious listening**, is used when you need to understand and remember both the general concept and all the details of the message. This mode requires more energy than the others because of the amount or complexity of material on which you must concentrate. When listening in this mode, your mind has no time to relax.

Skimming **Skimming** is used when you need to understand only the general concept of the message. When using this mode for listening, your mind has time to relax because you do not need to remember all the details being presented. Think of your mind as a computer. The amount of storage is vast but not limitless. Cluttering your mind with insignificant matter causes it to tire, which could cause you to forget the important points.

Scanning When **scanning**, you concentrate on details of specific interest to you instead of on the message's general concept. No energy is wasted trying to retain information that is not of specific value. One shortcoming in using this mode is that your mind may wander; you may miss material that is important.

KEEP AN OPEN MIND

NOTE 14.9
Don't allow biases to influence listening.

The speaker presents the message from his or her perspective. Respect this viewpoint by not allowing your own biases to block what is being said. Your listening ability may be impaired when you are not receptive to the message or when you have a strong emotional reaction to the speaker's use of impact words (also called color words). Another obstacle may be your expectation not to understand a speaker with a dialect different from yours. When you listen with an open mind, both you and the speaker will benefit. The speaker will believe that what he or she is saying is worthwhile, and you may acquire valuable information. Evaluate a speaker's message only after hearing the entire message. **Frozen evaluations**—quick, unwavering judgments—benefit no one.

USE FEEDBACK

NOTE 14.10
Positive feedback will improve the communication process.

Feedback is important. It is your response to the speaker. The speaker may volunteer more information if he or she receives positive feedback. For instance, a worker describing a problem in the office may expand on his or her comments when you offer feedback such as "Tell me more about . . ." or "Yes, but . . ." or even "Uh-huh." Asking questions to clarify the message also provides feedback. Erika Ludwig comments on the importance of feedback in the following Communication Quote.

COMMUNICATION QUOTE

Because Sauer-Danfoss is aggressively entering new markets to obtain a worldwide presence, communication between coworkers can be difficult. Our employees are often expressing themselves in their second or third language, and it is easy to capture their messages incorrectly. Listening closely, offering feedback, and asking questions are essential to conducting business globally.

—Erika Ludwig, Senior Internal Auditor, Sauer-Danfoss. (Photo courtesy of Erika Ludwig)

Paraphrasing can also be a form of feedback, one that can make the speaker feel as though he or she has not only been heard but also understood. Engaging in paraphrasing also helps listeners concentrate on both the words and the emotions of the speaker. If, for example, a classmate is angry because a team member is doing less than his or her share of work on a project, the classmate might angrily say, "He never does his share of the work, and he always gets away with it." Your feedback should help the speaker regain emotional control. A good paraphrased response might be, "You think he'll be rewarded for poor performance, and you feel as though you're doing more than your share on the project."

Some listening situations are not conducive to giving any type of feedback to the speaker. These situations include radio, television, and video presentations. Small group or one-to-one presentations lend themselves best to oral feedback. Each situation should be analyzed as to its appropriateness for feedback.

MINIMIZE NOTE TAKING

It may be wise to record complicated presentations for later review. Although your goal should be to have thorough notes, you will not be able to concentrate on listening if you attempt to record everything that is said. Instead, record key words and ideas in an outline. In oral communication situations that are not complex, record just the major points. Try to remember what is said without using notes.

NOTE 14.11
Taking notes may interfere with the listening process.

ANALYZE THE TOTAL MESSAGE

Watch the speaker's actions and facial expressions; listen to his or her tone of voice. A speaker can change the entire meaning of a message by raising an eyebrow or by changing the inflection of his or her voice. Such cues as these enable the listener to understand hidden messages.

DO NOT TALK OR INTERRUPT

An individual cannot talk and listen effectively at the same time. Listening should occur more often than speaking. When you are talking, you cannot use all the elements of effective listening. Interrupting a speaker or having side conversations is rude and reduces the effectiveness of the communication. Learn to distinguish between a mid-thought pause and the end of the speaker's comments.

NOTE 14.12
Talking and interrupting interfere with listening.

Dilbert

Barriers to Listening

A **listening barrier** is anything that interferes with the listening process. You should be aware of barriers so that you can avoid letting them interfere with your listening. Some of the more important barriers to listening are discussed here.

LEARNING OBJECTIVE
④ Describe barriers to effective listening.

PHYSICAL DISTRACTIONS

The individual responsible for setting up the meeting place in which the listening will occur should minimize physical distractions. However, you can take actions to limit this barrier by sitting at the front of the room, not sitting near a corridor or an open window, or not sitting next to an individual who will talk or whisper during the presentation.

NOTE 14.13
Be aware of physical distractions.

MENTAL DISTRACTIONS

NOTE 14.14
Don't let your mind wander when listening.

As a listener, you are responsible for giving your undivided attention to a speaker. You should avoid daydreaming or allowing your mind to wander. You can think approximately four times faster than the speaker can talk, so it is easy to begin thinking about other business or personal interests instead of paying attention to the speaker.

A very common distraction is mentally constructing a comment to make or a question to ask rather than concentrating on what is being said. A related mental distraction is forming an opinion or a rebuttal during a presentation. To listen effectively, keep an open mind—that is, hear *all* of what is said before making judgments.

HEALTH CONCERNS

Good health and well-being play a definite role in effective listening. When a listener is hungry, nauseous, or tired, he or she will find it difficult to listen. When these conditions exist, the speaker may wish to repeat the original message later.

NONVERBAL DISTRACTIONS

NOTE 14.15
Give the speaker positive feedback by avoiding negative nonverbal actions.

A listener may give a speaker negative nonverbal feedback. Facial expressions—frowning, yawning, raising an eyebrow, or closing the eyes—can convey a message of disinterest or disapproval. Glancing at a watch or a clock may tell the speaker that you are ready for the presentation to end. The lines of communication will remain open when these nonverbal distractions are avoided.

INAPPROPRIATE TIMING

A listener should ensure that a speaker can present his or her message at an appropriate time. A listener often knows if the time is appropriate. For example, a manager going through a plant may casually ask a worker, "Any problems?" If a supervisor is standing nearby and the manager knows the worker would be reluctant to speak in front of the supervisor, the worker might think the manager really does not want to listen. A more appropriate comment from the manager would be, "If you have any problems, I have an open-door policy and have reserved Wednesday afternoons to listen to employees." This would allow the speaker (the worker) to present his or her message at an appropriate time.

NOTE 14.16
A listener should give a speaker adequate time to present a message.

An individual presenting a message should be given adequate time so that he or she does not have to rush. It is the listener's responsibility to ensure that the speaker will have enough time to present the entire message. For example, if a manager has to leave for a meeting in 5 minutes and a supervisor enters the office to discuss a complex problem, the manager should make an appointment to meet with the supervisor at a later time. The manager should not expect the supervisor to condense the presentation into 5 minutes.

INEFFECTIVE SPEECH CHARACTERISTICS

NOTE 14.17
Work to overcome speech barriers.

A listener must be able to hear and understand a speaker in order to interpret the message. If the words are spoken at insufficient volume or at such a high pitch that the listener has trouble hearing the words, listening will be difficult, if not impossible. Other characteristic speech barriers include articulation, dialects, unusual pronunciations, jargon, regional speech patterns (accents), vocalization (tongue clicking, "ums"), and speech impairments. These barriers are difficult to overcome because listeners cannot review a spoken message in the same way they can review a written message. A comfortable atmosphere will cause a speaker to set a more relaxed pace and allow his or her message to be understood more easily. In addition, careful concentration may help a listener deal effectively with characteristic speech barriers.

Advantages of Effective Listening

LEARNING OBJECTIVE
(5) *Describe the advantages of effective listening.*

One of the best ways to acquire information is through effective listening. Effective listening will help you develop better attitudes. As mentioned in the following Communication Note, effective listening also can improve your relationships with others because they will realize that you are interested in them. Interested individuals will work diligently to communicate with you. This, in turn, will allow you to do a better job because you will have the support of the people around you. Effective listening will encourage individuals to tell you about minor problems before they become major problems. Businesses wishing to be perceived as customer-oriented must make the art of listening an integral part of their employee training.

COMMUNICATION NOTE

The Value of Listening Poor listening or not listening has a dollar value. Costs range from lost time, money, or productivity to poor relationships with customers, clients, and/or employees. Conversely, there is a positive dollar value in learning how to listen actively and empathetically, how to show that you are really listening and that you care. Skillful listening will increase the level of help and support you receive from employees, coworkers, managers, friends, and family.

Taken from "Listening Increases Support from Co-workers," by John Joyner, *Computing Canada,* October 19, 2001, 27(22), p. 31.

Nonverbal Communication

A **nonverbal message** is one that communicates without words. Nonverbal messages are an important part of the communication process because they provide added information the receiver can use in interpreting what is said. The extra information can add to or detract from the meaning of a message.

People constantly communicate through their conscious or unconscious nonverbal messages. As an example, suppose that every day on your way to work you meet the same person at the same place. Each morning as you pass each other you exchange greetings. Suddenly, one morning your greeting is met with indifference; the person does not acknowledge your presence. Later in the day someone asks whether you saw the passerby that morning and you recall your encounter. Would you be so aware of the encounter if the passerby had spoken to you as usual? Probably not. You were aware of the passerby this time because his or her actions differed from what you had determined to be congruent behavior. You used **benchmarking**—a comparison of "what is" against what you have come to expect as typical. You can use this same technique during conversations or business meetings. When a person's actions vary from what you have observed to be his or her positive nonverbal behavior, it may be time to ask whether the receiver has questions or concerns about what's being discussed or proposed.

NOTE 14.18
Nonverbal communication is a message without words.

NOTE 14.19
Establish a baseline to help interpret nonverbal cues.

Here is another example of how nonverbal messages affect other forms of communication: A prospective customer receives a poorly printed letter announcing a furniture sale. The poor printing is a nonverbal message suggesting carelessness. How quickly will the customer rush to the store for the sale? Which message is more effective—the written or the nonverbal?

The Importance of Nonverbal Communication

LEARNING OBJECTIVE
Explain the importance of nonverbal messages.
6

A person should be aware of the impact of nonverbal communication. Nonverbal messages may not always be intended; nevertheless, they clearly communicate with and influence people.

Nonverbal messages may aid or hinder communication. The following summarizes the more important characteristics of nonverbal communication:

NOTE 14.20
Nonverbal communication has several important characteristics.

- *The nonverbal communication can be unintentional.* The sender may be unaware that he or she is sending a nonverbal message and, consequently, may not be aware of the impact that message may have.
- *A nonverbal communication may be more honest than a verbal one.* Since the message may be transmitted unconsciously, the sender will not have planned it. Therefore, a nonverbal message can be more reliable than an oral or a written one that had been thought out ahead of time.
- *Nonverbal communication makes, or helps to make, a first impression.* First impressions are powerful. They often result in frozen evaluations, images that can be very difficult to alter.
- *Nonverbal communication is always present.* Neither oral nor written communication exists without nonverbal communication. Examples of nonverbal messages being sent even when the communication may not be face-to-face include tapping the phone receiver, loudly rearranging papers, or silence.

Although nonverbal messages are powerful, a listener should not become so intent on interpreting them that he or she fails to listen to the speaker's words.

Types of Nonverbal Communication

LEARNING OBJECTIVE
Identify different types of nonverbal messages and their impact on the communication process.
7

Nonverbal messages come in various forms. Some of the common types of nonverbal communication follow.

PHYSICAL APPEARANCE

Physical appearance is an important type of nonverbal communication. An individual will form a first impression from a letter's envelope, stationery, letterhead, format, and neatness. This first impression will definitely influence the receiver's reaction to the letter.

The physical appearance of a speaker influences an oral message as much as the appearance of a letter influences a written message. Listeners use physical appearance as a clue to the speaker's credibility. That is why a sloppily dressed salesperson will find it difficult, if not impossible, to sell expensive clothing.

NOTE 14.21
The appearance of written and oral messages creates first impressions.

Physical appearance also influences a receiver's perceptions of a speaker's socioeconomic status and judgment. For example, an individual who wears designer clothes, custom-made shoes, and expensive jewelry will transmit a nonverbal message. This nonverbal message will be perceived differently by receivers, depending on the occasion for which the individual is dressed. If the individual is going to lunch or dinner at an elegant restaurant, most people would perceive the person to be wealthy and successful. If the individual is washing a car or mowing a lawn, many people would perceive the person to be eccentric or to lack common sense.

BODY LANGUAGE

Whether used in conjunction with spoken words or viewed independently, your body sends messages to those with whom you communicate.

People transmit nonverbal messages through the actions of their bodies.

An advantage of using body language to respond to a message is that it conveys instant feedback to the sender. A smile is interpreted almost universally as an expression of friendliness and approval. A smile indicates satisfaction, but a frown shows disagreement. The eyes are also a powerful indicator. Failure to look a person in the eye when speaking may indicate shyness, dishonesty, or embarrassment. Eye contact may indicate confidence, agreement, or interest in the subject of a conversation. A raised eyebrow communicates the receiver's uncertainty. An individual who glances around while speaking is exhibiting nervousness or lack of interest.

Other forms of body language include posture and gestures. The way a person sits or stands communicates a nonverbal message. An individual standing or sitting erectly conveys confidence and pride, whereas a person slumping over may be perceived as being tired or depressed. If an individual leans toward another person during a conversation, body language indicates that the person likes or is interested in the other communicator. If the person leans away from the other person, the posture shows a dislike or disinterest in the other individual. Gestures and posture are two items to consider in mirroring, which is explained in the following Tips and Hints.

NOTE 14.22
Body language can change the meaning of an oral message.

NOTE 14.23
Posture conveys a nonverbal message.

Mirroring

Mirroring is based on the idea that people feel most comfortable with those who are like them. The higher the degree of comfort, the greater the level of trust and the greater the opportunity for the people involved to do business successfully. To mirror someone, you will want to be *similar* to him or her in as many of the following areas as possible:

- Clothing
- Energy level

- Gestures
- Head position and facial expressions
- Voice tone or tempo
- Vocabulary

The keys to mirroring successfully are to be subtle and to focus only on positive behaviors. With practice, mirroring can become a natural, spontaneous behavior.

NOTE 14.24
Handshakes communicate.

A handshake also communicates a nonverbal message. A person who firmly grips your hand demonstrates confidence, whereas an individual who squeezes your hand so tightly that it causes pain gives the impression of being overly aggressive or inconsiderate. A weak handshake may reflect insecurity or pessimism. Don't rush to judgment, though. A soft handshake could also be related to a person's culture, occupation, or a health concern. Native Americans, people with arthritis, surgeons, musicians, artists, and others may use a soft handshake by choice. Listen and watch for clues as to why an individual might use a particular type of handshake. The Web site at **http://www. rebrown.com/rebrown/handsh.htm** offers an interesting look at various types of handshakes and what they may be interpreted to mean.

Confidence, aggression, or insecurity may be conveyed through a handshake.

©IT STOCK INT'L/INDEX STOCK IMAGERY

It is practically impossible to communicate without some use of gestures. A gesture may be as simple as a thumbs-up to signify approval or a thumbs-down for disapproval. A gesture may be used to emphasize a critical point in an oral presentation. How interesting would a speech be if the only communicative motion was the opening and closing of the speaker's mouth?

Care should be taken in using gestures because, as pointed out in Chapter 2, different cultures interpret gestures in different ways. For instance, if a woman in southern Germany tilts her head to the side and leans forward to listen, she is considered attentive; but in northern Germany, she would be perceived as cringing and timid. To be considered attentive in northern Germany, she would sit up straight and look the speaker directly in the eye; in southern Germany, these actions would indicate that she is angry. Similar cultural differences apply to other nonverbal messages.

Body language, whether intentional or unintentional, can change the meaning of a verbal message. Unfortunately, most people are unaware of the messages they send through body language. To learn more about the messages you may be sending, follow the advice offered in the following Communication Note.

COMMUNICATION NOTE

Identifying Body Language Problems We are often unaware of our body language because it is composed of subtle habits that we have developed over the years. Our body language sends nonverbal cues that speak volumes.

Do you know what messages your body language is sending? If not, ask your significant other, close friend, or a trusted coworker to tell you which of your behaviors might be annoying to others. It will help you improve your communication style for better rapport and understanding.

Taken from "Communications Champ," by Debra J. Schmidt; *www.theLoyaltyBuilder.com*

SPACE

Communication is influenced by space. Space, as used in nonverbal communication, includes the size of a physical area, proximity to another person, and obstacles between you and the person with whom you are speaking.

The amount of space people control influences our attitudes and, therefore, inadvertently is a form of nonverbal communication. The size of a person's office is an indication of importance within the hierarchy of an organization; the larger the office, the higher the position.

A person in charge wants to keep his or her most trusted aide nearby. Therefore the proximity of an employee to a supervisor communicates nonverbally the importance of the employee within the organization. The employee's importance also may be indicated nonverbally by parking space location, by office size and location, or by seating location at meetings.

Research has shown that eliminating obstacles such as desks, chairs, and tables will improve oral communication between individuals. The communication will improve if both communicators are on the same physical level—sitting or standing. The distance between the communicators will also affect the communication. This distance will vary with individuals from different cultures. The purpose of the communication

NOTE 14.25
Space transmits a nonverbal message.

will determine the appropriate personal space between communicators. The table in the following Communication Note shows acceptable distances for personal space in the United States.

Distances for Personal Space in the United States

Distance	Purpose of Communication
½ to 1½ feet	Intimate communication with friends
1½ to 4 feet	Casual conversation with friends and coworkers
4 to 12 feet	Formal conversation with business associates
More than 12 feet	Speeches and presentations to groups

TIME

NOTE 14.26
Emphasis on time transmits a message.

Communicators must be aware that the amount of time devoted to a subject transmits a nonverbal message. If the president of a company, for instance, meets with one manager for ten minutes and another manager for two hours, a nonverbal message is being transmitted.

Punctuality relays a nonverbal message. A person who is always on time is perceived as being well organized. A person who is always late transmits a message that he or she is disorganized or that the appointment is unimportant. For instance, if two people of equal credentials were interviewing for a job and one arrived 15 minutes late for the interview, it is more likely that the punctual applicant would be hired.

The importance of time will vary among cultures. Punctuality is very important with individuals from most European countries; however, a 30-minute delay is customary in most Latin-American countries. Asians expect others to be punctual, but they themselves often will be late.

Summary of Learning Objectives

1. **Distinguish between hearing and listening.**

Hearing is a physical process; listening is a mental one. A person can hear something without listening to it. Listening involves comprehending and retaining the message.

2. **Describe the four elements of the listening process.**

The four elements of the listening process are hearing—the physiological process of the auditory nerves being stimulated by sound waves; filtering—the elimination of unwanted stimuli; interpreting—the listener's mind assigning meaning to the stimuli; and recalling—remembering at a later time the information that was interpreted earlier.

List the guidelines for effective listening.

Guidelines that may be followed to improve your listening are (1) concentrate on the message, (2) determine the purpose of the message, (3) keep an open mind, (4) use feedback, (5) minimize taking notes, (6) analyze the total message, and (7) do not talk or interrupt.

Describe barriers to effective listening.

Anything that interferes with the listening process is a barrier to effective listening. A physical distraction is any diversion that interferes with the listener's concentration on what is being said. A mental distraction occurs when a listener daydreams or permits his or her mind to wander from the subject being discussed. Health concerns that may affect listening include being hungry, sick, or tired. Nonverbal distractions include the listener looking at his or her watch, yawning, or frowning. Attempting to present a speech or hold a conversation at an inappropriate time can create a barrier to listening. A listener's understanding can be hindered by a speaker's heavy accent or dialect.

Describe the advantages of effective listening.

Effective listening will help to develop better attitudes, improve relationships with others, gain support from others, and enable you to learn about minor problems before they become major ones.

Explain the importance of nonverbal messages.

The sender of a nonverbal message may be unaware that a message is being sent and, therefore, be unaware of its effect on the receiver. Nonverbal messages may be more reliable than written or oral messages because they are usually unplanned. Nonverbal messages often cause the receiver to form a frozen evaluation of the sender. Nonverbal communication is always present.

Identify different types of nonverbal messages and their impact on the communication process.

The physical appearance of a written message influences a receiver by causing the receiver to form a first impression of a message before reading it. The physical appearance of an individual sends a nonverbal message—the way a person is dressed often influences the opinions of others. Body language—facial expressions, gestures, handshakes, and posture—also communicates nonverbal messages. Communication through body language is instantaneous. The size of the physical area, proximity to another person, and obstacles between you and the person to whom you are speaking are all examples of how space can be used to communicate messages. The amount of time spent with an individual and punctuality are examples of how time communicates nonverbal messages.

Discussion Questions

1. Distinguish between hearing and listening. Cite a personal example of an occasion when you heard but did not listen. (Objective 1)
2. Distinguish between filtering and interpreting. (Objective 2)

3. What advice could you give to a friend who confides in you that he or she has difficulty concentrating in a class taught by a faculty member for whom English is not a first language? (Objective 3)
4. How can a listener keep an open mind about the topic? (Objective 3)
5. Describe six barriers to listening. (Objective 4)
6. Good listeners can be described as patient and sincere; bad listeners can be described as self-centered and intolerant. What other words describe good listeners? Bad listeners? List at least three for each. (Objective 5)
7. List and explain the four characteristics of nonverbal messages. What nonverbal messages might students be sending when they begin to close books and notebooks and gather backpacks 5–10 minutes before the scheduled end of a class? (Objective 6)
8. Explain how physical appearance can affect written and oral messages. What messages might be sent by a tattoo? a scratched-out response on a job application? (Objective 7)
9. Is mirroring the same as mimicking? Explain. (Objective 7)
10. Discuss five ways nonverbal messages could be presented in a positive manner when interviewing for a supervisory position in a business organization. (Objective 7)

Application Exercises

1. **Teamwork.** As directed by your instructor, meet in a small group to discuss the following questions: (Objective 2)
   a. How do you feel when a teacher, manager, colleague, or service representative doesn't seem to be listening to you?
   b. How do you feel when these same people seem to be listening well?
   c. How do you feel when someone with whom you work, a sales associate, or a customer-service worker gives preference to a phone call rather than to you?
   Make a list of the feelings your group identifies and share them with the class. Then, discuss why people might give preference to a phone call rather than an in-person visitor.

2. **E-mail.** During the next conversation you have with a coworker, family member, or someone not from this class, use paraphrasing at least once. E-mail your instructor to describe the effect paraphrasing had on you and the other person. (Objective 3)

3. **Teamwork.** Bring a newspaper, magazine, or book to class.
   a. Working in a group of four, have one member read aloud for five minutes while the other three members listen—one using cautious listening, one skimming, and one scanning. Compare the results of the three listening efforts and report your results to the class.
   b. Repeat the exercise using different material. Have a fifth person make noise or cause some other distraction. Discuss how the distraction affected each person's ability to listen to the message (Objectives 3 and 4)

4. **Global. Teamwork.** Conduct an in-class debate on whether ineffective listening is strictly an American problem or whether it exists worldwide. Do the secondary research necessary to support your or your team's position. (Objective 4)

5. **Teamwork.** Conduct the following exercise with five people:

Raise your right hand and touch your pointer finger to your thumb to form a circle. Ask your listener to do the same. After he or she has done so, tell him or her to touch that circle to his or her chin. As he or she starts to do so, place your own finger-thumb circle on your right cheek.

How many of your listeners followed your nonverbal lead as opposed to your verbal instructions? Report your results and interpretation of them in a memo to your instructor. (Objective 6)

6. **Teamwork.** After the class has been divided into at least two teams, take turns acting out, without speaking, roles presented by the teacher. (Objective 7)

7. **Global.** Interview a foreign student or faculty member and ask him or her to indicate differences in interpretations of nonverbal messages that he or she has observed between Americans and people of his or her culture. Report your findings to the class. (Objective 7)

8. **Teamwork.** Form groups of four students. Shake hands with each member and then give either an oral or a written evaluation of the student's handshake. Your instructor may direct each group to develop a form for this purpose or have the class develop one form to be used by all groups. (Objective 7)

9. Observe students' and instructors' body language early in the week and late in the week. Record the differences in nonverbal communication. Are the differences easily apparent? (Objective 7)

10. **InfoTrac.** Listening is a valuable workplace skill, one that is getting more attention in the job interview process. Read InfoTrac article A93208697, "Listening Trumps Schmoozing. (Think Twice)," by Todd Raphael, from the October 2002 issue of *Workforce*. After reading the article, form a three-person group; designate one person as interviewer, one as candidate, and one as observer. Have the interviewer ask the candidate the four questions cited in the article. After the candidate has finished answering all four questions, the interviewer and observer should provide feedback on the candidate's verbal and nonverbal responses. Return to full-class format and discuss the results of the exercise. (Objectives 5 and 7)

There are Web exercises at **http://krizan.swlearning.com** to accompany this chapter.

Message Analysis

You work for Jason P. McDonald, a middle-aged, well-educated man who owns two card/gift shops, a security company, three fast-food restaurants, and a flower shop and garden center. Jason is creative and highly motivated. He credits his success, in part, to his ability to listen effectively. He wants his employees to share his view of how important it is to listen and plans to display attractively designed, framed quotes about listening in the work areas of his various businesses. He's asked you to select three quotes and to use the computer software you have available to create an appropriate design for each. He'll then decide which to have printed and framed. You've searched the Internet and prepared the following list of possible quotes. Now it's time to select the three you want to recommend and to create your design. Be sure you consider the diversity of Jason's businesses as you make your selections.

Try to listen carefully that you might not have to speak. —Quaker saying

The most basic of all human needs is the need to understand and be understood. The best way to understand people is to listen to them. —Ralph Nichols

History repeats itself because no one listens the first time. —Anonymous

It's my job to talk and yours to listen, but please, let me know if you finish before I do. —Anonymous

The greatest compliment that was ever paid me was when one asked me what I thought, and attended to my answer. —Henry David Thoreau

A good listener truly wants to know the speaker. —John Powell

You cannot truly listen to anyone and do anything else at the same time. —M. Scott Peck

If speaking is silver, then listening is gold. —Turkish proverb

Easy listening exists only on the radio. —David Barkan

Instead of listening to what is being said to them, many managers are already listening to what they are going to say. —Anonymous

It is the province of knowledge to speak, and it is the privilege of wisdom to listen. —Oliver Wendell Holmes

Opportunities are often missed because we are broadcasting when we should be listening. —Author unknown

Listening, not imitation, may be the sincerest form of flattery. —Dr. Joyce Brothers

No one ever listened themselves out of a job. —Calvin Coolidge

Good listeners, like precious gems, are to be treasured. —Walter Anderson

Courage is what it takes to stand up and speak; courage is also what it takes to sit down and listen. —Winston Churchill

Listening is the single skill that makes the difference between a mediocre and a great company. —Lee Iacocca

The beginning of wisdom is silence. The second stage is listening. —A Hebrew sage

Be a good listener. Your ears will never get you in trouble. —Frank Tyger

Know how to listen, and you will profit even from those who talk badly. —Plutarch

Grammar Workshop

Correct the grammar, spelling, punctuation, style, and word choice errors in the following sentences:

1. John and Becky Pearson was assisted by the blue blazers in cutting the ribbon at the J and B Electric grand-opening celebration last week.
2. Should aaron return the faulty ink cartridge back too the story, ore the manufacturer.
3. Only five percent of those whom responded to the survey indicated they felt undo pressure to reach the monthly sales quota.
4. I just finish reading you're book from cover-to-cover and I think its a great guide to french cooking.
5. Do you know if Frank has axed Stephen to give his prospective on the merger.
6. Walter spend the day washing and waxing his car, vacuuming his house, and fed his dog, cat, and bird.
7. When the painter finishes primming and painting the walls and the installers complete lying the carpets the Saxton's will move in to they're new home.
8. After you return from lunch stop by my office to discuss next years' budget, we can not differ the discussion another day.
9. The Store was unabled to make a profit, because much merchandise was stole.
10. Because Sallys' "to Do list was not on her desk she assumed it had been throne away accidently.

Oral Communication Essentials

15

Colleen Welty, Program Manager, Maui Family Social Services

LET'S TALK BUSINESS Whether making presentations to my staff, to collaborating agencies, to public health nurses, or at conferences, I've found the following techniques helpful:

[1] Have your notes typed in LARGE print on note cards; use only one side.

[2] Don't be totally dependent on visuals because equipment can fail.

[3] Wait to distribute handouts until you really want your audience looking at them rather than paying attention to you.

[4] Always arrive 15 minutes or so before you are scheduled to speak (as a courtesy to the program director and to help get your butterflies all flying in formation).

[5] Remember, your audience is watching you long before you start to speak.

[6] Organize your presentation so that it's easy for your audience to follow your points.

[7] Have fun! Tell a joke or compliment the audience.

PHOTO COURTESY OF COLEEN WELTY

Both written communication and oral communication are vital to your personal success and to the success of the business or organization where you work. Other parts of this book have been devoted to general foundations and principles of business communication and their application to written, interpersonal, and teamwork communication situations. In this chapter, you will learn how those foundations and principles relate to oral communication. Specifically, you will learn how to improve your voice and presence and how to prepare and deliver a formal oral presentation.

Depending on your position and level of responsibility within an organization, the amount of time you spend giving presentations will vary widely. Certain jobs require extensive oral communication. Sales representatives must make informative and persuasive presentations to prospective customers. Union negotiators must present convincing arguments for their proposals to management. Public relations specialists must organize and moderate news conferences. The list could go on, but the jobs listed illustrate the fact that effective presentations are a thread common to many careers. Your success will depend not only on *what* you say, but also on *how* you say it—on the quality of your voice and the strength of your presence. You must speak clearly, intelligently, and confidently.

NOTE 15.1
Some jobs involve extensive oral communication.

LEARNING OBJECTIVE
Improve the basic quality of your voice.

① Improving Your Voice Qualities

The starting point for enhancing your oral communication is to improve your speaking voice.

Proper Control of Breathing

High-quality sound with adequate volume depends on the proper use of one raw material—air. By taking a few deep breaths, you can relax your sound-producing organs and prepare them for speaking. By controlling the amount of air you inhale and exhale while speaking, you can improve the quality of the sounds you make.

NOTE 15.2
Controlled breathing helps produce rich, full sounds.

Controlled deep inhalation of air—called **abdominal** or **diaphragmatic breathing**—fills your lungs and provides ample air for speaking. Good posture controls the balance between your vocal cords and helps enrich your voice. When you inhale deeply, keep your shoulders low and level; expand your abdomen, lower back, and sides. The air should go all the way to the diaphragm—a muscle between the chest and the abdomen. When you are nervous, you may breathe shallowly and not fill your lungs. When this happens, you do not inhale enough air to produce rich, full sounds.

When you exhale to speak, the air should come from your diaphragm, pass your vocal cords, and fill the orifices in your head with enough force to cause the sounds to be rich and full. The orifices in your head—mouth, nose, and sinuses—are like echo chambers; they enrich the sound of your voice.

Proper Control of Jaw, Tongue, and Lips

NOTE 15.3
Avoid the troublesome t's.

The "troublesome t's" of tight jaw, tight tongue, and tight lips cause mumbled, muffled speech sounds that are hard to hear and difficult to understand. Pronunciation, enunciation, and clarity of sound depend on your jaw being flexible and your tongue and lips being loose and alive.

Practice freely flexing your jaw by saying *idea, up and down,* and *the sky is blue.* Now say those same expressions with a tightly clenched jaw. Notice how clenching your jaw muffles the sounds. For more jaw-flexing practice, count from 91 to 99, and say *fine*, *yes*, *no*, *pay*, *buy*, and *like* over and over.

For practice in freeing your tongue and making it come alive, say *either*, *left*, and *wealth*. Try to say the same words holding your tongue still. Now count from 21 to 29 and let your tongue move freely and loosely. Say *health*, *thin*, *think*, *alive*, and *luck*. Practicing these and similar words will increase the flexibility and mobility of your tongue.

To free your lips—important controllers of voice quality—say *when*, *where*, *be*, and *back*. See what happens to your enunciation when you try to say these words without moving your lips. Other words to practice that will help to free your lips are *west*, *window*, *puff*, *lisp*, and *lips*.

Deep breathing and controlled use of your jaw, tongue, and lips will enable you to achieve full, round tones—the voice quality displayed by announcers and broadcasters in the radio and television industries. Practice until deep breathing and keeping your jaw, tongue, and lips flexible come naturally.

NOTE 15.4
Practice breath control; keep your jaw, tongue, and lips flexible.

Using Your Voice Effectively

LEARNING OBJECTIVE
② *Use your voice effectively.*

Once you have control of the basic sound-making mechanisms, you are ready to improve the use of your voice. The important considerations in this improvement are pitch, volume, speed, tone, emphasis, enunciation, and pronunciation. These aspects of using your voice effectively can each be improved by using a tape or video recorder for self-analysis or by obtaining feedback from a family member, a friend, or others.

Pitch

Pitch refers to the highness or lowness of your voice. A voice that is too high or too low may be distracting to your listener or audience. Pitch has two important aspects:

- Finding your natural pitch and, assuming it is not too shrill or too deep, using it
- Varying your pitch while speaking to provide interest and emphasis

FIND YOUR NATURAL PITCH AND USE IT

To determine your natural pitch, yawn deeply three times. Then say aloud, "My natural pitch is. . . ." Yawn deeply, and say the words again. Your pitch should have become deeper, richer, and fuller. Yawn and repeat the words a third time. Let your voice rest for at least one minute. Now, once again say, "My natural pitch is. . . ." With this exercise you will have found your natural pitch.

To avoid damaging your vocal cords, find and use your natural pitch. If nervousness causes you to speak in a pitch higher than your natural one, you could strain your vocal cords. Speaking in a pitch that is artificially lower than your natural one could also cause you to strain your vocal cords. Strained vocal cords can result in a hoarse, raspy voice or a temporary voice loss.

NOTE 15.5
Use your natural pitch to avoid damaging your vocal cords.

If you think your pitch is too high or too low, consult a speech correction specialist. Most colleges have or can refer you to a speech correction specialist. With exercises prescribed by a professional, your natural pitch can be brought to a more attractive, pleasant level.

VARY YOUR PITCH WHILE SPEAKING

The second aspect of improving the use of your voice is to learn to vary your pitch while speaking. The sparkling, interesting, enthusiastic speaker varies the pitch of his or her voice and avoids the dullness of a monotone voice—a voice with a sameness in pitch level. Nothing will lose an audience faster than a monotonous voice, regardless of the quality of the content of the message.

NOTE 15.6
Varying your pitch adds life to your voice.

You can make your presentation style interesting and even exciting by using pitch variations effectively. Indicate comparisons by using the same pitch level; indicate contrasts by using varied pitch levels. "The market is up (moderate pitch), and its gains are solid (moderate pitch)" shows equal emphasis. "The market is up (high pitch), but its gains are not solid (low pitch)" shows contrast. Make a question clear and forceful by raising your pitch at the end. Emphasize the ending of a declarative sentence with a definite drop in pitch. When a speaker's voice rises at the end of a declarative sentence, he or she sounds tentative rather than confident.

Consciously varying your pitch while speaking is one of the most important ways to improve the effectiveness of your voice. Pitch variety holds your listeners' attention and helps them understand your messages.

Volume

A major aspect of using your voice effectively is **volume**—the intensity of sound. Proper volume control enables you to be heard appropriately by your listeners. Volume control also enables you to vary your emphasis to achieve dynamic, forceful oral communication.

USE THE APPROPRIATE VOLUME LEVEL

NOTE 15.7
You want to be heard without shouting.

The first goal of volume control is to be heard by every member of the audience. You want to project your voice, not shout. If your audience thinks you are shouting, you will have created a communication barrier.

Feedback is an important part of the communication process. You can obtain feedback about your volume level by asking whether you are being heard clearly. Another source of feedback is the nonverbal signals you get from your listeners. Does your audience seem to be getting restless? Are people straining to hear you? Is anyone cupping a hand behind an ear or covering both ears? If feedback indicates your volume level needs to be adjusted, do so immediately.

VARY YOUR VOLUME FOR EMPHASIS

NOTE 15.8
Give emphasis by varying your volume.

The second goal of voice volume control is to vary your volume level for emphasis. You can communicate strength, power, forcefulness, and excitement through louder speech. You can create a mood of sorrow, seriousness, respect, and sympathy by lowering the volume of your voice. Both methods can be used to attach importance and emphasis to what you are saying.

You can maintain the attention of an audience, regardless of its size, by varying the volume of your voice. In a one-to-one situation, your voice should be conversational; with a larger group, volume can show a wide range depending on your communication goals.

Speed

Changing the speed of your oral communication provides interest and emphasis. The monotone voice we all try to avoid uses not only the same pitch and volume level but also the same speed.

The rate at which you speak will vary with your topic and the size of your audience. Complex or technical material commands a slower pace than does routine or entertaining material. The slower pace allows the receiver time to concentrate on and absorb what is being said. Interactive communication will generally have a wider range (75 to 250 words a minute) than will one-way communication (75 to 150 words a minute). Rapid speech may impair enunciation and pronunciation. Try to achieve a balance between speed and clarity.

Speed can also be used for emphasis and to convey emotion. Stress selected parts of your message by speaking slowly. Convey excitement with a high rate of speed, seriousness with a slow rate. The important point is to vary your rate as you speak. Learning to phrase well will help with pacing and will make the message easy to understand.

NOTE 15.9
Match your speed to your message and audience.

Tone

Tone is possibly your most important voice quality. **Tone** is the way the message sounds to a receiver. Your tone can convey concern, irritation, confidence, tentativeness, excitement, calmness, disrespect, courtesy, detachment, and so forth. The same sentence, spoken with a different tone, can have a dramatically different meaning. The words, *I know what you mean*, can be said with a concerned tone, conveying understanding; with an irritated tone, conveying frustration; or with a skeptical tone, conveying mistrust.

Most business communication situations call for a friendly, objective, businesslike tone that conveys warmth, strength, and respect. You will not want to sound negative, overly formal, insincere, condescending, prejudiced, weak, or disrespectful. You should consciously determine the tone you use when you speak.

NOTE 15.10
Tone conveys meaning.

Emphasis

You can give emphasis to your oral communication by varying your pitch, volume, speed, and tone. The following exercise will help you vary your emphasis and give different meanings to the same words. Say each of the following sentences aloud, giving emphasis to the bold italicized word:

You can improve your voice. (Stresses who)

You *can* improve your voice. (Stresses ability)

You can *improve* your voice. (Stresses action)

You can improve *your* voice. (Stresses ownership)

You can improve your *voice*. (Stresses what)

Did you vary the emphasis in each sentence by using different pitches? volumes? speeds? Probably you used a combination of these techniques. Now, repeat each sentence in the exercise and emphasize the italicized word by varying your pitch. Next, say the sentences and vary your volume by saying the italicized words more loudly. Then, repeat the sentences and vary your rate by saying the italicized word slowly and the rest of the words quickly. Finally, say the sentences and vary your tone from a disinterested to a caring quality.

From your use of the different emphasis techniques, you can easily see how powerful voice variety can be. You can generate interest and communicate different meanings. You can strengthen the force, power, and effectiveness of your oral communication by using variations in your voice.

NOTE 15.11
Practice giving emphasis.

Enunciation

NOTE 15.12
Sound each word part clearly and accurately.

Enunciation refers to the manner in which you sound the parts of words. Sound each part of a word clearly and accurately. An example of correct enunciation is sounding clearly the *g's* in words ending in *ing*. Say *talking* instead of *talkin, going to* instead of *gonna,* and *studying* instead of *studyin.*

Slowing the rate at which you say individual words will help to correct errors in enunciation. Give each word its fair share of time so that each part can be sounded properly and each can be heard distinctly. Listeners should be able to recognize "Next we will examine" as four words, not one (*nextwewillexamine*). High-quality enunciation reflects favorably on your intelligence and credibility.

Pronunciation

NOTE 15.13
Join sounds correctly for proper pronunciation.

The way in which you join sounds to say a word is called **pronunciation**. You can make sounds distinctly (enunciate clearly) but still not pronounce a word correctly. The dictionary is your best source of information for correct pronunciation of individual words. The first pronunciation given in a dictionary is usually the preferred one. The second pronunciation is acceptable but less common.

As in the case of high-quality enunciation, the correctness of your pronunciation reflects on your intelligence and credibility. Your listeners expect you to speak correctly. Doing so minimizes the potential for a communication barrier and helps receivers focus on the content of your message. Good oral communicators pronounce words correctly. They say *library* instead of *libary, February* instead of *Febuary, was* instead of *wuz, again* instead of *agin, just* instead of *jist, because* instead of *becuz, to* instead of *ta, the* instead of *da,* and *our* instead of *ar.* If you are not sure how to pronounce a word, do not use it until you check a dictionary or learn from another person how to pronounce it correctly.

Analysis

NOTE 15.14
Analyze your voice to improve its effectiveness.

You can improve the effectiveness of your voice by analyzing its qualities and the way in which you use it. You can perform this analysis in several ways. You can record your voice on a tape recorder for self-analysis. You can ask a family member who speaks effectively and correctly to analyze your oral communication. You can ask an instructor at school for feedback, or you can seek the advice of a speech correction professional. Regardless of the method you choose, taking the time to analyze your voice qualities and to improve them where necessary will help make you a better oral communicator.

Strengthening Your Presence

LEARNING OBJECTIVE
③ *Strengthen your personal presence.*

You can further improve your oral communication by strengthening your personal presence. Your **presence** consists of your poise and bearing. It includes your tangible and intangible nonverbal communication. The important aspects of presence are confidence, enthusiasm, sincerity, friendliness, eye contact, body actions, and appearance.

Confidence

Whether you are talking to one person or several, your receiver(s) will sense the level of confidence you possess. For a strong presence, business professionals need the right amount of confidence—neither too little nor too much.

TOO LITTLE CONFIDENCE

In one-on-one situations, too little confidence is referred to as *nervousness*; when speaking to larger groups, it is called *stage fright.*

Speaking with too little confidence causes discomfort for both a speaker and an audience. A speaker's discomfort may be reflected in a quivering voice; shaking hands; perspiration; inability to think clearly; inability to respond to questions; or other unpleasant mental, emotional, or physical symptoms. Listeners will exhibit their discomfort through nonverbal cues or through side comments to others in the audience. Speakers who lack self-confidence may not be able to say what they want to say in the way they want to say it. As a result, they may lose credibility with their audience and reduce the effectiveness of the communication. Neither the speaker nor the audience will find the communication experience pleasant or productive.

For some individuals, too little confidence is caused by negative thinking and unrealistic expectations. Speakers should accept that they do not necessarily have to be admired or respected by everyone in the audience. In addition, they must realize that it is normal to misspeak occasionally; they must not allow such errors to reduce their confidence level.

NOTE 15.15
Lack of confidence causes stage fright.

TOO MUCH CONFIDENCE

Too much confidence can also inhibit oral communication effectiveness. The overconfident speaker projects a know-it-all attitude and a lack of concern for the audience. Your audience will respond negatively to overconfidence by rejecting you and your message.

NOTE 15.16
Overconfidence produces negative reactions.

AN EFFECTIVE LEVEL OF CONFIDENCE

Self-centeredness causes *both* underconfidence *and* overconfidence. Speakers who concentrate exclusively on themselves and do not consider their receivers will be perceived as having either too little confidence or too much. To achieve an effective confidence level, keep the emphasis on your listeners and use the you–viewpoint. You won't be too concerned about yourself if you are thinking about the needs, concerns, and interests of others.

NOTE 15.17
Concentrate on the audience and use the you–viewpoint.

Sales professionals like Rebecca McCall need to be confident and knowledgeable. As Rebecca mentions in the following Communication Quote, she focuses on her receiver as she prepares and delivers her sales message.

COMMUNICATION QUOTE

In my profession, I routinely have less than 2 minutes to communicate a sales message to a physician. In order to make an impact, I must be able to deliver a concise message that considers both the physician's communication style and his or her individual needs. If I am able to do this effectively, often that 2-minute sales message turns into a 5- or 10-minute exchange of ideas.

—Rebecca McCall, Pharmaceutical Sales Representative, Johnson & Johnson. (Photo courtesy of Rebecca McCall

Other ways of developing an effective level of confidence include careful preparation, diligent practice, and attention to your personal appearance. Sustain confidence by maintaining eye contact with your audience; talking in a strong, clear voice with sufficient volume; and observing and reacting to audience feedback.

Enthusiasm

NOTE 15.18
An enthusiastic speaker holds the listeners' attention.

Enthusiasm is contagious if it is genuine. When you are enthusiastic, your audience will become enthusiastic and positive about the ideas you express. Dullness can cause receivers to let their minds wander; it can even put some to sleep. Enthusiasm can excite listeners, spark their interest, and keep them alert.

You can project your enthusiasm by speaking with energy and animation. Variations in pitch, volume, and speed will assist in showing enthusiasm. Facial expressions such as smiles and raised eyebrows indicate enthusiasm. Eyes that are wide open, alive, and sparkling also show enthusiasm. Energetic and definite gestures and body movements help, too. Recognize the importance of building a positive, enthusiastic presence; practice every time you have an opportunity—in conversations, oral reports, discussions, and speeches.

Sincerity

NOTE 15.19
Being sincere strengthens credibility.

Effectiveness is enhanced if the audience perceives the speaker to be sincere. Inappropriate gestures or facial expressions reflect insincerity and an apparent lack of concern for an audience. In addition, an insincere speaker may have difficulty gaining or maintaining credibility. You communicate sincerity when the general tone of your oral presentation conveys that your message is important. Your message should be presented in a warm, friendly, and caring manner.

Friendliness

NOTE 15.20
Friendliness builds positive relationships with listeners.

The speaker who can project a congenial, pleasant, cordial, caring image—a warm friendliness—can relate more effectively to a listener or to an audience. Knowing that friendliness can significantly increase your effectiveness should motivate you to develop your ability to be gracious. A smiling face, a well-paced approach, and a genuine concern for feedback exhibit friendliness and an honest interest in your receivers. Concentrating on the needs and interests of your audience will help convey your friendliness.

Eye Contact

Appropriate eye contact reflects confidence, interest, honesty, and sincerity. Failure to establish eye contact reflects a lack of confidence and may cause you to project an image of weakness, insincerity, fear, and dishonesty.

Be sure the amount of eye contact you have with your audience is appropriate for the cultural mix in that audience. American audiences expect more eye contact than do Asians but less than French. Refer to Chapter 2 for more information about eye contact with receivers from various cultures.

When making a presentation, be sure to engage receivers in all areas of the room. Make each person feel that he or she is having a one-on-one conversation with you. Convey the impression that, although you need to talk to others in the audience, you will return to the individual again.

NOTE 15.21
Make every receiver feel important.

Body Actions

Some nonverbal signals that occur during oral communication fall under the heading of body actions. These nonverbal signals include facial expressions, posture, gestures, and body movements. Each of these topics will be reviewed briefly here. They are discussed in more detail in Chapter 14.

FACIAL EXPRESSIONS

Regardless of the words you say, your eyes and your face will convey your true feelings. Show your sincerity and friendliness in your facial expressions. As you practice for a presentation, look in the mirror to see whether you appear to be interested, enthusiastic, and friendly. If not, practice the necessary facial expressions until your nonverbal signals match your verbal message.

NOTE 15.22
Facial expressions will be read as your true feelings.

GESTURES

Your hands, arms, shoulders, and head can convey important supporting nonverbal signals. Sitting stiffly behind a desk or standing immobile behind a lectern results in a dull, uninteresting appearance. Use gestures to strengthen your verbal messages.

Gestures should be natural, not contrived. Raising the arms with palms facing upward, for example, can accent a verbal message that asks the rhetorical question, *What is the answer?* Pointing to an item on a visual aid helps stress the point being made.

Gestures should be varied, not repetitious. To develop gestures appropriate for you and the situation, practice in front of a mirror until you find movements that are natural and comfortable for you.

NOTE 15.23
Use natural gestures to strengthen your nonverbal message.

POSTURE

An upright, correct posture will improve your appearance and give you a feeling of confidence. You do not want to appear pompous or stiff but rather natural and comfortable. While standing, keep your weight evenly distributed on your feet. Do not lean on a lectern, table, or chair. When seated, keep your back straight. Do not slouch or hang one leg over a chair arm. Correct posture reflects self-confidence and shows respect for your listener.

NOTE 15.24
Good posture has internal and external benefits.

OTHER BODY MOVEMENTS

NOTE 15.25
All movements should be relaxed and natural.

Some body movement is important to hold attention and to relax your muscles. These movements should be graceful, unhurried, and natural. You can draw an audience's attention to a visual aid by turning your body toward it or walking to it. As with facial expressions and gestures, you can observe and practice your body movements in front of a mirror until they feel comfortable and convey the correct nonverbal message.

Appearance

The final aspect to consider in strengthening your presence is your appearance. Your personal appearance can be either a barrier or an asset to effective oral communication. Appearance is an important part of the total communication environment, particularly as a first impression.

NOTE 15.26
Strengthen your presence with a good personal appearance.

You have to accept and work with the raw material of your own basic appearance. What you do with what you have is what will influence your audience. Choose tasteful clothing. Be sure both your clothing and your accessories are appropriate for the occasion and the audience. You should be neatly groomed. Good appearance not only sets a favorable stage for oral communication, but it also serves to increase your confidence.

LEARNING OBJECTIVE
Classify delivery styles by type.

(4) Presentations

Business professionals often find it necessary to make oral presentations. The purpose of most oral presentations will be either (1) to inform the audience of certain facts, or (2) to persuade the audience to accept a point of view or take a certain action. Occasionally, you may be asked to deliver a presentation designed solely to entertain. Regardless of the purpose of a presentation, your career and your organization will benefit when you prepare and deliver it effectively.

Types of Oral Presentations

NOTE 15.27
Business presentations include briefings, reports, introductions, award presentations, and speeches.

Oral presentations in business take many forms. Depending on your position, you may be asked to brief a group of employees on the status of union negotiations or be asked to report to company officers on the market research your department has been conducting. You might be called on to introduce a speaker, present an award, speak to a class or student group, or give a presentation at a professional meeting. Generally, making such presentations will serve you and your organization well.

NOTE 15.28
Choose a delivery style appropriate for the situation.

Business presentations may be formal or informal, internal or external, short or long, delivered to small groups or to large ones. The situation will help guide you in selecting a delivery style. The four delivery styles from which you may choose are manuscript, memorized, impromptu, and extemporaneous. The features of each are described in the following paragraphs.

MANUSCRIPT

NOTE 15.29
A manuscript presentation is read to the audience.

A manuscript oral presentation is written word for word and then read to the audience. Used frequently in broadcast journalism, in high-level politics, or in situations where the audience is extremely large, this style is rare in business. Exceptions occur when precise wording is required, as during a crisis, or when a speaker must give several different presentations to various audiences within a short time frame. One of the difficulties associated with this presentation style is maintaining eye contact with the audience

Oral presentations are common in business.

without losing your place in the text. Speakers who read their manuscripts also risk having the pages become disordered. Finally, it is very difficult to prepare a manuscript that sounds conversational; writing for the ear is very different from writing for the eye.

MEMORIZED

As the name implies, a memorized oral presentation is one in which the speaker has memorized the content verbatim. This style virtually eliminates the need for notes, but the delivery may appear "canned." In addition, a speaker risks forgetting parts of the presentation or having his or her concentration broken by a question from the audience. A better method is to memorize parts (for example, the opening and closing) rather than the entire presentation.

NOTE 15.30
A memorized presentation is learned verbatim.

IMPROMPTU

A presentation given without the benefit of time to prepare is referred to as an impromptu oral presentation. For example, in a meeting of the company's sales force, a representative might be asked to say a few words about his or her experience in a specific territory. Remaining calm and thinking quickly are keys to doing a good job in an unexpected speaking situation.

NOTE 15.31
An impromptu presentation is one that has to be given with little or no preparation.

EXTEMPORANEOUS

An extemporaneous oral presentation is prepared and delivered from notes or an outline. The extemporaneous style works well in interactive small-group settings as well as in predominantly one-way large-group settings. It is a spontaneous, natural way to relate to an audience. It permits good eye contact, allows free movement, and enables the speaker to respond to audience feedback. This presentation method is the basis for the discussion in the rest of this chapter. The following Tips and Hints provide advice for speakers who work from note cards.

NOTE 15.32
An extemporaneous presentation is prepared and given from notes.

Working with Note Cards

[1] Use 3×5 note cards.

[2] Write each point or subpoint on a separate card. Include reminders or supporting information you need to explain or reinforce your point.

[3] Type or print only in uppercase letters; leave two or more blank lines between items.

[4] Use color-coding to signal the transition to a new point or to a visual aid.

[5] Number the cards sequentially.

[6] Punch a hole in the upper right corner if you are left-handed or in the upper left corner if you are right-handed. Insert a 1- or 1½-inch O-ring into the hole. Place the ring on the index finger or thumb of your nondominant hand. The cards should fit comfortably into the palm, and you should find it easy to move from one card to another without fear of dropping the set.

Keys for Successfully Preparing an Effective Oral Presentation

The foundation for a successful oral presentation is preparation. Speakers who do not prepare are telling the audience members they are unimportant, unworthy of the speaker's best effort. Thorough preparation builds a speaker's confidence and assures the audience of an interesting and informative presentation.

How much time does it take to prepare for a presentation? Although some speakers say they spend an hour preparing for each minute of oral presentation, no one formula works in every situation. The audience and the speaker's familiarity with the topic will influence preparation time. The steps in planning an oral presentation are described in the following sections.

DETERMINE YOUR PURPOSE

The first step in preparing for an oral presentation is to determine the purpose of the message. Stating the purpose in terms of the expected result will help to narrow your focus. When the primary purpose of an oral presentation is to inform, you want the audience to learn, to understand, or to know more about the topic. That is the expected result. When the primary purpose is to persuade, you want the audience either to adopt your viewpoint or to take specific action. That is the expected result. Here are some example purpose statements:

- To inform those attending Leigh Acala's retirement dinner about the contributions she made during her 20 years of service
- To inform the audience about recent market research for a product line
- To persuade employees to register as organ donors
- To persuade management to increase the employee discount from 10 to 15 percent

ANALYZE YOUR AUDIENCE

The second step in preparing an oral presentation is to decide exactly who will be in the audience and why. A captive audience is generally less receptive than one that attends voluntarily. Consider how the time of the presentation will affect the audience. People often get lethargic after a meal, can be tardy or slow to tune in for an early morning session, and become preoccupied near the end of the day. Speaking to an international audience outside the United States requires additional analysis, as noted in the following Communication Note.

COMMUNICATION NOTE

Speaking Outside the United States When developing a presentation and materials for an international audience, you must consider the customs of the host country, the expectations of the audience, and possible language and cultural barriers. The following suggestions and sources may be helpful:

- Do most of your research before leaving the United States. The embassy or consulate of the country to which you will travel is a good starting point. The State Department, the World Bank, the American Chamber of Commerce, and Voice of America are other possible sources. When you phone, introduce yourself and explain your situation. Ask about appropriate dress and greetings. Be sure to say your presentation will be given in English. If you have concerns that certain terms in your presentation may be misunderstood, ask about them. If you plan to use a foreign phrase, triple-check to be sure it means just what you want it to mean.

- Verbal humor doesn't translate well. Some cultures view humor as inappropriate in meetings or seminars. Visual humor such as cartoons and comic strips is much more widely acceptable as long as it does not have political overtones. If you use such a visual, read the caption for the audience and give them time to translate what you say.

- If you leave the stage during your presentation, remember that interpersonal space varies among cultures. You may want to interact with audience members, but they may view your proximity as an invasion of their personal space. The same caution applies to times when you share the stage with presenters from other cultures.

- Remember that the listener's culture will influence whether he or she asks questions. In some cultures, asking a question would imply that the speaker didn't explain the material well enough.

- If possible, arrive in the country early so you will have time to solicit a native's comments about your presentation.

Reprinted by permission of *Successful Meetings magazine.*

Analyze each member's knowledge, interests, attitudes, and emotional reaction regarding your topic. For large audiences, you may need to examine these factors in categories such as receivers' age, gender, profession, and so on. When speaking to an established small group within your organization, consider not only demographics but also politics. Learn the history of the group. Does the group interact formally or informally? Are members generally conservative or are they open to change? Who are the key decision makers? Who are the informal leaders? What concerns or objections might participants have? Build the oral presentation on your analysis of the audience.

GATHER SUPPORTING INFORMATION

NOTE 15.36
Gather information from a variety of sources.

When you have stated your purpose and analyzed the audience, you are ready to gather ideas and materials to support the development of your oral presentation. A good presentation typically has three to five main points; you will want to locate materials that support them. Conduct your research for an oral presentation in the same manner that you would if preparing for a written report. When preparing your speech use primary sources, print and electronic secondary sources, and/or personal experience for examples, illustrations, explanations, quotations, statistics, testimonials, comparisons, and analogies related to your topic. Use only credible sources and realistic examples. Be sure to record citation information for material drawn from copyrighted sources.

ORGANIZE YOUR PRESENTATION

NOTE 15.37
Organize your presentation based on your analysis of the audience.

As you gather information, you are apt to find that you have far more material than can be conveyed in the time you have available. Begin to organize your presentation by returning to your purpose and sorting your materials into three sets:

- Materials you **must** include (those closely related to your main idea)
- Materials you **should** include (those that support your main idea)
- Materials you **could** include (related background materials)

The "must" items will definitely be in your presentation, as will some from the "should" set. Information you do not use in your oral presentation will be helpful when responding to questions or during informal discussions that may occur as a result of the presentation.

Once the material is organized, you can determine which, if any, presentation aids to use.

SELECT APPROPRIATE PRESENTATION AIDS

NOTE 15.38
Choose presentation aids to strengthen your message.

Unlike a written report, which draws only on the receiver's sense of sight, an oral presentation can draw on sound, sight, touch, taste, and smell. Most speakers will find sound (audio) and sight (visual) most useful. Whether used separately or in combination (multimedia), presentation aids can be an asset in conveying a message. They can make it more understandable. As Amber Kellen notes in the following Communication Quote, visuals can spark interest, add variety, and help to hold an audience's attention. The Tips and Hints on page 429 suggest questions to be asked when de-

---

COMMUNICATION QUOTE

When asked to present material for my coworkers, I try to incorporate variety and audience interaction. Many of the presentations I give require the use of PowerPoint. Because text-only presentations are difficult for an audience to focus on, I use graphics, charts, and video-clips to enhance the content. I also build in interaction by asking the audience questions throughout the presentation.

—Amber Kellen, Programmer Analyst, General Mills. (Photo courtesy of Amber Kellen)

ciding to use a presentation aid. Selection and preparation of presentation aids is covered in Chapter 13.

TIPS AND HINTS

Deciding to Use a Presentation Aid

When deciding whether to use presentation aids, ask yourself the following questions:

- Will this aid make my message clearer?
- Will it be simple enough to be understood?

- Will it be worth the time it will take to develop?
- Will it enhance my message?

If your answer to any of these questions is no, you should not use the aid.

PREPARE YOUR PRESENTATION

You know your purpose. You have analyzed your audience. You have gathered supporting data and have prepared your presentation aids. You are now ready to put all this information together in a coherent oral presentation.

Some speakers write a full-text manuscript and then discard it after making notes from it. Other speakers work exclusively from an outline recorded on note cards or sheets of paper. However you arrive at your fully developed presentation, remember that it will have three parts:

[1] Opening

[2] Body

[3] Closing

The Opening An effective opening is crucial. The audience evaluates your credibility and capability as a speaker in the first few minutes and, regardless of what you do later, it is almost impossible to change that evaluation. A good first impression will serve you and your audience well throughout a presentation.

Use your opening to get audience attention and interest. Effective ways to open a presentation include a surprising statement, a quotation, an anecdote, a humorous story, a question, a problem statement, a historical reference, an impressive statistic, a visual aid, a reference to the situation, or an illustration. A humorous personal story may help you bond with an audience, but avoid leading with a prepared joke. When a joke fails, you risk losing your audience and undermining your self-confidence. Never use off-color humor or tell a story that embarrasses an audience member. Regardless of the method you choose, be sure the opening is brief and relates closely to your topic.

View the opening as an opportunity to show your audience why the topic is important, to give an overview of the talk, and to lead into the body of your presentation. Set the mood for the presentation and establish rapport between you and the audience. If the person who introduces you has not done so, tell the audience whether you will take questions during or after the presentation.

The Body Most of the information you present to the audience will be contained in the middle of the presentation—in the body. Plan this portion of your oral presentation carefully. Supplement your knowledge and experience with research and examples. Gather two or three times as much material as you think you will need, and use the best in your presentation.

NOTE 15.39
Each part of a presentation must be prepared carefully.

NOTE 15.40
Use the opening to capture interest, preview your topic, and establish rapport with the audience.

NOTE 15.41
The body contains most of the information.

A humorous anecdote strategically placed within the body of your presentation can help to lighten the mood of the audience, help to maintain listeners' interest, and reinforce an important point. See the following Communication Note for more information about using anecdotes.

COMMUNICATION NOTE

Anecdotes Statistics can connect a speaker to an audience intellectually but not as emotionally as stories do. Anecdotes make arguments easier to understand and remember; and, the easier information is to recall, the more likely people are to draw on it when making decisions. Stories are also less intimidating than numbers can be.

Unfortunately, there's no magic formula for selecting a good story—it's a speaker's judgment call. Good judgment suggests, however, that a story be respectful and interesting, without scaring or shaming the audience. In addition, the story must show that the speaker is human. It's that vulnerability or fallibility that creates a human connection. Finally, the story should have the audience with the feeling that the idea the anecdote supports is worthwhile and achievable.

Adapted from "Anecdotal Evidence," by Gary Hartzell; *School Library Journal, 49*(1), January 2003.

Decide which organizational pattern(s) work best for your topic and audience. As shown in the following Tips and Hints, you have several organizational patterns from which to choose. The Tips and Hints on page 431 offers guidelines for developing the body of a presentation.

TIPS AND HINTS

Selecting an Organizational Pattern

Speakers have several patterns from which to choose when they organize their presentations. Here are some frequently used patterns:

[1] **Cause and effect.** Show the relationship between events. Use this technique when attempting to persuade.

[2] **Comparison or contrast.** Show the similarities and dissimilarities of the subject matter on a category-by-category basis. This pattern can be used with informative, entertaining, or persuasive presentations.

[3] **Direct or indirect.** Start or end with the main point, depending on whether your receiver will perceive the message as good or bad news.

[4] **Problem and solution.** Describe the problem(s), then present the solution(s). This pattern is appropriate for persuasive messages.

[5] **Spatial relation.** Describe from top to bottom, bottom to top, left to right, right to left, inside to outside, outside to inside, room to room, desk to desk, or follow some other spatial flow pattern. Consider this pattern when making informative or entertaining speeches involving space.

[6] **Time sequence.** Review pertinent material from oldest to newest or from newest to oldest. This pattern works well for informative and persuasive messages because it allows the speaker to integrate valuable background information.

[7] **Topics and subtopics.** Organize the subject according to its logical parts. This pattern is especially useful for presentations designed to inform or entertain.

Developing the Body of an Oral Presentation

As you develop the body of an oral presentation, consider these guidelines:

[1] *Hold the listeners' attention.* Use short (less than 25 words) sentences built around active, present tense verbs. Keep your presentation audience-centered by using the you–viewpoint. Use examples and illustrations to create images for your listeners.

[2] *Emphasize your main points.* Use repetition, specificity, and mechanical means. Tell your listeners what is important by saying, "This is my most important point . . ." or "This, then, is the critical issue." You can also use audiovisual aids to give emphasis. Use statistics and examples to support main points. Make descriptions vivid.

[3] *Keep your presentation simple.* Audiences cannot comprehend complex, detailed information presented only orally. That kind of information should be presented in written form so that it can be studied and reread. Match your vocabulary to that of your audience. Avoid jargon and acronyms. Provide a smooth transition from one point to the next within the body. Limit uninterrupted talking (talking without any audience activity) to no more than 20 minutes.

[4] *Involve your listeners in the presentation.* Help them form images that support your points. Have the audience participate in small group discussions, exercises, and demonstrations.

The Closing In the closing, definitely let the audience know that you are ending. Summarize the main points of your presentation; specify what the audience should do; and part with the audience on a positive, professional note.

Use both verbal and nonverbal signals to let the audience know you are ending the oral presentation. Say, "In summary," "In closing," "To review," or "In conclusion." A more subtle way to signal closure is to pause and lower the pitch of your voice. Making a significant change in your stance relative to the lectern is another way.

The summary should be a very simple statement designed to recap the main points of your presentation. It may be followed by advice on how to use the information or by a clear statement of action the audience should take based on your presentation.

Your presentation should end on a positive, professional note. The techniques suggested for opening a presentation—a surprising statement, a quotation, an anecdote, a humorous story (carefully used), or an illustration—also work well for closing it, but

NOTE 15.42
End with a summary and call to action.

The Wizard of ID

be sure to choose a different technique. The closing is an important point of emphasis for your presentation. Be positive and optimistic. Be professional. Most important of all, use the you–viewpoint.

As you prepare, remember that there's no such thing as a "one size fits all" presentation. As noted in the following Communication Note, you may benefit from preparing several versions of your presentation.

REHEARSE YOUR PRESENTATION

Using the notes and presentation aids you have developed, rehearse your oral presentation. Plan your hand gestures and walking patterns. Practice how, when, and where you will move. Rehearsals will help you identify and correct distracting mannerisms such as those listed in the following Tips and Hints. Anticipate questions that might be asked. Identify three to five questions you hope will be asked and three to five that you hope won't be asked. Prepare to answer both sets.

If you will be speaking into a microphone, be sure you know how to use it effectively. Follow the suggestions in the Tips and Hints below. Microphones come in four styles: platform, handheld, lavaliere (clip and hanging), and remote. Platform microphones are the most restrictive; remote units are the least restrictive.

TIPS AND HINTS

Working with a Microphone

Follow these suggestions when using a microphone during a presentation:

[1] Adjust the mounting of a platform microphone to give 6 to 12 inches of space between it and your mouth. Stay within this range or sounds will be lost or distorted. Speak over rather than into the microphone. Remember that each time you turn your head to the right or left, sounds will be lost.

[2] Lavaliere microphones should be clipped or hung at midchest or above, but they should not touch the larynx. Remove pins, tie tacks, necklaces, or other items the microphone might brush against.

[3] Sound levels should be checked in advance and set to compensate for sounds absorbed by a room full of people. If you must check the microphone at the start of a presentation, do so by asking audience members to raise their hands if they cannot hear you well. You may also ask an audience member to stand or otherwise let you know of a sound problem. Blowing into the microphone, tapping on it, or asking, "Can you hear me?" are signs of amateurism.

[4] Remember to step away from, turn off, or remove the microphone after you have finished. Forgetting to do so may mean that your off-the-cuff remarks are heard by the entire audience.

To get feedback on your presentation, rehearse in front of a mirror or before friends, relatives, or colleagues. You can use an audio or a video recorder for this purpose as well. This practice will help you to decide which parts of your content and delivery need to be modified or fine-tuned. It also gives you experience in handling your audiovisual aids efficiently. It is the only way you can be sure of the length of your presentation. When a speaker goes beyond the expected time, audience members will leave—physically or mentally.

Rehearsing your oral presentation is essential to its success. Practice will increase your familiarity with the material and your confidence in delivering it. If you go into a presentation underprepared or unprepared, you will be preoccupied with yourself and your message and lose the opportunity to establish rapport with your audience.

NOTE 15.44
Get feedback on your content and delivery.

Keys for Successfully Delivering an Effective Oral Presentation

LEARNING OBJECTIVE
(6) *Demonstrate the techniques to be used when delivering an effective presentation.*

All the material you studied earlier in this chapter applies to the delivery of an oral presentation. You will want to use your voice effectively and project a strong presence. You will want to vary your pitch, volume, and speed for emphasis while speaking. You will want to enunciate sounds clearly and pronounce words correctly. Your poise and bearing should convey confidence, enthusiasm, sincerity, and friendliness. Establish appropriate eye contact with your audience, and use natural gestures. Your appearance should be appropriate for the audience and the situation.

You have prepared your oral presentation and now you are ready to deliver it. Here are keys to guide you in successfully delivering your oral presentation.

START POSITIVELY

NOTE 15.45
Become familiar with the site.

When you are scheduled to speak in an unfamiliar facility, visit it at least an hour in advance of your presentation. Acquaint yourself with the room arrangement, and determine whether everything you need is or will be in place before your presentation. Check the lectern and make sure it is the right height for you. Learn how to operate the equipment controls and the power supply and locate the room thermostat. Determine who can help if things go wrong.

Whether speaking in a new setting or in a familiar one, arrive five to ten minutes prior to your scheduled speaking time. Make a final check to ensure that the lighting, temperature, public address system, audiovisual equipment, lectern, and seating arrangement support and strengthen your presentation. Be sure your notes and visual aids are with you and in correct order. If possible, greet members of the audience as they arrive. Introduce yourself and get the names of as many attendees as you can. Smile and give the impression that you are enjoying yourself. This brief activity helps establish your credibility and should increase your confidence level.

When the program starts and you await your turn to speak, look pleasantly and confidently at the audience. At the appropriate time, move to the position designated for the speaker. If speaking in an auditorium or classroom-style setting, walk to the lectern with authority. If making a presentation in a conference room, follow the protocol of the group (move to the head of the table, stay seated, etc.). Whatever the setting, use your body language to tell the audience there is no place you would rather be than there with them. Take a moment to collect yourself. Arrange your notes and presentation aids.

NOTE 15.46
Establish rapport with the audience, then begin.

Once you have begun building rapport with your audience by establishing eye contact with them, begin your presentation. Go right to your opening; omit casual, unplanned remarks and platitudes such as, "It's my distinct pleasure to be here with such a distinguished group of professionals." It is good to memorize the first part, if not all, of the opening. In this way you can concentrate on the audience and your delivery and not have to worry about checking your notes.

Remember that your delivery is part performance and part content. Both must be well prepared for a successful delivery.

REMAIN CALM

NOTE 15.47
Handle stage fright by thinking positively and concentrating on the you–viewpoint.

Some speakers suffer from a phenomenon known as speaker anxiety or stage fright. Ironically, it's not the speaking that causes nerves, it is the fear of self-embarrassment. One way to handle nerves is to realize that even the most practiced and professional speakers have some apprehension about speaking to an audience. Don't be surprised if your heart rate accelerates or your palms become sweaty. Learn to relax. Sit comfortably, but keep your back straight. Remember that you will be more aware of your nervousness than your audience will be.

A second way of dealing with the stage fright that threatens to detract from a successful delivery is to use imagery. Picture yourself rising and moving to the speaking area. Hear yourself speak in a loud, clear, confident voice. See yourself using natural gestures. Picture the audience responding positively to your message. Remind yourself that you have prepared thoroughly.

Calm can be achieved once you have risen and moved to the area from which you will speak. Just before you begin, inconspicuously take a few deep breaths. Inhale slowly, hold your breath for four or five seconds, then exhale. Finally, concentrate on the you–viewpoint. Focus on the audience's needs, interests, and concerns. Remember that you are there to benefit your listeners and that they want you to succeed.

USE PRESENTATION AIDS EFFECTIVELY

You have chosen aids that complement your presentation and have designed them so that the audience can read or hear everything in them. You have practiced handling them efficiently. To use them effectively during your delivery, simply take advantage of your careful preparation. The Tips and Hints below and the one on page 436 contain advice for using presentation aids.

NOTE 15.48
Use presentation aids with poise and confidence.

If you have developed a packet of materials to share with your audience the day of the presentation, tell them so during your opening so they can relax and listen to what you have to say. To avoid having audience members focus on the handout during your presentation, distribute the materials after you finish speaking.

EVALUATE AUDIENCE FEEDBACK

Maintain good eye contact with the members of the audience so that you can secure feedback on how the presentation is progressing. Assess your listeners' changing reactions and make necessary adjustments to keep their attention and interest. Are you sure they can all hear you? If not, speak louder. Can they all see the visual aids? If not, make

NOTE 15.49
Adjust your presentation based on audience feedback.

TIPS AND HINTS

Using Transparencies

These suggestions will help you to use transparencies effectively:

[1] *Check equipment in advance.* Be sure the projector is at a comfortable height and placed on a vibration-free base. The projector lens and surface should be clean and dust-free. Locate the spare bulb. Be sure the power cord isn't a hazard to you or your audience. Focus and center the picture; be sure the image is readable from all parts of the room.

[2] *Place the screen on a diagonal, not directly behind you.* Tilt the screen toward the projector to ensure that the image is not larger on the top than on the bottom.

[3] *Face the audience, not the screen.* Be sure nothing comes between the projector and the screen, including you. Place the projector to your right if you are right-handed, to your left if you are left-handed. Be sure you have a surface on which to set your transparencies before and after you use them.

[4] *Place transparencies in sturdy frames.* Write notes on the frame to remind you of key points.

[5] *Use a pen, pencil, or similar device other than your finger to point to items on the transparency.* Movements are exaggerated by projection and may cause a distraction. Set the pointer down when not using it so that it does not distract the audience.

[6] *Darken the screen when nothing is being projected.* Turning off the projector can shorten the life of the bulb, so cover either the projection surface or the lens. Taping a small piece of cardboard above the lens makes darkening the screen convenient and inconspicuous.

Using Presentation Graphics Software

Following these guidelines will help you effectively use presentation software:

[1] *Know your equipment and software.* Be sure cords do not present a hazard to you or your audience. Try to rehearse with the equipment you will use when giving your presentation. Audiences get impatient with delays and feel their time is being wasted. Always have a backup plan in case equipment fails.

[2] *Position equipment so that you can see the monitor and use the computer while facing the audience.* Better yet, use a remote mouse. Doing so will free you to interact with your audience and minimize the need to move back to the computer every time you want to change a slide. Such movement interrupts the flow of your presentation and distracts your audience.

[3] *Don't just read the slides.* Provide more information than what appears on the screen.

[4] *Move slowly from slide to slide.* Electronic presentations tend to make you speak more quickly than usual.

[5] *Don't let the slide show be a distraction.* Audiences quickly grow tired of slide transitions, animations, and sounds. Remember, the audience should concentrate on you and your message.

[6] *Use blank (background only) screens where ideas will pause.* Begin with a title screen; end with a slide that recaps your major points, provides information on how to contact you, or shows only your slide show background pattern.

adjustments. Is their interest waning? If so, change your pace, pick up your enthusiasm, and start involving them in some way. Do they seem not to understand a point? If so, ask them questions, paraphrase, or ask a volunteer to explain his or her understanding of the point. Do members of the audience show signs of physical discomfort? If so, ask them about it and have the necessary adjustment made. Using the feedback you get from an audience can strengthen the effectiveness of an oral presentation.

END POSITIVELY

NOTE 15.50
End positively using a clear, strong voice.

Endings, like beginnings, are important points of emphasis. Deliver the closing with a clear, strong voice. Your poise and bearing should be at their best even if the body of your presentation did not meet your highest expectations. At this point, eye contact with the audience should be 100 percent. You should be focusing exclusively on your audience and using the you–viewpoint.

RESPOND TO QUESTIONS

Question-and-answer sessions are common in business presentation settings. In a large-group setting, questions are generally posed after the presentation has ended. In a small-group setting, questions may arise during or after the presentation depending on the audience or on the speaker's preference. When speaking to an audience of clients or to people holding positions higher than yours within your organization, it is best to answer questions as they are asked. In other settings, specify as part of your introduction or opening whether you will take questions during the presentation, after the presentation, or both.

Answering questions gives speakers an excellent opportunity to relate positively to the audience, to clarify and reemphasize points, and to alleviate any concerns the audience may have. Some questions may relate to the specifics of your content; others may be about a related topic or condition. Be prepared to answer both types. Following the guidelines in the Tips and Hints below will help your sessions go smoothly.

NOTE 15.51
Use question-and-answer sessions to strengthen your relationship with the audience.

TIPS AND HINTS

Question-and-Answer Sessions

During a question-and-answer session, you may encounter four types of questions: (1) information-seeking, (2) opinion-seeking, (3) hostile or negative, and (4) off-target. The following tips will help you make the experience a positive one for you and your audience:

[1] If time is limited, let your audience know in an inviting manner such as "We have about 25 minutes before this session ends; this would be a good time to ask questions."

[2] If no one asks a question, start the process yourself. Set the tone for a stimulating exchange by posing a clearly worded, concise question and then giving a brief (less than 30-second) direct response.

[3] When a question is asked, listen carefully. If necessary, repeat the question so that all may hear it. Determine the type of question, then formulate and give your answer.

[4] When answering, use a conversational style and look primarily at the person who asked the question.

[5] Deflect hostile or negative questions by rephrasing them before answering. Never argue with a questioner. Becoming defensive, hostile, or sarcastic not only tarnishes your image but also causes the audience to sympathize with the questioner. If someone asks a question unrelated to the topic, offer to meet with him or her after the presentation to discuss it.

[6] When answering a question, try to refer to topics covered during your presentation. This will reinforce and clarify.

[7] Be conscious of the nonverbal messages your gestures and body language convey as you respond to a question.

[8] Be prepared to end the session with a few brief remarks related to your presentation.

When you have finished, smile and graciously accept the applause or thanks the audience offers you. Later, reflect on the experience. Note what worked well and what you would like to improve.

Using the keys that have been presented in this section will help you to prepare and deliver effective business presentations in traditional settings. Not all speaking situations you encounter, however, will be traditional. Several such situations are described in the next section.

So far, material in this chapter has focused on how to make an individual presentation. Team presentations are also common in business. The Communication Note on page 438 offers suggestions for making successful team presentations.

Making a Team Presentation When speaking in groups of two or three, be sure to practice as a group. You must behave as a unified group, and this won't happen without practice. The planning process should address not only the formal presentation but also the questions/answer session.

While you are waiting to speak or after you have spoken, be sure to pay attention to your colleagues. You may be tempted to look at your notes or reflect on what you have said, but the key is to look interested in what the other person is saying. Looking at the audience and noting when members nod or frown is also useful; you can use the information to reinforce or explain a point later.

When it's time for questions and answers, involve all team members. The person who responds should keep his or her answer succinct and avoid over-talking in an effort to demonstrate expertise. Other members should avoid the temptation to add their own comments after a question has been answered.

Based on information in "Make 'em Sit Up and Listen," by Helen Osborne; *Estates Gazette*, February 9, 2002, p. 138.

LEARNING OBJECTIVE

Identify tasks and procedures associated with special presentation situations.

(7) Special Presentation Situations

Two additional speaking situations you may encounter during your career are discussed in this section—emceeing an event and introducing a speaker.

Emceeing an Event

The master of ceremonies, known informally as the **emcee**, plays a significant supporting role in the success of an event. It is his or her responsibility to ensure that the event begins, moves along, and ends in a timely fashion. He or she sets the tone for and maintains the continuity of the event.

NOTE 15.52
Emcees are responsible for setting and maintaining the flow of an event.

The specific duties performed by an emcee will be determined by those who plan the program. At the very least, an emcee will be expected to welcome the audience, introduce a series of speakers in a predetermined sequence, and end the program. Additional responsibilities may include introducing those seated at a head table, acknowledging dignitaries seated in the audience, assisting program participants, and serving as moderator of a question-and-answer session. The procedure for introducing a speaker is described in a separate section; the remaining duties are covered in the following paragraphs.

WELCOMING THE AUDIENCE

NOTE 15.53
Remember to introduce yourself.

The welcome, more than any other factor, will set the tone for the event. Begin by greeting the audience and then pausing briefly to allow conversations and activity to cease. Once you have gained the attention of the audience, give your name and welcome the group to the event. You might say, for example, "Good evening ladies and gentlemen. (pause) I'm Rita Rupert, your host for this year's Employee Recognition Dinner. Thank you for sharing this special night with us." Be sure to smile; scan the entire room; and speak in a clear, confident voice. Next, provide a brief overview of the agenda for the event. The entire welcome should take less than two minutes—no longer than five if you are also expected to prime the audience with a few humorous comments.

INTRODUCING THE HEAD TABLE

Although an emcee does not determine who sits where at a head table, he or she should follow a standard pattern for introducing those seated there. The pattern calls for moving from the emcee's far right to center, where the lectern is typically placed, then from the emcee's far left to center. Before beginning, the emcee should specify what each individual should do (rise, then be seated; rise, remain standing), and tell the audience to hold applause until all head table guests have been introduced. Correct pronunciation of each name is essential. The emcee should have good eye contact with the audience and occasionally look or gesture toward the people being introduced. The introductions should be simple and brief—name and title, role in the organization, or reason for being seated at the head table. If appropriate, the emcee could also make a light-hearted remark or tell an anecdote about each person. Format consistency is the key.

NOTE 15.54
Pronounce names carefully and correctly.

ACKNOWLEDGING DIGNITARIES

Those who plan the program may wish to have the emcee introduce some attendees not seated at the head table. These individuals may play a prominent role in the community or have some past, special tie to the group. Knowing in advance that each dignitary is actually at the event and where he or she is seated will make the process flow smoothly. Once again, the emcee should specify the actions to be taken by the audience and those being introduced. Names should be pronounced correctly. If several guests are to be introduced, decide how you will achieve smooth transition without being wordy. "Also with us tonight" and "Another special guest" are examples of introductory phrases that can be used as transitions.

NOTE 15.55
Recognize prominent attendees.

ASSISTING PROGRAM PARTICIPANTS

The emcee should introduce himself or herself to each program participant before the event begins. She or he should clarify seating arrangements, explain the sequence of events, verify the time the participant has been allocated, tend to special requests, and confirm the accuracy of personal information such as name pronunciation and title. In addition, the emcee should be sure that the sound system and other equipment are working properly. Also, he or she should be sure that a pitcher of water and several glasses are at or near the lectern. The emcee is responsible for assisting or knowing who has been assigned to assist the speaker with tasks such as distributing materials and operating equipment.

NOTE 15.56
Be courteous and efficient.

By keeping on schedule, the emcee assists not only those who participate in the program but also those who attend. If the participant exceeds the allotted time, the emcee must ask him or her to stop. Since the emcee is typically seated next to the lectern at a head table, passing a note saying "Your time has expired; please end now" should be sufficient. If the emcee is seated elsewhere, another method of signaling time must be devised. The emcee should select a method based on room and seating arrangements and then inform each participant of it.

NOTE 15.57
Extend thanks personally
and on behalf of the
group.

After the speaker finishes his or her presentation, the emcee should rise, extend personal thanks to the speaker, and then thank the speaker for the entire group. The personal remarks are made privately, as the emcee shakes the speaker's hand; formal thanks are given so the entire audience can hear. The formal thanks should identify the speaker by name and relate in some way to the topic. "Thank you, Dr. Fitzgerald, for sharing with us your ideas about the role of Internet commerce in today's global economy" completes the task in one sentence. Depending on the speaker and topic, a longer, perhaps humorous, statement would be appropriate.

MODERATING A QUESTION-AND-ANSWER SESSION

The primary tasks of an emcee during a question-and-answer session are to call for questions, repeat the questions after they have been asked, keep time, and thank the speaker.

After the presentation has ended and the speaker has been thanked for giving it, the emcee informs the audience of the time available and asks for questions. Often, this request will be met with silence. Audience members may need time to formulate their questions and summon the confidence to ask them. The emcee should give them this time by asking the first question. Doing so relieves the pressure that silence can place on both the audience and the speaker.

As audience members stand or raise their hands to be recognized, the emcee should acknowledge them, listen carefully to the question, and then repeat the question to ensure that all in the audience know what was asked. If the question is long, the emcee should paraphrase. If the question is complex, the emcee should divide it into logical subquestions and pose each separately.

In some settings, audience members are asked to write their questions on cards. The cards are collected and given to the emcee, who then reads them on behalf of the audience members. When this protocol is followed, the emcee should quickly scan the questions and select a fairly simple one as the first. While the speaker is responding, the emcee can decide which of the remaining questions will be asked and in what order. Similar questions may be paraphrased. Several questions should be thought-provoking. Of course, all questions should be in good taste.

When the allotted time has expired, the emcee thanks audience members for their questions and the speaker for responding to them.

CONCLUDING THE EVENT

Once all parts of the program have been completed, the emcee issues a general thanks to the entire group and bids them farewell. The remarks may include a brief summary of the events or a reference to the featured speaker's presentation. The emcee allows program participants to leave the stage area first and remains in the room until the majority of guests have left or are clearly engaged in conversation.

The emcee at a formal event serves the same purpose the host or hostess serves at a social event. He or she is responsible for ensuring that those who attend feel welcome and have an enjoyable time. That can occur only if the emcee recognizes that his or her role is important to the success of the event but that he or she is not the focus of the event. In other words, the emcee must maintain the you–viewpoint. This same unselfish approach must be used by the emcee or whoever introduces a speaker. Specific techniques for that task are covered in the following section.

Introducing a Speaker

When you are asked to introduce a speaker, accept the invitation with enthusiasm. The experience will give you a chance to enhance your own speaking ability and to provide a valuable service to the speaker and the audience.

The process you follow in preparing for and delivering a speaker's introduction will parallel that used for a longer presentation. You must identify your purpose, gather information, develop the presentation, rehearse, and deliver the introduction with skill and confidence. Although you might do so in an entertaining fashion, the primary purpose of an introduction is to inform audience members of who the speaker is, what the topic will be, why the topic is important to them, and what credentials qualify the speaker to make the presentation.

In some cases, the speaker will write his or her own introduction. When this occurs, the person designated to introduce the speaker should practice the introduction and give it with style and enthusiasm. When you are responsible for preparing the introduction, remember that the best source of information about a speaker is the speaker. As soon as you learn you will be making the introduction, obtain a copy of the speaker's resume. Review it and make a few notes to be used in your introduction. Consider consulting secondary sources for information about the topic. Ask program planners whether a formal question-and-answer session will be conducted and, if so, determine whether you or the emcee will serve as moderator. If program planners are flexible, ask the speaker to indicate whether questions should be asked as they arise or held until the presentation is completed. Include the information as part of your introduction.

Several days prior to the event, phone or meet with the speaker to gather additional information and to verify the accuracy and appropriateness of items you intend to use. Try to include more than facts and figures in your introduction. You will make the speaker seem more real if you include some personal information or an anecdote about him or her. Such information can be obtained from the speaker, from a friend or colleague of the speaker, or from your conversations with him or her.

As you prepare your introduction, remember that you have very little time—generally no more than two minutes—to make the audience eager to hear the speaker. Because your time before the audience will be brief, you could either memorize your presentation or give it extemporaneously. Whichever style you choose, be sure to practice. Do not, however, rehearse so much that you destroy the professional, self-confident, and friendly demeanor you wish to achieve.

On the day of the presentation, introduce yourself to the speaker long before you are to make the introduction. Confirm whether the speaker will remain seated or stand at your side while you make the introduction. When it is your turn to speak, rise, face the audience, smile, and begin to speak. Establish good eye contact with your audience. At some point during your introduction, look or gesture toward the speaker.

When you've finished your introduction, lead the applause (if appropriate), step to the side, greet the speaker with a handshake, and inconspicuously return to your seat. If applause is appropriate at the conclusion of the presentation, be the one to lead it. Convey your thanks to the speaker either as part of the program or in a more informal setting after the presentation ends.

Good preparation and attention to the basics of oral communication will help you deliver effective oral presentations.

NOTE 15.60
Draw material for an introduction from a variety of sources.

NOTE 15.61
Rehearse the introduction to be sure it is brief, informative, and inviting.

NOTE 15.62
Use nonverbal communication to acknowledge the speaker during your introduction.

Summary of Learning Objectives

(1) Improve the basic quality of your voice.

Speakers who want to improve the quality of their voice pay attention to the way in which they breathe. Inhaling deeply and exhaling so that air is forced from the diaphragm causes deep, rich sounds. Controlling the jaw, tongue, and lips relates to speaking clearly. The jaw should be flexible, the tongue and lips should be loose.

(2) Use your voice effectively.

Finding, using, and varying the natural pitch of your voice will protect your vocal cords from damage and will help to make your speech patterns interesting. Vary volume to be heard and to emphasize important points. Interest and emphasis are achieved by varying the speed at which a message is delivered. Tone is used to convey meaning; a businesslike tone that conveys warmth, strength, and respect is desirable. Speaking clearly and pronouncing words correctly are also important factors.

(3) Strengthen your personal presence.

Speakers who have good personal presence concentrate on their receivers, not on themselves. They are genuinely enthusiastic about the message they convey. They exhibit their friendliness and sincerity through their words and through nonverbal cues involving posture, eye contact, facial expressions, and gestures. Effective speakers choose clothing and accessories appropriate to the occasion and the audience.

(4) Classify delivery styles by type.

Presentations may be delivered in any of four styles: manuscript, memorized, impromptu, or extemporaneous. Manuscripts are written in full and read to the audience. Memorized presentations are written in full and delivered without notes. Impromptu presentations arise from situations; there is little or no time to prepare. Extemporaneous presentations are delivered from notes. Extemporaneous is the style preferred for business.

(5) Identify the steps to follow in preparing an oral presentation.

Determining the purpose of a presentation and analyzing the audience are the first two steps in preparing for an oral presentation. Gathering materials, organizing the presentation, and deciding whether to use presentation aids are additional steps. The presentation consists of an opening, a body, and a closing. Once the speaker has prepared the notes or outline from which the presentation will be given, he or she rehearses to get feedback about how to refine both content and delivery.

(6) Demonstrate the techniques to be used when delivering an effective presentation.

When the actual presentation occurs, the speaker should remain calm, begin positively, use presentation aids effectively, make adjustments based on audience feedback, end positively, and respond to questions from listeners.

Identify tasks and procedures associated with special presentation situations.

Emceeing an event and introducing a speaker are among the special speaking situations a business professional might encounter. Emcees are often called on to welcome participants and guests, introduce those seated at a head table, acknowledge special guests, assist program participants, moderate a question-and-answer session, and close an event. Sometimes an emcee introduces the featured speaker; at other times another participant has this privilege. Introductions must be brief yet informative.

Discussion Questions

1. What are the "troublesome t's"? How can they be managed? (Objective 1)
2. How does being nervous affect a speaker's ability to produce rich, full sounds? (Objective 2)
3. Explain how pitch can be used to show comparisons and contrasts. (Objective 2)
4. How can a speaker determine whether he or she is speaking at an appropriate volume? (Objective 2)
5. Define personal presence and explain the role it plays in effective oral communication. (Objective 3)
6. Describe how an audience might react to a speaker who has (a) too little confidence and (b) too much confidence. (Objective 3)
7. Draw from your experience in class, in a student organization, or in another group and discuss situations in which you have been called on to make presentations using each of the four delivery styles identified in this chapter. (Objective 4)
8. Discuss the impressions given by a speaker who does each of the following: (Objective 5)
   a. Speaks as he or she moves toward or leaves the podium or speaker's platform.
   b. Scans the audience by looking above members' heads.
   c. Sits on the meeting table or a desk while speaking.
   d. Keeps a hand in the pocket of his or her jacket and jingles the coins or keys kept there.
   e. Ends his or her presentation by saying, "Well, I guess that's it."

9. **Ethics.** While developing an oral report for a marketing class, Sara, one of your team members locates an article that fits perfectly with your topic. Sara suggests that the group take several paragraphs from the article and use them in the oral report without mentioning the source. How would you handle the situation? (Objective 5)
10. What advice would you give to a coworker who declines invitations to speak to professional and community groups because he or she is too scared? (Objective 6)
11. How should a speaker handle disruptions such as people arriving late or the sound of cell phones ringing? (Objective 6)
12. Discuss the role an emcee plays in the success of an event. (Objective 7)

Application Exercises

1. **Teamwork.** Work with one other student. Select a page from this book or some other source and have your partner read it aloud. After he or she finishes reading, comment on the volume, speed, pitch, and tone of the communication; note any enunciation or pronunciation errors that were made. Repeat the process with a different speaker and different material. (Objective 1)

2. Practice keeping your jaw, tongue, and lips flexible by saying the following sentences aloud three or more times each: (Objective 1)

> Loose lips sink ships.
> Shave a single shingle thin.
> Peter Piper picked a peck of pickling peppers.
> Hickory dickory dock, the mouse ran up the clock.
> She sells seashells by the seashore.

3. **E-mail.** Record your voice on a cassette tape recorder. Listen carefully to the recording and analyze your voice qualities in regard to pitch, volume, and speed. Summarize your findings in an e-mail to your instructor. Your message should include the following: (a) the way your voice sounds to you, (b) the strengths of your voice, (c) the weaknesses of your voice, and (d) a plan for improving your voice. (Objectives 1 and 2)

4. Give emphasis to the important points in the following paragraph by varying (a) your pitch; (b) your volume; (c) your speed; and (d) your pitch, volume, and speed in appropriate combinations: (Objective 2)

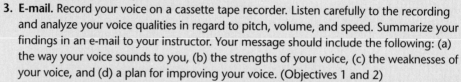

Your degree of success in providing leadership to others relates directly to your ability to speak clearly, intelligently, and confidently. Your effectiveness will depend on the quality of your voice and the strength of your presence.

5. Read the paragraph in Exercise 4 three times. Each time, vary your posture so you are (a) standing, head low, shoulders curved forward; (b) seated, almost reclining, with legs extended and crossed at the ankles; and (c) standing, shoulders squared, back straight. Which posture felt most comfortable? Which made you feel most confident? (Objective 3)

6. **Teamwork.** Sit back-to-back with another student in the class so that neither of you can use nonverbal cues to complete this exercise. Take turns saying the following sentence aloud three times: "Why were you late for the meeting?" Each time you speak the sentence, change your tone to reflect one of the following sentiments: concern, irritation, detachment. See whether your partner is able to determine which emotion you are conveying through your words. (Objective 3)

7. **Teamwork.** Form groups of five to seven students. Have each person in the group speak for one minute on one of the following topics:
   a. A hobby or personal interest.
   b. Whether PowerPoint is used too much (or too little) in classroom instruction.
   c. An important lesson learned from previous or current work experience.

   The speakers should practice trying to show a strong, positive personal presence. Listeners should provide constructive feedback. (Objective 3)

8. **Teamwork. E-mail.** Each member in a group of three should locate an article related to some aspect of business communication. Randomly assign the style (manuscript, memorized, or extemporaneous) by which each member will deliver a two-minute summary of the article. After all presentations have been given, discuss the strengths and weakness of each method from the perspective of the speaker and the audience. Summarize your conclusions in an e-mail to your instructor. (Objectives 4, 5, and 6)

9. **Teamwork. Global.** Work in groups of three to five students. Each group member should research, prepare, and deliver a two- to three-minute presentation about tipping customs in a country other than the United States. During each presentation, various listeners should give nonverbal cues for the speaker to interpret and respond to. After all group members have spoken, the listeners should provide constructive feedback. (Objectives 5 and 6)

10. Prepare and deliver a five-minute presentation on a topic approved by your instructor. Include one quote and one visual aid. (Objectives 5 and 6)

11. **InfoTrac. Teamwork. E-mail.** In spite of a speaker's best efforts, things can go wrong during a presentation, especially when technology is involved. The InfoTrac articles "Training, Low-Tech Style: When High-Tech Tools Fail, Be Ready with Flip Charts" and "Speaker's Notes: Successful Speakers Practice Expecting the Unexpected" explain some potential problems and offer suggestions on how to handle them. Access and read these articles (A94326766 and A93070475); then, do the following: (Objectives 5 and 6)

    a. Prepare one visual aid that shows the advantages and disadvantages of using flip charts and a second (different type) visual aid that offers tips for using and traveling with flip charts.

    b. Use the visuals created in 11a during a brief presentation to another group.

    c. Send an e-mail to your instructor in which you

       (1) Describe why a speaker's actions during the first minute after a problem arises are critical to handling the situation successfully.

       (2) Offer suggestions about what a speaker can do to prepare to handle problems.

12. Locate the annual report of a corporation in which you are interested. Use presentation software, or another method as your instructor directs, to present some aspect of the report to your class, who will act as the company's shareholders. Respond to questions from the audience. (Objectives 5 and 6)

13. **Teamwork. Global.** Work with six of your classmates to research the appropriate way to introduce people from a culture other than your own. Demonstrate for the class how you would introduce a head table that included political and business leaders from the United States and the country you selected. One group member should act as emcee; the others should be the head table guests. (Objective 7)

14. You have been invited to return to your high school and speak with business students about your school and your major. Prepare the opening to your presentation; include an anecdote or quote. As your instructor directs, deliver the opening to a small group or your entire class. (Objectives 5, 6, and 7)

15. **E-mail.** Project five years into the future and assume that you have accepted an invitation to speak about some aspect of your profession at a national meeting of one of its organizations. Write the introduction you would like given before your presentation. E-mail the text of the introduction to your instructor. (Objective 7).

There are Web exercises at **http://krizan.swlearning.com** to accompany this chapter.

Message Analysis

Revise and edit the following memo to reflect good organization and to ensure that its format and mechanics are accurate:

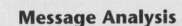

TO: *Managers*

FROM: *Alec Jacobs*

DATE: *March 12, 200–*

SUBJECT: ***Making Effective International Presentations***

In effective international presentations can results in misunderstandings, misinterpretations, and missed sales. To ensure that we make the most of our international opportunities, please follow these guidelines and share them with those in your units who make international business presentations.

1. Use simple, clear content. Word choice variety appeals to an American audience but can confuse a listener for whom English is a second language. If you use the team suggestions early in your presentation, stick with it rather than changing to advice or recommendations.

• Repeat your message several times during the presentation. Repeat—don't paraphrase. The extra time it takes will pay big dividends in audience retention and you'll reap the rewards of your efforts.

— Don't use, omit jargon, idiomatic expressions, and acronyms. That could confuse or insult your audience. Choose metaphors appropriate for the culture of your audience. Sports comparisons for baseball and golf may work well in Japan but flop in France.

3. Be deliberate in the way you use your voice. Speak in a normal presentation volume and us frequently and enunciate clearly but don't patronize.

5. When crating visuals, be aware of the way in which the colors and symbolls—including clip art—your select select will effect your audience.

Barb Schmidt will be creating a web site to address this topic. If you or your staff have personal suggestions or know of resources that should be included at the site, e-mail her at bschmidt.

Grammar Workshop

Correct the grammar, spelling, punctuation, style, and word choice errors in the following sentences:

1. Each of the resorts has an 18 whole golf coarse on sight or near by.
2. After useing Clear away for 6 weeks you will both notice that rinkles disappear and age spots fading
3. The A.M.A. has announced that they will present this years Outstanding Marketer award to Jacob Jackson principle in The Liberty Group.
4. Built in 2001 fore approximately $55.9 million dollars the River Road development contains 224 one, two, and three-bedroom apartments in seven three-story bldgs..
5. Everybody whom attended the demonstration were able to get their questions answered during the ten minute question:answer section that followed the 20 minute presentation.
6. For your convience I have inclosed a coupon good for a ten % discount which means you'll pay only 13.95 for a full-year of "the Money Manager's Guide'.
7. Known for service that is quick and quality repair work you're car will get the attention it deserves.
8. 4,400 companies-about 1/3 of those operating within the State has less then 5 hundred employees.
9. Roger Blake and his oldest daughter Cynthia have openned a public acctg firm in the Providence Bldg. On 2d street.
10. With 20 year's experience as a restaurant owner Cyril Wagner should have little difficulty establishing creditability as a caterer.

Part # 6

Employment Communication

16

The Job Search and Resume

O. Randall Powell, Vice President, Human Resources, The Valvoline Company

LET'S TALK BUSINESS An essential aspect of securing a new position is the initial communication with the prospective employer. A well-written cover letter and resume can generate interest, an interview, and ultimately a job offer.

Marketing oneself to an employer can be a frustrating and humbling experience; however, a consistent and diligent approach will be rewarded. The major focus in identifying prospective employers should be on the Internet and college placement offices. Nearly all public companies have job posting sites. The college placement office, while often overlooked and underutilized, can offer invaluable assistance to students and companies.

The initial contact with a company should be made according to its preference. Think of this as the initial screening requirement. A cover letter should state a clear work objective, provide contact and availability information, and indicate travel and relocation preferences. The resume should be one page and in chronological order. The cover letter and resume are extremely critical to generating interest for an interview. Without an interview, there will never be a job offer.

Your most important business communication will be about your employment. Randall Powell in Let's Talk Business emphasizes the importance of a well-written resume and application letter. During your life, you will spend most of your waking hours at work. Your work should be enjoyable, challenging, and rewarding. After completing this chapter and Chapter 17, you should have a plan for successfully obtaining employment—employment that best matches your interests, values, and qualifications. Also, in these chapters you will discover how to use the Internet to assist in finding a job and launching your career.

NOTE 16.1
Employment communication is your most important communication.

To obtain employment, you will conduct a job campaign. This campaign will include

- Analyzing your qualifications and job preferences
- Obtaining information about employment opportunities
- Developing resumes
- Writing application letters
- Interviewing for a job
- Preparing other employment communication

The first three steps in the job campaign are discussed in this chapter; the last three steps are discussed in Chapter 17.

Analyzing Your Qualifications and Job Preferences

LEARNING OBJECTIVE
1
Analyze your qualifications and job preferences for employment.

Because *you* are the product you are selling in your job campaign, you need to know yourself well. You will want to sell yourself honestly and fairly, but you should concentrate on your most positive features—your accomplishments, education, experience, and positive attributes. All communication with prospective employers should focus on how your skills and abilities can make a contribution in the position for which you are applying.

NOTE 16.2
Analyzing your qualifications means inventorying skills, attributes, and accomplishments.

Your first step when you begin a job search is to take an inventory of your qualifications, strengths, and interests. Then, you are ready to identify the types of positions in the job market that are a good match for you. Your campus career center is a good place to start. Ask to take an interest inventory or career decision-making test to assist you in focusing your job campaign. These career decision-making tests or assessment tools can help identify your strengths and weaknesses; pinpoint your interests and match them with your strengths; clarify your values and what matters to you, such as making money or feeling you make a difference in the world; look at the overlap among your strengths, interests, and values; and identify appropriate careers.

Analyzing your qualifications is an important part of your job campaign and includes an inventory of the skills, personal attributes, experiences, and accomplishments that you bring with you to the job marketplace. The results will be valuable as you construct your resume. Your resume will be your primary tool in securing interviews. The second part of your analysis examines job characteristics that are important to you. Researching the job market informs you of the kinds of jobs available in your field, as well as their requirements, and helps you decide the type of job you want. Your job campaign may be aimed at one particular solicited job—salesperson for Safeco Insurance Agency, for example—or it may involve sending unsolicited applications to a large number of potential employers. In either case, you will need to analyze your qualifications in relation to each job and its requirements.

NOTE 16.3
Emphasize facts about you and your accomplishments.

In most cases, you should begin your career inventory several months before you begin your employment search. In fact, inventorying your qualifications and career choices should begin well in advance of seeking employment. As a student, you would be wise to begin a prospective job file in your sophomore or junior year. Use it to file information that will be useful in your career inventory, career choice, and job search. For example, keep documents such as diplomas and awards; recognition letters, memoranda, or certificates of special accomplishments; part-time or full-time employment dates and record of earnings; and military experience records. In addition, note special training or assignments that demonstrate job skills.

In analyzing your qualifications, start by brainstorming (alone or possibly with friends and relatives) a list of facts about yourself and your accomplishments. The most important facts are evidence of your accomplishments—your achievements, honors, and knowledge. In addition, list your special qualities that could benefit a company. To complete your inventory, label five pages at the top as follows: "Individual Profile" at the top of the first page, "Education" on the next, "Experience" on the third, "References" on the fourth, and "Job Preferences" on the fifth page. These pages are worksheets to help you analyze your qualifications and strengths for the job market. At a good time of the day for you, find a quiet place and start thinking of facts about yourself. Suggestions for the kinds of facts to list are in the following sections. You will add information to these pages over a period of weeks or months, and they will provide a readily accessible source of information for you throughout your job search, application, and interview process. Figure 16.1 shows the five worksheet headings to use for these pages of your self-analysis.

FIGURE 16.1
Job Search Worksheets for Self-Analysis Inventory

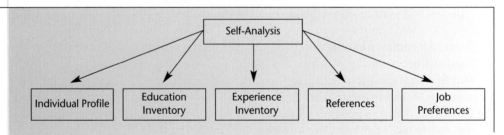

Individual Profile

NOTE 16.4
Develop your individual profile.

Start with the Individual Profile page because it will be the easiest category. Do not try to organize or evaluate the information at this point. The information on the Individual Profile sheet should include your name, temporary and/or permanent address, telephone number(s), and e-mail address. If you have a temporary address, give the expected end date for this address. You may want to include your fax number; and if you have an online resume, include its Uniform Resource Locator (URL).

Your Individual Profile should include a list of your interests and hobbies, community service activities, public-speaking experience, church activities, volunteer work, and organization memberships. As appropriate, include your accomplishments, offices held, experience gained, and honors or awards received.

On this Individual Profile page do not list your height, weight, birthdate, marital status, number of children, or religious affiliation. It is illegal for recruiters to use such information to select employees unless it is a requirement of the job; for example, age is relevant to job requirements if your position is to market or sell liquor because state law prohibits minors from holding such positions. An application for a modeling position may require a photograph.

In addition, list your special talents or skills, such as an ability to use specific software programs, write computer programs, or speak or write foreign languages. Next, list personal attributes that you would bring to a job, such as enthusiasm, a positive attitude, initiative, drive, sincerity, dependability, sense of humor, or adaptability. Include on your Individual Profile any personal information that might be of interest to an employer. For example, list your salary expectations, career objectives, and willingness to travel or relocate.

Some of the information from your Individual Profile will be used in preparing your resume. Other parts of it will assist you in choosing specific jobs, writing application letters, answering questions during interviews, and completing employment forms. Types of items to include on your Individual Profile inventory page are summarized in the following Communication Note.

COMMUNICATION NOTE

Types of Information on an Individual Profile Inventory:

Name	Church activities	Strong personal attributes
Community service	Special computer skills	Web site (if online resume)
Willingness to travel	E-mail address	Honors and awards
Address	Volunteer work	Salary expectations
Public speaking activities	Travel experience	Interests and hobbies
Skill with specific software	Fax number	Career objectives
Phone number	Organization memberships	Foreign language skills

---

Education

On the page labeled "Education," list the schools you have attended. For each school, list its name; its location; the dates you attended; your major; your minor; your grade-point average (GPA) in your major and overall; and the certificates, diplomas, or degrees you received. Indicate any special groupings of courses such as a series of office technology or management courses that qualify you for the position or positions in your job campaign. Enumerate computer software and hardware skills and specify any special projects you completed, such as a Web page. Describe teamwork experiences and group projects. List any education honors or awards received (such as outstanding student, membership in honorary organizations, dean's honor lists, certificates of recognition or appreciation, or scholarships). Specify any special research reports you have prepared. Indicate all extracurricular activities (such as professional organizations or service organization memberships, fraternity or sorority activities, intramural or intercollegiate athletics participation, community or special service activities, or study/travel abroad experiences). List any other information related to your education that might be of interest to an employer. Keep in mind that this is an inventory of your strengths for the job market—a laundry list of relevant items that can help you obtain a position

NOTE 16.5
List all your schools, key facts, and achievements.

that matches well with your career plans. The following Communication Note illustrates items from the Education inventory section.

Types of Information on an Education Inventory:

School names, locations, and dates	Computer software/hardware experiences
Diplomas, certificates, and degrees	Education honors and awards
Major and minor(s)	Membership in honorary organizations
Grade point average (GPA) or class rank	Honor roll and dean's list
Job-related courses	Certificates of recognition or appreciation
Special projects completed	Scholarships
Group projects (teamwork examples)	Professional organization memberships
Special research reports	Fraternity or sorority activities
Sports participation	Community service or other activities
Offices held	Leadership activities

Experience

NOTE 16.6
For each job, concentrate on responsibilities and accomplishments.

On the Experience page of your inventory, list all of your work experience—part time and full time. Keep in mind two basic categories as you reflect on each job you have held:

[1] Responsibilities.

[2] Accomplishments, such as achievements, knowledge or skills acquired, and contributions while performing the job.

Most persons make the mistake of listing only their job responsibilities on their resumes. Although employers are interested in the responsibilities you have had, they are more interested in how successfully you fulfilled those responsibilities. You should list all factual evidence of successful job performances (such as supervised ten employees, increased sales by 25 percent, conducted a presentation skills workshop, or earned a promotion to assistant manager). Remember to use action verbs to show your accomplishments. The first Communication Note on page 453 gives a list of action verbs.

List each job held, including any military service. For each, list your job title, name and location of employer, and dates of employment. Indicate your responsibilities and give evidence of your accomplishments. Specify what you learned while performing the job, any innovations you developed to improve job performance, sales quotas or other goals met, letters or other commendations received regarding your performance, promotions, or increases in responsibilities. List what you enjoyed most about each job, reasons why you left each job, and salaries received.

NOTE 16.7
Include applicable volunteer work.

Add any other work experience information you think might be helpful in your job campaign. You may include jobs held as a volunteer worker and internships, paid or unpaid. These jobs add to your list as experience. Including them is of special importance if you have little paid work experience. See the second Communication Note on page 453 for examples of items for both responsibilities and accomplishments for an Experience inventory.

Action Verb Examples:

accomplished	directed	mastered	redesigned
accounted for	documented	mediated	reduced
accumulated	earned	moderated	refined
adapted	established	modified	represented
administered	evaluated	monitored	researched
advised	gathered	motivated	resolved
analyzed	generated	negotiated	reviewed
applied	hired	obtained	revised
approved	identified	operated	scheduled
arranged	illustrated	ordered	secured
assembled	implemented	organized	selected
assigned	improved	originated	set up
assisted	increased	participated	simplified
attended	initiated	performed	sold
budgeted	inspected	persuaded	stimulated
built	installed	planned	summarized
collaborated	instructed	prepared	supervised
communicated	interpreted	presented	supported
computed	interviewed	presided	taught
conducted	invented	produced	tested
coordinated	investigated	promoted	trained
created	led	published	updated
decreased	listened	purchased	upgraded
delegated	made	recommended	validated
designed	managed	reconciled	wrote
developed	marketed	recruited	

Types of Experience Inventory Information:

Work experience—part time and full time	Volunteer positions held
Salary—beginning and ending	Dates of employment
Job title, employer, and supervisor	Letters or other commendations
Internships—paid or unpaid	Responsibilities
Employers' address and phone	Skills/knowledge gained
Evidence of accomplishments	Reasons for leaving positions
What you enjoyed most	Increases in responsibilities
Promotions	Military service

References

NOTE 16.8
List references who will give you favorable recommendations.

References should be individuals who know you or your work well and who are willing to write letters or talk to potential employers on your behalf. You should have at least three references and may have more if you have been employed many years. You can select as references those persons who know your character or who are former employers, current employers, professors, coworkers, or business contacts in positions similar to your career interest. Potential employers consider former or current employers the best types of references. At this point, simply list those potential references who will give you a favorable recommendation. Depending on the job you are seeking, you may use all or part of this list.

NOTE 16.9
Request permission from references to list them.

Before using anyone as a reference, ask him or her for permission. Once the person has agreed to be a reference for you, give him or her one of your current resumes, so that person can be familiar with your recent activities. Although you will need to deal honestly with any unfavorable information in your background, you are not required to list references who will hurt your chances for employment.

For each potential reference, list the person's name, title, position, organization, business (or home) address, business (or home) telephone number, fax number, and e-mail address. When you contact potential references for permission, be sure to ask where they would like to be contacted—at their business, home, or other location. Examples of inventory items for your References are shown on the following Communication Note.

COMMUNICATION NOTE

Types of Information on a References Inventory:

Employers—current and former
Persons who know your character
Persons agreeing to give a
  recommendation
Persons who will give positive
  recommendations
Professors
Coworkers

Business contacts in similar positions
Names, titles, and contact information
E-mail addresses
Business or home address
Each person's preference for contact—
  home, work, or other
Telephone numbers
Fax numbers

Job Preferences

NOTE 16.10
Analyze job characteristics important to you.

When you have completed a thorough analysis of your qualifications, you will be ready to seek information about employment opportunities. Begin identifying potential positions by analyzing your strengths and interests as they relate to the types of positions for your job search. Determine characteristics that are important for your long-term career objective (five or ten years from now). Here are sample questions to get you started:

- Do you like working indoors, outside an office environment, or in varied work environments?

- Do you want to work in a large company with a structured work environment, or do you prefer a small or less-structured company?

- Are stability and job security important to you?
- Do you enjoy influencing or persuading people?
- Do you enjoy teaching others?
- Do you value independence? challenge? chance for growth? opportunity for creativity?
- What salary range is acceptable?
- Are you willing to relocate? If so, to what geographic location?
- What are your long-term career goals?
- What types of positions are consistent with your career goals?

List those job characteristics that are important to you. Then, begin to research the market to learn about requirements and benefits for different types of positions that relate to your preferences. Read newspaper job advertisements, study company Web sites for businesses in your career field, and interview persons working in positions of interest. These sources will provide you with job characteristics and responsibilities to help you match your preferences with particular types of positions that interest you. The next Communication Note gives examples of information to consider for your Job Preferences inventory.

COMMUNICATION NOTE

Types of Information on a Job Preferences Inventory:

Short- and long-term career goals	Position responsibilities
Size of company	Acceptable salary range
Types of positions	Position advancement potential
Type of company	Job location preference
Job characteristics important to you	Job structure or independence

---

Now that you have completed an inventory of your strengths, interests, and preferences, you are ready to begin a search for employment opportunities that match your job preferences. The next section describes sources of information for locating a position.

Obtaining Information about Employment Opportunities

LEARNING OBJECTIVE
(2) *Describe five sources of information about job opportunities and job requirements.*

Finding positions for which you can apply generally requires an organized effort. You must determine available jobs and their requirements. You should include both *solicited* and *unsolicited* position openings in your job search.

A **solicited position** is a specific job for which employers are seeking applicants. These jobs are often listed on the Web by campus career centers, advertised in newspapers or journals, or announced through private or government placement agencies.

A job that is available but is unlisted or unadvertised is called an **unsolicited position**. These positions may be an important part of your job campaign. Unsolicited

NOTE 16.11
Positions are either solicited or unsolicited.

positions are obtained by direct contact with a company of your choice. You will learn of the availability of many of these positions through your network of friends, relatives, instructors, and acquaintances. Joining a professional association is important for networking with other individuals in your field. Examples of such professional associations include the Society for Human Resources Management (SHRM) for a career field in human resources, Management Information Systems Student Association (MISSA) for computer technology, or International Facilities Management Association (IFMA) for facilities management. Such a network can help provide you with information on available positions as well as keep you current in your career field.

An effective job campaign requires careful, documented research. You will want to use a variety of appropriate sources of information about the availability of jobs and about their requirements. This section of the chapter describes five sources.

Campus Career Centers

Your campus career center is a valuable source of information about jobs. Whether you are an undergraduate student looking for your first career position or a graduate seeking a change in employment, the campus career center can provide many services.

Among the placement services offered by most campus career centers are job-related publications, lists of job openings, arrangements for on-campus interviews with company representatives, maintenance of a credentials file, advice on the preparation of resumes and application letters, and guidance about or training for a job interview. These services are free or offered at minimal cost. The campus career center should be one of the first places you visit as you start your job campaign.

NOTE 16.12
Complete a search of job information sources.

NOTE 16.13
Visit your campus career center for career information and services.

Begin your job search with a visit to your campus career center.

©SPENCER GRANT/PHOTOEDIT

Of the publications available at the campus career center, the *Job Choices* series is one of the most helpful. This publication contains positions available across the nation. It lists the positions for which employers are seeking applicants and the educational requirements for those jobs. The employers are listed by geographical location, by occupational specialty, and by company name. From this list of employers, you can develop a prospect list of job opportunities in your field. The person to contact within each company is listed; this enables you to develop a mailing list for your job campaign.

Several other job-related books such as the *Occupational Outlook Handbook, Dictionary of Occupational Titles,* or job-related periodicals such as *Changing Times, High Technology,* or *Small Business Reporter* may be available at your campus career center. Trade association publications, government publications, and individual company publications may be available also. A CD-ROM software program *Job Power Source* can assist with your job search. This program or similar ones will help you set career goals, determine your work style, and find jobs.

NOTE 16.14
Job-related publications aid the job campaign.

Two major services of campus career centers are lists of specific job openings and, in larger schools and colleges, arrangements for on-campus interviews with company representatives. Generally, the lists of job openings are published and updated periodically. Campus career centers will post these listings on campus and may mail them to graduates. If you find an available position that interests you, request that the campus career center assist you with contacting the employer by sending your credentials or by arranging an on-campus interview.

To take advantage of your campus career center's services, register with that office. This registration will involve the careful, accurate, thorough, and neat completion of your credentials file. The credentials file contains information about your education and experience. Your Education and Experience inventory pages will be helpful in your preparation of credentials for your file. In addition, career center personnel may suggest that you contact references for letters of recommendation to be placed there.

NOTE 16.15
Register with the campus career center and complete your credentials file.

Completing your credentials file will serve you in your job search. The credentials file will be available to be duplicated and, with your permission or at your request, will enable the career center to provide this information to potential employers in a timely manner.

Many positions are obtained through the services of a campus career center. It should be your first source of information when you initiate a job search.

Networking Contacts

Networking through personal contacts can be an important part of your job search. Begin with a list of people you know. These individuals may be persons such as associates in professional associations and other organizations, friends, neighbors, relatives, former teachers and classmates, former military acquaintances, and persons with whom you have worked (in either paid or unpaid positions). Go through your list and place a check mark by those names that are most likely to know about employment opportunities or have contacts in your career field. Develop a telephone call sheet for these people. You will need to have columns for the person's name, telephone number, date called, and information gained. You have three goals to accomplish with your list of contacts:

NOTE 16.16
Personal networking provides valuable information about jobs and job openings.

[1] Gaining information about specific types of positions or companies.

[2] Identifying referrals for job contacts or introductions to people who may be helpful.

[3] Creating awareness that you are seeking employment opportunities.

Keep the purpose of these contacts to seek their guidance and advice—not to ask them for a job. Request a short meeting with the individual. Gaining the information that you need comes best person to person rather than by phone. The Communication Note that follows gives an outline for making calls to your contacts.

Calls to Networking Contacts:

Opening comments: Identify self and open with general, friendly comments such as "Hello, Jim. This is Joe Branson. I haven't talked with you since you returned from your vacation. How was the fishing?"

Creating awareness of job search: "Jim, I am currently investigating employment opportunities that will get me started toward my career goals. I know that you have considerable experience as an accountant, and this is the career that I would like to pursue."

Requesting a meeting and suggesting a time: "I would like an opportunity to schedule a half-hour meeting with you to learn about the job responsibilities, benefits, and opportunities for advancement. Would next Wednesday at 8 p.m. be convenient for you?"

Confirming the meeting and closing the call: "Thanks, Jim. Wednesday at 6:30 p.m. will work for me. I appreciate your taking time to meet with me to share information about your work. I know it will be helpful. I will see you next Wednesday."

These contacts may not know of job opportunities but may know someone in the career field. Getting the name of such a person enables you to make another contact to learn more about jobs related to your career objective. When you call, explain the purpose of your call (that you are interested in employment in this career field and that her or his name was suggested as someone knowledgeable of the field), and mention by name the person who suggested this contact. Having a mutual acquaintance who considered her or him as a knowledgeable contact creates a positive opening. Suggest a date and time for a short meeting to discuss careers in this field. At such a meeting, you may not only learn valuable information about this type of position but also you may learn of a job opening or get another contact name.

Networking with acquaintances to learn about careers and employment opportunities may seem time consuming; however, personal contacts and acquaintances often open the door for an interview that leads to a good position in a particular career field. In the Communications Quote by Michael Farr, he emphasizes the importance of not limiting your job search to solicited position openings because only a small percentage of openings are advertised. Most openings are filled through personal contacts.

Talking directly with people to whom you are referred by a mutual acquaintance gives you an opportunity to gain information that will give you an edge over other applicants. This networking figuratively "gets your foot in the door" and offers a higher potential for results than sending resumes as your first contact for employment. However, you should have copies of your resume with you when you meet with your network contacts. When appropriate, you will be ready to leave a resume with the contact.

The Internet

The Internet provides another means for seeking your career position and making worthwhile connections. The Web opens a new arena of job hunting for you! You can find a number of Web sites for accessing information on how to conduct a job search on the Web, how to develop and post an online resume, how to learn about the various companies, and which companies have openings in your field. Most career sites have fees paid by employers listing openings or individuals posting their resume. Be cautious, however, of large up-front fees. Know what you are receiving for a fee. If in doubt, consult your local Better Business Bureau.

To begin a cyberspace job search you must first have a computer and access to the Web. A good place to start your job search is on your campus career center's home page, which will have links to other job-related resources. The Communication Note lists Web sites that can be helpful in a job search. Locating positions on the Internet and posting your resume online can lead to job openings. However, don't rely on it as your only job search method. Using a variety of sources to locate employment opportunities increases your chance for success.

NOTE 16.18
Explore popular career center Web sites.

COMMUNICATION NOTE

Web Sites for Career Planning and Job Search:

http://www.BlastMyResume.com
http://www.careerbuilder.com
http://www.monstertrak.com
http://www.rileyguide.com
http://jobstar.org/tools/resume/index.cfm
http://www.jobfind.com
http://www.careermag.com

http://www.careerjournal.com
http://www.jobweb.com
http://usajobs.opm.gov
http://www.ajb.dni.us
http://www.collegegrad.com
http://internships.wetfeet.com
http://www.career.com

These are only a few of the Web site addresses for job searching online. You may contact your campus career center staff or Internet directory indexes for additional sites because new ones are added regularly and old ones sometimes change the Web-site location. As you surf the Internet and the many career-related sites, select sites that are current, look out for sales pitches, check the fees for listing your resume, be selective in contacting potential employers, and ask what type of confidentiality or privacy protection the site offers for your resume. A job search on the Web is just another tool to assist you in locating your career position.

NOTE 16.19
Check company Web sites for job openings.

Many companies have a Web page and often have information on their Web site about job openings and their application process; a number of companies now accept online applications. If you have identified specific companies as potential employers, locate their Web page. Using the company name or an abbreviated version of the name followed by *.com* may locate the Web home page. The **.com** ending signifies a commercial enterprise. A search by company name on an Internet directory or search engine such as google.com is another means of locating a company's Web site.

Newspaper and Journal Advertisements

NOTE 16.20
Classified ads are sources of job leads.

The classified advertisement sections of newspapers and many trade or professional journals are sources of information about job openings. You can obtain trade or professional journals for your field at your school library or public library. Also, you may access classified ads from the *Boston Globe, New York Times, Los Angeles Times, Chicago Tribune, Washington Post, San Jose Mercury,* and several other newspapers at **http://www.careerbuilder.com.** Job search information can be found also in *USA Today* at **http://www.usatoday.com** by searching for *Job Center.*

NOTE 16.21
Generally, journal ads are national in scope; newspaper ads are local.

Although journal job advertisements generally are national in scope, newspaper job advertisements are a source of information about specific positions in a given geographic area. Most classified advertisements of position openings also carry information about the job requirements and salary levels. By studying advertisements, you can determine available jobs in a geographic area, salary ranges, and job requirements. Most newspapers have several editions, and the job opening advertisements may vary from edition to edition. If you wish to relocate to Miami, for example, be aware that the edition of the *Miami Tribune* distributed within Miami will be likely to contain a more comprehensive listing of job openings than the edition distributed elsewhere. If you plan to relocate to a specific area, you may want to subscribe to one or more of the papers published there or access the online edition of the newspaper.

Private or Government Employment Agencies

NOTE 16.22
Private agencies can be sources of job listings.

Private employment agencies bring together job seekers and employers. Their services will be similar to those offered by your campus career center. Private employment agencies are in business both to provide these specialized services and to make a profit. Therefore, either the employee or the employer will have to pay the significant fee charged. Before using a private employment agency, be sure that you understand clearly what services are provided, how much the fee will be, and who is to pay the fee.

Another category of private employment agency is the nonprofit service of professional organizations. Some professional organizations publish job opening announcements, provide a hotline with recorded job listings, assist in linking job seekers and employers at professional conferences, and maintain a credentials file service. These services are usually offered at low or no cost to members. To determine services available to you from professional organizations, ask a professional in your field.

Public employment agencies can be found at all levels of government: federal, state, regional, and local. There is usually no charge for their services.

At the federal government level, the U.S. Office of Personnel Management administers an extensive employment service. There are hundreds of area federal employment offices throughout the United States that are sources of job opportunities within the U.S. government. You can locate your nearest federal employment office by contacting any federal government agency in your area. Also, at the federal level, there are job opportunities available in the United States Army, Navy, Marines, Coast Guard, and Air Force. These branches of the military service have recruiters in most local communities. The U.S. government's official Web site for jobs and employment information can be found at http://www.usajobs.opm.gov/. America's Job Bank also lists jobs that can be found in the 50 states and can be viewed at http://www.ajb.dni.us.

NOTE 16.23
Government employment agencies are job sources.

State governments provide employment services. These services are more extensive than the employment services provided by the federal government. They include employment opportunities both in the private sector and in the state government. Most states have regional employment offices throughout the state to serve local geographic areas. Usually, you can locate these services by looking under the name of your state in the telephone book, by contacting any state government office, or by searching the Web.

Local and regional government agencies provide employment services to link potential employees with positions within their agencies. Cities, counties, and regional service units are all sources of jobs. Usually, you can locate their employment or personnel offices by looking in the telephone book under the name of the government unit, city, county, or region.

NOTE 16.24
Local and regional employment offices provide information on job openings.

Many cities and chambers of commerce publish directories listing the names, addresses, and phone numbers of businesses in their localities. These directories often contain the names of top executives and departmental managers and are a good source for contacting individual businesses for possible unpublished job openings. Also, a search engine on the Web will help locate this information.

Other Sources

In an aggressive, vigorous job campaign, you will want to seek assistance from all sources. It is good initially to throw your net wide and then narrow your search. You may even want to advertise your job interests and qualifications in a newspaper or journal to obtain job leads, or you may contact the human resources office of companies with positions in your field.

Expect to spend several weeks or months in the job search process. Finding the right position is one of the most important activities that you will pursue. Keep a positive attitude and maintain confidence in yourself and the strengths that you can bring to an employer. Throughout the employment process, keep the focus on how your strengths and skills can make a contribution to the prospective employer.

NOTE 16.25
A job search takes several weeks or months; stay positive.

Preparing a Resume

A **resume** is a summary of your qualifications. It should be a clear, concise, positive review of who you are and what you have to offer an employer. Resumes should be written concisely and clearly because estimates show that employers spend only about 30 seconds per resume in their first screenings.

While most job applicants use a standard written resume, some use a videotape, CD, portfolio, or electronic resume. Assistance in creating a videotape resume for sales,

LEARNING OBJECTIVE
③ *Prepare targeted and general resumes in chronological, functional, or combination format.*

NOTE 16.26
A resume is a summary
of your qualifications.

NOTE 16.27
Some job applicants use
videotape, CD-ROM,
portfolio, or electronic
resumes.

NOTE 16.28
The primary purpose of
your resume is to obtain
a job interview.

NOTE 16.29
Use targeted resumes for
specific jobs.

NOTE 16.30
Use general resumes for
unsolicited jobs.

acting, and other selected job applications is available from some campus career centers and private employment services. Assistance in developing an attractive portfolio of items such as drawings, designs, writing samples, and projects for advertising, sales promotion, graphic arts, and other similar positions is available from individual faculty members and other professionals in your field. Particularly good course papers can be edited with faculty assistance and used in your portfolio. Some programs of study require a portfolio of work that demonstrates achievement. Selected items from such work can be useful in preparing a portfolio to help market your job skills.

Some applicants place their credentials on file with a resume database service. Employers seeking to fill positions can have direct online access to the database to search for candidates, or the service agency will do it for them. Both the candidate and the employer pay fees for this service.

Practically all applicants, however, must use standard written resumes if they are to be successful in securing job interviews. The rest of this chapter describes how to develop an effective written resume.

The primary purpose of a resume, along with an application letter, is to obtain a job interview. Fewer than one in ten employment applications results in an interview. Knowing that this statistic applies to all applicants can help you avoid feeling rejected as an individual. If your resume is better than your competitors' resumes in both appearance and content, you improve your chances of being that one person in ten who gets an interview. If you do not get an interview, you will not be hired.

Styles of Resumes

There are two basic types of traditional resumes: targeted and general. Either type can have a chronological, functional, or combination arrangement.

TARGETED RESUME

A **targeted resume** is prepared for a specific job application. It is individually keyed and printed, and it contains information to show specifically how you qualify for that one job. Accomplishments and skills on the resume can be tailored to requirements described for the position. In addition, for college courses completed within the last five years, list those that apply to responsibilities of the specific job.

A targeted resume is powerful and should be used for solicited job applications. A word processing program makes it easy to prepare, personalize, and update your resume.

GENERAL RESUME

A **general resume** is a description of your qualifications that can be used for any job related to your career objective and sent to more than one potential employer. It is appropriate for use when applying for unsolicited jobs that have similar characteristics. For example, if you apply for management trainee positions or a management internship position in several different companies with similar needs, you can send a general resume to prospective employers.

Formats for Resumes

The three basic resume formats are chronological, functional, and combination. The *chronological resume* is referred to also as a *traditional* or *traditional reverse chronological* resume. The *functional resume* may be called a *skills-oriented* or *nontraditional* resume.

The third format, the *combination resume*, uses features of both the chronological and functional resumes.

CHRONOLOGICAL FORMAT

A **chronological resume** has information in each section organized by date, with the most recent information listed first within each section. For example, in the section containing your experience, your current or most recent position is described first. The resume then describes each previous position, with the first position you held listed last. The same chronological approach is used in the sections for education, activities, community service, or any other section containing information accumulated over time.

Most employers prefer the chronological format because it gives the information they need in a familiar sequence and helps them compare resumes. If employers have to search too hard to find a vital bit of information about you, your application may go into the reject pile. This format enables employers to identify gaps in your work experience, as it emphasizes dates of employment, names and addresses of employers, job titles, and responsibilities. Both Figures 16.2 and 16.3 show a traditional chronological format for a resume. Figure 16.2 is a targeted resume sent in response to a position for an Assistant Property Manager for multi-family rental units. The job ad says that the preferred applicant should have excellent people skills, pay attention to detail, and have experience with sales and customer service. Figure 16.3 is a general resume. Both of the resumes represent a recent college graduate with part-time experience gained while attending school. In the first resume, Experience comes before Education because of work experience skills relevant to requirements of the targeted job. The Education section of the second student is stronger than Experience and, therefore, comes first on the resume.

NOTE 16.31
Chronological resumes are organized by date, with most recent listed first.

FUNCTIONAL FORMAT

A **functional resume** provides information in a format that emphasizes qualifications categorized by skills and knowledge and related accomplishments—in other words, by functions. Experiences and accomplishments are grouped under function or skill headings pertinent to your career objective. For example, headings used for functions may include *Management, Marketing* (or *Sales*), *Advertising, Communication,* or *Leadership.* This format is creative and is particularly appropriate for positions such as advertising, designing, or copy writing. Also, the functional format is useful to emphasize your strengths when you have already provided all the standard information to the employer in an application form.

The functional format for a resume works well for an individual who has been out of the job market for a number of years, has little employment experience, or has held several jobs and needs to combine them to make the presentation more concise or more favorable. An example of a resume in functional format is shown in Figure 16.4. This graduate has a strong experience record related to his career goal.

NOTE 16.32
The functional format emphasizes qualifications—skills, knowledge, and accomplishments.

COMBINATION FORMAT

Some applicants use a **combination resume**, which blends the strengths of the chronological format with the strengths of the functional format. Combination resumes work well for individuals with little work experience who are just entering the job market. Figure 16.5 displays a one-page combination resume for a recent college graduate with limited experience other than internship experience and part-time work while attending college.

NOTE 16.33
Combination resumes combine chronological and functional formats.

FIGURE 16.2
Chronological Format of
a One-Page Targeted
Resume

Shawn Watson
1234 Walkers' Way
Columbus, OH 43210
909.555.1212
swatson@email.net

Complete contact
information.

Objective for a specific
type of position.

OBJECTIVE
Property Management for multi-family unit residential property buildings

SUMMARY OF QUALIFICATIONS
- Graduated with a Bachelor of Arts in Business Administration (GPA, 3.8 out of 4)
- Earned 75% of my university tuition through part-time work with a major hotel
- Promoted from desk clerk to night manager; supervised 4 evening staff members
- Modified reservation computer data-entry procedures that reduced entry time by 30%
- Gained valuable people skills through meeting customer needs and motivating staff

Highlights data-entry
and people skills.

EXPERIENCE
Night Manager, Holiday Hotel, Sunset Avenue, Columbus, OH 43210
April 2002–Present

Most recent date first.

Responsibilities:
- Supervised 4 employees
- Maintained computerized accounting and reservation system
- Greeted and registered guests
- Balanced cash register receipts each night and made bank deposits

Major
accomplishments.

Major Accomplishments:
- Developed a batch data-entry system for computerized reservations
- Had no evening staff turnover during two years as night manager

Desk Clerk, Holiday Hotel, Sunset Avenue, Columbus, OH 43210
August 2001–March 2002

Responsibilities:
- Greeted and registered guests and assigned rooms
- Entered and verified data in guest registration database
- Completed guest checkouts and recorded cash receipts
- Handled multiple situations to ensure high-quality guest services

Major Accomplishments:
- Promoted to night manager
- Improved registration procedures that reduced guest check-in time by 5 minutes
- Gained communication and problem-solving skills

Appliance Sales and **Building Custodian,** XYZ Appliances, Middlesex Blvd., Columbus, OH 43206
August 2000–July 2001

Responsibilities:
- Sales clerk for kitchen appliances
- Evening custodial duties to clean and straighten store for the next day

Major Accomplishments:
- Recognized as top salesperson (out of a sales force of 4) for 3 of 6 months of employment
- Promoted from building custodian to salesperson

EDUCATION
B.S. in Business Administration, The Ohio State University, Columbus (May 2004)
Dean's Honor Roll 5 of 8 semesters
Major courses in business communication, financial management, and organizational planning

SPECIAL SKILLS
Experienced with computer software, including PowerPoint, Word, Excel, Access, and customized computer accounting systems

KATIE E. PARKER

451 Peninsula Way
Erie, PA 16523

General position
objective.

E-mail: *keparker@net.com*
Phone: (814) 555-2345

OBJECTIVE   An office administration position

EDUCATION   Lake Erie Community College, Erie, PA 16523
Associate of Arts Degree, June 2003
Administrative Management Major

Reverse order for
education and
experience.

Pertinent Classes:
• Administrative Management
• Principles of Management
• Communication for Management
• Business Telecommunication
• Microcomputer Applications for Administrative Personnel

Achievements:
• Ranked 5th in class of 200
• President, Administrative Management Club

Erie Technical College, Erie, PA 16523
Administrative Assistant Certificate Program, 1998

Limited experience.

EXPERIENCE   Student Assistant, Registrar's Office, Lake Erie Community College,
August 2002–June 2003
• Assisted students with transcript questions
• Assisted with development and maintenance of Registrar's Web
  home page
• Filed student records

Volunteer, Santa Theresa Hospital, Erie, PA 16523,
Summers, 2002–2003
• Served gift shop customers quickly and courteously
• Stocked and counted inventory

COMPUTER SKILLS

WordPerfect	FrontPage	Netscape
PowerPoint	Peachtree Accounting	Windows
Excel	Access	Web-page design

**SPECIAL SKILLS
AND ACTIVITIES**   Speak and write Spanish fluently
Experience as a high school exchange student in Mexico City,
    September 1998–May 1999

Multicultural
strengths.

Format for a Resume

The format you choose depends on the job you are seeking. Managers who review resumes and make decisions on who will be invited for an interview generally prefer
chronological resumes; therefore, they are more appropriate for most job campaigns.
Chronological resumes make it easy to recognize a continuous job history; and reasons
for gaps in the job history should be explained on the resume: 1999–2000, "Completed
a mission tour in China," "Studied for the CPA examination," or "Served as a full-time
parent after the birth of a child."

If you are applying for a position in a conservative organization or conservative
industry, such as banking, public accounting, or manufacturing, you should use the

NOTE 16.34
Each resume format fits
certain situations.

FIGURE 16.4
Functional Format of a
One-Page Resume for a
College Graduate with
Extensive Work
Experience

DENNIS HERNANDEZ
d.hernandz@home.net

Present Address
734 Perrin Drive
Detroit, MI 48289
Phone: 888.555.8743

Complete addresses
given.

Permanent Address (after 5/15/05)
Route 5, Box 345
Homestead, FL 33030-7123
Phone: 305.555.9215

Specific job objective.

CAREER OBJECTIVE—Human resources director for a Fortune 500 company

SKILLS DEVELOPED THROUGH EXPERIENCE

Skills by topics instead
of job.

Management Skills: Led a team of personnel classification specialists, classification assistants, and clerical support staff in classifying, managing, and organizing review and analysis of organizational staffing. Supervised recruitment, selection, and hiring of personnel to fill 25 vacant positions over three years. Administered personnel transfers and retirements. Received Certificate of Excellence for highest retention rate of 10 regional offices. Analyzed and revised work policies for the human resources department.

Skills as past tense
verbs.

Interpersonal Skills: Counseled employees in career decisions. Coordinated program for merit bonuses up to $15,000. Helped design voluntary termination program. Applied the Malcolm Baldrige Quality Criteria and Benchmarking to human resources operations to analyze work processes and implement reorganization.

Training and Development: Presented 10 seminars and counseled employees on education benefits. Developed cross-training seminars. Conducted leadership training.

Employee Health and Wellness: Supervised wellness activities. Administered insurance claims and counseled employees on health benefits. Published an employee wellness monthly newsletter.

EMPLOYMENT
2002 to present. **Human Resources Manager,** International Business Machines, 155 Ford Bypass, Detroit, MI 48290
2001, **Human Resources Consulting,** self-employed, Miami, FL 33146
2000, **Human Resources Specialist,** Martin Fabric Company, Pleasant Cove Drive, Miami, FL 33148

EDUCATION
Miami State University, Miami, FL 33148
BS Degree in Business Administration, May 1999
Human Resources Management Major
Managerial Computing Minor

Emphasizes job skills,
not education.

traditional chronological resume. If you are applying for a position in advertising, sales promotion, or entertainment, your best choice may be the nontraditional functional format. If you are a recent college graduate with little work experience, you may want to use the combination format.

Regardless of the type or format of resume you use, it should be a carefully prepared, accurate, attractive, high-quality representation of you. As has been indicated, it is the primary sales tool you will use to obtain an interview. Through the wording of the content of your resume, you are conveying to employers information about yourself that will help them determine how you fit their requirements for the position.

Preparing Your Resume

NOTE 16.35
Resumes have commonly
used sections.

With the information you developed when you analyzed your qualifications and the job market, you are now ready to prepare your resume. Follow the principles of busi-

MARY CAROL CHEN
P.O. Box 515
Coulterville, TN 37373
Home: 510.555.1751
E-mail: *mcchen@net.com*

> Objective for a job title.

OBJECTIVE
To obtain a position as a senior accountant

Summary of Qualifications
MBA degree in financial management. One-year accounting internship. Skills with computerized journal entry and financial reporting. Experience with commercial and customized accounting software. Set up and implemented an accounting system for a $500,000 net income real estate business.

> Accounting and finance highlighted.

Education
Owen School of Business, Vanderbilt University, Nashville, TN 37215
MBA in Financial Management, May 2004
4.0 GPA (4=A)

> Reverse chronological dates.

Murray State University, Murray, KY 42071
B.S. in Accounting, May 2003
3.98 GPA (4=A)

Paducah Community College, Paducah, KY 42003
A.A. in Office Administration, May 2001

Student Member of American Accounting Association (2001–2002)

Experience
2004–Present, Accountant, Finance Division, MYX Real Estate Properties, 1512 Charlsey Street, Nashville, TN 37215
2003, Accounting Intern (part time), Promble and Lane Pharmaceuticals, Nashville, TN 37215
2002, Accountant (part time), Polaris Realties, Inc., 215 Riverside, Paducah, KY 42001

> Skills grouped by categories.

ACCOUNTING
Experienced with maintaining computerized journals and ledgers, making correcting and closing entries, and preparing financial statements. Established and maintained an accounting system for a real estate company with approximately $500,000 net income.

COMPUTER SKILLS
Gained proficiency with a customized accounting computer system for a pharmaceutical company. Skilled in Peachtree, QuickBooks, Excel, Access, and Word software and SQL programming.

COMMUNICATION
Worked with a team of four accountants during accounting internship. Attended weekly Total Quality Management (TQM) team meetings and collaborated to improve accounting practices.

FINANCE
Conducted internal audits of cash receipts and disbursements.

Activities
> Leadership activities listed last.

Habitat for Humanity volunteer
Captain of intramural soccer team

FIGURE 16.5
Combination Format of a One-Page General Resume for a College Graduate with Limited Full-Time Experience

ness communication, but exercise creativity in presenting the best possible picture of yourself. The following are the major sections commonly addressed in preparation of a resume:

[1] Opening

[2] Education

[3] Experience

[4] Activities, honors, or special skills

[5] References

You may not need or want all these sections in your resume. Also, you may want to arrange them in some other order, or you may choose different or additional section headings such as Work History or Key Accomplishments. For example, if your experience is your strong point, it should be presented immediately following the opening. If you are a recent college graduate and have limited experience, have the education section follow the opening.

NOTE 16.36
Scanning a resume transfers it to a format for database entry.

More and more companies are scanning paper resumes into an electronic database. **Scanning a resume** means that the paper document is changed to an electronic format for computer storage and processing. Placing only your name on the first line and using a simple resume format that begins all or most items at the left margin improves its likelihood of being database compatible. Later in this chapter scannable resumes are discussed in greater detail. Before formatting a targeted paper resume, you can contact the human resources department of the prospective company to ask if they scan all resumes and, if so, any special formatting required.

Opening

NOTE 16.37
The opening includes a heading and an objective.

The opening of your resume should include a heading, your job and/or career objective, and, if appropriate, a summary of your qualifications. The purposes of the opening are to get potential employers to read the remainder of the resume, to inform them briefly of your interests and qualifications, and to make it easy for them to contact you.

HEADING

NOTE 16.38
The heading must include your name, address, telephone number, and e-mail address.

A resume heading includes information for contacting you. Your name, address, telephone number, and e-mail address are essential. You may want to include your fax number and a Web address to showcase a home page or reference an online resume. Be sure that your name is on a line by itself and is in the largest or darkest type. If you include a temporary school address and telephone number, give an ending date for that address and, in addition, give a permanent address. If you do not currently have a permanent address, you may use your parents' or a friend's address where your mail may be sent; or you could rent a post-office box.

A voice mail greeting on your telephone should be professional because potential employers will be telephoning your home. If you have a Web site, it should be professional and businesslike in case employers are assessing it. A prospective employer will receive an impression of you not only from the design of your home page but also by the content of this page and its links. Features or links that detract from a professional image will hurt rather than help. Remember that the majority of potential employers prefer a conservative, traditional resume. Here are three examples of resume headings:

[1]
MIKE ALVINO
malvino@nc.net
1910 Ginnway Drive
New Castle, DE 19720-2810
Telephone (302) 555-1933
Fax (302) 555-1930

[2]   **BRIETTA D'AMORE**
                              bdamore@mind.net

Current Address (until 5/30/06):   **Permanent Address:**
P.O. Box 826   917 Wellman Drive
Bridgeport, CT 06600-0835   Bridgeport, CT 06600-0826
(203) 555-9173   (203) 555-7845

[3]   **Shawn Watson**
                              1234 Dell Way
                             Pomona, CA 91768
                              909.555.1212
                            swatson@email.net

CAREER OBJECTIVE

Prospective employers like to see a Career Objective, sometimes called Objective, in the opening of a resume so they can tell whether their interests match yours. Your objective can be either specific or general. Use a specific objective for a targeted position and a general objective for a wider variety of positions that match your qualifications and work experience. For solicited positions, read the ad carefully to make sure that the career objective you write fits the position!

Keep the objective brief, clear, and direct. It tells the employer the type of position that you seek. Remember to use words carefully when preparing the objective. Here are examples:

Specific Career Objectives

[1] *Objective:* To obtain an internship in marketing with a Fortune 500 company.

[2] *Career Objective:* To obtain a position as a human resources director in the health care industry.

[3] *Objective:* An Administrative Assistant position with Third Street Bank.

General Career Objectives

[1] *Career Objective:* A challenging position in sales and marketing.

[2] *Career Objective:* A career-entry position leading to sales management. Long-term goal is to become a manager of a major department store.

[3] *Objective:* Payroll Specialist position with an opportunity for career advancement in an accounting department.

SUMMARY OF QUALIFICATIONS

This section provides a brief abstract of your qualifications. Other titles for this section are Qualifications Summary, Key Accomplishments, Major Achievements, Selected Achievements, and Summary of Accomplishments. In this section include *statements* or *phrases* that describe you and your accomplishments. Prepare your Summary of Qualifications section after you have completed the remainder of the resume so that you can select the most important facts to highlight in this section. Although including this section is optional, some employers like to see a summary statement in the opening of a resume so they can tell if your qualifications fit the position requirements.

NOTE 16.39
Make sure the Career Objective matches the position opening.

NOTE 16.40
A qualifications summary gives important achievements related to the objective.

Items should be specific to your career objective. Use parallel construction of statements. Strong action verbs make a good beginning for each statement (refer to the action verb list in the first part of this chapter). Inasmuch as possible, use numbers to report achievements. Here are examples:

[1]   **Summary of Qualifications**

Graduated with a Bachelor of Science in Business Administration with emphasis on computer information systems. Worked part time for four years in a variety of jobs from building custodian to hotel night manager-bookkeeper. Gained experience in working effectively with people and using a computerized reservation system.

[2]   **General Qualifications**

- Successful experience in retail sales.
- Three promotions for consistently exceeding quotas by 10%.
- Associate of Arts degree in retail sales management.
- Dean's Honor Roll for last four quarters.

[3]   **KEY ACCOMPLISHMENTS**

Supervised 5 employees.
Set up an accounting system for a $500,000 real estate business.
Negotiated a maintenance contract that saved the company $10,000 a year.
Served two terms as Vice Chair of the local real estate association.

Education

NOTE 16.41
Education may be the strongest section for a recent graduate.

Following your resume Opening, present your strongest qualifications. If you are, or soon will be, a college graduate and have limited experience, your education and related activities will be your strongest qualifications. If you have been employed and your work experiences match well with the job you are seeking, your Experience section should follow the Opening.

If you have or soon will be graduated from a postsecondary institution, it is unnecessary to review your high school record in the Education section. However, if while in high school you developed a job-related skill, you may want to include this skill. For example, if you are applying for a position in international business, you may want to state that while in high school you participated in a foreign exchange program and lived abroad for a year. Listing a high school is acceptable also if you wish to return to an area but no longer have a permanent residence address there.

Titles that you might use for this section are Education, Educational Qualifications, Educational Background, Specialized Education, Education and Credentials, Academic Preparation, Professional Education, Educational Data, and Educational Preparation. Remember that all headings at the same level should have parallel construction. If you attended several schools before earning a degree, consider using a statement such as "Degree included courses transferred from. . . ." rather than listing each school as a separate entry.

NOTE 16.42
Place the most recent information first on a chronological resume.

For the chronological resume, remember that the most recent information is listed first. In the Education section list the name and location of each school attended and the dates of attendance. Also, for each school show your degrees, major, and other selected information to reflect your achievements and extent of learning. Here are examples:

[1]   *Education*

University of North Dakota, Grand Forks, North Dakota
Bachelor of Science Degree, June 2005
Business Administration Major
Dean's Honor Roll last five semesters
GPA: 3.3 (4.0 = A)

[2]   *Educational Qualifications*

Dade County Community College, Miami, Florida
Associate of Arts in Office Administration (2001)
Courses specific to a position as office administrative assistant: Word processing, computer systems, keyboarding, business communication, and records management

Marshall High School, Marshall, Florida
College Preparatory Diploma (2000)
Ranked 10th in class of 100
Leadership Activities: Business Club (President), Hi-Y (Treasurer), Student Council (Secretary), Senior Yearbook Editor, Band, Basketball, American Field Service (AFS) Student to Japan

[3]   EDUCATIONAL PREPARATION

Central Washington University, Ellensburg, Washington
B.S. in Business Education, June 2006 (expected graduation)
Business Education Major and English Minor
GPA: 3.3 (major)

Experience

For applicants other than new graduates, employers rate work experience as the most important information in a resume. More decisions to grant or not to grant interviews are based on the quality of work experience than on any other basis.

Although all your work experience is important, the work experience that prepared you for the position you are seeking is especially important and should be highlighted. Your experience indicates your record of responsibility and accomplishments, provides the primary sources for references, and reflects your personality and personal preferences. When analyzing your qualifications and preparing an Experience inventory worksheet, you developed the information needed for the Experience section of your resume. Now you must decide how to present it most effectively.

Your accomplishments should be the focal point of your experience presentation, including what you learned from the experience, your achievements, and your contributions to each position. Your responsibilities for each position may also be listed briefly. Use appropriate action verbs in your listings of accomplishments and responsibilities. Use present tense verbs for current employment. For each position you should include dates of employment, job title, employer, and employer's address. Remember that for the chronological resume, you should list the most recent information first.

Depending on the format of your resume, your experience may be presented using a chronological, functional, or combination format. The following examples show how the same information might be presented in different formats:

NOTE 16.43
Experience is rated highly by employers.

NOTE 16.44
Focus on your accomplishments.

FIGURE 16.6
Example of the
Experience Section of a
Traditional Chronological
Resume

EXPERIENCE

Night Manager, Holiday Hotel, Sunset Avenue, Columbus, OH 43210 (2002–Present)

Responsibilities
- Supervise four employees.
- Greet and register guests.
- Maintain accounting and guest records.

Achievements
- Learned to work effectively with people.
- Gained skills in meeting difficult customer needs.
- Developed new guest accounting procedures that save an average of two hours of clerical time each night.

Part-time Work, Various Employers in the Columbus Area August 2000–March 2002

Responsibilities
- Hotel desk clerk, research assistant, appliance salesperson, and building custodian.

Achievements
- Promoted from hotel desk clerk to night manager.
- Learned research techniques while assisting professor in business communication study.
- Led appliance sales force of four in sales during three of six months of employment.
- Learned to work with a variety of people.

FIGURE 16.7
Example of the
Experience Section of a
Functional Resume

SKILLS DEVELOPED THROUGH EXPERIENCE

MANAGERIAL SKILLS	As a hotel night manager, developed skills in motivating employees and performing a variety of jobs. Assumed additional responsibilities readily. Improved employee productivity. Observed other managers and practiced their effective behavior.
COMMUNICATION SKILLS	Communicated clearly and concisely with employees and customers in many different situations.
	Developed ability to provide written and oral reports for financial and customer accounting data.
ACCOUNTING SKILLS	Developed thorough knowledge of double-entry book-keeping system. Became proficient in completing trial balances, balance sheets, profit and loss statements, and other financial statements.

FIGURE 16.8
Example of the
Experience Section of a
Combination Resume

**Night Manager, Holiday Hotel, Sunset Avenue, Columbus, OH 43210
April 2002–present**

Supervise four employees, greet and register guests, and maintain accounting and guest records.

MANAGEMENT

Developed new guest accounting procedures that save an average of two hours of clerical time each night, observed other managers and practiced their effective behavior, and improved employee productivity by developing a team concept.

COMMUNICATION

Learned to communicate clearly and concisely with employees and customers in different situations, developed written and oral reports for financial and customer accounting data, and gained skill in meeting difficult customer needs.

ACCOUNTING

Developed a thorough knowledge of double-entry bookkeeping and became proficient in completing trial balances, balance sheets, profit and loss statements, and other financial statements.

Part-time Work, Various Employers in the Columbus Area (2000–2002)

Held positions as hotel desk clerk, research assistant, appliance salesperson, and building custodian.

MANAGEMENT

Promoted from hotel desk clerk to night manager, led appliance sales force of four, and assumed responsibility for building maintenance.

COMMUNICATION

Learned to work with a variety of people.

ACCOUNTING

Balanced cash register receipts each night, prepared bank deposit for evening receipts, and made night bank deposit.

Activities, Honors, Special Skills, or Other Appropriate Titles

Include additional sections in your resume if your background justifies them. Any additional section that you include should be one that employers would consider positively. For example, if you were involved extensively in extracurricular activities during college, include a separate section on these activities immediately following the education section. Your background may justify a separate section on honors, special skills, computer competence, community services, published works, public presentations, military service, organization memberships, special interests, or any number of other possible categories. If you have a variety of activities, you may combine them into one section labeled simply Activities. The heading of the section should reflect the contents accurately. The important point is that you should not leave out any vital information that would enhance your resume. For the chronological resume, list the most recent activities first.

NOTE 16.45
Include special sections if
related to your qualifications for the job.

NOTE 16.46
Place special sections in
appropriate locations in
your resume.

Special sections should be placed near related information or at an appropriate point of emphasis. For example, a special section on academic honors should follow the Education section. A special interests section, because it is likely less important, should be placed at the end of the resume, just before the References. It is best not to list References in the last section of a resume; instead list them on a separate sheet. Briefly describe organizations that may be unfamiliar to readers (see Alpha Kappa Delta in the second example of the following special sections of resumes).

[1]   HONORS
Outstanding Employee, Bison Excavators, 2003
Boise Citizens' Sparkplug Award, 2002
Outstanding Young Woman in Idaho Award, 2001

[2]   EXTRACURRICULAR ACTIVITIES
President, Alpha Kappa Delta (Sociology honorary society), 2003–2004
Secretary-Treasurer, Alpha Kappa Delta, 2002
Social Chair, Alpha Kappa Delta, 2001
Northwood Representative, Cultural Awareness Program, 2001
Coach, Northwood Cross Country Team, 2000
Business Manager, *State College News*, 2000

[3]   ORGANIZATION MEMBERSHIPS
Coordinator of Marketing, Information Technology Association, 2002–Present
Administrative Management Association, 2000–2001 (Chapter Secretary, 2001)
Habitat for Humanity, 1999–2001
International Facilities Management Association, 1999–2000
Civitan Club, 1996–1998 (Club President, 1997; Area Governor, 1998)

[4]   SPECIAL SKILLS
Have proficiency in Microsoft computer software: PowerPoint, Word, Excel, Access, and FrontPage. Speak and write Spanish fluently. Speak and understand limited Mandarin and Japanese. Keyboard at 75 words per minute. Know how to use most electronic office equipment.

[5]   SPECIAL INTERESTS
Tennis, jogging, basketball, photography, and cooking.

[6]   INTERESTS
A gourmet cook and enjoy outdoor activities, including camping, basketball, and photography.

NOTE 16.47
Do not include informa-
tion an employer might
prefer not to have.

Employment laws prohibit employers from discriminating among applicants on the basis of race, color, religion, age, gender, disability, marital status, or national origin. Employers who have this information prior to selecting an applicant for a position leave themselves subject to charges of discrimination. Adding such information on resumes is not recommended. Omit information unrelated to the job you are seeking if you think a given employer would prefer not to have it. For example, do not include a photograph unless certain features are relevant to job performance; for example, a position as a model.

If a particular characteristic such as religious affiliation, race, national origin, sexual orientation, marital status, or disability relates to the job responsibilities and would strengthen your job application, you may include it. As illustrated in the Pardon My Planet cartoon, knowing what to include and what to leave out of a resume requires good judgment. For example, if you were applying for an administrative position with a Catholic Church headquarters office, letting the employer know that you are a member of the Catholic Church could be helpful. As a way to provide this type of information in your resume, you could list the church as one of your organization memberships, citing accomplishments related to your special qualification. Or, you could include the information in a special section devoted to your status. Another way is to mention the unique qualification in your application letter. Application letters are covered in Chapter 17.

NOTE 16.48
Present only the information that will strengthen your application.

Pardon My Planet

© VIC LEE. REPRINTED WITH SPECIAL PERMISSION OF KING FEATURES SYNDICATE.

References

Careful development of a list of references is a vital part of your job preparation. Although you want to list only references who will give you positive recommendations, you should list your most important previous employers. In addition, you may want to list college instructors, possibly high school teachers, and—in special circumstances— coworkers or character references. You may list different references for different job applications. Let the nature of the job and its requirements determine the references you think would be the most helpful to the potential employer.

Instead of taking up valuable space on your resume, develop a separate reference list to accompany your resume. Because it is a separate page, place contact information from your resume at the top of the References page. In certain areas of the country employers may want you to list the references on the resume; however, it is better to use this extra space for information about yourself. You do not need to list "references available on request" because employers know that you will provide references.

NOTE 16.49
List your most important previous employers as references.

NOTE 16.50
Provide full information, including a telephone number and an e-mail address.

You are encouraged to provide full information on your references on this list including addresses, telephone numbers, and e-mail addresses. For each reference—unless a reference directs you otherwise—list courtesy title (Mr., Ms., Mrs., or Dr.), name, position, organization, business address, business telephone number, and e-mail address.

Reference information should make it easy for a potential employer who finds your qualifications of interest to pick up the phone, call, and receive a favorable recommendation from one or more of your references. Here is an example of the way a reference list might appear:

REFERENCE LIST
Diane B. Smith
712 Southwood Drive, C-20
Danville, CA 94526
510.555.8873
dbsmith@dan.net

Dr. A. D. Ortiz, Professor Department of Accounting Middle State College Danville, CA 94526 510.555.9322 (Work) adortiz@msc.edu	Mr. Thomas Hopkins, Manager Uniform Fitting, Inc. 1844 Newport Blvd. Danville, CA 94526 510.555.1212 (Work) thopkins@ufi.com
Mrs. Rowena Kelsey Communications Consultant San Ramon Corporation 2387 Seboyeta Avenue Danville, CA 94526 510.555.7817 (Work) rkelsey@sanramon.com	Mr. Marion Sandoval, Manager Sandoval and Sandoval, CPAs 1234 Crownpoint Street Danville, CA 94526 510.555.7834 (Work) 510.555.7835 (Fax) msandoval@sands.com

(4) # Submitting Electronic Resumes

Computer technology provides varied resources for searching and applying for a job. An **electronic resume** is one that is transmitted in an electronic rather than paper format. Electronic resumes can be classified as either (1) scannable or (2) online.

Scannable Resumes

Large organizations, such as IBM, MCI, Motorola, American Airlines, Citibank, Coca-Cola, Southern California Edison, and UCLA, use applicant tracking computer systems in their human resources departments. The format of the scannable resume is one that can be transferred to a computer database by document imaging technology. Applicant electronic resumes posted to a job search Web site, resumes sent by e-mail, or even paper resumes can be scanned into a database.

Organizations with an applicant database tracking system scan resumes from potential employees (for either a solicited or unsolicited position) and place them in an electronic employment folder. The computer program then compares each resume with the job openings and job requirements and generates either a letter of invitation for an interview or a letter of rejection, depending on the final recommendation of the human resources personnel. Some companies that do not have their own computer systems for human resources lease the scanning services from providers. Online application systems are increasing in number, with organizations such as universities, as well as business organizations, beginning to make electronic job applications a part of the Human Resources section of their home Web site. For these sites, applicants usually complete all required information directly on the electronic forms posted on the Web.

Companies using electronic scanning store employee resumes in an electronic folder. These resumes are periodically updated with their job performance information. This database is used to locate candidates for job advancement. Therefore, if a firm with this type of database system hires you, remember to update your resume every six months and date your resume. Even if your employer does not maintain a job advancement database, you should update your resume at least once yearly. Add your most successful accomplishments for the year to your resume. Keeping an ongoing job file similar to the one you began with your job search can be helpful for promotion requests or a job change. Keep a record of major accomplishments, awards and recognition, and assignment changes in this file.

NOTE 16.53
Employees should keep their resumes updated.

Keywords

The scannable resume follows the traditional style and includes *keywords* throughout the resume, but particularly in the Summary of Qualifications and Experience sections. **Keywords** are generally nouns that describe you and are terms recognized and widely used in the targeted position career field. You should use around 20 to 25 keywords in a scannable resume. The following Communication Note gives examples of keywords.

NOTE 16.54
Keywords should be nouns specific to the position.

COMMUNICATION NOTE

Examples of Keywords for an Accounting Position:

Access database	Communication skills	Merit pay program
Accounts payable	Compensation	Month-end closing
Accounts receivable	Data entry	Multitasking
Accurate	Detail-minded	Open communication
Adaptable	Excel spreadsheet	Organizational skills
American Accounting Association	Financial Accounting Standards Board	Peachtree software
Analytical	Filing	PowerPoint
Audit	Financial reports	Presentation skills
B.S.	Industrious	Profit and loss statement
Bachelor of Arts	International Accounting Standards Board	Quick Books
Balance Sheet		Results-oriented
Certified Public Accountant (CPA)	Leadership	Tax accounting
	MBA	Team player
Closing entries	Ledger	Valuation
		Windows

NOTE 16.55
Keywords are words
commonly used in the
career field.

Because the keywords mark an electronic trail, you must learn the keywords that are used in the field for which you are applying so that you have a better chance of being selected for a job interview. Each time one of your keywords matches a keyword for the particular position, you have a "hit." The more "hits" you receive the better your chance for a job interview. Include only keywords that correctly and honestly describe you and your qualifications. Keywords related to job responsibilities can be included in job titles, department names, companies and organizations, degrees, special skills, and knowledge possessed by the applicant. Keywords pertaining to job requirements might be included in your class ranking, skills, experience, professional associations, licensure or certification, and interpersonal traits. An example of keywords for an individual working in the human resources area follows.

Keywords

Equal Employment Opportunity (EEO), American Disabilities Act (ADA), Society for Human Resources Management (SHRM), Merit Pay, Compensation and Benefits Program, Certified Facilitator and Instructor, Communicator, Master's in Business Administration (MBA), Malcolm Baldrige Quality Criteria, Benchmark Partners, Business Process Analysis, Planning and Organization, Job Analysis and Audit, Coordination of Team Initiatives, Organizational Review and Analysis, Job Classifications, Counseling, Supervision, Personnel Database, Applicant Database Tracking System, Data Analysis, MS Word, PowerPoint, Team Player, Self-starter, Willing to train, Enthusiastic, People Skills, Spanish Language Skills, Friendly, Trustworthy, Reliable, and Human Resources Manager.

Electronic and Scannable Resume Formats

Organization and appearance of the scannable resume are essential to the success of your job search. Your name should be on the first line by itself, followed by your address, telephone number, fax number, and e-mail address. The type font should be sans serif (such as Arial or Helvetica) and the font size between 10 and 14 points. Boldface may be acceptable, but avoid special fonts such as italicized, script, or underlined text. Also, avoid special spacing or formatting like double columns, tabs, graphics, and shading because these features may cause the scanner to read the information incorrectly. Some companies do have sophisticated scanning equipment that can read different fonts and styles; however, you cannot be sure of the kind of scanner the company is using unless you telephone them first. Your goal is a plain-vanilla resume.

Preferably, the scannable resume should be printed by a laser printer with black ink on smooth, white paper. If you have a two-page resume, do not staple the pages. When sending a paper copy of your resume, use a 9- by 12-inch mailing envelope to avoid folding the resume; the fold may cause the scanner to skip words.

NOTE 16.56
A call to a company can
verify its scannable for-
mat requirements.

To have your resume selected for human review in this computerized process, you must learn how the computer programming works. If you know your resume will be scanned, find out—from the company or another source—the nature of the computer program so you know what content to include. Figure 16.6 is an example of a scannable resume with keywords used throughout. This computer-friendly resume can be read easily and accurately by scanners as well as human eyes.

SHANA WILSON
1234 Dell Way
Pomona, CA 91768
909.555.1212
swilson@email.net

All items at left margin; plain fonts.

FIGURE 16.9
Chronological Format of a Targeted Scannable Resume

OBJECTIVE
Property manager for a progressive commercial and residential property company

SUMMARY OF QUALIFICATIONS
*Bachelor of Arts in Marketing, GPA: 3.8 based on 4-point system
*Asset management of $800,000 multi-family residential units
*Member of Certified Commercial Investment Management (CCIM)
*Specialized knowledge of e-commerce, sociocultural influences, and consumer behavior
*Detail oriented with positive people skills

Key words throughout.

Experience first emphasizes work record.

EXPERIENCE
Executive Manager, Home Properties, 1532 Greystone, Pomona, CA 91768, 2002 to Present

Responsibilities:
*Manage rent rolls, leasing, facility maintenance and improvement, and property promotions
*Analyze vacancy ratios and manage budget
*Exercise due diligence in notification of late fees and eviction notices

Uses asterisks to avoid special characters.

Accomplishments:
*Realized a 20 percent return on equity (ROE) over a two-year period
*Completed a feasibility analysis for five-year expansion plan

Marketing Assistant, Milwood Industries, PO Box 320, Porterville, CA 93257, 2000–2002

Responsibilities:
*Assisted in identification of marketing data needs
*Collected marketing data and proposed plans for promotional actions
*Developed market-product grids and estimated market size

Accomplishments:
*Researched potential global marketing opportunities
*Analyzed sociocultural influences on consumer behavior
*Assisted with development and management of electronic commerce (e-commerce)

EDUCATION
MBA, Marketing, University of California at Santa Barbara, CA 93106, May 2000
BS, Business Administration, California State University, Fresno, CA 93710, May 1999
Outstanding Marketing Student Award, 1999
Pertinent Courses: business communications, financial management, organizational management and planning, and marketing research

SPECIAL SKILLS
Experienced in computer software, including PowerPoint, Word, Excel, Access, and customized computerized accounting systems

Online Resumes

The Internet provides opportunities for accessing online career centers and company Web sites for posting your resume. The online resume posted on the Web is becoming an important tool in the workplace because many human resources departments are conducting searches on the Web for qualified applicants.

The style of this resume differs from the traditional or the scannable resume in that the contents can be "linked" to more detailed information about your work. The online resume can be thought of as a home page portfolio targeted to your career field. The home page can have links to move to other pages in your portfolio that show detailed examples of projects, proposals, and reports that you have developed. It is important to keep your Web site professional, as employers will be viewing the information that you have provided. Remember to avoid providing personal information on your Web site, including photos, as recruiters are legally barred from using this material in employment decisions.

When you post your resume to the Internet, your resume may be "shopped" to hundreds of employers at once. This can be good and result in several interviews; however, after you have accepted a position your resume may linger in cyberspace for several months or years.

Your online resume posted to your own Web page or on a job search Web site could be found by your savvy Web-smart current employer; this could result in your being called on the carpet and possibly fired. If you have had your resume posted on the Web, it is advisable to let your current employer know in order to avoid such a misunderstanding. Online applications completed for specific company or other organizational online application systems, however, have privacy protection.

Refining the Resume

You will be judged on the appearance of your resume; it is a potential employer's first impression of you. Though there are many helpful examples available, you should never simply try to make your information fit another person's resume format.

- Print your resume—use a laser printer if possible—on white, buff, or some other light color paper. Remember if your resume is to be scanned, you should use white paper. Use high-quality, clean, 8½- by 11-inch bond paper. Be sure your resume is neat, unwrinkled, and error free. The quality and clarity of its content will be a potential employer's impression of you.

- Arrange information simply but attractively. Use capitals or a different font size for major divisions of the resume. As discussed earlier, your goal for resumes that are to be scanned is to prepare a plain-vanilla resume (without unusual fonts or spacing). Because many companies now scan resumes into a database, using a simple format improves its chances of compatibility with a database file.

- Use action verbs and strong phrases rather than complete sentences. Emphasize relevant achievements, accomplishments, and special skills.

- Draft your resume carefully to show the employer that there is a clear match between your qualifications and job requirements. Remember it is important that you learn the jargon of the industry and use those keywords in your resume.

- Consider giving a draft of your resume to a classmate whom you don't know well and asking that person to review your resume. After two or three minutes of this review, ask him or her questions about your resume. If the reader cannot answer the questions or locate the answers quickly, the resume is ineffective.

- Proofread carefully; errors can result in the resume being eliminated from consideration. Have two other individuals review it to be sure it is accurate.
- Use a Summary of Qualifications to highlight your accomplishments. Many businesspeople prefer a one-page resume for new college graduates with limited experience. If your resume is two pages or longer, a Summary of Qualifications section is essential. If you know that an employer specifies the number of pages in applicants' resumes (such as, "Applicant resumes shall not exceed one page"), limit your resume length accordingly. In most cases limit the resume to one or two pages. Be sure that the information is not overcrowded or does not appear so dense as to discourage reading.
- Remember your objective for each job application is to construct the most powerful resume that you possibly can so you can convince the employer to give you an interview.

Following guidelines given in this chapter should enable you to create your own distinctive resume, one that will serve you well in your job search. Tailor items to the job requirements and make your message precise and powerful.

Summary of Learning Objectives

Analyze your qualifications and job preferences for employment.

In analyzing your qualifications, start by brainstorming facts about yourself. The most important facts are evidence of your accomplishments—achievements, honors, and knowledge. In addition, you develop an individual profile about yourself, your education, your experiences, a list of persons who can serve as your references, and your job preferences.

Describe five sources of information about job opportunities and job requirements.

Career positions can be either solicited or unsolicited. You can find job opportunities and job requirements through (1) job listings with campus career centers, (2) job referrals through a network of personal contacts, (3) classified ads in newspapers or journals, (4) announcements through private or government placement agencies, or (5) positions listed on the Internet. All of these resources except networking through personal contacts provide information on solicited positions. Unsolicited positions are ones obtained by direct contact with a company of your choice or advertising your job interests and qualifications through networking or in professional journals and newspapers.

Prepare targeted and general resumes in chronological, functional, or combination format.

A resume is a summary of your qualifications and must be clearly and concisely written. The primary purpose of a resume, along with an application letter, is to obtain a job interview. Resumes can be targeted to a specific position or prepared for a particular type of position in a career field. You may use a chronological, functional, or combination format to prepare either a targeted or a general resume. A chronological resume organizes information by date, with the most recent date listed first. A functional resume categorizes information by skills, knowledge, and related accomplishments and, thus, emphasizes qualifications. A combination format organizes some items by date but incorporates information categorized by skills, knowledge, and accomplishments. The five major sections common in resumes are the opening, education, experience, special activities or skills, and a reference page.

Prepare an electronic resume.

Electronic resumes are classified as either scannable or online. The format of a scannable resume should be simple, with all or most lines beginning at the left margin. Scanning a resume transfers it to a form compatible with an electronic database. A scannable resume should include 20 to 25 keywords. Keywords are usually nouns that label your qualifications in terms used in the career field. Because the keywords mark the electronic trail, you must learn the keywords that are used in the field for which you are applying so that you have a better chance for being selected for a job interview. The online resume can be developed on your computer and then uploaded to your own home page on the Web. The online computer resume is becoming an important tool in the workplace. Many human resources departments are conducting searches on the Web for qualified applicants and also may have their own online application system on their Web site to receive applicant information keyed directly onto electronic forms.

Discussion Questions

1. Explain why you should complete an inventory of your qualifications and job preferences before beginning your job search. (Objective 1)
2. Give examples of information to list on your Individual Profile inventory. (Objective 1)
3. Define *solicited position*. List where you could find a solicited position. (Objective 2)
4. What information should you list on your Experience inventory that will prepare you to write the Experience section of a resume? (Objectives 1 and 3)
5. Describe the information and services offered by campus career centers. (Objective 2)
6. How can the Internet be helpful in a job search? (Objective 2)
7. How does a targeted resume differ from a general resume? Which do you believe would be most effective and why? (Objective 3)
8. Explain the term *keywords* and their importance on your resume. (Objective 4)
9. Describe the chronological, functional, and combination resume formats and when each type would be most appropriately used. (Objective 3)
10. What is the difference between a scannable and an online resume? (Objective 4)

Application Exercises

1. Visit your campus career center and gather information on interest and personality tests they offer or recommend to help individuals determine their career interests. Take one of the tests, have the test evaluated, and write a report to your instructor on the findings. (Objective 1)
2. Interview a prospective employer to learn what qualities he or she would look for in an applicant who is a new college graduate. Design a PowerPoint presentation for your class on your findings. If PowerPoint software is not available, use word processing software to prepare an outline of your presentation as a handout. (Objective 1)

3. Analyze the professional organizations in your field of study. List those organizations in which you believe membership would strengthen your job candidacy. (Objective 2)

4. Using the information gained in Application Exercise 3, attend a meeting of a professional organization in which you think membership will strengthen your job candidacy. Write a memo to your instructor and make a presentation to your class giving the mission, purpose, and goals of the organization. Give information on the dues and the benefits of membership in the professional organization. (Objective 2)

5. **E-mail.** Attend a career fair or visit your campus career center and gather information on jobs available in your field. Send an e-mail to your instructor listing five possible positions for which you will be qualified once you graduate from school. (Objective 2)

6. **Ethics. Teamwork.** Read the scenario below; partner with a classmate to discuss the ethical questions following the scenario. Working together write an e-mail message to your instructor explaining your consensus about the ethics of the situation described in the scenario and what, if anything, Jason should do differently. (Objective 3)

Jason had searched for a job as a management trainee for the last three months since his graduation from a business administration program in the local community college. He had been interviewed for three positions but had received no job offers. He was beginning to feel desperate and decided that he had to do something to improve his chances for hiring. He had worked part time as a pizza delivery person while going to school but was fired from that position when he wrecked the delivery vehicle and was charged with reckless driving. He had included this position on his resume. When asked in the interview about his reason for leaving the position, he just said that he left because the pay was insufficient and that his supervisor was prejudiced against him because of his age—he was only 17 at the time.

   a. Is there any part of the above scenario that raises an ethical question? If so, what is it and what is the concern?

   b. Explain whether or not you believe this experience item on his resume could be a problem with Jason's lack of job offers. If so, should he remove it from his resume or take a different action?

   c. What advice would you give Jason that might eliminate any ethical concerns and improve his chances for a job offer?

7. **E-mail. Teamwork.** Form a group of two to three students and review the listings in the classified ads section of a local or regional newspaper. Assess the employment opportunities in relation to your career interests. Summarize your findings in a presentation to your class and an e-mail message or memo to your instructor. (Objective 2)

8. List the names of individuals in your personal network of friends, relatives, instructors, and acquaintances who you think could be valuable to you in a job search and develop a reference list. (Objectives 1 and 3)

9. Assume that you will graduate soon. Using actual information and assuming the course work, activities, and experience you will have between now and then, analyze your qualifications following the recommendations given in this chapter. (Objective 1)

10. Using the information gathered in Application Exercise 5, prepare a general resume in chronological format. (Objective 3)

11. **Internet.** Access job opportunities on the Internet for positions related to your career objective. Assess the job opportunities in terms of your interests in them. Write a letter to your instructor reporting your findings. (Objective 2)

12. Using the information gathered in Application Exercise 7, prepare a combination general resume that could be used with at least three of the advertised positions. Partner

with a classmate to proofread each other's resume. Submit your final copy of the resume with a copy of the applicable ads. (Objective 3)

13. Prepare a targeted resume in chronological format to apply for one of the positions you found on the Internet in Application Exercise 11. Partner with a classmate to proofread each other's resume. Submit your final copy of the resume with a copy of the applicable ad. (Objective 3)

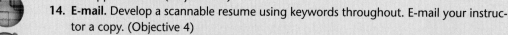

14. **E-mail.** Develop a scannable resume using keywords throughout. E-mail your instructor a copy. (Objective 4)

15. **InfoTrac.** Use InfoTrac to access an article in *PR Newswire,* October 15, 2002, about the value of temporary work (article No. A92844397). Read the article and answer the following questions: (Objectives 1 and 3)

   a. What kind of business is Accountemps? How could a business similar to this help you get started in your career field?

   b. Should temporary positions be listed on your resume? Why or why not?

   c. Go to Accountemps Web site and find three items of information about their services. Explain what you found.

16. Make a list of words that you believe to be keywords in Figure 16.9, a scannable resume illustrated in this chapter; the keywords relate to property management and marketing. (Objective 4)

Message Analysis

From the following Experience inventory, prepare the Experience section of a targeted resume of an individual applying for a human resources management position in an international company that does business in North and South America. After completing the Experience section, circle the 10 keywords that you believe to be applicable to this position.

Characteristics important in this company include a background of experience related to human resources management with special responsibilities for planning and budgeting for personnel and managing the applicant and employee database, a record of dependability and willingness to assume responsibility, development potential, international experiences, ability to speak and write the Spanish language, experience in training personnel, knowledge of and membership in an international human resources professional association.

MY EXPERIENCE RECORD

Hayward & Chappel Insurance Agency. Newark, California. 6/95–5/97. Customer Service Representative. Handled new policies and over 100 current policies. Update client files. Recommend improvements in the management of customer policies and translated training manual into Spanish. Train new service representatives. Brunswick Brothers, Inc. South American Division, San Ramon, California. May 1997–present. Financial Analyst and Human Resources. Organize and analyze general and administrative expenses. Update and maintained forecast. Conduct weekly training on worker's compensation reports. Evaluated and completed employment verifications. Use Spanish in working with clients as well as fellow colleagues in Argentina and Chile. 6/94–6/95. Lee and Sons Company. San Jose, California. Human Resources internship through San Jose State University. Recruited employees; developed training program and wrote project on how to train. Designed transfer program.

There are Web exercises at **http://krizan.swlearning.com** to accompany this chapter.

Grammar Workshop

Correct the grammar, spelling, punctuation, style, and word choice errors in the following sentences:

1. Analyses, classifying and selection of opportunities for appropriate markets is a important part of global marketing.
2. Women account for only seventeen % of undergraduate computer science majors at universities in the US.
3. One of the new printers in our office are broken.
4. The major advantage for telecommuting are as follows; savings in gasoline; reduction in pollution; and an decrease in traffic congestion.
5. Cohesive work groups has members that work togather towards a common goal.
6. The library of congress in Washington dc is the worlds' largest library.
7. Conflict becomes dysfunctional in a organization when it distracks from achieveing organization goals.
8. South Africa has a coast line along both the atlantic and pacific oceans.
9. To be a successfull Employee in the Software industry you must work eighty hours per week.
10. Digitel cameras have improved picture taking quality, and cost less than two years ago only.

17 Employment Communication and Interviewing

LEARNING OBJECTIVES

Write effective application letters for solicited and unsolicited positions.

Prepare for a successful job interview.

Compose a variety of follow-up letters and other employment-related messages.

Jim Logan, Human Resources Branch Manager, Civilian Personnel, U.S. Department of the Army

LET'S TALK BUSINESS Qualities that translate into a good employee, regardless of occupation, include the ability to get along with people, to stay calm under pressure, and to respond thoughtfully to daily problems. In addition, employers seek employees who can be trusted. Candidates for a position must possess the technical skills required by the position, but these skills alone will not assure success.

On the job, providing good customer service is essential. I believe that it is important to make your first exposure to a customer a success and then build on that positive beginning. Using the approach "How can we work together?" is a first step to building good relationships. Try to handle completion of some routine tasks face-to-face, and be sure to follow up on questions and provide assistance as requested.

PHOTO COURTESY OF JIM LOGAN

Chapter 16 covered the first three steps in your job campaign—analyzing your qualifications, obtaining information about employment, and developing a resume. You are now ready for the next three steps: writing application letters, interviewing for positions, and conducting follow-up communications. This chapter covers these steps. In Let's Talk Business Jim Logan describes characteristics that employers look for when interviewing to fill vacant positions and when evaluating personnel to promote employees. His comments reinforce the importance of interpersonal skills, as well as technical skills.

Writing Application Letters

LEARNING OBJECTIVE

1 *Write effective application letters for solicited and unsolicited positions.*

Once you complete your resume, you are ready to write a more personal sales message—an application letter. An **application letter** functions as a cover letter in the transmittal of your resume and gives you an opportunity to make important points that you cannot cover in a one- or two-page resume. A strong letter of application lends support to your resume—but does not repeat the same information. Guidelines given in Chapter 9 for persuasive messages will help you develop your application letter. Think of the cover letter that goes with the resume as a sales letter; the products are *your knowledge and skills* that can benefit the organization.

NOTE 17.1
An application letter is a sales letter for your knowledge and skills.

Application letters, as well as resumes, can be either general or targeted. Again, the choice depends on whether you are seeking a position for which applications are solicited or if it is an unsolicited position. If you apply for a specific position that has been advertised, use the targeted application letter. If you apply for an unsolicited position or do not know if an opening is available, use a general letter. For some situations you can combine a general resume and a targeted application letter into an effective application package. When sending applications to similar types of businesses, for example, you may use the same resume but personalize each letter with comments specific to the company.

NOTE 17.2
Application letters may be either general or targeted.

Chapter 16 suggests researching information about the company before preparing your resume; this advice applies to the resume, application letter, and interview. A targeted application letter can be much more effective if the message includes specific information that pertains to that company. Look in the local newspaper, national newspapers, and periodicals. Search the Internet. Locate the company's annual report. Ask knowledgeable community members about the company. Learn about the company's products, its customers, and its achievements. Call the company and ask for the name of the person who receives employment applications or the name of the human resources manager. In the section of this chapter titled "Preparing for a Job Interview," you will find specific Internet locations and publications that can help you learn more about specific companies.

NOTE 17.3
Learn about the company before writing a targeted application letter.

For an unsolicited general application or a targeted application for a position advertised with only a post office box for response, learn as much as you can about business operations and work responsibilities applicable to the type of position described. If the information appeals to you, the position described is probably consistent with your background and interests. Researching information about a specific company or a field of interest provides details that help you focus on the potential employer's needs. Knowledge of organization and position details enables you to explain your qualifications from the you–viewpoint. Highlight specific past accomplishments to show how hiring you will benefit the company. The focal point is not what you *have done*, but what you *can do* for the organization.

NOTE 17.4
An application letter
should be 1 to 1½ pages
in length.

The application letter should be from 1 to 1½ pages in length. In three or four paragraphs, a well-designed application letter accomplishes the four purposes listed below. Do these purposes look familiar? You saw them in Chapter 9 when you read about persuasive messages.

[1] **Attention:** Gain favorable attention and express your interest in the position.

[2] **Interest:** Market your qualifications; identify special strengths and attributes.

[3] **Desire:** Describe selected accomplishments that show how you can benefit the company.

[4] **Action:** Request an interview or propose a future meeting; make contact easy to schedule.

A successful application letter motivates a potential employer to read your resume with interest and to arrange an interview. To accomplish this goal, the letter and resume must create sufficient interest to separate you from the applicant pool and to invite you for a personal interview.

An Opening That Gains Attention

In a short opening paragraph (from one to five lines), you want to gain the favorable attention of your reader—motivate her or him to read the remainder of the application letter. In addition, you want to alert the reader to your interest in a position. This expression of interest is essential to provide orientation to the message and transition to details in the rest of the letter.

The opening can mention who referred you to this position. If the person has a respected and recognized name in the organization or in the same business field, mentioning the name can gain favorable attention. Other openings could indicate your knowledge about the position or the organization, explain why you are interested, or how you learned of the position. For example, you could say that you are applying for a position listed with your campus career center, advertised in the newspaper, recommended by a current employee of the organization, or posted on the Internet. For an unsolicited position, you could say that you are highly interested in employment if an opening occurs.

NOTE 17.6
A direct approach works
well for a targeted
application letter.

The opening of the letter can attract the potential employer's attention and can be creative or traditional. Creative openings, however, should be professional in tone and appearance and focus on gaining favorable attention. Your choice of opening will be based on applying the you–viewpoint, analyzing your reader, and considering the type of position that you seek. If the opening has been advertised, a direct approach can work well. If you are not sure if an opening is available, use the indirect approach. Here are examples of openings:

- Are you interested in a person with a solid record of accomplishment and a strong work ethic for your management trainee program? (*Gains attention by emphasizing applicant's strengths and identifying the position of interest.*)
- Please compare my qualifications with the job requirements for the auditor position that you advertised in the May issue of the *AAA Journal.* Consider me an applicant for the position. (*Emphasizes that qualifications match job requirements, identifies the position, and explains how you learned of the position.*)
- Creative! Knowledgeable! Organized! Just what you want in a new copywriter for Lo's Advertising Agency. (*Uses creative opening, emphasizes strengths, and identifies position of interest.*)

• Mr. Bill Mitchell, manager of your budget office, recommended that I apply for the position you have open for Assistant Budget Analyst in the Center for Community Affairs. Please note how well my qualifications, as described in the enclosed resume, match the job requirements of your opening. (*Names a company individual, specifies the position, and calls attention to the match between qualifications and job requirements.*)

Convincing an Employer That You Fit the Job

After the opening paragraph, the main body of an application letter should convince a potential employer that you fit the job requirements and that your employment will benefit the company. This is the most important part of your letter; it is here that you create interest in your qualifications and a desire to hire you.

In this section of an application letter, you should describe your most outstanding accomplishments that relate to the job requirements. This could be from your work experience, special expertise, or educational accomplishments. Briefly discuss your strengths and how they meet job requirements. When responding to a job advertisement, read the ad carefully and use the words in the letter that fit both you and the language in the ad. The order of content may vary in different application letters. The intent, however, is to compose a clear, concise, concrete, and convincing paragraph or two that will motivate the employer to look closely at your resume. Here are poor and good examples of the second part of an application letter:

NOTE 17.7
The letter creates interest in how you can benefit the company.

Poor:

I will be graduating with a Bachelor of Science degree in Business Administration with a major in marketing this June. This major included sales and marketing courses. I am confident that I have the expertise to be successful in sales. I will work hard to be a good employee. (*Repeats information from resume, includes vague promises rather than accomplishments, and does not link accomplishments to needs of the organization.*)

Good:

Mrs. Martinez, my solid record of experience in sales plus my marketing major match your requirements for an A to Z Hardware Marketing Representative. My accomplishments in the sales positions listed on my resume attest to my marketing skills. Each summer for the years 2000 through 2003, I received recognition as top sales person in the Western District (a five-state area). Employed full time in hardware sales during the summer and part time during the academic school year, I became familiar with hardware inventory and earned money to pay my educational expenses.

I have the personal qualities, as well as the education and experience, that could benefit your organization. I am an energetic, goal-oriented individual who works effectively in team efforts as well as through individual marketing contacts.

Promoting Action in the Close

NOTE 17.8
The letter closes with a positive, pleasant interview request.

NOTE 17.9
Make it easy to contact you for an interview.

Now you are ready to motivate the employer to take action—to read your resume and invite you to an interview. In most application letters, your goal is to get an interview. The best way to get an interview is to ask directly for it. This request should be made in a positive, pleasant manner.

The closing paragraph is the wrap-up. In the close of your application letter, you should make it easy for an employer to invite you to an interview by providing your telephone number and e-mail address and by offering to be at the employer's office at his or her convenience. Even if you do have limitations on your time flexibility—such as another interview scheduled for one day next week—you can usually arrange to change your schedule if the employer calls you. An alternate approach is to say that you will call in one or two weeks to check the status of your application. This statement is less passive than waiting to be called. Taking the initiative to follow up the interview with a call, if expressed courteously, is not likely to offend the prospective employer and may be viewed as a positive factor. Other closing comments should express thanks for consideration or indicate that you look forward to a response. The following examples show appropriate closings for application letters and give their positive aspects in parentheses.

- My experience in financial management, account development, and problem solving will enable me to make significant contributions to the continuing success of Loraine Foods. Please call me at (957) 555-1400 or e-mail me at eehew@nxvs.edu so that we can arrange an interview. I can meet at your convenience and look forward to discussing a future with your company. If hired for this position, you will find me to be a knowledgeable, energetic, and productive employee. (*Includes phone number and e-mail address, maintains a positive tone, asks for an interview at the interviewer's convenience, and reinforces strengths for the job.*)

- May I have an interview to discuss this opportunity with you, Ms. Bartel? I believe that I could become a valuable part of the team at the Lafayette Agency. You can reach me at (510) 555-1122 or e-mail me at ggdickson@zxy.edu. At your convenience, I can arrange to meet with you at your office. (*Specifically requests an interview, uses the person's name, emphasizes teamwork, provides contact information, and suggests willingness to accommodate the employer's schedule.*)

- Enclosed with this letter is my resume with contact information and further details of my qualifications and accomplishments. I would appreciate the opportunity to talk with you about how I would fit in with your organization. I will call you early next week to arrange an appointment convenient for your schedule. (*Shows initiative in contacting for an appointment at the employer's convenience, notes where contact information is found, and maintains a positive tone.*)

- I am excited about applying for an accounting position with Salvatore's Agency, a highly respected and long-standing name in public relations. Thank you for your time and consideration in reviewing my resume. You may reach me by telephone at (925) 555-1983 or by e-mail at jsn@srvqs.edu. Please call me to schedule an interview at your convenience. (*Indicates enthusiasm for the company and knowledge of its history, expresses thanks for consideration, makes contact information accessible, and courteously requests an interview.*)

Preparing an Application Letter

The application letters you use in your job campaign must meet the same high standards as resumes for neatness, accuracy, clarity, and conciseness. Application letters should be brief, generally no more than 1 to 1½ pages. As mentioned previously, research the company and learn about the organization before writing the letter and resume. Analyze your reader, use the you–viewpoint, apply the principles of business communication, and follow the guidelines given in Chapter 9 for persuasive messages. The following Tips and Hints summarize do's and don'ts of application letters.

NOTE 17.10
Use the you–viewpoint for an application letter.

TIPS AND HINTS
Application Letters

Format and Message Content	Appearance and Accuracy	General Tips
Print with laser printer: black print, Arial or Times Roman 12 pt. on white 8½- by 11-inch bond paper.	Present a clean, professional page appearance with sharp, easily read text.	Be positive in describing accomplishments but be honest and accurate.
Use modified-block or full-block letter style.	Don't use abbreviations within the message body.	Avoid gimmicks or attempts at humor.
Single space with double spacing between paragraphs.	Spell all words correctly and use correct grammar.	Avoid generalities and vague terms such as *etc.*
Use a name with the salutation, if possible; otherwise, use a subject line with simplified letter style.	Don't use stationery from your school or a company where you work or have worked.	Don't belittle your qualifications or speak negatively of another job, supervisor, or coworker.
Don't say *References available upon request.* This adds no information that the prospective employer doesn't know.	Don't photocopy the letter or resume, and don't fold for mailing.	Don't appeal to sympathy or what getting the job would do for you; base the application on qualifications that fit job requirements.
Highlight important accomplishments using bulleted items.	Verify recipient's correct name and title.	Wait until the interview to discuss salary.

Use 8½- by 11-inch bond paper for application letters. The paper should be the same quality and color as was used for your resume. Never use your current employer's stationery for an application letter. Use a 9- by 12-inch mailing envelope to avoid folding the letter and resume. Many organizations scan letters as well as resumes. Folds in the paper may cause the scanner to skip the words caught in the fold.

An application letter should be addressed to a specific person. If you need the name, call the organization and ask for the name and address of the person to whom your letter should be addressed. The letter should be individually prepared; even a general application letter for distribution to prospective employers should not be photocopied. If

NOTE 17.11
Application letters and resumes should not be folded for mailing.

NOTE 17.12
Address the letter to an individual or use simplified block format.

responding to a blind ad, use the simplified block letter format with a subject line (see Appendix A) rather than using "To Whom It May Concern" as the salutation.

A word processing program on your computer helps you prepare several letters and insert variable information in each one. Proofread an application letter carefully for the correct receiver's name, organization, and address. Remember to mention your enclosed resume. Keep copies of the letters and resumes sent to each potential employer.

Sample Application Letters

Figures 17.1 and 17.2 show a poor example and a good example of a general letter that could be addressed to human resources managers at several companies. Both of these letters were written to obtain an unsolicited job.

Figures 17.3 and 17.4 are poor and good examples of a targeted letter sent in response to a solicited job opening. Targeted letters usually are more powerful than general letters; in a targeted letter you can show specifically how your employment will benefit the employer.

NOTE 17.13
Proofread your letter carefully; it must be accurate.

NOTE 17.14
Targeted letters are more powerful than general letters.

LEARNING OBJECTIVE
② Prepare for a successful job interview.

Interviewing for a Job

The goal of your sending an application letter and resume is to obtain a job interview. When you are invited to come for an interview, start preparing for it. The interview can be one of the most important experiences in your life because it can determine the course of your career. You will want the interview to go as well as possible.

Preparing for a Job Interview

You have given thought and preparation through each step of your job search. You have analyzed your qualifications, examined the job market and job requirements, prepared your resume, and written application letters. Through this process you have learned about yourself, as well as the job market. In addition, you have organized this information so that you can talk about it efficiently and logically.

NOTE 17.15
The goal of the application letter and resume is an interview.

NOTE 17.16
A successful job quest requires careful preparation.

BE READY TO ANSWER QUESTIONS

The next step in your preparation is to anticipate questions that might be asked in an interview and to prepare generally the answers you will give. Have a friend or relative ask you the questions to give you practice answering.

Interview questions may be *traditional* or *behavioral style*. **Traditional** questions ask how you *would* handle a hypothetical situation or ask general questions to reveal your job-related attributes or opinions. In contrast, **behavioral** questions focus on specific past situations and how you *did* handle them. You will not know the style of interviewing beforehand; therefore, you must prepare for both the traditional and behavioral interviews. In fact, interviews often include a mix of questions—some traditional and some behavioral. Regardless of the style of questioning, the intent is for the potential employer to gather enough information to make a decision about the benefits that you would bring to the company or organization. The underlying question in the minds of the interviewers is, "Would this applicant be the best fit for the position and provide the greatest benefit to the organization?" Keep this in mind as you practice responding to a variety of interview questions so that you will be prepared to be your best in an interview.

NOTE 17.17
Practice answering anticipated interview questions.

NOTE 17.18
Interview questions may be behavioral or traditional.

Traditional Interview Questions Interviewers ask traditional questions to learn about your education, experience, career goals, and personal history and characteristics. Answers to these questions help the interviewer decide if you have the background, interests, and characteristics that fit the position. Consider possible questions and plan brief, but meaningful, positive responses that illustrate your past successes and accomplishments. The following list of traditional questions shows examples of interview questions.

NOTE 17.19
Responses should cover meaningful accomplishments.

Traditional Interview Questions

Personal History and Characteristics

[1] Tell me about yourself.

[2] What is your greatest strength?

[3] What is your greatest weakness?

[4] Who are your role models? Why?

[5] Where do you want to be in five years? Ten years?

[6] How do you handle stress?

[7] Give me three words that best describe you.

[8] What motivates you?

[9] Why are you interested in working for us?

[10] Why should we hire you rather than another candidate?

NOTE 17.20
Traditional questions ask how you *would* handle a situation.

Education

[11] Why did you choose to attend your college or university?

[12] Why did you choose your major? Minor?

[13] Tell me about your education at. . . .

[14] How does your college education or work experience relate to this job?

[15] Tell me about your course work. What courses did you like best? Least?

[16] Tell me about your extracurricular activities while you were in school.

[17] Tell me about your involvement with your professional organization.

[18] Do your grades accurately reflect your ability? Why or why not?

[19] Were you financially responsible for any portion of your college education?

[20] Do you have plans to get additional education?

Experience

[21] Why did you choose this field of work?

[22] What job-related skills have you developed?

[23] For what kind of supervisor do you like to work?

[24] Do you consider yourself ambitious?

[25] What do you think should determine the progress a person makes in a company?

[26] What does *teamwork* mean to you?

NEEDS WORK

1588 Northway Avenue
Nashville, TN 37233
January 21, 200-

Mr. Thomas Revney, President
Commerce National Bank
154 South Second Street
Nashville, TN 37220

No salutation with title and name.

I am interested in applying for a position with your bank. I was first in my graduating class when I completed a business major at the university in 1999. I left Nashville in 2000 and since then I have held various positions and believe that my education and experience will be valuable to your bank. I would like to come for an interview to discuss my qualifications.

No position type or major specified.

My career accomplishments include 3 years as a software installer, 5 years as a bank teller, and 2 years as a public relations director. Any business could use a person with these experiences. To add to my marketable skills, I periodically take training courses in computer programming and software development.

Accomplishments unrelated to organization needs.

If you are interested in someone with the high level of skills and knowledge that I have, I would be willing to join your bank for a salary in the range of $65,000 to $80,000 if advancement opportunities are able. Call me at 615.555.2515 and I will arrange a date and time to meet with you.

No you–viewpoint; premature salary statement.

Yours truly,

Marylou Marzano

Marylou Marzano

FIGURE 17.1
A *Poor* Example of a
General Application
Letter

[27] What did you do on your job at ____?

[28] Have you ever quit a job? Why?

[29] What did you like least in your job at ____ ?

[30] Have you done any volunteer work? What kind?

Career Goals

[31] How important is money to you?

[32] Do you like to work alone or with other people? Why?

[33] Are you willing to relocate?

[34] You are younger than most of the people you will supervise. What problems might this pose? How will you resolve them?

[35] Are you willing to travel?

[36] What salary do you expect to receive in this job?

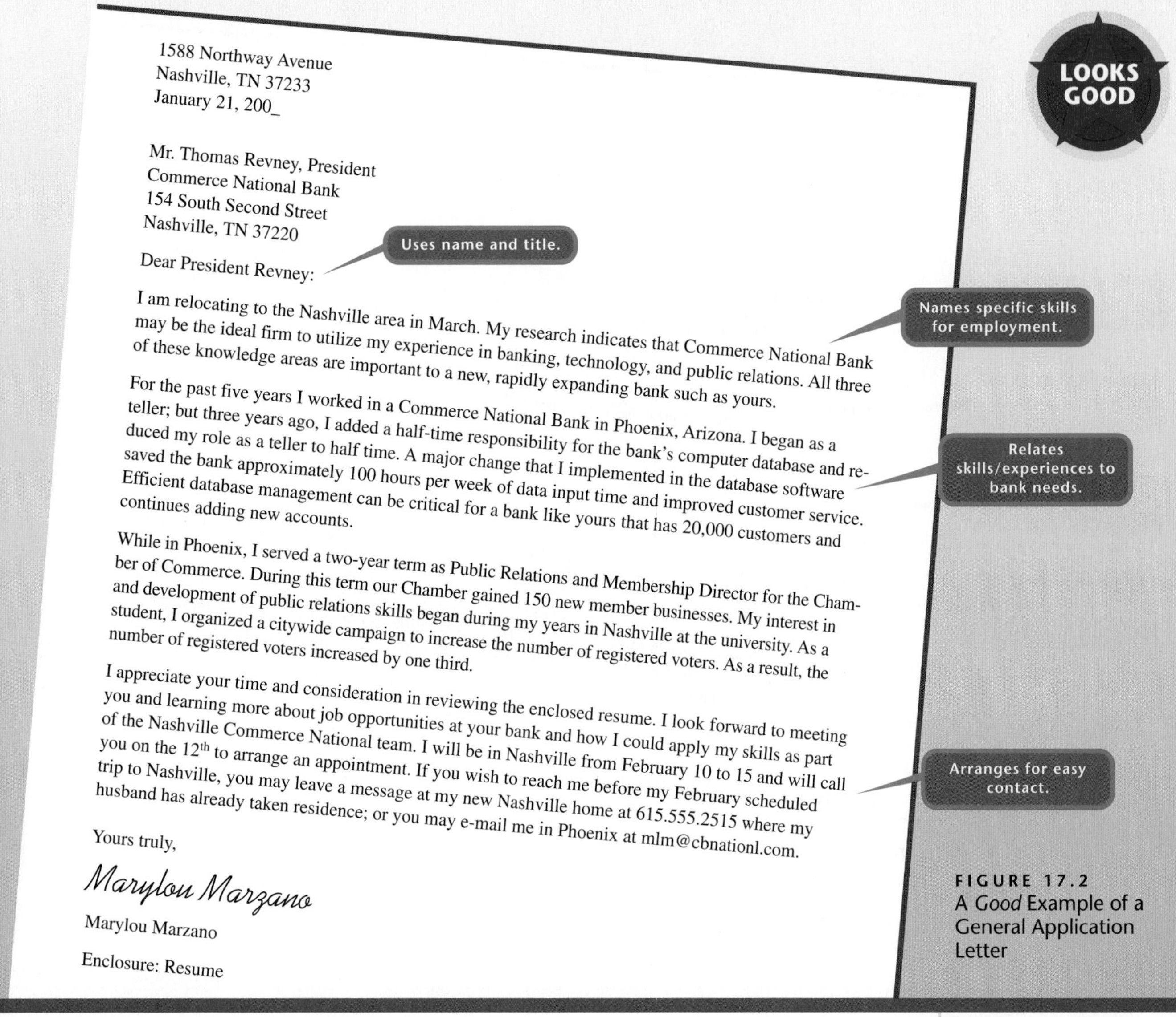

1588 Northway Avenue
Nashville, TN 37233
January 21, 200_

Mr. Thomas Revney, President
Commerce National Bank
154 South Second Street
Nashville, TN 37220

Dear President Revney:

Uses name and title.

I am relocating to the Nashville area in March. My research indicates that Commerce National Bank may be the ideal firm to utilize my experience in banking, technology, and public relations. All three of these knowledge areas are important to a new, rapidly expanding bank such as yours.

Names specific skills for employment.

For the past five years I worked in a Commerce National Bank in Phoenix, Arizona. I began as a teller; but three years ago, I added a half-time responsibility for the bank's computer database and reduced my role as a teller to half time. A major change that I implemented in the database software saved the bank approximately 100 hours per week of data input time and improved customer service. Efficient database management can be critical for a bank like yours that has 20,000 customers and continues adding new accounts.

Relates skills/experiences to bank needs.

While in Phoenix, I served a two-year term as Public Relations and Membership Director for the Chamber of Commerce. During this term our Chamber gained 150 new member businesses. My interest in and development of public relations skills began during my years in Nashville at the university. As a student, I organized a citywide campaign to increase the number of registered voters. As a result, the number of registered voters increased by one third.

I appreciate your time and consideration in reviewing the enclosed resume. I look forward to meeting you and learning more about job opportunities at your bank and how I could apply my skills as part of the Nashville Commerce National team. I will be in Nashville from February 10 to 15 and will call you on the 12th to arrange an appointment. If you wish to reach me before my February scheduled trip to Nashville, you may leave a message at my new Nashville home at 615.555.2515 where my husband has already taken residence; or you may e-mail me in Phoenix at mlm@cbnationl.com.

Arranges for easy contact.

Yours truly,

Marylou Marzano

Marylou Marzano

Enclosure: Resume

LOOKS GOOD

FIGURE 17.2
A *Good* Example of a General Application Letter

Behavioral Interview Questions Increasingly, businesses and other organizations use behavioral questions for all or most of the interview. These questions focus on how the applicant acted and behaved in past situations to predict how he or she will perform in the future. Employers support this style of interview because they have found that past behaviors are a good predictor of future behaviors. An added advantage is that answers centered on an actual event are less subjective and less likely to be only an answer the applicant believes the interviewer expects.

Prepare for behavioral interview questions by reviewing previous situations at school or at work and how you handled them. In particular, identify specific examples from past events that illustrate positive accomplishments and work attributes. Inasmuch as possible, practice stating these examples with data that illustrate outcomes. The following examples illustrate behavioral questions that you may be asked.

NOTE 17.21
Behavioral questions focus on how you *did* handle past situations.

NOTE 17.22
Identify past examples to illustrate your accomplishments.

NEEDS WORK

71 Greenbay Avenue
Milwaukee, WI 53066
March 17, 200-

Del Ray Department Store
Racine Mall
Racine, WI 53406

TO WHOM IT MAY CONCERN:

I heard that you have an opening for a credit manager and I wish to apply for it. I have just graduated from the university as you can see on my resuma. Being hired for this job will be a big boost to my career goal of management in retail merchandising.

I am the first person in my family to complete a B.S. degree; and now that I have finished my education, I want to give something back to my family by getting a good job with a company like yours. I worked part time while attending school, so I have work experience at food stores, department stores, etc. I am a hard worker; I grew up on the farm and could drive any kind of machinery.

I always got along with my teachers, coworkers, and supervisors, with the exception of one person; no one could get along with her. I am easygoing and like people, so I think that I could be successful working with people in a retail store.

Let me hear from you if you think that I could fill your position. If not, please keep my application on file for the first available job that you have that matches my education and experience. I want to work for your company.

Sincerely,

Gerald S. Penneybaker

Gerald S. Penneybaker

Callouts (left margin):
- Uses impersonal salutation.
- Uses the I–viewpoint; misspelled word.
- Does not relate to company needs.
- Conveys negative tone; unsure about skills.
- No contact information; conveys uncertainty.

FIGURE 17.3
A *Poor* Example of a Targeted Application Letter

Behavioral Interview Questions

[1] Describe a major problem you had with an employee at work and how you handled it. Describe why you did or did not confront this employee to resolve the problem.

[2] Describe a teamwork situation on a class project when a student on the team was not doing his or her work. Explain how you handled the situation. Explain what happened at the end of the project.

[3] Describe the most difficult challenge you have faced at work. Explain why you believe you met or failed to meet that challenge.

[4] Describe a situation in which you were successful (or unsuccessful) in motivating someone.

[5] Describe a situation at work or at school where you took the initiative. What was the result? How did you feel?

71 Greenbay Avenue
Milwaukee, WI 53066
March 17, 200-

Ms. Sandra Delgado, Manager
Del Ray Department Store
Racine Mall
Racine, WI 53406

Uses positive, direct approach.

Dear Ms. Delgado:

Your advertisement in the *Del Ray Times* of a Credit Manager vacancy appeals to me because the requirements for the position match well with my education and experiences. As your Credit Manager, I believe that I would make an immediate contribution to the continued success of Del Ray Department Store.

Matches skills to job requirements.

Your Requirements

B.S. degree in Business Finance

Experience in retail credit

Ability to work with people

Ability to solve problems

My Qualifications

- B.S. in Business Administration with a Finance specialty; received award as Outstanding Senior in Business Finance.
- 3 years part-time department store experience as Assistant Manager; had responsibility for credit approvals; held 3-year bad debts to a maximum of .2%.
- 3 summers work experience in a major retail food store.
- Good relationships with colleagues and supervisors; served 2 years as student council treasurer at the university.
- Managed fund-raising campaign that raised $15,000 for emergency loans for students with a B or above average who needed a short-term loan for tuition.

As requested, I have enclosed my resume with further details of my qualifications and accomplishments. I look forward to meeting with you to discuss how I would fit into your organization. You may contact me by phone at 608.555.3235 or e-mail at gspenney@umemt.net. I would like to come for an interview at your convenience.

Shows enclosure of resume.

Sincerely,

Gerald S. Penneybaker

Gerald S. Penneybaker

Enclosure: Resume

Makes contact easy; reinforces interest.

LOOKS GOOD

FIGURE 17.4
A *Good* Example of a Targeted Application Letter

[6] Tell me about a situation at work or at school when you were unsuccessful in accomplishing a task. What could you have done differently?

[7] From your previous work role, describe the responsibility that gave you the greatest satisfaction.

[8] Describe a day at work or at school when everything seemed to go wrong. How did you handle it?

[9] Tell me about a leadership role that you carried out at work or at school and how you handled it.

[10] Describe the most difficult person with whom you have worked. How did you handle the situation?

Answering Questions For all interviews your answers must be honest, sincere, positive, and enthusiastic. Be yourself, be polite, and be attentive. State your experiences and accomplishments in a specific and positive manner. Don't be modest about taking credit for your achievements; it is important to make these known. However, overstatement or embellishment is unlikely to get the positive reaction shown in the following cartoon.

"YOU DON'T HAVE MUCH EXPERIENCE, BUT I'M IMPRESSED BY HOW YOU'VE BLOWN IT OUT OF PROPORTION."

© 2004. Reprinted with courtesy of Bunny Hoest & Parade Magazine.

Relate your answers to the job for which you are applying. Take advantage of the opportunity to show your knowledge of the company and the position. Your answers should be brief, but not just yes or no. For example, you may be asked the question, "Do you have plans to get additional education?" You might say, "Yes, I think it is important to keep up-to-date. I am interested in taking short continuing education courses and, in a few years, working on an MBA degree." In response to, "What do you consider to be your weaknesses?" you might say after reflecting for a moment, "Well, some people may think I am reserved, but thinking before acting has helped me relate effectively to others." This example illustrates how to turn weaknesses into strengths.

If asked where you want to be in five years, respond with realistic opportunities within the organization. Have two or three positive responses for why the company should hire you. For example, you could say, "*My educational background in finance gives me a basic knowledge to become a credit manager. In my previous position as an assistant manager, I lowered the bad debt ratio from 1 percent to .2 percent. My success in managing credit approvals is an indication of how I can benefit your company by making sound credit decisions. I look forward to becoming part of your organization and expect a long-term mutually beneficial career relationship.*"

Often a general question asked early in an interview is "Tell us about yourself." Unless you have given prior thought to this request, the general nature of it can be disconcerting and leave you "clueless" where to begin and where to end! Keep the response relevant to your education and career development rather than relating a multitude of personal and family details. You could give reasons that led to your career choice, specific ways that your college or university education and any paid or voluntary work experience helped you progress toward your career goals, and reasons why this position is of interest to you. For example, you could say something from your experience similar to this example:

"During my senior year of high school, I began considering a career in public service when our school implemented a community service project as part of graduation requirements. I worked four hours per week in the mayor's office and was able to help plan and implement an after-school recreation program for inner-city youth. The satisfaction that I gained from this successful effort led to my attending Marshall State University because of its national reputation for offering an outstanding degree in public service. After graduation, I became excited when you advertised this position as Parks and Recreation Director. It seemed to be perfect timing, a match for my career goals, and a way to help others."

When considering how to respond to behavioral interview questions, think of two or three positive and negative experiences that you could use as examples of accomplishments related to the position for which you are applying. If asked to give an example of a negative experience, consider how something positive was gained. For example, *you may have worked with someone who was always late arriving at work. He worked the shift following yours at a fast-food restaurant in a part-time job that you held while attending the university. You could not leave your work at the restaurant until he arrived. After twice waiting for him resulted in being late to a university class, you met with him to resolve the problem in a way that was win-win for both of you. You learned that he did not have an alarm clock and often took a nap and overslept before coming to work. You agreed to give him a telephone call each day at a specific time until payday, at which time he agreed to buy an alarm clock. Before the year was over, you became good friends.*

Think of similar examples that could be used to respond to a question about a difficult person that you dealt with, a problem that you resolved, or a challenging situation. With thought, you should be able to come up with a few examples of turning a negative into a positive and strengths that have resulted in successes. Specific examples are more meaningful than general statements such as, "I have always been able to get along with coworkers."

NOTE 17.26
Think of a positive gained from a negative experience.

©FRANK SITEMAN/INDEX STOCK IMAGERY

Before the interview, anticipate questions and plan answers that showcase your strengths.

NOTE 17.27
Illegal questions could
result in discrimination
charges.

Handling Illegal Questions Civil rights legislation; Section 504 of the Rehabilitation Act; the Americans with Disabilities Act; the Age Discrimination in Employment Act; the Equal Employment Opportunity Act; and other federal, state, and local laws prohibit discriminatory practices in hiring and affect the content of acceptable pre-employment questions. A prospective employer who asks questions unrelated to job requirements and that may have a detrimental effect on groups of people protected from discrimination by legislation is susceptible to charges of discrimination in hiring. An applicant who is not hired may believe interview questions about age, gender, disability, race, ethnic background, or religion resulted in discrimination and may seek a legal remedy.

NOTE 17.28
Unacceptable interview
questions do not relate
to job requirements.

The following examples illustrate unacceptable questions that could gain knowledge not related to a bona fide occupational qualification for the position. This knowledge leaves the potential employer in a vulnerable position legally if persons not hired suspect the decision to be based on discrimination. Furthermore, the person interviewed may resent responding to questions of a personal nature that are unrelated to position requirements. After each of the following questions, the legislation or reason for unacceptability is shown along with the protected group(s).

Unacceptable Questions

How old are you? (*the Age Discrimination in Employment Act—persons over 40*)

You don't look like a native of this country. Where were you born? (*the Civil Rights Act and the Equal Employment Opportunity Act—ethnic background*)

Do you have adequate child care? Who will look after your children while you work? (*the Civil Rights Act—gender*)

Do you have any disabilities? (*the Americans with Disabilities Act and Section 504 of the Rehabilitation Act—persons with disabilities*)

Would you leave a photograph with us? (*the Civil Rights Act, the Equal Employment Opportunity Act, and the Age Discrimination in Employment Act—race, ethnic background, gender, or age*)

Where do you attend church? (*the Civil Rights Act, the Equal Employment Opportunity Act—religion*)

Such questions may not be illegal per se; but because various legislative acts prohibit discrimination against certain groups of people, the employer, if investigated for charges of discrimination, could be required to show that hiring practices were nondiscriminatory and related to job requirements. Obtaining pre-employment information that identifies characteristics of a protected group and that are unrelated to job requirements raises suspicion and makes it difficult to prove that discrimination was not a part of the hiring decision.

If directly linked to a job requirement, the question is legitimate. For example, if a minor applies for a job that legally requires the worker to be 18, an acceptable question about age would be, "This job requires that a person be 18 years of age. If hired, can you provide proof that you meet that requirement?" Also, a question about disability may be linked to job requirements; for example, "To perform this job requires you to be able to lift up to 50 pounds; do you have any condition that would prevent you from lifting this weight?" The person's appearance in a photograph can give evidence that the applicant is a member of a protected group, and a person's birthplace is a clue to national origin; thus, those questions are unacceptable. Asking for a photograph prior to employment could be acceptable for a position such as a model that requires a certain appearance. In any case, an employer may ask for a photograph for the files after the person is employed.

If asked legally unacceptable questions, how should you respond? Showing anger or irritation will not get the job; if you are strongly offended, you may not want the job. Only you can decide how you will respond. However, you are usually wise not to respond angrily. You have nothing to gain by displaying anger or irritation. Such questions are asked for one of two reasons: The interviewer does not realize the question is inappropriate or asks the question to get your reaction (a risky action on the part of the interviewer).

What are ways that you could respond to inappropriate or illegal questions? If asked about your age, you might smile and say, "Old enough to do the job and young enough to do it well." If asked who will care for your children, a woman could say, "Child care does not affect my being able to do the job," or smile and say, "I'm a good planner and my arrangements are not an issue." Then you can shift the topic back to the position. You can decide to answer the question, pleasantly evade the question, or say calmly that the question is not relevant to the job and shift to another topic.

NOTE 17.29
Displaying anger when asked an illegal question is usually unwise.

NOTE 17.30
Answer an illegal question or pleasantly side-step it and shift topics.

RESPONDING TO THE SALARY QUESTION

The salary question—the last one on the list of traditional interview questions—is an important one. The employer may have set a salary or a salary range for the position. You should try to get that information before the interview if you can. Also, you should try to learn before the interview what salaries are being paid for similar jobs in the employer's geographic area. Your campus career center may have salary information. Web sites with salary information include http://www.salary.com, http://www.salaryexpert.com, and http://www.careerjournal.com. On the careerjournal.com Web site, click the Salary/Hiring tab. Newspaper employment ads sometimes show salaries, too.

Try to avoid talking about salary until the final stages of the interview after you have made a good impression and are in a better position to negotiate. If pressed early in the interview for a specific answer, respond in a straightforward, objective manner. You might say, "In researching the job market, the range for this position seems to be between $ and $." Another response could be to ask the interviewer to give you the salary range that this company pays for the position so that you could weigh your answer carefully and give a response related to this specific position.

NOTE 17.31
Before the interview, locate information on salaries.

After you have the job offer is the time to discuss salary. In negotiating salary, reinforce the skills that you bring to the company. When considering a salary offer, ask about the total compensation package. Benefits such as health insurance, life insurance, retirement programs, leave time, and moving expenses to a new employment site can be important considerations. If the company does not agree to the amount you request, you can agree to their figure (if acceptable) and ask that your salary be reviewed for an increase in six months.

NOTE 17.32
If possible, wait to talk about salaries until you have a job offer.

PREPARING QUESTIONS ABOUT THE POSITION

Be ready to ask key questions of your own to the interviewer. Usually, near the end of the interview you will be asked if you have questions. Do not concentrate just on questions of personal benefit to you, such as ones about fringe benefits, retirement programs, vacation policies, and salary. Your questions might be about such subjects as job duties, the employee evaluation system, management philosophy, company progress

NOTE 17.33
Prepare key questions you can ask the interviewer.

Employment Communication and Interviewing   **CHAPTER 17**   **501**

and plans, promotion policies, and employee development programs. Below are examples of questions you may want to ask:

[1] Please describe the duties of the job for me.

[2] Would you describe the normal routine of this position? Describe a typical day.

[3] What kinds of job assignments might I expect the first six months on the job?

[4] How is job performance evaluated and how often?

[5] How much travel is normally expected? Is a car provided?

[6] Describe your relocation policy.

[7] Do you have plans for expansion?

[8] Does your company encourage further education?

[9] When do you expect to make a decision?

[10] Where do we go from here?

An effective exchange of information takes place in a successful job interview.

©ARIEL SKELLEY/CORBIS

RESEARCH THE COMPANY

NOTE 17.34
Learn about the organization before the interview.

Learn as much as you can about the company prior to the interview. Secure descriptive materials on the company and its industry from the company, your campus career center, the library, the chamber of commerce, the Better Business Bureau, a trade association, trade journals, or the Web. Chapter 16 and the first part of this chapter list some of the sources of information on organizations.

The Web has many sources of information. A business search engine such as http://www.business.com will provide a number of Web sites with information about a specific company by entering the company name. You can view Fortune 500 company profiles on http://www.fortune.com. Other sites such as http://www.fisonline.com give data on a large number of companies for a small fee and can provide information such as fact sheets and annual reports.

Through your public library, you can access several books and Web databases that have information about manufacturers and other businesses and industries. Examples of these databases are Dun and Bradstreet's *Million Dollar Directory* (for large-volume businesses) and *infoUSA*. The *Million Dollar Directory* may be viewed in book format in the reference section of the library or through an electronic database. It has 166,000 American companies that have more than $9 million dollars in sales or more than 180 total employees. The directory gives the location; phone number; number of employees; and names, titles, and short biographies of executives. Your librarian can help you locate these or similar materials. Libraries in some cities have copies on file of a number of company annual reports.

NOTE 17.35
Use the Internet and the library for information about employers.

Studying materials carefully to gain background knowledge of the organization will help you in the interview in two basic ways: It will aid your communication with the interviewer, and it will set you apart from the other interviewees who learned nothing about the company prior to an interview. Examples of questions you should research about the organization include the following:

[1] What is the size of the organization or company?

[2] What type of service or products does the company offer?

[3] What is the percent of annual sales growth in the last five years?

[4] What is the estimated number of employees?

[5] What are the strengths of the company?

[6] What is the organizational structure?

[7] Is the company an international company?

[8] What is the corporate culture of the company?

[9] What are the typical career paths and advancement opportunities in your field offered by the company?

[10] What is the salary range for the position?

[11] How long has the company been in business?

[12] What are the names of top company officers or executives? Human resources manager?

PREPARE YOURSELF PERSONALLY

Choose your clothes carefully, give attention to personal grooming, and avoid wearing heavy jewelry or strong colognes. Depending on the industry, men should remove earrings; both men and women should remove tongue studs. The interviewer(s) may be dressed in casual clothing; however, employers expect you to dress in a conservative business style for an interview. Wear the clothing at least once before the interview to be sure it is comfortable. Although appropriate dress varies from industry to industry, dressing conservatively for the interview keeps attention on your skills, not appearance. A suggested general guide follows:

NOTE 17.36
Give attention to grooming and dress for the interview.

Men

• Two-piece conservative suit in a solid color such as blue or gray.

• Long-sleeved white shirt with a tie in a plain or simple pattern.

• Polished shoes with socks that match the suit. Remember your belt should match your shoes.

Women

- Two-piece conservative suit with a knee-length or longer skirt in a solid color such as blue or gray. A business-style, well-fitted pantsuit is also appropriate.
- White blouse with modest jewelry.
- Polished shoes with plain hosiery.

Many companies are now suggesting to students that they dress in business or office casual for one of the interviews at the company. Because business casual varies greatly from company to company, follow these guidelines:

Men

- Sport coat and belted slacks
- Collared shirt
- Polished shoes and matching socks
- A tie is optional; however, you may want to carry one in your coat pocket

Women

- Sport coat and belted slacks
- Blouse
- Hosiery and polished shoes

Remember to be modest with the use of jewelry and cologne. Hair should be clean and well groomed. Job candidates should always dress professionally for an interview even if they know the employer will be wearing jeans.

NOTE 17.37
Leave early for the interview to allow for traffic delays.

Practice walking, sitting and rising, and shaking hands for the interview. Check in advance to be sure of the date, place, and name and title of the interviewer. If the location is unfamiliar, visit the place before the day of your interview. Plan your schedule so that you arrive early for the interview. Allow time for heavy traffic, a flat tire, or other delays.

Take a portfolio with the following materials: two copies of your resume; a copy of your transcript; examples of your course work and work projects; letters of reference; a reference list; and an application form with all the important details such as former employers, addresses, and phone numbers. In addition, take a pen and a small notebook to record notes about the position and the names of the people you have met. Ask for business cards so you will have accurate names, titles, and addresses and can send a letter of appreciation immediately after the interview.

NOTE 17.38
Reinforce your confidence by being well prepared.

Talk (mentally) to yourself and relax before the interview. Build your confidence by telling yourself that you have done all you can to prepare for the interview. You have anticipated questions and have prepared answers, you have learned about the company, and you have prepared yourself personally. You are ready for the interview.

Participating in an Interview

NOTE 17.39
Videotaping a practice interview helps you improve it.

View the interview as an opportunity to share your qualifications with an interested person who is knowledgeable in your career field. As part of your preparation, you can do a practice interview; videotape it, and evaluate your performance. The interview is important, but you are prepared; therefore, you should not be overly nervous. Some nervousness is natural and helpful to you; but too much nervousness makes a poor impression. Knowing that you are prepared will increase your confidence and help reduce nervousness.

Greet your interviewer warmly by name and pronounce the name correctly. Let the interviewer take the lead. If an offer is made to shake hands, do so with a firm grip and a smile. Sit when asked to do so. See your role as primarily responding to questions in a businesslike fashion. Keep appropriate eye contact with the interviewer. The amount of appropriate eye contact with interviewers varies depending on the interviewer's cultural background; 75 percent of the time is a good goal for interviews in North America. Other cultural variations that are important in interviews include verbal and nonverbal communication patterns (refer to Chapter 2 for further information on cultural variations in business communication).

The interviewer may intentionally challenge you by asking difficult questions or by appearing disinterested or even irritated. Be knowledgeable, calm, positive, gracious, and friendly. During the interview avoid appearing

- Overly aggressive or conceited
- Meek and mild
- Negative about past employers or other topics
- Unenthusiastic
- Too interested in money
- Too ambitious
- Humorless
- Too vague with answers
- Unappreciative of the interviewer's time

Don't smoke, chew gum, eat your lunch, lean back in your chair, lean on the interviewer's desk, act immature, tell jokes, or laugh nervously.

Be alert for signals that the interview is ending. The interviewer may slide her or his chair back, stand, or send you verbal signals. When the interview is over, express appreciation for the time and information given you. Indicate that you look forward to hearing from the interviewer. Ask when you will receive notice of the decision or when you may call about the decision. Shake hands, express thanks for the interview, and warmly tell the interviewer goodbye.

After the interview, evaluate your performance. Make written notes of those things that went well and those that you will change the next time you interview. Make a record of the information you learned about the job for comparison with other job opportunities. Record the correct spellings of the names and titles of those who interviewed you, and note what you will want to say in your follow-up communication.

Types of Interviews

Regardless of the interview type, interviews are scheduled usually at a mutually agreeable time for applicant and employer. One interview may cover two or more interview stages; some businesses will interview a candidate only once, maybe twice. Some interviews are conducted by telephone. With the increasing use of computers, video conferencing or an online computer system may be used for interviewing. One person or a group of individuals may interview you to assess your qualifications and determine if you are the best candidate to fit the position. The employee selection process is important to the organization as well as to the potential employee. Replacing

NOTE 17.40
Be warm, pleasant, and businesslike in the interview

NOTE 17.41
At the close, express appreciation for the interview.

NOTE 17.42
Evaluate the interview and record information for follow-up contacts.

NOTE 17.43
Interviews may cover one or two stages and use different media.

a worker who leaves after completing the hiring process doubles the cost of filling the position.

SCREENING INTERVIEWS

NOTE 17.44
Preliminary screening verifies your match to the position.

A **screening interview**, sometimes called a *preliminary interview,* is to verify that you meet the education, work experience, communication skills, and personality requirements for success in the position. Screening interviews may take place in the campus career center or in the employer's office. In some cases, a telephone or telephone conference-call interview may be used for screening.

NOTE 17.45
Screening may be a review of resumes and application letters.

A screening interview may start with traditional questions such as "Why are you interested in this position?" followed by behavioral interviewing questions. One or two human resources employees will conduct most of these interviews. If you make a favorable impression on the interviewer(s), you may be asked to a second interview. Not all employers hold screening interviews; the screening of resumes and application letters may suffice as the preliminary step before interviewing.

SUBSEQUENT INTERVIEWS

NOTE 17.46
After passing screening, you may have one or more interviews.

After you have passed the screening interview and/or screening of resumes and application letters, you may be invited to a company's office for one or more additional interviews. The subsequent interviews may include meeting with several individuals in the company separately and/or as a team on a panel. Panel or team interviews are conducted by a group of employees and may include a human resources representative, a potential supervisor, and potential colleagues. When interviewed by a panel, have eye contact with the questioner when responding to questions. Be prepared to answer questions from each interviewer. Always bring a paper and pencil with you so that you are prepared to write anything needed during the interview and to record the names of the interviewers.

TELEPHONE INTERVIEWS

NOTE 17.47
An interview may be conducted by telephone.

Prepare for a telephone interview in the same way as for a face-to-face interview, but you can use notes during the interview. Your notes for reference should be readily available by the telephone. Seat yourself comfortably and maintain a friendly, pleasant voice. A smile can be heard in your voice, so smile while speaking in the same manner that you would if the interviewer could see you. Being unable to see the speaker's nonverbal body language and facial expressions can make it more difficult to interpret the speaker's attitude toward your responses. Keeping a positive mental image of the interviewer will help your confidence.

VIDEO INTERVIEWS

NOTE 17.48
Video interviews may take place in a video conferencing center.

A newer form of interviewing uses a video conferencing system. Video interviews have become popular because they allow companies to interview new recruits at colleges more economically. If you are to participate in a video interview, your campus career center will provide you with the information on where the interview will take place. Many universities have their own video conferencing centers. Research offers a reassuring note for persons interviewed by video conferencing. Findings have shown that applicants rate slightly higher in video interviews than face-to-face. Interpretation of the findings are that the higher ratings may be due to belief in a need for bias correction, thus giving the benefit of the doubt to the applicant because of the assumption that he or she has little or no experience with video conference interviews.

ONLINE INTERVIEWS

Online interviewing uses a combination of video, camera, computer, and the Internet. Online interviewing may become more popular because of advancing technology. Either an individual or a team can conduct these interviews. Online interviewing enables employers to screen candidates rapidly and to cut interview costs. With a camera and microphone attached to the computer, online interviews become similar to video conferencing.

NOTE 17.49
The computer, microphone, and camera can create online interviews.

GROUP INTERVIEWS

With group interviews several people are interviewed at the same time for the same position(s). Companies use this method to determine how a potential employee will interact in a group situation and to evaluate the potential employee's interactive skills. Disney and various airline companies conduct group interviews.

NOTE 17.50
Group interviews test a person's interaction skills.

The organization's decision about making you an employment offer will result from the interview or series of interviews. You should consider whether or not you will accept an offer if one is made at the end of the interview. Regardless of the kind of job interview, the interview is a critical juncture in your job campaign. In most cases, any offer of employment would come a few days or weeks after interviewing. If you do receive an offer at the end of the interview, you may want to think about it at least overnight. You could indicate that you are very interested in the position and that, after careful consideration, you will call the next day with your answer. Ask the time of day that would be convenient for you to call, as well as the telephone number. If more time is needed, explain this and give a certain day of the week to call with your answer.

NOTE 17.51
For a job offered at the interview, you may call back with an answer.

Preparing Other Employment Communications

LEARNING OBJECTIVE
③ *Compose a variety of follow-up letters and other employment-related messages.*

Employment communication is not limited to resumes, application letters, and interviews. Other employment communication can include telephone calls, letters, e-mail, and in-person contacts. You may need to follow up on a pending application or communicate your acceptance of an invitation for an interview. You may want some kind of follow-up contact after an interview. It will be necessary to communicate your rejection or acceptance of a job offer. If you accept a job, you may need to resign from another job. Finally, you should express appreciation to all those who assisted you in your job campaign. Suggestions for composing these communications are given in the following sections of this chapter. These examples show the body of the letter only and do not include dates, inside addresses, salutations, and closings. All employment communication needs the appropriate format as shown in Appendix A. In addition, the Communication Quote by Bob Besten emphasizes the importance of clarity, brevity, and accuracy in business communication. These characteristics are essential for employment communication.

NOTE 17.52
Job-related communication may be in person, in writing, by phone, or by e-mail.

Following Up an Application

NOTE 17.53
Send a follow-up letter two weeks after receipt of your application.

If you think it has been too long since you heard about your application with an employer, you may want to initiate a follow-up contact after a couple of weeks. Remember, many unsolicited applications are not acknowledged. Your follow-up contact, depending on the circumstances, can be by letter, in person, or by telephone (be prepared to leave your message on an answering machine or in voice mail). Such a message would be neutral news for the employer; consequently, use the direct plan. Here is an example of such a follow-up message:

> *In March I sent you an application for a position in your marketing department. I am still very much interested in employment with Seagate Computer Sales.*
>
> *Since March, I have completed my Bachelor of Science degree in Business Administration with a major in Marketing. During May, I was selected as the outstanding member of the Marketing Club on campus.*
>
> *If you need any additional information, please telephone me at (716) 555-2995 or e-mail me at dyknow@ccuicon.edu. I look forward to interviewing for the position you have in marketing.*

Accepting an Interview Invitation

NOTE 17.54
Telephone and e-mail are commonly used for interview invitations.

Most interview invitations will be by telephone or e-mail. Be prepared to receive this kind of call or e-mail any time during your job campaign and to respond logically, clearly, and maturely. Check the voice mail message on your home telephone and the information on your e-mail account to be sure that they are professional. Your communication accepting an interview should use the direct plan (for positive news) and should (1) express appreciation, (2) indicate availability, and (3) convey a positive and optimistic attitude. Here is an example of content for either a written or an oral message:

> *Thank you for the opportunity to interview for the position in the accounting department. I am very much interested in meeting with you to discuss the position and my qualifications.*
>
> *I appreciate your asking me for three alternative dates. Because of my work and class schedules, the best interview dates are March 7, 9, or 10. Any of these three dates will be convenient for me.*
>
> *I look forward to visiting your offices and learning more about the auditing position.*

Following Up an Interview

A letter of appreciation is appropriate after an interview. If a company has been corresponding with you using e-mail, then it is acceptable that you send an e-mail letter of appreciation. This letter should be sent within one or two days following the interview. If you think you are still interested in the position, you should express that interest in the letter. If you are definitely not interested in the position, a letter of appreciation for the interview is still appropriate. In the latter case, in fairness to the employer, you should withdraw your candidacy. The letter in which you express your continuing interest should use the direct plan, and the letter in which you withdraw your candidacy should use the indirect plan. These letters should be brief, cordial, businesslike, and word processed. An example of a follow-up appreciation letter for a position you wish to obtain is shown in Figure 17.5.

NOTE 17.55
After an interview, send a letter of appreciation.

71 Greenbay Avenue
Milwaukee, WI 53066
April 1, 200-

Ms. Sandra Delgado, Manager
Del Ray Department Store
Racine Mall
Racine, WI 53406

Expresses appreciation for the interview.

Dear Ms. Delgado:

Thank you for the opportunity yesterday to interview for the position of Credit Manager for Del Ray Department Store. I appreciated the time that you and other members of your staff spent with me during the morning.

After meeting with you and your sales team, I am enthusiastic about the position and the growth opportunities that it offers. My experience in retail credit and previous problem-solving accomplishments, both with volunteer work and work experience while earning my Business Administration degree, match well with the responsibilities of the Credit Manager position.

Reinforces match of experience with the position.

I look forward to hearing your decision for filling the position. If you need additional information, please phone me at 608.555.3235 or send an e-mail to *gspenney@umemt.net.*

Sincerely,

Provides information for easy contact.

Gerald S. Penneybaker

Gerald S. Penneybaker

FIGURE 17.5
An Appreciation Letter as an Interview Follow-up

Accepting Employment

The communications offering employment and accepting employment most likely will be by telephone or in person, followed by confirming letters. A letter accepting employment is a positive communication and should use the direct plan: (1) The offer should be accepted, (2) any essential information about assuming the position should come next, and (3) an expression of appreciation should close the letter. An example of a confirming acceptance letter follows:

NOTE 17.56
Use the direct plan for a letter of employment acceptance.

This letter confirms my acceptance of the position as marketing representative with Marston Products, Inc. I understand that this position pays a salary of $2,750 per month and a 10 percent commission on sales.

I am eager to begin work with you. As agreed, I will report at 8 a.m. on June 20, 200– , to Mrs. Wanda L. Adams, Marketing Vice President, in Building A, Room 200.

Thank you for the opportunity to join the Marston team. I look forward to beginning a long and productive career with this progressive company.

Rejecting Employment

NOTE 17.57
An employment rejection should be brief, cordial, and businesslike.

As is the case with accepting employment, the first communication rejecting employment most likely will be by telephone. An indirect message following up an oral employment rejection may be appropriate. This letter should be brief, cordial, businesslike, and printed rather than handwritten. The body of a letter rejecting employment might look like this:

Thank you for offering me the position of customer service representative with Spectrum Laboratory. I appreciate your taking the time to interview me for the position and allowing me the time to consider your offer.

I have considered your offer and believe that the Spectrum Laboratory position would be interesting and challenging; however, I have decided to accept employment in a similar position at Access Laboratory, which is located closer to my home. I believe this is the best choice for me at this time.

I enjoyed the opportunity to meet you and your excellent staff. Please convey my thanks to all of the members of the interview team for their time and the courtesies extended to me.

Expressing Appreciation to References and Others

NOTE 17.58
Express appreciation for help given in a successful job campaign.

When you have completed a successful job campaign and accepted an employment offer, share the good news with your references. Also, it will be important to notify any placement service and others who assisted you. These expressions of appreciation for assistance may be by telephone, by e-mail, by letter, or in person.

Resigning from a Job

NOTE 17.59
A job resignation should be both oral in-person and written.

Once your job campaign is completed, it may be necessary to resign from your present position. It is best that your resignation not be a surprise for your employer. If you can, let your employer know that you have applied for another position while you are searching. If you think your employer would react negatively to your search for another position, you may want to keep your job search confidential.

Most resignations are given orally and in person and then followed by a written message. Usually, the employer will request that a resignation be submitted in writing. Be sure to give your employer the amount of notice required in company policy. Resignations are negative messages but are considered routine; therefore, they are written following a direct plan. Here is an example of a resignation letter written with a direct plan:

Please accept this letter as official resignation from my position as a human resources intern, effective Friday, January 15, 200–. I have accepted a position as a human resources benefits assistant with Belmont Telecommunications.

I have enjoyed working as an intern with this organization. The practical skills I obtained here have made me competitive in the job market as a new college graduate. I appreciate the experiences and support you and your staff provided.

In my new position in human resources, I look forward to continuing professional contacts.

Summary of Learning Objectives

Write effective application letters for solicited and unsolicited positions.

An application letter is a sales letter with *your knowledge and skills* as the products. The major parts of an application letter are the opening to gain attention, the summary of qualifications to convince the employer that you fit the job, and the request for an interview along with information that makes contact easy. Remember that the primary purpose of an application letter is to motivate a potential employer to read your resume and to invite you for an interview. Your sales focal point is to use past accomplishments to illustrate how your employment can benefit the organization.

Prepare for a successful job interview.

Preparing for an interview includes reviewing information gathered to this point; learning all you can about the company through research at the library, chamber of commerce, or the Web; preparing to ask and answer questions; dressing appropriately for the interview; and participating in the job interview.

Interview questions can be either traditional or behavioral. Traditional questions ask about your education and experience and how you *would* handle hypothetical situations, and behavioral questions focus on specific past situations and how you *did* handle them. Both types of questions are intended to determine how you will perform in the future.

The screening interview eliminates individuals who do not have the required education, work experience, communication skills, and other basic requirements for the position. Subsequent interviews may include meeting with several individuals in the organization separately and/or as a team on a panel. Interview types may include telephone, video, online, and group interviews. Telephone interviews may be used for screening or for final selection. A video interview uses a video conferencing system; and the online interview uses a combination of video, camera, computer, and the Internet. Group interviews involve several people being interviewed at the same time for the same position(s).

Compose a variety of follow-up letters and other employment-related messages.

Other employment messages that you should be able to prepare are as follows: a follow-up to an application letter, an interview acceptance letter, a thank-you letter after a job interview, a job acceptance letter, a letter rejecting employment, and a letter of resignation.

Discussion Questions

1. Discuss the purpose of application letters. Describe the two kinds of application letters. (Objective 1)
2. Describe briefly the four purposes accomplished by a well-designed application letter. (Objective 1)
3. What content should go in the closing paragraph of an application letter? (Objective 1)
4. How would you answer the question, "What do you consider your weaknesses?" (Objective 2)
5. How should you answer the question, "What salary do you expect for this position?" (Objective 2)
6. What is the difference between a traditional interview question and a behavioral question? (Objective 2)
7. Describe how you could gather information about a potential employer. Why is it important to have background information on a future employer? (Objective 2)
8. Describe what a man should wear to an interview. What is appropriate dress for a woman to wear to an interview? (Objective 2)
9. Describe three types of employment-related letters that you may write in addition to an application letter. (Objective 3)
10. Would you follow a direct or indirect plan in writing a letter accepting employment? Explain your answer. (Objective 3)

Application Exercises

1. Prepare the targeted application letter to accompany the targeted resume that you prepared for Chapter 16. (Objective 1) (*Hint:* Be sure your letter addresses all four purposes of a persuasive letter.)

2. **Global.** Explore business Web sites or your library resources and find a company with international opportunities. Write a general application letter expressing your interest in working for that company. (Objective 1)
3. Select and respond to ten traditional and ten behavioral interview questions from this chapter. (Objective 2)

4. **E-mail. Internet.** Use a Web site to locate salary information for a beginning accountant in the largest city in your state. In an e-mail to your teacher, explain what you learned about the salary; and give the Universal Resource Locator(s) (URLs) for the source(s) that you used to locate this information. (Objective 2)

5. **Teamwork. Ethics.** Form a group of two to three students. Decide what you believe would be the best way to respond to each of the unacceptable questions included in this chapter. Also, discuss ethical considerations for the interviewer and the applicant in regard to asking and responding to legally unacceptable questions. (Objective 2)

6. **Global.** If you were interviewing with a German company, describe how the following behavior might differ from interviewing with a company in the United States: (a) greeting the interviewer, (b) responding to questions, (c) closing remarks. (Objective 2)

7. **InfoTrac.** Use InfoTrac to access and read the short article "Thumbs Down on Green Hair" in *Career World* (article A90984051). Write a short paragraph about each of the five qualities the article says employers consider most important. In each paragraph, give a specific example of something that you did in the past that demonstrates one of these important qualities. (Objective 2)

8. **InfoTrac. Ethics.** Use InfoTrac to access and read article CJ85587780 and then answer the following questions: (Objective 2)
   a. How would you feel about the ethics of giving the mother-in-law response suggested for an illegal question about child care?

b. Review the biggest mistakes that job candidates make in an interview. Which one do you think would be the worst one for an applicant to make? Explain.

9. **E-mail.** Assume that you have received an e-mail invitation for an interview from the targeted application letter that you wrote in Application Exercise 1. The message suggested a date and time that would cause you to miss a final examination in one of your university courses. Prepare an e-mail response that indicates your acceptance of the invitation but suggests alternate times and/or dates for the interview. Send your e-mail message to your instructor. (Objective 3) (*Hint:* Use the indirect plan.)

10. **Teamwork.** With two classmates, role-play an interview for the position in the application letter that you wrote in Application Exercise 1. Take turns being the interviewer and applicant. After each of you have played the applicant role, work together to write a follow-up letter expressing appreciation for the interview and confirming your interest in the position. (Objective 3)

11. **Ethics. Teamwork.** Assume that you are employed with a company where you have worked for five years. Your experiences with the company have been generally positive, but you have not received the promotions and salary increases that you expected. Therefore, for the past three months, you have been sending letters of application and interviewing for another position. You have not told your present employer because you believe that you would lose your present job. However, your employer called you to his office today to tell you that he has a health problem and will be leaving in three weeks for a one-month overseas cruise based on his doctor's recommendation. He tells you that he has always depended on you and that he wants you to assume leadership of the company while he is gone. You are flattered by his offer, but you believe that it is in your best interest to leave the company and take a new position as soon as you find the right position. You still believe that if he knows that you plan to leave that he will ask you to leave so that he can fill your position with someone else. Partner with a classmate and discuss what you should do and say in response to your employer's request. Decide also what you believe the short-term and long-term effect will be of your response to the situation. (Objective 3)

12. Assume that you accepted another position the next week after the scenario described in Application Exercise 11. Write a letter of resignation from your present job. (Objective 3)

There are Web exercises at **http://krizan.swlearning.com** to accompany this chapter.

Message Analysis

List three problems with the following application letter. Rewrite it to strengthen the letter's effectiveness. Add details to your letter, as required, to improve it.

> *Please consider this letter an application for your company. I believe I could advance my career rapidly as an employee with a company such as yours. I am a quick learner and a hard worker. My business degree is a B.S. in Finance. I am good in accounting and really enjoy it. If you have an opening for anything, however, I am willing to take the job. What is the salary for a beginning accountant with your company? Please let me hear from you soon as I am eager to get a job and begin my career. I have work experience. I was a counter salesperson with McDonald's for three summers.*

Grammar Workshop

Correct the grammar, spelling, punctuation, style, and word choice errors in the following sentences:

1. A person whom has never interviewed will be most likely to be nervus in a interview.
2. Has the new employe adjusted to their job in the maleroom?
3. What affect do you think that the low math grade will have on your chanches for a job as a sales clerk?
4. The job market is tighter now, then it has been for the last several years.
5. One of the modems in the 201 classroom are broken.
6. The english grade on her transcrept should of helped her get the newsreporter job.
7. When did you return from your trip to Bangkok, and your trip to Queenland Australia?
8. Of the two employers ABC was the most family oriented business.
9. At the department level she was co-advisor of the MBA club; advising students in her office, and she taught job interviewing techniques.
10. Her contributions as a secretary is highly value by the Department.

Business English Seminars

Parts of Speech

Every word in a sentence has a use or function. Knowing word functions will enable you to select the right word, which in turn will help you communicate your ideas effectively. Your understanding of the parts of speech will aid you in selecting the right word at the right time. The eight parts of speech are as follows:

[1] **Verb.** A word or phrase that describes the action or state of being (or condition) of the subject

[2] **Noun.** A word that names a person, place, or thing

[3] **Pronoun.** A word that takes the place of a noun

[4] **Adjective.** A word that describes or modifies a noun or pronoun

[5] **Adverb.** A word that describes or modifies a verb, an adjective, or another adverb

[6] **Preposition.** A word that connects a noun or pronoun to other words in the sentence

[7] **Conjunction.** A word that joins words, phrases, or clauses

[8] **Interjection.** A word that expresses surprise, emotion, or strong feeling and is not related to other words in the sentence

Verbs

The verb is the most important part of speech in a sentence. It expresses an action or a state of being. Every complete sentence must have a verb. Some sentences—compound and complex—have more than one verb. (Compound and complex sentences are discussed in Seminar B.) When you are constructing sentences, remember that you should build each sentence around the verb.

Verb Types

Sentences are constructed using two types of verbs. The two types of verbs are action verbs and state-of-being verbs.

ACTION VERBS

An **action verb** expresses an act. It adds power and precision to your communication. *Hire, invest, join, negotiate, organize, praise, sell*, and thousands of other words are action verbs. The action verb is italicized in the following examples:

The company *liquidated* its assets.

Crude oil prices *rose* nearly $1 a barrel last week.

STATE-OF-BEING VERBS

A **state-of-being verb** expresses the five senses (*hear, smell, see, taste,* and *touch*). Other state-of-being verbs include *is, am, are, was, were, seem, appear, will be,* and *have been*. A state-of-being verb is also called a *linking verb*. These verbs join or link one part of a sentence to another. State-of-being verbs are less powerful and less precise than action verbs. The state-of-being verbs are in italics in the following examples:

The road repair *will be* completed in January.

The new office building *is* the tallest structure in the state.

NOTE SA.4
State-of-being verbs are used to link parts of sentences.

Verb Tense

Verb tense indicates the time that action occurs. Six verb tense forms are used to indicate time. The six tenses are categorized into two groups—simple tense and perfect tense.

NOTE SA.5
Verb tense indicates the time that action occurs.

SIMPLE TENSE

Simple tense includes present, past, and future. The time of action or state of being of each simple tense is designated by its name.

NOTE SA.6
The three simple tenses are present, past, and future.

Present Tense A **present tense verb** expresses action that is going on at the present time or action that is continuing or habitual. Present tense verbs may also be used to indicate general truths. Verbs showing present tense are in italics in the following examples:

The president *is presenting* his recommendation to the board. (present time)

Nancy *stocks* the fabric department at night. (continuing)

Fax machines *facilitate* communication within organizations. (general truths)

NOTE SA.7
Present tense expresses current and continuing action or general truths.

Past Tense A **past tense verb** indicates action that has been completed. Verbs in the past tense have two forms—regular and irregular. The past tense of regular verbs is formed by adding *-d* or *-ed*. The past tense of irregular verbs is formed by changing the root word. *Regular* and *irregular verbs* in the past tense are shown in italics in these examples:

Robert *learned* to operate the new cash register. (regular—*learn* [root word] + *ed*)

Robert *saved* 10 percent of his paycheck each month. (regular—*save* [root word] + *d*)

Karen *taught* Robert to operate the new cash register. (irregular—root word is *teach*)

NOTE SA.8
Past tense expresses completed action.

Future Tense A **future tense verb** is used to indicate actions that are expected to occur in the future. Future tense is formed by using *will* before the present tense form of the verb. The following sentences show verbs in the future tense in italics:

Will the company picnic *be held* on the 4th of July?

Roger *will retire* at the end of next year.

NOTE SA.9
Future tense expresses expected action.

PERFECT TENSE

NOTE SA.10
The three perfect tenses are present perfect, past perfect, and future perfect.

A **perfect tense verb** shows action that has been completed at the time the statement is made. The perfect tense requires a form of the verb *have*, along with the past participle of the main verb. (Participles are discussed at the end of this section.) The perfect tenses are present perfect, past perfect, and future perfect.

NOTE SA.11
Present perfect tense = *has* or *have* + past participle.

Present Perfect Tense A **present perfect tense verb** refers to an action begun in the past and completed in the present. Present perfect tense may also refer to habitual or repeated past action. This tense is formed by adding *has* or *have* to the past participle of the main verb. The following examples show verbs in the present perfect tense in italics:

> Mr. Thompson *has served* as the company president for 15 years.
> We *have watched* the Super Bowl together since its inception.
> The CEO *has written* many letters to the stockholders.

NOTE SA.12
Past perfect tense = *had* + past participle.

Past Perfect Tense A **past perfect tense verb** refers to an action that was completed before another event in the past occurred. This tense is formed by adding *had* to the past participle of the main verb. The verbs in the past perfect tense are in italics in the following examples:

> Mr. Thompson *had served* as the company president before his retirement.
> We *had watched* the Super Bowl together before Sharon moved to Chicago.
> The CEO *had written* many letters to the stockholders prior to the merger.

NOTE SA.13
Future perfect tense = *shall have* or *will have* + past participle.

Future Perfect Tense A **future perfect tense verb** is used to express an action that will be completed before a stated time in the future. This tense is formed by adding *shall have* or *will have* to the past participle of the main verb. Examples of verbs in the future perfect tense are in italics in the following sentences:

> Mr. Thompson *will have served* as the company president for 15 years on January 1, 2005.
> We *will have watched* the Super Bowl before we go to the NCAA basketball playoffs.
> By the end of the quarter, the CEO *will have written* many letters to the stockholders.

Verb Voice

Voice is the term used to indicate whether the subject is doing or receiving the action. Sentence meaning and emphasis are communicated through the proper use of verb voice. The two voices of verbs are active and passive.

NOTE SA.14
The two voices of verbs are active and passive.

ACTIVE VOICE

NOTE SA.15
The subject performs the action in the active voice.

When the subject of the sentence is performing the action, the verb is in the **active voice**. In business communication the active voice usually is preferred because it is more direct and concise. Sentences that use verbs in the active voice identify the one performing the action. The following examples demonstrate how the verbs, shown in italics, are used in the active voice:

Prior to going on vacation, Robert *hired* the technology specialist.

Echo *is applying* for the sales manager's position.

PASSIVE VOICE

A verb is in the **passive voice** when the subject of the sentence receives the action. The passive voice is used sparingly in business communication. It is used when the subject is unknown or when the writer wants to soften the message to avoid making an accusation. Another use of the passive voice is to emphasize the action rather than the person who performed the action. The passive voice can also be used to eliminate a gender pronoun.

NOTE SA.16
The subject receives the action in the passive voice.

Passive voice verbs require a form of *be* (*am, is, are, was, were, been*) as a helping verb, along with a past participle of the verb. Uses of verbs in the passive voice are shown in italics in the following examples:

Adrian *was informed* of his termination through an e-mail message. (Emphasis is on being informed rather than being terminated.)

The pallet of toys *was lifted* with a forklift. (The main point is what was lifted—the pallet of toys—not how it was lifted—with a forklift.)

The books *were audited* before the merger. (A biased statement was avoided by not saying, "He audited the books before the merger.")

Changing the verb voice from active to passive does not change the verb tense from present to past. The tense in the passive voice is expressed by its auxiliary (helping) verb. The following examples show verbs (in italics) in the passive voice in several different tenses:

Training sessions *are offered* each Thursday and Friday. (*passive voice*, present tense)

The company *offers* training sessions each Thursday and Friday. (*active voice*, present tense)

Training sessions *were offered* last summer. (*passive voice*, past tense)

The company *offered* training sessions last summer. (*active voice*, past tense)

Training sessions *will be offered* during the morning in the spring. (*passive voice*, future tense)

The company *will offer* training sessions during the morning in the spring. (*active voice*, future tense)

Verb Mood

Communicators use **verb moods** to express facts, commands, or conditions. The three moods are indicative, imperative, and subjunctive.

NOTE SA.17
The three verb moods are indicative, imperative, and subjunctive.

INDICATIVE MOOD

The **indicative mood** is used to make statements or to ask questions involving facts. Business writers use verbs in this mood more than in the imperative or subjunctive mood. Examples are in italics in these sentences:

What positions *will be available* in October?

The company *is expanding* into the northeast.

NOTE SA.18
Use indicative mood to ask questions or make factual statements.

IMPERATIVE MOOD

NOTE SA.19
Commands, instructions, and requests are in the imperative mood.

The **imperative mood** is used to give commands, give instructions, or make requests. Sentences in the imperative mood usually have *you* understood as the subject and, therefore, it is omitted. Verbs used in the imperative mood are shown in italics in the following sentences:

Please *submit* your prospectus to the board.

E-mail Katie about the acquisition.

SUBJUNCTIVE MOOD

NOTE SA.20
The subjunctive mood is used rarely.

The **subjunctive mood** can be used to express a wish or a doubt. This mood is rarely used today. Here are some examples; the subjunctive mood verbs are in italics:

Should the gas well *be productive*, we will build a new house. (doubt)

I wish it *would* quit raining. (wish)

Verbals

NOTE SA.21
The three verbals are the infinitive, the gerund, and the participle.

A **verbal** is a verb form used as a noun, an adjective, or an adverb. Verbals cannot function as verbs and do not express action or state of being. The three verbals are the infinitive, the gerund, and the participle.

INFINITIVE

NOTE SA.22
Infinitive = *to* + present tense of verb.

NOTE SA.23
Infinitives are used as nouns, adjectives, or adverbs.

The **infinitive** is formed by placing the word *to* in front of the present tense of the verb. Several examples are *to rent, to program*, and *to hire*. An infinitive can function as a noun, an adjective, or an adverb, but it can never be used as a verb. The infinitive is in italics and its use is in parentheses in each of the following sentences. (Some parts of speech are identified in examples in Seminar A and are discussed in depth in Seminar B.)

To remodel her kitchen is Judy's dream. (noun—subject)

Debra plans *to speak* at the annual conference in New York. (noun—direct object)

Natasha's job is *to greet* customers as they enter the store. (noun—predicate nominative)

Carmen's dream *to retire* early hinges on her investments. (adjective)

The tire company has agreed *to replace* defective tires. (adverb)

GERUND

NOTE SA.24
Gerunds are used only as nouns.

NOTE SA.25
Gerund = verb + *-ing*.

A **gerund** is a present tense verb form that can function only as a noun. It is formed by adding *-ing* to a verb. *Typing, hiring*, and *manufacturing* are examples of gerunds. Gerunds may be used in phrases consisting of a gerund, an object, and words modifying the object. In the following sentences the phrases are in italics, the gerunds are in bold, and their uses are in parentheses:

***Interviewing** prospective employees* is the responsibility of the human resources department. (subject)

Jessie's hobby is ***collecting** Elvis memorabilia*. (predicate nominative)

They enjoy ***going** to the movies*. (direct object)

He was awarded the prize for *driving the longest distance*. (object of preposition)

Mikki, *performing in the play*, is the youngest member of the cast. (appositive)

PARTICIPLE

A **participle** is a verb form that can be used as an adjective or as part of a verb phrase. The three types of participles are present, past, and perfect.

Present Participle The **present participle verb** is always formed by adding *-ing* to the present tense of a verb. The participial phrase is in italics, and the present participle is in bold in each of the following examples:

NOTE SA.26
Participles are used as adjectives or as parts of verb phrases.

Police arrested the *screaming pedestrian*. (adjective)

Martha is *saving her money* for a vacation in Europe. (verb phrase)

NOTE SA.27
Present participle = present tense verb + *-ing*.

Past Participle A **past participle verb** is usually formed by adding *-d* or *-ed* to the present tense of a regular verb. Irregular verbs form their past participles by changing the spelling of their root words. The past participle is in italics in each of the following examples:

NOTE SA.28
Past participle usually = present tense verb + *-d* or *-ed*.

Last week Nancy *moved* the ribbon display into the quick sale aisle. (verb—regular verb)

The language seminar will concentrate on *spoken* Spanish. (adjective—irregular verb)

NOTE SA.29
Sometimes the root word is changed.

Perfect Participle A **perfect participle verb** is always used as an adjective and is formed by combining *having* with the past participle. The perfect participles are in italics in the following sentences:

NOTE SA.30
The perfect participle is always an adjective.

Brad, *having displayed* too much anger, quickly left the room.

Patsy, *having resided* in Japan for 20 years, will experience difficulty in adjusting to the American culture.

NOTE SA.31
Perfect participle = *having* + past participle.

Nouns

A noun is a person, place, or thing. The two main groups of nouns are proper nouns and common nouns.

NOTE SA.32
Nouns are words that identify persons, places, and things.

Proper Nouns

A **proper noun** is a particular person, place, or thing. Proper nouns are always capitalized. *Mt. Rushmore, Yao Ming, Dallas,* and *USA Today* are examples of proper nouns.

NOTE SA.33
Proper nouns are specific.

Common Nouns

A **common noun** identifies a general class of persons, places, things, or ideas. Common nouns are not capitalized. Examples of common nouns are *employee, table, plate, sorrow, assets,* and *deposits.* The three classes of common nouns are concrete, abstract, and collective.

NOTE SA.34
Common nouns are general.

CONCRETE NOUNS

NOTE SA.35
Concrete nouns are precise.

A **concrete noun** identifies those things that you can see, touch, hear, taste, or smell. Words such as *director, dog, glass, computer, teacher*, and *truck* are concrete nouns. Concrete nouns are precise and easily understood, which makes them effective for business communication.

ABSTRACT NOUNS

NOTE SA.36
Abstract nouns are vague.

An **abstract noun** identifies an idea, emotion, quality, or belief. Examples of abstract nouns are *charity, disappointment, anger, love, surprise, attitude*, and *enthusiasm*. People's opinions and feelings differ in degree; therefore, abstract nouns are less precise than concrete nouns. Abstract nouns should be used infrequently in business communication because they are more difficult to understand than concrete nouns.

COLLECTIVE NOUNS

NOTE SA.37
Collective nouns identify a group.

A **collective noun** is a group of persons or a collection of things. It is normally treated as a singular noun because the group is acting as one body; however, a collective noun would be treated as a plural noun if the group members were acting as individuals. Collective nouns include *family, faculty, company, association, team*, and *band*.

Compound Nouns

NOTE SA.38
Compound nouns are multiple words used to name singular nouns.

A **compound noun** is two or more words used to identify one person, place, or thing. A compound noun may be written as one or more words, or it may be hyphenated. When in doubt, consult a dictionary for the correct spelling. Compound nouns can be classified under any of the three classes of common nouns. Examples of compound nouns in each class follow:

Concrete:	flight attendant, board member, mother-in-law
Abstract:	self-esteem, common sense, goodwill, life cycle
Collective:	garden club, board of directors, administrative staff

Plural Forms of Nouns

NOTE SA.39
A plural noun is normally formed by adding -s or -es to a singular noun.

A **plural noun** is used to identify two or more persons, places, or things. The plural of most nouns is formed by adding *-s* or *-es* to the singular form of the noun. Because there are so many ways of forming plurals, consult a dictionary if a question arises. Examples of different ways that nouns are formed as plurals include computer, *computers*; wolf, *wolves*; company, *companies*; portfolio, *portfolios*; sister-in-law, *sisters-in-law*; deer, *deer*; and potato, *potatoes*.

Possessive Forms of Nouns

NOTE SA.40
Possessive nouns show ownership.

A **possessive noun** is used to show possession or ownership. The possessive form of a noun is indicated by using an apostrophe. The following general guidelines will help you correctly form possessive nouns in written communication:

[1] The possessive of a singular noun not ending with an *s* or a *z* sound is formed by adding *apostrophe s*.

secretary's desk	company's executives

[2] The possessive of a singular noun ending with an *s* or a *z* sound is formed by adding *apostrophe s* to a noun with one syllable and by adding only an *apostrophe* to a noun with more than one syllable.

> Sims's plane   Kirkpatz' house

[3] The possessive of a plural noun ending with an *s* or a *z* sound is formed by adding an *apostrophe*.

> clients' rights   actors' guild

[4] The possessive of a compound noun is formed by placing the *apostrophe* or *apostrophe s* after the final word or word element.

> sergeant-at-arms's itinerary   all major generals' aides

[5] When two or more people share ownership of an object or objects, add an *apostrophe* or *apostrophe s* to the final name.

> Brian and Amy's truck   Tim and Stewartz' investments

[6] When two or more people each own separate objects, possession is indicated by adding an *apostrophe* or *apostrophe s* to each noun.

> Brian's and Amy's trucks   Tim's and Stewartz' investments

Pronouns

Pronouns are used in place of nouns. Pronouns make your writing more interesting because you do not repeat the noun. There are seven types of pronouns: personal, relative, interrogative, indefinite, demonstrative, reflexive, and intensive. Each type of pronoun performs a different function in a sentence.

Personal Pronouns

A **personal pronoun** is a substitute for a noun that refers to a specific person or thing. Personal pronouns change their form when they perform different functions and appear in different parts of a sentence. The different forms are called *cases*. The three types of personal pronoun cases are nominative, possessive, and objective.

NOMINATIVE CASE

The **nominative case** is used when the pronoun functions as the subject of a sentence or a clause. The nominative case is also called the *subjective case*. Singular personal pronouns in the nominative case are *I, you, he, she*, and *it*. Plural personal pronouns in the nominative case are *we, you*, and *they*. The nominative case is also used when the pronoun follows a linking verb. The italics in the following sentences illustrate the uses of nominative case pronouns:

> *I* will not attend the annual meeting. (subject of sentence)
> When *they* announce the new corporate structure, Shemika may search for another job. (subject of clause)
> It was *they* who surveyed the property. (*it*—subject of sentence; *they*—follows linking verb)

NOTE SA.41
Placement of an apostrophe and addition of -s to show possession depends on the noun and the ending sound.

NOTE SA.42
For compound nouns, possession is shown after the last word.

NOTE SA.43
Joint or individual possession of objects influences placement of *apostrophe* or *apostrophe s*.

NOTE SA.44
Pronouns replace nouns.

NOTE SA.45
The seven types of pronouns are personal, relative, interrogative, indefinite, demonstrative, reflexive, and intensive.

NOTE SA.46
Personal pronouns refer to specific people or things.

NOTE SA.47
Nominative case is used when the pronoun is the subject.

POSSESSIVE CASE

NOTE SA.48
Possessive case shows
ownership.

The **possessive case** is used when the pronoun shows possession or ownership. The possessive case does not need an apostrophe. Singular possessive pronouns are *my, mine, your, yours, his, her, hers*, and *its*. Plural possessive pronouns are *our, ours, your, yours, their*, and *theirs*. Several examples of pronouns in the possessive case are shown in italics in the following sentences:

> *His* car was involved in an accident. (shows whose car)
> What are *your* plans for this weekend? (shows whose plans)
> If the report is not *yours*, it must be *hers*. (shows whose report)
> *Our* vacation was changed because of the weather. (shows whose vacation)
> The company updated *its* logo. (shows whose logo)

OBJECTIVE CASE

NOTE SA.49
Objective case is used
when the pronoun is an
object.

The **objective case** is used when the pronoun functions as an object in a sentence, clause, or phrase. Singular pronouns in the objective case are *me, you, him, her*, and *it*. Plural objective pronouns are *us, you*, and *them*. The following sentences show in italics pronouns that are performing these functions:

> Shelia directed *me* to my seat in the stadium. (direct object of a sentence)
> Troy threw the pass *to him*. (object of preposition)
> When we saw *her*, Mary was driving an SUV. (direct object of a clause)

Relative Pronouns

NOTE SA.50
Relative pronouns link
clauses to nouns or
pronouns.

A **relative pronoun** connects a group of words containing a subject and verb (a clause) to a noun or pronoun. *Who, whom, whose, which*, and *that* are the relative pronouns. If the word to which the pronoun refers is a person, use *who, whom, whose*, or *that*. Use *who* when the pronoun referring to a person is in the nominative case and *whom* when the pronoun is in the objective case. Use *which* or *that* if the pronoun refers to a thing. Relative pronouns are in italics in the following sentences:

> The player *who* sacks the most quarterbacks will get the award.
> To *whom* shall we credit the sales?
> In case of a disagreement, *whose* story will you believe?
> The house, *which* was recently painted, is beautiful.
> The stock prices *that* were quoted were for Friday.

Interrogative Pronouns

NOTE SA.51
Interrogative pronouns
ask questions.

An **interrogative pronoun** is used within a question. *Who, whose, whom, which*, and *what* are the interrogative pronouns. Pronouns precede verbs in questions. Like other pronouns within sentences, they function as subjects, objects, modifiers, and subject complements. The italics in the following sentences illustrate how interrogative pronouns are used:

> *Who* cut Robert's hair? (subject)
> *Whose* department contributed the most to the flood victims? (modifier)
> *Whom* do you think the Cowboys will hire as a placekicker? (object)

Which bookkeeper handled Anderson's account? (modifier)

What was the basis for selecting the winners? (subject complement)

Indefinite Pronouns

An **indefinite pronoun** is used to make a general statement about individuals or things. Indefinite pronouns include *each, anyone, one, anything*, and *nobody*. The indefinite pronouns are in italics in the following sentences:

Each accountant is competent with spreadsheets.

Did *anyone* see the meteor shower last night?

One of the employees invests 10 percent of his paycheck in the stock market.

Is there *anything* that Amelia will not do?

Nobody can rely on an NFL team remaining in any city for ten years.

NOTE SA.52
Indefinite pronouns do not specify a particular person or thing.

Demonstrative Pronouns

A **demonstrative pronoun** is used to indicate a specific person, place, or thing. The four demonstrative pronouns are *this, these, that*, and *those*. Demonstrative pronouns are in italics in these sentences:

This project will require much work.

These tires will last much longer than the old ones.

Why did they select *that* plan for balancing the budget?

Are *those* the employees who earned the bonuses?

NOTE SA.53
Demonstrative pronouns substitute for specific nouns.

Compound Personal Pronouns

A **compound personal pronoun** has the suffix *self* or *selves*. A compound personal pronoun may be an intensive or reflexive pronoun. *Intensive pronouns* are used for emphasis, whereas *reflexive pronouns* reflect the action of the verb to the subject or to a noun or pronoun in the sentence. Examples of intensive and reflexive pronouns, in italics, follow:

The president *himself* welcomed each person to the celebration. (intensive—emphasizes a noun)

John will go to the bank *himself*. (intensive—emphasizes a noun)

The birds saw *themselves* reflected in the stream. (reflexive—refers to the subject, a pronoun)

NOTE SA.54
Compound personal pronouns are *intensive* or *reflexive*.

Adjectives

An **adjective** provides additional information about a noun or a pronoun. Adjectives make the meaning of the noun or pronoun more exact by answering such questions as *which one, how many*, and *what kind*. Adjectives also are called *modifiers*.

Adjectives may be regular or irregular. *Regular adjectives* generally are one-syllable words with *-er* or *-est* added when making comparisons. Irregular adjectives usually contain two or more syllables and use *less, least, more*, or *most* when making comparisons.

NOTE SA.55
Adjectives modify nouns and pronouns and make them more precise.

Degrees of Comparison in Adjectives

NOTE SA.56
The three degrees of comparison for adjectives are *positive, comparative,* and *superlative.*

Adjectives change form to show degrees of comparison. There are three degrees of comparison: positive, comparative, and superlative. Examples of the degrees of comparison of adjectives are shown in Figure SA.1.

FIGURE SA.1
Degrees of Comparison of Adjectives

Positive	Comparative	Superlative
cold	colder	coldest
easy	easier	easiest
cheerful	more cheerful	most cheerful
favorable	less favorable	least favorable

POSITIVE DEGREE

NOTE SA.57
Positive degree describes one noun.

The **positive degree** is used to describe one item or one group of items. The positive form is the form used in dictionary definitions. The adjective in the positive form is in italics in the following examples:

His computer has a *large* screen.

Floyd operates a *good* restaurant.

Her necklace is *expensive.*

COMPARATIVE DEGREE

NOTE SA.58
Comparative degree compares two nouns.

The **comparative degree** is used to show the difference between two items. The comparative degree is formed by adding *-er* to a regular adjective or by adding the words *more* or *less* to an irregular adjective. The adjectives used in the preceding examples in positive degree are shown in the following examples in the comparative degree:

His computer has a *larger* screen than yours.

Floyd operates a *better* restaurant than Mark.

Her necklace is *more expensive* than her bracelet.

SUPERLATIVE DEGREE

NOTE SA.59
Superlative degree compares three or more nouns.

The **superlative degree** is used to compare three or more items. It can also be used for emphasis. The superlative degree is formed by adding *-est* to a regular adjective or by adding *most* or *least* to an irregular adjective. The adjectives used in the previous two examples are now shown in the superlative degree:

His computer has the *largest* screen available.

Floyd operates the *best* restaurant in the area.

Her necklace is the *most expensive* piece of jewelry that she owns.

Absolute Adjectives

NOTE SA.60
Absolute adjectives are always in the superlative degree.

An **absolute adjective** is always in the superlative degree. Therefore, it cannot be compared. For example, if the design of a building is *perfect,* another building cannot have a *more perfect* design. Some absolute adjectives are *essential, unique, right, final, full, square, round, correct, never, dead,* and *empty.*

Compound Adjectives

A **compound adjective** is two or more words used together to describe a single noun or pronoun. Often compound adjectives are hyphenated; sometimes they are not. When compound adjectives are shown hyphenated in the dictionary, they are considered *permanent compounds* and should always be hyphenated. Compound nouns used as adjectives and shown as *open compounds* in the dictionary are not hyphenated. Compound adjectives not shown in the dictionary are referred to as *temporary compounds* and are hyphenated when they appear *before* the noun or pronoun they describe but are not hyphenated when they appear *after* the words they describe. Consult a dictionary for hyphenation of compound adjectives. Compound adjectives appear in italics in the following sentences:

> Mike is a *well-respected* attorney. (permanent compound adjective)
>
> Sylvia opened a *money market* account after she was promoted. (open compound adjective)
>
> *City-owned* vehicles are maintained by LaRoche Motors. (temporary compound adjective used before the noun)
>
> LaRoche Motors maintains all vehicles that are *city owned.* (temporary compound adjective used after the noun)

NOTE SA.61
Two or more adjectives used as one become a compound adjective.

Articles

Although classified as adjectives, *a, an*, and *the* are also called **articles**. The article *the* is used to denote specific nouns or pronouns. The articles *a* and *an* are used to denote general nouns or pronouns. The articles are in italics in the following examples:

> Zoe attended *the* rock concert.
>
> Zoe attended *a* concert.
>
> Zoe attended *an* uplifting concert.

When the word following the article begins with a consonant sound (*s*tore, *b*each, *c*ar, etc.), you use *a*; use *an* if the word begins with a vowel sound (*h*our, *e*gg, *e*xciting, etc.). Examples of articles used with words beginning with consonant and vowel sounds are shown in italics:

> Did you buy *a* dog?
>
> Cassandra is *an* honest individual.
>
> Carolyn did *an* excellent job in conducting the survey.

NOTE SA.62
A, an, and *the* are articles. *The* is specific. *A* and *an* are general.

Adverbs

Adverbs are modifiers that restrict, limit, or describe verbs, adjectives, or other adverbs. They answer questions such as *how, when, where, why, in what manner*, or *to what degree*. Many end in *-ly*. Examples of adverbs used as modifiers are shown in italics in the following sentences:

NOTE SA.63
Adverbs are used to modify verbs, adjectives, or other adverbs.

The sales dropped *drastically* during the month of November. (dropped *how?*)

A complete audit is conducted *annually*. (conducted *when?*)

The regional conference will be held *here*. (held *where?*)

The value of antique automobiles is increasing *extremely fast*. (increasing *how?* fast; *to what degree?* extremely)

Placement of Adverbs

NOTE SA.64
The placement of an adverb depends on how it is used in the sentence.

An adverb may be a single word (drive *carefully*), a phrase (drive *in a careful manner*), or a clause (drive *as carefully as you can*). A single-word adverb can be placed before or after the word it modifies. Prepositional and infinitive phrases and clauses that function as adverbs usually follow the word they modify. An **adverbial clause**, which is a dependent clause that acts as an adverb, precedes the independent clause in a sentence. Seminar B contains a detailed discussion of phrases and clauses.

Degrees of Adverbs

NOTE SA.65
Adverbs also have *positive, comparative,* and *superlative* degrees.

Some words that are used as adverbs as well as adjectives have positive, comparative, and superlative degrees of comparison. Examples of the degrees of comparison of adverbs are shown in Figure SA.2.

FIGURE SA.2
Degrees of Comparison of Adverbs

Positive	Comparative	Superlative
fast	faster	fastest
early	earlier	earliest
delightful	more delightful	most delightful
effective	less effective	least effective

Prepositions

NOTE SA.66
A preposition is a connector that needs an object.

A **preposition** connects a noun or pronoun to another word in a sentence. The noun or pronoun that follows the preposition is called the **object of the preposition**.

NOTE SA.67
A prepositional phrase contains the preposition and its object.

A word group containing a preposition and the object of the preposition is called a **prepositional phrase**. The following sentences illustrate prepositional phrases. The prepositions are in italics, and the object of each preposition is in bold.

Sales rose *in* all **segments** *of* the **economy** *during* the first **quarter** *of* the **year**.

The accountant sent an audit report *of* the **company** *to* the **president**.

Include a letter *of* **recommendation** *with* your **resume** when you send it *to* **employers**.

Functions of Prepositional Phrases

NOTE SA.68
Prepositional phrases work as adjectives and adverbs.

Prepositional phrases work as units in a sentence. They perform the functions of adjectives and adverbs and provide variety within the sentence. Examples of prepositional phrases that act as adjectives and adverbs are in italics in these examples:

The president *of the company* will arrive tomorrow. (The prepositional phrase as adjective modifies the noun *president*.)

Will you send the article *to the newspaper*? (The prepositional phrase as adverb modifies the verb *send*.)

LuAnn is going *to the lake with a friend*. (Both prepositional phrases act as adverbs. They modify the verb *is going*.)

Object of Preposition

As previously mentioned, the object of a preposition is a noun or pronoun that follows the preposition. The object of a preposition can be modified by an adjective; for example, "Belinda was proud of *her* grades."

Personal pronouns and *who* have unique objective forms. The objective form of *who* is *whom*. The personal pronouns are *me, us, you, him, her,* and *them*. The objects of the prepositions are in italics in these sentences:

NOTE SA.69
Objects of prepositions are nouns or pronouns and can be modified by adjectives.

With *whom* did you play the duet?

Did you send an e-mail message to *me*?

Charley drove the bus for *us*.

I saw you at the theater with *him* and *her*.

Yesterday, I received a letter from *you*.

Harry gave tomatoes to *them*.

Unnecessary Prepositions

Although prepositional phrases can be used effectively to make communication more interesting, a communicator must be careful to avoid unnecessary and, therefore, incorrect prepositions. Effective business communicators avoid inserting extra prepositions within a sentence or ending a sentence with a preposition.

NOTE SA.70
Omit unnecessary prepositions within sentences.

However, ending a sentence with a preposition is acceptable in oral communication if rearranging the sentence is awkward. Use only those prepositions that clarify a sentence. The prepositions *to, of, at, for,* and *up* are frequently used unnecessarily. Examples of these uses are shown in italics in the following sentences:

NOTE SA.71
Avoid ending a sentence with a preposition.

The team did not say where they were going *to*. (unnecessary preposition)
The team did not say where they were going.

The plate fell off *of* the table. (unnecessary preposition)
The plate fell off the table.

The mother did not know where her child was *at*. (unnecessary preposition)
The mother did not know where her child was.

Who is that phone call *for*? (incorrect)
For whom is that phone call?

He walked *up* to the statue and bowed *down* in respect.
(unnecessary prepositions)
He walked to the statue and bowed in respect.

Do you have any idea about what the meeting is? (awkward)
Do you have any idea what the meeting is about? (preferred)

Conjunctions

NOTE SA.72
Conjunctions are connectors without objects.

A **conjunction** is used to join words, phrases, and clauses. Conjunctions are also used to introduce clauses. Conjunctions are similar to prepositions in that they serve as connectors but are different in that they do not have objects. The three kinds of conjunctions are coordinate, correlative, and subordinate. Coordinate and correlative conjunctions join grammatically equal word elements; subordinate conjunctions join grammatically unequal word elements.

NOTE SA.73
The three types of conjunctions are *coordinate, correlative,* and *subordinate.*

Coordinate Conjunctions

NOTE SA.74
Coordinate conjunctions connect elements of equal rank.

A **coordinate conjunction** joins words, phrases, and independent clauses that are of equal importance or rank. Of equal importance or rank means that similar elements are connected; for example, adjectives are connected to adjectives and nouns are connected to nouns. The coordinate conjunctions are *and, but, or, nor, for, as,* and *yet.* The following examples show coordinate conjunctions (in italics) joining words, phrases, and independent clauses:

Both supervisors *and* cashiers attended the seminar. (joins nouns)

The wolf moved quickly *but* quietly. (joins adverbs)

The young man ran to the park *and* jumped over the fence to rescue his friend. (joins verbs)

They walked up one side *and* down the other. (joins prepositional phrases)

The dentist had a difficult time cleaning Jay's teeth, *for* the plaque had accumulated. (joins independent clauses)

Correlative Conjunctions

NOTE SA.75
A correlative conjunction is a pair of connectors that link sentence elements.

A **correlative conjunction** is paired with another correlative conjunction to connect two parallel words, phrases, or clauses. The most common correlative conjunction pairs are *both . . . and, either . . . or, neither . . . nor, not . . . but, not only . . . but also,* and *whether . . . or.* Examples, shown in italics, follow:

Earl *not only* earned a letter in baseball *but also* graduated with honors. (connects verb phrases)

Lori is a member of *both* the Civic Club *and* the Academic Club. (connects nouns)

Christie informed her mother that she would *either* wash the car *or* mow the yard. (connects clauses)

NOTE SA.76
Be sure that connected elements are parallel.

A common difficulty with using correlative conjunctions involves *parallelism.* Be sure that connected elements are equal or parallel in grammatical form or rank. A detailed discussion of parallelism is in Seminar B. The following sentences demonstrate a few parallelism errors. The correlative conjunctions are in italics.

By 11 o'clock Joe will *either* go to class *or* he will eat lunch. (Incorrect—*either* precedes the verb *go,* but *or* precedes the pronoun *he.*)

By 11 o'clock Joe will *either* go to class *or* eat lunch. (Correct—both conjunctions precede verbs.)

Mandy *not only* bought computers *but also* printers. (Incorrect—*not only* precedes the verb *bought* and *but also* precedes the noun *printers*.)

Mandy bought *not only* computers *but also* printers. (Correct—both conjunctions precede nouns.)

Subordinate Conjunctions

A **subordinate conjunction** joins a subordinate clause to the main clause; that is, a dependent clause to an independent clause. Some subordinate conjunctions are *after, although, because, before, since, when, while, where, if, whether, though,* and *until.* The subordinate conjunctions are in italics and the main clauses are in bold in the following examples:

> *Before you write the proposal,* **read the RFP very carefully**.
> **Julia was promoted to vice president** *because she was the most qualified.*
> **The grass turned green** *after it rained.*

NOTE SA.77
Subordinate conjunctions connect clauses of unequal rank.

Interjections

An **interjection** expresses strong emotion or feeling. It is not related grammatically to any other word in a sentence. Most interjections do not have any meaning if they are taken out of the message context. An interjection is normally punctuated with an exclamation point. Interjections are seldom used in business writing. They may be used in oral communication and in written advertising material. The interjections are in italics in the following examples:

> *No!* That is not right.
> *Wow!* Those flowers are beautiful.
> *Oops!* He spilled the tray of food.

NOTE SA.78
Interjections express strong emotions.

Application Exercises

1. Identify each verb and indicate whether it is an action or a state-of-being verb. Also indicate whether the verb is in active or passive voice.
   a. The inspection team did an outstanding job.
   b. Steve put the proposal on Ginny's desk after he completed reading it.
   c. The hummingbirds were seen for the first time last week.
   d. Antique collectors cherish things from the past.
   e. Did the computer operator detect the virus?
   f. The chairs were upholstered in a dreadful color on the advice of the office manager.
   g. The proposed regulation establishes limits on how long an airplane can be exposed to snow or freezing rain before being deiced again.
   h. The manager told the workers to go home early on Friday.
   i. The telecommunication office will be closed for the holiday on Monday.
   j. After the computers were purchased, they were shipped to Dallas.
2. Identify each verb or verb phrase and indicate whether it is in the indicative, imperative, or subjunctive mood:
   a. Warren looks at all opportunities to acquire more companies.

    b. The contractors worked together extremely well after the accident occurred.

    c. Stop the truck immediately.

    d. Who brought the doughnuts for the morning break?

    e. Come enjoy a glimpse of early Texas in the History Museum which includes a genealogical library.

    f. If the stock rises to $90, it will split.

    g. Market Day is held at the fairgrounds the first Saturday of each month from March through December.

3. Identify each verbal and indicate its form (infinitive, gerund, or participle):

    a. We are happy that you decided to join our organization.

    b. Tim asked his boss for an increase in salary.

    c. Having won the local contest, Henry will advance to the state level.

    d. The television network decided to take the lead in limiting pornography in its programs.

    e. Talking with friends, Fred missed the results of the race.

    f. Investments in mutual funds increased in the rapidly spiraling stock market.

    g. Instead of asking for help in unjamming the printer, Mindy broke it.

    h. Attending class is an important part of college life.

4. Determine the correct verb form and indicate the tense of the verbs that are italicized in the following sentences. Example: The announcement of the resignation *shake* the building. *Shook—past tense*

    a. Tomorrow we *went* to the movies.

    b. Late last night Candace *answers* the telephone.

    c. The price of BCK stock has fallen since it *will merge* with Realway.

    d. Last week the team *goes* to Boston.

    e. It *looked* warm outside, but it is cold.

    f. By the end of the decade, all of Bill and Cindy's children *will have went* to college.

    g. Next month Tari *began* working for Pyramid Grain.

    h. Geri and I *went* on vacation next month.

    i. The company *celebrates* its tenth anniversary next Tuesday.

    j. I *visited* the museum every week since moving to Chicago.

5. Identify each adjective and adverb in the following sentences, and indicate how the word is used (adjective or adverb). Indicate the word that each adjective or adverb modifies.

    a. Gasoline prices have been dropping steadily while oil prices have been rising.

    b. Bill was a trustworthy employee who performed his duties admirably.

    c. Profits were rapidly sliding, and stockholders were becoming increasingly alarmed.

    d. Officials of tax-exempt groups will soon face stiff new penalties.

    e. Networks buy new shows from Hollywood studios and later resell them to local television stations.

    f. The first storm of the season brought much snow.

    g. The law was carefully designed to prevent discrimination against people with disabilities.

    h. It's a good time to consider buying a new car.

    i. One good sign is that revenues have picked up dramatically.

    j. Why did Anne not graduate with her classmates?

6. Common errors occur in the following sentences. Find and correct the errors. Explain each correction.

    a. Do you know where the children are going to?

    b. The runoff from the rain cut deep into the topsoil.

    c. If I was nominated for the office, I would run a fair campaign.

    d. The new restaurant was builded on the corner of Sycamore and Vine.

    e. The workers will either accept the contract or they will strike.

    f. Jill is unable to go to lunch because she has went out of town.

    g. Where are you sending the truck to?

    h. The employees of Swift Truck Line hired an auditor to investigate the companies pension plan.

    i. John shaped and molded the image of African Americans worldwide.

    j. Between the NFL teams, the Cowboys have the higher salaries.

7. Identify the part of speech for each word in the following sentences:

    a. Wow! My stock tripled in value.

    b. Josh raked the leaves and put them into large bags.

    c. Worldwide, stocks rose in dollar terms.

    d. The government should do a thorough economic analysis of the deal's effect on farmers.

    e. Where did Robin go to school?

    f. Today's hike was longer and required some tricky footwork crossing a beaver dam.

    g. Rebates and other forms of price discounting will continue into the next decade.

    h. Prior to investing in stocks, an individual should have a thorough understanding of economics.

    i. Did the storm move through the area before midnight?

    j. Nowhere will you find a state with more pride in its history than Texas.

Message Analysis

Correct all grammatical errors in the following paragraphs:

> Paragraph component's include a topic sentence; supporting sentences; descriptive detales, and concluding sentence. Good writers very the lengths of sentences and paragraphs.
>
> The type and purpose of paragraphs determines the organization and sequins of detales. Messages that tell a story, describe, or pursuade follow specific organizational patterns and use direct or indirect approaches too writing.
>
> Opening paragraphs attracts the readers interest; closing paragraphs use memorable statements, look to the future, or call for action. These two paragraphs create the first and last impressions of the message.

Sentence Structure

NOTE SB.1
A sentence expresses a complete thought.

NOTE SB.2
Correct grammar provides clarity, precision, and credibility.

NOTE SB.3
The main parts of a sentence are the subject and the predicate.

NOTE SB.4
The subject tells who or what is being discussed.

NOTE SB.5
The complete subject includes all words related directly to the subject.

NOTE SB.6
The simple subject is the main noun or pronoun in the complete subject.

A **sentence** is a group of related words that has a subject and a predicate and expresses a complete thought. A sentence is the basic unit for organizing messages.

You can improve your ability to communicate by becoming familiar with sentence construction and learning how to organize sentence components. Construction of grammatically correct sentences improves your message clarity, expresses your meaning precisely, and increases your message credibility.

Parts of Sentences

A sentence expresses a statement, a command, a question, a wish, or an exclamation. The starting point in understanding how to structure sentences is to know their two essential parts: the subject and the predicate.

The Subject

The **subject** is the part of a sentence that tells who or what is being discussed. There are three types of subjects: complete, simple, and compound.

THE COMPLETE SUBJECT

The **complete subject** includes all words related directly to the subject. The complete subject is italicized in the following examples:

> *Jack* runs.
> *The five-year-old Jack* runs.
> *Willie* sleeps.
> *Willie, an eight-year-old dog,* sleeps most of the day.

THE SIMPLE SUBJECT

The **simple subject** of a sentence is the main noun or pronoun in the complete subject. The simple subject names *who* or *what* is performing the action, receiving the action, or existing in the state of being described in the sentence. The following examples show the simple subject in bold print and the complete subject in italics:

> *The five-year-old **Jack*** runs. (Jack names the *who* that performs the action of running.)

*The beautiful **pitcher** fell from the table.* (The pitcher names *what* fell.)

*The rose **garden** was planted by the local garden club.* (The garden names *what* received the action of planting.)

*The **ball** hit Marquis.* (The ball names *what* hit.)

*The **arboretum** is a quiet, peaceful place.* (The arboretum names *what* exists in the state of being described.)

THE COMPOUND SUBJECT

Two (or more) simple subjects connected by a coordinate conjunction form a **compound subject**. Coordinating conjunctions join equal or like ideas within a sentence; examples include *and, or, but, nor, for, yet,* and *so*. The following sentences have the compound subject in bold print and the complete subject in italics. The coordinating conjunction is underlined.

*The **doctor** <u>and</u> her **staff*** work to keep health care costs down.

*The **Firestix** <u>or</u> the **Wildcats*** will win the baseball tournament in Columbia, Missouri.

The Predicate

The **predicate** is the part of a sentence that tells something about the complete subject. The predicate consists of a verb with or without phrases or words that modify the verb, serve as its object, or complement the verb. The predicate may be complete, simple, or compound.

THE COMPLETE PREDICATE

The **complete predicate** includes the verb and all the words directly related to it. The following examples show the complete predicates italicized.

Jane *left.*

Basketball and football ticket prices *are increasing.*

Cats *eat slowly.*

The package *was sent by overnight express.*

Were you *comfortable in the 2001 Volvo?*

THE SIMPLE PREDICATE

The **simple predicate** is the main verb in the complete predicate. The verb expresses action or a state of being. The simple predicate is in bold print in these examples of italicized complete predicates:

The team ***left** quickly.* (*Left* expresses action.)

The package ***was sent** by overnight express.* (*Was sent* states the action.)

They ***feel** good.* (*Feel* expresses a state of being.)

She ***is** the last one to leave.* (*Is* expresses a state of being.)

THE COMPOUND PREDICATE

A **compound predicate** is formed when two (or more) simple predicates are connected by a coordinating conjunction. The compound predicate is in bold print in these examples of italicized complete predicates. The coordinating conjunction is underlined.

Cathy *sails* weekly <u>and</u> *races* monthly.

The college roommates *ate* dinner <u>and</u> *went* to a movie.

Manuel *walked* <u>or</u> *rode* the bus to school each day.

Subject and Predicate Identification

NOTE SB.12
Analyze sentences by first locating the simple predicate and then finding the subject.

Practice recognizing subjects and predicates to improve your understanding of sentence structure. Analyzing sentence structure is easier if you start by locating the simple predicate (the verb); then ask *who* or *what* to identify the subject. The following examples illustrate this approach:

The YMCA opened at 5 a.m. (The action word *opened* is the verb. What opened? The *YMCA* is the simple subject.)

Tan manages the computer store. (The action word *manages* is the verb. Who manages? *Tan* is the simple subject.)

Nikolas Pantuliano is 16 years old. (The verb *is* describes a state of being. Who is? *Nikolas Pantuliano* is the subject.)

The J. Paul Getty Trust Museum was interesting. (The state of being *was* is the verb. What was? The *museum* is the simple subject.)

Amalia and Eduardo worked together on a class project. (The action word *worked* is the verb. Who worked? The compound subject is *Amalia* <u>and</u> *Eduardo*.)

Ching-yu works at the theatre in the evening and attends school during the day. (The action words *works* <u>and</u> *attends* are the compound predicate. Who works and attends? *Ching-yu* is the simple subject.)

NOTE SB.13
In the usual sentence arrangement, the subject precedes the verb.

The most common sentence arrangement is for the subject to be followed by the verb (e.g., *Chuck rebuilt his Volkswagen*). A sentence in which the subject follows the verb is called an **inverted sentence**. Inverted sentences may ask a question or begin with *here* or *there*. The following examples, with the subject in bold print and the verb in italics, illustrate this inverted arrangement:

NOTE SB.14
In inverted sentences, the verb precedes the subject.

There *are* 20 **employees** in the front office.

Here *is* the **umbrella**.

Why *was* **he** absent?

To locate the subject and verb, restate the sentence in the standard order—subject, then verb, as in the following examples:

Inverted order: There *are* 20 **employees** in the front office.
Standard order: Twenty **employees** *are* in the front office.

Inverted order: Here *is* the **umbrella**.
Standard order: The **umbrella** *is* here.

Inverted order: Why *was* **he** absent?
Standard order: **He** *was* absent why?

In some of the previous examples, words or groups of words were ignored when the predicate and subject were being located. These parts of sentences will be considered in the sections that follow.

Objects and Subject Complements

Objects and subject complements are important parts of sentences. They help to complete the thought expressed by the subject and the simple predicate. Understanding the functions of objects and subject complements will assist you in avoiding grammatical errors.

OBJECTS

An **object** is a noun, a pronoun, a phrase, or clause used as a noun. Objects may be direct or indirect.

A **direct object** receives the action of the verb and helps complete the thought of the sentence. The direct object answers the *what* or *whom* question raised by the subject and verb. Examples of direct objects are shown in italics in the following sentences:

Cathy teaches the *piano*. (Cathy teaches what?)

Suzy is ill. (Only action verbs can take direct objects; is, a linking verb, links the subject with a word that describes Suzy, the subject. A modifier coming after a linking verb [also called a state-of-being verb] is called a *subject complement* and is explained in the next section of this Seminar.) See Seminar A, page 517 for linking or state-of-being verbs.

He ran *track* one semester. (He ran what?)

The recommendation assisted *Lauren Cole*. (The recommendation assisted whom?)

An **indirect object** receives the action that the verb makes on the direct object. The indirect object usually answers the question, "To whom is the action being directed?" Indirect objects are always located between the verb and the direct object. You cannot have an indirect object if you do not have a direct object. Neither the direct object nor the indirect object ever appears as a prepositional phrase. You can locate the indirect object by inverting the sentence and mentally inserting the word *to*. In the following two sentences the indirect object is in bold print and the direct object is in italics:

Kitty gives **Jon** the *saxophone*. (The saxophone is being given *to* Jon.)

Rob sold the **BYC member** a *laser sailboat*. (A laser sailboat was sold *to* the BYC member.)

SUBJECT COMPLEMENTS

The **subject complement** is (1) a noun or pronoun that renames the subject or (2) an adjective that modifies (describes) the subject. In both cases, the subject complement follows a linking verb in the sentence. A **linking verb** (such as, *is, was, has been, am, are*, and *seem*) indicates a state of being and does not show action. In each of the following examples, the subject and the subject complement are in italics and the linking verb is in bold:

Peter and *Lauren* **are** good *friends*. (*Friends* is a noun that renames *Peter* and *Lauren*.)

The *dog* **was** lazy. (*Lazy* is an adjective that modifies *dog*.)

Mary **has been** *ill*. (*Ill* is an adjective that modifies *Mary*.)

Betsy **is** my *sister*. (*Sister* is a noun that renames *Betsy*.)

NOTE SB.15
Objects and complements help complete the sentence thought.

NOTE SB.16
Direct objects receive the action of the verb.

NOTE SB.17
Indirect objects receive the action the verb makes on the direct object.

NOTE SB.18
Subject complements rename or modify the subject.

NOTE SB.19
Linking verbs do not show action.

Phrases, Clauses, and Fragments

Being able to identify groupings of words—referred to as *phrases* or *clauses*—is important for understanding sentence structure. Also, you should be able to recognize sentence fragments and make conscious decisions on whether or not you will use them.

PHRASES

NOTE SB.20
A phrase functions as a part of speech.

A **phrase** is a group of related words functioning as a part of speech. Phrases do not contain both a subject and a verb; phrases may contain one or the other or neither. Here are examples of phrases:

Verb phrases: will be mailing; have keyed; is considered; have been waiting

Noun phrases: my home address; the fall semester; Martin's sister; mother's flower garden

Prepositional phrases: to college; before the concert; under the table; for a good reason

Adjective phrases: pretty and smart; 15 years old; three dozen; soothing or calming

Participial phrases: having been promoted; seeing clearly; keying rapidly; waiting anxiously

Infinitive phrases: to play; to market; to promote; to elect

NOTE SB.21
Phrases can strengthen and add life to writing.

Using phrases as parts of speech—as adjectives, adverbs, and nouns—can make your writing more interesting. Phrases add variety and color. They can add strong words to your sentences and bring power to your writing. Finally, they can strengthen your writing by providing specific details and showing relationships. Note how the italicized phrases in the following examples add detail, variety, color, interest, power, and liveliness:

Mary Rose sings. (no phrases)

Mary Rose sings songs *in the shower.* (prepositional phrase)

Mary Rose sings *better-than-average soprano.* (adjective phrase)

Mary Rose, *a better-than-average soprano,* sings *contemporary songs.* (adjective phrase, noun phrase)

Mary Rose sings *to gain musical experience.* (infinitive phrase)

A *natural soprano,* Mary Rose sings *contemporary songs.* (adjective phrase, noun phrase)

Serenading softly, Mary Rose sings *contemporary songs.* (participial phrase, noun phrase)

Understanding the purpose of the phrase is also important. For example, prepositional phrases can serve both as adjectives and as adverbs. If a phrase serves as an adjective, it should be close to the noun it modifies to make the relationship clear:

Incorrect: The members present were *of the National Business Education Association.*

Correct: The members *of the National Business Education Association* were present.

The phrase *of the National Business Education Association* serves as an adjective and modifies the noun *members*. This relationship is clearly understood if the modifying phrase is close to the noun.

CLAUSES

A **clause** is a group of related words including both a subject and a predicate. There are two kinds of clauses: independent and dependent. An **independent clause**, sometimes referred to as the *main clause*, expresses a complete thought. It can stand alone as a separate sentence. In the following examples of independent clauses, the simple predicates are shown in bold print, and the simple subjects are italicized:

The *telephone* and the *fax* **are** important communication tools.

The business administration *program* **averaged** 150 graduates annually.

A **dependent clause**, also called a *subordinate clause*, does not express a complete thought; therefore, it cannot stand alone as a sentence. The dependent clause contains both a subject and a predicate but, because of its construction, depends upon another clause to complete the thought.

Most dependent clauses are introduced by a subordinate conjunction (such as *because, as soon as, if, since, while,* or *when*) or by a relative pronoun (such as *who, which,* or *that*). Look at the subordinating conjunction or relative pronoun (shown in bold), the simple subject (in bold italics), and the simple predicate (in regular italics) in these examples of dependent clauses:

if the *order* arrived by Monday

that the *class* is acceptable

The basic difference between dependent and independent clauses is the use of a subordinate conjunction or relative pronoun at the beginning of the clause. Adding a subordinate conjunction to the beginning of an independent clause would make it a dependent clause. On the other hand, if you were to omit the subordinate conjunction or relative pronoun at the beginning of the previous illustrations of dependent clauses, those clauses would become independent clauses:

The order arrived by Monday.

The class is acceptable.

Subordinate conjunctions and relative pronouns should be carefully selected; interchanging them reduces the precision of your message. Two commonly interchanged relative pronouns are *that* and *which*. Use *that* for clauses essential to the meaning of the sentence and *which* for clauses adding information that would not change the sentence meaning if omitted. The nonessential clause that is adding information should be set off with commas as shown below:

Correct: The course that I took last summer was difficult. (essential to identify the course)

Correct: BUS 564, which I took last summer, was difficult. (nonessential)

Use *who* or *whom* when referring to a person or persons. If the pronoun is the subject of a verb, use the word *who*; if the pronoun is used as an object, use *whom*. The sentences below show the relative pronoun in bold, the noun to which it refers in italics, and nonessential clauses set off by commas.

NOTE SB.22
A clause has both a subject and a predicate.

NOTE SB.23
Independent clauses can stand alone.

NOTE SB.24
Dependent clauses begin with subordinate conjunctions or relative pronouns; they cannot stand alone as sentences.

Correct:	Her *husband*, **who** was a graduate of Stanford, serves as mayor of the city. (who—subject of the verb *was*)
Correct:	*Anyone* **who** needs an education can get one. (who—subject of the verb *needs*)
Correct:	*Each* of the team players **who** left school last year graduates this year. (who—subject of the verb *left*)
Correct:	**Whom** did you see at the game? (You did see whom—object of the verb)
Incorrect:	Swimming brings calm to busy *people* **whom** need a stress reliever. (should be *who*—subject of verb *need*)

SENTENCE FRAGMENTS

NOTE SB.25
Sentence fragments are incomplete sentences and may or may not have meaning.

A **sentence fragment** is a group of words that may or may not have meaning. *Sentence fragment* is another name for an *incomplete sentence*. Note the following examples:

If the vacation is taken early (lacks meaning)
Congratulations! (has meaning in context)
Ernesto, having been promoted (lacks meaning)
Best wishes for success (has meaning in context)

NOTE SB.26
Some writers selectively use sentence fragments; others never use them.

Although the use of sentence fragments that have meaning in context is fairly common in business communication, the acceptability of their usage is debatable. Some business communicators think that the infrequent, selective use of meaningful sentence fragments gives life and personality to their messages. Other business communicators do not use sentence fragments because, technically, they are grammatically incorrect. You will need to make your own decision on this issue.

Sentence Patterns

NOTE SB.27
A common sentence pattern is subject → verb → object or complement.

A helpful approach to understanding sentence construction is to examine common basic sentence patterns. Although the English language is extremely flexible, the following patterns are the most frequently used:

[1] Subject → Verb

Elena → reads.

[2] Subject → Verb → Direct Object

Elena → reads → a novel.

[3] Subject → Verb → Indirect Object → Direct Object

Elena → reads → Cruz → a novel.

[4] Subject → Verb → Subject Complement

Gregory → is → lost.

[5] Here (or There) → Verb → Subject

Here → is → your snowboard.

Subject and Verb Agreement

One of the basic rules of sentence construction is that the subject and the verb must *agree in number*. If the subject is singular—refers to just one person or one thing—then the verb must be singular. If the subject is plural, the verb must also be plural. Your ability to identify the subject is essential to determining whether it is singular or plural. The subject and the verb are in italics in the following examples:

Singular: The *teacher was* late to class.
Plural: The *teachers were* on the program.
Singular: The *pilot flies* the helicopter.
Plural: The *pilots fly* the helicopters.

NOTE SB.28
The subject and verb must agree in number.

Recall that adding an -*s* to most subjects makes them plural and adding an -*s* to most verbs makes them singular. If you are not sure whether the subject is singular or plural (for example, a word like *athletics*), look in a dictionary. Then use the verb that agrees with the number of the subject.

Words between the subject and the verb (intervening words) must be ignored when determining the correct number of the subject. In the following examples the subject and the verb are in bold, and the word or words to be ignored are in italics:

Singular: The **man** *with the rackets* **is** the tennis player.
Plural: The **men** *with the rackets* **are** the tennis players.
Singular: The **computer**, *as well as the printers*, **was** new.
Plural: The **runners**, *other than Coach Bill*, **were** on time for the track meet.

Recall that a compound subject is two (or more) subjects connected by a coordinating conjunction. Some compound subjects take singular verbs and some take plural verbs. There are four possibilities:

[1] When compound subjects are connected by *and*, they are plural and require a plural verb.

[2] When compound subjects are connected by *or* or *nor* and both are singular, they take singular verbs.

[3] When compound subjects are connected by *or* or *nor* and both are plural, they take plural verbs.

[4] When compound subjects are connected by *or* or *nor* and one of the subjects is plural and one singular, the verb should agree with the number of the subject that is closer to it.

NOTE SB.29
Compound subjects may take singular or plural verbs.

The compound subjects are in bold print, and their correct verbs are in italics in these examples:

Plural: **Gloria** and **Catherine** *are* sisters.
Plural: The **pilot**, the **copilot**, and the **navigator** *fly* all the international flights.
Singular: Neither **Nancy** nor **Art** *is* going.

Plural:	**Tanks** and **guns** *are* essential for an army.
Plural:	**Jane** and the **children** *go* to the museum each week.
Singular:	**Tents** or a **cabin** *is* available for camping.
Plural:	A **cabin** or **tents** *are* available for camping.

Notice in the last example that the plural verb sounds better than the singular verb used in the previous sentence. In sentences with both singular and plural subjects, this is almost always true. Therefore, you might consider putting the plural subject closer to the verb.

NOTE SB.30
Some subjects appear to be plural but are singular.

Some words used as subjects are singular even though they may give the appearance of being plural. Examples of these words are *everybody, everyone, anybody, anyone, somebody, someone, nobody,* and *neither.* With these singular subjects, use singular verbs:

Singular:	Anyone is (not *are*) invited.
Singular:	Everybody is (not *are*) welcome.
Singular:	Each of the participants attends (not *attend*) a conference.
Singular:	Neither was (not *were*) late for the meeting.

Also, some words that end in *-s* are singular. Use singular verbs with those words:

Singular:	Athletics is an extracurricular activity.
Singular:	Mathematics is my favorite subject.
Singular:	Economics is an important field of study.

NOTE SB.31
Some subjects appear to be singular but are plural.

Other words appear to be singular but take a plural verb. *Data* and *criteria* are examples. The singular form of data is datum; the singular form of criteria is criterion. The singular forms of these two words are seldom used; but their plural counterparts are often mistaken for the singular form.

Plural:	Research data show that exercise is important.
Plural:	Before interviewing job applicants, be sure that selection criteria relate to job requirements.

NOTE SB.32
Book, magazine, or song titles ending in *-s* are singular.

The name of one song, book, company, magazine, or article is singular even though the name is plural:

Singular:	*People* is an interesting magazine.
Singular:	Starving Students, Inc., is located in Ft. Lauderdale.
Singular:	"Edelweiss" is an old song.

Subjects in plural form that are considered as a single unit or as a whole take singular verbs. Amounts, distances, and some compound subjects are examples of this:

Singular:	Ten feet is the distance to the end of the wall.
Singular:	Five to seven pounds is the average weight for a notebook computer.
Singular:	Turkey and dressing is a Thanksgiving favorite.

The words *few, both, many,* and *several* are considered plural and take plural verbs. For example:

Plural:	Few think that the car will be the best-selling convertible.
Plural:	Both were hired before graduation.
Plural:	Many select the 900 MHz cordless telephone.
Plural:	Several sing in the college choir.

Collective nouns such as *board, faculty,* and *audience* may be singular or plural. If the group is acting as one, the verb should be singular. If the group members are acting as individuals, the verb should be plural:

Singular:	The committee has written an academic code of honor this year.
Plural:	The committee represents different parts of the city.

Pronoun and Antecedent Agreement

To be grammatically correct in your communication, you will want to know and use another form of agreement—the *agreement of pronouns and their antecedents*. Recall that pronouns are noun substitutes. An **antecedent** is a word, phrase, or clause that is replaced by the pronoun. Most antecedents are nouns. The pronouns used as subjects, objects, or complements are *he, she, I, we, you, it, her, him, them,* and *they*. As a possessive, a pronoun is used as a modifier. Examples of possessive pronouns are *my, mine, our(s), your(s), his, her(s), its,* and *their(s)*. Possessive pronouns do not use an apostrophe to show possession. *Its* used as a possessive pronoun should not be written as *it's*, which is the contraction for *it is*.

Pronouns and their antecedents must agree in three ways: (1) in number, (2) in gender, and (3) in a clear relationship. In the following examples of agreement in number, the antecedent is in italics and the pronoun is in bold print:

Singular:	*Ruth* wrote the report, but **she** said that coworkers contributed ideas.
Plural:	*Robin* and *Dennis* reported on Monday, and **they** said the report is complete.
Singular:	The *company* began **its** production on January 1.
Plural:	Company *employees* began **their** work the previous November.
Singular:	*Everybody* sat at **his** or **her** desk.
Plural:	The *representatives* from that state vote as **their** constituents dictate.
Singular:	*Software, Inc.*, is opening **its** fifth store.
Plural:	All Software, Inc., *employees* believe **their** company will continue to grow.
Singular:	Either *Michelle* or *Anne* will sell **her** bicycle.
Plural:	Both *Michelle* and *Anne* will sell **their** bicycles.
Singular:	The *number* is high; **it** exceeds 100.
Plural:	A *number* of birds have eaten **their** bird seeds.

The next set of examples of pronouns and their antecedents shows agreement in gender. The antecedent is in italics and the pronoun is in bold print:

NOTE SB.33
Pronouns and their antecedents should agree.

NOTE SB.34
Pronouns are noun substitutes.

NOTE SB.35
Pronouns replace antecedents.

NOTE SB.36
Pronouns and their antecedents should agree in number.

NOTE SB.37
Pronouns and their antecedents should agree in gender.

Masculine:	*Rudolph* ran **his** best race at the Boston Marathon.
Feminine:	*Megan* cut **her** hair in a pageboy style today.
Mixed:	Every *man* and *woman* must send **his** or **her** vote before Wednesday's meeting.
Neuter:	The *meeting* begins when the president calls **it** to order.

NOTE SB.38
Pronouns and their
antecedents should
clearly relate.

Finally, there must be a clear relationship between a pronoun and its antecedent. Examples of unclear relationships and clear relationships follow:

Unclear:	Will attended the Las Vegas convention with his colleague, and he said the convention sales were low. (Antecedent not clear; who said the sales were low?)
Clear:	Will, who said the Las Vegas convention sales were low, attended this convention with his colleague.
Unclear:	Walter telephoned Professor Chang when he was on sabbatical. (Who was on sabbatical?)
Clear:	When Walter was on sabbatical, he telephoned Professor Chang.

Parallelism

NOTE SB.39
Sentence constructions
used for the same func-
tion should be parallel.

One other essential form of agreement for correct sentence structure is parallelism. **Parallelism** means having similar structure for words or word groups used in a similar fashion. Sentences that lack parallelism are unbalanced and awkward due to inconsistent structure.

NOTE SB.40
Use the same grammati-
cal form for parts that
serve the same function.

Parallelism is achieved by using the same grammatical form for the two or more parts of sentences that serve the same function. Using the same grammatical form means using noun with noun, adjective with adjective, verb with verb, adverb with adverb, phrase with phrase, or clause with clause. Parts of sentences serve the same function if they serve as a part of a series, a contrast, a comparison, a choice, or an expression of equality.

Different examples of parallelism are shown in the following illustrations. The parts of these sentences that are not parallel are shown in bold.

Series

NOTE SB.41
Parts of series should be
parallel.

Not parallel:	Designing a garden, **dues collection**, and **organization of a garden club** are essential to maintain current beautification activities. (*Designing a* garden is a participial phrase, *dues collection* is a noun phrase, and *organization of a garden club* is a noun phrase.)
Parallel:	*Designing a garden, collecting dues,* and *organizing a garden club* are essential to maintain current beautification activities. (All parts of the series are participial phrases.)
Not parallel:	Members of the class worked quickly, **with enthusiasm**, and **a display of skill**. (*Quickly* is an adverb; *with enthusiasm* is a prepositional phrase, and *a display of skill* is a noun phrase.)

Parallel:	Members of the class worked quickly, enthusiastically, and skillfully. (All parts of the series are adverbs.)
Not parallel:	The business communication seminar was (a) interesting, (b) **of benefit to participants**, and (c) **provided challenges**. (The series items are not parallel. Item a is an adjective, Item b has prepositional phrases, and Item c is a verb phrase-verb and its object.)
Parallel:	The business communication seminar was (a) **interesting**, (b) **beneficial**, and (c) **challenging**. (All parts of the series use adjectives describing the subject.)

Contrast

Not parallel:	Lydia speaks English eloquently but **many errors are in her writing**. (An active verb phrase contrasts with a linking verb clause.)
Parallel:	Lydia speaks English eloquently but *writes poorly*. (Both parts use an action verb and its modifiers.)

NOTE SB.42
Parts of contrasts should be parallel.

Comparison

Not parallel:	Your high volume sales season lasts longer than *Alliance Sporting Goods*. (The comparison is not clear—Is the season longer than the Alliance Sporting Goods? The necessary information to complete the comparison is omitted.)
Parallel:	Your high volume sales season lasts longer than the Alliance Sporting Goods' *high volume sales season*. (Both parts of the comparison now have similarly constructed noun phrases that clarify the comparison.)

NOTE SB.43
Parts of comparisons should be parallel.

Choice

Not parallel:	You may choose practicing piano, **to complete your lesson**, or **your room may be cleaned**. (The series has a gerund phrase, an infinitive phrase, and an independent clause.)
Parallel:	You may choose practicing piano, *completing your lesson*, or *cleaning your room*. (This series using three gerund phrases.)

NOTE SB.44
Parts of a choice should be parallel.

Expression of Equality

Not parallel:	Carmen Martinez tutored a fourth grade student and **fifth grade**. (The lack of the words *a fifth grade student* implies that Carmen tutors all of the fifth grade.)
Parallel:	Carmen Martinez tutored *a fourth grade student* and *a fifth grade student*. (The use of appropriate articles and modifiers in both places clarifies that two people were tutored.)

NOTE SB.45
Expressions of equality should be parallel.

The parallel constructions in these illustrations are precise, clear, and strong. Achieving parallelism in your sentences improves their readability. Because of their balance and consistency, parallel constructions communicate effectively as well as correctly.

Common Sentence Errors

NOTE SB.46
Avoid common sentence errors.

Dangling modifiers and double negatives are common sentence errors you want to avoid. Good writers also avoid split infinitives.

Dangling Modifiers

NOTE SB.47
Avoid dangling modifiers; place modifiers correctly.

A **dangling modifier** exists in a sentence if a phrase that limits or slightly changes the meaning of a word is misplaced and its relationship to that word is unclear. In other words, the modifying phrase is *dangling* if it is too far removed from the word it modifies. For clarity in your messages, avoid dangling modifiers. In each of the following examples, the modifier is in italics and the word to be modified is in bold print:

Incorrect: The human resources **manager** hesitated to explain the policy to the employee, *seemingly confused*. (Who is *seemingly confused*?)

Correct: The human resources **manager**, *seemingly confused*, hesitated to explain the policy to the employee. (Moving the modifier closer to **manager** clarifies the relationship.)

Incorrect: *While participating as a cheerleader for Northwood High,* the teacher gave **me** a new cheer. (Who was participating as a cheerleader?)

Correct: *While participating as a cheerleader for Northwood High,* **I** was given a new cheer by my teacher. (Modifier *While participating as a cheerleader for Northwood High,* now clearly modifies the subject, **I**, in the rephrased sentence.)

Double Negatives

NOTE SB.48
Avoid double negatives; do not use negative adverbs and negative verbs together.

A **double negative** is formed when a negative adverb (such as *no, not, hardly, barely,* or *scarcely*) is used in the same sentence with a negative verb (cannot, could not, won't, didn't, or other verbs plus *not*). Such constructions are illogical because their use actually forms a positive. Double negatives are grammatically unacceptable. In the following examples the negative adverbs are in bold print and the negative verbs are in italics:

Incorrect: I *couldn't* **hardly** understand what she said. (The negative verb *couldn't* and negative adverb **hardly** are used in the same sentence.)

Correct: I *could* **hardly** understand what she said. (The negative verb has been changed to positive.)

Incorrect: Finishing this course *won't* do **no** good for your grade point average. (The negative verb *won't* and negative adverb **no** are used in the same sentence.)

Correct: Finishing this course *will* do **no** good for your grade point average. (The negative verb *won't* has been changed to the positive verb *will*.)

Split Infinitives

NOTE SB.49
Avoid split infinitives; do not place words between *to* and a verb.

An infinitive is formed by placing the word *to* before a present tense verb (examples: *to accept, to agree,* and *to feel*). A **split infinitive** is formed when an adverb or other words are placed between the *to* and the verb (to *bravely* accept, to *barely* agree, to *warmly* feel). Split infinitives are not correct grammar. Avoid them when possible. In the following examples, the infinitives are in bold print and the adverbs or other words that split the infinitives are in italics:

Incorrect: The human resources department selected Pamela **to** *exclusively* **represent** her department at the company's annual conference. (The infinitive **to represent** has been split by the adverb *exclusively*.)

Correct: The human resources department selected Pamela exclusively **to represent** her department at the company's annual conference. (The adverb *exclusively* has been placed before the infinitive.)

Incorrect: Tina received an assignment **to** *as quickly as possible* **design** a presentation for ABC. (Several words, *as quickly as possible*, split the infinitive **to design**.)

Correct: Tina received an assignment **to design** a presentation for ABC *as quickly as possible*. (The words *as quickly as possible* have been moved to the end of the sentence so they do not split the infinitive.)

Some split infinitives seem to sound better than do technically correct versions. Usually, you can reword the sentence to avoid the problem. For example:

Technically correct: He decided **to change** *gradually* the procedures. (The wording *to change gradually* is awkward.)

Revision: He decided **to change** the procedures *gradually*. (The revision avoids the problem of a split infinitive.)

Functions of Sentences

Sentences can serve one of four basic functions. These four functions are described below:

NOTE SB.50
Sentences can serve as statements, questions, commands, or exclamations.

[1] *Statements.* Sentences that state ideas or facts are **declarative sentences** and are followed by a period. For example:

The executive board will meet on November 5.
I believe that the school year should be 11 months.

[2] *Questions.* Questions are called **interrogative sentences** and are followed by a question mark. For example:

Will you attend the party?
Where did Margo go after graduation?

[3] *Requests or Commands.* Commands or requests, also known as **imperative sentences**, are followed by a period. Usually *you* is understood as the subject in a command or request. For example:

[You] Please bring the file to our next meeting.
[You] Send the medical form to David Wu.

[4] *Expressions of Strong Emotion.* Exclamations or **exclamatory sentences** express strong emotion and are followed by an exclamation point. For example:

> Congratulations on your acceptance into the MBA program!
> Oh! I will miss you!

Types of Sentence Structures

NOTE SB.51
There are four sentence structures.

To construct correct sentences, you should know the four basic sentence structures. The technical names of these sentence structures are *simple sentence, compound sentence, complex sentence,* and *compound-complex sentence.* Sentence structures are classified by the number and kinds of clauses they have. You read about the two kinds of clauses—independent (main) and dependent (subordinate)—earlier in this seminar.

Varying sentence structure helps to make your messages interesting. Sentence structure can also place emphasis on an idea. Placing the idea in an independent clause emphasizes it, or by placing it in a dependent clause de-emphasizes it. The effective communicator understands and uses all four sentence structures.

The Simple Sentence

NOTE SB.52
Simple sentences contain one independent clause.

The **simple sentence** consists of a single independent clause and no dependent clauses. You will recall that an independent clause has both a subject and a predicate and expresses a complete thought. The independent clause does not begin with a subordinate conjunction or a relative pronoun. Simple sentences can have compound subjects or compound predicates and can include phrases. Here are examples of typical simple sentences:

> Tito swims. (simple sentence)
> Milton and John attend the same university. (simple sentence with compound subject)
> Sales of scanners doubled last year. (simple sentence with prepositional phrase)
> Because of the reporting date extension, we can edit and proofread our report again. (simple sentence with introductory prepositional phrase and compound predicate)
> Mr. Manrique, Executive Director of Ukropina Delivery, plans to retire next year. (simple sentence with descriptive phrases)

NOTE SB.53
Simple sentences are businesslike, but their overuse sounds choppy.

You can communicate an idea clearly using a simple sentence. This sentence structure gives the greatest emphasis to the idea because there are no distracting dependent clauses. The simple sentence is effective in composing business messages. It is a clear, concise, and efficient way of communicating—the simple sentence is businesslike. Overuse of simple sentences in a message, however, can result in choppy, singsong monotony—particularly if the sentences are all short. Note the choppiness in the following paragraph:

> I started the computer. I accessed the e-mail account. The MetaCrawler search engine was launched. The listing of Web sites was given. I located the URL for LOT Airlines' Web site.

To make your writing more interesting and to de-emphasize some ideas, you will want to use a mix of sentence structures. Understanding different sentence structures will help you vary sentence structure in your messages.

The Compound Sentence

The **compound sentence** contains two or more independent clauses (each with a subject and a predicate and no dependent clauses). In this sentence structure, two or more ideas share equal emphasis. Each independent clause could stand alone as a complete sentence because it expresses a complete thought. However, by pairing the ideas in one sentence, the ideas receive less emphasis than they would in separate simple sentences.

In the following examples, the subjects are in italics and the verbs are in bold. Note in these examples that the independent clauses in each compound sentence are joined with a comma and a coordinating conjunction or a semicolon:

> *Ronalee* **will take the train** to the conference, and *she* **will speak** on cellular biology at the 9 a.m. session.
>
> *Mr. March* **applied** for the position, but *he* **did not accept** the offer.
>
> *Janie* **is** a senior, *Jade* **is** a junior, and *Beau* **is** a freshman.
>
> *Kevin* **worked** for Blockbuster Video for three years; *Craig* **worked** for Boy Scouts of America for two years.

The use of the compound sentence structure enables you to give equal importance to two or more ideas. By putting them together in one sentence, you indicate a close relationship of the two ideas.

The Complex Sentence

The **complex sentence** has one independent clause and one or more dependent clauses. Remember that a dependent clause depends on the independent clause to make a complete thought—hence, the term *dependent clause*.

In the *complex sentence* structure, one or more ideas are subordinate to the main idea. The less important or negative ideas can be de-emphasized by placing them in dependent clauses; the main idea can be emphasized by placing it in the independent clause. Another advantage of the complex sentence is that the dependent clause can be used to explain, clarify, and strengthen the main idea. The dependent clauses commonly used in complex sentences are the following:

- Noun clauses—used as subjects and objects
- Adjective clauses—used to modify nouns and pronouns
- Adverb clauses—used to modify verbs

As you know, a dependent clause contains both a subject and a verb and is introduced with a subordinating conjunction (such as *because, although, while, as soon as, if, whether,* or *when*) or a relative pronoun (such as *who, which,* or *that*). In the following examples the dependent clauses are in italics:

> *Although 99 percent of American retail stores stay open all year,* most of them make more than half their profit during the November-December holiday season.
>
> *As soon as I receive the invoice,* I will remit payment.

NOTE SB.54
Compound sentences contain two or more independent clauses.

NOTE SB.55
Complex sentences contain one independent clause and one or more dependent clauses.

NOTE SB.56
Ideas can be emphasized and de-emphasized in complex sentences.

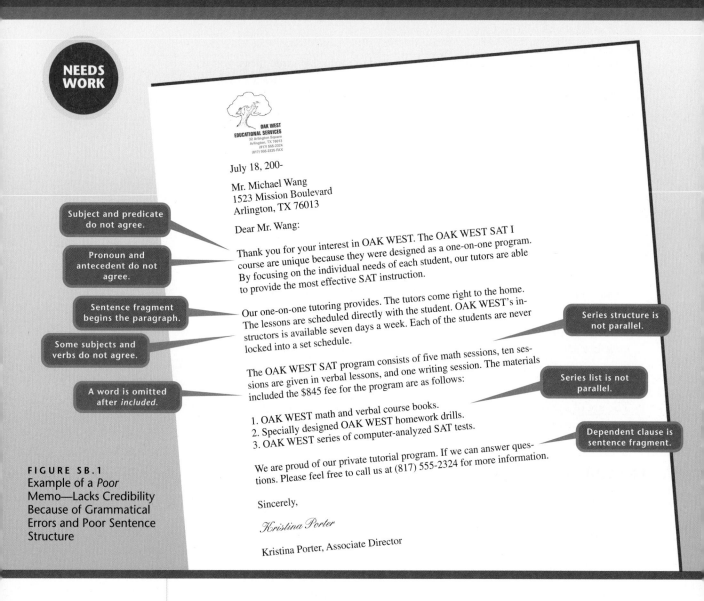

NEEDS WORK

Subject and predicate do not agree.

Pronoun and antecedent do not agree.

Sentence fragment begins the paragraph.

Some subjects and verbs do not agree.

A word is omitted after *included.*

Series structure is not parallel.

Series list is not parallel.

Dependent clause is sentence fragment.

OAK WEST EDUCATIONAL SERVICES
32 Arlington Square
Arlington, TX 76013
(817) 555-2324
(817) 555-2325 FAX

July 18, 200-

Mr. Michael Wang
1523 Mission Boulevard
Arlington, TX 76013

Dear Mr. Wang:

Thank you for your interest in OAK WEST. The OAK WEST SAT I course are unique because they were designed as a one-on-one program. By focusing on the individual needs of each student, our tutors are able to provide the most effective SAT instruction.

Our one-on-one tutoring provides. The tutors come right to the home. The lessons are scheduled directly with the student. OAK WEST's instructors is available seven days a week. Each of the students are never locked into a set schedule.

The OAK WEST SAT program consists of five math sessions, ten sessions are given in verbal lessons, and one writing session. The materials included the $845 fee for the program are as follows:

1. OAK WEST math and verbal course books.
2. Specially designed OAK WEST homework drills.
3. OAK WEST series of computer-analyzed SAT tests.

We are proud of our private tutorial program. If we can answer questions. Please feel free to call us at (817) 555-2324 for more information.

Sincerely,

Kristina Porter

Kristina Porter, Associate Director

FIGURE SB.1
Example of a *Poor* Memo—Lacks Credibility Because of Grammatical Errors and Poor Sentence Structure

You will want to know *that many call the independent clause the main clause.*

Mary Stanley, *who was Assistant Principal*, retired about 12 years ago.

All *who are being promoted* will receive raises.

When new graduates seek employment, they should use their networks of friends, acquaintances, and relatives.

The bright star *that we saw last night* was the planet Venus.

Complex sentences convey more than one idea. By its design, this structure causes some ideas to be de-emphasized and others to be emphasized.

Figure SB.1 and Figure SB.2 illustrate the importance of correct grammar and sentence structure in your communication; review these two examples of messages. Figure SB.1 is an example of a **poor** memo. Its writer will lose credibility because of the grammatical errors and poor sentence structure. Figure SB.2, a **good** version of the same memo, will gain credibility because of its correctness.

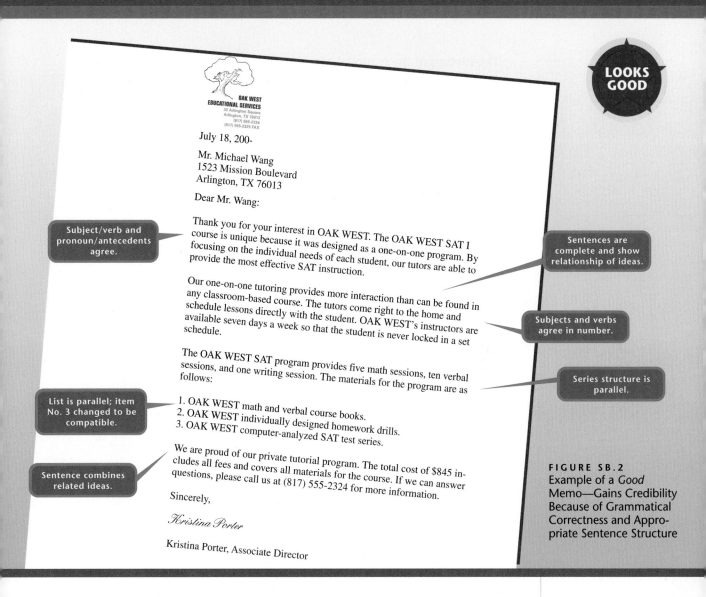

FIGURE SB.2
Example of a *Good* Memo—Gains Credibility Because of Grammatical Correctness and Appropriate Sentence Structure

Text in the figure:

OAK WEST EDUCATIONAL SERVICES
32 Arlington Square
Arlington, TX 76013
(817) 555-2324
(817) 555-2325 FAX

July 18, 200-

Mr. Michael Wang
1523 Mission Boulevard
Arlington, TX 76013

Dear Mr. Wang:

Thank you for your interest in OAK WEST. The OAK WEST SAT I course is unique because it was designed as a one-on-one program. By focusing on the individual needs of each student, our tutors are able to provide the most effective SAT instruction.

Our one-on-one tutoring provides more interaction than can be found in any classroom-based course. The tutors come right to the home and schedule lessons directly with the student. OAK WEST's instructors are available seven days a week so that the student is never locked in a set schedule.

The OAK WEST SAT program provides five math sessions, ten verbal sessions, and one writing session. The materials for the program are as follows:

1. OAK WEST math and verbal course books.
2. OAK WEST individually designed homework drills.
3. OAK WEST computer-analyzed SAT test series.

We are proud of our private tutorial program. The total cost of $845 includes all fees and covers all materials for the course. If we can answer questions, please call us at (817) 555-2324 for more information.

Sincerely,

Kristina Porter

Kristina Porter, Associate Director

Callout labels:
- LOOKS GOOD
- Subject/verb and pronoun/antecedents agree.
- Sentences are complete and show relationship of ideas.
- Subjects and verbs agree in number.
- Series structure is parallel.
- List is parallel; item No. 3 changed to be compatible.
- Sentence combines related ideas.

The Compound-Complex Sentence

The **compound-complex sentence** contains two or more independent clauses and one or more dependent clauses. The compound-complex sentence structure offers a business communicator the advantages of both the compound and complex sentences. Ideas can be related, emphasized, and de-emphasized in this complicated structure.

The compound-complex sentence structure, however, can become long and cumbersome. Business readers want to be able to understand a sentence on the first reading. For this reason, this sentence structure is used infrequently in business messages. In the following examples of compound-complex sentences, the dependent clauses are in italics and the independent clauses are in bold print.

When you take your next flight on a commercial airliner, **think about the fact that it was only 100 years ago that the first flight took place; and one man made this flight on a little 12-horsepower biplane.**

NOTE SB.57
Compound-complex sentences contain two or more independent clauses and one or more dependent clauses.

NOTE SB.58
Compound-complex sentences can be long and cumbersome.

The looting of the National Museum of Iraq, *which took place after the fall of the Saddam Hussein regime*, is one of the greatest cultural disasters in Middle Eastern history; 80 percent of the museum's priceless objects were stolen or destroyed.

Application Exercises

1. Key these sentences into a computer word-processing program. For each independent clause, italicize the complete subject (the subject with its modifiers); use bold for the complete predicate. Print a copy.
   a. Josh applied for a position as business manager.
   b. Boys and girls take the SAT test for college admission.
   c. The economy ranked as the top priority in a recent national poll.
   d. English skills are important in all occupations.
   e. Don, who received the outstanding principal award, is now the assistant superintendent for the high school district.
   f. Hobbyists, instead of software professionals, authored many early software packages.
   g. Stars circled by planets are quite rare.
   h. Newly uncovered Guatemalan hieroglyphs help explain Mayan history.
   i. X-ray film is headed for extinction; X-rays are going digital.
   j. Why can't you install the computer memory?
2. Using the copy of Application Exercise 1, circle the simple subject and the simple predicate in each independent and dependent clause.
3. List the letter of each of the following sentences. Write the direct objects and any indirect objects for that sentence beside the letter and write the word Direct or Indirect by each object.
   a. Jeannie sent the e-mail to Juan's account.
   b. Gordon gave Allen a haircut.
   c. Michael wrote an article about science.
   d. Angel Contreras gave Benito a book titled *Soy la Avon Lady and Other Stories.*
   e. Christopher Askew received an award for his singing.
4. Write or print the following sentences. Underline the linking verbs and circle or use bold print to identify the subject in the following sentences.
   a. Here is your coat.
   b. You look fabulous!
   c. I feel cold.
   d. He was ill last week.
   e. Julie has been out of the country for two weeks.
5. List the letters for the sentences in Application Exercise 4, and write the complete subject complement for each sentence.
6. List the letter of each of the following sentences. By each letter, write the word phrases in that sentence and label each one by the type of phrase.
   a. Jeffrey is the manager of an upscale restaurant.
   b. Jane likes to attend meetings.
   c. Billy laid the tile in the bathroom.
   d. Wanda walked by the store on her way home.
   e. Betty found Megan walking in the park.

7. List the letter for each of the following sentences. Beside each letter, write any dependent clause the sentence may contain, and indicate the sentence structure (i.e., simple, complex, compound, or compound-complex).

   a. When the question of ethics arose, the supervisor emphasized referring to the company code of ethics.

   b. Overseas shipments of freight are to be insured for full value if their value exceeds $1,000.

   c. Pay for men and women should be equal if the work performed is of comparable worth.

   d. Esther is well liked because she is a good listener when students need her.

   e. When the pizza is ready, let me know; I will ask our guests to come to the table.

   f. The College of Business Instructional Materials Center (IMC) is a full-service facility; when you need word processing, e-mail, fax service, or copying service, send your request to the IMC.

   g. The Nashville Ballet performed for the Arts Celebration; and the Shakespeare Theatre featured "Two Gentlemen of Verona," a 1972 Tony Award winner for best musical.

   h. "Ballet Under the Stars," a summer production that is performed in a city park, begins next week.

   i. Graphic aids help to make complex information understandable.

   j. Although not all the sales agents agreed, the home office changed the structure of the sales commissions.

8. List the letter for each sentence in Application Exercise 7. Write the independent (main) clause(s) beside each letter.

9. Write or print the following sentences using the correct verb form for each sentence.

   a. Forensics (is, are) required for the study of debate.

   b. Either Nancy or Peggy (is, are) going.

   c. *Communication Notes* (contain, contains) articles helpful to business writers.

   d. The committee (agree, agrees) with the new procedure.

   e. The board, rather than the officers, (vote, votes) on increasing fees.

   f. Neither Tien nor his friends (is, are) ready to report.

   g. Data (indicate, indicates) that our original plans were correct.

   h. Each of the members (want, wants) to see facts on the issue before deciding how to vote.

   i. Most of the guys (is, are) in the jazz band.

   j. What criteria (has, have) been established for selecting a new president?

10. Write or print the following sentences using the correct pronoun(s) for each sentence.

   a. All of the students had (their, his or her) lunches.

   b. Either Christina or Lucy left (their, her) coat at Julio's house.

   c. Global executives must learn to handle cultural differences in (her or his, their) own way.

   d. Each of the students introduced (their, his or her) dorm roommates.

   e. Every man or woman seeking employment should try to match opportunities with (their, her or his) qualifications.

11. Rewrite each sentence below to correct the lack of parallelism. Use correct punctuation for your rewritten sentences.

   a. CostCo's prices were lower than the Corner Store.

   b. The company paid its employees a high salary and giving them good health benefits.

    c. Shahz was strong, optimistic, and a woman of courage.

    d. International companies look for executives who can adapt to local customs and if they can speak the language.

    e. Tom and Daniel play baseball and basketball but are not playing soccer.

12. Examine the following sentences for the common sentence errors of dangling modifiers, double negatives, and split infinitives. List the letter of each sentence and write a corrected version of that sentence beside the letter.

    a. He wouldn't never deny that he had a good time.

    b. Sailing on the ocean, a beautiful sunset filled the sky.

    c. The attendance clerk wrote the note to specifically excuse the boy from class.

    d. Walking on the beach, the seashells fascinated me.

    e. You cannot pass this course if you do not hardly try to complete each lesson.

13. Write a short paragraph that includes an example of each of the four functions of sentences—statement, question, command or request, and exclamation.

14. Write a short paragraph that includes an example of each of the four basic sentence structures—simple sentence, compound sentence, complex sentence, and compound-complex sentence.

Message Analysis

Examine the following message. Rewrite the message and correct any grammatical or punctuation errors you find.

> A career advice service which appear in numberous newspapers accross the country now is offering a new service for newspapers. Newspapers can now partner with this service and include Web ID codes in it's job ads which give job seekers acsess to expanded job listings which have links to enable the job seeker to apply for the job directly online; employers have the option to target qualified candidates by placing an expanded listing with the the career Web cite online explaining additional details about qualifications for the position for which they are advertising. The job applicant cannot fail hardly to get the job, if they read the expanded listing, and are matching his or her qualifications to the job requirements.

Punctuation

When you speak, the tone of your voice, the gestures you make, and the pauses you insert help your listeners understand what you are saying. When you write, punctuation helps your readers understand your message. Punctuation tells your readers where one thought ends and the next begins; it helps emphasize ideas and clarify meaning. Writing without punctuation is comparable to building a house without a blueprint.

This seminar reviews the punctuation that occurs most often in business writing. The material is not designed to eliminate the need for reference manuals. When you have a question about punctuation, check a reliable source.

NOTE SC.1
Punctuation marks add emphasis and clarity to a message.

NOTE SC.2
Check reference sources when you are uncertain about punctuation.

Terminal Punctuation

The three punctuation symbols that are used to signal the end of a complete thought are the period, the question mark, and the exclamation mark.

The Period

The **period** is the most frequently used ending mark of punctuation. It signals the end of a declarative or an imperative sentence. A declarative sentence makes a statement; an imperative sentence gives a command:

> The policy will take effect March 1. (declarative)
> You may have the gift wrapped at no extra charge. (declarative)
> Lock the door when you leave. (imperative)
> Sign and date both copies of the contract. (imperative)

A **polite request**, sometimes called a *courteous request*, requires action rather than an oral or written response. The writer would rather have the reader devote time to doing what has been requested than to writing or calling to say yes or no. A polite request ends with a period:

> Won't you take a few moments now to complete and return the survey.
> Will you please adjust the volume.

The period is also used when the writer asks an **indirect question**—a statement about a question:

> I wonder when the new server will be installed.
> Manuel asked whether you and I are related.

NOTE SC.3
Periods are used to end
• Declarative and imperative sentences
• Polite requests that require action
• Indirect questions

The Question Mark

NOTE SC.4
Question marks are used to end direct questions.

A **question mark** should be used with an interrogative sentence. An interrogative sentence asks for or requires a definite response. The response may be a single word, or it may be one or more sentences:

> Have you mailed the invitations? (one-word response)
> What arrangements have you made for your trip to Seoul? (a response of one or more sentences)

When a series of questions has a common subject and predicate, each question is followed by a question mark. Unless the questions in a series are proper nouns or complete thoughts, capitalize only the first letter of the sentence:

> Have we determined when? where? why?
> Do you golf? play tennis? swim?
> Did you select maple? oak? cherry?

The Exclamation Mark

NOTE SC.5
Exclamation marks show strong emotion.

An **exclamation mark** is used with an exclamatory sentence—one that shows strong emotion. Because of the dramatic effect it creates, the exclamation mark is used sparingly in business correspondence:

> Yes! We submitted the low bid.
> Hurry! Make your reservation today.
> Excellent!
> Sharp's will not be undersold!

Choosing Terminal Punctuation

When deciding which terminal punctuation mark to use, ask these questions:

- Am I expressing a strong emotion? (If yes, use !)
- Am I asking the reader to give me a response? (If so, use ?)

If you answer no to both questions, use the period.

Primary Internal Punctuation

Terminal punctuation marks help guide your reader through your message. Internal punctuation marks help him or her through each sentence. The comma and the semicolon are the most frequently used internal punctuation marks.

The Comma

NOTE SC.6
Commas separate items in sentences.

NOTE SC.7
Too few or too many commas can hamper message clarity.

The comma plays an important role in business writing. A **comma** separates items in a sentence and helps the reader correctly interpret each thought. By learning how commas are used and by mastering the rules for their placement, you will become a more effective business writer. Using commas incorrectly—omitting them where needed or adding them where they are not needed—can hamper communication. Consider these examples:

After you have eaten the leftover meat the vegetables and the dairy products should be placed in the refrigerator. (commas have been omitted)

In this sentence, the absence of commas makes the reader wonder what is to be eaten and what is to be put into the refrigerator. Because the message is confusing, additional communication is necessary. The message becomes clear when a comma is inserted after the word *eaten* and between each item in the compound subject:

After you have eaten, the leftover meat, the vegetables, and the dairy products should be placed in the refrigerator.

In the following sentence, clarity is lost because four commas are used where none is needed:

This afternoon, we will meet with the chair, of the board, while her staff tours the new addition, to the factory. (commas are used where they are not needed)

The sentence should read as follows:

This afternoon we will meet with the chair of the board while her staff tours the new addition to the factory.

Although the original versions of these sentences are extreme examples of comma omission and misuse, they illustrate the need for caution when using commas. The best way to ensure correct use of commas is to justify their placement.

NOTE SC.8
Be sure to justify each comma you use.

CALENDAR DATES

A complete **calendar date** consists of a month, a day, and a year. Whenever a complete calendar date occurs within the body of a sentence, the year is set apart from the rest of the sentence by commas. When a complete calendar date occurs at the end of an independent clause or a sentence, the final comma is replaced by a semicolon or terminal punctuation. Commas are optional when the date consists of only the month and year. If the military or international date form is used, no commas are needed:

NOTE SC.9
Use commas with complete calendar dates.

On *June 17, 1932,* Carlson College held its first commencement ceremony. (Calendar date is complete.)

In *June 1932* Carlson College conducted its first commencement ceremony. (Commas optional when date consists only of month and year. *June, 1932,* is also correct.)

Carlson held its first commencement ceremony on *June 17, 1932.* (The calendar date is complete and ends the sentence.)

On *17 June 1932* Carlson College conducted its first commencement ceremony. (The military or international date form does not need commas.)

When a weekday is used with a calendar date, the date is set off by commas. The calendar date may be complete or incomplete:

Our office will be closed on *Friday, July 3,* to enable our staff to have an extended holiday. (Weekday with incomplete calendar date.)

The memorial was dedicated on *Tuesday, March 19, 2003.* (Weekday with complete calendar date.)

GEOGRAPHIC LOCATIONS

NOTE SC.10
Use commas with complete geographic locations.

A complete **geographic location** consists of a city and a state, province, or nation. When a geographic location is mentioned within a sentence, the name of the state, province, or nation is set apart from the rest of the sentence by commas. When an incomplete geographic location is named in a sentence, no commas are necessary:

The Olympic Games were held in Salt Lake City, *Utah*, during the winter of 2002. (Salt Lake City, Utah, is a complete geographic location.)

The new mall in *Silverdale* will open this fall. (The geographic location is incomplete.)

Have you ever visited *Acapulco, Mexico*? (The geographic location is complete; the question mark replaces the ending comma because the name of the country is the last item in the interrogative sentence.)

INDEPENDENT ADJECTIVES

NOTE SC.11
A comma replaces the word *and* between independent adjectives.

When two or more adjectives in a series independently modify the same noun, they are called **independent adjectives**. Commas are used to separate independent adjectives:

Avery is a *patient, caring, sincere* foster parent; Dyanne is a *well-known, well-respected* office automation consultant.

The adjectives in the first series independently describe Avery as a foster parent; those in the second series independently describe Dyanne as a consultant. The writer could have stated it this way:

Avery is a patient and caring and sincere foster parent; Dyanne is a well-known and well-respected office automation consultant.

Combining the adjectives, however, is more efficient for the writer and more pleasing to the reader. A good test of the need for commas and where they should be placed is to insert the word *and* between the adjectives. If the word *and* can be inserted without altering the meaning of the sentence, a comma should be used:

Sentence without punctuation: Reo gave a brief emotional acceptance speech.

Test: Reo gave a brief (and) emotional acceptance speech.

Correctly punctuated: Reo gave a brief, emotional acceptance speech.

The following example needs no commas. If we insert the word *and* between the adjectives, the sentence becomes awkward.

Sentence without punctuation: Roberto drives a shiny blue sports car. (The words *shiny*, *blue*, and *sports* describe the car, but they do so collectively, not independently.)

Test: Roberto drives a shiny (and) blue (and) sports car.

Correctly punctuated: Roberto drives a shiny blue sports car.

INDEPENDENT CLAUSES

NOTE SC.12
When two independent clauses are joined by a coordinating conjunction, place a comma before the conjunction.

When the independent clauses in a compound sentence are joined with a coordinating conjunction (*and, but, or, nor*), use a comma before the conjunction:

The car handles well, *and* it gets good mileage. (The coordinating conjunction joins independent clauses.)

The mountains and streams created a peaceful atmosphere, *but* Leona and Signe longed for the hustle and bustle of the city. (The coordinating conjunction joins the independent clauses.)

Jordan plays baseball and soccer. (No comma is needed because the coordinating conjunction *and* does not connect two independent clauses.)

INTRODUCTORY CLAUSES

When a dependent clause *introduces* an independent clause in a complex sentence, a comma is used to separate the clauses. Introductory clauses commonly begin with one of the following words:

NOTE SC.13
Use a comma after a dependent clause that introduces an independent clause.

after	before	until
although	if	when
as	since	whenever
because	unless	while

When the dependent clause does not introduce the independent clause, a comma is not used:

If you book your flight online, you will receive 500 bonus miles. (The dependent clause introduces the independent clause.)

After we receive your check, we will process your order. (The dependent clause introduces the independent clause.)

Be sure to replace the toner cartridge *before you leave.* (No comma is needed; the dependent clause does not introduce the independent clause.)

NONESSENTIAL ELEMENTS

Words, phrases, or clauses that are not necessary to the meaning or structure of a sentence are considered **nonessential elements**. Appositives, names used in direct address, introductory words, introductory phrases, nonrestrictive clauses, parenthetical expressions, and transitional expressions are all nonessential elements.

Each nonessential element requires one or more commas. A nonessential element that begins a sentence is followed by a comma. A nonessential element that ends an independent clause is followed by a comma or a semicolon; one that ends a sentence is followed by the appropriate terminal punctuation. A nonessential element that does not end an independent clause or a sentence is preceded and followed by a comma. To determine whether an item is nonessential, omit it from the sentence. If the meaning and structure of the sentence are complete, the item is nonessential.

NOTE SC.14
Nonessential elements require one or more commas.

APPOSITIVES

An **appositive** is a word or a phrase that immediately follows a noun and either explains or provides additional information about it. When this additional information is not necessary to the meaning of the sentence, it is separated from the rest of the sentence by commas:

NOTE SC.15
Use commas with nonessential appositives.

My oldest sister, *Sarah,* serves on the City Council. (The name Sarah is not essential to the meaning of the sentence; only one of the writer's sisters may be the oldest.)

My sister Sarah serves on the City Council. (The name is needed to indicate which of the writer's sisters serves on the Council.)

DIRECT ADDRESS

NOTE SC.16
Commas separate a direct address from the rest of the sentence.

In order to make a sentence sound more personal and conversational, senders may insert the receiver's name. When a name is used in this manner, it is referred to as a **direct address:**

Mr. Wilson, you'll receive many hours of enjoyment from your new treadmill.

Thank you, *Manjeet*, for your efforts on our behalf.

INTRODUCTORY WORDS

NOTE SC.17
An introductory word is followed by a comma.

An **introductory word** is the first word in a sentence; it leads the reader to the independent clause and is separated from the clause by a comma. *Obviously, generally,* and *unfortunately* are examples of introductory words; others are used in the following examples:

Yes, you may use my laptop. (The introductory word is not essential to the meaning or structure of the sentence.)

Currently, I am coaching a youth softball team. (The introductory word is not essential to the meaning or structure of the sentence.)

INTRODUCTORY PHRASES

NOTE SC.18
Commas are optional after introductory phrases.

An **introductory phrase** is a group of words that begins a sentence and introduces an independent clause. Introductory phrases may or may not be separated from an independent clause by a comma; the deciding factor is readability. If omitting the comma could cause reader confusion, include it. Some writers use a comma after an introductory phrase that has five or more words:

To earn a bonus you must exceed your sales goal by at least 20 percent. (No comma is necessary; the message is clear without the comma.)

By leaving now you will avoid rush-hour traffic. (No comma is necessary; the message is clear without the comma.)

Without warning, Juan turned and walked away. (Message clarity is improved by placing a comma after the introductory phrase.)

After entering your five-digit authorization code and hearing the progression tone, enter the area code and number. (Message clarity is improved by placing a comma after the long introductory phrase.)

NONRESTRICTIVE CLAUSES

NOTE SC.19
Nonrestrictive clauses provide additional information; use a comma before and after them.

Earlier in this section, you learned that an appositive provides additional information about a noun; a **nonrestrictive clause** has the same function. One feature distinguishes an appositive from a nonrestrictive clause: An appositive is a word or a phrase—not a clause.

Nonrestrictive clauses frequently begin with *who* or *which*. They are separated from the rest of a sentence by commas. Some writers prefer to use the word *which* to begin a nonrestrictive clause and the word *that* to begin a restrictive (essential) clause:

The play, *which was written by Rita Golden*, will be performed without intermission. (The clause is not essential to the meaning of the sentence.)

The payment *that was due March 15* is now three weeks late. (The clause is essential to the sentence.)

The people *who want to speak with you* are seated in the lobby. (The clause is essential to the sentence.)

Please inform Senator Barjo that, *although we have supported him in the past*, we will oppose him on the sales tax issue. (The clause is not essential to the meaning of the sentence. Note that this nonrestrictive clause does not begin with who or which.)

Sally, *who visited Mexico City last spring*, plans to vacation in Toronto this fall. (The clause does not restrict the meaning of the sentence.)

PARENTHETICAL EXPRESSIONS

When one or more words interrupt the flow of a sentence, a **parenthetical expression** is created. The expression is separated from the rest of the sentence by commas:

NOTE SC.20
Parenthetical expressions interrupt the flow of a sentence; they should be preceded and followed by a comma.

If you return on Monday, *however*, you will have time to visit the museum. (The word *however* interrupts the flow of the sentence.)

The white blossom, *although less common*, is as beautiful as the red. (The words *although less common* interrupt the flow of the sentence.)

The film is, *to quote the reviewer*, "extraordinary." (The words *to quote the reviewer* interrupt the flow of the sentence.)

TRANSITIONAL EXPRESSIONS

A word or phrase that links sentences or independent clauses is a **transitional expression**. When a transitional expression links two independent clauses, it is preceded by a semicolon and followed by a comma. When a transitional expression links two sentences, it is followed by a comma:

NOTE SC.21
Transitional expressions link independent clauses.

The wallpaper was printed in two different lots; *therefore*, the colors did not match. (The transitional expression links two independent clauses.)

Your newest catalog had not yet arrived when we placed our order. *As a result*, we were unable to use the new price in calculating the total cost of our order. (The transitional expression links two sentences.)

Words such as *however* and *therefore* and phrases such as *of course* and *as a result* may be either parenthetical or transitional. The key is how they are used in the sentence:

The invoice, *therefore*, has been approved for payment. (The word *therefore* interrupts the flow of the sentence—it is parenthetical.)

The remaining items in the order were delivered yesterday; *therefore*, the invoice has been approved for payment. (The word *therefore* is used as a transitional word linking two independent clauses.)

SERIES

When three or more words, phrases, or clauses form a subject, a verb, or an object, a **series** is created. Items in a series should be separated by commas. The final item is usually set apart from the others by the word *and* or the word *or*. For clarity, a comma should be used before the conjunction as well as between the other series items:

NOTE SC.22
Commas separate items in a series.

NOTE SC.23
The final item in a series follows a conjunction.

Sue, Dennis, and Cyndi will present our proposal. (The three names are part of a compound subject.)

Jason plays *bridge, chess, and backgammon.* (The items are the direct object of the verb plays.)

The campers will *canoe, hike, and swim.* (The verbs describe the actions of the campers.)

Up/down, near/far, and *thick/thin* are pairs of antonyms. (Each pair of words in the series is part of a compound subject.)

The Semicolon

The **semicolon** is used to separate. It may also be used to join.

NOTE SC.24
Semicolons may be used to separate and to join.

INDEPENDENT CLAUSES WITHOUT COORDINATING CONJUNCTIONS

NOTE SC.25
Semicolons join independent clauses when no conjunction is used.

A semicolon is used to connect two independent clauses not joined by a coordinating conjunction. The semicolon makes the reader aware of the close relationship between the independent clauses. Although each clause could be written as a separate sentence, joining them with a semicolon creates a smoother writing style:

Please sign and return the enclosed card; it requires no postage. (The clauses are closely related; no conjunction is used.)

Albert will edit the report; please send your corrections and suggestions to him. (The clauses are closely related; no conjunction is used.)

When a comma is mistakenly used to join independent clauses where no conjunction is present, a *comma splice* is created. Writers should be careful to avoid this error:

Paul has asked for a paternity leave, he and his wife have adopted a baby. (incorrectly punctuated; comma splice)

Paul has asked for a paternity leave; he and his wife have adopted a baby. (correctly punctuated; semicolon joins independent clauses)

INDEPENDENT CLAUSES WITH COORDINATING CONJUNCTIONS

NOTE SC.26
Semicolons should be used to join independent clauses that contain commas.

When independent clauses are joined by a coordinating conjunction and either or both of the clauses contain commas, clarity is achieved by using a semicolon (rather than a comma) before the conjunction that joins the two independent clauses. In the example that follows, the second sentence uses a semicolon and is clearer and easier to read:

Mr. Samkoff, Mr. Cromwell, and Mrs. Fritz will move to the new building on May 3, but Mr. Martin, Mrs. Hazel, and Mr. Kinnard will not relocate until May 8.

Mr. Samkoff, Mr. Cromwell, and Mrs. Fritz will move to the new building on May 3; Mr. Martin, Mrs. Hazel, and Mr. Kinnard will not relocate until May 8.

SERIES ITEMS CONTAINING COMMAS

NOTE SC.27
Use semicolons to separate long, complex series items that contain commas.

Using commas to separate items in a series could create confusion when one or more items within the series contain a comma. By using semicolons to separate the items within this type of series, the message is easier to interpret. In the example that follows, the second sentence—the one that uses semicolons to separate the series items—is much clearer:

> The group will visit Vienna, Austria, Paris, France, Munich, Germany, and Naples, Italy, during its two-week tour. (unclear)

> The group will visit Vienna, Austria; Paris, France; Munich, Germany; and Naples, Italy, during its two-week tour. (clear)

The comma and the semicolon are two punctuation marks that influence the clarity and readability of a message. Use them effectively to help your reader better understand your message.

Secondary Internal Punctuation

Several other punctuation marks are used within sentences to bring clarity, emphasis, and variety to writing. Those punctuation marks are discussed in this section.

The Apostrophe

As you write letters, memos, and reports, you will use the apostrophe in three ways: to form possessives, to form contractions, and to form plurals.

NOTE SC.28
Apostrophes are used to form possessives and contractions.

POSSESSIVES

A **possessive** shows ownership. Both nouns and pronouns may be expressed as possessives. Figure SC.1 shows the possessive form of several nouns and pronouns. Recall that only nouns use an apostrophe in their possessive form. The apostrophe is placed either before the *s* ('s) or after the *s* (s') depending on the noun. The context of the sentence will often provide a clue to placement of the apostrophe. Seminar A contains detailed information about forming possessives.

Word	Possessive	Word	Possessive
she (pronoun)	her office	employee (noun)	employee's folder
we (pronoun)	our contract	employees (noun)	employees' lounge
they (pronoun)	their proposal	Mike (noun)	Mike's office
he (pronoun)	his computer	perfume (noun)	perfume's scent
month (noun)	a month's salary	Dennis (noun)	Dennis' promotion

FIGURE SC.1
Possessive Forms

CONTRACTIONS

A **contraction** is a combination of two words in a shortened form. An apostrophe signals the omission of one or more letters in the contraction—*you're* for *you are, wouldn't* for *would not,* and *let's* for *let us.* Contractions are seldom used in business writing because they lack the formality desired in a permanent record. The opposite is true of *o'clock;* this contraction for *of the clock* is used when writers want formality.

When spoken, several contractions sound the same as possessive pronouns. These potentially confusing words are listed in Figure SC.2. If you are unsure about whether to use an apostrophe, remember this: A contraction *always* has an apostrophe.

NOTE SC.29
Contractions are seldom used in business correspondence.

Word	Meaning
its	possessive form of pronoun *it*
it's	contraction of *it is*
their	possessive form of pronoun *they* (before noun)
they're	contraction of *they are*
theirs	possessive form of the pronoun *they* (not before noun)
there's	contraction of *there is*
whose	possessive form of pronoun *who*
who's	contraction of *who is*
your	possessive form of pronoun *you*
you're	contraction of *you are*

PLURALS

For clarity, use an apostrophe to form the plural of a lowercase letter. Also use the apostrophe to form the plural of the uppercase letters A, I, M, and U. Without an apostrophe, these uppercase letters could be misread as words (As, Is, Us) or as an abbreviation (Ms):

> Place x's before all items that apply.
> How many A's did you earn last term?

The Colon

NOTE SC.30
Colons alert the reader that something of importance will follow.

The colon is often used as a clue to the reader that a *list*, an *explanation*, or an *example* will follow. The words that introduce the list should contain a subject and a predicate. The items following the colon may be words, phrases, or complete sentences. They may be displayed as part of the paragraph text or as a vertical list. The writer makes the placement decision based on the space available and the amount of emphasis to be placed on the items. A list will receive more attention than items presented in paragraph form. When displayed in paragraph form, items following a colon begin with a capital letter only when they are complete sentences; items in a list always begin with a capital letter. Items may be numbered in either style, but only one form should be used in the list:

> Bretta's reason for missing the meeting was simple: She was one of three passengers in the elevator when it stopped between the sixth and seventh floors. (explanation in paragraph form)

> Several factors influenced our decision: personnel, space, and equipment. (listing in paragraph form; common nouns)

NOTE SC.31
List in paragraph form.

> Three factors influenced our decision: (1) Additional personnel would be needed. (2) Space for expansion does not exist. (3) Our equipment is old and fragile. (explanatory list in paragraph form with numbered sentences)

> The decision was influenced by the following factors:

NOTE SC.32
List in vertical form.

> 1. The need for additional personnel
> 2. The lack of space for expansion
> 3. The condition of our equipment

> Our decision was influenced by personnel, space, and equipment factors. (No colon is used because the portion of the sentence before the series is not an independent clause.)

The colon has several other applications that occasionally occur in business writing. Those uses and an example of each are presented in Figure SC.3.

Use	Example
ratio	2:1 (2 to 1)
references	11:18–21 (volume:page numbers)
reference initials	DKH:jw (author:keyboarder)
salutations	Dear Mr. Waldorf: (mixed punctuation)
times	12:15 p.m. (hour:minutes)

The Dash

A **dash** is used to separate. When using word processing or desktop publishing software, writers create solid lines known as an *en dash* and an *em dash*. An *en dash* is a solid line used to separate the low and high elements of a numeric or an alphabetic range by taking the place of *to* or *through*. An *em dash* is a longer solid line used when a writer wants to show a sudden change in thought or to place emphasis on what follows.

NOTE SC.33
Dashes separate.

The en dash is created by keying a hyphen with no space before or after it and the items it separates. The em dash is created by keying two hyphens with no space before, between, or after them and the surrounding text. Because of its strength and impact, the em dash should be used less frequently than other marks of punctuation.

Bilin—a B+ student—plays catcher for the softball team. (em dash; sudden change of thought)

Only one product sold better than we predicted—the portfolio. (em dash; emphasis)

Items 1–5 focus on demographics; items 6–10, on opinions (en dash; numeric range)

When main floor seating is nearly full, open balconies A–C. (en dash; alphabetic range)

If en dashes and em dashes are not available, writers may use a single hyphen for an en dash and a double hyphen for an em dash. As with the en and em dashes, there is no space before, between, or after the hyphen(s) and related text.

The Diagonal

The **diagonal** (also called the *slant* or *slash*) frequently indicates a choice or an alternative. The diagonal is also used in creating fractions and may be used with some abbreviations. No space is used before or after the diagonal:

NOTE SC.34
The diagonal has several uses.

Do you want bagels and/or muffins at the meeting? (Either or both may be served.)

The new manager will select his/her administrative assistant. (The gender of the new employee is unknown.)

S/he will replace Arturo, who retires in May. (S/he is used to mean she or he and to eliminate gender bias.)

Tell them to proceed w/o delay. (without)

2/3 (fraction)

11 1/2 (mixed number; space before fraction)

When completing business forms, writers often use the diagonal as part of a date. The standard format is month/day/year; two character positions are allocated to each part. The emerging popularity of the international date style (day/month/year) and the confusion that could result make this format inappropriate for use in correspondence:

02/03/05 (February 3, 2005? March 2, 2005?)

The Ellipsis

An **ellipsis** is an intentional omission of words. An ellipsis is signaled by **ellipsis points**, a series of three periods separated from each other and from what precedes or follows them by one space. Ellipsis points are used for emphasis in advertising. In other forms of business writing, ellipsis points are used to indicate that words have been omitted from a direct quotation. When the ellipsis occurs at the end of a sentence, add the terminal punctuation:

The fluctuations in currency exchange rates are interesting . . . and worth watching.

The owner's manual says the picture should be ". . . clear and crisp."

Ethel choked back tears as she began her acceptance speech by saying, "I am truly honored . . . ." (end of sentence)

The Hyphen

The **hyphen** is used to bring things together, to show that two items are related. Because the purpose is to join, there is no space before or after a hyphen. Hyphens are commonly used in three ways: (1) to form compound words, (2) to join prefixes and suffixes to root words, and (3) to indicate where a word has been divided. The first two uses are more common and are explained in this section.

COMPOUND WORDS

The most frequent use of the hyphen is to form compound words. A **compound word** is two or more words used as one. Compound words may be nouns, verbs, or adjectives. Writing experts do not always agree on whether compound words should be hyphenated, written as two words, or written as one word; style preferences are continually changing. The best source of information about compound nouns and verbs is a current dictionary. The information presented in this section will help you determine when and how to hyphenate compound adjectives.

Compound adjectives may be permanent or temporary. Permanent compound adjectives include a hyphen as part of their dictionary entry; temporary compound adjectives do not. Permanent compound adjectives use a hyphen all the time; temporary compound adjectives contain a hyphen only when they come before a noun. Compound adjectives formed using an -*ly* adverb are never hyphenated:

Patricia Cornwell is a *well-known* author. (permanent compound)

Patricia Cornwell is *well-known* as an author. (permanent compound)

This is a highly entertaining short story. (temporary compound; -*ly* adverb compound)

The tasks are simple but *time consuming*. (temporary compound not before noun)

Dictionaries may vary. Always consult the current edition of a well-known dictionary.

Sometimes two or more hyphenated compound words with the same base word appear in a series. In this case the hyphen is used, but the base word may be omitted in all except the last item of the series. This procedure is called suspending a hyphen:

> Leah will describe our *short-* and *long-term* forecasting techniques. (The word *term* is omitted in the first compound word.)

> The announcement can be repeated at *5-, 15-,* or *30-minute* intervals. (The word *minute* is omitted in the first two compound words.)

PREFIXES

A **prefix** is one or more syllables added to the beginning of a word. Prefixes are followed by hyphens in a variety of situations. Figure SC.4 lists those situations and gives an example of each.

Prefix	Hyphenated	Example
ex	yes	ex-mayor; ex-officio
self	yes	self-addressed; self-sufficient
pre	generally not	preschool; preemployment
re	to distinguish from word with different meaning	re-form reform
non	generally not	noncompliant; nonresponsive
co	consult dictionary	co-owner; coworker
vice	consult dictionary	vice president; vice-chancellor

FIGURE SC.4
Hyphenating Prefixes

Whenever a prefix is added to a proper noun, the prefix is separated from the word by a hyphen:

> mid-May   trans-Alaska   self-motivated

Parentheses

Parentheses, like commas, may be used to separate nonessential information from the rest of a thought. If parentheses and commas were compared according to their strength, however, parentheses would be rated as weaker marks of punctuation. The information they contain may be so unimportant that the writer should consider eliminating it entirely. Names, dates, times, amounts, reference citations, abbreviations, area codes, phone numbers, addresses, and editorial comments are just a few of the items that may be enclosed within parentheses. If a writer chooses to use parentheses, certain requirements must be met:

[1] Both left and right parentheses must be used.

> Baron Clothiers, Inc. (BCI) accepts telephone orders between 7 a.m. and 4 p.m. (EST) Monday through Friday.

[2] Commas, semicolons, periods, or other punctuation marks should be used as needed within the parentheses.

NOTE SC.39
Items that are unimportant may be placed in parentheses.

The entree (salmon) will be served with a baked potato, broccoli with cheese sauce (or, if you prefer, lemon butter), and a colorful fruit garnish.

[3] The presence of parentheses should not affect the use of punctuation elsewhere in the statement or question.

After she retired (lucky woman!), Elsa moved to Idaho.

The Period

NOTE SC.40
Periods are used with
• Abbreviations
• Decimals
• Lists

Earlier in this chapter, you reviewed the use of the period as a mark of terminal punctuation. While that use of the period is certainly the most common, it is by no means the only use. This section focuses on other uses.

ABBREVIATIONS

Abbreviations are shortened forms of words, names, or phrases; their primary purpose is to save time and space. As a general rule, business writers restrict their use of abbreviations to those they believe their receivers will recognize.

The capitalization, punctuation, and spacing of abbreviations vary widely. Seminar D covers some of these issues. The most comprehensive source of information about abbreviations is a reference manual.

DECIMALS

A **decimal** is one method by which writers may express fractional components of a whole number. In business writing, use decimals when expressing money or measurements. Do not use a space before or after the decimal:

Safeway's rate for a 47-passenger coach is $1.10 a mile.

Kyle has averaged 10.3 points per game this season.

The second portage is the longest, 2.8 miles.

All units that vary from specification by more than .0025" must be rejected.

LISTS

NOTE SC.41
List formats vary.

When items in a list are identified by numbers or letters, a period is used. Lists may be formatted in three ways; all three apply to either numeric or alphabetic listings:

[1] In one format, the number is indented and the text wraps to the left margin. This is true whether the text runs over one line or many.

[2] In another format, both the number and any runover lines of the text begin at the left margin. This, also, is true whether the text runs over one line or many.

[3] Still another option is to key the number at the left margin and hang indent the text. This is true whether the text runs over one line or many.

A minimum of two spaces should follow the period. When using word processing software, simply tab to the next position on the preset tab grid, or use the feature that creates bullets and numbers for a list.

The Quotation Mark

NOTE SC.42
Quotation marks show exact wording, give special emphasis, or identify literary or artistic works.

A **quotation mark** serves three different purposes in written messages: (1) to indicate that the writer is using the exact words of another individual, (2) to emphasize words that are unique or have a special meaning in a particular message, or (3) to identify literary or artistic works. In all cases, quotation marks are used in pairs—one is placed at the beginning of the quote or item of information, while the other is placed at the end.

EXACT WORDS

Quotations may be indirect or direct. An **indirect quotation** paraphrases the words of a writer or speaker. A **direct quotation** uses the exact words of a writer. Quotation marks are used only with a direct quotation:

> Mrs. Larson said, "Third quarter sales exceeded expectations."
> Mrs. Larson said that third quarter sales exceeded expectations.

Using quotation marks to highlight someone's exact words works well if the quote is brief. When the quote is long, however, another display technique is more emphatic. If a direct quotation occupies less than four lines of type, place the text in quotation marks but do not indent the material:

NOTE SC.43
The length of a quote influences its display.

> In his inaugural address, Governor Snellgrover told the citizens of the state, "Education, jobs, and the environment are high-priority items." (short direct quotation)

If the quoted material occupies four or more lines of type, display it as a separate, single-spaced paragraph and indent the material from both the left and right margins. This indented format, together with information about the source of the material, makes quotation marks unnecessary:

> In his inaugural address, Governor Snellgrover told the citizens of the state
>> During my campaign I promised to work to maintain the quality of life that has made this state such a fine place in which to live. Education, jobs, and the environment are high-priority items. We must not lose what we have worked so hard to achieve; we must strive to make further gains.

EMPHASIS

Whenever you wish to emphasize a word or phrase, even if it is not part of a direct quote, consider displaying it in quotation marks. Humorous items, definitions, slang words or phrases, and technical terms used in nontechnical ways are good candidates for this type of emphasis. If words are emphasized with quotation marks too frequently, however, the benefits of this display are lost:

NOTE SC.44
Words in quotation marks receive emphasis.

> Although she wears a size 5 shoe, Robin is known to her friends as "Big Foot."
> Etc. is the abbreviation for the Latin phrase meaning "and so forth."

LITERARY AND ARTISTIC WORKS

Use quotation marks to set off the title of any section of a published work:

> Watch for John's article, "What is the Power Point?" in the December issue of *Best Practices*. (article in a magazine)
> "Houseplants" is the second chapter of Beth Bretaglia's book, *The Green Thumb Gardener*.

"Memory," a well-known song from the Broadway musical *Cats*, is one of the selections contained in *The Andrew Lloyd Webber Collection*. (song, musical, album)

WITH OTHER PUNCTUATION MARKS

Because quotation marks may be used to begin, end, or set off material within a statement or question, some guidelines must be set regarding the use of other punctuation when quotation marks are present. Figure SC.5 will be a helpful reference.

FIGURE SC.5
Quotation Marks with Other Punctuation Marks

Punctuation mark	Placement
period	inside quotation marks
comma	inside quotation marks
colon	outside quotation marks
semicolon	outside quotation marks
question mark	inside when quotation is a question; outside when the entire item is a question
exclamation point	inside when quotation is an exclamation; outside when the entire item is an exclamation

Three additional rules concerning the use of punctuation and quotation marks should be remembered in writing business letters, memos, and reports:

[1] Punctuation may be included in a quotation. If the quote is taken from a printed source, the punctuation should be included where the original author inserted it—even if it is incorrect.

[2] Ending punctuation may be placed before or after the quotation marks but never in both places. When a conflict exists, use the stronger mark of punctuation. Exclamation marks are stronger than both question marks and periods.

[3] Direct quotes that occur in the middle or near the end of other statements or questions are introduced by either a colon or a comma.

The following items illustrate how the placement guidelines and rules may be applied:

Did the performance appraisal contain this statement: "Sandra has become the department's expert in database management"? (The entire item is a question.)

Seth was so moved by the opera that he was the first to rise and shout, "Bravo!" (Only the quote is an exclamation.)

This badly damaged package was marked "Fragile"! (The entire sentence is an exclamation.)

The Underscore

The **underscore** is used to give special emphasis, especially when an italic font is not available.

The underscore is used to emphasize the titles of complete literary and artistic works. Literary works include books, magazines, and newspapers; artistic works include movies, plays, paintings, and sculptures. Displaying the titles of complete works in uppercase letters is also acceptable. As noted earlier in this chapter, titles of sections of these works are displayed in quotation marks:

NOTE SC.45
Underscores show special emphasis.

NOTE SC.46
Underscores may be used as a substitute for italics.

For faster service, call <u>1-800-555-CASH</u>. (emphasis)

The critics raved about <u>The Mist</u>, a French film recently released in the United States. (movie)

"Art in the Workplace" is the lead article in this month's issue of <u>Pizazz!</u> (magazine)

<u>Frenzy</u> is one of the sculptures on display at The Manx Museum. (sculpture)

Other Uses for Punctuation

Punctuation marks may be used in a number of other ways, among them as delimiters or dividers within mathematical formulas, telephone and fax numbers, e-mail addresses, and Internet URLs:

NOTE SC.47
Punctuation may be used as a delimiter or divider.

(707) 555-1234	707/555-2468	1.800.555.9876
$x = 3/(2y . 4)+5$	jp@tophat.org	http://www.vqun.com

Application Exercises

1. Carefully read each of the following items. Insert the terminal mark of punctuation that would be best in each situation. Choose periods, question marks, or exclamation marks.
   a. Theo asked whether he could leave 30 minutes early on Friday
   b. You're our *best* sales representative
   c. Have you created a Web page for your business
   d. The fire alarm is sounding
   e. When will R. J. be released from the hospital
   f. Will someone please replace the bulb in the projector in Room 20
   g. Elevator 2 will be out of service for three days
   h. Do you offer a discount to children and senior citizens
   i. Our medical plan does not cover cosmetic surgery
   j. Be sure to get a receipt

2. Locate the dates and geographic locations in the following sentences. Determine whether commas are needed, insert them where necessary, and give the reason for their use.
   a. Barbara lives and works in Calgary Alberta but often travels to Winnipeg Manitoba to consult with personnel at the corporate headquarters.
   b. Hotel reservations have been made for Sunday May 26 through Saturday June 1.
   c. Travel must be completed between February 15 and March 10.
   d. The bankruptcy petition was filed Thursday May 15 2002.
   e. The restaurant will be closed for remodeling from June 28 through July 9.
   f. In June 2006 Richard will retire and move to the home he and Phoebe are building in Lakeland Florida.
   g. The contract must be signed and returned by August 17.
   h. The cruise ship will depart from Miami Florida on January 12.
   i. In September 1998 Naples Florida formalized its Sister City agreement with Piemonte Italy.
   j. Seth's birthday is next Tuesday.

3. Read each of the following sentences and insert commas where necessary between independent adjectives. Some items may be correct.
   a. The Lunar New Year is the longest most important Chinese festival.
   b. The roller coaster ride was an unforgettable heart-stopping experience.
   c. Wooden furniture treated with dark mahogany stain helps create a warm welcoming atmosphere.
   d. The brightly lit room looked warm and inviting.
   e. Chuck's vintage motorcycle drew the attention and admiration of parade watchers.
   f. Please join us for a fascinating informative tour of the vineyard.
   g. The consultant provided us with a very clear picture of what needs to be done.
   h. The soft soothing music playing in the waiting room calmed the patients.
   i. The warm glowing embers of the fire lingered long after the campers were asleep.
   j. The laundry was unable to remove the stain from Sarah's dark blue wool suit.

4. Insert commas where needed in the following sentences, which may or may not contain independent or introductory clauses:
   a. When you are in New Orleans this summer be sure to visit the French Quarter.
   b. Take the package to the mail room when you go to lunch.
   c. The zoo director has requested both a photocopier and a fax machine but I think we should buy one unit that performs both functions.
   d. After you finish entering the data proofread the form carefully.
   e. The efficiency apartment is more affordable but I prefer the view and space in the studio unit.
   f. As we discussed yesterday your account will be credited for $57.
   g. When the technician arrives send him to Eric's office.
   h. Please verify the time and date of the next training session.
   i. Although Marge won the car her husband says he will be the one to drive it.
   j. Archie read the book last week and he plans to see the movie on Saturday.

5. Locate the nonessential elements in each of the following sentences and insert punctuation where needed. Indicate whether the nonessential element is an appositive, a direct address, an introductory word, an introductory phrase, a nonrestrictive clause, a parenthetical expression, or a transitional expression.
   a. I too have decided to retire.
   b. The new hotel which is located at Baron Avenue and East First Street has 950 guest rooms.
   c. Mr. Winston I look forward to meeting with you and your staff on the 19th.
   d. In the interest of customer safety we are recalling the Model 12.
   e. Interstate 94 which passes through Chicago is the best way to reach your destination.
   f. You will of course be fully vested in the retirement program.
   g. Yes two pedestrians witnessed the accident.
   h. The keynote speaker is Jackson Rutlege owner of Mocha Madness.
   i. Fortunately the negatives were not destroyed in the fire.
   j. Alexander forgot the map therefore he phoned to ask for directions.

6. Insert commas where necessary to separate series items in the following sentences:
   a. Corporations must begin to address social issues such as diversity work-family balance equal rights and the environment.
   b. People attending the concert may park in lot A D or F.
   c. Your business card should include your phone number your fax number and your e-mail address.
   d. The store in the lobby sells newspapers from Los Angeles Chicago Dallas and Miami.
   e. The lease specifies that we must shampoo the carpets wash the windows and clean the oven before we vacate the apartment.

f. Be sure to order more mugs hats and key chains.

g. Pam James and Ebony will have lunch with the candidate.

h. Rooms 316 317 and 318 will be remodeled next month.

i. The cafeteria is open for breakfast lunch and dinner.

j. The weather is especially nice during May June and July.

7. Insert commas and semicolons where necessary in each of the following sentences. Explain the reason for each punctuation mark.

   a. The principles on which the firm was based have not changed but the way in which those principles are implemented has changed.

   b. The written report is finished now we can concentrate on the oral presentation.

   c. The package was damaged during shipment therefore you are entitled to a full refund.

   d. Mo said that he would be working late every night this week he indicated however that he will not be working this Saturday.

   e. Will the next convention be in Dallas Texas Seattle Washington or Orlando Florida?

   f. Once the logo has been redesigned we'll reprint our stationery internal forms however will not be reprinted until our current inventory is depleted.

   g. The plaques have been delivered but they have not yet been engraved.

   h. Thanks to you Sandy the project was a success we appreciate your efforts.

   i. Sharon was angry when she learned of the defect she relaxed when she learned it would be repaired without cost.

   j. Hector Roche will describe the selection criteria Helene Alto will announce the results.

8. Insert terminal punctuation marks, commas, and semicolons where appropriate; some items may be correct.

   a. All representatives who exceed the quarterly sales goal will be eligible for the drawing.

   b. Ben Graves my dentist has joined Central Lakes Dental Associates.

   c. The Bookworm Club offers a wide selection of mystery novels: thrillers chillers and whodunnits

   d. The first part of the test went fairly well I think but I will need to review my English spelling and mathematics before returning for the next section of the examination.

   e. After reading ARE YOU UNDERINSURED? in your December issue I immediately phoned my agent and asked for a policy review.

   f. Robert Brown president of Brown Brothers Albert Pyroz personnel director at Dataform Sylvia Jacobsen owner of a consulting firm and Amanda Newel records manager at BZP Corporation were all members of the panel discussing mid-life career changes.

   g. You must use a pencil to record your responses otherwise the scanner will not be able to read them.

   h. If you want to explore the Internet without investing in a full-scale computer system consider purchasing a WebTV terminal.

   i. Congratulations Madeline

   j. The Bailey study which was conducted in California in 2002 challenges the results of earlier research.

   k. You must get the data to Olivia by noon on Friday or a decision on the waiver will be delayed until next week.

   l. Meteorologists do not control the weather they simply predict what is likely to occur.

   m. The contract calls for a bonus of 10 percent if construction is completed by June 23 2004.

   n. We will of course send a copy of the proposal to Sean.

   o. Cylene has a sincere positive attitude.

9. Decide whether the secondary internal punctuation marks have been used correctly in the following sentences. Make all changes that are necessary.
   a. Did Director Jackson ask "Why we want to replace the printer"?
   b. The visitors from abroad had difficulty understanding what Marvin meant by a "rock bottom price".
   c. Three options are available. 1 Enter into a contract with a service bureau. 2. Hire temporary workers. (3). Ask our employees to work overtime.
   d. The components were broken and had to be refused before shipping.
   e. Our business plan must contain short medium and long range financial projections.
   f. The grand opening (11/23/03] was a huge success!
   g. From 7 ... 9 p.m. Thursday, each student who brings his:her ID card to the theater will receive $1 1_2 off the posted ticket price and a coupon for a free box of popcorn.
   h. The brochure said we would get a whirl-wind tour of England and we did.
   i. Chapter 2, Sinks and Faucets, can be found on pages 126/134 of "Home Improvement Hints".
   j. On which of Janet Jackson's CDs would I find "Where Are You Now?"?

Message Analysis

Make the changes needed to ensure that the following letter is punctuated correctly. If you think that two sentences are closely related, replace the period and the capital letter that follows it with a semicolon and a lowercase letter.

Dear Mrs. Zylen:

Thank you for speaking at the March meeting of the Lakeview Garden Club. Your presentation was excellent.

After the meeting several members commented on how much they enjoyed your discussion of perennial gardening and the slides you used to emphasize your points. You certainly have been successful in blending size color and seasonality into your designs. Each garden reflects the unique personality of the home's owner while accommodating the ever present natural constraints of drainage light and soil richness.

Ms. Zylen please accept the enclosed gift certificate as a token of our appreciation for sharing your insight and experience with us. You can be sure that our knowledge 'grew' as a result of your presentation.

Style

The word *style* is used in several ways in business writing. A person's ability to organize and express ideas is called style. The format of a letter, memo, or report may be referred to as style. Reference manuals are sometimes called style manuals. In this seminar, **style** is used to mean the basic rules for number display, capitalization, and abbreviation that apply to business writing.

Writers should be as concerned about correct usage as they are about their basic writing skills. Correct usage—usually called mechanics—and good writing skills work together to

- Minimize the number of distractions in a message
- Bring consistency to communication
- Reflect well on the writer
- Have a positive effect on the reader

Reference manuals differ in the way they approach style items. Materials in this seminar are based on *HOW 10, A Handbook for Office Workers,* by Clark & Clark.

NOTE SD.1
Style refers to rules for correct usage.

Numbers

Numbers play a major role in our lives. They represent, describe, and locate people and objects. Because numbers are used so widely, attention must be given to expressing them correctly in business writing.

Business writers use general style when expressing numbers. **General style** is a blend of two styles known as *formal* and *technical*. In general style, numbers are represented in words when formality is needed and in figures when clarity is desired.

NOTE SD.2
General style is used for expressing numbers in business writing.

General Guidelines

Several guidelines relate to the way numbers are expressed. Some of these guidelines are used frequently in business writing, others are used rarely. This section describes those guidelines that have frequent application in business correspondence and reports.

WRITING WHOLE NUMBERS

Whole numbers greater than ten are written in figures. This guideline applies only to whole numbers—those that have no decimal or fractional parts:

NOTE SD.3
Write whole numbers greater than ten in figures.

The bill shows that Art made *three* long distance calls last month.

Because of the storm, Carol's flight was delayed *two* hours.

The manufacturer predicts that the van will get *19* mph in city driving conditions.

WRITING ROUND NUMBERS

NOTE SD.4
Using figures draws attention to large numbers.

Round numbers may be expressed in figures, in words, or as a combination of the two. To reduce the emphasis placed on a round number, use words. When emphasis is desired, use figures. Figures are often used in advertising for emphasis. Because numbers greater than a million may be difficult to read when expressed in figures, a writer may combine words and figures to achieve greater clarity:

The science museum hosted nearly *400,000* visitors since it opened.

The band spent more than *three hundred* days on the road last year.

The population of the country exceeds *15 million*.

BEGINNING A SENTENCE WITH A NUMBER

NOTE SD.5
Use words for numbers that begin sentences.

Numbers that begin a sentence are expressed in words. If the number is large, rewrite the sentence:

Five managers have requested early retirement.

Six thousand runners have registered for the marathon.

Thirteen thousand two hundred seventy-seven people attended the convention. (Awkward. See the following sentence.)

The convention attendance was *13,277*. (improved version)

WRITING NUMBERS CONSISTENTLY

NOTE SD.6
Make numbers easy to read.

Be consistent in expressing numbers, and strive for easy reading. When *related* numbers greater than and less than ten appear in the same sentence, use figures for all numbers. When *unrelated* numbers greater than and less than ten appear in the same sentence, follow the general guideline for writing whole numbers. Items in a series are always considered related:

Children *6* and under are admitted free; adults *65* and older receive a $2 discount. (related numbers)

Today's shipment included 20 pair of sneakers, 15 pair of sandals, and 5 purses. (related numbers)

The tour group consisted of *15 people* each of whom had at least *two suitcases*. (unrelated numbers)

If two numbers are adjacent to one another, as in a series, punctuation and spacing enhance readability. When one of two adjacent numbers is part of a compound modifier, the first number is written in words. If the first number cannot be written in one or two words, display it as a figure also:

The performance schedule includes *two 15-minute* intermissions. (adjacent numbers; compound modifier)

The developer plans to build *175 3-bedroom* condominiums north of Ridgeway. (large number as part of adjacent number; compound modifier)

When two unrelated numbers are adjacent to one another in a sentence, place a comma between them to make them easy to read:

By *1998, 15* of the franchises had been remodeled. (easy to read)

PUNCTUATING NUMBERS

In numbers with four or more digits, a comma is usually used. The comma is omitted in identification, model, serial, house, page, and telephone/fax numbers. It is also omitted in ZIP codes, years, decimal fractions, and metric measurements:

NOTE SD.7
Use commas in numbers with four or more digits.

1,113	1,250,671	ID No. 9336
217 Baker Court	Serial No. 8512-C	page 77
Cleveland, OH 44122-1856	2004	(715) 555-3821
.16824	3000 meters	Model 3700

Specific Guidelines

The general guidelines just presented will help you through many writing situations involving numbers. There are some specific guidelines, too, that should be mastered. As you read the material, you will encounter the term *ordinal*. **Ordinal** words or numbers show position in a series. *First, second, third, tenth*, and *seventy-fifth* are examples of ordinal words; *1st, 2nd, 3rd, 10th*, and *75th* are examples of ordinal numbers.

NOTE SD.8
Ordinals show position in a series.

ADDRESSES

House or building numbers except *one* are written in figures when used within the text of a message. As part of the mailing address in a letter or on an envelope, *all* house and building numbers are displayed in figures; *one* is not an exception. Numbered streets are written as word ordinals if ten or below and as figure ordinals in all other cases:

NOTE SD.9
Use figures for house and building numbers in mailing addresses.

NOTE SD.10
Use words for street names ten and under; otherwise, use figures.

One Ordean Road (in text)

1 Ordean Road (in a mailing address)

906 West Third Avenue

1212 65th Avenue West

10 North 32nd Avenue

DATES

Figures are used for the day and the year. If the day is used without a month or if the day precedes the month, ordinal numbers or words may be used:

NOTE SD.11
Use figures for the day and the year.

April 1904   May 28   January 1, 2007

the 1st and 15th (ordinal without a month)

the 2nd of October (ordinal number)

the eleventh of November (ordinal word)

Some writers use the international (military) date form, but it has not received widespread acceptance in American business correspondence. The international date form should be used in correspondence sent to receivers outside the United States. Select the form used in the country to which you are writing. Here are two common international date forms:

13 October 2004   2004.10.13 (year/month/day)

FRACTIONS

NOTE SD.12
Use words when a fraction stands alone; use figures when a fraction is part of a mixed number.

When a fraction appears alone, it is written in words. Use a hyphen between the numerator (top number) and denominator (bottom number) of a fraction written in words when the fraction is used as a compound adjective. When a fraction is part of a mixed number, express it in figures:

one fourth of the proceeds   a one-third share (adjective)

one thirty-second   7 3/5

Notice the space in the mixed number between the fraction and the whole number. Unless a typewriter or keyboard has a special key for fractions, this space is necessary for readability. Without the space the figure could be misread as 73/5 (seventy-three fifths).

MONEY

NOTE SD.13
Indefinite money amounts are written in words.

Money amounts are expressed in figures. If the money amount is a whole number, the decimal and zeros are omitted—even when whole and mixed dollar amounts occur in the same series. A comma is used in most money amounts of four digits or more. An indefinite amount of money should be written in words:

$7,093.32 $343 $6,000   several million dollars

The missing checks were for payments of $127.63, $250, and $325.50.

For amounts of money less than a dollar, use figures and spell the word *cents:*

1 cent   39 cents

On orders, invoices, and other business forms, the symbol ¢ may be used. If definite amounts of money greater and less than one dollar occur in the same sentence, use the $ symbol and a decimal where necessary:

The three lowest bids were $1.19, $1.03, and $.96 per unit.

ORDINALS

NOTE SD.14
Use only one- or two-word ordinals; in other cases, rewrite.

If an ordinal can be expressed in one or two words, spell it in full. If the ordinal exceeds one or two words, rewrite the sentence to avoid the need for an ordinal. This restriction applies only to ordinals that appear within the body of a sentence. Refer to the sections on addresses and dates under the Specific Guidelines heading in this seminar for the proper use of ordinals in those items:

The cast was exhausted after giving its *fifth* performance in three days.

The president gave a gold watch to Fred Benson, who was celebrating his *thirtieth* anniversary with the company.

Dilton's *one-hundred seventeenth* Customer Appreciation Sale will begin Monday, August 12. (Long ordinal; hard to read when written in words.)

Dilton's has held a Customer Appreciation Sale for *117* years; this year's sale will begin Monday, August 12. (Improved version; sentence has been rewritten to avoid the need for an ordinal.)

PERCENTAGES

In nontechnical business communication, write *percent* as a word, and express the number as a figure. Use the symbol % on forms or in statistical or technical tables. Include a zero before a decimal that does not begin with a zero:

25 percent	13¼ percent	76.2 percent	.05 percent	0.8 percent (in correspondence)
25%	13¼%	76.2%	.05%	0.8% (in statistical or technical tables)

NOTE SD.15
Use the word *percent* within text.

At the beginning of a sentence, spell the number or reword the sentence:

> *Six percent* of our budget is targeted for equipment purchases.
> We have targeted *6 percent* of our budget for equipment purchases.

TIME

To designate time with a.m. (midnight to noon) or p.m. (noon to midnight) use a figure; the colon and zeros are not needed for on-the-hour times. For formality, use a word before *o'clock*; for emphasis, use a figure before *o'clock*:

> The meeting time has been changed from *11 a.m.* to *1:30 p.m.*
> The reception will begin at *eight o'clock* this evening. (formality)

NOTE SD.16
Designate time in figures or words based on content.

In all cases, be sure the time of day is clear:

> The train will arrive at *5:30.* (in the morning or in the afternoon?)
> The train will arrive at *5:30 this afternoon.* (clear)

To avoid confusion, writers usually use *midnight* rather than 12 a.m. and *noon* rather than 12 p.m. Omit *a.m.* when using *noon* and omit *p.m.* when using *midnight.* Include 12 when noon or midnight is used in conjunction with another time; the figure is optional when the terms are used alone:

> The doors will be opened at *6 a.m.* and locked at *12 midnight.*
> Lunch will be served at noon.

Capitalization

Early in your education, you were taught to capitalize the first letter of a word that begins a sentence and the first letter of a proper noun. Few, if any, writers have difficulty with these practices. This section, therefore, will present other accepted rules for capitalization.

Academic Courses

When referring to a specific course, capitalize the first letter of the main word(s). Do not capitalize general subjects other than languages:

NOTE SD.17
Capitalize specific academic courses and languages.

> The spring schedule lists three sections of *Ethics and Technology.*
> Are you taking an ethics course this term?

Dr. Harwood teaches *Finance* 200, 315, and 450.

Dr. Harwood teaches *finance* courses.

History, Spanish, and *geography* are Benson's favorite subjects this term.

Compass Directions

NOTE SD.18
Compass directions that refer to a specific region should be capitalized.

Names of specific geographical regions are capitalized. Do not capitalize general directions:

Fran was born and raised in the *Northwest* but has decided to relocate to the *South.*

The Marks brothers have acquired the DeliMeat distributorship for the *Midwest.*

The parking lot on the *east* side of the building is being repaired. (a direction)

Drive three miles *south* on Highway G, then turn *west* on Route 12. (directions)

Government

NOTE SD.19
Full names of government agencies and their subsections are capitalized.

Principal words in the names of domestic and foreign government agencies, units, and organizations are capitalized:

Food and Drug Administration
Royal Canadian Mounted Police
United States Navy

Short forms of the names of national and international government bodies and their major divisions are generally capitalized. Writers should use short forms only when they are certain their readers will understand them:

the Court (United States Supreme Court)
the House (United States House of Representatives)
the Corps (United States Corps of Engineers)

The short forms of the names of state and local government bodies are not capitalized unless used in formal communication:

Rex bought a 20-acre tract of land adjacent to the county line. (general reference)
A city ordinance prohibits burning trash outdoors.

When in doubt about the capitalization of government and judicial body names, consult a reference book such as *HOW 10,* published by South-Western ITP.

Institutions and Organizations

NOTE SD.20
Capitalize the full name of an institution or organization according to its preference.

The full names of institutions (churches, libraries, hospitals, and schools) and organizations (associations, companies, and clubs) and their divisions or departments are capitalized. Capitalize *the* only when it is part of the official title. Follow the style established by the organization or institution as shown on its letterhead stationery or in other written communication:

Memorial Hospital has released the plans for its new addition.

The McCarren Library has a good selection of audio books.

Have you accepted the invitation to join Pi Sigma Epsilon?

Selina has accepted a job offer from The Prudential Insurance Company.

Audit Committee	but	the committee
Intensive Care Unit	but	the unit
Investor Services Division	but	the division

Time

The most common reference to time in business writing is a date, but time can also be a reference to seasons, holidays, or events. The names of days, months, specific special events, holidays, religious days, and historical events are always capitalized. The names of decades and centuries are generally not capitalized; season names, however, are capitalized when combined with a year:

Tuesday, August 3	Independence Day
Kwanzaa	Sidewalk Sale
twenty-first century	the mid-nineties
Winter Carnival	Fall 2003

NOTE SD.21
Dates are only one way to express time.

NOTE SD.22
Capitalize most references to time.

Titles

Titles are divided into two categories—occupational and official. Both titles are capitalized when used in a signature line or a mailing address. An occupational title is capitalized only when it is a specific job title. In correspondence text, however, the two are treated differently. An official title is capitalized when it comes before a personal name, unless the personal name has been added to clarify or describe (nonessential element set off by commas). An official title is generally not capitalized when it follows a personal name or replaces a personal name. The titles of state, national, and international officials are an exception; these titles are capitalized when they come before, come after, or are used in place of personal names:

NOTE SD.23
Capitalization of personal titles depends on how they are used.

The maintenance manager, P. J. Perkins, described the changes in the safety code. (name clarifies)

Acting Dean Jean Sanders will present the certificates. (specific job title)

Josefina Ortiz, city manager, reported on economic development activities. (title following name)

After vacationing in Florida, Ambassador Portor returned to France. (national title before a personal name)

The Emir hosted the dinner. (international title used in place of name)

Abbreviations

Abbreviations save space and time in business writing. Their use should be limited, however, to those that the reader will recognize and understand. If an abbreviation is to be used several times within a letter or report, the complete form—followed by the abbreviation in parentheses—should be used at the first instance. The reader will then understand the abbreviation when it occurs again:

NOTE SD.24
Use only those abbreviations your reader will understand.

The Student Conduct Committee (SCC) has filed its report. After the vice president has reviewed the SCC report, she will submit it to the Board of Governors.

Generally, an abbreviation follows the full-text format with respect to whether it is displayed in uppercase or lowercase letters—abbreviations for proper nouns use uppercase letters; abbreviations for common nouns use lowercase letters. Guidelines about whether to use or omit periods within the abbreviation are less clear. To be sure, consult a reference manual.

Acronyms and Initialisms

NOTE SD.25
Acronyms are pronounced as words; initialisms are not.

Acronyms and initialisms are special forms of abbreviations. **Acronyms** are words formed by using the first letter of each major word of a compound item. When abbreviations are formed from the first letter of major words in a compound item but the outcome is not pronounced as a word, the abbreviation is called an **initialism**. Business firms, government agencies, and professional groups are often known by their initialisms. Examples of both follow:

American Medical Association	becomes	AMA
Beginners All-purpose Symbolic Instruction Code	becomes	BASIC
Central Intelligence Agency	becomes	CIA
Consolidated Omnibus Budget Reconciliation Act	becomes	COBRA
Cost-of-living adjustment	becomes	COLA
Initial public offering	becomes	IPO
Personal Digital Assistant	becomes	PDA

Business and Association Names

NOTE SD.26
Spell generic business names when used alone in a sentence.

Abbreviated words are often part of the name of a business firm. *Assn.* for Association, *Co.* for Company, *Corp.* for Corporation, *Ltd.* for Limited, and *Inc.* for Incorporated are just a few examples. Abbreviate these items only when they are abbreviated in the business name; spell them in full when used independently within a sentence:

Adventure Travel Corporation
Financial analysts report that the *company* is sound.

Courtesy and Personal Titles

NOTE SD.27
Courtesy titles should be abbreviated when they occur before a name.

Courtesy title abbreviations such as *Mr.*, *Mrs.*, *Ms.*, and *Dr.* are used before a personal name:

Mr. Juan Estrada	*Ms.* Rose Pardue
Mrs. Celia Wood	*Dr.* Edward Robier

NOTE SD.28
The individual's preference should be respected when using titles.

Unless a woman's specific title is known, use *Ms.* A woman should tell her correspondents the title she prefers. When the person's preference is known, that title should be used. If a writer's first name may be used by members of either gender (Pat, Terry, Lee), the writer should include a personal title in the signature line. This procedure should also be followed if a writer uses only initials (A. K. Jones; B. W. O'Brien). This technique, as well as other options, is illustrated in Appendix A.

The personal titles *Junior* and *Senior* are abbreviated when they follow a name:

Kenneth Langford, *Jr.*   Hector Todd, *Sr.*

Measurements

Measurements may be abbreviated when they occur frequently in tables or business forms. When used, they are displayed in lowercase letters, with periods if they represent one word and without periods if they represent more than one word. In most business writing, measurements are spelled in full rather than abbreviated. Metric units of measurement are always written without periods. Common measurements and their abbreviations are shown in Figure SD.1.

NOTE SD.29
Spell measurements in general correspondence.

Measure	Abbreviation	Measure	Abbreviation
centimeter	cm	miles per hour	mph
foot	ft.	pound	lb.
gallon	gal.	pages per minute	ppm
kilogram	kg	words per minute	wpm

FIGURE SD.1
Measurement Abbreviations

Months/Days

Each of the months of the year and days of the week has a standard abbreviation:

Jan.	Apr.	July	Oct.
Feb.	May	Aug.	Nov.
Mar.	June	Sept./Sep.	Dec.

Sun.	Mon.	Tues. (Tue.)	Wed.	Thurs. (Thu.)	Fri.	Sat.
Su	M	Tu	W	Th	F	Sa

NOTE SD.30
Use abbreviations sparingly for months and days.

These abbreviations should be used only to save space on business forms; they should not be used in business reports or correspondence.

Personal Names

Abbreviations for personal names may take the form of an initial or a shortened form of the name:

C. Luisa Diaz   H. H. Kramer
Wm. Baxter   Jamie P. Adams-Roy

NOTE SD.31
Names may be abbreviated by using initials or a shortened form of the name.

An abbreviation is different from a nickname. An abbreviation is always shorter than its given name; it always ends with a period. Nicknames may be modifications of a given name (Katy for Katherine) or may be totally unrelated to the given name (George Herman "Babe" Ruth). Personal names should not be abbreviated unless space is limited, as in tabulations or enumerations. In business writing, restrict the use of nicknames to those that are modifications of given names (e.g., Don for Donald). Before abbreviating a person's name, be sure that the individual will not object to the use of the abbreviated form.

NOTE SD.32
Nicknames differ from abbreviations.

Professional Titles, Designations, and Degrees

NOTE SD.33
Abbreviate designations and academic degrees.

Many people choose to use their professional titles, designations, or degrees when conducting business. Whenever possible, write professional titles in full. Abbreviate designations and academic degrees:

Professor Bernard Lomax	Reverend Elizabeth Torvick
Tamara J. Webster, C.P.A.	J. J. Alvarez, R.N.
L. N. Lee, D.V.M.	Jessica Dunn, C.F.A.

NOTE SD.34
Use either a title or an academic degree abbreviation, not both.

When referring to a person who has the academic or medical credentials to be addressed as doctor, use either the title or the degree abbreviation, but not both. If the title is used, place the abbreviation *Dr.* before the name. If the abbreviation for the degree is used, place it after the name, and use a comma to separate the name from the abbreviation:

Dr. Jane Alexander   Jane Alexander, D.D.S.

States/Territories/Provinces

NOTE SD.35
Abbreviate names of states, territories, and provinces when they are part of a complete address.

The official two-letter postal abbreviations for state, territory, and province names should be used when part of a complete address. In all other cases, the name of the state, territory, or province should be spelled in full. A complete list of the two-letter postal abbreviations used in the United States and Canada is on page 600. Be sure to secure the postal address requirements of other countries to which you write.

Symbols

NOTE SD.36
Symbols are a form of abbreviation.

NOTE SD.37
Use only those symbols that your receiver will interpret correctly.

Symbols are a form of abbreviation. Figure SD.2 includes several standard symbols. A brief definition and an example of each are also provided. Symbols should be used sparingly in business writing. Include only those symbols that your readers will interpret correctly.

FIGURE SD.2
Frequently Used Symbols

Symbol	Definition	Example
&	ampersand (meaning *and*)	Dr. & Mrs. Wolff
*	asterisk (refers reader to a note)	Price*
		*subject to change without notice
@	at, each, per	17 @ $2.25 each
©	copyright	© South-Western College Publishing
®	registered trademark	Compaq®
°	degree	89°
/	diagonal, slash	and/or, s/he, http://, 5/11/02
¢	cents	79¢
$	dollars	$589.99
'	feet (apostrophe)	2'
"	inch (quotation mark)	10.2"
:	ratio (colon)	3:1
#	number (before figure)	#10
#	pounds (after figure)	100#
%	percent	75%
x	by or times (lowercase *x*)	2 x 4, 5 x 7
K	thousand	640K, $20K
<, >	less than, greater than	< 20, > 75

Time Zones

The world is divided into time zones. In Canada and the United States, each zone has its own abbreviation. In addition, one character in that abbreviation is changed to indicate whether those residing in the region are observing standard or daylight saving time:

EST	Eastern Standard Time	EDT	Eastern Daylight Time
CST	Central Standard Time	CDT	Central Daylight Time
MST	Mountain Standard Time	MDT	Mountain Daylight Time
PST	Pacific Standard Time	PDT	Pacific Daylight Time

Telephone directories typically include a map of North America and show the areas covered by each zone. When writers ask receivers to phone them, they often include the time zone in the message. Typically, the time zone is displayed in parentheses following the hours during which telephone calls are received—for example, 9 a.m. to 4 p.m. (EST).

NOTE SD.38
Time zones for both standard and daylight savings time are abbreviated.

Other Abbreviations

So many abbreviations are used in business that it is impractical to include all of them in this seminar. A brief list of some of the most commonly used terms is included in Figure SD.3.

NOTE SD.39
Consult references before abbreviating unfamiliar terms.

Term	Abbreviation	Term	Abbreviation
account	acct.	manager	mgr.
additional	addnl., add'l	merchandise	mdse.
also known as	a.k.a.	money order	MO
amount	amt.	month, months	mo., mos.
as soon as possible	ASAP	national	natl.
attached	att.	net weight	nt. wt.
average	avg.	not applicable	NA
balance	bal.	not available	NA
care of	c/o	optional	opt.
charge	chg.	organization	org.
collect on delivery	COD	original	orig.
continued	cont.	out of stock	OS or o.s.
courtesy copy	cc	over-the-counter	OTC
credit	cr.	package	pkg.
depreciation	depr.	page, pages	p., pp.
destination	dstn.	paid	pd.
discount	disc., dis.	parcel post	PP
division	div.	part, point	pt.
extension	ext., Ext.	port of entry	POE or p.o.e.
fiscal year	FY	prepaid	ppd.
for example	e.g.	purchase order	P.O., PO
forward	fwd.	quantity	qty.
freight	frt.	quarter, quarterly	qtr.
gross weight	gr. wt.	received	recd.
headquarters	HQ, hdqtrs.	requisition	req.
hour	hr.	respond, if you please	R.S.V.P., RSVP
institute	inst.	self-addressed, stamped envelope	SASE
international	intl., intnl.	standard	std.
inventory	invt.	statement	stmt.
invoice	inv.	wholesale	whsle.

FIGURE SD.3
Other Commonly Used Abbreviations

Notice that some of the abbreviations use capital letters; others use lowercase letters. Some of the abbreviations use periods, others do not. Because abbreviations are often associated with particular fields (e.g., education, law, medicine, transportation), you may encounter abbreviations with which you are unfamiliar. When this situation arises, consult a dictionary or reference manual.

Application Exercises

1. Circle the appropriate expression(s) for each number in the following items:
   a. Nearly (500/five hundred/5 hundred) students have preregistered for the (8-/eight-) week summer session.
   b. (3/Three) of the (15/fifteen) (2-/two-) drawer lateral file cabinets were dented during the move.
   c. Mail my reimbursement check to (523/Five Twenty-three/Five Hundred Twenty-three) (Second/2nd/2) Street South.
   d. The serial number on the Model (1222/1,222/twelve 22/twelve twenty-two) laser printer is (736,921-G/736921-G).
   e. PQG declared a (38-cent/thirty-eight cent/$.38) dividend.
   f. Officials estimate that more than (2,000,000/2 million/two million) people will attend the (three-/3-) day event.
   g. Please change my address from (763 - Fifth Avenue/763 - 5th Avenue/763 5th Avenue/763 Fifth Avenue) to (376 - Fifth Avenue/376 - 5th Avenue/376 5th Avenue/376 Fifth Avenue).
   h. The stock rose (1 1/4 / 11/4 / 1 and one-fourth) points in (two/2) days.
   i. By subscribing now, you'll get (15/fifteen) issues for the price of (10/ten), a savings of (50%/50 percent/fifty percent).
   j. We are a ($5 billion/five billion dollar/5 billion dollar) company that employs a total of (4,000/4 thousand/four thousand) people in (six/6) states.
2. Correct the number errors in the following sentences.
   a. Recall all Model 1,100 wrenches.
   b. Install 21 4-light fixtures in each bathroom.
   c. Deliver the package to Mark Muntz at 113 South 4th Street.
   d. The move must be completed by the 20 of May.
   e. 17 minutes later, the power was restored.
   f. Over three-fourths of the participants rated the seminar as above-average.
   g. Sam was successful in negotiating a $.03 cent discount.
   h. Order three lateral files three vertical files, and 10 dozen folders.
   i. On Wednesday, April 12th, Char Pullar will be in Cleveland for a book signing.
   j. Plan to arrive at least forty-five minutes prior to the concert.
3. Each of the following sentences requires corrections in capitalization. Some words shown in lowercase should be capitalized; some shown in capital letters should be in lowercase. Correct the errors.
   a. The Internal Revenue service has pledged to improve customer service.
   b. The centers for Disease Control (cdc) reported an outbreak of german measles in the Western Suburbs of Dallas.
   c. Mr. James C. Benton, Senior Accountant with st. Croix Chemical Company, will speak at next week's accounting club banquet.
   d. according to a recent Report from the American Council on Science and Health, fluoridation of drinking water is a very effective weapon against tooth decay.

    e. Students majoring in Spanish are encouraged to spend a Semester studying at a University in Valencia.

    f. The vice president will represent the President at the Nato meeting.

    g. the director's comments were well received; her Staff applauded.

    h. Each Summer, the residents of smithville gather at City park for a founder's day Picnic.

    i. After the election, mayor Bennett removed the door on his Office to show the citizens of parker that she had an "open door" policy.

    j. Stella, whose Bachelor's Degree is in Engineering, has applied for admission to the mba program at Central College.

4. Several company, organization, agency, and program names are listed here. By what abbreviation is each name most commonly known?

    a. America Online

    b. General Motors

    c. Occupational Safety and Health Administration

    d. Organization of Petroleum Exporting Countries

    e. United Auto Workers

5. Each of the following items contains at least one abbreviation. Decide whether each has been used correctly. If the abbreviation is incorrect, change it.

    a. Our 30-month cd has an A.P.Y. of 5.25 pct.

    b. Mr. @ Mrs. Harvey Wilcox, Jun., spent Sun. afternoon planning their Aug. trip to London.

    c. Hartford, Conn.; Pittsburgh, P.A., and Orono, ME are possible sites for our new branch office.

    d. Bagley # Sons, the co. for which Emi works, offers its employees a 10 percent disc. on the glassware it makes.

    e. Mstr. Alvin Atwater, c.f.o. at DataSource, Incorp., is vice president of the Albuquerque, New Mex. chapter.

Message Analysis

Edit the following message to reflect correct use of numbers, capitalization, abbreviations, and symbols:

> *7.March.03*
>
> *MS. Wan-ying Chu*
> *One West Maple Court*
> *Atlanta, GA 30321-4822*
>
> *Dear Miss Chu:*
>
> *TY for you're recent ltr re. your app. for employment as a Jr. Accts. Specialist with Bellows @ Magee, inc.*
>
> *your app. is one of over 100 we rec'd in response to our 2/3 ad in The gazette. Because the no. of applications we received is > we expected, the screening process has been delayed. The selection Committee is scheduled to meet on Tues., 3/12; once they have narrowed the # of candidates, we will contact references and arrange for interviews with the finalists.*
>
> *We appreciate your cont. int. in Bellows * Magee, inc.*
>
> *Yours truly,*
> *(Mrs.) Terry Mercado*
> *Personnel Administrator*

E

Word Usage

The words listed in this seminar are among those that can pose problems for writers. Some words are included because they are misused; some are included because they are often confused with other words. The words are listed alphabetically according to the first word in each set:

A LOT	(article/noun combination) many, much
ALLOT	(verb) to assign, give, or allocate
ALOT	misspelling of a lot
ADAPT	(verb) to adjust or modify
ADEPT	(adjective) skilled
ADOPT	(verb) to take and follow as one's own
ADVICE	(noun) suggestion, opinion, or recommendation
ADVISE	(verb) to counsel or recommend
AFFECT	(verb) to influence;
EFFECT	(verb) to bring about or cause to happen; to create (noun) result, outcome, or consequence
AGGRAVATE	(verb) to make something worse
IRRITATE	(verb) to create an annoying condition
ALL READY	(adjective) a state of complete readiness; prepared
ALREADY	(adverb) by or before the present time
ALL RIGHT	(adjective) satisfactory or acceptable
ALRIGHT	an informal spelling of all right; considered inappropriate for business writing
ALL TOGETHER	(adverb/adverb combination) wholly as a group; a summation
ALTOGETHER	(adverb) entirely or wholly
AMONG	(preposition) referring to three or more people or things
BETWEEN	(noun) used with plural nouns that can be counted; *and* is the conjunction to use with between
AMOUNT	(noun) used with "mass" nouns—things that can be measured but not counted
NUMBER	(noun) used with plural nouns and items that can be counted

ANXIOUS	(adjective) to show great concern, to be worried or apprehensive
EAGER	(adjective) to show enthusiasm or similar positive feeling
ANY ONE	(adjective/noun combination) *one* of a group of persons or things; always followed by *of*
ANYONE	(pronoun) any person
ANY WAY	(adjective/noun combination) no preference for method
ANYWAY	(adverb) in any case
ARBITRATE	(verb) to decide between two disagreeing people or groups
MEDIATE	(verb) to work to gain agreement between two disagreeing people or groups
AS	(conjunction) used to introduce a clause
LIKE	(preposition) similar to
ASSUME	(verb) to take for granted as true or to take on (as with an additional responsibility)
PRESUME	(verb) to anticipate with confidence
ASSURE	(verb) to promise or declare positively
ENSURE	(verb) to make something certain
INSURE	(verb) to protect against financial loss
BAD	(adjective) used with "sense" verbs—feel, hear, see, smell, taste, touch, etc)
BADLY	(adverb) used with action verbs
BIANNUAL	(adjective) twice a year
BIENNIAL	(adjective) every two years
BIMONTHLY	(adjective) every two months
SEMIMONTHLY	(adjective) twice a month
BRIEF	(adjective) referring to time
SHORT	(adjective) referring to time or to measurement
BRING	(verb) denotes movement toward the place occupied by the speaker/writer
TAKE	(verb) denotes movement away from the person or place
GET	(verb) refers to gaining possession
CAN	(verb) have the ability to do something
MAY	(verb) expresses permission to do something
CAN NOT	unacceptable in business writing
CANNOT	unable to do otherwise
CAPITAL	(noun) asset, uppercase letter; city in which government seat is located
CAPITOL	(noun) a state or national government building
CITE	(verb) to refer to or quote
SIGHT	(noun) relating to vision; refering to a spectacle or view (verb) to see, observe, or perceive
SITE	(noun) a place, an area, or a location

COMPARE	(verb) to examine similarities and differences
CONTRAST	(verb) to examine differences
COMPLEMENT	(verb) to complete or to enhance
COMPLIMENT	(verb) to praise
COMPOSED	(verb) to refer to the parts or components of something
COMPRISED	(verb) to refer to things included within something
CONSUL	(noun) a government official who resides in a foreign country for the purpose of representing the citizens of his or her home country
COUNCIL	(noun) an advisory group
COUNSEL	(verb) to give advice
	(noun) advice
CONTINUAL	(adjective) activity occurring with pauses or breaks
CONTINUOUS	(adjective) uninterrupted activity
CONVINCE	(verb) to bring someone to your point of view
PERSUADE	(verb) to induce someone to do something
DECENT	(adjective) in good taste
DESCENT	(noun) movement downward; ancestry
DISSENT	(noun) disagreement
DISBURSE	(verb) to pay
DISPERSE	(verb) to break up or spread
ELICIT	(verb) to bring out
ILLICIT	(adjective) unlawful or not permitted
EMINENT	(adjective) someone or something that stands out about others in quality or in position
IMMINENT	(adjective) likely to occur soon
FARTHER	(adjective) a greater distance
FURTHER	(verb) to more forward
	(adjective) additional or advanced
FEWER	(adjective) used with plural nouns and things that can be counted
LESS	(adjective) used most often to modify plural nouns involving time, distance, weight, and money
FLAIR	(noun) a natural talent or aptitude
FLARE	(verb) to blaze up or spread out
	(noun) a signal light
IF	(conjunction) used to establish or describe a condition
WHETHER	(conjunction) used with implicit or explicit alternatives
INVALUABLE	(adjective) priceless
VALUABLE	(adjective) has a desirable monetary value
IT'S	(contraction) it is
ITS	(pronoun) possessive form of it

LAST	(adjective) final, something at the end
LATEST	(adjective) something recent, the most current of a series
LAY	(verb) to put or to place
LIE	(verb) to recline or to rest
LED	(verb) past tense *lead*, meaning to provide direction
LEAD	(noun) a type of metal used when making pipes
LOOSE	(adjective) used to describe fit; it is the opposite of tight
LOSE	(verb) to misplace; it is the opposite of find
ME	(personal pronoun) objective case of the personal pronoun *I*
MYSELF	(reflexive pronoun) used in business writing only when you have been identified earlier in the sentence
MEDIA	(plural noun) several mass communication methods
MEDIUM	(singular noun) an individual mass communication method
PASSED	(verb) past tense or past participle of *pass*, meaning to go by or to circulate
PAST	(noun or adjective) time gone by or ended
PERPETRATE	(verb) to bring about or commit an act, such as a crime or injustice
PERPETUATE	(verb) to continue something indefinitely
PERSONAL	(adjective) private or individual
PERSONNEL	(noun) a group of workers or employees
PRECEDE	(verb) to go or to come before
PROCEED	(verb) to go forward with or to continue some action
PRINCIPAL	(noun) a leader; something or someone *chief* or *primary*
PRINCIPLE	(noun) a rule or a basic truth
SET	(verb) to place or to put
SIT	(verb) to take a seat or to remain in place
SHOULD	(helping verb) used only with first-person references; appropriate in formal writing
WOULD	(helping verb) preferred in business writing; used with all three pronoun persons
SOME TIME	(adjective/noun combination) a specific time
SOMETIME	(adverb) an indefinite time; occasionally
STATIONARY	(noun) in a fixed position
STATIONERY	(noun) writing paper
STATUE	(noun) a three-dimensional figure
STATUTE	(noun) a law or permanent rule
THAN	(conjunction) used as part of a comparison
THEN	(adverb) at that time

THAT	(pronoun) refers to persons, animals, or things; introduces restrictive clauses
WHICH	(pronoun) refers to animals or things; introduces nonrestrictive clauses
WHO	(pronoun) refers only to persons; may be used to introduce either a restrictive or a nonrestrictive clause
THOROUGH	(adjective) to the fullest level of detail
THROUGH	(proposition) to show movement into and out of, to specify methods, or to show completion
THRU	an informal variation of *through* that should not be used in business writing
TO	(preposition) movement or direction
TOO	(adverb) also or to an excessive degree
TOWARD	(preposition) in the direction of; use
TOWARDS	a secondary form of *toward*; avoid this usage in business writing
TRACK	(noun) a path
TRACT	(noun) a defined piece of land
WHO	(pronoun) used in questions to indicate what person or which persons
WHOM	(pronoun) used as an object of a verb or a preposition

Application Exercises

1. Select the appropriate word(s) in each of the following sentences:
   a. The speaker (complemented/complimented) the audience on (it's/its) ability to recognize the (principal/principle) idea of his speech.
   b. Vic has taken Gerry's (advice/advise) and offered to mediate the disagreement (among/between) Alex and Jamal.
   c. The (last/latest) issue of *Modern Textiles* is (laying/lying) on the table; the next issue will be available in two weeks.
   d. The IT staff has a (flair/flare) for (adapting/adopting) software programs that meet our needs.
   e. I (assume/presume) that the situation will be (aggravated/irritated) unless we take (farther/further) action.
   f. Maynard (continually/continuously) tries to (elicit/illicit) a positive response from the (stationary/stationery) company.
   g. (Some time/Sometime) next month, I will seek the (consul/council/counsel) of a (personal/personnel) trainer and try to (affect/effect) a change in my exercise pattern.
   h. Sarah (can/may) phone Adam and suggest he invite (fewer/less) people to this year's seminar (than/then) were invited last year.
   i. The legislature passed a (biannual/biennial) budget that includes money for (capital/capitol) expenditures.
   j. Edmond's (cite/sight/site) management team has (led/lead) the nation in productivity for the (passed/past) three years.

k. Edith said she had never seen (any one/anyone) as (anxious/eager) to (perpetrate/perpetuate) a bad habit as Milton.

l. Let me know when you are (thorough/through/thru) with Part A; we can (than/then) (precede/proceed) with Part B.

m. The (farther/further) we drove along the rutted dirt road, the more sure we were that the (track/tract) of land we bought was (bad/badly) overpriced.

n. Because the plant closing was (eminent/imminent), factory (personal/personnel) were given the opportunity to seek the (consul/council/counsel) of job training specialists.

o. Be sure to (cite/sight/site) the source of the data you use in preparing the (bi-monthly/semimonthly) report for January and February.

2. Find and correct the word-use errors in the following sentences. If a sentence has no errors, write correct.

a. The crowd was composed of a large amount of people whom had driven a brief distance to attend the concert.

b. Corrine adviced us there would be a lot of noise during the remodeling project that is to begin next Monday.

c. My schedule for Tuesday is full, but I'm sure we can find some time to meet on Wednesday or Thursday to discuss the consultant's advice.

d. Was it Jennifer who persuaded the principle to release the enrollment data to the media?

e. I asked Barry to loan me $50 so I can buy high-quality stationary to use in my job search.

f. We are anxious to see how well the furnishings in the outer office complement the decor of the conference room.

g. Phil was irritated because the crowd did not disburse after the council meeting adjourned.

h. Sally has tract down the problem—its a lose wire.

i. If we had to choose between the options, I would select A over B because of it's relationship to continuous process improvement.

j. Please bring the package to the Capital by noon so that Senator Billings may review it before this afternoon's hearing.

k. ABC has led the industry by providing top-quality products and high-quality service while earning a descent profit.

l. After you have analyzed the data, summarize your results and send a copy to Bill and myself.

m. It's like Barbara says, the latest person to arrive has to pay the tab!

n. The goal we have set for next year is to achieve greater balance between our desire for profit and our principals.

o. Although we will have less opportunities to work together, we may keep our friendship alive thorough social and recreational outlets.

Appendixes

Formats of Letters and Memos

LEARNING OBJECTIVES

① Describe the seven standard parts of a letter.

② Describe the appropriate use of supplementary parts of a letter.

③ Format business letters using the full block, modified block, and simplified block styles.

④ Address an envelope properly.

⑤ Format a memo properly.

⑥ Discuss the characteristics of appropriate stationery for letters, memos, and envelopes.

Your letters or memos should make an initial impression that will have a lasting effect on the receivers of your messages. The energy expended in writing good letters and memos is well spent when you select appropriate stationery and formats. The receiver will assume that you care and that you are knowledgeable about letter and memo writing when you use proper grammar, punctuation, spelling, stationery, and formats.

Letters

A **letter** is used to communicate a formal written message. The appearance of a letter is important because it makes the first impression on the reader; the content is important because it ensures that the reader understands and fully accepts your message. The appearance of a letter depends on the parts of a letter, punctuation style, letter format, and stationery. In this appendix, you will learn how to improve the appearance of a letter; you will be taught how to organize and write the content of a letter in Chapters 6, 7, 8, 9, and 17.

Uses of Letters

Letters are used to communicate written messages to individuals outside an organization. Letters are also used to communicate formal written messages to employees within an organization.

Standard Parts of a Letter

The number and location of letter parts depend on the format you select. As shown in Figure APA.1, most letters contain seven standard parts: heading, inside address, salutation, body, complimentary close, signature block, and reference initials.

HEADING

The first standard part of a letter is the **heading**, which consists of the letterhead and the dateline or the return address and a dateline. All business organizations should use letterhead stationery for the first page of a letter. A **letterhead** contains the name of the

1. HEADING

Jason's Professional Cleaning Service

2569 Davis Lane
Columbus, OH 43215-1246

(614) 555-2479   FAX (614) 555-5172

Commercial, Residential, Industrial Carpet Cleaning, Floor Stripping and Waxing,
Over 25 years experience

Dateline

2. INSIDE ADDRESS
XXXXXXXXXXXXXXXX
XXXXXXXXXXXXXXXX

3. SALUTATION
XXXXXXXXXXXXXXXXXXXXXXXXXXXXXXXXXXXXXXXXXXXXXXXXXXXXXXX
X   X
X   X
X   X
X   X
X   X
X   4. BODY   X
X   X
X   X
X   X
X   X
X   X
X   X
XXXXXXXXXXXXXXXXXXXXXXXXXXXXXXXXXXXXXXXXXXXXXXXXXXXXXXX

5. COMPLIMENTARY CLOSE

6. SIGNATURE BLOCK
XXXXXXXXXXXXXXXX

7. REFERENCE INITIALS

company and its complete address. It may contain a phone number; fax number; e-mail address; originating department; originator's title; founding date; organizational slogan, emblem, or logo; and other information that the organization deems appropriate. The amount of information in a letterhead will depend on the type of organization sending the letter. However, a letterhead should use no more than two vertical inches of stationery space. Although a letterhead usually is placed at the top of the page, part of the information may be at the bottom of the page. For example, the street address and telephone number or another location may be shown at the bottom of letterhead stationery. The letterhead may be printed in more than one color. Examples of letterheads are shown in Figure APA.2.

The **dateline** contains the month, day, and year that the letter is written. The month should be spelled in full. Figures are not used for the month (e.g., 6/09/05)

LEARNING OBJECTIVE

① *Describe the seven standard parts of a letter.*

because there is no universal agreement as to whether the day or month appears first. Dates may be in one of the following two styles:

June 9, 200–

9 June 200–

Notice that there is no punctuation when the day appears before the month in the dateline. Placing the month before the day is the style used by most American business organizations. Placing the day first is the preferred style for international and military use.

The horizontal placement of the dateline (or the keyed return address and dateline) depends on the letter format. The vertical placement of the dateline varies depending on the length of the letter. The dateline usually is keyed two or more lines below the printed letterhead or is keyed two inches from the top edge of the page.

When a return address is keyed at the top of a personal business letter, the dateline is keyed on the line below it. When the return address appears below the signature block of a personal business letter, the date usually is placed between lines 10 and 15.

Letterhead stationery is used only for the first page of a letter. Stationery of the same color and quality, but without the letterhead, is used for continuation pages. The heading on each additional page begins on line seven, leaving a top margin of one inch (six lines). The continuation page heading should contain the first line of the inside address, the page number, and the date. Two popular formats for continuation page headings are

Mr. Herbert Hughes   3   July 22, 200–

or

Mr. Herbert Hughes
Page 3
July 22, 200–

The body of the letter continues a double space (two lines) below this heading. At least one complete paragraph of the letter should be carried over to a continuation page. If a complete paragraph cannot be carried over, revise the letter so that it is only one page. Individual words are never divided between pages. Divide a paragraph only if you can leave at least two lines on the preceding page and carry over at least two lines to the following page. Leave at least a one-inch margin at the bottom of the first page.

INSIDE ADDRESS

The **inside address** includes the receiver's courtesy title (Ms., Miss, Mrs., Mr., Dr., etc.), name, street address (or some other specific mailing designation, such as post office box number), city, state, and ZIP code. Abbreviations should be avoided in street addresses (e.g., use *Avenue* instead of *Ave.*; use *Road* instead of *Rd.*). The two-letter U.S. postal abbreviation should be used in complete mailing addresses. United States and Canadian two-letter postal abbreviations are shown in Figure APA.3. The ZIP code is keyed one space after the postal abbreviation.

The **ZIP code** is a five-digit code that identifies areas within the United States and its possessions. In 1985 the U.S. Postal Service introduced the **ZIP + 4** system. This system uses the original ZIP code plus a hyphen and four additional numbers. This expanded code should be used when it is known because it speeds the delivery of mail. It enables the Postal Service to sort mail on high-speed automated equipment for specific streets, specific buildings, or even to specific floors within buildings. The ZIP code for an address can be obtained from a ZIP code directory provided by the U.S. Postal Service.

Other countries, such as Canada and Germany, also use mail codes. Canada's six-character codes use alternating numbers and letters (e.g., T2K5S3). In Germany the city identification code is keyed prior to the name of the city (e.g., 53105 Bonn).

The inside address is always keyed flush with the left margin and usually follows the date. The length of the letter determines the number of blank lines between the date and the inside address. Normally, the first line of the inside address is keyed three to five lines below the date.

Two-Letter Postal Abbreviations

U.S. State, District, and Territory Names

Name	Two-Letter Abbreviation	Name	Two-Letter Abbreviation
Alabama	AL	Montana	MT
Alaska	AK	Nebraska	NE
Arizona	AZ	Nevada	NV
Arkansas	AR	New Hampshire	NH
California	CA	New Jersey	NJ
Colorado	CO	New Mexico	NM
Connecticut	CT	New York	NY
Delaware	DE	North Carolina	NC
District of Columbia	DC	North Dakota	ND
Florida	FL	Ohio	OH
Georgia	GA	Oklahoma	OK
Guam	GU	Oregon	OR
Hawaii	HI	Pennsylvania	PA
Idaho	ID	Puerto Rico	PR
Illinois	IL	Rhode Island	RI
Indiana	IN	South Carolina	SC
Iowa	IA	South Dakota	SD
Kansas	KS	Tennessee	TN
Kentucky	KY	Texas	TX
Louisiana	LA	Utah	UT
Maine	ME	Vermont	VT
Maryland	MD	Virgin Islands	VI
Massachusetts	MA	Virginia	VA
Michigan	MI	Washington	WA
Minnesota	MN	West Virginia	WV
Mississippi	MS	Wisconsin	WI
Missouri	MO	Wyoming	WY

Canadian Provinces and Territories

Name	Two-Letter Abbreviation	Name	Two-Letter Abbreviation
Alberta	AB	Nova Scotia	NS
British Columbia	BC	Ontario	ON
Manitoba	MB	Prince Edward Island	PE
New Brunswick	NB	Quebec	PQ
Newfoundland	NF	Saskatchewan	SK
Northwest Territories	NT	Yukon Territory	YT

SALUTATION

The **salutation** is the greeting that begins the message. Examples of correct and incorrect salutations for letters to specific individuals include the following:

Correct	Incorrect
Dear Ms. Shelton:	Dear Rita Shelton:
Dear Rita:	Dear Ms. Rita:
Dear Jack and Tanya:	Dear McClendons:

Examples of correct and incorrect salutations in writing the same letter to many people include the following:

Correct	Incorrect
Dear Customers:	Dear Gentlemen:
Ladies and Gentlemen:	Dear Ladies and Gentlemen:

The content of the salutation depends on the first line of the inside address. When a letter is addressed to a company and contains an attention line (discussed on page 602), the salutation is directed to the company and not to the person in the attention line. The formality of the salutation depends on the relationship between the sender and the receiver of the letter. A general guide is to use the name that you would use if you met the person or persons face to face. If the first line of the inside address is singular, the salutation must be singular; if the first line is plural, the salutation must be plural.

The salutation is keyed flush with the left margin and placed a double space below the last line of the inside address or attention line, if used. A colon follows the salutation in a business letter if mixed punctuation is used; no punctuation follows the salutation if open punctuation is used. Mixed and open punctuation styles are discussed on page **605**. The salutation is omitted in the simplified block format (see page 608).

BODY

The **body** is the message section of the letter. It begins a double space below the salutation. The body is single-spaced within paragraphs and double-spaced between paragraphs. The paragraphs may be indented or blocked, depending on the letter format selected. Normally, the first and last paragraphs of a letter are shorter than the other paragraphs.

COMPLIMENTARY CLOSE

The **complimentary close** ends the message. Frequently used complimentary closes include the following:

Sincerely,   Sincerely yours,   Cordially,

The complimentary close is keyed a double space below the last line of the body of the letter. The first character of the close should begin at the same horizontal point as the first character of the date. Only the first character of the first word in the complimentary close is capitalized. The complimentary close is followed by a comma if mixed punctuation is used and by no punctuation if open punctuation is used. The simplified block letter omits the complimentary close.

SIGNATURE BLOCK

The **signature block** contains the writer's signed name, keyed name, and title. The name is keyed four spaces (lines) below the complimentary close. A courtesy title in the signature block is optional. It may be included, in parentheses, when the gender of the writer is unclear (e.g., Pat, Kim, or Lynn). The name and position title may appear on the same line or on separate lines, depending on the length of each item. If the name and position title are on the same line, a comma separates them. The sender of the message signs the letter in the space between the complimentary close and the keyed name. The signature normally does not include the courtesy title even if it is keyed in the signature block.

REFERENCE INITIALS

The initials of the message originator and the keyboard operator make up the **reference initials**. If the originator is the same person who signs the letter, his or her initials are optional. When the message originator keys the letter, no reference initials are necessary. If the originator's initials are given, they are separated from those of the keyboard operator by a colon or a diagonal. The originator's initials should be uppercase and the keyboard operator's lowercase. The reference initials are flush with the left margin on the line below the sender's title. Examples of reference initials are the following:

ev

NRE:pd

JHT/ras

LEARNING OBJECTIVE

Describe the appropriate use of supplementary parts of a letter.

②

Supplementary Parts of a Letter

In addition to the seven standard parts, letters may contain one or more supplementary parts. These parts include the attention line, subject line, company name in signature block, enclosure notation, copy notation, and postscript.

ATTENTION LINE

When a company name is used as the first line of the inside address, the **attention line** can be used to direct the letter to a person, position title, or department within the company. Using a person's name in the first line of the inside address is preferred over using an attention line.

When used, the attention line should be a double space below the last line of the inside address. It may be keyed with all capital letters or a combination of initial capital and lowercase letters. The word *Attention* should not be abbreviated. Separating the word *Attention* from the rest of the attention line with a colon is optional. The salutation agrees with the first line of the address and not the attention line. An example of an inside address with an attention line follows:

College Station Medical Center
1604 Rock Prairie Road
College Station, TX 77842-1437

Attention: Radiology

Ladies and Gentlemen:

SUBJECT LINE

The **subject line** identifies the main topic of the letter. It is considered part of the body of the letter. The subject line should be short—less than one line—and it should not be a complete sentence. The key words contained in a subject line help office personnel to sort and route incoming mail and to code documents for storage and retrieval.

The subject line is keyed a double space below the salutation. It may be centered, flush with the left margin, or indented the same number of spaces as the paragraphs. It may be keyed in all capitals or keyed with initial capitals and lowercase letters. If the word *Subject* is used, a colon follows it. If an attention line appears in the same letter, use the same format for both lines. A letter that includes a subject line is shown in Figure APA.4.

A **reference line** is sometimes used instead of a subject line (Re: Contract 1065-940). It is used to direct the reader to source documents or files. A reference line is keyed a double space below the inside address.

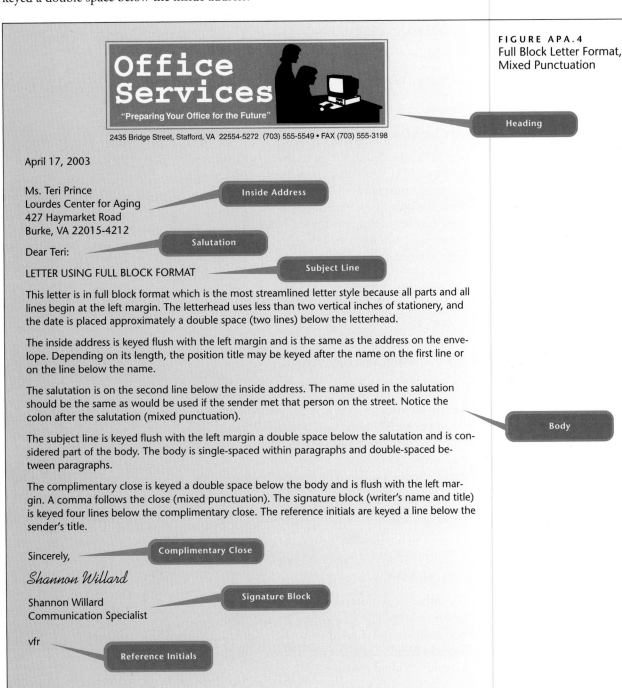

Heading

Inside Address

Salutation

Subject Line

Body

Complimentary Close

Signature Block

Reference Initials

Office Services
"Preparing Your Office for the Future"

2435 Bridge Street, Stafford, VA 22554-5272 (703) 555-5549 • FAX (703) 555-3198

April 17, 2003

Ms. Teri Prince
Lourdes Center for Aging
427 Haymarket Road
Burke, VA 22015-4212

Dear Teri:

LETTER USING FULL BLOCK FORMAT

This letter is in full block format which is the most streamlined letter style because all parts and all lines begin at the left margin. The letterhead uses less than two vertical inches of stationery, and the date is placed approximately a double space (two lines) below the letterhead.

The inside address is keyed flush with the left margin and is the same as the address on the envelope. Depending on its length, the position title may be keyed after the name on the first line or on the line below the name.

The salutation is on the second line below the inside address. The name used in the salutation should be the same as would be used if the sender met that person on the street. Notice the colon after the salutation (mixed punctuation).

The subject line is keyed flush with the left margin a double space below the salutation and is considered part of the body. The body is single-spaced within paragraphs and double-spaced between paragraphs.

The complimentary close is keyed a double space below the body and is flush with the left margin. A comma follows the close (mixed punctuation). The signature block (writer's name and title) is keyed four lines below the complimentary close. The reference initials are keyed a line below the sender's title.

Sincerely,

Shannon Willard

Shannon Willard
Communication Specialist

vfr

COMPANY NAME IN SIGNATURE BLOCK

The name of the company may be keyed in all capital letters a double space below the complimentary close. The company name is placed in the signature block when the letter is in the nature of a contract or when plain paper is used rather than letterhead stationery. The first character of the company name is aligned with the first character of the complimentary close. An example of a company name in the signature block follows:

Sincerely,
O'MALLEY ENGINEERING

Richard O'Malley

Richard O'Malley, President

This addition is not commonly used with letterhead stationery.

ENCLOSURE OR ATTACHMENT NOTATION

Any item included in the envelope other than the letter, such as a check, invoice, or photograph, is considered an **enclosure**. When something is included with a letter, an enclosure notation should be keyed a single or double space below the reference initials (flush with the left margin). The enclosures may be identified, or the number of enclosures may be put in parentheses. When an enclosure is attached to the letter, use *Attachment* or *Att.* in place of the enclosure notation. Examples of enclosure and attachment notations are as follows:

Enclosure: Abstract
Enclosures (3)
Enc. 3
Attachment
Attachment: Donation receipt

COPY NOTATION

A **copy notation** is used when a copy of a letter is being sent to someone other than the addressee. The copy notation may appear as *cc* for *courtesy copy* or *c* for *copy*. The copy notation is keyed flush with the left margin and a double space below the reference initials (or enclosure notation if used). The names of the individuals or groups to receive the copies should be keyed after the notation. Examples of copy notations include the following:

cc: Tim Miller
cc: Roger Schoenfeldt
     Holly Rudolph
c: Accounting

A **blind copy notation** is used when it is unnecessary or inappropriate for an addressee to know that a copy of the letter is being sent to other individuals. The blind copy notation is indicated only on copies of the letter or memo, *not* on the original. Place the blind copy notation where the regular copy notation normally appears. An example of a blind copy notation is

bcc: Becky LaBlanc

POSTSCRIPT

A **postscript** may be used to add a personal comment or to emphasize an important point discussed in the body of the letter. It should *not* be used to add an important point omitted from the body of the letter. The postscript should follow the last notation and be formatted in the same style as the paragraphs of the message. If the paragraphs are indented, the postscript should also be indented. A postscript may be handwritten. The notation "P.S." is usually omitted.

Punctuation Styles

The two styles of punctuation commonly used in business letters are mixed and open. The most popular style is mixed punctuation. **Mixed punctuation** requires a colon after the salutation and a comma after the complimentary close.

Letters using **open punctuation** omit the colon after the salutation and the comma after the complimentary close. Open punctuation is becoming more accepted but is still less popular than mixed punctuation.

Letter Formats

LEARNING OBJECTIVE
③ *Format business letters using the full block, modified block, and simplified block styles.*

The format helps create the reader's first impression of your letter. Organizations usually designate the format for their letters, but in some circumstances they may permit the originator to select the format. The most frequently used formats are full block, modified block, and simplified block.

FULL BLOCK

The **full block format** is becoming very popular. It can be keyed rapidly because none of the parts of the letter is indented. Figure APA.4 shows a full block format letter.

MODIFIED BLOCK

The date (or the return address and date), complimentary close, and signature block begin at the horizontal center of the page in the **modified block format**. There are two versions of the modified block format: (1) body of the letter with blocked paragraphs and (2) body of the letter with indented paragraphs. Letters using the modified block format are shown in Figures APA.5 and APA.6.

SIMPLIFIED BLOCK

The **simplified block format** is a modern, efficient letter format that eliminates the salutation and complimentary close. It is often used when addressed to a company rather than an individual, when the gender of the receiver is unknown, or when marital status of a female receiver is unknown. Figure APA.7 shows a letter in the simplified block format.

Placement

A carefully arranged letter resembles a picture in a frame. The letter should have a border of blank space to form a frame. The width of this frame will vary with the length of the letter, but it should normally be at least one inch on each side. Today, with most offices using word processing software, a letter can be adjusted easily to give it an attractive appearance. Some organizations are justifying their line lengths (making the right margin even). This gives the letter an attractive and somewhat more formal appearance.

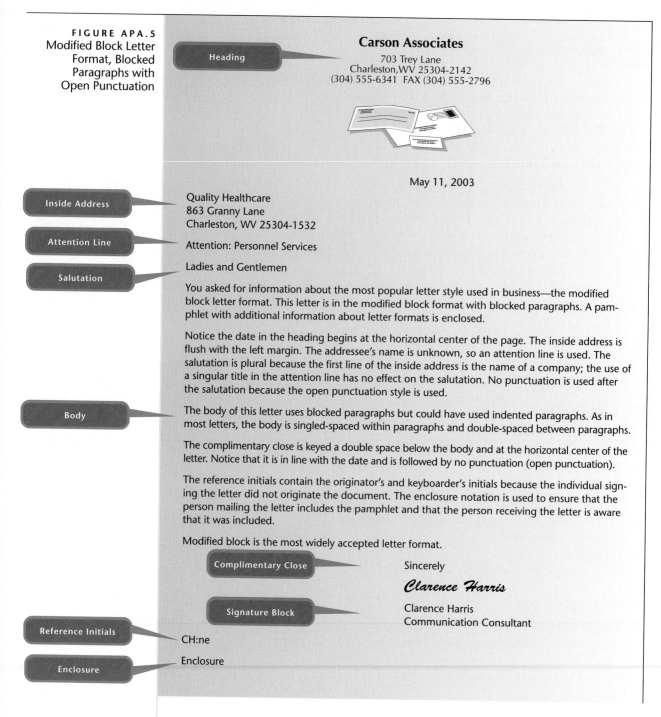

Heading

Carson Associates
703 Trey Lane
Charleston, WV 25304-2142
(304) 555-6341 FAX (304) 555-2796

May 11, 2003

Inside Address

Quality Healthcare
863 Granny Lane
Charleston, WV 25304-1532

Attention Line

Attention: Personnel Services

Salutation

Ladies and Gentlemen

You asked for information about the most popular letter style used in business—the modified block letter format. This letter is in the modified block format with blocked paragraphs. A pamphlet with additional information about letter formats is enclosed.

Notice the date in the heading begins at the horizontal center of the page. The inside address is flush with the left margin. The addressee's name is unknown, so an attention line is used. The salutation is plural because the first line of the inside address is the name of a company; the use of a singular title in the attention line has no effect on the salutation. No punctuation is used after the salutation because the open punctuation style is used.

Body

The body of this letter uses blocked paragraphs but could have used indented paragraphs. As in most letters, the body is singled-spaced within paragraphs and double-spaced between paragraphs.

The complimentary close is keyed a double space below the body and at the horizontal center of the letter. Notice that it is in line with the date and is followed by no punctuation (open punctuation).

The reference initials contain the originator's and keyboarder's initials because the individual signing the letter did not originate the document. The enclosure notation is used to ensure that the person mailing the letter includes the pamphlet and that the person receiving the letter is aware that it was included.

Modified block is the most widely accepted letter format.

Complimentary Close

Sincerely

Clarence Harris

Signature Block

Clarence Harris
Communication Consultant

Reference Initials

CH:ne

Enclosure

Enclosure

Personal Business Letters

A **personal business letter** is written by an individual when conducting business of a personal nature. An application for employment, a request for information, and a comment about services received are examples of personal business letters. A good grade of paper should be used for this type of letter. A full block style or modified block style with mixed or open punctuation is suitable. The return address of the sender should be

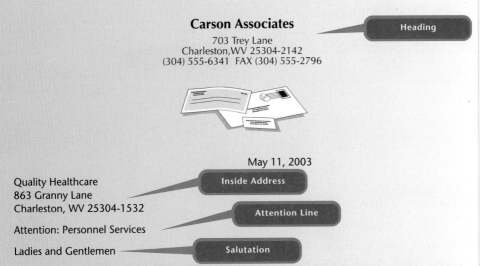

Carson Associates
703 Trey Lane
Charleston,WV 25304-2142
(304) 555-6341 FAX (304) 555-2796

[Heading]

May 11, 2003

Quality Healthcare
863 Granny Lane
Charleston, WV 25304-1532

[Inside Address]

Attention: Personnel Services

[Attention Line]

Ladies and Gentlemen

[Salutation]

You asked for information about the modified block letter format. This letter is in the modified block format with indented paragraphs. You will notice that it is identical to the modified block except that the first word in each paragraph is indented one-half inch. When a subject line is used, it may be centered or indented one-half inch to match the paragraphs. A pamphlet with additional information about letter formats is enclosed.

The date in the heading begins at the horizontal center of the page, whereas the inside address is flush with the left margin. No punctuation is used after the salutation because the open punctuation style is used.

The body of this letter uses indented paragraphs but could have used blocked paragraphs. As in most letters, the body is singled-spaced within paragraphs and double-spaced between paragraphs.

[Body]

The complimentary close is keyed a double space below the body and at the horizontal center of the letter. Notice that it is in line with the date and is followed by no punctuation (open punctuation).

The reference initials contain the originator's and keyboarder's initials because the individual signing the letter did not prepare the document. The enclosure notation is used to ensure that the person mailing the letter includes the pamphlet and that the person receiving the letter is aware that it was included.

Modified block is a well-accepted letter format that is popular in many organizations.

Sincerely

[Complimentary Close]

Clarence Harris

Clarence Harris
Communication Consultant

[Signature Block]

CH:ne

[Reference Initials]

Enclosure

[Enclosure]

placed two inches from the top edge of the paper. The date should be keyed on the line below the return address; however, the date is not considered a part of the return address. The simplified block format is not recommended for application letters because many individuals interpret the lack of a salutation as being impersonal. Figure APA.8 shows a personal business letter.

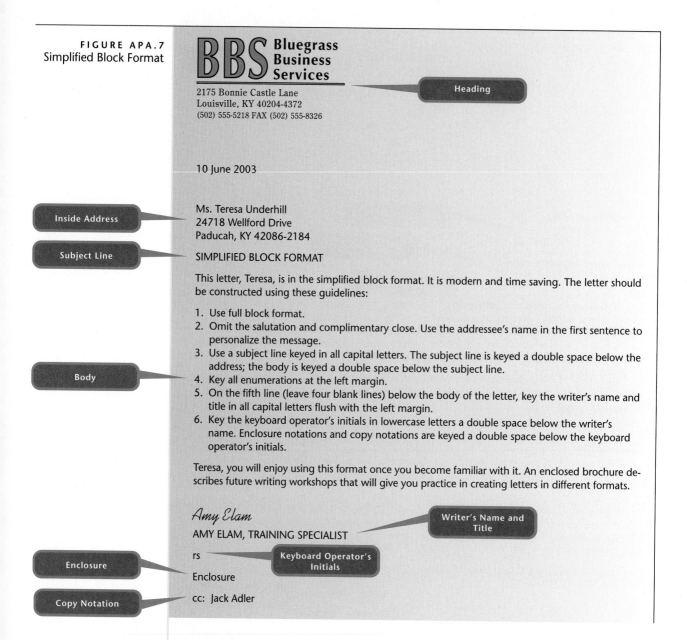

FIGURE APA.7
Simplified Block Format

BBS **Bluegrass Business Services**

Heading

2175 Bonnie Castle Lane
Louisville, KY 40204-4372
(502) 555-5218 FAX (502) 555-8326

10 June 2003

Inside Address

Ms. Teresa Underhill
24718 Wellford Drive
Paducah, KY 42086-2184

Subject Line

SIMPLIFIED BLOCK FORMAT

This letter, Teresa, is in the simplified block format. It is modern and time saving. The letter should be constructed using these guidelines:

1. Use full block format.
2. Omit the salutation and complimentary close. Use the addressee's name in the first sentence to personalize the message.
3. Use a subject line keyed in all capital letters. The subject line is keyed a double space below the address; the body is keyed a double space below the subject line.

Body

4. Key all enumerations at the left margin.
5. On the fifth line (leave four blank lines) below the body of the letter, key the writer's name and title in all capital letters flush with the left margin.
6. Key the keyboard operator's initials in lowercase letters a double space below the writer's name. Enclosure notations and copy notations are keyed a double space below the keyboard operator's initials.

Teresa, you will enjoy using this format once you become familiar with it. An enclosed brochure describes future writing workshops that will give you practice in creating letters in different formats.

Amy Elam
AMY ELAM, TRAINING SPECIALIST

Writer's Name and Title

rs

Keyboard Operator's Initials

Enclosure

Enclosure

Copy Notation

cc: Jack Adler

International Business Correspondence

Business letter formats used by writers in other countries are similar to those used by business letter writers in the United States. When corresponding with someone in a foreign country, you must be knowledgeable about differences in letter formatting that may cause misunderstandings. For instance, the date March 9, 2000, would be written as 3/9/00 in the United States, but written as 9.3.2000 in Germany. Figure APA.9 shows a sample business letter written in German, and Figure APA.10 shows the same letter written in English.

There are other differences between German and American letter formatting: The street name comes before the house number, the city name follows the mailing code, the dateline is always flush right, and the salutation is a double space below the subject

858 Church Road
Pittsburg, KS 66762
April 17, 2003

Heading

Dr. Ron Clement
453 Grouse Lane
Pittsburg, KS 66762

Inside Address

Dear Ron:

Salutation

This is a personal business letter keyed in modified block format with indented paragraphs. The personal business letter may use any of the three accepted formats.

The heading contains the sender's address immediately above the date. This address is keyed and not printed, as it would be in letterhead stationery. Notice that the individual sending the letter omits his or her name in the heading. A general guide is to place the heading two inches from the top edge of the paper, but this varies with the length of the letter.

The inside address is flush with the left margin four to six lines below the dateline. The inside address is the receiver's address, which also appears on the envelope.

Body

The salutation is a double space (two lines) below the inside address. When mixed punctuation is used, key a colon (not a comma) after the salutation because this letter is business and not personal in content.

Supplementary parts (attention lines, subject lines, enclosures, etc.) are used as in regular business letters. The body of the letter contains the message that the sender is transmitting to the receiver. The body should be single-spaced within paragraphs and double-spaced between paragraphs.

The writer signs in the space between the complimentary close and the signature block. Normally, a personal business letter does not contain reference initials because the sender keys the letter.

Sincerely,

Complimentary Close

Gary Smart

Signature Block

Gary Smart

line. Germans are more formal than Americans in their communication; writers include titles such as Dr., Mr., Mrs., or Ms. in the salutation and rarely address someone by his or her first name.

Envelopes

Envelope paper should be the same color and quality as the letterhead stationery. The envelope must be of adequate size to hold the letter and any enclosures or attachments without unnecessary folding. The return address, mailing address, and envelope notations are the three things that may be included on an envelope. Correctly addressed envelopes are shown in Figure APA.11.

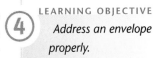

LEARNING OBJECTIVE
Address an envelope properly.

Return Address

The **return address** is the sender's address. It is keyed in capitals in the upper left corner of the envelope. It should contain the sender's address as shown on the letterhead. Often the sender's name will be keyed immediately above a preprinted business return

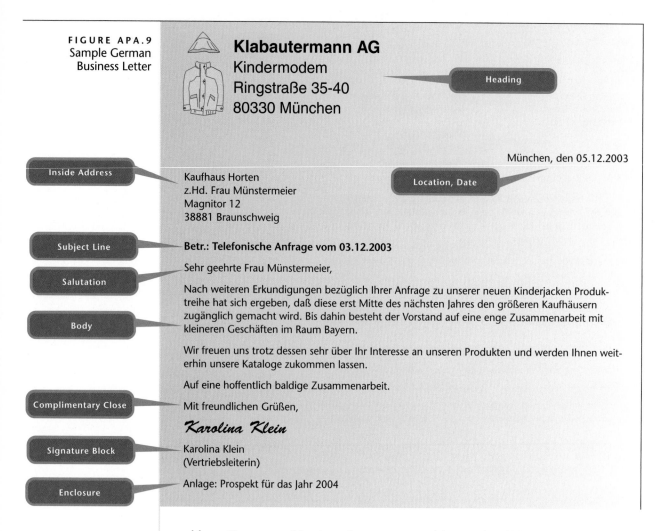

FIGURE APA.9
Sample German
Business Letter

Klabautermann AG
Kindermodem
Ringstraße 35-40
80330 München

Heading

München, den 05.12.2003

Inside Address

Kaufhaus Horten
z.Hd. Frau Münstermeier
Magnitor 12
38881 Braunschweig

Location, Date

Subject Line

Betr.: Telefonische Anfrage vom 03.12.2003

Salutation

Sehr geehrte Frau Münstermeier,

Body

Nach weiteren Erkundigungen bezüglich Ihrer Anfrage zu unserer neuen Kinderjacken Produktreihe hat sich ergeben, daß diese erst Mitte des nächsten Jahres den größeren Kaufhäusern zugänglich gemacht wird. Bis dahin besteht der Vorstand auf eine enge Zusammenarbeit mit kleineren Geschäften im Raum Bayern.

Wir freuen uns trotz dessen sehr über Ihr Interesse an unseren Produkten und werden Ihnen weiterhin unsere Kataloge zukommen lassen.

Auf eine hoffentlich baldige Zusammenarbeit.

Complimentary Close

Mit freundlichen Grüßen,

Karolina Klein

Signature Block

Karolina Klein
(Vertriebsleiterin)

Enclosure

Anlage: Prospekt für das Jahr 2004

address. For personal business letters, return addresses should be printed on labels or keyed on plain envelopes.

Mailing Address

The mailing address contains the receiver's name and address as shown in the inside address. The address should not exceed five lines, and all lines should be blocked. The ZIP code or ZIP + 4 (preferably) should be used in all addresses. The last line of the inside address must contain only the city, state, and ZIP code.

The first line of the address should be keyed one-half inch to the left of the horizontal center of the envelope and on line 14 or 15 of a No. 10 envelope or on line 12 of a No. 6¾ envelope.

Envelope Notations

Two types of envelope notations are used. Special mailing instructions should be keyed in all capital letters a double space below the postage stamp or meter mark. These Postal Service requirements permit electronic scanning and sorting of mail. Mailing instructions include SPECIAL DELIVERY, SPECIAL HANDLING, REGISTERED, and CERTIFIED.

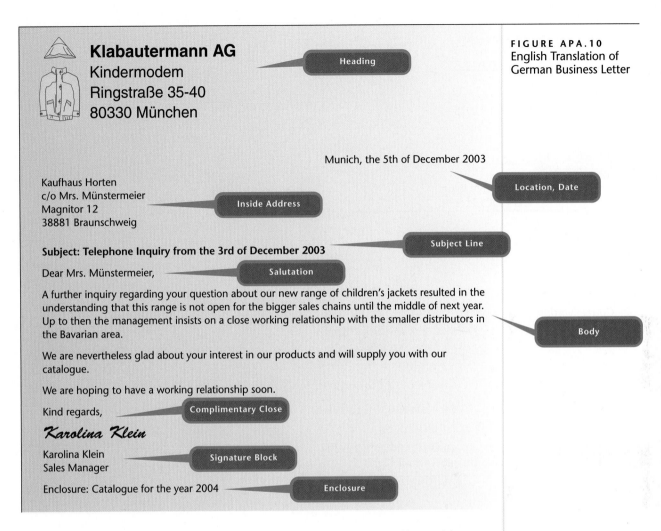

FIGURE APA.10
English Translation of German Business Letter

The letter shown in the figure contains the following labeled parts:

Klabautermann AG
Kindermodem
Ringstraße 35-40
80330 München

— Heading

Munich, the 5th of December 2003

— Location, Date

Kaufhaus Horten
c/o Mrs. Münstermeier
Magnitor 12
38881 Braunschweig

— Inside Address

Subject: Telephone Inquiry from the 3rd of December 2003

— Subject Line

Dear Mrs. Münstermeier,

— Salutation

A further inquiry regarding your question about our new range of children's jackets resulted in the understanding that this range is not open for the bigger sales chains until the middle of next year. Up to then the management insists on a close working relationship with the smaller distributors in the Bavarian area.

We are nevertheless glad about your interest in our products and will supply you with our catalogue.

We are hoping to have a working relationship soon.

— Body

Kind regards,

— Complimentary Close

Karolina Klein

Karolina Klein
Sales Manager

— Signature Block

Enclosure: Catalogue for the year 2004

— Enclosure

Instructions to individuals handling the receiver's mail are keyed in all capital letters a double space below the return address. These notations include CONFIDENTIAL, HOLD FOR ARRIVAL, PERSONAL, and PLEASE FORWARD.

Memos

The most common form of written message for communication within an organization is the **memorandum**, or *memo* as it usually is called. Memos have grown in popularity as organizations have become larger and as communications within organizations have become more complex. Memos are normally less formal and shorter than letters.

LEARNING OBJECTIVE
5
Format a memo properly.

Uses of Memos

Memos are used in a variety of ways. They may be used to communicate upward to superiors, downward to subordinates, laterally to peers, and diagonally to other members of a network. Information of all kinds can be conveyed from one department to another through the use of memos. They are used to announce such things as times and

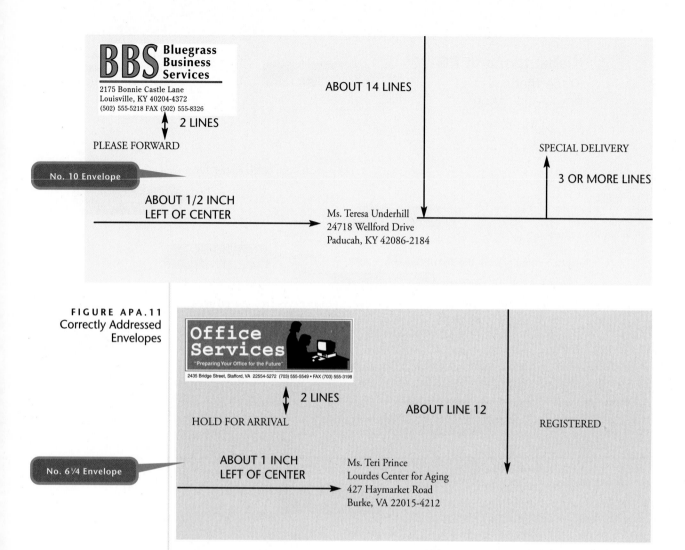

FIGURE APA.11
Correctly Addressed Envelopes

dates of upcoming meetings as well as results of previous meetings, proposed or actual changes in policies or procedures, reports of activities, and instructions.

Advantages of Memos

Using memos has several advantages. One advantage is that the same memo can be addressed to several individuals. If you want to send the same memo to specific employees, you can list all the names and place a check mark after a different name on each copy. Or, you can list all the names and request that the memo be routed from the first-named person through the last-named person. Entire groups can be addressed in a memo and individual copies can be given to each member of the group, or the memo may be placed on a bulletin board. Examples of ways to address memos properly follow:

Specific Individuals

TO: Jim Thomas
     Teresa Underhill
     George Williams

TO: See Distribution List Below

Entire Groups

TO: Human Resources Department Employees

In the last example, See Distribution List Below, the names on the distribution list would be listed at the left margin two lines below the text of the memo under a section entitled Distribution List.

A second advantage of using memos is that they are less formal than letters and may require less time to compose. Memos should be clear and accurate, but they usually do not have to be as polished as letters. Memos may be handwritten to save time.

Another advantage of using a memo is that it provides a written record of the message. Written messages make a more lasting impression than do oral messages.

Formats of Memos

Memos may be prepared using a formal or a simplified format. The same organization may use more than one format for its memos, or it may specify the format that will be used throughout the organization.

A formal memo may be prepared on a preprinted form that contains the headings TO:, FROM:, DATE:, and SUBJECT:, or on letterhead stationery with headings keyed when the memo is keyed. In addition, most word processing software packages permit the user to select a preformatted memo form from a built-in template or macro. A simplified memo may be keyed on plain paper or letterhead stationery. The format of a simplified memo is the same as a simplified block letter, except that the address is omitted. A formal memo prepared using a Microsoft Word memo template is shown in Figure APA.12; a simplified memo appears in Figure APA.13.

Special Forms of Memos

Business firms have developed various kinds of memo forms to perform specific functions within an organization. One is a **round-trip memo**, which is also called a *message-reply memo*. It usually consists of multiform paper, carbon or carbonless, on which the sender can complete the heading and the message portion. The sender can then remove a copy for her or his files before sending the memo. The receiver may add a reply and remove a copy before returning the memo to the original sender. An example of this kind of memo is shown in Figure APA.14.

Stationery

LEARNING OBJECTIVE

6 *Discuss the characteristics of appropriate stationery for letters, memos, and envelopes.*

Stationery used for letters or memos will influence the impression formed by the receiver of the message. The type of stationery that is used will be determined by the purpose of the message. For example, the stationery used for closing a major business transaction should be of a higher quality than the stationery used for announcing an upcoming sale to credit card customers. Some organizations also use a lower quality paper for memos.

Weight

The weight of paper plays a part in impressing the receiver of your message. The stationery most commonly used for business letters is 20-pound bond. The weight measurement is determined by the weight of four reams of $8\frac{1}{2}$- by 11-inch paper. One ream usually contains 500 sheets.

Taylor Enterprises

Company Name

Memo

To: All Employees
From: Janet Wilkins, Administrative Specialist *JW*
Date: 03/17/04
Re: Characteristics of Formal Memos

Heading

Many questions have arisen concerning proper construction and use of formal memos. The following guidelines should answer these questions.

Formal memos contain several unique characteristics. Some of these characteristics follow:

1. A memo should have a preprinted or keyed heading consisting of **TO:**, **FROM:**, **DATE:**, and **SUBJECT:** or **Re.**

2. The individual sending the memo may or may not use a business title. The sender normally does not use a complete signature. An individual's first name or initials are usually written after the keyed name on the **FROM** line in the heading.

3. The memo is not centered vertically as is a letter.

Body

4. Memos, whether formal or simplified, are normally short and contain only one topic; that topic is indicated in the subject line. If more than one topic is needed, separate memos are sent.

5. The body of the memo is in block style beginning a double space below the heading. The body is single-spaced.

6. Informal writing style is appropriate for memos. First person, I, is commonly used as in letters.

Remember that memos should be concise and easy to read; they should not contain any irrelevant information.

Reference Initials

fp

Size

Most business letters are prepared on **standard-size paper**, $8^1/_2$- by 11-inch. Letters from business executives are sometimes placed on $7^1/_4$- by 10-inch high-quality stationery called **executive stationery**. Standard-size paper ($8^1/_2$- by 11-inch) and **half-sheet paper** ($8^1/_2$- by $5^1/_2$-inch) are the two most common sizes of paper used for formal memos. The paper-saving advantage of using half sheets is often outweighed by the disadvantage of locating the smaller sheet when it is filed with standard-size paper. Simplified memos are prepared on standard-size paper.

Color

Color is another important consideration in selecting business stationery. White is the most popular color and is acceptable for all correspondence. Recently, there has been a

March 17, 2004

All Employees

CHARACTERISTICS OF SIMPLIFIED MEMOS

Many questions have arisen concerning proper construction and use of memos. The following guidelines should answer these questions.

Simplified memos contain several characteristics which are unique. Some of these characteristics follow:

1. Full sheets of either plain paper or letterhead stationery are used to prepare simplified memos.

2. All spacing guidelines for a simplified letter also apply to the simplified memo. The only difference is that no address is used in the simplified memo.

3. Personal titles are not used, but a business title or department name may be used.

4. Memos, whether formal or simplified, are normally short and contain only one topic; that topic is indicated in the subject line. If more than one topic is needed, separate memos are sent.

5. Informal writing style is appropriate for memos. First person, I, is commonly used along with inferences and jargon.

6. Reference initials, enclosure notations, copy notations, and second-page headings are used as in letters.

Remember that memos should be concise and easy to read; they should contain only relevant information. Either the formal memo or simplified memo format is acceptable for our interoffice communication.

Janet Wilkins

Janet Wilkins, Administrative Specialist

fp

trend toward using other paper colors. Selecting the appropriate stationery color is extremely important to the image of the company. The type of industry certainly must be a determining factor in selecting paper color. For example, Mary Kay Cosmetics uses pink (its theme color) throughout its product line, including its stationery. On the other hand, a lumber company may very effectively use light wood-grained stationery. Some companies use different colored memo forms to identify originating departments.

Quality

The quality of stationery is determined by the amount of rag content in the paper. The **rag content** is the amount and type of fiber (usually cotton) used in the composition of the paper. High-quality stationery usually has 25 percent or more rag content. High-quality stationery also has a watermark showing the name of the company

To	From
	Randi Nance LaRoche Creations Hammond, LA 70403-2174

MESSAGE

SUBJECT	DATE

SIGNED

REPLY

DATE

SIGNED

that manufactures the paper or the emblem of the organization that uses the stationery. Letters should be prepared on high-quality stationery; all pages should be of the same weight, color, quality, and size. The advantages of using high-quality stationery for letters include superior appearance, excellent texture, and long life without chemical breakdown. Memos should be prepared on less-expensive grades of paper.

Envelope Paper

Although the previously cited factors are important, they do not represent the end of the stationery selection process. Envelopes, too, must be given consideration. Envelope paper should be of the same weight, color, and quality as the letterhead stationery. Also, envelopes should be in proportion to the size of the stationery. For example, standard $8^1/_2$- by 11-inch stationery requires No. 10 ($9^1/_2$- by $4^1/_8$-inch) envelopes; executive stationery is $7^1/_4$- by 10-inch and requires No. 7 ($7^1/_2$- by $3^7/_8$-inch) envelopes.

Written messages convey a positive or negative image of an organization. The stationery selected to carry these messages should share importance with the composition of the messages.

Summary of Learning Objectives

① Describe the seven standard parts of a letter.

The seven standard parts of a letter are as follows: (1) heading—consists of a letterhead and the dateline or the return address and a dateline; (2) inside address—includes the receiver's courtesy title, name, street address, city, state, and ZIP code; (3) salutation—the greeting that begins the message; (4) body—the message section of the letter; (5) complimentary close—a phrase used to end a message; (6) signature block—contains the writer's signed name, keyed name, and title; and (7) reference initials—the initials of the message originator and/or the keyboard operator.

Describe the appropriate use of supplementary parts of a letter.

Uses for supplementary parts of a letter are as follows: (1) attention line—directs the letter to a person, position title, or department within a company; (2) subject line—identifies the main topic of a letter; (3) company name in signature block—appears when the letter is used as a contract; (4) enclosure notation—indicates the inclusion of material other than the letter in an envelope; (5) copy notation—identifies others receiving the letter; and (6) postscript—used to add personal comment or to emphasize an important point discussed in the letter.

Format business letters using the full block, modified block, and simplified block styles.

Letters written in the full block format have the dateline, inside address, salutation, body, complimentary close, signature block, and reference initials begin at the left margin. Modified block letters have the date, complimentary close, and signature block begin at the horizontal center of the page; whereas, everything else begins at the left margin. Paragraphs in modified block letters may be blocked or indented. Simplified block letters are prepared in the block format. The salutation and complimentary close are omitted but the receiver's name appears in the first line of the message. In addition, simplified block letters have the subject line and the writer's name and title in all capital letters. The writer's name and title are both keyed on the same line four spaces below the body of the letter.

Address an envelope properly.

The return address—the sender's address as shown on the letterhead—is keyed in all capital letters in the upper-left corner of the envelope. The mailing address, the receiver's name and address as shown in the inside address, is keyed in about $1/2$ inch left of the center and on about line 14 of a No. 10 envelope or line 12 of a No. $6^3/4$ envelope. Mailing instructions for the postal service should be placed a double space below the postage stamp. Mailing instructions to individuals handling the receiver's mail should be a double space below the return address. Mailing and delivery instructions should be in all capital letters.

Format a memo properly.

Memos can be prepared using a formal or a simplified format. A formal memo may be prepared on a preprinted form that contains the headings TO:, FROM:, DATE:, and SUBJECT:, or on letterhead stationery with headings keyed when the memo is prepared. The format of a simplified memo is the same as that of a simplified block letter, except that the address is omitted.

6 Discuss the characteristics of appropriate stationery for letters, memos, and envelopes.

The most commonly used stationery is 20-pound bond. Most correspondence is prepared on standard-size paper, $8^1/_2$- by 11-inch, but may be prepared on executive stationery, $7^1/_2$- by 10-inch, or half-sheet paper, $8^1/_2$- by $5^1/_2$-inch. White is the most popular color for stationery, but colored stationery is acceptable. The rag content determines the quality of the stationery. Letters are prepared on higher quality stationery than are memos. The envelopes and stationery should be the same quality and color. The envelope should be an appropriate size for the stationery.

Document Format— APA and MLA

LEARNING
OBJECTIVES

①

Document reference sources in text citations following APA format.

②

Prepare a complete list of reference sources using APA format.

③

Document reference sources in text citations following MLA format.

④

Prepare a complete list of reference sources using MLA format.

Giving proper credit when using words or ideas from other sources is emphasized in Chapter 3. This appendix gives guidelines for formatting citations within formal papers, reports, and manuscripts and preparing the list of sources at the end of the document. Two widely used style manuals that can be used to give consistency for citing sources in written work are the *Publication Manual of the American Psychological Association* (APA) and the *MLA Handbook for Writers of Research Papers* (MLA). In this appendix, you will find examples of different types of source documents formatted according to both APA and MLA style guidelines.

Documentation Format—APA

Documentation of citations that conform to APA style uses the author's surname and date for in-text citations and an end-of-document alphabetic reference list of all sources cited within the text. The APA style is used in the fields of psychology, behavioral, and social sciences, including business and education. APA examples in this seminar conform to the fifth edition of the APA style manual, published by the American Psychological Association, 750 First Street, NE, Washington, DC 20002-4242. The APA Web page may be found at http://www.apa.org; an order for the *Publication Manual of the American Psychological Association* should be e-mailed to order@apa.org.

Reference Citations in Text

① LEARNING OBJECTIVE
Document reference sources in text citations following APA format.

Within document text, APA style includes a citation with the author's surname and year of publication or author's surname, year, and page number where the information can be found in the original source. Readers go to the Reference List to obtain complete information necessary to locate the source document. A quoted item from source material requires the author's surname, year, and page number for the citation. The following examples illustrate in-text citations of work by one author or multiple authors:

Kridel (2002) describes the high capacities of 3G and flash memory.

Flash memory is moving into all kinds of portable devices (Kridel, 2002).

"A flash memory card is not much different from everyday RAM," according to Kridel (2002, p. 80).

Japanese society expects a high level of individual conformity with detailed norms (Schneider & Silverman, 2000).

"The United States, Japan, and Germany are the three largest industrial economies in the world" (Sundaram, Bradley, Schipani, & Walsh, 2000, p. 111).

The last example shows a work cited with four authors. According to APA, a citation of a work with two authors should use both surnames each time the work is cited. For three to five authors, all authors are cited the first time, but only the first author followed by et al. and the year are included in subsequent citations. The above citation has four authors and would be shown in subsequent text citations as follows:

Governance boards mediate and manage stakeholder trade-offs (Sundaram et al., 2000).

Sundaram et al. (2000) states that governance boards mediate and manage stakeholder trade-offs.

The following examples show group names as authors and works with no authors. Group names are spelled out unless an abbreviation is easily recognizable. If the name is long, give the full name the first time; but if the abbreviation is understandable, abbreviate it for subsequent citations. For works with no author, cite the first few words of the reference list entry (usually the title) and the year. The title of an article or chapter would be in double quotation marks; and a journal, book, brochure, or report title would be italicized.

University of Kentucky (2004) catalog states. . . .

First citation as follows; subsequent citations use USDA and date:

Small farms in the United States are disappearing at a rapid pace (United States Department of Agriculture [USDA], 2003).

No author; abbreviated title with date:

Changes in the arts venue brought in new leadership ("Arts World Changes," 2004).

Cite personal interviews, telephone conversations, e-mail messages, letters, or memos in the text only. Such personal communications are not recoverable by others and, therefore, are not included in the reference list. The following examples show two ways that personal communication information can be cited in the document text:

M. G. Lane (personal communication, March 17, 2004) reported that. . . .

These statistics were verified (M. G. Lane, personal communication, March 17, 2004).

LEARNING OBJECTIVE

②

Prepare a complete list of reference sources using APA format.

Reference List or Bibliography

A **reference list** is a list of works cited in the text of a particular paper, report, or manuscript; whereas, a **bibliography** is a list of sources cited in the text plus other works that give additional information on the topic of the paper. The APA style format applies to both types of lists.

For a reference list at the end of a paper, all references cited in the text must be included in the list, and all resources in the reference list must be cited at least once in the text. For a bibliography, all in-text citations must appear in the bibliography; but all resources in the bibliography would not be cited in the text.

The reference list at the end of a document begins on a new page with the title *References* or *Reference List* at the top margin. This list shows all information necessary to identify and retrieve each source.

The following guidelines will assist you with the development of an APA style reference list.

[1] The list contains information on all of the works that have been cited in the document.

[2] You should carefully check all dates and spellings of each source. Reference data must be correct and complete to enable readers to retrieve and use the source.

[3] The reference list begins on a separate page with the list of source information beginning a double space after the title *References* or *Reference List*.

[4] Each entry uses a *hanging indent* format. A **hanging indent** begins the first line of the entry at the left margin with other lines of the entry indented half an inch. Manuscripts prepared for publication double space the reference list; however, other types of papers and reports usually have single spacing for each reference item with double spacing between items.

[5] The entries are in alphabetical order by the surname of the first author or by title if the entry has no author.

[6] In the title, capitalize only the first word and proper nouns. This capitalization applies to book titles, as well as chapter or article titles in other publications. However, each word in magazine and journal names is capitalized in the same manner as is used normally for the publication name.

[7] The names of books, magazines, and journals should be in italics.

[8] For books, reports, brochures, and other non-periodical publications, give the location and publisher's name. Use the city and state for location of the publisher. Baltimore, Boston, Chicago, Los Angeles, New York, Philadelphia, San Francisco, and other widely recognized cities do not require the state to be given because their location is known without further identification.

[9] Electronic resources include many kinds of publications. As a general rule, Internet resources in the reference list give the author (if known), a title or description, date, and the Uniform Resource Locator (URL).

Figure APB.1 shows examples of entries in an APA style reference list.

Internet Citations

Internet documents may be articles from newspapers, newsletters, or journals; research papers or reports, online books or brochures, or Web pages. Electronic library resources may come from electronic databases. Direct readers as closely as possible to the source document and be sure that the URL address works.

Specific information for citing electronic references using APA style formatting can be found at http://www.apastyle.org/elecmedia.html. Reference examples are given for Internet articles based on a print source, articles from electronic journals, Internet newsletters, electronic documents with no author and no publication date, documents from university Web sites, and journal articles from a library electronic database.

In-text citations of resources obtained from the Internet follow the same pattern as for other sources. The citation includes the author's name or portion of the title followed by a document date, or (n.d.) if there is no document date. The URL does not appear in the in-text citation.

FIGURE APB.1
APA Reference List

References

Internet article based on print source (no author)
→ Arts world changes for the better [Electronic version]. (2004). *Journal of Fine Arts, 5,* 12–14.

Newspaper article (one author)
→ Earnest, L. (2004, January 21). Investments: Diversification. *Kansas City Star,* p. B4.

Magazine article (one author)
→ Kridel, T. (2002, November). Trading spaces: The power of flash memory. *Laptop Mobile Solutions for Business & Life,* 78–86.

Encyclopedia article (one author)
→ Lorenz, J. R. (2002). Commodity exchange. In *The World Book Encyclopedia* (Vol. 20, pp. 495–497). Chicago: World Book, Inc.

Unpublished paper presented at a meeting
→ Mead, T. C. (2004, January). *Researching business communication practices of CEOs.* Paper presented at the meeting of the Association of Business Communication, San Diego, CA.

Internet-only journal article
→ Miller, A. (2003). Mission impossible: Increasing female enrollment in computer science. *Online Computer World, 6.* Retrieved November 25, 2004, from *http://www.elecjournals/ocw.volume6/ejj0030.html.*

Journal article
→ Moore, W. (2002, December). Economics brought to life. *Business Education Forum, 57*(2), 36–37.

Newsletter article from electronic database
→ On-the-job interview: Survey shows value of temporary work as prelude to full-time job. (2002, October 15). *PR Newswire.* Retrieved November 10, 2002, from the InfoTrac College Edition database.

CD-ROM encyclopedia article
→ Perry, J. T. (2002). Mindscapes. *Microsoft Encarta 2000* [CD-ROM]. Redmond, WA: Microsoft.

Book (two authors)
→ Schneider, L., & Silverman, A. (2000). *Global sociology* (2nd ed.). Boston: McGraw-Hill Higher Education.

Chapter in edited book (four authors)
→ Sundaram, A. K., Bradley, M., Schipani, C. A., & Walsh, J. P. (2000). Comparative corporate governance and global corporate strategy. In R. E. Grosse (Ed.), *Thunderbird on global business strategy* (pp. 110–150). New York: John Wiley & Sons, Inc.

Governmental agency Internet datafile
→ U.S. Census Bureau. (n.d.). *Population profile of the United States: 2000* [Internet release]. Retrieved January 1, 2003, from *http://www.census.gov/population/www/pop-profile/profile2000.html.*

University publication
→ University of Kentucky. (2004). *Graduate catalog.* Lexington, KY: University of Kentucky Press.

Corporate document
→ VCR Corporation of America. (2003, February). 2002 annual report (Report No. 15). Washington, DC: Author.

Dictionary entry
→ *Webster's new world dictionary of the American language.* (2001). New York: Warner.

Documentation Format—MLA

The MLA style was developed by the Modern Language Association of America. The MLA style is used by writers in government, business, industry, the professions, and the media. MLA style is currently used by more than 125 scholarly and literary journals, newsletters, and magazines with circulation over one thousand. In addition, the MLA guidelines are used by hundreds of smaller periodicals and by many university and commercial presses. In 2003, the *MLA Handbook for Writers of Research Papers,* 6th edition, was authored by Joseph Gibaldi. The *MLA Handbook* may be ordered from the MLA Web page which is located at http://www.mla.org. Documentation guidelines for the Modern Language Association are not published on the Web.

Reference Citation in Text

LEARNING OBJECTIVE
(3) *Document reference sources in text citations following MLA format.*

Periodically, you will use primary and secondary sources in writing. Individuals must be given proper credit whenever their works are used by others. When you use the MLA style, you may use parenthetical citations in the text and an alphabetical list of cited works that appears at the end of the document. The parenthetical citations in the text use the author-page method such as (Biggs, 128). This style of citation identifies the source for readers and enables them to locate the source of information in the Works Cited list at the end of the document. The titles of longer works should be highlighted by underlining or by placing them in italics throughout the text.

Works Cited List

LEARNING OBJECTIVE
(4) *Prepare a complete list of reference sources using MLA format.*

The Works Cited list at the end of the document provides the information necessary to identify each source and to retrieve the material. This list should contain all the works that are cited in the text.

The following guidelines will assist you with the development of the MLA style Works Cited list:

[1] The list contains information on all of the works that have been cited in the document.

[2] The most common title for the list is *Works Cited*; however, other titles used for the list include *Bibliography, Literature Cited, Works Consulted,* and *Annotated Bibliography.*

[3] The Works Cited list is placed at the end of the document.

[4] The Works Cited list should begin on a separate page; and each page should be numbered, continuing with the page numbers of the text.

[5] The title, *Works Cited,* should be centered an inch from the top of the page with a double space between the title and the first reference entry.

[6] Begin each entry flush with the left margin. Indent each subsequent line one-half inch from the left margin.

[7] Arrange entries in alphabetical order by the author's last name.

Refer to Figure APB.2 for an example of the use of the MLA documentation style.

Internet Citations

The *MLA Handbook for Writers of Research Papers* has complete guidelines that cover citing World Wide Web sources. Entries for types of Web sources include Scholarly Project, Professional Site, Personal Site, Book, Poem, Article in a Reference Database, Article in a Journal, Article in a Magazine, Work From a Subscription Service, and Posting to a Discussion List. Please refer to Figure APB.2 for examples of how to cite information from a Web site on the Internet, an online magazine article, and an online newspaper article.

Works Cited

Internet article based on print source (no author)

"Arts World Changes for the Better." *Journal of Fine Arts* 5 (2004): 12–14 <http://www.musu.edu/jfa.html>.

Newspaper article (one author)

Earnest, Larry. "Investments: Diversification." *Kansas City Star* 21 Jan. 2004: B4.

Magazine article (one author)

Kridel, Tim. "Trading Spaces: The Power of Flash Memory." *Laptop Mobile Solutions for Business & Life.* 1 Nov. 2002: 78–86.

Encyclopedia article (one author)

Lorenz, Jerry R. "Commodity Exchange." *The World Book Encyclopedia.* Chicago: World Book, Inc., 2002.

Unpublished paper presented at a meeting

Mead, Tammy. "Researching Business Communication Practices of CEOs." 2004 Association of Business Communication Regional Meeting.

Internet-only journal article

Miller, Andrea. "Mission Impossible: Increasing Female Enrollment in Computer Science." *Online Computer World* 25 Nov. 2003, <http://www.elecjournals/ocw.volume6/ejj0030.html>.

Journal article

Moore, Wayne. "Economics Brought to Life." *Business Education Forum* 12 (2002): 36–37.

Newsletter article from electronic database

"On-the-Job Interview: Survey Shows Value of Temporary Work as Prelude to Full-Time Job." *PR Newswire* Oct. 2002: 16–18. InfoTrac College Edition. 10 Nov. 2002 <http://www.infotrac-college.com>.

CD-ROM encyclopedia article

Perry, James. "Mindscapes." *Microsoft Encarta 2000.* CD-ROM. Redmond, WA: Microsoft, 2002.

Book (two authors)

Schneider, Linda, and Arnold Silverman. *Global Sociology* (2nd ed.) Boston: McGraw-Hill Higher Education, 2000.

Chapter in edited book (four authors)

Sundaram, Anant K., Michael Bradley, Cindy A. Schipani, and James P. Walsh. "Comparative Corporate Governance and Global Corporate Strategy." *Thunderbird on Global Business Strategy.* Ed. Robert E. Grosse. New York: John Wiley & Sons, 2000. 110–150.

Governmental agency Internet datafile

United States Census Bureau. *Population Profile of the United States: 2000.* 1 Jan. 2003. <http://www.census.gov/population/www/pop-profile/profile2000.html>.

University publication

University of Kentucky. *Graduate Catalog.* Lexington, KY: University of Kentucky Press, 2004.

Corporate document

VCR Corporation of America. *2000 Annual Report.* Washington, DC: VCR Corporation of America.

Dictionary entry

Webster's New World Dictionary of the American Language. New York: Warner, 2001.

Example Formal Report

The title page.

EMPLOYEE INTEREST
IN A
COMPANY-SPONSORED FITNESS PROGRAM

States the subject of the report.

Prepared for

Tells to whom it is being submitted.

Jillian Erp

Human Resources Director

Prepared by

Tells who is submitting it.

Hank Thorp

Human Resources Specialist

Nomar Printing Company

Identifies the organization.

June 15, 200–

Gives the date of submission.

EMPLOYEE INTEREST
IN A
COMPANY-SPONSORED FITNESS PROGRAM

Nomar Printing Company

220 North Highway 367
Boise, ID 83705
(208) 555-0227 FAX (208) 555-1008

March 12, 2003

Authorization message (not discussed in the text).

TO: Hank Thorp
           Human Resources Specialist

FROM: Jillian Erp $\mathcal{JE}$
           Human Resources Director

SUBJECT: **Research Authorization**

Gives authority to conduct the study.

The Human Resources Committee has read, discussed, and approved your proposal to survey Nomar employees about their interest in a company-sponsored fitness program. As you point out in your proposal, our plans to renovate and expand our facilities offer a unique opportunity to investigate ways in which we can improve the quality of work life for our employees, especially in light of declining productivity levels over the past few years.

The Committee has set a July 15 deadline for the report and approved a $1,500 budget for your use in designing, field testing, printing, distributing, and analyzing the surveys. The Committee asks, however, that you submit the survey questionnaire for approval prior to final distribution.

Gives relevant information, such as deadline and funding.

Please contact me if I or the Committee can be of assistance.

rt

iii

Nomar Printing Company

220 North Highway 367
Boise, ID 83705
(208) 555-0227 FAX (208) 555-1008

June 15, 2003

> Transmittal message.

TO: Jillian Erp
         Human Resources Director

FROM: Hank Thorp   *HT*
         Human Resources Specialist

SUBJECT: **Employee Interest Survey—Company-Sponsored Fitness Program**

> Sets the context and transmits the report.

As we agreed in March, I have surveyed a representative sample of Nomar employees to determine their interest in a company-sponsored fitness program, including the possibility of a company-sponsored fitness center. Here is the report of that study.

> Provides highlights of the study.

Response to the survey was outstanding; over 80 percent replied. The results suggest that there is strong interest in a company-sponsored fitness program. The concept of an on-site fitness center was also viewed positively.

> Summarizes the recommendations.

Based on the findings of the survey, I recommend that we develop proposals for a fitness program that includes an on-site fitness center.

I would appreciate your sharing this report with the HR Committee. If you would like me to discuss the results with the Committee members, please let me know.

dkh

iv

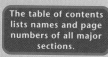

The table of contents lists names and page numbers of all major sections.

TABLE OF CONTENTS

v

The list of illustrations contains the titles and page numbers of all visuals used in the report.

LIST OF ILLUSTRATIONS

TABLES

FIGURES

EXECUTIVE SUMMARY

Nomar plans to renovate and expand its current facilities. This growth provides the company with an opportunity to investigate ways in which employees' work life quality can be improved. A fitness program, possibly one including an on-site fitness center, is one of the options available to the company.

Research has shown that health and productivity are related and that work is one of the three top sources of stress for adults in the United States. Physical exercise has been identified as an effective method for controlling stress. Access to an on-site fitness center can be useful in reducing stress and raising productivity if the center offers a variety of activities in which employees may voluntarily participate.

In order to determine employee interest in a company-sponsored fitness program and an on-site fitness center, 500 employees were surveyed using a stratified random sample data-gathering technique. Over 80 percent of those surveyed responded.

Data collected through the survey show that Nomar employees are interested in improving their fitness and that they currently participate in a variety of activities. Those surveyed show strong support for a company-sponsored fitness program; a majority also favor construction of an on-site fitness center. The findings suggest that a center would be used regularly.

Based on the results of this survey, Nomar should pursue development of a company-sponsored fitness program that includes an on-site fitness center.

I. INTRODUCTION

Background

The daily routines, quotas, and deadlines under which most workers at Nomar Printing operate go hand in hand with stress buildup. Depending on the individual, work-related stress can be perceived as intolerable and threatening or as normal and stimulating. If individual workers have planned leisure activities that allow for the release of such daily stressors, then supposedly all is well within the working community. One area of concern, though, is the amount of time workers devote to gaining and maintaining a good fitness level. Without regular exercise, the workforce can become increasingly unmotivated or physically ill.

Statement of the Problem

Productivity at Nomar has declined steadily over the past three years despite increased wages.

Purpose of the Study

A representative of Allied Insurance, Nomar's health care provider, has suggested that offering employees a fitness program might improve productivity. The purpose of the study was to determine whether Nomar's employees are interested in a company-sponsored fitness program.

Scope

This study is limited to full-time, regular employees of Nomar who have been with the company at least one year.

II. RELATED LITERATURE

"Stress is unavoidable" (Krazen, 1999, p. 48). This was one of the conclusions in a study conducted by the Winthrow Group in 1999. The report of this study pointed out that stress can be produced by any demands placed on a person or any changes in his or her life. Money, interpersonal relationships, and job satisfaction are identified in the report as the top three sources of stress for adults in the United States.

While stress cannot be avoided, it can be minimized. Dr. Joshua Carey of the Quincy Institute for Better Health states in a recent *Journal of Stress Science* article:

> Physical exercise seems to be effective in controlling stress. A planned exercise program will minimize physical *and* emotional reactions to pressure; it will help keep blood pressure, heart rate, and cholesterol at acceptable levels (Carey, 2001, pp. 78–79).

The concept that stress can be reduced through exercise is not new. In the mid-1980s, published articles suggested that exercise was linked with better health. Ethan-Rolle monitored the energy levels of 150 adults between the ages of 35 and 45. During the two years of her

1

research, she found that "physical activities such as walking, jogging, biking, and aerobics diminished stress and fatigue" (Ethan-Rolle, 1986, p. 103).

The strong relationship between exercise and stress reduction has important implications for business and industry. In 1996, the Sanders Corporation converted a portion of an unused warehouse into a physical fitness center for its employees. During the next five years, the company traced worker health, productivity levels, and facility use. The report prepared at the end of the research period indicated that Sanders' workers were in better health, productivity had increased, and the popularity of the facility had risen steadily (*West Coast Business,* 2002, p. 6c).

Not all the news is good, however. Some firms that have begun corporate wellness programs report that "workers are 'suspicious' of companies that try to become involved in aspects of their private lives" (Haugen, 1999, p. 38). To minimize the effects of suspicion, Haugen recommends that wellness programs be voluntary and that they include options to meet the varying interests and needs of employees (Haugen, 1999, p. 41). A similar study involving office workers in New York City (Trent, 2002, p. 118) yielded comparable results.

> The procedures section describes the steps taken in conducting the study.

III. PROCEDURES

After the literature was reviewed, a questionnaire was designed, field tested, and revised. The questionnaire, which contained ten items, was designed to gather information about employees' current exercise patterns and their interest in a company-sponsored fitness program. A copy of the questionnaire, which was approved by the HR Committee on April 24, is in the Appendix.

In order to get responses from a cross-section of Nomar employees, a stratified random sample data gathering technique was used. With the help of personnel from the Human Resources Management Department and the Information Systems Department, questionnaires were distributed with the May 12 paychecks of 500 full-time Nomar employees who had been with the company for at least one year. Employees were asked to complete the survey and return it to the Human Resources Management Department within five working days. A second distribution was made on May 26 to those employees who did not respond to the initial mailing.

> In formal reports that are simple and brief, analysis can be combined with findings.

IV. FINDINGS AND ANALYSIS

Responses were received from 408 of the 500 employees surveyed. This high response rate (81.6 percent) is one indication of the employees' interest in their health. The majority of the respondents (228; 55.9 percent) were men. Respondents ranged in age from 19 to 68; the median age of the respondents was 41. Respondents were fairly evenly distributed across all employment length categories with the average length of employment being 11 years.

Nearly two thirds (266; 65.2 percent) of the respondents felt they would like to be more fit. When asked why they were interested in improving their fitness level, 211 (51.7 percent) indicated they wanted to improve their health, 101 (24.8 percent) wanted to improve their physical appearance, and the remaining 96 (23.5 percent) wanted to have more energy. The national trend toward health and fitness is reflected in the distribution of these responses. Data do not reflect whether this high interest in fitness is related to busy, stress-producing lifestyles.

Just over a third (143; 35 percent) of the employees who returned surveys currently participate in regular programs designed to maintain or improve their health. As shown in Table 1, employees participate in unstructured activities such as swimming, walking, and weight training as well as structured activities such as aerobics and exercise classes.

Findings are presented objectively.

TABLE 1   EXERCISE PROGRAMS IN WHICH NOMAR EMPLOYEES PARTICIPATE (N=408)

Activity	Respondents Participating*
Walking	308
Weight Training	141
Aerobics	121
Swimming	95
Jogging	77
Exercise Classes	62
Racquetball	38
Cycling	16
Other	7
No Response	4

*Respondents could check multiple activities.

Illustrations are numbered by type and use descriptive titles.

When data were examined to determine the effect of age, gender, and length of employment, no significant differences were found but observable differences were noted. Regardless of how long they have worked at Nomar, employees of both sexes and all ages participate in the activities listed in Table 1. Men and women between the ages of 19 and 30 run, cycle, and do aerobics while those 50 and older prefer to walk and swim. Readers should note, however, that the survey did not solicit information about how frequently employees participated in the various activities.

Employees were asked to indicate their level of interest in a company-sponsored fitness program. Considering the strong interest in fitness that was expressed in earlier responses, it is not surprising that 287 (70.3 percent) of those returning surveys indicated that their interest in a company-sponsored fitness program was "Very High" or "High." (See Table 2).

The analysis shows important relationships.

TABLE 2   EMPLOYEE INTEREST IN A COMPANY-SPONSORED FITNESS PROGRAM (N=408)

Interest Level	Number	Percent
Very High	113	27.7
High	174	42.6
Moderate	66	16.2
Low	31	7.6
Very Low	24	5.9

When asked about the type of activities they would like to see included if the company developed a fitness program, respondents expressed a preference for an on-site walking/jogging path and an on-site fitness center. These responses loosely parallel the workers' current activity patterns. Refer to Table 3 for further information.

TABLE 3 PREFERRED FITNESS PROGRAM ACTIVITIES (N=408)

Activity	Number Selecting*	Percent
Classes	173	42.4
On-site Fitness Center	284	69.6
On-site Walking/Jogging Path	301	73.8
Paid Health Club Membership	37	9.1

*Respondents could check more than one item.

Additional analysis showed that 22 of those employees indicating they would like to have paid health club memberships also favored an on-site fitness center. The data do not reveal whether those who favored paid health club memberships are currently members of fitness centers or whether they would forego those memberships if the company were to establish an on-site center.

Those respondents who indicated they would like to have an on-site fitness center included in a company-sponsored fitness program were asked how often they anticipated using such a facility. As shown in Figure 1, a majority of these workers said they would use the facility on a regular basis.

Figure 1. Projected Fitness Center Use

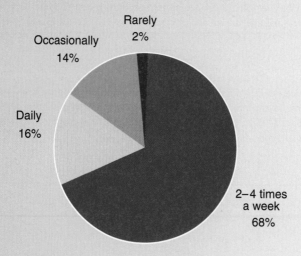

Those who indicated they would use an on-site fitness center were also asked to indicate the time of day at which they anticipated using the center. Findings suggest that use would be distributed fairly evenly across the before work, lunch break, and after-work time frames. Location and the availability of lockers and showers would likely influence use patterns. Refer to Figure 2.

Figure 2. Anticipated Times of Use

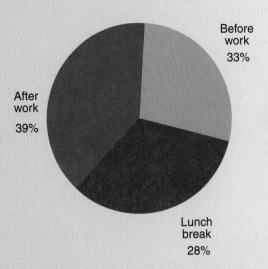

V. CONCLUSIONS AND RECOMMENDATIONS

> Conclusions are drawn from the analysis of the findings.

Conclusions

1. Nomar employees are interested in becoming fit and/or maintaining their personal fitness.

2. Nomar employees, regardless of age or gender, engage in both structured and unstructured fitness activities.

3. Nomar employees are interested in having a company-sponsored fitness program.

4. A company-sponsored fitness program should include an on-site fitness center and an on-site walking/jogging path.

Recommendations

> Recommendations are based on the study's conclusions.

1. Nomar should develop a company-sponsored fitness program.

2. Nomar should investigate the feasibility of establishing an on-site fitness center and on-site walking/jogging path.

3. Employees should be consulted regarding the facilities/activities they would like to see included in an on-site fitness center.

APPENDIX

SURVEY QUESTIONNAIRE

An appendix contains supportive supplementary material that is related to the study.

NOMAR PRINTING COMPANY
Employee Interest Survey

Please complete the following survey, fold it to highlight the address, and return it by May 19. The number on the form will be used only to do a second mailing (if necessary). Once a sufficient number of responses has been received, data linking surveys and respondents will be destroyed.

No. _____

DEMOGRAPHIC DATA

Please check the most appropriate response or supply the requested information.

1. How long have you worked at Nomar?

   ❏ 1–5 years
   ❏ 6–10 years
   ❏ 11–15 years
   ❏ 16 years or more

2. What is your gender?   ❏ Male   ❏ Female

3. What is your age? _____

FITNESS INTERESTS

Please check the most appropriate response or supply the requested information. For some items, you may check more than one response.

4. Would you like to be more fit?   ❏ Yes   ❏ No

5. If your answer to Question 4 was Yes, why are you interested in being more fit?

   ❏ Better health
   ❏ Improved appearance
   ❏ More energy

6. In which of the following activities do you currently participate? Check all that apply.

   ❏ Aerobics
   ❏ Cycling
   ❏ Exercise classes
   ❏ Jogging
   ❏ Racquetball
   ❏ Swimming
   ❏ Walking
   ❏ Weight training
   ❏ Other

7. Please indicate the extent of your interest in a company-sponsored fitness program.

   ❑ Very high
   ❑ High
   ❑ Moderate
   ❑ Low
   ❑ Very low

8. If the company were to develop and sponsor a *fitness* program, which of the following items would you like to see included? Check all that apply.

   ❑ Classes (e.g., Health and Nutrition, Aerobics, Yoga)
   ❑ On-site fitness center (e.g., exercise equipment, free weights, etc.)
   ❑ Paid membership in private health club
   ❑ Walking/jogging path on the premises

9. If you checked *on-site fitness center* in item 8, how often would you anticipate using the facility?

   ❑ Rarely
   ❑ Occasionally
   ❑ 2–4 times a week
   ❑ Daily

10. At what time of day would you be most likely to use the facility?

   ❑ Before work
   ❑ During lunch break
   ❑ After work

Thank you for your input. Please fold and return by *May 19* to:

> Hank Thorp
> Human Resources Management Department
> 146 Building C

The reference list includes citations for all materials used as sources for the study.

REFERENCE LIST

REFERENCE LIST

Carey, Joshua. "Exercise Promotes Better Health." *Journal of Stress Science* 26:7 (February 2001): 78–79.

Ethan-Rolle, Madeleine E. "Run for Your Life." *Today's Healthy Living* 19 (June 7, 1986): 103.

Haugen, R. P. "Are Stress Reduction Programs Stressful?" *Today's Healthy Living* 22 (January 31, 1989): 38–41.

Krazen, C. B. *The Winthrow Group Report on Stress*, Report 108. Altoona, PA: Winthrow, 1999.

"Sanders on Top of Fitness Scene." *West Coast Business*, 17 December 2002: 6c.

Trent, Willis M. "Insurer Has Fitness Policy." *NYC Today* 35 (March 31, 2002): 118.

Index

R

ab·ro·ga·tion (æbrəgéiʃən) *n.* the act of abrogating (e.g. a law) [fr. L. *abrogatio (abrogationis)*]

ab·rupt (əbrʌ́pt) *adj.* sudden, unexpected, *an abrupt halt* ‖ steep, precipitous ‖ rough, brusque in manner ‖ disconnected, *an abrupt style* [fr. L. *abrumpere (abruptus)*, to break away]

A·bruz·zi e Mo·li·se (ɑbrúːttsiːemɔ́liːze) a region (area 5,954 sq. miles, pop. 1,221,900) in central Italy, formed of the provinces of Aquila, Campobasso, Chieti, Pescara and Teramo, lying in the highest and wildest part of the Apennines (Gran Sasso d'Italia, 9,560 ft), and bounded on the east by the Adriatic: olives, vines, almonds, sheep, hydroelectric power, oil

Ab·sa·lom (æbsələm) the third and best-loved son of David, king of Judah (11 Samuel xiii-xix)

ABSCAM (æbsxǽm) an investigation conducted by the Federal Bureau of Investigation in 1978–80. Seven U.S. Congressmen and various state and local officials were convicted of bribery, conspiracy, and related charges after FBI agents impersonating an Arab sheikh and his associates had videotaped government officials accepting bribes. Critics accused the FBI of entrapment, but the courts ruled that the FBI acted within legal limits

ab·scess (æbses) *n.* a localized collection of pus occurring anywhere in the body **ab·scessed** *adj.* [fr. L. *abscessus*, a going away]

ab·scis·sa (æbsísə) *n.* (*math.*) the horizontal or x-coordinate in a plane coordinate system [L. = (part) cut off]

ab·scis·sion (æbsíʒən) *n.* a cutting off [fr. L. *abscissio (abscissionis)*]

ab·scond (æbskɔ́nd) *v.i.* to flee secretly, esp. to escape the law [fr. L. *abscondere*, to hide]

ab·sence (æbsəns) *n.* a being away ‖ a failure to be present ‖ lack, *absence of proof* [F.]

absence of mind inattention, mental abstraction

ab·sent (æbsənt) *adj.* away, not present ‖ abstracted, *an absent air* [F.]

ab·sent (æbsént) *v. refl.* to keep (oneself) away, *to absent oneself from a meeting* **ab·sen·tee** (æbsənti:) *n.* a person who is absent **ab·sen·tee·ism** *n.* persistent absence from work, usually without good reason [F. *absenter*]

absentee landlord a proprietor who does not live on his estate and care for his tenants but merely exploits his property

ab·sent·ly (æbsəntli:) *adv.* in an absent way, inattentively

ab·sent·mind·ed (æbsəntmáindid) *adj.* preoccupied and for that reason not paying attention to what one is doing

ab·sinthe, ab·sinth (æbsinθ) *n.* the plant wormwood ‖ a strongly alcoholic liqueur made from high-proof brandy, wormwood and other aromatics [F.]

ab·sis·sic acid (æbsísik) (*chem.*) [C₁₅H₂₀O₄] organic inhibitor of plant growth marketed as Dormin. *abbr* ABA

ab·so·lute (æbsəlu:t) 1. *adj.* whole, complete ‖ pure, *absolute alcohol* ‖ having unrestricted power, *an absolute ruler* ‖ not conditioned by, or dependent upon, anything else ‖ (*gram.*) of a case not determined by any other word in the sentence (*ABLATIVE) ‖ (*philos.*) existing independently of any cause outside itself and of our sense perceptions 2. *n.* something that is absolute **the Absolute** the self-existent, the First Cause, God [F. *absolut*]

absolute address location of stored information in a digital computer

absolute alcohol ethyl alcohol containing not less than 99% pure ethyl alcohol by weight

absolute altimeter radio or similar apparatus designed to indicate the true vertical height of an aircraft above the terrain

absolute code (*computer*) code for an absolute address

absolute dud (*mil.*) a nuclear weapon that fails to explode when launched at, or emplaced on, a target

absolute expansion the true expansion of a liquid irrespective of the expansion of the containing vessel

absolute film *ABSTRACT FILM

absolute humidity the humidity of the air measured by the number of grams of water vapor present in one cubic meter of the air

absolute music music which does not illustrate or depict (in contrast to program music)

absolute pitch the pitch of a note as determined by a simple frequency, not a combination

---

Guide words showing the alphabetical range of entries on the page

Pronunciation respelling See Part 2.

Foreign pronunciation See Part 2.

Etymology See Part 5.

Field label See Part 4A.

Stress-marked derivative See Part 1D.

Unsyllabicated main entry See Part 1A.

Spelling variants See Part 1B.

Multiple definitions in several parts of speech See Part 3A.

Cross-reference to related term See Part 3C.

Defining cross-reference See Part 3C.

PRONUNCIATION KEY USED IN THIS DICTIONARY

(Continued)

ʃ	fi*sh*, a*c*tion, fi*ss*ion
t	*t*ime, we*t*, le*tt*er
θ	*th*ick, tru*th*
ð	mo*th*er, *th*ough
ʌ	d*u*ck, t*ou*gh, r*u*dder
ə:	b*ir*d, l*ear*n
u	b*u*ll, c*u*shion, b*oo*k
uə	p*oor*, s*ewer*
u:	f*oo*d, tr*u*e
ju:	*u*nite, conf*u*se
v	*v*erb, o*v*er, wa*v*e
w	*w*ell, *w*aver
x	lo*ch*
j	*y*outh, *y*ellow
z	*z*oom, ro*s*e

Foreign Sounds

y	l*u*ne
ɔ̃	b*on*
ɑ̃	*an*
ɛ̃	v*in*
œ̃	br*un*

Stress

The symbol ′ marks the primary stress in pronouncing the word. The syllable in which the primary stress symbol appears is pronounced with greater emphasis than other syllables.

The symbol ˌ marks the secondary stress of a word. The syllable under which this symbol appears is pronounced with less emphasis than the syllable with primary stress.